2016 Edition

Directory of State Court Clerks and County Courthouses

**State Court Clerks • County Courthouses • County Clerks
State Supreme Court Justices • State Vital Records Offices**

LEADERSHIP DIRECTORIES, INC.

www.leadershipdirectories.com
info@leadershipdirectories.com

New York Office
1407 Broadway, Suite 318
New York, NY 10018
(212) 627-4140
Fax (212) 645-0931

Washington, DC Office
1667 K Street, NW, Suite 801
Washington, DC 20006
(202) 347-7757
Fax (202) 628-3430

Leadership Directories, Inc.

DIRECTORY OF STATE COURT CLERKS AND COUNTY COURTHOUSES

2016 Edition

Brian Beth, *Content Manager*
Brian Combs, *Senior Content Manager, Municipal and Technical Support Specialist*

William W. Cressey, *Chairman of the Board*
Gretchen Teichgraeber, *President and Chief Executive Officer*
James M. Petrie, *Secretary*

Sales, Marketing, and Customer Service
Tom Silver, *Senior Vice President, Sales and Marketing*
Imogene Akins Hutchinson, *Vice President, Brand Development*
Jacqueline Johnson, *Fulfillment Manager*
Michele Anderson; Laurie Consoli; Anne Marie Del Vecchio; Heather Donegal; Ed Faas; Melissa Kaus; Jack Levengard; Jim Marcus; William Schneider; Nancy Scholem; Judy Smith; Wanda Speight-Bridgers

Products and Content
Sue Healy, *Senior Vice President, Products and Content*
Tom Zurla, *Assistant Vice President, Content*
Carmela Makabali, *Senior Director, Content and Database Management*
Harris Beringer, *Product Manager*
Dave Marmon, *Senior Product Specialist*
Gareth Sparks, *Manager, Content Development and Quality*

Information Technology
Brian F. Hanley, *Chief Information Officer*
Jill McLoughlin, *Project Leader/DBA*
Rabeya Khandaker, *Senior Software Engineer*
Cynthia Cordova, *Network Administrator*

Administration and Finance
James Gee, *Vice President for Administration and Treasurer*
Shai Tzach, *Controller*
Diane Calogrides, *Office Assistant (NY)*
Elvis A. Perez

ISBN: 978-0-87289-180-7

Printed in the United States of America.

The *Directory of State Court Clerks and County Courthouses* is published annually by Leadership Directories, Inc., 1407 Broadway, Suite 318, New York, NY 10018.

For additional information, including details about other Leadership Directories, Inc. publications, please call (212) 627-4140.

Leadership Directories
www.leadershipdirectories.com

Directory of State Court Clerks and County Courthouses

**State Court Clerks • County Courthouses • County Clerks
State Supreme Court Justices • State Vital Records Offices**

Basic Structure of the U.S. Court System

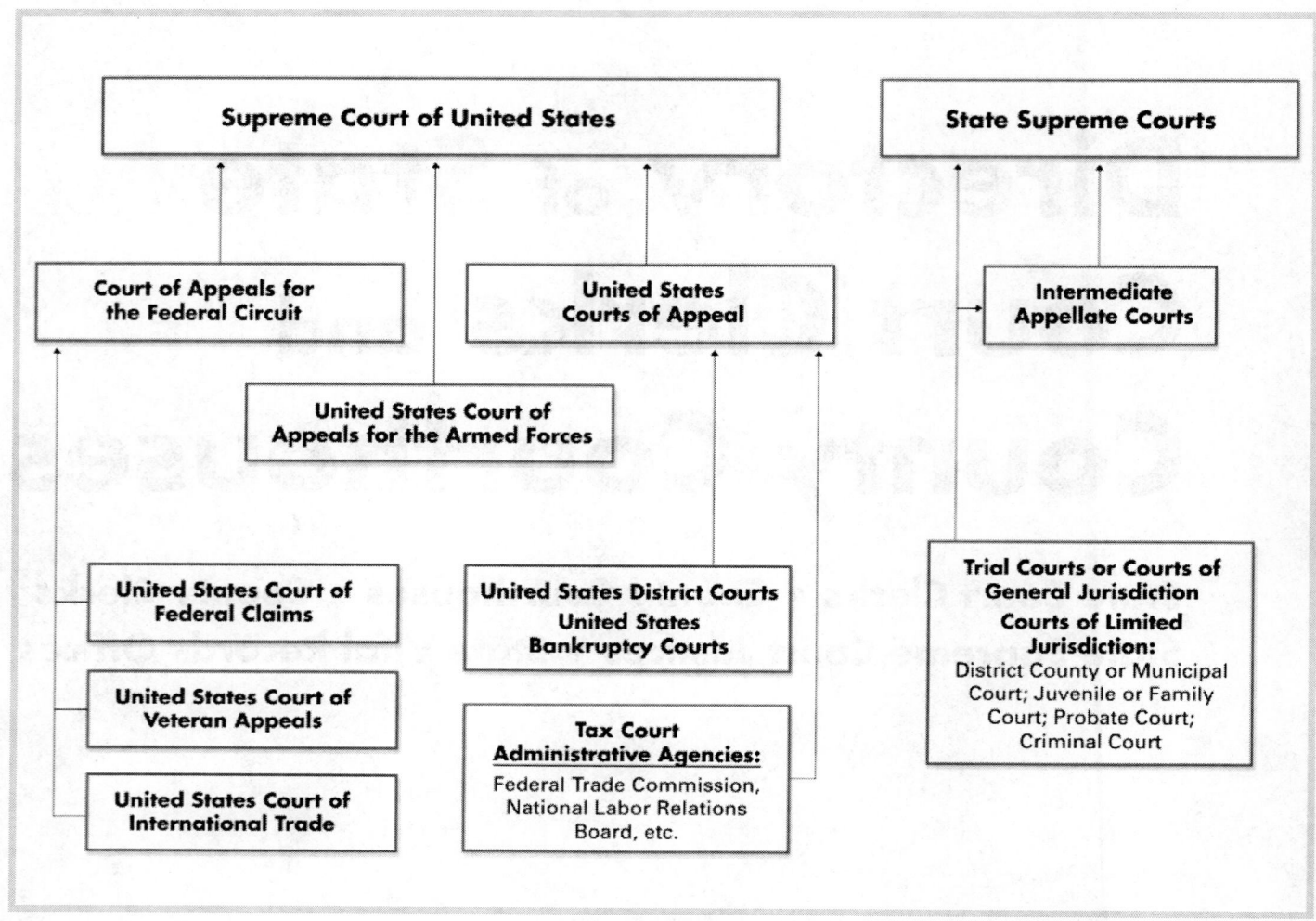

Table of Contents

Introduction vii

How to Use the Directory of State Court
  Clerks and County Courthouses ix

State Court Charts. 1
Alabama 3
Alaska 4
Arizona 5
Arkansas 6
California 7
Colorado 8
Connecticut. 9
Delaware 10
District of Columbia 11
Florida. 12
Georgia 13
Hawaii 14
Idaho 15
Illinois 16
Indiana. 17
Iowa. 18
Kansas. 19
Kentucky. 20
Louisiana 21
Maine 22
Maryland. 23
Massachusetts 24
Michigan. 25
Minnesota 26
Mississippi 27
Missouri 28
Montana 29
Nebraska. 30
Nevada. 31
New Hampshire. 32
New Jersey 33
New Mexico 34
New York. 35
North Carolina 36
North Dakota. 37
Ohio. 38
Oklahoma 39
Oregon. 40
Pennsylvania 41
Puerto Rico 42
Rhode Island 43

South Carolina 44
South Dakota. 45
Tennessee 46
Texas 47
Utah. 48
Vermont. 49
Virginia 50
Washington 51
West Virginia. 52
Wisconsin 53
Wyoming. 54

State and County Courts 55
Alabama 57
Alaska 65
Arizona 71
Arkansas 75
California 87
Colorado 95
Connecticut. 107
Delaware 111
District of Columbia 113
Florida. 115
Georgia 123
Hawaii 139
Idaho 141
Illinois 147
Indiana. 159
Iowa. 169
Kansas. 181
Kentucky. 201
Louisiana 223
Maine 231
Maryland. 235
Massachusetts 239
Michigan. 243
Minnesota 255
Mississippi 265
Missouri 279
Montana 289
Nebraska. 299
Nevada. 309
New Hampshire. 313
New Jersey 315
New Mexico 321
New York. 327
North Carolina 341

Table of Contents - continued

State and County Courts - continued

North Dakota. 351
Ohio. 357
Oklahoma 369
Oregon. 377
Pennsylvania 383
Puerto Rico 399
Rhode Island 401
South Carolina 403
South Dakota. 409
Tennessee 417
Texas 433
Utah. 485
Vermont. 489
Virginia 491
Washington 503
West Virginia. 507
Wisconsin 517
Wyoming. 525

State Probate, Recording, and Notary Offices 531

Offices of Vital Statistics 537

Corporate and UCC Filings 549

Introduction

Leadership Directories is pleased to present the fully updated 2016 edition of the *Directory of State Court Clerks and County Courthouses.*

The 2016 edition of the *Directory of State Court Clerks and County Courthouses* is complete with 465 new email addresses and 146 updates to key phone and fax numbers, providing vital contact information for 411 new individuals who have taken positions in the nation's state and county courthouses since publication of the 2015 edition.

The Directory of State Court Clerks and County Courthouses Content Overview

The *Directory of State Court Clerks and County Courthouses* is a handy reference for reaching court clerks. It features the names, addresses, and phone numbers for each state's supreme court, appellate court, and trial court clerks. Each state's listing is broken down by county and includes information for both the clerk of the court for the trial court in that county as well as the municipal county clerk. In many states, the same person holds both positions. In other states, they are two separate positions. The clerk of the trial court is generally an appointed position, while the county clerk is usually an elected position. The clerk of the trial court is the keeper of the records for that particular court. The county clerk is typically responsible for recording of deeds and other property interests (liens), tax assessment and collection, and probate matters.

The directory also includes state judiciary websites, a listing of state attorneys general, state offices of vital statistics, and a state-by-state guide to obtaining corporate and UCC filings.

The Directory of State Court Clerks and County Courthouses Section-by-Section

State Courts

- A hierarchical visualization of the state court structure distinguishing trial level from appellate level, with clear indication of the route of appeal
- Description of case jurisdiction, trial types, and number of judges for each court within the state system
- Chief Justice and Supreme Court Justices
- Clerk of the Supreme Court, with name, address and phone
- State Court System website
- Court Administrative Director, with name, address and phone
- State Website and State Capitol phone
- Governor, Attorney General, and Secretary of State, each listed with name, address and phone
- Head of Vital Statistics, with name, address and phone

The Directory of State Court Clerks and County Courthouses
Section-by-Section—continued

State Court Clerks and County Courthouses

- State supreme courts, appellate court, and trial court for all 50 U.S. states plus the District of Columbia and Puerto Rico, with address, phone, fax, and website
- Supreme and appellate court clerks, clerks of trial courts, and county clerks with full name, title, and detailed contact information including email
- Lists of counties covered by each court

State Probate and Recording Offices

- State-by-state reference of the offices responsible for handling probate and recording matters, including estates and wills; deed and mortgage recording; and certificate of notary

State Offices of Vital Statistics

- Offices of Vital Statistics for each state, with address, phone, fax, and website, plus details on prices and processes for ordering copies of vital records

Corporate and UCC Filings

- A handy reference of phone numbers with each state for contacting offices that provides information on corporate filings, annual reports, UCC filings, limited partnerships, trademark availabilities, and notaries

Thank you for purchasing the 2016 edition of *Directory of State Court Clerks and County Courthouses*. We invite you to visit our website or call us to provide comments, learn more about Leadership Directories' various publications, or to find out more about the companion book to *Directory of State Court Clerks and County Courthouses*, the *Federal–State Court Directory*. We also send our sincere appreciation to the countless contacts within courts, judges' chambers, and county offices who assist us on a continuous basis by providing updated information for our directories.

How to Use the Directory of State Court Clerks and County Courthouses

State Courts

To the right is a sample of a page from the State Courts section. Use this guide to help you understand the layout of information on these pages.

See corresponding numbers on example.

1 Listing begins with the state name.

2 The Chief Justice of the State Supreme Court.

3 Justices of the State Supreme Court are listed in alphabetical order.

4 Supreme Court Clerk with full contact details

5 Website for State court system

6 Main court administrator with exact title and full contact details

7 Governor with full contact details

8 State website and main capitol phone

9 State Attorney General with full contact details

10 Secretary of State with full contact details

11 Head of state vital statistics with exact title and full contact details

12 Structural chart of state court system

13 Guide for reading state court chart, indicating appellate level, trial level, and route of appeal

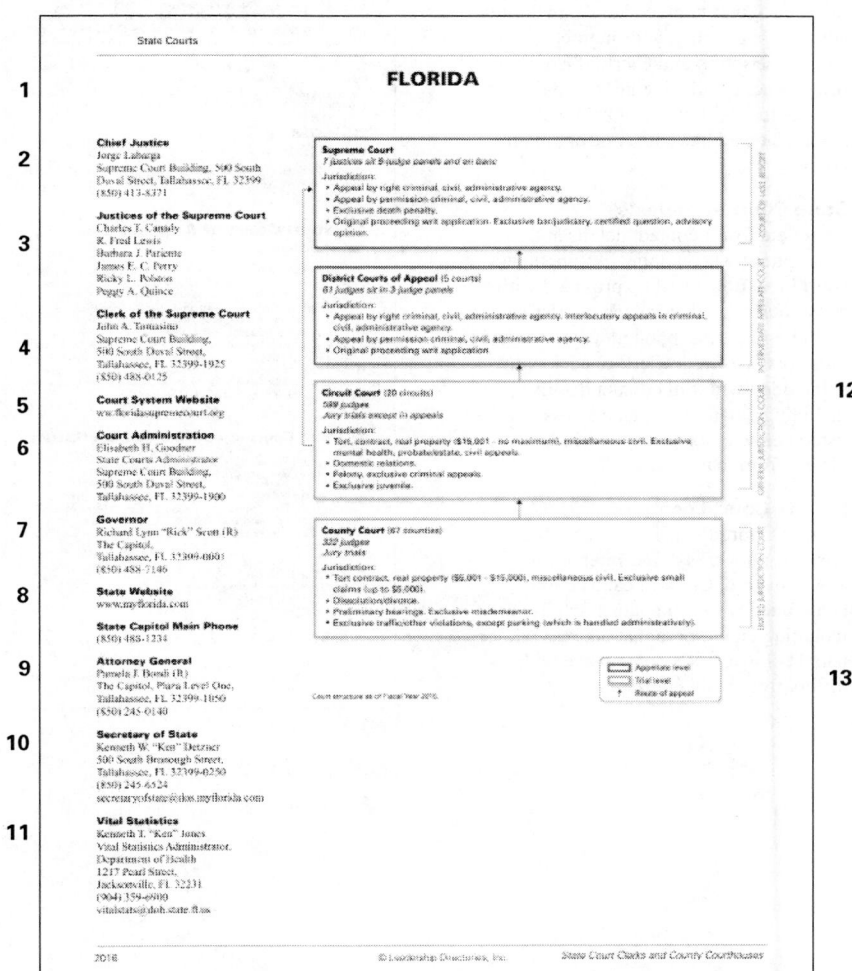

(continued on next page)

State and County Courts

To the right is a sample of a page from the State and County Courts section. Use this guide to help you understand the layout of information on these pages.

See corresponding numbers on example.

1 State Name

Each state is introduced with a description of the structure of the court system.

2 State Supreme Court

Supreme Court contact details, including address, phone, fax, and Internet, plus court description and Clerk of Court with full contact details, including email; note that address will be listed below clerk's name when address differs from main court.

3 State Court of Appeals

Appellate Court contact details and description; when applicable, appellate court breakdown will be provided with full contact details for each district's court, including address, phone, fax, and Internet, plus areas covered. Clerk of each court is included with full contact details, including email; note that address will be listed below clerk's name when address differs from main court.

4 County Court Locations

County Court contact details, including address, phone, fax, and Internet, plus areas covered. Clerk of each court is included with full contact details, including email; note that address will be listed below clerk's name when address differs from main court.

1

State Court Clerks and County Courthouses

Missouri Court Clerks and Courthouses

The trial courts of general jurisdiction in Missouri are called circuit courts, which consist of several divisions. There are 45 judicial circuits, each circuit consisting of at least one county. Each county has a county clerk and a circuit court clerk. The circuit court clerks are listed below

2

Missouri Supreme Court

Supreme Court Building, 207 West High Street, Jefferson City, MO 65101
P.O. Box 150, Jefferson City, MO 65102
Tel: (573) 751-4144 Fax: (573) 751-7514
Internet: www.courts.mo.gov

The Supreme Court consists of a chief justice and six judges who are appointed by the Governor from a list of candidates submitted by a nonpartisan Appellate Judicial Commission. Appointed judges face a retention vote in the next general election occurring after one year in office for a twelve-year term. The chief justice is elected by peer vote for a two-year term. Retirement is mandatory at age seventy; however, retired judges may be assigned to serve in state courts. The Supreme Court has exclusive appellate jurisdiction in all cases involving federal or Missouri constitutional law, federal treaties or statutes, Missouri revenue laws, and in any case involving the death penalty or life imprisonment. The Court exercises appellate jurisdiction over cases transferred from the Missouri Court of Appeals. The Court has rule-making authority over the lower courts and regulates admission to the state bar.

Court Staff

Fax: (573) 751-7514

Clerk of Court **Bill L. Thompson** . . . . (573) 751-4144
E-mail: bill.thompson@courts.mo.gov

3

Missouri Court of Appeals

Tel: (417) 895-6811 Fax: (417) 895-6817

The judges of the Court of Appeals are initially appointed by the Governor from a list of candidates submitted by a nonpartisan Appellate Judicial Commission. They must then stand for retention in the next general election occurring at least one year after their appointment. Retention elections are held every twelve years. The chief judges are elected by peer vote in each district for a term determined by the district. The method of selection varies with each district, as does the length of term. Retirement is at age seventy, but retired judges may serve as senior judges in any Missouri court, as assigned by the Supreme Court. The Court of Appeals has appellate jurisdiction over civil and criminal cases, except those within the exclusive jurisdiction of the Missouri Supreme Court.

Missouri Court of Appeals, Eastern District

One Post Office Square, 815 Olive Street, St. Louis, MO 63101
Tel: (314) 539-4300 Fax: (314) 539-4354
Internet: www.courts.mo.gov

Areas Covered: Counties of Audrain, Cape Girardeau, Clark, Franklin, Gasconade, Jefferson, Knox, Lewis, Lincoln, Madison, Marion, Monroe, Montgomery, Osage, Perry, Pike, Ralls, St. Charles, St. Francois, St. Genevieve, St. Louis, St. Louis City, Scotland, Shelby, Warren and Washington

Court Staff

Clerk of Court **Laura Thielmeier Roy** . . . . (314) 539-4300
E-mail: laura.roy@courts.mo.gov

Missouri Court Clerks and Courthouses *continued*

Missouri Court of Appeals, Southern District

John Q. Hammons Building, 300 Hammons Parkway,
Springfield, MO 65806
Tel: (417) 895-6811 Fax: (417) 895-6617
Internet: www.courts.mo.gov

Areas Covered: Counties of Barry, Barton, Bollinger, Butler, Camden, Carter, Cedar, Christian, Crawford, Dade, Dallas, Dent, Douglas, Dunklin, Greene, Hickory, Howell, Iron, Jasper, Laclede, Lawrence, McDonald, Maries, Mississippi, New Madrid, Newton, Oregon, Ozark, Pemiscot, Phelps, Polk, Pulaski, Reynolds, Ripley, Scott, Shannon, Saint Clair, Stoddard, Stone, Taney, Texas, Wayne, Webster and Wright

Court Staff

Clerk of Court **Sandra L. Skinner** . . . . (417) 895-6811
E-mail: sandra.skinner@courts.mo.gov

Missouri Court of Appeals, Western District

1300 Oak Street, Kansas City, MO 64106-2970
Tel: (816) 889-3600 Fax: (816) 889-3668

Areas Covered: Counties of Adair, Andrew, Atchison, Bates, Benton, Boone, Buchanan, Caldwell, Callaway, Cass, Chariton, Clay, Clinton, Carroll, Cole, Cooper, Daviess, DeKalb, Gentry, Grundy, Henry, Holt, Howard, Harrison, Jackson, Johnson, Lafayette, Linn, Livingston, Macon, Mercer, Miller, Moniteau, Morgan, Nodaway, Platte, Putnam, Pettis, Randolph, Ray, Saline, Schuyler, Sullivan, Vernon and Worth

Court Staff

Clerk of Court **Terence G. Lord** . . . . (816) 889-3600
E-mail: lord@courts.mo.gov

County-By-County

4

Adair County

Circuit Clerk

2nd Judicial Circuit Court
Circuit Clerk, Adair County **Linda S. Decker** . . . . (660) 665-2552
106 West Washington Street,   Fax: (660) 665-3420
Kirksville, MO 63501

Andrew County

Circuit Clerk

5th Judicial Circuit Court
Circuit Clerk, Andrew County **Tena Christmas** . . . . (816) 324-4221
Main Street, Savannah, MO 64485   Fax: (816) 324-5667

Atchison County

Circuit Clerk

4th Judicial Circuit Court
Circuit Clerk, Atchison County **Lorie Hall** . . . . . . (660) 744-2700
P.O. Box 280, Rock Port, MO 64482   Fax: (660) 744-6100
(continued on next page)

State Court Clerks and County Courthouses   © Leadership Directories, Inc.   2016

State Courts

ALABAMA

Chief Justice
Roy S. Moore
300 Dexter Avenue,
Montgomery, AL 36104-3741
(334) 229-0700

Justices of the Supreme Court
Michael F. Bolin
Tommy Elias Bryan
James Allen Main
Glenn Murdock
Tom Parker
Greg Shaw
Lyn Stuart
Alisa Kelli Wise

Clerk of the Supreme Court
Julia J. Weller
300 Dexter Avenue,
Montgomery, AL 36104-3741
(334) 229-0700

Court System Website
www.judicial.alabama.gov

Court Administration
Rich Hobson
Administrative Director of Courts
300 Dexter Avenue,
Montgomery, AL 36104-3741
(334) 954-5080

Governor
Robert Julian Bentley (R)
600 Dexter Avenue,
Montgomery, AL 36130
(334) 242-7210

State Website
www.alabama.gov

State Capitol Main Phone
(334) 242-7100

Attorney General
Luther J. Strange (R)
501 Washington Avenue,
Montgomery, AL 36130
(334) 242-7300

Secretary of State
John H. Merrill
P.O. Box 5616,
Montgomery, AL 36103-5616
(334) 242-7200

Vital Statistics
Cathy (Molchan) Donald
Director, Center for Health Statistics,
Alabama Department of Public Health
RSA Tower, 201 Monroe Street,
Suite 1168, Montgomery, AL 36104
(334) 206-5426
cathy.molchan@adph.state.al.us

Supreme Court
9 justices sit in 5-judge panels of 5 and en banc
Assigns cases to the Court of Civil Appeals

Jurisdiction:
- Appeal by right tort, contract, and real property, probate ($50,000 - no maximum), limited administrative agency.
- Appeal by permission criminal, civil, administrative agency. Interlocutory appeals in criminal, civil, administrative agency.
- Death penalty appeal by permission.
- Original proceeding writ application. Exclusive bar/judiciary, certified questions, advisory opinion.

COURT OF LAST RESORT

Court of Civil Appeals
5 judges sit en banc

Jurisdiction:
- Appeal by right in civil ($0 - $50,000), administrative agency.
- Original proceeding writ application.

Court of Criminal Appeals
5 judges sit en banc

Jurisdiction:
- Appeal by right criminal, juvenile. Interlocutory appeals in criminal, juvenile.
- Death penalty appeal by right, writ application.
- Original proceeding writ application.

INTERMEDIATE APPELLATE COURT

Circuit Court (41 circuits)
144 judges
Jury trials

Jurisdiction:
- Tort, contract, real property ($3,000 - no maximum). Exclusive civil appeals.
- Domestic relations.
- Felony, misdemeanor, and criminal appeals.
- Juvenile.

GENERAL JURISDICTION COURT

District Court (67 districts)
106 judges
No jury trials

Jurisdiction:
- Tort, contract, real property ($3,000 - $10,000). Exclusive small claims (up to $3,000).
- Paternity, custody, support, visitation, adoption.
- Preliminary hearings, misdemeanor.
- Juvenile.
- Traffic infractions.

Probate Court (68 courts)
68 judges
No jury trials

Jurisdiction:
- Exclusive mental health, probate/estate. Real Property.
- Adoption.

Municipal Court (273 courts)
279 judges
No jury trials

Jurisdiction:
- Misdemeanor.
- Exclusive ordinance violations. Traffic infractions, parking.

LIMITED JURISDICTION COURT

Court structure as of Fiscal Year 2015.

▭	Appellate level
▭	Trial level
↑	Route of appeal

ALASKA

Chief Justice
Craig F. Stowers
303 K Street,
Anchorage, AK 99501-2084
(907) 264-0612

Justices of the Supreme Court
Joel H. Bolger
Dana Fabe
Peter J. Maassen
Daniel E. Winfree

Clerk of the Supreme Court
Marilyn May
Boney Memorial Courthouse,
303 K Street,
Anchorage, AK 99501-2084
(907) 264-0608

Court System Website
www.courts.alaska.gov

Court Administration
Christine E. Johnson
Administrative Director
Boney Memorial Courthouse,
303 K Street,
Anchorage, AK 99501-2099
(907) 264-0547

Governor
William M. "Bill" Walker (I)
State Capitol, Third Floor,
Juneau, AK 99801
(907) 465-3500
bill.walker@alaska.gov

State Website
www.alaska.gov

State Capitol Main Phone
(907) 465-2111

Attorney General
Craig Richards
P.O. Box 110300
Juneau, AK 99811-0300
(907) 465-2133
craig.richards@alaska.gov

Lieutenant Governor
Byron I. Mallott
State Capitol Building, 3rd Floor,
Juneau, AK 99801
(907) 465-3520
byron.mallott@alaska.gov

Vital Statistics
Andrew Jessen
Bureau Chief, Bureau of Vital Statistics,
Division of Public Health
P.O. Box 110675, Juneau, AK 99811
(907) 465-8643
andrew.jessen@alaska.gov

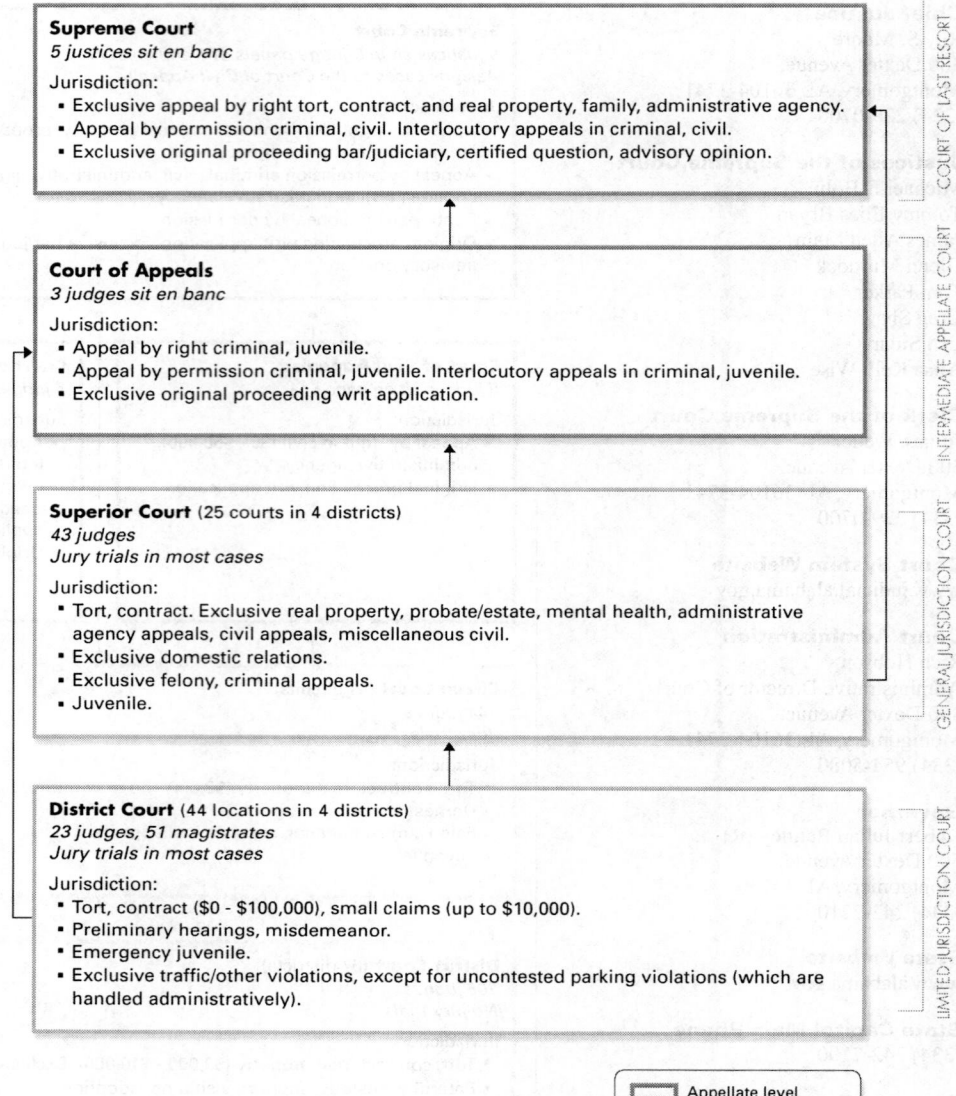

Supreme Court
5 justices sit en banc
Jurisdiction:
- Exclusive appeal by right tort, contract, and real property, family, administrative agency.
- Appeal by permission criminal, civil. Interlocutory appeals in criminal, civil.
- Exclusive original proceeding bar/judiciary, certified question, advisory opinion.

Court of Appeals
3 judges sit en banc
Jurisdiction:
- Appeal by right criminal, juvenile.
- Appeal by permission criminal, juvenile. Interlocutory appeals in criminal, juvenile.
- Exclusive original proceeding writ application.

Superior Court (25 courts in 4 districts)
43 judges
Jury trials in most cases
Jurisdiction:
- Tort, contract. Exclusive real property, probate/estate, mental health, administrative agency appeals, civil appeals, miscellaneous civil.
- Exclusive domestic relations.
- Exclusive felony, criminal appeals.
- Juvenile.

District Court (44 locations in 4 districts)
23 judges, 51 magistrates
Jury trials in most cases
Jurisdiction:
- Tort, contract ($0 - $100,000), small claims (up to $10,000).
- Preliminary hearings, misdemeanor.
- Emergency juvenile.
- Exclusive traffic/other violations, except for uncontested parking violations (which are handled administratively).

COURT OF LAST RESORT

INTERMEDIATE APPELLATE COURT

GENERAL JURISDICTION COURT

LIMITED JURISDICTION COURT

Court structure as of Fiscal Year 2015.

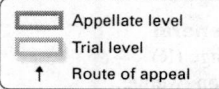
Appellate level
Trial level
↑   Route of appeal

ARIZONA

Chief Justice
W. Scott Bales
Arizona State Courts Building,
1501 West Washington Street, Suite 434,
Phoenix, AZ 85007-3222
(602) 452-3534

Justices of the Supreme Court
Rebecca White Berch
Robert M. Brutinel
A. John Pelander
Ann Scott Timmer

Clerk of the Supreme Court
Janet Johnson
Arizona State Courts Building,
1501 West Washington Street,
Phoenix, AZ 85007
(602) 452-3396

Court System Website
www.azcourts.gov

Court Administration
David K. Byers
Administrative Director
Arizona State Courts Building,
1501 West Washington Street,
Phoenix, AZ 85007
(602) 452-3301

Governor
Douglas A. "Doug" Ducey (R)
State Capitol, Executive Tower,
1700 West Washington Street, 9th Floor,
Phoenix, AZ 85007
(602) 542-4331

State Website
www.az.gov

State Capitol Main Phone
(602) 542-4331

Attorney General
Mark Brnovich (R)
1275 West Washington,
Phoenix, AZ 85007
(602) 542-5025

Secretary of State
Michele Reagan
State Capitol, West Wing,
1700 West Washington Street, 7th Floor,
Phoenix, AZ 85007
(602) 542-0681

Vital Statistics
Krystal Colburn
Deputy Bureau Chief, Office of Vital
Records, Division of Public Health
Services
P.O. Box 3887, Phoenix, AZ 85030-3887
(602) 364-1225
krystal.colburn@azdhs.gov

Supreme Court
5 justices sit en banc

Jurisdiction:
- Appeal by right criminal, tort, contract, and real property, probate, family.
- Appeal by permission criminal, civil, administrative agency. Interlocutory appeals in criminal, civil, administrative agency.
- Exclusive death penalty.
- Original proceeding writ application. Exclusive bar/judiciary, certified question.

COURT OF LAST RESORT

Court of Appeals
22 judges sit in panels

Jurisdiction:
- Appeal by right criminal, civil, limited administrative agency. Interlocutory appeals in criminal, civil, limited administrative agency.
- Appeal by permission administrative agency. Interlocutory appeals in administrative agency.
- Original proceeding writ application.

INTERMEDIATE APPELLATE COURT

Superior Court (15 counties)
177 judges*
Jury trials

Jurisdiction:
- Tort, contract, real property ($5,000 to $10,000 - no maximum). Exclusive probate/estate, mental health, civil appeals, miscellaneous civil.
- Domestic relations.
- Exclusive felony, criminal appeals. Misdemeanor.
- Juvenile.

Tax Court
Superior court judge serves

Jurisdiction:
- Administrative agency appeals.

GENERAL JURISDICTION COURT

Justice of the Peace Court (88 precincts)
88 judges
Jury trials except in small claims

Jurisdiction:
- Tort, contract, real property ($0 - $5,000 to $10,000), non-domestic relations restraining order. Exclusive small claims (up to $2,500).
- Civil protection order.
- Preliminary hearings, misdemeanor.
- Traffic/other violations.

Municipal Court (84 courts)
154 judges
Jury trials

Jurisdiction:
- Non-domestic relations restraining order.
- Civil protection order.
- Misdemeanor.
- Traffic/other violations.

LIMITED JURISDICTION COURT

*There are also approximately 98 full- and part-time judges pro tempore, commissioners, and hearing officers in the Superior Court.

Court structure as of Fiscal Year 2015.

☐ Appellate level
☐ Trial level
↑ Route of appeal

ARKANSAS

Chief Justice
James R. "Jim" Hanna
Justice Building, 625 Marshall Street,
First Floor North,
Little Rock, AR 72201
(501) 682-6873

Justices of the Supreme Court
Karen R. Baker
Paul E. Danielson
Courtney Hudson (Henry) Goodson
Josephine Linker Hart
Rhonda Wood
Robin F. Wynne

Clerk of the Supreme Court
Stacy Pectol
Justice Building, 625 Marshall Street,
Little Rock, AR 72201
(501) 682-6849

Court System Website
courts.arkansas.gov

Court Administration
James D. Gingerich
Director, Arkansas Administrative Office
of the Courts
Justice Building, 625 Marshall Street,
Suite 1100, Little Rock, AR 72201-1020
(501) 682-9400

Governor
W. Asa Hutchinson (R)
State Capitol Building, Room 250,
Little Rock, AR 72201
(501) 682-2345

State Website
www.arkansas.gov

State Capitol Main Phone
(501) 682-3000

Attorney General
Leslie Rutledge (R)
323 Center Street, Suite 200,
Little Rock, AR 72201-2610
(501) 682-2007

Secretary of State
LTC J. Timothy "Tim" Griffin,
USAR (R)
State Capitol, Suite 270,
Little Rock, AR 72201
(501) 682-2144

Vital Statistics
Lynda Lehing
Branch Chief, Health Statistics Branch,
Arkansas Department of Health [ADH]
4815 West Markham Street,
Little Rock, AR 72205
(501) 661-2231
lynda.lehing@arkansas.gov

Supreme Court
7 justices sit en banc (1 chief justice, 6 associate justices)

Jurisdiction:
- Appeal by permission criminal, appeal by right criminal, civil, administrative agency.
- Exclusive revenue (tax). Interlocutory appeals in criminal, civil, administrative agency.
- Exclusive death penalty.
- Exlusice original proceeding writ application, bar/judiciary, certified question.

COURT OF LAST RESORT

Court of Appeals
12 judges sit in 3-judge panels and en banc (1 chief judge, 11 judges)

Jurisdiction:
- Appeal by right criminal, civil, administrative agency.

INTERMEDIATE APPELLATE COURT

Circuit Court (28 circuits)
121 judges
Jury trials

Jurisdiction:
- Tort, contract, real property ($100 - no maximum), miscellaneous civil. Exclusive probate/estate, mental health, civil appeals.
- Exclusive domestic relations.
- Exclusive felony, criminal appeals. Misdemeanor.
- Exclusive juvenile.

GENERAL JURISDICTION COURT

State District Court (16 courts)
67 departments
25 judges
No jury trials

Jurisdiction:
- Preliminary felony, misdemeanor.
- Civil cases involving contracts, property damage (up to $25,000).
- Small claims (up to $5,000).

Local District Court (77 courts)
178 departments
90 judges
No jury trials

Jurisdiction:
- Minor civil and criminal.
- Small claims (up to $5,000).

LIMITED JURISDICTION COURT

Court structure as of Fiscal Year 2015.

Appellate level
Trial level
↑ Route of appeal

CALIFORNIA

Chief Justice
Tani G. Cantil-Sakauye
350 McAllister Street,
San Francisco, CA 94102
(415) 865-7000

Justices of the Supreme Court
Ming W. Chin
Carol A. Corrigan
Mariano-Florentino "Tino" Cuéllar
Leondra R. Kruger
Goodwin Liu
Kathryn Mickle Werdegar

Clerk of the Supreme Court
Frank McGuire
Court Executive Officer
350 McAllister Street, Room 1295,
San Francisco, CA 94102
(415) 865-7000 ext. 57015

Court System Website
www.courtinfo.ca.gov

Court Administration
Martin A. Hoshino
Administrative Director of the Courts
455 Golden Gate Avenue,
San Francisco, CA 94102-3688
(415) 865-4200

Governor
Edmund Gerald "Jerry" Brown, Jr. (D)
State Capitol, Suite 1173,
Sacramento, CA 95814
(916) 445-2841

State Website
www.ca.gov

State Capitol Main Phone
(800) 807-6755

Attorney General
Kamala Devi Harris (D)
1300 I Street, Sacramento, CA 95814
(916) 324-5437

Secretary of State
Alejandro "Alex" Padilla (D)
1500 11th Street,
Sacramento, CA 95814
(916) 653-7244
alejandro.padilla@sausd.us

Vital Statistics
Tony Agurto
Vital Statistics State Registrar,
California Department of Public Health
[CDPH], Health and Human Services
Agency [CHHS]
P.O. Box 997377, MS 0500,
Sacramento, CA 95899-7377
(510) 620-3129
tony.agurto@cdph.ca.gov

Supreme Court
7 justices sit en banc
Jurisdiction:
- Appeal by permission criminal, civil, administrative agency.
- Exclusive death penalty.
- Original proceeding writ application. Exclusive bar/judiciary, certified question.

COURT OF LAST RESORT

Courts of Appeal (6 districts)
105 justices sit in panels
Jurisdiction:
- Appeal by right criminal, civil, administrative agency.
- Appeal by permission criminal, civil, administrative agency. Interlocutory appeals in criminal, civil, administrative agency.
- Original proceeding writ application.

INTERMEDIATE APPELLATE COURT

Superior Court (58 counties)
1,598 judges
Jury trials except in appeals, domestic relations, and juvenile cases
Jurisdiction:
- Tort, contract, real property ($25,000 - no maximum), miscellaneous civil. Exclusive small claims (up to $7,500), probate/estate, mental health, civil appeals. [Limited jurisdiction: tort, contract, real property ($0 - $25,000).]
- Exclusive domestic relations.
- Exclusive criminal.
- Exclusive juvenile.
- Exclusive traffic/other violations.

GENERAL JURISDICTION COURT

Court structure as of Fiscal Year 2015.

Appellate level
Trial level
↑   Route of appeal

COLORADO

Chief Justice
Nancy E. Rice
2 East Fourteenth Avenue,
Denver, CO 80203
(720) 625-5460

Justices of the Supreme Court
Brian Boatright
Nathan B. Coats
Allison H. Eid
Richard Lance Gabriel
Gregory J. Hobbs, Jr.
William W. Hood, III
Monica Marie Márquez

Clerk of the Supreme Court
Christopher T. Ryan
Ralph L. Carr Judicial Center,
2 East Fourteenth Avenue,
Denver, CO 80203
(303) 837-3790

Court System Website
www.courts.state.co.us

Court Administration
Gerald A. "Jerry" Marroney
State Court Administrator
1300 Broadway, Suite 1200,
Denver, CO 80203
(720) 625-5801

Governor
John W. Hickenlooper (D)
136 State Capitol,
Denver, CO 80203-1792
(303) 866-2471

State Website
www.colorado.gov

State Capitol Main Phone
(303) 866-5000

Attorney General
Cynthia H. Coffman (R)
1300 Broadway, 10th Floor,
Denver, CO 80203
(720) 508-6000

Secretary of State
Wayne W. Williams
1700 Broadway, 2nd Floor,
Denver, CO 80290
(303) 894-2200

Vital Statistics
Ronald S. Hyman
State Registrar, Center for Health
and Environmental Information and
Statistics, Colorado Department of
Public Health and Environment
4300 Cherry Creek Drive, South, HS-
VRD-VR-A1, Denver, CO 80246-1530
(303) 692-2164

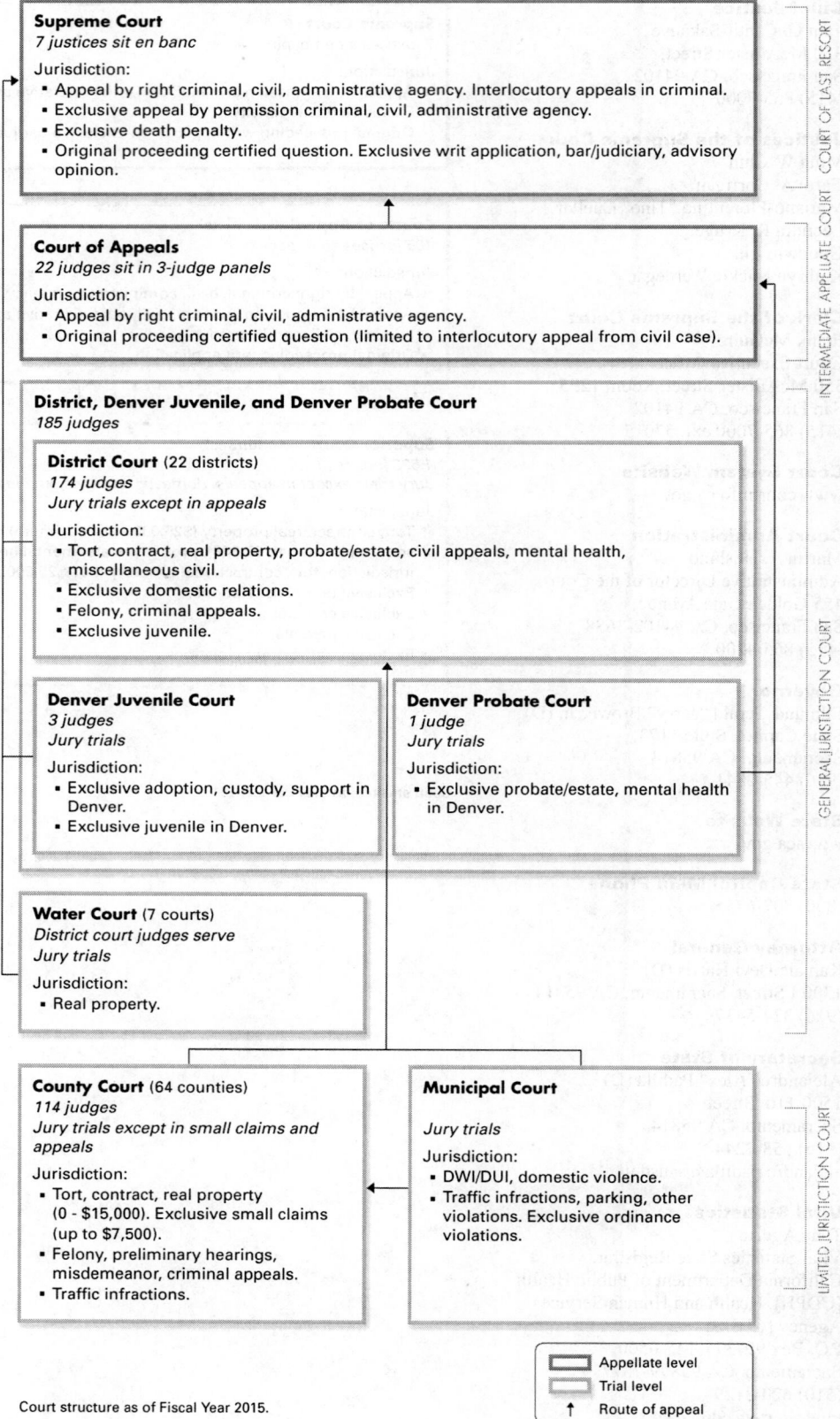

Supreme Court
7 justices sit en banc

Jurisdiction:
- Appeal by right criminal, civil, administrative agency. Interlocutory appeals in criminal.
- Exclusive appeal by permission criminal, civil, administrative agency.
- Exclusive death penalty.
- Original proceeding certified question. Exclusive writ application, bar/judiciary, advisory opinion.

Court of Appeals
22 judges sit in 3-judge panels

Jurisdiction:
- Appeal by right criminal, civil, administrative agency.
- Original proceeding certified question (limited to interlocutory appeal from civil case).

District, Denver Juvenile, and Denver Probate Court
185 judges

District Court (22 districts)
174 judges
Jury trials except in appeals

Jurisdiction:
- Tort, contract, real property, probate/estate, civil appeals, mental health, miscellaneous civil.
- Exclusive domestic relations.
- Felony, criminal appeals.
- Exclusive juvenile.

Denver Juvenile Court
3 judges
Jury trials

Jurisdiction:
- Exclusive adoption, custody, support in Denver.
- Exclusive juvenile in Denver.

Denver Probate Court
1 judge
Jury trials

Jurisdiction:
- Exclusive probate/estate, mental health in Denver.

Water Court (7 courts)
District court judges serve
Jury trials

Jurisdiction:
- Real property.

County Court (64 counties)
114 judges
Jury trials except in small claims and appeals

Jurisdiction:
- Tort, contract, real property (0 - $15,000). Exclusive small claims (up to $7,500).
- Felony, preliminary hearings, misdemeanor, criminal appeals.
- Traffic infractions.

Municipal Court

Jury trials

Jurisdiction:
- DWI/DUI, domestic violence.
- Traffic infractions, parking, other violations. Exclusive ordinance violations.

COURT OF LAST RESORT

INTERMEDIATE APPELLATE COURT

GENERAL JURISDICTION COURT

LIMITED JURISDICTION COURT

Court structure as of Fiscal Year 2015.

Appellate level
Trial level
↑   Route of appeal

CONNECTICUT

Chief Justice
Chase Theodora Rogers
Supreme Court Building,
231 Capitol Avenue, Hartford, CT 06106
(860) 757-2200

Justices of the Supreme Court
Carmen Elisa Espinosa
Dennis G. Eveleigh
Andrew J. McDonald
Richard N. Palmer
Richard A. Robinson
Christine S. Vertefeuille
Peter T. Zarella

Clerk of the Supreme Court
Paul S. Hartan
Supreme Court Building,
231 Capitol Avenue, Hartford, CT 06106
(860) 757-2200

Court System Website
www.jud.ct.gov

Court Administration
Patrick L. Carroll, III
Chief Court Administrator
Supreme Court Building,
231 Capitol Avenue, Hartford, CT 06106
(860) 757-2100

Governor
Dannel P. "Dan" Malloy (D)
State Capitol, 210 Capitol Avenue,
Hartford, CT 06106
(860) 566-4840
governor.malloy@po.state.ct.us

State Website
www.ct.gov

State Capitol Main Phone
(800) 406-1527

Attorney General
George C. Jepsen (D)
55 Elm Street, Hartford, CT 06106
(860) 808-5318

Secretary of State
Denise W. Merrill (D)
State Capitol, 210 Capitol Avenue,
Room 104, Hartford, CT 06106
(860) 509-6200

Vital Statistics
Jane Purtill
Vital Records Director,
Population Health Statistics and
Surveillance Branch
410 Capitol Avenue, Mail Stop 11VRS,
Hartford, CT 06134
(860) 509-7895
jane.purtill@ct.gov

Supreme Court
7 justices sit en banc

Jurisdiction:
- Appeal by right criminal, civil, administrative agency.
- Appeal by permission criminal, and civil.
- Exclusive death penalty appeal by right.
- Exclusive original proceeding judicial qualification.

Appellate Court
9 judges sit in 3-judge panels and en banc

Jurisdiction:
- Appeal by right criminal, civil, administrative agency.
- Appeal by permission limited administrative agency. Interlocutory appeals in administrative agency.

Superior Court (13 districts and 20 geographical areas for civil, domestic relations, criminal, and traffic matters; 13 districts for juvenile matters; and 7 housing session locations)
174 judges
Jury trials in most cases

Jurisdiction:
- Mental health, miscellaneous civil. Exclusive tort, contract, real property rights, small claims (up to $5,000), administrative agency appeals (except workers' compensation).
- Support, custody, paternity. Exclusive marriage dissolution.
- Exclusive criminal.
- Juvenile.
- Exclusive traffic/other violations, except for uncontested parking (which is handled administratively).

Probate Court (60 courts)
55 judges
No jury trials

Jurisdiction:
- Mental health, miscellaneous civil. Exclusive probate/estate.
- Support, custody, paternity. Exclusive adoption.
- Juvenile.

COURT OF LAST RESORT

INTERMEDIATE APPELLATE COURT

GENERAL JURISDICTION COURT

LIMITED JURISDICTION COURT

Court structure as of Fiscal Year 2015.

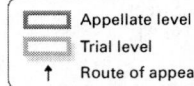

	Appellate level
	Trial level
↑	Route of appeal

DELAWARE

Chief Justice
Leo E. Strine, Jr.
57 The Green, Dover, DE 19901-0476
(302) 651-3902

Justices of the Supreme Court
Randy J. Holland
Collins J. "C.J." Seitz
Karen Valihura
James T. Vaughn, Jr.

Clerk of the Supreme Court
Cathy L. Howard
Elbert N. Carvel State Office Building,
820 North French Street,
Wilmington, DE 19801
(302) 739-4155

Court System Website
www.courts.state.de.us

Court Administration
Patricia W. Griffin
State Court Administrator
1 South Race Street,
Georgetown, DE 19947
(302) 856-5406

Governor
Jack A. Markell (D)
Tatnall Building, 2nd Floor,
Dover, DE 19901
(302) 744-4101
jack.markell@state.de.us

State Website
www.delaware.gov

State Capitol Main Phone
(800) 464-4357

Attorney General
Matthew P. "Matt" Denn (D)
Carvel State Office Building,
820 North French Street,
Wilmington, DE 19801
(302) 577-8400
matthew.denn@state.de.us

Secretary of State
Jeffrey W. "Jeff" Bullock
401 Federal Street, Suite 3,
Dover, DE 19901
(302) 739-4111

Vital Statistics
Brenda (Abele) Conner
Vital Statistics Director, Division of
Public Health [DPH]
Jesse Cooper Building,
417 Federal Street, Dover, DE 19901
(302) 744-4748
brenda.conner@state.de.us

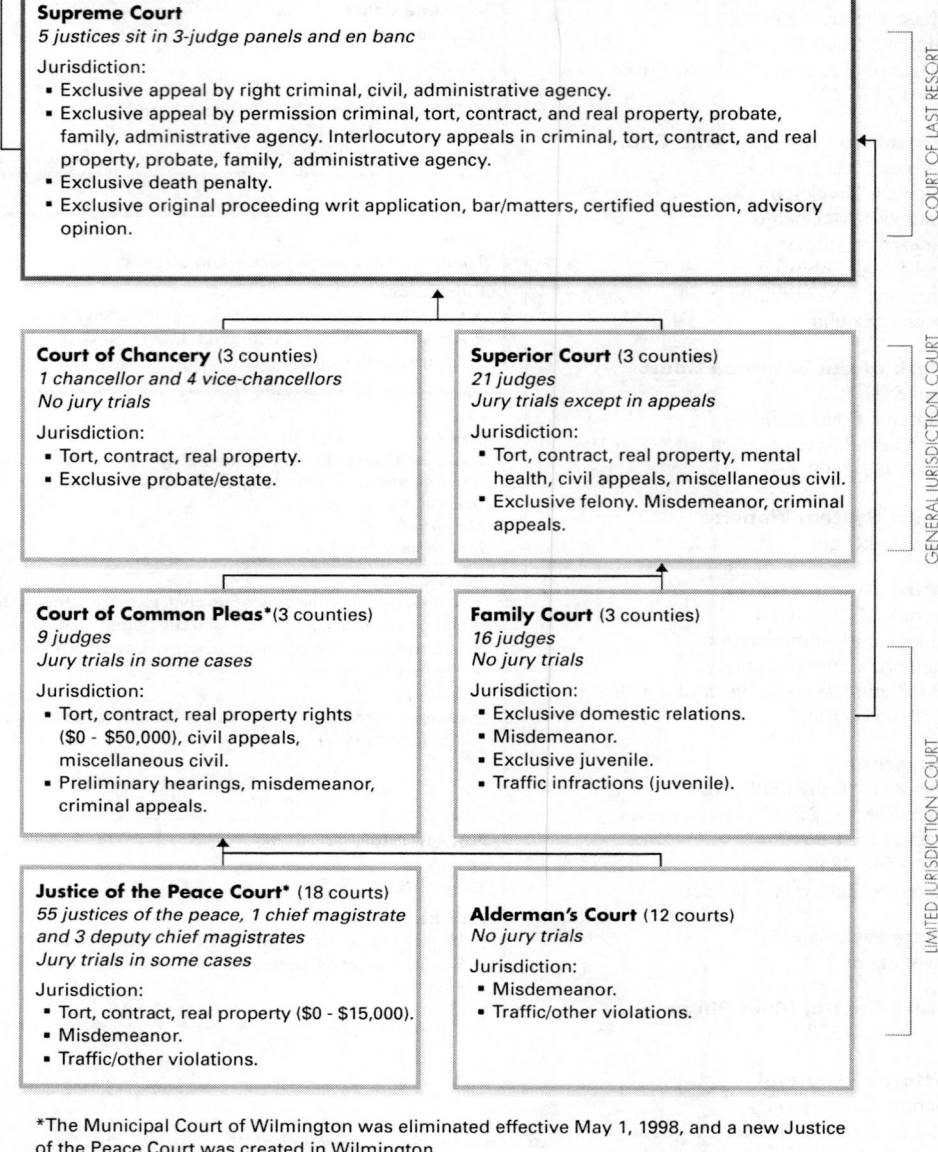

Supreme Court
5 justices sit in 3-judge panels and en banc
Jurisdiction:
- Exclusive appeal by right criminal, civil, administrative agency.
- Exclusive appeal by permission criminal, tort, contract, and real property, probate, family, administrative agency. Interlocutory appeals in criminal, tort, contract, and real property, probate, family, administrative agency.
- Exclusive death penalty.
- Exclusive original proceeding writ application, bar/matters, certified question, advisory opinion.

COURT OF LAST RESORT

Court of Chancery (3 counties)
1 chancellor and 4 vice-chancellors
No jury trials
Jurisdiction:
- Tort, contract, real property.
- Exclusive probate/estate.

Superior Court (3 counties)
21 judges
Jury trials except in appeals
Jurisdiction:
- Tort, contract, real property, mental health, civil appeals, miscellaneous civil.
- Exclusive felony. Misdemeanor, criminal appeals.

GENERAL JURISDICTION COURT

Court of Common Pleas* (3 counties)
9 judges
Jury trials in some cases
Jurisdiction:
- Tort, contract, real property rights ($0 - $50,000), civil appeals, miscellaneous civil.
- Preliminary hearings, misdemeanor, criminal appeals.

Family Court (3 counties)
16 judges
No jury trials
Jurisdiction:
- Exclusive domestic relations.
- Misdemeanor.
- Exclusive juvenile.
- Traffic infractions (juvenile).

Justice of the Peace Court* (18 courts)
55 justices of the peace, 1 chief magistrate and 3 deputy chief magistrates
Jury trials in some cases
Jurisdiction:
- Tort, contract, real property ($0 - $15,000).
- Misdemeanor.
- Traffic/other violations.

Alderman's Court (12 courts)
No jury trials
Jurisdiction:
- Misdemeanor.
- Traffic/other violations.

LIMITED JURISDICTION COURT

*The Municipal Court of Wilmington was eliminated effective May 1, 1998, and a new Justice of the Peace Court was created in Wilmington.

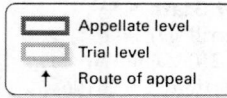
Appellate level
Trial level
↑ Route of appeal

Court structure as of Fiscal Year 2015.

DISTRICT OF COLUMBIA

Chief Judge — Court of Appeals
Eric T. Washington
Historic Courthouse, 430 E Street NW,
Room 319, Washington, DC 20001
(202) 879-2771

Appeals Court Associate Judges
Corinne Ann Beckwith
Anna Blackburne-Rigsby
John R. Fisher
Catharine "Kate" Friend Easterly
Stephen H. Glickman
Todd S. Kim (Designate)
Roy W. McLeese, III
Phyllis D. Thompson

Clerk of Court of Appeals
Julio A. Castillo
430 E Street NW,
Washington, DC 20001
(202) 879-2725

Court System Website
www.dcappeals.gov

Appeals Court Administration
Reginald Turner
Administration Director,
430 E Street NW,
Washington, DC 20001
(202) 879-2738

Mayor
Muriel Bowser (D)
John A. Wilson Building,
1350 Pennsylvania Avenue, NW,
Suite 316, Washington, DC 20004
(202) 727-6300

DC Website
www.dc.gov

DC Main Phone
(202) 737-4404

Attorney General
Karl A. Racine (D)
441 4th Street NW,
Washington, DC 20001
(202) 727-3400

Secretary of DC
Lauren C. Vaughan
1350 Pennsylvania Avenue, NW,
Room 419, Washington, DC 20004
(202) 727-6306

Vital Statistics
Terra Abrams
Vital Records Registrar, Center for
Policy, Planning and Evaluation, DOH
825 North Capitol Street, NE, 2nd Floor,
Washington, DC 20002
(202) 442-9029
terra.abrams@dc.gov

Court of Appeals
9 judges sit in 3-judge panels and en banc

Jurisdiction:
- Exclusive appeal by right criminal, civil, administrative agency. Interlocutory appeals in criminal, civil, administrative agency.
- Exclusive appeal by permission misdemeanor, small claims.
- Exclusive original proceeding writ application, bar/judiciary, certified question.

COURT OF LAST RESORT

Superior Court
58 judges, 24 magistrates*
Jury trials

Jurisdiction:
- Exclusive civil ($5,001 - no maximum). Small claims (up to $5,000).
- Exclusive domestic relations.
- Exclusive criminal.
- Exclusive juvenile.
- Exclusive traffic/other violations, except for most parking cases (which are handled administratively).

GENERAL JURISDICTION COURT

*Does not include senior judges that serve on a part-time basis.

Court structure as of Fiscal Year 2015.

Appellate level
Trial level
↑   Route of appeal

FLORIDA

Chief Justice
Jorge Labarga
Supreme Court Building, 500 South
Duval Street, Tallahassee, FL 32399
(850) 413-8371

Justices of the Supreme Court
Charles T. Canady
R. Fred Lewis
Barbara J. Pariente
James E. C. Perry
Ricky L. Polston
Peggy A. Quince

Clerk of the Supreme Court
John A. Tomasino
Supreme Court Building,
500 South Duval Street,
Tallahassee, FL 32399-1925
(850) 488-0125

Court System Website
ww.floridasupremecourt.org

Court Administration
Elisabeth H. Goodner
State Courts Administrator
Supreme Court Building,
500 South Duval Street,
Tallahassee, FL 32399-1900

Governor
Richard Lynn "Rick" Scott (R)
The Capitol,
Tallahassee, FL 32399-0001
(850) 488-7146

State Website
www.myflorida.com

State Capitol Main Phone
(850) 488-1234

Attorney General
Pamela J. Bondi (R)
The Capitol, Plaza Level One,
Tallahassee, FL 32399-1050
(850) 245-0140

Secretary of State
Kenneth W. "Ken" Detzner
500 South Bronough Street,
Tallahassee, FL 32399-0250
(850) 245-6524
secretaryofstate@dos.myflorida.com

Vital Statistics
Kenneth T. "Ken" Jones
Vital Statistics Administrator,
Department of Health
1217 Pearl Street,
Jacksonville, FL 32231
(904) 359-6900
vitalstats@doh.state.fl.us

Supreme Court
7 justices sit 5-judge panels and en banc
Jurisdiction:
- Appeal by right criminal, civil, administrative agency.
- Appeal by permission criminal, civil, administrative agency.
- Exclusive death penalty.
- Original proceeding writ application. Exclusive bar/judiciary, certified question, advisory opinion.

COURT OF LAST RESORT

District Courts of Appeal (5 courts)
61 judges sit in 3-judge panels
Jurisdiction:
- Appeal by right criminal, civil, administrative agency. Interlocutory appeals in criminal, civil, administrative agency.
- Appeal by permission criminal, civil, administrative agency.
- Original proceeding writ application.

INTERMEDIATE APPELLATE COURT

Circuit Court (20 circuits)
599 judges
Jury trials except in appeals
Jurisdiction:
- Tort, contract, real property ($15,001 - no maximum), miscellaneous civil. Exclusive mental health, probate/estate, civil appeals.
- Domestic relations.
- Felony, exclusive criminal appeals.
- Exclusive juvenile.

GENERAL JURISDICTION COURT

County Court (67 counties)
322 judges
Jury trials
Jurisdiction:
- Tort contract, real property ($5,001 - $15,000), miscellaneous civil. Exclusive small claims (up to $5,000).
- Dissolution/divorce.
- Preliminary hearings. Exclusive misdemeanor.
- Exclusive traffic/other violations, except parking (which is handled administratively).

LIMITED JURISDICTION COURT

Court structure as of Fiscal Year 2015.

☐ Appellate level
☐ Trial level
↑ Route of appeal

       State Court Clerks and County Courthouses

GEORGIA

Chief Justice
Hugh P. Thompson
State Judicial Building
40 Capitol Street, Room 507,
Atlanta, GA 30334-9003
(404) 656-3472

Justices of the Supreme Court
Robert Benham
Keith R. Blackwell
Carol W. Hunstein
P. Harris Hines
Harold D. Melton
David E. Nahmias

Clerk of the Supreme Court
Therese S. "Tee" Barnes
State Judicial Building,
244 Washington Street, SW, Room 572,
Atlanta, GA 30334
(404) 656-3470

Court System Website
www.gasupreme.us

Court Administration
Cynthia Hinrichs Clanton (Acting)
Director, Administrative Office of the
Georgia Courts
244 Washington Street, SW, Suite 300,
Atlanta, GA 30334
(404) 656-5171

Governor
Nathan Deal (R)
203 State Capitol, Atlanta, GA 30334
(404) 656-1776

State Website
www.georgia.gov

State Capitol Main Phone
(404) 656-2000

Attorney General
Samuel S. "Sam" Olens (R)
40 Capitol Square, SW,
Atlanta, GA 30334
(404) 483-2477

Secretary of State
Brian P. Kemp (R)
214 State Capitol, Atlanta, GA 30334
(404) 656-2881

Vital Statistics
Donna Moore
Vital Records Director,
Department of Public Health [DPH]
(404) 679-4702
donna.moore@dph.ga.gov

Supreme Court
7 justices sit en banc

Jurisdiction:
- Appeal by right criminal, civil, administrative agency.
- Appeal by permission criminal, civil, administrative agency. Interlocutory appeals in criminal, civil, administrative agency.
- Exclusive death penalty.
- Exclusive original proceeding habeas corpus writ, bar/judiciary, certified question, advisory opinion.

Capitol felonies; constitutional issues title to land; wills, equity and divorce

Court of Appeals (4 divisions)
12 judges sit in 3-judge panels

Jurisdiction:
- Appeal by right criminal, civil, administrative agency.
- Appeal by permission criminal, civil, administrative agency. Interlocutory appeals in criminal, civil, administrative agency.

Superior Court (159 counties, 49 circuits)
209 judges authorized
Jury trials

Jurisdiction:
- Tort, contract, probate/wills/intestate, civil appeals, miscellaneous civil. Exclusive real property.
- Exclusive domestic relations.
- Misdemeanor. Exclusive felony, criminal appeals.
- Traffic infractions, ordinance violations.

Only for counties with population over 96,000 where probate judge is attorney practicing at least 7 years.

Civil Court (Bibb and Richmond counties)
4 judges
Jury trials

Jurisdiction:
- Tort, contract [$0 - $25,000 (Bibb Co.); $0 - $45,000 (Richmond Co.)].
- Preliminary hearings, misdemeanor.

County Recorder's Court
(4 courts)
14 judges
No jury trials

Jurisdiction:
- Preliminary hearings, misdemeanors.
- Traffic/other violations.

Probate Court (159 circuits)
159 judges, 12 associate judges
Jury trials only in counties with populations greater than 96,000

Jurisdiction:
Exclusive mental health,
- probate/estate.
Preliminary hearings,
- misdemeanor.

State Court (70 courts)
123 judges
Jury trials

Jurisdiction:
- Tort, contract, civil appeals, miscellaneous civil.
- Preliminary hearings, misdemeanor.
- Traffic infractions.

Magistrate Court
(159 courts)
159 chief magistrates, and 333 magistrates
No jury trials

Jurisdiction:
- Small claims (up to $15,000).
- Preliminary hearings, misdemeanor.
- Ordinance violations.

Municipal Courts* (370 courts)
352 judges
No jury trials

Jurisdiction:
- Small claims (up to $15,000) in Columbus Co.
- Tort, contract ($0 - $25,000 Bibb Co.); ($0 - $45,000 Richmond Co.).
- Preliminary hearings, misdemeanor.
- Traffic/other violations.

Juvenile Court (159 courts)
138 judges
In Ogeechee circuit, 4 of the full-time judges are superior court judges who hear juvenile court cases.
No jury trials

Jurisdiction:
- Custody.
- Juvenile.
- Traffic infractions.

*A small number of special courts authorized by the Georgia constitution, have limited civil or criminal jurisdiction throughout a designated county.

COURT OF LAST RESORT
INTERMEDIATE APPELLATE COURT
GENERAL JURISDICTION COURT
LIMITED JURISDICTION COURT

☐ Appellate level
☐ Trial level
↑ Route of appeal

Court structure as of Fiscal Year 2015.

HAWAII

Chief Justice
Mark E. Recktenwald
Ali'iolani Hale, 417 South King Street,
Honolulu, HI 96813-2902
(808) 539-4735

Justices of the Supreme Court
Sabrina McKenna
Paula A. Nakayama
Richard W. Pollack
Michael D. Wilson

Clerk of the Supreme Court
Rochelle R. Hasuko
Ali'iolani Hale, 417 South King Street,
Room 103, Honolulu, HI 96813-2902
(808) 539-4919

Court System Website
www.courts.state.hi.us

Court Administration
Rodney A. Maile
Administrative Director of the Courts
Ali'iolani Hale, 417 South King Street,
Room 206A, Honolulu, HI 96813-2902
(808) 539-4900
rodney.a.maile@courts.hawaii.gov

Governor
David Y. Ige (D)
State Capitol, Honolulu, HI 96813
(808) 586-8201

State Website
www.hawaii.gov

State Capitol Main Phone
(808) 586-2211

Attorney General
David M. Louie
425 Queen Street, Honolulu, HI 96813
(808) 586-1282
david.m.louie@hawaii.gov

Lieutenant Governor
Shan S. Tsutsui (D)
State Capitol, Honolulu, HI 96813
(808) 586-0255
shan.tsutsui@hawaii.gov

Vital Statistics
Alvin Onaka, PhD
State Registrar and Chief, Office of
Health Status Monitoring [OHSM]
P.O. Box 3378, Honolulu, HI 96801
(808) 586-4600
alvino@hawaii.edu

Supreme Court
5 justices sit en banc

Jurisdiction:
- Appeal by right criminal, civil, administrative agency.
- Exclusive appeal by permission criminal, civil, administrative agency. Interlocutory appeals in criminal, civil, administrative agency.
- Original proceeding writ application, certified question. Exclusive bar/judiciary.

Intermediate Court of Appeals
6 judges sit in 3-judge panels

Jurisdiction:
- Appeal by right criminal, civil, administrative agency. Interlocutory in criminal, civil, administrative agency.
- Original proceeding writ application, certified question.

Circuit Court and Family Court (4 circuits)
32 circuit judges, 6 of which are designated Family Court judges, plus 17 District Family Court judges
Jury trials

Jurisdiction:
- Tort contract, real property ($10,000 - no maximum) [concurrent from $10,000 - $25,000], miscellaneous civil. Mental health, probate/estate, administrative agency appeals.
- Exclusive domestic relations.
- Juvenile.
- Traffic infractions.

District Court (4 circuits)
22 judges, 41 Per Diem Judges
No jury trials

Jurisdiction:
- Tort, contract, real property ($0 - $25,000) [concurrent from $10,000 - $25,000 (civil nonjury)], miscellaneous civil. Exclusive small claims up to ($5,000) unless residential security deposit case.
- Preliminary hearings, misdemeanor.
- Traffic infractions. Exclusive parking, ordinance violations.

COURT OF LAST RESORT

INTERMEDIATE APPELLATE COURT

GENERAL JURISDICTION COURT

LIMITED JURISDICTION COURT

Court structure as of Fiscal Year 2015.

Appellate level
Trial level
↑   Route of appeal

IDAHO

Chief Justice
Roger S. Burdick
P.O. Box 83720, Boise, ID 83720-0101
(208) 334-3464

Justices of the Supreme Court
Daniel T. Eismann
Joel D. Horton
Jim Jones
Warren E. Jones

Clerk of the Supreme Court
Stephen W. Kenyon
P.O. Box 83720, Boise, ID 83720-0101
(208) 334-2210

Court System Website
www.isc.idaho.gov

Court Administration
Linda Copple Trout
Administrative Director of the Courts
P.O. Box 83720, Boise, ID 83720-0101
(208) 334-2246

Governor
C. L. "Butch" Otter (R)
P. O. Box 83720, Boise, ID 83720
(208) 334-2100

State Website
www.idaho.gov

State Capitol Main Phone
(208) 334-2100

Attorney General
Lawrence G. Wasden (R)
P.O. Box 83720, Boise, ID 83720-0010
(208) 334-2400

Secretary of State
Lawerence E. Denney
P.O. Box 83720, Boise, ID 83720-0080
(208) 334-2300
ldenney@sos.idaho.gov

Vital Statistics
James Aydelotte
Health Policy and Vital Statistics
Bureau Chief, Public Health Division,
Department of Health and Welfare
450 West State Street,
Boise, ID 83720-0036
(208) 334-4969
aydelotj@dhw.idaho.gov

Supreme Court
5 justices sit en banc
Assigns cases to the Court of Appeals

Jurisdiction:
- Appeal by right criminal, civil. Exclusive administrative agency.
- Exclusive appeal by permission criminal, civil, administrative agency. Interlocutory appeals in criminal, civil, administrative agency.
- Exclusive death penalty.
- Original proceeding writ application. Exclusive bar discipline/eligibility, judicial qualification, certified question.

Court of Appeals
4 judges sit in 3-judge panels and en banc

Jurisdiction:
- Appeal by right criminal, civil.

District Court (7 districts)
44 district judges
Jury trials

Jurisdiction:
- Tort, contract, real property rights ($10,000 - no maximum), probate/estate, mental health, miscellaneous civil.
- Domestic relations.
- Exclusive felony and criminal appeals. Misdemeanor.
- Juvenile.

Magistrates Division
94 full-time magistrate judges
Jury trials

Jurisdiction:
- Tort, contract, real property rights ($0 - $10,000), small claims (up to $5,000), probate/estate, mental health, miscellaneous civil.
- Domestic relations.
- Preliminary hearings, misdemeanor.
- Juvenile.
- Exclusive traffic/other violations.

COURT OF LAST RESORT

INTERMEDIATE APPELLATE COURT

GENERAL JURISDICTION COURT

LIMITED JURISDICTION COURT

Notes: The Magistrates Division of the District Court functions as a limited jurisdiction court. There are an additional 44 senior judges that serve the judicial branch.

Court structure as of Fiscal Year 2015.

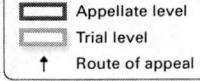

☐ Appellate level
☐ Trial level
↑ Route of appeal

ILLINOIS

Chief Justice
Rita B. Garman
1819 - 4th Avenue,
Rock Island, IL 61201
(309) 794-3608

Justices of the Supreme Court
Anne M. Burke
Charles E. Freeman
Lloyd A. Karmeier
Thomas L. Kilbride
Mary Jane Theis
Robert R. Thomas

Clerk of the Supreme Court
Carolyn Taft Grosboll
Supreme Court Building,
200 East Capitol Avenue,
Springfield, IL 62701
(217) 782-2035

Court System Website
www.state.il.us/court

Court Administration
Michael J. Tardy
Director, Administrative Office of the
Illinois Courts
222 North LaSalle Street, 13th Floor,
Chicago, IL 60601
(217) 558-4490

Governor
Bruce V. Rauner (R)
207 State Capitol Building,
Springfield, IL 62706
(217) 782-6830

State Website
www.illinois.gov

State Capitol Main Phone
(217) 782-2000

Attorney General
Lisa Madigan (D)
500 South Second Street,
Springfield, IL 62706
(217) 782-9000

Secretary of State
Jesse White (D)
213 State Capitol Building,
Springfield, IL 62756
(217) 782-2201

Vital Statistics
Joseph "Joe" Aiello
Division Chief, Division of Vital
Records, Illinois Department of Public
Health [IDPH]
925 East Ridgely Avenue,
Springfield, IL 62702
(217) 785-3163

Supreme Court
7 justices sit en banc

Jurisdiction:
- Appeal by right criminal, civil, administrative agency. Interlocutory appeals in criminal, civil, administrative agency.
- Appeal by permission in criminal, civil, administrative agency. Interlocutory appeals in criminal, civil, administrative agency.
- Exclusive death penalty.
- Original proceeding writ application. Exclusive bar admission, bar discipline/eligibility, certified question.

COURT OF LAST RESORT

Appellate Court (5 districts)
54 authorized judges, with 12 circuit court judges assigned to the appellate court, sit in 3-judge panels

Jurisdiction:
- Appeal by right criminal, civil, limited administrative agency. Interlocutory appeals in criminal, civil, limited administrative agency.
- Appeal by permission criminal, civil, limited administrative agency. Interlocutory appeals in criminal, civil, limited administrative agency.
- Original proceeding writ application.

INTERMEDIATE APPELLATE COURT

Circuit Court (23 circuits)
525 circuit judges, 382 associate judges
Jury trials permissible in most cases

Jurisdiction:
- Exclusive civil (including administrative agency appeals), small claims (up to $10,000).
- Exclusive domestic relations.
- Exclusive criminal.
- Exclusive juvenile.
- Exclusive traffic/other violations.

GENERAL JURISDICTION COURT

Court structure as of Fiscal Year 2015.

☐ Appellate level
☐ Trial level
↑ Route of appeal

INDIANA

Chief Justice
Loretta Hogan Rush
200 West Washington Street,
Indianapolis, IN 46204-3466
(317) 232-2540

Justices of the Supreme Court
Steven H. David
Brent E. Dickson
Mark S. Massa
Robert D. Rucker

Clerk of the Supreme Court
Kevin S. Smith
200 West Washington Street,
Indianapolis, IN 46204-2732
(317) 232-2540

Court System Website
www.courts.in.gov

Court Administration
Lilia G. Judson
Executive Director
30 South Meridian Street, Suite 500
Indianapolis, IN 46204-3568
(317) 232-2542

Governor
Mike Pence (R)
P.O. Box 1038, Anderson, IN 46015
(317) 232-4567

State Website
www.in.gov

State Capitol Main Phone
(317) 232-1000

Attorney General
Gregory F. "Greg" Zoeller (R)
302 West Washington Street, 5th Floor,
Indianapolis, IN 46204
(317) 232-6201

Secretary of State
Connie Lawson (R)
201 Statehouse, 200 West Washington
Street, Indianapolis, IN 46204-2790
(317) 232-6532
sos@sos.in.gov

Vital Statistics
Brian Carnes
State Registrar, Health Care Quality and
Regulatory Services Commission
P.O. Box 7125, Indianapolis, IN 46206
(317) 233-7523
bcarnes@isdh.in.gov

Supreme Court
5 justices sit en banc
Jurisdiction:
- Appeal by right felony, tort, contract, and real property, probate, family.
- Appeal by permission criminal, civil, administrative agency.
- Exclusive death penalty.
- Exclusive original proceeding writ application, bar/judiciary, certified question.

Court of Appeals (5 districts)
15 judges sit in 3-judge panels
Jurisdiction:
- Appeal by right criminal, civil, limited administrative agency.
- Appeal by permission interlocutory appeals in criminal, civil, limited administrative agency.

Tax Court
1 judge
Jurisdiction:
- Appeal by right revenue (tax).

Superior, Circuit, and Probate Court
315 judges

Superior Court*
210 judges
Jury trials except small claims, probate/estate, mental health, domestic relations, and juvenile
Jurisdiction:
- Tort, contract, real property, small claims (up to $6,000), mental health, probate/estate, civil appeals, miscellaneous civil.
- Domestic relations.
- Felony, misdemeanor, criminal appeals, preliminary hearings.
- Juvenile.
- Traffic infractions.

Circuit Court (91 circuits)
104 judges
Jury trials except small claims
Jurisdiction:
- Tort, contract, real property, small claims (up to $6000), mental health, probate/estate, civil appeals, miscellaneous civil.
- Domestic relations.
- Felony, misdemeanor, criminal appeals, preliminary hearings.
- Juvenile.
- Traffic infractions.

Probate Court
(St. Joseph)
1 judge
Jury trials
Jurisdiction:
- Probate/estate, miscellaneous civil.
- Adoption.
- Miscellaneous criminal.
- Juvenile.

City and Town Court
69 judges

City Court (47 courts)
44 judges
Jury trials
Jurisdiction:
- Tort, contract ($0-$500 to $3,000), small claims (up to $3,000).
- Misdemeanor.
- Traffic/other violations.

Town Court (27 courts)
25 judges
Jury trials
Jurisdiction:
- Misdemeanor.
- Traffic/other violations.

Small Claims Court of Marion County (9 courts)
9 judges
No jury trials
Jurisdiction:
- Small claims (up to $6,000), miscellaneous civil.

COURT OF LAST RESORT

INTERMEDIATE APPELLATE COURT

GENERAL JURISDICTION COURT

LIMITED JURISDICTION COURT

* Effective January 1, 1996, all Municipal Courts became Superior Court. Effective January 1, 2009, all County Courts merged with Superior Court.

[ ] Appellate level
[ ] Trial level
↑ Route of appeal

Court structure as of Fiscal Year 2015.

IOWA

Chief Justice
Mark S. Cady
P.O. Box 507, Fort Dodge, IA 50501
(515) 281-5911

Justices of the Supreme Court
Brent R. Appel
Daryl L. Hecht
Edward M. Mansfield
Thomas D. Waterman
David S. Wiggins
Bruce Zager

Clerk of the Supreme Court
Donna Humphal
Iowa Judicial Building,
1111 East Court Avenue,
Des Moines, IA 50319
(515) 281-5911

Court System Website
www.iowacourts.gov

Court Administration
David K. Boyd
State Court Administrator
Iowa Judicial Building,
1111 East Court Avenue,
Des Moines, IA 50319
(515) 281-5241

Governor
Terry E. Branstad (R)
1007 East Grand Avenue,
Des Moines, IA 50319
(515) 281-5211

State Website
www.iowa.gov

State Capitol Main Phone
(515) 281-5011

Attorney General
Thomas J. "Tom" Miller (D)
Hoover Building, 2nd Floor,
Des Moines, IA 50319
(515) 281-8373

Secretary of State
Paul D. Pate (R)
State Capitol, 1007 East Grand Avenue,
Room 105, Des Moines, IA 50319-0146
(515) 281-5204

Vital Statistics
Melissa R. Bird
Bureau Chief, Bureau of Health
Statistics, Iowa Department of Public
Health [IDPH]
Lucas State Office Building, 321 East
12th Street, Des Moines, IA 50319-0075
(515) 281-6762

COURT OF LAST RESORT

Supreme Court
7 justices sit en banc
Assigns cases to the Court of Appeals

Jurisdiction:
- Appeal by right criminal, civil, administrative agency.
- Exclusive appeal by permission criminal, civil, administrative agency. Interlocutory appeals in criminal, civil, administrative agency.
- Original proceeding writ application. Exclusive bar/judiciary, certified question, advisory opinion.

INTERMEDIATE APPELLATE COURT

Court of Appeals
9 judges sit in 3-panels and en banc

Jurisdiction:
- Appeal by right criminal, civil, administrative agency. Interlocutory appeals in criminal, civil, administrative agency.
- Original proceeding writ application.

GENERAL JURISDICTION COURT

District Court (8 districts in 99 counties)
114 authorized district judges, 69 district associate judges, 38 senior judges,
5 associate juvenile judges, 118 part-time magistrates, and 1 associate probate judge
Jury trials except in small claims, juvenile, equity cases, city and county ordinance
violations, mental health cases

Jurisdiction:
- Exclusive civil. Small claims (up to $5,000).
- Exclusive domestic relations.
- Exclusive criminal.
- Exclusive juvenile.
- Exclusive traffic/other violations, except for uncontested parking.

Court structure as of Fiscal Year 2015.

Appellate level
Trial level
↑ Route of appeal

KANSAS

Chief Justice
Lawton R. Nuss
389 Kansas Judicial Center,
301 SW Tenth Avenue,
Topeka, KS 66612-1507
(785) 296-4898

Justices of the Supreme Court
Carol A. Beier
William Daniel Biles
Lee Alan Johnson
Marla J. Luckert
Eric S. Rosen
Caleb Stegall

Clerk of the Supreme Court
Heather L. Smith
Clerk of the Appellate Courts
374 Kansas Judicial Center,
301 SW Tenth Avenue,
Topeka, KS 66612-1507
(785) 296-3229

Court System Website
www.kscourts.org

Court Administration
Nancy Maydew Dixon
Judicial Administrator
Kansas Judicial Center, 301 SW Tenth
Avenue, Topeka, KS 66612

Governor
Samuel Dale "Sam" Brownback (R)
State Capitol, 2nd Floor,
Topeka, KS 66612-1590
(785) 368-8500

State Website
www.kansas.gov

State Capitol Main Phone
(785) 296-5059

Attorney General
Derek Schmidt (R)
120 Southwest 10th Avenue, 2nd Floor,
Topeka, KS 66612-1597
(785) 296-2215

Secretary of State
Kris W. Kobach (R)
Memorial Hall, 120 S.W. 10th Avenue,
Topeka, KS 66612-1594
(785) 296-4575

Vital Statistics
Dr. Elizabeth "Lou" Saadi, PhD
State Registrar, Office of Vital
Statistics, Kansas Department of Health
and Environment [KDHE]
Curtis State Office Building,
1000 Southwest Jackson Street,
Suite 120, Topeka, KS 66612-2221
(785) 296-1400

Supreme Court
7 justices sit en banc

Jurisdiction:
- Appeal by right criminal, tort, contract, and real property, probate, family, administrative agency.
- Appeal by permission criminal, civil, administrative agency. Interlocutory appeals in criminal, civil, administrative agency.
- Exclusive death penalty.
- Original proceeding writ application. Exclusive bar/judiciary, certified question, advisory opinion.

COURT OF LAST RESORT

Court of Appeals
14 judges

Jurisdiction:
- Appeal by right criminal, civil, limited administrative agency. Interlocutory appeals in criminal, limited administrative agency.
- Appeal by permission interlocutory appeals in tort, contract, and real property, probate, family.
- Original proceeding limited writ application.

INTERMEDIATE APPELLATE COURT

District Court (31 districts)
244 judges (includes 73 magistrates)
Jury trials except in small claims

Jurisdiction:
- Exclusive civil (including civil appeals). Small claims (up to $4,000).
- Exclusive domestic relations.
- DWI/DUI. Exclusive felony, misdemeanor, criminal appeals.
- Exclusive juvenile.
- Traffic infractions.

GENERAL JURISDICTION COURT

Municipal Court (388 cities)
255 judges
No jury trials

Jurisdiction:
- DWI/DUI.
- Traffic infractions. Exclusive ordinance violations, parking.

LIMITED JURISDICTION COURT

Court structure as of Fiscal Year 2015.

☐ Appellate level
☐ Trial level
↑ Route of appeal

KENTUCKY

Chief Justice
John D. Minton, Jr.
231 State Capitol, 700 Capital Avenue,
Frankfort, KY 40601
(502) 564-4162

Justices of the Supreme Court
Lisabeth Hughes Abramson
David A. Barber
Bill Cunningham
Michelle M. Keller, RN
Mary C. Noble
Daniel J. Venters

Clerk of the Supreme Court
Susan Stokley Clary
Court Administrator, General Counsel
and Clerk of the Supreme Court
State Capitol Building, 700 Capital Ave,
Room 235, Frankfort, KY 40601
(502) 564-4176

Court System Website
www.kycourts.net

Court Administration
Laurie K. Dudgeon
Director, Kentucky Administrative
Office of the Courts
100 Millcreek Park,
Frankfort, KY 40601
(502) 573-2350

Governor
Steven L. "Steve" Beshear (D)
100 State Capitol, 700 Capital Avenue,
Suite 100, Frankfort, KY 40601
(502) 564-2611

State Website
www.kentucky.gov

State Capitol Main Phone
(502) 564-2500

Attorney General
Jack Conway (D)
State Capitol, 700 Capitol Avenue,
Suite 118, Frankfort, KY 40601
(502) 696-5300

Secretary of State
Alison (Lundergan) Grimes (D)
P.O. Box 718, Frankfort, KY 40601
(502) 564-3490

Vital Statistics
Christina Stewart
Manager, Office of Vital Statistics,
Cabinet for Health and Family Services
275 East Main Street,
Frankfort, KY 40601
(502) 564-4212

Supreme Court
7 justices sit en banc
Jurisdiction:
- Appeal by right felony (limited to 20 yr+ sentence), workers' compensation. Interlocutory appeals in felony, workers' compensation.
- Appeal by permission criminal, civil, administrative agency. Interlocutory appeals in criminal, civil, administrative agency.
- Exclusive death penalty.
- Original proceeding writ application. Exclusive bar/judiciary, certified question, advisory opinion.

COURT OF LAST RESORT

Court of Appeals
14 judges sit in 3-judge panels, (sit en banc in a policy-making capacity)
Jurisdiction:
- Appeal by right criminal (limited to less than 20 year sentence), civil, limited administrative agency.
- Appeal by permission misdemeanor, civil, limited administrative agency. Interlocutory appeals in misdemeanor, civil, limited administrative agency.
- Original proceeding limited writ application.

INTERMEDIATE APPELLATE COURT

Circuit Court (57 judicial circuits)
102 judges plus domestic relations commissioners
Jury trials except in appeals
Jurisdiction:
- Tort, contract, real property ($4,001 - no maximum), interstate support, probate/estate. Exclusive civil appeals, miscellaneous civil.
- Domestic relations.
- Misdemeanor. Exclusive felony, criminal appeals.
- Juvenile.

Family Court (71 counties)
51 judges
Jury trials
Jurisdiction:
- Domestic relations.
- Domestic violence.
- Juvenile.
- Civil (contract, probate).

GENERAL JURISDICTION COURT

District Court (60 judicial districts)
116 judges plus trial commissioners
Jury trials in most cases
Jurisdiction:
- Tort, contract, real property ($0 - $4,000), probate/estate. Exclusive mental health, small claims (up to $1,500).
- Domestic relations.
- Preliminary hearings, misdemeanor.
- Juvenile.
- Exclusive traffic/other violations.

LIMITED JURISDICTION COURT

Note: There are also 60 senior status judges that can serve on any court except the Supreme Court.

Court structure as of Fiscal Year 2015.

☐ Appellate level
☐ Trial level
↑ Route of appeal

LOUISIANA

Chief Justice
Bernette Joshua Johnson
400 Royal Street,
New Orleans, LA 70130
(504) 310-2359

Justices of the Supreme Court
Marcus R. Clark
Greg Gerard Guidry
Jefferson D. Hughes, III
Jeannette Theriot Knoll
John L. Weimer

Clerk of the Supreme Court
John Tarlton Olivier
400 Royal Street, Suite 4200,
New Orleans, LA 70130-2104
(504) 310-2300

Court System Website
www.lasc.org

Court Administration
Sandra Vujnovich
Judicial Administrator
400 Royal Street, Suite 1190,
New Orleans, LA 70130
(504) 310-2550

Governor
Piyush "Bobby" Jindal (R)
P.O. Box 94004,
Baton Rouge, LA 70804-9004
(225) 342-7015

State Website
www.louisiana.gov

State Capitol Main Phone
(225) 342-6600

Attorney General
James D. "Buddy" Caldwell (R)
P.O. Box 94005,
Baton Rouge, LA 70804-9005
(225) 326-6708

Secretary of State
John Thomas "Tom" Schedler (R)
8585 Archives Avenue,
Baton Rouge, LA 70809
(225) 922-2880

Vital Statistics
Devin George
State Registrar and Center Director,
Center of State Registrar and Vital
Records, Department of Health and
Hospitals [DHH]
P.O. Box 60630,
New Orleans, LA 70160
(504) 593-5100

Supreme Court
7 justices sit en banc
Jurisdiction:
- Appeal by right limited criminal, civil, administrative agency.
- Appeal by permission criminal, civil, administrative agency. Interlocutory appeals in criminal, civil, administrative agency.
- Exclusive death penalty.
- Original proceeding application for writ. Exclusive bar/judiciary, certified question.

COURT OF LAST RESORT

Court Appeals (5 courts)
53 judges sit in 3-judge panels
Jurisdiction:
- Appeal by right criminal, civil, administrative agency.
- Original proceeding application for writ.

INTERMEDIATE APPELLATE COURT

District Court
218 judges, 11 commissioners

District Court (64 parishes)
218 judges, 11 commissioners
Jury trials in most cases
Jurisdiction:
- Tort, contract, real property, mental health. Exclusive probate/estate, civil trial court appeals, miscellaneous civil.
- Domestic relations.
- Misdemeanor. Exclusive felony, criminal appeals.
- Juvenile.
- Traffic infractions.

Juvenile Court (4 courts)
14 judges
No jury trials
Jurisdiction:
- Mental health.
- Support, adoption.
- Juvenile.

Family Court (1 in East Baton Rouge)
4 judges
No jury trials
Jurisdiction:
- Mental health.
- Domestic relations.
- Domestic violence.
- Juvenile.

GENERAL JURISDICTION COURT

Justice of the Peace Court
(~382 courts)
~382 justices of the peace
No jury trials
Jurisdiction:
- Tort, contract ($0 - $5000), small claims (up to $2,000).
- Traffic/other violations.

Mayor's Court
(~250 courts)
~250 judges (mayors)
No jury trials
Jurisdiction:
- Traffic/other violations.

City and Parish Courts
(52 courts)
73 judges
No jury trials
Jurisdiction:
- Tort, contract ($0 - $50,000, varies by court), small claims (up to $3,000), civil appeals.
- Paternity.
- Preliminary hearings, misdemeanor.
- Juvenile.
- Traffic/other violations.

LIMITED JURISDICTION COURT

Court structure as of Fiscal Year 2015.

- Appellate level
- Trial level
- ↑ Route of appeal

MAINE

Chief Justice
Leigh I. Saufley
Main Supreme Judicial Court,
205 Newbury Street, Room 139,
Portland, ME 04101-4125
(207) 822-4286

Justices of the Supreme Court
Donald G. Alexander
Ellen A. Gorman
Jeffrey L. Hjelm
Thomas E. Humphrey (Designate)
Joseph M. Jabar
Andrew M. Mead

Clerk of the Supreme Court
Matthew E. Pollack
Maine Supreme Judicial Court,
205 Newbury Street, Room 139,
Portland, ME 04101-4125
(207) 822-4146

Court System Website
www.courts.state.me.us

Court Administration
James T. Glessner
State Court Administrator
P.O. Box 4820,
Portland, ME 04112-4820
(207) 822-0710

Governor
Paul R. LePage (R)
One State House Station,
Augusta, ME 04333
(207) 287-3531

State Website
www.maine.gov

State Capitol Main Phone
(207) 264-9494

Attorney General
Janet T. Mills (D)
Six State House Station,
Augusta, ME 04333
(207) 626-8800

Secretary of State
Matthew Dunlap (D)
Nash Building, 148 State House Station,
2nd Floor, Augusta, ME 04333-0148
(207) 626-8400

Vital Statistics
Marty Henson
Data, Research & Vital Statistics Office
Director, Maine Center for Disease
Control and Prevention, Department of
Health and Human Services [DHHS]
244 Water Street, Augusta, ME 04330
(207) 287-3771

Supreme Judicial Court Sitting as Law Court
7 justices sit in 3-judge panels and en banc

Jurisdiction:
- Exclusive appeal by right criminal, civil, limited administrative agency. Interlocutory appeals in criminal, civil, administrative agency.
- Exclusive appeal by permission criminal (limited to extradition, 1 yr+ sentence), limited administrative agency.
- Exclusive original proceeding application for writ, bar/judiciary, certified question.

COURT OF LAST RESORT

District Court (29 locations)
36 judges plus 8 family law magistrates
No jury trials

Jurisdiction:
- Tort, contract, real property rights ($0 - no maximum). Exclusive small claims (up to $4,500), mental health.
- Exclusive domestic relations (except for adoption).
- Felony, preliminary hearings, misdemeanor.
- Exclusive juvenile.
- Traffic infractions, ordinance violations. Exclusive parking.

Superior Court (19 locations)
17 justices
Jury trials in some cases

Jurisdiction:
- Tort, contract, real property, civil appeals, miscellaneous civil.
- Felony, misdemeanor, criminal appeals.

GENERAL JURISDICTION COURT

Probate Court (16 counties)
16 part-time judges
No jury trials

Jurisdiction:
- Exclusive probate/estate jurisdiction.
- Exclusive adoption.

LIMITED JURISDICTION COURT

Note: The Administrative Court was eliminated effective March 15, 2001, with the caseload absorbed by the District Court.

Court structure as of Fiscal Year 2015.

Appellate level
Trial level
↑ Route of appeal

MARYLAND

Chief Judge — Court of Appeals
Mary Ellen Barbera
Judicial Center, 50 Maryland Avenue,
Rockville, MD 20850
(240) 777-9320

Judges of the Appeals Court
Sally D. Adkins
Lynne A. Battaglia
Clayton Greene, Jr.
Glenn T. Harrell, Jr.
Robert N. McDonald
Shirley M. Watts

Clerk of the Appeals Court
Bessie M. Decker
Robert C. Murphy Courts of Appeal
Building, 361 Rowe Boulevard,
Annapolis, MD 21401
(410) 260-1500

Court System Website
www.mdcourts.gov

Court Administration
Pamela Q. Harris
State Court Administrator
Maryland Judicial Ctr, 580 Taylor Ave,
Annapolis, MD 21401
(410) 260-1295

Governor
Lawrence J. "Larry" Hogan, Jr.
State Capitol, 100 State Circle,
Annapolis, MD 21401
(410) 974-3901

State Website
www.maryland.gov

State Capitol Main Phone
(410) 974-3901

Attorney General
Brian E. Frosh (D)
200 Saint Paul Place,
Baltimore, MD 21202-2021
(410) 576-6300

Secretary of State
John Casper Wobensmith
State House, 16 Francis Street,
Annapolis, MD 21401
(410) 974-5521

Vital Statistics
Geneva G. Sparks
Vital Records Deputy Director, Vital
Statistics Administration, Department of
Health and Mental Hygiene [DHMH]
6550 Reistertown Road,
Baltimore, MD 21215
(410) 764-3186

Court of Appeals
7 judges sit en banc

Jurisdiction:
- Limited appeal by right civil. Limited interlocutory appeals in civil.
- Appeal by permission criminal, civil, administrative agency. Interlocutory appeals in criminal, civil, administrative agency.
- Exclusive death penalty.
- Original proceeding writ application. Exclusive bar/judiciary, certified question.

COURT OF LAST RESORT

Court of Special Appeals
13 judges sit in 3-judge panels and en banc

Jurisdiction:
- Appeal by right criminal, civil, administrative agency. Interlocutory appeals in criminal, civil, administrative agency.
- Appeal by permission criminal, civil.
- Original proceeding writ application.

INTERMEDIATE APPELLATE COURT

Circuit Court (8 circuits in 24 counties)
161 judges
Jury trials in most cases

Jurisdiction:
- Tort, contract, real property ($5,000 - no maximum), probate/estate, miscellaneous civil. Exclusive mental health, civil appeals.
- Domestic relations.
- Felony, misdemeanor. Exclusive criminal appeals.
- Exclusive juvenile.

GENERAL JURISDICTION COURT

District Court (12 districts in 24 counties)
125 judges (plus 1 chief judge with administrative duties)
No jury trials

Jurisdiction:
- Tort, contract ($5,000 - $30,000), real property, miscellaneous civil. Exclusive small claims (up to $5,000).
- Civil protection/restraining orders.
- Felony, preliminary hearings, misdemeanor.
- Exclusive traffic/other violations.

Orphan's Court (23 counties)
68 judges
No jury trials

Jurisdiction:
- Probate/estate, except where such cases are handled by circuit court in Montgomery and Harford counties.

LIMITED JURISDICTION COURT

Court structure as of Fiscal Year 2015.

☐ Appellate level
☐ Trial level
↑ Route of appeal

MASSACHUSETTS

Chief Justice
Ralph D. Gants
One Pemberton Square,
Boston, MA 02108-1735
(617) 557-1020

Justices of the Supreme Court
Margot Botsford
Robert J. Cordy
Fernande R. V. "Nan" Duffly
Geraldine S. Hines
Barbara A. Lenk
Francis X. Spina

Clerk of the Supreme Court
Francis V. Kenneally
Clerk for the Commonwealth
One Pemberton Square, Suite 2500,
Boston, MA 02108-1750
(617) 557-1165

Court System Website
www.mass.gov/courts/sjc

Court Administration
Thomas Ambrosino
Executive Director
One Pemberton Square, Suite 2500,
Boston, MA 02108-1750
(617) 557-1194

Governor
Charles D. "Charlie" Baker, Jr. (R)
State House, Executive Office,
Room 360, Boston, MA 02133
(617) 725-4005

State Website
www.mass.gov

State Capitol Main Phone
(671) 725-4000

Attorney General
Maura Healey (D)
One Ashburton Place,
Boston, MA 02108-1518
(617) 727-2200

Secretary of the Commonwealth
William Francis Galvin (D)
McCormack Building,
One Ashburton Place, Room 1611,
Boston, MA 02108-1518
(617) 727-7030

Vital Statistics
Antonio "Tony" Sousa
Director, Bureau of Health
Information Research Statistics and
Evaluation, Department of Public Health
250 Washington Street, 6th Floor,
Boston, MA 02108
(617) 740-2617

Supreme Judicial Court
7 justices sit in 5-judge panels and en banc*

Jurisdiction:
- Appeal by permission criminal, civil, administrative agency. Appeal by right criminal (limited to 1st degree murder). Interlocutory appeals in criminal, civil, administrative agency.
- Exclusive original proceeding application for writ, bar/judiciary, certified question, advisory opinion.

Appeals Court
25 justices sit in 3-judge panels*

Jurisdiction:
- Appeal by right criminal, exclusive appeal by right, civil, administrative agency.
- Appeal by permission interlocutory appeals in criminal, civil, administrative agency.

Superior Court Department (14 divisions)
80 justices
Jury trials

Jurisdiction:
- Tort, contract, real property ($25,000 - no maximum), civil appeals, miscellaneous civil.
- Civil protection/restraining orders.
- Felony, misdemeanor.

District Court Department (62 divisions)
162 justices
Jury trials

Jurisdiction:
- Tort, contract, real property ($0 - $25,000), small claims (up to $7,000), mental health, civil appeals, miscellaneous civil.
- Civil protection/restraining orders.
- Felony, preliminary hearings, misdemeanor.
- Traffic/other violations.

Boston Municipal Court Department
(8 divisions)
30 justices
Jury trials

Jurisdiction:
- Tort, contract, real property rights ($0 - $25,000), small claims (up to $7,000), mental health, civil appeals, miscellaneous civil.
- Civil protection/restraining orders.
- Felony, preliminary hearings, misdemeanor.
- Traffic/other violations.

Juvenile Court Department
(11 divisions)
39 justices
Jury trials

Jurisdiction:
- Guardianship.
- Adoption.
- Juvenile.

Housing Court Department
(5 divisions)
10 justices
Jury trials except in small claims

Jurisdiction:
- Contract, small claims (up to $7,000).
- Preliminary hearings, misdemeanor.
- Ordinance violations.

Land Court Department
(1 statewide court)
7 justices
No jury trials

Jurisdiction:
- Mortgage foreclosure, real property.

Probate & Family Court Department
(14 divisions)
48 justices
No jury trials

Jurisdiction:
- Exclusive probate/estate, miscellaneous civil.
- Domestic relations. Exclusive divorce/dissolution.
- Juvenile dependency.

COURT OF LAST RESORT

INTERMEDIATE APPELLATE COURT

GENERAL JURISDICTION COURT

LIMITED JURISDICTION COURT

Note: All departments (general and limited jurisdiction trial courts) make up the Trial Court of Massachusetts. The Administrative Office of the Trial Court reports caseload data by Department; thus, each Department is treated as a unique jurisdiction reporting unit.

*The justices also sit individually in the "single justice" side of the court, on a rotating basis.

Court structure as of Fiscal Year 2015.

☐ Appellate level
☐ Trial level
↑ Route of appeal

MICHIGAN

Chief Justice
Robert P. Young, Jr.
Cadillac Place,
3034 West Grand Boulevard,
Suite 8-500,
Detroit, MI 48202-6034
(313) 972-3250

Justices of the Supreme Court
Richard H. Bernstein
Stephen J. Markman
Bridget McCormack
David Viviano
Brian K. Zahra

Clerk of the Supreme Court
Larry Royster
P.O. Box 30052, Lansing, MI 48909
(517) 373-0120

Court System Website
www.courts.mi.gov

Court Administration
John A. Hohman, Jr.
State Court Administrator
P.O. Box 30048, Lansing, MI 48909
(517) 373-0128

Governor
Richard D. "Rick" Snyder (R)
P.O. Box 30013, Lansing, MI 48909
(517) 373-3400

State Website
www.michigan.gov

State Capitol Main Phone
(517) 373-1837

Attorney General
William D. "Bill" Schuette (R)
P.O. Box 30212, Lansing, MI 48909
(517) 373-1110

Secretary of State
Ruth Johnson (R)
Richard H. Austin Building,
430 West Allegan Street, 4th Floor,
Lansing, MI 48918-8900
(517) 373-2511

Vital Statistics
Glenn Copeland
Vital Records and Health Statistics State
Registrar, Public Health Administration
Chief Administrative Office, Department
of Community Health [MDCH]
201 Townsend Street,
Lansing, MI 48913
(517) 335-8677

Supreme Court
7 justices sit en banc
Jurisdiction:
- Appeal by permission criminal, civil, administrative agency. Interlocutory appeals in criminal, civil, administrative agency.
- Exclusive original proceeding bar/judiciary, certified question, advisory opinion.

Court of Appeals (4 districts)
28 judges sit in 3-judge panels
Jurisdiction:
- Exclusive appeal by right criminal, civil, administrative agency.
- Appeal by permission criminal, civil, administrative agency. Interlocutory appeals in criminal, civil, administrative agency.
- Exclusive original proceeding application for writ.

Court of Claims
(this is a function of the 30th Circuit Court)
4 judges
No jury trials
- Jurisdiction:
  Administrative agency appeals involving claims against the state.

Circuit Court* (57 courts)**
233 judges
Jury trials except in domestic relations
Jurisdiction:
- Tort, contract, real property ($25,001 - no maximum), probate/estate, mental health, administrative agency appeals, miscellaneous civil. Exclusive civil trial court appeals.
- Exclusive domestic relations.
- Felony, criminal appeals.
- Juvenile.

District Court (90 Districts)
295 judges
Jury trials in most cases
Jurisdiction:
- Tort, contract, real property ($0 - $25,000), small claims (up to $3,000).
- Felony, preliminary hearings, misdemeanor.
- Ordinance violations.

Probate Court (73 courts)
132 judges
Jury trials in some cases
Jurisdiction:
- Probate/estate, mental health.

Municipal Court (4 courts)
4 judges
Jury trials in most cases
Jurisdiction:
- Tort, contract, real property ($0 - $1,500; $0 - $3,000 if approved by local funding unit), small claims (up to $100; up to $600 if approved).
- Preliminary hearings, misdemeanor.
- Traffic/other violations.

COURT OF LAST RESORT

INTERMEDIATE APPELLATE COURT

GENERAL JURISDICTION COURT

LIMITED JURISDICTION COURT

*The Recorder's Court of Detroit merged with the Circuit Court effective October 1, 1997.
**A Family Division of Circuit Court became operational on January 1, 1998.

Court structure as of Fiscal Year 2015.

☐	Appellate level
☐	Trial level
↑	Route of appeal

MINNESOTA

Chief Justice
Lorie Skjerven Gildea
25 Rev. Dr. Martin Luther King, Jr. Blvd,
St. Paul, MN 55155
(651) 297-7650

Justices of the Supreme Court
G. Barry Anderson
Christopher J. Dietzen
David Lillehaug
Alan C. Page
David R. Stras
Wilhelmina M. Wright

Clerk of the Supreme Court
AnnMarie S. O'Neill
Clerk of the Appellate Courts and
Supreme Court Administrator
25 Rev. Dr. Martin Luther King, Jr. Blvd,
St. Paul, MN 5515
(651) 297-5529

Court System Website
www.mncourts.gov

Court Administration
Jeffrey "Jeff" Shorba
State Court Administrator
135 Minnesota Judicial Center,
25 Rev. Dr. Martin Luther King, Jr. Blvd,
St. Paul, MN 55155
(651) 296-2474

Governor
Mark Dayton (DFL)
130 State Capitol,
75 Rev. Dr. Martin Luther King, Jr. Blvd,
St. Paul, MN 55155
(651) 201-3400

State Website
www.mn.gov

State Capitol Main Phone
(651) 201-3400

Attorney General
Lori R. Swanson (DFL)
1400 Bremer Tower, 445 Minnesota
Street, St. Paul, MN 55101
(651) 296-6196

Secretary of State
Steve Simon (DFL)
180 State Office Building, 100 Rev. Dr.
Martin Luther King, Jr. Blvd,
St. Paul, MN 55155-1299
(651) 296-2803

Vital Statistics
Steven Elkins, State Registrar
P.O. Box 64499,
St. Paul, MN 55164-0499
(651) 201-5980

COURT OF LAST RESORT

Supreme Court
7 justices sit en banc

Jurisdiction:
- Appeal by right felony, civil administrative agency.
- Appeal by permission criminal, civil, limited administrative agency.
- Original proceeding application for writ, certified question. Exclusive bar discipline/eligibility, advisory opinion.

INTERMEDIATE APPELLATE COURT

Court of Appeals
19 judges sit in 3-judge panels en banc

Jurisdiction:
- Appeal by right criminal, civil, workers' compensation. Interlocutory appeals in criminal, civil, workers' compensation.
- Appeal by permission criminal, civil. Exclusive workers' compensation. Interlocutory appeals in criminal, civil, workers' compensation.
- Original proceeding application for writ, certified question.

GENERAL JURISDICTION COURT

District Court (10 districts)
289 judges
Jury trials except in small claims and non-extended juvenile jurisdiction cases

Jurisdiction:
- Exclusive civil (conciliation division: $0 - $7,500).
- Exclusive domestic relations.
- Exclusive criminal.
- Exclusive juvenile.
- Exclusive traffic/other violations.

Court structure as of Fiscal Year 2015.

▭	Appellate level
▭	Trial level
↑	Route of appeal

MISSISSIPPI

Chief Justice
William L. Waller, Jr.
P.O. Box 117, Jackson, MS 39205-0117
(601) 359-2139

Justices of the Supreme Court
David A. Chandler
Josiah D. Coleman
Jess H. Dickinson
Leslie D. King
James W. "Jim" Kitchens
Ann Hannaford Lamar
Randy G. "Bubba" Pierce
Michael K. Randolph

Clerk of the Supreme Court
Muriel Ellis
P.O. Box 117, Jackson, MS 39205
(601) 359-2175

Court System Website
www.mssc.state.ms.us

Court Administration
Hubbard T. "Hubby" Saunders, IV
Supreme Court Administrator
P.O. Box 117, Jackson, MS 39205
(601) 359-2182

Governor
Phil Bryant (R)
P.O. Box 139, Jackson, MS 39205
(601) 359-3150

State Website
www.mississippi.gov

State Capitol Main Phone
(601) 359-3100

Attorney General
James Matthew "Jim" Hood (D)
P.O. Box 220, Jackson, MS 39205
(601) 359-3680

Secretary of State
C. Delbert Hosemann, Jr. (R)
P.O. Box 136, Jackson, MS 39205-0136
(601) 359-6342
delbert.hosemann@sos.ms.gov

Vital Statistics
Judy Moulder
Director, Vital Records Office,
Office of Health Administration
570 East Woodrow Wilson,
Jackson, MS 39215-1700
(601) 576-7961
judy.moulder@msdh.state.ms.us

Supreme Court
9 justices sit in 3-judge panels and en banc
Assigns cases to the Court of Appeals

Jurisdiction:
- Appeal by right criminal, civil, administrative agency. Interlocutory appeals in criminal, civil, administrative agency.
- Exclusive appeal by permission criminal, civil, administrative agency. Interlocutory appeals in criminal, civil, administrative agency.
- Exclusive death penalty.
- Original proceeding application for writ. Exclusive bar/judiciary, certified question, advisory opinion.

Court of Appeals (5 districts)
10 judges sit in 3-judge panels and en banc

Jurisdiction:
- Appeal by right criminal, civil, administrative agency. Interlocutory appeals in criminal, civil, administrative agency.
- Original proceeding application for writ.

Circuit Court (22 districts)
53 judges
Jury trials

Jurisdiction:
- Tort, contract, real property ($201 - no maximum), civil law appeals.
- Criminal.

Chancery Court (20 districts)
49 judges
Jury trials (limited)

Jurisdiction:
- Tort, contract, real property ($0 - no maximum), probate/estate, mental health, civil equity appeals.
- Domestic relations.
- Juvenile (if no County Court).
- Appeals from Justice and Municipal Courts (if no County Court).

County Court (21 courts)
30 judges
Jury trials (limited)

Jurisdiction:
- Tort, contract, real property ($0 - $200,000), civil appeals. Probate/estate and mental health (as assigned by Chancery Court).
- Domestic relations (as assigned by Chancery Court).
- Preliminary hearings, misdemeanor.
- Juvenile.

Justice Court (82 courts)
197 judges
Jury trials

Jurisdiction:
- Small claims ($0 - $3,500).
- Preliminary hearings, misdemeanor.

Municipal Court (226 courts)
227 judges
No jury trials

Jurisdiction:
- Preliminary hearings, misdemeanor.
- Traffic/other violations.

COURT OF LAST RESORT

INTERMEDIATE APPELLATE COURT

GENERAL JURISDICTION COURT

LIMITED JURISDICTION COURT

The Family Court was abolished July 1, 1999 and merged into County Court.

Appellate level
Trial level
↑ Route of appeal

Court structure as of Fiscal Year 2015.

MISSOURI

Chief Justice
Mary Rhodes Russell
Supreme Court Building, 207 West High
Street, Jefferson City, MO 65101
(573) 751-6880

Justices of the Supreme Court
Patricia Breckenridge
George W. Draper, III
Zel Martin Fischer
Laura Denvir Stith
Richard B. Teitelman
Paul Wilson

Clerk of the Supreme Court
Bill L. Thompson
P.O. Box 150, Jefferson City, MO 65102
(573) 751-4144

Court System Website
www.courts.mo.gov

Court Administration
Kathy S. Lloyd
State Courts Administrator
P.O. Box 104480,
Jefferson City, MO 65110
(573) 526-8803

Governor
Jeremiah W. "Jay" Nixon (D)
P.O. Box 720, Jefferson City, MO 65102
(573) 751-3222

State Website
www.mo.gov

State Capitol Main Phone
(573) 751-2000

Attorney General
Chris Koster (D)
P.O. Box 899, Jefferson City, MO 65102
(573) 751-3321
attorney.general@ago.mo.gov

Secretary of State
Jason Kander (D)
P.O. Box 140252,
Kansas City, MO 64114
(573) 751-1880

Vital Statistics
Craig Ward
State Vital Records Registrar,
Epidemiology for Public Health Practice
Section, Department of Health and
Senior Services [DHSS]
P.O. Box 570, Jefferson City, MO 65102
(573) 526-0348

Supreme Court
7 judges
Jurisdiction:
- Appeal by right limited criminal, civil, administrative agency. Interlocutory appeals in criminal, civil, administrative agency.
- Appeal by permission criminal, civil, administrative agency. Interlocutory appeals in criminal, civil, administrative agency.
- Exclusive death penalty.
- Original proceeding application for writ. Exclusive bar/judiciary.

Court of Appeals (3 districts)
32 judges sit in 3-judge panels
Jurisdiction:
- Appeal by right criminal, civil, administrative agency. Interlocutory appeals in criminal, civil, administrative agency.
- Original proceeding application for writ.

Circuit Court (45 circuits)
141 circuit judges, 193 associate circuit judges, 32 commissioners and deputy commisioners
Jury trials in most cases
Jurisdiction:
- Exclusive civil (circuit division: $0 - $no maximum; associate division: $0 - $25,000), small claims (up to $3,000).
- Exclusive domestic relations.
- Exclusive criminal.
- Exclusive juvenile.
- Traffic/other violations.

Municipal Court (467 divisions)
476 municipal judges
Jury trials in Springfield Municipality only
Jurisdiction:
- Traffic/other violations.

Court structure as of Fiscal Year 2015.

COURT OF LAST RESORT
INTERMEDIATE APPELLATE COURT
GENERAL JURISDICTION COURT
LIMITED JURISDICTION COURT

☐ Appellate level
☐ Trial level
↑ Route of appeal

MONTANA

Chief Justice
Mike McGrath
Justice Building,
215 North Sanders, Helena, MT 59620
(406) 444-5490

Justices of the Supreme Court
Beth Baker
Patricia Cotter
Laurie McKinnon
Jim Rice
James Jeremiah "Jim" Shea
Michael E. Wheat

Clerk of the Supreme Court
Ed Smith
P.O. Box 203003,
Helena, MT 59620-3001
(406) 444-3858

Court System Website
www.montanacourts.org

Court Administration
Beth McLaughlin
P.O. Box 203002,
Helena, MT 59620-3002
(406) 841-2966

Governor
Steve Bullock (D)
P.O. Box 200801,
Helena, MT 59620-0801
(406) 444-3111

State Website
www.mt.gov

State Capitol Main Phone
(406) 444-3111

Attorney General
Timothy C. "Tim" Fox (R)
P.O. Box 201401,
Helena, MT 59620-1401
(406) 444-2026

Secretary of State
Linda McCulloch (D)
P.O. Box 202801,
Helena, MT 59620-2801
(406) 444-4195

Vital Statistics
Karin Ferlicka
Vital Records State Registrar,
Department of Public Health and
Human Services [DPHHS]
111 North Sanders, Room 6,
Helena, MT 59604
(406) 444-4250
hhsvitalrecords@mt.gov

Supreme Court
7 justices sit in 5-judge panels and en banc
Jurisdiction:
- Exclusive appeal by right criminal, civil, administrative agency. Interlocutory appeals in criminal, civil, administrative agency.
- Exclusive death penalty.
- Exclusive original proceeding application for writ, certified question, advisory opinion.

COURT OF LAST RESORT

Water Court
1 chief judge, 1 associate judge, water masters as needed
No jury trials
Jurisdiction:
- Real property, limited to adjudication of existing water rights.

District Court (56 counties)
46 judges
Jury trials
Jurisdiction:
- Tort, contract, real property rights. Exclusive mental health, estate, civil appeals, miscellaneous civil.
- Exclusive domestic relations.
- Misdemeanor. Exclusive felony, criminal appeals.
- Juvenile.

Workers' Compensation Court
1 judge
No jury trials
Jurisdiction:
- Limited to workers' compensation disputes.

GENERAL JURISDICTION COURT

Justice Court (61 courts)
66 justices of the peace
Jurisdiction:
- Tort, contract, real property rights ($0 - $7,000), small claims ($3,000).
- Preliminary hearings, misdemeanor.
- Traffic infractions, parking.

City Court (84 courts)
87 judges
Jurisdiction:
- Tort, contract, real property rights ($0 - $7,000).
- Preliminary hearings, misdemeanor.
- Traffic infractions. Exclusive ordinance violations.

Municipal Court (6 courts)
8 judges
Jury trials
Jurisdiction:
- Tort, contract, real property rights ($0 - $7,000).
- Preliminary hearings, misdemeanor.
- Traffic infractions, parking.

LIMITED JURISDICTION COURT

Court structure as of Fiscal Year 2015.

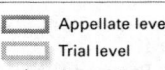

☐ Appellate level
☐ Trial level
↑ Route of appeal

NEBRASKA

Chief Justice
Michael G. Heavican
P.O. Box 98910, Lincoln, NE 68509
(402) 471-3738

Justices of the Supreme Court
William B. Cassel
William M. Connolly
Michael McCormack
Lindsey Miller-Lerman
Kenneth C. Stephan
John F. Wright

Clerk of the Supreme Court
Teresa A. "Terri" Brown
Clerk of Supreme Court and
Court of Appeals
2413 State Capitol Building,
1445 K Street, Lincoln, NE 68509
(402) 471-3731

Court System Website
www.supremecourt.ne.gov

Court Administration
Corey R. Steel
State Court Administrator
P.O. Box 98910, Lincoln, NE 68509
(402) 471-3730

Governor
John Peter "Pete" Ricketts (R)
P.O. Box 94848,
Lincoln, NE 68509-4848
(402) 471-2244

State Website
www.nebraska.gov

State Capitol Main Phone
(402) 471-2311

Attorney General
Douglas J. "Doug" Peterson (R)
P. O. Box 98920, Lincoln, NE 98920
(402) 471-2682
jon.bruning@nebraska.gov

Secretary of State
John A. Gale (R)
2300 State Capitol, P.O. Box 94608,
Lincoln, NE 68509-4608
(402) 471-1572
john.gale@nebraska.gov

Vital Statistics
Stan Cooper
Vital Records Director,
Division of Public Health
1033 O Street, Suite 130,
Lincoln, NE 68508
(402) 471-0915
stan.cooper@nebraska.gov

Supreme Court
7 justices sit en banc

Jurisdiction:
- Appeal by right criminal, civil, administrative agency. Interlocutory appeals in criminal, civil, administrative agency.
- Exclusive appeal by permission criminal, civil, administrative agency. Interlocutory appeals in criminal, civil, administrative agency.
- Exclusive death penalty.
- Original proceeding application for writ, bar discipline/eligibility.

COURT OF LAST RESORT

Court of Appeals
6 judges sit in 3-judge panels

Jurisdiction:
- Appeal by right criminal, civil, administrative agency. Interlocutory appeals in criminal, civil, administrative agency.

INTERMEDIATE APPELLATE COURT

District Court (12 districts)
56 judges
Jury trials excpt in appeals

Jurisdiction:
- Tort, contract, real property ($52,001 - no maximum), civil appeals, miscellaneous civil. Exclusive mental health.
- Domestic relations.
- Misdemeanor. Exclusive felony, criminal appeals, miscellaneous criminal.

GENERAL JURISDICTION COURT

Separate Juvenile Court
(3 counties)
11 *judges*
No jury trials

Jurisdiction:
- Custody, support.
- Juvenile.

County Court (12 districts)
58 judges
Jury trials except in juvenile and small claims

Jurisdiction:
- Tort, contract, real property rights ($0 - $52,000), small claims ($3,500). Exclusive probate/estate.
- Exclusive adoption. Domestic relations.
- Preliminary hearings, misdemeanor.
- Juvenile.
- Traffic/other violations.

Workers' Compensation Court
7 judges
No jury trials

Jurisdiction:
- Administrative agency appeals.

LIMITED JURISDICTION COURT

Court structure as of Fiscal Year 2015.

Appellate level
Trial level
↑   Route of appeal

NEVADA

Chief Justice
James W. Hardesty
Supreme Court Building, 201 South
Carson Street, Carson City, NV 89701
(775) 684-1590

Justices of the Supreme Court
Michael A. Cherry
Michael L. Douglas
Mark Gibbons
Ronald Parraguirre
Kristina "Kris" Pickering
Nancy M. Saitta

Clerk of the Supreme Court
Tracie Lindeman
Supreme Court Building,
201 South Carson Street, Suite 201,
Carson City, NV 89701-4702
(775) 684-1600

Court System Website
www.nevadajudiciary.us

Court Administration
Robin Sweet
State Court Administrator
Supreme Court Building,
201 South Carson Street, Suite 250,
Carson City, NV 89701-4702
(775) 684-1717

Governor
Brian E. Sandoval (R)
101 North Carson Street,
Carson City, NV 89701
(775) 684-5670

State Website
www.nv.gov

State Capitol Main Phone
(775) 684-1000

Attorney General
Adam Paul Laxalt (R)
100 North Carson Street,
Carson City, NV 89701-4717
(775) 684-1100

Secretary of State
Barbara K. Cegavske (R)
State Capitol Bldg, 101 North Carson St,
Suite 3, Carson City, NV 89701-4786
(775) 684-5708

Vital Statistics
Steven "Steve" Gilbert
Vital Statistics Program Officer,
Health Division, Department of Health
and Human Services [DHHS]
4150 Technology Way,
Carson City, NV 89706
(775) 684-4242

Supreme Court
7 justices sit in 3-judge panels en banc

Jurisdiction:
- Exclusive appeal by right criminal, civil, administrative agency. Interlocutory appeals in criminal, civil, administrative agency.
- Exclusive death penalty.
- Exclusive original proceeding application for writ, bar admission, bar discipline/eligibility, certified questions.

COURT OF LAST RESORT

Court of Appeals
3 judges

Jurisdiction:
- Exclusive appeal by right criminal, civil, administrative agency. Interlocutory appeals in criminal, civil, administrative agency.
- Exclusive death penalty.
- Exclusive original proceeding application for writ, bar admission, bar discipline/eligibility, certified questions.

INTERMEDIATE APPELLATE COURT

District Court (10 districts)
82 judges
Jury trials in most cases

Jurisdiction:
- Tort, contract, real property ($10,001 - no maximum). Exclusive mental health, probate/estate, civil appeals, miscellaneous civil.
- Exclusive domestic relations.
- Felony, misdemeanor.*
- Exclusive criminal appeals.
- Exclusive juvenile.

GENERAL JURISDICTION COURT

Justice Court (43 towns)
75 justices of the peace
(8 of these also serve as Municipal Court judges)
Jury trials except in small claims, traffic and parking cases

Jurisdiction:
- Tort, contract, real property rights ($0 - $10,000), small claims up to $5,000).
- Preliminary hearings, misdemeanor.*
- Traffic infractions, parking.

Municipal Court
(17 incorporated cities/towns)
30 judges (8 of these also serve as Justice Court Judges)
Jury trials except in small claims, traffic, parking and ordinance violation cases

Jurisdiction:
- Small claims (up to $2,500).
- Misdemeanor.*
- Traffic infractions, parking. Exclusive ordinance violations.

LIMITED JURISDICTION COURT

*District Court hears gross misdemeanor anors cases; Justice & Municipal Courts hear misdemeanors with fines under $1,000 and/or sentence of less than six months.

Court structure as of Fiscal Year 2015.

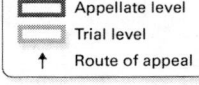

Appellate level
Trial level
↑ Route of appeal

NEW HAMPSHIRE

Chief Justice
Linda S. Dalianis
One Charles Doe Drive,
Concord, NH 03301
(603) 271-2646

Justices of the Supreme Court
James P. "Jim" Bassett
Carol Ann Conboy
Gary E. Hicks
Robert J. Lynn

Clerk of the Supreme Court
Eileen Fox
Supreme Court Building,
One Charles Doe Drive,
Concord, NH 03301-6160
(603) 271-2646

Court System Website
www.courts.state.nh.us

Court Administration
Donald D. Goodnow, Esq.
Director, Administrative Office of the
Courts of New Hampshire
Two Charles Doe Drive,
Concord, NH 03301-6179
(603) 271-2521

Governor
Margaret Wood "Maggie" Hassan (D)
107 North Main Street,
Concord, NH 03301
(603) 271-2121

State Website
www.nh.gov

State Capitol Main Phone
(603) 271-1110

Attorney General
Joseph A. Foster (D)
33 Capitol Street,
Concord, NH 03301-639
(603) 271-1202

Secretary of State
William M. "Bill" Gardner (D)
State House, 107 North Main Street,
Room 204, Concord, NH 03301
(603) 271-3242

Vital Statistics
Stephen M. Wurtz
State Registrar, Division of Vital
Records Administration, Office of the
Secretary of State
71 South Fruit Street,
Concord, NH 03301
(603) 271-4655
stephen.wurtz@sos.nh.gov

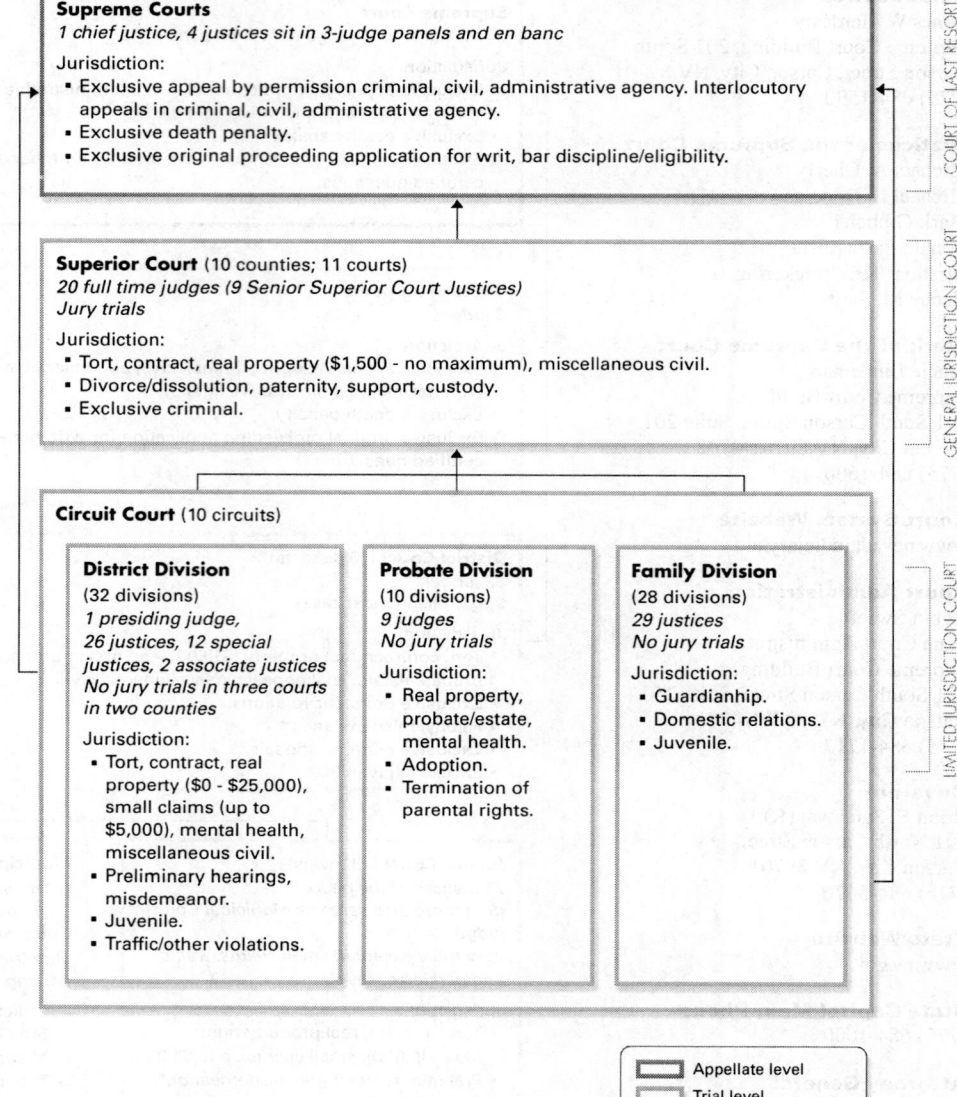

Supreme Courts
1 chief justice, 4 justices sit in 3-judge panels and en banc
Jurisdiction:
- Exclusive appeal by permission criminal, civil, administrative agency. Interlocutory appeals in criminal, civil, administrative agency.
- Exclusive death penalty.
- Exclusive original proceeding application for writ, bar discipline/eligibility.

Superior Court (10 counties; 11 courts)
20 full time judges (9 Senior Superior Court Justices)
Jury trials
Jurisdiction:
- Tort, contract, real property ($1,500 - no maximum), miscellaneous civil.
- Divorce/dissolution, paternity, support, custody.
- Exclusive criminal.

Circuit Court (10 circuits)

District Division
(32 divisions)
1 presiding judge, 26 justices, 12 special justices, 2 associate justices No jury trials in three courts in two counties
Jurisdiction:
- Tort, contract, real property ($0 - $25,000), small claims (up to $5,000), mental health, miscellaneous civil.
- Preliminary hearings, misdemeanor.
- Juvenile.
- Traffic/other violations.

Probate Division
(10 divisions)
9 judges
No jury trials
Jurisdiction:
- Real property, probate/estate, mental health.
- Adoption.
- Termination of parental rights.

Family Division
(28 divisions)
29 justices
No jury trials
Jurisdiction:
- Guardianhip.
- Domestic relations.
- Juvenile.

COURT OF LAST RESORT

GENERAL JURISDICTION COURT

LIMITED JURISDICTION COURT

Court structure as of Fiscal Year 2015.

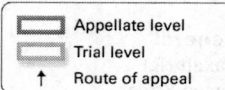
Appellate level
Trial level
↑   Route of appeal

State Court Clerks and County Courthouses

NEW JERSEY

Chief Justice
Stuart Rabner
P.O. Box 023, Trenton, NJ 08625-0023
(609) 292-2448

Justices of the Supreme Court
Barry T. Albin
David Bauman (Designate)
Mary Catherine Cuff (Acting)
Faustino J. "F.J." Fernandez-Vina
Jaynee LaVecchia
Anne M. Patterson
Lee A. Solomon

Clerk of the Supreme Court
Mark Neary
P.O. Box 970, Trenton, NJ 08625-0970
(609) 292-4837

Court System Website
www.njcourts.com

Court Administration
Glenn A. Grant
Administrative Director (Acting)
P.O. Box 037, Trenton, NJ 08625-0037
(609) 984-0275

Governor
Christopher J. "Chris" Christie (R)
P.O. Box 001, Trenton, NJ 08625
(609) 292-6000

State Website
www.newjersey.gov

State Capitol Main Phone
(609) 292-2121

Attorney General
John Jay Hoffman
Attorney General (Acting)
P.O. Box 080, Justice Complex,
Trenton, NJ 08625
(609) 292-4930

Secretary of State
Kimberly A. "Kim" Guadagno
125 W. State Street, Trenton, NJ 08625
(609) 777-0884

Vital Statistics
Vincent Arrisi
Vital Statistics State Registrar,
Department of Health
P.O. Box 360, Trenton, NJ 08625-0360
(609) 292-4087

Supreme Court
7 justices sit en banc

Jurisdiction:
- Appeal by right criminal, civil, administrative agency. Interlocutory appeals in criminal, civil, administrative agency.
- Appeal by permission interlocutory appeals in criminal, civil, administrative agency.
- Exclusive original proceeding, bar/judiciary, certified question.

Appellate Division of Superior Court (8 parts)
32 judges sit in two- and three-judge panels

Jurisdiction:
- Appeal by right criminal, civil, administrative agency.
- Appeal by permission, interlocutory appeals in criminal, civil, administrative agency.

Superior Court (15 vicinages in 21 counties)
Approximately 360 judges
Jury trials in most cases

Jurisdiction:
- Exclusive civil ($0 - no maximum; special civil part: $0 - $15,000). Small claims (up to $3,000; up to $5,000 for security deposit demand cases).
- Exclusive domestic relations.
- Felony. Exclusive criminal appeals.
- Exclusive juvenile.

Municipal Court (539 courts, of which 21 are multi-municipal)
560 judges
No jury trials

Jurisdiction:
- Felony,* misdemeanor.
- Exclusive traffic/other violations.

Tax Court
12 judges
No jury trials

Jurisdiction:
- Administrative agency appeals, tax cases.

COURT OF LAST RESORT

INTERMEDIATE APPELLATE COURT

GENERAL JURISDICTION COURT

LIMITED JURISDICTION COURT

*Felony cases are handled on first appearance in the Municipal Courts and then are transferred through the county Prosecutor's office to the Superior Court.

Court structure as of Fiscal Year 2015.

☐ Appellate level
☐ Trial level
↑ Route of appeal

NEW MEXICO

Chief Justice
Barbara J. Vigil
P.O. Box 848, Santa Fe, NM 87504-0848
(505) 827-4883

Justices of the Supreme Court
Richard C. Bosson
Edward L. Chavez
Charles W. Daniels
Petra Jimenez Maes

Clerk of the Supreme Court
Joey Moya
P.O. Box 848, Santa Fe, NM 87504-0848
(505) 827-4860

Court System Website
www.nmcourts.com

Court Administration
Arthur W. Pepin
Administrative Office of the Courts
Director
Supreme Court Building,
237 Don Gaspar Avenue, Room 25,
Santa Fe, NM 87501
(505) 827-4800

Governor
Susana Martinez (R)
State Capitol Building,
490 Old Santa Fe Trail, Room 400,
Santa Fe, NM 87501
(505) 476-2200

State Website
www.newmexico.gov

State Capitol Main Phone
(800) 825-6639

Attorney General
Hector H. Balderas, CFE (D)
P.O. Drawer 1508,
Santa Fe, NM 87504-1508
(575) 770-7995

Secretary of State
Dianna J. Duran (R)
New Mexico State Capitol,
325 Don Gaspar, Suite 300,
Santa Fe, NM 87503
(505) 827-3600

Vital Statistics
Mark Kassouf
Vital Records and Health Statistics
Bureau Chief, Epidemiology and
Response Division
PO Box 25767, Albuquerque, NM 87125
(505) 827-0121

Supreme Court
5 justices sit en banc

Jurisdiction:
- Appeal by right felony, other criminal, limited administrative agency. Interlocutory appeals in felony, administrative agency.
- Appeal by permission criminal, civil, administrative agency. Interlocutory appeals in criminal, civil, administrative agency.
- Exclusive death penalty.
- Original proceeding application for writ. Exclusive bar discipline/eligibility, judicial qualification, certified question.

COURT OF LAST RESORT

Court of Appeals
10 judges sit in 3-judge panels

Jurisdiction:
- Appeal by right criminal, limited administrative agency. Exclusive civil.
- Appeal by permission criminal, civil. Interlocutory appeals in criminal, civil.

INTERMEDIATE APPELLATE COURT

District Court (13 districts)
94 judges
Jury trials

Jurisdiction:
- Tort, contract, real property, probate/estate. Exclusive mental health, civil appeals, miscellaneous civil.
- Exclusive domestic relations.
- Felony, misdemeanor. Exclusive criminal appeals.
- Exclusive juvenile.

GENERAL JURISDICTION COURT

Magistrate Court (54 courts)
67 judges
Jury trials in some cases

Jurisdiction:
- Small claims (up to $10,000).
- Preliminary hearings, misdemeanor.
- Traffic infractions.

Bernalillo County Metropolitan Court
19 judges
Jury trials in some cases

Jurisdiction:
- Small claims (up to $10,000).
- Preliminary hearings, misdemeanor.
- Traffic/other violation.

Municipal Court (80 courts)
82 judges
No jury trials

Jurisdiction:
- Misdemeanor.
- Traffic/other violations.

Probate Court (33 counties)
33 judges
No jury trials

Jurisdiction:
- Probate/estate (uncontested cases).

LIMITED JURISDICTION COURT

Court structure as of Fiscal Year 2015.

- Appellate level
- Trial level
- ↑ Route of appeal

NEW YORK

Chief Judge — Court of Appeals
Jonathan Lippman
Court of Appeals Hall, 20 Eagle Street,
Albany, NY 12207
(518) 455-7840

Judges of the Appeals Court
Sheila Abdus-Salaam
Eugene Fahey
Eugene F. Pigott, Jr.
Susan Phillips Read
Jenny Rivera
Leslie E. Stein

Clerk of the Appeals Court
Andrew W. Klein
Court of Appeals Hall, 20 Eagle Street,
Albany, NY 12207-1095
(518) 455-7700

Court System Website
www.nycourts.gov

Court Administration
Lawrence K. Marks
Chief Administrative Judge of the Courts
25 Beaver Street, New York, NY 10004
(212) 428-2120

Governor
Andrew Mark Cuomo (D)
State Capitol, Albany, NY 12224
(518) 474-8390

State Website
www.ny.gov

State Capitol Main Phone
(518) 474-8390

Attorney General
Eric T. Schneiderman (D)
120 Broadway,
New York, NY 10271-0332
(518) 474-7330

Secretary of State
Cesar A. Perales
One Commerce Plaza,
99 Washington Avenue,
Albany, NY 12231-0001
(518) 474-0050

Vital Statistics
Guy Warner
Vital Records Section Director,
Information Systems and Health
Statistics Group, New York State
Department of Health [NYSDOH]
P.O. Box 2602, Albany, NY 12220-2602
(518) 474-5245
vr@health.ny.gov

Court of Appeals
7 judges sit en banc
Jurisdiction:
- Appeal by right civil, administrative agency. Interlocutory appeals in civil, administrative agency.
- Appeal by permission criminal, civil, administrative agency. Interlocutory appeals in criminal, civil, administrative agency.
- Exclusive original proceeding judicial qualification, certified question.

COURT OF LAST RESORT

Appellate Divisions of Supreme Court (4 departments)
51 justices sit in 5-judge panels
Jurisdiction:
- Appeal by right criminal, civil, administrative agency. Interlocutory appeals in criminal, civil, administrative agency.
- Appeal by permission criminal, civil, administrative agency. Interlocutory appeals in criminal, civil, administrative agency.
- Exclusive original proceeding application for writ, bar/judiciary.

Appellate Terms of Supreme Court (2 departments)
10 justices sit in 3-judge panels
Jurisdiction:
- Appeal by right criminal, civil. Interlocutory appeal in criminal, civil.
- Appeal by permission criminal, juvenile.
- Interlocutory appeals in criminal, juvenile.

INTERMEDIATE APPELLATE COURT

Supreme and County Court 326 justices, 134 judges

Supreme Court (12 districts)
328 justices

Jury trials

Jurisdiction:
- Tort, contract, real property, miscellanous civil.
- Exclusive marriage dissolution.
- Felony, misdemeanor.

County Court (57 counties outside NYC)
129 judges (50 serve the Surrogates' Court and 6 serve the Family Court)
Jury trials

Jurisdiction:
- Tort, contract, real property ($0 - $25,000), civil appeals, miscellanous civil.
- Criminal.

GENERAL JURISDICTION COURT

Court of Claims (1 court)
26 judges

No jury trials

Jurisdiction:
- Tort, contract, real property, involving the state.

Family Court
(62 counties)
127 judges plus 6 judges from the County Court and 81 quasi-judicial staff
No jury trials

Jurisdiction:.
- Guardianship.
- Domestic relations.
- Exclusive domestic violence.
- Exclusive juvenile.

Surrogates' Court
(62 counties)
31 surrogates plus 50 judges from the County Court
Jury trials in probate/estate

Jurisdiction:
- Probate/estate.
- Adoption.

District and City Court 208 judges

District Court (Nassau and Suffolk counties)
50 judges
Jury trials except in traffic
Jurisdiction:
- Tort, contract, real property ($0 - $15,000), small claims (up to $5,000).
- Felony, preliminary hearings, misdemeanor.
- Traffic infractions, ordinance violations.

City Court (79 courts in 61 cities)
162 judges
Jury trials for highest level misdemeanor
Jurisdiction:
- Tort, contract, real property ($0 - $15,000), small claims (up to $5,000).
- Felony, preliminary hearings, misdemeanor.
- Traffic infractions, ordinance violations.

Civil Court of the City of New York
120 judges
Jury trials
Jurisdiction:
- Tort, contract, real property ($0 - $25,000), small claims (up to $5,000), miscellaneous civil.

Criminal Court of the City of New York
107 judges
Jury trials for highest level misdemeanor
Jurisdiction:
- Preliminary hearings, misdemeanor.
- Traffic infractions, ordinance violations.

Town and Village Justice Court (1,487 courts)
2,570 justices
Jury trials in most cases
Jurisdiction:
- Tort, contract, real property ($0 - $3,000), small claims (up to $3,000),
- Preliminary hearings, misdemeanor.
- Traffic /other violations. violations.

LIMITED JURISDICTION COURT

☐ Appellate level
☐ Trial level
↑ Route of appeal

Court structure as of Fiscal Year 2015.

NORTH CAROLINA

Chief Justice
Mark D. Martin
P.O. Box 1841, Raleigh, NC 27602
(919) 831-5712

Justices of the Supreme Court
Cheri Beasley
Robert H. Edmunds, Jr.
Sam J. "Jimmy" Ervin, IV
Robin E. Hudson
Barbara Jackson
Paul M. Newby

Clerk of the Supreme Court
Christie Speir Cameron Roeder
P.O. Box 1841, Raleigh, NC 27602
(919) 831-5700

Court System Website
www.nccourts.org

Court Administration
Marion Warren
Director, Administrative Office of the
Courts of North Carolina
P.O. Box 2448, Raleigh, NC 27602
(919) 890-1391

Governor
Patrick L. "Pat" McCrory (R)
20301 Mail Service Center,
Raleigh, NC 27699-0301
(919) 814-2000

State Website
www.nc.gov

State Capitol Main Phone
(919) 733-1110

Attorney General
Roy A. Cooper (D)
9001 Mail Service Center,
Raleigh, NC 27699-9001
(919) 716-6400

Secretary of State
Elaine Folk Marshall (D)
P.O. Box 29622,
Raleigh, NC 27626-0622
(919) 807-2008

Vital Statistics
Catherine Ryan
Vital Records Director and State
Registrar (Acting), Division of Public
Health, Department of Health and
Human Services [DHHS]
225 North McDowell Street,
Raleigh, NC 27603-1382
(919) 733-3526

Supreme Court
7 justices sit en banc
Jurisdiction:
- Appeal by right criminal, civil, administrative agency. Interlocutory appeals in criminal, civil, administrative agency.
- Appeal by permission criminal, civil, administrative agency. Interlocutory appeals in criminal, civil, administrative agency.
- Exclusive death penalty.
- Original proceeding application for writ, bar/judiciary. Exclusive advisory opinion.

COURT OF LAST RESORT

Court of Appeals
15 judges sit in 3-judge panels
Jurisdiction:
- Appeal by right criminal, civil, administrative agency.
- Appeal by permission criminal, civil, administrative agency. Interlocutory appeals in criminal, civil, administrative agency.
- Original proceeding application for writ, bar/judiciary.

INTERMEDIATE APPELLATE COURT

Superior Court (50 districts for administrative purposes; 65 districts for elective purposes)
112 judges (including 13 special judges) and 100 clerks serve as ex officio judges of probate with jurisdiction in estate cases and with certain other judicial authorities
Jury trials
Jurisdiction:
- Tort, contract, real property ($10,001 - no maximum), miscellaneous civil. Exclusive probate/estate, civil appeals.
- Criminal.

GENERAL JURISDICTION COURT

District Court (41 districts for administrative purposes; 40 districts for elective purposes)
270 judges and 654 magistrates
Jury trials in civil cases only
Jurisdiction:
- Tort, contract, real property ($0 - $10,000) miscellaneous civil. Exclusive small claims (up to $5,000), mental health.
- Exclusive domestic relations.
- Preliminary hearings, misdemeanor.
- Exclusive juvenile.
- Traffic/other violations.

LIMITED JURISDICTION COURT

Court structure as of Fiscal Year 2015.

Appellate level
Trial level
↑ Route of appeal

NORTH DAKOTA

Chief Justice
Gerald W. VandeWalle
State Capitol, Judicial Wing,
Dept 180, 600 East Boulevard Avenue,
Bismarck, ND 58505-0530
(701) 328-2221

Justices of the Supreme Court
Daniel J. Crothers
Carol Ronning Kapsner
Lisa K. Fair McEvers
Dale V. Sandstrom

Clerk of the Supreme Court
Penny Miller
State Capitol, Judicial Wing,
600 East Boulevard Avenue, 1st Floor,
Bismarck, ND 58505-0530
(701) 328-2221

Court System Website
www.ndcourts.gov

Court Administration
Sally A. Holewa
State Court Administrator
State Capitol, Judicial Wing,
600 East Boulevard Avenue,
Bismarck, ND 58505-0530
(701) 328-4216

Governor
John S. "Jack" Dalrymple, III (R)
State Capitol, 600 East Boulevard Ave,
Department 101,
Bismarck, ND 58505-0001
(701) 328-2200

State Website
www.nd.gov

State Capitol Main Phone
(701) 328-2000

Attorney General
Wayne Stenehjem (R)
State Capitol, 600 East Boulevard Ave,
1st Floor, Department 125,
Bismarck, ND 58505-0040
(701) 328-2210

Secretary of State
Alvin A. "Al" Jaeger (R)
State Capitol, 600 East Boulevard Ave,
Dept 108, Bismarck, ND 58505-0500
(701) 328-2900

Vital Statistics
Darin J. Meschke
Vital Records Division Director, Dept
of Health, State of North Dakota
600 East Boulevard Avenue, Dept. 301,
Bismarck, ND 58505-0001
(701) 328-2360

Supreme Court
5 justices sit en banc
Assigns cases to the Temporary Court of Appeals

Jurisdiction:
- Appeal by right criminal, civil, administrative agency. Interlocutory appeals in criminal, civil, administrative agency.
- Original proceeding application for writ. Exclusive bar/judiciary, certified question, advisory opinion.

Temporary Court of Appeals*
3 judges sit in panel

Jurisdiction:
- Appeal by right criminal, civil, administrative agency. Interlocutory appeals in criminal, civil, administrative agency.
- Original proceeding application for writ.

District Court (8 judicial districts in 53 counties)
46 judges, 8 judicial referees
Jury trials in many cases

Jurisdiction:
- Exclusive civil.
- Exclusive domestic relations.
- Criminal.
- Exclusive juvenile.
- Traffic/other violations.

Municipal Court (104 municipalities)
74 judges
No jury trials

Jurisdiction:
- DWI/DUI.
- Traffic/other violations.

COURT OF LAST RESORT

INTERMEDIATE APPELLATE COURT

GENERAL JURISDICTION COURT

LIMITED JURISDICTION COURT

*Note: A temporary Court of Appeals was established July 1, 1987, to exercise appellate and original jurisdiction as delegated by the Supreme Court. Authorization for the Court of Appeals extends to January 1, 2017.

Court structure as of Fiscal Year 2015.

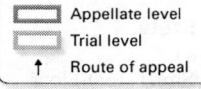

Appellate level
Trial level
↑ Route of appeal

OHIO

Chief Justice
Maureen O'Connor
65 South Front Street,
Columbus, OH 43215-3431
(614) 387-9060

Justices of the Supreme Court
Judith L. French
Sharon L. Kennedy
Judith Ann Lanzinger
Terrence O'Donnell
William O'Neill
Paul E. Pfeifer

Clerk of the Supreme Court
Sandra Grosko
65 South Front Street,
Columbus, OH 43215-3431
(614) 387-9530

Court System Website
www.supremecourtofohio.gov

Court Administration
Michael L. Buenger
Administrative Director
65 South Front Street,
Columbus, OH 43215-3431
(614) 387-9500

Governor
John Richard Kasich (R)
Vern Riffe Center, 77 South High Street,
30th Floor, Columbus, OH 43215-6123
(614) 466-3555

State Website
www.ohio.gov

State Capitol Main Phone
(614) 466-3357

Attorney General
Richard Michael "Mike" DeWine (R)
30 East Broad Street, 17th Floor,
Columbus, OH 43215-0421
(614) 466-4320

Secretary of State
Jon A. Husted (R)
180 East Broad Street, 16th Floor,
Columbus, OH 43215-3793
(614) 466-2655

Vital Statistics
Judith B. "Judy" Nagy
ital Statistics State Registrar,
Department of Health [ODH]
P.O. Box 15098,
Columbus, OH 43215-0098
(614) 466-0538
judy.nagy@odh.ohio.gov

Supreme Court
7 justices sit en banc

Jurisdiction:
- Appeal by right criminal, civil, administrative agency.
- Exclusive appeal by permission criminal, civil, limited administrative agency. Interlocutory appeals in criminal, civil, administrative agency.
- Exclusive death penalty.
- Original proceeding application for writ. Exclusive bar/judiciary, certified question.

COURT OF LAST RESORT

Court of Appeals (12 courts)
69 judges sit in 3-judge panels

Jurisdiction:
- Appeal by right criminal, civil, administrative agency. Interlocutory appeals in criminal, civil, administrative agency.
- Original proceeding application for writ.

INTERMEDIATE APPELLATE COURT

Court of Common Pleas (88 courts)
244 judges
Jury trials in most cases

Jurisdiction:
- Tort, contract, real property ($500 - no maximum), administrative agency appeals, miscellaneous civil. Exclusive mtal health, probate/estate.
- Exclusive domestic relations.
- Felony, misdemeanor.
- Exclusive juvenile.
- Traffic/other violations (juvenile only).

GENERAL JURISDICTION COURT

Municipal Court (126 courts)
215 judges
Jury trials in most cases

Jurisdiction:
- Tort, contract, real property ($0 - $15,000), small claims (up to $3,000), miscellaneous civil.
- Criminal.
- Traffic infractions, ordinance violations.

County Court (22 courts)
37 judges
Jury trials in most cases

Jurisdiction:
- Tort, contract, real property ($0 - $15,000), small claims (up to $3,000), miscellaneous civil.
- Criminal.
- Traffic infractions, ordinance violations.

Court of Claims
Judges assigned by the Chief Justice
Jury trials in some cases

Jurisdiction:
- Civil (actions against the state, victims of crime cases).

Mayors Court (310 courts)

No jury trials

Jurisdiction:
- DWI/DUI, other misdemeanors.
- Traffic/other violations.

LIMITED JURISDICTION COURT

Court structure as of Fiscal Year 2015.

☐ Appellate level
☐ Trial level
↑ Route of appeal

OKLAHOMA

Chief Justice
John F. Reif
State Capitol, 2300 North Lincoln Blvd,
Room 204, Oklahoma City, OK 73105
(405) 521-3843

Justices of the Supreme Court
Douglas L. Combs, Vice Chief Justice
Tom Colbert
James E. Edmondson
Noma Gurich
Yvonne Kauger
Steven W. Taylor
Joseph M. Watt
James Winchester

Clerk of the Supreme Court
Michael S. Richie
Oklahoma Judicial Center,
2100 North Lincoln Boulevard, Suite 2,
Oklahoma City, OK 73105-4907
(405) 556-9400

Court System Website
www.oscn.net

Court Administration
Michael D. Evans
Administrative Director
1915 North Stiles Avenue, Suite 305,
Oklahoma City, OK 73105
(405) 522-7878

Governor
Mary Fallin (R)
2300 North Lincoln Boulevard,
Suite 212, Oklahoma City, OK 73105
(405) 521-2342

State Website
www.ok.gov

State Capitol Main Phone
(405) 521-2011

Attorney General
E. Scott Pruitt (R)
313 Northeast 21st Street,
Oklahoma City, OK 73105
(405) 521-3921

Secretary of State
Chris Benge
101 State Capitol, 2300 North Lincoln
Blvd, Oklahoma City, OK 73105-4897
(405) 521-3912

Vital Statistics
Kelly Baker, MPH
State Registrar and Director, Center for
Health Statistics, OSDH
P.O. Box 53551,
Oklahoma City, OK 73152
(405) 271-2224

COURT OF LAST RESORT

Supreme Court
9 justices sit en banc
Assigns cases to the Court of Civil Appeals

Jurisdiction:
- Appeal by right civil, administrative agency. Interlocutory appeals in civil, administrative agency.
- Appeal by permission civil, administrative agency. Interlocutory appeals in civil, administrative agency.
- Exclusive original proceeding bar/judiciary, certified question.

Court of Criminal Appeals
5 judges sit en banc

Jurisdiction:
- Exclusive appeal by right criminal, juvenile. Interlocutory appeals in criminal, juvenile.
- Exclusive appeal by permission criminal, juvenile. Interlocutory appeals in criminal, juvenile.
- Exclusive death penalty.
- Original proceeding application for writ.

INTERMEDIATE APPELLATE COURT

Court of Civil Appeals (4 divisions)
12 judges sit in 3-judge panels

Jurisdiction:
- Appeal by right civil, administrative agency. Interlocutory appeals in civil, administrative agency.
- Original proceeding application for writ.

GENERAL JURISDICTION COURT

District Court (77 courts in 26 districts)
73 district, 77 associate district, and 89 special judges
Jury trials

Jurisdiction:
- Exclusive civil (except administrative agency appeals), small claims (up to $6,000).
- Exclusive domestic relations.
- Exclusive criminal.
- Exclusive juvenile.
- Traffic infractions, ordinance violations.

LIMITED JURISDICTION COURT

Court of Tax Review
3 District Court judges serve
No jury trials

Jurisdiction:
- Administrative agency appeals.

Municipal Court Not of Record (352 courts)
~360 full- and part-time judges
Jury trials

Jurisdiction:
- Traffic/other violations.

Municipal Criminal Court of Record (2 courts)
~7 full-time judges
Jury trials

Jurisdiction:
- Traffic/other violations.

Note: Oklahoma has a workers' compensation court, which hears complaints that are handled exclusively by administrative agencies in other states.

Court structure as of Fiscal Year 2015.

☐ Appellate level
☐ Trial level
↑ Route of appeal

OREGON

Chief Justice
Thomas A. "Tom" Balmer
State Supreme Court Building,
1163 State St, Salem, OR 97301-2563
(503) 986-5717

Justices of the Supreme Court
Richard C. Baldwin
David V. Brewer
Rives Kistler
Jack L. Landau
Virginia L. Linder
Martha L. Walters

Clerk of the Supreme Court
Rebecca J. "Becky" Osborne
Appellate Courts Records Administrator
Supreme Court Building, 1163 State St,
Salem, OR 97301-2563
(503) 986-5589

Court System Website
www.courts.oregon.gov/ojd

Court Administration
Kingsley W. Click
State Court Administrator
Supreme Court Building, 1163 State St,
Salem, OR 97301-2563
(503) 986-5500

Governor
Kate Brown (D)
160 State Capitol, 900 Court Street, NE,
Salem, OR 97301-4047
(503) 378-3111

State Website
www.oregon.gov

State Capitol Main Phone
(503) 378-3111

Attorney General
Ellen F. Rosenblum (D)
Justice Building, 1162 Court Street, NE,
Salem, OR 97301-4096
(503) 378-4400

Secretary of State
Jeanne Atkins (D)
136 State Capitol, Salem, OR 97310
(503) 986-1523

Vital Statistics
Jennifer A. Woodward
Section Manager/State Registrar, Vital
Records - Center for Health Statistics
800 Northeast Oregon Street,
Portland, OR 97232
(971) 673-1180
jennifer.a.woodward@state.or.us

Supreme Court
7 justices sit en banc

Jurisdiction:
- Exclusive appeal by right revenue (tax).
- Exclusive appeal by permission criminal, civil, limited administrative agency.
- Exclusive death penalty.
- Exclusive original proceeding application for writ, bar/judiciary, certified question, advisory opinion.

COURT OF LAST RESORT

Court of Appeals
13 judges sit in 3-judge panels and en banc

Jurisdiction:
- Exclusive appeal by right criminal, civil, limited administrative agency.

INTERMEDIATE APPELLATE COURT

Tax Court
1 judge
No jury trials

Jurisdiction:
- Administrative agency appeals.

Circuit Court (27 judicial districts in 36 counties; 36 courts)
174 judges
Jury trials for most case types

Jurisdiction:
- Exclusive tort, contract, real property, probate/estate, civil appeals, civil miscellaneous. Small claims (up to $7,500), mental health.
- Exclusive domestic relations (except adoption).
- Exclusive felony, criminal appeals. Misdemeanor.
- Juvenile. Exclusive termination of parental rights.
- Traffic/other violations.

GENERAL JURISDICTION COURT

County Court (7 courts)
7 judges
No jury trials

Jurisdiction:
- Probate/estate, mental health.
- Adoption.
- Juvenile (except termination of parental rights).

Justice Court
(32 courts/21 counties)
30 justices of the peace
Jury trials for some case types

Jurisdiction:
- Landlord/tenant, small claims (up to $7,500).
- Misdemeanor.
- Traffic/other violations.

Municipal Court
(144 courts)
230 judges
Jury trials for some case types

Jurisdiction:
- Misdemeanor.
- Traffic/other violations.

LIMITED JURISDICTION COURT

Note: Effective January 15, 1998 all District Courts were eliminated and District judges became Circuit judges.

Court structure as of Fiscal Year 2015.

☐	Appellate level
☐	Trial level
↑	Route of appeal

PENNSYLVANIA

Chief Justice
Thomas G. Saylor
200 North Third Street,
Harrisburg, PA 17101
(717) 772-1599

Justices of the Supreme Court
Max Baer
J. Michael Eakin
Correale F. Stevens
Debra Todd

Clerk of the Supreme Court
Irene Bizzoso
Prothonotary
P.O. Box 62575,
Harrisburg, PA 17106
(717) 787-6181

Court System Website
www.pacourts.us

Court Administration
Zygmont A. Pines
Court Administrator
1515 Market Street, Suite 1414,
Philadelphia, PA 19102
(215) 560-6300

Governor
Thomas W. "Tom" Wolf (D)
Main Capitol Building,
Harrisburg, PA 17120
(717) 787-2500

State Website
www.pa.gov

State Capitol Main Phone
(717) 787-2500

Attorney General
Kathleen Granahan Kane (D)
Strawberry Square, 16th Floor,
Harrisburg, PA 17120
(717) 787-3391

Secretary of State
Pedro A. Cortés
302 North Office Building,
Harrisburg, PA 17120
(717) 787-8727

Vital Statistics
Lana Adams
Health Statistics and Research State
Center Director, Department of Health
101 South Mercer Street,
New Castle, PA 16103
(717) 783-2548
lanadams@pa.gov

Supreme Court
7 justices sit en banc
Jurisdiction:
- Appeal by right criminal, civil, administrative agency. Interlocutory appeals in criminal, civil, administrative agency.
- Appeal by permission criminal, civil, administrative agency. Interlocutory appeals in criminal, civil, administrative agency.
- Exclusive death penalty.
- Original proceeding application for writ. Exclusive bar/judiciary, certified question.

COURT OF LAST RESORT

Commonwealth Court*
9 judges sit in 3-judge panels and en banc
Jurisdiction:
- Appeal by right criminal, civil, administrative agency. Interlocutory appeals in criminal, civil, administrative agency.
- Appeal by permission criminal, civil, limited administrative agency. Interlocutory appeals in criminal, civil, administrative agency.
- Original proceeding application for writ.

Superior Court
15 judges sit in 3-judge panels and en banc
Jurisdiction:
- Appeal by right criminal, civil. Interlocutory appeal in criminal, civil.
- Appeal by permission criminal, civil. Interlocutory appeal in criminal, civil.
- Original proceeding application for writ.

INTERMEDIATE APPELLATE COURT

Court of Common Pleas (60 districts in 67 counties)
545 judges
Jury trials in most cases
Jurisdiction:
- Tort, contract, real property, probate/estate, administrative agency appeals, miscellaneous civil.
- Domestic relations.
- Felony, miscellaneous criminal.
- Exclusive juvenile.

GENERAL JURISDICTION COURT

Philadelphia Municipal Court**
27 judges
No jury trials
Jurisdiction:
- Landlord/tenant, real property ($0 - $15,000), small claims (up to $10,000), miscellaneous civil.
- Felony, preliminary hearings, misdemeanor.
- Ordinance violations.

Magisterial District Judge Court***
(522 courts)
522 judges
No jury trials
Jurisdiction:
- Small claims (up to $8,000).
- Felony, preliminary hearings, misdemeanor.
- Traffic/other violations.

LIMITED JURISDICTION COURT

*Commonwealth Court hears cases brought by and against the Commonwealth.
**Effective 2013, the Philadelphia Traffic Court merged with the Philadelphia Municipal Court.
***Effective January 1, 2005, the Pittsburgh Municipal Court merged with the Allegheny County Magisterial District Judge Court.

Court structure as of Fiscal Year 2015.

Appellate level
Trial level
↑ Route of appeal

PUERTO RICO

Chief Justice
Liana Fiol Matta Hon
P.O. Box 9022392,
San Juan, PR 00902-2392
(787) 721-6625

Justices of the Supreme Court
Robert Cintron Feliberti
Luis Estrella Martinez
Eric V. Kolthoff Caraballo
Rafael L. Martinez Torres
Mildred G. Pabon Charneco
Edgardo Rivera Garcia
Maite Oronoz Rodriguez
Anabelle Rodriguez Rodriguez

Clerk of the Supreme Court
Aida Ileana Oquendo
P.O. Box 9022392,
San Juan, PR 00902-2392
(787) 641-6600 ext. 2072

Court System Website
www.ramajudicial.pr

Court Administration
Sonia Colon Velez Ivette
Administrative Director of the Courts
P.O. Box 9022392,
San Juan, PR 00902-2392
(787) 641-6600

Governor
Alejandro J. García Padilla (PDP)
403 Constitution Avenue,
San Juan, PR 00906
(787) 725-7234

State Website
www.pr.gov

State Capitol Main Phone
(787) 721-7000

Attorney General
César R. Miranda
P.O. Box 909192,
San Juan, PR 00902-9192
(787) 721-2900 ext. 2747

Secretary of State
Dr. David Bernier
P.O. Box 9023271,
San Juan, PR 00902-3271
(787) 722-2121

Vital Statistics
Wanda C. Llovet Diaz
Demographic Registry Director,
Health Department
P.O. Box 11854, San Juan, PR 00917
(787) 767-9120 ext. 2402

COURT OF LAST RESORT

Supreme Court
1 presiding justice, 7 associate justices
Jurisdiction:
- Appeal by right criminal, civil, administrative agency.
- Appeal by permission criminal, civil, administrative agency. Interlocutory appeals in criminal, civil, administrative agency.
- Original proceeding application for writ. Exclusive bar/judiciary, certified questions.

INTERMEDIATE APPELLATE COURT

Court of Appeals
38 judges sit in 3-judge panels
Jurisdiction:
- Appeal by right civil, administrative agency. Exclusive criminal.
- Appeal by permission criminal, civil, administrative agency. Interlocutory appeals in criminal, civil, administrative agency.
- Original proceeding application for writ.

GENERAL JURISDICTION COURT

Court of First Instance
13 regions, 337 judges

Superior Division
258 judges
Jury trials in felony cases
Jurisdiction:
- Tort, contract, real property, probate/estate, administrative agency appeals.
- Domestic relations.
- Exclusive felony. Preliminary hearings, misdemeanor.
- Juvenile.

Municipal Division
79 judges
No jury trials
Jurisdiction:
- Tort, contract, real property ($0 - $3,000), small claims (up to $5,000), miscellaneous civil.
- Non-criminal traffic (infraction), ordinance violations.

Note: The Judicial Law 2001, renamed the Judicial Reform Act of 1994, changed the name of the intermediate appellate court from the Circuit Court of Appeals to the Court of Appeals and abolished the District Division of the Court of First Instance. The District Division was abolished in 2002, and its functions were transferred to the Superior Division.

Court structure as of Fiscal Year 2015.

Appellate level
Trial level
↑   Route of appeal

RHODE ISLAND

Chief Justice
Paul A. Suttell
Frank Licht Judicial Complex,
250 Benefit Street, Providence, RI 02903
(401) 222-3943

Justices of the Supreme Court
Francis X. Flaherty
Maureen McKenna Goldberg
Gilbert V. Indeglia
William P. Robinson, III

Clerk of the Supreme Court
Debra Saunders
Frank Licht Judicial Complex,
250 Benefit Street, Providence, RI 02903
(401) 222-3272

Court System Website
www.courts.ri.gov

Court Administration
J. Joseph Baxter, Jr.
State Court Administrator
Frank Licht Judicial Complex,
250 Benefit Street, Providence, RI 02903
(401) 222-3266

Governor
Gina M. Raimondo (D)
222 State House, Providence, RI 02908
(401) 222-2080
gina.raimondo@governor.ri.gov

State Website
www.ri.gov

State Capitol Main Phone
(401) 222-2000

Attorney General
Peter F. Kilmartin (D)
150 South Main Street,
Providence, RI 02903
(401) 274-4400

Secretary of State
Nellie M. Gorbea (D)
State House, 82 Smith Street,
Room 217, Providence, RI 02903
(401) 222-2357
ngorbea@sos.ri.gov

Vital Statistics
Colleen Fontana
State Registrar Chief, Office of Vital
Records, Department of Health
Cannon Building, Three Capitol Hill,
Providence, RI 02908-5097
(401) 222-2812
colleen.fontana@health.ri.gov

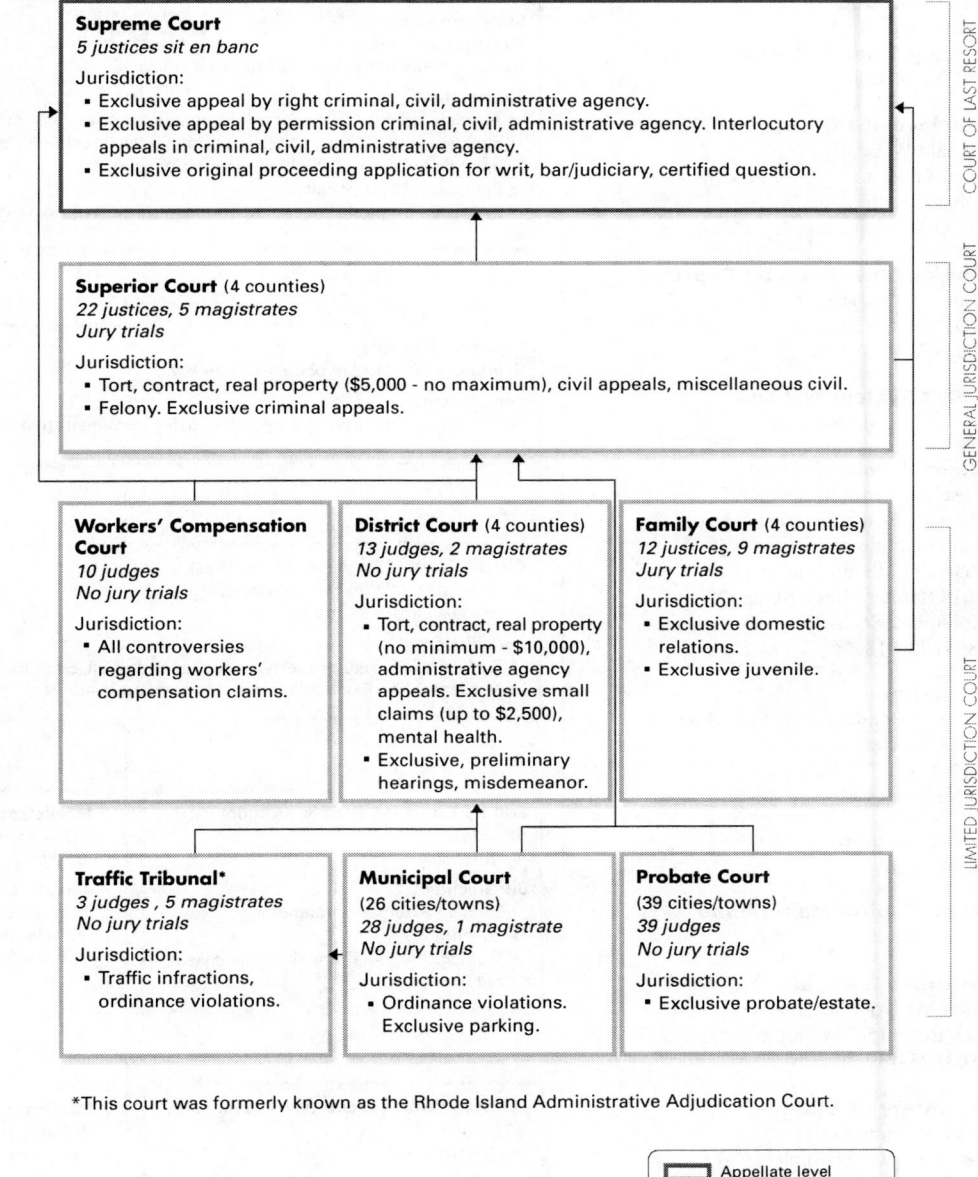

Supreme Court
5 justices sit en banc

Jurisdiction:
- Exclusive appeal by right criminal, civil, administrative agency.
- Exclusive appeal by permission criminal, civil, administrative agency. Interlocutory appeals in criminal, civil, administrative agency.
- Exclusive original proceeding application for writ, bar/judiciary, certified question.

Superior Court (4 counties)
22 justices, 5 magistrates
Jury trials

Jurisdiction:
- Tort, contract, real property ($5,000 - no maximum), civil appeals, miscellaneous civil.
- Felony. Exclusive criminal appeals.

Workers' Compensation Court
10 judges
No jury trials

Jurisdiction:
- All controversies regarding workers' compensation claims.

District Court (4 counties)
13 judges, 2 magistrates
No jury trials

Jurisdiction:
- Tort, contract, real property (no minimum - $10,000), administrative agency appeals. Exclusive small claims (up to $2,500), mental health.
- Exclusive, preliminary hearings, misdemeanor.

Family Court (4 counties)
12 justices, 9 magistrates
Jury trials

Jurisdiction:
- Exclusive domestic relations.
- Exclusive juvenile.

Traffic Tribunal*
3 judges , 5 magistrates
No jury trials

Jurisdiction:
- Traffic infractions, ordinance violations.

Municipal Court
(26 cities/towns)
28 judges, 1 magistrate
No jury trials

Jurisdiction:
- Ordinance violations. Exclusive parking.

Probate Court
(39 cities/towns)
39 judges
No jury trials

Jurisdiction:
- Exclusive probate/estate.

COURT OF LAST RESORT

GENERAL JURISDICTION COURT

LIMITED JURISDICTION COURT

*This court was formerly known as the Rhode Island Administrative Adjudication Court.

Court structure as of Fiscal Year 2015.

☐ Appellate level
☐ Trial level
↑ Route of appeal

SOUTH CAROLINA

Chief Justice
Jean Hoefer Toal
P.O. Box 12456, Columbia, SC 29201
(803) 734-1584

Justices of the Supreme Court
Donald W. Beatty
Kaye G. Hearn
John W. Kittredge
Costa M. Pleicones

Clerk of the Supreme Court
Daniel E. Shearouse
P.O. Box 11330, Columbia, SC 29211
(803) 734-1080

Court System Website
www.judicial.state.sc.us

Court Administration
Rosalyn Woodson Frierson
Director, South Carolina Court
Administration
John C. Calhoun Building,
1015 Sumter Street, Suite 200,
Columbia, SC 29201
(803) 734-1800

Governor
Nimrata Randhawa "Nikki" Haley (R)
1205 Pendleton Street,
Columbia, SC 2920
(803) 734-2100

State Website
www.sc.gov

State Capitol Main Phone
(803) 896-0000

Attorney General
Alan McCrory Wilson (R)
P.O. Box 11549, Columbia, SC 29211
(803) 734-3970

Secretary of State
Mark Hammond (R)
Edgar Brown Building,
1205 Pendleton Street, Suite 525,
Columbia, SC 29201
(803) 734-2156

Vital Statistics
Angie Saleeby
Vital Records Division Director, Public
Health Statistics, Department of Health
and Environmental Control [DHEC]
2600 Bull Street, Columbia, SC 29201
(803) 898-3324

Supreme Court
5 justices sit en banc
Assigns cases to the Court of Appeals
Jurisdiction:
- Appeal by right criminal, civil. Interlocutory appeals in criminal, civil.
- Exclusive appeal by permission criminal, civil, administrative agency. Interlocutory appeals in criminal, civil, administrative agency.
- Exclusive death penalty.
- Exclusive original proceeding application for writ, bar/judiciary, certified question.

COURT OF LAST RESORT

Court of Appeals
9 judges sit in 3-judge panels and en banc
Jurisdiction:
- Appeal by right criminal, civil. Exclusive administrative agency.

INTERMEDIATE APPELLATE COURT

Circuit Court (16 circuits, 46 counties)
49 judges and 21 masters-in-equity
Jury trials except in appeals
Jurisdiction:
- Tort, contract, real property, miscellaneous civil. Exclusive civil appeals.
- Misdemeanor. Exclusive felony, criminal appeals.

GENERAL JURISDICTION COURT

Family Court (16 circuits, 46 counties)
58 judges
No jury trials
Jurisdiction:
- Exclusive domestic relations.
- Juvenile.
- Traffic/other violations (juvenile cases only).

Magistrate Court (46 counties)
317 magistrates
Jury trials
Jurisdiction:
- Small claims (up to $7,500).
- Preliminary hearings, misdemeanor.
- Traffic/other violations.

Probate Court (46 courts, 46 counties)
46 judges
No jury trials
Jurisdiction:
- Exclusive probate/estate, mental health.

Municipal Court (~200 courts)
329 judges
Jury trials
Jurisdiction:
- Preliminary hearings, misdemeanor.
- Traffic/other violations.

LIMITED JURISDICTION COURT

Court structure as of Fiscal Year 2015.

- Appellate level
- Trial level
- ↑ Route of appeal

SOUTH DAKOTA

Chief Justice
David Gilbertson
State Capitol Building,
500 East Capitol Avenue,
Pierre, SD 57501
(605) 773-4881

Justices of the Supreme Court
Janine Kern
Glen A. Severson
Lori S. Wilbur
Steven L. Zinter

Clerk of the Supreme Court
Shirley A. Jameson-Fergel
State Capitol Building,
500 East Capitol Avenue,
Pierre, SD 57501
(605) 773-3511

Court System Website
www.sdjudicial.com

Court Administration
Greg Sattizahn
State Court Administrator
State Capitol Building,
500 East Capitol Avenue,
Pierre, SD 57501-5070
(605) 773-3474

Governor
Dennis M. Daugaard (R)
500 East Capitol Avenue,
Pierre, SD 57501
(605) 773-3212

State Website
www.sd.gov

State Capitol Main Phone
(605) 773-3011

Attorney General
Martin J. "Marty" Jackley (R)
1302 East Highway 14,
Pierre, SD 57501-8501
(605) 773-3215

Secretary of State
Shantel Krebs (R)
500 East Capitol Avenue, Suite 204,
Pierre, SD 57501-5070
(605) 773-3537

Vital Statistics
Mariah Pokorny
State Registrar of Vital Records,
Department of Health
600 East Capitol Avenue,
Pierre, SD 57501-2536
(605) 773-4961
mariah.pokorny@state.sd.us

Supreme Court
5 justices sit en banc

Jurisdiction:
- Exclusive appeal by right criminal, civil, administrative agency.
- Exclusive appeal by permission criminal, civil, administrative agency. Interlocutory appeals in criminal, civil, administrative agency.
- Exclusive death penalty.
- Exclusive original proceeding application for writ, bar/judiciary, certified question, advisory opinion.

COURT OF LAST RESORT

↑

Circuit Court (7 circuits)
41 judges
Jury trials except in small claims

Jurisdiction:
- Tort, contract, real property ($12,000 - no maximum), small claims (up to $12,000).
- Exclusive, domestic relations.
- Criminal.
- Exclusive juvenile.
- Exclusive traffic/other violations (except uncontested parking, which is handled administratively).

GENERAL JURISDICTION COURT

↑

Magistrate Court (7 circuits)
13 magistrate judges
Jury trials

Jurisdiction:
- Tort, contract, real property ($0 - $10,000), small claims (up to $12,000).
- Preliminary hearings, misdemeanor.

LIMITED JURISDICTION COURT

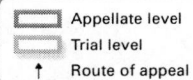

- Appellate level
- Trial level
- ↑ Route of appeal

Court structure as of Fiscal Year 2015.

TENNESSEE

Chief Justice
Sharon Gail Lee
P.O. Box 444,
Knoxville, TN 37901-0444
(865) 594-6121

Justices of the Supreme Court
Jeffrey S. Bivins
Cornelia A. Clark
Holly M. Kirby
Gary R. Wade

Clerk of the Supreme Court
James M. Hivner
Supreme Court Building,
401 Seventh Avenue North,
Nashville, TN 37219-1407
(615) 253-1470

Court System Website
www.tncourts.gov

Court Administration
Deborah Taylor Tate
Administrative Director
600 Nashville City Center,
511 Union Street, Suite 600,
Nashville, TN 37219
(615) 741-2687

Governor
William Edward "Bill" Haslam (R)
State Capitol, First Floor,
Nashville, TN 37243
(615) 741-2001

State Website
www.tn.gov

State Capitol Main Phone
(615) 741-2001

Attorney General
Herbert H. Slatery, III
P.O. Box 20207, Nashville, TN 37202
(615) 741-3491

Secretary of State
Tré Hargett (R)
State Capitol, First Floor,
Nashville, TN 37243-0305
(615) 741-2819
tre.hargett@tn.gov

Vital Statistics
R. Benton McDonough
State Registrar and Vital Records Office
Director, Department of Health
Central Services Building,
421 Fifth Avenue North, Floor One,
Nashville, TN 37243
(615) 532-2600
r.benton.mcdonough@tn.gov

COURT OF LAST RESORT

Supreme Court
5 justices sit en banc

Jurisdiction:
- Exclusive appeal by right workers' compensation.
- Appeal by permission criminal, civil, administrative agency. Interlocutory appeals in criminal, civil, administrative agency.
- Death penalty.
- Exclusive original proceeding bar admission, bar discipline/eligibility, certified question.

INTERMEDIATE APPELLATE COURT

Court of Appeals (3 divisions)
12 judges sit in 3-judge panels

Jurisdiction:
- Exclusive appeal by right civil, limited administrative agency.
- Appeal by permission, civil, administrative agency. Interlocutory appeals in civil, administrative agency.

Court of Criminal Appeals (3 divisions)
12 judges sit in 3-judge panels

Jurisdiction:
- Exclusive appeal by right criminal.
- Appeal by permission criminal. Interlocutory appeals in criminal.
- Death penalty.
- Exclusive original proceeding limited application for writ.

GENERAL JURISDICTION COURT

Circuit, Criminal, Chancery and Probate Court (31 districts)
120 judges, 33 chancellors

Circuit Court
(95 counties)
84 judges
Jury trials

Jurisdiction:
- Tort, contract, real property ($50 - no maximum), probate/estate, civil appeals.
- Domestic relations.
- Criminal.

Chancery Court
33 chancellors
Jury trials

Jurisdiction:
- Tort, contract, real property ($50 - no maximum), probate/estate, civil appeals.
- Domestic relations.

Probate Court
2 judges
No jury trials

Jurisdiction:
- Probate/estate, civil appeals.

Criminal Court
33 judges
Jury trials

Jurisdiction:
- Criminal.

LIMITED JURISDICTION COURT

Juvenile Court (98 courts)
109 judges, 45 magistrates
No jury trials

Jurisdiction:
- Mental health.
- Support, custody, paternity.
- Juvenile.

General Sessions Court
(93 counties; 2 additional counties have a trial justice court)
182 judges
No jury trials

Jurisdiction:
- Landlord/tenant, probate/estate mental health. Exclusive small claims (up to $25,000).
- Marriage dissolution, support, custody.
- Preliminary hearings, misdemeanor.
- Juvenile.
- Traffic/other violations.

Municipal Court
(228 courts)
228 judges
No jury trials

Jurisdiction:
- Preliminary hearings, misdemeanor.
- Traffic/other violations.

Court structure as of Fiscal Year 2015.

▭	Appellate level
▭	Trial level
↑	Route of appeal

TEXAS

Chief Justice
Nathan L. Hecht
P.O. Box 12248,
Capitol Station, Austin, TX 78711
(512) 463-1348

Justices of the Supreme Court
Jeffrey S. "Jeff" Boyd
Jeffrey V. "Jeff" Brown
John Devine
Paul W. Green
Eva M. Guzman
Phil Johnson
Debra H. Lehrmann
Don R. Willett

Clerk of the Supreme Court
Blake A. Hawthorne
P.O. Box 12248, Austin,
TX 78711-2248
(512) 463-1312

Court System Website
www.courts.state.tx.us

Court Administration
David Slayton
Administrative Director
P.O. Box 12066, Austin,
TX 78711-2066
(512) 463-1625

Governor
Greg Abbott (R)
P.O. Box 12428, Austin, TX 78711
(512) 463-2000

State Website
www.texas.gov

State Capitol Main Phone
(512) 463-2000

Attorney General
Ken Paxton (R)
P.O. Box 12548, Austin,
TX 78711-2548
(512) 463-2100

Secretary of State
Carlos H. Cascos, CPA, CGFM
State Capitol, P.O. Box 12697,
Austin, TX 78711
(512) 463-5770

Vital Statistics
Geraldine Harris
State Registrar, Center For Health
Statistics
P.O. Box 12040, Austin,
TX 78711-2040
(512) 776-2068
geraldine.harris@dshs.state.tx.us

Supreme Court
9 justices sit en banc
Jurisdiction:
- Exclusive appeal by permission civil, administrative agency.
- Original proceeding application for writ, certified question. Exclusive bar/judiciary.

Court of Criminal Appeals
9 judges sit en banc
Jurisdiction:
- Exclusive appeal by permission criminal.
- Exclusive death penalty.
- Original proceeding application for writ, certified question.

COURT OF LAST RESORT

Court of Appeals (14 courts)
80 justices sit in 3-judge panels
Jurisdiction:
- Appeal by right criminal, civil, administrative agency. Interlocutory appeals in criminal, civil, administrative agency.
- Original proceeding application for writ.

INTERMEDIATE APPELLATE COURT

District Courts* (454 courts)
459 courts, 459 judges

District Court (441 courts)
446 courts, 446 judges
Jury trials
Jurisdiction:
- Tort, contract, real property ($201 - no maximum), probate/estate, miscellaneous civil. Exclusive administrative agency appeal.
- Domestic relations.
- Felony, misdemeanor.
- Juvenile.

Criminal District Court
(13 courts)
13 judges
Jury trials
Jurisdiction:
- Felony, misdemeanor.

GENERAL JURISDICTION COURT

County-Level Courts (504 courts)
511 Courts, 511 judges

Constitutional County Court (254 courts)
254 judges
Jury trials
Jurisdiction:
- Tort, contract, real property ($200 - $10,000), probate/estate, mental health, civil trial court appeals, miscellaneous civil.
- Misdemeanor, criminal appeals.
- Juvenile.
- Traffic infractions.

Probate Court
(18 courts)
18 judges
Jury trials
Jurisdiction:
- Probate/estate, mental health.

Statutory County Court
(239 courts, 89 counties)
239 judges
Jury trials
Jurisdiction:
- Tort, contract, real property ($200 - $10,000), probate/estate, mental health, civil trial court appeals, miscellaneous civil.
- Misdemeanor, criminal appeals.
- Juvenile.
- Traffic infractions.

Municipal Court*
(926 cities)
1,273 judges
Jury trials
Jurisdiction:
- Misdemeanor.
- Traffic infractions. Exclusive ordinance violations.

Justice Courts* (807 courts)
807 judges
Jury trials
Jurisdiction:
- Tort, contract, real property ($0 - $10,000), small claims (up to $10,000).
- Misdemeanor.
- Traffic infractions, parking.

LIMITED JURISDICTION COURT

*Some Municipal and Justice of the Peace courts may appeal to the District court.

Court structure as of Fiscal Year 2015.

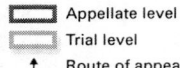
☐ Appellate level
☐ Trial level
↑ Route of appeal

UTAH

Chief Justice
Matthew B. Durrant
P.O. Box 140210,
Salt Lake City, UT 84114-0210
(801) 238-7937

Justices of the Supreme Court
Christine M. Durham
Constandinos "Deno" Himonas
Thomas Rex "Tom" Lee
Jill N. Parrish

Clerk of the Supreme Court
Andrea Martinez
P.O. Box 140210,
Salt Lake City, UT 84114-0210
(801) 238-7974

Court System Website
www.utcourts.gov

Court Administration
Daniel J. "Dan" Becker
State Court Administrator
P.O. Box 140241,
Salt Lake City, UT 84114-0241
(801) 578-3806

Governor
Gary Richard Herbert (R)
P.O. Box 142220,
Salt Lake City, UT 84114-2220
(801) 538-1000

State Website
www.utah.gov

State Capitol Main Phone
(801) 538-3000

Attorney General
Sean D. Reyes
P.O. Box 142320,
Salt Lake City, UT 84114-2320
(801) 366-0260

Lieutenant Governor
Spencer J. Cox
Utah State Capitol, Suite 220,
Salt Lake City, UT 84114
(801) 538-1048

Vital Statistics
Janice Houston
State Registrar and Director, Office of
Vital Records, Center for Health Data
P.O. Box 141012,
Salt Lake City, UT 84114-1012
(801) 538-6262
jlhouston@utah.gov

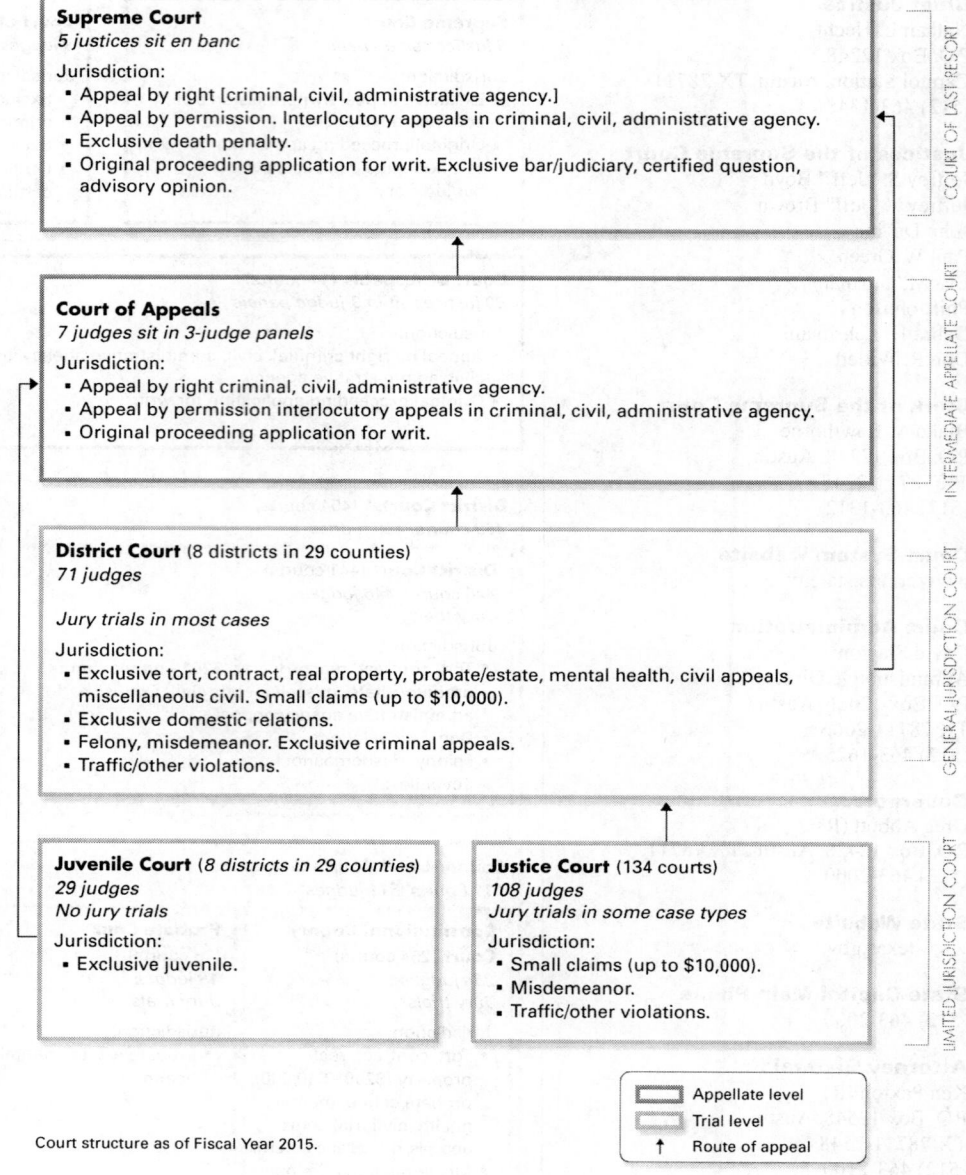

Supreme Court
5 justices sit en banc
Jurisdiction:
- Appeal by right [criminal, civil, administrative agency.]
- Appeal by permission. Interlocutory appeals in criminal, civil, administrative agency.
- Exclusive death penalty.
- Original proceeding application for writ. Exclusive bar/judiciary, certified question, advisory opinion.

Court of Appeals
7 judges sit in 3-judge panels
Jurisdiction:
- Appeal by right criminal, civil, administrative agency.
- Appeal by permission interlocutory appeals in criminal, civil, administrative agency.
- Original proceeding application for writ.

District Court (8 districts in 29 counties)
71 judges

Jury trials in most cases
Jurisdiction:
- Exclusive tort, contract, real property, probate/estate, mental health, civil appeals, miscellaneous civil. Small claims (up to $10,000).
- Exclusive domestic relations.
- Felony, misdemeanor. Exclusive criminal appeals.
- Traffic/other violations.

Juvenile Court (*8 districts in 29 counties*)
29 judges
No jury trials
Jurisdiction:
- Exclusive juvenile.

Justice Court (134 courts)
108 judges
Jury trials in some case types
Jurisdiction:
- Small claims (up to $10,000).
- Misdemeanor.
- Traffic/other violations.

COURT OF LAST RESORT

INTERMEDIATE APPELLATE COURT

GENERAL JURISDICTION COURT

LIMITED JURISDICTION COURT

Court structure as of Fiscal Year 2015.

- ☐ Appellate level
- ☐ Trial level
- ↑ Route of appeal

VERMONT

Chief Justice
Paul L. Reiber
109 State Street,
Montpelier, VT 05609-0801
(802) 828-4784

Justices of the Supreme Court
John A. Dooley
Harold E. Eaton, Jr.
Beth Robinson
Marilyn S. Skoglund

Clerk of the Supreme Court
Patricia Gabel
Court Administrator and Clerk of Court
111 State Street,
Montpelier, VT 05609-0801
(802) 828-3278

Court System Website
www.vermontjudiciary.org

Court Administration
Patricia Gabel
Court Administrator and Clerk of Court
111 State Street,
Montpelier, VT 05609-0801
(802) 828-3278

Governor
Peter E. Shumlin (D)
Pavilion Office Building,
109 State Street, Fifth Floor,
Montpelier, VT 05609-0101
(802) 828-3333

State Website
www.vermont.gov

State Capitol Main Phone
(802) 828-1110

Attorney General
William H. "Bill" Sorrell (D)
Pavilion Office Building, 109 State St,
Montpelier, VT 05609-1001
(802) 828-3173
bsorrell@atg.state.vt.us

Secretary of State
James C. "Jim" Condos (D)
128 State Street, Montpelier, VT 05633
(802) 828-2148
secretary@sec.state.vt.us

Vital Statistics
Cynthia Hooley
Vital Records Section Chief, Health
Department, Agency of Human Services
PO Box 70, Burlington, VT 05402-0070
(802) 651-1636
cynthia.hooley@state.vt.us

Supreme Court
5 justices sit en banc

Jurisdiction:
- Exclusive appeal by right criminal, civil, administrative agency. Interlocutory appeals in criminal, civil, administrative agency.
- Exclusive appeal by permission criminal, civil, administrative agency. Interlocutory appeals in criminal, civil, administrative agency.
- Exclusive original proceeding bar admission, bar discipline/eligibility, certified question.

COURT OF LAST RESORT

Superior Court
34 superior judges, 14 probate judges, 5 magistrates, 28 assistant judges

Civil Division
14 counties, 32 superior judges, 5 magistrates, 28 assistant judges (shared)
Jury trials

Jurisdiction:
- Civil appeals, civil miscellaneous.

Criminal Division
14 counties, 32 superior judges, 5 magistrates, 28 assistant judges (shared)
Jury trials

Jurisdiction:
- Felonies and misdemeanors.
- Municipal appeals.
- License suspensions.

Family Division
14 counties, 32 superior judges, 5 magistrates, 28 assistant judges (shared)
No jury trials

Jurisdiction:
- Child support, visitation, protective services.
- Mental health.
- Divorce and annulment.

Environmental Division
Statewide, 2 superior judges
No jury trials

Jurisdiction:
- Administrative agency appeals.

Probate Division
14 counties, 14 judges
No jury trials

Jurisdiction:
- Wills, estates, trusts.
- Adoption and appointment of guardians.
- Certifications.
- Civil miscellaneous.

GENERAL JURISDICTION COURT

Vermont Judicial Bureau
2 hearing officers
No jury trials

Jurisdiction:
- Other civil violations.
- Traffic infractions, ordinance violations.

LIMITED JURISDICTION COURT

Note: On July 1, 2010 the courts of Vermont were unified into five divisions under the administrative control of the Supreme Court.

Court structure as of Fiscal Year 2015.

☐ Appellate level
☐ Trial level
↑ Route of appeal

VIRGINIA

Chief Justice
Donald W. Lemons
100 North Ninth Street,
Richmond, VA 23219
(804) 225-2183

Justices of the Supreme Court
S. Bernard Goodwyn
D. Arthur Kelsey
Elizabeth A. McClanahan
LeRoy F. Millette, Jr.
William C. "Bill" Mims
Cleo Elaine Powell
Lawrence L. Koontz, Jr., Senior Justice
Elizabeth B. Lacy, Senior Justice
Charles S. Russell, Senior Justice

Clerk of the Supreme Court
Patricia L. Harrington
100 North Ninth Street,
Richmond, VA 2321
(804) 786-2251

Court System Website
www.courts.state.va.us

Court Administration
Karl R. Hade
Executive Secretary
Supreme Court Bldg, 100 North Ninth
Street, 3rd Floor, Richmond, VA 23219
(804) 786-6455

Governor
Terence Richard "Terry" McAuliffe (D)
P.O. Box 1475, Richmond, VA 23218
(804) 786-2211

State Website
www.virginia.gov

State Capitol Main Phone
(804) 786-0000

Attorney General
Mark R. Herring (D)
900 East Main Street
Richmond, VA 23219
(804)786-2071

Secretary of the Commonwealth
Levar Stoney
P.O. Box 2454, Richmond, VA 23218
(804) 786-2441

Vital Statistics
Janet Rainey
Vital Records Division Director,
Department of Health [VDH], Health
and Human Resources Secretariat
2001 Maywill Street,
Richmond, VA 23230
(804) 662-6245

Supreme Court of Appeals
5 justices sit en banc

Jurisdiction:
- Exclusive appeal by permission criminal, civil, administrative agency. Interlocutory appeals in criminal, civil, administrative agency.
- Exclusive original proceeding application for writ, bar/judiciary, certified question.

COURT OF LAST RESORT

Circuit Court (55 counties, 31 circuits)
70 judges
Jury trials

Jurisdiction:
- Tort, contract, real property ($300 - no maximum). Exclusive probate/estate, mental health, civil appeals.
- Domestic relations.
- Misdemeanor. Exclusive felony, criminal appeals.
- Juvenile.

GENERAL JURISDICTION COURT

Magistrate Court
(55 counties)
158 magistrates
Jury trials

Jurisdiction:
- Small claims ($0 - $5,000), mental health.
- Emergency civil protection/restraining orders.
- Preliminary hearings, misdemeanor.
- Juvenile.
- Traffic infractions.

Family Court (27 circuits)
45 judges
No jury trials

Jurisdiction:
- Domestic relations.
- Domestic violence.

Municipal Court

Jury trials

Jurisdiction:
DWI/DUI.
- Traffic infractions.
- Exclusive parking, ordinance violations.

LIMITED JURISDICTION COURT

Court structure as of Fiscal Year 2015.

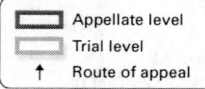

☐	Appellate level
☐	Trial level
↑	Route of appeal

WASHINGTON

Chief Justice
Barbara A. Madsen
P.O. Box 40929,
Olympia, WA 98504-0929
(360) 357-2037

Justices of the Supreme Court
Charles W. Johnson, Associate Chief
Justice
Mary E. Fairhurst
Steven C. González
Sheryl McCloud
Susan Owens
Debra L. Stephens
Charles K. Wiggins
Mary Yu

Clerk of the Supreme Court
Ronald R. Carpenter
P.O. Box 40929,
Olympia, WA 98504-0929
(360) 357-2077

Court System Website
www.courts.wa.gov

Court Administration
Callie T. Dietz
Administrator
P.O. Box 41170,
Olympia, WA 98504-1170
(360) 357-2121

Governor
Jay Robert Inslee (D)
P.O. Box 40002,
Olympia, WA 98504-0002
(360) 902-4111

State Website
www.access.wa.gov/

State Capitol Main Phone
(360) 753-5000

Attorney General
Robert W. "Bob" Ferguson (D)
P.O. Box 40100,
Olympia, WA 98504-0100
(360) 753-6200

Secretary of State
Kim Wyman, CERA (R)
PO Box 40220,
Olympia, WA 98504-0220
(360) 902-4499

Vital Statistics
Jennifer Tebaldi
Epidemiology, Health Statistics & Public
Health Laboratories Asst Sec, DOH
PO Box 47811,
Olympia, WA 98504-7811
(360) 236-4204

Supreme Court
9 justices sit en banc

Jurisdiction:
- Appeal by permission criminal, civil, administrative agency. Interlocutory appeals in criminal, civil, administrative agency.
- Exclusive death penalty.
- Original proceeding application for writ. Exclusive bar/judiciary, certified question.

Court of Appeals (3 courts/divisions)
22 judges sit in 3-judge panels

Jurisdiction:
- Exclusive appeal by right criminal, civil, administrative agency.
- Appeal by permission, interlocutory appeals in criminal, civil, administrative agency.
- Original proceeding application for writ.

Superior Court (32 districts in 39 counties)
185 judges (and 48 full-time court commissioners, 7.93 part-time commissioners)
Jury trials

Jurisdiction:
- Tort, contract. Exclusive real property, probate/estate, mental health, civil appeals, miscellaneous civil.
- Exclusive domestic relations.
- Exclusive felony, criminal appeals.
- Exclusive juvenile.

Municipal Court (~81 courts)
111 judges (including 12 court commissioners and magistrates)
Jury trials except in traffic infractions and parking violations

Jurisdiction:
- Misdemeanor.
- Traffic/other violations.

District Court* (~44 courts)
118 judges (including 10 court commissioners and magistrates)
Jury trials except in traffic infractions and parking violations

Jurisdiction:
- Tort, contract ($0 - $75,000). Exclusive small claims (up to $5,000).
- Preliminary hearings, misdemeanor.
- Traffic/other violations.

COURT OF LAST RESORT

INTERMEDIATE APPELLATE COURT

GENERAL JURISDICTION COURT

LIMITED JURISDICTION COURT

*District Court provides services to municipalities that do not have a Municipal Court.

Court structure as of Fiscal Year 2015.

☐ Appellate level
☐ Trial level
↑ Route of appeal

WEST VIRGINIA

Chief Justice
Margaret L. Workman
State Capitol Complex,
Charleston, WV 25302
(304) 558-2606

Justices of the Supreme Court
Brent D. Benjamin
Robin Jean Davis
Menis E. Ketchum, II
Allen H. Loughry, II

Clerk of the Supreme Court
Rory L. Perry, II
Capitol Complex,
1900 Kanawha Blvdd East,
Room E-317, Charleston, WV 25305
(304) 558-2601

Court System Website
www.state.wv.us/wvsca

Court Administration
Steven D. Canterbury
Administrative Director
Capitol Complex,
1900 Kanawha Blvd East, Building 1,
Room E-100, Charleston, WV 25305
(304) 558-0145

Governor
Earl Ray Tomblin (D)
State Capitol Building, 1900 Kanawha
Boulevard East, Charleston, WV 25305
(304) 558-2000

State Website
www.wv.gov

State Capitol Main Phone
(304) 558-3456

Attorney General
Patrick Morrisey (R)
State Capitol Complex, Building 1,
Room E-26, Charleston, WV 25305
(304) 558-2021

Secretary of State
Natalie E. Tennant (D)
State Capitol Complex, Building One,
1900 Kanawha Blvd, East, Suite 157K,
Charleston, WV 25305-0770
(304) 558-6000

Vital Statistics
Gary L. Thompson
State Registrar and Assistant Director,
Health Statistics Center, Department of
Health and Human Resources [DHHR]
350 Capitol Street, Room 165,
Charleston, WV 25301
(304) 558-2931

Supreme Court of Appeals
5 justices sit en banc

Jurisdiction:
- Exclusive appeal by permission criminal, civil, administrative agency. Interlocutory appeals in criminal, civil, administrative agency.
- Exclusive original proceeding application for writ, bar/judiciary, certified question.

COURT OF LAST RESORT

Circuit Court (55 counties, 31 circuits)
70 judges
Jury trials

Jurisdiction:
- Tort, contract, real property ($300 - no maximum). Exclusive probate/estate, mental health, civil appeals.
- Domestic relations.
- Misdemeanor. Exclusive felony, criminal appeals.
- Juvenile.

GENERAL JURISDICTION COURT

Magistrate Court
(55 counties)
158 magistrates
Jury trials

Jurisdiction:
- Small claims ($0 - $5,000), mental health.
- Emergency civil protection/restraining orders.
- Preliminary hearings, misdemeanor.
- Juvenile.
- Traffic infractions.

Family Court (27 circuits)
45 judges
No jury trials

Jurisdiction:
- Domestic relations.
- Domestic violence.

Municipal Court

Jury trials

Jurisdiction:
DWI/DUI.
- Traffic infractions.
- Exclusive parking, ordinance violations.

LIMITED JURISDICTION COURT

Court structure as of Fiscal Year 2015.

☐ Appellate level
☐ Trial level
↑ Route of appeal

       State Court Clerks and County Courthouses

WISCONSIN

Chief Justice
Patience Drake Roggensack
P.O. Box 1688,
Madison, WI 53701-1688
(608) 266-1888

Justices of the Supreme Court
Shirley S. Abrahamson
Ann Walsh Bradley
N. Patrick Crooks
Michael J. Gableman
David T. Prosser
Annette Kingsland Ziegler

Clerk of the Supreme Court
Diane Fremgen
P.O. Box 1688,
Madison, WI 53701-1688
(608) 266-1880

Court System Website
www.wicourts.gov

Court Administration
J. Denis Moran
Director of State Courts (Interim)
P.O. Box 1688,
Madison, WI 53701-1688
(608) 266-6828

Governor
Scott K. Walker (R)
State Capitol, 115 East Capitol,
Madison, WI 53702
(608) 266-1212

State Website
www.wisconsin.gov

State Capitol Main Phone
(608) 266-1212

Attorney General
Brad Schimel (R)
P.O. Box 7857, Madison, WI 53707
(608) 266-1221

Secretary of State
Douglas La Follette (D)
P.O. Box 7848,
Madison, WI 53707-7848
(608) 266-8888

Vital Statistics
Rebecca Biel, Vital Records Section
Chief (Interim), Public Health Division,
Department of Health Services
P.O. Box 309, Madison, WI 53701-0309
(608) 267-9171
rebecca.biel@wisconsin.com

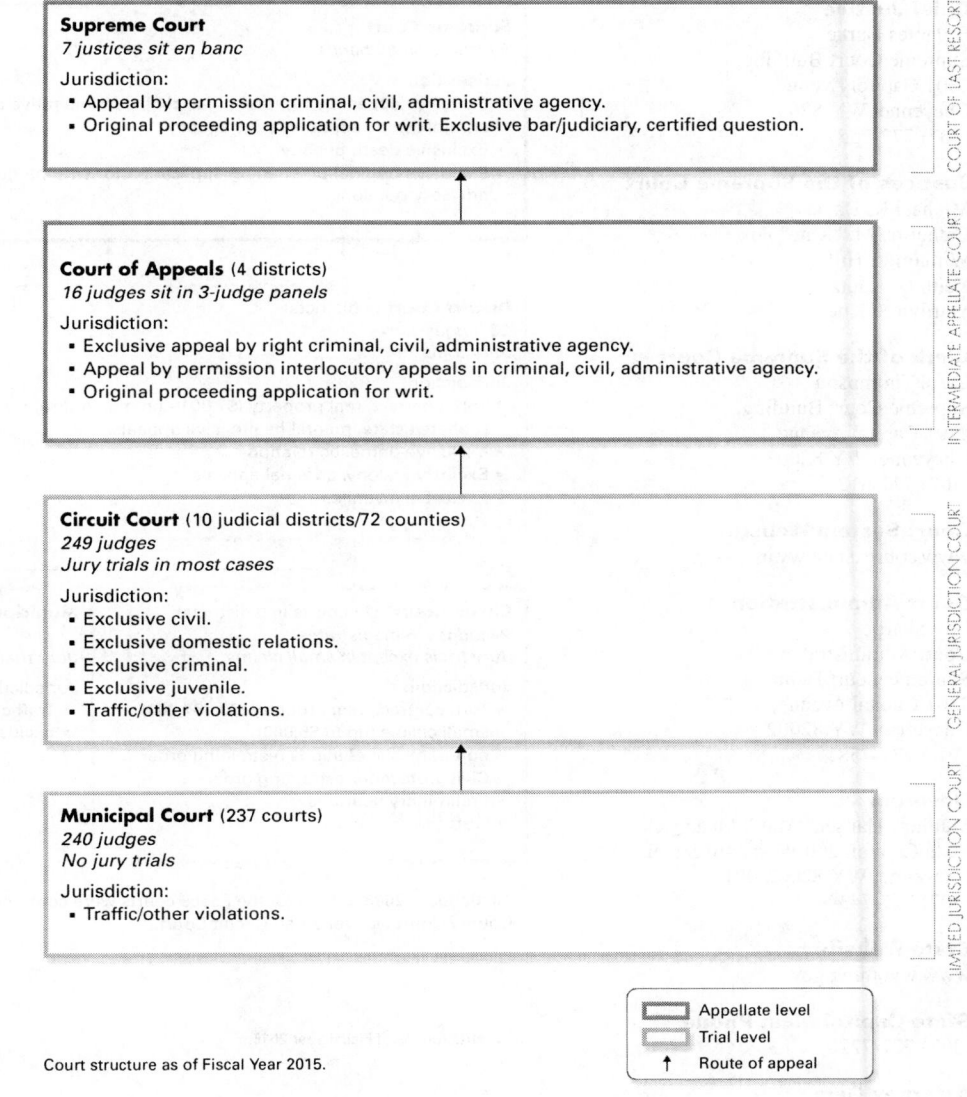

Supreme Court
7 justices sit en banc
Jurisdiction:
- Appeal by permission criminal, civil, administrative agency.
- Original proceeding application for writ. Exclusive bar/judiciary, certified question.

Court of Appeals (4 districts)
16 judges sit in 3-judge panels
Jurisdiction:
- Exclusive appeal by right criminal, civil, administrative agency.
- Appeal by permission interlocutory appeals in criminal, civil, administrative agency.
- Original proceeding application for writ.

Circuit Court (10 judicial districts/72 counties)
249 judges
Jury trials in most cases
Jurisdiction:
- Exclusive civil.
- Exclusive domestic relations.
- Exclusive criminal.
- Exclusive juvenile.
- Traffic/other violations.

Municipal Court (237 courts)
240 judges
No jury trials
Jurisdiction:
- Traffic/other violations.

COURT OF LAST RESORT
INTERMEDIATE APPELLATE COURT
GENERAL JURISDICTION COURT
LIMITED JURISDICTION COURT

Court structure as of Fiscal Year 2015.

Appellate level
Trial level
↑ Route of appeal

WYOMING

COURT OF LAST RESORT

Chief Justice
E. James Burke
Supreme Court Building,
2301 Capitol Avenue,
Cheyenne, WY 82002
(307) 777-7557

Justices of the Supreme Court
Michael K. Davis
Catherine M. "Kate" Fox
William U. Hill
Keith G. Kautz
Marilyn S. Kite

Clerk of the Supreme Court
Carol Thompson
Supreme Court Building,
2301 Capital Avenue,
Cheyenne, WY 82002
(307) 777-6129

Court System Website
www.courts.state.wy.us

Court Administration
Lily Sharpe
Court Administrator
Supreme Court Building,
2301 Capital Avenue,
Cheyenne, WY 82002
(307) 777-7581

Governor
Matthew Hansen "Matt" Mead (R)
State Capitol, 200 West 24th Street,
Cheyenne, WY 82002-0010
(307) 777-7434

State Website
www.wyoming.gov

State Capitol Main Phone
(307) 777-7220

Attorney General
Peter K. Michael
Attorney General (Interim)
123 State Capitol, Cheyenne, WY 82002
(307) 777-7841

Secretary of State
Edward F. Murray, III (R)
State Capitol, 200 West 24th Street,
Room 106, Cheyenne, WY 82002-0020
(307) 777-7378

Vital Statistics
James M. "Jim" McBride
Vital Statistics Services Manager,
Wyoming Department of Health [WDH]
401 Hathaway Building, 2300 Capitol
Avenue, Cheyenne, WY 82002
(307) 777-6040

Supreme Court
5 justices sit en banc

Jurisdiction:
- Exclusive appeal by right criminal, civil, administrative agency. Interlocutory appeals in criminal, civil, administrative agency.
- Exclusive death penalty.
- Exclusive original proceeding application for writ, bar/judiciary, certified question, advisory opinion.

District Court (9 districts)
23 judges
Jury trials

Jurisdiction:
- Tort, contract, real property ($7,001 - no maximum), civil miscellaneous. Exclusive probate/estate, mental health, civil appeals.
- Exclusive domestic relations.
- Exclusive felony, criminal appeals.
- Exclusive juvenile.

Circuit Court* (24 courts in 9 districts)
24 judges, 6 magistrates
Jury trials except in small claims

Jurisdiction:
- Tort, contract, real property ($0 - $7,000), small claims (up to $5,000), non-domestic relations restraining order.
- Civil protection/restraining order.
- Preliminary hearings.
- Traffic infractions.

Municipal Court

Jury trials

Jurisdiction:
- Traffic infractions, parking.
- Exclusive ordinance violations.

*In January 2003, Justice of the Peace courts were combined with County courts, and County Court was renamed Circuit Court.

Court structure as of Fiscal Year 2015.

COURT OF LAST RESORT · GENERAL JURISDICTION COURT · LIMITED JURISDICTION COURT

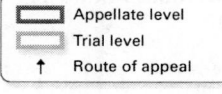

	Appellate level
	Trial level
↑	Route of appeal

State Court Clerks and County Courthouses

Alabama Court Clerks and Courthouses

The trial courts of general jurisdiction in Alabama are called circuit courts. There are 41 judicial circuits, each circuit consisting of one or more counties. There is a separate district court (limited jurisdiction) in each county. In most counties, the clerk of the circuit court also serves as clerk of the district courts in that circuit.

Alabama Supreme Court

300 Dexter Avenue, Montgomery, AL 36104-3741
Tel: (334) 229-0700 Fax: (334) 229-0522
Internet: http://judicial.alabama.gov
Internet: http://judicial.alabama.gov/supreme.cfm

The Supreme Court consists of a chief justice and eight associate justices who are elected in statewide partisan elections for six-year terms. Vacancies are filled on an interim basis by the Governor. The Supreme Court has general supervisory authority over all courts in the state and the authority to review any judgment of any other court in the state. The Court has exclusive appellate jurisdiction in actions involving title to or possession of land, in civil cases when the amount exceeds $50,000 and in all appeals involving utility rates approved by the Alabama Public Service Commission. The Court may review decisions of the Alabama Court of Criminal Appeals or the Court of Civil Appeals, as well as all decisions involving capital cases.

Court Staff
Clerk of the Supreme Court **Julia J. Weller** . . . . (334) 229-0700
Fax: (334) 229-0522

Alabama Court of Civil Appeals

300 Dexter Avenue, Montgomery, AL 36104-3741
Tel: (334) 229-0733 Fax: (334) 229-0530
Internet: http://judicial.alabama.gov/civil.cfm

The Court of Civil Appeals, created by the Alabama State Legislature in 1969, consists of a presiding judge and four judges who are elected in statewide partisan elections for six-year terms. The presiding judge is selected based on seniority, and vacancies are filled on an interim basis by the Governor. The Court of Civil Appeals is a court of intermediate appeals in Alabama. The Court has exclusive appellate jurisdiction in all civil cases when the amount in controversy does not exceed $50,000 and also has exclusive appellate jurisdiction in domestic relations cases, workers' compensation cases and all administrative cases (excluding those involving the Alabama Public Service Commission).

Court Staff
Clerk of Court **Rebecca C. Oates** . . . . (334) 229-0733
E-mail: roates@appellate.state.al.us

Alabama Court of Criminal Appeals

300 Dexter Avenue, Montgomery, AL 36104-3741
Tel: (334) 229-0751 Fax: (334) 229-0521
Internet: http://judicial.alabama.gov/criminal.cfm

The Court of Criminal Appeals is a five-judge court consisting of a presiding judge and four judges who are elected in statewide partisan elections for six-year terms. The presiding judge is elected by peer vote. Vacancies on the Court are temporarily filled by gubernatorial appointment. The Court of Criminal Appeals is a court of intermediate appeals in Alabama. The Court has exclusive appellate jurisdiction over all misdemeanors, including violations of municipal ordinances, all felonies, and all post conviction writs in criminal cases.

Alabama Court Clerks and Courthouses *continued*

Court Staff
Clerk of Court **D. Scott Mitchell** . . . . (334) 229-0751

County-By-County

Autauga County

Circuit Clerk

Nineteenth Judicial District
8935 US Highway 231, Wetumpka, AL 36092

Circuit Clerk, Autauga County **William W. Moncrief** . . . . (334) 358-6801
134 North Court Street, Room 114,
Prattville, AL 35057

Baldwin County

Circuit Clerk

Twenty-Eighth Judicial District
312 Courthouse Square, Suite 22, Bay Minette, AL 35507

Circuit Clerk **Jody W. Campbell** . . . . (251) 937-9561
312 Courthouse Square, Suite 10,
Bay Minette, AL 35507
E-mail: jody.campbell@alacourt.gov

Barbour County

Circuit Clerk

Third Judicial District
303 East Broad Street, Eufaula, AL 36027

Circuit Clerk, Barbour County **David S. Nix** . . . . (334) 775-8366
One Court Square, Clayton, AL 35016
E-mail: david.nix@alacourt.gov

Bibb County

Circuit Clerk

Fourth Judicial District
P.O. Box 475, Centreville, AL 35042

Circuit Clerk, Bibb County **Gayle Bearden** . . . . (205) 926-3103
35 Court Square East, Centreville, AL 35042
E-mail: gayle.bearden@alacourt.gov

Blount County

Circuit Clerk

Forty-First Judicial District
220 Second Avenue East, Room 207, Oneonta, AL 35121

Circuit Clerk **Michael E. Criswell** . . . . (205) 625-4153
220 Second Avenue East, Room 208,
Oneonta, AL 35121

(continued on next page)

Bullock County

Circuit Clerk

Third Judicial District
303 East Broad Street, Eufaula, AL 36027

Circuit Clerk, Bullock County **RaShawn Harris** . . . . (334) 738-2280
217 North Prairie, Union Springs, AL 36089
E-mail: rashawn.harris@alacourt.gov

Butler County

Circuit Clerk

Second Judicial District
700 Court Square, Greenville, AL 36037

Circuit Clerk, Butler County **Mattie Gomillion** . . . . (334) 382-3521
700 Court Square, Greenville, AL 36037

Calhoun County

Circuit Clerk

Seventh Judicial District
25 West 11th Street, Anniston, AL 36201

Circuit Clerk, Calhoun County **Eli Henderson** . . . . (256) 231-1750
25 West 11th Street, Anniston, AL 36201
E-mail: eli.henderson@alacourt.gov

Chambers County

Circuit Clerk

Fifth Judicial Circuit
101 East Rosa Parks Avenue, Tuskegee, AL 35083

Circuit Clerk, Chambers County **Lisa Burdette** . . . . (334) 864-4348
2 South Lafayette Street, Lafayette, AL 36862
E-mail: lisa.burdette@alacourt.gov

Cherokee County

Circuit Clerk

Ninth Judicial District
300 Grand Avenue, Suite 403, Fort Payne, AL 35967

Circuit Clerk, Cherokee County **Dwayne Amos** . . . . (256) 927-3637
100 Main Street, Centre, AL 35960
E-mail: dwayne.amos@alacourt.gov

Chilton County

Circuit Clerk

Nineteenth Judicial District
8935 US Highway 231, Wetumpka, AL 36092

Circuit Clerk, Chilton County **Glenn D. McGriff** . . . . (205) 755-4275
500 Second Avenue North,
Clayton, AL 35046
E-mail: glenn.mcgriff@alacourt.gov

Choctaw County

Circuit Clerk

First Judicial District
One Court Street, Chatom, AL 35518

Circuit Clerk, Choctaw County **Donna Murphy** . . . . (251) 275-3363
117 South Mulberry Street,
Butler, AL 35904
E-mail: donna.murphy@alacourt.gov

Clarke County

Circuit Clerk

First Judicial District
One Court Street, Chatom, AL 35518

Circuit Clerk, Clarke County **Summer Scruggs** . . . . (251) 275-3363
114 Court Street, Grove Hill, AL 35451
E-mail: summer.scruggs@alacourt.gov

Clay County

Circuit Clerk

Fortieth Judicial District
P.O. Box 212, Ashland, AL 36251

Circuit Clerk, Clay County **Jeffery L. Colburn** . . . . (256) 354-2926
P.O. Box 816, Ashland, AL 36251

Cleburne County

Circuit Clerk

Seventh Judicial District
25 West 11th Street, Anniston, AL 36201

Circuit Clerk, Cleburne County **Jerry P. Owen** . . . . (256) 463-2651
120 Vickery Street, Heflin, AL 36264

Coffee County

Circuit Clerk

Twelfth Judicial District
230 M Court, Elba, AL 36323
120 West Church Street, Troy, AL 36081

Circuit Clerk, Coffee County **James M. Counts** . . . . (334) 897-2954
230 M Court, Elba, AL 36323   Tel: (334) 347-2519

Colbert County

Circuit Clerk

Thirty-First Judicial Circuit
201 North Main Street, Tuscumbia, AL 35574
Tel: (256) 386-8526

Circuit Clerk **Nancy L. Hearn** . . . . (256) 386-5854
201 North Main Street, Tuscumbia, AL 35574
E-mail: nancy.hearn@alacourt.gov

Conecuh County

Circuit Clerk

Thirty-Fifth Judicial Circuit
111 Court Street, Monroeville, AL 36461

Circuit Clerk, Conecuh County **David F. Jackson** . . . . (251) 578-2066
111 Court Street, Monroeville, AL 36461
E-mail: david.jackson@alacourt.gov

Coosa County

Circuit Clerk

Fortieth Judicial District
P.O. Box 212, Ashland, AL 36251

Circuit Clerk, Coosa County **Jeffrey A. Wood** . . . . (256) 377-4988
P.O. Box 96, Rockford, AL 35136

Covington County

Circuit Clerk

Twenty-Second Judicial District
1K North Court Square, Andalusia, AL 36420

Circuit Clerk **Amy Jones** . . . . (334) 428-2520
1K North Court Square, Andalusia, AL 36420
E-mail: amy.jones@alacourt.gov

Crenshaw County

Circuit Clerk

Second Judicial District
700 Court Square, Greenville, AL 36037

Circuit Clerk, Crenshaw County **Jeannie Gibson** . . . . (334) 335-6575
South Glenwood Avenue, Luverne, AL 36049
E-mail: jeannie.gibson@alacourt.gov

Cullman County

Circuit Clerk

Thirty-Second Judicial Circuit
500 Second Avenue SW, Cullman, AL 35055
Tel: (256) 775-4654

Circuit Clerk **Lisa McSwain** . . . . (256) 775-4654
500 Second Avenue SW, Cullman, AL 35055
E-mail: lisa.mcswain@alacourt.gov

Dale County

Circuit Clerk

Thirty-Third Judicial District
100 East Court Square, Ozark, AL 36360
200 North Commerce Street, Geneva, AL 36340
Tel: (334) 774-5003   Tel: (334) 684-5620

Circuit Clerk, Dale County **Delores Woodham** . . . . (334) 774-5003
100 East Court Square, Ozark, AL 36360
E-mail: delores.woodham@alacourt.gov

Dallas County

Circuit Clerk

Fourth Judicial District
P.O. Box 475, Centreville, AL 35042

Circuit Clerk, Dallas County **Cheryl S. Ratcliff** . . . . (334) 874-2523
105 Lauderdale Street, Selma, AL 35701
E-mail: cheryl.ratcliff@alacourt.gov

DeKalb County

Circuit Clerk

Ninth Judicial District
300 Grand Avenue, Suite 403, Fort Payne, AL 35967

Circuit Clerk, DeKalb County **Palma B. Simpson** . . . . (256) 845-8525
300 Grand Avenue, Fort Payne, AL 35967
E-mail: palma.simpson@alacourt.gov

Elmore County

Circuit Clerk

Nineteenth Judicial District
8935 US Highway 231, Wetumpka, AL 36092

Circuit Clerk, Elmore County **Brian Justiss** . . . . (334) 567-1123
8935 US Highway 231, Wetumpka, AL 36092
E-mail: brian.justiss@alacourt.gov

Escambia County

Circuit Clerk

Twenty-First Judicial District
P.O. Box 795, Brewton, AL 36427

Circuit Clerk **John Fountain** . . . . (251) 867-0225
314 Belleville Avenue, Brewton, AL 36427
P.O. Box 856, Brewton, AL 35427
E-mail: john.fountain@alacourt.gov

Etowah County

Circuit Clerk

Sixteenth Judicial District
801 Forrest Avenue, Suite 303, Gadsden, AL 35901

Circuit Clerk **Samantha Johnson** . . . . (256) 549-2181
801 Forrest Avenue, Gadsden, AL 35901

Fayette County

Circuit Clerk

Twenty-Fourth Judicial Circuit
113 Temple Avenue, Fayette, AL 35555

Circuit Clerk, Fayette County **Samantha Howard** . . . . (205) 932-4617
113 Temple Avenue, Fayette, AL 35555
E-mail: samantha.howard@alacourt.gov

(continued on next page)

Franklin County

Circuit Clerk

Thirty-Fourth Judicial District
410 Jackson Avenue North, Russellville, AL 35653
Tel: (256) 332-8861

Circuit Clerk **Anita M. Scott** . . . . (256) 332-8861
410 Jackson Avenue North,
Russellville, AL 35653
E-mail: anita.scott@alacourt.gov

Geneva County

Circuit Clerk

Thirty-Third Judicial District
100 East Court Square, Ozark, AL 36360
200 North Commerce Street, Geneva, AL 36340
Tel: (334) 774-5003 Tel: (334) 684-5620

Circuit Clerk, Geneva County **Gale Laye** . . . . (334) 684-5620
200 North Commerce Street,
Geneva, AL 36340
E-mail: gale.laye@alacourt.gov

Greene County

Circuit Clerk

Seventeenth Judicial District
P.O. Drawer 290, Livingston, AL 35470

Circuit Clerk, Greene County **Mattie D. Atkins** . . . . (205) 372-3598
400 Morrow Avenue, Eutaw, AL 35642
E-mail: mattie.atkins@alacourt.gov

Hale County

Circuit Clerk

Fourth Judicial District
P.O. Box 475, Centreville, AL 35042

Circuit Clerk, Hale County **Catrinna Perry** . . . . (334) 624-4334
1001 Main Street, Greensboro, AL 35744
E-mail: catrinna.perry@alacourt.gov

Henry County

Circuit Clerk

Twentieth Judicial District
114 North Oates Street, Dothan, AL 36302

Circuit Clerk, Henry County **Shirlene Vickers** . . . . (334) 585-2753
101 Court Square, Abbeville, AL 36310
E-mail: shirlene.vickers@alacourt.gov

Houston County

Circuit Clerk

Twentieth Judicial District
114 North Oates Street, Dothan, AL 36302

Circuit Clerk, Houston County **Carla H. Woodall** . . . . (334) 677-4805
114 North Oates Street, Dothan, AL 36302
E-mail: carla.woodall@alacourt.gov

Jackson County

Circuit Clerk

Thirty-Eighth Judicial District
102 Laurel Street, Scottsboro, AL 35768

Circuit Clerk **William K. Ferrell** . . . . (256) 574-9320
102 Laurel Street, Scottsboro, AL 35768

Jefferson County

Circuit Clerk

Tenth Judicial District
716 Richard Arrington Boulevard North, Suite 600,
Birmingham, AL 35203

Circuit Clerk **Anne-Marie Adams** . . . . (205) 325-5360
716 N. Richard Arrington, Jr. Boulevard,
Birmingham, AL 35203
E-mail: annemarie.adams@alacourt.gov

Circuit Clerk - Bessemer Division

Tenth Judicial District
716 Richard Arrington Boulevard North, Suite 600,
Birmingham, AL 35203

Circuit Clerk, Bessemer Division **Benny Watson** . . . . (205) 497-8510
1801 Third Avenue, Bessemer, AL 35020

Lamar County

Circuit Clerk

Twenty-Fourth Judicial Circuit
113 Temple Avenue, Fayette, AL 35555

Circuit Clerk, Lamar County **Mary Ann Jones** . . . . (205) 695-7193
330 First Street NE, Vernon, AL 35592
E-mail: mary.jones@alacourt.gov

Lauderdale County

Circuit Clerk

Eleventh Judicial Circuit
200 Court Street, 5th Floor, Florence, AL 35630

Circuit Clerk **Melissa Hibbett-Homan** . . . . (256) 760-5831
200 South Court Street, Florence, AL 35631
P.O. Box 776, Florence, AL 35631

Lawrence County

Circuit Clerk

Thirty-Sixth Judicial District
14451 Market Street, Suite 230, Moulton, AL 35650-1452

Circuit Clerk **Sandra P. Ligon** . . . . (256) 974-2438
14451 Market Street, Moulton, AL 35650-1452
E-mail: sandra.ligon@alacourt.gov

Lee County

Circuit Clerk

Thirty-Seventh Judicial District
Lee County Justice Center, 2311 Gateway Drive, Opelika, AL 36801

Circuit Clerk **Mary Roberson** . . . . (334) 749-7141
Lee County Justice Center, 2311 Gateway Drive,
Room 104, Opelika, AL 36801
E-mail: mary.roberson@alacourt.gov

Limestone County

Circuit Clerk

Thirty-Ninth Judicial District
P.O. Box 486, Athens, AL 35612

Circuit Clerk **Brad Curnutt** . . . . (256) 233-6406
200 Washington Street West, First Floor,
Athens, AL 35611
E-mail: brad.curnutt@alacourt.gov

Lowndes County

Circuit Clerk

Second Judicial District
700 Court Square, Greenville, AL 36037

Circuit Clerk, Lowndes County **Ruby Jones-Thomas** . . . . (334) 548-2252
One Washington Street, Hayneville, AL 36040-0876

Macon County

Circuit Clerk

Fifth Judicial Circuit
101 East Rosa Parks Avenue, Tuskegee, AL 35083

Circuit Clerk, Macon County **David R. Love** . . . . (334) 724-2614
101 East Rosa Parks Avenue,
Tuskegee, AL 35083
E-mail: david.love@alacourt.gov

Madison County

Circuit Clerk

Twenty-Third Judicial Circuit
100 North Side Square, Huntsville, AL 35801

Circuit Clerk **Jane C. Smith** . . . . (256) 532-3390
100 North Side Square, Huntsville, AL 35801
E-mail: jane.smith@alacourt.gov

Marengo County

Circuit Clerk

Seventeenth Judicial District
P.O. Drawer 290, Livingston, AL 35470

Circuit Clerk, Marengo County **Kenny Freeman** . . . . (334) 295-2219
101 East Coats Avenue, Linden, AL 36748
E-mail: kenny.freeman@alacourt.gov

Marion County

Circuit Clerk

Twenty-Fifth Judicial Circuit
132 Military Street, Hamilton, AL 35570

Circuit Clerk, Marion County **Shelia Cochran** . . . . (205) 921-7451
132 Military Street, Hamilton, AL 35570

Marshall County

Circuit Clerk

Twenty-Seventh Judicial District
133 South Emmet Street, Albertville, AL 35950

Circuit Clerk **Cheryl Pierce** . . . . (256) 571-7785
133 South Emmet Street, Suite 201,
Albertville, AL 35950

Mobile County

Circuit Clerk

Thirteenth Judicial Circuit
205 Government Street, Mobile, AL 35544

Circuit Clerk **Jo Schwarzauer** . . . . (251) 574-8806
205 Government Street, Suite 913,
Mobile, AL 35544
E-mail: jo.schwarzauer@alacourt.gov

Monroe County

Circuit Clerk

Thirty-Fifth Judicial Circuit
111 Court Street, Monroeville, AL 36461

Circuit Clerk, Monroe County **William R. McMillan** . . . . . (251) 743-2283
Courthouse Square, Monroeville, AL 36460

Montgomery County

Circuit Clerk

Fifteenth Judicial Circuit
251 South Lawrence Street, Montgomery, AL 36104
Tel: (334) 832-1357

Circuit Clerk **Tiffany B. McCord** . . . . (334) 832-1260
251 South Lawrence Street,
Montgomery, AL 36104
E-mail: tiffany.mccord@alacourt.gov

Morgan County

Circuit Clerk

Eighth Judicial District
P.O. Box 668, Decatur, AL 35502

Circuit Clerk **Chris Priest** . . . . (256) 351-4649
P.O. Box 668, Decatur, AL 35502
302 Lee Street, Decatur, AL 35502
E-mail: chris.priest@alacourt.gov

(continued on next page)

Perry County

Circuit Clerk

Fourth Judicial District
P.O. Box 475, Centreville, AL 35042

Circuit Clerk, Perry County **Mary C. Moore** . . . . (334) 683-6106
  P.O. Box 505, Marion, AL 35756
  E-mail: mary.moore@alacourt.gov

Pickens County

Circuit Clerk

Twenty-Fourth Judicial Circuit
113 Temple Avenue, Fayette, AL 35555

Circuit Clerk, Pickens County **Bobby W. Cowart** . . . . (205) 367-2050
  20 Phoenix Avenue, Carrollton, AL 35447
  E-mail: bobby.cowart@alacourt.gov

Pike County

Circuit Clerk

Twelfth Judicial District
230 M Court, Elba, AL 36323
120 West Church Street, Troy, AL 36081

Circuit Clerk, Pike County **Jamie Scarbrough** . . . . (334) 566-4622
  120 West Church Street, Troy, AL 36081
  E-mail: jamie.scarbrough@alacourt.gov

Randolph County

Circuit Clerk

Fifth Judicial Circuit
101 East Rosa Parks Avenue, Tuskegee, AL 35083

Circuit Clerk, Randolph County **Christopher R. May** . . . . (256) 357-4551
  One Main Street, Wedowee, AL 36278

Russell County

Circuit Clerk

Twenty-Sixth Judicial Circuit
P.O. Box 820, Phenix City, AL 36868

Circuit Clerk **Kathy S. Coulter** . . . . (334) 298-0516
  P.O. Box 820, Phenix City, AL 36868   Fax: (334) 297-6250
  E-mail: kathy.coulter@alacourt.gov

St. Clair County

Circuit Clerk

Thirtieth Judicial Circuit
100 Sixth Avenue, Suite 400, Ashville, AL 35953

Circuit Clerk **Annette Manning Hall** . . . . (205) 594-2184 (Ashville)
  100 Sixth Avenue, Suite 400,   Tel: (205) 338-2511
  Ashville, AL 35953   (Pell City)
  1815 Cogswell Avenue, Suite 217,
  Pell City, AL 35125
  E-mail: annette.hall@alacourt.gov

Shelby County

Circuit Clerk

Eighteenth Judicial District
P.O. Box 1136, Columbiana, AL 35051

Circuit Clerk **Mary H. Harris** . . . . (205) 669-3779
  112 North Main Street, Columbiana, AL 35051
  P.O. Box 1810, Columbiana, AL 35051
  E-mail: mary.harris@alacourt.gov

Sumter County

Circuit Clerk

Seventeenth Judicial District
P.O. Drawer 290, Livingston, AL 35470

Circuit Clerk, Sumter County **DeVon A. James** . . . . (205) 652-2291
  Franklin St. Court Square,
  Livingston, AL 35470
  P.O. Drawer 290, Livingston, AL 35740
  E-mail: devon.james@alacourt.gov

Talladega County

Circuit Clerk

Twenty-Ninth Judicial District
148 East Street North, Talladega, AL 35161
P.O. Box 6137, Talladega, AL 35160

Circuit Clerk **Brian York** . . . . (256) 761-2102
  148 East Street North, Talladega, AL 35161
  E-mail: brian.york@alacourt.gov

Tallapoosa County

Circuit Clerk

Fifth Judicial Circuit
101 East Rosa Parks Avenue, Tuskegee, AL 35083

Circuit Clerk, Tallapoosa County **Patrick Craddock** . . . . . . (334) 864-4348
  125 North Broadnax, Dadeville, AL 36853
  E-mail: patrick.craddock@alacourt.gov

Tuscaloosa County

Circuit Clerk

Sixth Judicial Circuit
714 Greensboro Avenue, Tuscaloosa, AL 35401

Circuit Clerk **Margaria H. Bobo** . . . . (205) 349-3870
  714 Greensboro Avenue, Tuscaloosa, AL 35401

Walker County

Circuit Clerk

Fourteenth Judicial District
P.O. Box 1603, Jasper, AL 35501

Circuit Clerk **Susan D. Odom** . . . . (205) 384-7268
  P.O. Box 1389, Jasper, AL 35502
  19th Street/2nd Avenue, Jasper, AL 35502
  E-mail: susan.odom@alacourt.gov

Washington County

Circuit Clerk

First Judicial District
One Court Street, Chatom, AL 35518

Circuit Clerk, Washington County **Valerie Knapp** . . . . (251) 847-2239
P.O. Box 548, Chatom, AL 35518

Wilcox County

Circuit Clerk

Fourth Judicial District
P.O. Box 475, Centreville, AL 35042

Circuit Clerk, Wilcox County **Ralph W. Ervin** . . . . (334) 682-4126
12 Waters Street, Camden, AL 35725
E-mail: ralph.ervin@alacourt.gov

Winston County

Circuit Clerk

Twenty-Fifth Judicial Circuit
132 Military Street, Hamilton, AL 35570

Circuit Clerk, Winston County **John D. Snoddy** . . . . (205) 489-5533
25166 Highway 195, Double Springs, AL 35553
E-mail: john.snoddy@alacourt.gov

Counties Within Judicial Districts

Circuit Court, 1st Judicial Circuit
Areas Covered: Choctaw, Clarke, and Washington Counties.

Circuit Court, 2nd Judicial Circuit
Areas Covered: Butler, Crenshaw, and Lowndes Counties.

Circuit Court, 3rd Judicial Circuit
Areas Covered: Barbour and Bullock Counties.

Circuit Court, 4th Judicial Circuit
Areas Covered: Bibb, Dallas, Hale, Perry, and Wilcox Counties.

Circuit Court, 5th Judicial Circuit
Areas Covered: Chambers, Macon, Randolph, and Tallapoosa Counties.

Circuit Court, 6th Judicial Circuit
Areas Covered: Tuscaloosa County.

Circuit Court, 7th Judicial Circuit
Areas Covered: Calhoun and Cleburne Counties.

Circuit Court, 8th Judicial Circuit
Areas Covered: Morgan County.

Circuit Court, 9th Judicial Circuit
Areas Covered: Cherokee and DeKalb Counties.

Circuit Court, 10th Judicial Circuit
Areas Covered: Jefferson County.

Circuit Court, 11th Judicial Circuit
Areas Covered: Lauderdale County.

Circuit Court, 12th Judicial Circuit
Areas Covered: Coffee and Pike Counties.

Circuit Court, 13th Judicial Circuit
Areas Covered: Mobile County.

Circuit Court, 14th Judicial Circuit
Areas Covered: Walker County.

Circuit Court, 15th Judicial Circuit
Areas Covered: Montgomery County.

Circuit Court, 16th Judicial Circuit
Areas Covered: Etowah County.

Circuit Court, 17th Judicial Circuit
Areas Covered: Greene, Marengo, and Sumter Counties.

Circuit Court, 18th Judicial Circuit
Areas Covered: Shelby County.

Circuit Court, 19th Judicial Circuit
Areas Covered: Autauga, Chilton, and Elmore Counties.

Circuit Court, 20th Judicial Circuit
Areas Covered: Henry and Houston Counties.

Circuit Court, 21st Judicial Circuit
Areas Covered: Escambia County.

Circuit Court, 22nd Judicial Circuit
Areas Covered: Covington County.

Circuit Court, 23rd Judicial Circuit
Areas Covered: Madison County.

Circuit Court, 24th Judicial Circuit
Areas Covered: Fayette, Lamar, and Pickens Counties.

Circuit Court, 25th Judicial Circuit
Areas Covered: Marion and Winston Counties.

Circuit Court, 26th Judicial Circuit
Areas Covered: Russell County.

Circuit Court, 27th Judicial Circuit
Areas Covered: Marshall County.

(continued on next page)

Alabama Court Clerks and Courthouses *continued*

Circuit Court, 28th Judicial Circuit
Areas Covered: Baldwin County.

Circuit Court, 29th Judicial Circuit
Areas Covered: Talladega County.

Circuit Court, 30th Judicial Circuit
Areas Covered: St. Clair and Blount Counties.

Circuit Court, 31st Judicial Circuit
Areas Covered: Colbert County.

Circuit Court, 32nd Judicial Circuit
Areas Covered: Cullman County.

Circuit Court, 33rd Judicial Circuit
Areas Covered: Dale and Geneva Counties.

Circuit Court, 34th Judicial Circuit
Areas Covered: Franklin County.

Circuit Court, 35th Judicial Circuit
Areas Covered: Conecuh and Monroe Counties.

Circuit Court, 36th Judicial Circuit
Areas Covered: Lawrence County.

Circuit Court, 37th Judicial Circuit
Areas Covered: Lee County.

Circuit Court, 38th Judicial Circuit
Areas Covered: Jackson County.

Circuit Court, 39th Judicial Circuit
Areas Covered: Limestone County.

Circuit Court, 40th Judicial Circuit
Areas Covered: Clay and Coosa Counties.

Circuit Court, 41st Judicial Circuit
Areas Covered: Blount County.

Alaska Court Clerks and Courthouses

Alaska has a unified and centrally administered judicial system. This system is divided into four judicial districts. The trial court of general jurisdiction in Alaska is called the Superior Court. Given below is a city-by-city listing of superior court clerk offices. For recorders' offices, see http://dnr.alaska.gov/ssd/recoff/distlist.cfm.

Alaska Supreme Court

Boney Memorial Courthouse, 303 K Street, Anchorage, AK 99501-2084
Tel: (907) 264-0612 Fax: (907) 264-0878
E-mail: supreme_court@appellate.courts.state.ak.us
Internet: http://courts.alaska.gov

The Supreme Court consists of a chief justice and four justices who are appointed by the Governor from nominees of the Alaska Judicial Council and are subject to a retention vote for a ten-year term on a nonpartisan ballot in the first general election held more than three years after the appointment. The chief justice is elected by a peer vote to serve a non-consecutive three-year term. The Supreme Court has final appellate jurisdiction in civil and criminal cases. The Court hears appeals of final judgments entered by the Alaska Superior Court in any civil action. The Court may review decisions of the Alaska Court of Appeals involving criminal cases. The Court has administrative authority over all courts and the practice of law in the state.

Court Staff

Clerk of the Appellate Courts **Marilyn May** . . . . (907) 264-0608
  E-mail: mmay@akcourts.us

Alaska Court of Appeals

Boney Memorial Courthouse, 303 K Street, Anchorage, AK 99501-2084
Tel: (907) 264-0612 Fax: (907) 264-0878
Internet: http://courts.alaska.gov/appcts.htm

The Court of Appeals, created by the Alaska State Legislature in 1980, consists of a chief judge and two judges. The chief judge serves a consecutive two-year term and is appointed by the chief justice of the Alaska Supreme Court. The judges are appointed by the Governor from nominees submitted by the Alaska Judicial Council and are subject to a retention vote for an eight-year term in the first general election held more than three years after the appointment. The Court of Appeals has appellate jurisdiction in actions and proceedings commenced in the Alaska Superior Court, including appeals from judgments in criminal cases, juvenile delinquency cases, habeas corpus matters and cases involving probation and parole decisions. The Court also has jurisdiction to review sentences imposed by either the Alaska Superior Court or District Court and discretionary review of District Court appeals to the Alaska Superior Court.

Court Staff

Clerk of the Appellate Courts **Marilyn May** . . . . (907) 264-0608
  E-mail: mmay@akcourts.us

City-By-City Listing of Trial Court Offices

Ambler

Note: Served by Kotzebue.

Anchorage

Court Clerk

Third Judicial District
825 West Fourth Avenue, Anchorage, AK 99501

District Clerk, Anchorage **Cynthia Lee** . . . . (907) 264-0480
  825 West Fourth Avenue,
  Anchorage, AK 99501-2004
  E-mail: clee@akcourts.us

Angoon

Court Clerk

First Judicial District
415 Main Street, Ketchikan, AK 99901-6399

District Clerk, Angoon **Elaine Kookesh** . . . . (907) 788-3229
  P.O. Box 250, Angoon, AK 99820-0250   Fax: (907) 788-3108
  E-mail: ekookesh@akcourts.us

Aniak

Court Clerk

Fourth Judicial District
101 Lacey Street, Fairbanks, AK 99701

District Clerk, Aniak **Jean Ekemo** . . . . (907) 675-4325
  P.O. Box 147, Aniak, AK 99557-0147
  E-mail: jekemo@akcourts.us

Barrow

Court Clerk

Second Judicial District
P.O. Box 270, Barrow, AK 99723-0270

District Clerk, Barrow (Acting) **Misa Uluaave** . . . . (907) 852-4800
  P.O. Box 270, Barrow, AK 99723-0270

Bethel

Court Clerk

Fourth Judicial District
101 Lacey Street, Fairbanks, AK 99701

District Clerk, Bethel **Natalie Alexie** . . . . (907) 543-2298
  P.O. Box 130, Bethel, AK 99559-0130
  E-mail: nalexie@akcourts.us

Chevak

Court Clerk

Fourth Judicial District
101 Lacey Street, Fairbanks, AK 99701

District Clerk, Chevak **Elizabeth Howarts** . . . . (907) 858-7232
  P.O. Box 238, Chevak, AK 99563

(continued on next page)

Alaska Court Clerks and Courthouses *continued*

Cordova

Court Clerk

Third Judicial District
825 West Fourth Avenue, Anchorage, AK 99501

District Clerk, Cordova **Kay Adams** . . . . (907) 424-7312
  P.O. Box 0898, Cordova, AK 99574-0898
  E-mail: kadams@akcourts.us

Craig

Court Clerk

First Judicial District
415 Main Street, Ketchikan, AK 99901-6399

District Clerk, Craig **Kimberly Rice** . . . . (907) 826-3306
  P.O. Box 646, Craig, AK 99921-0646   Fax: (907) 826-3904
  E-mail: krice@akcourts.us

Delta Junction

Court Clerk

Fourth Judicial District
101 Lacey Street, Fairbanks, AK 99701

District Clerk, Delta Junction **Sandra Dighton** . . . . (907) 895-4211
  P.O. Box 401, Delta Junction, AK 99737-0401
  E-mail: sdighton@akcourts.us

Dillingham

Court Clerk

Third Judicial District
825 West Fourth Avenue, Anchorage, AK 99501

District Clerk, Dillingham **Tatiana O'Conor** . . . . (907) 842-5215
  P.O. Box 909, Dillingham, AK 99576-0909

Emmonak

Court Clerk

Fourth Judicial District
101 Lacey Street, Fairbanks, AK 99701

District Clerk, Emmonak **Billy Westlock** . . . . (907) 949-1748
  P.O. Box 176, Emmonak, AK 99581

Fairbanks

Court Clerk

Fourth Judicial District
101 Lacey Street, Fairbanks, AK 99701

District Clerk, Fairbanks **Ruth Meier** . . . . (907) 452-9277
  101 Lacey Street, Fairbanks, AK 99701
  E-mail: rmeier@akcourts.us

Alaska Court Clerks and Courthouses *continued*

Fort Yukon

Court Clerk

Fourth Judicial District
101 Lacey Street, Fairbanks, AK 99701

District Clerk, Fort Yukon **(Vacant)** . . . . (907) 662-2336
  P.O. Box 211, Fort Yukon, AK 99740

Galena

Court Clerk

Fourth Judicial District
101 Lacey Street, Fairbanks, AK 99701

District Clerk, Galena **Pamela Pitka** . . . . (907) 656-1322
  P. O. Box 167, Galena, AK 99741

Gambell

Note: Served by Nome.

Glennallen

Court Clerk

Third Judicial District
825 West Fourth Avenue, Anchorage, AK 99501

District Clerk, Glennallen **Linda Woodcock** . . . . (907) 822-3405
  Ahtna Building, MIle 115 Richardson Highway,
  Glennallen, AK 99588-0086
  P.O. Box 86, Glennallen, AK 99588-0086
  E-mail: lwoodcock@akcourts.us

Haines

Court Clerk

First Judicial District
415 Main Street, Ketchikan, AK 99901-6399

District Clerk, Haines **Bonnie Hedrick** . . . . (907) 766-2801
  P.O. Box 169, Haines, AK 99827-0169   Fax: (907) 766-3148
  E-mail: bhedrick@akcourts.us

Healy

Note: Served by Nenana.

Homer

Court Clerk

Third Judicial District
825 West Fourth Avenue, Anchorage, AK 99501

District Clerk, Homer **Darcy Gredway** . . . . (907) 235-8171
  Building A, 3670 Lake Street,
  Homer, AK 99603-7686

Hoonah

Court Clerk

First Judicial District
415 Main Street, Ketchikan, AK 99901-6399

District Clerk, Hoonah **Billy Miller** . . . . (907) 945-3668
   P.O. Box 430, Hoonah, AK 99829-0430   Fax: (907) 945-3637
   E-mail: bmiller@akcourts.us

Juneau

Court Clerk

First Judicial District
415 Main Street, Ketchikan, AK 99901-6399

District Clerk, Juneau **Sharon Heidersdorf** . . . . (907) 463-4700
   P.O. Box 114100, Juneau, AK 99811-4100   Tel: (907) 463-3788
   E-mail: sheidersdorf@akcourts.us

Kake

Court Clerk

First Judicial District
415 Main Street, Ketchikan, AK 99901-6399

District Clerk, Kake **Mike Jackson** . . . . (907) 785-3651
   P.O. Box 100, Kake, AK 99830
   E-mail: mjackson@akcourts.us

Kenai

Court Clerk

Third Judicial District
825 West Fourth Avenue, Anchorage, AK 99501

District Clerk, Kenai **Deirdre Cheek** . . . . (907) 283-3110
   125 Trading Bay Drive, Kenai, AK 99611-7717
   E-mail: dcheek@akcourts.us

Ketchikan

Court Clerk

First Judicial District
415 Main Street, Ketchikan, AK 99901-6399

District Clerk, Ketchikan **Stacey Hallstrom** . . . .(907) 225-3195
   415 Main Street, Room 400,   Fax: (907) 225-7849
   Ketchikan, AK 99901-6399
   E-mail: shallstrom@akcourts.us

Kiana

Note: Served by Kotzebue.

Kobuk

Note: Served by Kotzebue.

Kodiak

Court Clerk

Third Judicial District
825 West Fourth Avenue, Anchorage, AK 99501

District Clerk, Kodiak **Suzanne Cowley** . . . .(907) 486-1600
   204 Mission Road, Room 124,
   Kodiak, AK 99615-7312
   E-mail: scowley@akcourts.us

Kotzebue

Court Clerk

Second Judicial District
P.O. Box 270, Barrow, AK 99723-0270

District Clerk, Kotzebue **James Kwon** . . . . (907) 442-3208
   P.O. Box 317, Kotzebue, AK 99752-0317
   E-mail: jkwon@akcourts.us

McGrath

Note: Served by Aniak.

Naknek

Court Clerk

Third Judicial District
825 West Fourth Avenue, Anchorage, AK 99501

District Clerk, Naknek **Laurie Marvin** . . . .(907) 246-4240
   Bristol Bay Borough Building, 1 Main Street,
   Naknek, AK 99633-0229
   P.O. Box 229, Naknek, AK 99633-0229
   E-mail: lmarvin@akcourts.us

Nenana

Court Clerk

Fourth Judicial District
101 Lacey Street, Fairbanks, AK 99701

District Clerk, Nenana **Samantha Thompson** . . . .(907) 832-5430
   P.O. Box 449, Nenana, AK 99760-0449
   E-mail: sthompson@akcourts.us

Nome

Court Clerk

Second Judicial District
P.O. Box 270, Barrow, AK 99723-0270

District Clerk, Nome **Brodie Kimmel** . . . . (907) 443-5216
   P.O. Box 1110, Nome, AK 99762-1110
   113 Front Street, Room 230,
   Nome, AK 99762-1110
   E-mail: bkimmel@akcourts.us

Noorvik

Note: Served by Kotzebue.

(continued on next page)

Palmer

Court Clerk

Third Judicial District
825 West Fourth Avenue, Anchorage, AK 99501

District Clerk, Palmer **Debra Miller**...................(907) 746-8181
435 South Denali Street, Palmer, AK 99645-6437
E-mail: dmiller@akcourts.us

Pelican

Note: Served by Sitka.

Petersburg

Court Clerk

First Judicial District
415 Main Street, Ketchikan, AK 99901-6399

District Clerk, Petersburg **Brandy Boggs**.............. (907) 772-3824
P.O. Box 1009, Petersburg, AK 99833-1009   Fax: (907) 772-3018
E-mail: bboggs@akcourts.us

Point Hope

Note: Served by Kotzebue.

Quinhagak

Note: Served by Bethel.

St. Mary's

Court Clerk

Fourth Judicial District
101 Lacey Street, Fairbanks, AK 99701

District Clerk, St. Mary's **Winnifred Xavier**............(907) 438-2912
P.O. Box 269, Saint Mary's, AK 99658
E-mail: wxavier@akcourts.us

St. Paul Island

Note: Served by Seward.

Sand Point

Note: Served by Valdez.

Savoonga

Note: Served by Nome.

Selawik

Note: Served by Kotzebue.

Seward

Court Clerk

Third Judicial District
825 West Fourth Avenue, Anchorage, AK 99501

District Clerk, Seward **Jennifer Sommerville** .... (907) 224-3075
Box 1929, Seward, AK 99664-1929

Shungnak

Note: Served by Kotzebue.

Sitka

Court Clerk

First Judicial District
415 Main Street, Ketchikan, AK 99901-6399

District Clerk, Sitka **Jonie Calhoun** .... (907) 747-3291
304 Lake Street, Room 203,   Fax: (907) 747-6690
Sitka, AK 99835-7759
E-mail: jcalhoun@akcourts.us

Skagway

Court Clerk

First Judicial District
415 Main Street, Ketchikan, AK 99901-6399

District Clerk, Skagway **Susan Reed**..................(907) 983-2368
P.O. Box 495, Skagway, AK 99840   Fax: (907) 983-3801
E-mail: sreed@akcourts.us

Tanana

Note: Served by Galena.

Tok

Court Clerk

Fourth Judicial District
101 Lacey Street, Fairbanks, AK 99701

District Clerk, Tok **Lauren Burnham** .... (907) 883-5171
P.O. Box 187, Tok, AK 99780-0187
E-mail: lburnham@akcourts.us

Unalakleet

Court Clerk

Second Judicial District
P.O. Box 270, Barrow, AK 99723-0270

District Clerk, Unalakleet **Heidi Ivanoss**.............. (907) 624-3015
P.O. Box 250, Unalakeet, AK 99684-0250

Unalaska

Court Clerk

Third Judicial District
825 West Fourth Avenue, Anchorage, AK 99501

District Clerk, Unalaska **Rebecca Duffy** . . . . (907) 581-1379
  P.O. Box 245, Unalaska, AK 99685

Valdez

Court Clerk

Third Judicial District
825 West Fourth Avenue, Anchorage, AK 99501

District Clerk, Valdez **Lisa Anderson** . . . . (907) 835-2266
  Box 127, Valdez, AK 99686-0127
  E-mail: landerson@akcourts.us

Whittier

Note: Served by Anchorage.

Wrangell

Court Clerk

First Judicial District
415 Main Street, Ketchikan, AK 99901-6399

District Clerk, Wrangell **Leanna Nash** . . . . (907) 874-2311 ext. 13
  P.O. Box 869, Wrangell, AK 99929-0869
  E-mail: lnash@akcourts.us

Yakutat

Court Clerk

First Judicial District
415 Main Street, Ketchikan, AK 99901-6399

District Clerk, Yakutat **Mary Kay Germain** . . . . (907) 784-3274
  P.O. Box 426, Yakutat, AK 99689-0426   Fax: (907) 784-3257

Arizona Court Clerks and Courthouses

The trial courts of general jurisdiction in Arizona are called Superior Courts. There is one Superior Court per county, each court exercising countywide jurisdiction. Listed below for each county are the Clerk of Superior Court and the County Recorder.

Supreme Court of Arizona

Arizona State Courts Building, 1501 West Washington Street, Phoenix, AZ 85007
Tel: (602) 452-3300
Internet: http://www.azcourts.gov

The Supreme Court of Arizona consists of a chief justice and four justices who are appointed by the Governor for initial two-year terms. Subsequent terms of six years are by retention vote in the first general election after two years. The chief justice is elected by peer vote to a five-year term. Retirement is mandatory at age seventy; however, the chief justice may assign retired justices as needed. The Supreme Court has final appellate jurisdiction over all other courts in the state (except in some actions arising in Justice and Municipal Courts) and exclusive appellate jurisdiction in cases involving the death penalty. The Court has discretionary review of decisions made by the Arizona Court of Appeals, and has exclusive jurisdiction in cases between counties.

Court Staff
Clerk of the Court **Janet Johnson** . . . . (602) 452-3396

Arizona Court of Appeals

The Arizona Court of Appeals hears and decides cases in three-judge panels. Judges are appointed by the Governor for initial two-year terms and are then subject to retention votes every six years. The chief judge and vice chief judge of each of the two divisions are elected annually by peer vote. Retirement is mandatory at age seventy; however, the Chief Justice of the Arizona Supreme Court may assign retired judges to serve as needed, usually for a period of six months. The Court of Appeals exercises appellate jurisdiction over cases appealed from the Arizona Superior Court, except those cases involving the death penalty, which must be appealed directly to the Arizona Supreme Court. In addition, the Arizona Court of Appeals, Division One has statewide responsibility to review decisions of the Industrial Commission, unemployment compensation appeals from the Arizona Department of Economic Security, and the Arizona Tax Court.

Arizona Court of Appeals, Division One

Arizona State Courts Building, 1501 West Washington Street, Phoenix, AZ 85007
Tel: (602) 542-4821 Fax: (602) 542-4833
Internet: www.azcourts.gov

Areas Covered: Counties of Apache, Coconino, La Paz, Maricopa, Mohave, Navajo, Yavapai and Yuma

Court Staff
Clerk of the Court **Ruth A. Willingham** . . . . (602) 542-4821
  E-mail: rwillingham@appeals.az.gov

Arizona Court of Appeals, Division Two

North Building, State Office Complex, 400 West Congress Street, Room 200, Tucson, AZ 85701-1374
Tel: (520) 628-6954 Fax: (520) 628-6959
Internet: www.apltwo.ct.state.az.us

Areas Covered: Counties of Cochise, Gila, Graham, Greenlee, Pima, Pinal and Santa Cruz

Court Staff
Clerk of the Court **Jeffrey P. Handler** . . . . (520) 628-6954
  E-mail: handler@appeals2.az.gov

County-By-County

Apache County

Clerk of the Court

Apache County Superior Court
70 West 3rd South, Saint Johns, AZ 85936-0667
Tel: (928) 337-7555 Fax: (928) 337-7586

Clerk of Court **Annell Hounshell** . . . . (928) 337-7550
  E-mail: clerk@apacheclerk.net   Fax: (928) 337-2771

County Recorder

Office of the Recorder
P.O. Box 425, Saint Johns, AZ 85936
Tel: (928) 337-7514

Recorder **LeNora Y. Fulton** . . . . (928) 337-7514
  E-mail: lfulton@co.apache.az.us

Cochise County

Clerk of the Court

Cochise County Superior Court
100 Quality Hill, Bisbee, AZ 85603
P.O. Drawer CK, Bisbee, AZ 85603
Tel: (520) 432-8570 Fax: (520) 432-4850

Clerk of Court **Mary Ellen Dunlap** . . . . (520) 432-8570
  E-mail: madunlap@courts.az.gov

County Recorder

Office of the Recorder
Building B, 1415 Melody Lane, Bisbee, AZ 85603
Tel: (520) 432-8350 Fax: (520) 432-8368

Recorder **Christine Rhodes** . . . . (520) 432-8350
  E-mail: crhodes@cochise.az.gov

Coconino County

Clerk of the Court

Coconino County Superior Court
200 North San Francisco Street, Flagstaff, AZ 86001
Tel: (928) 679-7600

Clerk of Court **Valerie Wyant** . . . . (928) 679-7600

(continued on next page)

Arizona Court Clerks and Courthouses *continued*

County Recorder

Office of the Recorder
110 East Cherry Avenue, Flagstaff, AZ 86001
Tel: (928) 679-7850 Fax: (928) 679-7851

Recorder **Patty Hansen** .... (928) 679-7850
 E-mail: phansen@coconino.az.gov

Gila County

Clerk of the Court

Gila County Superior Court
1400 East Ash Street, Globe, AZ 85501
Tel: (928) 425-3231 (Globe Courthouse)
Tel: (928) 474-3978 (Payson Courthouse)

Clerk of Court **Anita Escobedo**...................... (928) 474-3978

County Recorder

Office of the Recorder
1400 East Ash Street, Globe, AZ 85501
Tel: (928) 402-8740 Fax: (928) 425-9270

Recorder **Sadie Jo Bingham** .... (928) 402-8735
 E-mail: sbingham@gilacountyaz.gov

Graham County

Clerk of the Court

Graham County Superior Court
800 West Main Street, Safford, AZ 85546
Tel: (928) 428-3310

Clerk of Court **Darlee Maylen**...................... (928) 428-3100
 E-mail: dmaylen@graham.az.gov

County Recorder

Office of the Recorder
921 Thatcher Boulevard, 2nd Floor, Thatcher, AZ 85546
P.O. Box 747, Safford, AZ 85548
Tel: (928) 428-3560 Fax: (928) 428-8828

Recorder **Wendy John** .... (928) 792-5031
 E-mail: wjohn@graham.az.gov

Greenlee County

Clerk of the Court

Greenlee County Superior Court
223 5th Street, Clifton, AZ 85533
Tel: (928) 865-3872 Fax: (928) 865-5358

Clerk of Court **Pamela "Pam" Pollock** .... (928) 865-4242
 E-mail: ppollock@courts.az.gov

County Recorder

Office of the Recorder
P.O. Box 1625, Clifton, AZ 85533
Tel: (928) 865-2632 Fax: (928) 865-4417

Recorder **Berta Manuz**........................... (928) 865-2632
 E-mail: bmanuz@co.greenlee.az.us

Arizona Court Clerks and Courthouses *continued*

La Paz County

Clerk of the Court

La Paz County Superior Court
1316 Kofa Avenue, Suite 607, Parker, AZ 85344

Clerk of Court **Megan Spielman** .... (928) 669-6131

County Recorder

Office of the Recorder
1112 Joshua Avenue, Room 201, Parker, AZ 85344
Tel: (928) 669-6136 Fax: (928) 669-5638

Recorder **Shelly Baker** .... (928) 669-6136
 E-mail: recorder@co.la-paz.az.us

Maricopa County

Clerk of the Court

Maricopa County Superior Court
Central Court Building, 201 West Jefferson, Phoenix, AZ 85003-2243
Tel: (602) 506-3204

Clerk of Court **Michael K. Jeanes** .... (602) 372-5375

County Recorder

Office of the Recorder
West Court Bldg., 111 South Third Avenue, Suite 103,
Phoenix, AZ 85003
Fax: (602) 506-3273

Recorder **Helen Purcell**........................... (602) 506-3535
 E-mail: hpurcell@risc.maricopa.gov

Mohave County

Clerk of the Court

Mohave County Superior Court
401 East Spring Street, Kingman, AZ 86401
P.O. Box 7000, Kingman, AZ 86402
Tel: (928) 753-0713

Clerk of Court **Virlynn Tinnell** .... (928) 753-0713 ext. 4037

County Recorder

Office of the Recorder
700 West Beale Street, Kingman, AZ 86402-0070
P.O. Box 70, Kingman, AZ 86402-0070
Tel: (928) 753-0701

Recorder **Carol Meier** .... (928) 753-0701
 E-mail: carol.meier@mohavecounty.us

Navajo County

Clerk of the Court

Navajo County Superior Court
Navajo County Governmental Complex, 100 East Carter Drive,
South Highway 77, Holbrook, AZ 86025
P.O. Box 668, Holbrook, AZ 86025
Tel: (928) 524-4223 Tel: (928) 524-4246

Clerk of Court **Deanne Romo** .... (928) 524-4188

County Recorder

Office of the Recorder
100 East Code Talkers Drive, South Highway 77, Holbrook, AZ 86025
Tel: (928) 524-4194 Fax: (928) 524-4308

Recorder **Laurette Justman** . . . . (928) 524-4194
   E-mail: laurie.justman@navajocountyaz.gov

Pima County

Clerk of the Court

Pima County Superior Court
110 West Congress Street, Tucson, AZ 85701
Tel: (520) 724-3200 Fax: (520) 798-3531

Clerk of Court **Toni Hellon** . . . . (520) 724-3201

County Recorder

Office of the County Recorder
County Courthouse, 115 North Church Avenue, 1st Floor,
Tucson, AZ 85701
Fax: (520) 623-1785

Recorder **F. Ann Rodriguez** . . . . (520) 724-4350
   E-mail: fann.rodriguez@recorder.pima.gov

Pinal County

Clerk of the Court

Pinal County Superior Court
971 Jason Lopez Circle, Building A, Florence, AZ 85132
Tel: (520) 866-5400 Fax: (520) 866-5401

Clerk of Court **Amanda Stanford** . . . . (520) 866-5300
                                               Fax: (520) 866-5320

County Recorder

Recorder's Office
Building E, 31 North Pinal Street, Florence, AZ 85132
Tel: (520) 866-6830 Fax: (520) 866-6831
Internet: http://pinalcountyaz.gov/recorder/pages/home.aspx

County Recorder **Virginia Ross** . . . . (520) 866-6830
   E-mail: virginia.ross@pinalcountyaz.gov

Santa Cruz County

Clerk of the Court

Santa Cruz County Superior Court
2150 North Congress Drive, Nogales, AZ 85621
Tel: (520) 375-7730

Clerk of Court **Juan Pablo Guzman** . . . . (520) 375-7700

County Recorder

Office of the Recorder
2150 North Congress Drive, Suite 101, Nogales, AZ 85621
Tel: (520) 375-7990

Recorder **Suzanne Sainz** . . . . (520) 375-7990
   E-mail: ssainz@co.santa-cruz.az.us

Yavapai County

Clerk of the Court

Yavapai County Superior Court
120 South Cortez Street, Prescott, AZ 86303
Tel: (928) 771-3483 Fax: (928) 771-3389

Clerk of Court **Donna McQuality** . . . . (928) 771-3483

County Recorder

Office of the County Recorder
1015 Fair Street, Prescott, AZ 86305-1852
Tel: (928) 771-3244 Fax: (928) 771-3258
E-mail: web.recorder@co.yavapai.az.us

Recorder **Leslie M. Hoffman** . . . . (928) 771-3244

Yuma County

Clerk of the Court

Yuma County Superior Court
250 West 2nd Street, Yuma, AZ 85364
Tel: (928) 817-4083 Fax: (928) 817-4091

Clerk of Court **Lynn Fazz** . . . . (928) 817-4222
   E-mail: lfazz@courts.az.gov

County Recorder

Office of the Recorder
410 South Maiden Lane, Suite B, Yuma, AZ 85364-2311
Tel: (928) 373-6020 Fax: (928) 373-6024

Recorder **Robyn Stallworth Pouquette** . . . . (928) 373-6020
   E-mail: robyn.pouquette@yumacountyaz.gov

Arkansas Court Clerks and Courthouses

General jurisdiction courts in Arkansas are called circuit courts. There are 23 circuits, with each circuit consisting of at least one county. Listed below are clerks of the circuit courts and county court clerks. In some counties both positions are held by one clerk.

Arkansas Supreme Court

Justice Building, 625 Marshall Street, First Floor North, Room 130, Little Rock, AR 72201
Tel: (501) 682-6849 Tel: (501) 682-2147 (Supreme Court Library)
Fax: (501) 682-6877 (Supreme Court Library)
Internet: www.courts.state.ar.us
E-mail: arsclib@arkansas.gov

The Supreme Court consists of a chief justice and six justices who are elected statewide for eight-year terms in partisan elections. Vacancies are filled temporarily by the Governor; however, appointees are not eligible to run for the position in the next general election. Retirement is mandatory at age seventy. The Supreme Court has appellate jurisdiction over cases from the Arkansas Courts involving interpretation of the state constitution; elections; attorney and judicial discipline; a prior decision by the Supreme Court; and criminal cases in which a sentence of life or the death penalty is imposed. The Court may also review decisions from the Arkansas Court of Appeals.

Court Staff
Clerk of the Court **Stacey Pectol** . . . . (501) 682-6849
  E-mail: stacey.pectol@arkansas.gov

Arkansas Court of Appeals

Justice Building, 625 Marshall Street, Little Rock, AR 72201
Tel: (501) 682-7460 Fax: (501) 682-7494
Internet: www.courts.state.ar.us

The Court of Appeals, established in 1978, consists of a chief judge and eleven judges who are elected in partisan elections to eight-year terms from the seven Court of Appeals districts in the state. The chief judge is appointed by the chief justice of the Arkansas Supreme Court for a consecutive four-year term. Retirement is mandatory at age seventy; however, retired judges may serve by assignment of the chief justice. The Court of Appeals has appellate jurisdiction over the Arkansas Circuit and Chancery Courts except in those cases appealed directly to the Arkansas Supreme Court.

Court Staff
Clerk of the Court **Stacey Pectol** . . . . (501) 682-6845
  E-mail: stacey.pectol@arkansas.gov

County-By-County

Arkansas County

Circuit Clerk

Eleventh East Judicial Circuit
101 Court Square, De Witt, AR 72042

Circuit Clerk, Arkansas County **Sarah Merchant** . . . . (870) 946-4219
  101 Court Square, De Witt, AR 72042   Fax: (870) 946-1394
  302 South College, Stuttgart, AR 72160
  E-mail: arcocircuitclerk@ymail.com

County Clerk

Office of the County Clerk
101 Court Square, De Witt, AR 72042
Tel: (870) 946-4349 Fax: (870) 946-4399

County Clerk **Melissa Wood** . . . . (870) 946-4349
  E-mail: arcoclerkmelissa@centurytel.net

Ashley County

Circuit Clerk

Tenth Judicial Circuit
210 South Main Street, Monticello, AR 71655

Circuit Clerk, Ashley County **Vickie Stell** . . . . (870) 853-2030
  205 East Jefferson Street, Hamburg, AR 71646   Fax: (870) 853-2034

County Clerk

Office of the County Clerk
205 East Jefferson Street, #5, Hamburg, AR 71646
Tel: (870) 853-2020 Fax: (870) 853-2082

County Clerk **Christie Martin** . . . . (870) 853-2020
  E-mail: ashleycoclerk@sbcglobal.net

Baxter County

Circuit and County Clerk

Fourteenth Judicial Circuit
301 East Sixth Street, Mountain Home, AR 72653

Circuit Clerk, Baxter County **Canda Reese** . . . . (870) 425-3475
  One East Seventh Street,   Fax: (870) 424-5105
  Mountain Home, AR 72653
  E-mail: canda.reese@baxtercounty.org

Benton County

Circuit Clerk

Nineteenth West Judicial Circuit
102 Northeast "A" Street, Bentonville, AR 72712

Circuit Clerk, Benton County **Brenda DeShields** . . . . (479) 271-1015
  102 Northeast "A" Street, Bentonville, AR 72712   Fax: (479) 271-5719
  E-mail: bdeshields@co.benton.ar.us

County Clerk

Office of the County Clerk
215 East Central Avenue, Room 217, Bentonville, AR 72712
Tel: (479) 271-1013

County Clerk **Tena O'Brien** . . . . (479) 271-1013
  E-mail: tena.obrien@BentonCountyAR.gov

Boone County

Circuit Clerk

Fourteenth Judicial Circuit
301 East Sixth Street, Mountain Home, AR 72653

Circuit Clerk, Boone County **Rhonda Watkins** . . . . (870) 741-5560
  100 North Main Street, Harrison, AR 72601   Fax: (870) 741-4335
  E-mail: rwatkins@boonecounty-ar.gov

(continued on next page)

Arkansas Court Clerks and Courthouses *continued*

County Clerk

Office of the County Clerk
100 North Main Street, Suite 201, Harrison, AR 72601
Tel: (870) 741-8428 Fax: (870) 741-9724

County Clerk **Crystal Graddy** . . . . (870) 741-8428

Bradley County

Circuit Clerk

Tenth Judicial Circuit
210 South Main Street, Monticello, AR 71655

Circuit Clerk, Bradley County **Cindy Wagnon** . . . . (870) 226-2272
100 East Cedar Street, Warren, AR 71671   Fax: (870) 226-8416

County Clerk

Office of the County Clerk
101 East Cedar Street, Warren, AR 71671
Tel: (870) 226-3464 Fax: (870) 226-8404

County Clerk **Karen Belin** . . . . (870) 226-3464
E-mail: bradleyclerk@arkansasclerks.com

Calhoun County

Circuit and County Clerk

Thirteenth Judicial Circuit
101 North Washington Street, El Dorado, AR 71730

Circuit and County Clerk, Calhoun County
Alma Davis . . . . (870) 798-2517
P.O. Box 1175, Hampton, AR 71744   Fax: (870) 798-2428
E-mail: hogskinholidays@hotmail.com

Carroll County

Circuit Clerk

Nineteenth East Judicial Circuit
210 West Church Avenue, Berryville, AR 72616

Circuit Clerk, Carroll County **Ramona Wilson** . . . . (870) 423-2422
210 West Church Avenue, Berryville, AR 72616   Fax: (870) 423-4796

County Clerk

Office of the County Clerk
210 West Church Avenue, Berryville, AR 72616
Tel: (870) 423-2022 Fax: (870) 423-7400

County Clerk **Jamie Correia** . . . . (870) 423-2022
E-mail: jcorreiaclerk@outlook.com

Chicot County

Circuit Clerk

Tenth Judicial Circuit
210 South Main Street, Monticello, AR 71655

Circuit Clerk, Chicot County **Josephine T. Griffin** . . . . (870) 265-8010
108 Main Street, Lake Village, AR 71653   Fax: (870) 265-8012
E-mail: jgriffinchicotcc@att.net

Arkansas Court Clerks and Courthouses *continued*

County Clerk

Office of the County Clerk
108 Main Street, Lake Village, AR 71653
Tel: (870) 265-8000 Fax: (870) 265-8018

County Clerk **Pam Donaldson** . . . . (870) 265-8000
E-mail: chicotclerk@arkansasclerks.com

Clark County

Circuit Clerk

Ninth East Judicial Circuit
401 Clay Street, Arkadelphia, AR 71923

Circuit Clerk, Clark County **Martha Jo Smith** . . . . (870) 246-4281
401 Clay Street, Arkadelphia, AR 71923   Fax: (870) 246-1419

County Clerk

Office of the County Clerk
401 Clay Street, Arkadelphia, AR 71923
Tel: (870) 246-4491 Fax: (870) 246-6505

County Clerk **Rhonda L. Cole** . . . . (870) 246-4491
E-mail: rhonda@clarkcountyarkansas.com

Clay County

Circuit Clerk

Second Judicial Circuit
200 West Hale Avenue, Osceola, AR 72370

Circuit Clerk, Clay County **Janet Luff Kilbreath** . . . . (870) 598-2524
151 South Second Street, Piggott, AR 72454   Fax: (870) 598-1107
E-mail: claycce@centurytel.net

County Clerk

Office of the County Clerk
151 South Second Avenue, Piggott, AR 72454
Tel: (870) 598-2813 Fax: (870) 598-2815

County Clerk **Pat Poole** . . . . (870) 598-2813
E-mail: clay123@centurytel.net

Cleburne County

Circuit Clerk

Sixteenth Judicial Circuit
107 West Main Street, Mountain View, AR 72560

Circuit Clerk, Cleburne County **Karen Giles** . . . . (501) 362-8149
301 West Main Street, Heber Springs, AR 72543   Fax: (501) 362-4650

County Clerk

Office of the County Clerk
301 West Main Street, Heber Springs, AR 72543
Tel: (501) 362-4620 Fax: (501) 362-4622

County Clerk **Paul Muse** . . . . (501) 362-4620
E-mail: cleburneclerk@arkansasclerks.com

Cleveland County

Circuit and County Clerk

Thirteenth Judicial Circuit
101 North Washington Street, El Dorado, AR 71730

Circuit and County Clerk, Cleveland County
  Jimmy Cummings . . . . (870) 325-6902
  20 Magnolia Street, Rison, AR 71665   Fax: (870) 325-6144
  E-mail: ccclerk4@yahoo.com

Columbia County

Circuit Clerk

Thirteenth Judicial Circuit
101 North Washington Street, El Dorado, AR 71730

Circuit Clerk, Columbia County **Phyllis Disotell** . . . . (870) 235-3700
  One Court Square, Magnolia, AR 71753   Fax: (870) 235-3786

County Clerk

Office of the County Clerk
One Court Square, Magnolia, AR 71753
Tel: (870) 235-3774 Fax: (870) 235-3723

County Clerk **Sherry Bell** . . . . (870) 235-3774
  E-mail: countyclerk@countyofcolumbia.net

Conway County

Circuit Clerk

Fifteenth Judicial Circuit
108 Union Street, Dardanelle, AR 72834

Circuit Clerk, Conway County **Darlene Massingill** . . . . . . (501) 354-9617
  115 South Moose Street, Morrilton, AR 72110   Fax: (501) 354-9612

County Clerk

Office of the County Clerk
115 South Moose Street, Morrilton, AR 72110
Tel: (501) 354-9621 Fax: (501) 354-9610

County Clerk **Debbie Hartman** . . . . (501) 354-9621
  E-mail: dhartman@conwaycounty.org

Craighead County

Circuit Clerk

Second Judicial Circuit
200 West Hale Avenue, Osceola, AR 72370

Circuit Clerk, Craighead County **Candice Edwards** . . . . . . (870) 933-4530
  511 South Main Street, Jonesboro, AR 72403   Fax: (870) 933-4534
  E-mail: cedwards@craigheadcounty.org

County Clerk

Office of the County Clerk
511 South Main Street, Jonesboro, AR 72401
Tel: (870) 933-4520 Fax: (870) 933-4514
E-mail: craigheadclerk@arkansasclerks.com

County Clerk **Kade Holliday** . . . . (870) 933-4520
  E-mail: kholliday@craigheadcounty.org

Crawford County

Circuit Clerk

Twenty-First Judicial Circuit
300 Main Street, Van Buren, AR 72956

Circuit Clerk, Crawford County **Sharon Blount-Baker** . . . (479) 474-1821
  300 Main Street, Van Buren, AR 72956   Fax: (479) 471-0622
  E-mail: sblountbaker@crawford-county.org

County Clerk

Office of the County Clerk
300 Main Street, Van Buren, AR 72956
Tel: (479) 474-1312 Fax: (479) 471-3236

County Clerk **Teresa Armer** . . . . (479) 474-1312
  E-mail: tarmer@crawfordcounty.org

Crittenden County

Circuit Clerk

Second Judicial Circuit
200 West Hale Avenue, Osceola, AR 72370

Circuit Clerk, Crittenden County **Terry Hawkins** . . . . (870) 739-3248
  100 Court Street, Marion, AR 72364   Fax: (870) 739-3287

County Clerk

Office of the County Clerk
100 Court Street, Marion, AR 72364
Tel: (870) 739-4434 Fax: (870) 739-3072

County Clerk **Paula Brown** . . . . (870) 739-4434
  E-mail: crittendenclerk@arkansasclerks.com

Cross County

Circuit Clerk

First Judicial Circuit
313 South Izard Street, Forrest City, AR 72336

Circuit Clerk, Cross County **Rhonda J. Sullivan** . . . . (870) 238-5720
  705 East Union Street, Wynne, AR 72396   Fax: (870) 238-5722

County Clerk

Office of the County Clerk
705 East Union, Wynne, AR 72396
Tel: (870) 238-5735 Fax: (870) 238-5739

County Clerk **Melanie Davis Winkler** . . . . (870) 238-5735
  E-mail: mwinkler@crosscountyar.org

Dallas County

Circuit and County Clerk

Thirteenth Judicial Circuit
101 North Washington Street, El Dorado, AR 71730

Circuit Clerk, Dallas County **Susie Williams** . . . . (870) 352-2307
  202 Third Street West, Fordyce, AR 71742   Fax: (870) 352-7179
  E-mail: susie.williams@arkansas.gov

(continued on next page)

Desha County

Circuit Clerk

Tenth Judicial Circuit
210 South Main Street, Monticello, AR 71655

Circuit Clerk, Desha County **Minnie Haywood** . . . . (870) 877-2411
Desha County Courthouse, Robert S. Moore Street,   Fax: (870) 877-3407
Arkansas City, AR 71630

County Clerk

Office of the County Clerk
604 Robert S. Moore Avenue, Arkansas City, AR 71630
Tel: (870) 877-2323 Fax: (870) 877-3413

County Clerk **Valerie Donaldson** . . . . (870) 877-2323
E-mail: countyclerk@deshacounty.org

Drew County

Circuit Clerk

Tenth Judicial Circuit
210 South Main Street, Monticello, AR 71655

Circuit Clerk, Drew County **Sandy Erlanson** . . . . (870) 460-6250
210 South Main Street, Monticello, AR 71655   Fax: (870) 460-6255
E-mail: drewcountycircuitclerk@yahoo.com

County Clerk

Office of the County Clerk
210 South Main Street, Monticello, AR 71655
Tel: (870) 460-6260 Fax: (870) 460-6246

County Clerk **Lyna Gulledge** . . . . (870) 460-6260
E-mail: drewclerk@arkansasclerks.com

Faulkner County

Circuit Clerk

Twentieth Judicial Circuit
801 Locust Street, Conway, AR 72034

Circuit Clerk, Faulkner County
Rhonda Long Wharton . . . . (501) 450-4913
801 Locust Street, Conway, AR 72034   Fax: (501) 450-4948
E-mail: rwharton@faulknercounty.org

County Clerk

Office of the County Clerk
801 Locust Street, Conway, AR 72034
Tel: (501) 450-4909 Fax: (501) 450-4938

County Clerk **Margaret Darter** . . . . (501) 450-4909
E-mail: margaret.darter@faulknercounty.org

Franklin County

Circuit Clerk

Fifth Judicial Circuit
100 West Main Street, Russellville, AR 72811

Circuit Clerk, Franklin County **Wilma Brushwood** . . . . . . (479) 667-3818
211 West Commercial Street,   Fax: (479) 667-5174
Ozark, AR 72949
E-mail: franklincocircuit@centurytel.net

County Clerk

Office of the County Clerk
211 West Commercial Street, Ozark, AR 72949
Tel: (479) 667-3607 Fax: (479) 667-3611

County Clerk **DeAnna Schmalz** . . . . (479) 667-3607
E-mail: franklincoclerk@fra.countyservice.net

Fulton County

Circuit and County Clerk

Sixteenth Judicial Circuit
107 West Main Street, Mountain View, AR 72560

Circuit and County Clerk, Fulton County
Vickie Bishop . . . . (870) 895-3310
123 South Main Street, Salem, AR 72576   Fax: (870) 895-3383
E-mail: vickiefcclerk@centurytel.net

Garland County

Circuit Clerk

Eighteenth East Judicial Circuit
607 Ouachita Avenue, Hot Springs, AR 71901

Circuit Clerk, Garland County **Jeannie Pike** . . . . (501) 622-3630
501 Ouachita Street, Hot Springs, AR 71901   Fax: (501) 609-9043
E-mail: jpike@garlandcounty.org

County Clerk

Office of the County Clerk
501 Ouachita Avenue, Hot Springs, AR 71901
Tel: (501) 622-3610 Fax: (501) 624-0665

County Clerk **Sarah Smith** . . . . (501) 622-3610
E-mail: Sasmith@garlandcounty.org

Grant County

Circuit and County Clerk

Seventh Judicial Circuit
210 Locust Street, Malvern, AR 72104

Circuit and County Clerk, Grant County **Carol Ewing** . . . . (870) 942-2631
101 West Center, Room 106,   Fax: (870) 942-3564
Sheridan, AR 72150
E-mail: gcclerk@seark.net

Greene County

Circuit Clerk

Second Judicial Circuit
200 West Hale Avenue, Osceola, AR 72370

Circuit Clerk, Greene County **Jan Griffin** . . . . (870) 239-6330
320 West Court Street, Paragould, AR 72450   Fax: (870) 239-3550
E-mail: greenecirclerk@paragould.net

County Clerk

Office of the County Clerk
320 West Court Street, Paragould, AR 72450
Tel: (870) 239-6311 Fax: (870) 239-6320

County Clerk **Phyllis Rhynes** . . . . (870) 239-6311
E-mail: greeneclerk@arkansasclerks.com

Hempstead County

Circuit Clerk

Eighth North Judicial Circuit
400 South Washington Street, Hope, AR 71801

Circuit Clerk, Hempstead County **Gail Wolfenbarger** .... (870) 777-2384
  400 South Washington Street,   Fax: (870) 777-7827
  Hope, AR 71801

County Clerk

Office of the County Clerk
400 South Washington Street, Hope, AR 71802
P.O. Box 1420, Hope, AR 71801
Tel: (870) 777-2241 Fax: (870) 777-7829

County Clerk **Sandra Rodgers** .... (870) 777-7800
  E-mail: countyclerk@hempsteadcountyar.com

Hot Spring County

Circuit Clerk

Seventh Judicial Circuit
210 Locust Street, Malvern, AR 72104

Circuit Clerk, Hot Spring County **Mayme Brown** .... (501) 332-2281
  210 Locust Street, Malvern, AR 72104
  E-mail: mbrown@hotspringcounty.org

County Clerk

Office of the County Clerk
210 Locust Street, Malvern, AR 72104
Tel: (501) 332-2291 Fax: (501) 332-2221

County Clerk **Sandy Boyette**........................(501) 332-2291
  E-mail: sboyette@hotspringcounty.org

Howard County

Circuit Clerk

Ninth West Judicial Circuit
351 North Second Street, Ashdown, AR 71822

Circuit Clerk, Howard County **Angie Lewis**............ (870) 845-7506
  421 North Main Street, Nashville, AR 71852   Fax: (870) 845-7505
  E-mail: angie.lewis@arkansas.gov

County Clerk

Office of the County Clerk
421 North Main Street, Nashville, AR 71852
Tel: (870) 845-7502 Fax: (870) 845-7505

County Clerk **Brenda Washburn**....................(870) 845-7502
  E-mail: howardclerk@arkansasclerks.com

Independence County

Circuit Clerk

Sixteenth Judicial Circuit
107 West Main Street, Mountain View, AR 72560

Circuit Clerk, Independence County
  Deborah "Debbie" Finley .... (870) 793-8833
  192 East Main Street, Batesville, AR 72501   Fax: (870) 793-8888

County Clerk

Office of the County Clerk
192 East Main Street, Batesville, AR 72501
Tel: (870) 793-8828 Fax: (870) 793-8831

County Clerk **Tracey Nast Mitchell** .... (870) 793-8828
  E-mail: independenceclerk@arkansasclerks.com

Izard County

Circuit and County Clerk

Sixteenth Judicial Circuit
107 West Main Street, Mountain View, AR 72560

Circuit Clerk, Izard County **Rhonda Halbrook**.........(870) 368-4316
  Main and Lunen Street, Melbourne, AR 72556   Fax: (870) 368-4748

Jackson County

Circuit Clerk

Third Judicial Circuit
108 South Marr Street, Pocahontas, AR 72455

Circuit Clerk, Jackson County **Vera Brann** .... (870) 523-7423
  208 Main Street, Newport, AR 72112   Fax: (870) 523-3682

County Clerk

Office of the County Clerk
208 Main Street, Newport, AR 72112
Tel: (870) 523-7420 Fax: (870) 523-7406

County Clerk **Melanie Clark** .... (870) 523-7420
  E-mail: jacksoncountyclerk@gmail.com

Jefferson County

Circuit Clerk

Eleventh West Judicial Circuit
101 West Barraque Street, Pine Bluff, AR 71601

Circuit Clerk, Jefferson County **Lafayette Woods** .... (870) 541-5312
  101 West Barraque Street,   Fax: (870) 541-5351
  Pine Bluff, AR 71601

County Clerk

Office of the County Clerk
101 West Barraque Street, Pine Bluff, AR 71601
Tel: (870) 541-5322 Fax: (870) 541-2977

County Clerk **Patricia Johnson** .... (870) 541-5322
  E-mail: pjohnson.jcclerk@sbcglobal.net

Johnson County

Circuit Clerk

Fifth Judicial Circuit
100 West Main Street, Russellville, AR 72811

Circuit Clerk, Johnson County **Alicia Nowotny** .... (479) 754-2977
  215 West Main Street, Clarksville, AR 72830   Fax: (479) 754-4235

(continued on next page)

Arkansas Court Clerks and Courthouses continued

County Clerk

Office of the County Clerk
Courthouse, Main Street, Clarksville, AR 72830
Tel: (479) 754-3967 Fax: (479) 754-3967

County Clerk **Michelle Frost** . . . . (479) 754-3967
   E-mail: johnsonclerk@arkansasclerks.com

Lafayette County

Circuit Clerk

Eighth South Judicial Circuit
400 Laurel Street, Texarkana, AR 71854

Circuit Clerk, Lafayette County **Mary Joe Rogers** . . . . . . (870) 921-4878
   Three Courthouse Square,   Fax: (870) 921-4879
   Lewisville, AR 71845
   E-mail: lafcocirclerk@whti.net

County Clerk

Office of the County Clerk
Two Courthouse Square, Lewisville, AR 71845
Tel: (870) 921-4633 Fax: (870) 921-4505

County Clerk **Regenia Morton** . . . . (870) 921-4633
   E-mail: lafayetteclerk@arkansasclerks.com

Lawrence County

Circuit Clerk

Third Judicial Circuit
108 South Marr Street, Pocahontas, AR 72455

Circuit Clerk, Lawrence County **Stacie Sullivan** . . . . (870) 886-1112
   315 West Main Street, Walnut Ridge, AR 72476   Fax: (870) 886-1128

County Clerk

Office of the County Clerk
315 West Main Street, Walnut Ridge, AR 72476
P.O. Box 526, Walnut Ridge, AR 72476
Tel: (870) 886-1111 Fax: (870) 886-1122

County Clerk **Tina Stowers** . . . . (870) 886-1111
   E-mail: lawrenceclerk@arkansasclerks.com

Lee County

Circuit Clerk

First Judicial Circuit
313 South Izard Street, Forrest City, AR 72336

Circuit Clerk, Lee County **Mary Ann Wilkinson** . . . . (870) 295-7710
   15 East Chestnut Street, Marianna, AR 72360   Fax: (870) 295-7712
   E-mail: maryannwilkinson1@att.net

County Clerk

Office of the County Clerk
15 East Chestnut Street, Marianna, AR 72360
Tel: (870) 295-7715 Fax: (870) 295-7766

County Clerk **Lynsey Russell** . . . . (870) 295-7715
   E-mail: leeclerk@arkansasclerks.com

Lincoln County

Circuit Clerk

Eleventh West Judicial Circuit
101 West Barraque Street, Pine Bluff, AR 71601

Circuit Clerk, Lincoln County **Cindy Glover** . . . . (870) 628-3154
   300 South Drew Street, Star City, AR 71667   Fax: (870) 628-5545
   E-mail: lincocircuitclerk@centurytel.net

County Clerk

Office of the County Clerk
300 South Drew, Star City, AR 71667
Tel: (870) 628-5114 Fax: (870) 628-5794

County Clerk **Katherine Lawson** . . . . (870) 628-5114
   E-mail: lincolnclerk@arkansasclerks.com

Little River County

Circuit Clerk

Ninth West Judicial Circuit
351 North Second Street, Ashdown, AR 71822

Circuit Clerk, Little River County **Andrea Billingsley** . . . . (870) 898-7212
   351 North Second Street, Ashdown, AR 71822   Fax: (870) 898-5783
   E-mail: lrcircuitclerk@lit.countyservice.net

County Clerk

Office of the County Clerk
351 North Second Street, Ashdown, AR 71822
Tel: (870) 898-7210 Fax: (870) 898-7207

County Clerk **Deanna Sivley** . . . . (870) 898-7210
   E-mail: deanas3@sbcglobal.net

Logan County

Circuit Clerk

Fifteenth Judicial Circuit
108 Union Street, Dardanelle, AR 72834

Circuit Clerk, Logan County **Everly Kellar** . . . . (479) 963-2164
   25 West Walnut Steet, Paris, AR 72855   Fax: (479) 963-3304

County Clerk

Office of the County Clerk
25 West Walnut Street, Paris, AR 72855
Tel: (479) 963-2618 Fax: (479) 963-9017

County Clerk **Peggy Fitzjurls** . . . . (479) 963-2618
   E-mail: countyclerksofc@centurytel.net

Lonoke County

Circuit Clerk

Twenty-Third Judicial Circuit
301 North Center Street, Lonoke, AR 72086

Circuit Clerk, Lonoke County **Deborah Oglesby** . . . . (501) 676-2316
   301 North Center Street, Lonoke, AR 72086   Fax: (501) 676-3014

Arkansas Court Clerks and Courthouses *continued*

County Clerk

Office of the County Clerk
301 North Center Street, Lonoke, AR 72086
P.O. Box 188, Lonoke, AR 72086
Tel: (501) 676-2368 Fax: (501) 676-3038

County Clerk **Dawn Porterfield** . . . .(501) 676-2368
E-mail: dporterfield@lonokecountyclerk.org

Madison County

Circuit Clerk

Fourth Judicial Circuit
280 North College Avenue, Fayetteville, AR 72701

Circuit Clerk, Madison County **Phyllis Villines** . . . . (479) 738-2215
201 West Main Street, Huntsville, AR 72740   Fax: (479) 738-1544
E-mail: mccourt@madisoncounty.net

County Clerk

Office of the County Clerk
201 West Main, Huntsville, AR 72740
Tel: (479) 738-2747 Fax: (479) 738-1544

County Clerk **Faron Ledbetter** . . . . (479) 738-2747
E-mail: madisonclerk@arkansasclerks.com

Marion County

Circuit and County Clerk

Fourteenth Judicial Circuit
301 East Sixth Street, Mountain Home, AR 72653

Circuit Clerk, Marion County **Dee Carlton** . . . .(870) 449-6226
Courthouse Square, Yellville, AR 72687   Fax: (870) 449-4979
E-mail: clerkmarioncounty@yahoo.com

Miller County

Circuit Clerk

Eighth South Judicial Circuit
400 Laurel Street, Texarkana, AR 71854

Circuit Clerk, Miller County **Mary Pankey** . . . .(870) 774-4501
400 Laurel Street, Suite 109,   Fax: (870) 772-5293
Texarkana, AR 71854

County Clerk

Office of the County Clerk
400 Laurel Street, Suite 105, Texarkana, AR 71854
Tel: (870) 774-1501 Fax: (870) 774-3090

County Clerk **Stephanie Harvin** . . . . (870) 774-1501
E-mail: Steph.Harvin@millercountyar.org

Mississippi County

Circuit Clerk

Second Judicial Circuit
200 West Hale Avenue, Osceola, AR 72370

Circuit Clerk, Mississippi County **Leslie Mason** . . . . (870) 762-2332
200 West Walnut Street, Blytheville, AR 72315   Fax: (870) 762-8148

Arkansas Court Clerks and Courthouses *continued*

County Clerk

Office of the County Clerk
200 West Walnut Street, Blytheville, AR 72315
Tel: (870) 762-2411 Fax: (870) 763-0150

County Clerk **Janice Currie** . . . . (870) 762-2411
E-mail: mississippiclerk@arkansasclerks.com

Monroe County

Circuit Clerk

First Judicial Circuit
313 South Izard Street, Forrest City, AR 72336

Circuit Clerk, Monroe County **Alice F. Smith** . . . .(870) 747-3615
123 Madison Street, Clarendon, AR 72029   Fax: (870) 747-3710
E-mail: mccirclerk@centurytel.net

County Clerk

Office of the County Clerk
123 Madison Street, Clarendon, AR 72029
Tel: (870) 747-3632 Fax: (870) 747-5961

County Clerk **Tina Wofford** . . . . (870) 747-3632
E-mail: monroeclerk@arkansasclerks.com

Montgomery County

Circuit and County Clerk

Eighteenth West Judicial Circuit
507 Church Street, Mena, AR 71953

Circuit and County Clerk, Montgomery County
Debbie Baxter . . . . (870) 867-3521
105 Highway 270 East, Suite 10,   Fax: (870) 867-2177
Mount Ida, AR 71957
E-mail: montgomeryclerk@arkansasclerks.com

Nevada County

Circuit Clerk

Eighth North Judicial Circuit
400 South Washington Street, Hope, AR 71801

Circuit Clerk, Nevada County **Rita Reyenga** . . . .(870) 887-2511
215 East Second Street, Prescott, AR 71857   Fax: (870) 887-1911

County Clerk

Office of the County Clerk
215 East Second Street, Prescott, AR 71857
Tel: (870) 887-2710 Fax: (870) 887-5795

County Clerk **Julie Oliver** . . . . (870) 887-2710
E-mail: nevadaclerk@arkansasclerks.com

Newton County

Circuit and County Clerk

Fourteenth Judicial Circuit
301 East Sixth Street, Mountain Home, AR 72653

Circuit and County Clerk, Newton County
Donnie Davis . . . . (870) 446-5125
100 East Court Street, Jasper, AR 72641   Fax: (870) 446-5755

(continued on next page)

Ouachita County

Circuit Clerk

Thirteenth Judicial Circuit
101 North Washington Street, El Dorado, AR 71730

Circuit Clerk, Ouachita County **Betty R. Wilson** . . . . (870) 837-2230
   145 Jefferson Street, SW, Camden, AR 71701   Fax: (870) 837-2252

County Clerk

Office of the County Clerk
145 Jefferson Street SW, Camden, AR 71701
Tel: (870) 837-2220 Fax: (870) 837-2217

County Clerk **Britt Williford** . . . . (870) 837-2220
   E-mail: ouachitaclerk@arkansasclerks.com

Perry County

Circuit and County Clerk

Sixth Judicial Circuit
401 West Markham Street, Little Rock, AR 72201

Circuit and County Clerk, Perry County
   Persundra Hood . . . . (501) 889-5126
   310 West Main Street, Perryville, AR 72126   Fax: (501) 889-5759

Phillips County

Circuit Clerk

First Judicial Circuit
313 South Izard Street, Forrest City, AR 72336

Circuit Clerk, Phillips County **Lynn Stillwell** . . . . (870) 338-5515
   620 Cherry Street, Helena, AR 72342   Fax: (870) 338-5513

County Clerk

Office of the County Clerk
620 Cherry Street, Room 202, Helena, AR 72342
Tel: (870) 338-5505 Fax: (870) 338-5509

County Clerk **Linda White** . . . . (870) 338-5505
   E-mail: phillipsclerk@arkansasclerks.com

Pike County

Circuit Clerk

Ninth West Judicial Circuit
351 North Second Street, Ashdown, AR 71822

Circuit Clerk, Pike County **Sebrina Williams** . . . . (870) 285-2231
   P.O. Box 219, Murfreesboro, AR 71958   Fax: (870) 285-3281

County Clerk

Office of the County Clerk
One Courthouse Square, Murfreesboro, AR 71958
Tel: (870) 285-2743 Fax: (870) 285-3281

County Clerk **Sandy Campbell** . . . . (870) 285-2743
   E-mail: pikeclerk@arkansasclerks.com

Poinsett County

Circuit Clerk

Second Judicial Circuit
200 West Hale Avenue, Osceola, AR 72370

Circuit Clerk, Poinsett County **Misty Richardson** . . . . (870) 578-4420
   401 Market Street, Harrisburg, AR 72432   Fax: (870) 578-4427
   E-mail: misty.richardson@arkansas.gov

County Clerk

Office of the County Clerk
401 Market Street, Harrisburg, AR 72432
Tel: (870) 578-4410 Fax: (870) 578-2441

County Clerk **Teresa Rouse** . . . . (870) 578-4410

Polk County

Circuit Clerk

Eighteenth West Judicial Circuit
507 Church Street, Mena, AR 71953

Circuit Clerk, Polk County **Sharon Simmons** . . . . (479) 394-8100
   507 Church Street, Mena, AR 71953   Fax: (479) 394-8170
   E-mail: sharon.circuit@sbcglobal.net

County Clerk

Office of the County Clerk
507 Church Street, Mena, AR 71953
Tel: (479) 394-8123 Fax: (479) 394-8115

County Clerk **Terri Harrison** . . . . (479) 394-8123
   E-mail: polkcountyclerk@yahoo.com

Pope County

Circuit Clerk

Fifth Judicial Circuit
100 West Main Street, Russellville, AR 72811

Circuit Clerk, Pope County **Diane Wilcox** . . . . (479) 968-7499
   100 West Main Street, Russellville, AR 72811   Fax: (479) 880-8463
   E-mail: fernpopecounty@centurytel.net

County Clerk

Office of the County Clerk
101 West Main Street, Russellville, AR 72801
Tel: (479) 968-6064 Fax: (479) 967-2291

County Clerk **Laura McGuire** . . . . (479) 968-6064
   E-mail: popeclerk@arkansasclerks.com

Prairie County

Circuit and County Clerk

Seventeenth Judicial Circuit
1600 East Booth Road, Searcy, AR 72143

Circuit and County Clerk, Prairie County
   Vanessa Peters . . . . (870) 256-4434
   200 Courthouse Square, Suite 104,
   Des Arc, AR 72040
   E-mail: prairieclerk@arkansasclerks.com

Pulaski County

Circuit and County Clerk

Sixth Judicial Circuit
401 West Markham Street, Little Rock, AR 72201

Circuit and County Clerk, Pulaski County **Larry Crane** . . . (501) 340-8500
   Pulaski County Courthouse,   Fax: (501) 340-8240
   401 West Markham Street, Room 100,
   Little Rock, AR 72201
   E-mail: larry.crane@pulaskiclerk.com

Randolph County

Circuit Clerk

Third Judicial Circuit
108 South Marr Street, Pocahontas, AR 72455

Circuit Clerk, Randolph County **Debbie Wise** . . . . (870) 892-5522
   107 West Broadway, Pocahontas, AR 72455   Fax: (870) 892-8794
   E-mail: randolphcircuitclerk@yahoo.com

County Clerk

Office of the County Clerk
101 East Broadway, Suite A, Pocahontas, AR 72455
Tel: (870) 892-5822 Fax: (870) 892-5829

County Clerk **Rhonda Blevins** . . . . (870) 892-5822
   E-mail: randolphclerk@arkansasclerks.com

Saline County

Circuit Clerk

Twenty-Second Judicial Circuit
200 North Main Street, Benton, AR 72015

Circuit Clerk, Saline County **Myka Bonosample** . . . . (501) 303-5615

County Clerk

Office of the County Clerk
215 North Main, Suite 5, Benton, AR 72015
Tel: (501) 303-5630 Fax: (501) 776-2412

County Clerk **Doug Curtis** . . . . (501) 303-5630
   E-mail: doug.curtis@salinecounty.org

Scott County

Circuit and County Clerk

Fifteenth Judicial Circuit
108 Union Street, Dardanelle, AR 72834

Circuit and County Clerk, Scott County
   Barbara Whiteley . . . . (479) 637-2642
   100 West First Street, Waldron, AR 72958   Fax: (479) 637-0124

Searcy County

Circuit and County Clerk

Twentieth Judicial Circuit
801 Locust Street, Conway, AR 72034

Circuit Clerk, Searcy County **Debbie Loggins** . . . . (870) 448-3807
   P.O. Box 998, Marshall, AR 72034   Fax: (870) 448-5005
   E-mail: searcyclerk@gmail.com

Sebastian County

Circuit Clerk

Twelfth Judicial Circuit
901 South B Street, Fort Smith, AR 72901

Circuit Clerk, Sebastian County **Denora Coomer** . . . . (479) 782-1046
   901 South B Street, Fort Smith, AR 72901   Fax: (479) 784-1580
   E-mail: dcoomer@co.sebastian.ar.us

County Clerk

Office of the County Clerk
35 South Sixth Street, Room 102, Fort Smith, AR 72901
P.O. Box 1089, Fort Smith, AR 72902
Tel: (479) 782-5065 Fax: (479) 784-1567

County Clerk **Sharon Brooks** . . . . (479) 782-5065
   E-mail: sbrooks@co.sebastian.ar.us

Sevier County

Circuit Clerk

Ninth West Judicial Circuit
351 North Second Street, Ashdown, AR 71822

Circuit Clerk, Sevier County **Kathy Smith** . . . . (870) 584-3055
   115 North Third Street, DeQueen, AR 71832   Fax: (870) 642-3119
   E-mail: kathy.smith@arkansas.gov

County Clerk

Office of the County Clerk
115 North Third Street, Room 102, DeQueen, AR 71832
Tel: (870) 642-2852 Fax: (870) 642-3896

County Clerk **Debbie Akin** . . . . (870) 642-2852
   E-mail: sevierclerk@arkansasclerks.com

Sharp County

Circuit and County Clerk

Third Judicial Circuit
108 South Marr Street, Pocahontas, AR 72455

Circuit and County Clerk, Sharp County **Tommy Estes** . . . (870) 994-7361
   718 Ash Flat Drive, Ash Flat, AR 72513   Fax: (870) 994-7712
   E-mail: sharpclerk@centurytel.net

St. Francis County

Circuit Clerk

First Judicial Circuit
313 South Izard Street, Forrest City, AR 72336

Circuit Clerk, St. Francis County **Bette S. Green** . . . . (870) 261-1715
   500 North Third Street, Augusta, AR 72006   Fax: (870) 261-1723
   313 South Izard Street, Forrest City, AR 72336

County Clerk

Office of the County Clerk
313 South Izard Street, Forrest City, AR 72335
Tel: (870) 261-1725 Fax: (870) 630-1210

County Clerk **Emily R. Holley** . . . . (870) 261-1725
   E-mail: stfranciscoclerkofc@cablelynx.com

(continued on next page)

Arkansas Court Clerks and Courthouses *continued*

Stone County

Circuit and County Clerk

Sixteenth Judicial Circuit
107 West Main Street, Mountain View, AR 72560

Circuit and County Clerk, Stone County
 Angie Hudspeth-Wade .... (870) 269-3271
 107 West Main Street, Mountain View, AR 72560   Fax: (870) 269-2303

Union County

Circuit Clerk

Thirteenth Judicial Circuit
101 North Washington Street, El Dorado, AR 71730

Circuit Clerk, Union County **Cheryl Cochran-Wilson** .... (870) 864-1940
 101 North Washington Street,   Fax: (870) 864-1994
 El Dorado, AR 71730

County Clerk

Office of the County Clerk
101 North Washington Avenue, Suite 102, El Dorado, AR 71730
Tel: (870) 864-1910 Fax: (870) 864-1927

County Clerk **Shannon Phillips** .... (870) 864-1910
 E-mail: unioncountyclerk@ymail.com

Van Buren County

Circuit and County Clerk

Office of the Circuit and County Clerk
273 Main Street, Suite 2, Clinton, AR 72031
Tel: (501) 745-4140 Fax: (501) 745-7400

Circuit and County Clerk **Ester Bass** .... (501) 745-4140
 E-mail: vanburenclerk@arkansasclerks.com

Washington County

Circuit Clerk

Fourth Judicial Circuit
280 North College Avenue, Fayetteville, AR 72701

Circuit Clerk, Washington County **Kyle Sylvester** .... (479) 444-1538
 280 North College Avenue,   Fax: (479) 444-1537
 Fayetteville, AR 72701

County Clerk

Office of the County Clerk
280 North College, Room 300, Fayetteville, AR 72701
Tel: (479) 444-1711 Fax: (479) 575-0385

County Clerk **Becky Lewallen** .... (479) 444-1711
 E-mail: washingtonclerk@arkansasclerks.com

White County

Circuit Clerk

Seventeenth Judicial Circuit
1600 East Booth Road, Searcy, AR 72143

Circuit Clerk, White County **Tami King** .... (501) 279-6223
 300 North Spruce Street, Searcy, AR 72143

Arkansas Court Clerks and Courthouses *continued*

County Clerk

Office of the County Clerk
315 North Spruce Street, Searcy, AR 72143
Tel: (501) 279-6204 Fax: (501) 279-6260

County Clerk **Carla Ervin** .... (501) 279-6204
 E-mail: whitecounty.clerk@yahoo.com

Woodruff County

Circuit Clerk

First Judicial Circuit
313 South Izard Street, Forrest City, AR 72336

Circuit Clerk, Woodruff County **Jean Carter** .... (870) 347-2391
 500 North Third Street, Augusta, AR 72006   Fax: (870) 347-8703

County Clerk

Office of the County Clerk
500 North Third Street, Augusta, AR 72006
Tel: (870) 347-2871 Fax: (870) 347-2608

County Clerk **Kelly Peebles** .... (870) 347-2871
 E-mail: Kellypeebles@hotmail.com

Yell County

Circuit and County Clerk

Fifteenth Judicial Circuit
108 Union Street, Dardanelle, AR 72834

Circuit and County Clerk, Yell County
 Shannon Stanberry Barnett .... (479) 495-4850
 101 East Fifth Street, Danville, AR 72833   Fax: (479) 495-4875
 E-mail: yellclerk@arkansasclerks.com

Counties Within Judicial Districts

Circuit Court, 1st Circuit

Areas Covered: Cross, Lee, Monroe, Phillips, St. Francis, and Woodruff Counties.

Circuit Court, 2nd Circuit

Areas Covered: Clay, Craighead, Crittenden, Greene, Mississippi, and Poinsett Counties.

Circuit Court, 3rd Circuit

Areas Covered: Jackson, Lawrence, Randolph, and Sharp Counties.

Circuit Court, 4th Circuit

Areas Covered: Madison and Washington Counties.

Circuit Court, 5th Circuit

Areas Covered: Franklin, Johnson, and Pope Counties.

Circuit Court, 6th Circuit

Areas Covered: Perry and Pulaski Counties.

Circuit Court, 7th Circuit

Areas Covered: Grant and Hot Springs Counties.

Circuit Court, 8th Circuit (North)
Areas Covered: Hempstead and Nevada Counties.

Circuit Court, 8th Circuit (South)
Areas Covered: Lafayette and Miller Counties.

Circuit Court, 9th Circuit (East)
Areas Covered: Clark County.

Circuit Court, 9th Circuit (West)
Areas Covered: Howard, Little River, Pike and Sevier Counties.

Circuit Court, 10th Circuit
Areas Covered: Bradley, Chicot, Desha, and Drew Counties.

Circuit Court, 11th Circuit (East)
Areas Covered: Arkansas County.

Circuit Court, 11th Circuit (West)
Areas Covered: Jefferson and Lincoln Counties.

Circuit Court, 12th Circuit
Areas Covered: Sebastian County.

Circuit Court, 13th Circuit
Areas Covered: Calhoun, Cleveland, Columbia, Dallas, Ouachita, and Union Counties.

Circuit Court, 14th Circuit
Areas Covered: Boone, Marion, and Newton Counties.

Circuit Court, 15th Circuit
Areas Covered: Conway, Logan, Scott, and Yell Counties.

Circuit Court, 16th Circuit
Areas Covered: Cleburne, Fulton, Independence, Izard, and Stone Counties.

Circuit Court, 17th Circuit
Areas Covered: Prairie and White Counties.

Circuit Court, 18th Circuit (East)
Areas Covered: Garland County.

Circuit Court, 18th Circuit (West)
Areas Covered: Montgomery and Polk Counties.

Circuit Court, 19th Circuit (East)
Areas Covered: Carroll County.

Circuit Court, 19th Circuit (West)
Areas Covered: Benton County.

Circuit Court, 20th Circuit
Areas Covered: Faulkner, Searcy, and Van Buren Counties.

Circuit Court, 21st Circuit
Areas Covered: Crawford County.

Circuit Court, 22nd Circuit
Areas Covered: Saline County.

Circuit Court, 23rd Circuit
Areas Covered: Lonoke County.

California Court Clerks and Courthouses

The trial courts of general jurisdiction in California are called superior courts. There is one Superior Court (with divisional offices) per county. In California, the county clerk/recorder and superior court clerk (executive officer) positions are separate. Listed below for each county is contact information for the county clerk/recorder. For Superior Court locations and phone numbers, see the California Judiciary website – www.courts.ca.gov.

California Supreme Court

350 McAllister Street, Room 1295, San Francisco, CA 94102
Tel: (415) 865-7000 Tel: (213) 830-7050 (Los Angeles Office)
Tel: (916) 653-0284 (Sacramento Office) Fax: (415) 865-7183
Internet: www.courtinfo.ca.gov

The Supreme Court consists of a chief justice and six associate justices appointed by the Governor and confirmed by the Commission on Judicial Appointments. After confirmation, justices serve until the next gubernatorial election and then run unopposed on a nonpartisan ballot for election to twelve year terms. The Supreme Court has original jurisdiction in mandamus, certiorari, prohibition and habeas corpus proceedings. The Court may review decisions of the California Courts of Appeal, and the Court has final appellate jurisdiction over all cases in which a judgment of death has been pronounced. The Court also reviews the recommendations of the Commission on Judicial Performance and the State Bar of California concerning the removal and suspension of judges and attorneys for misconduct.

Court Staff
Court Executive Officer **Frank McGuire** . . . . . . (415) 865-7000 ext. 57015

California Court of Appeal

Internet: www.courts.ca.gov

The California Courts of Appeal are comprised of six districts, three of which are separated into divisions. Each division (or district, if there are no divisions) has a presiding justice. All justices of the Courts of Appeal are initially appointed by the Governor and confirmed by the Commission on Judicial Appointments. After confirmation, justices serve until the next gubernatorial election, at which time they run unopposed on a nonpartisan ballot for election to the remaining portion of the term. A full term is twelve years. The Courts of Appeal have jurisdiction in cases on appeal from the California Superior Courts, except when judgment of death has been pronounced and in other cases as prescribed by statute.

California Court of Appeal, First Appellate District

350 McAllister Street, San Francisco, CA 94102
Tel: (415) 865-7300 Fax: (415) 865-7309
Internet: www.courts.ca.gov/1dca.htm

Areas Covered: Counties of Alameda, Contra Costa, Del Norte, Humboldt, Lake, Marin, Mendocino, Napa, San Francisco, San Mateo, Solano and Sonoma

Court Staff
Fax: (415) 865-7209

Clerk/Administrator **Diana Herbert** . . . . (415) 865-7264
E-mail: diana.herbert@jud.ca.gov

California Court of Appeal, Second Appellate District

Ronald Reagan State Building, 300 South Spring Street, Room 2217, Los Angeles, CA 90013
Tel: (213) 830-7000 Fax: (213) 897-2430
Internet: www.courts.ca.gov/2dca.htm

Areas Covered: Counties of Los Angeles, San Luis Obispo, Santa Barbara and Ventura

Court Staff
Clerk of Court **Joseph A. Lane** . . . . (213) 830-7000
E-mail: joseph.lane@jud.ca.gov

California Court of Appeal, Third Appellate District

914 Capitol Mall, Fourth Floor, Sacramento, CA 95814
Tel: (916) 654-0209
Internet: www.courts.ca.gov/3dca.htm

Areas Covered: Counties of Alpine, Amador, Butte, Calaveras, Colusa, El Dorado, Glenn, Lassen, Modoc, Mono, Nevada, Placer, Plumas, Sacramento, San Joaquin, Shasta, Sierra, Siskiyou, Sutter, Tehama, Trinity, Yolo and Yuba

Court Staff
Clerk/Administrator **Deena C. Fawcett** . . . . (916) 654-0209
E-mail: deena.fawcett@jud.ca.gov

California Court of Appeal, Fourth Appellate District

750 B Street, Suite 300, San Diego, CA 92101
Tel: (619) 744-0760 Fax: (619) 645-2495
Internet: www.courts.ca.gov/4dca.htm

Areas Covered: Counties of Imperial, Inyo, Orange, Riverside, San Bernardino and San Diego

Court Staff
Clerk of the Court/Administrator **Kevin J. Lane** . . . . (619) 744-0760

California Court of Appeal, Fifth Appellate District

2424 Ventura Street, Fresno, CA 93721
Tel: (559) 445-5491 Fax: (559) 445-5769
Internet: www.courts.ca.gov/5dca.htm

Areas Covered: Counties of Fresno, Kern, Kings, Madera, Mariposa, Merced, Stanislaus, Tulare and Tuolumne

Court Staff
Court Administrator/Clerk of the Court
Charlene Ynson . . . . (559) 445-5491
E-mail: charlene.ynson@jud.ca.gov

California Court of Appeal, Sixth Appellate District

333 West Santa Clara Street, Suite 1060, San Jose, CA 95113
Tel: (408) 277-1004 Fax: (408) 277-9916
Internet: www.courts.ca.gov/6dca.htm

Areas Covered: Counties of Monterey, San Benito, Santa Clara and Santa Cruz

(continued on next page)

California Court Clerks and Courthouses *continued*

Court Staff
Clerk of the Court **Dan Potter** . . . . (408) 277-1004

County-By-County

Alameda County

County Clerk/Recorder

Auditor-Controller Agency
County Administration Building, 1221 Oak Street, Room 249,
Oakland, CA 94612
Fax: (510) 272-6502 (Auditor-Controller)
Fax: (510) 272-6382 (Clerk-Recorder)
Internet: www.acgov.org/auditor

Auditor-Controller/Clerk-Recorder **Steve Manning** . . . . . . (510) 272-6565
  E-mail: steve.manning@acgov.org

Alpine County

County Clerk

Office of the County Clerk
99 Water Street, Markleeville, CA 96120
Tel: (530) 694-2281 Fax: (530) 694-2491

County Clerk **Teola L. Tremayne** . . . . (530) 694-2281
  E-mail: ttremayne@alpinecountyca.gov

County Recorder

Office of the Assessor/Recorder
99 Water Street, Markleeville, CA 96120
Tel: (530) 694-2283 Fax: (530) 694-2491

Assessor/Recorder **Donald O'Connor** . . . . (530) 694-2283
  E-mail: doconnor@alpinecountyca.gov

Amador County

County Clerk/Recorder

Office of the County Clerk/Recorder
810 Court Street, Jackson, CA 95642
Tel: (209) 223-6468 Fax: (209) 223-6467

County Clerk/Recorder **Kimberly L. Grady** . . . . (209) 223-6468
  E-mail: elections@amadorgov.org

Butte County

County Clerk/Recorder

County Clerk-Recorder
25 County Center Drive, Suite 110, Oroville, CA 95965
Tel: (530) 538-7691 Fax: (530) 538-7975
E-mail: clerk@buttecounty.net
Internet: http://clerk-recorder.buttecounty.net

County Clerk-Recorder and Registrar of Voters
  Candace J. "Candy" Grubbs . . . . (530) 538-7691
  E-mail: cgrubbs@buttecounty.net

California Court Clerks and Courthouses *continued*

Calaveras County

County Clerk/Recorder

Office of the County Clerk/Recorder
891 Mountain Ranch Road, San Andreas, CA 95249
Tel: (209) 754-6371 Fax: (209) 754-6733

County Clerk/Recorder **Rebecca Turner** . . . . (209) 754-6371
  E-mail: elections@co.calaveras.ca.us

Colusa County

County Clerk/Recorder

Office of the County Clerk and Recorder
546 Jay Street, Suite 200, Colusa, CA 95932
Tel: (530) 458-0500 Fax: (530) 458-0512

County Clerk and Recorder **Rose Gallo-Vasquez** . . . . (530) 458-0500
  E-mail: clerkinfo@countyofcolusa.org

Contra Costa County

County Clerk/Recorder

Office of the County Clerk/Recorder
555 Escobar Street, Martinez, CA 94553
Fax: (925) 335-7893

Clerk/Recorder **Joseph Canciamilla** . . . . (925) 335-7899
  E-mail: joe.canciamilla@cr.cccounty.us

Del Norte County

County Clerk/Recorder

Office of the County Clerk/Recorder
981 H Street, Suite 160, Crescent City, CA 95531
Tel: (707) 464-7216 Fax: (707) 465-0321

County Clerk/Recorder **Alissia D. Northrup** . . . . (707) 464-7216
  E-mail: anorthrup@co.del-norte.ca.us

El Dorado County

County Clerk/Recorder

Office of the County Clerk/Recorder
360 Fair Lane, Placerville, CA 95667
Tel: (530) 621-5490 Fax: (530) 621-2147

County Clerk/Recorder **William E. Schultz** . . . . (530) 621-5490
  E-mail: recorderclerk@edcgov.us

Fresno County

County Clerk

Office of the County Clerk/Registrar of Voters
2221 Kern Street, Fresno, CA 93721-2613
Tel: (559) 600-2575 (Clerk)
Tel: (559) 600-8683 (Elections) Fax: (559) 488-3279
E-mail: clerk-elections@co.fresno.ca.us
Internet: www.co.fresno.ca.us/elections

County Clerk/Registrar of Voters **Brandi L. Orth** . . . . (559) 600-2575
  E-mail: borth@co.fresno.ca.us

California Court Clerks and Courthouses *continued*

County Recorder

Office of the Assessor/Recorder
Hall of Records, 2281 Tulare Street, Room 201, Fresno, CA 93721
Fax: (559) 600-1482

Assessor/Recorder **Paul A. Dictos** . . . . (559) 600-6879

Glenn County

County Clerk/Recorder

Office of the County Clerk/Recorder
516 West Sycamore Street, Willows, CA 95988
Tel: (530) 934-6412   Fax: (530) 934-6571

County Clerk/Recorder **Sheryl Thur** . . . . (530) 934-6412
E-mail: elections@countyofglenn.net

Humboldt County

County Clerk/Recorder

Office of the County Clerk/Recorder
825 Fifth Street, Fifth Floor, Eureka, CA 95501
Tel: (707) 445-7593   Fax: (707) 445-7430

County Clerk/Recorder **Kelly Sanders** . . . . (707) 445-7593
E-mail: ehayes@co.humboldt.ca.us

Imperial County

County Clerk/Recorder

Office of the County Clerk/Recorder
940 West Main Street, Suite 202, El Centro, CA 92243
Tel: (442) 265-1076 (Clerk)   Tel: (442) 265-1077 (Recorder)
Fax: (442) 265-1091

County Clerk/Recorder **Chuck Storey** . . . .(442) 265-1076
E-mail: clerkrec@co.imperial.ca.us

Inyo County

County Clerk/Recorder

Office of the County Clerk/Recorder
168 North Edwards Street, Independence, CA 93526
Tel: (760) 878-0222   Fax: (760) 878-1805

County Clerk **Kammi Foote**. . . . .(760) 878-0222
E-mail: kfoote@inyocounty.us

Kern County

County Clerk

Office of the Auditor-Controller-County Clerk
Administrative Center, 1115 Truxtun Ave., Bakersfield, CA 93301-4617
Fax: (661) 868-3560
Internet: www.co.kern.ca.us/auditor

Auditor-Controller-County Clerk **Mary Bedard** . . . . (661) 868-3599
E-mail: bedardm@co.kern.ca.us

California Court Clerks and Courthouses *continued*

County Recorder

Office of the Assessor-Recorder
Administrative Center, 1115 Truxtun Avenue, 3rd Floor,
Bakersfield, CA 93301-4839
Fax: (661) 868-3209
Internet: www.recorder.co.kern.ca.us

Assessor/Recorder **Jon Lifquist** . . . . (661) 868-3485

Kings County

County Clerk/Recorder

Office of the County Clerk/Recorder
1400 West Lacey Boulevard, Hanford, CA 93230
Tel: (559) 582-3211   Fax: (559) 582-6639

County Clerk/Recorder **Christina McKay** . . . . . . (559) 582-3211 ext. 2470
E-mail: christina.mckay@co.kings.ca.us

Lake County

County Clerk

Office of the County Clerk
255 North Forbes Street, Lakeport, CA 95453
Tel: (707) 263-2311   Fax: (707) 263-2310

County Clerk **Cathy Saderlund** . . . .(707) 263-2311
E-mail: auditoremail@co.lake.ca.us

County Recorder

Office of the Assessor-Recorder
255 North Forbes Street, Lakeport, CA 95453
Tel: (707) 263-2293 (Recorder's Office)
Tel: (707) 263-2302 (Assessor's Office)   Fax: (707) 263-3703

Assessor-Recorder **Richard A. Ford** . . . .(707) 263-2302
E-mail: assessor@co.lake.ca.us

Lassen County

County Clerk/Recorder

Office of the County Clerk/Recorder
221 South Roop Street, Suite 5, Susanville, CA 96130
Tel: (530) 251-8217   Fax: (530) 257-3480

County Clerk/Recorder **Julie Bustamante** . . . . (530) 251-8217
E-mail: lcclerk@co.lassen.ca.us

Los Angeles County

County Clerk/Recorder

Office of the Registrar-Recorder/County Clerk
12400 Imperial Highway, Norwalk, CA 90650-8357
Tel: (562) 466-1310 (Information)
TTY: (562) 462-2259   Fax: (562) 929-4790
Internet: www.lavote.net

Registrar-Recorder/County Clerk **Dean C. Logan** . . . .(562) 462-2716
E-mail: dlogan@rrcc.lacounty.gov

(continued on next page)

California Court Clerks and Courthouses *continued*

Birth, Death, and Marriage Records

Office of the Registrar-Recorder/County Clerk
12400 Imperial Highway, Norwalk, CA 90650-8357
Tel: (562) 466-1310 (Information)
TTY: (562) 462-2259 Fax: (562) 929-4790
Internet: www.lavote.net

Assistant Manager, Vital Records **Julia Melendez** . . . . (562) 462-2983

Business Filings and Registration

Office of the Registrar-Recorder/County Clerk
12400 Imperial Highway, Norwalk, CA 90650-8357
Tel: (562) 466-1310 (Information)
TTY: (562) 462-2259 Fax: (562) 929-4790
Internet: www.lavote.net

Manager, Business Filings and Registration **Darla Neal** . . . (562) 462-2057

Document Analysis and Recording

Office of the Registrar-Recorder/County Clerk
12400 Imperial Highway, Norwalk, CA 90650-8357
Tel: (562) 466-1310 (Information)
TTY: (562) 462-2259 Fax: (562) 929-4790
Internet: www.lavote.net

Manager, Document Recording Division **Jaime Pailma** . . . (562) 462-2889
   E-mail: jpailma@rrcc.lacounty.gov

Real Estate Records

Office of the Registrar-Recorder/County Clerk
12400 Imperial Highway, Norwalk, CA 90650-8357
Tel: (562) 466-1310 (Information)
TTY: (562) 462-2259 Fax: (562) 929-4790
Internet: www.lavote.net

Manager, Real Estate Records **Deborah Johnson** . . . . (562) 462-2001

Madera County

County Clerk/Recorder

Office of the County Clerk/Recorder
200 West Fourth Street, Madera, CA 93637
Tel: (559) 675-7720 Fax: (559) 675-7870

County Clerk/Recorder **Rebecca Martinez** . . . . (559) 675-7720
   E-mail: CountyClerkInfo@Madera-County.com

Marin County

County Clerk/Recorder

Office of the Assessor-Recorder-County Clerk
3501 Civic Center Drive, Rooms 208 (Assessor), 232 (Recorder), and 234
(Clerk), San Rafael, CA 94903
Tel: (415) 499-7215 (Assessor) Tel: (415) 499-6092 (Recorder)
Tel: (415) 499-6152 (County Clerk) Fax: (415) 499-6542 (Assessor)
Fax: (415) 499-7893 (Recorder) Fax: (415) 499-7184 (County Clerk)
E-mail: assessor@co.marin.ca.us
E-mail: recorder@co.marin.ca.us
E-mail: countyclerk@co.marin.ca.us

Assessor-Recorder-County Clerk
   Richard N. "Rich" Benson . . . . (415) 499-7198
   E-mail: rbenson@marincounty.org

California Court Clerks and Courthouses *continued*

Mariposa County

County Clerk

Office of the County Clerk
4982 10th Street, Mariposa, CA 95338
Tel: (209) 966-2007 Fax: (209) 966-6496

County Clerk **Keith M. Williams** . . . . (209) 966-2007
   E-mail: kwilliams@mariposacounty.org

County Recorder

Office of the Assessor and Recorder
4982 10th Street, Mariposa, CA 95338
Tel: (209) 966-5719 Fax: (209) 966-5147

Assessor-Recorder **Becky Crafts** . . . . (209) 966-5719
   E-mail: bcrafts@mariposacounty.org

Mendocino County

County Clerk/Recorder

Office of the County Assessor/Clerk/Recorder
501 Low Gap Road, Room 1020, Ukiah, CA 95482
Tel: (707) 234-6822 Fax: (707) 463-4257

County Assessor/Clerk/Recorder **Susan M. Ranochak** . . . (707) 234-6822
   E-mail: acr@co.mendocino.ca.us

Merced County

County Clerk/Recorder

Office of the County Clerk
2222 M Street, Merced, CA 95340
Tel: (209) 385-7627 Fax: (209) 385-7626

County Clerk **Barbara "Barb" Levey** . . . . (209) 385-7627

Modoc County

County Clerk/Recorder

Office of the County Clerk/Recorder
108 East Modoc Street, Alturas, CA 96101
Tel: (530) 233-6205 Fax: (530) 233-6666

County Clerk/Recorder **Stephanie Wellemeyer** . . . . (530) 233-6205
   E-mail: recorder@co.modoc.ca.us

Mono County

County Clerk/Recorder

Office of the County Clerk/Recorder
74 North School Street, Bridgeport, CA 93517
Tel: (760) 932-5530 Tel: (760) 932-5531 Fax: (760) 932-5531

County Clerk/Recorder **Bob Musil** . . . . (760) 932-5530
   E-mail: bmusil@mono.ca.gov

Monterey County

County Clerk/Recorder

Office of the Assessor-County Clerk-Recorder
168 West Alisal Street, 1st Floor, Salinas, CA 93901
P.O. Box 570, Salinas, CA 93902
Fax: (831) 755-5435
E-mail: assessor@co.monterey.ca.us
Internet: www.co.monterey.ca.us/assessor (Assessor)
Internet: www.co.monterey.ca.us/recorder (Recorder-County Clerk)

Assessor-County Clerk-Recorder **Stephen L. Vagnini** . . . . (831) 755-5803
E-mail: vagninis@co.monterey.ca.us

Napa County

County Clerk/Recorder

Office of the County Clerk/Recorder
900 Coombs Street, Room 116, Napa, CA 94559
Tel: (707) 253-4247 (Clerk)
Tel: (707) 253-4105 (Recorder) Fax: (707) 259-8149
E-mail: recorder-clerk@countyofnapa.org

County Clerk/Recorder **John Tuteur** . . . . (707) 253-4459
E-mail: john.tuteur@countyofnapa.org

Nevada County

County Clerk/Recorder

Office of the County Clerk/Recorder
950 Maidu Avenue, Suite 210, Nevada City, CA 95959
Fax: (530) 265-9842 Tel: (530) 265-1221

County Clerk/Recorder **Gregory J. Diaz** . . . . (530) 265-1221
E-mail: nc.recorder@co.nevada.ca.us

Orange County

County Clerk/Recorder

Office of the County Clerk-Recorder
12 Civic Center Plaza, Room 101 and 106, Santa Ana, CA 92701
Tel: (714) 834-2500 Fax: (714) 834-2675
Internet: www.ocrecorder.com

Clerk-Recorder **Hugh Nguyen** . . . . (714) 834-2248
E-mail: hugh.nguyen@ocgov.com

Placer County

County Clerk/Recorder

Office of the County Clerk-Recorder-Registrar of Voters
2954 Richardson Drive, Auburn, CA 95603
Tel: (530) 886-5600 Fax: (530) 886-5687
E-mail: clerk@placer.ca.gov

County Clerk-Recorder-Registrar of Voters
Jim McCauley . . . . (530) 886-5650
E-mail: jmccaule@placer.ca.gov

Plumas County

County Clerk/Recorder

Office of the County Clerk/Recorder
520 Main Street, Room 102, Quincy, CA 95971
Tel: (530) 283-6218 Tel: (530) 283-6256 Fax: (530) 283-6155
E-mail: clerkrecorder@countyofplumas.com

County Clerk/Recorder **Kathleen "Kathy" Williams** . . . . . (530) 283-6218
E-mail: kathywilliams@countyofplumas.com

Riverside County

County Clerk/Recorder

Office of the Assessor-County Clerk-Recorder
County Administrative Center, 4080 Lemon Street, First, Fifth, and Sixth
Floors, Riverside, CA 92501
P.O. Box 751, Riverside, CA 92502-0751
Tel: (951) 955-6200 (Assessor)
Tel: (951) 486-7000 (County Clerk-Recorder)
E-mail: accrmail@asrclkrec.com
Internet: http://riverside.asrclkrec.com

Assessor-County Clerk-Recorder **Peter Aldana** . . . . (951) 955-6200

Sacramento County

County Clerk/Recorder

Office of the County Clerk/Recorder
600 8th Street, Sacramento, CA 95814
P.O. Box 839, Sacramento, CA 95812-0839
Tel: (916) 874-6334
Internet: www.ccr.saccounty.net

Clerk/Recorder **Donna Allred** . . . . (916) 874-6334
E-mail: sacrec@saccounty.net

San Benito County

County Clerk/Recorder

Office of the County Clerk
481 Fourth Street, Room 206, Hollister, CA 95023
Tel: (831) 636-4046 Fax: (831) 635-9340

County Clerk/Auditor/Recorder **Joe Paul Gonzalez** . . . . . (831) 636-4046
E-mail: acurro@cosb.us

San Bernardino County

County Clerk/Recorder

Office of the Assessor-Recorder-County Clerk
172 West Third Street, San Bernardino, CA 92415-0310
Tel: (909) 387-8306 Fax: (909) 387-6718
Internet: www.sbcounty.gov/assessor

Assessor-Recorder-County Clerk **Bob Dutton** . . . . (909) 387-8306

(continued on next page)

California Court Clerks and Courthouses *continued*

San Diego County

County Clerk/Recorder

Office of the Assessor-Recorder-County Clerk
County Administration Center, 1600 Pacific Highway, Suite 103, Mail
Stop A-4, San Diego, CA 92101-2480 (Assessor)
Tel: (619) 236-3771 (Assessor) Fax: (619) 557-4056 (Assessor)
Tel: (619) 237-0502 (Recorder/County Clerk)
Fax: (619) 557-4155 (Recorder/County Clerk)
Internet: www.sdarcc.com

Assessor-Recorder-County Clerk
  Ernest J. Dronenburg, Jr. . . . . (619) 531-5507
  E-mail: arcc.fgg@sdcounty.ca.gov

San Francisco County

County Clerk

Office of the County Clerk
1 Dr. Carlton B. Goodlett Place, Room 168, San Francisco, CA 94102
Tel: (415) 554-4950 Fax: (415) 554-4951
Internet: www.sfgov.org/countyclerk

County Clerk **Naomi Kelly** . . . . (415) 554-4955
  E-mail: county.clerk@sfgov.org

County Recorder

Office of the Assessor/Recorder
City Hall, Rm. 190, 1 Dr. Carlton B. Goodlett Place,
San Francisco, CA 94102
Fax: (415) 554-7915
E-mail: assessor@sfgov.org

Assessor/Recorder **Carmen Chu** . . . . (415) 554-5502
  E-mail: assessor@sfgov.org

San Joaquin County

County Clerk/Recorder

Office of the Recorder-County Clerk
44 North San Joaquin Street, Suite 230, Stockton, CA 95202
Fax: (209) 468-8040

Recorder-County Clerk **Kenneth Blakemore** . . . . (209) 468-2630
  E-mail: kblakemore@sjgov.org

San Luis Obispo County

County Clerk/Recorder

Office of the County Clerk-Recorder
1055 Monterey Street, Suite D120, San Luis Obispo, CA 93408
Tel: (805) 781-5080 Fax: (805) 781-1111
Internet: www.slocounty.ca.gov/clerk.htm

County Clerk-Recorder **Tommy Gong** . . . . (805) 781-5080

California Court Clerks and Courthouses *continued*

San Mateo County

County Clerk/Recorder

Office of the Assessor-County Clerk-Recorder
555 County Center, 3rd Floor, Redwood City, CA 94063
Tel: (650) 363-4500 Fax: (650) 363-1903 (Assessor's Office)
Fax: (650) 599-7458 (Clerk's Office)
Fax: (650) 363-4843 (Recorder's Office)
Internet: www.smcare.org

Assessor-County Clerk-Recorder **Mark Church** . . . . (650) 363-4988
  E-mail: mchurch@smcare.org

Santa Barbara County

County Clerk/Recorder

Office of the County Clerk-Recorder-Assessor
105 East Anapamu Street, Room 204, Santa Barbara, CA 93101
P.O. Box 159, Santa Barbara, CA 93102-0159
Fax: (805) 568-3247
Internet: www.sbcvote.com

County Clerk-Recorder-Assessor
  Joseph Edward Holland . . . . (805) 568-2550
  E-mail: holland@co.santa-barbara.ca.us

Santa Clara County

County Clerk/Recorder

Office of the Clerk-Recorder
70 West Hedding Street, San Jose, CA 95110-1705
Tel: (408) 299-5688

County Clerk/Recorder
  Regina M. "Gina" Alcomendras . . . . (408) 299-5621
  E-mail: gina.alcomendras@rec.sccgov.org

Santa Cruz County

County Clerk

Office of the County Clerk
701 Ocean Street, Room 210, Santa Cruz, CA 95060
Tel: (831) 454-2060 Fax: (831) 454-2445
Internet: www.sccoclerk.com
Internet: www.votescount.com (Elections)

County Clerk **Gail L. Pellerin** . . . . (831) 454-2419
  E-mail: gail.pellerin@santacruzcounty.us

County Recorder

Office of the County Assessor
701 Ocean Street, First Floor, Santa Cruz, CA 95060
Tel: (831) 454-2002 Fax: (831) 454-2495
E-mail: asr@santacruzcounty.us
Internet: www.co.santa-cruz.ca.us/asr/index.htm

Assessor/Recorder **Sean Saldavia** . . . . (831) 454-2002
  E-mail: sean.saldavia@santacruzcounty.us

Shasta County

County Clerk

Office of the County Clerk
1643 Market Street, Redding, CA 96001
Tel: (530) 225-5730 Fax: (530) 225-5454

County Clerk **Cathy Darling Allen** . . . . (530) 225-5730
  E-mail: countyclerk@co.shasta.ca.us

County Recorder

Office of the Assessor-Recorder
1450 Court Street, Suite 208, Redding, CA 96001
Tel: (530) 225-5671 (Recorder's Office)
Tel: (530) 225-3600 (Assessor's Office)
Fax: (530) 225-5152 (Recorder's Office)
Fax: (530) 225-5673 (Assessor's Office)

Assessor-Recorder **Leslie Morgan** . . . . (530) 225-5671
  E-mail: lmorgan@co.shasta.ca.us

Sierra County

County Clerk/Recorder

Office of the County Clerk/Recorder
100 Courthouse Square, Room 11, Downieville, CA 95936

County Clerk/Recorder **Heather Foster** . . . . (530) 289-3295
  E-mail: hfoster@sierracounty.ws

Siskiyou County

County Clerk

Office of the County Clerk
510 North Main Street, Yreka, CA 96097
Fax: (530) 841-4110 Tel: (530) 842-8084

County Clerk/Registrar **Colleen Setzer** . . . . (530) 842-8084
  E-mail: colleen@sisqvotes.org

County Recorder

Office of the Assessor-Recorder
311 Fourth Street, Room 108, Yreka, CA 96097
Tel: (530) 842-8065 (Recorder's Office)
Tel: (530) 842-8036 (Assessor's Office) Fax: (530) 842-8059

Assessor-Recorder **Mike Mallory** . . . . (530) 842-8065
  E-mail: mmallory@co.siskiyou.ca.us

Solano County

County Clerk

Office of the Treasurer-Tax Collector-County Clerk
675 Texas Street, Suite 1900, Fairfield, CA 94533
Tel: (707) 784-7910 (Clerk's Office)
Tel: (707) 784-6295 (Treasurer's Office)
Tel: (707) 784-7485 ((Tax Collector)) Fax: (707) 784-6311
E-mail: ttccc@solanocounty.com

Treasurer/Tax Collector/County Clerk
  Charles A. Lomeli . . . . (707) 784-6295
  E-mail: calomeli@solanocounty.com

County Recorder

Office of the Assessor/Recorder
675 Texas Street, Suite 2700, Fairfield, CA 94533
Tel: (707) 784-6200 Fax: (707) 784-6209
E-mail: assessor@solanocounty.com

Assessor/Recorder **Marc C. Tonnesen** . . . . (707) 784-6203
  E-mail: mctonnesen@solanocounty.com

Sonoma County

County Clerk/Recorder

**Office of the County Clerk-Recorder-Assessor-Registrar
of Voters**
585 Fiscal Drive, Room 104F, Santa Rosa, CA 95403
Fax: (707) 565-1364
Internet: www.sonoma-county.org/cra

County Clerk-Recorder-Assessor-Registrar of Voters
  William F. "Bill" Rousseau . . . . (707) 565-1877
  E-mail: thecountyclerk@sonoma-county.org

Stanislaus County

County Clerk/Recorder

Office of the Clerk-Recorder
1021 I Street, Suite 101, Modesto, CA 95354
P.O. Box 1008, Modesto, CA 95353
Fax: (209) 525-5804 (Clerk-Recorder)
Fax: (209) 525-5802 (Registrar of Voters)
Internet: www.stancounty.com/clerkrecorder
Internet: www.stanvote.com

Clerk-Recorder/Registrar of Voters **Lee Lundrigan** . . . .(209) 525-5200
  E-mail: stanvote@stancounty.com   Tel: (209) 525-5250

Sutter County

County Clerk/Recorder

Office of the County Clerk/Recorder
433 Second Street, Yuba City, CA 95991
Tel: (530) 822-7134 Fax: (530) 822-7214

County Clerk/Recorder **Donna Johnston** . . . . (530) 822-7134
  E-mail: djohnston@co.sutter.ca.us

Tehama County

County Clerk/Recorder

Office of the County Clerk/Recorder
633 Washington Street, Room 11, Red Bluff, CA 96080
Tel: (530) 527-3350 Fax: (530) 527-1745
E-mail: recorder@co.tehama.ca.us

County Clerk/Recorder **Jennifer Vise** . . . . (530) 527-3350
  E-mail: jvise@co.tehama.ca.us

Trinity County

County Clerk/Recorder

Office of the County Clerk/Recorder
11 Court Street, Weaverville, CA 96093
Tel: (530) 623-1215 Fax: (530) 623-8398

County Clerk/Recorder/Assessor **Shanna S. White** . . . . . . (530) 623-1215
  E-mail: recorder@trinitycounty.org

(continued on next page)

California Court Clerks and Courthouses *continued*

Tulare County

County Clerk/Recorder

Office of the County Assessor/Clerk-Recorder
221 South Mooney Boulevard, Room 103, Visalia, CA 93291-4593
Fax: (559) 740-4329

County Assessor/Clerk-Recorder **Roland P. Hill** . . . . (559) 636-5051

Tuolumne County

County Clerk

Office of the County Clerk
2 South Green Street, Sonora, CA 95370
Tel: (209) 533-5573 Fax: (209) 694-8931

County Clerk and Auditor/Controller
  Deborah Bautista Second Floor . . . . (209) 533-5573
  E-mail: dbautista@co.tuolumna.ca.us

County Recorder

Office of the Recorder
2 South Green Street, Sonora, CA 95370
Tel: (209) 533-5531 (Recorder's Office)
Tel: (209) 533-5535 (Assessor's Office)
Fax: (209) 533-6543 (Recorder's Office)
Fax: (209) 533-5674 (Assessor's Office)

Assistant Recorder **Carol Jackson** . . . . (209) 533-5531
  E-mail: recorder@tuolumnecounty.ca.gov

Ventura County

County Clerk/Recorder

Office of the County Clerk and Recorder
County Government Center, Administration Bldg., 800 S. Victoria Ave.,
Main Plaza, Ventura, CA 93009-1260
Tel: (805) 654-2263 (County Clerk Division)
Tel: (805) 654-3665 (Recorder's Office)
Tel: (805) 654-2781 (Elections Division) Fax: (805) 654-2392
Internet: http://recorder.countyofventura.org/

County Clerk and Recorder **Mark A. Lunn** . . . . (805) 654-2266
  E-mail: mark.lunn@ventura.org   Fax: (805) 654-2392

Yolo County

County Clerk/Recorder

Office of the County Clerk/Recorder
625 Court Street, Room B01, Woodland, CA 95695
Tel: (530) 666-8130 Fax: (530) 666-8109

County Clerk/Recorder **Freddie Oakley** . . . . (530) 666-8130
  E-mail: cntyclrk@yolorecorder.org

Yuba County

County Clerk/Recorder

Office of the County Clerk/Recorder
915 Eigth Street, Suite 107, Marysville, CA 95901
Tel: (530) 749-7851 Fax: (530) 749-7854

County Clerk/Recorder **Terry A. Hansen** . . . . (530) 749-7851
  E-mail: clerk@co.yuba.ca.us

Colorado Court Clerks and Courthouses

The trial courts of general jurisdiction in Colorado are called district courts. There are 22 judicial districts, each district consisting of at least one county. Listed below are the Clerks of Court and the County Clerk/Recorder for each county.

Colorado Supreme Court

Ralph L. Carr Judicial Center, 2 East Fourteenth Avenue, Denver, CO 80203
Tel: (720) 625-5150 Tel: (720) 625-5100 (Supreme Court Library)
Internet: http://www.courts.state.co.us

The Supreme Court consists of a chief justice and six justices who are appointed by the Governor from a list of candidates submitted by the Supreme Court Nominating Commission. Justices serve initial two-year terms and thereafter stand for retention in general elections for ten-year terms. The chief justice, who is elected by peer vote for a nonspecific term, is the executive head of the judicial system. Retirement is mandatory at age seventy-two; however, retired justices may serve as senior judges by assignment of the state court administrator. The Supreme Court has initial appellate jurisdiction over cases where a statute has been declared unconstitutional by a district court, decisions or actions of the Colorado Public Utilities Commission, habeas corpus, water priorities, and the election code. The Court also has certiorari review over appeals initiated in the Colorado Court of Appeals and District Courts.

Court Staff
Clerk of the Court **Christopher T. Ryan** . . . . (303) 837-3790
E-mail: christopher.ryan@judicial.state.co.us

Colorado Court of Appeals

Ralph L. Carr Judicial Center, 2 East Fourteenth Avenue, Denver, CO 80203
Tel: (720) 625-5150 Fax: (720) 625-5148
Internet: www.courts.state.co.us/Courts/Court_Of_Appeals/Index.cfm

The Court of Appeals consists of a chief judge and twenty judges who are appointed by the Governor from a list of candidates submitted by the Supreme Court Nominating Commission. The Court sits in divisions of three judges each on a rotating basis as assigned by the chief judge. Judges serve initial two-year terms and then stand for retention of office in general elections for eight-year terms. The chief judge is appointed by the chief justice of the Colorado Supreme Court to serve a non-specified term. Retirement is mandatory at age seventy-two; however, retired judges may serve as senior judges by assignment of the state court administrator. The Court of Appeals has initial appellate jurisdiction over appeals from final judgments of the Colorado District Courts and Denver Probate and Juvenile Courts, except for those matters which come under the direct jurisdiction of the Colorado Supreme Court. The Court also reviews the decisions of twenty six state administrative agencies.

Court Staff
Clerk of the Court **Christopher T. Ryan** . . . . (303) 837-3767
E-mail: christopher.ryan@judicial.state.co.us

Denver Juvenile Court

520 West Colfax Avenue, Room 125, Denver, CO 80204
Tel: (720) 337-0570

Court Staff
Clerk of Court **Matthew Forbes** . . . . (720) 337-0570
E-mail: matthew.forbes@judicial.state.co.us

Colorado Court Clerks and Courthouses continued

Denver Probate Court

1437 Bannock Street, Room 230, Denver, CO 80202
Tel: (720) 865-8310 ext. 5

Court Staff
Clerk of Court **Amber Roth** . . . . (720) 865-8310 ext. 5
E-mail: amber.roth@judicial.state.co.us

County-By-County

Adams County

County Clerk/Recorder

Office of the County Clerk and Recorder
4430 South Adams County Parkway, Brighton, CO 80601-8203
Tel: (720) 523-6020 Fax: (720) 523-6059

County Clerk and Recorder **Stan Martin** . . . . (720) 523-6015

Court Clerk

Seventeenth Judicial District
1100 Judicial Center Drive, Brighton, CO 80601

Clerk of Court, Adams County **Suzanne Fredrickson** . . . . (303) 659-1161
1100 Judicial Center Drive,   Fax: (303) 654-3216
Brighton, CO 80601
E-mail: suzanne.fredrickson@judicial.state.co.us

Alamosa County

County Clerk/Recorder

Office of the Clerk and Recorder
402 Edison Avenue, Alamosa, CO 81101
Tel: (719) 589-6681 Fax: (719) 589-6118

Clerk and Recorder **Melanie Woodward** . . . . (719) 589-6681
E-mail: mwoodward@alamosacounty.org

Court Clerk

Twelfth Judicial District
702 Fourth Street, Alamosa, CO 81101

Clerk of Court, Alamosa County **Shirley M. Skinner** . . . . (719) 589-4996
702 Fourth Street, Alamosa, CO 81101
E-mail: alamosaclerk@judicial.state.co.us

Arapahoe County

County Clerk/Recorder

Office of the Clerk and Recorder
5334 South Prince Street, Littleton, CO 80120-1136
Fax: (303) 794-4625
E-mail: clerk@co.arapahoe.co.us
Internet: www.co.arapahoe.co.us/departments/cr

Clerk and Recorder **Matthew Crane** . . . . (303) 795-4200
E-mail: clerk@arapahoegov.com

(continued on next page)

Colorado Court Clerks and Courthouses *continued*

Court Clerk

Eighteenth Judicial District
7325 South Potomac Street, Centennial, CO 80112

Clerk of Court, Arapahoe County **Tammy L. Herivel** . . . . . (303) 649-6355
7325 South Potomac Street, Fax: (303) 792-2401
Centennial, CO 80112
E-mail: tammy.herivel@judicial.state.co.us

Archuleta County

County Clerk/Recorder

Office of the Clerk and Recorder
449 San Juan Street, Pagosa Springs, CO 81147
Tel: (970) 264-8350 Fax: (970) 264-8357

Clerk and Recorder **June Madrid** . . . . (970) 264-8350
E-mail: jmadrid@archuletacounty.org

Court Clerk

Sixth Judicial District
1060 East Second Avenue, Room 106, Durango, CO 81301
Tel: (970) 247-2304

Clerk of Court, Archuleta County **Debbie Tully** . . . . (970) 264-8160
449 San Juan Street, Pagosa Springs, CO 81147   Fax: (970) 264-8161
E-mail: debbie.tully@judicial.state.co.us

Baca County

County Clerk/Recorder

Office of the Clerk and Recorder
741 Main Street, Springfield, CO 81073
Tel: (719) 523-4372 Fax: (719) 523-4881

Clerk and Recorder **Sharon Dubois** . . . . (719) 523-4372
E-mail: bacaclerk@bacacountyco.gov

Court Clerk

Fifteenth Judicial District
301 South Main, Suite 300, Lamar, CO 81052

Clerk of Court, Baca County **Jamie Smith** . . . . (719) 523-4555
714 Main Street, Suite 5, Springfield, CO 81073   Fax: (719) 523-4552
E-mail: jamie.smith@judicial.state.co.us

Bent County

County Clerk/Recorder

Office of the Clerk and Recorder
725 Bent Avenue, Las Animas, CO 81054
Tel: (719) 456-2009 Fax: (719) 456-0375

Clerk and Recorder **Patti Nickell** . . . . (719) 456-2009
E-mail: patti.nickell@bentcounty.net

Court Clerk

Sixteenth Judicial District
13 West Third Street, Room 207, La Junta, CO 81050

Clerk of Court, Bent County **Robyn Dunham** . . . . (719) 456-1353
725 Bent, Las Animas, CO 81054
E-mail: robyn.dunham@judicial.state.co.us

Colorado Court Clerks and Courthouses *continued*

Boulder County

County Clerk/Recorder

Office of the County Clerk and Recorder
1750 33rd Street, Suite 101, Boulder, CO 80301
Fax: (303) 413-7750
E-mail: clerkandrecorder@bouldercounty.org

County Clerk and Recorder **Hillary Hall** . . . . (303) 413-7700
E-mail: hhall@bouldercounty.org

Court Clerk

Twentieth Judicial District
1777 Sixth Street, Boulder, CO 80302

Clerk of Court, Boulder County **Debra Crosser** . . . . (303) 441-3766
1777 Sixth Street, Boulder, CO 80302
P.O. Box 4249, Boulder, CO 80306
E-mail: debra.crosser@judicial.state.co.us

Broomfield County

County Clerk/Recorder

Office of the Clerk and Recorder
One DesCombes Drive, Broomfield, CO 80020
Tel: (303) 464-5898 Fax: (303) 438-6228

Clerk and Recorder **Jim F. Candelarie** . . . . (303) 438-6332
E-mail: jcandelarie@broomfield.org

Court Clerk

Seventeenth Judicial District
1100 Judicial Center Drive, Brighton, CO 80601

Clerk of Court, Broomfield County **Dina Jones** . . . . (720) 887-2100
17 Des Combre Drive, Broomfield, CO 80020
E-mail: dina.jones@judicial.state.co.us

Chaffee County

County Clerk/Recorder

Office of the Clerk and Recorder
104 Crestone Avenue, Salida, CO 81201
Tel: (719) 539-4004 Fax: (719) 539-8588

Clerk and Recorder **Lori Mitchell** . . . . (719) 539-4004
E-mail: lmitchell@chaffeecounty.org

Court Clerk

Eleventh Judicial District
142 Crestone, Salida, CO 81201

Clerk of Court, Chaffee County **Karen Prosser** . . . . (719) 539-2561
142 Crestone, Salida, CO 81201   Fax: (719) 539-6281
P.O. Box 279, Salida, CO 81201
E-mail: karen.prosser@judicial.state.co.us

Cheyenne County

County Clerk/Recorder

Office of the Clerk and Recorder
51 South First Street, Cheyenne Wells, CO 80810
Tel: (719) 767-5685 Fax: (719) 767-8730

Clerk and Recorder **Patricia Daugherty** . . . . (719) 767-5685
E-mail: cheyclerk@gmail.com

Court Clerk

Fifteenth Judicial District
301 South Main, Suite 300, Lamar, CO 81052

Clerk of Court, Cheyenne County **Vicki Allen** . . . . (719) 767-5649
51 South First Street, Cheyenne Wells, CO 80810   Fax: (719) 767-5671
P.O. Box 696, Cheyenne Wells, CO 80810
E-mail: vicki.allen@judicial.state.co.us

Clear Creek County

County Clerk/Recorder

Office of the Clerk and Recorder
405 Argentine Street, Georgetown, CO 80444
Tel: (303) 679-2339 Fax: (303) 679-2416

Clerk and Recorder **Pam Phipps** . . . . (303) 679-2339
E-mail: clerk@co.clear-creek.co.us

Court Clerk

Fifth Judicial District
405 Argentine, Georgetown, CO 80444
Tel: (303) 679-4220

Clerk of Court, Clear Creek County **Tammy Lewis** . . . . . . (303) 679-4220
405 Argentine, Georgetown, CO 80444   Fax: (303) 569-3274
P.O. Box 367, Georgetown, CO 80444

Conejos County

County Clerk/Recorder

Office of the Clerk and Recorder
6683 County Road 13, Conejos, CO 81129
Tel: (719) 376-5422 Fax: (719) 376-5997

Clerk and Recorder **Lawrence D. Gallegos** . . . . (719) 376-5422
E-mail: lawrence.gallegos@co.conejos.co.us

Court Clerk

Twelfth Judicial District
702 Fourth Street, Alamosa, CO 81101

Clerk of Court, Conejos County **Jennifer L. Guillen** . . . . . (719) 376-5465
6683 County Road 13, Conejos, CO 81129
P.O. Box 128, Conejos, CO 81129
E-mail: conejosclerk@judicial.state.co.us

Costilla County

County Clerk/Recorder

Office of the Clerk and Recorder
400 Gasper Street, San Luis, CO 81152
Tel: (719) 937-7671 Fax: (719) 672-3781

Clerk and Recorder **Karen Garcia** . . . . (719) 937-7671
E-mail: kgarcia@colorado.edu

Court Clerk

Twelfth Judicial District
702 Fourth Street, Alamosa, CO 81101

Clerk of Court, Costilla County **Jennifer L. Guillen** . . . . . (719) 672-3681
304 Main Street, San Luis, CO 81152
E-mail: costillaclerk@judicial.state.co.us

Crowley County

County Clerk/Recorder

Office of the Clerk and Recorder
631 Main Street, Ordway, CO 81063
Tel: (719) 267-5225 Fax: (719) 267-4608

Clerk and Recorder **Lucile Nichols** . . . . (719) 267-5225
E-mail: lnichols@crowleycounty.net

Court Clerk

Sixteenth Judicial District
13 West Third Street, Room 207, La Junta, CO 81050

Clerk of Court, Crowley County **Andrea Cruz** . . . . (719) 267-4468
110 East Sixth, Room 303,   Fax: (719) 267-3753
Ordway, CO 81063
E-mail: andrea.cruz@judicial.state.co.us

Custer County

County Clerk/Recorder

Office of the Clerk and Recorder
205 South Sixth Street, Westcliffe, CO 81252
Tel: (719) 783-2441 Fax: (719) 783-2885 Tel: (719) 783-0441

Clerk and Recorder **Kelley Camper** . . . . (719) 783-2441
E-mail: ccclerk@centurytel.net

Court Clerk

Eleventh Judicial District
142 Crestone, Salida, CO 81201

Clerk of Court, Custer County **Linda C. Urwiller** . . . . (719) 783-2274
205 South Sixth Street, Westcliffe, CO 81252   Fax: (719) 783-2995
P.O. Box 60, Westcliffe, CO 81252
E-mail: linda.urwiller@judicial.state.co.us

Delta County

County Clerk/Recorder

Office of the Clerk and Recorder
501 Palmer Street, Suite 211, Delta, CO 81416
Tel: (970) 874-2150 Fax: (970) 874-2161

Clerk and Recorder **Teri A. Stephenson** . . . . (970) 874-2150
E-mail: tstephenson@deltacounty.com

Court Clerk

Seventh Judicial District
200 East Virginia Avenue, Second Floor, Gunnison, CO 81230
Tel: (970) 541-3500

Clerk of Court, Delta County **Mandy S. Allen** . . . . (970) 874-6280
501 Palmer, Room 338, Delta, CO 81416   Fax: (970) 874-4306
E-mail: mandy.allen@judicial.state.co.us

Denver County

County Clerk/Recorder

Office of the Clerk and Recorder
201 West Colfax, Department 101, Denver, CO 80202
E-mail: clerkandrecorder@denvergov.org
Internet: www.denverclerkandrecorder.org

Clerk and Recorder **Debra Johnson** . . . . (720) 913-1311
E-mail: clerkandrecorder@denvergov.org

(continued on next page)

Colorado Court Clerks and Courthouses *continued*

Court Clerk

Second Judicial District
1437 Bannock Street, Room 256, Denver, CO 80202 (Civil, Domestic and Felony matters)
520 West Colfax Avenue, Room 135, Denver, CO 80204

Clerk of Court, Denver County **Sabra A. Millett** . . . . (720) 865-8301
1437 Bannock Street, Room 256,
Denver, CO 80202
E-mail: sabra.millett@judicial.state.co.us

Dolores County

County Clerk/Recorder

Office of the Clerk and Recorder
409 North Main Street, Dove Creek, CO 81324
Tel: (970) 677-2381   Fax: (970) 677-4144

Clerk and Recorder **LaRita Randolph** . . . . (970) 677-2381
E-mail: dolorescounty@hotmail.com

Court Clerk

Twenty Second Judicial District
109 West Main, Room 210, Cortez, CO 81321

Clerk of Court, Dolores County
Anne Deyell-Lawrence . . . . (970) 677-2258
409 North Main, Cortez, CO 81321   Fax: (970) 677-4156
P.O. Box 511, Cortez, CO 81321

Douglas County

County Clerk/Recorder

Office of the County Clerk and Recorder
301 Wilcox Street, 2nd Floor, Castle Rock, CO 80104
Tel: (303) 660-7469   Fax: (303) 814-2750

County Clerk and Recorder **Merlin Klotz** . . . . (303) 660-7446

Court Clerk

Eighteenth Judicial District
7325 South Potomac Street, Centennial, CO 80112

Clerk of Court, Douglas County **Cheryl Lane** . . . . (720) 437-6200
4000 Justice Way, Room 2009,   Fax: (303) 688-1962
Castle Rock, CO 80109

Eagle County

County Clerk/Recorder

Office of the Clerk and Recorder
500 Broadway, Suite 101, Eagle, CO 81631
Tel: (970) 328-8710   Fax: (970) 328-8716

Clerk and Recorder **Teak J. Simonton** . . . . (970) 328-8728
E-mail: teak.simonton@eaglecounty.us

Court Clerk

Fifth Judicial District
405 Argentine, Georgetown, CO 80444
Tel: (303) 679-4220

Clerk of Court, Eagle County **Jackie Cooper** . . . . (970) 328-8584
885 Chambers Avenue, Eagle, CO 81631   Fax: (970) 328-6328
P.O. Box 597, Eagle, CO 81631
E-mail: jackie.cooper@judicial.state.co.us

Colorado Court Clerks and Courthouses *continued*

El Paso County

County Clerk/Recorder

Office of the Clerk and Recorder
1675 West Garden of the Gods Road, Colorado Springs, CO 80907
Fax: (719) 520-6212

Clerk and Recorder **Chuck Broerman** . . . . (719) 520-6202

Court Clerk

Fourth Judicial District
270 South Tejon, Colorado Springs, CO 80901
Tel: (719) 452-5000 (Colorado Springs)
Tel: (719) 689-2574 (Cripple Creek)

Clerk of Court, El Paso County **Lynette D. Cornelius** . . . . (719) 452-5000
270 South Tejon, Colorado Springs, CO 80901   Fax: (719) 452-5010
P.O. Box 2980, Colorado Springs, CO 80903
E-mail: lynette.collins@judicial.state.co.us

Elbert County

County Clerk/Recorder

Office of the Clerk and Recorder
215 Comanche Street, Kiowa, CO 80117
Tel: (303) 621-3127   Fax: (303) 621-3168

Clerk and Recorder **Dallas Schroeder** . . . . (303) 621-3116
E-mail: dallas.schroeder@elbertcounty-co.gov

Court Clerk

Eighteenth Judicial District
7325 South Potomac Street, Centennial, CO 80112

Clerk of Court, Elbert County **Cheryl Lane** . . . . (303) 621-2131
751 Ute Street, Kiowa, CO 80117   Fax: (303) 621-2722
P.O. Box 232, Kiowa, CO 80117

Fremont County

County Clerk/Recorder

Office of the Clerk and Recorder
615 Macon Avenue, Room 102, Canon City, CO 81212
Tel: (719) 276-7330   Fax: (719) 276-7338

Clerk and Recorder **Katie Barr** . . . . (719) 276-7330
E-mail: katie.barr@fremontco.com

Court Clerk

Eleventh Judicial District
142 Crestone, Salida, CO 81201

Clerk of Court, Fremont County
Deborah Sather-Stringari . . . . (719) 204-2204
136 Justice Center Road, Canon City, CO 81212   Fax: (719) 204-2275
E-mail: deborah.sather-stringari@judicial.state.co.us

Garfield County

County Clerk/Recorder

Office of the Clerk and Recorder
108 Eighth Street, Suite 200, Glenwood Springs, CO 81601
Tel: (970) 384-3700   Fax: (970) 947-1078

Clerk and Recorder **Jean Alberico** . . . . (970) 384-3700
E-mail: jalberico@garfield-county.com

Court Clerk

Ninth Judicial District
109 Eighth Street, Suite 104, Glenwood Springs, CO 81601
Tel: (970) 945-5075

Clerk of Court, Garfield County **James C. Bradford** . . . . . (970) 945-5075
109 Eighth Street, Suite 104,   Fax: (970) 945-8756
Glenwood Springs, CO 81601
E-mail: james.bradford@judicial.state.co.us

Gilpin County

County Clerk/Recorder

Office of the Clerk and Recorder
203 Eureka Street, Central City, CO 80427
Tel: (303) 582-5321 Fax: (303) 565-1797

Clerk and Recorder **Colleen Stewart** . . . . (303) 582-5321 ext. 2180
E-mail: gcclerk@co.gilpin.co.us

Court Clerk

First Judicial District
100 Jefferson County Parkway, Golden, CO 80401

Clerk of Court, Gilpin County **Terri Meredith** . . . . (303) 582-5522
2960 Dory Hill Road, Suite 200,   Fax: (303) 528-3112
Golden, CO 80403
E-mail: terri.meredith@judicial.state.co.us

Grand County

County Clerk/Recorder

Office of the Clerk and Recorder
308 Byers Avenue, Hot Sulphur Springs, CO 80451
Tel: (970) 725-3110 Fax: (970) 725-0100

Clerk and Recorder **Sara L. Rosene** . . . . (970) 725-3110
E-mail: srosene@co.grand.co.us

Court Clerk

Fourteenth Judicial District
1955 Shield Dr., Steamboat Springs, CO 80477

Clerk of Court, Grand County **Heather J. Harms** . . . . (970) 725-3357
307 Moffat Avenue,
Hot Sulphur Springs, CO 80451
P.O. Box 192, Hot Sulphur Springs, CO 80451
E-mail: heather.harms@judicial.state.co.us

Gunnison County

County Clerk/Recorder

Office of the Clerk and Recorder
221 North Wisconsin Street, Suite #C, Gunnison, CO 81230
Tel: (970) 641-1516 Fax: (970) 641-7956

Clerk and Recorder **Kathy Simillion** . . . . (970) 641-1516
E-mail: ksimillion@gunnisoncounty.org

Court Clerk

Seventh Judicial District
200 East Virginia Avenue, Second Floor, Gunnison, CO 81230
Tel: (970) 541-3500

Clerk of Court, Gunnison County **Betsy Nesbitt** . . . . (970) 641-3500
200 East Virginia Avenue,   Fax: (970) 641-6876
Gunnison, CO 81230
E-mail: betsy.nesbitt@judicial.state.co.us

Hinsdale County

County Clerk

Office of the Clerk
317 North Henson Street, Lake City, CO 81235
Tel: (970) 944-2228 Fax: (970) 944-2202

Clerk **Linda Pavich Ragle** . . . . (970) 944-2228
E-mail: hinsdaleclerk@yahoo.com

Court Clerk

Seventh Judicial District
200 East Virginia Avenue, Second Floor, Gunnison, CO 81230
Tel: (970) 541-3500

Clerk of Court, Hinsdale County **Joan Anastasion** . . . . . . (970) 944-2227
317 Henson, Lake City, CO 81235   Fax: (970) 944-2289
P.O. Box 245, Lake City, CO 81235
E-mail: joan.anastasion@judicial.state.co.us

Huerfano County

County Clerk/Recorder

Office of the Clerk and Recorder
401 Main Street, Suite 204, Walsenburg, CO 81089
Tel: (719) 738-2380 Fax: (719) 738-2060

Clerk and Recorder **Nancy Cruz** . . . . (719) 738-2380
E-mail: nancy@huerfano.us

Court Clerk

Third Judicial District
401 Main Street, Walsenburg, CO 81089
Tel: (719) 738-1040

Clerk of Court, Huerfano County
Lorraine A. Cisneros . . . . (719) 738-1040
401 Main Street, Room 304,
Walsenburg, CO 81089
E-mail: lorraine.cisneros@judicial.state.co.us

Jackson County

County Clerk/Recorder

Office of the Clerk and Recorder
396 LaFever Street, Walden, CO 80480
Tel: (970) 723-4334 Fax: (970) 723-3214

Clerk and Recorder **Hayle M. Johnson** . . . . (970) 723-4334
E-mail: jc_clerk@hotmail.com

Court Clerk   *MR. Rightson 66-668*

Eighth Judicial District
201 La Porte Avenue, Suite 100, Fort Collins, CO 80521
Tel: (970) 494-3500

Clerk of Court, Jackson County **Salli Johnroe** . . . . (970) 723-4363
396 Lafever Street, Walden, CO 80480
E-mail: salli.johnroe@judicial.state.co.us

(continued on next page)

Colorado Court Clerks and Courthouses *continued*

Jefferson County

County Clerk/Recorder

Office of the Clerk and Recorder
100 Jefferson County Parkway, Golden, CO 80419
Fax: (303) 271-8197

County Clerk and Recorder **Faye Griffin** . . . . (303) 271-8168

Court Clerk

First Judicial District
100 Jefferson County Parkway, Golden, CO 80401

Clerk of Court, Jefferson County **Shana Kloek** . . . . (303) 271-6175
100 Jefferson Parkway, Golden, CO 80401
E-mail: shana.kloek@judicial.state.co.us

Kiowa County

County Clerk/Recorder

Office of the Clerk and Recorder
1305 Goff Street, Eads, CO 81036
Tel: (719) 438-5421   Fax: (719) 438-5327

Clerk and Recorder **Delisa Weeks** . . . . (719) 438-5421
E-mail: delisa.weeks@state.co.us

Court Clerk

Fifteenth Judicial District
301 South Main, Suite 300, Lamar, CO 81052

Clerk of Court, Kiowa County **Elaine Lindholm** . . . . (719) 438-5558
1305 Goff Street, Eads, CO 81036   Fax: (719) 438-5300
P.O. Box 353, Eads, CO 81036

Kit Carson County

County Clerk/Recorder

Office of the Clerk and Recorder
251 16th Street, Suite 203, Burlington, CO 80807
Tel: (719) 346-8638   Fax: (719) 346-8721

Clerk and Recorder **Susan Corliss** . . . . (719) 346-8638 ext. 301
E-mail: clerkandrecorder@kitcarsoncounty.org

Court Clerk

Thirteenth Judicial District
110 North Riverview Road, Room 200, Sterling, CO 80751

Clerk of Court, Kit Carson County **Sharlene K. Mills** . . . . (719) 346-5524
251 Sixteenth Street, Suite 301,   Fax: (719) 346-7805
Burlington, CO 80807
E-mail: sharlene.mills@judicial.state.co.us

La Plata County

County Clerk/Recorder

Office of the Clerk and Recorder
98 Everett Street, Suite C, Durango, CO 81303
Tel: (970) 382-6281   Fax: (970) 259-5413

Clerk and Recorder **Tiffany Lee Parker** . . . . (970) 382-6281
E-mail: tiffany.parker@co.laplata.co.us

Colorado Court Clerks and Courthouses *continued*

Court Clerk

Sixth Judicial District
1060 East Second Avenue, Room 106, Durango, CO 81301
Tel: (970) 247-2304

Clerk of Court, La Plata County **Debra J. Craig** . . . . (970) 247-2304
1060 East Second Avenue, Room 106,   Fax: (970) 247-4348
Durango, CO 81301
E-mail: debi.craig@judicial.state.co.us

Lake County

County Clerk/Recorder

Office of the Clerk and Recorder
505 Harrison Avenue, Leadville, CO 80461
Tel: (719) 486-1410

Clerk and Recorder **Patricia A. "Patty" Berger** . . . . (719) 486-1410
E-mail: pberger@co.lake.co.us

Court Clerk

Fifth Judicial District
405 Argentine, Georgetown, CO 80444
Tel: (303) 679-4220

Clerk of Court, Lake County **Brenda Knoll** . . . . (719) 486-0535
505 Harrison Avenue, Leadville, CO 80461   Fax: (719) 486-5006
P.O. Box 55, Leadville, CO 80461
E-mail: brenda.knoll@judicial.state.co.us

Larimer County

County Clerk/Recorder

Clerk and Recorder's Office
200 West Oak Street, 1st Floor, Fort Collins, CO 80522
Tel: (970) 498-7852   Fax: (970) 498-7830
Internet: www.co.larimer.co.us/clerk

County Clerk and Recorder **Angela Myers** . . . . (970) 498-7852
E-mail: myersag@co.larimer.co.us

Court Clerk

Eighth Judicial District
201 La Porte Avenue, Suite 100, Fort Collins, CO 80521
Tel: (970) 494-3500

Clerk of Court, Larimer County **Sherlyn K. Sampson** . . . (970) 494-3501
201 La Porte Avenue, Suite 100,
Fort Collins, CO 80521
E-mail: sherlyn.sampson@judicial.state.co.us

Las Animas County

County Clerk/Recorder

Office of the Clerk and Recorder
First & Maple Street, Room 205, Trinidad, CO 81082
Tel: (719) 846-3314   Fax: (719) 845-2573

Clerk and Recorder **Patricia M. "Peach" Vigil** . . . . (719) 846-3314

Colorado Court Clerks and Courthouses *continued*

Court Clerk

Third Judicial District
401 Main Street, Walsenburg, CO 81089
Tel: (719) 738-1040

District Administrator/Clerk of the Court
Bob Kreiman . . . . (719) 846-3316
200 East First Street, Room 304,
Trinidad, CO 81082
E-mail: bob.kreiman@judicial.state.co.us

Lincoln County

County Clerk/Recorder

Office of the Clerk and Recorder
103 Third Avenue, Hugo, CO 80821
Tel: (719) 743-2444 Fax: (719) 743-2524

Clerk and Recorder **Corinne M. Lengel** . . . . (719) 743-2444
E-mail: lcclerk@lincolncountyco.us

Court Clerk

Eighteenth Judicial District
7325 South Potomac Street, Centennial, CO 80112

Clerk of Court, Lincoln County **Kimberly Graham** . . . . . . (719) 743-2455
103 Third Street, Hugo, CO 80821   Fax: (719) 743-2636
P.O. Box 128, Hugo, CO 80821
E-mail: kimberly.graham@judicial.state.co.us

Logan County

County Clerk/Recorder

Office of the Clerk and Recorder
315 Main Street, Sterling, CO 80751
Tel: (970) 522-1544 Fax: (970) 522-2063

Clerk and Recorder **Pamela M. Bacon** . . . . (970) 522-1544
E-mail: baconp@logancountyco.gov

Court Clerk

Thirteenth Judicial District
110 North Riverview Road, Room 200, Sterling, CO 80751

Clerk of Court, Logan County **Sara Harms** . . . . (970) 522-6565
110 North Riverview Road, Room 200,   Fax: (970) 522-6566
Sterling, CO 80751
E-mail: sara.harms@judicial.state.co.us

Mesa County

County Clerk/Recorder

Office of the Clerk and Recorder
200 South Spruce Street, Grand Junction, CO 81501
Tel: (970) 244-1885 Fax: (970) 255-5039

Clerk and Recorder **Sheila Reiner** . . . . (970) 244-1896
E-mail: sheila.reiner@mesacounty.us

Court Clerk

Twenty First Judicial District
125 North Spruce, Grand Junction, CO 81502
Tel: (970) 257-3637

Clerk of Court, Mesa County **Charlene Benton** . . . . (970) 257-3660
125 North Spruce, Grand Junction, CO 81502
E-mail: charlene.benton@judicial.state.co.us

Colorado Court Clerks and Courthouses *continued*

Mineral County

County Clerk/Recorder

Office of the Clerk and Recorder
1201 North Main Street, Creede, CO 81330
Tel: (719) 658-2440 Fax: (719) 658-0358

Clerk and Recorder **Eryn K. Wintz** . . . . (719) 658-2440
E-mail: mineralcountyclerk@hotmail.com

Court Clerk

Twelfth Judicial District
702 Fourth Street, Alamosa, CO 81101

Clerk of Court, Mineral County
Hollie G. Wheelwright . . . . (719) 658-2575
North First Street, Creede, CO 81130
P.O. Box 337, Creede, CO 81130
E-mail: mineralclerk@judicial.state.co.us

Moffat County

County Clerk/Recorder

Office of the Clerk and Recorder
221 West Victory Way, Suite 200, Craig, CO 81625
Tel: (970) 824-9104 Fax: (970) 826-3413

Clerk and Recorder **Lila Herod** . . . . (970) 824-9104
E-mail: lherod@moffatcounty.net

Court Clerk

Fourteenth Judicial District
1955 Shield Dr., Steamboat Springs, CO 80477

Clerk of Court, Moffat County **Diana L. Meyer** . . . . (970) 824-8254
221 West Victory Way, Suite 300,
Craig, CO 81625
E-mail: diana.meyer@judicial.state.co.us

Montezuma County

County Clerk/Recorder

Office of the Clerk and Recorder
140 West Main Street, Suite One, Cortez, CO 81321
Tel: (970) 565-3728 Fax: (970) 564-0215

Clerk and Recorder **Kim Percell** . . . . (970) 565-3728
E-mail: kpercell@co.montezuma.co.us

Court Clerk

Twenty Second Judicial District
109 West Main, Room 210, Cortez, CO 81321

Clerk of Court, Montezuma County **Felicia Canzona** . . . . (970) 565-1111
109 West Main, Room 210,   Fax: (970) 565-8516
Cortez, CO 81321
E-mail: montezumaclerk@judicial.state.co.us

Montrose County

County Clerk/Recorder

Office of the Clerk and Recorder
320 South First Street, Room 101, Montrose, CO 81401
Tel: (970) 249-3362 Fax: (970) 252-4553

Clerk and Recorder **Tressa Guynes** . . . . (970) 249-3362
E-mail: tguynes@montrosecounty.net

(continued on next page)

Colorado Court Clerks and Courthouses *continued*

Court Clerk

Seventh Judicial District
200 East Virginia Avenue, Second Floor, Gunnison, CO 81230
Tel: (970) 541-3500

Clerk of Court, Montrose County **Jodi A. Hanson** . . . . . . (970) 252-4300
  Montrose County Justice Center,
  1200 North Grand Avenue, Bin A,
  Montrose, CO 81401
  E-mail: jodi.hanson@judicial.state.co.us

Morgan County

County Clerk/Recorder

Office of the Clerk and Recorder
231 Ensign Street, Fort Morgan, CO 80701
Tel: (970) 542-3521 Fax: (970) 542-3553 (Recording and Elections)
Fax: (970) 542-3525 (Motor Vehicle)
E-mail: clerkmorganc@co.morgan.co.us

Clerk and Recorder **Susan Bailey** . . . . (970) 542-3521
  E-mail: sbailey@co.morgan.co.us

Court Clerk

Thirteenth Judicial District
110 North Riverview Road, Room 200, Sterling, CO 80751

Clerk of Court, Morgan County **Cathlene J. Marshall** . . . (970) 542-3435
  400 Warner Street, Fort Morgan, CO 80701   Fax: (970) 542-3436
  E-mail: cathlene.marshall@judicial.state.co.us

Otero County

County Clerk/Recorder

Office of the Clerk and Recorder
13 West Third Street, La Junta, CO 81050
Tel: (719) 383-3020 Fax: (719) 383-2922
E-mail: ssisnroy@oterogov.org

Clerk and Recorder **Sharon Sisnroy** . . . . (719) 383-3020
  E-mail: ssisnroy@oterogov.org

Court Clerk

Sixteenth Judicial District
13 West Third Street, Room 207, La Junta, CO 81050

Clerk of Court, Otero County **Caryl Pearce** . . . . (719) 384-4951
  13 West Third, Room 207,   Fax: (719) 384-4991
  La Junta, CO 81050
  E-mail: caryl.pearce@judicial.state.co.us

Ouray County

County Clerk/Recorder

Office of the Clerk and Recorder
541 Fourth Street, Ouray, CO 81427
P.O. Box C, Ouray, CO 81427
Tel: (970) 325-4961 Fax: (970) 325-0452

Clerk and Recorder **Michelle Ann Nauer** . . . . (970) 325-4961
  E-mail: mnauer@ouraycountyco.gov

Colorado Court Clerks and Courthouses *continued*

Court Clerk

Seventh Judicial District
200 East Virginia Avenue, Second Floor, Gunnison, CO 81230
Tel: (970) 541-3500

Clerk of Court, Ouray County **Jane E. Holmes** . . . . (970) 325-4405
  541 South Fourth Street, Ouray, CO 81427   Fax: (970) 325-7364
  E-mail: jane.holmes@judicial.state.co.us

Park County

County Clerk/Recorder

Office of the Clerk and Recorder
501 Main Street, Fairplay, CO 80440
Tel: (719) 836-4333 Fax: (719) 836-4348

Clerk and Recorder **Debra Green** . . . . (719) 836-4333
  E-mail: pcclerk@parkco.us

Court Clerk

Eleventh Judicial District
142 Crestone, Salida, CO 81201

Clerk of Court, Park County **Kathy Jones** . . . . . . (719) 836-2940 ext. 228
  300 Fourth Street, Fairplay, CO 80440   Fax: (719) 836-2892
  P.O. Box 190, Fairplay, CO 80440
  E-mail: kathy.jones@judicial.state.co.us

Phillips County

County Clerk/Recorder

Office of the Clerk and Recorder
221 South Interocean Avenue, Holyoke, CO 80734
Tel: (970) 854-3131 Fax: (970) 854-4745

Clerk and Recorder **Madene "Beth" Zilla** . . . . (970) 854-3131
  E-mail: beth.zilla@phillipscounty.co

Court Clerk

Thirteenth Judicial District
110 North Riverview Road, Room 200, Sterling, CO 80751

Clerk of Court, Phillips County **Joy Strack** . . . . (970) 854-3279
  221 South Interocean, Holyoke, CO 80734   Fax: (970) 854-3179
  E-mail: joy.strack@judicial.state.co.us

Pitkin County

County Clerk/Recorder

Office of the Clerk and Recorder
530 East Main Street, First Floor, Aspen, CO 81611
Tel: (970) 920-5180 Fax: (970) 920-5196

Clerk and Recorder **Janice Vos Caudill** . . . . (970) 429-2710
  E-mail: janice.vos@pitkincounty.com

Court Clerk

Ninth Judicial District
109 Eighth Street, Suite 104, Glenwood Springs, CO 81601
Tel: (970) 945-5075

Clerk of Court, Pitkin County **Jonna Goldstone** . . . . (970) 925-7635
  506 East Main, Suite 300,   Fax: (970) 925-6349
  Aspen, CO 81611
  E-mail: jonna.goldstone@judicial.state.co.us

Prowers County

County Clerk/Recorder

Office of the Clerk and Recorder
301 South Main Street, Suite 210, Lamar, CO 81052
Tel: (719) 336-8011   Fax: (719) 336-5306

Clerk and Recorder **Jana Coen** . . . . (719) 336-8011
E-mail: jcoen@prowerscounty.net

Court Clerk

Fifteenth Judicial District
301 South Main, Suite 300, Lamar, CO 81052

Clerk of Court, Prowers County **Diane Crow** . . . . (719) 336-8946
301 South Main, Suite 300,   Tel: (719) 336-8976
Lamar, CO 81052
E-mail: diane.crow@judicial.state.co.us

Pueblo County

County Clerk/Recorder

Office of the Clerk and Recorder
215 West 10th Street, Pueblo, CO 81003
Tel: (719) 583-6507   Fax: (719) 583-4894

Clerk and Recorder **Gilbert Ortiz, Jr.** . . . . (719) 583-6507
E-mail: ortiz@co.pueblo.co.us

Court Clerk

Tenth Judicial District
320 West Tenth Street, Pueblo, CO 81003

Clerk of Court, Pueblo County **Janet Thielemier** . . . . (719) 583-7000
320 West Tenth Street, Pueblo, CO 81003
E-mail: janet.thielemier@judicial.state.co.us

Rio Blanco County

County Clerk/Recorder

Office of the Clerk and Recorder
555 Main Street, Meeker, CO 81641
Tel: (970) 878-9460   Fax: (970) 878-3587

Clerk and Recorder **Boots Campbell** . . . . (970) 878-9460
E-mail: clerk@rbc.us

Court Clerk

Ninth Judicial District
109 Eighth Street, Suite 104, Glenwood Springs, CO 81601
Tel: (970) 945-5075

Clerk of Court, Rio Blanco County **Susan Mills** . . . . (970) 878-5622
555 Main Street, Meeker, CO 81641   Tel: (970) 878-4295
P.O. Box 1150, Meeker, CO 81641
E-mail: susan.mills@judicial.state.co.us

Rio Grande County

County Clerk/Recorder

Office of the Clerk and Recorder
965 Sixth Street, Del Norte, CO 81332
Tel: (719) 657-3334   Fax: (719) 657-2621

Clerk and Recorder **Cindy Hill** . . . . (719) 657-3334
E-mail: clerk@riograndecounty.org

Court Clerk

Twelfth Judicial District
702 Fourth Street, Alamosa, CO 81101

Clerk of Court, Rio Grande County (Acting)
  Hollie G. Wheelwright . . . . (719) 657-3394
925 Sixth Street, Room 204,
Del Norte, CO 81132
E-mail: riograndeclerk@judicial.state.co.us

Routt County

County Clerk/Recorder

Office of the Clerk and Recorder
522 Lincoln Avenue, Steamboat Springs, CO 80477
Tel: (970) 870-5556   Fax: (970) 870-1329

Clerk and Recorder **Kim Bonner** . . . . (970) 870-5556
E-mail: clerk@co.routt.co.us

Court Clerk

Fourteenth Judicial District
1955 Shield Dr., Steamboat Springs, CO 80477

Clerk of Court, Routt County **Maryann Ninger** . . . . (970) 879-5020
1955 Shield Drive, Steamboat Springs, CO 80487
P.O. Box 773117, Steamboat Springs, CO 80487
E-mail: maryann.ninger@judicial.state.co.us

Saguache County

County Clerk/Recorder

Office of the Clerk and Recorder
501 Fourth Street, First Floor, Saguache, CO 81149
Tel: (719) 655-2512   Fax: (719) 655-2730
E-mail: clerkrecorder@saguachecounty-co.gov

Clerk and Recorder **Carla Gomez** . . . . (719) 655-2512
E-mail: cgomez@saguachecounty-co.gov

Court Clerk

Twelfth Judicial District
702 Fourth Street, Alamosa, CO 81101

Clerk of Court, Saguache County **Brandie Taylor** . . . . (719) 655-2522
501 Christy Avenue, Saguache, CO 81149
E-mail: saguacheclerk@judicial.state.co.us

San Juan County

County Clerk/Recorder

Office of the Clerk and Recorder
1557 Greene Street, Silverton, CO 81433
Tel: (970) 387-5671

Clerk and Recorder **Ladonna L. Jaramillo** . . . . (970) 387-5671
E-mail: ladonna.jaramillo@sanjuancountycolorado.
us

Court Clerk

Sixth Judicial District
1060 East Second Avenue, Room 106, Durango, CO 81301
Tel: (970) 247-2304

Clerk of Court, San Juan County **Cassandra Roof** . . . . (970) 387-5790
1557 Greene Street, Silverton, CO 81433   Fax: (970) 387-0295
P.O. Box 900, Silverton, CO 81433
E-mail: cassandra.roof@judicial.state.co.us

(continued on next page)

Colorado Court Clerks and Courthouses *continued*

San Miguel County

County Clerk/Recorder

Office of the Clerk and Recorder
305 West Colorado Avenue, First Floor, Telluride, CO 81435
Tel: (970) 728-3954 Fax: (970) 728-4808
E-mail: clerkandrecorder@sanmiguelcounty.org

Clerk and Recorder **Kathleen Erie** . . . .(970) 728-3954
 E-mail: kathleene@sanmiguelcounty.org

Court Clerk

Seventh Judicial District
200 East Virginia Avenue, Second Floor, Gunnison, CO 81230
Tel: (970) 541-3500

Clerk of Court, San Miguel County **Bryan Yug** . . . . (970) 369-3310
 305 West Colorado, Telluride, CO 81435   Fax: (970) 728-6216
 P.O. Box 919, Telluride, CO 81435
 E-mail: bryan.yug@judicial.state.co.us

Sedgwick County

County Clerk/Recorder

Office of the Clerk and Recorder
315 Cedar Street, Suite 220, Julesburg, CO 80737
Tel: (970) 474-3346 Fax: (970) 474-0954

Clerk and Recorder **Christy M. Beckman** . . . .(970) 474-3346
 E-mail: cbeckman@sedgwickcountygov.net

Court Clerk

Thirteenth Judicial District
110 North Riverview Road, Room 200, Sterling, CO 80751

Clerk of Court, Sedgwick County **Susan S. Kinnison** . . . .(970) 474-3627
 118 West Third Street, Julesburg, CO 80737   Fax: (970) 474-2026
 E-mail: susan.kinnison@judicial.state.co.us

Summit County

County Clerk/Recorder

Office of the Clerk and Recorder
208 East Lincoln Avenue, Breckenridge, CO 80424
Tel: (970) 453-3470 Fax: (970) 453-3540

Clerk and Recorder **Kathleen Neel** . . . .(970) 453-3470
 E-mail: kathyn@co.summit.co.us

Court Clerk

Fifth Judicial District
405 Argentine, Georgetown, CO 80444
Tel: (303) 679-4220

Clerk of Court, Summit County **Kari Bryan** . . . . (970) 547-2611
 501 North Park Avenue, Breckenridge, CO 80424   Fax: (970) 453-1134
 P.O. Box 185, Breckenridge, CO 80424
 E-mail: kari.bryan@judicial.state.co.us

Colorado Court Clerks and Courthouses *continued*

Teller County

County Clerk/Recorder

Office of the Clerk and Recorder
101 West Bennett Avenue, Cripple Creek, CO 80813
Tel: (719) 689-2951 Fax: (719) 686-8030

Clerk and Recorder **Krystal Brown** . . . .(719) 689-2951
 E-mail: brownk@co.teller.co.us

Court Clerk

Fourth Judicial District
270 South Tejon, Colorado Springs, CO 80901
Tel: (719) 452-5000 (Colorado Springs)
Tel: (719) 689-2574 (Cripple Creek)

Clerk of Court, Teller County **Janell Sciacca** . . . . . (719) 689-2574 ext. 2
 101 West Bennett Avenue,
 Cripple Creek, CO 80903
 P.O. Box 997, Cripple Creek, CO 80813
 E-mail: janell.sciacca@judicial.state.co.us

Washington County

County Clerk/Recorder

Office of the Clerk and Recorder
150 Ash Avenue, First Floor, Akron, CO 80720
Tel: (970) 345-6565 Fax: (970) 345-6607

Clerk and Recorder **Garland M. Wahl** . . . .(970) 345-6565
 E-mail: gwahl@co.washington.co.us

Court Clerk

Thirteenth Judicial District
110 North Riverview Road, Room 200, Sterling, CO 80751

Clerk of Court, Washington County **Sandra K. Farris** . . . . (970) 345-2756
 26861 Highway 34, Akron, CO 80720   Fax: (970) 345-2829
 P.O. Box 455, Akron, CO 80720
 E-mail: sandra.farris@judicial.state.co.us

Weld County

County Clerk/Recorder

Office of the Clerk and Recorder
1402 North 17th Avenue, Greeley, CO 80631
Tel: (970) 353-3840 Fax: (970) 353-1964

Clerk and Recorder **Carly S. Koppes** . . . .(970) 304-6530
 E-mail: ckoppes@co.weld.co.us

Court Clerk

Nineteenth Judicial District
901 Ninth Avenue, Greeley, CO 80632

Clerk of Court, Weld County **Catherine L. Walker** . . . . . .(970) 475-2402
 901 Ninth Avenue, Greeley, CO 80632
 P.O. Box 2038, Greeley, CO 80632

Colorado Court Clerks and Courthouses *continued*

Yuma County

County Clerk/Recorder

Office of the Clerk and Recorder
310 Ash Street, Suite F, Wray, CO 80758
Tel: (970) 332-5809 Fax: (970) 332-5919
E-mail: yumacountyclerk@co.yuma.co.us

Clerk and Recorder **Beverly Ann Wenger** . . . . (970) 332-5809
   E-mail: yumacountyclerk@co.yuma.co.us

Court Clerk

Thirteenth Judicial District
110 North Riverview Road, Room 200, Sterling, CO 80751

Clerk of Court, Yuma County **Jo Clemons** . . . . (970) 332-4118
   310 Ash Street, Yuma, CO 80758   Fax: (970) 332-4119
   P.O. Box 347, Wray, CO 80758

Counties Within Judicial Districts

District Court, 1st District
Areas Covered: Gilpin and Jefferson Counties.

District Court, 2nd District
Areas Covered: Denver County.

District Court, 3rd District
Areas Covered: Huerfano and Las Animas Counties.

District Court, 4th District
Areas Covered: El Paso and Teller Counties.

District Court, 5th District
Areas Covered: Clear Creek, Eagle, Lake, and Summit Counties.

District Court, 6th District
Areas Covered: Archuleta, La Plata, and San Juan Counties.

District Court, 7th District
Areas Covered: Delta, Gunnison, Hinsdale, Montrose, Ouray, and San Miguel Counties.

District Court, 8th District
Areas Covered: Jackson and Larimer Counties.

District Court, 9th District
Areas Covered: Garfield, Pitkin, and Rio Blanco Counties.

District Court, 10th District
Areas Covered: Pueblo County.

District Court, 11th District
Areas Covered: Chaffee, Custer, Fremont, and Park Counties.

District Court, 12th District
Areas Covered: Alamosa, Conejos, Costilla, Mineral, Rio Grande, and Saguache Counties.

Colorado Court Clerks and Courthouses *continued*

District Court, 13th District
Areas Covered: Kit Carson, Logan, Morgan, Phillips, Sedgwick, Washington, and Yuma Counties.

District Court, 14th District
Areas Covered: Grand, Moffat, and Routt Counties.

District Court, 15th District
Areas Covered: Baca, Cheyenne, Kiowa, and Prowers Counties.

District Court, 16th District
Areas Covered: Bent, Crowley, and Otero Counties.

District Court, 17th District
Areas Covered: Adams and Broomfield Counties.

District Court, 18th District
Areas Covered: Arapahoe, Douglas, Elbert, and Lincoln Counties.

District Court, 19th District
Areas Covered: Weld County.

District Court, 20th District
Areas Covered: Boulder County.

District Court, 21st District
Areas Covered: Mesa County.

District Court, 22nd District
Areas Covered: Dolores and Montezuma Counties.

Connecticut Court Clerks and Courthouses

The trial courts of general jurisdiction in Connecticut are part of the Superior Court system. The Superior Court consists of 16 districts and 23 geographical areas for civil and criminal matter, 13 districts for juvenile matters, and seven housing session locations. The 16 district and 23 geographical area courts are listed below.

Connecticut Supreme Court

Supreme Court Building, 231 Capitol Avenue, Hartford, CT 06106
Tel: (860) 757-2200 Fax: (860) 757-2217
Internet: www.jud.ct.gov

The Supreme Court consists of a chief justice and six associate justices who are appointed to eight-year terms by the General Assembly upon nomination of the Governor from a list compiled by the Judicial Selection Commission. The chief justice is appointed by the Governor and approved by the General Assembly to serve an eight-year term. Retirement is mandatory at age seventy; however, justices who voluntarily retire early may continue to serve the court as senior justices until they reach age 70. The Supreme Court has exclusive appellate jurisdiction over certain cases from the Connecticut Superior Court. These cases include appeals involving the validity of a state statute or state constitutional provision, conviction for a capital felony and other specified felonies, review of a death sentence, a dispute over an election or primary, reprimand or censure of a probate judge, judicial removal or suspension of a judge and decisions of the Judicial Review Council.

Court Staff

Chief Clerk **Paul S. Hartan** . . . . (860) 757-2200
E-mail: paul.hartan@conn.app.jud.ct.gov

Connecticut Appellate Court

75 Elm Street, Hartford, CT 06106
Tel: (860) 713-2192 Fax: (860) 713-2216
Internet: www.jud.ct.gov

The Appellate Court, established in 1983, consists of a chief judge and nine judges who are appointed to eight-year terms by the Connecticut General Assembly upon nomination of the Governor from a list compiled by the Judicial Selection Commission. A chief judge is appointed by and serves at the pleasure of the chief justice of the Connecticut Supreme Court. Retirement is mandatory at age seventy; however, judges who voluntarily retire before that time may continue to serve the Court as judge trial referees. The Appellate Court has appellate jurisdiction over the Connecticut Superior Court and Probate Court except when the Connecticut Supreme Court has exclusive jurisdiction.

Note: Filings should be addressed to: Connecticut Appellate Court, 231 Capitol Ave, Hartford, CT 06106.

Court Staff

Fax: (860) 757-2217

Chief Clerk **Paul S. Hartan** . . . . (860) 757-2200
231 Capitol Avenue, Hartford, CT 06106
E-mail: paul.hartan@conn.app.jud.ct.gov

Connecticut Court Clerks and Courthouses *continued*

Connecticut Superior Court

Ansonia - Milford Judicial District

14 West River Street, Milford, CT 06460
Tel: (203) 877-4293

Areas Covered: Towns of Ansonia, Beacon Falls, Derby, Milford, Orange, Oxford, Seymour, Shelton, and West Haven.

Court Staff

Chief Clerk **James Quinn** . . . . (203) 877-4293

Danbury Judicial District

146 White Street, Danbury, CT 06810
Tel: (203) 207-8600 Fax: (203) 207-8642

Areas Covered: Towns of Bethel, Brookfield, Danbury, New Fairfield, Newtown, Redding, Ridgefield, and Sherman.

Court Staff

Chief Clerk **Louis A. Pace, Jr.** . . . . (203) 207-8600

Fairfield Judicial District

1061 Main Street, Bridgeport, CT 06604
Tel: (203) 579-6527 Fax: (203) 382-8406

Areas Covered: Towns of Bridgeport, Easton, Fairfield, Monroe, Stratford and Trumbull.

Court Staff

Chief Clerk **Donald Mastrony** . . . . (203) 579-6527

Hartford Judicial District

95 Washington Street, Hartford, CT 06106
Tel: (860) 548-2700 Fax: (860) 548-2711

Areas Covered: Towns of Avon, Bloomfield, Canton, East Granby, East Hartford, East Windsor, Enfield, Farmington, Glastonbury, Granby, Hartford, Manchester, Marlborough, Simsbury, South Windsor, Suffield, West Hartford, Windsor, and Windsor Locks.

Court Staff

Chief Clerk **Robin C. Smith** . . . . (860) 548-2700

Litchfield Judicial District

15 West Street, Litchfield, CT 06759
Tel: (860) 567-0885 Fax: (860) 567-4779

Areas Covered: Towns of Barkhamsted, Bethlehem, Bridgewater, Canaan, Colebrook, Cornwall, Goshen, Hartland, Harwinton, Kent, Litchfield, Morris, New Hartford, New Milford, Norfolk, North Canaan, Roxbury, Salisbury, Sharon, Thomaston, Torrington, Warren, Washington and Winchester.

Court Staff

Chief Clerk **Brandon Pelegano** . . . . (860) 567-0885

(continued on next page)

Middlesex Judicial District

1 Court Street, Middletown, CT 06457
Tel: (860) 343-6400 Fax: (860) 343-6423

Areas Covered: Towns of Chester, Clinton, Cromwell, Deep River, Durham, East Haddam, East Hampton, Essex, Haddam, Killingworth, Middlefield, Middletown, Old Saybrook, Portland and Westbrook.

Court Staff
Chief Clerk **Jonathan W. Field** . . . . (860) 343-6400

New Britain Judicial District

20 Franklin Square, New Britain, CT 06051
Tel: (860) 515-5050

Areas Covered: Towns of Berlin, Bristol, Burlington, New Britain, Newington, Plainville, Plymouth, Rocky Hill, Southington, and Wethersfield.

Court Staff
Chief Clerk **Cynthia DeGoursey** . . . . (860) 515-5180

Connecticut Tax Session
Tax and Administrative Appeals Court, 20 Franklin Square, Room 310, New Britain, CT 06051
Tel: (860) 515-5145 Fax: (860) 515-5145

Court Staff
Court Officer **Anastasia Gordanopoulos** . . . . (860) 515-5145
Court Officer **Stephen Goldschmidt** . . . . (860) 515-5145

New Haven Judicial District

235 Church Street, New Haven, CT 06510
Tel: (203) 503-6830

Areas Covered: Towns of Bethany, Branford, Cheshire, East Haven, Guilford, Hamden, Madison, Meriden, New Haven, North Branford, North Haven, Wallingford and Woodbridge.

Court Staff
Chief Clerk **William Sadek** . . . . (203) 503-6800

New London Judicial District

70 Huntington Street, New London, CT 06320
Tel: (860) 442-2977

Areas Covered: Towns of Bozrah, Colchester, East Lyme, Franklin, Griswold, Groton, Lebanon, Ledyard, Lisbon, Lyme, Montville, New London, North Stonington, Norwich, Old Lyme, Preston, Salem, Sprague, Stonington, Voluntown and Waterford.

Court Staff
Chief Clerk **David S. Gage** . . . . (860) 443-5363

Stamford-Norwalk Judicial District

123 Hoyt Street, Stamford, CT 06905
Tel: (203) 965-5315

Areas Covered: Towns of Darien, Greenwich, New Canaan, Norwalk, Stamford, Weston, Westport and Wilton.

Court Staff
Chief Clerk **Ann-Margaret Archer** . . . . (203) 965-5308

Tolland Judicial District

69 Brooklyn Street, Vernon, CT 06066
Tel: (860) 896-4930

Areas Covered: Towns of Andover, Bolton, Columbia, Coventry, Ellington, Hebron, Mansfield, Somers, Stafford, Tolland, Union, Vernon and Willington.

Court Staff
Chief Clerk **Roy Smith, Jr.** . . . . (860) 896-4920

Waterbury Judicial District

300 Grand Street, Waterbury, CT 06702
Tel: (203) 591-3340

Areas Covered: Towns of Middlebury, Naugatuck, Prospect, Southbury, Waterbury, Watertown, Wolcott and Woodbury.

Court Staff
Chief Clerk **Philip H. Groth** . . . . (203) 591-3300

Windham Judicial District

155 Church Street, Putnam, CT 06260
Tel: (860) 779-8500

Areas Covered: Towns of Ashford, Brooklyn, Canterbury, Chaplin, Eastford, Hampton, Killingly, Plainfield, Pomfret, Putnam, Scotland, Sterling, Thompson, Windham and Woodstock.

Court Staff
Chief Clerk **Karen A. Berris** . . . . (860) 928-7749

Geographical Area Courts

Geographical Area 1 at Stamford
123 Hoyt Street, Stamford, CT 06905
Tel: (203) 965-5208 (Clerk's Office)

Geographical Area 2 at Bridgeport
172 Golden Hill Street, Bridgeport, CT 06604
Tel: (203) 579-6568 (Clerk's Office)

Geographical Area 3 at Danbury
146 White Street, Danbury, CT 06810
Tel: (203) 207-8600 (Clerk's Office)

Geographical Area 4 at Waterbury
400 Grand Street, Waterbury, CT 06702
Tel: (203) 236-8100 (Clerk's Office)

Geographical Area 5 at Derby
106 Elizabeth Street, Derby, CT 06418
Tel: (203) 735-7438 (Clerk's Office)

Geographical Area 7 at Meriden
54 West Main Street, Meriden, CT 06451
Tel: (203) 238-6130 (Clerk's Office)

Geographical Area 9 at Middletown
1 Court Street, Middletown, CT 06457-3377
Tel: (860) 343-6445 (Clerk's Office)

Geographical Area 10 at New London
112 Broad Street, New London, CT 06320
Tel: (860) 443-8343 (Clerk's Office)

Geographical Area 11 at Danielson
120 School Street, Danielson, CT 06239
Tel: (860) 779-8480 (Clerk's Office)

Geographical Area 12 at Manchester
410 Center Street, Manchester, CT 06040
Tel: (860) 647-1091 (Clerk's Office)

Geographical Area 13 at Enfield
111 Phoenix Avenue, Enfield, CT 06082
Tel: (860) 741-3727 (Clerk's Office)

Geographical Area 14 at Hartford
101 Lafayette Street, Hartford, CT 06106
Tel: (860) 566-1630 (Clerk's Office)

Geographical Area 15 at New Britain
20 Franklin Square, New Britain, CT 06051
Tel: (860) 515-5080 (Clerk's Office)

Geographical Area 17 at Bristol
131 North Main Street, Bristol, CT 06010
Tel: (860) 582-8111 (Clerk's Office)

Geographical Area 18 at Bantam
80 Doyle Road, Litchfield, CT 06750
Tel: (860) 567-3942 (Clerk's Office)

Geographical Area 19 at Rockville
20 Park Street, Vernon, CT 06066
Tel: (860) 870-3200 (Clerk's Office)

Geographical Area 20 at Norwalk
17 Belden Avenue, Norwalk, CT 06850
Tel: (203) 849-3580 (Clerk's Office)

Geographical Area 21 at Norwich
1 Courthouse Square, Norwich, CT 06360
Tel: (860) 889-7338 (Clerk's Office)

Geographical Area 22 at Milford
14 West River Street, Milford, CT 06460
Tel: (203) 874-1116 (Clerk's Office)

Geographical Area 23 at New Haven
121 Elm Street, New Haven, CT 06510
Tel: (203) 789-7461 (Clerk's Office)

Delaware Court Clerks and Courthouses

The trial courts of general jurisdiction in Delaware is the Superior Court. Most matters involving the incorporation of out-of-state companies in the State are heard in the Court of Chancery.

Delaware Supreme Court

Elbert N. Carvel State Office Building, 820 North French Street, Wilmington, DE 19801
Tel: (302) 577-8425 Fax: (302) 577-3702
Internet: http://courts.delaware.gov/supreme/

The Supreme Court of Delaware consists of a chief justice and four justices who are appointed for twelve-year terms by the Governor with the consent of the Delaware State Senate from a list of candidates provided by the Judicial Nominating Commission. The Supreme Court has final appellate jurisdiction over all civil cases from the Delaware Chancery, Superior and Family Courts and over criminal cases in which the penalty is death, imprisonment over one month, or a fine exceeding $100. The Court also has original jurisdiction over certain extraordinary writs.

Court Staff

Clerk of the Court **Cathy L. Howard**.................(302) 739-4155
  E-mail: Cathy.Howard@state.de.us   Fax: (302) 739-3751

Delaware Court of Chancery

New Castle County Courthouse, 500 North King Street, Suite 1551, Wilmington, DE 19801-3734
Tel: (302) 255-0544 Fax: (302) 255-2213

The Court of Chancery consists of one chancellor and four vice chancellors. The chancellor and vice chancellors are nominated by the Governor and must be confirmed by the Senate for 12-year terms. The Delaware Court of Chancery is a non-jury trial court that serves as Delaware's court of original and exclusive equity jurisdiction, and adjudicates a wide variety of cases involving trusts, real property, guardianships, civil rights, and commercial litigation. The chancellor and vice chancellors must be learned in the law and must be Delaware citizens.

Court Staff

Court Administrator **Karlis P. Johnson**...............(302) 255-0544
Operations Manager, Kent County **Lois B. Holland**......(302) 736-2242
  38 The Green, Dover, DE 19901
  E-mail: lois.holland@state.de.us
Operations Manager, Sussex County **Katrina Kruger**.....(302) 856-5775
  34 The Circle, Georgetown, DE 19947
  E-mail: katrina.kruger@state.de.us

Superior Court of Delaware

New Castle County Courthouse, 500 North King Street, Wilmington, DE 19801
Tel: (302) 255-0800 Fax: (302) 255-2264

Court Staff

Prothonotary, Kent County **Lisa Robinson**............(302) 735-1909
  414 Federal Street, Room 140,   Fax: (302) 739-6717
  Dover, DE 19901
  E-mail: lisa.robinson@state.de.us
Prothonotary, New Castle County **Sharon Agnew**
  Suite 500....................................(302) 255-0700
  E-mail: marcelle.adams@state.de.us   Fax: (302) 255-2264
Prothonotary, Sussex County **Joyce Collins**...........(302) 854-6959
  1 The Circle, Room 214, Georgetown, DE 19947   Fax: (302) 856-5739
  E-mail: joyce.collins@state.de.us

District of Columbia Court Clerks and Courthouses

The trial court of general jurisdiction in the District of Columbia is called the Superior Court, which consists of one unified court which has jurisdiction throughout the District of Columbia. Operations of the Superior court are organized into the Family Court Operations, Civil, Criminal, Probate, Special Operations, Multi-Door Dispute Resolution, Family Court Services, and Domestic Violence divisions.

District of Columbia Court of Appeals

430 E Street NW, Washington, DC 20001
Tel: (202) 879-2700 Fax: (202) 626-8840
Internet: www.dcappeals.gov

The Court of Appeals consists of a chief judge and eight associate judges who are appointed for fifteen-year terms by the President of the United States with approval of the United States Senate from a list compiled by the District of Columbia Judicial Nomination Commission. The chief judge is designated by the Judicial Nomination Commission from among the active judges for a four-year term. The Court sits in three-judge panels rotating within three divisions unless a hearing or rehearing before the full Court is ordered. Retirement is mandatory at age seventy-four; however, senior judges may serve by assignment. The Court of Appeals has jurisdiction over appeals from the Superior Court of the District of Columbia and, to the extent provided by law, jurisdiction to review orders and decisions of administrative agencies of the district. The Court's decisions are final regarding nonstatutory common law; however, all decisions concerning statutes of the United States relevant to District of Columbia and the U.S. Constitution may be appealed to the United States Supreme Court.

Court Staff
Clerk of Court **Julio A. Castillo** . . . . (202) 879-2725
   E-mail: jcastillo@dcappeals.gov

Superior Court of the District of Columbia

Moultrie Courthouse, 500 Indiana Avenue, NW, Room 2500,
Washington, DC 20001
Tel: (202) 879-1400
Internet: http://www.dccourts.gov/dccourts/superior/index.jsp

Court Staff
Clerk of the Court **Duane B. Delaney** . . . . (202) 879-1400

Florida Court Clerks and Courthouses

The trial courts of general jurisdiction in Florida are called circuit courts. There are 20 judicial circuits, each circuit consisting of at least one county. The clerks in each county function both as Clerk of the Circuit Court and County Clerk.

Florida Supreme Court

Supreme Court Building, 500 South Duval Street,
Tallahassee, FL 32399-1925
Tel: (850) 488-0125
E-mail: supremecourt@flcourts.org
Internet: www.floridasupremecourt.org

The Supreme Court consists of a chief justice and six justices who are appointed for six-year terms. Vacancies are filled by the Governor from a list of names submitted by a judicial nominating commission. Justices must stand for retention on a nonpartisan ballot in the next general election occurring at least one year after appointment. Retention elections are held every six years thereafter. The senior justice who has not previously served is selected as chief justice to serve a two-year term. Retirement is mandatory at age seventy. The Supreme Court has exclusive jurisdiction over criminal appeals involving the death penalty, bond validation and certificates of indebtedness, and shall review actions of statewide agencies related to rates or service of utilities.

Court Staff
Clerk of the Court **John A. Tomasino** . . . . (850) 488-0125

Florida District Courts of Appeal

2000 Drayton Drive, Tallahassee, FL 32399
Tel: (850) 487-1000 Fax: (850) 488-7989
Internet: www.flcourts.org

The judges of the Florida District Courts of Appeal are elected for six-year terms on a non-partisan ballot in general elections held in their respective districts. The Courts sit on panels of three judges each. Vacancies are filled by the governor from a list of names submitted by the Judicial Nominating Commission. New appellate judges stand for retention in the first general election occurring at least one year after appointment. The chief judges are elected by peer vote for two-year terms. Retirement is mandatory at age seventy. The District Courts of Appeal have jurisdiction over civil and criminal appeals, including those taken as a matter of rights from final judgments of trial courts, review of administrative actions not directly appealable to another court or as prescribed by law, and interlocutory orders as provided by Florida Supreme Court rules.

Florida District Court of Appeal, First District

2000 Drayton Drive, Tallahassee, FL 32399
Tel: (850) 487-1000 Fax: (850) 488-7989
Internet: www.1dca.org

Areas Covered: Counties of Alachua, Baker, Bay, Bradford, Calhoun, Clay, Columbia, Dixie, Duval, Escambia, Franklin, Gadsden, Gilchrist, Gulf, Hamilton, Holmes, Jackson, Jefferson, Lafayette, Leon, Levy, Liberty, Madison, Nassau, Okaloosa, Santa Rosa, Suwannee, Taylor, Union, Wakulla, Walton and Washington

Court Staff
Clerk of the Court **Jon S. Wheeler** . . . . (850) 717-8100
E-mail: wheelerj@1dca.org

Florida District Court of Appeal, Second District

1700 North Tampa Street, Tampa, FL 33601
P.O. Box 327, Lakeland, FL 33802-0327
Tel: (863) 499-2290 Fax: (863) 413-2649
E-mail: 2dca@wpgate.courts.state.fl.us

Areas Covered: Counties of Charlotte, Collier, DeSoto, Glades, Hardee, Hendry, Highlands, Hillsborough, Lee, Manatee, Pasco, Pinellas, Polk and Sarasota

Court Staff
Clerk of the Court **James R. Birkhold** . . . . (863) 499-2290
E-mail: birkholj@flcourts.org

Florida District Court of Appeal, Third District

2001 SW 117th Avenue, Miami, FL 33175-1716
Tel: (305) 229-3200 Fax: (305) 229-3206
E-mail: 3dca@flcourts.org
Internet: www.3dca.flcourts.org

Areas Covered: Counties of Dade and Monroe

Court Staff
Clerk of the Court **Mary Cay Blanks** . . . . (305) 229-3200
E-mail: 3dca@flcourts.org

Florida District Court of Appeal, Fourth District

1525 Palm Beach Lakes Boulevard, West Palm Beach, FL 33401
Tel: (561) 242-2000
Internet: www.4DCA.org

Areas Covered: Counties of Broward, Indian River, Martin, Okeechobee, Palm Beach and St. Lucie

Court Staff
Clerk **Lonn Weissblum** . . . . (561) 242-2000
E-mail: weissbluml@flcourts.org

Florida District Court of Appeal, Fifth District

300 South Beach Street, Daytona Beach, FL 32114
Tel: (386) 947-1500 Fax: (386) 947-1565
E-mail: 5dca@flcourts.org

Areas Covered: Counties of Brevard, Citrus, Flagler, Hernando, Lake, Marion, Orange, Osceola, Putnam, St. Johns, Seminole, Sumter and Volusia

Court Staff
Clerk of Court **Joanne P. Simmons** . . . . (386) 255-8600
E-mail: simmonsj@flcourts.org

(continued on next page)

Florida Court Clerks and Courthouses *continued*

County-By-County

Alachua County

County Clerk

Clerk of the Court and Comptroller
201 East University Avenue, Gainesville, FL 32601
Fax: (352) 338-3201

Clerk of the Court and Comptroller **J.K. Irby** . . . . (352) 374-3636

Baker County

County Clerk

Office of the Clerk of the Courts
339 East Macclenny Avenue, Suite 113, Macclenny, FL 32063
Tel: (904) 259-8113   Fax: (904) 259-4176

Clerk of the Courts **Stacie Harvey** . . . . (904) 259-8113
    E-mail: clerk@bakercountyfl.org

Bay County

County Clerk

Office of the Clerk of the Court
300 East Fourth Street, Panama City, FL 32401
Tel: (850) 763-9061   Fax: (850) 747-5188

Clerk of the Court and Comptroller **Bill Kinsaul** . . . . (850) 763-9061
    E-mail: webbaycoclerk@baycoclerk.com

Bradford County

County Clerk

Office of the Clerk of the Court
945 North Temple Avenue, Starke, FL 32091
Tel: (904) 966-6281   Fax: (904) 966-6256

Clerk of Court **Ray Norman** . . . . (904) 966-6281
    E-mail: ray_norman@bradford-co-fla.org

Brevard County

County Clerk

Office of the Clerk of the Circuit Court
400 South St., Titusville, FL 32780
Tel: (321) 637-5413   Fax: (321) 264-6940
Internet: www.brevardclerk.us

Clerk of the Circuit Court **Scott Ellis** . . . . (321) 637-5413
    E-mail: scott.ellis@brevardclerk.us   Fax: (321) 267-6940

Broward County

County Clerk

Broward County Clerk of the Courts
201 South East Sixth Street, Fort Lauderdale, FL 33301
Tel: (954) 831-6565
Internet: www.clerk-17th-flcourts.org

Clerk of Court **Howard C. Forman** . . . . (954) 831-6565

Florida Court Clerks and Courthouses *continued*

Calhoun County

County Clerk

Office of the Clerk of Court
20859 Central Avenue East, Room 130, Blountstown, FL 32424
Tel: (850) 674-4545   Fax: (850) 674-5553

Clerk of the Court and Comptroller **Carla Hand** . . . . (850) 674-4545
    E-mail: chand@calhounclerk.com

Charlotte County

County Clerk

Office of the Clerk of the Circuit Court
350 East Marion Avenue, Punta Gorda, FL 33950
Tel: (941) 505-4716

Clerk of the Circuit Court **Barbara T. Scott** . . . . (941) 505-4716
    E-mail: casweb@co.charlotte.fl.us

Citrus County

County Clerk

Office of the Clerk of the Courts
110 North Apopka Avenue, Inverness, FL 34450
Tel: (352) 341-6424   Fax: (352) 341-6584

Clerk of the Circuit Court and Comptroller
    Angela Vick . . . . (352) 341-6424
    E-mail: clerkofcourts@clerk.citrus.fl.us

Clay County

County Clerk

Office of the Clerk of the Circuit Court
825 North Orange Avenue, Green Cove Springs, FL 32043
Tel: (904) 284-6317   Tel: (904) 269-6317   Fax: (904) 284-6390
Fax: (904) 269-6390

Clerk of the Circuit Court **Tara S. Green** . . . . (904) 284-6317
    E-mail: greent@clayclerk.com

Collier County

County Clerk

Office of the Clerk of the Courts
3315 Tamiami Trail East, Second Floor, Naples, FL 34112
Tel: (239) 252-2745   Fax: (239) 252-2755
Internet: www.collierclerk.com

Clerk of the Court **Dwight E. Brock** . . . . (239) 252-2745
    E-mail: CollierClerk@collierclerk.com

Columbia County

County Clerk

Office of the Clerk of the Courts
173 NE Hernando Avenue, Lake City, FL 32055
Tel: (386) 758-1041   Fax: (386) 719-7457

Clerk of the Court **P. DeWitt Cason** . . . . (386) 758-1041
    E-mail: pdcason@columbiaclerk.com

De Soto County

County Clerk

Office of the Clerk of the Circuit Court
115 East Oak Street, Room 101, Arcadia, FL 34266
Tel: (863) 993-4876 Fax: (863) 993-4669

Clerk of the Circuit Court **Mitzie W. McGavic** . . . . (863) 993-4876
  E-mail: mitzie.mcgavic@desotoclerk.com

Dixie County

County Clerk

Office of the Clerk of the Courts
214 NE Highway 351, Cross City, FL 32628
Tel: (352) 498-1200 Fax: (352) 498-1201

Clerk of the Court and Comptroller **Dana Johnson** . . . . . . (352) 498-1200
  E-mail: djohnson@dixieclerk.com

Duval County

County Clerk

Duval County Clerk of Courts
Duval County Courthouse, 501 West Adams Street, Room 103,
Jacksonville, FL 32202
Internet: www.duvalclerk.com

Clerk of the Circuit and County Courts
  Ronnie Fussell . . . . (904) 255-2000
  E-mail: ronnie.fussell@duvalclerk.com

Escambia County

County Clerk

Office of the Clerk of the Circuit Court and Comptroller
190 Governmental Center, Pensacola, FL 32502
Tel: (850) 595-4310
Internet: www.escambiaclerk.com

Clerk of the Circuit Court and Comptroller
  Pam Childers . . . . (850) 595-4310

Flagler County

County Clerk

Office of the Clerk of the Courts
Kim C. Hammond Justice Center, Building 1, 1769 East Moody
Boulevard, Bunnell, FL 32210
Tel: (386) 313-4400 Fax: (386) 313-4101

Clerk of the Circuit Court **Gail Wadsworth** . . . . (386) 313-4409
  E-mail: clerk@flaglerclerk.com

Franklin County

County Clerk

Office of the Clerk of the Courts
33 Market Street, Suite 203, Apalachicola, FL 32320
Tel: (850) 653-8861 Fax: (850) 653-2261

Clerk of the Courts **Marcia M. Johnson** . . . . (850) 653-8861
  E-mail: mmjohnson@franklinclerk.com

Gadsden County

County Clerk

Office of the Clerk of the Circuit Court
10 East Jefferson Street, Quincy, FL 32351
Tel: (850) 875-8601 Fax: (850) 875-8612

Clerk of the Circuit Court **Nicholas Thomas** . . . . (850) 875-8601
  E-mail: clerkofcourt@gadsdenclerk.com

Gilchrist County

County Clerk

Office of the Clerk of the Courts
112 South Main Street, Trenton, FL 32693
Tel: (352) 463-3170 Fax: (352) 463-3166 Tel: (800) 267-3182

Clerk of the Circuit Court and Comptroller
  Todd Newton . . . . (352) 463-3170
  E-mail: tnewton@gilchrist.fl.us

Glades County

County Clerk

Office of the Clerk of the Court
500 Avenue J, Moore Haven, FL 33471
Tel: (863) 946-6010 Fax: (863) 946-0560

Clerk of the Court and Comptroller **Sandra Brown** . . . . . . (863) 946-6010
  E-mail: sbrown@gladesclerk.com

Gulf County

County Clerk

Office of the Clerk of the Courts
1000 Cecil G. Costin, Sr. Boulevard, Room 148, Port Saint Joe, FL 32456
Tel: (850) 229-6112 Tel: (850) 639-5068 Fax: (850) 229-9252

Clerk of Court **Rebecca L. "Becky" Norris** . . . . (850) 229-6112 ext. 1101
  E-mail: info@gulfclerk.com

Hamilton County

County Clerk

Office of the Clerk of the Circuit Court
207 NE First Street, Room 106, Jasper, FL 32052
Tel: (386) 792-1288 Fax: (386) 792-3524

Clerk of Circuit Court **Greg Godwin** . . . . (386) 792-1288
  E-mail: hamiltonclerk@flcjn.net

Hardee County

County Clerk

Office of the Clerk of the Courts
417 West Main Street, Wauchula, FL 33873
Tel: (863) 773-4174 Fax: (863) 773-4422

Clerk of the Circuit Court **Victoria L. Rogers** . . . . (863) 773-4174
  E-mail: victoria.rogers@hardeecounty.net

(continued on next page)

Hendry County

County Clerk

Office of the Clerk of the Courts
25 Hickpochee Avenue, LaBelle, FL 33975
Tel: (863) 675-5217 Fax: (863) 675-5238

Clerk of the Courts **Barbara S. Butler** .... (863) 675-5201
    E-mail: clerk@hendryclerk.org

Hernando County

County Clerk

Office of the Clerk of the Circuit Court
20 North Main Street, Room 130, Brooksville, FL 34601
Tel: (352) 754-4201 Fax: (352) 754-4247

Clerk of the Circuit Court and Comptroller
    Don Barbee, Jr. .... (352) 754-4201
    E-mail: dbarbee@hernandocounty.us

Highlands County

County Clerk

Office of the Clerk of the Courts
590 South Commerce Avenue, Sebring, FL 33870
Tel: (863) 402-6768 Fax: (863) 402-6835

Clerk of the Courts **Robert W. "Bob" Germain** .... (863) 402-6565
    E-mail: clerk@hcclerk.org

Hillsborough County

County Clerk

Office of the Clerk of the Circuit Court
George E. Edgecomb Courthouse, 800 Twiggs Street, Tampa, FL 33602
Tel: (813) 276-8100 Fax: (813) 272-6518
E-mail: clerkadmin@hillsclerk.com

Clerk of the Circuit Court **Pat Collier Frank** .... (813) 276-8100
    E-mail: frankp@hillsclerk.com

Holmes County

County Clerk

Office of the Clerk of the Courts
201 North Oklahoma Street, Suite 302, Bonifay, FL 32425
Tel: (850) 547-1100 Fax: (850) 547-6630

Clerk of the Court and Comptroller **Kyle Hudson** .... (850) 547-1100
    E-mail: kyle.hudson@holmesclerk.com

Indian River County

County Clerk

Office of the Clerk of the Circuit Court
2000 16th Avenue, Vero Beach, FL 32960
Tel: (772) 770-5185 Fax: (772) 770-5008

Clerk of the Circuit Court **Jeffrey R. Smith** ....(772) 770-5185 ext. 3160
    E-mail: clerk@clerk.indian-river.org

Jackson County

County Clerk

Office of the Clerk of the Circuit Court
4445 Lafayette Street, Marianna, FL 32446
Tel: (850) 482-9552 Fax: (850) 482-7849

Clerk of the Circuit Court and Comptroller
    Dale Rabon Guthrie .... (850) 482-9552
    E-mail: clerkmail@jacksonclerk.com

Jefferson County

County Clerk

Office of the Clerk of the Courts
One Courthouse Circle, Monticello, FL 32344
Tel: (850) 342-0218 Fax: (850) 342-0222

Clerk of the Courts **Kirk Reams** .... (850) 342-0218 ext. 232
    E-mail: kreams@jeffersonclerk.com

Lafayette County

County Clerk

Office of the Clerk of the Courts
120 West Main Street, Mayo, FL 32066
Tel: (386) 294-1600 Fax: (386) 294-4231

Clerk of the Court and Comptroller **Ricky Lyons** .... (386) 294-1600
    E-mail: rlyons@lafayetteclerk.com

Lake County

County Clerk

Office of the Clerk of Circuit Court
550 West Main Street, Tavares, FL 32778
Tel: (352) 742-4102 Fax: (352) 742-4110
E-mail: webmaster@lakecountyclerk.org
Internet: www.lakecountyclerk.org

Clerk of Circuit Court **Neil Kelly** .... (352) 742-4102

Lee County

County Clerk

Office of the Clerk of the Circuit Court
Justice Center, 1700 Monroe Street, 2nd Floor, Fort Myers, FL 33901
Tel: (239) 533-2555
Internet: www.leeclerk.org
E-mail: leeclerk_info@leeclerk.org

Clerk of the Circuit Court **Linda Doggett** .... (239) 533-2555

Leon County

County Clerk

Office of the Clerk of the Courts
301 South Monroe Street, Room 100, Tallahassee, FL 32301
Tel: (850) 577-4000 Fax: (850) 577-4013

Clerk of the Courts **Bob Inzer** .... (850) 577-4000
    E-mail: bbinzer@leoncountyfl.gov

Levy County

County Clerk

Office of the Clerk of the Circuit Court
355 South Court Street, Bronson, FL 32621
Tel: (352) 486-5266 Tel: (800) 733-5389 Fax: (352) 486-5166

Clerk of the Circuit Court **Danny J. Shipp** . . . . (352) 486-5266
  E-mail: shipp-danny@circuit8.org

Liberty County

County Clerk

Office of the Clerk of the Courts
10811 NW SR 20, Bristol, FL 32321
Tel: (850) 643-2215 Fax: (850) 643-2866
E-mail: info@libertyclerk.com

Clerk of the Court and Comptroller
  Kathleen E. "Kathy" Brown . . . . (850) 643-2215
  E-mail: kbrown@libertyclerk.com

Madison County

County Clerk

Office of the Clerk of the Courts
125 SW Range Avenue, Madison, FL 32340
Tel: (850) 973-1500 Fax: (850) 973-2059

Clerk of the Court and Comptroller **Tim Sanders** . . . . (850) 973-1500
  E-mail: tsanders@madisonclerk.com

Manatee County

County Clerk

Office of the Clerk of the Circuit Court
1115 Manatee Avenue W, Bradenton, FL 34206
Tel: (941) 749-1800 Fax: (941) 741-4082
Internet: www.manateeclerk.com

Clerk of the Circuit Court **Richard B. "Chips" Shore** . . . . (941) 749-1800
  E-mail: chips.shore@manateeclerk.com

Marion County

County Clerk

Office of the Clerk of the Court
110 Northwest First Avenue, Ocala, FL 34475
Tel: (352) 671-5604 Fax: (352) 671-5600
Internet: www.marioncountyclerk.org

Clerk of the Court **David R. Ellspermann** . . . . (352) 671-5604

Martin County

County Clerk

Office of the Clerk of the Circuit Court
100 East Ocean Boulevard, Stuart, FL 34994
Tel: (772) 288-5576 Fax: (772) 288-5548

Clerk of the Circuit Court and County Comptroller
  Carolyn Timmann . . . . (772) 288-5576
  E-mail: ctimmann@martin.fl.us

Miami-Dade County

County Clerk

Office of the Clerk of the Courts
Dade County Courthouse, 73 W. Flagler St., Room 242, Miami, FL 33130
P.O. Box 011711, Miami, FL 33101
Fax: (305) 349-7403
Internet: www.miami-dadeclerk.com

Clerk **Harvey Ruvin** . . . . (305) 349-7333
  E-mail: clerk@miami-dadeclerk.com

Monroe County

County Clerk

Office of the Clerk of the Circuit Court
500 Whitehead Street, Key West, FL 33040
Tel: (305) 295-3130 Fax: (305) 295-3663

Clerk of the Circuit Court **Amy Heavilin** . . . . (305) 295-3130
  E-mail: aheavilin@monroe-clerk.com

Nassau County

County Clerk

Office of the Clerk of the Courts
76347 Veteran's Way, Suite 456, Yulee, FL 32097
Tel: (904) 548-4600 Tel: (800) 958-3496 Fax: (904) 548-4508

Clerk of the Circuit and County Courts
  John A. Crawford . . . . (904) 548-4600
  E-mail: jcrawford@nassauclerk.com

Okaloosa County

County Clerk

Office of the Clerk of the Circuit Court
101 East James Lee Boulevard, Crestview, FL 32536
Tel: (850) 689-5000 Fax: (850) 689-8071

Clerk of the Circuit Court **J.D. Peacock** . . . . (850) 689-5000 ext. 4301
  E-mail: jpeacock@co.okaloosa.fl.us

Okeechobee County

County Clerk

Office of the Clerk of the Circuit Court
312 Northwest 3rd Street, Okeechobee, FL 34972
Tel: (863) 763-2131 Fax: (863) 763-1557

Clerk of the Circuit Court **Sharon Robertson** . . . . (863) 763-2131
  E-mail: srobertson@clerk.co.okeechobee.fl.us

Orange County

County Clerk

Office of the Clerk of the Courts
425 North Orange Avenue, Orlando, FL 32801
P.O. Box 4994, Orlando, FL 32802-4994
Tel: (407) 836-2000
Internet: www.myorangeclerk.com

Clerk of Courts **Eddie Fernández** . . . . (407) 836-2000

(continued on next page)

Osceola County

County Clerk

Clerk of Circuit Court
2 Courthouse Square, Suite 2000, Kissimmee, FL 34741
Tel: (407) 742-3500 Fax: (407) 742-3699
Internet: www.osceolaclerk.com

Clerk of the Courts **Armando Ramirez** . . . .(407) 742-3500

Palm Beach County

County Clerk

Office of the Clerk and Comptroller
205 North Dixie Highway, West Palm Beach, FL 33401
E-mail: clerkweb@mypalmbeachclerk.com

Clerk and Comptroller **Sharon R. Bock** . . . . (561) 355-2996

Pasco County

County Clerk

Office of the Clerk of the Circuit Court
38053 Live Oak Avenue, Dade City, FL 33523
Tel: (352) 521-4274
Internet: www.pascoclerk.com

County Clerk and Comptroller **Paula O'Neil** . . . .(352) 521-4274
   E-mail: poneil@pascoclerk.com

Pinellas County

County Clerk

Office of the Clerk of the Circuit Court
315 Court Street, 4th Floor, Clearwater, FL 33756
Tel: (727) 464-3341 Fax: (727) 453-3589
E-mail: clerkinfo@co.pinellas.fl.us
Internet: www.pinellasclerk.org

Clerk of the Court **Ken Burke** . . . . (727) 464-3341
   E-mail: kburke@co.pinellas.fl.us

Polk County

County Clerk

Office of the Clerk of the Circuit Court/County Comptroller's Office
P.O. Box 988, Bartow, FL 33831
Tel: (863) 534-4540 Fax: (863) 534-4089
Internet: www.polkcountyclerk.net

Clerk of Courts/Comptroller **Stacy Butterfield** . . . . (863) 534-4540

Putnam County

County Clerk

Office of the Clerk of the Courts
410 St. Johns Avenue, Palatka, FL 32177
Tel: (386) 329-0361 Fax: (386) 329-0888

Clerk of the Courts **Tim Smith** . . . . (386) 329-0361
   E-mail: timsmith@putnam-fl.com

St. Johns County

County Clerk

Office of the Clerk of the Courts
4010 Lewis Speedway, St. Augustine, FL 32084
Tel: (904) 819-3600 Fax: (904) 819-3661

Clerk of the Circuit Court **Cheryl Strickland** . . . . (904) 819-3600

St. Lucie County

County Clerk

Office of the Clerk of the Circuit Court
201 South Indian River Drive, Fort Pierce, FL 34950
Tel: (772) 462-6900
Internet: www.stlucieclerk.com

Clerk of the Circuit Court **Joseph E. "Joe" Smith** . . . . . .(772) 462-6900
   E-mail: joe@stlucieclerk.com

Santa Rosa County

County Clerk

Office of the Clerk of Court and Comptroller
6495 Caroline Street, Suite A, Milton, FL 32570
Tel: (850) 983-1973 Fax: (850) 983-1986

Clerk of Court and Comptroller **Donald C. Spencer** . . . . . (850) 983-1973
   E-mail: spencerd@flcjn.net

Sarasota County

County Clerk

Office of the Clerk of the Circuit Court and County Comptroller
2000 Main Street, Sarasota, FL 34237
Tel: (941) 861-7400
Internet: www.sarasotaclerk.com
Fax: (941) 861-7738

Clerk of the Circuit Court and County Comptroller
   Karen E. Rushing . . . . (941) 861-7400
   E-mail: krushing@scgov.net

Seminole County

County Clerk

Office of the Clerk of Courts
301 North Park Avenue, Sanford, FL 32771
Tel: (407) 665-4313 Fax: (407) 330-7193

Clerk of the Circuit Court **Maryanne Morse** . . . . (407) 665-4313

Sumter County

County Clerk

Office of the Clerk of the Courts
215 East McCollum Avenue, Bunnell, FL 33513
Tel: (352) 569-6600 Fax: (352) 569-6623

Clerk of the Courts **Gloria R. Hayward** . . . . (352) 569-6600
   E-mail: sumterclerk@earthlink.net

Suwannee County

County Clerk

Office of the Clerk of the Circuit Court
200 South Ohio Avenue, Live Oak, FL 32064
Tel: (386) 362-0500 Fax: (386) 362-0567

Clerk of Court **Barry A. Baker** . . . . (386) 362-0516
E-mail: bbaker@suwclerk.org

Taylor County

County Clerk

Office of the Clerk of the Courts
108 North Jefferson Street, Suite 102, Perry, FL 32347
Tel: (850) 838-3506 Fax: (850) 838-3549

Clerk of the Court and Comptroller
Annie Mae Murphy . . . . (850) 838-3506
E-mail: amurphy@taylorcountygov.com

Union County

County Clerk

Office of the Clerk of the Court
55 West Main Street, Room 103, Lake Butler, FL 32054
Tel: (386) 496-3711 Fax: (386) 496-1718

Clerk of Court and Comptroller
Kellie Hendricks Connell . . . . (386) 496-3711
E-mail: kconnell@flclerks.com

Volusia County

County Clerk

Office of the Clerk of the Circuit Court
101 North Alabama Avenue, DeLand, FL 32724
Fax: (386) 822-5711
E-mail: clerk@clerk.org

Clerk of the Circuit Court **Diane M. Matousek** . . . . (386) 736-5915
E-mail: clerk@clerk.org

Wakulla County

County Clerk

Office of the Clerk of the Courts
3056 Crawfordville Highway, Crawfordville, FL 32327
Tel: (850) 926-0905 Fax: (850) 926-0938

Clerk of Courts **Brent Xavier Thurmond** . . . . (850) 926-0905
E-mail: bxt@wakullaclerk.com

Walton County

County Clerk

Office of the Clerk of the Courts
571 U.S. Highway 90 East, DeFuniak Springs, FL 32435
Tel: (850) 892-8115 Fax: (850) 892-8130

Clerk of the Courts and Comptroller **Alex Alford** . . . . (850) 892-8115
E-mail: alfalex@co.walton.fl.us

Washington County

County Clerk

Office of the Clerk of the Courts
1331 South Boulevard, Chipley, FL 32428
Tel: (850) 638-6289 Fax: (850) 638-6288

Clerk of the Courts and Comptroller **Lora C. Bell** . . . . (850) 638-6289
E-mail: lbell@washingtonclerk.com

Counties Within Judicial Districts

Circuit Court, 1st Judicial Circuit
Areas Covered: Escambia, Okaloosa, Santa Rosa, and Walton Counties.

Circuit Court, 2nd Judicial Circuit
Areas Covered: Franklin, Gadsden, Jefferson, Leon, Liberty, and Wakulla Counties.

Circuit Court, 3rd Judicial Circuit
Areas Covered: Columbia, Dixie, Hamilton, Lafayette, Madison, Suwannee, and Taylor Counties.

Circuit Court, 4th Judicial Circuit
Areas Covered: Clay, Duval, and Nassau Counties.

Circuit Court, 5th Judicial Circuit
Areas Covered: Citrus, Hernando, Lake, Marion, and Sumter Counties.

Circuit Court, 6th Judicial Circuit
Areas Covered: Pasco and Pinellas Counties.

Circuit Court, 7th Judicial Circuit
Areas Covered: Flagler, Putnam, St. Johns, and Volusia Counties.

Circuit Court, 8th Judicial Circuit
Areas Covered: Alachua, Baker, Bradford, Gilchrist, Levy, and Union Counties.

Circuit Court, 9th Judicial Circuit
Areas Covered: Orange and Osceola Counties.

Circuit Court, 10th Judicial Circuit
Areas Covered: Hardee, Highlands, and Polk Counties.

Circuit Court, 11th Judicial Circuit
Areas Covered: Dade County.

Circuit Court, 12th Judicial Circuit
Areas Covered: De Soto, Manatee, and Sarasota Counties.

Circuit Court, 13th Judicial Circuit
Areas Covered: Hillsborough County.

Circuit Court, 14th Judicial Circuit
Areas Covered: Bay, Calhoun, Gulf, Holmes, Jackson, and Washington Counties.

(continued on next page)

Florida Court Clerks and Courthouses *continued*

Circuit Court, 15th Judicial Circuit

Areas Covered: Palm Beach County.

Circuit Court, 16th Judicial Circuit

Areas Covered: Monroe County.

Circuit Court, 17th Judicial Circuit

Areas Covered: Broward County.

Circuit Court, 18th Judicial Circuit

Areas Covered: Brevard and Seminole Counties.

Circuit Court, 19th Judicial Circuit

Areas Covered: Indian River, Martin, Okeechobee, and St. Lucie Counties.

Circuit Court, 20th Judicial Circuit

Areas Covered: Charlotte, Collier, Glades, Hendry, and Lee Counties.

Georgia Court Clerks and Courthouses

The trial courts of general jurisdiction in Georgia are called Superior Courts. There is a Clerk of the Superior Court in each of Georgia's 159 counties. In most counties, the clerk of the superior court also functions as clerk of the state court (Court of limited jurisdiction). Property records are handled by the superior court clerk.

Supreme Court of Georgia

State Judicial Building, 244 Washington Street, SW, Room 572, Atlanta, GA 30334
Tel: (404) 656-3470 Fax: (404) 656-2253
E-mail: scinfo@gasupreme.us
Internet: www.gasupreme.us

The Supreme Court, established by the Georgia State Legislature in 1845, consists of a chief justice, presiding justice, and five justices. The chief justice and presiding justice, who handle administrative matters for the Court, are elected by peer vote to two-year terms. All justices are elected in statewide, nonpartisan elections for six-year terms. Retirement is mandatory at age seventy-five or on the last day of the term during which the justice turns seventy, whichever is later. The Supreme Court has exclusive appellate jurisdiction in all cases involving the United States or Georgia constitutions, the constitutionality of a law or ordinance, and contested elections. The Court has general appellate jurisdiction in areas of land title, equity, divorce and alimony, the validity or construction of wills, capital felonies, extraordinary remedies, or cases referred to it by the Court of Appeals of Georgia or the United States Court of Appeals for the Eleventh Circuit.

Court Staff
Clerk of the Court **Therese S. "Tee" Barnes** . . . . (404) 656-3470

Court of Appeals of Georgia

47 Trinity Avenue, SW, Suite 501, Atlanta, GA 30334
Tel: (404) 656-3450

The Court of Appeals, established by a constitutional amendment in 1906, consists of a chief judge, four presiding judges and seven associate judges. The judges elect one of their own members as chief judge for a two-year term. The chief judge assigns judges to four equal divisions and designates presiding judges for one-year terms for each division. Cases are assigned to each judge in each division on an equal basis, via a random assignment wheel for civil, criminal, discretionary applications and interlocutory applications. The Court of Appeals of Georgia is required by the State Constitution to dispose of every case at the term for which it is entered on the Court's docket for hearing or at the next term. All judges are elected in statewide, nonpartisan elections for six-year terms. Vacancies are temporarily filled by the Governor from a list of candidates provided by the Judicial Nominating Commission. Retirement is mandatory at age seventy-five or on the last day of the six-year term during which the judge turns seventy, whichever is later. The Court of Appeals has appellate jurisdiction in all civil and criminal matters where exclusive jurisdiction or general appellate jurisdiction is not reserved to the Supreme Court of Georgia by the Constitution, or conferred on other courts. The Court hears cases involving appeals from torts, contracts, malpractice, workers compensation, juvenile cases and all criminal cases excepting those in which the sentence of death was imposed or could be imposed.

Court Staff
Clerk and Court Administrator **Stephen E. Castlen** . . . . . (404) 656-3450

County-By-County

Appling County

Superior Court Clerk

Brunswick Judicial Circuit
701 H Street, Brunswick, GA 31520
Tel: (912) 554-7364

Clerk of Court, Appling County **F. Floyd Hunter** . . . . (912) 367-8126
  69 Tippins Street, Suite 103,   Fax: (912) 367-8180
  Baxley, GA 31513

Atkinson County

Superior Court Clerk

Alapaha Judicial Circuit
201 North Davis Street, Nashville, GA 31639

Clerk of Court, Atkinson County **Wilson Paulk** . . . . (912) 422-3343
  305 South Main Street, Pearson, GA 31642   Fax: (912) 422-7025

Bacon County

Superior Court Clerk

Waycross Judicial Circuit
101 South Peterson Avenue, Douglas, GA 31533
Tel: (912) 384-0587

Clerk of Court, Bacon County **Sherry Tillman** . . . . (912) 632-4915
  502 West 12th Street, Alma, GA 31510   Fax: (912) 632-6545

Baker County

Superior Court Clerk

South Georgia Judicial Circuit
Decatur County Courthouse, 112 West Water Street, Mezzanine Level, Bainbridge, GA 39817
Tel: (229) 246-1111
Internet: www.southgeorgiajudicialcircuit.com

Clerk of Court, Baker County **Betty Bush** . . . . (229) 734-3004
  167 Baker Place, Newton, GA 39870   Fax: (229) 734-7770
  P.O. Box 10, Newton, GA 39870-0010

Baldwin County

Superior Court Clerk

Ocmulgee Judicial Circuit
P.O. Box 728, Madison, GA 30650

Clerk of Court, Baldwin County
  Rosemary Fordham Phillips . . . . (478) 445-6324
  121 North Wilkinson Street, Suite 209,   Fax: (478) 445-6039
  Milledgeville, GA 31061
  P.O. Box 987, Milledgeville, GA 31059

(continued on next page)

Banks County

Superior Court Clerk

Piedmont Judicial Circuit
652 Barrow Park Drive, Winder, GA 30680
Internet: www.10thjudicialdistrictga.com/Piedmont.html

Clerk of Court, Banks County **Tim Harper** . . . .(706) 677-6243
P.O. Box 337, Homer, GA 30547   Fax: (706) 677-6294
E-mail: tim.harper@gsccca.org

Barrow County

Superior Court Clerk

Piedmont Judicial Circuit
652 Barrow Park Drive, Winder, GA 30680
Internet: www.10thjudicialdistrictga.com/Piedmont.html

Clerk of Court, Barrow County **Regina B. McIntyre** . . . . .(770) 867-8993
652 Barrow Park Drive, Suite B,   Fax: (770) 867-4800
Winder, GA 30680
E-mail: rmcintyre@barrowga.org

Bartow County

Superior Court Clerk

Cherokee Judicial Circuit
135 West Cherokee Avenue, Cartersville, GA 30120

Clerk of Court, Bartow County **Gary Bell** . . . .(770) 387-5025
135 West Cherokee Avenue, Suite 233,   Fax: (770) 387-5611
Cartersville, GA 30120

Ben Hill County

Superior Court Clerk

Cordele Judicial Circuit
510 North 7th Street, Cordele, GA 31010
Tel: (229) 271-4722 Fax: (229) 271-4714

Clerk of Court, Ben Hill County **Betty Lynn Johnson** . . .(229) 426-5135
P.O. Box 1104, Fitzgerald, GA 31750   Fax: (229) 426-5487

Berrien County

Superior Court Clerk

Alapaha Judicial Circuit
201 North Davis Street, Nashville, GA 31639

Clerk of Court, Berrien County **Shawna C. Hughes** . . . . .(229) 686-5506
201 North Davis Street, Room 230,   Fax: (229) 543-1032
Nashville, GA 31639

Bibb County

Superior Court Clerk

Macon Judicial Circuit
601 Mulberry Street, Macon, GA 31202

Clerk of Court, Bibb County **Erica Woodford** . . . .(478) 621-6527
601 Mulberry Street, Room 216,   Fax: (478) 621-6033
Macon, GA 31202
E-mail: ewoodford@co.bibb.ga.us

Bleckley County

Superior Court Clerk

Oconee Judicial Circuit
P.O. Box 4248, Eastman, GA 31023

Clerk of Court, Bleckley County **Dianne C. Brown** . . . . . .(478) 934-3210
112 North Second Street, Cochran, GA 31014   Fax: (478) 934-6671
P.O. Box 272, Cochran, GA 31014

Brantley County

Superior Court Clerk

Waycross Judicial Circuit
101 South Peterson Avenue, Douglas, GA 31533
Tel: (912) 384-0587

Clerk of Court, Brantley County **Lera C. Crews** . . . .(912) 462-5635
117 Brantley Street, Nahunta, GA 31553   Fax: (912) 462-6247
E-mail: quailpen@btconline.net

Brooks County

Superior Court Clerk

Southern Judicial Circuit
P.O. Box 2227, Moultrie, GA 31776
Tel: (229) 616-7474 Fax: (229) 616-7447
Internet: www.southernjudicialcircuit.com

Clerk of Court, Brooks County **Ginger Shiver** . . . .(229) 263-4747
P.O. Box 630, Quitman, GA 31643   Fax: (229) 263-5050

Bryan County

Superior Court Clerk

Atlantic Judicial Circuit
P.O. Box 713, Hinesville, GA 31310
Tel: (912) 368-2250

Clerk of Court, Bryan County **Rebecca G. Crowe** . . . .(912) 653-3872
151 South College Street, Pembroke, GA 31321 Fax: (912) 653-3870
E-mail: becky.crowe@gsccca.org

Bulloch County

Superior Court Clerk

Ogeechee Judicial Circuit
P.O. Box 326, Statesboro, GA 30458
Tel: (912) 764-6095 Fax: (912) 489-3148
Internet: www.ogeecheecircuit.org

Clerk of Court, Bulloch County **Heather B. McNeal** . . . . .(912) 764-9009
20 Siebald Street, Statesboro, GA 30458   Fax: (912) 764-5953

Burke County

Superior Court Clerk

Augusta Judicial Circuit
735 James Brown Boulevard, Augusta, GA 30901

Clerk of Court, Burke County
Sherri J. Cochran Cates . . . .(706) 554-2279
111 East 16th Street, Waynesboro, GA 30830   Fax: (706) 554-7887
E-mail: sherri.cochran@gsccca.org

Butts County

Superior Court Clerk

Towaliga Judicial Circuit
One Courthouse Square, Forsyth, GA 31029
Tel: (478) 994-7658

Clerk of Court, Butts County **Rhonda T. Smith** . . . . (770) 775-8215
26 Third Street, Jackson, GA 30233   Fax: (770) 504-1359

Calhoun County

Superior Court Clerk

South Georgia Judicial Circuit
Decatur County Courthouse, 112 West Water Street, Mezzanine Level,
Bainbridge, GA 39817
Tel: (229) 246-1111
Internet: www.southgeorgiajudicialcircuit.com

Clerk of Court, Calhoun County **Karen Taylor** . . . . (229) 849-2715
P.O. Box 69, Morgan, GA 39866-0069   Fax: (229) 849-0072

Camden County

Superior Court Clerk

Brunswick Judicial Circuit
701 H Street, Brunswick, GA 31520
Tel: (912) 554-7364

Clerk of Court, Camden County **Joy Lynn Turner** . . . . (912) 576-5631
210 East Fourth Street, Woodbine, GA 31569   Fax: (912) 576-5648
P.O. Box 550, Woodbine, GA 31569

Candler County

Superior Court Clerk

Middle Judicial Circuit
107 South Main Street, Swainsboro, GA 30401

Clerk of Court, Candler County **Linda F. Sewell** . . . . (912) 685-5257
355 South Broad Street, Metter, GA 30439   Fax: (912) 685-2946

Carroll County

Superior Court Clerk

Coweta Judicial Circuit
72 Greenville Street, Newnan, GA 30263

Clerk of Court, Carroll County **Alan Lee** . . . . (770) 830-5830
323 Newman Street, Carrollton, GA 30117   Fax: (770) 214-3584

Catoosa County

Superior Court Clerk

Lookout Mountain Judicial Circuit
P.O. Box 1185, LaFayette, GA 30728
Tel: (706) 638-1695 Fax: (706) 638-1654
Internet: www.lmjc.net

Clerk of Court, Catoosa County **Fancy Moran** . . . . (706) 935-4231
7694 Nashville Street, Ringgold, GA 30736

Charlton County

Superior Court Clerk

Waycross Judicial Circuit
101 South Peterson Avenue, Douglas, GA 31533
Tel: (912) 384-0587

Clerk of Court, Charlton County **Wendy Whitaker** . . . . . . (912) 496-2354
100 North Third Street, Folkston, GA 31537   Fax: (912) 496-3882

Chatham County

Superior Court Clerk

Eastern Judicial Circuit
133 Montgomery Street, Savannah, GA 31401
Tel: (912) 652-7200 Fax: (912) 652-7380
Internet: www.chathamcounty.org/superiorcourt.html

Clerk of Court, Chatham County **Daniel W. Massey** . . . . . (912) 652-7197

Chattahoochee County

Superior Court Clerk

Chattahoochee Judicial Circuit
100 10th Street, Columbus, GA 31901

Clerk of Court, Chattahoochee County **Laura Marion** . . . . (706) 989-3424
379 Broad Street, Cusseta, GA 31805   Fax: (706) 989-1508

Chattooga County

Superior Court Clerk

Lookout Mountain Judicial Circuit
P.O. Box 1185, LaFayette, GA 30728
Tel: (706) 638-1695 Fax: (706) 638-1654
Internet: www.lmjc.net

Clerk of Court, Chattooga County
Sam L. "Laan" Cordle, Jr. . . . . (706) 857-0706
10035 Commerce Street, Summerville, GA 30747   Fax: (706) 857-0686

Cherokee County

Superior Court Clerk

Blue Ridge Judicial Circuit
90 North Street, Canton, GA 30114

Clerk of Court, Cherokee County **Patty Baker** . . . . (678) 493-6511
E-mail: pbaker@cherokeega.com

Clarke County

Superior Court Clerk

Western Judicial Circuit
P.O. Box 8064, Athens, GA 30603

Clerk of Court, Clarke County **Beverly Logan** . . . . (706) 613-3190
325 East Washington Street, Room 450,   Fax: (706) 613-3189
Athens, GA 30601
E-mail: beverly.logan@gsccca.org

(continued on next page)

Clay County

Superior Court Clerk

Pataula Judicial Circuit
235 East Lee Street, Dawson, GA 39842
Tel: (912) 995-4994

Clerk of Court, Clay County **Deanna K. Bertrand** . . . .(229) 768-2631
  210 Washington Street, Fort Gaines, GA 39851   Fax: (229) 768-3047
  P.O. Box 550, Fort Gaines, GA 39851
  E-mail: superiorcourtclerk@claycountyga.org

Clayton County

Superior Court Clerk

Clayton Judicial Circuit
9151 Tara Boulevard, Jonesboro, GA 30236
Tel: (770) 477-3415
Internet: www.co.clayton.ga.us/superior_court/index.htm

Clerk of Court, Clayton County **Jacquline D. Willis** . . . . . (770) 477-4565
  E-mail: magistratecourtclerk@co.clayton.ga.us

Clinch County

Superior Court Clerk

Alapaha Judicial Circuit
201 North Davis Street, Nashville, GA 31639

Clerk of Court, Clinch County **Mary Ruth Handley** . . . . . (912) 487-5854
  25 Court Square, Suite C, Homerville, GA 31634   Fax: (912) 487-3083

Cobb County

Superior Court Clerk

Cobb Judicial Circuit
32 Waddell Street, Marietta, GA 30090

Clerk of Court, Cobb County **Jay C. Stephenson** . . . .(770) 528-1300
  32 Waddell Street, Marietta, GA 30090   Fax: (770) 528-1382

Coffee County

Superior Court Clerk

Waycross Judicial Circuit
101 South Peterson Avenue, Douglas, GA 31533
Tel: (912) 384-0587

Clerk of Court, Coffee County **Angela Spell-Hutto** . . . . . .(912) 384-2865
  101 South Peterson Avenue, Suite 218B,   Fax: (912) 393-3252
  Douglas, GA 31533

Colquitt County

Superior Court Clerk

Southern Judicial Circuit
P.O. Box 2227, Moultrie, GA 31776
Tel: (229) 616-7474 Fax: (229) 616-7447
Internet: www.southernjudicialcircuit.com

Clerk of Court, Colquitt County **Lynn G. Purvis** . . . . (229) 616-7420
  Nine South Main Street, Room 214,   Fax: (229) 616-7029
  Moultrie, GA 31768

Columbia County

Superior Court Clerk

Augusta Judicial Circuit
735 James Brown Boulevard, Augusta, GA 30901

Clerk of Court, Columbia County **Cindy Mason** . . . . (706) 312-7139
  640 Ronald Reagan Drive,   Fax: (706) 312-7152
  Evans, GA 30809
  E-mail: cindy.mason@gsccca.org

Cook County

Superior Court Clerk

Alapaha Judicial Circuit
201 North Davis Street, Nashville, GA 31639

Clerk of Court, Cook County **April M. Garrett** . . . . (229) 896-7717
  212 North Hutchinson Avenue,   Fax: (229) 896-7589
  Adel, GA 31620

Coweta County

Superior Court Clerk

Coweta Judicial Circuit
72 Greenville Street, Newnan, GA 30263

Clerk of Court, Coweta County **Cindy G. Brown** . . . .(770) 254-2690
  72 Greenville Street, Newnan, GA 30263   Fax: (770) 716-4868

Crawford County

Superior Court Clerk

Macon Judicial Circuit
601 Mulberry Street, Macon, GA 31202

Clerk of Court, Crawford County **Ryan Johnson** . . . .(478) 836-3328
  P.O. Box 1037, Roberta, GA 31078   Fax: (478) 836-9170

Crisp County

Superior Court Clerk

Cordele Judicial Circuit
510 North 7th Street, Cordele, GA 31010
Tel: (229) 271-4722 Fax: (229) 271-4714

Clerk of Court, Crisp County **Jean H. Rogers** . . . .(229) 271-4726
  P.O. Box 747, Cordele, GA 31010   Fax: (229) 271-4737

Dade County

Superior Court Clerk

Lookout Mountain Judicial Circuit
P.O. Box 1185, LaFayette, GA 30728
Tel: (706) 638-1695 Fax: (706) 638-1654
Internet: www.lmjc.net

Clerk of Court, Dade County **Kathy D. Page** . . . .(706) 657-4778
  255 West Crabtree Street, Suite 103,   Fax: (706) 657-8284
  Trenton, GA 30752
  P.O. Box 417, Trenton, GA 30752

Dawson County

Superior Court Clerk

Northeastern Judicial Circuit
P.O. Box 1435, Gainesville, GA 30503

Clerk of Court, Dawson County **Justin Power** . . . . (706) 344-3510
  25 Tucker Avenue, Suite 106,   Fax: (706) 344-3511
  Dawsonville, GA 30534

Decatur County

Superior Court Clerk

South Georgia Judicial Circuit
Decatur County Courthouse, 112 West Water Street, Mezzanine Level,
Bainbridge, GA 39817
Tel: (229) 246-1111
Internet: www.southgeorgiajudicialcircuit.com

Clerk of Court, Decatur County **Cecilia Willis** . . . . (229) 248-3025
  Decatur County Courthouse, 112 West Water Street,   Fax: (229) 248-3029
  Bainbridge, GA 39817
  P.O. Box 336, Bainbridge, GA 39818-0336

DeKalb County

Superior Court Clerk

Stone Mountain Judicial Circuit
410 DeKalb County Courthouse, Decatur, GA 30030
Tel: (404) 371-4901 Fax: (404) 371-2002
Internet: www.co.dekalb.ga.us/superior/index.htm

Clerk of Court, DeKalb County **Debra Deberry** . . . . (404) 371-2836
                                      Fax: (404) 371-2635

Dodge County

Superior Court Clerk

Oconee Judicial Circuit
P.O. Box 4248, Eastman, GA 31023

Clerk of Court, Dodge County **Rhett Walker** . . . . (478) 374-2871
  5401 Anson Avenue, Eastman, GA 31023   Fax: (478) 374-3035
  E-mail: rhett.walker@gsccca.org

Dooly County

Superior Court Clerk

Cordele Judicial Circuit
510 North 7th Street, Cordele, GA 31010
Tel: (229) 271-4722 Fax: (229) 271-4714

Clerk of Court, Dooly County **Betty Colter** . . . . (229) 268-4234
  P.O. Box, Vienna, GA 31092   Fax: (229) 268-1427

Dougherty County

Superior Court Clerk

Dougherty Judicial Circuit
225 Pine Avenue, Suite 123, Albany, GA 31701
P.O. Box 1827, Albany, GA 31702

Clerk of Court, Dougherty County **Evonne Mull** . . . . (229) 431-2198
  225 Pine Avenue, Room 126,
  Albany, GA 31701

Douglas County

Superior Court Clerk

Douglas Judicial Circuit
8700 Hospital Drive, Douglasville, GA 30134

Clerk of Court, Douglas County **Tammy Howard** . . . . (770) 920-7252
  8700 Hospital Drive, Douglasville, GA 30134   Fax: (770) 920-7561
  E-mail: clerksuperiorcourt@co.douglas.ga.us

Early County

Superior Court Clerk

Pataula Judicial Circuit
235 East Lee Street, Dawson, GA 39842
Tel: (912) 995-4994

Clerk of Court, Early County **Emily A. Wilbourn** . . . . (229) 723-3033
  P.O. Box 849, Blakely, GA 31723   Fax: (229) 723-4411

Echols County

Superior Court Clerk

Southern Judicial Circuit
P.O. Box 2227, Moultrie, GA 31776
Tel: (229) 616-7474 Fax: (229) 616-7447
Internet: www.southernjudicialcircuit.com

Clerk of Court, Echols County **Paula Goss** . . . . (229) 559-5642
  P.O. Box 213, Statenville, GA 31648   Fax: (229) 559-5792
  E-mail: paula.goss@echols.gsccca.org

Effingham County

Superior Court Clerk

Ogeechee Judicial Circuit
P.O. Box 326, Statesboro, GA 30458
Tel: (912) 764-6095 Fax: (912) 489-3148
Internet: www.ogeecheecircuit.org

Clerk of Court, Effingham County
  Elizabeth Z. Hursey . . . . (912) 754-2146
  901 North Pine Street, Springfield, GA 31329   Fax: (912) 754-6023
  E-mail: ehursey@effinghamcounty.org

Elbert County

Superior Court Clerk

Northern Judicial Circuit
P.O. Box 645, Elberton, GA 30635

Clerk of Court, Elbert County **Pat V. Anderson** . . . . (706) 283-2005
  12 South Oliver Street, Elberton, GA 30635   Fax: (706) 213-7286
  E-mail: pat.anderson@gsccca.org

Emanuel County

Superior Court Clerk

Middle Judicial Circuit
107 South Main Street, Swainsboro, GA 30401

Clerk of Court, Emanuel County **Kristin C. Hall** . . . . (478) 237-8911
  125 South Main Street, Swainsboro, GA 30401   Fax: (478) 237-1220
  P.O. Box 627, Swainsboro, GA 30401

(continued on next page)

Evans County

Superior Court Clerk

Atlantic Judicial Circuit
P.O. Box 713, Hinesville, GA 31310
Tel: (912) 368-2250

Clerk of Court, Evans County **Kathy P. Hendrix** .... (912) 739-3868
    100 Courthouse Square, Claxton, GA 30417   Fax: (912) 739-2504

Fannin County

Superior Court Clerk

Appalachian Judicial Circuit
50 North Main Street, Jasper, GA 30143

Clerk of Court, Fannin County **Dana Chastain** .... (706) 632-2039
    P.O. Box 1300, Blue Ridge, GA 30513

Fayette County

Superior Court Clerk

Griffin Judicial Circuit
One Center Drive, Fayetteville, GA 30214

Clerk of Court, Fayette County **Sheila Studdard** .... (770) 716-4290
    One Center Drive, Fayetteville, GA 30214   Fax: (770) 716-4868
    E-mail: sstuddard@fayettecountyga.gov

Floyd County

Superior Court Clerk

Rome Judicial Circuit
Three Government Plaza, Suite 101, Rome, GA 30161
Tel: (706) 291-5192

Clerk of Court, Floyd County **Barbara Penson** .... (706) 291-5190
    Three Government Plaza, Suite 101,   Fax: (706) 235-0035
    Rome, GA 30161

Forsyth County

Superior Court Clerk

Bell-Forsyth Judicial Circuit
100 Courthouse Square, Cumming, GA 30040
Tel: (770) 205-4660 Fax: (770) 205-4661

Clerk of Court, Forsyth County **Greg G. Allen** .... (770) 781-2120
    E-mail: ggallen@forsythco.com   Fax: (770) 886-2858

Franklin County

Superior Court Clerk

Northern Judicial Circuit
P.O. Box 645, Elberton, GA 30635

Clerk of Court, Franklin County
    Melissa Blakely Holbrook .... (706) 384-2514
    9592 Lavonia Road, Carnesville, GA 30521   Fax: (706) 384-4384
    P.O. Box 70, Carnesville, GA 30521

Fulton County

Superior Court Clerk

Atlanta Judicial Circuit
Superior Court of Fulton County, 136 Pryor Street, Atlanta, GA 30303

Clerk of Court, Fulton County
    Cathelene "Tina" Robinson .... (404) 613-5313
    Superior Court of Fulton County,   Fax: (404) 332-0391
    136 Pryor Street, Suite C-640,
    Atlanta, GA 30303

Gilmer County

Superior Court Clerk

Appalachian Judicial Circuit
50 North Main Street, Jasper, GA 30143

Clerk of Court, Gilmer County **Glenda Sue Johnson** ... (706) 635-4462
    One Broad Street, Suite 102,
    Ellijay, GA 30540

Glascock County

Superior Court Clerk

Toombs Judicial Circuit
P.O. Box 480, Thomson, GA 30824

Clerk of Court, Glascock County **Carla Stevens** .... (706) 598-2084
    62 East Main Street, Gibson, GA 30810   Fax: (706) 598-2577
    E-mail: carla.stevens@gsccca.org

Glynn County

Superior Court Clerk

Brunswick Judicial Circuit
701 H Street, Brunswick, GA 31520
Tel: (912) 554-7364

Clerk of Court, Glynn County **Lola B. Jamsky** .... (912) 554-7272
    701 H Street, Brunswick, GA 31520   Fax: (912) 267-5625

Gordon County

Superior Court Clerk

Cherokee Judicial Circuit
135 West Cherokee Avenue, Cartersville, GA 30120

Clerk of Court, Gordon County **Grant Walraven** .... (706) 629-9533
    100 South Wall Street, Calhoun, GA 30701   Fax: (706) 629-2139
    E-mail: gwalraven@gordoncounty.org

Grady County

Superior Court Clerk

South Georgia Judicial Circuit
Decatur County Courthouse, 112 West Water Street, Mezzanine Level,
Bainbridge, GA 39817
Tel: (229) 246-1111
Internet: www.southgeorgiajudicialcircuit.com

Clerk of Court, Grady County **Debbie Kines** .... (229) 377-2912
    Grady County Courthouse, 250 North Broad Street,   Fax: (229) 377-7078
    Box 8, Cairo, GA 39828

Greene County

Superior Court Clerk

Ocmulgee Judicial Circuit
P.O. Box 728, Madison, GA 30650

Clerk of Court, Greene County **Deborah D. Jackson** .... (706) 453-3340
113 North Main Street, Suite 109,   Fax: (706) 453-9179
Greensboro, GA 30642

Gwinnett County

Superior Court Clerk

Gwinnett Judicial Circuit
75 Langley Drive, Lawrenceville, GA 30046
Tel: (770) 822-8580   Fax: (770) 822-8566
Internet: www.gwinnettcourts.com

Clerk of Court, Gwinnett County
   Richard T. Alexander, Jr. .... (770) 822-8100

Habersham County

Superior Court Clerk

Mountain Judicial Circuit
P.O. Box 485, Clarkesville, GA 30523

Clerk of Court, Habersham County **David C. Wall** .... (706) 754-2923
555 Monroe Street, First Floor,   Fax: (706) 839-6351
Clarkesville, GA 30523
E-mail: clerkofcourt@habershamga.com

Hall County

Superior Court Clerk

Northeastern Judicial Circuit
P.O. Box 1435, Gainesville, GA 30503

Clerk of Court, Hall County **Charles Baker** .... (770) 531-7025
225 Green Street, SE, Gainesville, GA 30501   Fax: (770) 531-7070
E-mail: cbaker@hallcounty.org

Hancock County

Superior Court Clerk

Ocmulgee Judicial Circuit
P.O. Box 728, Madison, GA 30650

Clerk of Court, Hancock County **LeShauna Jackson** .... (706) 444-6644
P.O. Box 451, Sparta, GA 31087   Fax: (706) 444-5685

Haralson County

Superior Court Clerk

Tallapoosa Judicial Circuit
100 Prior Street, Cedartown, GA 30125
Tel: (770) 749-6790

Clerk of Court, Haralson County **Becky S. Robinson** .... (770) 646-2005
P.O. Box 849, Buchanan, GA 30113   Fax: (770) 646-8827

Harris County

Superior Court Clerk

Chattahoochee Judicial Circuit
100 10th Street, Columbus, GA 31901

Clerk of Court, Harris County **Stacy K. Haralson** .... (706) 628-4944
102 North College Street, Hamilton, GA 31811   Fax: (706) 628-7039

Hart County

Superior Court Clerk

Northern Judicial Circuit
P.O. Box 645, Elberton, GA 30635

Clerk of Court, Hart County **Frankie Gray** .... (706) 376-7189
185 West Franklin Street, Room 1,   Fax: (706) 376-1277
Hartwell, GA 30643
E-mail: frankie.gray@gsccca.org

Heard County

Superior Court Clerk

Coweta Judicial Circuit
72 Greenville Street, Newnan, GA 30263

Clerk of Court, Heard County **Bryan Owensby** .... (706) 675-3301
215 East Court Street, Franklin, GA 30217   Fax: (706) 675-6138

Henry County

Superior Court Clerk

Flint Judicial Circuit
One Courthouse Square, McDonough, GA 30253
Tel: (770) 288-8022
Internet: www.co.henry.ga.us/SuperiorCourt/

Clerk of Court, Henry County **Barbara A. Harrison** ..... (770) 288-8022
   E-mail: bharrison@co.henry.ga.us   Fax: (770) 898-7573

Houston County

Superior Court Clerk

Houston Judicial Circuit
201 North Perry Parkway, Perry, GA 31069

Clerk of Court, Houston County **Carolyn V. Sullivan** .... (478) 218-4720
201 North Perry Parkway,   Fax: (478) 218-4735
Perry, GA 31069

Irwin County

Superior Court Clerk

Tifton Judicial Circuit
P.O. Box 1369, Tifton, GA 31793
Tel: (229) 386-7904   Fax: (229) 386-7977
Internet: www.tiftoncircuit.com

Clerk of Court, Irwin County **Nancy Ross** .... (229) 468-5356
Ocilla, GA 31774   Fax: (229) 468-9753

(continued on next page)

Jackson County

Superior Court Clerk

Piedmont Judicial Circuit
652 Barrow Park Drive, Winder, GA 30680
Internet: www.10thjudicialdistrictga.com/Piedmont.html

Clerk of Court, Jackson County **Camie W. Thomas** . . . . . (706) 387-6246
  5000 Jackson Parkway, Suite 150,   Fax: (706) 387-6273
  Jefferson, GA 30549
  E-mail: cthomas@jacksoncountygov.com

Jasper County

Superior Court Clerk

Ocmulgee Judicial Circuit
P.O. Box 728, Madison, GA 30650

Clerk of Court, Jasper County **Dan Jordan** . . . .(706) 468-4901
  126 West Green Street, Suite 110,   Fax: (706) 468-4946
  Monticello, GA 31064

Jeff Davis County

Superior Court Clerk

Brunswick Judicial Circuit
701 H Street, Brunswick, GA 31520
Tel: (912) 554-7364

Clerk of Court, Jeff Davis County **Myra Murphy** . . . .(912) 375-6615
  14 Jeff Davis Street, Hazelhurst, GA 31539   Fax: (912) 375-6637

Jefferson County

Superior Court Clerk

Middle Judicial Circuit
107 South Main Street, Swainsboro, GA 30401

Clerk of Court, Jefferson County **Anne Durden** . . . .(478) 625-7922
  202 East Broad Street, Gainesville, GA 30434   Fax: (478) 625-4037
  P.O. Box 151, Gainesville, GA 30434

Jenkins County

Superior Court Clerk

Ogeechee Judicial Circuit
P.O. Box 326, Statesboro, GA 30458
Tel: (912) 764-6095   Fax: (912) 489-3148
Internet: www.ogeecheecircuit.org

Clerk of Court, Jenkins County **Elizabeth T. Landing** . . . .(478) 982-4683
  P.O. Box 659, Millen, GA 30442   Fax: (478) 982-1274

Johnson County

Superior Court Clerk

Dublin Judicial Circuit
P.O. Box 2100, Dublin, GA 31040

Clerk of Court, Johnson County **Patricia Glover** . . . . (478) 864-3484
  P.O. Box 321, Wrightsville, GA 31096   Fax: (478) 864-1343

Jones County

Superior Court Clerk

Ocmulgee Judicial Circuit
P.O. Box 728, Madison, GA 30650

Clerk of Court, Jones County **Bart W. Jackson** . . . .(478) 986-6671
  110 South Jefferson Street,   Fax: (478) 986-2030
  Gray, GA 31032

Lamar County

Superior Court Clerk

Towaliga Judicial Circuit
One Courthouse Square, Forsyth, GA 31029
Tel: (478) 994-7658

Clerk of Court, Lamar County
  Robert "Frank" Abbott . . . . (770) 358-5145
  326 Thomaston Street, Box 7,   Fax: (770) 358-5814
  Barnesville, GA 30204

Lanier County

Superior Court Clerk

Alapaha Judicial Circuit
201 North Davis Street, Nashville, GA 31639

Clerk of Court, Lanier County **Deborah Clark** . . . .(229) 482-3594
  56 West Main Street, Suite 5,   Fax: (229) 482-8333
  Lakeland, GA 31635

Laurens County

Superior Court Clerk

Dublin Judicial Circuit
P.O. Box 2100, Dublin, GA 31040

Clerk of Court, Laurens County **Jackie Dalton** . . . .(478) 272-3210
  101 North Jefferson Street,   Fax: (478) 275-2595
  Dublin, GA 31040
  P.O. Box 2028, Dublin, GA 31040

Lee County

Superior Court Clerk

Southwestern Judicial Circuit
P.O. Box 784, Americus, GA 31709
Internet: www.southwesterncircuit.com

Clerk of Court, Lee County **Sara Clark** . . . .(229) 759-6018
  100 Leslie Highway, Leesburg, GA 31763   Fax: (229) 438-6049
  E-mail: sara.clark@gsccca.org

Liberty County

Superior Court Clerk

Atlantic Judicial Circuit
P.O. Box 713, Hinesville, GA 31310
Tel: (912) 368-2250

Clerk of Court, Liberty County **F. Barry Wilkes** . . . .(912) 876-3625
  112 North Main Street, Hinesville, GA 31313   Fax: (912) 369-5463
  E-mail: clerk@libertycountyga.com

Lincoln County

Superior Court Clerk

Toombs Judicial Circuit
P.O. Box 480, Thomson, GA 30824

Clerk of Court, Lincoln County
Amanda "Mandy" Doss .... (706) 359-5505
210 Humphrey Street, Lincolnton, GA 30817   Fax: (706) 359-5027
E-mail: adoss@lincolncountyga.com

Long County

Superior Court Clerk

Atlantic Judicial Circuit
P.O. Box 713, Hinesville, GA 31310
Tel: (912) 368-2250

Clerk of Court, Long County **Sherry Long** .... (912) 545-2123
10 McDonald Street, Ludowici, GA 31316   Fax: (912) 545-2020

Lowndes County

Superior Court Clerk

Southern Judicial Circuit
P.O. Box 2227, Moultrie, GA 31776
Tel: (229) 616-7474 Fax: (229) 616-7447
Internet: www.southernjudicialcircuit.com

Clerk of Court, Lowndes County
Beth Copeland Greene .... (229) 333-5126
108 East Central Avenue, Valdosta, GA 31601   Fax: (229) 333-7637

Lumpkin County

Superior Court Clerk

Enotah Judicial Circuit
65 Courthouse Street, Blairsville, GA 30512

Clerk of Court, Lumpkin County
Rita Harkins ....(706) 864-3736 ext. 300
99 Courthouse Hill, Suite D,   Fax: (706) 864-5298
Dahlonega, GA 30533
E-mail: rita.harkins@gsccca.org

Macon County

Superior Court Clerk

Southwestern Judicial Circuit
P.O. Box 784, Americus, GA 31709
Internet: www.southwesterncircuit.com

Clerk of Court, Macon County **Juanita M. Laidler** ...... (478) 472-7661
121 South Sumter Street, Oglethorpe, GA 31068   Fax: (478) 472-4775
P.O. Box 337, Oglethorpe, GA 31068
E-mail: juanita.laidler@gsccca.org

Madison County

Superior Court Clerk

Northern Judicial Circuit
P.O. Box 645, Elberton, GA 30635

Clerk of Court, Madison County
Michelle H. Strickland .... (706) 795-6310
91 Albany Avenue, Danielsville, GA 30633   Fax: (706) 795-2209
P.O. Box 247, Danielsville, GA 30633
E-mail: michelle.strickland@gsccca.org

Marion County

Superior Court Clerk

Chattahoochee Judicial Circuit
100 10th Street, Columbus, GA 31901

Clerk of Court, Marion County **Joy Smith** .... (229) 649-7321
100 North Broad Street, Buena Vista, GA 31803   Fax: (229) 649-7931

McDuffie County

Superior Court Clerk

Toombs Judicial Circuit
P.O. Box 480, Thomson, GA 30824

Clerk of Court, McDuffie County
Connie H. Cheatham .... (706) 595-2134
337 Main Street, Thomson, GA 30824   Fax: (706) 595-9150
E-mail: connie.cheatham@gsccca.org

McIntosh County

Superior Court Clerk

Atlantic Judicial Circuit
P.O. Box 713, Hinesville, GA 31310
Tel: (912) 368-2250

Clerk of Court, McIntosh County
Saundra "Bootie" Goodrich .... (912) 437-6641
312 Northway, Darien, GA 31305   Fax: (912) 437-6673

Meriwether County

Superior Court Clerk

Coweta Judicial Circuit
72 Greenville Street, Newnan, GA 30263

Clerk of Court, Meriwether County
Kyemeshia T. "Kye" Gibson .... (706) 672-4416
P.O. Box 160, Greenville, GA 30222   Fax: (706) 672-9465

Miller County

Superior Court Clerk

Pataula Judicial Circuit
235 East Lee Street, Dawson, GA 39842
Tel: (912) 995-4994

Clerk of Court, Miller County **Gail Johnson** .... (229) 758-4102
155 South First Street, Room 103,   Fax: (229) 758-6585
Colquitt, GA 39837

(continued on next page)

Mitchell County

Superior Court Clerk

South Georgia Judicial Circuit
Decatur County Courthouse, 112 West Water Street, Mezzanine Level,
Bainbridge, GA 39817
Tel: (229) 246-1111
Internet: www.southgeorgiajudicialcircuit.com

Clerk of Court, Mitchell County **Adayne B. Broome** .... (229) 336-2022
11 West Broad Street, Camilla, GA 31730-0427   Fax: (229) 336-9866
P.O. Box 427, Camilla, GA 31730-0427

Monroe County

Superior Court Clerk

Towaliga Judicial Circuit
One Courthouse Square, Forsyth, GA 31029
Tel: (478) 994-7658

Clerk of Court, Monroe County **Lynn W. Ham** .... (478) 994-7022
15 West Main Street, Forsyth, GA 31029   Fax: (478) 994-7053

Montgomery County

Superior Court Clerk

Oconee Judicial Circuit
P.O. Box 4248, Eastman, GA 31023

Clerk of Court, Montgomery County **Keith Hamilton** .... (912) 583-4401
400 South Railroad Avenue,   Fax: (912) 583-4343
Mount Vernon, GA 30445
P.O. Box 331, Mount Vernon, GA 30445

Morgan County

Superior Court Clerk

Ocmulgee Judicial Circuit
P.O. Box 728, Madison, GA 30650

Clerk of Court, Morgan County **Jody M. Moss** .... (706) 342-3605
384 Hancock Street, Madison, GA 30650   Fax: (706) 343-6462
E-mail: jmoss@morganga.org

Murray County

Superior Court Clerk

Conasauga Judicial Circuit
205 North Selvidge Street, Dalton, GA 30720

Clerk of Court, Murray County **Connie Reed** .... (706) 695-2932
121 North Third Avenue, Chatsworth, GA 30705   Fax: (706) 517-9672
P.O. Box 1000, Chatsworth, GA 30705

Muscogee County

Superior Court Clerk

Chattahoochee Judicial Circuit
100 10th Street, Columbus, GA 31901

Clerk of Court, Muscogee County **Linda Pierce** .... (706) 653-4353
100 10th Street, 2nd Floor,   Fax: (706) 653-4359
Columbus, GA 31901

Newton County

Superior Court Clerk

Alcovy Judicial Circuit
303 South Hammond Drive, Monroe, GA 30655

Clerk of Court, Newton County **Linda Hays** ....(770) 784-2035
1132 Usher Street, Room 338,   Fax: (770) 788-3717
Covington, GA 30014
E-mail: lhays@co.newton.ga.us

Oconee County

Superior Court Clerk

Western Judicial Circuit
P.O. Box 8064, Athens, GA 30603

Clerk of Court, Oconee County
Angela Elder-Johnson .... (706) 769-3940
23 North Main Street, Watkinsville, GA 30677   Fax: (706) 769-3948

Oglethorpe County

Superior Court Clerk

Northern Judicial Circuit
P.O. Box 645, Elberton, GA 30635

Clerk of Court, Oglethorpe County
Kelli Paradise Smith ....(706) 743-5731
111 West Main Street, Lexington, GA 30648   Fax: (706) 743-5335
E-mail: kelli.smith@gsccca.org

Paulding County

Superior Court Clerk

Paulding Judicial Circuit
280 Constitution Boulevard, Room 3047, Dallas, GA 30132
Tel: (678) 363-2900 Fax: (678) 363-2902
Internet: www.paulding.gov/index.aspx?nid=205

Clerk of Court, Paulding County **Treva W. Shelton** ......(770) 443-7527
E-mail: tshelton@paulding.gov   Fax: (770) 505-3863

Peach County

Superior Court Clerk

Macon Judicial Circuit
601 Mulberry Street, Macon, GA 31202

Clerk of Court, Peach County **Joe Wilder** ....(478) 825-5331
Fort Valley, GA 31030   Fax: (478) 825-8662
E-mail: joe.wilder@gsccca.org

Pickens County

Superior Court Clerk

Appalachian Judicial Circuit
50 North Main Street, Jasper, GA 30143

Clerk of Court, Pickens County **Gail Brown** ....(706) 253-8763
52 North Main Street, Jasper, GA 30143

Pierce County

Superior Court Clerk

Waycross Judicial Circuit
101 South Peterson Avenue, Douglas, GA 31533
Tel: (912) 384-0587

Clerk of Court, Pierce County **Thomas W. Sauls** . . . . (912) 449-2020
3550 U.S. Highway 84, Blackshear, GA 31516   Fax: (912) 449-2106

Pike County

Superior Court Clerk

Griffin Judicial Circuit
One Center Drive, Fayetteville, GA 30214

Clerk of Court, Pike County **Carolyn Williams** . . . . (770) 567-2000
100 Barnesville Street, Zebulon, GA 30295   Fax: (770) 567-2017
E-mail: carolyn.williams@pike.gsccca.org

Polk County

Superior Court Clerk

Tallapoosa Judicial Circuit
100 Prior Street, Cedartown, GA 30125
Tel: (770) 749-6790

Clerk of Court, Polk County **Shelia Wells** . . . . (770) 749-2114
P.O. Box 948, Cedartown, GA 30125   Fax: (770) 749-2148

Pulaski County

Superior Court Clerk

Oconee Judicial Circuit
P.O. Box 4248, Eastman, GA 31023

Clerk of Court, Pulaski County **Peggy G. Fauscett** . . . . . . (478) 783-1911
350 Commerce Street, Hawkinsville, GA 31036   Fax: (478) 892-3308
E-mail: peggy.fauscett@pulaskico.com

Putnam County

Superior Court Clerk

Ocmulgee Judicial Circuit
P.O. Box 728, Madison, GA 30650

Clerk of Court, Putnam County **Sheila H. Perry** . . . . (706) 485-4501
100 South Jefferson Avenue, Suite 236,   Fax: (706) 485-2875
Eatonton, GA 31024
E-mail: sheila.perry@gsccca.org

Quitman County

Superior Court Clerk

Pataula Judicial Circuit
235 East Lee Street, Dawson, GA 39842
Tel: (912) 995-4994

Clerk of Court, Quitman County
   Rebecca S. "Becky" Fendley . . . . (229) 334-2578
111 Main Street, Suite 2, Georgetown, GA 39854   Fax: (229) 334-3991

Rabun County

Superior Court Clerk

Mountain Judicial Circuit
P.O. Box 485, Clarkesville, GA 30523

Clerk of Court, Rabun County **Holly Henry Perry** . . . . (706) 782-3615
25 Courthouse Square, Suite 105,   Fax: (706) 782-1391
Clayton, GA 30525
E-mail: hollyehenryperry@yahoo.com

Randolph County

Superior Court Clerk

Pataula Judicial Circuit
235 East Lee Street, Dawson, GA 39842
Tel: (912) 995-4994

Clerk of Court, Randolph County **Kay Arnold** . . . . (229) 732-2216
208 Court Street, Cuthbert, GA 39840   Fax: (229) 732-5881

Richmond County

Superior Court Clerk

Augusta Judicial Circuit
735 James Brown Boulevard, Augusta, GA 30901

Clerk of Court, Richmond County **Elaine C. Johnson** . . . (706) 821-1837
530 Greene Street, Room 503,   Fax: (706) 821-2448
Augusta, GA 30901
E-mail: ejohnson3@comcast.net

Rockdale County

Superior Court Clerk

Rockdale Judicial Circuit
922 Court Street, Conyers, GA 30012
Tel: (770) 278-7690

Clerk of Court, Rockdale County **Ruth A. Wilson** . . . . (770) 278-7900
P.O. Box 938, Conyers, GA 30012   Fax: (770) 929-4110

Schley County

Superior Court Clerk

Southwestern Judicial Circuit
P.O. Box 784, Americus, GA 31709
Internet: www.southwesterncircuit.com

Clerk of Court, Schley County **Kathy S. Royal** . . . . (229) 937-5581
14 South Broad Street, Ellaville, GA 31806   Fax: (229) 937-5588

Screven County

Superior Court Clerk

Ogeechee Judicial Circuit
P.O. Box 326, Statesboro, GA 30458
Tel: (912) 764-6095   Fax: (912) 489-3148
Internet: www.ogeecheecircuit.org

Clerk of Court, Screven County **Janis Reddick** . . . . (912) 564-2614
216 Mims Road, Sylvania, GA 30467   Fax: (912) 564-2622

(continued on next page)

Seminole County

Superior Court Clerk

Pataula Judicial Circuit
235 East Lee Street, Dawson, GA 39842
Tel: (912) 995-4994

Clerk of Court, Seminole County **Earlene Bramlett** . . . . . (229) 524-2525
  200 South Knox Avenue, Donalsonville, GA 39845   Fax: (229) 524-8883

Spalding County

Superior Court Clerk

Griffin Judicial Circuit
One Center Drive, Fayetteville, GA 30214

Clerk of Court, Spalding County **Marcia L. Norris** . . . . (770) 467-4745
  132 East Solomon Street, Griffin, GA 30223   Fax: (770) 467-4478
  P.O. Box 1046, Griffin, GA 30223

Stephens County

Superior Court Clerk

Mountain Judicial Circuit
P.O. Box 485, Clarkesville, GA 30523

Clerk of Court, Stephens County **Tim Quick** . . . . (706) 886-9496
  70 North Alexander Street, Suite 202,   Fax: (706) 886-5710
  Toccoa, GA 30577
  E-mail: tquick@stephenscountyga.com

Stewart County

Superior Court Clerk

Southwestern Judicial Circuit
P.O. Box 784, Americus, GA 31709
Internet: www.southwesterncircuit.com

Clerk of Court, Stewart County **Patti B. Smith** . . . . (229) 838-6220
  P.O. Box 910, Lumpkin, GA 31815   Fax: (229) 838-4505
  E-mail: patti.smith@gsccca.org

Sumter County

Superior Court Clerk

Southwestern Judicial Circuit
P.O. Box 784, Americus, GA 31709
Internet: www.southwesterncircuit.com

Clerk of Court, Sumter County **Nancy C. Smith** . . . . (229) 928-4537
  500 West Lamar Street, Suite 1,   Fax: (229) 928-4539
  Americus, GA 31709
  P.O. Box 333, Americus, GA 31709
  E-mail: nancy.smith@gsccca.org

Talbot County

Superior Court Clerk

Chattahoochee Judicial Circuit
100 10th Street, Columbus, GA 31901

Clerk of Court, Talbot County
  Penny Dillingham-Mahone . . . . (706) 665-3239
  26 South Washington Avenue,   Fax: (706) 665-8637
  Talbotton, GA 31827

Taliaferro County

Superior Court Clerk

Toombs Judicial Circuit
P.O. Box 480, Thomson, GA 30824

Clerk of Court, Taliaferro County **Sandra S. Greene** . . . . (706) 456-2123
  113 Monument Street, Crawfordville, GA 30631   Fax: (706) 456-2749
  E-mail: sandra.greene@gsccca.org

Tattnall County

Superior Court Clerk

Atlantic Judicial Circuit
P.O. Box 713, Hinesville, GA 31310
Tel: (912) 368-2250

Clerk of Court, Tattnall County **Debbie Crews** . . . . (912) 557-6716
  100 North Main Street, Reidsville, GA 30453   Fax: (912) 557-4861

Taylor County

Superior Court Clerk

Chattahoochee Judicial Circuit
100 10th Street, Columbus, GA 31901

Clerk of Court, Taylor County **Robert E. Taunton, Jr.** . . . . (478) 862-5594
  P.O. Box 248, Butler, GA 31006   Fax: (478) 862-5334

Telfair County

Superior Court Clerk

Oconee Judicial Circuit
P.O. Box 4248, Eastman, GA 31023

Clerk of Court, Telfair County **Belinda Thomas** . . . . (229) 868-6525
  19 East Oak Street, Suite C,   Fax: (229) 868-7956
  McRae, GA 31055

Terrell County

Superior Court Clerk

Pataula Judicial Circuit
235 East Lee Street, Dawson, GA 39842
Tel: (912) 995-4994

Clerk of Court, Terrell County **Janice Bryant** . . . . (229) 995-2631
  235 East Lee Street, Dawson, GA 39842   Fax: (229) 995-6453

Thomas County

Superior Court Clerk

Southern Judicial Circuit
P.O. Box 2227, Moultrie, GA 31776
Tel: (229) 616-7474 Fax: (229) 616-7447
Internet: www.southernjudicialcircuit.com

Clerk of Court, Thomas County
  David G. Hutchings, Jr. . . . . (229) 225-4108
  325 North Madison Street,   Fax: (229) 225-4110
  Thomasville, GA 31792
  P.O. Box 1995, Thomasville, GA 31799
  E-mail: david.hutchings@gsccca.org

Tift County

Superior Court Clerk

Tifton Judicial Circuit
P.O. Box 1369, Tifton, GA 31793
Tel: (229) 386-7904 Fax: (229) 386-7977
Internet: www.tiftoncircuit.com

Clerk of Court, Tift County **Gwen Pate** . . . . (229) 386-7816
   P.O. Box 354, Tifton, GA 31793   Fax: (229) 386-7813
   E-mail: gwen.pate@tiftcounty.org

Toombs County

Superior Court Clerk

Middle Judicial Circuit
107 South Main Street, Swainsboro, GA 30401

Clerk of Court, Toombs County **Chess Fountain** . . . .(912) 526-3501
   100 Courthouse Square, Lyons, GA 30436   Fax: (912) 912-1004

Towns County

Superior Court Clerk

Enotah Judicial Circuit
65 Courthouse Street, Blairsville, GA 30512

Clerk of Court, Towns County **Cecil Dye** . . . . (706) 896-2130
   48 River Street, Suite E, Hiawassee, GA 30546   Fax: (706) 896-1772

Treutlen County

Superior Court Clerk

Dublin Judicial Circuit
P.O. Box 2100, Dublin, GA 31040

Clerk of Court, Treutlen County **Connie Sumner** . . . . (912) 529-4215
   639 Second Street South, Suite 301,   Fax: (912) 529-6737
   Soperton, GA 30457

Troup County

Superior Court Clerk

Coweta Judicial Circuit
72 Greenville Street, Newnan, GA 30263

Clerk of Court, Troup County **Jackie Taylor** . . . .(706) 883-1740
   100 Ridley Avenue, LaGrange, GA 30241   Fax: (706) 883-1724
   P.O. Box 866, LaGrange, GA 30241
   E-mail: jackie.taylor@gsccca.org

Turner County

Superior Court Clerk

Tifton Judicial Circuit
P.O. Box 1369, Tifton, GA 31793
Tel: (229) 386-7904 Fax: (229) 386-7977
Internet: www.tiftoncircuit.com

Clerk of Court, Turner County **Mary Lee Green** . . . . (229) 567-2011
   219 East College Avenue, Room 3,   Fax: (229) 567-0450
   Ashburn, GA 31714

Twiggs County

Superior Court Clerk

Dublin Judicial Circuit
P.O. Box 2100, Dublin, GA 31040

Clerk of Court, Twiggs County **Patti H. Grimsley** . . . .(478) 945-3350
   P.O. Box 234, Jefferson, GA 31044   Fax: (478) 945-6751
   425 Railroad Street, Jefferson, GA 31044

Union County

Superior Court Clerk

Enotah Judicial Circuit
65 Courthouse Street, Blairsville, GA 30512

Clerk of Court, Union County **Judy Odom** . . . . (706) 439-6022
   65 Courthouse Street, Suite 5,   Fax: (706) 439-6026
   Blairsville, GA 30512

Upson County

Superior Court Clerk

Griffin Judicial Circuit
One Center Drive, Fayetteville, GA 30214

Clerk of Court, Upson County **Teresa Harper** . . . . (706) 647-7835
   Courthouse Annex Bldg, 116 Main Street,   Fax: (706) 647-8999
   Thomaston, GA 30286
   P.O. Box 469, Thomaston, GA 30286
   E-mail: tharper@upsoncountyga.org

Walker County

Superior Court Clerk

Lookout Mountain Judicial Circuit
P.O. Box 1185, LaFayette, GA 30728
Tel: (706) 638-1695 Fax: (706) 638-1654
Internet: www.lmjc.net

Clerk of Court, Walker County **Carter Brown** . . . . (706) 638-1742
   P.O. Box 1125, LaFayette, GA 30728   Fax: (706) 638-2869
   E-mail: carter.brown@lmjc.net

Walton County

Superior Court Clerk

Alcovy Judicial Circuit
303 South Hammond Drive, Monroe, GA 30655

Clerk of Court, Walton County **Kathy K. Trost** . . . .(770) 266-1774
   303 South Hammond Drive, Suite 335,   Fax: (770) 267-1304
   Monroe, GA 30655
   E-mail: kathy.trost@gsccca.org

Ware County

Superior Court Clerk

Waycross Judicial Circuit
101 South Peterson Avenue, Douglas, GA 31533
Tel: (912) 384-0587

Clerk of Court, Ware County **Melba Fiveash** . . . .(912) 287-4340
   800 Church Street, Suite 124,   Fax: (912) 287-2498
   Waycross, GA 31501
   E-mail: mfiveash@warecounty.com

(continued on next page)

Georgia Court Clerks and Courthouses *continued*

Warren County

Superior Court Clerk

Toombs Judicial Circuit
P.O. Box 480, Thomson, GA 30824

Clerk of Court, Warren County **Shirley T. Cheeley** . . . . . . (706) 465-2262
   100 Main Street, Warrenton, GA 30828   Fax: (706) 465-0232
   E-mail: shirley.cheeley@gsccca.org

Washington County

Superior Court Clerk

Middle Judicial Circuit
107 South Main Street, Swainsboro, GA 30401

Clerk of Court, Washington County **Joy H. Conner** . . . . . . (478) 552-3186
   P.O. Box 231, Sandersville, GA 31082   Fax: (478) 553-9969

Wayne County

Superior Court Clerk

Brunswick Judicial Circuit
701 H Street, Brunswick, GA 31520
Tel: (912) 554-7364

Clerk of Court, Wayne County **Elouise Ogden** . . . . (912) 427-5930
   174 North Brunswick Street,   Fax: (912) 427-5939
   Jesup, GA 31546
   P.O. Box 920, Jesup, GA 31598
   E-mail: elouise.ogden@wayne.gsccca.org

Webster County

Superior Court Clerk

Southwestern Judicial Circuit
P.O. Box 784, Americus, GA 31709
Internet: www.southwesterncircuit.com

Clerk of Court, Webster County **Tina Blankenship** . . . . . . (229) 828-3525
   6330 Hamilton Street, Room 102,   Fax: (229) 828-6961
   Preston, GA 31824
   P.O. Box 117, Preston, GA 31824
   E-mail: tina.blankenship@gsccca.org

Wheeler County

Superior Court Clerk

Oconee Judicial Circuit
P.O. Box 4248, Eastman, GA 31023

Clerk of Court, Wheeler County **Carol W. Bragg** . . . .(912) 568-7137
   119 West Pearl Street, Alamo, GA 30411   Fax: (912) 568-7453
   P.O. Box 38, Alamo, GA 30411

White County

Superior Court Clerk

Enotah Judicial Circuit
65 Courthouse Street, Blairsville, GA 30512

Clerk of Court, White County **Dena M. Adams** . . . .(706) 865-2613
   59 South Main Street, Suite B,   Fax: (706) 865-7749
   Cleveland, GA 30528

Georgia Court Clerks and Courthouses *continued*

Whitfield County

Superior Court Clerk

Conasauga Judicial Circuit
205 North Selvidge Street, Dalton, GA 30720

Clerk of Court, Whitfield County **Melica Kendrick** . . . . . . (706) 275-7450
   205 North Selvidge Street,   Fax: (706) 275-7456
   Dalton, GA 30720

Wilcox County

Superior Court Clerk

Cordele Judicial Circuit
510 North 7th Street, Cordele, GA 31010
Tel: (229) 271-4722 Fax: (229) 271-4714

Clerk of Court, Wilcox County **Wanda F. Hawkins** . . . . . .(229) 467-2442
   103 North Broad Street, Abbeville, GA 31001   Fax: (229) 467-2886

Wilkes County

Superior Court Clerk

Toombs Judicial Circuit
P.O. Box 480, Thomson, GA 30824

Clerk of Court, Wilkes County **Mildred Peeler** . . . . (706) 678-2423
   23 East Court Street, Room 205,   Fax: (706) 678-2115
   Washington, GA 30673
   E-mail: mpeeler@wilkes.gsccca.org

Wilkinson County

Superior Court Clerk

Ocmulgee Judicial Circuit
P.O. Box 728, Madison, GA 30650

Clerk of Court, Wilkinson County **Cinda S. Bright** . . . . . . (478) 946-2221
   100 Bacon Street, Irwinton, GA 31042   Fax: (478) 946-1497
   P.O. Box 250, Irwinton, GA 31042

Worth County

Superior Court Clerk

Tifton Judicial Circuit
P.O. Box 1369, Tifton, GA 31793
Tel: (229) 386-7904 Fax: (229) 386-7977
Internet: www.tiftoncircuit.com

Clerk of Court, Worth County **Brenda Hicks** . . . . (229) 776-8205
   201 North Main Street, Room 13,   Fax: (229) 776-8232
   Sylvester, GA 31791

Counties Within Judicial Districts

Superior Court, Alapaha Judicial Circuit
Areas Covered: Atkinson, Berrien, Clinch, Cook, and Lanier Counties.

Superior Court, Alcovy Judicial Circuit
Areas Covered: Newton and Walton Counties.

Superior Court, Appalachian Judicial Circuit
Areas Covered: Fannin, Gilmer, and Pickens Counties.

Superior Court, Atlanta Judicial Circuit

Areas Covered: Fulton County.

Superior Court, Atlantic Judicial Circuit

Areas Covered: Bryan, Evans, Liberty, Long, McIntosh, and Tattnall Counties.

Superior Court, Augusta Judicial Circuit

Areas Covered: Burke, Columbia, and Richmond Counties.

Superior Court, Bell-Forsyth Judicial Circuit

Areas Covered: Forsyth County.

Superior Court, Blue Ridge Judicial Circuit

Areas Covered: Cherokee County.

Superior Court, Brunswick Judicial Circuit

Areas Covered: Appling, Camden, Glynn, Jeff Davis, and Wayne Counties.

Superior Court, Chattahoochee Judicial Circuit

Areas Covered: Harris, Marion, Muscogee, Talbot, and Taylor Counties.

Superior Court, Cherokee Judicial Circuit

Areas Covered: Bartow and Gordon Counties.

Superior Court, Clayton Judicial Circuit

Areas Covered: Clayton County.

Superior Court, Cobb Judicial Circuit

Areas Covered: Cobb County.

Superior Court, Conasauga Judicial Circuit

Areas Covered: Murray and Whitfield Counties.

Superior Court, Cordele Judicial Circuit

Areas Covered: Ben Hill, Crisp, Dooly, and Wilcox Counties.

Superior Court, Coweta Judicial Circuit

Areas Covered: Carroll, Coweta, Heard, Meriwether, and Troup Counties.

Superior Court, Dougherty Judicial Circuit

Areas Covered: Dougherty County.

Superior Court, Douglas Judicial Circuit

Areas Covered: Douglas County.

Superior Court, Dublin Judicial Circuit

Areas Covered: Johnson, Laurens, Treutlen, and Twiggs Counties.

Superior Court, Easter Judicial Circuit

Areas Covered: Chatham County.

Superior Court, Enotah Judicial Circuit

Areas Covered: Union, Towns, Lumpkin, and White Counties.

Superior Court, Flint Judicial Circuit

Areas Covered: Henry County.

Superior Court, Griffin Judicial Circuit

Areas Covered: Fayette, Pike, Spalding, and Upson Counties.

Superior Court, Gwinnett Judicial Circuit

Areas Covered: Gwinnett County.

Superior Court, Houston Judicial Circuit

Areas Covered: Houston County.

Superior Court, Lookout Mountain Judicial Circuit

Areas Covered: Catoosa, Chattooga, Dade, and Walker Counties.

Superior Court, Macon Judicial Circuit

Areas Covered: Bibb, Crawford, and Peach Counties.

Superior Court, Middle Judicial Circuit

Areas Covered: Candler, Emanuel, Jefferson, Toombs, and Washington Counties.

Superior Court, Mountain Judicial Circuit

Areas Covered: Habersham, Rabun, and Stephens Counties.

Superior Court, Northeastern Judicial Circuit

Areas Covered: Dawson and Hall Counties.

Superior Court, Northern Judicial Circuit

Areas Covered: Elbert, Franklin, Hart, Madison, and Oglethorpe Counties.

Superior Court, Ocmulgee Judicial Circuit

Areas Covered: Baldwin, Greene, Hancock, Jasper, Jones, Morgan, Putnam, and Wilkinson Counties.

Superior Court, Oconee Judicial Circuit

Areas Covered: Bleckley, Dodge, Montgomery, Pulaski, Telfair, and Wheeler Counties.

Superior Court, Ogeechee Judicial Circuit

Areas Covered: Bulloch, Effingham, Jenkins, and Screven Counties.

Superior Court, Pataula Judicial Circuit

Areas Covered: Clay, Early, Miller, Quitman, Randolph, Seminole, and Terrell Counties.

Superior Court, Paulding Judicial Circuit

Areas Covered: Paulding County.

Superior Court, Piedmont Judicial Circuit

Areas Covered: Banks, Barrow, and Jackson Counties.

(continued on next page)

Georgia Court Clerks and Courthouses *continued*

Superior Court, Rockdale Judicial Circuit

Areas Covered: Rockdale County.

Superior Court, Rome Judicial Circuit

Areas Covered: Floyd County.

Superior Court, South Georgia Judicial Circuit

Areas Covered: Baker, Calhoun, Decatur, Grady, and Mitchell Counties.

Superior Court, Southern Judicial Circuit

Areas Covered: Brooks, Colquitt, Echols, Lowndes, and Thomas Counties.

Superior Court, Southwestern Judicial Circuit

Areas Covered: Lee, Macon, Schley, Stewart, Sumter, and Webster Counties.

Superior Court, Stone Mountain Judicial Circuit

Areas Covered: DeKalb County.

Superior Court, Tallapoosa Judicial Circuit

Areas Covered: Haralson and Polk Counties.

Superior Court, Tifton Judicial Circuit

Areas Covered: Irwin, Tift, Turner, and Worth Counties.

Superior Court, Toombs Judicial Circuit

Areas Covered: Glascock, Lincoln, McDuffie, Taliaferro, Warren, and Wilkes Counties.

Superior Court, Towaliga Judicial Circuit

Areas Covered: Butts, Lamar, and Monroe Counties.

Superior Court, Waycross Judicial Circuit

Areas Covered: Bacon, Brantley, Charlton, Coffee, Pierce, and Ware Counties.

Superior Court, Western Judicial Circuit

Areas Covered: Clarke and Oconee Counties.

Hawaii Court Clerks and Courthouses

The trial courts of general jurisdiction in Hawaii are called circuit courts. There are four circuits, each with at least one county. Appeals from a circuit court are sent directly to the State Supreme Court, which on its discretion can assign certain cases to an appellate panel, the Intermediate Court of Appeals. Listed below are the circuit courts.

Hawaii Supreme Court

Ali'iolani Hale, 417 South King Street, Room 103,
Honolulu, HI 96813-2902
Tel: (808) 539-4919 Fax: (808) 539-4928
Internet: www.state.hi.us/jud/

The Supreme Court consists of a chief justice and four associate justices who are appointed for ten-year terms by the Governor with the consent of the Hawaii State Senate from a list compiled by the Judicial Selection Commission. The Supreme Court has appellate jurisdiction over all questions of law or fact brought before it from any other agency or court. The Court has exclusive jurisdiction in the examination, licensing and discipline of attorneys and has superintending control over all inferior courts.

Court Staff
Chief Clerk of the Court **Rochelle R. Hasuko** . . . . (808) 539-4919
  E-mail: rochelle.hasuko@courts.hawaii.gov

Intermediate Court of Appeals of Hawaii

426 Queen Street, Room 201, Honolulu, HI 96813-2914
Tel: (808) 539-4750 Fax: (808) 539-4644

The Intermediate Court of Appeals, established by the Hawaii State Legislature in 1979, consists of a chief judge and five associate judges. The judges are appointed for ten-year terms by the Governor, with the consent of the Hawaii State Senate, from a list compiled by the Judicial Selection Commission. The chief judge is selected through a merit selection plan for a ten-year term. The Intermediate Court of Appeals has concurrent jurisdiction with the Hawaii Supreme Court with the exception of examinations, licensing and discipline of attorneys and questions reserved by a federal appellate court, which fall under the Hawaii Supreme Court's exclusive jurisdiction.

Court Staff
Appellate Clerk **Alison M. Hanamoto** . . . . (808) 539-4611
  E-mail: alison.m.hanamoto@courts.state.hi.us
Appellate Clerk **Shirley Toyama** . . . . (808) 539-4750
  E-mail: shirley.toyama@courts.state.hi.us

Hawaii Circuit Courts

Note: There is no Fourth Judicial Circuit. The Fourth Circuit, which represented a portion of the island of Hawaii, was eliminated in 1943 when it merged into the Third Circuit.

First Judicial Circuit

777 Punchbowl Street, Honolulu, HI 96813

Areas Covered: Honolulu County.

Court Staff
Chief Court Administrator **Lori N. Okita** . . . . (808) 539-4333
  E-mail: lori.okita@courts.hawaii.gov   Fax: (808) 539-4322

Second Judicial Circuit

2145 Main Street, Wailuku, HI 96793

Areas Covered: Maui County.

Court Staff
Chief Court Administrator **Sandy S. Kozaki** Suite 106 . . . (808) 244-2930
  E-mail: sandy.kozaki@courts.hawaii.gov   Fax: (808) 244-2932

Third Judicial Circuit

777 Kilauea Avenue, Hilo, HI 96720

Areas Covered: Hawaii County.

Court Staff
Chief Court Administrator **Lester D. Oshiro** . . . . (808) 961-7435
  E-mail: lester.oshiro@courts.hawaii.gov   Fax: (808) 961-7577

Fifth Judicial Circuit

3970 Kaana Street, Lihue, HI 96766

Areas Covered: Kauai County.

Court Staff
Chief Court Administrator **David Lam** . . . . (808) 482-2308
  E-mail: david.lam@courts.hawaii.gov   Fax: (808) 482-2510

Idaho Court Clerks and Courthouses

The trial courts of general jurisdiction in Idaho are called district courts. There are seven judicial districts, each district consisting of several counties. The listing below consists of county clerks. The court clerk serves under the county clerk.

Idaho Supreme Court

Supreme Court Building, 451 West State Street, Boise, ID 83702
P.O. Box 83720, Boise, ID 83720-0101
Tel: (208) 334-2210 Fax: (208) 334-2616
Internet: www.isc.idaho.gov

The Supreme Court consists of a chief justice and four justices, who are elected in statewide, nonpartisan elections for six-year terms. The chief justice is elected by peer vote to a four-year term. Vacancies are filled by the Governor from a list of candidates provided by the Judicial Council or by election. The Supreme Court has appellate jurisdiction over decisions of the Idaho Court of Appeals, interim rulings and final judgments of the Idaho District Courts, decisions of the Public Utilities Commission and the Industrial Commission, and criminal cases imposing sentences of capital punishment. The Court has original jurisdiction to hear claims against the state, to issue writs and to decide disciplinary actions against attorneys. The Court exercises general supervisory and administrative control over the trial courts.

Court Staff
Clerk of Courts **Stephen W. Kenyon** . . . . (208) 334-2210
  E-mail: skenyon@idcourts.net

Idaho Court of Appeals

451 West State Street, Boise, ID 83702-0101
P.O. Box 83720, Boise, ID 83720-0101
Tel: (208) 334-5170 Fax: (208) 334-2526
Internet: http://isc.idaho.gov

The Court of Appeals, established in 1981, consists of a chief judge and two judges who are elected to six-year terms in statewide nonpartisan elections. Vacancies are filled temporarily by the Governor from a list of candidates provided by the Judicial Council. Temporary judges are subject to a retention vote in the next general election for a full, six-year term. The chief judge is appointed by the Idaho Supreme Court to serve a two-year term. Retirement is mandatory at age seventy. The Court of Appeals has appellate jurisdiction over cases assigned by the Idaho Supreme Court. The Court may not hear cases involving the original jurisdiction of the Supreme Court, recommendatory orders of the Bar Commission or the Judicial Council, appeals from imposition of capital punishment or appeals from the Industrial Commission or Public Utilities Commission.

Court Staff
Clerk of Courts **Stephen W. Kenyon** . . . . (208) 334-5170
  E-mail: skenyon@idcourts.net   Fax: (208) 334-2616

Idaho Court Clerks and Courthouses *continued*

County-By-County

Ada County

County Clerk

Office of the Clerk/Auditor/Recorder
200 West Front Street, Room 1196, Boise, ID 83702
Tel: (208) 287-6000 (Clerk) Tel: (208) 287-6860 (Elections)
Tel: (208) 287-6840 (Recorder) Fax: (208) 287-6909

Clerk/Auditor/Recorder **Christopher D. "Chris" Rich** . . . . (208) 287-6886
  E-mail: aurichcd@adaweb.net

Adams County

County Clerk

Office of the Clerk/Auditor/Recorder
201 Industrial Avenue, Council, ID 83612
P.O. Box 48, Council, ID 83612
Tel: (208) 253-4561 Fax: (208) 253-4880

Clerk/Auditor/Recorder **Sherry Ward** . . . . (208) 253-4561
  E-mail: sward@co.adams.id.us

Bannock County

County Clerk

Office of the Clerk/Auditor/Recorder
Bannock County Courthouse, 624 East Center, Room 104,
Pocatello, ID 83201
Tel: (208) 236-7358 Fax: (208) 236-7345

Clerk/Auditor/Recorder **Robert Poleki** . . . . (208) 236-7358
  E-mail: robertp@bannockcounty.us

Bear Lake County

County Clerk

Office of the Clerk
Seven East Center, Paris, ID 83261
P.O. Box 190, Paris, ID 83261
Tel: (208) 945-2212 Fax: (208) 945-2248

Clerk **Cindy Garner** . . . . (208) 945-2212
  E-mail: blcgarner@dcdi.net

Benewah County

County Clerk

Office of the Clerk/Auditor/Recorder
701 West College Avenue, St. Maries, ID 83861
Tel: (208) 245-3212 Fax: (208) 245-9152

Clerk/Auditor/Recorder **Deanne Bramblett** . . . . (208) 245-3212
  E-mail: dbramblett@benewahcounty.org

(continued on next page)

Bingham County

County Clerk

Office of the Clerk/Auditor/Recorder
501 North Maple, Blackfoot, ID 83221
Tel: (208) 782-3160

Clerk/Auditor/Recorder **Pam Eckhardt** . . . . (208) 782-3160
E-mail: peckhardt@co.bingham.id.us

Blaine County

County Clerk

Office of the Clerk/Auditor/Recorder
206 First Avenue South, Suite 200, Hailey, ID 83333
Tel: (208) 788-5505 Fax: (208) 788-5501

Clerk/Auditor/Recorder **JoLynn Drage** . . . . (208) 788-5505
E-mail: jdrage@co.blaine.id.us

Boise County

County Clerk

Office of the Clerk/Auditor/Recorder
P.O. Box 1300, Idaho City, ID 83631
Tel: (208) 392-4431 Fax: (208) 392-4473

Clerk/Auditor/Recorder **Mary T. Prisco** . . . .(208) 392-4431 ext. 125
E-mail: mprisco@co.boise.id.us

Bonner County

County Clerk

Office of the Clerk/Auditor/Recorder
215 South 1st Avenue, Sandpoint, ID 83864
Tel: (208) 265-1432 Fax: (888) 960-4885

Clerk/Auditor/Recorder **Michael W. Rosedale** . . . .(208) 265-1432
E-mail: mrosedale@bonnercountyid.gov

Bonneville County

County Clerk

Office of the Clerk/Auditor/Recorder
605 North Capital Avenue, Room 204, Idaho Falls, ID 83402
Tel: (208) 529-1350 ext. 1355 Fax: (208) 529-1311

Clerk/Auditor/Recorder **Ron Longmore** . . . . (208) 529-1350 ext. 1355
E-mail: rlongmore@co.bonneville.id.us

Boundary County

County Clerk

Office of the Clerk/Auditor/Recorder
6452 Kootenai St, Bonners Ferry, ID 83805
P.O. Box 419, Bonners Ferry, ID 83805
Tel: (208) 267-2242 Fax: (208) 267-7814

Clerk/Auditor/Recorder **Glenda Poston** . . . . (208) 267-2242
E-mail: gposton@boundarycountyid.org

Butte County

County Clerk

Office of the Clerk/Auditor/Recorder
County Courthouse, Arco, ID 83213-0737
P.O. Box 737, Arco, ID 83213
Tel: (208) 527-3021 Fax: (208) 527-3295

Clerk/Auditor/Recorder **Shelly Shaffer** . . . . (208) 527-3021
E-mail: butteclerk@atcnet.net

Camas County

County Clerk

Office of the Clerk
Camas County Courthouse, 501 Soldier Road, Fairfield, ID 83327
Tel: (208) 764-2242 Fax: (208) 764-2349

Clerk **Korri Blodgett** . . . .(208) 764-2242
E-mail: kblodgett@rtci.net

Canyon County

County Clerk

Canyon County District Court
1115 Albany Street, Caldwell, ID 83605
Tel: (208) 454-7570

Clerk of the Court and Clerk/Auditor/Recorder
Chris Yamamoto . . . . (208) 454-7570
E-mail: canyoncountyclerk@canyonco.org

Caribou County

County Clerk

Office of the Clerk/Auditor/Recorder
Caribou County Courthouse, 159 South Main Street, Room 202,
Soda Springs, ID 83276
P.O. Box 775, Soda Springs, ID 83276
Tel: (208) 547-4324 Fax: (208) 547-4759

Clerk/Auditor/Recorder **Denise Horsley** . . . . (208) 547-4324
E-mail: dhorsley@co.caribou.id.us

Cassia County

County Clerk

Office of the Clerk/Auditor/Recorder
1559 Overland Avenue, Burley, ID 83318
Tel: (208) 878-5231 Fax: (208) 878-5830

Clerk/Auditor/Recorder **Joseph W. Larsen** . . . .(208) 878-5231
E-mail: cassiaclerk@cassiacounty.org

Clark County

County Clerk

Office of the County Clerk
320 West Main, Dubois, ID 83423
P.O. Box 205, Dubois, ID 83423
Tel: (208) 374-5304 Fax: (208) 374-5609
E-mail: clerk5c@mudlake.net

County Clerk **Velvet Killian** . . . . (208) 374-5304
E-mail: clerk5c@mudlake.net

Clearwater County

Clerk of the Court and County Clerk

Clearwater County District Court
Clearwater County Courthouse, 150 Michigan Avenue, Orofino, ID 83544
Tel: (208) 476-5596   Tel: (208) 476-0239

Clerk of the Court and County Clerk/Auditor/Recorder
Carrie Bird . . . . (208) 476-5615
E-mail: cbird@idcourts.net

Custer County

County Clerk

Office of the Clerk/Auditor/Recorder
801 East Main Avenue, Challis, ID 83226
P.O. Box 385, Challis, ID 83226
Tel: (208) 879-2360   Fax: (208) 879-5246

Clerk/Auditor/Recorder **Laura Baker** . . . . (208) 879-2360
E-mail: lbaker@co.custer.id.us

Elmore County

County Clerk

Office of the Clerk/Auditor/Recorder
150 South Fourth East Street, Mountain Home, ID 83647
Tel: (208) 587-2130

Clerk/Auditor/Recorder **Barbara Steele** . . . . (208) 587-2130
E-mail: bsteele@elmorecounty.org

Franklin County

County Clerk

Office of the Clerk/Auditor/Recorder
39 West Oneida, Preston, ID 83263
Tel: (208) 852-1090   Fax: (208) 852-1094

Clerk/Auditor/Recorder **Shauna T. Geddes** . . . . (208) 852-1090
E-mail: stgeddes@plmw.com

Fremont County

County Clerk

Office of the Clerk/Auditor/Recorder
151 West First North Street, Suite 12 , St. Anthony, ID 83445
Tel: (208) 624-7332   Fax: (208) 624-7335

Clerk/Auditor/Recorder **Abbie D. Mace** . . . . (208) 624-7332
E-mail: amace@co.fremont.id.us

Gem County

County Clerk

Office of the Clerk/Auditor/Recorder
415 East Main, Emmett, ID 83617
Tel: (208) 365-4561   Fax: (208) 365-7795

Clerk/Auditor/Recorder **Shelly Tilton** . . . . (208) 365-4561
E-mail: clerk@co.gem.id.us

Gooding County

County Clerk

Office of the Clerk/Auditor/Recorder
624 Main Street, Gooding, ID 83330
P.O. Box 417, Gooding, ID 83330
Tel: (208) 934-4841   Fax: (208) 934-5019

Clerk/Auditor/Recorder **Denise Gill** . . . . (208) 934-4841
E-mail: dgill@co.gooding.id.us

Idaho County

County Clerk

Idaho County District Court
320 West Main Street, Grangeville, ID 86530
Tel: (208) 983-2776   Fax: (208) 983-2376

Clerk of the Court and County Clerk/Auditor
Kathy M. Ackerman . . . . (208) 983-2751
E-mail: kackerman@idahocounty.org   Fax: (208) 983-1428

Jefferson County

County Clerk

Office of the Clerk/Auditor/Recorder
210 Courthouse Way, Suite 100 , Rigby, ID 83442
Tel: (208) 745-7756   Fax: (208) 745-8703

Clerk/Auditor/Recorder **Colleen Poole** . . . . (208) 745-7756
E-mail: cpoole@co.jefferson.id.us

Jerome County

County Clerk

Office of the Clerk/Auditor/Recorder
300 North Lincoln, Jerome, ID 83338
Tel: (208) 644-2600   Fax: (208) 644-2609

Clerk/Auditor/Recorder **Michelle Emerson** . . . . (208) 644-2600
E-mail: memerson@co.jerome.id.us

Kootenai County

County Clerk

Office of the Clerk/Auditor/Recorder
451 Government Way, Coeur d'Alene, ID 83814
P.O. Box 9000, Coeur d'Alene, ID 83816-9000
Tel: (208) 446-1650

Clerk/Auditor/Recorder **Jim Brannon** . . . . (208) 446-1650
E-mail: jbrannon@kcgov.us

Latah County

Clerk of the Court and County Clerk

Latah County District Court
Latah County Courthouse, Fifth and Van Buren Street, Moscow, ID 83843
P.O. Box 8068, Moscow, ID 83843
Tel: (208) 883-2255   Fax: (208) 883-2259

Clerk of the Court and County Clerk/Auditor/Recorder
Henrianne Westberg . . . . (208) 883-2249
                                                         Fax: (208) 883-7203

(continued on next page)

Idaho Court Clerks and Courthouses *continued*

Lemhi County

County Clerk

Office of the Clerk/Auditor/Recorder
206 Courthouse Drive, Salmon, ID 83467
Tel: (208) 756-2815 ext. 221 Fax: (208) 756-8424

Clerk/Auditor/Recorder **Terri Morton** . . . . (208) 756-2815 ext. 221
    E-mail: clerk@lemhicountyidaho.org

Lewis County

Clerk of the Court and County Clerk

Idaho County District Court
320 West Main Street, Grangeville, ID 86530
Tel: (208) 983-2776 Fax: (208) 983-2376

Clerk of the Court and County Clerk/Auditor
    Kathy M. Ackerman . . . . (208) 983-2751
    E-mail: kackerman@idahocounty.org   Fax: (208) 983-1428

Lincoln County

County Clerk

Office of the Clerk/Auditor/Recorder
111 West B Street, Suite C , Shoshone, ID 83352
Tel: (208) 886-7641 ext. 101 Fax: (208) 886-2798

Clerk/Auditor/Recorder **Brenda Farnworth** . . . . . (208) 886-7641 ext. 101

Madison County

County Clerk

Office of the Clerk/Auditor/Recorder
134 East Main Street, Rexburg, ID 83440
P.O. Box 389, Rexburg, ID 83440
Tel: (208) 359-6200 Fax: (208) 356-8396

Clerk/Auditor/Recorder **Kim Muir** . . . . (208) 359-6200
    E-mail: kmuir@co.madison.id.us

Minidoka County

County Clerk

Office of the Clerk/Auditor/Recorder
715 G Street, Rupert, ID 83350
Tel: (208) 436-9511 Fax: (208) 436-9061

Clerk/Auditor/Recorder **Patty Temple** . . . . (208) 436-9511
    E-mail: ptemple@co.minidoka.id.us

Nez Perce County

County Clerk

Nez Perce County District Court
1230 Main Street, Nezperce, ID 83501
P.O. Box 896, Nezperce, ID 83501
Tel: (208) 799-3040 Fax: (208) 799-3058

Clerk of the Court and County Clerk/Auditor/Recorder
    Patty Weeks . . . . (208) 799-3020
    E-mail: pattyweeks@co.nezperce.id.us   Fax: (208) 799-3070

Idaho Court Clerks and Courthouses *continued*

Oneida County

County Clerk

Office of the Clerk/Auditor/Recorder
10 Court Street, Malad City, ID 83252
Tel: (208) 766-4116 ext. 100 Fax: (208) 766-2448

Clerk/Auditor/Recorder **Lon Colton** . . . . (208) 766-4116 ext. 3
    E-mail: lcolton@co.oneida.id.us

Owyhee County

County Clerk

Office of the Clerk/Auditor/Recorder
20381 State Highway 78, Murphy, ID 83650
P.O. Box 128, Murphy, ID 83650
Tel: (208) 495-2421 Fax: (208) 495-1173

Clerk/Auditor/Recorder **Angie Barkell** . . . . (208) 495-2421
    E-mail: abarkell@co.owyhee.id.us

Payette County

County Clerk

Office of the Clerk
1130 Third Avenue North, Room 104, Payette, ID 83661
Tel: (208) 642-6000 Fax: (208) 642-6011

County Clerk **Betty Dressen** . . . . (208) 642-6000 ext. 1127
    E-mail: bdressen@payettecounty.org

Power County

County Clerk

Office of the Clerk/Auditor/Recorder
543 Bannock Avenue, American Falls, ID 83211
Tel: (208) 226-7611 Fax: (208) 226-7612

Clerk/Auditor/Recorder **Sharee Sprague** . . . . (208) 226-7611
    E-mail: ssprague@co.power.id.us

Shoshone County

County Clerk

Office of the Clerk/Auditor/Recorder
700 Bank Street, Wallace, ID 83873
Tel: (208) 752-1264 Fax: (208) 752-1896

Clerk/Auditor/Recorder **Peggy White** . . . . (208) 752-1264
    E-mail: pwhite@co.shoshone.id.us

Teton County

County Clerk

Office of the Clerk/Auditor/Recorder
150 Courthouse Drive, Driggs, ID 83422
Tel: (208) 354-8780 Fax: (208) 354-8410

Clerk/Auditor/Recorder **Mary Lou Hansen** . . . . (208) 354-8780
    E-mail: clerk@co.teton.id.us

Idaho Court Clerks and Courthouses *continued*

Twin Falls County

County Clerk

Office of the Clerk/Auditor/Recorder
630 Addison Avenue West, 2nd Floor, Twin Falls, ID 83303
P.O. Box 126, Twin Falls, ID 83303
Tel: (208) 736-4004 Fax: (208) 736-4182

Clerk/Auditor/Recorder **Kristina Glascock** . . . . (208) 736-4004
  E-mail: kglascock@co.twin-falls.id.us

Valley County

County Clerk

Office of the Clerk/Auditor/Recorder
219 North Main Street, Cascade, ID 83611
Tel: (208) 382-7100 Fax: (208) 382-7107

Clerk/Auditor/Recorder **Doug Miller** . . . . (208) 382-7102
  E-mail: dmiller@co.valley.id.us

Washington County

County Clerk

Office of the Clerk/Auditor/Recorder
256 East Court, Weiser, ID 83672
Tel: (208) 414-2092 Fax: (208) 414-3925

Clerk/Auditor/Recorder **Betty J. Thomas** . . . . (208) 414-2092
  E-mail: wcclerk@co.washington.id.us

Counties Within Judicial Districts

Circuit Court, 1st Judicial Circuit
Areas Covered: Benewah, Bonner, Boundary, Kootenai, and Shoshone Counties.

Circuit Court, 2nd Judicial Circuit
Areas Covered: Clearwater, Idaho, Latah, Lewis, and Nez Perce Counties.

Circuit Court, 3rd Judicial Circuit
Areas Covered: Adams, Canyon, Gem, Owyhee, Payette, and Washington Counties.

Circuit Court, 4th Judicial Circuit
Areas Covered: Ada, Boise, Elmore, and Valley Counties.

Circuit Court, 5th Judicial Circuit
Areas Covered: Blaine, Camas, Cassia, Gooding, Jerome, Lincoln, Minidoka, and Twin Falls Counties.

Circuit Court, 6th Judicial Circuit
Areas Covered: Bannock, Bear Lake, Caribou, Franklin, Oneida, and Power Counties.

Circuit Court, 7th Judicial Circuit
Areas Covered: Bingham, Bonneville, Butte, Clark, Custer, Fremont, Jefferson, Lemhi, Madison, and Teton Counties.

Illinois Court Clerks and Courthouses

The trial courts of general jurisdiction in Illinois are called circuit courts. There are 22 judicial circuits, each circuit consisting of at least once county plus a Circuit Court for Cook County. Each county has a County Clerk and a Circuit Court Clerk. Circuit Clerks are listed below.

Illinois Supreme Court

Supreme Court Building, 200 East Capitol Avenue, Springfield, IL 62701
Tel: (217) 782-2035 TTY: (217) 524-8132
Internet: www.state.il.us/court

The Supreme Court consists of a chief justice and six justices who are initially elected in partisan elections in one of five judicial districts for a ten-year term. After the first election, justices run for retention in nonpartisan elections in their respective judicial districts for ten-year terms. Three justices are elected from the First Judicial District, and one justice each is elected from the Second through Fifth Judicial Districts. The chief justice is elected by peer vote for a three-year term. A judge is automatically retired at the expiration of the term in which the judge attains the age of seventy-five. The Supreme Court has discretionary original jurisdiction in cases relating to revenue, mandamus, prohibition or habeas corpus, and exclusive jurisdiction over matters of redistricting the Illinois General Assembly and the ability of the Governor to hold office. Generally, the Court considers direct appeals from the Illinois Circuit Courts in cases involving capital punishment and where a statute has been held unconstitutional, and discretionary appeals from the Illinois Appellate Court. The Court has general administrative control over all courts in the state.

Court Staff
Clerk of Court **Carolyn Taft Grosboll** . . . . (217) 782-2035
    E-mail: cgrosboll@illinoiscourts.gov

Illinois Appellate Court

The Illinois Appellate Court is comprised of five districts, some of which are subdivided into divisions. The justices of the Appellate Court are initially elected in partisan elections in their respective districts for ten-year terms. Vacancies may be temporarily filled by Illinois Supreme Court appointment. A presiding justice is elected in each division by peer vote to a one-year term. Retirement is mandatory at the age of seventy-five; however, retired justices may be assigned by the Supreme Court to serve on a temporary basis. The Appellate Court hears appeals of decisions of the Illinois Circuit Courts, except those cases heard directly by the Illinois Supreme Court. The Court may exercise any original jurisdiction it finds necessary and reviews administrative actions as provided by law.

Illinois Appellate Court, First District

160 North LaSalle Street, Suite 1400, Chicago, IL 60601
Tel: (312) 793-5415 Fax: (312) 793-4408
Internet: www.state.il.us/court/appellatecourt

Areas Covered: County of Cook

Court Staff
Clerk of the Court **Steven M. Ravid** . . . . (312) 793-5950
    E-mail: sravid@illinoiscourts.gov

Illinois Appellate Court, Second District

Appellate Court Building, 55 Symphony Way, Elgin, IL 60120-5558
Tel: (847) 695-3750 Fax: (847) 695-4949
Internet: www.state.il.us/court/appellatecourt

Areas Covered: Counties of Boone, Carroll, DeKalb, DuPage, Jo Daviess, Kane, Kendall, Lake, Lee, McHenry, Ogle, Stephenson and Winnebago

Court Staff
Clerk of Court **Robert J. Mangan** . . . . (847) 695-3750
    E-mail: rmangan@court.state.il.us

Illinois Appellate Court, Third District

1004 Columbus Street, Ottawa, IL 61350
Tel: (815) 434-5050
Internet: www.state.il.us/court/appellatecourt

Areas Covered: Counties of Bureau, Fulton, Grundy, Hancock, Henderson, Henry, Iroquois, Kankakee, Knox, La Salle, Marshall, McDonough, Mercer, Peoria, Putnam, Rock Island, Stark, Tazewell, Warren, Whiteside and Will

Court Staff
Clerk of the Court **Barbara Trumbo** . . . . (815) 434-5050
    E-mail: btrumbo@illinoiscourts.gov

Illinois Appellate Court, Fourth District

Appellate Court Building, 201 West Monroe, Springfield, IL 62794
P.O. Box 19206, Springfield, IL 62794-9206
Tel: (217) 782-2586
Internet: www.state.il.us/court/appellatecourt

Areas Covered: Counties of Adams, Brown, Calhoun, Cass, Champaign, Clark, Coles, Cumberland, DeWitt, Douglas, Edgar, Ford, Greene, Jersey, Livingston, Logan, Macon, Macoupin, Mason, McLean, Menard, Morgan, Moultrie, Piatt, Pike, Sangamon, Schuyler, Scott, Vermilion and Woodford

Court Staff
Clerk of the Court **Carla Bender** . . . . (217) 782-2586
    E-mail: cbender@court.state.il.us

Illinois Appellate Court, Fifth District

P.O. Box 867, Mount Vernon, IL 62864-0018
Tel: (618) 242-3120
Internet: www.state.il.us/court/appellatecourt

Areas Covered: Counties of Alexander, Bond, Christian, Clay, Clinton, Crawford, Edwards, Effingham, Fayette, Franklin, Gallatin, Hamilton, Hardin, Jackson, Jasper, Jefferson, Johnson, Lawrence, Madison, Marion, Massac, Monroe, Montgomery, Perry, Pope, Pulaski, Randolph, Richland, Saline, Shelby, St Clair, Union, Wabash, Washington, Wayne, White and Williamson

Court Staff
Clerk of the Court **John J. Flood** . . . . (618) 242-3120
    E-mail: jflood@court.state.il.us

(continued on next page)

Illinois Court Clerks and Courthouses *continued*

County-By-County

Adams County

Circuit Clerk

Eighth Judicial Circuit
521 Vermont Street, Quincy, IL 62301
Tel: (217) 277-2055 Fax: (217) 277-2072
Internet: www.state.il.us/court/CircuitCourt/CircuitMap/8th.asp

Clerk of Court, Adams County **Lori Geschwandner** . . . . . (217) 277-2100
521 Vermont Street, Quincy, IL 62301   Fax: (217) 277-2116

Alexander County

Circuit Clerk

First Judicial Circuit
200 West Jefferson, Marion, IL 62959
P.O. Box 940, Marion, IL 62959
Tel: (618) 997-1234 Fax: (618) 993-6618
Internet: www.state.il.us/court/CircuitCourt/CircuitMap/1st.asp

Clerk of Court, Alexander County **Paul Jones** . . . . (618) 734-0107
2000 Washington Avenue,   Fax: (618) 734-7003
Cairo, IL 62914

Bond County

Circuit Clerk

Third Judicial Circuit
155 North Main Street, Suite 405, Edwardsville, IL 62025
Tel: (618) 296-4884 Fax: (618) 692-7475
Internet: www.state.il.us/court/CircuitCourt/CircuitMap/3rd.asp

Clerk of Court, Bond County **Rex Catron** . . . . (618) 664-3208
200 West College, Greenville, IL 62246-1057   Fax: (618) 664-2257

Boone County

Circuit Clerk

Seventeenth Judicial Circuit
400 West State Street, Suite 215, Rockford, IL 61101
Tel: (815) 319-4800 Fax: (815) 319-4808
Internet: www.state.il.us/court/CircuitCourt/CircuitMap/17th.asp
Internet: www.illinois17th.com

Clerk of Court, Boone County **Linda Anderson** . . . . (815) 544-0371
601 North Main Street, Room 303,   Fax: (815) 547-9213
Belvidere, IL 61008
E-mail: circuitclerk@boonecountyil.org

Brown County

Circuit Clerk

Eighth Judicial Circuit
521 Vermont Street, Quincy, IL 62301
Tel: (217) 277-2055 Fax: (217) 277-2072
Internet: www.state.il.us/court/CircuitCourt/CircuitMap/8th.asp

Clerk of Court, Brown County **Rhonda Johnson** . . . . (217) 773-2713
One Court Street, Mount Sterling, IL 62353   Fax: (217) 773-2433

Illinois Court Clerks and Courthouses *continued*

Bureau County

Circuit Clerk

Thirteenth Judicial Circuit
119 West Madison Street, Ottawa, IL 61350
Tel: (815) 434-0786 Fax: (815) 434-6062
Internet: www.state.il.us/court/CircuitCourt/CircuitMap/13th.asp

Clerk of Court, Bureau County
Mary Romanelli Dremann . . . . (815) 872-2001
700 South Main Street, Princeton, IL 61356   Fax: (815) 872-0027

Calhoun County

Circuit Clerk

Eighth Judicial Circuit
521 Vermont Street, Quincy, IL 62301
Tel: (217) 277-2055 Fax: (217) 277-2072
Internet: www.state.il.us/court/CircuitCourt/CircuitMap/8th.asp

Clerk of Court, Calhoun County **Yvonne Macauley** . . . . . (618) 576-2451
Main and County Roads, Hardin, IL 62047   Fax: (618) 576-9541

Carroll County

Circuit Clerk

Fifteenth Judicial Circuit
106 South Fifth Street, Suite 306A, Oregon, IL 61061
Tel: (815) 732-1197 Fax: (815) 732-1198
Internet: www.state.il.us/court/CircuitCourt/CircuitMap/15th.asp
Internet: www.15thjudicialcircuit.com/

Clerk of Court, Carroll County **Sherri A. Miller** . . . . (815) 244-0230
301 North Main Street, Mount Carroll, IL 61053   Fax: (815) 244-3869
E-mail: smiller@illinoiscourts.gov

Cass County

Circuit Clerk

Eighth Judicial Circuit
521 Vermont Street, Quincy, IL 62301
Tel: (217) 277-2055 Fax: (217) 277-2072
Internet: www.state.il.us/court/CircuitCourt/CircuitMap/8th.asp

Clerk of Court, Cass County **Cheri Kay Garner** . . . . (217) 452-7225
P.O. Box 203, Virginia, IL 62691   Fax: (217) 452-7219

Champaign County

Circuit Clerk

Sixth Judicial Circuit
10 South Main, Suite 12, Sullivan, IL 61951
Tel: (217) 762-4521 Fax: (217) 728-8551
Internet: www.state.il.us/court/CircuitCourt/CircuitMap/6th.asp

Clerk of Court, Champaign County **Katie Blakeman** . . . . . (217) 384-3725
101 East Main Street, Urbana, IL 61801   Fax: (217) 384-3879

Illinois Court Clerks and Courthouses *continued*

Christian County

Circuit Clerk

Fourth Judicial Circuit
221 South Seventh Street, Vandalia, IL 62471
Tel: (618) 283-2030 Fax: (618) 283-9741
Internet: www.fourthcircuitil.com

Clerk of Court, Christian County **Julie Mayer** . . . . (217) 824-4966
  P.O. Box 617, Taylorville, IL 62568   Fax: (217) 824-5030

Clark County

Circuit Clerk

Fifth Judicial Circuit
501 Archer Avenue, Marshall, IL 62441
Tel: (217) 826-3943 Fax: (217) 826-2646
Internet: www.state.il.us/court/CircuitCourt/CircuitMap/5th.asp

Clerk of Court, Clark County **Kathy Ramsey** . . . . (217) 826-2811
  501 Archer Avenue, Marshall, IL 62441   Fax: (217) 826-1391

Clay County

Circuit Clerk

Fourth Judicial Circuit
221 South Seventh Street, Vandalia, IL 62471
Tel: (618) 283-2030 Fax: (618) 283-9741
Internet: www.fourthcircuitil.com

Clerk of Court, Clay County **Crystal Ballard** . . . . (618) 665-3523
  111 Chestnut, Louisville, IL 62858-0100   Fax: (618) 665-3543

Clinton County

Circuit Clerk

Fourth Judicial Circuit
221 South Seventh Street, Vandalia, IL 62471
Tel: (618) 283-2030 Fax: (618) 283-9741
Internet: www.fourthcircuitil.com

Clerk of Court, Clinton County **Rod Kloezkner** . . . . (618) 594-2415
  850 Fairfax, Carlyle, IL 62231-0407   Fax: (618) 594-0197

Coles County

Circuit Clerk

Fifth Judicial Circuit
501 Archer Avenue, Marshall, IL 62441
Tel: (217) 826-3943 Fax: (217) 826-2646
Internet: www.state.il.us/court/CircuitCourt/CircuitMap/5th.asp

Clerk of Court, Coles County **Melissa Hurst** . . . . (217) 348-0516
  P.O. Box 48, Charleston, IL 61920   Fax: (217) 348-7324

Cook County

Circuit Clerk

Circuit Court of Cook County
50 West Washington Street, Chicago, IL 60602
Tel: (312) 603-6000 Fax: (312) 603-5366
Internet: www.cookcountycourt.net

Clerk of Circuit Court **Dorothy Brown** . . . . (312) 603-5031
  E-mail: courtclerk@cookcountycourt.com

Illinois Court Clerks and Courthouses *continued*

Crawford County

Circuit Clerk

Second Judicial Circuit
911 Casey Avenue, Suite HI-05, Mount Vernon, IL 62864
Tel: (618) 244-8036 Fax: (618) 244-8038
Internet: www.illinoissecondcircuit.info/

Clerk of Court, Crawford County
  Angela "Angie" Reinoehl . . . . (618) 544-3512
  P.O. Box 655, Robinson, IL 62454-0655   Fax: (618) 546-5628
  E-mail: circuitclerk@crawfordcountycentral.com

Cumberland County

Circuit Clerk

Fifth Judicial Circuit
501 Archer Avenue, Marshall, IL 62441
Tel: (217) 826-3943 Fax: (217) 826-2646
Internet: www.state.il.us/court/CircuitCourt/CircuitMap/5th.asp

Clerk of Court, Cumberland County (Interim)
  Denny Shupe . . . . (217) 849-3601
  P.O. Box 145, Toledo, IL 62468   Fax: (217) 849-2655

DeKalb County

Circuit Clerk

Sixteenth Judicial Circuit
37W777 Route 38, Suite 301, St. Charles, IL 60175
Tel: (630) 232-3440 Fax: (630) 406-7121
Internet: www.state.il.us/court/CircuitCourt/CircuitMap/16th.asp
Internet: www.illinois16thjudicialcircuit.org

Clerk of Court, DeKalb County **Maureen Josh** . . . . (815) 895-7135
  133 West State Street, Sycamore, IL 60178   Fax: (815) 895-7140

DeWitt County

Circuit Clerk

Sixth Judicial Circuit
10 South Main, Suite 12, Sullivan, IL 61951
Tel: (217) 762-4521 Fax: (217) 728-8551
Internet: www.state.il.us/court/CircuitCourt/CircuitMap/6th.asp

Clerk of Court, DeWitt County **Pamela Barnes** . . . . (217) 935-7751
  201 West Washington Street,   Fax: (217) 935-3310
  Clinton, IL 61727

Douglas County

Circuit Clerk

Sixth Judicial Circuit
10 South Main, Suite 12, Sullivan, IL 61951
Tel: (217) 762-4521 Fax: (217) 728-8551
Internet: www.state.il.us/court/CircuitCourt/CircuitMap/6th.asp

Clerk of Court, Douglas County **Julie Mills** . . . . (217) 253-2352
  401 South Center Street, Tuscola, IL 61953   Fax: (217) 253-9006

(continued on next page)

Illinois Court Clerks and Courthouses *continued*

DuPage County

Circuit Clerk

Eighteenth Judicial Circuit
505 North County Farm Road, Room 2015, Wheaton, IL 60187-3907
Tel: (630) 407-8901 Fax: (630) 407-8836
Internet: www.state.il.us/court/CircuitCourt/CircuitMap/18th.asp
Internet: www.dupageco.org/courts

Clerk of Court, DuPage County **Chris Kachiroubas** . . . . . (630) 407-8700
  505 North County Farm Road,   Fax: (630) 407-8575
  Wheaton, IL 60187-3907

Edgar County

Circuit Clerk

Fifth Judicial Circuit
501 Archer Avenue, Marshall, IL 62441
Tel: (217) 826-3943 Fax: (217) 826-2646
Internet: www.state.il.us/court/CircuitCourt/CircuitMap/5th.asp

Clerk of Court, Edgar County **Karen Halloran** . . . . (217) 466-7447
  115 West Court Street, Paris, IL 61944   Fax: (217) 466-7443

Edwards County

Circuit Clerk

Second Judicial Circuit
911 Casey Avenue, Suite HI-05, Mount Vernon, IL 62864
Tel: (618) 244-8036 Fax: (618) 244-8038
Internet: www.illinoissecondcircuit.info/

Clerk of Court, Edwards County **Patsy Taylor** . . . . (618) 445-2016
  50 East Main Street, Albion, IL 62806-1262   Fax: (618) 445-4943

Effingham County

Circuit Clerk

Fourth Judicial Circuit
221 South Seventh Street, Vandalia, IL 62471
Tel: (618) 283-2030 Fax: (618) 283-9741
Internet: www.fourthcircuitil.com

Clerk of Court, Effingham County **John Niemerg** . . . . (217) 342-4065
  120 East Jefferson, Effingham, IL 62401-0586   Fax: (217) 342-6183

Fayette County

Circuit Clerk

Fourth Judicial Circuit
221 South Seventh Street, Vandalia, IL 62471
Tel: (618) 283-2030 Fax: (618) 283-9741
Internet: www.fourthcircuitil.com

Clerk of Court, Fayette County **Kathy Emerick** . . . . (618) 283-5009
  221 South Seventh Street, Vandalia, IL 62471   Fax: (618) 283-4490

Illinois Court Clerks and Courthouses *continued*

Ford County

Circuit Clerk

Eleventh Judicial Circuit
104 West Front Street, Bloomington, IL 61701
Tel: (309) 888-5254 Fax: (309) 862-8215
Internet: www.state.il.us/court/CircuitCourt/CircuitMap/11th.asp

Clerk of Court, Ford County **Kim Evans** . . . . (217) 379-2641
  200 West State, Paxton, IL 60957-0080   Fax: (217) 379-3445
  P.O. Box 80, Paxton, IL 60957-0080

Franklin County

Circuit Clerk

Second Judicial Circuit
911 Casey Avenue, Suite HI-05, Mount Vernon, IL 62864
Tel: (618) 244-8036 Fax: (618) 244-8038
Internet: www.illinoissecondcircuit.info/

Clerk of Court, Franklin County **Nancy Hobbs** . . . . (618) 439-2011
  P.O. Box 485, Benton, IL 62812-2264   Fax: (618) 439-4119

Fulton County

Circuit Clerk

Ninth Judicial Circuit
130 South Lafayette Street, Suite 30, Macomb, IL 61455
Tel: (309) 837-9278 Fax: (309) 833-3547

Clerk of Court, Fulton County **Mary C. Hampton** . . . . (309) 547-3041
  P.O. Box 152, Lewistown, IL 61542   Fax: (309) 547-3674

Gallatin County

Circuit Clerk

Second Judicial Circuit
911 Casey Avenue, Suite HI-05, Mount Vernon, IL 62864
Tel: (618) 244-8036 Fax: (618) 244-8038
Internet: www.illinoissecondcircuit.info/

Clerk of Court, Gallatin County **Brittney Capeheart** . . . . . (618) 269-3140
  P.O. Box 249, Shawneetown, IL 62984-0249   Fax: (618) 269-4324

Greene County

Circuit Clerk

Seventh Judicial Circuit
200 South Ninth Street, Springfield, IL 62701
Tel: (217) 753-6360 Fax: (217) 753-6357
Internet: www.state.il.us/court/CircuitCourt/CircuitMap/7th.asp

Clerk of Court, Greene County **Shirley Thornton** . . . . (217) 942-3421
  519 North Main Street, Carrollton, IL 62016   Fax: (217) 942-5431
  E-mail: sthornton@illinoiscourts.gov

Grundy County

Circuit Clerk

Thirteenth Judicial Circuit
119 West Madison Street, Ottawa, IL 61350
Tel: (815) 434-0786 Fax: (815) 434-6062
Internet: www.state.il.us/court/CircuitCourt/CircuitMap/13th.asp

Clerk of Court, Grundy County **Karen Slattery** . . . . (815) 941-3258
   111 East Washington Street, Room 30,   Fax: (815) 941-3265
   Morris, IL 60450

Hamilton County

Circuit Clerk

Second Judicial Circuit
911 Casey Avenue, Suite HI-05, Mount Vernon, IL 62864
Tel: (618) 244-8036 Fax: (618) 244-8038
Internet: www.illinoissecondcircuit.info/

Clerk of Court, Hamilton County **Beth Sandusky** . . . . (618) 643-3224
   100 South Jackson Street,   Fax: (618) 643-3455
   Mcleansboro, IL 62859-1490

Hancock County

Circuit Clerk

Ninth Judicial Circuit
130 South Lafayette Street, Suite 30, Macomb, IL 61455
Tel: (309) 837-9278 Fax: (309) 833-3547

Clerk of Court, Hancock County **John Neally** . . . . (217) 357-2616
   P.O. Box 189, Carthage, IL 62321   Fax: (217) 357-2231

Hardin County

Circuit Clerk

Second Judicial Circuit
911 Casey Avenue, Suite HI-05, Mount Vernon, IL 62864
Tel: (618) 244-8036 Fax: (618) 244-8038
Internet: www.illinoissecondcircuit.info/

Clerk of Court, Hardin County **Nancy Pennell** . . . . (618) 287-2735
   P.O. Box 308, Elizabethtown, IL 62931-0308   Fax: (618) 287-2713

Henderson County

Circuit Clerk

Ninth Judicial Circuit
130 South Lafayette Street, Suite 30, Macomb, IL 61455
Tel: (309) 837-9278 Fax: (309) 833-3547

Clerk of Court, Henderson County **Sandra D. Keane** . . . . (309) 867-3121
   P.O. Box 546, Oquawka, IL 61469   Fax: (309) 867-3207

Henry County

Circuit Clerk

Fourteenth Judicial Circuit
210 Fifteenth Street, Rock Island, IL 61201
Tel: (309) 558-3289 Fax: (309) 558-3263
Internet: www.state.il.us/court/CircuitCourt/CircuitMap/14th.asp

Clerk of Court, Henry County **Jackie Oberg** . . . . (309) 937-3572
   307 West Center Street, Cambridge, IL 61238   Fax: (309) 937-3990

Iroquois County

Circuit Clerk

Twenty First Judicial Circuit
450 East Court Street, Kankakee, IL 60901
Tel: (815) 937-2915 Fax: (815) 937-3903
Internet: http://www.co.kankakee.il.us/21stJudicial/index.html

Clerk of Court, Iroquois County **Lisa Hines** . . . . (815) 432-6950
   550 South 10th Street, Watseka, IL 60970   Fax: (815) 432-9333

Jackson County

Circuit Clerk

First Judicial Circuit
200 West Jefferson, Marion, IL 62959
P.O. Box 940, Marion, IL 62959
Tel: (618) 997-1234 Fax: (618) 993-6618
Internet: www.state.il.us/court/CircuitCourt/CircuitMap/1st.asp

Clerk of Court, Jackson County **Cindy R. Svanda** . . . . (618) 687-7300
   P.O. Box 730, Murphysboro, IL 62966   Fax: (618) 684-6378

Jasper County

Circuit Clerk

Fourth Judicial Circuit
221 South Seventh Street, Vandalia, IL 62471
Tel: (618) 283-2030 Fax: (618) 283-9741
Internet: www.fourthcircuitil.com

Clerk of Court, Jasper County **Jamie Blake** . . . . (618) 783-2524
   100 West Jourdan, Newton, IL 62448-1973   Fax: (618) 783-8626

Jefferson County

Circuit Clerk

Second Judicial Circuit
911 Casey Avenue, Suite HI-05, Mount Vernon, IL 62864
Tel: (618) 244-8036 Fax: (618) 244-8038
Internet: www.illinoissecondcircuit.info/

Clerk of Court, Jefferson County **Randy Pollard** . . . . (618) 244-8007
   P.O. Box 1266, Mount Vernon, IL 62864-1266   Fax: (618) 244-8029

Jersey County

Circuit Clerk

Seventh Judicial Circuit
200 South Ninth Street, Springfield, IL 62701
Tel: (217) 753-6360 Fax: (217) 753-6357
Internet: www.state.il.us/court/CircuitCourt/CircuitMap/7th.asp

Clerk of Court, Jersey County **Charles E. Huebener** . . . . . (618) 498-5571
   201 West Pearl, Jerseyville, IL 62052   Fax: (618) 498-6128

(continued on next page)

Jo Daviess County

Circuit Clerk

Fifteenth Judicial Circuit
106 South Fifth Street, Suite 306A, Oregon, IL 61061
Tel: (815) 732-1197 Fax: (815) 732-1198
Internet: www.state.il.us/court/CircuitCourt/CircuitMap/15th.asp
Internet: www.15thjudicialcircuit.com/

Clerk of Court, Jo Daviess County **Sharon A. Wand** .... (815) 777-0037
330 North Bench Street, Galena, IL 61036   Fax: (815) 776-9146

Johnson County

Circuit Clerk

First Judicial Circuit
200 West Jefferson, Marion, IL 62959
P.O. Box 940, Marion, IL 62959
Tel: (618) 997-1234 Fax: (618) 993-6618
Internet: www.state.il.us/court/CircuitCourt/CircuitMap/1st.asp

Clerk of Court, Johnson County **Ryan O'Neal** .... (618) 658-4751
P.O. Box 517, Vienna, IL 62995   Fax: (618) 658-2908

Kane County

Circuit Clerk

Sixteenth Judicial Circuit
37W777 Route 38, Suite 301, St. Charles, IL 60175
Tel: (630) 232-3440 Fax: (630) 406-7121
Internet: www.state.il.us/court/CircuitCourt/CircuitMap/16th.asp
Internet: www.illinois16thjudicialcircuit.org

Clerk of Court, Kane County
Thomas "Tom" Hartwell .... (630) 232-3413
540 South Randall Road, St. Charles, IL 60174   Fax: (630) 208-2172

Kankakee County

Circuit Clerk

Twenty First Judicial Circuit
450 East Court Street, Kankakee, IL 60901
Tel: (815) 937-2915 Fax: (815) 937-3903
Internet: http://www.co.kankakee.il.us/21stJudicial/index.html

Clerk of Court, Kankakee County **Sandra Cianci** .... (815) 936-5701
450 East Court Street, Kankakee, IL 60901   Fax: (815) 939-8830
E-mail: scianci@k3county.net

Kendall County

Circuit Clerk

Sixteenth Judicial Circuit
37W777 Route 38, Suite 301, St. Charles, IL 60175
Tel: (630) 232-3440 Fax: (630) 406-7121
Internet: www.state.il.us/court/CircuitCourt/CircuitMap/16th.asp
Internet: www.illinois16thjudicialcircuit.org

Clerk of Court, Kendall County **Becky Morganegg** ..... (630) 553-4183
807 West john Street, Yorkville, IL 60560   Fax: (630) 553-4964

Knox County

Circuit Clerk

Ninth Judicial Circuit
130 South Lafayette Street, Suite 30, Macomb, IL 61455
Tel: (309) 837-9278 Fax: (309) 833-3547

Clerk of Court, Knox County **Kelly A. Cheesman** .... (309) 345-3859
200 South Cherry Street, Galesburg, IL 61401   Fax: (309) 345-0098

Lake County

Circuit Clerk

Nineteenth Judicial Circuit
18 North County Street, Waukegan, IL 60085
Tel: (847) 377-3600
E-mail: courts@lakecountyil.gov
Internet: www.state.il.us/court/CircuitCourt/CircuitMap/19th.asp
Internet: www.19thcircuitcourt.state.il.us

Clerk of Court, Lake County **Keith Brin** .... (847) 377-3380
18 North County Street, Waukegan, IL 60085   Fax: (847) 360-6409

LaSalle County

Circuit Clerk

Thirteenth Judicial Circuit
119 West Madison Street, Ottawa, IL 61350
Tel: (815) 434-0786 Fax: (815) 434-6062
Internet: www.state.il.us/court/CircuitCourt/CircuitMap/13th.asp

Clerk of Court, LaSalle County **Andrew F. Skoog** .... (815) 434-8671
119 West Madison, Ottawa, IL 61350   Fax: (815) 433-9198

Lawrence County

Circuit Clerk

Second Judicial Circuit
911 Casey Avenue, Suite HI-05, Mount Vernon, IL 62864
Tel: (618) 244-8036 Fax: (618) 244-8038
Internet: www.illinoissecondcircuit.info/

Clerk of Court, Lawrence County **Peggy Frederick** ...... (618) 943-2815
1100 State Street, Lawrenceville, IL 62439-2390   Fax: (618) 943-5205

Lee County

Circuit Clerk

Fifteenth Judicial Circuit
106 South Fifth Street, Suite 306A, Oregon, IL 61061
Tel: (815) 732-1197 Fax: (815) 732-1198
Internet: www.state.il.us/court/CircuitCourt/CircuitMap/15th.asp
Internet: www.15thjudicialcircuit.com/

Clerk of Court, Lee County **Denise A. McCaffrey** .... (815) 284-5237
309 South Galena, Dixon, IL 61021   Fax: (815) 288-5615
P.O. Box 329, Dixon, IL 61021

Livingston County

Circuit Clerk

Eleventh Judicial Circuit
104 West Front Street, Bloomington, IL 61701
Tel: (309) 888-5254 Fax: (309) 862-8215
Internet: www.state.il.us/court/CircuitCourt/CircuitMap/11th.asp

Clerk of Court, Livingston County **Judith K. Cremer** .... (815) 844-2602
110 North Main Street, Pontiac, IL 61764   Fax: (815) 844-2322

Logan County

Circuit Clerk

Eleventh Judicial Circuit
104 West Front Street, Bloomington, IL 61701
Tel: (309) 888-5254 Fax: (309) 862-8215
Internet: www.state.il.us/court/CircuitCourt/CircuitMap/11th.asp

Clerk of Court, Logan County **Mary Kelley** .... (217) 735-2376
601 Broadway, Lincoln, IL 62656   Fax: (217) 732-1231

Macon County

Circuit Clerk

Sixth Judicial Circuit
10 South Main, Suite 12, Sullivan, IL 61951
Tel: (217) 762-4521 Fax: (217) 728-8551
Internet: www.state.il.us/court/CircuitCourt/CircuitMap/6th.asp

Clerk of Court, Macon County **Lois A. Durbin** .... (217) 424-1454
253 East Wood Street, Decatur, IL 62523   Fax: (217) 424-1350

Macoupin County

Circuit Clerk

Seventh Judicial Circuit
200 South Ninth Street, Springfield, IL 62701
Tel: (217) 753-6360 Fax: (217) 753-6357
Internet: www.state.il.us/court/CircuitCourt/CircuitMap/7th.asp

Clerk of Court, Macoupin County **Mike Mathis** .... (217) 854-3211
201 East Main Street, Carlinville, IL 62626   Fax: (217) 854-7361

Madison County

Circuit Clerk

Third Judicial Circuit
155 North Main Street, Suite 405, Edwardsville, IL 62025
Tel: (618) 296-4884 Fax: (618) 692-7475
Internet: www.state.il.us/court/CircuitCourt/CircuitMap/3rd.asp

Clerk of Court, Madison County **Mark Vonnida** .... (618) 692-6240
155 North Main Street, Edwardsville, IL 62025   Fax: (618) 692-0676

Marion County

Circuit Clerk

Fourth Judicial Circuit
221 South Seventh Street, Vandalia, IL 62471
Tel: (618) 283-2030 Fax: (618) 283-9741
Internet: www.fourthcircuitil.com

Clerk of Court, Marion County **Ronda Yates** .... (618) 548-3856
100 Main Street, Salem, IL 62881-0130   Fax: (618) 740-0118

Marshall County

Circuit Clerk

Tenth Judicial Circuit
324 Main Street, Room 215, Peoria, IL 61602-1363
Tel: (309) 672-6047 Fax: (309) 672-6957
Internet: www.state.il.us/court/CircuitCourt/CircuitMap/10th.asp

Clerk of Court, Marshall County **Gina M. Noe** .... (309) 246-6435
122 North Prairie, Lacon, IL 61540   Fax: (309) 246-2173

Mason County

Circuit Clerk

Eighth Judicial Circuit
521 Vermont Street, Quincy, IL 62301
Tel: (217) 277-2055 Fax: (217) 277-2072
Internet: www.state.il.us/court/CircuitCourt/CircuitMap/8th.asp

Clerk of Court, Mason County **Michael Roat** .... (309) 543-6619
125 North Plum, Havana, IL 62644   Fax: (309) 543-4214

Massac County

Circuit Clerk

First Judicial Circuit
200 West Jefferson, Marion, IL 62959
P.O. Box 940, Marion, IL 62959
Tel: (618) 997-1234 Fax: (618) 993-6618
Internet: www.state.il.us/court/CircuitCourt/CircuitMap/1st.asp

Clerk of Court, Massac County **Larry Grace** .... (618) 524-5011
P.O. Box 152, Metropolis, IL 62960   Fax: (618) 524-4850

McDonough County

Circuit Clerk

Ninth Judicial Circuit
130 South Lafayette Street, Suite 30, Macomb, IL 61455
Tel: (309) 837-9278 Fax: (309) 833-3547

Clerk of Court, McDonough County **Kimberly Wilson** ... (309) 837-4889
P.O. Box 348, Macomb, IL 61455   Fax: (309) 833-4493
E-mail: kwilson@illinoiscourts.gov

McHenry County

Circuit Clerk

Twenty Second Judicial Circuit
2200 North Seminary Avenue, Woodstock, IL 60098
Tel: (815) 334-4385 Fax: (815) 338-0248
Internet: www.state.il.us/court/CircuitCourt/CircuitMap/22nd.asp

Clerk of Court, McHenry County **Katherine M. Keefe** ... (815) 334-4000
2200 North Seminary Avenue,   Fax: (815) 338-8583
Woodstock, IL 60098

(continued on next page)

Illinois Court Clerks and Courthouses *continued*

McLean County

Circuit Clerk

Eleventh Judicial Circuit
104 West Front Street, Bloomington, IL 61701
Tel: (309) 888-5254 Fax: (309) 862-8215
Internet: www.state.il.us/court/CircuitCourt/CircuitMap/11th.asp

Clerk of Court, McLean County **Don R. Everhart** . . . . (309) 888-5324
 104 West Front Street, Bloomington, IL 61701   Fax: (309) 888-5281

Menard County

Circuit Clerk

Eighth Judicial Circuit
521 Vermont Street, Quincy, IL 62301
Tel: (217) 277-2055 Fax: (217) 277-2072
Internet: www.state.il.us/court/CircuitCourt/CircuitMap/8th.asp

Clerk of Court, Menard County **Penny Hoke** . . . . (217) 632-2615
 P.O. Box 466, Petersburg, IL 62675   Fax: (217) 632-4124

Mercer County

Circuit Clerk

Fourteenth Judicial Circuit
210 Fifteenth Street, Rock Island, IL 61201
Tel: (309) 558-3289 Fax: (309) 558-3263
Internet: www.state.il.us/court/CircuitCourt/CircuitMap/14th.asp

Clerk of Court, Mercer County **Jeff G. Benson** . . . . (309) 582-7122
 100 Southeast 3rd Street, Aledo, IL 61231   Fax: (309) 582-7121

Monroe County

Circuit Clerk

Twentieth Judicial Circuit
10 Public Square, Belleville, IL 62220
Tel: (618) 277-7325 Fax: (618) 277-1398
Internet: www.state.il.us/court/CircuitCourt/CircuitMap/20th.asp

Clerk of Court, Monroe County **Sandra Sauget** . . . . (618) 939-8681
 100 South Main Street, Room 115,   Fax: (618) 939-1929
 Waterloo, IL 62298-1322

Montgomery County

Circuit Clerk

Fourth Judicial Circuit
221 South Seventh Street, Vandalia, IL 62471
Tel: (618) 283-2030 Fax: (618) 283-9741
Internet: www.fourthcircuitil.com

Clerk of Court, Montgomery County **Holly Lemons** . . . . . (217) 532-9546
 120 North Main, Hillsboro, IL 62049   Fax: (217) 532-9614

Illinois Court Clerks and Courthouses *continued*

Morgan County

Circuit Clerk

Seventh Judicial Circuit
200 South Ninth Street, Springfield, IL 62701
Tel: (217) 753-6360 Fax: (217) 753-6357
Internet: www.state.il.us/court/CircuitCourt/CircuitMap/7th.asp

Clerk of Court, Morgan County **Theresa Lonergan** . . . . . . (217) 243-5419
 300 West State Street, Jacksonville, IL 62650   Fax: (217) 243-2009

Moultrie County

Circuit Clerk

Sixth Judicial Circuit
10 South Main, Suite 12, Sullivan, IL 61951
Tel: (217) 762-4521 Fax: (217) 728-8551
Internet: www.state.il.us/court/CircuitCourt/CircuitMap/6th.asp

Clerk of Court, Moultrie County **Cynthia J. Braden** . . . . . (217) 728-4622
 10 South Main Street, Suite 7,   Fax: (217) 728-7833
 Sullivan, IL 61951

Ogle County

Circuit Clerk

Fifteenth Judicial Circuit
106 South Fifth Street, Suite 306A, Oregon, IL 61061
Tel: (815) 732-1197 Fax: (815) 732-1198
Internet: www.state.il.us/court/CircuitCourt/CircuitMap/15th.asp
Internet: www.15thjudicialcircuit.com/

Clerk of Court, Ogle County **Kim Stahl** . . . . (815) 732-3201 ext. 205
 106 South Fifth Street, Suite 300,   Fax: (815) 732-6273
 Oregon, IL 61061
 E-mail: circuitclerk@oglecounty.org

Peoria County

Circuit Clerk

Tenth Judicial Circuit
324 Main Street, Room 215, Peoria, IL 61602-1363
Tel: (309) 672-6047 Fax: (309) 672-6957
Internet: www.state.il.us/court/CircuitCourt/CircuitMap/10th.asp

Clerk of Court, Peoria County **Robert Spears** . . . . (309) 672-6989
 324 Main Street, Room G22,   Fax: (309) 672-6228
 Peoria, IL 61602-1363

Perry County

Circuit Clerk

Twentieth Judicial Circuit
10 Public Square, Belleville, IL 62220
Tel: (618) 277-7325 Fax: (618) 277-1398
Internet: www.state.il.us/court/CircuitCourt/CircuitMap/20th.asp

Clerk of Court, Perry County **Kim Kellerman** . . . . (618) 357-6726
 P.O. Box 219, Pinckneyville, IL 62274-0219   Fax: (618) 357-8336

Piatt County

Circuit Clerk

Sixth Judicial Circuit
10 South Main, Suite 12, Sullivan, IL 61951
Tel: (217) 762-4521 Fax: (217) 728-8551
Internet: www.state.il.us/court/CircuitCourt/CircuitMap/6th.asp

Clerk of Court, Piatt County **Charles A. Barre** . . . . (217) 762-5906
  10 South Main, Sullivan, IL 61951   Fax: (217) 762-8394

Pike County

Circuit Clerk

Eighth Judicial Circuit
521 Vermont Street, Quincy, IL 62301
Tel: (217) 277-2055 Fax: (217) 277-2072
Internet: www.state.il.us/court/CircuitCourt/CircuitMap/8th.asp

Clerk of Court, Pike County **Debbie Dugan** . . . .(217) 285-6612
  100 East Washington, Pittsfield, IL 62363   Fax: (217) 285-4726

Pope County

Circuit Clerk

First Judicial Circuit
200 West Jefferson, Marion, IL 62959
P.O. Box 940, Marion, IL 62959
Tel: (618) 997-1234 Fax: (618) 993-6618
Internet: www.state.il.us/court/CircuitCourt/CircuitMap/1st.asp

Clerk of Court, Pope County **Sean Goins** . . . .(618) 683-3941
  Main Street, Grantsburg, IL 62938   Fax: (618) 683-3018
  P.O. Box 438, Grantsburg, IL 62938

Pulaski County

Circuit Clerk

First Judicial Circuit
200 West Jefferson, Marion, IL 62959
P.O. Box 940, Marion, IL 62959
Tel: (618) 997-1234 Fax: (618) 993-6618
Internet: www.state.il.us/court/CircuitCourt/CircuitMap/1st.asp

Clerk of Court, Pulaski County **Cindy Kennedy** . . . . (618) 748-9300
  500 Illinois Avenue, Mound City, IL 62963   Fax: (618) 748-9329

Putnam County

Circuit Clerk

Tenth Judicial Circuit
324 Main Street, Room 215, Peoria, IL 61602-1363
Tel: (309) 672-6047 Fax: (309) 672-6957
Internet: www.state.il.us/court/CircuitCourt/CircuitMap/10th.asp

Clerk of Court, Putnam County **Cathy J. Oliveri** . . . . (815) 925-7016
  120 North 4th Street, Hennepin, IL 61327   Fax: (815) 925-7492

Randolph County

Circuit Clerk

Twentieth Judicial Circuit
10 Public Square, Belleville, IL 62220
Tel: (618) 277-7325 Fax: (618) 277-1398
Internet: www.state.il.us/court/CircuitCourt/CircuitMap/20th.asp

Clerk of Court, Randolph County **Sherry Johnson** . . . . . . (618) 826-3116
  One Taylor Street, Room 302,   Fax: (618) 826-3761
  Chester, IL 62233-0329

Richland County

Circuit Clerk

Second Judicial Circuit
911 Casey Avenue, Suite HI-05, Mount Vernon, IL 62864
Tel: (618) 244-8036 Fax: (618) 244-8038
Internet: www.illinoissecondcircuit.info/

Clerk of Court, Richland County **Zach Holder** . . . .(618) 392-2151
  103 West Main Street, Room 21,   Fax: (618) 392-5041
  Olney, IL 62450-2170

Rock Island County

Circuit Clerk

Fourteenth Judicial Circuit
210 Fifteenth Street, Rock Island, IL 61201
Tel: (309) 558-3289 Fax: (309) 558-3263
Internet: www.state.il.us/court/CircuitCourt/CircuitMap/14th.asp

Clerk of Court, Rock Island County **Tammy Weikert** . . . . (309) 786-4451
  210 Fifteenth Street, Rock Island, IL 61201   Fax: (309) 786-3029

Saline County

Circuit Clerk

First Judicial Circuit
200 West Jefferson, Marion, IL 62959
P.O. Box 940, Marion, IL 62959
Tel: (618) 997-1234 Fax: (618) 993-6618
Internet: www.state.il.us/court/CircuitCourt/CircuitMap/1st.asp

Clerk of Court, Saline County **Randy Nyberg** . . . . (618) 253-5096
  10 East Poplar, Harrisburg, IL 62946-1553   Fax: (618) 253-3904

Sangamon County

Circuit Clerk

Seventh Judicial Circuit
200 South Ninth Street, Springfield, IL 62701
Tel: (217) 753-6360 Fax: (217) 753-6357
Internet: www.state.il.us/court/CircuitCourt/CircuitMap/7th.asp

Clerk of Court, Sangamon County **Anthony P. Libri** . . . . . (217) 753-6674
  200 South Ninth Street, Room 405,   Fax: (217) 753-6665
  Springfield, IL 62701

(continued on next page)

Schuyler County

Circuit Clerk

Eighth Judicial Circuit
521 Vermont Street, Quincy, IL 62301
Tel: (217) 277-2055 Fax: (217) 277-2072
Internet: www.state.il.us/court/CircuitCourt/CircuitMap/8th.asp

Clerk of Court, Schuyler County **Elaine Boyd** . . . . (217) 322-4633
  P.O. Box 80, Rushville, IL 62681   Fax: (217) 322-6164

Scott County

Circuit Clerk

Seventh Judicial Circuit
200 South Ninth Street, Springfield, IL 62701
Tel: (217) 753-6360 Fax: (217) 753-6357
Internet: www.state.il.us/court/CircuitCourt/CircuitMap/7th.asp

Clerk of Court, Scott County **Stacy J. Evans** . . . . (217) 742-5217
  35 East Market Street, Winchester, IL 62694   Fax: (217) 742-5853

Shelby County

Circuit Clerk

Fourth Judicial Circuit
221 South Seventh Street, Vandalia, IL 62471
Tel: (618) 283-2030 Fax: (618) 283-9741
Internet: www.fourthcircuitil.com

Clerk of Court, Shelby County **Susan Arthur** . . . . (217) 774-4212
  P.O. Box 469, Shelbyville, IL 62565-0469   Tel: (217) 774-4109

St. Clair County

Circuit Clerk

Twentieth Judicial Circuit
10 Public Square, Belleville, IL 62220
Tel: (618) 277-7325 Fax: (618) 277-1398
Internet: www.state.il.us/court/CircuitCourt/CircuitMap/20th.asp

Clerk of Court, St. Clair County **Kahalah A. Clay** . . . . (618) 277-6832
  10 Public Square, Belleville, IL 62220   Fax: (618) 277-1562

Stark County

Circuit Clerk

Tenth Judicial Circuit
324 Main Street, Room 215, Peoria, IL 61602-1363
Tel: (309) 672-6047 Fax: (309) 672-6957
Internet: www.state.il.us/court/CircuitCourt/CircuitMap/10th.asp

Clerk of Court, Stark County **Marian E. Purtscher** . . . . . . (309) 286-5941
  130 Main Street, Toulon, IL 61483   Fax: (309) 286-4039

Stephenson County

Circuit Clerk

Fifteenth Judicial Circuit
106 South Fifth Street, Suite 306A, Oregon, IL 61061
Tel: (815) 732-1197 Fax: (815) 732-1198
Internet: www.state.il.us/court/CircuitCourt/CircuitMap/15th.asp
Internet: www.15thjudicialcircuit.com/

Clerk of Court, Stephenson County **Bonnie K. Curran** . . . (815) 235-8266
  15 North Galena Avenue, Second Floor,   Fax: (815) 233-1576
  Freeport, IL 61032
  E-mail: bcurran@co.stephenson.il.us

Tazewell County

Circuit Clerk

Tenth Judicial Circuit
324 Main Street, Room 215, Peoria, IL 61602-1363
Tel: (309) 672-6047 Fax: (309) 672-6957
Internet: www.state.il.us/court/CircuitCourt/CircuitMap/10th.asp

Clerk of Court, Tazewell County **Lincoln Hobson** . . . . (309) 477-2214
  342 Court Street, Pekin, IL 31554   Fax: (309) 353-7801

Union County

Circuit Clerk

First Judicial Circuit
200 West Jefferson, Marion, IL 62959
P.O. Box 940, Marion, IL 62959
Tel: (618) 997-1234 Fax: (618) 993-6618
Internet: www.state.il.us/court/CircuitCourt/CircuitMap/1st.asp

Clerk of Court, Union County **Lorraine Moreland** . . . . . . (618) 833-5913
  309 West Market Street, Room 101,   Fax: (618) 833-5223
  Jonesboro, IL 62952-0360

Vermilion County

Circuit Clerk

Fifth Judicial Circuit
501 Archer Avenue, Marshall, IL 62441
Tel: (217) 826-3943 Fax: (217) 826-2646
Internet: www.state.il.us/court/CircuitCourt/CircuitMap/5th.asp

Clerk of Court, Vermilion County **Dennis R. Gardner** . . . (217) 554-7700
  Seven North Vermilion Street,   Fax: (217) 554-7728
  Danville, IL 61832

Wabash County

Circuit Clerk

Second Judicial Circuit
911 Casey Avenue, Suite HI-05, Mount Vernon, IL 62864
Tel: (618) 244-8036 Fax: (618) 244-8038
Internet: www.illinoissecondcircuit.info/

Clerk of Court, Wabash County **Angela K. Crum** . . . . (618) 262-5362
  401 Market Street, Mount Carmel, IL 62863   Fax: (618) 263-4441

Warren County

Circuit Clerk

Ninth Judicial Circuit
130 South Lafayette Street, Suite 30, Macomb, IL 61455
Tel: (309) 837-9278 Fax: (309) 833-3547

Clerk of Court, Warren County **Denise Schreck** . . . . (309) 734-5179
100 West Broadway, Monmouth, IL 61462   Fax: (309) 734-4151

Washington County

Circuit Clerk

Twentieth Judicial Circuit
10 Public Square, Belleville, IL 62220
Tel: (618) 277-7325 Fax: (618) 277-1398
Internet: www.state.il.us/court/CircuitCourt/CircuitMap/20th.asp

Clerk of Court, Washington County
Cynthia Barcewski . . . . (618) 327-4800
101 East St. Louis Street, Nashville, IL 62263-1100   Fax: (618) 327-3583

Wayne County

Circuit Clerk

Second Judicial Circuit
911 Casey Avenue, Suite HI-05, Mount Vernon, IL 62864
Tel: (618) 244-8036 Fax: (618) 244-8038
Internet: www.illinoissecondcircuit.info/

Clerk of Court, Wayne County **Sharon L. Gualdoni** . . . . . (618) 842-7684
307 East Main Street, Fairfield, IL 62837-0096   Fax: (618) 842-2556

White County

Circuit Clerk

Second Judicial Circuit
911 Casey Avenue, Suite HI-05, Mount Vernon, IL 62864
Tel: (618) 244-8036 Fax: (618) 244-8038
Internet: www.illinoissecondcircuit.info/

Clerk of Court, White County **Kelly Fulkerson** . . . . (618) 382-2321
301 East Main Street, Carmi, IL 62821-0310   Fax: (618) 382-2322
E-mail: cclerk@whitecounty-il.gov

Whiteside County

Circuit Clerk

Fourteenth Judicial Circuit
210 Fifteenth Street, Rock Island, IL 61201
Tel: (309) 558-3289 Fax: (309) 558-3263
Internet: www.state.il.us/court/CircuitCourt/CircuitMap/14th.asp

Clerk of Court, Whiteside County **Susan Ottens** . . . . (815) 772-5188
200 East Knox Street, Morrison, IL 61270   Fax: (815) 772-5187

Will County

Circuit Clerk

Twelfth Judicial Circuit
14 West Jefferson Street, Joliet, IL 60432
Tel: (815) 727-8540 Fax: (815) 727-8817
Internet: www.state.il.us/court/CircuitCourt/CircuitMap/12th.asp

Clerk of Court, Will County **Pamela J. McGuire** . . . . (815) 727-8585
14 West Jefferson Street, Suite 212,   Fax: (815) 727-8896
Joliet, IL 60432

Williamson County

Circuit Clerk

First Judicial Circuit
200 West Jefferson, Marion, IL 62959
P.O. Box 940, Marion, IL 62959
Tel: (618) 997-1234 Fax: (618) 993-6618
Internet: www.state.il.us/court/CircuitCourt/CircuitMap/1st.asp

Clerk of Court, Williamson County **Stuart Hall** . . . . (618) 997-1301
200 West Jefferson, Marion, IL 62959   Fax: (618) 998-9401

Winnebago County

Circuit Clerk

Seventeenth Judicial Circuit
400 West State Street, Suite 215, Rockford, IL 61101
Tel: (815) 319-4800 Fax: (815) 319-4808
Internet: www.state.il.us/court/CircuitCourt/CircuitMap/17th.asp
Internet: www.illinois17th.com

Clerk of Court, Winnebago County **Tom Klein** . . . . (815) 319-4500
400 West State Street, Rockford, IL 61101   Fax: (815) 319-4571
E-mail: circuit_clerk@wincoil.us

Woodford County

Circuit Clerk

Eleventh Judicial Circuit
104 West Front Street, Bloomington, IL 61701
Tel: (309) 888-5254 Fax: (309) 862-8215
Internet: www.state.il.us/court/CircuitCourt/CircuitMap/11th.asp

Clerk of Court, Woodford County **Carol J. Newtson** . . . . (309) 467-3312
115 North Main Street, Eureka, IL 61530   Fax: (309) 467-7377

Counties Within Judicial Districts

Circuit Court, 1st Judicial Circuit

Areas Covered: Alexander, Jackson, Johnson, Massac, Pope, Pulaski, Saline, Union, and Williamson Counties.

Circuit Court, 2nd Judicial Circuit

Areas Covered: Crawford, Edwards, Franklin, Gallatin, Hamilton, Hardin, Jefferson, Lawrence, Richland, Wabash, Wayne, and White Counties.

Circuit Court, 3rd Judicial Circuit

Areas Covered: Bond and Madison Counties.

(continued on next page)

Circuit Court, 4th Judicial Circuit
Areas Covered: Christian, Clay, Clinton, Effingham, Fayette, Jasper, Marion, Montgomery, and Shelby Counties.

Circuit Court, 5th Judicial Circuit
Areas Covered: Clark, Coles, Cumberland, Edgar, and Vermilion Counties.

Circuit Court, 6th Judicial Circuit
Areas Covered: Champaign, DeWitt, Douglas, Macon, Moultrie, and Piatt Counties.

Circuit Court, 7th Judicial Circuit
Areas Covered: Greene, Jersey, Macoupin, Morgan, Sangamon, and Scott Counties.

Circuit Court, 8th Judicial Circuit
Areas Covered: Adams, Brown, Calhoun, Cass, Mason, Menard, Pike, and Schuyler Counties.

Circuit Court, 9th Judicial Circuit
Areas Covered: Fulton, Hancock, Henderson, Knox, McDonough, and Warren Counties.

Circuit Court, 10th Judicial Circuit
Areas Covered: Marshall, Peoria, Putnam, Stark, and Tazewell Counties.

Circuit Court, 11th Judicial Circuit
Areas Covered: Ford, Livingston, Logan, McLean, and Woodford Counties.

Circuit Court, 12th Judicial Circuit
Areas Covered: Will County.

Circuit Court, 13th Judicial Circuit
Areas Covered: Bureau, Grundy, and LaSalle Counties.

Circuit Court, 14th Judicial Circuit
Areas Covered: Henry, Mercer, Rock Island, and Whiteside Counties.

Circuit Court, 15th Judicial Circuit
Areas Covered: Carroll, Jo Daviess, Lee, Ogle, and Stephenson Counties.

Circuit Court, 16th Judicial Circuit
Areas Covered: Kane County.

Circuit Court, 17th Judicial Circuit
Areas Covered: Boone and Winnebago Counties.

Circuit Court, 18th Judicial Circuit
Areas Covered: DuPage County.

Circuit Court, 19th Judicial Circuit
Areas Covered: Lake County.

Circuit Court, 20th Judicial Circuit
Areas Covered: Monroe, Perry, Randolph, St. Clair, and Washington Counties.

Circuit Court, 21st Judicial Circuit
Areas Covered: Iroquois and Kankakee Counties.

Circuit Court, 22nd Judicial Circuit
Areas Covered: McHenry County.

Circuit Court, 23rd Judicial District
Areas Covered: Dekalb and Kendall Counties.

Circuit Court, Cook County Judicial Circuit
Areas Covered: Cook County.

Indiana Court Clerks and Courthouses

The trial courts of general jurisdiction in Indiana are called Circuit Courts, with Superior Courts serving as divisions of the Circuit Court. There is a Circuit Court in each of the 92 Indiana counties. The Clerk serves as both the Circuit Clerk and the County Clerk. The County Recorder is a separate position.

Indiana Supreme Court

200 West Washington Street, Indianapolis, IN 46204-2732
Tel: (317) 232-2540 Fax: (317) 232-8372
Internet: www.in.gov/judiciary/supreme

The Supreme Court consists of a chief justice and four associate justices who are appointed for initial two-year terms by the Governor from a list supplied by the Judicial Nominating Commission. Justices are then subject to a retention vote in the next statewide general election for a ten-year term. The chief justice is selected by the Judicial Nominating Commission to serve a consecutive five-year term. The Supreme Court has original exclusive jurisdiction over cases involving admission to the practice of law; discipline and disbarment of those admitted to the practice of law; unauthorized practice of law; discipline, removal, or retirement of judges; exercise of jurisdiction by other courts; appeals from judgments imposing a sentence of death or life imprisonment; appeals from the denial of post-conviction relief in which the sentence was death; and appealable cases where a state or federal statute has been declared unconstitutional.

Court Staff

Supreme Court Administrator **Kevin S. Smith** . . . . (317) 232-2540
   E-mail: kevin.smith@courts.in.gov
Clerk of the Supreme and Appellate Courts
   Kevin S. Smith . . . . (317) 232-2540
   E-mail: kevin.smith@courts.in.gov   Fax: (317) 232-8365

Indiana Court of Appeals

200 West Washington Street, Indianapolis, IN 46204
Tel: (317) 232-6906 Fax: (317) 233-4627
Internet: www.in.gov/judiciary/appeals

Each District of the Court of Appeals in Indiana consists of a presiding judge and two judges, who are appointed for initial two-year terms by the Governor from a list supplied by the Judicial Nominating Commission. Following the initial two-year term, judges face a retention vote in their districts for a ten-year term. The Court of Appeals has appellate jurisdiction over all cases except for those where the Indiana Supreme Court has exclusive jurisdiction. The Court also reviews final decisions of administrative agencies. The First, Second and Third Districts of the Court of Appeals hear appeals from specific geographic areas. The Court of Appeals for the Fourth District hears every fourth case from the First, Second and Third Districts, while the Court of Appeals for the Fifth District hears every fifth case.

Court Staff

Administrator for the Court of Appeals
   Steven F. Lancaster . . . . (317) 232-4197
   Note: Until October 1, 2015.
   E-mail: steven.lancaster@courts.in.gov
Clerk of the Supreme and Appellate Courts
   Kevin S. Smith . . . . (317) 232-1930
   State House, 200 W. Washington St.,   Fax: (317) 232-8365
   Indianapolis, IN 46204
   E-mail: kevin.smith@courts.in.gov

Indiana Court of Appeals, First District

State House, 200 West Washington Street, Indianapolis, IN 46204
Tel: (317) 232-6906 Fax: (317) 233-4627

Areas Covered: Counties of Bartholomew, Boone, Brown, Clark, Clay, Crawford, Daviess, Dearborn, Decatur, Dubois, Fayette, Floyd, Fountain, Franklin, Gibson, Greene, Hancock, Harrison, Hendricks, Henry, Jackson, Jefferson, Jennings, Johnson, Knox, Lawrence, Martin, Monroe, Montgomery, Morgan, Ohio, Orange, Owen, Parke, Perry, Pike, Posey, Putnam, Randolph, Ripley, Rush, Scott, Shelby, Spencer, Sullivan, Switzerland, Union, Vanderburgh, Vermillion, Vigo, Warrick, Washington and Wayne

Indiana Court of Appeals, Second District

State House, 200 West Washington Street, Indianapolis, IN 46204
Tel: (317) 232-6906 Fax: (317) 233-4627

Areas Covered: Counties of Adams, Blackford, Carroll, Cass, Clinton, Delaware, Grant, Hamilton, Howard, Huntington, Jay, Madison, Marion, Miami, Tippecanoe, Tipton, Wabash, Wells and White

Indiana Court of Appeals, Third District

200 West Washington Street, Indianapolis, IN 46204
Tel: (317) 232-6906 Fax: (317) 233-4627

Areas Covered: Counties of Allen, Benton, DeKalb, Elkhart, Fulton, Jasper, Kosciusko, LaGrange, Lake, LaPorte, Marshall, Newton, Noble, Porter, Pulaski, St. Joseph, Starke, Steuben, Warren and Whitley

Indiana Court of Appeals, Fourth District

200 West Washington Street, Indianapolis, IN 46204
Tel: (317) 232-6906 Fax: (317) 233-4627

The Court of Appeals, Fourth District hears every fourth case from the Courts of Appeals for the First, Second and Third Districts.

Indiana Court of Appeals, Fifth District

200 West Washington Street, Indianapolis, IN 46204
Tel: (317) 232-6906 Fax: (317) 233-4627

The Court of Appeals, Fifth District hears every fifth case from the Courts of Appeals for the First, Second and Third Districts.

Indiana Tax Court

115 West Washington Street, 960 South, Indianapolis, IN 46204-2241
Tel: (317) 232-4694 Fax: (317) 232-0644
Internet: www.courts.in.gov/tax

Areas Covered: Counties of Allen, Jefferson, Lake, Marion, St. Joseph, Vigo and Vanderburgh

Established effective July 1, 1986, the Indiana Tax Court has exclusive jurisdiction over any case that arises under the Indiana tax laws. The Court also has exclusive jurisdiction over cases that are initial appeals of final determinations made by the Indiana Department of State Revenue or the Indiana Board of Tax Review. In addition, the Court has jurisdiction over certain appeals from the Department of Local Government Finance. The Court also hears appeals of inheritance tax determinations from the courts of probate jurisdiction. Decisions of the Tax Court may be appealed directly to the Indiana Supreme Court.

Court Staff

Court Administrator **Karyn D. Graves** . . . . (317) 232-4694
   E-mail: karyn.graves@courts.in.gov

(continued on next page)

Indiana Court Clerks and Courthouses *continued*

Clerk of the Supreme and Appellate Courts
  Kevin S. Smith . . . . (317) 232-1930
    E-mail: kevin.smith@courts.in.gov   Fax: (317) 232-8365

County-By-County

Adams County

Circuit Court Clerk

Adams County Circuit Court
112 South Second Street, Decatur, IN 46733
Tel: (260) 724-5307 Tel: (260) 724-5308

Clerk of Court **James Voglewede** . . . . (260) 724-5309
    E-mail: clerk@co.adams.in.us

Allen County

Circuit Court Clerk

Allen County Circuit Court
715 South Calhoun Street, Room 300, Fort Wayne, IN 46802
Tel: (260) 449-7602 Fax: (260) 449-7652

Clerk of Court **Lisbeth A. "Lisa" Borgmann** . . . . (260) 449-7245

Bartholomew County

Circuit Court Clerk

Bartholomew County Circuit Court
234 Washington Street, Columbus, IN 47201
Tel: (812) 379-1605 Tel: (812) 379-1764

Clerk of Court **Jay Phelps** . . . . (812) 379-1600

Benton County

Circuit Court Clerk

Benton County Circuit Court
706 East Fifth Street, Fowler, IN 47944
Tel: (765) 884-0370 Fax: (765) 884-2027

Clerk of Court **Natalie Kidd** . . . . (765) 884-0930

Blackford County

Circuit Court Clerk

Blackford County Circuit Court
110 West Washington, Hartford City, IN 47348
Tel: (765) 348-2901 Fax: (765) 348-7213

Clerk of Court **Derinda Shady** . . . . (765) 348-1130
    E-mail: dshady@blackfordcounty.com

Boone County

Circuit Court Clerk

Boone County Circuit Court
One Courthouse Square, Lebanon, IN 46052
Tel: (765) 482-0530 Fax: (765) 483-4420
Internet: http://www.boonecounty.in.gov/circuit

Clerk of Court **Jessica Fouts** . . . . (765) 482-3510

Indiana Court Clerks and Courthouses *continued*

Brown County

Circuit Court Clerk

Brown County Circuit Court
20 East Main Street, Nashville, IN 47448
P.O. Box 85, Nashville, IN 47448

Clerk of Court **Brenda Woods** . . . . (812) 988-5512

Carroll County

Circuit Court Clerk

Carroll County Circuit Court
P.O. Box 28, Delphi, IN 46923
101 West Main Street, Delphi, IN 46923

Clerk of Court **Andrea Miller** . . . . (765) 564-4485

Cass County

Circuit Court Clerk

Cass County Circuit Court
200 Court Park, Logansport, IN 46947

Clerk of Court **Beth Liming** . . . . (574) 753-7740

Clark County

Circuit Court Clerk

Clark County Circuit Court
501 East Court Avenue, Jeffersonville, IN 47130

Clerk of Court **Susan Popp** . . . . (812) 285-6244
    E-mail: spopp@co.clark.in.us

Clay County

Circuit Court Clerk

Clay County Circuit Court
609 East National Avenue, Brazil, IN 47834
Tel: (812) 448-9036 Fax: (812) 448-8255

Clerk of Court **Victoria J. "Vickie" Wheeler** . . . . (812) 448-9025

Clinton County

Circuit Court Clerk

Clinton County Circuit Court
355 Courthouse Square, Frankfort, IN 46041
Tel: (765) 659-6345

Clerk of Court **Sherri Crews** . . . . (765) 659-6335

Crawford County

Circuit Court Clerk

Crawford County Circuit Court
715 Judicial Plaza Drive, English, IN 47118
Tel: (812) 338-3113 Fax: (812) 338-2341

Clerk of Court **Edna Brown** . . . . (812) 338-2565

Daviess County

Circuit Court Clerk

Daviess County Circuit Court
200 East Walnut Street, Washington, IN 47501
Tel: (812) 254-8670 Fax: (812) 254-8683

Clerk of Court **Janice M. Williams** . . . .(812) 254-8664
Fax: (812) 254-8698

Dearborn County

Circuit Court Clerk

Dearborn County Circuit Court
215 West High Street, Lawrenceburg, IN 47025
Tel: (812) 537-8865 Fax: (812) 537-8765

Clerk of Court **Rick Probst** . . . . (812) 537-8867
E-mail: rprobst@dearborncounty.in.gov

Decatur County

Circuit Court Clerk

Decatur County Circuit Court
150 Courthouse Square, Suite 206, Greensburg, IN 47240
Tel: (812) 663-8455 Fax: (812) 663-7957

Clerk of Court **Adina A. Roberts** . . . . (812) 663-8223
E-mail: clerk@decaturcounty.in.gov

DeKalb County

Circuit Court Clerk

DeKalb County Circuit Court
100 South Main Street, Auburn, IN 46706
Tel: (260) 925-2764 Fax: (260) 925-5126

Clerk of Court **Martha "Marty" Grimm** . . . . (260) 925-0912

Delaware County

Circuit Court Clerk

Delaware County Circuit Court
100 West Washington Street, Muncie, IN 47305
Tel: (765) 747-7780 Fax: (765) 741-5792

Clerk of Court **Michael A. King** . . . . (765) 747-7726 ext. 223
E-mail: making@co.delaware.in.us

Dubois County

Circuit Court Clerk

Dubois County Circuit Court
One Courthouse Square, Jasper, IN 47546
Tel: (812) 481-7020 Fax: (812) 481-7030

Clerk of Court **Bridgette N. Jarboe** . . . . (812) 481-7035
E-mail: clerk@duboiscountyin.org

Elkhart County

Circuit Court Clerk

Elkhart County Circuit Court
101 North Main Street, Goshen, IN 46526
Tel: (574) 535-6425

Clerk of Court **Wendy Hudson** . . . . (574) 535-6430

Fayette County

Circuit Court Clerk

Fayette County Circuit Court
401 North Central Avenue, Connersville, IN 47331
Tel: (765) 825-1331 Fax: (765) 825-7307

Clerk of Court **Melinda Sudhoff** . . . .(765) 825-1813
E-mail: clerk@co.fayette.in.us

Floyd County

Circuit Court Clerk

Floyd County Circuit Court
311 Hauss Square, Room 413, New Albany, IN 47150
Tel: (812) 948-5455 Fax: (812) 948-4735

Clerk of Court **Christina "Christi" Eurton** . . . .(812) 948-5415
E-mail: ceurton@floydcountyin.gov

Fountain County

Circuit Court Clerk

Fountain County Circuit Court
301 Fourth Street, Covington, IN 47932
P.O. Box 97, Covington, IN 47932
Tel: (765) 793-3301 Fax: (765) 793-5002

Clerk of Court **Jessica Woodrow** . . . .(765) 793-2192

Franklin County

Circuit Court Clerk

Franklin County Circuit Court
459 Main Street, Franklin, IN 47012
Tel: (765) 647-4186 Fax: (765) 647-4970

Clerk of Court **Karla Bauman** . . . .(765) 647-5111
E-mail: clerk@franklincounty.in.gov

Fulton County

Circuit Court Clerk

Fulton County Circuit Court
815 Main Street, Rochester, IN 46975
Tel: (574) 223-4339 Fax: (574) 224-4340

Clerk of Court **Teri Furnivall** . . . . (574) 223-4824
(continued on next page)

Gibson County

Circuit Court Clerk

Gibson County Circuit Court
101 North Main Street, Princeton, IN 47670
Tel: (812) 385-4885 Fax: (812) 385-3089

Clerk of Court **Jim Morrow** . . . . (812) 386-6474
 E-mail: jmorrow@gibsoncounty-in.gov   Fax: (812) 385-5025

Grant County

Circuit Court Clerk

Grant County Circuit Court
101 East Fourth Street, Marion, IN 46952-4057
Tel: (765) 664-5527 Fax: (765) 668-6541

Clerk of Court **J. Mark Florence** . . . . (765) 668-8121
 E-mail: clerk@grantcounty.net

Greene County

Circuit Court Clerk

Greene County Circuit Court
P.O. Box 231, Bloomfield, IN 47424-0231
Tel: (812) 384-4325 Fax: (812) 384-8458

Clerk of Court **Susan Fowler** . . . . (812) 384-8532

Hamilton County

Circuit Court Clerk

Hamilton County Circuit Court
One Hamilton Square, Noblesville, IN 46060
Tel: (317) 776-9635 Fax: (317) 776-8220

Clerk of Court **Tammy Baitz** . . . . (317) 776-9629

Hancock County

Circuit Court Clerk

Hancock County Circuit Court
9 East Main Street, Greenfield, IN 46140
Tel: (317) 477-1107 Fax: (317) 477-1711

Clerk of Court **Marcia Moore** . . . . (317) 477-1109

Harrison County

Circuit Court Clerk

Harrison County Circuit Court
300 North Capitol Avenue, Corydon, IN 47112
Tel: (812) 738-2191 Fax: (812) 738-7502

Clerk of Court **Sally Whitis** . . . . (812) 738-4289
 E-mail: sallywhite@harrisoncounty.in.gov

Hendricks County

Circuit Court Clerk

Hendricks County Circuit Court
One Courthouse Square, Danville, IN 46122
Tel: (317) 745-9271 Fax: (317) 745-9256

Clerk of Court **Debbie Hoskins** . . . . (317) 745-9388
 51 West Main Street, #104,   Fax: (317) 718-8364
 Danville, IN 46112

Henry County

Circuit Court Clerk

Henry County Circuit Court
1215 Race Street, New Castle, IN 47362
Tel: (765) 529-1403 Fax: (765) 599-2498

Clerk of Court **Debra Walker** . . . . (765) 529-6401
 E-mail: dwalker@henryco.net

Howard County

Circuit Court Clerk

Howard County Circuit Court
104 North Buckeye Street, Kokomo, IN 46901
Tel: (765) 456-2202 Fax: (765) 456-2016

Clerk of Court **Kimmerly "Kim" Wilson** . . . . (765) 456-2204

Huntington County

Circuit Court Clerk

Huntington County Circuit Court
201 North Jefferson Street, Huntington, IN 46750
Tel: (260) 358-4814 Fax: (260) 358-4813

Clerk of Court **Kittie Keiffer** . . . . (260) 358-4817
 E-mail: kittie.keiffer@huntington.in.us

Jackson County

Circuit Court Clerk

Jackson County Circuit Court
111 South Main Street, Brownstown, IN 47220
Tel: (812) 358-6133 Fax: (812) 358-4689

Clerk of Court **Amanda Cunningham Lowery** . . . . (812) 358-6117

Jasper County

Circuit Court Clerk

Jasper County Circuit Court
115 West Washington Street, Rensselaer, IN 47978-2890
Tel: (219) 866-4941 Fax: (219) 866-4943

Clerk of Court **Vickie Bozell** . . . . (219) 866-4926

© Leadership Directories, Inc.

Jay County

Circuit Court Clerk

Jay County Circuit Court
120 North Court Street, Portland, IN 47371-2116
Tel: (260) 726-6950 Fax: (260) 726-6951

Clerk of Court **Ellen Coats** . . . . (260) 726-6915
   E-mail: ecoats@co.jay.in.us   Fax: (260) 726-6922

Jefferson County

Circuit Court Clerk

Jefferson County Circuit Court
300 East Main Street, Madison, IN 47250-3537
Tel: (812) 265-8930 Fax: (812) 265-8946

Clerk of Court **Karen Mannix** . . . . (812) 265-8924

Jennings County

Circuit Court Clerk

Jennings County Circuit Court
P.O. Box 386, Vernon, IN 47282
Tel: (812) 352-3082 Fax: (812) 352-3085

Clerk of Court **Mary Dorsett Kilgore** . . . .(812) 352-3070

Johnson County

Circuit Court Clerk

Johnson County Circuit Court
5 East Jefferson Street, Franklin, IN 46131
Tel: (317) 346-4400 Fax: (317) 736-3996

Clerk of Court **Sue Anne "Susie" Misiniec** . . . . (317) 346-4450

Knox County

Circuit Court Clerk

Knox County Circuit Court
111 North Seventh Street, Vincennes, IN 47591
Tel: (812) 885-2527 Fax: (812) 886-9414

Clerk of Court **Terri Allen** . . . .(812) 885-2521

Kosciusko County

Circuit Court Clerk

Kosciusko County Circuit Court
121 North Lake Street, Warsaw, IN 46580
Tel: (574) 372-2403 Fax: (574) 372-2406

Clerk of Court **Ann Torpy** . . . .(574) 372-2334

LaGrange County

Circuit Court Clerk

LaGrange County Circuit Court
105 North Detroit Street, LaGrange, IN 46761
Tel: (260) 499-6358 Fax: (260) 499-6448

Clerk of Court **Bonnie Brown** . . . .(260) 499-6372

Lake County

Circuit Court Clerk

Lake County Circuit Court
2293 North Main Street, Crown Point, IN 46307
Tel: (219) 755-3488 Fax: (219) 755-3484

Clerk of Court **Michael Brown** . . . . (219) 755-3461

LaPorte County

Circuit Court Clerk

LaPorte County Circuit Court
813 Lincoln Way, LaPorte, IN 46350
Tel: (219) 326-6808 Fax: (219) 324-0147

Clerk of Court **Lynne F. Spevak** . . . . (219) 326-6808
   813 Lincolnway, Suite 105,
   LaPorte, IN 46350
   E-mail: lspevak@laportecounty.org

Lawrence County

Circuit Court Clerk

Lawrence County Circuit Court
916 15th Street, Bedford, IN 47421
Tel: (812) 275-2421 Fax: (812) 275-1044

Clerk of Court **Myron Rainey** . . . . (812) 275-7543

Madison County

Circuit Court Clerk

Madison County Circuit Court
16 East Ninth Street, Anderson, IN 46016
Tel: (765) 641-9436 Fax: (765) 640-4216

Clerk of Court **Darlene Likens** . . . .(765) 641-9443

Marion County

Circuit Court Clerk

Marion County Circuit Court
200 East Washington Street, Indianapolis, IN 46204
Tel: (317) 327-4010 Tel: (317) 327-4473

Clerk of Court **Myla Eldridge** . . . . (317) 327-4740

Marshall County

Circuit Court Clerk

Marshall County Circuit Court
501 North Center Street, Plymouth, IN 46563-1707
Tel: (574) 935-8780 Fax: (574) 936-4703

Clerk of Court **Deborah Van DeMark** . . . . (574) 936-8922
   211 West Madison Street, Plymouth, IN 46563   Fax: (574) 936-8893

(continued on next page)

Martin County

Circuit Court Clerk

Martin County Circuit Court
129 Main Street, Shoals, IN 47581-0370
P.O. Box 370, Shoals, IN 47581-0370
Fax: (812) 247-3901

Clerk of Court **Julie Fithian** . . . . (812) 247-2791
  E-mail: clerk@martincounty.in.gov

Miami County

Circuit Court Clerk

Miami County Circuit Court
25 North Broadway, Peru, IN 46970
Tel: (765) 472-3901 Fax: (765) 472-2189

Clerk of Court **Tawna Leffel Sands** . . . . (765) 472-3901 ext. 256

Monroe County

Circuit Court Clerk

Monroe County Circuit Court
301 North College Avenue, Bloomington, IN 47404
Tel: (812) 349-2615 Fax: (812) 349-2791

Clerk of Court **Linda Robbins** . . . . (812) 349-2614
  E-mail: lrobbins@co.monroe.in.us   Fax: (812) 349-2610

Montgomery County

Circuit Court Clerk

Montgomery County Circuit Court
100 East Main Street, Crawfordsville, IN 47933-1715
Tel: (765) 364-6450 Fax: (765) 364-7251

Clerk of Court **Jennifer Bentley** . . . . (765) 364-6430
  E-mail: clerk@montgomeryco.net

Morgan County

Circuit Court Clerk

Morgan County Circuit Court
P.O. Box 1556, Martinsville, IN 46151
Tel: (765) 342-1020 Fax: (765) 342-1090

Clerk of Court **Stephanie Elliott** . . . . (765) 342-1025

Newton County

Circuit Court Clerk

Newton County Circuit Court
P.O. Box 101, Ketland, IN 47951
Tel: (219) 474-5131 Fax: (219) 474-6751

Clerk of Court **Janis M. Wilson** . . . . (219) 474-6081
  E-mail: jwilson@newtoncounty.in.gov

Noble County

Circuit Court Clerk

Noble County Circuit Court
101 North Orange Street, Albion, IN 46701
Tel: (260) 636-2128 Fax: (260) 636-3053

Clerk of Court **Michelle Mawhorter** . . . . (260) 636-2736

Ohio County

Circuit Court Clerk

Ohio County Circuit Court
413 Main Street, Rising Sun, IN 47040
Tel: (812) 438-3410 Fax: (812) 438-2017

Clerk of Court **Jamie Stegemiller** . . . . (812) 438-2610

Orange County

Circuit Court Clerk

Orange County Circuit Court
1 Court Street, Paoli, IN 47454
Tel: (812) 723-2411 Fax: (812) 723-4603

Clerk of Court **Beth Jones** . . . . (812) 723-2649

Owen County

Circuit Court Clerk

Owen County Circuit Court
P.O. Box 146, Spencer, IN 47460
Tel: (812) 829-5030 Fax: (812) 829-5147

Clerk of Court **Jeff Brothers** . . . . (812) 829-5015

Parke County

Circuit Court Clerk

Parke County Circuit Court
116 West High Street, Rockville, IN 47872
Tel: (765) 569-5671 Fax: (765) 569-4005

Clerk of Court **Diana Hazlett** . . . . (765) 569-5132
  E-mail: pcclerk@parkecounty-in.gov

Perry County

Circuit Court Clerk

Perry County Circuit Court
2219 Payne Street, Tell City, IN 47586
Tel: (812) 547-7048 Fax: (812) 547-5424

Clerk of Court **Amanda F. Mogan** . . . . (812) 547-3741

Pike County

Circuit Court Clerk

Pike County Circuit Court
P.O. Box 467, Petersburg, IN 47567
Tel: (812) 354-6026 Fax: (812) 354-3552

Clerk of Court **Carol Austin** . . . . (812) 354-6025

Porter County

Circuit Court Clerk

Porter County Circuit Court
16 Lincolnway, Valparaiso, IN 46383
Tel: (219) 465-3425 Fax: (219) 465-3647

Clerk of Court **Karen M. Martin** . . . . (219) 465-3450

Posey County

Circuit Court Clerk

Posey County Circuit Court
P.O. Box 745, Mt. Vernon, IN 47620
Tel: (812) 838-1302 Fax: (812) 838-1345

Clerk of Court **Betty Postletheweight** . . . . (812) 838-1306
    E-mail: betty.postletheweight@poseycountyin.gov

Pulaski County

Circuit Court Clerk

Pulaski County Circuit Court
112 East Main Street, Suite 310, Winamac, IN 46996
Tel: (574) 946-3851 Fax: (574) 946-6585

Clerk of Court **Tasha Foerg** . . . . (574) 946-6038

Putnam County

Circuit Court Clerk

Putnam County Circuit Court
One Courthouse Square, Greencastle, IN 46135
Tel: (765) 653-5315 Fax: (765) 653-4870

Clerk of Court **Heather Gilbert** . . . . (765) 653-2648

Randolph County

Circuit Court Clerk

Randolph County Circuit Court
100 South Main Street, Winchester, IN 47394
Tel: (765) 584-4011 Fax: (765) 584-7186

Clerk of Court **Laura J. Martin** . . . . (765) 584-4214
    E-mail: laura.martin@randolphcountyin.net

Ripley County

Circuit Court Clerk

Ripley County Circuit Court
P.O. Box 445, Versailles, IN 47042
Tel: (812) 689-6226 Fax: (812) 689-6104

Clerk of Court **MaryAnn McCoy** . . . . (812) 689-6115
    E-mail: mamccoy@ripleycounty.com

Rush County

Circuit Court Clerk

Rush County Circuit Court
101 East Second Street, Rushville, IN 46173-1887
Tel: (765) 932-2078 Fax: (765) 932-2357

Clerk of Court **Deborah Richardson** . . . . (765) 932-2086
    E-mail: clerk@rushcounty.in.gov

Scott County

Circuit Court Clerk

Scott County Circuit Court
One East McClain Avenue, Scottsburg, IN 47170
Tel: (812) 752-8430 Fax: (812) 752-8431

Clerk of Court **Missy Applegate** . . . . (812) 752-8420
    E-mail: scottcoclerk@iglou.com

Shelby County

Circuit Court Clerk

Shelby County Circuit Court
407 South Harrison Street, Shelbyville, IN 46176
Tel: (317) 392-6360 Fax: (317) 392-6496

Clerk of Court **Vicki Franklin** . . . . (317) 392-6320

Spencer County

Circuit Court Clerk

Spencer County Circuit Court
P.O. Box 152, Rockport, IN 47635
Tel: (812) 649-6025 Fax: (812) 649-6499

Clerk of Court **GayAnn Harney** . . . . (812) 649-6028
    E-mail: clerk@spencercounty.in.gov

St. Joseph County

Circuit Court Clerk

St. Joseph County Circuit Court
101 South Main Street, South Bend, IN 46601
Tel: (574) 235-9551 Fax: (574) 245-6618

Clerk of Court **Terri Rethlake** . . . . (574) 235-9635

Starke County

Circuit Court Clerk

Starke County Circuit Court
P.O. Box 395, Knox, IN 46534
Tel: (574) 772-9146 Fax: (574) 772-9120

Clerk of Court **Vicki Cooley** . . . . (574) 772-9128
    E-mail: clerk75@co.starke.in.us

(continued on next page)

Steuben County

Circuit Court Clerk

Steuben County Circuit Court
55 South Public Square, Angola, IN 46703
Tel: (260) 668-1000 Fax: (260) 665-1913

Clerk of Court **Shelly Herbert** . . . . (260) 668-1000

Sullivan County

Circuit Court Clerk

Sullivan County Circuit Court
100 Courthouse Square, Sullivan, IN 47882
Tel: (812) 268-4411 Fax: (812) 268-4870

Clerk of Court **Peggy Goodman** . . . . (812) 268-4657

Switzerland County

Circuit Court Clerk

Switzerland County Circuit Court
212 West Main Street, Vevay, IN 47043
Tel: (812) 427-4415 Fax: (812) 427-4438

Clerk of Court **Gayle Sullivan** . . . . (812) 427-3175
                                                       Fax: (812) 427-4408

Tippecanoe County

Circuit Court Clerk

Tippecanoe County Circuit Court
301 Main Street, Lafayette, IN 47901
Tel: (765) 423-9343 Fax: (765) 423-9116

Clerk of Court **Christa Coffey** . . . . (765) 423-9326
    E-mail: ccoffey@tippecanoe.in.gov

Tipton County

Circuit Court Clerk

Tipton County Circuit Court
101 East Jefferson, Tipton, IN 46072
Tel: (765) 675-2791 Fax: (765) 675-6436

Clerk of Court **Debbie Tragesser** . . . . (765) 675-2795
    E-mail: debbie.tragesser@courts.in.gov

Union County

Circuit Court Clerk

Union County Circuit Court
26 West Union Street, Liberty, IN 47353
Tel: (765) 458-5934 Fax: (765) 458-5263

Clerk of Court **Loree Persinger** . . . . (765) 458-6121

Vanderburgh County

Circuit Court Clerk

Vanderburgh County Circuit Court
825 Sycamore Street, Evansville, IN 47708
Tel: (812) 435-5195 Fax: (812) 435-5459

Clerk of Court **Debra Stucki** . . . . (812) 435-5160

Vermillion County

Circuit Court Clerk

Vermillion County Circuit Court
255 South Main, Newport, IN 47966
Tel: (765) 492-5320 Fax: (765) 492-5325

County Clerk **Florinda Pruitt** . . . . (765) 492-5350
    E-mail: florinda.pruitt@vermillioncounty.in.gov

Vigo County

Circuit Court Clerk

Vigo County Circuit Court
33 South Third Street, Terre Haute, IN 47807
Tel: (812) 462-3241 Fax: (812) 232-4995

Clerk of Court **David Crockett** . . . . (812) 462-3211

Wabash County

Circuit Court Clerk

Wabash County Circuit Court
49 West Hill Street, Wabash, IN 46992
Tel: (260) 563-0661 Fax: (260) 569-1374

Clerk of Court **Elaine J. Martin** . . . . (260) 563-0661 ext. 230
    69 West Hill Street, Wabash, IN 46992   Fax: (260) 569-1352

Warren County

Circuit Court Clerk

Warren County Circuit Court
125 North Monroe Street, Williamsport, IN 47993
Tel: (765) 762-3604 Fax: (765) 762-1692

Clerk of Court **Deb Hiatt** . . . . (765) 762-3510

Warrick County

Circuit Court Clerk

Warrick County Circuit Court
One County Square, Boonville, IN 47601
Tel: (812) 897-6130 Fax: (812) 897-6137

Clerk of Court **Sarah E. Redman** . . . . (812) 897-6160
    E-mail: clerk@warrickcounty.gov

Indiana Court Clerks and Courthouses *continued*

Washington County

Circuit Court Clerk

Washington County Circuit Court
99 Public Square, Salem, IN 47167
Tel: (812) 883-5302 Fax: (812) 883-1933

Clerk of Court **Shirley Batt** . . . . (812) 883-5748
  E-mail: clerk@washingtoncountyin.gov

Wayne County

Circuit Court Clerk

Wayne County Circuit Court
301 East Main Street, Richmond, IN 47374-4200
Tel: (765) 973-9266 Fax: (765) 973-9250

Clerk of Court **Debra Berry** . . . . (765) 973-9220
  E-mail: clerk@co.wayne.in.us

Wells County

Circuit Court Clerk

Wells County Circuit Court
102 Market Street, Bluffton, IN 46714
Tel: (260) 824-6485 Fax: (260) 824-6488

Clerk of Court **Yvette Runkle** . . . . (260) 824-6479
  E-mail: clerk@wellscounty.org

White County

Circuit Court Clerk

White County Circuit Court
110 North Main Street, Monticello, IN 47960
Tel: (574) 583-5032 Fax: (574) 583-1532

Clerk of Court **Paula Lantz** . . . . (574) 583-7032

Whitley County

Circuit Court Clerk

Whitley County Circuit Court
101 West Van Buren Street, Columbia City, IN 46725
Tel: (260) 248-3115 Fax: (260) 248-3166

Clerk of Court **Debbie Beers** . . . . (260) 248-3102
  E-mail: wcclerk1@whitleygov.com

Iowa Court Clerks and Courthouses

The trial courts of general jurisdiction in Iowa are called district courts. There are eight judicial districts, each district including several counties. The Clerk of the Court functions both as Clerk of the District Court and County Clerk.

Iowa Supreme Court

Iowa Judicial Building, 1111 East Court Avenue, Des Moines, IA 50319
Tel: (515) 281-5174 Fax: (515) 281-3043
Internet: www.iowacourts.gov

The Supreme Court consists of a chief justice and six associate justices who are appointed by the Governor from a list of nominees selected by a judicial nominating commission. Justices face a retention vote for an eight-year term in the first general election following at least one year of service. The chief justice is elected by peer vote for an eight-year term. Retirement is mandatory at age seventy-two; however, retired justices may serve as senior judges with temporary assignments until age seventy-eight. The Supreme Court has general appellate jurisdiction in civil and criminal cases including questions concerning the constitutionality of a legislative or executive act. The Court hears or transfers to the Iowa Court of Appeals all cases appealed from the Iowa District Court, except those concerning real estate interests when the amount involves less than $5000 (or small claims actions when the amount in controversy is $5000 or less) unless the trial judges certifies that the cause is one in which appeals should be allowed. The Court has original jurisdiction in such cases as reapportionment, bar discipline, and the issuance of temporary injunctions. The Court also exercises administrative control and supervisory control over the trial courts.

Court Staff
Clerk of the Supreme Court **Donna Humphal** . . . . (515) 281-5911
Fax: (515) 242-6164

Iowa Court of Appeals

Iowa Judicial Building, 1111 East Court Avenue, Des Moines, IA 50319
Tel: (515) 281-5221 Fax: (515) 281-8371
Internet: www.iowacourts.gov

The Court of Appeals consists of a chief judge and eight judges who are appointed by the Governor from a list of nominees selected by a judicial nomination commission. Judges face a retention vote for a six-year term in the first general election after at least one year of service. The chief judge is elected by peer vote for a two-year term. Retirement is mandatory at age seventy-two; however, retired judges may serve as senior judges with temporary assignments until age eighty. The Court of Appeals has appellate jurisdiction over all civil and criminal actions, post-conviction remedy proceedings, small claims actions, writs, orders and other proceedings. The Court hears only those cases which are transferred to it by the Iowa Supreme Court.

Court Staff
Clerk of the Courts **Donna Humpal** . . . . (515) 281-5911
E-mail: donna.humpal@iowacourts.gov
Staff Attorney **Carla Scholten** . . . . (515) 281-7287
E-mail: carla_scholten@iowacourts.gov

County-By-County

Adair County

Clerk of the Court
Fifth Judicial District
Polk County Courthouse, 500 Mulberry Street, Room 411,
Des Moines, IA 50309
Tel: (515) 286-3198

Clerk of Court, Adair County **Stacey Armstrong** . . . . (641) 743-2445
400 Public Square, Greenfield, IA 50849
E-mail: stacey.armstrong@iowacourts.gov

Adams County

Clerk of the Court
Fifth Judicial District
Polk County Courthouse, 500 Mulberry Street, Room 411,
Des Moines, IA 50309
Tel: (515) 286-3198

Clerk of Court, Adams County **Jackie Saville** . . . . (641) 322-4711
500 Ninth Street, Corning, IA 50841
E-mail: jackie.saville@iowacourts.gov

Allamakee County

Clerk of the Court
First Judicial District
316 East Fifth Street, Waterloo, IA 50703
Tel: (319) 833-3332

Clerk of Court, Allamakee County **Elizabeth Nuss** . . . . . . (563) 568-6351
Allamakee County Courthouse,
110 Allamakee Street, Waukon, IA 52172
E-mail: elizabeth.nuss@iowacourts.gov

Appanoose County

Clerk of the Court
Eighth Judicial District
211 East Fourth Street, Ottumwa, IA 52501
Tel: (641) 684-6502

Clerk of Court, Appanoose County
Mary Jean Houser . . . . (641) 856-6101
201 North 12th Street, Centerville, IA 52544
E-mail: appanoose.county.clerk@iowacourts.gov

Audubon County

Clerk of the Court
Fourth Judicial District
Pottawattamie County Courthouse, 227 South Sixth Street,
Fourt Floor, Room 413, Council Bluffs, IA 51501
Tel: (712) 328-5733

Clerk of Court, Audubon County **Kim Johnson** . . . . (712) 563-4275
318 Leroy Street, Room 6,
Audubon, IA 50025
E-mail: kim.johnson@iowacourts.gov

(continued on next page)

Benton County

Clerk of the Court

Sixth Judicial District
P.O. Box 5488, Cedar Rapids, IA 52406
Tel: (319) 398-3920 ext. 1100

Clerk of Court, Benton County **Cynthia Forsyth** . . . .(319) 472-2766
111 East Fourth Street, Vinton, IA 52349
E-mail: cynthia.forsyth@iowacourts.gov

Black Hawk County

Clerk of the Court

First Judicial District
316 East Fifth Street, Waterloo, IA 50703
Tel: (319) 833-3332

Clerk of Court, Black Hawk County **Waynette Saul** . . . . .(319) 833-3331
Black Hawk County Courthouse,
316 East Fifth Street, Waterloo, IA 50703
E-mail: waynette.saul@iowacourts.gov

Boone County

Clerk of the Court

Second Judicial District
220 North Washington Avenue, Mason City, IA 50401
Tel: (641) 494-3611

Clerk of Court, Boone County
Patricia "Patty" Freund . . . .(515) 433-0561
Boone County Courthouse, 201 State Street,
Boone, IA 50036
E-mail: patricia.freund@iowacourts.gov

Bremer County

Clerk of the Court

Second Judicial District
220 North Washington Avenue, Mason City, IA 50401
Tel: (641) 494-3611

Clerk of Court, Bremer County **Julie Kneip** . . . .(319) 352-1059
415 East Bremer Avenue, Waverly, IA 50677
E-mail: julie.kneip@iowacourts.gov

Buchanan County

Clerk of the Court

First Judicial District
316 East Fifth Street, Waterloo, IA 50703
Tel: (319) 833-3332

Clerk of Court, Buchanan County **Waynette Saul** . . . .(319) 334-2196
Buchanan County Courthouse, 210 Fifth Street,
Independence, IA 50644
E-mail: waynette.saul@iowacourts.gov

Buena Vista County

Clerk of the Court

Third Judicial District
Woodbury County Courthouse, Seventh and Douglas, Room 210,
Sioux City, IA 51101

Clerk of Court, Buena Vista County **Joann Kinnetz** . . . . .(712) 749-2546
215 East Fifteenth Street, Storm Lake, IA 50588
E-mail: joann.kinnetz@iowacourts.gov

Butler County

Clerk of the Court

Second Judicial District
220 North Washington Avenue, Mason City, IA 50401
Tel: (641) 494-3611

Clerk of Court, Butler County **Debra Bausman** . . . .(319) 267-2487
Butler County Courthouse, 428 Sixth Street,   Fax: (319) 267-2488
Allison, IA 50602
E-mail: debra.bausman@iowacourts.gov

Calhoun County

Clerk of the Court

Second Judicial District
220 North Washington Avenue, Mason City, IA 50401
Tel: (641) 494-3611

Clerk of Court, Calhoun County **Donna Geery** . . . .(712) 297-8122
416 Fourth Street, Suite 5,   Fax: (712) 297-5082
Rockwell City, IA 50579
E-mail: donna.geery@iowacourts.gov

Carroll County

Clerk of the Court

Second Judicial District
220 North Washington Avenue, Mason City, IA 50401
Tel: (641) 494-3611

Clerk of Court, Carroll County **Linda Frank** . . . .(712) 792-4327
Carroll County Courthouse, 114 East Sixth Street,
Carroll, IA 51401
E-mail: linda.frank@iowacourts.gov

Cass County

Clerk of the Court

Fourth Judicial District
Pottawattamie County Courthouse, 227 South Sixth Street,
Fourt Floor, Room 413, Council Bluffs, IA 51501
Tel: (712) 328-5733

Clerk of Court, Cass County **Sheila Kunze** . . . .(712) 243-2105
Five West Seventh Street, Atlantic, IA 50022
E-mail: sheila.kunze@iowacourts.gov

Cedar County

Clerk of the Court

Seventh Judicial District
Scott County Courthouse, 416 West Fourth Street, Davenport, IA 52801
Tel: (563) 326-8783

Clerk of Court, Cedar County **Julie Carlin** . . . . (563) 886-2101
   400 Cedar Street, Tipton, IA 52772
   E-mail: julie.carlin@iowacourts.gov

Cerro Gordo County

Clerk of the Court

Second Judicial District
220 North Washington Avenue, Mason City, IA 50401
Tel: (641) 494-3611

Clerk of Court, Cerro Gordo County **Karen Purcell** . . . . . . (641) 424-6431
   220 North Washington Avenue,
   Mason City, IA 50401
   E-mail: karen.purcell@iowacourts.gov

Cherokee County

Clerk of the Court

Third Judicial District
Woodbury County Courthouse, Seventh and Douglas, Room 210,
Sioux City, IA 51101

Clerk of Court, Cherokee County (Acting)
   Lisa Grashoff . . . . (712) 225-6744
   520 West Main Street, Cherokee, IA 51012
   E-mail: lisa.grashoff@iowacourts.gov

Chickasaw County

Clerk of the Court

First Judicial District
316 East Fifth Street, Waterloo, IA 50703
Tel: (319) 833-3332

Clerk of Court, Chickasaw County **Damian Baltes** . . . . . . (641) 394-2754
   Chickasaw County Courthouse,
   Eight East Prospect Street,
   Hampton, IA 50659
   E-mail: damian.baltes@iowacourts.gov

Clarke County

Clerk of the Court

Fifth Judicial District
Polk County Courthouse, 500 Mulberry Street, Room 411,
Des Moines, IA 50309
Tel: (515) 286-3198

Clerk of Court, Clarke County **Linda Graves** . . . . (641) 342-6096
   100 South Main Street, Osceola, IA 50213
   E-mail: linda.graves@iowacourts.gov

Clay County

Clerk of the Court

Third Judicial District
Woodbury County Courthouse, Seventh and Douglas, Room 210,
Sioux City, IA 51101

Clerk of Court, Clay County **Laurie Janssen** . . . . (712) 262-4335
   215 West Fourth Street, Spencer, IA 51301
   E-mail: laurie.janssen@iowacourts.gov

Clayton County

Clerk of the Court

First Judicial District
316 East Fifth Street, Waterloo, IA 50703
Tel: (319) 833-3332

Clerk of Court, Clayton County **Linny Emrich** . . . . (563) 245-2204
   Clayton County Courthouse, 111 High Street,
   Elkader, IA 52043
   E-mail: linny.emrich@iowacourts.gov

Clinton County

Clerk of the Court

Seventh Judicial District
Scott County Courthouse, 416 West Fourth Street, Davenport, IA 52801
Tel: (563) 326-8783

Clerk of Court, Clinton County **Kim Hess** . . . . . (563) 243-6213 ext. 4230
   612 North Second Street, Clinton, IA 52732

Crawford County

Clerk of the Court

Third Judicial District
Woodbury County Courthouse, Seventh and Douglas, Room 210,
Sioux City, IA 51101

Clerk of Court, Crawford County **Karen Kahl** . . . . (712) 263-4310
   1202 Broadway, Denison, IA 51442
   E-mail: karen.kahl@iowacourts.gov

Dallas County

Clerk of the Court

Fifth Judicial District
Polk County Courthouse, 500 Mulberry Street, Room 411,
Des Moines, IA 50309
Tel: (515) 286-3198

Clerk of Court, Dallas County **Marsha McDermott** . . . . . (515) 993-6968
   801 Court Street, Adel, IA 50003
   E-mail: marsha.mcdermott@iowacourts.gov

Davis County

Clerk of the Court

Eighth Judicial District
211 East Fourth Street, Ottumwa, IA 52501
Tel: (641) 684-6502

Clerk of Court, Davis County **Mary Jean Houser** . . . . (641) 664-2011
   100 Courthouse Square, Bloomfield, IA 52537
   E-mail: davis.county.clerk@iowacourts.gov

(continued on next page)

Decatur County

Clerk of the Court

Fifth Judicial District
Polk County Courthouse, 500 Mulberry Street, Room 411,
Des Moines, IA 50309
Tel: (515) 286-3198

Clerk of Court, Decatur County **Traci Tharp** . . . . (641) 446-4331
207 North Main, Leon, IA 50144
E-mail: traci.tharp@iowacourts.gov

Delaware County

Clerk of the Court

First Judicial District
316 East Fifth Street, Waterloo, IA 50703
Tel: (319) 833-3332

Clerk of Court, Delaware County **Linny Emrich** . . . . (563) 927-4942
Delaware County Courthouse, 301 East Main Street,
Manchester, IA 52057
E-mail: linny.emrich@iowacourts.gov

Des Moines County

Clerk of the Court

Eighth Judicial District
211 East Fourth Street, Ottumwa, IA 52501
Tel: (641) 684-6502

Clerk of Court, Des Moines County
Christine Brakeville . . . . (319) 753-8262
513 North Main, Burlington, IA 52601
E-mail: desmoines.county.clerk@iowacourts.gov

Dickinson County

Clerk of the Court

Third Judicial District
Woodbury County Courthouse, Seventh and Douglas, Room 210,
Sioux City, IA 51101

Clerk of Court, Dickinson County **Marcia Eckerman** . . . . (712) 336-1138
1802 Hill Avenue, Suite 2506,
Spirit Lake, IA 51360
E-mail: marcia1.eckerman@iowacourts.gov

Dubuque County

Clerk of the Court

First Judicial District
316 East Fifth Street, Waterloo, IA 50703
Tel: (319) 833-3332

Clerk of Court, Dubuque County **Kevin Firnstahl** . . . . (563) 245-2204
720 Central Avenue, Dubuque, IA 52004-1220
P.O. Box 1220, Dubuque, IA 52004-1220
E-mail: kevin.firnstahl@iowacourts.gov

Emmet County

Clerk of the Court

Third Judicial District
Woodbury County Courthouse, Seventh and Douglas, Room 210,
Sioux City, IA 51101

Clerk of Court, Emmet County **Cynthia Kelly** . . . . (712) 362-3325
609 First Avenue North, Estherville, IA 51334
E-mail: cynthia.kelly@iowacourts.gov

Fayette County

Clerk of the Court

First Judicial District
316 East Fifth Street, Waterloo, IA 50703
Tel: (319) 833-3332

Clerk of Court, Fayette County **Elizabeth Nuss** . . . . (563) 422-5695
114 North Vine Street, West Union, IA 52175
E-mail: elizabeth.nuss@iowacourts.gov

Floyd County

Clerk of the Court

Second Judicial District
220 North Washington Avenue, Mason City, IA 50401
Tel: (641) 494-3611

Clerk of Court, Floyd County **Julie Kneip** . . . . (641) 228-7777
101 South Main Street, Suite 305,   Fax: (641) 228-7772
Charles City, IA 50616
E-mail: julie.kneip@iowacourts.gov

Franklin County

Clerk of the Court

Second Judicial District
220 North Washington Avenue, Mason City, IA 50401
Tel: (641) 494-3611

Clerk of Court, Franklin County **Debra Bausman** . . . . (641) 456-5626
12 First Avenue NW, Suite 203,   Fax: (641) 456-5628
Hampton, IA 50441
E-mail: debra.bausman@iowacourts.gov

Fremont County

Clerk of the Court

Fourth Judicial District
Pottawattamie County Courthouse, 227 South Sixth Street,
Fourt Floor, Room 413, Council Bluffs, IA 51501
Tel: (712) 328-5733

Clerk of Court, Fremont County **Robin Shirley** . . . . (712) 374-2232
Courthouse Square, Sibley, IA 51526
E-mail: robin.shirley@iowacourts.gov

Greene County

Clerk of the Court

Second Judicial District
220 North Washington Avenue, Mason City, IA 50401
Tel: (641) 494-3611

Clerk of Court, Greene County
Patricia "Patty" Freund . . . . (515) 386-2516
Greene County Courthouse,   Fax: (515) 386-2321
114 North Chestnut Street,
Jefferson, IA 50129
E-mail: patricia.freund@iowacourts.gov

Grundy County

Clerk of the Court

First Judicial District
316 East Fifth Street, Waterloo, IA 50703
Tel: (319) 833-3332

Clerk of Court, Grundy County **Waynette Saul** . . . . (319) 824-5220
Grundy County Courthouse, 706 G. Avenue,
Grundy Center, IA 50638
E-mail: waynette.saul@iowacourts.gov

Guthrie County

Clerk of the Court

Fifth Judicial District
Polk County Courthouse, 500 Mulberry Street, Room 411,
Des Moines, IA 50309
Tel: (515) 286-3198

Clerk of Court, Guthrie County **Leisa Imboden** . . . . (641) 747-3415
200 North Fifth Street, Guthrie Center, IA 50115
E-mail: leisa.imboden@iowacourts.gov

Hamilton County

Clerk of the Court

Second Judicial District
220 North Washington Avenue, Mason City, IA 50401
Tel: (641) 494-3611

Clerk of Court, Hamilton County
Janelle Groteluschen . . . . (515) 832-9600
2300 Superior Street, Webster City, IA 50595   Fax: (515) 832-9519
E-mail: janelle.groteluschen@iowacourts.gov

Hancock County

Clerk of the Court

Second Judicial District
220 North Washington Avenue, Mason City, IA 50401
Tel: (641) 494-3611

Clerk of Court, Hancock County **Lori Hasfjord** . . . . (641) 923-3421
855 State Street, Garner, IA 50438
E-mail: lori.hasfjord@iowacourts.gov

Hardin County

Clerk of the Court

Second Judicial District
220 North Washington Avenue, Mason City, IA 50401
Tel: (641) 494-3611

Clerk of Court, Hardin County **Diane Ryerson** . . . . (641) 858-2328
1215 Edington Avenue, Suite 7,   Fax: (641) 858-2320
Eldora, IA 50627
E-mail: diane.ryerson@iowacourts.gov

Harrison County

Clerk of the Court

Fourth Judicial District
Pottawattamie County Courthouse, 227 South Sixth Street,
Fourt Floor, Room 413, Council Bluffs, IA 51501
Tel: (712) 328-5733

Clerk of Court, Harrison County **Vicki Krohn** . . . . (712) 644-2665
Harrison County Courthouse,
111 North Second Avenue,
Logan, IA 51546
E-mail: vicki.krohn@iowacourts.gov

Henry County

Clerk of the Court

Eighth Judicial District
211 East Fourth Street, Ottumwa, IA 52501
Tel: (641) 684-6502

Clerk of Court, Henry County **Linda Fear** . . . . (319) 385-3150
100 East Washington Street,
Mount Pleasant, IA 52641
E-mail: henry.county.clerk@iowacourts.gov

Howard County

Clerk of the Court

First Judicial District
316 East Fifth Street, Waterloo, IA 50703
Tel: (319) 833-3332

Clerk of Court, Howard County **Damian Baltes** . . . . (563) 547-2661
Howard County Courthouse, 137 North Elm Street,
Cresco, IA 52136
E-mail: damian.baltes@iowacourts.gov

Humboldt County

Clerk of the Court

Second Judicial District
220 North Washington Avenue, Mason City, IA 50401
Tel: (641) 494-3611

Clerk of Court, Humboldt County
Janelle Groteluschen . . . . (515) 332-1806
203 Main Street, Dakota City, IA 50529   Fax: (515) 332-7100
E-mail: janelle.groteluschen@iowacourts.gov

(continued on next page)

Ida County

Clerk of the Court

Third Judicial District
Woodbury County Courthouse, Seventh and Douglas, Room 210,
Sioux City, IA 51101

Clerk of Court, Ida County **Cheryl A. Kaskey** . . . . (712) 364-2628
  401 Moorehead Street, Ida Grove, IA 51445
  E-mail: cheryl.kaskey@iowacourts.gov

Iowa County

Clerk of the Court

Sixth Judicial District
P.O. Box 5488, Cedar Rapids, IA 52406
Tel: (319) 398-3920 ext. 1100

Clerk of Court, Iowa County **Cynthia Forsyth** . . . .(319) 642-3914
  901 Court Avenue, Marengo, IA 52301
  E-mail: cynthia.forsyth@iowacourts.gov

Jackson County

Clerk of the Court

Seventh Judicial District
Scott County Courthouse, 416 West Fourth Street, Davenport, IA 52801
Tel: (563) 326-8783

Clerk of Court, Jackson County **Kim Hess** . . . . .(563) 243-6213 ext. 4230
  201 West Platt Street, Maquoketa, IA 52060

Jasper County

Clerk of the Court

Fifth Judicial District
Polk County Courthouse, 500 Mulberry Street, Room 411,
Des Moines, IA 50309
Tel: (515) 286-3198

Clerk of Court, Jasper County **Carol Sage** . . . . (641) 792-9161
  101 First Street North, Newton, IA 50208
  E-mail: carol.sage@iowacourts.gov

Jefferson County

Clerk of the Court

Eighth Judicial District
211 East Fourth Street, Ottumwa, IA 52501
Tel: (641) 684-6502

Clerk of Court, Jefferson County **Barbara Droz** . . . . (641) 472-3454
  51 West Briggs, Fairfield, IA 52556
  E-mail: jefferson.county.clerk@iowacourts.gov

Johnson County

Clerk of the Court

Sixth Judicial District
P.O. Box 5488, Cedar Rapids, IA 52406
Tel: (319) 398-3920 ext. 1100

Clerk of Court, Johnson County **Kim Montover** . . . .(319) 356-6060
  417 South Clinton Street, Iowa City, IA 52244-2510
  E-mail: kim.montover@iowacourts.gov

Jones County

Clerk of the Court

Sixth Judicial District
P.O. Box 5488, Cedar Rapids, IA 52406
Tel: (319) 398-3920 ext. 1100

Clerk of Court, Jones County **Roxanne Repstein** . . . . (319) 462-4342
  500 West Main Street, Anamosa, IA 52205
  E-mail: roxanne.repstein@iowacourts.gov

Keokuk County

Clerk of the Court

Eighth Judicial District
211 East Fourth Street, Ottumwa, IA 52501
Tel: (641) 684-6502

Clerk of Court, Keokuk County **Janietta Criswell** . . . .(641) 622-2210
  101 South Main Street, Sigourney, IA 52591
  E-mail: keokuk.county.clerk@iowacourts.gov

Kossuth County

Clerk of the Court

Third Judicial District
Woodbury County Courthouse, Seventh and Douglas, Room 210,
Sioux City, IA 51101

Clerk of Court, Kossuth County **Mary Ellen Munn** . . . . . .(515) 295-3240
  114 West State Street, Algona, IA 50511
  E-mail: mary.munn@iowacourts.gov

Lee County

Clerk of the Court

Eighth Judicial District
211 East Fourth Street, Ottumwa, IA 52501
Tel: (641) 684-6502

Clerk of Court, Lee County **Susan McCarty** . . . . .(319) 524-2433 (South)
  25 North Seventh Street, Keokuk, IA 52632 (South)   Tel: (319) 372-3523
  701 Avenue F, Fort Madison, IA 52627 (North)   (North)
  E-mail: northlee.county.clerk@iowacourts.gov

Linn County

Clerk of the Court

Sixth Judicial District
P.O. Box 5488, Cedar Rapids, IA 52406
Tel: (319) 398-3920 ext. 1100

Clerk of Court, Linn County **Roxanne Repstein** . . . . (319) 398-3411
  Third Avenue Bridge, Cedar Rapids, IA 52406
  E-mail: roxanne.repstein@iowacourts.gov

Louisa County

Clerk of the Court

Eighth Judicial District
211 East Fourth Street, Ottumwa, IA 52501
Tel: (641) 684-6502

Clerk of Court, Louisa County **Melissa Schoonover** . . . . (319) 523-4541
  117 South Main, Wapello, IA 52653
  E-mail: louisa.county.clerk@iowacourts.gov

Lucas County

Clerk of the Court

Fifth Judicial District
Polk County Courthouse, 500 Mulberry Street, Room 411,
Des Moines, IA 50309
Tel: (515) 286-3198

Clerk of Court, Lucas County **Vicky Black** . . . . (641) 774-4421
916 Braden Street, Chariton, IA 50049
E-mail: vicky.black@iowacourts.gov

Lyon County

Clerk of the Court

Third Judicial District
Woodbury County Courthouse, Seventh and Douglas, Room 210,
Sioux City, IA 51101

Clerk of Court, Lyon County **Stephanie Wollmuth** . . . . . (712) 472-8530
206 South Second Avenue,
Rock Rapids, IA 51246-0072
E-mail: stephanie.wollmuth@iowacourts.gov

Madison County

Clerk of the Court

Fifth Judicial District
Polk County Courthouse, 500 Mulberry Street, Room 411,
Des Moines, IA 50309
Tel: (515) 286-3198

Clerk of Court, Madison County **Pam Slings** . . . . (515) 462-4451
Madison County Courthouse,
112 North John Wayne Drive,
Winterset, IA 50273
E-mail: janice.bowers@iowacourts.gov

Mahaska County

Clerk of the Court

Eighth Judicial District
211 East Fourth Street, Ottumwa, IA 52501
Tel: (641) 684-6502

Clerk of Court, Mahaska County **Teresa Augustine** . . . . . (641) 673-7786
106 South First Street, Oskaloosa, IA 52577
E-mail: teresa.augustine@iowacourts.gov

Marion County

Clerk of the Court

Fifth Judicial District
Polk County Courthouse, 500 Mulberry Street, Room 411,
Des Moines, IA 50309
Tel: (515) 286-3198

Clerk of Court, Marion County **Carol Sage** . . . . (641) 828-2207 ext. 6
214 East Main Street, Knoxville, IA 50138
E-mail: carol.sage@iowacourts.gov

Marshall County

Clerk of the Court

Second Judicial District
220 North Washington Avenue, Mason City, IA 50401
Tel: (641) 494-3611

Clerk of Court, Marshall County **Carol Haney** . . . . (641) 754-1608
One East Main Street, Marshalltown, IA 50158
E-mail: carol.haney@iowacourts.gov

Mills County

Clerk of the Court

Fourth Judicial District
Pottawattamie County Courthouse, 227 South Sixth Street,
Fourt Floor, Room 413, Council Bluffs, IA 51501
Tel: (712) 328-5733

Clerk of Court, Mills County **Kim Carter** . . . . (712) 527-4880
418 Sharp Street, Glenwood, IA 51534
E-mail: kim.carter@iowacourts.gov

Mitchell County

Clerk of the Court

Second Judicial District
220 North Washington Avenue, Mason City, IA 50401
Tel: (641) 494-3611

Clerk of Court, Mitchell County **Karen Purcell** . . . . (641) 732-3726
918 North Second Street, Suite 100,   Fax: (641) 732-3728
Osage, IA 50461
E-mail: karen.purcell@iowacourts.gov

Monona County

Clerk of the Court

Third Judicial District
Woodbury County Courthouse, Seventh and Douglas, Room 210,
Sioux City, IA 51101

Clerk of Court, Monona County **Karen Kahl** . . . . (712) 423-2491
610 Iowa Avenue, Onawa, IA 51040
E-mail: jean.ulven@iowacourts.gov

Monroe County

Clerk of the Court

Eighth Judicial District
211 East Fourth Street, Ottumwa, IA 52501
Tel: (641) 684-6502

Clerk of Court, Monroe County **Ann Taylor** . . . . (641) 932-5212
10 Benton Avenue East, Albia, IA 52531
E-mail: ann.taylor@iowacourts.gov

(continued on next page)

Montgomery County

Clerk of the Court

Fourth Judicial District
Pottawattamie County Courthouse, 227 South Sixth Street,
Fourt Floor, Room 413, Council Bluffs, IA 51501
Tel: (712) 328-5733

Clerk of Court, Montgomery County **Kim Carter** . . . . (712) 623-4986
105 Coolbaugh Street, Red Oak, IA 51566
E-mail: kimberly.carter@iowacourts.gov

Muscatine County

Clerk of the Court

Seventh Judicial District
Scott County Courthouse, 416 West Fourth Street, Davenport, IA 52801
Tel: (563) 326-8783

Clerk of Court, Muscatine County **Jeff Tollenaer** . . . . (563) 263-6511
401 East Third Street, Muscatine, IA 52761
E-mail: jeff.tollenaer@iowacourts.gov

O'Brien County

Clerk of the Court

Third Judicial District
Woodbury County Courthouse, Seventh and Douglas, Room 210,
Sioux City, IA 51101

Clerk of Court, O'Brien County **Laurie Janssen** . . . . (712) 957-3255
155 South Hayes Avenue, Primghar, IA 51245
E-mail: jeffrey.roos@iowacourts.gov

Osceola County

Clerk of the Court

Third Judicial District
Woodbury County Courthouse, Seventh and Douglas, Room 210,
Sioux City, IA 51101

Clerk of Court, Osceola County **Stephanie Wollmuth** . . . (712) 754-3595
300 Seventh Street, Sibley, IA 51249
E-mail: stephanie.wollmuth@iowacourts.gov

Page County

Clerk of the Court

Fourth Judicial District
Pottawattamie County Courthouse, 227 South Sixth Street,
Fourt Floor, Room 413, Council Bluffs, IA 51501
Tel: (712) 328-5733

Clerk of Court, Page County **Robin Shirley** . . . . (712) 542-3214
112 East Main Street, Clarinda, IA 51632
E-mail: robin.shirley@iowacourts.gov

Palo Alto County

Clerk of the Court

Third Judicial District
Woodbury County Courthouse, Seventh and Douglas, Room 210,
Sioux City, IA 51101

Clerk of Court, Palo Alto County **Mary Ellen Munn** . . . . . (712) 852-3603
1010 Broadway, Emmetsburg, IA 50536
E-mail: mary.munn@iowacourts.gov

Plymouth County

Clerk of the Court

Third Judicial District
Woodbury County Courthouse, Seventh and Douglas, Room 210,
Sioux City, IA 51101

Clerk of Court, Plymouth County **Peggy Frericks** . . . . (712) 546-4215
215 Fourth Avenue SE, Le Mars, IA 51031
E-mail: peggy.frericks@iowacourts.gov

Pocahontas County

Clerk of the Court

Second Judicial District
220 North Washington Avenue, Mason City, IA 50401
Tel: (641) 494-3611

Clerk of Court, Pocahontas County **Carol Williams** . . . . . . (712) 335-4208
Pocahontas County Courthouse, 99 Court Square,   Fax: (712) 335-5045
Pocahontas, IA 50574-1695
E-mail: carol.williams@iowacourts.gov

Polk County

Clerk of the Court

Fifth Judicial District
Polk County Courthouse, 500 Mulberry Street, Room 411,
Des Moines, IA 50309
Tel: (515) 286-3198

Clerk of Court, Polk County **Randy Osborn** . . . . (515) 286-3769
Polk County Courthouse, Fifth and Mulberry,
Des Moines, IA 50301
E-mail: randy.osborn@iowacourts.gov

Pottawattamie County

Clerk of the Court

Fourth Judicial District
Pottawattamie County Courthouse, 227 South Sixth Street,
Fourt Floor, Room 413, Council Bluffs, IA 51501
Tel: (712) 328-5733

Clerk of Court, Pottawattamie County **Ruth Godfrey** . . . . . (712) 328-5759
Pottawattamie County Courthouse,
227 South Sixth Street, Fourth Floor,
Council Bluffs, IA 51501
E-mail: ruth.godfrey@iowacourts.gov

Poweshiek County

Clerk of the Court

Eighth Judicial District
211 East Fourth Street, Ottumwa, IA 52501
Tel: (641) 684-6502

Clerk of Court, Poweshiek County **Janietta Criswell** . . . . . (641) 623-5644
P.O. BOX 218, Montezuma, IA 50171
E-mail: poweshiek.county.clerk@iowacourts.gov

Ringgold County

Clerk of the Court

Fifth Judicial District
Polk County Courthouse, 500 Mulberry Street, Room 411,
Des Moines, IA 50309
Tel: (515) 286-3198

Clerk of Court, Ringgold County **Jackie Saville** . . . . (641) 464-3234
109 West Madison, Mount Ayr, IA 50854
E-mail: jackie.saville@iowacourts.gov

Sac County

Clerk of the Court

Second Judicial District
220 North Washington Avenue, Mason City, IA 50401
Tel: (641) 494-3611

Clerk of Court, Sac County **Donna Geery** . . . . (712) 662-7791
100 East State Street, Sac City, IA 50583   Fax: (712) 662-4718
E-mail: donna.geery@iowacourts.gov

Scott County

Clerk of the Court

Seventh Judicial District
Scott County Courthouse, 416 West Fourth Street, Davenport, IA 52801
Tel: (563) 326-8783

Clerk of Court, Scott County **Julie Carlin** . . . . (563) 326-8743
Scott County Courthouse, 400 West Fourth Street,
Davenport, IA 52801
E-mail: julie.carlin@iowacourts.gov

Shelby County

Clerk of the Court

Fourth Judicial District
Pottawattamie County Courthouse, 227 South Sixth Street,
Fourt Floor, Room 413, Council Bluffs, IA 51501
Tel: (712) 328-5733

Clerk of Court, Shelby County **Vicki Krohn** . . . . (712) 755-5543
Shelby County Courthouse, 612 Court Street,
Third floor, Harlan, IA 51537
E-mail: vicki.krohn@iowacourts.gov

Sioux County

Clerk of the Court

Third Judicial District
Woodbury County Courthouse, Seventh and Douglas, Room 210,
Sioux City, IA 51101

Clerk of Court, Sioux County **Deb Fischer** . . . . (712) 737-2286
210 Central Avenue SW, Orange City, IA 51041
E-mail: deb.fischer@iowacourts.gov

Story County

Clerk of the Court

Second Judicial District
220 North Washington Avenue, Mason City, IA 50401
Tel: (641) 494-3611

Clerk of Court, Story County **Diane Tott** . . . . (515) 382-7410
1315 South B. Avenue, Nevada, IA 50201
E-mail: diane.tott@iowacourts.gov

Tama County

Clerk of the Court

Sixth Judicial District
P.O. Box 5488, Cedar Rapids, IA 52406
Tel: (319) 398-3920 ext. 1100

Clerk of Court, Tama County **Connie Rohach** . . . . (641) 484-3381
100 West High Street, Toledo, IA 52342
E-mail: connie.rohach@iowacourts.gov

Taylor County

Clerk of the Court

Fifth Judicial District
Polk County Courthouse, 500 Mulberry Street, Room 411,
Des Moines, IA 50309
Tel: (515) 286-3198

Clerk of Court, Taylor County **Jackie Saville** . . . . (712) 523-2095
Taylor County Courthouse, 405 Jefferson Street,
Bedford, IA 50833
E-mail: jackie.saville@iowacourts.gov

Union County

Clerk of the Court

Fifth Judicial District
Polk County Courthouse, 500 Mulberry Street, Room 411,
Des Moines, IA 50309
Tel: (515) 286-3198

Clerk of Court, Union County **Allison Danilovich** . . . . (641) 782-7315
Union County Courthouse, 300 North Pine, Suite 6,
Creston, IA 50801
E-mail: allison.danilovich@iowacourts.gov

(continued on next page)

Iowa Court Clerks and Courthouses *continued*

Van Buren County

Clerk of the Court

Eighth Judicial District
211 East Fourth Street, Ottumwa, IA 52501
Tel: (641) 684-6502

Clerk of Court, Van Buren County **Barbara Droz** . . . . (319) 293-3108
905 Broad Street, Keosauqua, IA 52565
E-mail: vanburen.county.clerk@iowacourts.gov

Wapello County

Clerk of the Court

Eighth Judicial District
211 East Fourth Street, Ottumwa, IA 52501
Tel: (641) 684-6502

Clerk of Court, Wapello County **Deb Littlejohn** . . . . (641) 683-0060
101 West Fourth Street, Ottumwa, IA 52501
E-mail: deb.littlejohn@iowacourts.gov

Warren County

Clerk of the Court

Fifth Judicial District
Polk County Courthouse, 500 Mulberry Street, Room 411,
Des Moines, IA 50309
Tel: (515) 286-3198

Clerk of Court, Warren County **Cathie Hullinger** . . . . (515) 961-1033
Warren County Courthouse,
115 North Howard Street, Indianola, IA 50125
E-mail: cathie.hullinger@iowacourts.gov

Washington County

Clerk of the Court

Eighth Judicial District
211 East Fourth Street, Ottumwa, IA 52501
Tel: (641) 684-6502

Clerk of Court, Washington County **Julie Johnson** . . . . . . (319) 653-7741
224 West Main, Washington, IA 52353
E-mail: julie.johnson@iowacourts.gov

Wayne County

Clerk of the Court

Fifth Judicial District
Polk County Courthouse, 500 Mulberry Street, Room 411,
Des Moines, IA 50309
Tel: (515) 286-3198

Clerk of Court, Wayne County **Traci Tharp** . . . . (641) 872-2264
101 North Franklin, Corydon, IA 50060
E-mail: traci.tharp@iowacourts.gov

Iowa Court Clerks and Courthouses *continued*

Webster County

Clerk of the Court

Second Judicial District
220 North Washington Avenue, Mason City, IA 50401
Tel: (641) 494-3611

Clerk of Court, Webster County **Janelle Groteluschen** . . . (515) 576-7115
701 Central Avenue, Fort Dodge, IA 50501   Fax: (515) 576-0555
E-mail: janelle.groteluschen@iowacourts.gov

Winnebago County

Clerk of the Court

Second Judicial District
220 North Washington Avenue, Mason City, IA 50401
Tel: (641) 494-3611

Clerk of Court, Winnebago County **Lori Hasfjord** . . . . (641) 585-4520
126 South Clark Street, Forest City, IA 50436
E-mail: lori.hasfjord@iowacourts.gov

Winneshiek County

Clerk of the Court

First Judicial District
316 East Fifth Street, Waterloo, IA 50703
Tel: (319) 833-3332

Clerk of Court, Winneshiek County **Elizabeth Nuss** . . . . . (563) 382-2469
Winneshiek County Courthouse,
201 West Main Street, Decorah, IA 52101
E-mail: elizabeth.nuss@iowacourts.gov

Woodbury County

Clerk of the Court

Third Judicial District
Woodbury County Courthouse, Seventh and Douglas, Room 210,
Sioux City, IA 51101

Clerk of Court, Woodbury County **Amy Berntson** . . . . (712) 233-8945
620 Douglas Street, Room 101,
Sioux City, IA 51101
E-mail: amy.berntson@iowacourts.gov

Worth County

Clerk of the Court

Second Judicial District
220 North Washington Avenue, Mason City, IA 50401
Tel: (641) 494-3611

Clerk of Court, Worth County **Lori Hasfjord** . . . . (641) 324-2840
12 First Avenue NW, Hampton, IA 50441   Fax: (641) 324-2360
E-mail: lori.hasfjord@iowacourts.gov

Wright County

Clerk of the Court

Second Judicial District
220 North Washington Avenue, Mason City, IA 50401
Tel: (641) 494-3611

Clerk of Court, Wright County **Janelle Groteluschen** . . . (515) 532-3113
115 North Main Street, Clarion, IA 50525   Fax: (515) 532-2343
E-mail: janelle.groteluschen@iowacourts.gov

Counties Within Judicial Districts

District Court, 1st District

Areas Covered: Allamakee, Black Hawk, Buchanan, Chickasaw, Clayton, Delaware, Dubuque, Fayette, Grundy, Howard, and Winneshiek Counties.

District Court, 2nd District

Areas Covered: Boone, Bremer, Butler, Calhoun, Carroll, Cerro Gordo, Floyd, Franklin, Greene, Hamilton, Hancock, Hardin, Humboldt, Marshall, Mitchell, Pocahontas, Sac, Story, Webster, Winnebago, Worth, and Wright Counties.

District Court, 3rd District

Areas Covered: Buena Vista, Cherokee, Clay, Crawford, Dickinson, Emmet, Ida, Lyon, Kossuth, Monona, O'Brien, Osceola, Palo Alto, Plymouth, Sioux, and Woodbury Counties.

District Court, 4th District

Areas Covered: Audubon, Cass, Fremont, Harrison, Mills, Montgomery, Page, Pottawattamie, and Shelby Counties.

District Court, 5th District

Areas Covered: Adair, Adams, Clarke, Dallas, Decatur, Guthrie, Jasper, Lucas, Madison, Marion, Polk, Ringgold, Taylor, Union, Warren, and Wayne Counties.

District Court, 6th District

Areas Covered: Benton, Iowa, Johnson, Jones, Linn, and Tama Counties.

District Court, 7th District

Areas Covered: Cedar, Clinton, Jackson, Muscatine, and Scott Counties.

District Court, 8th District

Areas Covered: Appanoose, Davis, Des Moines, Henry, Jefferson, Keokuk, Lee, Louisa, Mahaska, Monroe, Poweshiek, Van Buren, Wapello, and Washington Counties.

Kansas Court Clerks and Courthouses

The trial courts of general jurisdiction in Kansas are called district courts. There are 31 districts with at least one county per district. Each county includes a County Clerk and a Clerk of the District Court.

Kansas Supreme Court

374 Kansas Judicial Center, 301 SW Tenth Avenue, Topeka, KS 66612-1507
Tel: (785) 296-3229 Fax: (785) 296-7076
Internet: www.kscourts.org
Internet: http://www.kscourts.org/kansas-courts/supreme-court/justice-bios/default.asp

The Supreme Court consists of a chief justice and six justices who are appointed by the Governor from nominations submitted by a Supreme Court nominating commission. Newly-appointed justices serve initial one-year terms and then face a retention vote for a six-year term in the next general election. The justice with the most seniority serves as chief justice. Retirement is mandatory at age seventy or at the end of the current term; however, retired justices may be appointed by the Supreme Court to serve temporary assignments. The Supreme Court has original jurisdiction in proceedings in quo warranto, mandamus, and habeas corpus. Cases involving the death penalty and off-grid are appealed directly to the Supreme Court. The Court may also review decisions of the Kansas Court of Appeals.

Court Staff
Clerk of the Appellate Courts **Heather L. Smith** . . . . (785) 296-3229

Kansas Court of Appeals

Kansas Judicial Center, 301 SW Tenth Avenue, Topeka, KS 66612-1502
Tel: (785) 296-3229 Fax: (785) 296-7079
Internet: www.kscourts.org

The Court of Appeals consists of a chief judge and eleven judges who are appointed by the Governor from nominations submitted by a Supreme Court nominating commission. Judges serve four-year terms and then stand for retention in the next general election. The chief judge is selected by the Kansas Supreme Court. Judges may not stand for retention after age seventy-five; however, retired judges may serve by assignment of the Kansas Supreme Court. The Court of Appeals has statewide jurisdiction over appeals in civil and criminal matters arising in the Kansas District Court, except where the Kansas Supreme Court has exclusive jurisdiction.

Court Staff
Clerk of the Appellate Courts **Heather L. Smith** . . . . (785) 296-3229
Fax: (785) 296-1028

County-By-County

Allen County

County Clerk

Office of the County Clerk
One North Washington Avenue, Iola, KS 66749
Tel: (620) 365-1407 Fax: (620) 365-1441

County Clerk **Sherrie L. Riebel** . . . . (620) 365-1407
E-mail: coclerk@allencounty.org

Kansas Court Clerks and Courthouses *continued*

District Clerk

Thirty-First Judicial District
One North Washington, Room B, Iola, KS 66749

Clerk of the District Court, Allen County
Dina Morrison . . . . (620) 365-1425
One North Washington, Iola, KS 66749 Fax: (620) 365-1429
E-mail: dinamorrison@acdc.kscoxmail.com

Anderson County

County Clerk

Office of the County Clerk
100 East Fourth Avenue, Garnett, KS 66032
Tel: (785) 448-6841 Fax: (785) 448-3205

County Clerk **Phyllis Gettler** . . . . (785) 448-6841
E-mail: pgettler@andersoncountyks.org

District Clerk

Fourth Judicial District
110 South Sixth Street, Burlington, KS 66839

Clerk of the District Court, Anderson County
Carla Skiles . . . . (785) 448-6886
100 East Fourth, Garnett, KS 66032 Fax: (785) 448-3230
P.O. Box 305, Garnett, KS 66032
E-mail: districtcourt@embarqmail.com

Atchison County

County Clerk

Office of the County Clerk
423 North Fifth Street, Atchison, KS 66002
Tel: (913) 804-6030 Fax: (913) 367-0227

County Clerk **Pauline M. Lee** . . . . (913) 804-6030
E-mail: at_county_clerk@wan.kdor.state.ks.us

District Clerk

First Judicial District
601 South Third Street, Leavenworth, KS 66048

Clerk of the District Court, Atchison County
Donna Oswald . . . . (913) 804-6066
423 North Fifth Street, Atchison, KS 66002 Fax: (913) 367-1171
P.O. Box 408, Atchison, KS 66002
E-mail: doswald@atcodistcourt.org

Barber County

County Clerk

Office of the County Clerk
120 East Washington Avenue, Medicine Lodge, KS 67104
Tel: (620) 886-3961 Fax: (620) 886-5425

County Clerk **Debbie Wesley** . . . . (620) 886-3961
E-mail: bacoclerk4@cyberlodg.com

District Clerk

Thirtieth Judicial District
130 North Spruce, Kingman, KS 67068
P.O. Box 495, Kingman, KS 67068

Clerk of the District Court, Barber County
Ann McNett . . . . (620) 886-5639
118 East Washington, Medicine Lodge, KS 67104 Fax: (620) 886-5854
E-mail: amcnett@barber.ks.gov

(continued on next page)

Kansas Court Clerks and Courthouses *continued*

Barton County

County Clerk

Office of the County Clerk
1400 Main Street, Room 202, Great Bend, KS 67530
Tel: (620) 793-1835 Fax: (620) 793-1990

County Clerk **Donna J. Zimmerman** . . . . (620) 793-1835
E-mail: clerk@bartoncounty.org

District Clerk

Twentieth Judicial District
1400 Main, Great Bend, KS 67530

Clerk of the District Court, Barton County
Heather Ward . . . . (620) 793-1856
1400 Main, Room 306, Great Bend, KS 67530   Fax: (620) 793-1860
E-mail: hwbtdistcrt@cpcis.net

Bourbon County

County Clerk

Office of the County Clerk
210 South National Avenue, Fort Scott, KS 66701
Tel: (620) 223-3880 Fax: (620) 223-5832

County Clerk **Kendell Mason** . . . . (620) 223-3880 ext. 14
E-mail: countyclerk@bourboncountyks.org

District Clerk

Sixth Judicial District
P.O. Box 350, Mound City, KS 66056

Clerk of the District Court, Bourbon County
Rhonda Cole . . . . (620) 223-0780
210 South National, Fort Scott, KS 66701   Fax: (620) 223-5303
P.O. Box 868, Fort Scott, KS 66701
E-mail: recole@cebridge.net

Brown County

County Clerk

Office of the County Clerk
601 Oregon Street, Second Floor, Hiawatha, KS 66434
Tel: (785) 742-2581 Fax: (785) 742-7705

County Clerk **Debbie Parker** . . . . (785) 742-2581
E-mail: dparker@brcoks.org

District Clerk

Twenty-Second Judicial District
601 Oregon, Hiawatha, KS 66434
P.O. Box 417, Hiawatha, KS 66434

Clerk of the District Court, Brown County **Joy Moore** . . . (785) 742-7481
601 Oregon, Hiawatha, KS 66434   Fax: (785) 742-3506
P.O. Box 417, Hiawatha, KS 66434
E-mail: jmoore@brdistcrt.org

Butler County

County Clerk

Office of the County Clerk
205 West Central Avenue, El Dorado, KS 67042
Tel: (316) 322-4239 Fax: (316) 321-1011

County Clerk **Don Engels** . . . . (316) 322-4239
E-mail: dengels@bucoks.com

Kansas Court Clerks and Courthouses *continued*

District Clerk

Thirteenth Judicial District
201 West Pine, Suite B, El Dorado, KS 67042

Clerk of the District Court, Butler County
Janell Jessup . . . . (316) 322-4370
201 West Pine, Suite 101, El Dorado, KS 67042   Fax: (316) 321-9486
E-mail: bcdcclerk@bcdc.kscoxmail.com

Chase County

County Clerk

Office of the County Clerk
P.O. Box 529, Cottonwood Falls, KS 66845
Tel: (620) 273-6423 Fax: (620) 273-6617

County Clerk **Brande Studer** . . . . (620) 273-6423
E-mail: cs_county_clerk@wan.kdor.state.ks.us

District Clerk

Fifth Judicial District
430 Commercial, Emporia, KS 66801

Clerk of the District Court, Chase County
Barbara Davis . . . . (620) 273-6319
300 Pearl, Cottonwood Falls, KS 66845   Fax: (620) 273-6890
P.O. Box 529, Cottonwood Falls, KS 66845
E-mail: csclerk@5thjd.org

Chautauqua County

County Clerk

Office of the County Clerk
215 North Chautauqua Street, Sedan, KS 67361
Tel: (620) 725-5800 Fax: (620) 725-5801

County Clerk **Janice A. Fine** . . . . (620) 725-5800
E-mail: cqclerk@yahoo.com

District Clerk

Fourteenth Judicial District
300 East Main Street, Independence, KS 67301

Clerk of the District Court, Chautauqua County
Cynthia Weaver . . . . (620) 725-5870
215 North Chautauqua Street, Box 306,   Fax: (620) 725-3027
Sedan, KS 67361
E-mail: cqcodct@sbcglobal.net

Cherokee County

County Clerk

Office of the County Clerk
110 West Maple Street, Columbus, KS 66725
Tel: (620) 429-2042 Fax: (620) 429-1042

County Clerk **Rodney D. Edmondson** . . . . (620) 429-2042
E-mail: ck_county_clerk@wan.kdor.state.ks.us

District Clerk

Eleventh Judicial District
111 East Forest Street, Girard, KS 66743

Clerk of the District Court, Cherokee County
Terry Cizerle . . . . (620) 429-3880
110 West Maple, Columbus, KS 66725   Fax: (620) 429-1130
P.O. Box 189, Columbus, KS 66725
E-mail: tcizerle@11thjd.org

Cheyenne County

County Clerk

Office of the County Clerk
212 East Washington Street, Saint Francis, KS 67756
Tel: (785) 332-8800 Fax: (785) 332-8825

County Clerk **Deb Lindsten** . . . . (785) 332-8800
E-mail: cn_county_clerk@wan.kdor.state.ks.us

District Clerk

Fifteenth Judicial District
300 North Court, Colby, KS 67701
P.O. Box 805, Colby, KS 67701

Clerk of the District Court, Cheyenne County
Natalie Stahlecker . . . . (785) 332-8850
212 East Washington, Saint Francis, KS 67756   Fax: (785) 332-8851
P.O. Box 646, Saint Francis, KS 67756
E-mail: cndist@stfks.net

Clark County

County Clerk

Office of the County Clerk
913 Highland Street, Ashland, KS 67831
Tel: (620) 635-2813 Fax: (620) 635-2051

County Clerk **Rebecca Mishler** . . . . (620) 635-2813
E-mail: cacoclrk@ucom.net

District Clerk

Sixteenth Judicial District
101 West Spruce, Dodge City, KS 67801
P.O. Box 197, Dodge City, KS 67801

Clerk of the District Court, Clark County
Sherre Harrington . . . . (620) 635-2753
913 Highland, Ashland, KS 67831   Fax: (620) 635-2155
P.O. Box 790, Ashland, KS 67831
E-mail: cadistct@ucom.net

Clay County

County Clerk

Office of the County Clerk
712 Fifth Street, Suite 102, Clay Center, KS 67432
Tel: (785) 632-2552 Fax: (785) 632-5856

County Clerk **Kayla Wang** . . . . (785) 632-2552
E-mail: cyclerk@claycountykansas.org

District Clerk

Twenty-First Judicial District
100 Courthouse Plaza, Manhattan, KS 66505

Clerk of the District Court, Clay County
Melissa Stellner . . . . (785) 632-3443
712 Fifth Street, Suite 204,   Fax: (785) 632-2651
Clay Center, KS 67432
E-mail: mstellner@claycountykansas.org

Cloud County

County Clerk

Office of the County Clerk
811 Washington Street, Concordia, KS 66901
Tel: (785) 243-8110 Fax: (785) 243-8123

County Clerk **Shella Thoman** . . . . (785) 243-8110
E-mail: clerk@cloudcountyks.org

District Clerk

Twelfth Judicial District
214 C Street, Washington, KS 66968

Clerk of the District Court, Cloud County
Lea D. Throckmorton . . . . (785) 243-8124
811 Washington, Suite P, Concordia, KS 66901   Fax: (785) 243-8188
E-mail: leaw@12jd.org

Coffey County

County Clerk

Office of the County Clerk
110 South Sixth Street, Burlington, KS 66839
Tel: (620) 364-2191 Fax: (620) 364-8975

County Clerk **Angie Kirchner** . . . . (620) 364-2191
E-mail: angiek@coffeycountyks.org

District Clerk

Fourth Judicial District
110 South Sixth Street, Burlington, KS 66839

Clerk of the District Court, Coffey County
Alexandria L. Cox . . . . (620) 364-8628
110 South Sixth Street, Suite 102,   Fax: (620) 364-8535
Burlington, KS 66839
E-mail: districtcourt@coffeycountyks.org

Comanche County

County Clerk

Office of the County Clerk
201 South New York Avenue, Coldwater, KS 67029
Tel: (620) 582-2361 Fax: (620) 582-2426

County Clerk **Alice Smith** . . . . (620) 582-2361
E-mail: cm_county_clerk@wan.kdor.state.ks.us

District Clerk

Sixteenth Judicial District
101 West Spruce, Dodge City, KS 67801
P.O. Box 197, Dodge City, KS 67801

Clerk of the District Court, Comanche County
Penny Wells . . . . (620) 582-2182
201 South New York, Coldwater, KS 67029   Fax: (620) 582-2603
P.O. Box 722, Coldwater, KS 67029
E-mail: cmcourtclerk@gmaxx.us

(continued on next page)

Cowley County

County Clerk

Office of the County Clerk
Cowley County South Annex, 321 East 10 Avenue, Winfield, KS 67156
Tel: (620) 221-5400 Fax: (620) 221-5498

County Clerk **Karen Defore** . . . . (620) 221-5495
  E-mail: kdefore@cowleycounty.org

District Clerk

Nineteenth Judicial District
311 East Ninth, Winfield, KS 67156

Clerk of the District Court, Cowley County
  Marilyn Leith . . . . (620) 221-5480 (Winfield)
  311 East Ninth, Winfield, KS 67156   Tel: (620) 441-4520
  P.O. Box 472, Winfield, KS 67156   (Arkansas City)
  City Hall Building, Arkansas City, KS 67005   Fax: (620) 442-7213
  P.O. Box 1152, Arkansas City, KS 67005   (Arkansas City)
  E-mail: mleith@cowleycourt.com

Crawford County

County Clerk

Office of the County Clerk
111 East Forest Avenue, Second Floor, Girard, KS 66743
Tel: (620) 724-6115 Tel: (888) 504-8683 Fax: (620) 724-6007

County Clerk **Donald P. Pyle** . . . . (620) 724-6115
  E-mail: countyclerk@ckt.net

District Clerk

Eleventh Judicial District
111 East Forest Street, Girard, KS 66743

Clerk of the District Court, Crawford
  County **Pamela Hicks** . . . . (620) 724-6212 (Girard Division)
  111 East Forest Street, Girard, KS 66743   Tel: (620) 231-0380
  P.O. Box 69, Girard, KS 66743   (Pittsburg Division)
  602 North Locust, Pittsburg, KS 66762   Fax: (620) 231-0316
  E-mail: phicks@11thjd.org   (Pittsburg Division)

Decatur County

County Clerk

Office of the County Clerk
120 East Hall Street, Oberlin, KS 67749
Tel: (785) 475-8102 Fax: (785) 475-8130

County Clerk **Colleen Geihsler** . . . . (785) 475-8102
  E-mail: Colleen_geih@yahoo.com

District Clerk

Seventeenth Judicial District
101 South Kansas, Norton, KS 67654
P.O. Box 70, Norton, KS 67654

Clerk of the District Court, Decatur County
  Janet Meitl . . . . (785) 475-8107
  120 East Hall Street, Box 89,   Fax: (785) 475-8170
  Oberlin, KS 67749
  E-mail: dcdcourt@ruraltel.net

Dickinson County

County Clerk

Office of the County Clerk
109 East First Street, Abilene, KS 67410
P.O. Box 248, Abilene, KS 67410
Tel: (785) 263-3774 Fax: (785) 263-2045

County Clerk **Barbara M. Jones** . . . . (785) 263-3774
  E-mail: dk_county_clerk@wan.kdor.state.ks.us

District Clerk

Eighth Judicial District
200 South Third, Marion, KS 66861

Clerk of the District Court, Dickinson County
  Cindy MacDonald . . . . (785) 263-3142
  109 East First, Abilene, KS 67410   Fax: (785) 263-4407
  P.O. Box 127, Abilene, KS 67410
  E-mail: cmacdonald@8thjd.com

Doniphan County

County Clerk

Office of the County Clerk
120 East Chestnut Street, South Side, First Floor, Troy, KS 66087
Tel: (785) 985-3513 Fax: (785) 985-3723

County Clerk **Peggy Franken** . . . . (785) 985-3513
  E-mail: dp_county_clerk@wan.kdor.state.ks.us

District Clerk

Twenty-Second Judicial District
601 Oregon, Hiawatha, KS 66434
P.O. Box 417, Hiawatha, KS 66434

Clerk of the District Court, Doniphan County
  Michelle Smith . . . . (785) 985-3582
  120 East Chestnut, Troy, KS 66087   Fax: (785) 985-2402
  P.O. Box 295, Troy, KS 66087
  E-mail: dpdc@carsoncomm.com

Douglas County

County Clerk

Office of the County Clerk
1100 Massachusetts Street, First Floor, Lawrence, KS 66044
Tel: (785) 832-5167 Fax: (785) 832-5192

County Clerk **Jamie Shew** . . . . (785) 832-5167
  E-mail: jshew@douglas-county.com

District Clerk

Seventh Judicial District
111 East 11th, Lawrence, KS 66044

Clerk of the District Court, Douglas County
  Douglas Hamilton . . . . (785) 832-5333
  111 East 11th, Lawrence, KS 66044   Fax: (785) 832-5174
  E-mail: dhamilton@douglas-county.com

Edwards County

County Clerk

Office of the County Clerk
312 South Massachusetts Avenue, Kinsley, KS 67547
Tel: (620) 659-3000 Fax: (620) 659-2583

County Clerk **Gina Schuette** . . . . (620) 659-3000
E-mail: edwardsclerk@edwards.kscoxmail.com

District Clerk

Twenty-Fourth Judicial District
715 Broadway, Larned, KS 67550
P.O. Box 270, Larned, KS 67550

Clerk of the District Court, Edwards County
Linda Atteberry . . . . (620) 659-2442
312 Massachusetts, Kinsley, KS 67547   Fax: (620) 659-2998
P.O. Box 232, Kinsley, KS 67547
E-mail: edsdistct@edwards.kscoxmail.com

Elk County

County Clerk

Office of the County Clerk
225 East Washington Street, Howard, KS 67349
Tel: (620) 374-2490 Tel: (877) 504-2490 Fax: (620) 374-2771

County Clerk **Vicky D. Wedman** . . . . (620) 374-2490
E-mail: ekclerk@sktc.net

District Clerk

Thirteenth Judicial District
201 West Pine, Suite B, El Dorado, KS 67042

Clerk of the District Court, Elk County **Erin Meader** . . . . (620) 374-2370
127 North Pine, Howard, KS 67349   Fax: (620) 374-3531
P.O. Box 306, Howard, KS 67349
E-mail: ekcourt@yahoo.com

Ellis County

County Clerk

Office of the County Clerk
1204 Fort Street, Hays, KS 67601
Tel: (785) 628-9410 Fax: (785) 628-9413

County Clerk **Donna J. Maskus** . . . . (785) 628-9410
E-mail: dclerk@ellisco.net

District Clerk

Twenty-Third Judicial District
1204 Fort Street, Hays, KS 67601
P.O. Box 8, Hays, KS 67601

Clerk of the District Court, Ellis County
Amanda Truan . . . . (785) 628-9415
1204 Fort Street, Hays, KS 67601   Fax: (785) 628-8415
P.O. Box 8, Hays, KS 67601
E-mail: agates@23rdjudicial.org

Ellsworth County

County Clerk

Office of the County Clerk
210 North Kansas Avenue, Ellsworth, KS 67439
Tel: (785) 472-4161 Fax: (785) 472-3818

County Clerk **Shelly Dvopat** . . . . (785) 472-4161
E-mail: ewclerk@kansas.com

District Clerk

Twentieth Judicial District
1400 Main, Great Bend, KS 67530

Clerk of the District Court, Ellsworth County
Peggy Svaty . . . . (785) 472-4052
210 North Kansas Avenue,   Fax: (785) 472-5712
Ellsworth, KS 67439
E-mail: ewpas@cpcis.net

Finney County

County Clerk

Office of the County Clerk
311 North Ninth Street, Garden City, KS 67846
Tel: (620) 272-3575 Fax: (620) 272-3890

County Clerk **Elsa Ulrich** . . . . (620) 272-3524
E-mail: eulrich@finneycounty.org

District Clerk

Twenty-Fifth Judicial District
425 North Eighth Street, Garden City, KS 67846
P.O. Box 798, Garden City, KS 67846

Clerk of the District Court, Finney County
Christine Blake . . . . (620) 271-6120
425 North Eighth Street, Garden City, KS 67846   Fax: (620) 271-6140
P.O. Box 798, Garden City, KS 67846
E-mail: cblake@finneycounty.org

Ford County

County Clerk

Office of the County Clerk
100 Gunsmoke Street, Fourth Floor, Dodge City, KS 67801
Tel: (620) 227-4670 Fax: (620) 227-4699

County Clerk **Sharon Seibel** . . . . (620) 227-4553
E-mail: sseibel@fordcounty.net

District Clerk

Sixteenth Judicial District
101 West Spruce, Dodge City, KS 67801
P.O. Box 197, Dodge City, KS 67801

Clerk of the District Court, Ford County
Rhonda Whitney . . . . (620) 227-4609
101 West Spruce, Dodge City, KS 67801   Fax: (620) 227-6799
E-mail: rwhitney@16thdistrict.net

(continued on next page)

Franklin County

County Clerk

Office of the County Clerk
315 South Main Street, Ottawa, KS 66067
Tel: (785) 229-3410

County Clerk **Janet Paddock** . . . . (785) 229-3410
 E-mail: jpaddock@franklincoks.org

District Clerk

Fourth Judicial District
110 South Sixth Street, Burlington, KS 66839

Clerk of the District Court, Franklin County
 Linda S. Meier . . . . (785) 242-6000
 301 South Main, Ottawa, KS 66067   Fax: (785) 242-5970
 P.O. Box 637, Ottawa, KS 66067
 E-mail: lmeier@franklincoks.org

Geary County

County Clerk

Office of the County Clerk
200 East Eigth Street, Junction City, KS 66441
Tel: (785) 238-3912 Fax: (785) 238-5419

County Clerk **Rebecca Bossemeyer** . . . . (785) 238-3912
 E-mail: rebecca.bossemeyer@gearycounty.org

District Clerk

Eighth Judicial District
200 South Third, Marion, KS 66861

Clerk of the District Court, Geary County **Patty Aska** . . . . (785) 762-5221
 138 East Eighth, Junction City, KS 66441   Fax: (785) 762-4420
 E-mail: paska@8thjd.com

Gove County

County Clerk

Office of the County Clerk
520 Washington Street, Suite 105, Gove, KS 67736
Tel: (785) 938-2300 Fax: (785) 938-2305

County Clerk **Doug Press** . . . . (785) 938-2300
 E-mail: go_county_clerk@wan.kdor.state.ks.us

District Clerk

Twenty-Third Judicial District
1204 Fort Street, Hays, KS 67601
P.O. Box 8, Hays, KS 67601

Clerk of the District Court, Gove County
 Teresa Lewis . . . . (785) 938-2310
 420 Broad Street, Gove, KS 67736   Fax: (785) 938-2312
 P.O. Box 97, Gove, KS 67736
 E-mail: gcdc@ruraltel.net

Graham County

County Clerk

Office of the County Clerk
410 North Pomeroy Street, Hill City, KS 67642
Tel: (785) 421-3453 Fax: (785) 421-6374

County Clerk **Jana Irby** . . . . (785) 421-3453
 E-mail: grahcocl@ruraltel.net

District Clerk

Seventeenth Judicial District
101 South Kansas, Norton, KS 67654
P.O. Box 70, Norton, KS 67654

Clerk of the District Court, Graham County
 Donna Elliott . . . . (785) 421-3458
 410 North Pomeroy, Hill City, KS 67642   Fax: (785) 421-5463
 E-mail: ghdc@ruraltel.net

Grant County

County Clerk

Office of the County Clerk
108 South Glenn Street, Ulysses, KS 67880
Tel: (620) 356-1335 Fax: (620) 356-3081

County Clerk **Sheila Brown** . . . . (620) 356-1335
 E-mail: clerk@pld.com

District Clerk

Twenty-Sixth Judicial District
200 East Sixth, Hugoton, KS 67951

Clerk of the District Court, Grant County
 Reid Richardson . . . . (620) 356-1526
 108 South Glenn, Ulysses, KS 67880   Fax: (620) 353-2131
 E-mail: gcdistct@pld.com

Gray County

County Clerk

Office of the County Clerk
300 South Main Street, Room 104, Cimarron, KS 67835
Tel: (620) 855-3618 Fax: (620) 855-3107

County Clerk **Ashley Rogers** . . . . (620) 855-3618
 E-mail: arogers@grayco.org

District Clerk

Sixteenth Judicial District
101 West Spruce, Dodge City, KS 67801
P.O. Box 197, Dodge City, KS 67801

Clerk of the District Court, Gray County
 Angela Bowlin . . . . (620) 855-3812
 300 South Main, Cimarron, KS 67835   Fax: (620) 855-7037
 P.O. Box 487, Cimarron, KS 67835
 E-mail: gycodist@ucom.net

Greeley County

County Clerk

Office of the County Clerk
616 Second Street, Tribune, KS 67879
Tel: (620) 376-4256 Fax: (620) 376-4255
E-mail: gl.county.clerk@wan.kdor.state.ks.us

County Clerk **Jerri Young** . . . . (620) 376-4256
 E-mail: gcclerk@fairpoint.net

District Clerk

Twenty-Fifth Judicial District
425 North Eighth Street, Garden City, KS 67846
P.O. Box 798, Garden City, KS 67846

Clerk of the District Court, Greeley County
Debra Riley..(620) 376-4292
616 Second Avenue, Tribune, KS 67879   Fax: (620) 376-2351
P.O. Box 516, Tribune, KS 67879
E-mail: gldistct@sunflowertelco.com

Greenwood County

County Clerk

Office of the County Clerk
311 North Main Street, Suite 3, Eureka, KS 67045
Tel: (620) 583-8121 Fax: (620) 583-8124

County Clerk **Kathy Robison**.......................(620) 583-8121
E-mail: gw_county_clerk@wan.kdor.state.ks.us

District Clerk

Thirteenth Judicial District
201 West Pine, Suite B, El Dorado, KS 67042

Clerk of the District Court, Greenwood County
Tami Evenson ....(620) 583-8153
311 North Main, Eureka, KS 67045   Fax: (620) 583-6818
E-mail: tevenson@fox-net.net

Hamilton County

County Clerk

Office of the County Clerk
219 North Main Street, Syracuse, KS 67878
Tel: (620) 384-5629 Fax: (620) 384-5853

County Clerk **Angie Moser** ....(620) 384-5629
E-mail: hmcoclerk@wbsnet.org

District Clerk

Twenty-Fifth Judicial District
425 North Eighth Street, Garden City, KS 67846
P.O. Box 798, Garden City, KS 67846

Clerk of the District Court, Hamilton County
Glenda Cheatum..................................(620) 384-5159
219 North Main, Syracuse, KS 67878   Fax: (620) 384-7806
P.O. Box 745, Syracuse, KS 67878
E-mail: dcourt@wbsnet.org

Harper County

County Clerk

Office of the County Clerk
201 North Jennings Avenue, Second Floor, Anthony, KS 67003
Tel: (620) 842-5555 Fax: (620) 842-3455

County Clerk **Cheryl Adelhardt** ....(620) 842-5555
E-mail: clerk@harpercountyks.gov

District Clerk

Thirtieth Judicial District
130 North Spruce, Kingman, KS 67068
P.O. Box 495, Kingman, KS 67068

Clerk of the District Court, Harper County
Tracy Aleshire ....(620) 842-3721
201 North Jennings, Anthony, KS 67003   Fax: (620) 842-6025
P.O. Box 467, Anthony, KS 67003
E-mail: taleshire@harpercountyks.gov

Harvey County

County Clerk

Office of the County Clerk
800 North Main Street, Newton, KS 67114
P.O. Box 687, Newton, KS 67114
Tel: (316) 284-6840 Fax: (316) 284-6856

County Clerk **Rick Piepho** ....(316) 284-6840
E-mail: rpiepho@harveycounty.com

District Clerk

Ninth Judicial District
Eighth and Main Streets, Newton, KS 67114
P.O. Box 665, Newton, KS 67114

Clerk of the District Court, Harvey County
L. Deena Jones ....(316) 284-6824
Eighth and Main Streets, Newton, KS 67114   Fax: (316) 283-4601
P.O. Box 665, Newton, KS 67114
E-mail: deenaj@9thdistct.net

Haskell County

County Clerk

Office of the County Clerk
300 South Inman Street, Sublette, KS 67877
Tel: (620) 675-2263 Fax: (620) 675-2681

County Clerk **Pamela Carrion** ....(620) 675-2263
E-mail: hspc@unitedwireless.com

District Clerk

Twenty-Sixth Judicial District
200 East Sixth, Hugoton, KS 67951

Clerk of the District Court, Haskell County
Toni Martin......................................(620) 675-2671
300 South Inman, Sublette, KS 67877   Fax: (620) 675-8599
P.O. Box 146, Sublette, KS 67877
E-mail: hsdictct@pld.com

Hodgeman County

County Clerk

Office of the County Clerk
500 Main Street, Jetmore, KS 67854
Tel: (620) 357-6421 Fax: (620) 357-6313

County Clerk **Sarah Rains**.........................(620) 357-6421
E-mail: hg_county_clerk@wan.kdor.state.ks.us

(continued on next page)

Kansas Court Clerks and Courthouses *continued*

District Clerk

Twenty-Fourth Judicial District
715 Broadway, Larned, KS 67550
P.O. Box 270, Larned, KS 67550

Clerk of the District Court, Hodgeman County
Laura Cure .... (620) 357-6522
500 Main, Jetmore, KS 67854   Fax: (620) 357-6216
P.O. Box 187, Jetmore, KS 67854
E-mail: hgdistct@fairpoint.net

Jackson County

County Clerk

Office of the County Clerk
400 New York Avenue, Room 201, Holton, KS 66436
Tel: (785) 364-2891 Fax: (785) 364-4204

County Clerk **Kathy L. Mick** .... (785) 364-2891
E-mail: jacountyclerk@yahoo.com

District Clerk

Second Judicial District
P.O. Box 327, Oskaloosa, KS 66066

Clerk of the District Court, Jackson County
Colleen A. Reamer .... (785) 364-2191
400 New York, Room 311,   Fax: (785) 364-3804
Holton, KS 66436
E-mail: reamercolleen@hotmail.com

Jefferson County

County Clerk

Office of the County Clerk
300 Jefferson Street, Oskaloosa, KS 66066
Tel: (785) 863-2272 Fax: (785) 863-3135

County Clerk **Linda M. Buttron** .... (785) 863-2272
E-mail: lbuttron@jfcountyks.com

District Clerk

Second Judicial District
P.O. Box 327, Oskaloosa, KS 66066

Clerk of the District Court, Jefferson County
Connie Milner .... (785) 863-2461
300 Jefferson, Oskaloosa, KS 66066   Fax: (785) 863-2369
P.O. Box 327, Oskaloosa, KS 66066
E-mail: cmilner@embarqmail.com

Jewell County

County Clerk

Office of the County Clerk
307 North Commercial Street, Mankato, KS 66956
Tel: (785) 378-4020 Fax: (785) 378-3037

County Clerk **Carla J. Waugh** .... (785) 378-4020
E-mail: jw_county_clerk@wan.kdor.state.ks.us

District Clerk

Twelfth Judicial District
214 C Street, Washington, KS 66968

Clerk of the District Court, Jewell County
Dixie L. Dethloff .... (785) 378-4030
307 North Commercial, Mankato, KS 66956   Fax: (785) 378-4035
E-mail: dixiea@12jd.org

Kansas Court Clerks and Courthouses *continued*

Johnson County

County Clerk

Department of Records and Tax Administration [RTA]
111 South Cherry Street, Olathe, KS 66061
Tel: (913) 715-0775 Fax: (913) 715-0800
E-mail: rta_info@jocogov.org
Internet: http://rta.jocogov.org/

Director **John A. Bartolac** .... (913) 715-0775
E-mail: john.bartolac@jocogov.org

District Clerk

Tenth Judicial District
100 North Kansas Avenue, Olathe, KS 66061

Clerk of the District Court, Johnson County
Sandra McCurdy .... (913) 715-3350
100 North Kansas Avenue,   Fax: (913) 715-3401
Olathe, KS 66061
E-mail: sandra.mccurdy@jocogov.org

Kearny County

County Clerk

Office of the County Clerk
304 North Main Street, Lakin, KS 67860
Tel: (620) 355-6422 Fax: (620) 355-7382

County Clerk **Jana Jenkinson** .... (620) 355-6422
E-mail: ke_county_clerk@wan.kdor.state.ks.us

District Clerk

Twenty-Fifth Judicial District
425 North Eighth Street, Garden City, KS 67846
P.O. Box 798, Garden City, KS 67846

Clerk of the District Court, Kearny County
Catherine Cole .... (620) 355-6481
304 North Main, Lakin, KS 67860   Fax: (620) 355-7462
P.O. Box 64, Lakin, KS 67860
E-mail: kecodc@pld.com

Kingman County

County Clerk

Office of the County Clerk
130 North Spruce Street, Kingman, KS 67068
Tel: (620) 532-2521 Fax: (620) 532-5082

County Clerk **Carol Noblit** .... (620) 532-2521

District Clerk

Thirtieth Judicial District
130 North Spruce, Kingman, KS 67068
P.O. Box 495, Kingman, KS 67068

Clerk of the District Court, Kingman County
Staci L. Jackson .... (620) 532-5151
130 North Spruce, Kingman, KS 67068   Fax: (620) 532-2952
P.O. Box 495, Kingman, KS 67068
E-mail: stacij@kmdistrictcourt.kscoxmail.com

Kiowa County

County Clerk

Office of the County Clerk
211 East Florida Avenue, Greensburg, KS 67054
Tel: (620) 723-3366 Fax: (620) 723-3234

County Clerk **Kristi Cooper** . . . . (620) 723-3366
 E-mail: kristi.cooper@kiowacountyks.org

District Clerk

Sixteenth Judicial District
101 West Spruce, Dodge City, KS 67801
P.O. Box 197, Dodge City, KS 67801

Clerk of the District Court, Kiowa County
 Debra Schmidt . . . . (620) 723-3317
 211 East Florida, Greensburg, KS 67054   Fax: (620) 723-2970
 E-mail: debra.schmidt@kiowacountyks.org

Labette County

County Clerk

Office of the County Clerk
501 Merchant Street, Oswego, KS 67356
Tel: (620) 795-2138 Fax: (620) 795-2928

County Clerk **Peggy Minor** . . . . (620) 795-2138
 E-mail: pminor@labettecounty.com

District Clerk

Eleventh Judicial District
111 East Forest Street, Girard, KS 66743

Clerk of the District Court, Labette
 County **Terri Thurman** . . . . (620) 795-4533 (Oswego Division)
 517 Merchant Street, Oswego, KS 67356   Tel: (620) 421-4120
 201 South Central, Parsons, KS 67357   (Parsons Division)
 E-mail: lbcoclerks@sbcglobal.net   Fax: (620) 421-3633
          (Parsons Division)

Lane County

County Clerk

Office of the County Clerk
144 South Lane Street, Dighton, KS 67839
Tel: (620) 397-5356 Fax: (620) 397-5419

County Clerk **Stephanie Benzel** . . . . (620) 397-5356

District Clerk

Twenty-Fourth Judicial District
715 Broadway, Larned, KS 67550
P.O. Box 270, Larned, KS 67550

Clerk of the District Court, Lane County
 Marlene Rupp . . . . (620) 397-2805
 144 South Lane, Dighton, KS 67839   Fax: (620) 397-5526
 P.O. Box 188, Dighton, KS 67839
 E-mail: ledistct@st-tel.net

Leavenworth County

County Clerk

Office of the County Clerk
300 Walnut Street, Suite 106, Leavenworth, KS 66048
Tel: (913) 684-0421 Fax: (913) 680-1489

County Clerk **Janet Klasinski** . . . . (913) 684-0421
 E-mail: jklasinski@leavenworthcounty.org

District Clerk

First Judicial District
601 South Third Street, Leavenworth, KS 66048

Clerk of the District Court, Leavenworth County
 Janet Westbrook . . . . (913) 684-0700
 601 South Third Street, Suite 3051,   Fax: (913) 684-0492
 Leavenworth, KS 66048
 E-mail: jwestbrook@leavenworthcounty.org

Lincoln County

County Clerk

Office of the County Clerk
216 East Lincoln Avenue, Lincoln, KS 67455
Tel: (785) 524-4757 Fax: (785) 524-5008

County Clerk **Dawn M. Harlow** . . . . (785) 524-4757
 E-mail: lcclerk@lincolncoks.org

District Clerk

Twelfth Judicial District
214 C Street, Washington, KS 66968

Clerk of the District Court, Lincoln County
 Jo Hachmeister . . . . (785) 524-4057
 216 East Lincoln Avenue, Lincoln, KS 67455   Fax: (785) 524-3204
 E-mail: joh@12jd.org

Linn County

County Clerk

Office of the County Clerk
315 Main Street, Mound City, KS 66056
Tel: (913) 795-2668 Fax: (913) 795-2889

County Clerk **David L. Lamb** . . . . (913) 795-2668
 E-mail: dlamb@linncountyks.com

District Clerk

Sixth Judicial District
P.O. Box 350, Mound City, KS 66056

Clerk of the District Court, Linn County
 Kelly R. Gibson . . . . (913) 795-2660
 318 Chestnut, Mound City, KS 66056   Fax: (913) 795-2004
 P.O. Box 350, Mound City, KS 66056
 E-mail: gibsonlndc@earthlink.net

Logan County

County Clerk

Office of the County Clerk
710 West Second Street, Oakley, KS 67748
Tel: (785) 671-4244 Fax: (785) 671-3341

County Clerk **Crystal Rucker** . . . . (785) 671-4244
 E-mail: lg_county_clerk@wan.kdor.state.ks.us

(continued on next page)

District Clerk

Fifteenth Judicial District
300 North Court, Colby, KS 67701
P.O. Box 805, Colby, KS 67701

Clerk of the District Court, Logan County
  Sonya Gallagher . . . . (785) 671-3654
  710 West Second, Oakley, KS 67748   Fax: (785) 671-3517

Lyon County

County Clerk

Office of the County Clerk
430 Commercial Street, Emporia, KS 66801
Tel: (620) 341-3245 Fax: (620) 341-3415

County Clerk **Tammy Vopat** . . . . (620) 341-3245
  E-mail: lyclerk@lyoncounty.org

District Clerk

Fifth Judicial District
430 Commercial, Emporia, KS 66801

Clerk of the District Court, Lyon County
  R. Christine Brammer . . . . (620) 341-3280
  430 Commercial, Emporia, KS 66801   Fax: (620) 341-3497
  E-mail: dstclerk@5thjd.org

Marion County

County Clerk

Office of the County Clerk
200 South Third Street, Suite 104, Marion, KS 66861
Tel: (620) 382-2185 Tel: (800) 305-8851 Fax: (620) 382-8815

County Clerk **Tina D. Spencer** . . . . (620) 382-2185
  E-mail: coclerk@marioncoks.net

District Clerk

Eighth Judicial District
200 South Third, Marion, KS 66861

Clerk of the District Court, Marion County
  Jan Helmer . . . . (620) 382-2104
  200 South Third, Suite 201,   Fax: (620) 382-2259
  Marion, KS 66861
  E-mail: jhelmer@8thjd.com

Marshall County

County Clerk

Office of the County Clerk
1201 Broadway Street, Marysville, KS 66508
Tel: (785) 562-5361 Fax: (785) 562-5262

County Clerk **Sonya L. Stohs** . . . . (785) 562-5361
  E-mail: msctyclk@bluevalley.net

District Clerk

Twenty-Second Judicial District
601 Oregon, Hiawatha, KS 66434
P.O. Box 417, Hiawatha, KS 66434

Clerk of the District Court, Marshall County
  Nancy Koch . . . . (785) 562-5301
  1201 Broadway, Marysville, KS 66508   Fax: (785) 562-2458
  P.O. Box 149, Marysville, KS 66508
  E-mail: mcdc@bluevalley.net

McPherson County

County Clerk

Office of the County Clerk
117 North Maple Street, McPherson, KS 67460
Tel: (620) 241-3656 Fax: (620) 241-1168

County Clerk **Cathy A. Schmidt** . . . . (620) 241-3656
  E-mail: cschmidt@mcphersoncountyks.us

District Clerk

Ninth Judicial District
Eighth and Main Streets, Newton, KS 67114
P.O. Box 665, Newton, KS 67114

Clerk of the District Court, McPherson County
  Cindy Teter . . . . (620) 241-3422
  117 North Maple Street, McPherson, KS 67460   Fax: (620) 241-1372
  P.O. Box 1106, McPherson, KS 67460
  E-mail: cindyt@9thdistct.net

Meade County

County Clerk

Office of the County Clerk
200 North Fowler Street, Meade, KS 67864
Tel: (620) 873-8700 Fax: (620) 873-8713

County Clerk **Janet Hale** . . . . (620) 873-8700
  E-mail: jhale@meadeco.org

District Clerk

Sixteenth Judicial District
101 West Spruce, Dodge City, KS 67801
P.O. Box 197, Dodge City, KS 67801

Clerk of the District Court, Meade County
  Decinda Heinz . . . . (620) 873-8750
  200 North Fowler, Meade, KS 67864   Fax: (620) 873-8759
  P.O. Box 623, Meade, KS 67864
  E-mail: decinda.heinz@sbcglobal.net

Miami County

County Clerk

Office of the County Clerk
201 South Pearl Street, Suite 102, Paola, KS 66071
Tel: (913) 294-3976 Fax: (913) 294-9544

County Clerk **Janet White** . . . . (913) 294-3976
  E-mail: countyclerk@miamicountyks.org

District Clerk

Sixth Judicial District
P.O. Box 350, Mound City, KS 66056

Clerk of the District Court, Miami County
  Stephanie Gerken . . . . (913) 294-3326
  120 South Pearl, Paola, KS 66071   Fax: (913) 294-2535
  P.O. Box 187, Paola, KS 66071

Mitchell County

County Clerk

Office of the County Clerk
111 South Hersey Avenue, Beloit, KS 67420
Tel: (785) 738-3652   Fax: (785) 738-5524

County Clerk **Christine "Chris" Treaster** . . . .(785) 738-3652
   E-mail: mitchell_co@nckcn.com

District Clerk

Twelfth Judicial District
214 C Street, Washington, KS 66968

Clerk of the District Court, Mitchell County
   Pam Thiessen . . . . (785) 738-3753
   115 South Hersey, Beloit, KS 67420   Fax: (785) 738-4101
   E-mail: pamt@12jd.org

Montgomery County

County Clerk

Office of the County Clerk
217 East Myrtle Street, Independence, KS 67301
Tel: (620) 330-1200   Fax: (620) 330-1202

County Clerk **Charlotte A. Scott-Schmid** . . . . (620) 330-1200
   E-mail: csschmidt@mgcountyks.org

District Clerk

Fourteenth Judicial District
300 East Main Street, Independence, KS 67301

Clerk of the District Court, Montgomery County
   Bonnie James . . . . (620) 330-1070
   300 East Main Street, Suite 201,   Fax: (620) 331-6120
   Independence, KS 67301

Morris County

County Clerk

Office of the County Clerk
501 West Main Street, Suite Nine, Council Grove, KS 66846
Tel: (620) 767-5518   Fax: (620) 767-6789

County Clerk **Michelle Garrett** . . . . (620) 767-5518
   E-mail: morris@tctelco.net

District Clerk

Eighth Judicial District
200 South Third, Marion, KS 66861

Clerk of the District Court, Morris County
   Kathleen Rohloff . . . .(620) 767-6838
   501 West Main, Council Grove, KS 66846   Fax: (620) 767-6488

Morton County

County Clerk

Office of the County Clerk
1025 Morton Street, Elkhart, KS 67950
Tel: (620) 697-2157   Fax: (620) 697-2159

County Clerk **Gina Castillo** . . . . (620) 697-2157
   E-mail: mortoncountyclerk@elkhart.com

District Clerk

Twenty-Sixth Judicial District
200 East Sixth, Hugoton, KS 67951

Clerk of the District Court, Morton County
   Mellisa Lewis . . . .(620) 697-2563
   1025 Morton, Elkhart, KS 67950   Fax: (620) 697-4289
   P.O. Box 825, Elkhart, KS 67950
   E-mail: mtcodist@elkhart.com

Nemaha County

County Clerk

Office of the County Clerk
607 Nemaha Street, Seneca, KS 66538
Tel: (785) 336-2170   Fax: (785) 336-3373

County Clerk **Mary Kay Schultejans** . . . . (785) 336-2170
   E-mail: nmclerk@carsoncomm.com

District Clerk

Twenty-Second Judicial District
601 Oregon, Hiawatha, KS 66434
P.O. Box 417, Hiawatha, KS 66434

Clerk of the District Court, Nemaha County
   Patricia Heideman . . . .(785) 336-2146
   607 Nemaha, Seneca, KS 66538   Fax: (785) 336-6450
   E-mail: nmcourt@carsoncomm.com

Neosho County

County Clerk

Office of the County Clerk
100 South Main Street, Suite 102, Erie, KS 66733
Tel: (620) 244-3811   Fax: (620) 244-3810

County Clerk **Randal E. Neely** . . . . (620) 244-3811
   E-mail: nococlerk@neoshocounty.kscoxmail.com

District Clerk

Thirty-First Judicial District
One North Washington, Room B, Iola, KS 66749

Clerk of the District Court, Neosho
   County **Angela Walters** . . . . (620) 431-5700 (Chanute Division)
   102 South Lincoln, Chanute, KS 66720   Tel: (620) 244-3831
   P.O. Box 889, Chanute, KS 66720   (Erie Division)
   100 South Main, Erie, KS 66733   Fax: (620) 244-3830
   P.O. Box 19, Erie, KS 66733   (Erie Division)
   E-mail: anwalters@cableone.net

Ness County

County Clerk

Office of the County Clerk
202 West Sycamore Street, Ness City, KS 67560
Tel: (785) 798-2401   Fax: (785) 798-3180

County Clerk **Renee S. Kerr** . . . . (785) 798-2401
   E-mail: ns_county_clerk@wan.kdor.state.ks.us

(continued on next page)

District Clerk

Twenty-Fourth Judicial District
715 Broadway, Larned, KS 67550
P.O. Box 270, Larned, KS 67550

Clerk of the District Court, Ness County
Joby Henning . . . . (785) 798-3693
100 South Kansas, Ness City, KS 67560
P.O. Box 445, Ness City, KS 67560   Fax: (785) 798-3348
E-mail: nsdistct@gbta.net

Norton County

County Clerk

Office of the County Clerk
105 South Kansas Avenue, Norton, KS 67654
Tel: (785) 877-5710   Fax: (785) 877-5794

County Clerk **Robert D. Wyatt** . . . . (785) 877-5710
E-mail: nt_county_clerk@wan.kdor.state.ks.us

District Clerk

Seventeenth Judicial District
101 South Kansas, Norton, KS 67654
P.O. Box 70, Norton, KS 67654

Clerk of the District Court, Norton County
Darla Engel . . . . (785) 877-5720
101 South Kansas, Norton, KS 67654   Fax: (785) 877-5722
P.O. Box 70, Norton, KS 67654
E-mail: ntdc@ruraltel.net

Osage County

County Clerk

Office of the County Clerk
717 Topeka Avenue, Lyndon, KS 66451
Tel: (785) 828-4812   Fax: (785) 828-4749

County Clerk **Rhond Beets** . . . . (785) 828-4812
E-mail: os_county_clerk@wan.kdor.state.ks.us

District Clerk

Fourth Judicial District
110 South Sixth Street, Burlington, KS 66839

Clerk of the District Court, Osage County
Charna Williams . . . . (785) 828-4713
717 Topeka Avenue, Lyndon, KS 66451   Fax: (785) 828-4704
P.O. Box 549, Lyndon, KS 66451
E-mail: charnaos@embarqmail.com

Osborne County

County Clerk

Office of the County Clerk
423 West Main Street, Osborne, KS 67473
Tel: (785) 346-2431   Fax: (785) 346-5252

County Clerk **Vienna Janis** . . . . (785) 346-2431
E-mail: obcoclerk@ruraltel.net

District Clerk

Seventeenth Judicial District
101 South Kansas, Norton, KS 67654
P.O. Box 70, Norton, KS 67654

Clerk of the District Court, Osborne County
Sheryl Gorsuch . . . . (785) 346-5911
423 West Main, Osborne, KS 67473   Fax: (785) 346-5992
P.O. Box 160, Osborne, KS 67473
E-mail: obcodc@ruraltel.net

Ottawa County

County Clerk

Office of the County Clerk
307 North Concord Street, Suite 102, Minneapolis, KS 67467
Tel: (785) 392-2279   Fax: (785) 392-2011

County Clerk **Mary P. Arganbright** . . . . (785) 392-2279
E-mail: occlerk@nckcn.com

District Clerk

Twenty-Eighth Judicial District
300 West Ash, Salina, KS 67402
P.O. Box 1760, Salina, KS 67402

Clerk of the District Court, Ottawa County
Sara L. Thompson . . . . (785) 392-2917
307 North Concord, Minneapolis, KS 67467   Fax: (785) 392-3626
E-mail: clerktwo@nckcn.com

Pawnee County

County Clerk

Office of the County Clerk
715 Broadway, Larned, KS 67550
Tel: (620) 285-3721   Fax: (620) 285-2559

County Clerk **Ruth M. Searight** . . . . (620) 285-3721
E-mail: pn_county_clerk@wan.kdor.state.ks.us

District Clerk

Twenty-Fourth Judicial District
715 Broadway, Larned, KS 67550
P.O. Box 270, Larned, KS 67550

Clerk of the District Court, Pawnee County
Kay M. Schartz . . . . (620) 285-6937
715 Broadway, Larned, KS 67550   Fax: (620) 285-3665
P.O. Box 270, Larned, KS 67550
E-mail: pndistct@pawnee.kscoxmail.com

Phillips County

County Clerk

Office of the County Clerk
301 State Street, Phillipsburg, KS 67661
Tel: (785) 543-6825   Fax: (785) 543-6827

County Clerk **Linda McDowell** . . . . (785) 543-6825
E-mail: pl_county_clerk@wan.kdor.state.ks.us

District Clerk

Seventeenth Judicial District
101 South Kansas, Norton, KS 67654
P.O. Box 70, Norton, KS 67654

Clerk of the District Court, Phillips County
Debra Grammon .... (785) 543-6830
301 State Street, Phillipsburg, KS 67661   Fax: (785) 543-6832
P.O. Box 564, Phillipsburg, KS 67661
E-mail: plcocdc@ruraltel.net

Pottawatomie County

County Clerk

Office of the County Clerk
207 North First Street, Westmoreland, KS 66549
Tel: (785) 457-3314   Fax: (785) 457-3507

County Clerk **Nancy E. McCarter** .... (785) 457-3314
E-mail: nmccarter@pottcounty.org

District Clerk

Second Judicial District
P.O. Box 327, Oskaloosa, KS 66066

Clerk of the District Court, Pottawatomie County
Sara Helget .... (785) 457-3392
107 North First Street, Westmoreland, KS 66549   Fax: (785) 457-2107
P.O. Box 129, Westmoreland, KS 66549
E-mail: ptdistct@kscourts.net

Pratt County

County Clerk

Office of the County Clerk
300 South Ninnescah Street, Second Floor, Pratt, KS 67124
Tel: (620) 672-4110   Fax: (620) 672-9541

County Clerk **Sherry Kruse** .... (620) 672-4110
E-mail: skruse@prattcounty.org

District Clerk

Thirtieth Judicial District
130 North Spruce, Kingman, KS 67068
P.O. Box 495, Kingman, KS 67068

Clerk of the District Court, Pratt County
Shawna Kiley .... (620) 672-4100
300 South Ninnescah, Pratt, KS 67124   Fax: (620) 672-2902
P.O. Box 984, Pratt, KS 67124

Rawlins County

County Clerk

Office of the County Clerk
607 Main Street, Suite C, Atwood, KS 67730
Tel: (785) 626-3351   Fax: (785) 626-9019

County Clerk **Rachel Finley** .... (785) 626-3351
E-mail: ra_county_clerk@wan.kdor.state.ks.us

District Clerk

Fifteenth Judicial District
300 North Court, Colby, KS 67701
P.O. Box 805, Colby, KS 67701

Clerk of the District Court, Rawlins County
Sierra Lowry .... (785) 626-3465
607 Main, Room F, Atwood, KS 67730   Fax: (785) 626-3350

Reno County

County Clerk

Office of the County Clerk
206 West First Avenue, Hutchinson, KS 67501
Tel: (620) 694-2934   Fax: (620) 694-2534

County Clerk **Donna Patton** .... (620) 694-2934
E-mail: donna.patton@renogov.org

District Clerk

Twenty-Seventh Judicial District
206 West First Street, 3rd Floor, Hutchinson, KS 67501

Clerk of the District Court, Reno County **Pam Moses** .... (620) 694-2956
206 West First Street, 3rd Floor,   Fax: (620) 694-2958
Hutchinson, KS 67501
E-mail: pam.moses@renogov.org

Republic County

County Clerk

Office of the County Clerk
1815 M Street, Belleville, KS 66935
Tel: (785) 527-7231   Fax: (785) 527-2668

County Clerk **Kathleen L. Marsicek** .... (785) 527-7231
E-mail: kmarsicek@republiccounty.org

District Clerk

Twelfth Judicial District
214 C Street, Washington, KS 66968

Clerk of the District Court, Republic County
Kristen L. Kling .... (785) 527-7234
1815 M Street, Belleville, KS 66935   Fax: (785) 527-5029
P.O. Box 8, Belleville, KS 66935
E-mail: krisk@12jd.org

Rice County

County Clerk

Office of the County Clerk
101 West Commercial Street, Lyons, KS 67554
Tel: (620) 257-2232   Fax: (620) 257-3039

County Clerk **Alicia Showalter** .... (620) 257-2232
E-mail: ashow@ricecocthse.com

District Clerk

Twentieth Judicial District
1400 Main, Great Bend, KS 67530

Clerk of the District Court, Rice County **Jane Hrabik** .... (620) 257-2383
101 West Commercial Street, 3rd Floor,   Fax: (620) 257-3826
Lyons, KS 67554
E-mail: rcdiscrt@ricecocthse.com

(continued on next page)

Riley County

County Clerk

Office of the County Clerk
110 Courthouse Plaza, First Floor, Room B118, Manhattan, KS 66502
Tel: (785) 565-6200 Fax: (785) 537-6394

County Clerk **Rich Vargo** . . . . (785) 537-6301
E-mail: rvargo@rileycountyks.gov

District Clerk

Twenty-First Judicial District
100 Courthouse Plaza, Manhattan, KS 66505

Clerk of the District Court, Riley County
Katherine Oliver . . . . (785) 537-6364
100 Courthouse Plaza, Manhattan, KS 66505   Fax: (785) 537-6382
P.O. Box 158, Manhattan, KS 66505
E-mail: koliver@rileycountyks.gov

Rooks County

County Clerk

Office of the County Clerk
115 North Walnut Street, Second Floor, Stockton, KS 67669
Tel: (785) 425-6391 Fax: (785) 425-6015
E-mail: ro_county_clerk@wan.kdor.state.ks.us

County Clerk **Clara Strutt** . . . . (785) 425-6391
E-mail: ro_county_clerk@wan.kdor.state.ks.us

District Clerk

Twenty-Third Judicial District
1204 Fort Street, Hays, KS 67601
P.O. Box 8, Hays, KS 67601

Clerk of the District Court, Rooks County
Connie Stithem . . . . (785) 425-6718
115 North Walnut, Stockton, KS 67669   Fax: (785) 425-6568
P.O. Box 532, Stockton, KS 67669
E-mail: cstithem@rooksdc.org

Rush County

County Clerk

Office of the County Clerk
715 Elm Street, La Crosse, KS 67548
Tel: (785) 222-2731 Fax: (785) 222-3559

County Clerk **Corinne Baldwin** . . . . (785) 222-2731
E-mail: rh_county_clerk@wan.kdor.state.ks.us

District Clerk

Twenty-Fourth Judicial District
715 Broadway, Larned, KS 67550
P.O. Box 270, Larned, KS 67550

Clerk of the District Court, Rush County
Pamela J. Davis . . . . (785) 222-2718
715 Elm, La Crosse, KS 67548   Fax: (785) 222-2748
E-mail: rhdistct@gbta.net

Russell County

County Clerk

Office of the County Clerk
401 North Main Street, Russell, KS 67665
Tel: (785) 483-4641 Fax: (785) 483-5725

County Clerk **Mary K. Nuss** . . . . (785) 483-4641
E-mail: russellcoclerk@ruraltel.net

District Clerk

Twentieth Judicial District
1400 Main, Great Bend, KS 67530

Clerk of the District Court, Russell County
Laura Seirer . . . . (785) 483-5641
Fourth and Main Street, Russell, KS 67665   Fax: (785) 483-2448
P.O. Box 876, Russell, KS 67665
E-mail: lseirer@ruraltel.net

Saline County

County Clerk

Office of the County Clerk
300 West Ash Street, Room 215, Salina, KS 67401
Tel: (785) 309-5820 Fax: (785) 309-5826

County Clerk **Donald R. "Don" Merriman** . . . . (785) 309-5820
E-mail: don.merriman@saline.org

District Clerk

Twenty-Eighth Judicial District
300 West Ash, Salina, KS 67402
P.O. Box 1760, Salina, KS 67402

Clerk of the District Court, Saline County
Teresa Drane . . . . (785) 309-5831
300 West Ash, Salina, KS 67402   Fax: (785) 309-5845
P.O. Box 1760, Salina, KS 67402
E-mail: teresa.lueth@saline.org

Scott County

County Clerk

Office of the County Clerk
303 Court Street, Scott City, KS 67871
Tel: (620) 872-2420 Tel: (620) 872-7165 Fax: (620) 872-7145

County Clerk **Alice Brokofsky** . . . . (620) 872-2420
E-mail: sc_county_clerk@wan.kdor.state.ks.us

District Clerk

Twenty-Fifth Judicial District
425 North Eighth Street, Garden City, KS 67846
P.O. Box 798, Garden City, KS 67846

Clerk of the District Court, Scott County **Sandra Eitel** . . . (620) 872-7208
303 Court Street, Scott City, KS 67871   Fax: (620) 872-3683
E-mail: scdc@wbsnet.org

Sedgwick County

County Clerk

Office of the County Clerk
525 N. Main St., Room 211, Wichita, KS 67203
Tel: (316) 660-9249   Fax: (316) 383-7961

County Clerk **Kelly Arnold** . . . . (316) 660-9222
E-mail: sgclerk@sedgwick.gov

District Clerk

Eighteenth Judicial District
525 North Main, Wichita, KS 67203

Clerk of the District Court, Sedgwick County
Bernie Lumbreras . . . . (316) 660-5801
525 North Main, Wichita, KS 67203   Fax: (316) 941-5361
E-mail: blumbrer@dc18.org

Seward County

County Clerk

Office of the County Clerk
515 North Washington Avenue, Suite 100, Liberal, KS 67901
Tel: (620) 626-3355   Fax: (620) 626-3211

County Clerk **Stacia D. Long** . . . . (620) 626-3355
E-mail: slong@sewardcountyks.org

District Clerk

Twenty-Sixth Judicial District
200 East Sixth, Hugoton, KS 67951

Clerk of the District Court, Seward County
Koleen Nosekabel . . . . (620) 626-3375
415 North Washington, Suite 103,   Fax: (620) 626-3302
Liberal, KS 67901
E-mail: swcdc@swko.net

Shawnee County

County Clerk

Office of the County Clerk
200 SE Seventh Street, Room 107, Topeka, KS 66603
Tel: (785) 251-4155   Fax: (785) 251-4912
E-mail: countyclerk@snco.us

County Clerk **Cynthia A. "Cyndi" Beck** . . . . (785) 251-4155
E-mail: cyndi.beck@snco.us

District Clerk

Third Judicial District
200 SE Seventh Street, Topeka, KS 66603

Clerk of the District Court, Shawnee County
Angela M. Callahan . . . . (785) 251-4422
200 SE Seventh Street, Suite 209,   Fax: (785) 251-4908
Topeka, KS 66603
E-mail: acallahan@shawneecourt.org

Sheridan County

County Clerk

Office of the County Clerk
925 Ninth Street, Second Floor, Hoxie, KS 67740
Tel: (785) 675-3361   Fax: (785) 675-3487

County Clerk **Heather Bracht** . . . . (785) 675-3361
E-mail: sdcoclk@ruraltel.net

District Clerk

Fifteenth Judicial District
300 North Court, Colby, KS 67701
P.O. Box 805, Colby, KS 67701

Clerk of the District Court, Sheridan County
Rhonda White . . . . (785) 675-3451
925 Ninth Street, Hoxie, KS 67740   Fax: (785) 675-2256
P.O. Box 753, Hoxie, KS 67740

Sherman County

County Clerk

Office of the County Clerk
813 Broadway, Room 102, Goodland, KS 67735
Tel: (785) 890-4806   Fax: (785) 890-4809

County Clerk **Ashley Mannis** . . . . (785) 890-4808
E-mail: amannis@shermancounty.org

District Clerk

Fifteenth Judicial District
300 North Court, Colby, KS 67701
P.O. Box 805, Colby, KS 67701

Clerk of the District Court, Sherman County
Linda Bowen . . . . (785) 890-4850
813 Broadway, Room 201,   Fax: (785) 890-4858
Goodland, KS 67735
E-mail: shcodc@st-tel.net

Smith County

County Clerk

Office of the County Clerk
218 South Grant Street, Smith Center, KS 66967
Tel: (785) 282-5110   Fax: (785) 282-5114

County Clerk **Sharon K. Wolters** . . . . (785) 282-5110
E-mail: sm_county_clerk@wan.kdor.state.ks.us

District Clerk

Seventeenth Judicial District
101 South Kansas, Norton, KS 67654
P.O. Box 70, Norton, KS 67654

Clerk of the District Court, Smith County **Karen Blank** . . . (785) 282-5140
218 South Grant, Smith Center, KS 66967   Fax: (785) 282-5145
P.O. Box 273, Smith Center, KS 66967
E-mail: smcodc@ruraltel.net

(continued on next page)

Stafford County

County Clerk

Office of the County Clerk
209 North Broadway, Second Floor, Saint John, KS 67576
Tel: (620) 549-3509   Fax: (620) 549-3481

County Clerk **Nita J. Keenan** . . . . (620) 549-3509
E-mail: coclerk@gbta.net

District Clerk

Twentieth Judicial District
1400 Main, Great Bend, KS 67530

Clerk of the District Court, Stafford County
Renee Salem . . . . (620) 549-3296
209-215 North Broadway,   Fax: (620) 549-3298
Saint John, KS 67576
P.O. Box 365, Saint John, KS 67576
E-mail: rsalem@embarqmail.com

Stanton County

County Clerk

Office of the County Clerk
201 North Main Street, Johnson, KS 67855
Tel: (620) 492-2140   Fax: (620) 492-2688

County Clerk **Sandra "Sandy" Barton** . . . . (620) 492-2140
E-mail: st_county_clerk@wan.kdor.state.ks.us

District Clerk

Twenty-Sixth Judicial District
200 East Sixth, Hugoton, KS 67951

Clerk of the District Court, Stanton County
Bonnie Parks . . . . (620) 492-2180
201 North Main Box 913,   Fax: (620) 492-6410
Johnson, KS 67855
E-mail: stcourt@pld.com

Stevens County

County Clerk

Office of the County Clerk
200 East Sixth Street, Hugoton, KS 67951
Tel: (620) 544-2541   Fax: (620) 544-4094

County Clerk **Pam Bensel** . . . . (620) 544-2541
E-mail: sv_county_clerk@wan.kdor.state.ks.us

District Clerk

Twenty-Sixth Judicial District
200 East Sixth, Hugoton, KS 67951

Clerk of the District Court, Stevens County
Kelsee Burnett . . . . (620) 544-2484
200 East Sixth, Hugoton, KS 67951   Fax: (620) 544-2528
E-mail: svcodist@pld.com

Sumner County

County Clerk

Office of the County Clerk
501 North Washington Avenue, Room 101, Wellington, KS 67152
Tel: (620) 326-3395   Fax: (620) 326-2116

County Clerk **Debra A. Norris** . . . . (620) 326-3395
E-mail: dnorris@co.sumner.ks.us

District Clerk

Thirtieth Judicial District
130 North Spruce, Kingman, KS 67068
P.O. Box 495, Kingman, KS 67068

Clerk of the District Court, Sumner County
Barbara Whitham . . . . (620) 326-5936
501 North Washington, Wellington, KS 67152   Fax: (620) 326-5365
P.O. Box 399, Wellington, KS 67152
E-mail: dcclerk@sutv.com

Thomas County

County Clerk

Office of the County Clerk
300 North Court Avenue, Colby, KS 67701
Tel: (785) 460-4500   Fax: (785) 460-4503

County Clerk **Shelly A. Harms** . . . . (785) 460-4500
E-mail: tcc01@st-tel.net

District Clerk

Fifteenth Judicial District
300 North Court, Colby, KS 67701
P.O. Box 805, Colby, KS 67701

Clerk of the District Court, Thomas County
Kim Schwarz . . . . (785) 460-4540
300 North Court, Colby, KS 67701   Fax: (785) 460-2291
P.O. Box 805, Colby, KS 67701
E-mail: kschwarz@thomascounty.us

Trego County

County Clerk

Office of the County Clerk
216 North Main Street, WaKeeney, KS 67672
Tel: (785) 743-5773   Fax: (785) 743-5594

County Clerk **Lori Augustine** . . . . (785) 743-5773
E-mail: clerk@ruraltel.net

District Clerk

Twenty-Third Judicial District
1204 Fort Street, Hays, KS 67601
P.O. Box 8, Hays, KS 67601

Clerk of the District Court, Trego County
Tiffany Gillespie . . . . (785) 743-2148
216 North Main, WaKeeney, KS 67672   Fax: (785) 743-2726
E-mail: tcdc@ruraltel.net

Wabaunsee County

County Clerk

Office of the County Clerk
215 Kansas Avenue, Alma, KS 66401
Tel: (785) 765-2421 Fax: (785) 765-3704

County Clerk **Jennifer A. Savage** . . . . (785) 765-2421
E-mail: jensavage@embarqmail.com

District Clerk

Second Judicial District
P.O. Box 327, Oskaloosa, KS 66066

Clerk of the District Court, Wabaunsee County
Krisena Silva . . . . (785) 765-2406
215 Kansas, Alma, KS 66401   Fax: (785) 765-2487
E-mail: wabcourt@wdcourt.com

Wallace County

County Clerk

Office of the County Clerk
P.O. Box 70, Sharon Springs, KS 67758
Tel: (785) 852-4282 Fax: (785) 852-5283

County Clerk **Jacalyn Mai** . . . . (785) 852-4282
E-mail: wa_county_clerk@wan.kdor.state.ks.us

District Clerk

Fifteenth Judicial District
300 North Court, Colby, KS 67701
P.O. Box 805, Colby, KS 67701

Clerk of the District Court, Wallace County
Allison A. Thon . . . . (785) 852-4289
313 Main, Sharon Springs, KS 67758   Fax: (785) 852-4271
P.O. Box 8, Sharon Springs, KS 67758
E-mail: wacodcc@sunflowertelco.com

Washington County

County Clerk

Office of the County Clerk
214 C Street, Washington, KS 66968
Tel: (785) 325-2974 Tel: (888) 955-2974 Fax: (785) 325-2303

County Clerk **Denae Jueneman** . . . . (785) 325-2974
E-mail: WS_County_Clerk@wan.kdor.state.ks.us

District Clerk

Twelfth Judicial District
214 C Street, Washington, KS 66968

Clerk of the District Court, Washington County
Shirley A. Marrs . . . . (785) 325-2381
214 C Street, Washington, KS 66968   Fax: (785) 325-2557
E-mail: shirleym@12jd.org

Wichita County

County Clerk

Office of the County Clerk
206 South Fourth Street, Leoti, KS 67861
Tel: (620) 375-2731 Fax: (620) 375-4350

County Clerk **Carol Cary** . . . . (620) 375-2731
E-mail: coclerk@wbsnet.org

District Clerk

Twenty-Fifth Judicial District
425 North Eighth Street, Garden City, KS 67846
P.O. Box 798, Garden City, KS 67846

Clerk of the District Court, Wichita County
Korina Wedel . . . . (620) 375-4454
206 South Fourth, Leoti, KS 67861   Fax: (620) 375-2999
P.O. Box 968, Leoti, KS 67861
E-mail: wcdcourt@wbsnet.org

Wilson County

County Clerk

Office of the County Clerk
615 Madison Street, Room 104, Fredonia, KS 66736
Tel: (620) 378-2186 Fax: (620) 378-3841

County Clerk **Rhonda D. Willard** . . . . (620) 378-2186
E-mail: wilsoncoclerk1@twinmounds.com

District Clerk

Thirty-First Judicial District
One North Washington, Room B, Iola, KS 66749

Clerk of the District Court, Wilson County
Janel M. Downey . . . . (620) 378-4533
615 Madison, Room 214, Fredonia, KS 66736   Fax: (620) 378-4531
E-mail: janeldowney@gmail.com

Woodson County

County Clerk

Office of the County Clerk
105 West Rutledge Street, Room 103, Yates Center, KS 66783
Tel: (620) 625-8605 Fax: (620) 625-8670

County Clerk **Denice Julian** . . . . (620) 625-8605
E-mail: coclerk@woodsoncounty.net

District Clerk

Thirty-First Judicial District
One North Washington, Room B, Iola, KS 66749

Clerk of the District Court, Woodson County
Lisa Page . . . . (620) 625-8610
105 West Rutledge, Yates Center, KS 66783   Fax: (620) 625-8674
E-mail: lisa_page@woodsoncounty.net

Wyandotte County

County Clerk

Unified Clerk
Municipal Office Bldg., 701 N. Seventh St., Suite 323,
Kansas City, KS 66101
Fax: (913) 573-5299
Internet: www.wycokck.org/dept.aspx?id=350&menu_id=554

Unified Government County Clerk **Bridgette Cobbins** . . . (913) 573-5260
E-mail: bcobbins@wycokck.org

(continued on next page)

District Clerk

Twenty-Ninth Judicial District
710 North Seventh Street, Kansas City, KS 66101

Clerk of the District Court, Wyandotte County
Kathleen Collins . . . . (913) 573-2946
710 North Seventh Street, Kansas City, KS 66101   Fax: (913) 281-4354
E-mail: kcollins@wycokck.org

Counties Within Judicial Districts

District Court, 1st District
Areas Covered: Atchison and Leavenworth Counties.

District Court, 2nd District
Areas Covered: Jackson, Jefferson, Pottawatomie, and Wabaunsee Counties.

District Court, 3rd District
Areas Covered: Shawnee County.

District Court, 4th District
Areas Covered: Anderson, Coffey, Franklin, and Osage Counties.

District Court, 5th District
Areas Covered: Chase and Lyon Counties.

District Court, 6th District
Areas Covered: Bourbon, Linn, and Miami Counties.

District Court, 7th District
Areas Covered: Douglas County.

District Court, 8th District
Areas Covered: Dickinson, Geary, Marion, and Morris Counties.

District Court, 9th District
Areas Covered: Harvey and McPherson Counties.

District Court, 10th District
Areas Covered: Johnson County.

District Court, 11th District
Areas Covered: Cherokee, Crawford and Labette Counties.

District Court, 12th District
Areas Covered: Cloud, Jewell, Lincoln, Mitchell, Republic, and Washington Counties.

District Court, 13th District
Areas Covered: Butler, Elk, and Greenwood Counties.

District Court, 14th District
Areas Covered: Chautauqua and Montgomery Counties.

District Court, 15th District
Areas Covered: Cheyenne, Logan, Sheridan, Sherman, Rawlins, Thomas, and Wallace Counties.

District Court, 16th District
Areas Covered: Clark, Comanche, Ford, Gray, Kiowa, and Meade Counties.

District Court, 17th District
Areas Covered: Decatur, Graham, Norton, Osborne, Phillips, and Smith Counties.

District Court, 18th District
Areas Covered: Sedgwick County.

District Court, 19th District
Areas Covered: Cowley County.

District Court, 20th District
Areas Covered: Barton, Ellsworth, Rice, Russell, and Stafford Counties.

District Court, 21st District
Areas Covered: Clay and Riley Counties.

District Court, 22nd District
Areas Covered: Brown, Doniphan, Marshall, and Nemaha Counties.

District Court, 23rd District
Areas Covered: Ellis, Gove, Rooks, and Trego Counties.

District Court, 24th District
Areas Covered: Edwards, Hodgeman, Lane, Ness, Pawnee, and Rush Counties.

District Court, 25th District
Areas Covered: Finney, Greeley, Hamilton, Kearny, Scott, and Wichita Counties.

District Court, 26th District
Areas Covered: Grant, Haskell, Morton, Seward, Stanton, and Stevens Counties.

District Court, 27th District
Areas Covered: Reno County.

District Court, 28th District
Areas Covered: Ottawa and Saline Counties.

District Court, 29th District
Areas Covered: Wyandotte County.

District Court, 30th District
Areas Covered: Barber, Harper, Kingman, Pratt, and Sumner Counties.

Kansas Court Clerks and Courthouses *continued*

District Court, 31st District

Areas Covered: Allen, Neosho, Wilson, and Woodson Counties.

Kentucky Court Clerks and Courthouses

The trial courts of general jurisdiction in Kentucky are called circuit courts. There are 57 circuits, each circuit consisting of at least one county. Each county includes both a Circuit (trial court) Clerk and a County Clerk.

Kentucky Supreme Court

State Capitol Building, 700 Capital Avenue, Room 235, Frankfort, KY 40601
Tel: (502) 564-5444 Fax: (502) 564-2665
Internet: www.kycourts.net

The Supreme Court consists of seven justices who are elected in nonpartisan elections in separate districts throughout the state for eight-year terms. Temporary appointments may be made by the Governor to fill vacancies. The chief justice is elected by peer vote for a four-year term and serves as the administrative head of the state's court system. The Supreme Court exercises appellate jurisdiction over civil and criminal matters, with direct review over sentences of death, life imprisonment, or imprisonment of more than twenty years.

Court Staff

Court Administrator, General Counsel and Clerk of the
    Supreme Court **Susan Stokley Clary** . . . . (502) 564-4176
    E-mail: susanclary@kycourts.net

Kentucky Court of Appeals

360 Democratic Drive, Frankfort, KY 40601
Tel: (502) 573-7920 Fax: (502) 573-6795
Internet: www.aoc.state.ky.us

The Court of Appeals consists of fourteen judges who are divided into panels of three to review and decide cases. Two judges are elected in nonpartisan elections in each of the seven Supreme Court districts for eight-year terms. The chief judge is elected by peer vote for a four-year term. Temporary appointments may be made by the Governor to fill vacancies. The Court of Appeals has appellate jurisdiction over final and interlocutory judgments, convictions, orders or decrees of the Kentucky Circuit Court unless such actions involve a judgment dissolving marriage or were rendered in an appeal from the Kentucky District Court. The Court also reviews decisions of administrative agencies.

Court Staff

Clerk of the Court **Samuel Givens, Jr.** . . . . (502) 573-7920
    E-mail: samg@kycourts.net

County-By-County

Adair County

Circuit Clerk

Twenty-Ninth Judicial Circuit
201 Campbellsville Street, Suite 299, Columbia, KY 42728
Tel: (270) 384-7122 Fax: (270) 384-0259

Clerk of the Court, Adair County **Dennis Loy** . . . . (270) 384-2626
    201 Campbellsville Street, Suite 101,   Fax: (270) 384-4299
    Columbia, KY 42728
    E-mail: dennisloy@kycourts.net

County Clerk

Office of the County Clerk
424 Public Square, Suite 3, Columbia, KY 42728
Tel: (270) 384-2801 Fax: (270) 384-4805

County Clerk **Sheila Blair** . . . . (270) 384-2801
    E-mail: sheila.blair@ky.gov

Allen County

Circuit Clerk

Forty-Ninth Judicial Circuit
Simpson County Justice Center, 101 Court Street,
Franklin, KY 42135-0509
Tel: (270) 586-8058 Fax: (270) 586-0731

Clerk of the Court, Allen County **Todd B. Calvert** . . . . (270) 237-3561
    Allen County Judicial Center,   Fax: (270) 237-9120
    200 West Main Street, Scottsville, KY 42164
    E-mail: toddcalvert@kycourts.net

County Clerk

Office of the County Clerk
201 West Main Street, Room 6, Scottsville, KY 42164
Tel: (270) 237-3706 Fax: (270) 237-9206

County Clerk **Elaine Williams** . . . . (270) 237-3706
    E-mail: elaine.williams@ky.gov

Anderson County

Circuit Clerk

Fifty-Third Judicial Circuit
401 Main Street, Suite 401, Shelbyville, KY 40065
Tel: (502) 647-5234 Fax: (502) 647-5386

Clerk of the Court, Anderson County
    Pamela J. Robinson . . . . (502) 839-3508
    Anderson County Courthouse,   Fax: (502) 839-4995
    151 South Main Street, Lawrenceburg, KY 40234

County Clerk

Office of the County Clerk
100 South Main Street, Lawrenceburg, KY 40342
Tel: (502) 839-3041 Fax: (502) 839-3043

County Clerk **Jason Denny** . . . . (502) 839-3041
    E-mail: jason.denny2@ky.gov

Ballard County

Circuit Clerk

First Judicial Circuit
114 Wellington Street, Hickman, KY 42050
P.O. Box 167, Hickman, KY 42050-0167

Clerk of Court, Ballard County **Holly Oldham Dunker** . . . (270) 335-5123
    132 North Fourth Street, Wickliffe, KY 42087-0265   Fax: (270) 335-3849
    P.O. Box 265, Wickliffe, KY 42087
    E-mail: hollydunker@kycourts.net

(continued on next page)

County Clerk

Office of the County Clerk
132 North Fourth Street, Wickliffe, KY 42087
P.O. Box 145, Wickliffe, KY 42087
Tel: (270) 335-5168   Fax: (270) 335-3081
E-mail: bcclerk@brtc.net

County Clerk **Lynn W. Lane** . . . . (270) 335-5168
   E-mail: lynnw.layne2@ky.gov

Barren County

Circuit Clerk

Forty-Third Judicial Circuit
300 Courthouse Square, Glasgow, KY 42141
Tel: (270) 651-2744   Fax: (270) 651-7051

Clerk of the Court, Barren County **Krissie Coe Fields** . . . (270) 651-2561
   100 Courthouse Square, Glasgow, KY 42142-1359   Fax: (270) 651-6203
   P.O. Box 1359, Glasgow, KY 42141-1359
   E-mail: krissiefields@kycourts.net

County Clerk

Office of the County Clerk
117 North Public Square, Suite 1A, Glasgow, KY 42141
Tel: (270) 651-3783   Fax: (270) 651-1083

County Clerk **Joanne London** . . . . (270) 651-3783
   E-mail: joanne.london@ky.gov

Bath County

Circuit Clerk

Twenty-First Judicial Circuit
P.O. Box 1267, Mt. Sterling, KY 40353
Tel: (859) 498-0488   Fax: (859) 498-2665

Clerk of the Court, Bath County **Claudette Faudere** . . . . . (606) 674-2186
   Bath County Courthouse Annex,   Fax: (606) 674-3996
   19 East Main Street, Owingsville, KY 40360-0558
   E-mail: claudettefaudere@kycourts.net

County Clerk

Office of the County Clerk
17 West Main Street, Owingsville, KY 40360
P.O. Box 609, Owingsville, KY 40360
Tel: (606) 674-2613   Fax: (606) 674-9526

County Clerk **Roger Coyle** . . . . (606) 674-2613
   E-mail: roger.coyle@ky.gov

Bell County

Circuit Clerk

Forty-Fourth Judicial Circuit
Farmer Helton Judicial Center, 101 Park Avenue, Suite 210,
Pineville, KY 40977
Tel: (606) 337-5949   Fax: (606) 337-9455

Clerk of the Court, Bell County **Colby Slusher** . . . . (606) 337-2942
   Farmer Helton Judicial Center,   Fax: (606) 337-8850
   101 West Park Avenue, Pineville, KY 40977-0307
   E-mail: colbyslusher@kycourts.net

County Clerk

Office of the County Clerk
101 Courthouse Square, Suite 200, Pineville, KY 40977
P.O. Box 157, Pineville, KY 40977
Tel: (606) 337-6143   Fax: (606) 337-5415

County Clerk **Debbie Gambrel** . . . . (606) 337-6143
   E-mail: debbie.gambrel@ky.gov

Boone County

Circuit Clerk

Fifty-Fourth Judicial Circuit
6025 Rogers Lane, Suite 444, Burlington, KY 41005
Tel: (859) 817-5800   Fax: (859) 817-5819

Clerk of the Court, Boone County **Dianne Murray** . . . . . . (859) 334-2286
   Boone County Justice Center, 6025 Rogers Lane,   Fax: (859) 334-3650
   Burlington, KY 41005
   E-mail: diannemurray@kycourts.net

County Clerk

Office of the County Clerk
2950 East Washington Street, First Floor, Burlington, KY 41005
P.O. Box 874, Burlington, KY 41005
Tel: (859) 334-2108   Fax: (859) 334-2193

County Clerk **Kenny R. Brown** . . . . (859) 334-2108
   E-mail: kenny.brown@boonecountyky.org

Bourbon County

Circuit Clerk

Fourteenth Judicial Circuit
Scott County Justice Center, 119 North Hamilton Street,
Georgetown, KY 40324
Tel: (502) 570-0947   Fax: (502) 570-0949

Clerk of the Court, Bourbon County **Beverly Smits** . . . . . (859) 987-2624
   310 Main Street, Paris, KY 40362   Fax: (859) 987-6049
   P.O. Box 740, Paris, KY 40362-0740
   E-mail: beverlysmits@kycourts.net

County Clerk

Office of the County Clerk
301 Main Street, Suite 106, Paris, KY 40361
P.O. Box 312, Paris, KY 40361
Tel: (859) 987-2142   Fax: (859) 987-5660

County Clerk **Richard Stipp Eads** . . . . (859) 987-2142
   E-mail: richard.eads@ky.gov

Boyd County

Circuit Clerk

Thirty-Second Judicial Circuit
P.O. Box 417, Catlettsburg, KY 41129
Tel: (606) 739-6122   Fax: (606) 739-5186

Clerk of the Court, Boyd County **Linda Kay Baker** . . . . . . (606) 739-4131
   2800 Louisa Street, Catlettsburg, KY 41129   Fax: (606) 739-5793
   E-mail: lindabaker@kycourts.net

County Clerk

Office of the County Clerk
2800 Louisa Street, Catlettsburg, KY 41129
P.O. Box 523, Catlettsburg, KY 41129
Tel: (606) 739-5116 Fax: (606) 739-0430

County Clerk **Debbie A. Jones** . . . . (606) 739-5116
  E-mail: debbiejones@zoominternet.net

Boyle County

Circuit Clerk

Fiftieth Judicial Circuit
Boyle County Courthouse, 321 West Main, Second Floor,
Danville, KY 40422
Tel: (859) 239-7009 Fax: (859) 239-7033

Clerk of the Court, Boyle County **Joni H. Terry** . . . . (859) 239-7442
  Boyle County Courthouse, 321 West Main,   Fax: (859) 239-7000
  Danville, KY 40422
  E-mail: joniterry@kycourts.net

County Clerk

Office of the County Clerk
321 West Main Street, Room 123, Danville, KY 40422
Tel: (859) 238-1110 Fax: (859) 238-1114

County Clerk **Trille Bottom** . . . . (859) 238-1110
  E-mail: trille.bottom@ky.gov

Bracken County

Circuit Clerk

Nineteenth Judicial Circuit
100 West Third Street, Maysville, KY 41056
Tel: (606) 564-9736 Fax: (606) 564-0308

Clerk of the Court, Bracken County **Kathy Free** . . . . (606) 735-3328
  116 West Miami Street,   Fax: (606) 735-3900
  Brooksville, KY 41004-0205
  P.O. Box 205, Brooksville, KY 41004-0205
  E-mail: kathyfree@kycourts.net

County Clerk

Office of the County Clerk
116 West Miami Street, Brooksville, KY 41004
P.O. Box 147, Brooksville, KY 41004
Tel: (606) 735-2952 Fax: (606) 735-2687

County Clerk **Rae Jean Poe** . . . . (606) 735-2952
  E-mail: raejean.poe@ky.gov

Breathitt County

Circuit Clerk

Thirty-Ninth Judicial Circuit
P.O. Box 946, Jackson, KY 41339-0946
Tel: (606) 666-7130

Clerk of the Court, Breathitt County **James E. Turner** . . . (606) 666-5768
  Breathitt County Justice Center, 1131 Main Street,   Fax: (606) 666-4893
  Jackson, KY 41339
  E-mail: jamesturner@kycourts.net

County Clerk

Office of the County Clerk
1137 Main Street, Jackson, KY 41339
Tel: (606) 666-3800 ext. 707 Fax: (606) 666-3817

County Clerk **Harold Hutchinson** . . . . (606) 666-3800 ext. 707
  E-mail: harold.hutchinson@ky.gov

Breckinridge County

Circuit Clerk

Forty-Sixth Judicial Circuit
Meade County Courthouse, 516 Hillcrest Drive, Brandenburg, KY 40108
Tel: (270) 422-7800 Fax: (270) 422-7801

Clerk of the Court, Breckinridge County
  Cindy Rhodes . . . . (270) 756-2239
  Breckinridge County Justice   Fax: (270) 756-1129
  Center, 111 West Second Street,
  Hardinsburg, KY 40143-0111
  E-mail: cindyrhodes@kycourts.net

County Clerk

Office of the County Clerk
208 Main Street, Hardinsburg, KY 40143
P.O. Box 538, Hardinsburg, KY 40143
Tel: (270) 756-2246 Fax: (270) 756-1569

County Clerk **Jill Irwin** . . . . (270) 756-2246
  E-mail: jill.irwin@ky.gov

Bullitt County

Circuit Clerk

Fifty-Fifth Judicial Circuit
P.O. Box 97, Shepherdsville, KY 40165
Tel: (502) 543-4776 Fax: (502) 543-7134

Clerk of the Court, Bullitt County **Paulita A. Keith** . . . . . . (502) 543-7104
  Bullitt County Judicial Center,   Fax: (502) 543-7158
  250 Frank E. Simon Avenue,
  Shepherdsville, KY 40165-0746
  E-mail: paulitakeith@kycourts.net

County Clerk

Office of the County Clerk
149 North Walnut Street, Shepherdsville, KY 40165
P.O. Box 6, Shepherdsville, KY 40165
Fax: (502) 543-9121

County Clerk **Kevin Mooney** . . . . (502) 955-6369
  E-mail: info@bullittcountyclerk.com

Butler County

Circuit Clerk

Thirty-Eighth Judicial Circuit
P.O. Box 169, Hartford, KY 42347
Tel: (270) 298-7250 Fax: (270) 298-3646

Clerk of the Court, Butler County **Melissa Cardwell** . . . . . (270) 526-5631
  Butler County Courthouse, 110 North Main Street,   Fax: (270) 526-6763
  Morgantown, KY 42261-0625
  E-mail: melissacardwell@kycourts.net

(continued on next page)

Kentucky Court Clerks and Courthouses *continued*

County Clerk

Office of the County Clerk
110 North Main Street, Morgantown, KY 42261
P.O. Box 449, Morgantown, KY 42261
Tel: (270) 526-5676 Fax: (270) 526-2658

County Clerk **Sherry Johnson** . . . . (270) 526-5676
  E-mail: sherrye.johnson@ky.gov

Caldwell County

Circuit Clerk

Fifty-Sixth Judicial Circuit
P.O. Box 790, Eddyville, KY 42038-0790
Tel: (270) 388-5182 Fax: (270) 388-0869

Clerk of the Court, Caldwell County **Danny Hooks** . . . . . . (270) 365-6884
  Caldwell County Courthouse Annex,   Fax: (270) 365-9171
  105 West Court Street, Princeton, KY 42445
  E-mail: dannyhooks@kycourts.net

County Clerk

Office of the County Clerk
100 East Market Street, Room 23, Princeton, KY 42445
Tel: (270) 365-6754 Fax: (270) 365-7447
E-mail: coclerk@caldwellcourthouse.com

County Clerk **Toni Watson** . . . . (270) 365-6754
  E-mail: toni.watson@ky.gov

Calloway County

Circuit Clerk

Forty-Second Judicial Circuit
Marshall Circuit and District Courts, 80 Judicial Drive, Unit 215,
Benton, KY 42025
Tel: (270) 527-1480 Fax: (270) 527-7516

Clerk of the Court, Calloway County **Linda Avery** . . . . (270) 753-2714
  Calloway County Judicial Building,   Fax: (270) 759-9822
  312 North Fourth Street, Murray, KY 42071
  E-mail: lindaavery@kycourts.net

County Clerk

Office of the County Clerk
101 South Fifth Street, Suite 5, Murray, KY 42071
Tel: (270) 753-3923 Fax: (270) 759-9611

County Clerk **Antonia Faulkner** . . . . (270) 753-3923
  E-mail: antonia.faulkner@ky.gov

Campbell County

Circuit Clerk

Seventeenth Judicial Circuit
330 York Street, Newport, KY 41071
Tel: (859) 292-6303 Fax: (859) 431-0816

Clerk of the Court, Campbell County
  Taunya Nolan Jack . . . . (859) 292-6305
  330 York Street, Newport, KY 41071   Fax: (859) 292-6593

Kentucky Court Clerks and Courthouses *continued*

County Clerk

Office of the County Clerk
1098 Monmouth Street, Newport, KY 41072
Tel: (859) 292-3845 Fax: (859) 292-0615

County Clerk **Jim Luersen** . . . . (859) 292-3885
  E-mail: jluersen@campbellcountyky.org

Carlisle County

Circuit Clerk

First Judicial Circuit
114 Wellington Street, Hickman, KY 42050
P.O. Box 167, Hickman, KY 42050-0167

Clerk of Court, Carlisle County **Kevin Hoskins** . . . . (270) 628-5425
  U.S. Highway 62, Bardwell, KY 42023-0198   Fax: (270) 628-5456
  P.O. Box 337, Bardwell, KY 42023-0337
  E-mail: kevinhoskins@kycourts.net

County Clerk

Office of the County Clerk
985 US Highway 62, Bardwell, KY 42023
P.O. Box 176, Bardwell, KY 42023
Tel: (270) 628-3233 Fax: (270) 628-0191

County Clerk **Michael E. Toon** . . . . (270) 628-3233
  E-mail: michael.toon@ky.gov

Carroll County

Circuit Clerk

Fifteenth Judicial Circuit
Grant County Judicial Center, 224 South Main Street,
Williamstown, KY 41097
Tel: (859) 824-7516 Fax: (859) 824-6494

Clerk of the Court, Carroll County **Laman L. Stark** . . . . . (502) 732-4305
  802 Clay Street, Carrollton, KY 41008   Fax: (502) 732-8138
  E-mail: lamanstark@kycourts.net

County Clerk

Office of the County Clerk
440 Main Street, Carrollton, KY 41008
Tel: (502) 732-7005 Fax: (502) 732-7007

County Clerk **Alice W. Marsh** . . . . (502) 732-7005
  E-mail: alice.marsh@ky.gov

Carter County

Circuit Clerk

Thirty-Seventh Judicial Circuit
100 East Main Street, Grayson, KY 41143-1302
Tel: (606) 474-5191 Fax: (606) 474-0710

Clerk of the Court, Carter County **Larry D. Thompson** . . . (606) 474-5191
  Carter County Justice Center, 100 East Main Street,   Fax: (606) 474-8826
  Grayson, KY 41143-1302
  E-mail: larrythompson@kycourts.net

County Clerk

Office of the County Clerk
300 West Main Street, Room 232, Grayson, KY 41143
Tel: (606) 474-5188 Fax: (606) 474-2719

County Clerk **Mike Johnston** . . . . (606) 474-5188
  E-mail: mike.johnston@ky.gov

Casey County

Circuit Clerk

Twenty-Ninth Judicial Circuit
201 Campbellsville Street, Suite 299, Columbia, KY 42728
Tel: (270) 384-7122 Fax: (270) 384-0259

Clerk of the Court, Casey County **Craig L. Overstreet** . . . (606) 787-6510
  Casey County Judicial Center,   Fax: (606) 787-2497
  231 Courthouse Square, Liberty, KY 42539-0147
  E-mail: craigoverstreet@kycourts.net

County Clerk

Office of the County Clerk
625 Courthouse Square, Liberty, KY 42539
P.O. Box 310, Liberty, KY 42539
Tel: (606) 787-6471 Fax: (606) 787-9155

County Clerk **Casey Davis** . . . . (606) 787-6471
  E-mail: casey.davis@ky.gov

Christian County

Circuit Clerk

Third Judicial Circuit
Christian County Justice Center, 100 Justice Way, Hopkinsville, KY 42240
Tel: (270) 889-6537 Fax: (270) 889-6006

Clerk of the Court **Gary Haddock** . . . . (270) 889-6539
  E-mail: garyhaddock@kycourts.net   Fax: (270) 889-6564

County Clerk

Office of the County Clerk
511 South Main Street, Suite 11, Hopkinsville, KY 42240
Tel: (270) 887-4107 Fax: (270) 887-4186

County Clerk **Michael A. Kem** . . . . (270) 887-4107
  E-mail: michael.kem@ky.gov

Clark County

Circuit Clerk

Twenty-Fifth Judicial Circuit
Madison County Courthouse, 101 West Main Street,
Richmond, KY 40475-0819
Tel: (859) 624-4750

Clerk of the Court, Clark County **Paula S. Joslin** . . . . (859) 737-7264
  Governor James Clark Judicial Center,   Fax: (859) 737-7005
  17 Cleveland Avenue, Winchester, KY 40392-0687
  E-mail: paulajoslin@kycourts.net

County Clerk

Office of the County Clerk
34 South Main Street, Winchester, KY 40391
P.O. Box 4060, Winchester, KY 40392
Tel: (859) 745-0280 Fax: (859) 745-4251

County Clerk **Michelle Turner** . . . . (859) 745-0280
  E-mail: michelles.turner@ky.gov

Clay County

Circuit Clerk

Forty-First Judicial Circuit
Clay County Justice Center, 316 Main Street, Suite 320,
Manchester, KY 40962
Tel: (606) 598-5251 Fax: (606) 598-4113

Clerk of the Court, Clay County **James S. Phillips** . . . . . . (606) 598-3663
  Clay County Justice Center, 316 Main Street,   Fax: (606) 598-4047
  Suite 108, Manchester, KY 40962
  E-mail: jamesphillips@kycourts.net

County Clerk

Office of the County Clerk
102 Richmond Road, Suite 101, Manchester, KY 40962
Tel: (606) 598-2544 Fax: (606) 599-0603

County Clerk **Michael Baker** . . . . (606) 598-2544
  E-mail: michaeld.baker@ky.gov

Clinton County

Circuit Clerk

Fortieth Judicial Circuit
112 Courthouse Square, Burkesville, KY 42717-0395
Tel: (270) 864-5192 Fax: (270) 864-1418

Clerk of the Court, Clinton County **Jake Staton** . . . . (270) 387-6424
  Clinton County Courthouse,   Fax: (270) 387-8154
  100 South Cross Street, Suite 212,
  Albany, KY 42602
  E-mail: jakestaton@kycourts.net

County Clerk

Office of the County Clerk
100 South Cross Street, Albany, KY 42602
Tel: (606) 387-5943 Fax: (606) 387-5258

County Clerk **Shelia Booher** . . . . (606) 387-5943
  E-mail: shelia.booher@ky.gov

Crittenden County

Circuit Clerk

Fifth Judicial Circuit
Webster County Courthouse, 35 US Highway, 41A-S, Dixon, KY 42409
Tel: (270) 639-5506 Fax: (270) 389-1572

Clerk of the Court, Crittenden County **Melissa Guill** . . . . . (270) 965-4200
  107 South Main Street, Suite 202,   Fax: (270) 965-4572
  Marion, KY 42064
  E-mail: melissaguill@kycourts.net

(continued on next page)

County Clerk

Office of the County Clerk
107 South Main Street, Suite 203, Marion, KY 42064
Tel: (270) 965-3403 Fax: (270) 965-3447

County Clerk **Carolyn Byford** . . . . (270) 965-3403
E-mail: carolyn.byford@ky.gov

Cumberland County

Circuit Clerk

Fortieth Judicial Circuit
112 Courthouse Square, Burkesville, KY 42717-0395
Tel: (270) 864-5192 Fax: (270) 864-1418

Clerk of the Court, Cumberland County
Nancy L. Brewington . . . . (270) 864-2611
Cumberland County Justice   Fax: (270) 864-1227
Center, 112 Courthouse Square,
Burkesville, KY 42717-0395
E-mail: nancybrewington@kycourts.net

County Clerk

Office of the County Clerk
601 Courthouse Square, Burkesville, KY 42717
P.O. Box 275, Burkesville, KY 42717
Tel: (270) 864-3726 Fax: (270) 864-5884

County Clerk **Kim King** . . . . (270) 864-3726
E-mail: kim.king@ky.gov

Daviess County

Circuit Clerk

Sixth Judicial Circuit
Holbrook Judicial Center, 100 East Second Street, Owensboro, KY 42301
Tel: (270) 687-7329 Fax: (270) 687-7999

Clerk of the Court **Susan W. Tierney** . . . . (270) 687-7220
E-mail: susantierney@kycourts.net

County Clerk

Office of the County Clerk
212 Street Ann Street, Owensboro, KY 42302
P.O. Box 609, Owensboro, KY 42302
Tel: (270) 685-8434 Fax: (270) 686-7111

County Clerk **David "Oz" Osborne** . . . . (270) 685-8434
E-mail: david.osbourne@ky.gov

Edmonson County

Circuit Clerk

Thirty-Eighth Judicial Circuit
P.O. Box 169, Hartford, KY 42347
Tel: (270) 298-7250 Fax: (270) 298-3646

Clerk of the Court, Edmonson County
Tanya R. Hodges . . . . (270) 597-2584
Edmonson County Courthouse,   Fax: (270) 597-2884
110 Cross Main Street,
Brownsville, KY 42210-0739
E-mail: tanyaluttrell@kycourts.net

County Clerk

Office of the County Clerk
108 South Main Street, Brownsville, KY 42210
P.O. Box 830, Brownsville, KY 42210
Tel: (270) 597-2624 Fax: (270) 597-9714

County Clerk **Kevin Alexander** . . . . (270) 597-2624
E-mail: kevin.alexander@ky.gov

Elliott County

Circuit Clerk

Thirty-Seventh Judicial Circuit
100 East Main Street, Grayson, KY 41143-1302
Tel: (606) 474-5191 Fax: (606) 474-0710

Clerk of the Court, Elliot County **William Jason Ison** . . . (606) 738-5238
Elliott County Courthouse Annex,   Fax: (606) 738-6962
100 Court and Main Streets,
Sandy Hook, KY 41171-0788

County Clerk

Office of the County Clerk
100 Court and Main Streets, Sandy Hook, KY 41171
P.O. Box 225, Sandy Hook, KY 41171
Tel: (606) 738-5421 Fax: (606) 738-4462

County Clerk **Sheila L. Blevins** . . . . (606) 738-5421
E-mail: sheilal.blevins@ky.gov

Estill County

Circuit Clerk

Twenty-Third Judicial Circuit
59 Main Street, Beattyville, KY 41311
Tel: (606) 464-2648 Fax: (606) 464-8229

Clerk of the Court, Estill County
Stephanie L. Brinegar . . . . (606) 723-3970
Estill County Courthouse, 130 Main Street,   Fax: (606) 723-1158
Irvine, KY 40336
E-mail: stephaniebrinegar@kycourts.net

County Clerk

Office of the County Clerk
130 Main Street, Room 102, Irvine, KY 40336
P.O. Box 59, Irvine, KY 40336
Tel: (606) 723-5156 Fax: (606) 723-5108

County Clerk **Sherry L. Fox** . . . . (606) 723-5156
E-mail: sherry.fox@ky.gov

Fayette County

Circuit Clerk

Twenty-Second Judicial Circuit
Fayette County Courthouse, 150 North Limestone, Lexington, KY 40507
Tel: (859) 246-2533 Fax: (859) 246-2139

Clerk of the Court, Fayette County **Vincent Riggs** . . . . (859) 246-2277
Robert F. Stephens Circuit Courthouse,   Fax: (859) 246-2530
150 North Limestone, Room D-118,
Lexington, KY 40507

County Clerk

Office of the County Clerk
162 E. Main St., Lexington, KY 40507
Fax: (859) 231-9619
Internet: www.fayettecountyclerk.com/

County Clerk **Donald W. "Don" Blevins, Jr.**...........(859) 253-3344
  E-mail: info@fayettecountyclerk.com

Fleming County

Circuit Clerk

Nineteenth Judicial Circuit
100 West Third Street, Maysville, KY 41056
Tel: (606) 564-9736 Fax: (606) 564-0308

Clerk of the Court, Fleming County **Amy Saunders**.....(606) 845-7011
  Fleming County Courthouse, 100 Court Square,   Fax: (606) 849-2400
  Flemingsburg, KY 41041

County Clerk

Office of the County Clerk
100 Court Square, Flemingsburg, KY 41041
Tel: (606) 845-8461 Fax: (606) 845-0212

County Clerk **Jarrod R. Fritz**......................(606) 845-8461
  E-mail: jarrod.fritz@ky.gov

Floyd County

Circuit Clerk

Thirty-First Judicial Circuit
Floyd County Justice Center, 127 South Lake Drive,
Prestonsburg, KY 41653
Tel: (606) 889-1900 Fax: (606) 889-1902

Clerk of the Court, Floyd County **Douglas Ray Hall**.....(606) 889-1672
  Floyd County Justice Center, 127 South Lake Drive,   Fax: (606) 889-1666
  Prestonsburg, KY 41653

County Clerk

Office of the County Clerk
149 South Central Avenue, Room 1, Prestonsburg, KY 41653
P.O. Box 1089, Prestonsburg, KY 41653
Tel: (606) 886-3816 Fax: (606) 886-8089

County Clerk **Chris D. Waugh**......................(606) 886-3816
  E-mail: chrisd.waugh@ky.gov

Franklin County

Circuit Clerk

Forty-Eighth Judicial Circuit
Franklin County Courthouse, 222 St. Clair, Frankfort, KY 40601
Tel: (502) 564-8383 Fax: (502) 564-0096

Clerk of the Court, Franklin County **Sally Jump**........(502) 564-8380
  Franklin County Circuit Court Clerk, 222 St. Clair,   Fax: (502) 564-8188
  Frankfort, KY 40601
  E-mail: sallyjump@kycourts.net

County Clerk

Office of the County Clerk
315 West Main Street, Frankfort, KY 40602
P.O. Box 338, Frankfort, KY 40602
Tel: (502) 875-8702 Fax: (502) 875-8718

County Clerk **Jeff Hancock**........................(502) 875-8702
  E-mail: jeff.hancock@ky.gov

Fulton County

Circuit Clerk

First Judicial Circuit
114 Wellington Street, Hickman, KY 42050
P.O. Box 167, Hickman, KY 42050-0167

Clerk of Court, Fulton County **Sarah Johnson**.........(270) 236-3944
  114 East Wellington Street,   Fax: (270) 236-3729
  Hickman, KY 42050-0198
  P.O. Box 198, Hickman, KY 42050-0198
  E-mail: sarahjohnson@kycourts.net

County Clerk

Office of the County Clerk
2216 Myron Cory Drive, Hickman, KY 42050
P.O. Box 126, Hickman, KY 42050
Tel: (270) 236-2727 Fax: (270) 236-2522

County Clerk **Betty Abernathy**.....................(270) 236-2727
  E-mail: betty.abernathy@ky.gov

Gallatin County

Circuit Clerk

Fifty-Fourth Judicial Circuit
6025 Rogers Lane, Suite 444, Burlington, KY 41005
Tel: (859) 817-5800 Fax: (859) 817-5819

Clerk of the Court, Gallatin County **Pam McIntyre**......(859) 567-5241
  Gallatin County Courthouse, 100 Main Street,   Fax: (859) 567-7420
  Warsaw, KY 41095-0256
  E-mail: pammcintyre@kycourts.net

County Clerk

Office of the County Clerk
102 West High Street, Warsaw, KY 41095
P.O. Box 1309, Warsaw, KY 41095
Tel: (859) 567-5411 Fax: (859) 567-5444

County Clerk **Tracy Miles**.........................(859) 567-5411
  E-mail: tracy.miles@ky.gov

Garrard County

Circuit Clerk

Thirteenth Judicial Circuit
101 North Main Street, Nicholasville, KY 40356
Tel: (859) 885-6722 Fax: (859) 881-5252

Clerk of the Court, Garrard County **Dana Hensley**......(859) 792-2961
  54 Stanford Street, Lancaster, KY 40444   Fax: (859) 792-6414

(continued on next page)

County Clerk

Office of the County Clerk
15 Public Square, Suite 5, Lancaster, KY 40444
Tel: (859) 792-3071 Fax: (859) 792-6751
E-mail: garrardcoclerk@yahoo.com

County Clerk **Kevin Montgomery** . . . . (859) 792-3071
 E-mail: kevin.montgomery@ky.gov

Grant County

Circuit Clerk

Fifteenth Judicial Circuit
Grant County Judicial Center, 224 South Main Street,
Williamstown, KY 41097
Tel: (859) 824-7516 Fax: (859) 824-6494

Clerk of the Court, Grant County **Tina Melton** . . . . (859) 824-4467
 Grant County Judicial Center,   Fax: (859) 824-0183
 224 South Main Street, Williamstown, KY 41097
 E-mail: tinamelton@kycourts.net

County Clerk

Office of the County Clerk
107 North Main Street, Williamstown, KY 41097
Tel: (859) 824-3321 Fax: (859) 824-3367

County Clerk **Tabatha Clemons** . . . . (859) 824-3321
 E-mail: tabatha.clemons@ky.gov

Graves County

Circuit Clerk

Fifty-Second Judicial Circuit
Graves County Courthouse, 100 East Broadway, Second Floor,
Mayfield, KY 42066
Tel: (270) 247-8726 Fax: (270) 247-7679

Clerk of the Court, Graves County **Heather Winfrey** . . . . .(270) 247-1733
 Graves County Courthouse, 100 East Broadway,   Fax: (270) 247-7358
 Suite 1, Mayfield, KY 42066
 E-mail: heatherwinfrey@kycourts.net

County Clerk

Office of the County Clerk
101 East South Street, Suite 2, Mayfield, KY 42066
Tel: (270) 247-1676 Fax: (270) 247-1274

County Clerk **Barry Kennemore** . . . . (270) 247-1676
 E-mail: barry.kennemore@ky.gov

Grayson County

Circuit Clerk

Forty-Sixth Judicial Circuit
Meade County Courthouse, 516 Hillcrest Drive, Brandenburg, KY 40108
Tel: (270) 422-7800 Fax: (270) 422-7801

Clerk of the Court, Grayson County **Stacie Blain** . . . . (270) 259-3040
 Grayson County Judicial Center,   Fax: (270) 259-9866
 500 Carroll Gibson Boulevard,
 Leitchfield, KY 42754
 E-mail: stacieblain@kycourts.net

County Clerk

Office of the County Clerk
10 Public Square, Leitchfield, KY 42754
Tel: (270) 259-3201 Fax: (270) 259-9264

County Clerk **Sherry Weedman** . . . . (270) 259-3201
 E-mail: sherry.weedman@ky.gov

Green County

Circuit Clerk

Eleventh Judicial Circuit
Taylor County Justice Center, 300 East Main Street, Suite 301,
Campbellsville, KY 42718
Tel: (270) 465-6603 Fax: (270) 469-4804

Clerk of the Court, Green County **John Frank** . . . . (270) 932-5631
 200 West Court Street, Greensburg, KY 42743   Fax: (270) 932-6468
 E-mail: johnfrank@kycourts.net

County Clerk

Office of the County Clerk
203 West Court Street, Greensburg, KY 42743
Tel: (270) 932-5386 Fax: (270) 932-6241

County Clerk **Billy Joe Lowe** . . . . (270) 932-5386
 E-mail: billyjoe.lowe@ky.gov

Greenup County

Circuit Clerk

Twentieth Judicial Circuit
Courthouse Annex, 101 Harrison Street, Greenup, KY 41144-0676
Tel: (606) 473-7165 Fax: (606) 473-6665

Clerk of the Court, Greenup County **Allen Kent Reed** . . . (606) 473-9869
 Greenup County Courthouse Annex,   Fax: (606) 473-7388
 101 Harrison Street, Greenup, KY 41144-0676
 E-mail: allenreed@kycourts.net

County Clerk

Office of the County Clerk
301 Main Street, Greenup, KY 41144
P.O. Box 686, Greenup, KY 41144
Tel: (606) 473-7394 Fax: (606) 473-5354

County Clerk **Patricia "Pat" Hieneman** . . . . (606) 473-7394
 E-mail: patricia.hieneman@ky.gov

Hancock County

Circuit Clerk

Thirty-Eighth Judicial Circuit
P.O. Box 169, Hartford, KY 42347
Tel: (270) 298-7250 Fax: (270) 298-3646

Clerk of the Court, Hancock County **Noel J. Quinn** . . . . . (270) 927-8144
 Hancock County Judicial Center,   Fax: (270) 927-8629
 310 Hawesville School Drive,
 Hawesville, KY 42348-0250
 E-mail: noelquinn@kycourts.net

County Clerk

Office of the County Clerk
225 Main Cross Street, Hawesville, KY 42348
P.O. Box 146, Hawesville, KY 42348
Tel: (270) 927-6117 Fax: (270) 927-8639

County Clerk **Trina Ogle**..........................(270) 927-6117
  E-mail: trina.ogle@ky.gov

Hardin County

Circuit Clerk

Ninth Judicial Circuit
Hardin County Justice Center, 120 East Dixie Avenue,
Elizabethtown, KY 42701-1487
Tel: (270) 766-5039 Fax: (270) 766-5253

Clerk of the Court **Loretta Crady** ....(270) 766-5000
  E-mail: lorettacrady@kycourts.net   Fax: (270) 766-5243

County Clerk

Office of the County Clerk
14 Public Square, Elizabethtown, KY 42702
P.O. Box 1030, Elizabethtown, KY 42702
Tel: (270) 765-2171 Fax: (270) 765-6193

County Clerk **Debbie Donnelly**.....................(270) 765-2171
  E-mail: debbie.donnelly@ky.gov

Harlan County

Circuit Clerk

Twenty-Sixth Judicial Circuit
P.O. Box 799, Harlan, KY 40831-0799
Tel: (606) 573-3242 Fax: (606) 573-1280

Clerk of the Court, Harlan County (Interim)
  Colby Slusher....................................(606) 573-7114
  Harlan County Justice Center,   Fax: (606) 573-5895
  129 South First Street, Harlan, KY 40831-0190

County Clerk

Office of the County Clerk
210 East Central Street, Suite 205, Harlan, KY 40831
P.O. Box 670, Harlan, KY 40831
Tel: (606) 573-3636 Fax: (606) 573-0064

County Clerk **Donna G. Hoskins** ....(606) 573-3636
  E-mail: donna.hoskins@ky.gov

Harrison County

Circuit Clerk

Eighteenth Judicial Circuit
Harrison County Justice Center, 115 Court Street, Cynthiana, KY 41031
Tel: (859) 234-3431 Fax: (859) 234-6878

Clerk of the Court, Harrison County **Teresa Furnish** .....(859) 234-1914
  115 Court Street, Suite 1, Cynthiana, KY 41031   Fax: (859) 234-6787
  E-mail: teresafurnish@kycourts.net

County Clerk

Office of the County Clerk
111 South Main Street, Suite 102, Cynthiana, KY 41031
Tel: (859) 234-7130 Fax: (859) 234-8049

County Clerk **Linda B. Furnish** ....(859) 234-7130
  E-mail: linda.furnish@ky.gov

Hart County

Circuit Clerk

Tenth Judicial Circuit
Nelson County Justice Center, 200 Nelson County Plaza,
Bardstown, KY 40004-2100
Tel: (502) 348-7313 Fax: (502) 348-2702

Clerk of the Court, Hart County **Rita Doyle**...........(270) 524-5181
  117 East South Street, Munfordville, KY 42765   Fax: (270) 524-7202
  P.O. Box 248, Munfordville, KY 42765
  E-mail: ritadoyle@kycourts.net

County Clerk

Office of the County Clerk
200 Main Street, Munfordville, KY 42765
P.O. Box 277, Munfordville, KY 42765
Tel: (270) 524-2751 Fax: (270) 524-0458

County Clerk **Lisa Hensley** ....(270) 524-2751
  E-mail: lisa.hensley@ky.gov

Henderson County

Circuit Clerk

Fifty-First Judicial Circuit
5 North Main Street, Henderson, KY 42450
Tel: (270) 869-0460 Fax: (270) 869-0120

Clerk of the Court, Henderson County **Ruth London** ....(270) 826-2405
  5 North Main Street, Henderson, KY 42450   Fax: (270) 831-2710
  E-mail: ruthlondon@kycourts.net

County Clerk

Office of the County Clerk
20 North Main Street, Henderson, KY 42420
P.O. Box 374, Henderson, KY 42419
Tel: (270) 826-3906 Fax: (270) 826-9677

County Clerk **Renesa Abner** ....(270) 826-3906
  E-mail: renesa.abner@ky.gov

Henry County

Circuit Clerk

Twelfth Judicial Circuit
Oldham County Courthouse, 100 West Main Street,
La Grange, KY 40031-1116
Tel: (502) 222-1692 Fax: (502) 222-5684

Clerk of the Court, Henry County **Gina Lyle** ....(502) 845-2868
  30 North Main Street, New Castle, KY 40050   Fax: (502) 845-2969
  P.O. Box 359, New Castle, KY 40050
  E-mail: ginalyle@kycourts.net

(continued on next page)

County Clerk

Office of the County Clerk
27 South Property Road, New Castle, KY 40050
P.O. Box 615, New Castle, KY 40050
Tel: (502) 845-5705 Fax: (502) 845-5708

County Clerk **Shanda Archer** . . . . (502) 845-5705
  E-mail: shanda.archer@ky.gov

Hickman County

Circuit Clerk

First Judicial Circuit
114 Wellington Street, Hickman, KY 42050
P.O. Box 167, Hickman, KY 42050-0167

Clerk of Court, Hickman County **Cinda Yates** . . . . (270) 653-3901
  109 Washington Street, Clinton, KY 42031   Fax: (270) 653-3989
  E-mail: cindayates@kycourts.net

County Clerk

Office of the County Clerk
110 East Clay Street, Suite E, Clinton, KY 42031
Tel: (270) 653-2131 Fax: (270) 653-2831

County Clerk **James "Jimbo" Berry** . . . . (270) 653-2131
  E-mail: jimbo.berry@ky.gov

Hopkins County

Circuit Clerk

Fourth Judicial Circuit
Hopkins County Judicial Center, 120 East Center Street, Box 1,
Madisonville, KY 42431
Tel: (270) 824-7422 Fax: (270) 824-7051

Clerk of the Court **Karen L. McKnight** . . . . (270) 824-7502
  E-mail: karenmcknight@kycourts.net   Fax: (270) 824-7032

County Clerk

Office of the County Clerk
24 Union Street, Madisonville, KY 42431
Tel: (270) 821-7361 Fax: (270) 821-3270

County Clerk **Keenan Cloern** . . . . (270) 821-7361
  E-mail: keenan.cloern@ky.gov

Jackson County

Circuit Clerk

Forty-First Judicial Circuit
Clay County Justice Center, 316 Main Street, Suite 320,
Manchester, KY 40962
Tel: (606) 598-5251 Fax: (606) 598-4113

Clerk of the Court, Jackson County **Doris Kay Ward** . . . . . (606) 287-7783
  Jackson County Judicial Center, 100 First Street,   Fax: (606) 287-3277
  McKee, KY 40447-0084
  E-mail: dorisward@kycourts.net

County Clerk

Office of the County Clerk
108 Courthouse Square, McKee, KY 40447
P.O. Box 339, McKee, KY 40447
Tel: (606) 287-7800 Fax: (606) 287-4505

County Clerk **Donald "Duck" Moore** . . . . (606) 287-7800
  E-mail: jcclerk@prtcnet.org   Fax: (606) 287-4505

Jefferson County

Circuit Clerk

Thirtieth Judicial Circuit
700 West Jefferson Street, Louisville, KY 40202-4737
Tel: (502) 595-4103 Fax: (502) 595-3496

Circuit Court Clerk, Jefferson County
  David L. Nicholson . . . . (502) 595-3055
  600 West Jefferson Street,   Fax: (502) 595-4629
  Louisville, KY 40202
  E-mail: dnicholson@kycourts.net

County Clerk

Office of the County Clerk
County Courthouse, 527 W. Jefferson St., Suite 105, Louisville, KY 40202
Tel: (502) 574-5700 Fax: (502) 574-5566

County Clerk **Barbara "Bobbie" Holsclaw** . . . . (502) 574-5680
  E-mail: barbara.holsclaw@louisvilleky.gov

Jessamine County

Circuit Clerk

Thirteenth Judicial Circuit
101 North Main Street, Nicholasville, KY 40356
Tel: (859) 885-6722 Fax: (859) 881-5252

Clerk of the Court, Jessamine County **H. Douglas Fain** . . . (859) 885-4531
  107 North Main Street, Nicholasville, KY 40356   Fax: (859) 887-0425

County Clerk

Office of the County Clerk
101 North Main Street, Nicholasville, KY 40356
Tel: (859) 885-4161 Fax: (859) 885-5837

County Clerk **Johnny Collier** . . . . (859) 885-4161
  E-mail: johnny.collier@ky.gov

Johnson County

Circuit Clerk

Twenty-Fourth Judicial Circuit
Johnson County Judicial Center, 908 Third Street, Paintsville, KY 41240
Tel: (606) 297-9586 Fax: (606) 297-9588

Clerk of the Court, Johnson County **Penny Adams** . . . . . . (606) 297-9567
  Johnson County Judicial Center,   Tel: (606) 297-9573
  908 Third Street, Suite 109,
  Paintsville, KY 41240
  E-mail: pennyadams@kycourts.net

County Clerk

Office of the County Clerk
230 Court Street, Suite 124, Paintsville, KY 41240
Tel: (606) 789-2557 Fax: (606) 789-2559

County Clerk **Sallee "Conley" Holbrook** . . . . (606) 789-2557
  E-mail: sallee.conley-holbrook@ky.gov

Kenton County

Circuit Clerk

Sixteenth Judicial Circuit
Kenton County Justice Center, 230 Madison Avenue,
Covington, KY 41011
Tel: (859) 292-6531 Fax: (859) 292-6384

Clerk of the Court, Kenton County
John C. Middleton . . . . (859) 292-6521
230 Madison Avenue, Third Floor,   Fax: (859) 292-6611
Covington, KY 41011
E-mail: johnmiddleton@kycourts.net

County Clerk

Office of the County Clerk
303 Court Street, Room 103, Covington, KY 41012
P.O. Box 1109, Covington, KY 41012
Tel: (859) 392-1652 Fax: (859) 392-1642

County Clerk **Gabrielle Summe** . . . . (859) 392-1652
E-mail: gabrielle.summe@ky.gov

Knott County

Circuit Clerk

Thirty-Sixth Judicial Circuit
53 West Main Street, Hindman, KY 41822
Tel: (606) 785-3842 Fax: (606) 785-9096

Clerk of the Court, Knott County **Judy Collins** . . . . (606) 785-5021
Knott County Justice Center, 100 Justice Drive,   Fax: (606) 785-3994
Hindman, KY 41822-1317
E-mail: judycollins@kycourts.net

County Clerk

Office of the County Clerk
54 West Main Street, Hindman, KY 41822
P.O. Box 446, Hindman, KY 41822
Tel: (606) 785-5651 Fax: (606) 785-0996

County Clerk **Kennith Gayheart** . . . . (606) 785-5651
E-mail: kenneth.gayheart@ky.gov

Knox County

Circuit Clerk

Twenty-Seventh Judicial Circuit
P.O. Box 1209, London, KY 40743-1209
Tel: (606) 330-2147 Fax: (606) 330-2145

Clerk of the Court, Knox County **Greg Helton** . . . . (606) 546-3075
Knox County Courthouse Annex, 401 Court Square,   Fax: (606) 546-7949
Barbourville, KY 40906-0760
E-mail: greghelton@kycourts.net

County Clerk

Office of the County Clerk
401 Court Square, Suite 102, Barbourville, KY 40906
Tel: (606) 546-3568 Fax: (606) 546-3589

County Clerk **Mike Corey** . . . . (606) 546-3568
E-mail: mike.corey@ky.gov

LaRue County

Circuit Clerk

Tenth Judicial Circuit
Nelson County Justice Center, 200 Nelson County Plaza,
Bardstown, KY 40004-2100
Tel: (502) 348-7313 Fax: (502) 348-2702

Clerk of the Court, LaRue County **Larry C. Bell** . . . . (270) 358-3421
209 West High Street, Hodgenville, KY 42748   Fax: (270) 358-3731
P.O. Box 191, Hodgenville, KY 42748
E-mail: larrybell@kycourts.net

County Clerk

Office of the County Clerk
209 West High Street, Suite 3, Hodgenville, KY 42748
Tel: (270) 358-3544 Fax: (270) 358-4528

County Clerk **Linda C. Carter** . . . . (270) 358-3544 ext. 1011
E-mail: lindac.carter@ky.gov

Laurel County

Circuit Clerk

Twenty-Seventh Judicial Circuit
P.O. Box 1209, London, KY 40743-1209
Tel: (606) 330-2147 Fax: (606) 330-2145

Clerk of the Court, Laurel County **Roger Schott** . . . . (606) 330-2079
Laurel County Judicial Center,   Fax: (606) 330-2084
305 South Main Street, London, KY 40743-1798
E-mail: rogerschott@kycourts.net

County Clerk

Office of the County Clerk
101 South Main Street, Room 203, London, KY 40741
Tel: (606) 864-5158 Fax: (606) 864-7369

County Clerk **Dean Johnson** . . . . (606) 864-5158
E-mail: dean.johnson@ky.gov

Lawrence County

Circuit Clerk

Twenty-Fourth Judicial Circuit
Johnson County Judicial Center, 908 Third Street, Paintsville, KY 41240
Tel: (606) 297-9586 Fax: (606) 297-9588

Clerk of the Court, Lawrence County **Jodi Parsley** . . . . . . (606) 638-4215
Lawrence County Courthouse Annex,   Tel: (606) 638-0264
122 Main Cross Street, Louisa, KY 41230-0847
E-mail: jodiparsley@kycourts.net

County Clerk

Office of the County Clerk
122 South Main Cross Street, Louisa, KY 41230
Tel: (606) 638-4108 Fax: (606) 638-0638

County Clerk **Chris Jobe** . . . . (606) 638-4108
E-mail: chris.jobe@ky.gov

(continued on next page)

Lee County

Circuit Clerk

Twenty-Third Judicial Circuit
59 Main Street, Beattyville, KY 41311
Tel: (606) 464-2648 Fax: (606) 464-8229

Clerk of the Court, Lee County **Emma C. Adams** . . . . (606) 464-8400
Lee County Courthouse, 256 Main Street,   Fax: (606) 464-0144
Beattyville, KY 41311-2005
E-mail: emmaadams@kycourts.net

County Clerk

Office of the County Clerk
256 Main Street, Beattyville, KY 41311
P.O. Box 556, Beattyville, KY 41311
Tel: (606) 464-4115 Fax: (606) 464-4102

County Clerk **Russell Stamper** . . . . (606) 464-4115
E-mail: russell.stamper@ky.gov

Leslie County

Circuit Clerk

Forty-First Judicial Circuit
Clay County Justice Center, 316 Main Street, Suite 320,
Manchester, KY 40962
Tel: (606) 598-5251 Fax: (606) 598-4113

Clerk of the Court, Leslie County
Carmolitta Morgan-Pace . . . . (606) 672-2503
Leslie County Courthouse, 22010 Main Street,   Fax: (606) 672-5128
Hyden, KY 41749-1750

County Clerk

Office of the County Clerk
22010 Main Street, Hyden, KY 41749
P.O. Box 916, Hyden, KY 41749
Tel: (606) 672-2193 Fax: (606) 672-4264
E-mail: leslieclerk@tds.net

County Clerk **James Lewis** . . . . (606) 672-2193
E-mail: james1.lewis@ky.gov

Letcher County

Circuit Clerk

Forty-Seventh Judicial Circuit
Letcher County Courthouse, 156 Main Street, Suite 205,
Whitesburg, KY 41858
Tel: (606) 633-2259 Fax: (606) 633-2866

Clerk of the Court, Letcher County **Margaret Nichols** . . . (606) 633-7559
Letcher County Circuit Court Clerk,   Fax: (606) 633-5864
156 Main Street, Suite 201,
Whitesburg, KY 41858
E-mail: margaretnichols@kycourts.net

County Clerk

Office of the County Clerk
156 Main Street, Suite 102, Whitesburg, KY 41858
Tel: (606) 633-2432 Fax: (606) 632-9282

County Clerk **Winston Meade** . . . . (606) 633-2432
E-mail: winston.meade@ky.gov

Lewis County

Circuit Clerk

Twentieth Judicial Circuit
Courthouse Annex, 101 Harrison Street, Greenup, KY 41144-0676
Tel: (606) 473-7165 Fax: (606) 473-6665

Clerk of the Court, Lewis County **Kathy Hardy** . . . . (606) 796-3053
Lewis County Justice Center, 94 Second Street,   Fax: (606) 796-3030
Vanceburg, KY 41179-0070
P.O. Box 70, Vanceburg, KY 41179-0070
E-mail: kathyhardy@kycourts.net

County Clerk

Office of the County Clerk
112 Second Street, Vanceburg, KY 41179
P.O. Box 129, Vanceburg, KY 41179
Tel: (606) 796-3062 Fax: (606) 796-6511
E-mail: lewiscoclerk@yahoo.com

County Clerk **Glenda K. Himes** . . . . (606) 796-3062
E-mail: glenda.himes@ky.gov

Lincoln County

Circuit Clerk

Twenty-Eighth Judicial Circuit
50 Public Square, 3rd Floor, Somerset, KY 42501
Tel: (606) 677-4098 Tel: (606) 677-4182

Clerk of the Court, Lincoln County **Teresa Reed** . . . . (606) 365-2535
101 East Main Street, Stanford, KY 40484   Fax: (606) 365-3389
E-mail: teresareed@kycourts.net

County Clerk

Office of the County Clerk
301 North 3rd Street, Stanford, KY 40484
Tel: (606) 365-4570 Fax: (606) 365-4572

County Clerk **George Spoonamore, Jr.** . . . . (606) 365-4570
E-mail: george.spoonamore@ky.gov

Livingston County

Circuit Clerk

Fifty-Sixth Judicial Circuit
P.O. Box 790, Eddyville, KY 42038-0790
Tel: (270) 388-5182 Fax: (270) 388-0869

Clerk of the Court, Livingston County
Deborah Harp Knoth . . . . (270) 928-2172
Livingston County Justice Center,   Fax: (270) 928-2976
122 West Adair Street, Smithfield, KY 42081-0160

County Clerk

Office of the County Clerk
321 Court Street, Smithland, KY 42081
P.O. Box 400, Smithland, KY 42081
Tel: (270) 928-2162 Fax: (270) 928-2211

County Clerk **Sonya Williams** . . . . (270) 928-2162
E-mail: sonya.williams@ky.gov

Logan County

Circuit Clerk

Seventh Judicial Circuit
200 West Fourth Street, Russellville, KY 42276-0667
P.O. Box 667, Russellville, KY 42276-0667
Tel: (270) 726-2242 Fax: (270) 725-8575

Clerk of the Court, Logan County **Sherry Wilkins** . . . . (270) 726-2424
329 West Fourth Street, Russellville, KY 42276   Fax: (270) 726-7893
P.O. Box 420, Russellville, KY 42276
E-mail: sherrywilkins@kycourts.net

County Clerk

Office of the County Clerk
229 West Third Street, Russellville, KY 42276
P.O. Box 358, Russellville, KY 42276
Tel: (270) 726-6061 Fax: (270) 726-4355

County Clerk **Scottie Harper** . . . . (270) 726-6061
E-mail: scottie.harper@ky.gov

Lyon County

Circuit Clerk

Fifty-Sixth Judicial Circuit
P.O. Box 790, Eddyville, KY 42038-0790
Tel: (270) 388-5182 Fax: (270) 388-0869

Clerk of the Court, Lyon County **Rebecca Howard** . . . . . . (270) 388-7231
Lyon County Judicial Center, 500 West Dale,   Fax: (270) 388-9135
Eddyville, KY 42038-0565
E-mail: rebeccahoward@kycourts.net

County Clerk

Office of the County Clerk
236 Commerce Street, Eddyville, KY 42038
P.O. Box 310, Eddyville, KY 42038
Tel: (270) 388-2331 Fax: (270) 388-0634

County Clerk **Sarah Defew** . . . . (270) 388-2331
E-mail: sarah.defew@ky.gov

Madison County

Circuit Clerk

Twenty-Fifth Judicial Circuit
Madison County Courthouse, 101 West Main Street,
Richmond, KY 40475-0819
Tel: (859) 624-4750

Clerk of the Court, Madison County **Darlene Snyder** . . . . (859) 624-4793
Madison County Courthouse, 101 West Main Street,   Fax: (859) 624-4746
Richmond, KY 40475-0819
E-mail: darlenesnyder@kycourts.net

County Clerk

Office of the County Clerk
101 West Main Street, Suite 7, Richmond, KY 40475
P.O. Box 1270, Richmond, KY 40476
Tel: (859) 624-4703 Fax: (859) 624-4954

County Clerk **Kenny Barger** . . . . (859) 624-4703
E-mail: kenny.barger@ky.gov

Magoffin County

Circuit Clerk

Thirty-Sixth Judicial Circuit
53 West Main Street, Hindman, KY 41822
Tel: (606) 785-3842 Fax: (606) 785-9096

Clerk of the Court, Magoffin County
Tonya Arnett Ward . . . . (606) 439-2215
Magoffin County Justice Center,   Fax: (606) 349-2209
100 East Maple Street, Salyersville, KY 14165-0147
E-mail: tonyaward@kycourts.net

County Clerk

Office of the County Clerk
249 Mountain Parkway Drive, Salyersville, KY 41465
P.O. Box 1535, Salyersville, KY 41465
Tel: (606) 349-2216 Fax: (606) 349-2328

County Clerk **Renee Shepherd** . . . . (606) 349-2216
E-mail: renee.shepherd@ky.gov

Marion County

Circuit Clerk

Eleventh Judicial Circuit
Taylor County Justice Center, 300 East Main Street, Suite 301,
Campbellsville, KY 42718
Tel: (270) 465-6603 Fax: (270) 469-4804

Clerk of the Court, Marion County **Kim T. May** . . . . (270) 692-2681
121 North Spalding Avenue,   Fax: (270) 692-3097
Lebanon, KY 40033
E-mail: kimmay@kycourts.net

County Clerk

Office of the County Clerk
223 North Spalding Avenue, Suite 102, Lebanon, KY 40033
Tel: (270) 692-2651 Fax: (270) 692-9811

County Clerk **Chad G. Mattingly** . . . . (270) 692-2651
E-mail: chad.mattingly@ky.gov

Marshall County

Circuit Clerk

Forty-Second Judicial Circuit
Marshall Circuit and District Courts, 80 Judicial Drive, Unit 215,
Benton, KY 42025
Tel: (270) 527-1480 Fax: (270) 527-7516

Clerk of the Court, Marshall County **Carla Marshall** . . . . . (270) 527-1721
Marshall County Judicial Building,   Fax: (270) 527-5865
80 Judicial Drive, Unit 101,
Benton, KY 42025
E-mail: carlamarshall@kycourts.net

County Clerk

Office of the County Clerk
1101 Main Street, Benton, KY 42025
Tel: (270) 527-4740 Fax: (270) 527-4738

County Clerk **Tim York** . . . . (270) 527-4740
E-mail: tim.york@ky.gov

(continued on next page)

Martin County

Circuit Clerk

Twenty-Fourth Judicial Circuit
Johnson County Judicial Center, 908 Third Street, Paintsville, KY 41240
Tel: (606) 297-9586 Fax: (606) 297-9588

Clerk of the Court, Martin County **Jack Horn** . . . . (606) 298-3508
  Martin County Courthouse, 14 Court Street,   Tel: (606) 298-4202
  Inez, KY 41224-0430
  E-mail: jackhorn@kycourts.net

County Clerk

Office of the County Clerk
100 Main Street, Inez, KY 41224
P.O. Box 460, Inez, KY 41224
Tel: (606) 298-2810 Fax: (606) 298-0143

County Clerk **Carol Sue Mills** . . . . (606) 298-2810
  E-mail: carol.mills@ky.gov

Mason County

Circuit Clerk

Nineteenth Judicial Circuit
100 West Third Street, Maysville, KY 41056
Tel: (606) 564-9736 Fax: (606) 564-0308

Clerk of the Court, Mason County **Kirk Tolle** . . . . (606) 564-4340
  100 West Third Street, Maysville, KY 41056   Fax: (606) 564-0932
  E-mail: kirktolle@kycourts.net

County Clerk

Office of the County Clerk
27 West Third Street, Maysville, KY 41056
P.O. Box 234, Maysville, KY 41056
Tel: (606) 564-3341 Fax: (606) 564-8979

County Clerk **Stephanie G. Schumacher** . . . . (606) 564-3341
  E-mail: stephanieg.schumacher@ky.gov

McCracken County

Circuit Clerk

Second Judicial Circuit
McCracken County Courthouse, 301 South Sixth Street,
Paducah, KY 42003

Clerk of the Court, McCracken County **Kim Channell** . . . (270) 575-7280
  E-mail: kimchannell@kycourts.net   Fax: (270) 575-7029

County Clerk

Office of the County Clerk
301 South Sixth Street, Paducah, KY 42003
P.O. Box 609, Paducah, KY 42002
Tel: (270) 444-4700 Fax: (270) 444-4704

County Clerk **Julie Griggs** . . . . (270) 444-4700
  E-mail: julie.griggs@ky.gov

McCreary County

Circuit Clerk

Thirty-Fourth Judicial Circuit
Whitley County Courthouse, 100 Main Street,
Williamsburg, KY 40769-0329
Tel: (606) 549-0825 Fax: (606) 539-3933

Clerk of the Court, McCreary County **Othel King** . . . . (606) 376-5041
  McCreary County Courthouse, 1 North Main Street,   Fax: (606) 376-8844
  Whitley City, KY 42653-0040

County Clerk

Office of the County Clerk
One North Main Street, Whitley City, KY 42653
P.O. Box 699, Whitley City, KY 42653
Tel: (606) 376-2411 Fax: (606) 376-3898

County Clerk **Eric Haynes** . . . . (606) 376-2411
  E-mail: eric.haynes@ky.gov

McLean County

Circuit Clerk

Forty-Fifth Judicial Circuit
136 South Main Street, Greenville, KY 42345
Tel: (270) 338-5930 Fax: (270) 338-6915

Clerk of the Court, McLean County
  Stephanie J, King-Logsdon . . . . (270) 273-3966
  136 South Main Street, Greenville, KY 42345   Fax: (270) 273-5918

County Clerk

Office of the County Clerk
210 Main Street, Calhoun, KY 42327
P.O. Box 57, Calhoun, KY 42327
Tel: (270) 273-3082 Fax: (270) 273-5084

County Clerk **Stacy Patrick** . . . . (270) 273-3082
  E-mail: stacy.patrick@ky.gov

Meade County

Circuit Clerk

Forty-Sixth Judicial Circuit
Meade County Courthouse, 516 Hillcrest Drive, Brandenburg, KY 40108
Tel: (270) 422-7800 Fax: (270) 422-7801

Clerk of the Court, Meade County **Evelyn D. Medley** . . . . (270) 422-4961
  Meade County Courthouse, 516 Hillcrest Drive,   Fax: (270) 422-2147
  Brandenburg, KY 40108
  E-mail: evelynmedley@kycourts.net

County Clerk

Office of the County Clerk
516 Hillcrest Drive, Brandenburg, KY 40108
P.O. Box 614, Brandenburg, KY 40108
Tel: (270) 422-2152 Fax: (270) 422-2158

County Clerk **Judy Jordan** . . . . (270) 422-2152
  E-mail: judy.jordan@ky.gov

Menifee County

Circuit Clerk

Twenty-First Judicial Circuit
P.O. Box 1267, Mt. Sterling, KY 40353
Tel: (859) 498-0488 Fax: (859) 498-2665

Clerk of the Court, Menifee County
   Karen Wells-Sorrell . . . .(606) 768-2461
   Menifee County Courthouse, 12 Main Street,   Fax: (606) 768-2462
   Frenchburg, KY 40322-0172

County Clerk

Office of the County Clerk
12 Main Street, Frenchburg, KY 40322
P.O. Box 123, Frenchburg, KY 40322
Tel: (606) 768-3512 Fax: (606) 768-6738

County Clerk **Brenda Carty** . . . .(606) 768-3512
   E-mail: brenda.carty@ky.gov

Mercer County

Circuit Clerk

Fiftieth Judicial Circuit
Boyle County Courthouse, 321 West Main, Second Floor,
Danville, KY 40422
Tel: (859) 239-7009 Fax: (859) 239-7033

Clerk of the Court, Mercer County **Beth Neal** . . . . (859) 734-8452
   Mercer County Circuit Court Clerk,   Fax: (859) 734-8454
   207 West Lexington Street,
   Harrodsburg, KY 40330
   E-mail: bethneal@kycourts.net

County Clerk

Office of the County Clerk
207 West Lexington Street, Harrodsburg, KY 40330
P.O. Box 426, Harrodsburg, KY 40330
Tel: (859) 734-6310 Fax: (859) 734-6309

County Clerk **Chris Horn** . . . .(859) 734-6310
   E-mail: chris.horn@ky.gov

Metcalfe County

Circuit Clerk

Forty-Third Judicial Circuit
300 Courthouse Square, Glasgow, KY 42141
Tel: (270) 651-2744 Fax: (270) 651-7051

Clerk of the Court, Metcalfe County
   Tommy A. Garrett . . . .(270) 432-3663
   Metcalfe County Courthouse,   Fax: (270) 432-4437
   201 East Stockton Street,
   Edmonton, KY 42129-0027
   P.O. Box 27, Edmonton, KY 42129
   E-mail: tommygarrett@kycourts.net

County Clerk

Office of the County Clerk
100 East Stockton Street, Edmonton, KY 42129
P.O. Box 25, Edmonton, KY 42129
Tel: (270) 432-4821 Fax: (270) 432-5176
E-mail: metclerk@scrtc.com

County Clerk **Carol England Chaney** . . . .(270) 432-4821
   E-mail: carol.england@ky.gov

Monroe County

Circuit Clerk

Fortieth Judicial Circuit
112 Courthouse Square, Burkesville, KY 42717-0395
Tel: (270) 864-5192 Fax: (270) 864-1418

Clerk of the Court, Monroe County **Joyce Emberton** . . . .(270) 487-5480
   Monroe County Justice Center,   Fax: (270) 487-0068
   300 North Main Street, Tompkinsville, KY 42167
   E-mail: joyceemberton@kycourts.net

County Clerk

Office of the County Clerk
200 North Main Street, Suite D, Tompkinsville, KY 42167
Tel: (270) 487-5471 Fax: (270) 487-5976
E-mail: monroecountyclerk@mchsi.com

County Clerk **Teresa McMillin Sheffield** . . . .(270) 487-5471
   E-mail: teresa.sheffield@ky.gov

Montgomery County

Circuit Clerk

Twenty-First Judicial Circuit
P.O. Box 1267, Mt. Sterling, KY 40353
Tel: (859) 498-0488 Fax: (859) 498-2665

Clerk of the Court, Montgomery County
   Tanya P. Terry . . . .(859) 498-5966
   Montgomery County Courthouse, 1 Court Street,   Fax: (859) 498-9341
   Mount Sterling, KY 40353-0327
   E-mail: tanyaterry@kycourts.net

County Clerk

Office of the County Clerk
One Court Street, Suite 2, Mount Sterling, KY 40353
Tel: (859) 498-8700 Fax: (859) 498-8729

County Clerk **Chris Cockrell** . . . .(859) 498-8700
   E-mail: chris.cokkrell@ky.gov

Morgan County

Circuit Clerk

Thirty-Seventh Judicial Circuit
100 East Main Street, Grayson, KY 41143-1302
Tel: (606) 474-5191 Fax: (606) 474-0710

Clerk of the Court, Morgan County **Donna Pelfrey** . . . . . .(606) 743-3763
   Morgan County Courthouse, 518 Main Street,   Fax: (606) 743-2633
   West Liberty, KY 41472-0085
   E-mail: donnapelfrey@kycourts.net

County Clerk

Office of the County Clerk
450 Prestonsburg Street, Room 1A, West Liberty, KY 41472
P.O. Box 26, West Liberty, KY 41472
Tel: (606) 743-3949 Fax: (606) 743-2111

County Clerk **Randy Williams** . . . .(606) 743-3949
   E-mail: rwclerk@mrtc.com

(continued on next page)

Muhlenberg County

Circuit Clerk

Forty-Fifth Judicial Circuit
136 South Main Street, Greenville, KY 42345
Tel: (270) 338-5930 Fax: (270) 338-6915

Clerk of the Court, Muhlenberg County
Camron Laycock . . . . (270) 338-4850
Muhlenberg County Judicial Building,   Fax: (270) 338-0177
136 South Main Street, Greenville, KY 42345
E-mail: camronlaycock@kycourts.net

County Clerk

Office of the County Clerk
100 South Main Street, Greenville, KY 42345
P.O. Box 525, Greenville, KY 42345
Tel: (270) 338-1441 Fax: (270) 338-1774

County Clerk **Gaylan L. Spurlin** . . . . (270) 338-1441
E-mail: gaylanl.spurlin@ky.gov

Nelson County

Circuit Clerk

Tenth Judicial Circuit
Nelson County Justice Center, 200 Nelson County Plaza,
Bardstown, KY 40004-2100
Tel: (502) 348-7313 Fax: (502) 348-2702

Clerk of the Court, Nelson County **Diane Thompson** . . . . (502) 348-3648
Nelson County Justice Center,
200 Nelson County Plaza,
Bardstown, KY 40004-2100
E-mail: dianethompson@kycourts.net

County Clerk

Office of the County Clerk
113 East Stephen Foster Avenue, Bardstown, KY 40004
Tel: (502) 348-1820 Fax: (502) 348-1822

County Clerk **Elaine A. Filiatreau** . . . . (502) 348-1820
E-mail: elaine.filiatreau@ky.gov

Nicholas County

Circuit Clerk

Eighteenth Judicial Circuit
Harrison County Justice Center, 115 Court Street, Cynthiana, KY 41031
Tel: (859) 234-3431 Fax: (859) 234-6878

Clerk of the Court, Nicholas County **Sandye Watkins** . . . (859) 289-2336
125 Main Street, Carlisle, KY 40311-0109   Fax: (859) 289-6141
P.O. Box 109, Carlisle, KY 40311-0109
E-mail: sandyewatkins@kycourts.net

County Clerk

Office of the County Clerk
125 East Main Street, Carlisle, KY 40311
P.O. Box 227, Carlisle, KY 40311
Tel: (859) 289-3730 Fax: (859) 289-3709

County Clerk **Martha L. Moss** . . . . (859) 289-3730
E-mail: martha.moss@ky.gov

Ohio County

Circuit Clerk

Thirty-Eighth Judicial Circuit
P.O. Box 169, Hartford, KY 42347
Tel: (270) 298-7250 Fax: (270) 298-3646

Clerk of the Court, Ohio County **Shannon Kirtley** . . . . . . (270) 298-3671
Ohio County Community Center,   Fax: (270) 298-9565
130 East Washington Street,
Hartford, KY 42347-0067

County Clerk

Office of the County Clerk
301 South Main Street, Suite 201, Hartford, KY 42347
Tel: (270) 298-4423 Fax: (270) 298-4426

County Clerk **Bess T. Ralph** . . . . (270) 298-4423
E-mail: bess.ralph@ky.gov

Oldham County

Circuit Clerk

Twelfth Judicial Circuit
Oldham County Courthouse, 100 West Main Street,
La Grange, KY 40031-1116
Tel: (502) 222-1692 Fax: (502) 222-5684

Clerk of the Court, Oldham County **Rick Rash** . . . . (502) 222-9837
Oldham County Courthouse, 100 West Main Street,   Fax: (502) 222-3047
La Grange, KY 40031-1116
E-mail: rickrash@kycourts.net

County Clerk

Office of the County Clerk
100 West Jefferson Street, La Grange, KY 40031
Tel: (502) 222-0047 Fax: (502) 222-3210

County Clerk **Julie K. Barr** . . . . (502) 222-0047
E-mail: julie.barr@ky.gov

Owen County

Circuit Clerk

Fifteenth Judicial Circuit
Grant County Judicial Center, 224 South Main Street,
Williamstown, KY 41097
Tel: (859) 824-7516 Fax: (859) 824-6494

Clerk of the Court, Owen County **Margaret Forsee** . . . . . (502) 484-2232
401 South Main Street, Owenton, KY 40359-0473   Fax: (502) 484-0625
P.O. Box 473, Owenton, KY 40359-0473
E-mail: margaretforsee@kycourts.net

County Clerk

Office of the County Clerk
136 West Bryan Street, Owenton, KY 40359
Tel: (502) 484-2213 Fax: (502) 484-1002

County Clerk **Laurel P. Stivers** . . . . (502) 484-2213
E-mail: laurel.stivers@ky.gov

Owsley County

Circuit Clerk

Twenty-Third Judicial Circuit
59 Main Street, Beattyville, KY 41311
Tel: (606) 464-2648 Fax: (606) 464-8229

Clerk of the Court, Owsley County **A. Michael Mays** .... (606) 593-6226
Owsley County Courthouse, 1 North Court Street,   Fax: (606) 593-6343
Booneville, KY 41314-0130

County Clerk

Office of the County Clerk
One Main Street, Booneville, KY 41314
P.O. Box 500, Booneville, KY 41314
Tel: (606) 593-5735 Fax: (606) 593-5737

County Clerk **Shanna Oliver** .... (606) 593-5735
E-mail: shanna.oliver@ky.gov

Pendleton County

Circuit Clerk

Eighteenth Judicial Circuit
Harrison County Justice Center, 115 Court Street, Cynthiana, KY 41031
Tel: (859) 234-3431 Fax: (859) 234-6878

Clerk of the Court, Pendleton County
Michael D. Redden .... (859) 654-3347
Pendleton County Judicial Center,   Fax: (859) 654-3405
120 Ridgeway Avenue, Falmouth, KY 41040-0069
E-mail: michaelredden@kycourts.net

County Clerk

Office of the County Clerk
233 Main Street, Room 1, Falmouth, KY 41040
P.O. Box 112, Falmouth, KY 41040
Tel: (859) 654-2143 Fax: (859) 654-5600

County Clerk **Rita Spencer** .... (859) 654-2143
E-mail: rita.spencer@ky.gov

Perry County

Circuit Clerk

Thirty-Third Judicial Circuit
Perry County Hall of Justice, 545 Main Street, Hazard, KY 41701-7433
Tel: (606) 435-6004 Fax: (606) 435-6110

Clerk of the Court, Perry County **Charles Patterson** ..... (606) 435-6000
Perry County Hall of Justice, 545 Main Street,   Fax: (606) 435-6143
Hazard, KY 41701-7433
E-mail: charlespatterson@kycourts.net

County Clerk

Office of the County Clerk
481 Main Street, Suite 150, Hazard, KY 41701
P.O. Box 150, Hazard, KY 41702
Tel: (606) 436-4614 Fax: (606) 439-0557

County Clerk **Haven King** .... (606) 436-4614
E-mail: haven.king@ky.gov

Pike County

Circuit Clerk

Thirty-Fifth Judicial Circuit
Pike County Judicial Center, 175 Main Street, Pikeville, KY 41501-1002
Tel: (606) 433-7554 Fax: (606) 433-7029

Clerk of the Court, Pike County **Anna Pinson Spears** ... (606) 433-7557
Pike County Hall of Justice, 175 Main Street,   Fax: (606) 433-7044
Pikeville, KY 41501-1002
E-mail: annapinson@kycourts.net

County Clerk

Office of the County Clerk
146 Main Street, Pikeville, KY 41501
P.O. Box 631, Pikeville, KY 41501
Tel: (606) 432-6211 Fax: (606) 432-6222

County Clerk **Rhonda Taylor** .... (606) 432-6211
E-mail: rhonda.taylor@ky.gov

Powell County

Circuit Clerk

Thirty-Ninth Judicial Circuit
P.O. Box 946, Jackson, KY 41339-0946
Tel: (606) 666-7130

Clerk of the Court, Powell County
Patricia Darlene Drake .... (606) 663-4141
Powell County Courthouse, 525 Washington Street,   Fax: (606) 663-2710
Stanton, KY 40380-0578

County Clerk

Office of the County Clerk
525 Washington Street, Room 109, Stanton, KY 40380
P.O. Box 193, Stanton, KY 40380
Tel: (606) 663-6444 Fax: (606) 663-6406

County Clerk **Rhonda Allen Barnett** .... (606) 663-6444
E-mail: rhondaa.barnett@ky.gov

Pulaski County

Circuit Clerk

Twenty-Eighth Judicial Circuit
50 Public Square, 3rd Floor, Somerset, KY 42501
Tel: (606) 677-4098 Tel: (606) 677-4182

Clerk of the Court, Pulaski County **George F. Flynn** ..... (606) 677-4029
Pulaski County Court of Justice, 50 Public Square,   Fax: (606) 677-4002
Somerset, KY 42501
E-mail: georgeflynn@kycourts.net

County Clerk

Office of the County Clerk
100 North Main Street, Room 208, Somerset, KY 42501
P.O. Box 739, Somerset, KY 42502
Tel: (606) 679-2042 Fax: (606) 678-0073

County Clerk **Linda Burnett** .... (606) 679-2042
E-mail: linda.burnett@ky.gov

(continued on next page)

Robertson County

Circuit Clerk

Eighteenth Judicial Circuit
Harrison County Justice Center, 115 Court Street, Cynthiana, KY 41031
Tel: (859) 234-3431 Fax: (859) 234-6878

Clerk of the Court, Robertson County **Tabitha Tilton** . . . . (606) 724-5993
127 East Walnut Street,   Fax: (606) 724-5721
Mount Olivet, KY 41064-0063
P.O. Box 63, Mount Olivet, KY 41064-0063
E-mail: tabithatilton@kycourts.net

County Clerk

Office of the County Clerk
26 Court Street, Mount Olivet, KY 41064
P.O. Box 75, Mount Olivet, KY 41064
Tel: (606) 724-5212 Fax: (606) 724-5022

County Clerk **Stephanie A. Bogucki** . . . . (606) 724-5212
E-mail: stephanie.bogucki@ky.gov

Rockcastle County

Circuit Clerk

Twenty-Eighth Judicial Circuit
50 Public Square, 3rd Floor, Somerset, KY 42501
Tel: (606) 677-4098 Tel: (606) 677-4182

Clerk of the Court, Rockcastle County
Eliza Jane York . . . . (606) 256-2581
Rockcastle County Courthouse Annex,   Fax: (606) 256-4569
205 East Main Stree, Room 102,
Mount Vernon, KY 40456
E-mail: elizayork@kycourts.net

County Clerk

Office of the County Clerk
205 East Main Street, Room 6, Mount Vernon, KY 40456
Tel: (606) 256-2831 Fax: (606) 256-4302

County Clerk **Danetta Ford Allen** . . . . (606) 256-2831
E-mail: danetta.allen@ky.gov

Rowan County

Circuit Clerk

Twenty-First Judicial Circuit
P.O. Box 1267, Mt. Sterling, KY 40353
Tel: (859) 498-0488 Fax: (859) 498-2665

Clerk of the Court, Rowan County **Jim Barker** . . . .(606) 783-8505
Rowan County Judicial Center,   Fax: (606) 783-8504
700 West Main Street, Morehead, KY 40351
E-mail: jimbarker@kycourts.net

County Clerk

Office of the County Clerk
600 WestMain Street, Room 102, Morehead, KY 40351
Tel: (606) 784-5212 Fax: (606) 784-2923

County Clerk **Kim Davis** . . . .(606) 784-5212
E-mail: kimberlyb.davis@ky.gov

Russell County

Circuit Clerk

Fifty-Seventh Judicial Circuit
Wayne County Justice Center, 100 West Columbia Avenue,
Monticello, KY 42633
Tel: (606) 340-8159 Fax: (606) 340-8168

Clerk of the Court, Russell County **Tony D. Kerr** . . . .(270) 343-2185
Russell County Judicial Center,   Fax: (270) 343-5808
202 Monument Square, Suite 106,
Jamestown, KY 42629
E-mail: tonykerr@kycourts.net

County Clerk

Office of the County Clerk
410 Monument Square, Jamestown, KY 42629
P.O. Box 397, Jamestown, KY 42629
Tel: (270) 343-2125 Fax: (270) 343-4700

County Clerk **Sue Popplewell-Brockman** . . . . (270) 343-2125

Scott County

Circuit Clerk

Fourteenth Judicial Circuit
Scott County Justice Center, 119 North Hamilton Street,
Georgetown, KY 40324
Tel: (502) 570-0947 Fax: (502) 570-0949

Clerk of the Court, Scott County **Karen Boehm** . . . .(502) 863-0474
Scott County Justice Center,   Fax: (502) 863-9089
119 North Hamilton Street,
Georgetown, KY 40324
E-mail: karenboehm@kycourts.net

County Clerk

Office of the County Clerk
101 East Main Street, Georgetown, KY 40324
Tel: (502) 863-7875 Fax: (502) 863-7898

County Clerk **Rebecca M. Johnson** . . . . (502) 863-7875
E-mail: rebeccam.johnson@ky.gov

Shelby County

Circuit Clerk

Fifty-Third Judicial Circuit
401 Main Street, Suite 401, Shelbyville, KY 40065
Tel: (502) 647-5234 Fax: (502) 647-5386

Clerk of the Court, Shelby County **Lowry S. Miller** . . . . . .(502) 633-1287
Shelby County Judicial Center, 401 Main Street,   Fax: (502) 633-0146
Suite 101, Shelbyville, KY 40065

County Clerk

Office of the County Clerk
501 Washington Street, Shelbyville, KY 40066
P.O. Box 819, Shelbyville, KY 40066
Tel: (502) 633-4410 Fax: (502) 633-7887

County Clerk **Sue Carole Perry** . . . .(502) 633-4410
E-mail: suecarole.perry@ky.gov

Simpson County

Circuit Clerk

Forty-Ninth Judicial Circuit
Simpson County Justice Center, 101 Court Street,
Franklin, KY 42135-0509
Tel: (270) 586-8058 Fax: (270) 586-0731

Clerk of the Court, Simpson County
 Mary Thomas Vincent . . . . (270) 586-4241
 Simpson County Justice Center, Fax: (270) 586-0265
 101 North Court Street, Franklin, KY 42135-0261

County Clerk

Office of the County Clerk
103 West Cedar Street, Franklin, KY 42134
P.O. Box 268, Franklin, KY 42135
Tel: (270) 586-8161 Fax: (270) 586-6464

County Clerk **Bobby C. Phillips, Jr.** . . . . (270) 586-8161
 E-mail: bobby.phillips@ky.gov

Spencer County

Circuit Clerk

Fifty-Third Judicial Circuit
401 Main Street, Suite 401, Shelbyville, KY 40065
Tel: (502) 647-5234 Fax: (502) 647-5386

Clerk of the Court, Spencer County
 Becky M. Robinson . . . . (502) 477-3220
 Spencer County Courthouse, 27 East Main Street, Fax: (502) 477-9368
 Taylorsville, KY 40071-0280
 E-mail: beckyrobinson@kycourts.net

County Clerk

Office of the County Clerk
Two West Main Street, Taylorsville, KY 40071
P.O. Box 544, Taylorsville, KY 40071
Tel: (502) 477-3215 Fax: (502) 477-3216

County Clerk **Lynn Hesselbrock** . . . . (502) 477-3215
 E-mail: lynnhesselbrock@spencercountyky.gov

Taylor County

Circuit Clerk

Eleventh Judicial Circuit
Taylor County Justice Center, 300 East Main Street, Suite 301,
Campbellsville, KY 42718
Tel: (270) 465-6603 Fax: (270) 469-4804

Clerk of the Court, Taylor County **Rodney Burress** . . . . . . (270) 465-6686
 300 East Main Street, Campbellsville, KY 42718 Fax: (270) 789-4356

County Clerk

Office of the County Clerk
203 North Court Street, Suite 5, Campbellsville, KY 42718
Tel: (270) 465-6677 Fax: (270) 789-1144

County Clerk **Mark Carney** . . . . (270) 465-6677
 E-mail: mark.carney@ky.gov

Todd County

Circuit Clerk

Seventh Judicial Circuit
200 West Fourth Street, Russellville, KY 42276-0667
P.O. Box 667, Russellville, KY 42276-0667
Tel: (270) 726-2242 Fax: (270) 725-8575

Clerk of the Court, Todd County **J. Mark Cowherd** . . . . . (270) 265-2343
 204 West Main Street, Elkton, KY 42220 Fax: (270) 265-2122
 P.O. Box 337, Elkton, KY 42220

County Clerk

Office of the County Clerk
202 East Washington Street, Elkton, KY 42220
P.O. Box 307, Elkton, KY 42220
Tel: (270) 265-9966 ext. 203 Fax: (270) 265-2588

County Clerk **Kimberly R. "Kim" Chapman** . . . . (270) 265-9966 ext. 203
 E-mail: kimberlyr.chapman@ky.gov

Trigg County

Circuit Clerk

Fifty-Sixth Judicial Circuit
P.O. Box 790, Eddyville, KY 42038-0790
Tel: (270) 388-5182 Fax: (270) 388-0869

Clerk of the Court, Trigg County **Pam W. Perry** . . . . (270) 522-6270
 Trigg County Justice Center, 41 Main Street, Fax: (270) 522-5828
 Cadiz, KY 42211-0673
 E-mail: pamperry@kycourts.net

County Clerk

Office of the County Clerk
38 Main Street, Cadiz, KY 42211
P.O. Box 1310, Cadiz, KY 42211
Tel: (270) 522-6661 Fax: (270) 522-6662

County Clerk **Dorris McGill** . . . . (270) 522-6661
 E-mail: dorris.mcgill@ky.gov

Trimble County

Circuit Clerk

Twelfth Judicial Circuit
Oldham County Courthouse, 100 West Main Street,
La Grange, KY 40031-1116
Tel: (502) 222-1692 Fax: (502) 222-5684

Clerk of the Court, Trimble County **Stacy M. Bruner** . . . . (502) 255-3213
 30 Highway 42 East, Bedford, KY 40006 Fax: (502) 255-4953
 P.O. Box 248, Bedford, KY 40006
 E-mail: stacybruner@kycourts.net

County Clerk

Office of the County Clerk
30 Highway 42 East, Bedford, KY 40006
P.O. Box 262, Bedford, KY 40006
Tel: (502) 255-7174 Fax: (502) 255-7045

County Clerk **Tina Browning** . . . . (502) 255-7174
 E-mail: tina.browning@ky.gov

(continued on next page)

Union County

Circuit Clerk

Fifth Judicial Circuit
Webster County Courthouse, 35 US Highway, 41A-S, Dixon, KY 42409
Tel: (270) 639-5506 Fax: (270) 389-1572

Clerk of the Court, Union County **Sue W. Beaven** . . . . . . (270) 389-2264
   121 South Morgan Street, Morganfield, KY 42437   Fax: (270) 389-9887
   P.O. Box 59, Morganfield, KY 42437
   E-mail: suebeaven@kycourts.net

County Clerk

Office of the County Clerk
100 West Main Street, Morganfield, KY 42437
P.O. Box 119, Morganfield, KY 42437
Tel: (270) 389-1334 Fax: (270) 389-9135

County Clerk **Trey Peak** . . . . (270) 389-1334
   E-mail: trey.peak@ky.gov

Warren County

Circuit Clerk

Eighth Judicial Circuit
Warren County Justice Center, 1001 Center Street,
Bowling Green, KY 42101
Tel: (270) 746-7400 Fax: (270) 746-7501

Clerk of the Court **Brandi Duvall** . . . . (270) 746-7400
   E-mail: brandiduvall@kycourts.net

County Clerk

Office of the County Clerk
429 East Tenth Street, Suite 100, Bowling Green, KY 42101
P.O. Box 478, Bowling Green, KY 42102
Tel: (270) 842-9416 Fax: (270) 843-5319

County Clerk **Lynette Yates** . . . . (270) 842-9416
   E-mail: lynette.yates@ky.gov

Washington County

Circuit Clerk

Eleventh Judicial Circuit
Taylor County Justice Center, 300 East Main Street, Suite 301,
Campbellsville, KY 42718
Tel: (270) 465-6603 Fax: (270) 469-4804

Clerk of the Court, Washington County **JoAnne Miller** . . . (270) 336-3761
   100 East Main Street, Suite 100,   Fax: (270) 336-9824
   Springfield, KY 40069
   E-mail: joannemiller@kycourts.net

County Clerk

Office of the County Clerk
111 North Cross Main, Springfield, KY 40069
P.O. Box 446, Springfield, KY 40069
Tel: (859) 336-5425 Fax: (859) 336-5408

County Clerk **Glenn Black** . . . . (859) 336-5425
   E-mail: glenn.black@ky.gov

Wayne County

Circuit Clerk

Fifty-Seventh Judicial Circuit
Wayne County Justice Center, 100 West Columbia Avenue,
Monticello, KY 42633
Tel: (606) 340-8159 Fax: (606) 340-8168

Clerk of the Court, Wayne County **Patricia Lay** . . . . (606) 348-5841
   Wayne County Circuit Court Clerk,   Fax: (606) 348-4225
   100 West Columbia Avenue, Suite 101,
   Monticello, KY 42633
   E-mail: patricialay@kycourts.net

County Clerk

Office of the County Clerk
55 North Main Street, Suite 106, Monticello, KY 42633
Tel: (606) 348-5721 Fax: (606) 348-8303

County Clerk **Josephine Gregory** . . . . (606) 348-5721
   E-mail: josephine.gregory@ky.gov

Webster County

Circuit Clerk

Fifth Judicial Circuit
Webster County Courthouse, 35 US Highway, 41A-S, Dixon, KY 42409
Tel: (270) 639-5506 Fax: (270) 389-1572

Clerk of the Court, Webster County **Amy A. Villines** . . . . . (270) 639-9160
   35 U.S. Highway 41A South,   Fax: (270) 639-6757
   Dixon, KY 42409
   P.O. Box 290, Dixon, KY 42409
   E-mail: amyvillines@kycourts.net

County Clerk

Office of the County Clerk
25 US Highway 41-A South, Dixon, KY 42409
P.O. Box 19, Dixon, KY 42409
Tel: (270) 639-7006 Fax: (270) 639-7029

County Clerk **Valerie Franklin** . . . . (270) 639-7006
   E-mail: valerie.franklin@ky.gov

Whitley County

Circuit Clerk

Thirty-Fourth Judicial Circuit
Whitley County Courthouse, 100 Main Street,
Williamsburg, KY 40769-0329
Tel: (606) 549-0825 Fax: (606) 539-3933

Clerk of the Court, Whitley-Williamsburg County
   Gary W. Barton . . . . (606) 549-2973
   Whitley County Judicial Center, 100 Main Street,   Fax: (606) 549-3393
   Williamsburg, KY 40769-0329
   E-mail: garybarton@kycourts.net

County Clerk

Office of the County Clerk
200 Main Street, Suite 2, Williamsburg, KY 40769
P.O. Box 8, Williamsburg, KY 40769
Tel: (606) 549-6002 Fax: (606) 549-2790

County Clerk **Kay Schwartz** . . . . (606) 549-6002
   E-mail: kay.schwartz@ky.gov

Kentucky Court Clerks and Courthouses *continued*

Wolfe County

Circuit Clerk

Thirty-Ninth Judicial Circuit
P.O. Box 946, Jackson, KY 41339-0946
Tel: (606) 666-7130

Clerk of the Court, Wolfe County **Debra Sparks** . . . . (606) 668-3736
  Wolfe County Judicial Center, 133 Main Street,   Fax: (606) 668-3198
  Campton, KY 41301-0296

County Clerk

Office of the County Clerk
10 Court Street, Campton, KY 41301
P.O. Box 400, Campton, KY 41301
Tel: (606) 668-3515 Fax: (606) 668-3492

County Clerk **Steve Oliver** . . . . (606) 668-3515
  E-mail: stevef.oliver@ky.gov

Woodford County

Circuit Clerk

Fourteenth Judicial Circuit
Scott County Justice Center, 119 North Hamilton Street,
Georgetown, KY 40324
Tel: (502) 570-0947 Fax: (502) 570-0949

Clerk of the Court, Woodford County
  Christie Edwards . . . . (859) 873-3711
  130 Court Street, Versailles, KY 40383   Fax: (859) 879-8531
  E-mail: christieedwards@kycourts.net

County Clerk

Office of the County Clerk
103 South Main Street, Suite 120, Versailles, KY 40383
Tel: (859) 873-3421 Fax: (859) 873-6985

County Clerk **Sandra V. Jones** . . . . (859) 873-3421
  E-mail: sandra.jones@ky.gov

Counties Within Judicial Circuits

Circuit Court, 1st Circuit
Areas Covered: Fulton and Hickman Counties.

Circuit Court, 2nd Circuit
Areas Covered: McCracken County.

Circuit Court, 3rd Circuit
Areas Covered: Christian County.

Circuit Court, 4th Circuit
Areas Covered: Hopkins County.

Circuit Court, 5th Circuit
Areas Covered: Crittenden, Union, and Webster Counties.

Circuit Court, 6th Circuit
Areas Covered: Daviess County.

Kentucky Court Clerks and Courthouses *continued*

Circuit Court, 7th Circuit
Areas Covered: Logan and Todd Counties.

Circuit Court, 8th Circuit
Areas Covered: Warren County.

Circuit Court, 9th Circuit
Areas Covered: Hardin County.

Circuit Court, 10th Circuit
Areas Covered: Hart and LaRue Counties.

Circuit Court, 11th Circuit
Areas Covered: Green, Marion, Taylor, and Washington Counties.

Circuit Court, 12th Circuit
Areas Covered: Henry, Oldham, and Trimble Counties.

Circuit Court, 13th Circuit
Areas Covered: Garrard, Jessamine and Lincoln Counties.

Circuit Court, 14th Circuit
Areas Covered: Bourbon, Scott, and Woodford Counties.

Circuit Court, 15th Circuit
Areas Covered: Carroll, Grant, and Owen Counties.

Circuit Court, 16th Circuit
Areas Covered: Kenton County.

Circuit Court, 17th Circuit
Areas Covered: Campbell County.

Circuit Court, 18th Circuit
Areas Covered: Harrison, Nicholas, Pendleton, and Robertson Counties.

Circuit Court, 19th Circuit
Areas Covered: Bracken, Fleming, and Mason Counties.

Circuit Court, 20th Circuit
Areas Covered: Greenup and Lewis Counties.

Circuit Court, 21st Circuit
Areas Covered: Bath, Menifee, Montgomery, and Rowan Counties.

Circuit Court, 22nd Circuit
Areas Covered: Fayette County.

Circuit Court, 23rd Circuit
Areas Covered: Estill, Lee, and Owsley Counties.

Circuit Court, 24th Circuit
Areas Covered: Johnson, Lawrence, and Martin Counties.

(continued on next page)

Circuit Court, 25th Circuit
Areas Covered: Clark and Madison Counties.

Circuit Court, 26th Circuit
Areas Covered: Harlan County.

Circuit Court, 27th Circuit
Areas Covered: Knox and Laurel Counties.

Circuit Court, 28th Circuit
Areas Covered: Pulaski and Rockcastle Counties.

Circuit Court, 29th Circuit
Areas Covered: Adair and Casey Counties.

Circuit Court, 30th Circuit
Areas Covered: Jefferson County.

Circuit Court, 31st Circuit
Areas Covered: Floyd County.

Circuit Court, 32nd Circuit
Areas Covered: Boyd County.

Circuit Court, 33rd Circuit
Areas Covered: Perry County.

Circuit Court, 34th Circuit
Areas Covered: McCreary and Whitley Counties.

Circuit Court, 35th Circuit
Areas Covered: Pike County.

Circuit Court, 36th Circuit
Areas Covered: Knott and Magoffin Counties.

Circuit Court, 37th Circuit
Areas Covered: Carter, Elliott, and Morgan Counties.

Circuit Court, 38th Circuit
Areas Covered: Butler, Edmonson, Hancock, and Ohio Counties.

Circuit Court, 39th Circuit
Areas Covered: Breathitt, Powell, and Wolfe Counties.

Circuit Court, 40th Circuit
Areas Covered: Clinton, Russell and Wayne Counties.

Circuit Court, 41st Circuit
Areas Covered: Clay, Jackson, and Leslie Counties.

Circuit Court, 42nd Circuit
Areas Covered: Calloway County.

Circuit Court, 43rd Circuit
Areas Covered: Barren and Metcalfe Counties.

Circuit Court, 44th Circuit
Areas Covered: Bell County.

Circuit Court, 45th Circuit
Areas Covered: McLean and Muhlenberg Counties.

Circuit Court, 46th Circuit
Areas Covered: Breckinridge, Grayson, and Meade Counties.

Circuit Court, 47th Circuit
Areas Covered: Letcher County.

Circuit Court, 48th Circuit
Areas Covered: Franklin County.

Circuit Court, 49th Circuit
Areas Covered: Allen and Simpson Counties.

Circuit Court, 50th Circuit
Areas Covered: Boyle and Mercer Counties.

Circuit Court, 51st Circuit
Areas Covered: Henderson County.

Circuit Court, 52nd Circuit
Areas Covered: Graves County.

Circuit Court, 53rd Circuit
Areas Covered: Anderson, Shelby, and Spencer Counties.

Circuit Court, 54th Circuit
Areas Covered: Boone and Gallatin Counties.

Circuit Court, 55th Circuit
Areas Covered: Bullitt County.

Circuit Court, 56th Circuit
Areas Covered: Caldwell, Livingston, Lyon, and Trigg Counties.

Circuit Court, 57th Circuit
Areas Covered: Nelson County.

Circuit Court, 58th Circuit
Areas Covered: Marshall County.

Circuit Court, 59th Circuit
Areas Covered: Ballard and Carlisle Counties.

Circuit Court, 60th Circuit
Areas Covered: Cumberland and Monroe Counties.

Louisiana Court Clerks and Courthouses

The trial courts of general jurisdiction in Louisiana are called district courts. There are 42 judicial districts, each district consisting of at least one parish (county), plus the Civil District Court of Orleans Parish. The clerk in each parish functions both as District Court Clerk and Parish Clerk.

Supreme Court of Louisiana

400 Royal Street, Suite 4200, New Orleans, LA 70130-2104
Tel: (504) 310-2300
Internet: www.lasc.org

The Supreme Court consists of a chief justice and six justices who are elected on a nonpartisan basis from seven districts throughout the state for ten-year terms. The most senior justice is selected as chief justice and serves until retirement, which is mandatory at age seventy (seventy-five if elected under an earlier constitution). Vacancies are filled within one year by a special election called by the Governor. The Supreme Court has appellate jurisdiction over cases in which an ordinance or law has been declared unconstitutional or the death penalty has been imposed. The Court has exclusive original jurisdiction over disbarment proceedings and petitions for discipline of judges. The Court has discretionary review over decisions of the Louisiana Courts of Appeal and trial courts.

Court Staff

Clerk of the Court **John Tarlton Olivier** . . . . (504) 310-2300
   E-mail: jolivier@lasc.org

Louisiana Courts of Appeal

Internet: www.lasc.org

The Courts of Appeal are courts of intermediate appellate jurisdiction over all civil cases. The courts also have jurisdiction over all criminal cases triable by a jury, except for those in which the death penalty has been imposed. The jurisdiction of the courts is limited to matters of law in criminal cases and questions of fact and law in civil cases. The courts hear appeals from the Louisiana Family, District and Juvenile Courts; they also may issue writs when necessary. There are five judicial circuits in Louisiana, with a court of appeal in each circuit. These circuits, in turn, are divided into at least three districts. The judges are elected in nonpartisan elections in their respective districts and serve for ten years. The chief judge of each court is the most senior member of its court and may serve in this capacity as long as he serves on the court. Retirement is mandatory at the age of seventy; however, retired judges may serve by assignment of the Supreme Court. A judge who reaches the mandatory age while in office, may complete the term. Each court sits in panels of three judges, but may sit in larger panels when necessary.

Louisiana Court of Appeal, First Circuit

1600 North Third Street, Baton Rouge, LA 70802
P.O. Box 4408, Baton Rouge, LA 70821-4408
Tel: (225) 382-3000 Fax: (225) 382-3010
E-mail: webmaster@la-fcca.org
Internet: www.la-fcca.org

Areas Covered: Parishes of Ascension, Assumption, East Baton Rouge, East Feliciana, Iberville, Lafourche, Livingston, Pointe Coupee, St. Helena, St. Mary, St. Tammany, Tangipahoa, Terrebonne, Washington, West Baton Rouge and West Feliciana

Court Staff

Clerk of Court **Christine L. Crow** . . . . (225) 382-3000
   E-mail: ccrow@la-fcca.org

Louisiana Court of Appeal, Second Circuit

Pike Hall, Jr. Courthouse, 430 Fannin Street, Shreveport, LA 71101-5537
Tel: (318) 227-3700 Fax: (318) 227-3735
Internet: www.lacoa2.org

Areas Covered: Parishes of Bienville, Bossier, Caddo, Caldwell, Claiborne, DeSoto, East Carroll, Franklin, Jackson, Lincoln, Madison, Morehouse, Ouachita, Red River, Richland, Tensas, Union, Webster, West Carroll and Winn

Court Staff

Clerk of the Court and Court Administrator
   Lillian Evans Richie . . . .(318) 227-3702
   E-mail: lrichie@la2nd.org   Fax: (318) 227-3735

Louisiana Court of Appeal, Third Circuit

1000 Main Street, Lake Charles, LA 70615
P.O. Box 16577, Lake Charles, LA 70616
Tel: (337) 433-9403 Fax: (337) 491-2590
Internet: www.la3circuit.org

Areas Covered: Parishes of Acadia, Allen, Avoyelles, Beauregard, Calcasieu, Cameron, Catahoula, Concordia, Evageline, Grant, Iberia, Jefferson Davis, Lafayette, La Salle, Natchitoches, Rapides, Sabine, St. Landry, St. Martin, Vermilion and Vernon

Court Staff

Clerk of the Court **Charles Kelly McNeely** . . . . (337) 493-3012

Louisiana Court of Appeal, Fourth Circuit

400 Royal Street, New Orleans, LA 70130-2199
Tel: (504) 412-6001
Internet: www.la4th.org

Areas Covered: Parishes of Orleans, Plaquemines and St. Bernard

Court Staff

Clerk of Court **Danielle A. Schott** . . . . (504) 412-6001
   E-mail: das@la4th.org

Louisiana Court of Appeal, Fifth Circuit

101 Derbigny Street, Gretna, LA 70053
P.O. Box 489, Gretna, LA 70054
Tel: (504) 376-1400 Fax: (504) 376-1498
Internet: www.fifthcircuit.org

Areas Covered: Parishes of Jefferson, St. Charles, St. James and St. John the Baptist

Court Staff

Clerk of the Court **Cheryl Q. Landrieu** . . . . (504) 376-1400
   E-mail: clandrieu@fifthcircuit.org   Fax: (504) 376-1498

New Orleans First City Court

421 Loyola Avenue, Room 201, New Orleans, LA 70112
Tel: (504) 407-0400 Fax: (504) 592-9281

Court Staff

Clerk of Court **Ellen M. Hazeur** . . . . (504) 407-0400

(continued on next page)

New Orleans Second City Court

225 Morgan Street, Room 206, New Orleans, LA 70114
Tel: (504) 407-0435 Fax: (504) 366-2970

Court Staff
Clerk of Court **Darron Lombard** . . . . (504) 407-0435

Parish-By-Parish

Acadia Parish

Court Clerk

15th Judicial District Court of Louisiana
P.O. Box 1366, Crowley, LA 70527 (Acadia Office)
P.O. Box 3368, Lafayette, LA 70502 (Lafayette Office)
Tel: (337) 788-8814 (Acadia) Tel: (337) 269-5756 (Lafayette)
Fax: (337) 269-5737 (Lafayette)

Clerk of Court, Acadia Parish
 Robert T. "Robby" Barousse . . . . (337) 788-8881
P.O. Box 922, Crowley, LA 70527   Fax: (337) 788-1048
E-mail: robby@acadiaparishclerk.com

Allen Parish

Court Clerk

33rd Judicial District Court of Louisiana
Clerk of Court, Allen Parish **Gerald W. Harrington** . . . . . (337) 639-4351
 400 West Sixth Avenue, Oberlin, LA 70655   Fax: (337) 639-2030
 P.O. Box 248, Oberlin, LA 70655
 E-mail: apcofc@centurytel.net

Ascension Parish

Court Clerk

23rd Judicial District Court of Louisiana
Clerk of Court, Ascension Parish **Bridget Hanna** . . . . (225) 621-8400
 815 East Worthy, Gonzales, LA 70737   Fax: (225) 621-8403
 E-mail: bhanna@ascensionclerk.com

Assumption Parish

Court Clerk

23rd Judicial District Court of Louisiana
Clerk of Court, Assumption Parish **Darlene Landry** . . . . . . (985) 369-6653
 4809 Highway 1, Napoleonville, LA 70390   Fax: (985) 369-2032
 P.O. Box 249, Napoleonville, LA 70390
 E-mail: dlandry@assumptionclerk.com

Avoyelles Parish

Court Clerk

12th Judicial District Court of Louisiana
Clerk of Court, Avoyelles Parish **Connie B. Couvillon** . . . (318) 253-7523
 P.O. Box 196, Marksville, LA 71351   Fax: (318) 253-7578
 E-mail: cbc02@bellsouth.net

Beauregard Parish

Court Clerk

36th Judicial District Court of Louisiana
Clerk of Court, Beauregard Parish **Brian Lestage** . . . . (337) 463-8595
 201 West First Street, DeRidder, LA 70634   Fax: (337) 462-3196
 E-mail: beauregardcoc@att.net

Bienville Parish

Court Clerk

2nd Judicial District Court of Louisiana
Clerk of Court, Bienville Parish
 James W. "Jim" Martin . . . . (318) 263-2123
 100 Courthouse Drive, Room 100,   Fax: (318) 263-7426
 Arcadia, LA 71001
 E-mail: jimmartin@bienvilleparish.org

Bossier Parish

Court Clerk

26th Judicial District Court of Louisiana
P.O. Box 310, Benton, LA 71006
Tel: (318) 965-2336

Clerk of Court, Bossier Parish **Cynthia J. Johnston** . . . . . (318) 965-2336
 204 Burt Boulevard, Benton, LA 71006   Fax: (318) 965-1299
 E-mail: cindy.johnston@bossierclerk.com

Caddo Parish

Court Clerk

1st Judicial District Court of Louisiana
501 Texas Street, Shreveport, LA 71101-5408
Tel: (318) 226-6780

Clerk of Court, Caddo Parish **Gary Loftin** . . . . (318) 226-6780
 501 Texas Street, Room 103,
 Shreveport, LA 71101-5408
 E-mail: clerk@caddoclerk.com

Calcasieu Parish

Court Clerk

14th Judicial District Court of Louisiana
1001 Lakeshore Drive, Lake Charles, LA 70601
P.O. Box 3210, Lake Charles, LA 70602
Tel: (337) 721-3100 Tel: (337) 437-3332

Clerk of Court, Calcasieu Parish **H. Lynn Jones** . . . . (337) 437-3550
 1000 Ryan Street, Lake Charles, LA 70601   Fax: (337) 437-3804
 P.O. Box 1030, Lake Charles, LA 70602
 E-mail: lynnjones@calclerkofcourt.com

Caldwell Parish

Court Clerk

37th Judicial District Court of Louisiana
Clerk of Court, Caldwell Parish **Eugene Dunn** . . . . (318) 649-2272
 201 Main Street, Suite 1, Columbia, LA 71418   Fax: (318) 649-2037
 E-mail: caldclerk@bellsouth.net

Cameron Parish

Court Clerk

38th Judicial District Court of Louisiana
Clerk of Court, Cameron Parish **Carl Broussard** . . . . (337) 775-5316
  119 Smith Circle, Room 21,   Fax: (337) 775-7172
  Cameron, LA 70631
  P.O. Box 549, Cameron, LA 70631

Catahoula Parish

Court Clerk

7th Judicial District Court of Louisiana
Clerk of Court, Catahoula Parish **Janet Payne** . . . .(318) 744-5222
  301 Bushley Street, Harrisonburg, LA 71340   Fax: (318) 744-5488
  P.O. Box 654, Harrisonburg, LA 71340
  E-mail: jtpayne184@yahoo.com

Claiborne Parish

Court Clerk

2nd Judicial District Court of Louisiana
Clerk of Court, Claiborne Parish **James P. Gladney** . . . . . (318) 927-9601
  512 East Main Street, Homer, LA 71040   Fax: (318) 927-2345
  E-mail: claib212@bellsouth.net

Concordia Parish

Court Clerk

7th Judicial District Court of Louisiana
Clerk of Court, Concordia Parish
  Clyde R. Webber, Jr. . . . . (318) 336-4204
  4001 Carter Street, Room 5,
  Vidalia, LA 71373
  E-mail: clydewebber@aol.com

DeSoto Parish

Court Clerk

42nd Judicial District Court of Louisiana
Clerk of Court, DeSoto Parish **Jeremy Evans** . . . . (318) 872-3110
  101 Texas Street, Mansfield, LA 71052   Fax: (318) 872-4202
  E-mail: jeremye@desotoparishclerk.org

East Baton Rouge Parish

Court Clerk

19th Judicial District Court of Louisiana
Clerk of Court, East Baton Rouge Parish
  Doug Welborn . . . . (225) 389-3960
  222 St. Louis Street, Baton Rouge, LA 70802   Fax: (225) 389-5594
  P.O. Box 1991, Baton Rouge, LA 70821-1991
  E-mail: dwelborn@ebrclerkofcourt.org

East Carroll Parish

Court Clerk

6th Judicial District Court of Louisiana
Clerk of Court, East Carroll Parish
  Beatrice Allen Carter . . . . (318) 559-2399
  400 First Street, Suite 3,   Fax: (318) 559-0037
  Lake Providence, LA 71254
  E-mail: eastcarrollparis@bellsouth.net

East Feliciana Parish

Court Clerk

20th Judicial District Court of Louisiana
Clerk of Court, East Feliciana Parish **David Dart** . . . . (225) 683-5145
  12305 St. Helena Street, Clinton, LA 70722   Fax: (225) 683-3556
  P.O. Box 599, Clinton, LA 70722
  E-mail: david@eastfelicianaclerk.org

Evangeline Parish

Court Clerk

13th Judicial District Court of Louisiana
200 Court Street, Ville Platte, LA 70586
Tel: (337) 363-5671

Clerk of Court, Evangeline Parish
  Randall "Randy" Deshotel . . . . (337) 363-5671
  200 Court Street, Ville Platte, LA 70586   Fax: (337) 363-5780
  P.O. Box 347, Ville Platte, LA 70586-0347
  E-mail: evangelinecoc@yahoo.com

Franklin Parish

Court Clerk

5th Judicial District Court of Louisiana
Clerk of Court, Franklin Parish **Ann Johnson** . . . . (318) 435-5133
  P.O. Box 1564, Winnsboro, LA 71295   Fax: (318) 435-6792
  6550 Main Street, Winnsboro, LA 71295
  E-mail: ann@fpclerk.com

Grant Parish

Court Clerk

35th Judicial District Court of Louisiana
Clerk of Court, Grant Parish (Acting) **L. Davis Silk** . . . . . . (318) 627-3246
  200 Main Street, Colfax, LA 71417   Fax: (318) 627-3201
  E-mail: elraycoc@aol.com

Iberia Parish

Court Clerk

16th Judicial District Court of Louisiana
Clerk of Court, Iberia Parish **Mike Thibodeaux** . . . .(337) 365-7282
  300 Iberia Street, New Iberia, LA 70562
  P.O. Box 12010, New Iberia, LA 70562
  E-mail: iberiaclerk@bellsouth.net

Iberville Parish

Court Clerk

18th Judicial District Court of Louisiana
Clerk of Court, Iberville Parish
  J. Gerald "Bubbie" Dupont, Jr. . . . . (225) 687-5160
  58050 Meriam Street, Plaquemine, LA 70764-0423   Fax: (225) 687-5260
  P.O. Box 423, Plaquemine, LA 70765-0423
  E-mail: clerk@ibervilleclerk.com

(continued on next page)

Jackson Parish

Court Clerk

2nd Judicial District Court of Louisiana
Clerk of Court, Jackson Parish **Ann B. Walsworth** ...... (318) 259-2424
  P.O. Box 730, Jonesboro, LA 71251   Fax: (318) 395-0386
  E-mail: awalsworth@jacksonparishclerk.org

Jefferson Parish

Court Clerk

24th Judicial District Court of Louisiana
Clerk of Court, Jefferson Parish **Jon A. Gegenheimer** ... (504) 364-2900
  General Government Building,   Fax: (504) 362-6355
  200 Derbigny Street, Suite 5600,
  Gretna, LA 70053
  P.O. Box 10, Gretna, LA 70051-0010
  E-mail: jgegenheimer@jpclerkofcourt.us

Jefferson Davis Parish

Court Clerk

31st Judicial District Court of Louisiana
Clerk of Court, Jefferson Davis Parish
  Richard Arceneaux .... (337) 824-1160
  300 North State Street, Room 106,   Fax: (337) 824-1354
  Jennings, LA 70546
  P.O. Box 799, Jennings, LA 70546
  E-mail: rick@jeffdavisclerk.com

Lafayette Parish

Court Clerk

15th Judicial District Court of Louisiana
P.O. Box 1366, Crowley, LA 70527 (Acadia Office)
P.O. Box 3368, Lafayette, LA 70502 (Lafayette Office)
Tel: (337) 788-8814 (Acadia) Tel: (337) 269-5756 (Lafayette)
Fax: (337) 269-5737 (Lafayette)

Clerk of Court, Lafayette Parish **Louis J. Perret** .... (337) 291-6400
  800 South Buchanan, Lafayette, LA 70501-6853   Fax: (337) 291-6392
  E-mail: ljperret@lpclerk.com

Lafourche Parish

Court Clerk

17th Judicial District Court of Louisiana
Clerk of Court, Lafourche Parish **Vernon Rodrigue** ...... (985) 447-4841
  P.O. Box 818, Thibodaux, LA 70302-0818   Fax: (985) 447-5800
  E-mail: vautin@lafourcheclerk.com

LaSalle Parish

Court Clerk

28th Judicial District Court of Louisiana
Clerk of Court, LaSalle Parish **Steve D. Andrews** .... (318) 992-2158
  1050 Courthouse Street, Jena, LA 71342   Fax: (318) 992-2157
  E-mail: sandrewslasclerk@centurytel.net

Lincoln Parish

Court Clerk

3rd Judicial District Court of Louisiana
Clerk of Court, Lincoln Parish **Linda Cook** .... (318) 251-5130
  100 West Texas Avenue, Ruston, LA 71270   Fax: (318) 255-6004
  P.O. Box 924, Ruston, LA 71273-0924
  E-mail: lindat@lincolnparish.org

Livingston Parish

Court Clerk

21st Judicial District Court of Louisiana
Clerk of Court, Livingston Parish
  Thomas "Tom" Sullivan, Jr. .... (225) 686-2216 ext. 1100
  20180 Iowa Street, Livingston, LA 70754   Fax: (225) 686-1867
  P.O. Box 1150, Livingston, LA 70754
  E-mail: tsullivan@livclerk.org

Madison Parish

Court Clerk

6th Judicial District Court of Louisiana
Clerk of Court, Madison Parish **Marion Hopkins** .... (318) 574-0655
  100 North Cedar Street, Tallulah, LA 71282   Fax: (318) 574-3961
  P.O. Box 1710, Tallulah, LA 71282
  E-mail: mpcofc@bellsouth.net

Morehouse Parish

Court Clerk

4th Judicial District Court of Louisiana
Clerk of Court, Morehouse Parish **Carol Jones** .... (318) 281-3343
  100 East Madison, Bastrop, LA 71220   Fax: (318) 281-3775
  E-mail: morehouseclerk@gmail.com

Natchitoches Parish

Court Clerk

10th Judicial District Court of Louisiana
Clerk of Court, Natchitoches Parish **Louie Bernard** ...... (318) 352-8152
  P.O. Box 476, Natchitoches, LA 71458-0476   Fax: (318) 352-9321
  E-mail: lbernard@cp-tel.net

Orleans Parish – Civil

Court Clerk

41st Judicial District Court of Louisiana
Clerk of Court, Recorder of Conveyances and Recorder
  of Mortgages, Orleans Parish (Civil District)
  Dale N. Atkins .... (504) 407-0134
  421 Loyola Avenue, Room 402,   Fax: (504) 592-9128
  New Orleans, LA 70112
  1340 Poydras Street, Fourth Floor,
  New Orleans, LA 70112
  E-mail: daleatk@orleanscdc.com

Orleans Parish – Criminal

Court Clerk

41st Judicial District Court of Louisiana
Clerk of Court, Orleans Parish (Criminal District)
Arthur A. Morrell...........................(504) 658-9000
2700 Tulane Avenue, New Orleans, LA 70119   Fax: (504) 658-9183
E-mail: aamorrell@nola.gov

Orleans Parish – Recorder of Mortgages

Court Clerk

41st Judicial District Court of Louisiana
Clerk of Court, Recorder of Conveyances and Recorder
of Mortgages, Orleans Parish (Civil District)
Dale N. Atkins................................(504) 407-0134
421 Loyola Avenue, Room 402,   Fax: (504) 592-9128
New Orleans, LA 70112
1340 Poydras Street, Fourth Floor,
New Orleans, LA 70112
E-mail: daleatk@orleanscdc.com

Orleans Parish – Recorder of Conveyances

Court Clerk

41st Judicial District Court of Louisiana
Clerk of Court, Recorder of Conveyances and Recorder
of Mortgages, Orleans Parish (Civil District)
Dale N. Atkins................................(504) 407-0134
421 Loyola Avenue, Room 402,   Fax: (504) 592-9128
New Orleans, LA 70112
1340 Poydras Street, Fourth Floor,
New Orleans, LA 70112
E-mail: daleatk@orleanscdc.com

Ouachita Parish

Court Clerk

4th Judicial District Court of Louisiana
Clerk of Court, Ouachita Parish **Louise Bond**..........(318) 327-1444
300 St John Street, Monroe, LA 71201   Fax: (318) 327-1462
E-mail: opcclbond@aol.com

Plaquemines Parish

Court Clerk

25th Judicial District Court of Louisiana
301 Main Street, Belle Chasse, LA 70037
P.O. Box 40, Belle Chasse, LA 70037
Tel: (504) 297-5180 Fax: (504) 297-5195

Clerk of Court, Plaquemines Parish
Dorothy "Dot" Lundin..........................(504) 297-5182
P.O. Box 40, Belle Chasse, LA 70037
E-mail: dlundin@clerk25th.com

Pointe Coupee Parish

Court Clerk

18th Judicial District Court of Louisiana
Clerk of Court, Pointe Coupee Parish
Lanell Swindler Landry.......................(225) 638-9596
P.O. Box 38, New Roads, LA 70760   Fax: (225) 638-9590
E-mail: pcclerk@yahoo.com

Rapides Parish

Court Clerk

9th Judicial District Court of Louisiana
701 Murray Street, Alexandria, LA 71309
P.O. Box 1431, Alexandria, LA 71309
Tel: (318) 473-8153

Clerk of Court, Rapides Parish **Robin L. Hooter**........(318) 473-8153
701 Murray Street, Alexandria, LA 71309   Fax: (318) 473-4667
P.O. Box 952, Alexandria, LA 71309
E-mail: rlhooter@rapidesclerk.org

Red River Parish

Court Clerk

39th Judicial District Court of Louisiana
Clerk of Court, Red River Parish **Stuart R. Shaw**.......(318) 932-6741
615 East Carrol Street, Coushatta, LA 71019   Fax: (318) 932-3126
P.O. Box 485, Coushatta, LA 71019
E-mail: stuart@redriverclerk.com

Richland Parish

Court Clerk

5th Judicial District Court of Louisiana
Clerk of Court, Richland Parish **Stacie S. Williamson**...(318) 728-4171
708 Julia Street, Suite 103,   Fax: (318) 728-7020
Rayville, LA 71269
P.O. Box 119, Rayville, LA 71269
E-mail: richlandparishcc@bellsouth.net

Sabine Parish

Court Clerk

11th Judicial District Court of Louisiana
Clerk of Court, Sabine Parish **Tammy Foster**...........(318) 256-6223
400 South Capitol Street, Room 102,   Fax: (318) 256-9037
Many, LA 71449
E-mail: sabineclerk@bellsouth.net

St. Bernard Parish

Court Clerk

34th Judicial District Court of Louisiana
Clerk of Court, St. Bernard Parish **Randy Nunez**.......(504) 271-3434
9061 West Judge Perez Drive,   Fax: (504) 278-4380
Chalmette, LA 70043
P.O. Box 1746, Chalmette, LA 70044
E-mail: rsn@stbclerk.com

St. Charles Parish

Court Clerk

29th Judicial District Court of Louisiana
Clerk of Court, St. Charles Parish **Lance Marino**........(985) 783-6632
St. Charles Parish Courthouse, 15045 River Road,   Fax: (985) 783-2005
Hahnville, LA 70057
P.O. Box 424, Hahnville, LA 70057
E-mail: stcharlescoc@bellsouth.net

(continued on next page)

Louisiana Court Clerks and Courthouses *continued*

St. Helena Parish

Court Clerk

21st Judicial District Court of Louisiana
Clerk of Court, St. Helena Parish **Mildred T. Cyprian** . . . . (225) 222-4514
  369 Sitman Street, Greensburg, LA 70441   Fax: (225) 222-3443
  P.O. Box 308, Greensburg, LA 70441
  E-mail: mildredcyprian@yahoo.com

St. James Parish

Court Clerk

23rd Judicial District Court of Louisiana
Clerk of Court, St. James Parish
  Edmond E. Kinler, Jr. . . . . (225) 562-2270
  5800 Louisiana Highway 44,   Fax: (225) 562-2383
  Convent, LA 70723
  P.O. Box 63, Convent, LA 70723
  E-mail: mamclerk@yahoo.com

St. John the Baptist Parish

Court Clerk

40th Judicial District Court of Louisiana
Clerk of Court, St. John The Baptist Parish
  Eliana DeFrancesch . . . . (985) 497-3331 ext. 2103
  2393 Highway 18, Edgard, LA 70049
  E-mail: edefrancesch@stjohnclerk.org

St. Landry Parish

Court Clerk

27th Judicial District Court of Louisiana
Clerk of Court, St. Landry Parish **Charles Jagneaux** . . . . (337) 942-5606
  118 South Court Street, Opelousas, LA 70570   Tel: (337) 642-7265
  P.O. Box 750, Opelousas, LA 70570
  E-mail: stlancoc@bellsouth.net

St. Martin Parish

Court Clerk

16th Judicial District Court of Louisiana
Clerk of Court, St. Martin Parish **Becky P. Patin** . . . . (337) 394-2210
  415 St. Martin Street, Saint Martinville, LA 70582
  P.O. Box 308, Saint Martinville, LA 70582
  E-mail: beckypatin@stmartinparishclerkofcourt.com

St. Mary Parish

Court Clerk

16th Judicial District Court of Louisiana
Clerk of Court, St. Mary Parish **Cliff Dressel** . . . . (337) 828-4100
  500 Main Street, Franklin, LA 70538-1231
  P.O. Box 1231, Franklin, LA 70538-1231
  E-mail: stmaryclerk@teche.net

Louisiana Court Clerks and Courthouses *continued*

St. Tammany Parish

Court Clerk

22nd Judicial District Court of Louisiana
701 North Columbia Street, Covington, LA 70433
P.O. Box 1090, Covington, LA 70434 (St. Tammany Parish)
P.O. Box 607, Franklinton, LA 70438 (Washington Parish)
Tel: (985) 809-8700 (St. Tammany Parish)
Tel: (985) 839-7821 (Washington Parish)

Clerk of Court, St. Tammany Parish **Malise Prieto** . . . . . . (985) 809-8700
  701 North Columbia Street,
  Covington, LA 70433
  P.O. Box 1090, Covington, LA 70434
  E-mail: madameclerk@yahoo.com

Tangipahoa Parish

Court Clerk

21st Judicial District Court of Louisiana
Clerk of Court, Tangipahoa Parish **Julian E. Dufreche** . . . (985) 748-4146
  P.O. Box 667, Amite, LA 70422   Fax: (985) 748-6503
  E-mail: jdufreche@tangiclerk.org

Tensas Parish

Court Clerk

6th Judicial District Court of Louisiana
Clerk of Court, Tensas Parish **Ernest I. Sikes** . . . . (318) 766-3921
  201 Hancock Street, Saint Joseph, LA 71366   Fax: (318) 766-3926
  P.O. Box 78, Saint Joseph, LA 71366
  E-mail: tensasclerk@bellsouth.net

Terrebonne Parish

Court Clerk

32nd Judicial District Court of Louisiana
P.O. Box 1569, Houma, LA 70361
Tel: (504) 868-5660

Clerk of Court, Terrebonne Parish
  Theresa A. Robichaux . . . . (985) 868-5660
  P.O. Box 1569, Houma, LA 70361   Fax: (985) 868-5143
  E-mail: theresa.robichaux@yahoo.com

Union Parish

Court Clerk

3rd Judicial District Court of Louisiana
Clerk of Court, Union Parish **Dodi Dodd Eubanks** . . . . . . (318) 368-3055
  100 East Bayou Street, Suite 105,   Fax: (318) 368-3861
  Farmerville, LA 71241
  E-mail: upclerk@bayou.com

Vermilion Parish

Court Clerk

15th Judicial District Court of Louisiana
P.O. Box 1366, Crowley, LA 70527 (Acadia Office)
P.O. Box 3368, Lafayette, LA 70502 (Lafayette Office)
Tel: (337) 788-8814 (Acadia) Tel: (337) 269-5756 (Lafayette)
Fax: (337) 269-5737 (Lafayette)

Clerk of Court, Vermilion Parish
Diane Meaux Broussard . . . . (337) 898-1992
100 North State Street, Suite 101,   Fax: (337) 898-9803
Abbeville, LA 70510
E-mail: vermilionclerk@cox-internet.com

Vernon Parish

Court Clerk

30th Judicial District Court of Louisiana
Clerk of Court, Vernon Parish **Willie Deon, Jr.** . . . . (337) 238-1384
215 South Fourth Street, Leesville, LA 71446   Fax: (337) 238-9902
P.O. Box 40, Leesville, LA 71496-0040
E-mail: vernonclerk@bellsouth.net

Washington Parish

Court Clerk

22nd Judicial District Court of Louisiana
701 North Columbia Street, Covington, LA 70433
P.O. Box 1090, Covington, LA 70434 (St. Tammany Parish)
P.O. Box 607, Franklinton, LA 70438 (Washington Parish)
Tel: (985) 809-8700 (St. Tammany Parish)
Tel: (985) 839-7821 (Washington Parish)

Clerk of Court, Washington Parish **Johnny D. Crain** . . . . . (985) 839-4663
Washington and Main Street,   Fax: (985) 839-3116
Franklinton, LA 70438
P.O. Box 607, Franklinton, LA 70438
E-mail: washparcoc@yahoo.com

Webster Parish

Court Clerk

26th Judicial District Court of Louisiana
P.O. Box 310, Benton, LA 71006
Tel: (318) 965-2336

Clerk of Court, Webster Parish **Holli Vining** . . . . (318) 371-0366
410 Main Street, Minden, LA 71055   Fax: (318) 371-0226
P.O. Box 370, Minden, LA 71055
E-mail: hollivining@yahoo.com

West Baton Rouge Parish

Court Clerk

18th Judicial District Court of Louisiana
Clerk of Court- West Baton Rouge Parish
Mark Graffeo . . . . (225) 383-0378
850 8th Street, Port Allen, LA 70767   Fax: (225) 383-3694
P.O. Box 107, Port Allen, LA 70767
E-mail: mark.graffeo@wbrclerk.org

West Carroll Parish

Court Clerk

5th Judicial District Court of Louisiana
Clerk of Court, West Carroll Parish **Robyn Creech** . . . . . . (318) 428-3281
305 East Main Street, Room 101,   Fax: (318) 428-9896
Oak Grove, LA 71263
P.O. Box 1078, Oak Grove, LA 71263
E-mail: wcclerk@bellsouth.net

West Feliciana Parish

Court Clerk

20th Judicial District Court of Louisiana
Clerk of Court, West Feliciana Parish
Felicia Ann Hendl . . . . (225) 635-3794
4785 Prosperity Street, St. Francisville, LA 70775   Fax: (225) 635-3770
P.O. Box 1843, St. Francisville, LA 70775
E-mail: wfelicianaclerk@bellsouth.net

Winn Parish

Court Clerk

8th Judicial District Court of Louisiana
Clerk of Court, Winn Parish **Donald E. "Don" Kelley** . . . (318) 628-3515
119 West Main Street, Room 103,   Fax: (318) 628-3527
Winnfield, LA 71483
E-mail: winncoc@suddenlinkmail.com

Counties Within Judicial Districts

District Court, 1st Judicial District
Areas Covered: Caddo Parish.

District Court, 2nd Judicial District
Areas Covered: Claiborne, Bienville, and Jackson Parishes.

District Court, 3rd Judicial District
Areas Covered: Lincoln and Union Parishes.

District Court, 4th Judicial District
Areas Covered: Morehouse and Ouachita Parishes.

District Court, 5th Judicial District
Areas Covered: Franklin, Richland, and West Carroll Parishes.

District Court, 6th Judicial District
Areas Covered: East Carroll, Madison, and Tensas Parishes.

District Court, 7th Judicial District
Areas Covered: Catahoula Parish, and Concordia Parishes.

District Court, 8th Judicial District
Areas Covered: Winn Parish.

District Court, 9th Judicial District
Areas Covered: Rapides Parish.

(continued on next page)

Louisiana Court Clerks and Courthouses *continued*

District Court, 10th Judicial District
Areas Covered: Natchitoches Parish.

District Court, 11th Judicial District
Areas Covered: Sabine Parish.

District Court, 12th Judicial District
Areas Covered: Avoyelles Parish.

District Court, 13th Judicial District
Areas Covered: Evangeline Parish.

District Court, 14th Judicial District
Areas Covered: Calcasieu Parish.

District Court, 15th Judicial District
Areas Covered: Acadia, Lafayette, and Vermilion Parishes.

District Court, 16th Judicial District
Areas Covered: St. Martin, Iberia, and St. Mary Parishes.

District Court, 17th Judicial District
Areas Covered: Lafourche Parish.

District Court, 18th Judicial District
Areas Covered: Iberville Parishes, Pointe Coupee, and West Baton Rouge Parishes.

District Court, 19th Judicial District
Areas Covered: East Baton Rouge Parish.

District Court, 20th Judicial District
Areas Covered: East Feliciana Parish and West Feliciana Parishes.

District Court, 21st Judicial District
Areas Covered: Livingston, St. Helena, and Tangipahoa Parishes.

District Court, 22nd Judicial District
Areas Covered: St. Tammany Parish and Washington Parishes.

District Court, 23rd Judicial District
Areas Covered: Ascension, Assumption, and St. James Parishes.

District Court, 24th Judicial District
Areas Covered: Jefferson Parish.

District Court, 25th Judicial District
Areas Covered: Plaquemines Parish.

District Court, 26th Judicial District
Areas Covered: Bossier Parish and Webster Parishes.

District Court, 27th Judicial District
Areas Covered: St. Landry Parish.

Louisiana Court Clerks and Courthouses *continued*

District Court, 28th Judicial District
Areas Covered: La Salle Parish.

District Court, 29th Judicial District
Areas Covered: St. Charles Parish.

District Court, 30th Judicial District
Areas Covered: Vernon Parish.

District Court, 31st Judicial District
Areas Covered: Jefferson Davis Parish.

District Court, 32nd Judicial District
Areas Covered: Terrebonne Parish.

District Court, 33rd Judicial District
Areas Covered: Allen Parish.

District Court, 34th Judicial District
Areas Covered: St. Bernard Parish.

District Court, 35th Judicial District
Areas Covered: Grant Parish.

District Court, 36th Judicial District
Areas Covered: Beauregard Parish.

District Court, 37th Judicial District
Areas Covered: Caldwell Parish.

District Court, 38th Judicial District
Areas Covered: Cameron Parish.

District Court, 39th Judicial District
Areas Covered: Red River Parish.

District Court, 40th Judicial District
Areas Covered: St. John the Baptist Parish.

District Court, 41st Judicial District
Areas Covered: Orleans Parish.

District Court, 42nd Judicial District
Areas Covered: De Soto Parish.

Maine Court Clerks and Courthouses

The trial courts of general jurisdiction in Maine are called superior courts. There are 16 courts, one for each county. Each county has a Superior Court Clerk and a County Clerk. Note: The State of Maine has no intermediate appellate court.

Supreme Judicial Court of Maine

Maine Supreme Judicial Court, 205 Newbury Street, Room 139, Portland, ME 04101-4125
Tel: (207) 822-4146
Internet: www.courts.state.me.us

The Supreme Judicial Court, established in 1820, consists of a chief justice and six associate justices who are appointed by the Governor with consent of the Maine State Legislature for seven-year terms. Three justices are appointed by the chief justice to serve as the Sentence Review Panel for the review of criminal sentences of one year or more. The Supreme Judicial Court hears appeals of civil and criminal cases from the Maine Superior Court, appeals from final judgments, orders and decrees of the Maine Probate Court, appeals of decisions of the Maine Public Utilities Commission and the Workers' Compensation Board, interlocutory criminal appeals and appeals of decisions from a single justice of the Court. The Court makes decisions regarding legislative apportionment and renders advisory opinions concerning important questions of law when requested by the Governor or State Legislature.

Court Staff
Clerk **Matthew E. Pollack** . . . . (207) 822-4146
   E-mail: matthew.pollack@courts.maine.gov

County-By-County

Androscoggin County

Superior Court Clerk

Maine Superior Court
Clerk of Court, Androscoggin County **Linda Mason** . . . . . (207) 783-5458
   Two Turner Street, Auburn, ME 04212
   P.O. Box 3660, Auburn, ME 04212
   E-mail: linda.mason@courts.maine.gov

County Clerk

Office of the County Clerk
Two Turner Street, Auburn, ME 04210
Tel: (207) 784-8390 Fax: (207) 782-5367

County Clerk **Patricia Fournier** . . . . (207) 784-8390
   E-mail: pfournier@androscoggincountymaine.gov

Aroostook County

Superior Court Clerk

Maine Superior Court
Clerk of Court, Aroostook County **Diane Glidden** . . . . (207) 498-8125
   144 Sweden Street, Suite 101,
   Caribou, ME 04736
   E-mail: diane.glidden@courts.maine.gov

County Clerk

Office of the County Administrator
144 Sweden Street, Suite 1, Caribou, ME 04736
Tel: (207) 493-3318 Fax: (207) 493-3491

County Clerk **Douglas F. "Doug" Beaulieu** . . . . (207) 493-3318
   E-mail: doug@aroostook.me.us

Cumberland County

Superior Court Clerk

Maine Superior Court
Clerk of Court, Cumberland County **Sally Bourget** . . . . . . (207) 822-4109
   205 Newbury Street, Portland, ME 04112
   P.O. Box 412, Portland, ME 04112
   E-mail: sally.bourget@courts.maine.gov

County Clerk

Office of the County Manager/Clerk
142 Federal Street, Room 102, Portland, ME 04101-4196
Fax: (207) 871-8292

County Manager/Clerk **Peter J. Crichton** . . . . (207) 871-8380
   E-mail: crichton@cumberlandcounty.org

Franklin County

Superior Court Clerk

Maine Superior Court
Clerk of Court, Franklin County **Laureen Pratt** . . . . (207) 778-3346
   140 Farm Street, Farmington, ME 04938

County Clerk

Office of the County Clerk
140 Main Street, Suite 3, Farmington, ME 04938
Tel: (207) 778-6614 Fax: (207) 778-5899

County Clerk **Julie Magoon** . . . . (207) 778-6614
   E-mail: jmagoon@franklincountyme.com

Hancock County

Superior Court Clerk

Maine Superior Court
Clerk of Court, Hancock County **Terry Harding** . . . . (207) 667-7176
   50 State Street, Ellsworth, ME 04605
   E-mail: terry.harding@courts.maine.gov

County Clerk

Office of the County Administrator
50 State Street, Suite 7, Ellsworth, ME 04605
Tel: (207) 667-9542 Fax: (207) 667-1412

County Administrator **Eugene Conlogue** . . . . (207) 667-9542

Kennebec County

Superior Court Clerk

Maine Superior Court
Clerk of Court, Kennebec County **Michele Lumbert** . . . . . (207) 624-5800
   95 State Street, Augusta, ME 04330
   E-mail: michele.lumbert@courts.maine.gov

(continued on next page)

County Administrator

Office of the County Administrator
125 State Street, Augusta, ME 04330
Tel: (207) 622-0971 Fax: (207) 623-4083

County Administrator **Robert G. Devlin** . . . . (207) 622-0971 ext. 255
    E-mail: bgdevlin@kennebecso.com

Knox County

Superior Court Clerk

Maine Superior Court
Clerk of Court, Knox County **Eileen Bridges** . . . . (207) 594-2576
    62 Union Street, Rockland, ME 04841
    E-mail: eileen.bridges@courts.maine.gov

County Administrator

Office of the County Administrator
62 Union Street, Rockland, ME 04841
Tel: (207) 594-0420 Fax: (207) 594-0443

County Administrator **Andrew L. Hart** . . . . (207) 594-0420
    E-mail: ahart@knoxcountymaine.gov

Lincoln County

Superior Court Clerk

Maine Superior Court
Clerk of Court, Lincoln County **Bethany Gabrey** . . . . (207) 882-7517
    32 High Street, Wiscasset, ME 04578
    P.O. Box 249, Wiscasset, ME 04578
    E-mail: bethany.gabrey@courts.maine.gov

County Administrator

Office of the County Administrator
32 High Street, Wiscasset, ME 04578
P.O. Box 249, Wiscasset, ME 04578
Tel: (207) 882-6311 Fax: (207) 882-4320

County Administrator **John O'Connell** . . . . (207) 882-6311
    E-mail: administrator@lincolncountymaine.me

Oxford County

Superior Court Clerk

Maine Superior Court
Clerk of Court, Oxford County **Michelle Howe** . . . . (207) 743-8936
    26 Western Avenue, South Paris, ME 04281
    P.O. Box 179, South Paris, ME 04281
    E-mail: michelle.howe@courts.maine.gov

County Clerk

Office of the County Clerk
26 Western Avenue, South Paris, ME 04281
Tel: (207) 743-6359 Fax: (207) 743-1545

County Clerk **Scott Cole** . . . . (207) 743-6359
    E-mail: scole@oxfordcounty.org

Penobscot County

Superior Court Clerk

Maine Superior Court
Clerk of Court, Penobscot County **Penny Reckards** . . . . . . (207) 561-2300
    78 Exchange Street, Bangor, ME 04401
    E-mail: penny.reckards@courts.maine.gov

County Administrator

Office of the County Administrator
97 Hammond Street, Bangor, ME 04401
Tel: (207) 942-8535 Fax: (207) 945-6027

County Administrator **William "Bill" Collins** . . . . . . (207) 942-8535 ext. 1
    E-mail: bcollins@penobscot-county.net

Piscataquis County

Superior Court Clerk

Maine Superior Court
Clerk of Court, Piscataquis County **Lisa Richardson** . . . . . (207) 564-2240
    159 East Main Street, Suite 21,
    Dover Foxcroft, ME 04426
    E-mail: lisa.richardson@courts.maine.gov

County Manager

Office of the County Manager
163 East Main Street, Dover Foxcroft, ME 04426
Tel: (207) 564-2161 Fax: (207) 564-3022

County Manager **Thomas K. Lizotte** . . . . (207) 564-2161
    E-mail: countymanager@piscataquis.us

Sagadahoc County

Superior Court Clerk

Maine Superior Court
Clerk of Court, Sagadahoc County **Anita Alexander** . . . . . (207) 443-9733
    752 High Street, Bath, ME 04530

County Administrator

Office of the County Administrator
752 High Street, Bath, ME 04530
Tel: (207) 443-8200 Fax: (207) 443-8213

County Administrator **Pamela A. Hile** . . . . (207) 443-8200
    E-mail: administrator@sagcounty.com

Somerset County

Superior Court Clerk

Maine Superior Court
Clerk of Court, Somerset County **Susan Furbush** . . . . (207) 474-5161
    41 Court Street, Skowhegan, ME 04976
    P.O. Box 725, Skowhegan, ME 04976
    E-mail: susan.furbush@courts.maine.gov

County Administrator

Office of the County Administrator
41 Court Street, Skowhegan, ME 04976
Tel: (207) 474-9861 Fax: (207) 474-7405

County Administrator **Dawn DiBlasi** . . . . (207) 474-9861
    E-mail: ddiblasi@somersetcounty-me.org

Waldo County

Superior Court Clerk

Maine Superior Court
Clerk of Court, Waldo County **Brooke Otis** . . . . (207) 338-1940
    137 Church Street, Belfast, ME 04915
    E-mail: brooke.otis@courts.maine.gov

Maine Court Clerks and Courthouses *continued*

County Clerk

Office of the County Clerk
39B Spring Street, Belfast, ME 04915
Tel: (207) 338-3282   Fax: (207) 338-6788

County Clerk **Barbara L. Arseneau** . . . . (207) 338-3282
    E-mail: countyclerk@waldocountyme.gov

Washington County

Superior Court Clerk

Maine Superior Court
Clerk of Court, Washington County
    Pamela McPherson . . . . (207) 255-3326
    47 Court Street, Machias, ME 04654
    P.O. Box 526, Machias, ME 04654

County Manager

Office of the County Manager
85 Court Street, Machias, ME 04654
P.O. Box 297, Machias, ME 04654
Tel: (207) 255-3127   Fax: (207) 255-3313

County Manager **Betsy Fitzgerald** . . . . (207) 255-3127
    E-mail: manager@washingtoncountymaine.com

York County

Superior Court Clerk

Maine Superior Court
Clerk of Court, York County (Acting) **Tamara Rueda** . . . . (207) 324-5122
    45 Kennebunk Road, Alfred, ME 04002
    P.O. Box 160, Alfred, ME 04002
    E-mail: tamara.rueda@courts.maine.gov

County Manager

Office of the County Manager
149 Jordan Springs Road, Alfred, ME 04002
Tel: (207) 324-1571   Fax: (207) 324-9494

County Manager **Gregory Zinser** . . . . (207) 459-2312
    E-mail: gtzinser@co.york.me.us

Maryland Court Clerks and Courthouses

The trial courts of general jurisdiction in Maryland are called circuit courts. There are eight judicial circuits, each circuit consisting of at least one county. In each county there is a clerk of the circuit court and a county clerk or administrator who has administrative duties.

Court of Appeals of Maryland

Robert C. Murphy Courts of Appeal Building, 401 Bosley Avenue, Towson, MD 21204
Tel: (410) 260-1500 Tel: (800) 926-2583 (Toll Free)
Internet: www.mdcourts.gov

The Court of Appeals, created by the Maryland Constitution in 1776, is divided into seven appellate judicial circuits and consists of a chief judge and six judges; one elected in each appellate circuit. Judges are initially appointed by the Governor and confirmed by the Maryland State Senate. Appointed judges face a retention vote after one year in a general election for a ten-year term. The chief judge is designated by the Governor as the constitutional administrative head of the Maryland court system and serves until the end of his term. Retirement is mandatory at age seventy; however, retired judges may be recalled for temporary assignment. The Court of Appeals has exclusive appellate jurisdiction in criminal cases when judgment of death has been pronounced or when a question certified under the Uninformed Certified Questions of Law Act is involved. The Court exercises discretionary review of cases pending in or decided by the Court of Special Appeals of Maryland. The Court has rule-making and supervisory control over the lower courts and regulates admission to the bar and the conduct of its members and members of the bench.

Court Staff
Clerk of Court **Bessie M. Decker** . . . . (410) 260-1500
  E-mail: bessie.decker@mdcourts.gov

Court of Special Appeals of Maryland

Robert C. Murphy Courts of Appeal Building, 361 Rowe Boulevard, 2nd Floor, Annapolis, MD 21401
Tel: (410) 260-1450
Tel: (888) 200-7444 (Direct line from Washington, DC (Toll-free))
Internet: www.mdcourts.gov

The Court of Special Appeals, established in 1966, is divided into the same seven appellate judicial circuits as the Court of Appeals of Maryland and consists of a chief judge and twelve judges. One judge is appointed from each circuit. The remaining six judges are appointed at large. Judges are initially appointed by the Governor and confirmed by the Maryland State Senate, and they run for retention for ten-year terms at the next general election occurring at least one year after the appointment. The chief judge is appointed by the Governor and serves until the end of his or her term. Retirement is mandatory at age seventy; however, retired judges may be recalled for temporary assignments. The Court of Special Appeals has exclusive initial appellate jurisdiction over any reviewable judgment, decree, order or other action of the Maryland Circuit Court or Orphans' Court except as provided by law.

Court Staff
Clerk of the Court **Gregory Hilton** . . . . (410) 260-1459
  E-mail: greg.hilton@mdcourts.gov

County-By-County

Allegany County

Court Clerk

Allegany County Circuit Court
Courthouse, 30 Washington Street, Cumberland, MD 21502
Tel: (301) 777-5923 TTY: (301) 777-5825
Tel: (800) 988-9087 (Toll-Free in Maryland)

Clerk of Court **Dawne D. Lindsey** . . . . (301) 777-5923
  E-mail: dawne.lindsey@mdcourts.gov

Anne Arundel County

Court Clerk

Anne Arundel County Circuit Court
7 Church Circle, Annapolis, MD 21401
Tel: (410) 222-1397 TTY: (410) 222-1429
Tel: (888) 246-0615 (Toll-free in Maryland)

Clerk of Court **Robert P. "Bob" Duckworth** . . . . (410) 222-1397
  E-mail: robert.duckworth@mdcourts.gov

Baltimore City

Court Clerk

Baltimore City Circuit Court
Clarence M. Mitchell, Jr. Courthouse, 100 North Calvert Street, Baltimore, MD 21202
Courthouse East, 111 North Calvert Street, Baltimore, MD 21202
Tel: (410) 333-3722 TTY: (410) 333-4389

Clerk of Court **Lavinia G. Alexander** . . . . (443) 333-3733

Baltimore County

Court Clerk

Baltimore County Circuit Court
County Courts Building, 401 Bosley Avenue, Towson, MD 21204
Tel: (410) 887-2601 Tel: (800) 938-5802 (Toll-free in Maryland)
Fax: (410) 887-3062

Clerk of Court **Julie Ensor** . . . . (410) 887-2998
  E-mail: julie.ensor@mdcourts.gov

Calvert County

Court Clerk

Calvert County Circuit Court
Courthouse, 175 Main Street, Prince Frederick, MD 20678
Tel: (410) 535-1660 TTY: (410) 535-4392
Tel: (888) 535-0113 (Toll-free in Maryland)

Clerk of Court **Kathy P. Smith** . . . . (410) 535-1660
  E-mail: kathy.smith@mdcourts.gov

(continued on next page)

Caroline County

Court Clerk

Caroline County Circuit Court
Court House, 109 Market Street, Denton, MD 21629
Tel: (410) 479-1811

Clerk of Court **F. Dale Miner** . . . . (410) 479-1811

Carroll County

Court Clerk

Carroll County Circuit Court
55 North Court Street, Westminster, MD 21157
Tel: (410) 386-8710 TTY: (800) 735-2258
Tel: (888) 786-0039 (Toll-free in Maryland) Fax: (410) 876-0822

Clerk of the Court **Donald B. Sealing II** . . . .(410) 386-8710
E-mail: donald.sealing@mdcourts.gov

Cecil County

Court Clerk

Cecil County Circuit Court
129 East Main Street, Elkton, MD 21921
Tel: (410) 996-1021 TTY: (410) 398-2097
Tel: (800) 287-0576 (Toll-free in Maryland) Fax: (410) 392-6032

Clerk of Court **Charlene Notarcola** . . . . (410) 996-3023
E-mail: derrick.lowe@mdcourts.gov

Charles County

Court Clerk

Charles County Circuit Court
200 Charles Street, P.O. Box 970, La Plata, MD 20646
Tel: (301) 932-3201 Tel: (301) 870-2659 TTY: (301) 753-4258
Tel: (888) 932-2072 (Toll-free in Maryland) Fax: (301) 932-3206

Clerk of Court **Sharon L. "Sherri" Hancock** . . . .(301) 932-3201
E-mail: sharon.hancock@mdcourts.gov

Dorchester County

Court Clerk

Dorchester County Circuit Court
206 High Street, P.O. Box 150, Cambridge, MD 21613
Tel: (410) 228-0481 TTY: (800) 735-2258
Tel: (800) 340-9186 (Toll-free in Maryland)

Clerk of Court **Amy J. Craig** . . . . (410) 228-0481
E-mail: amy.craig@mdcourts.gov

Frederick County

Court Clerk

Frederick County Circuit Court
100 West Patrick Street, Frederick, MD 21701
Tel: (301) 600-1976 TTY: (800) 735-2258
Tel: (800) 341-8797 (Toll-free in Maryland)

Clerk of Court **Sandra K. Dalton** . . . . (301) 600-1976
E-mail: sandra.dalton@mdcourts.gov

Garrett County

Court Clerk

Garrett County Circuit Court
203 South 4th Street, Room 109, P.O. Box 447, Oakland, MD 21550
Tel: (301) 334-1937 TTY: (301) 334-5027
Tel: (800) 989-9760 (Toll-free in Maryland) Fax: (301) 334-5017

Clerk of Court **Timothy W. Miller** . . . . (301) 334-1942
E-mail: tim.miller@mdcourts.gov

Harford County

Court Clerk

Harford County Circuit Court
20 West Courtland Street, Bel Air, MD 21014
Tel: (410) 638-3426 Tel: (410) 879-2000
Tel: (800) 989-8296 (Toll-free in Maryland)

Clerk of Court **James Reilly** . . . . (410) 838-4952
E-mail: james.reilly@mdcourts.gov

Howard County

Court Clerk

Howard County Circuit Court
8360 Court Avenue, Ellicott City, MD 21045
Tel: (410) 313-2111 TTY: (410) 313-3840
Tel: (888) 313-0197 (Toll-free in Maryland)

Clerk of Court **Wayne A. Robey** . . . .(410) 313-2160
E-mail: wayne.robey@mdcourts.gov

Kent County

Court Clerk

Kent County Circuit Court
103 North Cross Street, Chestertown, MD 21620
Tel: (410) 778-7460 TTY: (410) 778-0608
Tel: (800) 989-2520 (Toll-free in Maryland)

Clerk of Court **Mark L. Mumford** . . . . (240) 778-7460
E-mail: kentcc@courts.state.md.us

Montgomery County

Court Clerk

Montgomery County Circuit Court
Maryland Judicial Center, 50 Maryland Avenue, Rockville, MD 20850
Tel: (240) 777-9400 TTY: (240) 777-9500
Tel: (888) 287-0593 (Toll-free in Maryland)

Clerk of Court **Barbara H. Meiklejohn** . . . .(240) 777-9400
E-mail: barbara.meiklejohn@mdcourts.gov

Prince George's County

Court Clerk

Prince George's County Circuit Court
Court House, 14735 Main Street, Upper Marlboro, MD 20772
Tel: (410) 952-3318 TTY: (301) 952-3925
Tel: (800) 937-1335 (Toll-free in Maryland)

Clerk of Court **Marilynn M. Bland** . . . . (301) 952-3318
E-mail: marilynn.bland@mdcourts.gov

Maryland Court Clerks and Courthouses *continued*

Queen Anne's County

Court Clerk

Queen Anne's County Circuit Court
100 Courthouse Square, Centreville, MD 21617
Tel: (410) 758-1773   TTY: (410) 758-6739
Tel: (800) 987-7591 (Toll-free in Maryland)

Clerk of Court **Scott MacGlashan** . . . . (410) 758-1773 ext. 116
E-mail: scott.macglashan@mdcourts.gov

St. Mary's County

Court Clerk

St. Mary's County Circuit Court
41605 Courthouse Drive, Leonardtown, MD 20650
Tel: (301) 475-7844   TTY: (301) 475-6597
Tel: (800) 988-5052 (Toll-free in Maryland)

Clerk of Court **Joan W. Williams** . . . . (301) 475-7844
E-mail: joan.williams@mdcourts.gov

Somerset County

Court Clerk

Somerset County Circuit Court
Court House, 30512 Prince William Street, Princess Anne, MD 21853
Tel: (410) 845-4840   Tel: (800) 341-2206 (Toll-free in Maryland)

Clerk of Court **Charles T. Horner** . . . . (410) 845-4840

Talbot County

Court Clerk

Talbot County Circuit Court
Court House, 11 North Washington Street, Suite 16, Easton, MD 21601
Tel: (410) 770-6801   Tel: (800) 339-3403 (Toll-free in Maryland)
Fax: (410) 770-6802

Clerk of Court **Mary Ann Shortall** . . . . (410) 822-2611
E-mail: maryann.shortall@mdcourts.gov

Washington County

Court Clerk

Washington County Circuit Court
24 Summit Avenue, Hagerstown, MD 21740
P.O. Box 229, Hagerstown, MD 21741
Tel: (301) 733-8660   TTY: (301) 791-2632
Tel: (800) 937-2062 (Toll-free in Maryland) Fax: (301) 791-1151

Clerk of Court **Dennis J. Weaver** . . . . (301) 733-8660
E-mail: dennis.weaver@mdcourts.gov

Wicomico County

Court Clerk

Wicomico County Circuit Court
101 North Division Street, Courthouse, Room 105, Salisbury, MD 21801
P.O. Box 198, Salisbury, MD 21803-0198
Tel: (410) 543-6551 ext. 207   TTY: (410) 548-3268
Tel: (800) 989-6592 (Toll-free in Maryland) Fax: (410) 546-8590

Clerk of Court **Mark S. Bowen** . . . . (410) 543-6551 ext. 159
E-mail: mark.bowen@mdcourts.gov

Maryland Court Clerks and Courthouses *continued*

Worcester County

Court Clerk

Worcester County Circuit Court
Court House, One West Market Street, Room 104, P.O. Box 40,
Snow Hill, MD 21863
Tel: (410) 632-0600   Tel: (800) 340-0691 (Toll-free in Maryland)

Clerk of Court **Susan Braniecki** . . . . (410) 632-5660

Counties Within Judicial Circuits

Circuit Court, 1st Judicial Circuit
Areas Covered: Dorchester, Somerset, Wicomico, and Worcester
Counties.

Circuit Court, 2nd Judicial Circuit
Areas Covered: Caroline, Cecil, Kent, Queen Anne's, and Talbot
Counties.

Circuit Court, 3rd Judicial Circuit
Areas Covered: Baltimore and Harford Counties.

Circuit Court, 4th Judicial Circuit
Areas Covered: Allegany, Garrett, and Washington Counties.

Circuit Court, 5th Judicial Circuit
Areas Covered: Anne Arundel, Carroll, and Howard Counties.

Circuit Court, 6th Judicial Circuit
Areas Covered: Frederick and Montgomery Counties.

Circuit Court, 7th Judicial Circuit
Areas Covered: Calvert, Charles, Prince George's, and St. Mary's
Counties.

Circuit Court, 8th Judicial Circuit
Areas Covered: Baltimore City.

Massachusetts Court Clerks and Courthouses

The Massachusetts court system includes the Supreme Judicial Court, the Appeals Court, and the Trial Court of the Commonwealth. The Trial Court is the court of general jurisdiction and consists of the administrative office and seven departments plus the Offices of the Commission of Probation and the Jury Commissioner. The Clerks of Court for the Superior Court for each of the 14 counties is given below; this is followed by a listing of the 21 offices of the Registry of Deeds.

Massachusetts Supreme Judicial Court

John Adams Courthouse, One Pemberton Square, Suite 2500,
Boston, MA 02108-1750
Tel: (617) 557-1000 Fax: (617) 723-3577
Internet: www.mass.gov/courts/sjc

The Supreme Judicial Court consists of a chief justice and six associate justices who are appointed by the Governor with the consent of the Massachusetts Executive Council to serve until age seventy. The Supreme Judicial Court has concurrent appellate jurisdiction with the Massachusetts Appeals Court over civil and criminal matters in all lower courts. The Court has original appellate jurisdiction in cases of first degree murder and in cases that the Supreme Judicial Court or the Appeals Court certifies for direct review or one that has broad public concern. The Court may render advisory opinions to the State Legislature, the Governor, and the Executive Council.

Court Staff

Clerk for the Commonwealth **Francis V. Kenneally** . . . . . . (617) 557-1020
    E-mail: francis.kenneally@sjc.state.ma.us   Fax: (617) 557-1145
Clerk of the Supreme Judicial Court, Suffolk County
    Maura Sweeney Doyle . . . .(617) 557-1180
    John Adams Courthouse, One Pemberton Square,   Fax: (617) 523-1540
    First Floor, Suite 1300, Boston, MA 02108
    E-mail: maura.doyle@sjc.state.ma.us

Massachusetts Appeals Court

John Adams Courthouse, One Pemberton Square, Suite 3500,
Boston, MA 02108-1705
Tel: (617) 725-8106
Internet: www.mass.gov/courts/appealscourt

The Appeals Court consists of a chief justice and 24 associate justices who are appointed by the Governor with the consent of the Massachusetts Governor's Council to serve until age seventy. The justices sit in panels of three or more as determined by the chief justice of the Appeals Court. The Appeals Court has concurrent appellate jurisdiction with the Supreme Judicial Court in civil and equity matters, administrative determinations and proceedings related to extraordinary writs, and in criminal matters except appeals from first degree murder convictions. The Court has appellate jurisdiction over final decisions of the Massachusetts Employee Relations Board, the Appellate Tax Board and the Department of Industrial Accidents.

Court Staff

Clerk of the Appeals Court **Joseph F. Stanton** . . . . (617) 725-8106
    E-mail: joseph.stanton@appct.state.ma.us

County-By-County

Barnstable County

Clerk of Court

Superior Court Department
Suffolk County Courthouse, Three Pemberton Square, Boston, MA 02108

Clerk of Court, Barnstable County
    Scott W. Nickerson . . . .(508) 375-6684
    Barnstable Superior Court, 3195 Main Street,
    Barnstable, MA 02630
    P.O. Box 425, Barnstable, MA 02630

Berkshire County

Clerk of Court

Superior Court Department
Suffolk County Courthouse, Three Pemberton Square, Boston, MA 02108

Clerk of Court, Berkshire County
    Deborah S. Capeless . . . . (413) 499-7487
    76 East Street, Pittsfield, MA 01201

Bristol County

Clerk of Court

Superior Court Department
Suffolk County Courthouse, Three Pemberton Square, Boston, MA 02108

Clerk of Court, Bristol County **Marc J. Santos** . . . . (508) 823-6588
    Nine Court Street, Room 13,
    Taunton, MA 02780

Dukes County

Clerk of Court

Superior Court Department
Suffolk County Courthouse, Three Pemberton Square, Boston, MA 02108

Clerk of Court, Dukes County **Joseph Sollitto, Jr.** . . . . . . (508) 627-4668
    P.O. Box 1267, Edgartown, MA 02539   Fax: (508) 627-7571
    Courthouse, Main Street, Edgartown, MA 02539

Essex County

Clerk of Court

Superior Court Department
Suffolk County Courthouse, Three Pemberton Square, Boston, MA 02108

Clerk of Court, Essex County **Thomas H. Driscoll, Jr.** . . . . (978) 744-5500
    J. Michael Ruane Judicial Center, 56 Federal Street,   Fax: (978) 741-0691
    Salem, MA 01970

Franklin County

Clerk of Court

Superior Court Department
Suffolk County Courthouse, Three Pemberton Square, Boston, MA 02108

Clerk of Court, Franklin County
    Susan K. Emond . . . .(413) 774-5535 ext. 248
    Franklin Superior Court, 425 Main Street,   Fax: (413) 774-4770
    Greenfield, MA 01302
    P.O. Box 1573, Greenfield, MA 01302

(continued on next page)

Hampden County

Clerk of Court

Superior Court Department

Suffolk County Courthouse, Three Pemberton Square, Boston, MA 02108

Clerk of Court, Hampden County **Laura S. Gentile** . . . . . . (413) 735-6016
Hampden Superior Court, 50 State Street,
Springfield, MA 01102-0559
P.O. Box 559, Springfield, MA 01102-0559

Hampshire County

Clerk of Court

Superior Court Department

Suffolk County Courthouse, Three Pemberton Square, Boston, MA 02108

Clerk of Court, Hampshire County
Harry Jekanowski . . . . (413) 584-5810 ext. 293
Hampshire Superior Court, 15 Gothic Street,   Fax: (413) 586-8217
Northampton, MA 01061
P.O. Box 119, Northampton, MA 01061

Middlesex County

Clerk of Court

Superior Court Department

Suffolk County Courthouse, Three Pemberton Square, Boston, MA 02108

Clerk of Court, Middlesex County
Michael A. Sullivan . . . . (781) 939-2700
200 TradeCenter, Woburn, MA 01801

Nantucket County

Clerk of Court

Superior Court Department

Suffolk County Courthouse, Three Pemberton Square, Boston, MA 02108

Clerk of Court, Nantucket County
Mary Elizabeth Adams . . . . (508) 228-2559
16 Broad Street, Nantucket, MA 02554   Fax: (508) 228-3725
P.O. Box 967, Nantucket, MA 02554

Norfolk County

Clerk of Court

Superior Court Department

Suffolk County Courthouse, Three Pemberton Square, Boston, MA 02108

Clerk of Court, Norfolk County **Walter F. Timilty** . . . . (781) 326-1600
Norfolk Superior Court, 650 High Street,
Dedham, MA 02026

Plymouth County

Clerk of Court

Superior Court Department

Suffolk County Courthouse, Three Pemberton Square, Boston, MA 02108

Clerk of Court, Plymouth County
Robert S. Creedon, Jr. . . . . (508) 747-8565
52 Obery Street, Suite 2041,
Plymouth, MA 02360

Suffolk County (Civil)

Clerk of Court

Superior Court Department

Suffolk County Courthouse, Three Pemberton Square, Boston, MA 02108

Clerk of Court (Civil), Suffolk County
Michael Joseph Donovan . . . . (617) 788-8175
Suffolk County Courthouse,
Three Pemberton Square, Boston, MA 02108

Suffolk County (Criminal)

Clerk of Court

Superior Court Department

Suffolk County Courthouse, Three Pemberton Square, Boston, MA 02108

Clerk of Court (Criminal), Suffolk County
Maura A. Hennigan . . . . (617) 788-8160
Suffolk County Courthouse,   Tel: (617) 788-7798
Three Pemberton Square, Boston, MA 02108

Worcester County

Clerk of Court

Superior Court Department

Suffolk County Courthouse, Three Pemberton Square, Boston, MA 02108

Clerk of Court, Worcester County
Dennis P. McManus . . . . (508) 831-2000
225 Main Street, Worcester, MA 01608

Offices of Registry of Deeds

Barnstable Office

3195 Main Street, Barnstable, MA 02630
Tel: (508) 362-7733 Fax: (508) 362-5065

Register of Deeds **John F. Meade** . . . . (508) 362-7733
E-mail: jmeade@barnstabledeeds.org
Assistant Register of Deeds **David Murphy** . . . . (508) 362-7733
E-mail: dmurphy@barnstablecounty.org

Dukes Office

81 Main Street, Edgartown, MA 02539
P.O. Box 5231, Edgartown, MA 02539
Tel: (508) 627-4025 Fax: (508) 627-7821
E-mail: registry@dukescounty.org

Register of Deeds **Dianne E. Powers** . . . . (508) 627-4025
E-mail: dianne.powers@sec.state.ma.us

Fall River Bristol Office

441 North Main Street, Fall River, MA 02720
Tel: (508) 673-1651 Fax: (508) 673-7633

Register of Deeds **Bernard J. McDonald III** . . . . (508) 673-2910
E-mail: bernard.mcdonald@sec.state.ma.us
Assistant Register of Deeds **John P. Collias** . . . . (508) 673-2910
E-mail: john.collias@sec.state.ma.us   Fax: (508) 673-7633

Franklin Office

30 Olive Street, Suite 2, Greenfield, MA 01301
P.O. Box 1495, Greenfield, MA 01301
Tel: (413) 772-0239 Fax: (413) 774-7150
E-mail: franklinrod@sec.state.ma.us

Register of Deeds **Scott A. Cote** . . . . (413) 772-0239
  E-mail: scott.cote@sec.state.ma.us

Hampden Office

50 State Street, Springfield, MA 01103 (Springfield Office)
59 Court Street, Westfield, MA 01085 (Westfield Office)
Tel: (413) 755-1722 (Springfield Office)
Fax: (413) 731-8190 (Springfield Office)
Tel: (413) 568-2290 (Westfield Office)
Fax: (413) 568-4869 (Westfield Office)
E-mail: hcrodsd@sec.state.ma.us

Register of Deeds **Donald E. Ashe** . . . . (413) 755-1722
  E-mail: donald.ashe@sec.state.ma.us

Hampshire Office

33 King Street, Northampton, MA 01060
Tel: (413) 584-3637 Fax: (413) 584-4136
E-mail: hampshirereg@sec.state.ma.us

Register of Deeds **Mary Olberding** . . . . (413) 584-3637
  E-mail: mary.olberding@sec.state.ma.us

Middle Berkshire Office

44 Bank Row, Pittsfield, MA 01201
Tel: (413) 443-7438 Fax: (413) 448-6025

Register of Deeds **Patricia M. Harris** . . . . (413) 443-7438
  E-mail: patricia.harris@sec.state.ma.us

Nantucket Office

16 Broad Street, Nantucket, MA 02554
Tel: (508) 228-7250 Fax: (508) 325-5331

Register of Deeds **Jennifer H. Ferreira** . . . . (508) 228-7250
  E-mail: jen.ferreira@sec.state.ma.us

Norfolk Office

649 High Street, Dedham, MA 02026-0069
P.O. Box 69, Dedham, MA 02026-0069
Tel: (781) 461-6122 Fax: (781) 461-4742
Internet: www.norfolkdeeds.org

Register of Deeds **William P. O'Donnell** . . . . (781) 461-6122

Northern Berkshire Office

65 Park Street, Adams, MA 01220
Tel: (413) 743-0035 Fax: (413) 741-1003
E-mail: nbrd@sec.state.ma.us

Register of Deeds **Frances T. Brooks** . . . . (413) 743-0035
  E-mail: frances.brooks@sec.state.ma.us

Northern Bristol Office

11 Court Street, Taunton, MA 02780
Tel: (508) 822-0502 Fax: (508) 880-4975
E-mail: registry@tauntondeeds.com

Registry of Deeds **Barry J. Amaral** . . . . (508) 822-0502
  E-mail: barry.amaral@sec.state.ma.us

Northern Essex Office

354 Merrimack Street, Lawrence, MA 01843
Tel: (978) 683-2745 Fax: (978) 688-4679

Register of Deeds **M. Paul Iannuccillo** . . . . (978) 683-2745
  E-mail: paul.iannuccillo@sec.state.ma.us

Northern Middlesex Office

360 Gorham Street, Lowell, MA 01852
Tel: (978) 322-9000 Fax: (978) 322-9001
E-mail: lowelldeeds@comcast.net

Register of Deeds **Richard P. Howe, Jr.** . . . . (978) 322-9000

Northern Worcester Office

166 Boulder Drive, Suite 202, Fitchburg, MA 01420
Tel: (978) 342-2637 Fax: (978) 345-2865
E-mail: fitchreg@sec.state.ma.us

Register of Deeds **Kathleen Daigneault** . . . . (978) 342-2637
  E-mail: kathleen.daigneault@sec.state.ma.us

Plymouth Office

50 Obery Street, Plymouth, MA 02361
Tel: (508) 830-9200 Fax: (508) 830-9280

Register of Deeds **John R. Buckley, Jr.** . . . . (508) 830-9200
  E-mail: john.buckley@sec.state.ma.us

Southern Berkshire Office

334 Maine Street, Suite 2, Great Barrington, MA 01230-1894
Tel: (413) 528-0146 Fax: (413) 528-6878
E-mail: sbrd@sec.state.ma.us

Register of Deeds **Wanda M. Beckwith** . . . . (413) 528-0146
  E-mail: wanda.beckwith@sec.state.ma.us

Southern Bristol Office

25 North 6th Street, New Bedford, MA 02740
Tel: (508) 993-2605 Fax: (508) 997-4250
E-mail: nbregistry@gis.net

Register of Deeds **J. Mark Treadup** . . . . (508) 993-2605
  E-mail: mark.treadup@sec.state.ma.us   Fax: (508) 997-4250

Southern Essex Office

Shetland Park, 45 Congress Street, Suite 4100, Salem, MA 01970
Tel: (978) 741-1704 Fax: (978) 744-5865
E-mail: southernessexcustomerservice@sec.state.ma.us

Register of Deeds **John L. O'Brien** . . . . (978) 741-0201

(continued on next page)

Massachusetts Court Clerks and Courthouses *continued*

Southern Middlesex Office

208 Cambridge Street, Cambridge, MA 02141-0068
P.O. Box 68, Cambridge, MA 02141-0068
Tel: (617) 679-6310 Fax: (617) 494-9083
E-mail: middlesexsouth@sec.state.ma.us

Register of Deeds **Maria C. Curtatone** . . . . (617) 679-6300
   E-mail: maria.curtatone@sec.state.ma.us

Suffolk Office

24 New Chardon Street, Boston, MA 02114-9660
P.O. Box 9660, Boston, MA 02114-9660
Tel: (617) 788-6250 Fax: (617) 720-4163
E-mail: suffolk.deeds@sec.state.ma.us

Register of Deeds **Francis "Mickey" Roache** . . . .(617) 788-6250
   E-mail: francis.roache@sec.state.ma.us

Worcester Office

90 Front Street, Worcester, MA 01608
Tel: (508) 798-7717 Fax: (508) 798-7746

Register of Deeds **Anthony J. Vigliotti** . . . . (508) 798-7717
   E-mail: anthony.vigliotti@sec.state.ma.us

Michigan Court Clerks and Courthouses

The trial courts of general jurisdiction in Michigan are called circuit courts. There are 57 judicial circuits, each circuit consisting of at least one county. The listing that follows provides for each county the County Clerk which functions as the clerk of the county and the clerk of the circuit court.

Michigan Supreme Court

Hall of Justice, 925 West Ottawa, Lansing, MI 48909
P.O. Box 30052, Lansing, MI 48909
Tel: (517) 373-0120
Internet: http://courts.michigan.gov/courts/michigansupremecourt/pages

The Supreme Court consists of seven justices who are nominated by political parties and elected in nonpartisan elections for eight-year terms. The chief justice is elected by peer vote for a consecutive two-year term. The Supreme Court has discretionary review of cases from the Michigan Court of Appeals and other state courts. Cases are appealed to the Supreme Court by filing an application for leave to appeal with the Court which has the authority to grant or deny any application. In addition to its judicial duties, the Court is responsible for the general administrative supervision of all courts in the state. The Court also establishes rules for practice and procedure in all courts.

Court Staff
Clerk of Court **Larry Royster** . . . . (517) 373-0120
    E-mail: roysterl@courts.mi.gov

Michigan Court of Appeals

925 West Ottawa, Lansing, MI 48915
P.O. Box 30022, Lansing, MI 48909-7522
Tel: (517) 373-0786 Tel: (313) 972-5678 (Detroit Office)
Tel: (616) 456-1167 (Grand Rapids Office)
Tel: (248) 524-8700 (Troy Office)

The Court of Appeals, established in 1963, is comprised of four districts from which twenty-eight judges are elected in nonpartisan elections for six-year terms. The Chief Judge is designated by the Michigan Supreme Court. Chief Judge Pro Tem is selected by the Chief Judge. The Court sits in panels of three judges each. The Court of Appeals has appellate jurisdiction in both civil and criminal cases from Michigan Circuit Courts.

Court Staff
Chief Clerk of Court **Jerome "Jerry" Zimmer** . . . . (517) 373-2252
    E-mail: jzimmer@courts.mi.gov
District Clerk, First District **John P. Lowe** . . . . (313) 972-5678
    Cadillac Place, 3020 West Grand Boulevard,
    Suite 14-300, Detroit, MI 48202-6020
District Clerk, Second District **Angela DiSessa** . . . . (248) 524-8700
    201 West Big Beaver Road, Suite 800,
    Troy, MI 48084
District Clerk, Third District **Lori Zarzecki** . . . . (616) 456-1167
    State of Michigan Office Bldg., 350 Ottawa, NW,
    Grand Rapids, MI 49503-2349
    E-mail: lzarzecki@courts.mi.gov
District Clerk, Fourth District **Kimberly S. Hauser** . . . . . . (517) 373-0786
    P.O. Box 30022, Lansing, MI 48909
    925 West Ottawa Street, Lansing, MI 48913
    E-mail: khauser@courts.mi.gov

Michigan Court Clerks and Courthouses *continued*

Michigan Court of Claims

925 West Ottawa, Lansing, MI 48909
P.O. Box 30185, Lansing, MI 48909-7522
Tel: (517) 373-0807

Court Staff
Clerk **Jerome "Jerry" Zimmer** . . . .(517) 373-0807

County-By-County

Alcona County

County Clerk

Twenty Third Judicial Circuit
120 North Grove, Standish, MI 48658
Tel: (989) 846-6131 Fax: (989) 846-6757

County Clerk, Alcona County **Patricia Truman** . . . . (989) 724-9410
    106 Fifth Street, Harrison, MI 48740   Fax: (989) 724-9419
    P.O. Box 308, Harrison, MI 48740

Alger County

County Clerk

Eleventh Judicial Circuit
300 Walnut Street, Manistique, MI 49854
Tel: (906) 341-3655 Fax: (906) 341-8291

County Clerk/Clerk of Court, Alger County
    Mary ann Froberg . . . .(906) 387-2076
    101 Court Street, Munising, MI 49862   Fax: (906) 387-2156
    E-mail: mfroberg@algercourthouse.com

Allegan County

County Clerk

Forty Eighth Judicial Circuit
113 Chestnut Street, Allegan, MI 49010
Tel: (269) 673-0300

County Clerk **Joyce Watts** . . . . (269) 673-0450
    113 Chestnut Street, Allegan, MI 49010   Tel: (269) 673-0300
                                            (Courthouse)
                                      Fax: (269) 673-0298

Alpena County

County Clerk

Twenty Sixth Judicial Circuit
720 West Chisholm, Suite 1, Alpena, MI 49707
Tel: (989) 354-9573 Fax: (989) 354-9643

County Clerk, Alpena County **Bonnie Friedrichs** . . . . (989) 354-9520
    720 West Chisholm, Suite 2,   Fax: (989) 354-9644
    Alpena, MI 49707
    E-mail: friedrib@alpenacounty.org

(continued on next page)

Antrim County

County Clerk

Thirteenth Judicial Circuit
328 Washington Street, Suite 300, Traverse City, MI 49684
Tel: (231) 922-4701 Fax: (231) 922-4519

County Clerk/Clerk of Court, Antrim County
Sheryl Guy . . . . (231) 533-6353
P.O. Box 520, Bellaire, MI 49615   Fax: (231) 533-6935
E-mail: clerk@antrimcounty.org

Arenac County

County Clerk

Twenty Third Judicial Circuit
120 North Grove, Standish, MI 48658
Tel: (989) 846-6131 Fax: (989) 846-6757

County Clerk, Arenac County **Ricky Rockwell** . . . . (989) 846-4626
P.O. Box 747, Standish, MI 48658   Fax: (989) 846-9194
120 North Grove, Standish, MI 48658

Baraga County

County Clerk

Twelfth Judicial Circuit
401 East Houghton Avenue, Houghton, MI 49931
Tel: (906) 482-5420 Fax: (906) 483-0364
Internet: www.houghtoncounty.net/directory-12jcc.shtml

County Clerk/Clerk of Court, Baraga County
Wendy Tollefson-Goodreau . . . . (906) 524-6183
16 North Third Street, Lanse, MI 49946

Barry County

County Clerk

Fifth Judicial Circuit
220 West State Street, Hastings, MI 49058
Tel: (269) 945-1286 Fax: (269) 945-1299

County Clerk/Clerk of Court **Pamela Palmer** . . . . (269) 945-1285
220 West State Street, Hastings, MI 49058   Fax: (269) 945-0209
E-mail: ppalmer@barryco.org

Bay County

County Clerk

Eighteenth Judicial Circuit
1230 Washington Avenue, Bay City, MI 48708
Tel: (989) 895-4265 Fax: (989) 895-4099
Internet: www.baycounty-mi.gov/CircuitCourt

County Clerk **Cynthia Luczak** . . . . (989) 895-4280
515 Center Avenue, Suite 101,   Fax: (989) 895-4284
Bay City, MI 48708
E-mail: luczakc@baycounty.net

Benzie County

County Clerk

Nineteenth Judicial Circuit
415 Third Street, Manistee, MI 49660
Tel: (231) 723-6664 Fax: (231) 723-1645

County Clerk, Benzie County **Dawn Olney** . . . . (231) 882-9671
448 Court Place, Beulah, MI 49617
E-mail: dolney@benzieco.net

Berrien County

County Clerk

Second Judicial Circuit
811 Port Street, Saint Joseph, MI 49085
Tel: (269) 983-7111
E-mail: trialcourt@berriencounty.org

County Clerk/Clerk of Court **Sharon Tyler** . . . . . (269) 983-7111 ext. 8368
811 Port Street, Saint Joseph, MI 49085   Fax: (269) 982-8642
E-mail: records@berriencounty.org

Branch County

County Clerk

Fifteenth Judicial Circuit
31 Division Street, Coldwater, MI 49036
Tel: (517) 279-4304 Fax: (517) 279-5110
E-mail: circuitcourt@countyofbranch.com

County Clerk/Clerk of Court **Terry A. Kubasiak** . . . . (517) 279-4306
31 Division Street, Coldwater, MI 49036   Fax: (517) 278-5627

Calhoun County

County Clerk

Thirty Seventh Judicial Circuit
County Justice Center, 161 East Michigan Avenue,
Battle Creek, MI 49014-4066
Tel: (269) 969-6530 Fax: (269) 969-6663
Internet: http://www.calhouncountymi.gov/government/circuit_court/

County Clerk **Anne B. Norlander** . . . . (269) 781-0730
315 West Green Street, Marshall, MI 49068   Tel: (269) 969-6530
County Justice Center, 161 East Michigan Avenue,   (Courthouse)
Battle Creek, MI 49014-4066 (Courthouse)   Fax: (269) 781-0720
E-mail: anorlander@calhouncountymi.gov

Cass County

County Clerk

Forty Third Judicial Circuit
60296 M-62, Cassopolis, MI 49031
Tel: (269) 445-4412

County Clerk **Monica Kennedy** . . . . (269) 445-4464
120 North Broadway, Room 123,   Tel: (269) 445-4416
Cassopolis, MI 49031   (Courthouse)
P.O. Box 355, Cassopolis, MI 49031 (Mail)
60296 M-62, Cassopolis, MI 49031 (Courthouse)

Charlevoix County

County Clerk

Thirty Third Judicial Circuit
Charlevoix County Building, 301 State Street, Charlevoix, MI 49720
Tel: (231) 547-7243 Fax: (231) 547-7264
Internet: www.charlevoixcounty.org/circuitcourt.asp

County Clerk **Cheryl Potter Browe**...................(231) 547-7200
  203 West Antrim, Charlevoix, MI 49720   Tel: (231) 547-7243
  Charlevoix County Building, 301 State Street,   (Courthouse)
  Charlevoix, MI 49720 (Courthouse)   Fax: (231) 547-7217
  E-mail: clerk@charlevoixcounty.org

Cheboygan County

County Clerk

Fifty Third Judicial Circuit
870 South Main Street, Cheboygan, MI 49721
Tel: (231) 627-8818
Internet: www.cheboygancounty.net/53rd_circuit_court/

County Clerk, Cheboygan County **Mary Ellen Tryban**....(231) 627-8808
  870 South Main Street, Cheboygan, MI 49721   Tel: (231) 627-8818
  P.O. Box 70, Cheboygan, MI 49721   (Courthouse)
  E-mail: clerk@cheboygancounty.net

Chippewa County

County Clerk

Fiftieth Judicial Circuit
319 Court Street, Sault Sainte Marie, MI 49783
Tel: (906) 635-6338 Fax: (906) 635-6385

County Clerk **Catherine Maleport** ....(906) 635-6300
  319 Court Street, Sault Sainte Marie, MI 49783   Tel: (906) 635-6338
  E-mail: cmaleport@chippewacountymi.gov   (Courthouse)

Clare County

County Clerk

Fifty Fifth Judicial Circuit
401 West Cedar Avenue, Gladwin, MI 48624
Tel: (989) 426-9237 Fax: (989) 426-4493

County Clerk, Clare County **Pamela Mayfield**..........(989) 539-7131
  P.O. Box 438, Harrison, MI 48625   Fax: (989) 539-6616
  225 West Main Street, Harrison, MI 48625
  E-mail: mayfieldp@clareco.net

Clinton County

County Clerk

Twenty Ninth Judicial Circuit
100 East State Street, Suite 4500, St. Johns, MI 48879
Tel: (989) 224-5130 Fax: (989) 224-5102
E-mail: circuit@clinton-county.org

County Clerk, Clinton County **Diane Zuker** ....(989) 224-5140
  100 East State Street, Suite 2600,   Fax: (989) 227-6421
  St. Johns, MI 48879
  E-mail: clerk@clinton-county.org

Crawford County

County Clerk

Forty Sixth Judicial Circuit
800 Livingston Boulevard, Gaylord, MI 49735
Tel: (989) 731-7500
Internet: www.circuit46.org

County Clerk, Crawford County **Sandra Moore**.........(989) 344-3206
  200 West Michigan Avenue,   Fax: (989) 344-3223
  Grayling, MI 49738-1741
  E-mail: smoore@crawfordco.org

Delta County

County Clerk

Forty Seventh Judicial Circuit
310 Ludington Street, Escanaba, MI 49829
Tel: (906) 789-5103 Fax: (906) 789-5104
E-mail: circuit@deltacountymi.org

County Clerk **Nancy J. Kolich**.....................(906) 789-5105
  310 Ludington Street, Escanaba, MI 49829   Fax: (906) 789-5196
  E-mail: clerk@deltacountymi.org

Dickinson County

County Clerk

Forty First Judicial Circuit
705 South Stephenson Street, Iron Mountain, MI 49801
Tel: (906) 774-2266 Fax: (906) 779-0587
Internet: www.dickinsoncountymi.gov/?41stcircuit

County Clerk, Dickinson County **Dolly L. Cook**.........(906) 774-0988
  705 South Stephenson Street,   Fax: (906) 774-4660
  Iron Mountain, MI 49801

Eaton County

County Clerk

Fifty Sixth Judicial Circuit
1045 Independence Boulevard, Charlotte, MI 48813
Tel: (517) 543-4335

County Clerk **Diana Bosworth** ....(517) 543-2426
  1045 Independence Boulevard,   Fax: (517) 541-0666
  Charlotte, MI 48813
  E-mail: countyclerk@eatoncounty.org

Emmet County

County Clerk

Fifty Seventh Judicial Circuit
200 Division Street, Suite 100, Petoskey, MI 49770
Tel: (231) 348-1748 Fax: (231) 348-0619

County Clerk **Juli Wallin** ....(231) 348-1744
  200 Division Street, Suite 130,   Fax: (231) 348-0602
  Petoskey, MI 49770
  E-mail: jwallin@emmetcounty.org

(continued on next page)

Genesee County

County Clerk

Seventh Judicial Circuit
Genesee County Courthouse, 900 South Saginaw Street, Flint, MI 48502
Tel: (810) 257-3252
Internet: www.co.genesee.mi.us/circuitcourt/index.htm

County Clerk/Clerk of Court **John J. Gleason** . . . . (810) 257-3224
   Genesee County Courthouse,
   900 South Saginaw Street,
   Flint, MI 48502
   E-mail: jgleason@co.genesee.mi.us

Gladwin County

County Clerk

Fifty Fifth Judicial Circuit
401 West Cedar Avenue, Gladwin, MI 48624
Tel: (989) 426-9237   Fax: (989) 426-4493

County Clerk, Gladwin County
   Laura Brandon-Maveal . . . .(989) 426-9237
   401 West Cedar Avenue, Gladwin, MI 48624   Fax: (989) 426-6917
   E-mail: countyclerk@gladwinco.com

Gogebic County

County Clerk

Thirty Second Judicial Circuit
200 North Moore Street, Bessemer, MI 49911
Tel: (906) 663-4211   Fax: (906) 667-1102
Internet: www.gogebic.org/circuit.htm

County Clerk, Gogebic County **Gerry Pelissero** . . . .(906) 663-4518
   200 North Moore Street, Bessemer, MI 49911   Tel: (906) 663-4211
   E-mail: gpelissero@gogebic.org   (Courthouse)
                                                          Fax: (906) 663-4660

Grand Traverse County

County Clerk

Thirteenth Judicial Circuit
328 Washington Street, Suite 300, Traverse City, MI 49684
Tel: (231) 922-4701   Fax: (231) 922-4519

County Clerk/Clerk of Court, Grand Traverse County
   Bonnie Scheely . . . . (231) 922-4760
   400 Boardman Avenue, Traverse City, MI 49684
   328 Washington Street, Traverse City, MI 49684
   (Courthouse)
   E-mail: gtcclerk@co.grand-traverse.mi.us

Gratiot County

County Clerk

Twenty Ninth Judicial Circuit
100 East State Street, Suite 4500, St. Johns, MI 48879
Tel: (989) 224-5130   Fax: (989) 224-5102
E-mail: circuit@clinton-county.org

County Clerk, Gratiot County **Carol Vernon** . . . .(989) 875-5215
   214 East Center Street, Ithaca, MI 48847   Tel: (989) 875-5224
                                                          Fax: (989) 875-5254

Hillsdale County

County Clerk

First Judicial Circuit
29 North Howell, Hillsdale, MI 49242
Tel: (517) 437-4321   Fax: (517) 437-3121

County Clerk/Clerk of Court **Marney M. Kast** . . . .(517) 437-3391
   29 North Howell, Room 1,
   Hillsdale, MI 49242

Houghton County

County Clerk

Twelfth Judicial Circuit
401 East Houghton Avenue, Houghton, MI 49931
Tel: (906) 482-5420   Fax: (906) 483-0364
Internet: www.houghtoncounty.net/directory-12jcc.shtml

County Clerk/Clerk of Court, Houghton County
   Patricia Janke . . . . (906) 482-1150
   401 East Houghton Avenue,
   Houghton, MI 49931

Huron County

County Clerk

Fifty Second Judicial Circuit
County Building, 250 East Huron Avenue, Room 207,
Bad Axe, MI 48413
Tel: (989) 269-7112   Fax: (989) 269-0005
Internet: www.co.huron.mi.us/Circuit.asp

County Clerk **Lori Neal-Wonsowicz** . . . .(989) 269-9942
   County Building, 250 East Huron Avenue,   Fax: (989) 269-6160
   Room 201, Bad Axe, MI 48413
   E-mail: neall@co.huron.mi.us

Ingham County

County Clerk

County Clerk's Office
341 South Jefferson Street, 1st Floor, Mason, MI 48854
313 West Kalamazoo Street, Lansing, MI 48933 (Branch Office)
P.O. Box 179, Mason, MI 48854
Tel: (517) 676-7201   Fax: (517) 676-7254
Internet: www.ingham.org/cl

County Clerk **Barb Byrum** . . . .(517) 483-6454

Ionia County

County Clerk

Eighth Judicial Circuit
639 North State Street, Stanton, MI 48888
100 West Main Street, Ionia, MI 48846 (Ionia Office)
Tel: (989) 831-7363   Tel: (616) 527-5315 (Ionia Office)
Fax: (989) 831-7428   Fax: (616) 527-5381 (Ionia Office)
Internet: www.montcalm.org/8thcircuit.asp

County Clerk/Clerk of Court, Ionia County
   Tonda Rich . . . . (616) 527-5322
   100 West Main Street, Ionia, MI 48846   Fax: (616) 527-8201

Iosco County

County Clerk

Twenty Third Judicial Circuit
120 North Grove, Standish, MI 48658
Tel: (989) 846-6131   Fax: (989) 846-6757

County Clerk, Iosco County **Nancy J. Huebel** . . . .(989) 362-3497
  422 West Lake Street, Tawas City, MI 48764   Fax: (989) 984-1012
  P.O. Box 838, Tawas City, MI 48764
  E-mail: nhuebel@ioscocounty.org

Iron County

County Clerk

Forty First Judicial Circuit
705 South Stephenson Street, Iron Mountain, MI 49801
Tel: (906) 774-2266   Fax: (906) 779-0587
Internet: www.dickinsoncountymi.gov/?41stcircuit

County Clerk, Iron County **Diane Hilberg** . . . . (906) 875-3221
  Two South Sixth Street, Suite 9,
  Crystal Falls, MI 49920-1413
  E-mail: dhilberg@iron.org

Isabella County

County Clerk

Twenty First Judicial Circuit
300 North Main Street, Mt. Pleasant, MI 48858
Tel: (989) 772-0911   Fax: (989) 779-8022

County Clerk **Minde Lux** . . . .(989) 772-0911 ext. 205
  200 North Main, Mt. Pleasant, MI 48858
  E-mail: clerk@isabellacounty.org

Jackson County

County Clerk

Fourth Judicial Circuit
312 South Jackson Street, Jackson, MI 49201
Tel: (517) 788-4268   Fax: (517) 788-4691

County Clerk/Clerk of Court **Amanda L. Riska** . . . . (517) 788-4268
  312 South Jackson Street, Jackson, MI 49201
  E-mail: ariska@co.jackson.mi.us

Kalamazoo County

County Clerk

Ninth Judicial Circuit
Kalamazoo County Building, 201 West Kalamazoo Avenue,
Kalamazoo, MI 49007
Tel: (269) 383-8837   Fax: (269) 383-8647

County Clerk/Clerk of Court
  Timothy A. "Tim" Snow . . . .(269) 383-8840
  Kalamazoo County Building,
  201 West Kalamazoo Avenue,
  Kalamazoo, MI 49007
  E-mail: tasnow@kalcounty.com

Kalkaska County

County Clerk

Forty Sixth Judicial Circuit
800 Livingston Boulevard, Gaylord, MI 49735
Tel: (989) 731-7500
Internet: www.circuit46.org

County Clerk, Kalkaska County **Deborah Hill** . . . . (231) 258-3300
  605 North Birch Street, Kalkaska, MI 49646   Fax: (231) 258-3337
  E-mail: dhill@kalkaskacounty.org

Kent County

County Clerk

Seventeenth Judicial Circuit
180 Ottawa Avenue, NW, Grand Rapids, MI 49503
Tel: (616) 632-5137   Fax: (616) 632-5130

County Clerk **Mary Hollinrake** . . . . (616) 632-7640
  180 Ottawa Avenue, NW, Grand Rapids, MI 49503   Fax: (616) 632-7645
  300 Monroe Avenue NW, Grand Rapids, MI 49503
  (Clerk's office)
  E-mail: mary.hollinrake@kentcountymi.gov

Keweenaw County

County Clerk

Twelfth Judicial Circuit
401 East Houghton Avenue, Houghton, MI 49931
Tel: (906) 482-5420   Fax: (906) 483-0364
Internet: www.houghtoncounty.net/directory-12jcc.shtml

County Clerk/Clerk of Court, Keweenaw County
  Julie Carlson . . . . (906) 337-2229
  5095 Fourth Street, Eagle River, MI 49950   Fax: (906) 337-2795

Lake County

County Clerk

Fifty First Judicial Circuit
304 East Ludington Avenue, Ludington, MI 49431
Tel: (231) 845-0516   Fax: (231) 845-7779

County Clerk, Lake County **Shelly Myers** . . . . (231) 745-4641
  800 Tenth Street, Baldwin, MI 49304   Fax: (231) 745-8632
  E-mail: clerk@co.lake.mi.us

Lapeer County

County Clerk

Fortieth Judicial Circuit
255 Clay Street, Lapeer, MI 48446
Tel: (810) 245-4816

County Clerk **Theresa Spencer** . . . .(810) 667-0356
  225 Clay Street, Lapeer, MI 48446   Tel: (810) 245-4816
                                               (Courthouse)
                                          Fax: (810) 667-0362

(continued on next page)

Leelanau County

County Clerk

Thirteenth Judicial Circuit
328 Washington Street, Suite 300, Traverse City, MI 49684
Tel: (231) 922-4701   Fax: (231) 922-4519

County Clerk/Clerk of Court, Leelanau County
  Michelle L. Crocker . . . . (231) 256-9824
  8257 East Government Center Drive, Suite 103,   Fax: (231) 256-8295
  Suttons Bay, MI 49682

Lenawee County

County Clerk

Thirty Ninth Judicial Circuit
425 North Main Street, Adrian, MI 49221
Tel: (517) 264-4597
Internet: www.lenawee.mi.us/circuit_court.html

County Clerk **Roxann Holloway** . . . . (517) 264-4599
  425 North Main Street, Adrian, MI 49221   Tel: (517) 264-4597
  E-mail: roxann.holloway@lenawee.mi.us   (Courthouse)

Livingston County

County Clerk

Forty Fourth Judicial Circuit
204 South Highlander Way, Suite 5, Howell, MI 48843
Tel: (517) 546-8079   Fax: (517) 546-0048

County Clerk **Margaret M. Dunleavy** . . . . (517) 546-9816
  204 South Highlander Way, Suite 4,   Fax: (517) 548-4219
  Howell, MI 48843
  E-mail: circuitcourtclerk@co.livingston.mi.us

Luce County

County Clerk

Eleventh Judicial Circuit
300 Walnut Street, Manistique, MI 49854
Tel: (906) 341-3655   Fax: (906) 341-8291

County Clerk/Clerk of Court, Luce County
  Sharon Price . . . . (906) 293-5521
  407 West Harrie Street, Newberry, MI 49868   Fax: (906) 293-0050

Mackinac County

County Clerk

Eleventh Judicial Circuit
300 Walnut Street, Manistique, MI 49854
Tel: (906) 341-3655   Fax: (906) 341-8291

County Clerk/Clerk of Court, Mackinac County
  Mary Kay Tamlyn . . . . (906) 643-7300
  100 Marley Street, Room 10,   Fax: (906) 643-7302
  St. Ignace, MI 49781

Macomb County

County Clerk

Sixteenth Judicial Circuit
40 North Main Street, Mount Clemens, MI 48043
Tel: (586) 469-5351

County Clerk **Carmella Sabaugh** . . . . (586) 469-5351
  40 North Main, First Floor,
  Mount Clemens, MI 48043

Manistee County

County Clerk

Nineteenth Judicial Circuit
415 Third Street, Manistee, MI 49660
Tel: (231) 723-6664   Fax: (231) 723-1645

County Clerk, Manistee County **Jill Nowak** . . . . (231) 723-3331
  415 Third Street, Manistee, MI 49660   Fax: (231) 723-1492
  E-mail: clerk@manisteecountymi.gov

Marquette County

County Clerk

Twenty Fifth Judicial Circuit
234 West Baraga, Marquette, MI 49855
Tel: (906) 225-8205   Fax: (906) 225-8216

County Clerk **Linda Talsma** . . . . (906) 225-8330
  234 West Baraga, Marquette, MI 49855   Fax: (906) 228-1572
  E-mail: countyclerk@mqtco.org

Mason County

County Clerk

Fifty First Judicial Circuit
304 East Ludington Avenue, Ludington, MI 49431
Tel: (231) 845-0516   Fax: (231) 845-7779

County Clerk, Mason County **Cheryl Kelly** . . . . (231) 843-8202
  304 East Ludington Avenue,   Tel: (231) 845-0516
  Ludington, MI 49431   (Courthouse)
  E-mail: ckelly@masoncounty.net   Fax: (231) 843-1972

Mecosta County

County Clerk

Forty Ninth Judicial Circuit
400 Elm Street, Big Rapids, MI 49307
Tel: (231) 592-0780   Fax: (231) 592-0100
E-mail: 49circt@co.mecosta.mi.us
Internet: www.co.mecosta.mi.us/circuit.asp

County Clerk, Mecosta County **Marcee Purcell** . . . . (231) 592-0783
  400 Elm Street, Big Rapids, MI 49307   Fax: (231) 592-0193
  E-mail: mcclerk@co.mecosta.mi.us

Menominee County

County Clerk

Forty First Judicial Circuit
705 South Stephenson Street, Iron Mountain, MI 49801
Tel: (906) 774-2266 Fax: (906) 779-0587
Internet: www.dickinsoncountymi.gov/?41stcircuit

County Clerk, Menominee County **Marc Kleiman** . . . . (906) 863-8532
839 10th Avenue, Menominee, MI 49858

Midland County

County Clerk

Forty Second Judicial Circuit
301 West Main Street, Midland, MI 48640
Tel: (989) 832-6735 Fax: (989) 832-6610
Internet: http://www.co.midland.mi.us/departments/home.php?id=4

| County Clerk **Ann Manary** . . . .(989) 832-6739 |
220 West Ellsworth Street,	Tel: (989) 832-6735
Midland, MI 48640-5194 (Courthouse)	(Courthouse)
301 West Main Street, Midland, MI 48640	Fax: (989) 832-6680

Missaukee County

County Clerk

Twenty Eighth Judicial Circuit
437 East Division Street, Cadillac, MI 49601
Tel: (231) 779-9790 Fax: (231) 779-9230
E-mail: circuitcourt@wexfordcounty.org

County Clerk, Missaukee County
Carolyn Flore . . . .(231) 839-4967 ext. 204
111 South Canal, Lake City, MI 49651   Fax: (231) 839-3684
P.O. Box 800, Lake City, MI 49651
E-mail: clerk@missaukee.org

Monroe County

County Clerk

Thirty Eighth Judicial Circuit
106 East First Street, Monroe, MI 48161
Tel: (734) 240-7020 Fax: (734) 240-7132

County Clerk **Sharon Lemasters** . . . . (734) 240-7020
106 East First Street, Monroe, MI 48161   Fax: (734) 240-7045

Montcalm County

County Clerk

Eighth Judicial Circuit
639 North State Street, Stanton, MI 48888
100 West Main Street, Ionia, MI 48846 (Ionia Office)
Tel: (989) 831-7363 Tel: (616) 527-5315 (Ionia Office)
Fax: (989) 831-7428 Fax: (616) 527-5381 (Ionia Office)
Internet: www.montcalm.org/8thcircuit.asp

County Clerk/Clerk of Court, Montcalm County
Kristen Millard . . . .(989) 831-3520
639 North State Street, Stanton, MI 48888
P.O. Box 296, Stanton, MI 48888

Montmorency County

County Clerk

Twenty Sixth Judicial Circuit
720 West Chisholm, Suite 1, Alpena, MI 49707
Tel: (989) 354-9573 Fax: (989) 354-9643

County Clerk, Montmorency County
Cheryl A. Neilsen . . . . (989) 785-8022
P.O. Box 789, Atlanta, MI 49709   Fax: (989) 785-8023

Muskegon County

County Clerk

Fourteenth Judicial Circuit
990 Terrace Street, Muskegon, MI 49442
Tel: (231) 724-6251 Fax: (231) 724-6695

County Clerk/Clerk of Court **Nancy Waters** . . . .(231) 724-6221
141 East Apple Avenue, 2nd Floor,   Fax: (231) 724-6262
Muskegon, MI 49442

Newaygo County

County Clerk

Twenty Seventh Judicial Circuit
1092 Newell Street, White Cloud, MI 49349
Tel: (231) 689-7252 Fax: (231) 689-7015

County Clerk, Newaygo County **Laurel J. Breuker** . . . . . . (231) 689-7235
1092 Newell Street, White Cloud, MI 49349   Tel: (231) 689-7269
1087 Newell Street, White Cloud, MI 49349   Fax: (231) 689-7241
(Clerk's office)
P.O. Box 885, White Cloud, MI 49349 (Clerk's
office)
E-mail: laurie@co.newaygo.mi.us

Oakland County

County Clerk

Sixth Judicial Circuit
1200 North Telegraph Road, Pontiac, MI 48341
Tel: (248) 452-2159 Fax: (248) 975-9877
Internet: www.oakgov.com/circuit

County Clerk **Lisa Anne Brown** . . . . (248) 858-0581
1200 North Telegraph Road,
Pontiac, MI 48341
E-mail: clerk@oakgov.com

Oceana County

County Clerk

Twenty Seventh Judicial Circuit
1092 Newell Street, White Cloud, MI 49349
Tel: (231) 689-7252 Fax: (231) 689-7015

County Clerk, Oceana County **Rebecca J. Griffin** . . . . (231) 873-4328
100 State Street, Suite M-1,
Hart, MI 49420
E-mail: readie@oceana.mi.us

(continued on next page)

Michigan Court Clerks and Courthouses *continued*

Ogemaw County

County Clerk

Thirty Fourth Judicial Circuit
806 West Houghton Avenue, West Branch, MI 48661
Tel: (989) 345-0215 Fax: (989) 345-3959

County Clerk, Ogemaw County **Gary Klacking** . . . . (989) 345-0215
806 West Houghton Avenue,
West Branch, MI 48661

Ontonagon County

County Clerk

Thirty Second Judicial Circuit
200 North Moore Street, Bessemer, MI 49911
Tel: (906) 663-4211 Fax: (906) 667-1102
Internet: www.gogebic.org/circuit.htm

County Clerk, Ontonagon County **Stacy Preiss** . . . . (906) 884-4255
725 Greenland, Ontonagon, MI 49953

Osceola County

County Clerk

Forty Ninth Judicial Circuit
400 Elm Street, Big Rapids, MI 49307
Tel: (231) 592-0780 Fax: (231) 592-0100
E-mail: 49circt@co.mecosta.mi.us
Internet: www.co.mecosta.mi.us/circuit.asp

County Clerk, Osceola County **Karen Bluhm** . . . . (231) 832-3261
301 West Upton, Reed City, MI 49677
E-mail: oscclerk1@charterinternet.com

Oscoda County

County Clerk

Twenty Third Judicial Circuit
120 North Grove, Standish, MI 48658
Tel: (989) 846-6131 Fax: (989) 846-6757

County Clerk, Oscoda County **Jeri Winton** . . . . (989) 826-1110
311 South Morenci Street,   Fax: (989) 826-1136
Mio, MI 48647
P.O. Box 355, Cassopolis, MI 49031
E-mail: jwinton@oscodacountymi.com

Otsego County

County Clerk

Forty Sixth Judicial Circuit
800 Livingston Boulevard, Gaylord, MI 49735
Tel: (989) 731-7500
Internet: www.circuit46.org

County Clerk, Otsego County
  Susan I. "Suzy" DeFeyter . . . . (989) 731-7504
225 West Main Street, Harrison, MI 48625   Fax: (989) 731-7519
800 Livingston Boulevard,
Gaylord, MI 49735 (Courthouse)
E-mail: sdefeyter@otsegocountymi.gov

Michigan Court Clerks and Courthouses *continued*

Ottawa County

County Clerk

Twentieth Judicial Circuit
414 North Washington Avenue, Suite 300, Grand Haven, MI 49417
Tel: (616) 846-8320 Fax: (616) 846-8179
E-mail: circuitcourt@miottawa.org
Internet: www.miottawa.org/CourtsLE/20thcircuit/

County Clerk **Justin F. Roebuck** . . . . (616) 846-8315
12220 Fillmore Street, Room 130,   Fax: (616) 994-4538
West Olive, MI 49460 (Clerk's office)
414 North Washington Avenue, Suite 300,
Grand Haven, MI 49417
E-mail: countyclerk@miottawa.org

Presque Isle County

County Clerk

Fifty Third Judicial Circuit
870 South Main Street, Cheboygan, MI 49721
Tel: (231) 627-8818
Internet: www.cheboygancounty.net/53rd_circuit_court/

County Clerk, Presque Isle County **Ann Marie Main** . . . . . (989) 734-3288
151 East Huron Avenue, Rogers City, MI 49779   Fax: (989) 734-7635
P.O. Box 110, Rogers City, MI 49799
E-mail: piclerk@picounty.org

Roscommon County

County Clerk

Thirty Fourth Judicial Circuit
806 West Houghton Avenue, West Branch, MI 48661
Tel: (989) 345-0215 Fax: (989) 345-3959

County Clerk, Roscommon County
  Michelle Stevenson . . . . (989) 275-5923
500 Lake Street, Roscommon, MI 48653   Fax: (989) 275-8640
E-mail: clerk@roscommoncounty.net

Saginaw County

County Clerk

Tenth Judicial Circuit
111 South Michigan Avenue, Saginaw, MI 48602
Tel: (989) 790-5470 Fax: (989) 793-8180

County Clerk/Clerk of Court **Susan Kaltenbach** . . . . (989) 790-5251
111 South Michigan Avenue, Room 101,
Saginaw, MI 48602

Sanilac County

County Clerk

Twenty Fourth Judicial Circuit
60 West Sanilac, Sandusky, MI 48471
Tel: (810) 648-2120 Fax: (810) 648-5466

County Clerk **Denise McGuire** . . . . (810) 648-3212
60 West Sanilac, Sandusky, MI 48471   Fax: (810) 648-5466
E-mail: dmcguire@voyager.net

Schoolcraft County

County Clerk

Eleventh Judicial Circuit
300 Walnut Street, Manistique, MI 49854
Tel: (906) 341-3655 Fax: (906) 341-8291

County Clerk/Clerk of Court, Schoolcraft County
  Beth Edwards . . . . (906) 341-3618
  300 Walnut Street, Room 164,
  Manistique, MI 49854
  E-mail: clerk@schoolcraftcounty.us

Shiawassee County

County Clerk

Thirty Fifth Judicial Circuit
208 North Shiawassee Street, Corunna, MI 48817
Tel: (989) 743-2239 Fax: (989) 743-2602

County Clerk **Lauri Braid** . . . . (989) 743-2242
  208 North Shiawassee Street,   Tel: (989) 743-2239
  Corunna, MI 48817   (Courthouse)
  E-mail: lbraid@shiawassee.net   Fax: (989) 743-2241

St. Clair County

County Clerk

Thirty First Judicial Circuit
200 North Moore Street, Bessemer, MI 49911
Tel: (810) 985-2031 Fax: (810) 985-2030

County Clerk **Jay DeBoyer** . . . . (810) 985-2200
  200 North Moore Street, Bessemer, MI 49911   Tel: (810) 985-2031
                                                           (Circuit Court)
                                                      Fax: (810) 985-4796

St. Joseph County

County Clerk

Forty Fifth Judicial Circuit
125 Main Street, Centreville, MI 49032
Tel: (269) 467-5500 Fax: (269) 467-5628
Internet: www.stjosephcountymi.org/circuit/

County Clerk **Pattie S. Bender** . . . . (269) 467-5531
  125 Main Street, Centreville, MI 49032   Fax: (269) 467-5628

Tuscola County

County Clerk

Fifty Fourth Judicial Circuit
440 North State Street, Caro, MI 48723
Tel: (989) 673-3330 Fax: (989) 672-2169
Internet: www.tuscolacounty.org/circuit%20court/

County Clerk **Jodi S. Fetting** . . . . (989) 672-3780
  440 North State Street, Caro, MI 48723   Fax: (989) 672-4266
  E-mail: clerk@tuscolacounty.org

Van Buren County

County Clerk

Thirty Sixth Judicial Circuit
212 Paw Paw Street, Second Floor, Paw Paw, MI 49079
Tel: (269) 657-8218 Fax: (269) 657-8298
Internet: www.vbco.org/government0312.asp

County Clerk **Tina Leary** . . . . (269) 657-8218
  212 Paw Paw Street, Paw Paw, MI 49079   Fax: (269) 657-8298
  E-mail: learyt@vbco.org

Washtenaw County

County Clerk

Twenty Second Judicial Circuit
101 East Huron, Ann Arbor, MI 48107
Tel: (734) 222-3270 Fax: (734) 222-3077
E-mail: tcadmin@ewashtenaw.org
Internet: http://washtenawtrialcourt.org/

County Clerk **Lawrence Kestenbaum** . . . . (734) 222-6700
  P.O. Box 8645, Ann Arbor, MI 48107   Fax: (734) 222-6700
  200 North Main, Ann Arbor, MI 48107
  101 East Huron, Ann Arbor, MI 48107
  (Courthouse)

Wayne County

County Clerk

Third Judicial Circuit
Coleman A. Young Municipal Center, Two Woodward Avenue,
Detroit, MI 48226
Tel: (313) 224-5261 Fax: (313) 224-6070
Internet: www.3rdcc.org

County Clerk/Clerk of Court **Cathy M. Garrett** . . . . (313) 224-6262
  Coleman A. Young Municipal Center,
  Two Woodward Avenue, Rooms 201 and 207,
  Detroit, MI 48226
  E-mail: cgarrett@co.wayne.mi.us

Wexford County

County Clerk

Twenty Eighth Judicial Circuit
437 East Division Street, Cadillac, MI 49601
Tel: (231) 779-9790 Fax: (231) 779-9230
E-mail: circuitcourt@wexfordcounty.org

County Clerk, Wexford County **Elaine L. Richardson** . . . . (231) 779-9450
  437 East Division Street, Cadillac, MI 49601   Fax: (231) 779-0447
  E-mail: clerk@wexfordcounty.org

Counties Within Judicial Circuits

Circuit Court, 1st Circuit
Areas Covered: Hillsdale County.

Circuit Court, 2nd Circuit
Areas Covered: Berrien County.

Circuit Court, 3rd Circuit
Areas Covered: Wayne County.

(continued on next page)

Circuit Court, 4th Circuit
Areas Covered: Jackson County.

Circuit Court, 5th Circuit
Areas Covered: Barry County.

Circuit Court, 6th Circuit
Areas Covered: Oakland County.

Circuit Court, 7th Circuit
Areas Covered: Genesee County.

Circuit Court, 8th Circuit
Areas Covered: Ionia and Montcalm Counties.

Circuit Court, 9th Circuit
Areas Covered: Kalamazoo County.

Circuit Court, 10th Circuit
Areas Covered: Saginaw County.

Circuit Court, 11th Circuit
Areas Covered: Alger, Luce, Mackinac, and Schoolcraft Counties.

Circuit Court, 12th Circuit
Areas Covered: Baraga, Houghton, and Keweenaw Counties.

Circuit Court, 13th Circuit
Areas Covered: Antrim, Grand Traverse, and Leelanau Counties.

Circuit Court, 14th Circuit
Areas Covered: Muskegon County.

Circuit Court, 15th Circuit
Areas Covered: Branch County.

Circuit Court, 16th Circuit
Areas Covered: Macomb County.

Circuit Court, 17th Circuit
Areas Covered: Kent County.

Circuit Court, 18th Circuit
Areas Covered: Bay County.

Circuit Court, 19th Circuit
Areas Covered: Benzie and Manistee Counties.

Circuit Court, 20th Circuit
Areas Covered: Ottawa County.

Circuit Court, 21st Circuit
Areas Covered: Isabella County.

Circuit Court, 22nd Circuit
Areas Covered: Washtenaw County.

Circuit Court, 23rd Circuit
Areas Covered: Alcona, Arenac, Iosco, and Oscoda Counties.

Circuit Court, 24th Circuit
Areas Covered: Sanilac County.

Circuit Court, 25th Circuit
Areas Covered: Marquette County.

Circuit Court, 26th Circuit
Areas Covered: Alpena and Montmorency Counties.

Circuit Court, 27th Circuit
Areas Covered: Newaygo and Oceana Counties.

Circuit Court, 28th Circuit
Areas Covered: Missaukee and Wexford Counties.

Circuit Court, 29th Circuit
Areas Covered: Clinton and Gratiot Counties.

Circuit Court, 30th Circuit
Areas Covered: Ingham County.

Circuit Court, 31st Circuit
Areas Covered: St. Clair County.

Circuit Court, 32nd Circuit
Areas Covered: Gogebic and Ontonagon Counties.

Circuit Court, 33rd Circuit
Areas Covered: Charlevoix County.

Circuit Court, 34th Circuit
Areas Covered: Ogemaw and Roscommon Counties.

Circuit Court, 35th Circuit
Areas Covered: Shiawassee County.

Circuit Court, 36th Circuit
Areas Covered: Van Buren County.

Circuit Court, 37th Circuit
Areas Covered: Calhoun County.

Circuit Court, 38th Circuit
Areas Covered: Monroe County.

Circuit Court, 39th Circuit
Areas Covered: Lenawee County.

Michigan Court Clerks and Courthouses *continued*

Circuit Court, 40th Circuit

Areas Covered: Lapeer County.

Circuit Court, 41st Circuit

Areas Covered: Dickinson, Iron, and Menominee Counties.

Circuit Court, 42nd Circuit

Areas Covered: Midland County.

Circuit Court, 43rd Circuit

Areas Covered: Cass County.

Circuit Court, 44th Circuit

Areas Covered: Livingston County.

Circuit Court, 45th Circuit

Areas Covered: St. Joseph County.

Circuit Court, 46th Circuit

Areas Covered: Crawford, Kalkaska, and Otsego Counties.

Circuit Court, 47th Circuit

Areas Covered: Delta County.

Circuit Court, 48th Circuit

Areas Covered: Allegan County.

Circuit Court, 49th Circuit

Areas Covered: Mecosta and Osceola Counties.

Circuit Court, 50th Circuit

Areas Covered: Chippewa County.

Circuit Court, 51st Circuit

Areas Covered: Lake and Mason Counties.

Circuit Court, 52nd Circuit

Areas Covered: Huron County.

Circuit Court, 53rd Circuit

Areas Covered: Cheboygan and Presque Isle Counties.

Circuit Court, 54th Circuit

Areas Covered: Tuscola County.

Circuit Court, 55th Circuit

Areas Covered: Clare and Gladwin Counties.

Circuit Court, 56th Circuit

Areas Covered: Eaton County.

Circuit Court, 57th Circuit

Areas Covered: Emmet County.

Minnesota Court Clerks and Courthouses

The trial courts of general jurisdiction in Minnesota are called district courts. There are 10 judicial districts, each consisting of at least one county. The clerks of the District Court in each county are called court administrators.

Minnesota Supreme Court

Minnesota Judicial Center, 25 Rev. Dr. Martin Luther King, Jr. Boulevard, St. Paul, MN 55155
Tel: (651) 297-7650 Tel: (651) 296-2254 (Attorney Registrations)
Fax: (651) 297-5636
Internet: www.mncourts.gov

The Supreme Court consists of a chief justice and six associate justices who are elected in statewide, nonpartisan elections for six-year terms. Vacancies are filled by the Governor. Newly appointed justices serve until the next general election occurring at least one year after appointment, at which time they may run for the position. Retirement is mandatory at age seventy; however, retired justices may be temporarily assigned to serve in any state court. The Supreme Court has original appellate jurisdiction over first degree murder convictions, legislative contest appeals, and appeals from the Minnesota Tax Court and Workers' Compensation Court of Appeals. The Court has discretionary review of decisions of the Minnesota Court of Appeals. The Court also has supervisory control over the lower courts and authority to regulate admission to the bar and review grievance complaints against attorneys.

Court Staff

Clerk of the Appellate Courts and Supreme Court
Administrator **AnnMarie S. O'Neill** . . . . (651) 297-5529
Fax: (651) 297-4149

Minnesota Court of Appeals

Minnesota Judicial Center, 25 Rev. Dr. Martin Luther King, Jr. Boulevard, St. Paul, MN 55155
Tel: (651) 297-1000 Fax: (651) 297-8779
Internet: www.mncourts.gov

The Court of Appeals, established by a constitutional amendment which went into effect in 1983, consists of nineteen judges who are elected in statewide, nonpartisan elections to six-year terms. The Court sits in three-judge panels with rotating memberships. Vacancies are filled by the Governor. The chief judge is appointed by the Governor to serve a three-year term. Retirement is mandatory at age seventy; however, retired judges may be assigned to serve in any court except the Minnesota Supreme Court. The Court of Appeals has appellate jurisdiction over final decisions of the trial courts except decisions of conciliation courts and first degree murder convictions, appeals from administrative agency decisions, and appeals from the Minnesota Commissioner of Economic Security.

Court Staff

Clerk of the Appellate Courts and Supreme Court
Administrator **AnnMarie S. O'Neill** . . . . (651) 297-5529
Fax: (651) 297-4149

County-By-County

Aitkin County

Court Administrator

Ninth Judicial District
616 America Avenue NW, Suite 250, Bemidji, MN 56601
Tel: (218) 755-4500 Fax: (218) 755-4502

Court Administrator, Aitkin County **Bonnie LeCocq** . . . . . (218) 927-7350
  209 Second Street NW, Room 242A,　　　　　　Fax: (218) 927-4535
  Aitkin, MN 56431
  E-mail: bonnie.lecocq@courts.state.mn.us

Anoka County

Court Administrator

Tenth Judicial District
7533 Sunwood Drive NW, Suite 306, Ramsey, MN 55303

Court Administrator, Anoka County **Lori Meyer** . . . . (763) 422-7350
  325 East Main Street, Anoka, MN 55303-2489　　Fax: (763) 422-6919

Becker County

Court Administrator

Seventh Judicial District
725 Courthouse Square, Room 406, St. Cloud, MN 56303

Court Administrator, Becker County **Jan Cossette** . . . . . . (218) 846-7305
  915 Lake Avenue, Detroit Lakes, MN 56501　　Fax: (218) 847-7620

Beltrami County

Court Administrator

Ninth Judicial District
616 America Avenue NW, Suite 250, Bemidji, MN 56601
Tel: (218) 755-4500 Fax: (218) 755-4502

Court Administrator, Beltrami County
  Robert Fommerville . . . . (218) 333-4120
  Beltrami County Judicial Center,　　　　　　Fax: (218) 333-4209
  600 Minnesota Avenue NW, Suite 108,
  Benidji, MN 56601-3068
  E-mail: robert.fommerville@courts.state.mn.us

Benton County

Court Administrator

Seventh Judicial District
725 Courthouse Square, Room 406, St. Cloud, MN 56303

Court Administrator, Benton County **Timothy Roberts** . . . (218) 846-7305
  615 Highway 23, Foley, MN 56329　　　　　　Fax: (218) 847-7620
  E-mail: timothy.roberts@courts.state.mn.us

(continued on next page)

Big Stone County

Court Administrator

Eighth Judicial District
505 Becker Avenue SW, Suite 107, Willmar, MN 56201
Tel: (320) 231-6570 Fax: (320) 231-6577

Court Administrator, Big Stone County
Sandee Tollefson . . . . (320) 839-2536
Big Stone County Courthouse,   Fax: (320) 839-2537
20 Second Street SE, Suite 107,
Ortonville, MN 56278
E-mail: sandee.tollefson@courts.state.nm.us

Blue Earth County

Court Administrator

Fifth Judicial District
11 Civic Center Plaza, Mankato, MN 56001

Court Administrator, Blue Earth County **Kelly Iverson** . . . (507) 304-4650
401 Carver Road, Mankato, MN 56002-0347   Fax: (507) 304-4700
P.O. Box 0347, Mankato, MN 56002-0347
E-mail: kelly.iverson@courts.state.mn.us

Brown County

Court Administrator

Fifth Judicial District
11 Civic Center Plaza, Mankato, MN 56001

Court Administrator, Brown County **Carol Weikle** . . . . (507) 233-6670
14 South State Street, New Ulm, MN 56073-0248   Fax: (507) 359-9562
P.O. Box 248, New Ulm, MN 56073-0248
E-mail: carol.weikle@courts.state.mn.us

Carlton County

Court Administrator

Sixth Judicial District
100 North 5th Avenue West, Room 139, Duluth, MN 55802
Internet: www.mncourts.gov/district/6

Court Administrator, Carlton County (Acting)
Amy Turnquist . . . . (218) 384-9578
301 Walnut Street, Carlton, MN 55718
E-mail: amy.turnquist@courts.state.mn.us

Carver County

Court Administrator

First Judicial District
1620 South Frontage Road, Suite 200, Hastings, MN 55033

Court Administrator, Carver County **Vicky Carlson** . . . . . . (952) 361-1420
604 East Fourth Street, Chaska, MN 55318   Fax: (952) 361-1491
E-mail: vicky.carlson@courts.state.mn.us

Cass County

Court Administrator

Ninth Judicial District
616 America Avenue NW, Suite 250, Bemidji, MN 56601
Tel: (218) 755-4500 Fax: (218) 755-4502

Court Administrator, Cass County
Robert Fommerville . . . . (218) 547-1904
300 Minnesota Avenue, Walker, MN 56484   Fax: (218) 927-4535
P.O. Box 3000, Walker, MN 56484
E-mail: robert.fommerville@courts.state.mn.us

Chippewa County

Court Administrator

Eighth Judicial District
505 Becker Avenue SW, Suite 107, Willmar, MN 56201
Tel: (320) 231-6570 Fax: (320) 231-6577

Court Administrator, Chippewa County
Cheryl Eckhardt . . . . (320) 269-7774
629 North Eleventh Street, Suite 9,   Fax: (320) 269-7733
Montevideo, MN 56265
E-mail: cheryl.eckhardt@courts.state.mn.us

Chisago County

Court Administrator

Tenth Judicial District
7533 Sunwood Drive NW, Suite 306, Ramsey, MN 55303

Court Administrator, Chisago County
Kathleen Karnowski . . . . (651) 213-8650
313 North Main Street, Center City, MN 55012   Fax: (651) 213-8651
E-mail: kathleen.karnowski@courts.state.mn.us

Clay County

Court Administrator

Seventh Judicial District
725 Courthouse Square, Room 406, St. Cloud, MN 56303

Court Administrator, Clay County **Jan Cossette** . . . . (218) 299-5065
915 Lake Avenue, Detroit Lakes, MN 56501   Fax: (218) 299-7307

Clearwater County

Court Administrator

Ninth Judicial District
616 America Avenue NW, Suite 250, Bemidji, MN 56601
Tel: (218) 755-4500 Fax: (218) 755-4502

Court Administrator, Clearwater County
Camille Bessler . . . . (218) 694-6177
Clearwater County District Court,   Fax: (218) 694-6213
213 Main Avenue, Room 303,
Bagley, MN 56621

Cook County

Court Administrator

Sixth Judicial District
100 North 5th Avenue West, Room 139, Duluth, MN 55802
Internet: www.mncourts.gov/district/6

Court Administrator, Cook County (Acting)
Diane Herrick-Schmidt . . . . (218) 387-3610
411 West Second Street, Grand Marais, MN 55604   Fax: (218) 387-3007

Cottonwood County

Court Administrator

Fifth Judicial District
11 Civic Center Plaza, Mankato, MN 56001

Court Administrator, Cottonwood County
Cheryl Peters . . . . (507) 831-4551
401 Carver Road, Mankato, MN 56002-0347   Fax: (507) 831-1425
E-mail: cheryl.peters@courts.state.mn.us

Crow Wing County

Court Administrator

Ninth Judicial District
616 America Avenue NW, Suite 250, Bemidji, MN 56601
Tel: (218) 755-4500 Fax: (218) 755-4502

Court Administrator, Crow Wing County
Bonnie LeCocq . . . . (218) 824-1310
Crow Wing County Judicial Center,   Fax: (218) 824-1311
213 Laurel Street, Suite 11,
Brainerd, MN 56401
E-mail: bonnie.lecocq@courts.state.mn.us

Dakota County

Court Administrator

First Judicial District
1620 South Frontage Road, Suite 200, Hastings, MN 55033

Court Administrator, Dakota County **Carolyn Renn** . . . . . . (651) 438-8100
Dakota County Judicial Center, 1560 Highway 55,
Hastings, MN 55033

Dodge County

Court Administrator

Third Judicial District
1696 Greenview Drive SW, Rochester, MN 55902
Tel: (507) 206-2300 Fax: (507) 285-7476

Court Administrator, Dodge County **Lea Hall** . . . . (507) 635-6260
22 - East Sixth Street, Department 12,
Mantorville, MN 55955

Douglas County

Court Administrator

Seventh Judicial District
725 Courthouse Square, Room 406, St. Cloud, MN 56303

Court Administrator, Douglas County **Rhonda Bot** . . . . . . (320) 762-3033
305 Eighth Avenue West, Alexandria, MN 56308   Fax: (320) 762-8863
E-mail: rhonda.bot@courts.state.mn.us

Faribault County

Court Administrator

Fifth Judicial District
11 Civic Center Plaza, Mankato, MN 56001

Court Administrator, Faribault County **Vicky Driscoll** . . . . (507) 526-6273
415 North Main, Blue Earth, MN 56013-0130   Fax: (507) 526-3054
P.O. Box 130, Blue Earth, MN 56013-0130
E-mail: vicky.driscoll@courts.state.mn.us

Fillmore County

Court Administrator

Third Judicial District
1696 Greenview Drive SW, Rochester, MN 55902
Tel: (507) 206-2300 Fax: (507) 285-7476

Court Administrator, Fillmore County
James Attwood . . . . (507) 765-3356
101 Fillmore Street, Preston, MN 55965

Freeborn County

Court Administrator

Third Judicial District
1696 Greenview Drive SW, Rochester, MN 55902
Tel: (507) 206-2300 Fax: (507) 285-7476

Court Administrator, Freeborn County **Kristine Maiers** . . . (507) 377-5163
411 South Broadway, Albert Lea, MN 56007
E-mail: kristine.maiers@courts.state.mn.us

Goodhue County

Court Administrator

First Judicial District
1620 South Frontage Road, Suite 200, Hastings, MN 55033

Court Administrator, Goodhue County **Yvonne Black** . . . . (651) 267-4800
Goodhue County Justice Center,   Fax: (651) 267-4989
4554 West Sixth Street, Red Wing, MN 55066
E-mail: yvonne.black@courts.state.mn.us

Grant County

Court Administrator

Eighth Judicial District
505 Becker Avenue SW, Suite 107, Willmar, MN 56201
Tel: (320) 231-6570 Fax: (320) 231-6577

Court Administrator, Grant County **Diane K. Fox** . . . . (218) 685-8282
10 Second Street NE, Elbow Lake, MN 56531-1007   Fax: (218) 685-5349
E-mail: diane.fox@courts.state.mn.us

Hennepin County

Court Administrator

Fourth Judicial District
300 South 6th Street, Minneapolis, MN 55487

District Administrator, Hennepin County
Mark Thompson . . . . (612) 348-2040
E-mail: mark.thompson@courts.state.mn.us

(continued on next page)

Minnesota Court Clerks and Courthouses *continued*

Houston County

Court Administrator

Third Judicial District
1696 Greenview Drive SW, Rochester, MN 55902
Tel: (507) 206-2300 Fax: (507) 285-7476

Court Administrator, Houston County **Darlene Larson** ... (507) 725-5806
306 South Marshall, Suite 2100,
Caledonia, MN 55921-1324
E-mail: darlene.larson@courts.state.mn.us

Hubbard County

Court Administrator

Ninth Judicial District
616 America Avenue NW, Suite 250, Bemidji, MN 56601
Tel: (218) 755-4500 Fax: (218) 755-4502

Court Administrator, Hubbard County **Camille Bessler** ... (218) 732-5286
301 Court Avenue, Park Rapids, MN 56470   Fax: (218) 732-0137

Isanti County

Court Administrator

Tenth Judicial District
7533 Sunwood Drive NW, Suite 306, Ramsey, MN 55303

Court Administrator, Isanti County **Tracy Gullerud** ...... (763) 689-2292
555 Eighteenth Avenue SW,
Cambridge, MN 55008
E-mail: tracy.gullerud@courts.state.mn.us

Itasca County

Court Administrator

Ninth Judicial District
616 America Avenue NW, Suite 250, Bemidji, MN 56601
Tel: (218) 755-4500 Fax: (218) 755-4502

Court Administrator, Itasca County **Sean Jones** .... (218) 327-2870
Itasca County District Court, 123 Fourth Street NE,   Fax: (218) 327-2897
Grand Rapids, MN 55744
E-mail: sean.jones@courts.state.mn.us

Jackson County

Court Administrator

Fifth Judicial District
11 Civic Center Plaza, Mankato, MN 56001

Court Administrator, Jackson County **Connie Belgard** ... (507) 847-4400
405 Fourth Street, Jackson, MN 56143   Fax: (507) 847-5433
E-mail: connie.belgard@courts.state.mn.us

Kanabec County

Court Administrator

Tenth Judicial District
7533 Sunwood Drive NW, Suite 306, Ramsey, MN 55303

Court Administrator, Kanabec County
Sharon Schubert ....(320) 679-6400
209 Second Street NW, Aitkin, MN 56431   Fax: (320) 679-6411
E-mail: rosemary.nelson@courts.state.mn.us

Minnesota Court Clerks and Courthouses *continued*

Kandiyohi County

Court Administrator

Eighth Judicial District
505 Becker Avenue SW, Suite 107, Willmar, MN 56201
Tel: (320) 231-6570 Fax: (320) 231-6577

Court Administrator, Kandiyohi County
Debra Mueske ....(320) 231-6206
Kandiyohi County Courthouse,   Fax: (320) 231-6276
505 Becker Avenue SW, Willmar, MN 56201
E-mail: debra.mueske@courts.state.mn.us

Kittson County

Court Administrator

Ninth Judicial District
616 America Avenue NW, Suite 250, Bemidji, MN 56601
Tel: (218) 755-4500 Fax: (218) 755-4502

Court Administrator, Kittson County
Teresa McDonnell ....(218) 843-3632
Kittson County District Court,   Fax: (218) 843-3634
410 South Fifth Street, Suite 204,
Hallock, MN 56728
E-mail: teresa.mcdonnell@courts.state.mn.us

Koochiching County

Court Administrator

Ninth Judicial District
616 America Avenue NW, Suite 250, Bemidji, MN 56601
Tel: (218) 755-4500 Fax: (218) 755-4502

Court Administrator, Koochiching County **Sean Jones** ... (218) 283-1160
Koochiching County District Court,   Fax: (218) 283-1162
715 Fourth Street, International Falls, MN 56649
E-mail: sean.jones@courts.state.mn.us

Lac qui Parle County

Court Administrator

Eighth Judicial District
505 Becker Avenue SW, Suite 107, Willmar, MN 56201
Tel: (320) 231-6570 Fax: (320) 231-6577

Court Administrator, Lac qui Parle County
Cheryl Eckhardt ....(320) 598-3536
600 Sixth Street, Suite 11,   Fax: (320) 598-3915
Madison, MN 56256
E-mail: cheryl.eckhardt@courts.state.nm.us

Lake County

Court Administrator

Sixth Judicial District
100 North 5th Avenue West, Room 139, Duluth, MN 55802
Internet: www.mncourts.gov/district/6

Court Administrator, Lake County (Acting)
Diane Herrick-Schmidt ....(218) 384-8330
301 Walnut Street, Carlton, MN 55718   Fax: (218) 834-8397

Lake of the Woods County

Court Administrator

Ninth Judicial District
616 America Avenue NW, Suite 250, Bemidji, MN 56601
Tel: (218) 755-4500 Fax: (218) 755-4502

Court Administrator, Lake of the Woods County
  Sean Jones . . . . (218) 634-1451
  Lake of the Woods County District Court,   Fax: (218) 634-9444
  206 Eighth Avenue SE, Room 250,
  Baudette, MN 56623
  E-mail: sean.jones@courts.state.mn.us

Le Sueur County

Court Administrator

First Judicial District
1620 South Frontage Road, Suite 200, Hastings, MN 55033

Court Administrator, Le Sueur County **Joanne Kopet**. . . .(507) 357-2251
  Le Sueur County Courthouse,   Fax: (507) 357-6433
  888 South Park Avenue, Le Center, MN 56057
  E-mail: joanne.kopet@courts.state.mn.us

Lincoln County

Court Administrator

Fifth Judicial District
11 Civic Center Plaza, Mankato, MN 56001

Court Administrator, Lincoln County **Wendy Rost** . . . . . . (507) 694-1355
  319 North Rebecca Street,   Fax: (507) 694-1717
  Ivanhoe, MN 56142
  E-mail: wendy.rost@courts.state.mn.us

Lyon County

Court Administrator

Fifth Judicial District
11 Civic Center Plaza, Mankato, MN 56001

Court Administrator, Lyon County **Karen Bierman** . . . . . . (507) 537-6734
  Lyon County Government Center, 607 West Main,   Fax: (507) 537-6150
  Marshall, MN 56258
  E-mail: karen.bierman@courts.state.mn.us

Mahnomen County

Court Administrator

Ninth Judicial District
616 America Avenue NW, Suite 250, Bemidji, MN 56601
Tel: (218) 755-4500 Fax: (218) 755-4502

Court Administrator, Mahnomen County
  Camille Bessler . . . . (218) 935-2251
  311 North Main, Mahnomen, MN 56557   Fax: (218) 935-2851

Marshall County

Court Administrator

Ninth Judicial District
616 America Avenue NW, Suite 250, Bemidji, MN 56601
Tel: (218) 755-4500 Fax: (218) 755-4502

Court Administrator, Marshall County
  Teresa McDonnell . . . . (218) 745-4921
  Marshall County District Court, 208 East Colvin,   Fax: (218) 745-4343
  Suite 18, Warren, MN 56762
  E-mail: teresa.mcdonnell@courts.state.mn.us

Martin County

Court Administrator

Fifth Judicial District
11 Civic Center Plaza, Mankato, MN 56001

Court Administrator, Martin County **Connie Belgard** . . . . (507) 238-3205
  Martin County Security Building, 201 Lake Avenue,   Fax: (507) 238-1913
  Fairmont, MN 56031
  E-mail: connie.belgard@courts.state.mn.us

McLeod County

Court Administrator

First Judicial District
1620 South Frontage Road, Suite 200, Hastings, MN 55033

Court Administrator, McLeod County **Karen Messner** . . . (320) 864-1281
  McLeod County Courthouse,   Fax: (320) 864-5905
  830 Eleventh Street East, Glencoe, MN 55336
  E-mail: karen.messner@courts.state.mn.us

Meeker County

Court Administrator

Eighth Judicial District
505 Becker Avenue SW, Suite 107, Willmar, MN 56201
Tel: (320) 231-6570 Fax: (320) 231-6577

Court Administrator, Meeker County **Debra Mueske**. . . . .(320) 693-5230
  325 North Sibley, Litchfield, MN 55355   Fax: (320) 693-5254
  E-mail: debra.mueske@courts.state.mn.us

Mille Lacs County

Court Administrator

Seventh Judicial District
725 Courthouse Square, Room 406, St. Cloud, MN 56303

Court Administrator, Mille Lacs County **George Lock** . . . (320) 983-8313
  225 Sixth Avenue SE, Milaca, MN 56353   Fax: (320) 983-8384
  E-mail: george.lock@courts.state.mn.us

Morrison County

Court Administrator

Seventh Judicial District
725 Courthouse Square, Room 406, St. Cloud, MN 56303

Court Administrator, Morrison County **Rhonda Bot** . . . . . (320) 632-0327
  213 First Avenue Southeast,   Fax: (320) 632-0340
  Little Falls, MN 56345
  E-mail: rhonda.bot@courts.state.mn.us

(continued on next page)

Mower County

Court Administrator

Third Judicial District
1696 Greenview Drive SW, Rochester, MN 55902
Tel: (507) 206-2300 Fax: (507) 285-7476

Court Administrator, Mower County **Kristine Bartness** . . . (507) 437-9465
    201 Second Avenue NE, Austin, MN 55912

Murray County

Court Administrator

Fifth Judicial District
11 Civic Center Plaza, Mankato, MN 56001

Court Administrator, Murray County **Denise Brandel** . . . . (507) 836-6148
    2500 Twenty Eighth Street,   Fax: (507) 836-6019
    Slayton, MN 56172-0057
    P.O. Box 57, Slayton, MN 56172-0057
    E-mail: denise.brandel@courts.state.mn.us

Nicollet County

Court Administrator

Fifth Judicial District
11 Civic Center Plaza, Mankato, MN 56001

Court Administrator, Nicollet County **Carol Weikle** . . . . . . (507) 931-6800
    501 South Minnesota Avenue,   Fax: (507) 931-4278
    St. Peter, MN 56082
    P.O. Box 496, St. Peter, MN 56082
    E-mail: carol.weikle@courts.state.mn.us

Nobles County

Court Administrator

Fifth Judicial District
11 Civic Center Plaza, Mankato, MN 56001

Court Administrator, Nobles County **Denise Brandel** . . . . (507) 372-8263
    1530 Airport Road, Worthington, MN 56187   Fax: (507) 372-4994
    P.O. Box 547, Worthington, MN 56187
    E-mail: denise.brandel@courts.state.mn.us

Norman County

Court Administrator

Ninth Judicial District
616 America Avenue NW, Suite 250, Bemidji, MN 56601
Tel: (218) 755-4500 Fax: (218) 755-4502

Court Administrator, Norman County **Camille Bessler** . . . (218) 784-5458
    Norman County District Court,   Fax: (218) 784-3110
    16 East Third Avenue East,
    Ada, MN 56510

Olmsted County

Court Administrator

Third Judicial District
1696 Greenview Drive SW, Rochester, MN 55902
Tel: (507) 206-2300 Fax: (507) 285-7476

Court Administrator, Olmsted County **Chuck Kjos** . . . . (507) 206-2400
    151 Fourth Street SE, Rochester, MN 55904
    E-mail: chuck.kjos@courts.state.mn.us

Otter Tail County

Court Administrator

Seventh Judicial District
725 Courthouse Square, Room 406, St. Cloud, MN 56303

Court Administrator, Otter Tail County **Jan Cossette** . . . . (218) 998-8420
    121 West Junius Avenue, Room 310,   Fax: (218) 998-8438
    Fergus Falls, MN 56537

Pennington County

Court Administrator

Ninth Judicial District
616 America Avenue NW, Suite 250, Bemidji, MN 56601
Tel: (218) 755-4500 Fax: (218) 755-4502

Court Administrator, Pennington County
    Kathy Narlock . . . . (218) 683-7023
    Pennington County District Court, 101 North Main,   Fax: (218) 681-0907
    Thief River Falls, MN 56701
    E-mail: kathy.narlock@courts.state.mn.us

Pine County

Court Administrator

Tenth Judicial District
7533 Sunwood Drive NW, Suite 306, Ramsey, MN 55303

Court Administrator, Pine County **Lu Ann Blegen** . . . . (320) 691-1500
    635 Northridge Drive NW, Suite 320,   Fax: (320) 591-1524
    Pine City, MN 55063
    E-mail: luann.blegen@courts.state.mn.us

Pipestone County

Court Administrator

Fifth Judicial District
11 Civic Center Plaza, Mankato, MN 56001

Court Administrator, Pipestone County
    Denise Brandel . . . . (507) 825-6730
    416 South Hiawatha, Pipestone, MN 56164   Fax: (507) 825-6733
    P.O. Box 337, Pipestone, MN 56164
    E-mail: denise.brandel@courts.state.mn.us

Polk County

Court Administrator

Ninth Judicial District
616 America Avenue NW, Suite 250, Bemidji, MN 56601
Tel: (218) 755-4500 Fax: (218) 755-4502

Court Administrator, Polk County **Kathy Narlock** . . . . (218) 281-2332
    Polk County Justice Center, 816 Marin Avenue,   Fax: (218) 281-2204
    Suite 210, Crookston, MN 56716
    E-mail: kathy.narlock@courts.state.mn.us

Minnesota Court Clerks and Courthouses *continued*

Pope County

Court Administrator

Eighth Judicial District
505 Becker Avenue SW, Suite 107, Willmar, MN 56201
Tel: (320) 231-6570 Fax: (320) 231-6577

Court Administrator, Pope County **Sandee Tollefson** .... (320) 634-5222
  130 East Minnesota, Suite 309,   Fax: (320) 634-5527
  Glenwood, MN 56334
  E-mail: sandee.tollefson@courts.state.mn.us

Ramsey County

Court Administrator

Second Judicial District
15 West Kellogg Boulevard, St. Paul, MN 55102
Tel: (651) 266-8266

District Administrator, Ramsey County
  Heather Kendall .... (651) 266-8276
  E-mail: heather.kendall@courts.state.mn.us   Fax: (651) 266-8278

Red Lake County

Court Administrator

Ninth Judicial District
616 America Avenue NW, Suite 250, Bemidji, MN 56601
Tel: (218) 755-4500 Fax: (218) 755-4502

Court Administrator, Red Lake County **Kathy Narlock** ... (218) 253-4281
  Red Lake County District Court,   Fax: (218) 253-4287
  124 Main Avenue NW, Red Lake Falls, MN 56750
  P.O. Box 339, Red Lake Falls, MN 56750
  E-mail: kathy.narlock@courts.state.mn.us

Redwood County

Court Administrator

Fifth Judicial District
11 Civic Center Plaza, Mankato, MN 56001

Court Administrator, Redwood County **Patty Amberg**....(507) 637-4020
  250 South Jefferson,   Fax: (507) 637-4021
  Redwood Falls, MN 56283-0130
  E-mail: patty.amberg@courts.state.mn.us

Renville County

Court Administrator

Eighth Judicial District
505 Becker Avenue SW, Suite 107, Willmar, MN 56201
Tel: (320) 231-6570 Fax: (320) 231-6577

Court Administrator, Renville County **Susan T. Stahl** .... (320) 523-3680
  Renville County Courthouse, 500 East Depue,   Fax: (320) 523-3689
  Third Level, Olivia, MN 56277
  E-mail: susan.stahl@courts.state.mn.us

Minnesota Court Clerks and Courthouses *continued*

Rice County

Court Administrator

Third Judicial District
1696 Greenview Drive SW, Rochester, MN 55902
Tel: (507) 206-2300 Fax: (507) 285-7476

Court Administrator, Rice County **Hans Holland** .... (507) 332-6107
  218 NW Third Street, Suite 300,
  Faribault, MN 55021
  E-mail: hans.holland@courts.state.mn.us

Rock County

Court Administrator

Fifth Judicial District
11 Civic Center Plaza, Mankato, MN 56001

Court Administrator, Rock County **Denise Brandel**...... (507) 283-5020
  204 East Brown Street, Luverne, MN 56156-0745   Fax: (507) 283-5017
  P.O. Box 745, Luverne, MN 56156-0745
  E-mail: denise.brandel@courts.state.mn.us

Roseau County

Court Administrator

Ninth Judicial District
616 America Avenue NW, Suite 250, Bemidji, MN 56601
Tel: (218) 755-4500 Fax: (218) 755-4502

Court Administrator, Roseau County
  Teresa McDonnell .... (218) 463-2541
  606 Fifth Avenue SW, Room 20,   Fax: (218) 463-1889
  Roseau, MN 56751
  E-mail: teresa.mcdonnell@courts.state.mn.us

Scott County

Court Administrator

First Judicial District
1620 South Frontage Road, Suite 200, Hastings, MN 55033

Court Administrator, Scott County **Heather Kendall** ..... (952) 496-8200
  Scott County Justice Center,   Fax: (952) 496-8211
  200 Fourth Avenue West,
  Shakopee, MN 55379-1220
  E-mail: heather.kendall@courts.state.mn.us

Sherburne County

Court Administrator

Tenth Judicial District
7533 Sunwood Drive NW, Suite 306, Ramsey, MN 55303

Court Administrator, Sherburne County **Pat Kuka** .... (763) 765-4600
  13880 Business Center Drive,
  Elk River, MN 55330

Sibley County

Court Administrator

First Judicial District
1620 South Frontage Road, Suite 200, Hastings, MN 55033

Court Administrator, Sibley County **Karen Messner** ..... (507) 237-4051
  400 Court Street, Gaylord, MN 55334   Fax: (507) 237-4062
  E-mail: karen.messner@courts.state.mn.us

(continued on next page)

Minnesota Court Clerks and Courthouses *continued*

St. Louis County

Court Administrator

Sixth Judicial District
100 North 5th Avenue West, Room 139, Duluth, MN 55802
Internet: www.mncourts.gov/district/6

Court Administrator, St. Louis County
    Amy Turnquist . . . . (218) 726-2460 (Duluth)
    100 North Fifth Avenue West,   Tel: (218) 749-7106
    Duluth, MN 55802-1285   (Virginia)
    1810 East Twelfth Avenue,
    Hibbing, MN 55746-1680
    300 Fifth Avenue South, Virginia, MN 55792-2666
    E-mail: amy.turnquist@courts.state.mn.us

Stearns County

Court Administrator

Seventh Judicial District
725 Courthouse Square, Room 406, St. Cloud, MN 56303

Court Administrator, Stearns County **Timothy Roberts** . . . (320) 656-3620
    725 Courthouse Square, St. Cloud, MN 56303   Fax: (320) 656-3626
    E-mail: timothy.roberts@courts.state.mn.us

Steele County

Court Administrator

Third Judicial District
1696 Greenview Drive SW, Rochester, MN 55902
Tel: (507) 206-2300   Fax: (507) 285-7476

Court Administrator, Steele County **Robin Hoefley** . . . . . . (507) 444-7700
    111 East Main Street, Owatonna, MN 55060
    E-mail: robin.hoefley@courts.state.mn.us

Stevens County

Court Administrator

Eighth Judicial District
505 Becker Avenue SW, Suite 107, Willmar, MN 56201
Tel: (320) 231-6570   Fax: (320) 231-6577

Court Administrator, Stevens County
    Sandee Tollefson . . . . (320) 208-6640
    Stevens County Courthouse,   Fax: (320) 589-7288
    400 Colorado Avenue, Suite 307,
    Morris, MN 56267
    E-mail: sandee.tollefson@courts.state.mn.us

Swift County

Court Administrator

Eighth Judicial District
505 Becker Avenue SW, Suite 107, Willmar, MN 56201
Tel: (320) 231-6570   Fax: (320) 231-6577

Court Administrator, Swift County **Debra Mueske** . . . . . . (320) 843-2744
    Swift County Courthouse,   Fax: (320) 843-4124
    301 14th Avenue Street North, Suite 6,
    Benson, MN 56215
    E-mail: debra.mueske@courts.state.mn.us

Minnesota Court Clerks and Courthouses *continued*

Todd County

Court Administrator

Seventh Judicial District
725 Courthouse Square, Room 406, St. Cloud, MN 56303

Court Administrator, Todd County **George Lock** . . . . (320) 732-7800
    221 First Avenue South, Long Prairie, MN 56347   Fax: (320) 732-2506
    E-mail: george.lock@courts.state.mn.us

Traverse County

Court Administrator

Eighth Judicial District
505 Becker Avenue SW, Suite 107, Willmar, MN 56201
Tel: (320) 231-6570   Fax: (320) 231-6577

Court Administrator, Traverse County **Diane K. Fox** . . . . . (320) 563-4343
    Traverse County Courthouse,   Fax: (320) 563-4311
    702 Second Avenue North,
    Wheaton, MN 56296
    E-mail: diane.fox@courts.state.mn.us

Wabasha County

Court Administrator

Third Judicial District
1696 Greenview Drive SW, Rochester, MN 55902
Tel: (507) 206-2300   Fax: (507) 285-7476

Court Administrator, Wabasha County **Julie Welt** . . . . (507) 565-3524
    848 17 Street East, Suite 4,
    Wabasha, MN 55981
    E-mail: julie.welt@courts.state.mn.us

Wadena County

Court Administrator

Seventh Judicial District
725 Courthouse Square, Room 406, St. Cloud, MN 56303

Court Administrator, Wadena County **Rhonda Bot** . . . . . . (218) 631-7633
    415 Jefferson Street South,   Fax: (218) 631-7635
    Wadena, MN 56482
    E-mail: rhonda.bot@courts.state.mn.us

Waseca County

Court Administrator

Third Judicial District
1696 Greenview Drive SW, Rochester, MN 55902
Tel: (507) 206-2300   Fax: (507) 285-7476

Court Administrator, Waseca County **Hans Holland** . . . . . (507) 835-0540
    307 North State Street, Waseca, MN 56093
    E-mail: hans.holland@courts.state.mn.us

Washington County

Court Administrator

Tenth Judicial District
7533 Sunwood Drive NW, Suite 306, Ramsey, MN 55303

Court Administrator, Washington County
Annette Fritz . . . . (651) 430-6263
14949 62nd Street North, Stillwater, MN 55082
P.O. Box 3802, Stillwater, MN 55082
E-mail: annette.fritz@courts.state.mn.us

Watonwan County

Court Administrator

Fifth Judicial District
11 Civic Center Plaza, Mankato, MN 56001

Court Administrator, Watonwan County **Kelly Iverson** . . . . (507) 375-1238
710 Second Avenue South,   Fax: (507) 375-5010
Saint James, MN 56081
P.O. Box 518, Saint James, MN 56081
E-mail: kelly.iverson@courts.state.mn.us

Wilkin County

Court Administrator

Eighth Judicial District
505 Becker Avenue SW, Suite 107, Willmar, MN 56201
Tel: (320) 231-6570 Fax: (320) 231-6577

Court Administrator, Wilkin County **Diane K. Fox** . . . . (218) 643-7172
Wilkin County Courthouse, 300 South Fifth Street,   Fax: (218) 643-7167
Breckenridge, MN 56520
P.O. Box 219, Breckenridge, MN 56520
E-mail: diane.fox@courts.state.nm.us

Winona County

Court Administrator

Third Judicial District
1696 Greenview Drive SW, Rochester, MN 55902
Tel: (507) 206-2300 Fax: (507) 285-7476

Court Administrator, Winona County **Sally Cumiskey** . . . . (507) 457-6385
171 West Third Street, Winona, MN 55987
E-mail: sally.cumiskey@courts.state.mn.us

Wright County

Court Administrator

Tenth Judicial District
7533 Sunwood Drive NW, Suite 306, Ramsey, MN 55303

Court Administrator, Wright County
Monica Tschumper . . . . (763) 682-7539
10 Second Street NW, Buffalo, MN 55313   Fax: (763) 682-7300
E-mail: monica.tschumper@courts.state.mn.us

Yellow Medicine County

Court Administrator

Eighth Judicial District
505 Becker Avenue SW, Suite 107, Willmar, MN 56201
Tel: (320) 231-6570 Fax: (320) 231-6577

Court Administrator, Yellow Medicine County
Cheryl Eckhardt . . . .(320) 564-3325
Yellow Medicine County Courthouse,   Fax: (320) 564-4435
415 Ninth Avenue, Suite 103,
Granite Falls, MN 56241
E-mail: cheryl.eckhardt@courts.state.mn.us

Counties Within Judicial Districts

District Court, 1st Judicial District
Areas Covered: Carver, Dakota, Goodhue, LeSueur, McLeod, Scott, and Sibley Counties.

District Court, 2nd Judicial District
Areas Covered: Ramsey County.

District Court, 3rd Judicial District
Areas Covered: Dodge, Fillmore, Freeborn, Houston, Mower, Olmsted, Rice, Steele, Wabasha, Waseca, and Winona Counties.

District Court, 4th Judicial District
Areas Covered: Hennepin County.

District Court, 5th Judicial District
Areas Covered: Blue Earth, Brown, Cottonwood, Faribault, Jackson, Lincoln, Lyon, Martin, Murray, Nicollet, Nobles, Pipestone, Redwood, Rock, and Watonwan Counties.

District Court, 6th Judicial District
Areas Covered: Carlton, Cook, Lake, and St. Louis Counties.

District Court, 7th Judicial District
Areas Covered: Becker, Benton, Clay, Douglas, Mille Lacs, Morrison, Otter Tail, Stearns, Todd, and Wadena Counties.

District Court, 8th Judicial District
Areas Covered: Big Stone, Chippewa, Grant, Kandiyohi, Lac qui Parle, Meeker, Pope, Renville, Stevens, Swift, Traverse, Wilkin, and Yellow Medicine Counties.

District Court, 9th Judicial District
Areas Covered: Aitkin, Beltrami, Cass, Clearwater, Crow Wing, Hubbard, Itasca, Kittson, Koochiching, Lake of the Woods, Mahnomen, Marshall, Norman, Pennington, Polk, Red Lake, and Roseau Counties.

District Court, 10th Judicial District
Areas Covered: Anoka, Chisago, Isanti, Kanabec, Pine, Sherburne, Washington, and Wright Counties

Mississippi Court Clerks and Courthouses

The trial courts of general jurisdiction in Mississippi consist of circuit courts and chancery courts. There are 22 circuit court districts, each district consisting of at least one county, and 20 chancery court districts, each composed of at least one county. Each county has a Circuit Clerk and a Chancery Clerk. The Circuit Clerk is in charge of the civil and criminal docket. The Chancery Clerk is in charge of the recording of deeds, probate matters, and divorce and guardianship.

Mississippi Supreme Court

Carroll Gartin Justice Building, 450 High Street, Jackson, MS 39201
P.O. Box 117, Jackson, MS 39205
Tel: (601) 359-3697 Fax: (601) 359-2443
E-mail: sctclerk@mssc.state.ms.us
Internet: www.mssc.state.ms.us

The Supreme Court consists of nine justices who are elected in one of three districts for eight-year terms and sit in divisions of three justices each. The Governor appoints temporary justices to fill vacancies, and these appointees serve until the first general election occurring more than nine months after the initial appointment. The longest serving justice is selected as chief justice, and the next two senior justices are selected as presiding justices. The Supreme Court exercises appellate jurisdiction over the lower state courts. The Court also exercises jurisdiction over all matters relating to the state bar.

Court Staff

Clerk of the Court **Muriel Ellis** . . . .(601) 359-2175
    E-mail: sctclerk@mssc.state.ms.us   Fax: (601) 359-2407

Court of Appeals of the State of Mississippi

450 High Street, Jackson, MS 39201
Tel: (601) 576-4665 Fax: (601) 576-4708
Internet: www.courts.ms.gov

The judges of the Mississippi Court of Appeals are elected for eight-year terms on a nonpartisan ballot; each court of appeals district elects two judges to serve on the court. The chief judge is appointed by the Chief Justice of the Mississippi Supreme Court. The chief judge, in turn, appoints the two presiding judges of the Court of Appeals. Established by statute in 1995, the Mississippi Court of Appeals hears cases deflected from the Supreme Court. However, the Supreme Court retains cases involving the death penalty, utility rates, bar matters, annexations, bond issues, election contests, and statutes that have been ruled unconstitutional by a lower court. Decisions by the Court of Appeals are final, except for those accepted by a writ of certiorari to the Supreme Court.

Court Staff

Clerk of the Court **Muriel Ellis** . . . .(601) 359-2175
                                                      Fax: (601) 359-2407

County-By-County

Adams County

Circuit Clerk

Sixth Judicial District
P.O. Box 1383, Natchez, MS 39121

Circuit Clerk, Adams County **Edward C. Walker** . . . .(601) 446-6326
    P.O. Box 1224, Natchez, MS 39121   Fax: (601) 445-7955
    E-mail: ewalker@adamscountyms.gov

Chancery Clerk

Office of the Chancery Clerk
P.O. Box 1006, Natchez, MS 39121
Tel: (601) 446-6684 Fax: (601) 445-7913
E-mail: chanceryclerk@adamscounty.gov

Chancery Clerk **Thomas J. O'Beirne** . . . . (601) 446-6684
    E-mail: chanceryclerk@adamscountyms.gov

Alcorn County

Circuit Clerk

First Judicial District
P.O. Drawer 1100, Tupelo, MS 38802

Circuit Clerk, Alcorn County **Joe Caldwell** . . . . (662) 286-7740
    P.O. Box 430, Corinth, MS 38835   Fax: (662) 286-7767
    600 Waldron Street, Corinth, MS 38834
    E-mail: jcaldwell@co.alcorn.ms.us

Chancery Clerk

Office of the Chancery Clerk
500 Waldron Street, Corinth, MS 38834
Tel: (662) 286-7700 Fax: (662) 286-7706

Chancery Clerk **Bobby Marolt** . . . .(662) 286-7700
    E-mail: bmarolt@co.alcorn.ms.us

Amite County

Circuit Clerk

Sixth Judicial District
P.O. Box 1383, Natchez, MS 39121

Circuit Clerk, Amite County **Debbie Reid Kirkland** . . . . . (601) 657-8932
    P.O. Box 312, Liberty, MS 39645   Fax: (601) 657-1082
    E-mail: ciclerk@amitecountyms.gov

Chancery Clerk

Office of the Chancery Clerk
Courthouse Square, 242 West Main Street, Liberty, MS 39645
Tel: (601) 657-8022 Fax: (601) 657-8288
Internet: www.amitecounty.ms/elected-offices/chancery-clerk

Chancery Clerk **Ronny Taylor** . . . . (601) 657-8022
    E-mail: rtaylor@amitecountyms.gov

(continued on next page)

Attala County

Circuit Clerk

Fifth Judicial District
P.O. Box 721, Kosciusko, MS 39090

Circuit Clerk, Attala County **Wanda Fancher** . . . .(662) 289-1471
  118 West Washington Street,   Fax: (662) 289-7666
  Kosciusko, MS 39090
  E-mail: circuitclerk@attalacounty.net

Chancery Clerk

Office of the Chancery Clerk
230 West Washington Street, Kosciusko, MS 39090
Tel: (662) 289-2921 Fax: (662) 289-7662
E-mail: chanceryclerk@attalacounty.net

Chancery Clerk **Gerry Taylor** . . . . (662) 289-2921
  E-mail: chanceryclerk@attalacounty.net

Benton County

Circuit Clerk

Third Judicial District
One Courthouse Square, Oxford, MS 38655

Circuit Clerk, Benton County **Kathy M. Graves** . . . .(662) 224-6310
  P.O. Box 262, Ashland, MS 38603   Fax: (662) 224-6312
  190 Ripley Avenue, Ashland, MS 38603
  E-mail: circlk@bentoncountyms.gov

Chancery Clerk

Office of the Chancery Clerk
P.O. Box 218, Ashland, MS 38603
Tel: (662) 224-6300
E-mail: chanceryclerk@bentoncountyms.gov

Chancery Clerk **Marlene McKenzie** . . . . (662) 224-6300
  E-mail: chanceryclerk@bentoncountyms.gov

Bolivar County

Circuit Clerk

Eleventh Judicial District
P.O. Box 478, Cleveland, MS 38732

Circuit Clerk, Bolivar County
  Marilyn L. Kelly. . . . .(662) 759-6521 (First District)
  P.O. Box 205, Rosedale, MS 38769 (First District)   Tel: (662) 843-2061
  200 South Court Street, Cleveland, MS 38732   (Second District)
  (Second District)   Fax: (662) 846-2943
  P.O. Box 670, Cleveland, MS 38732 (Second   (Second District)
  District)
  E-mail: mkelly@co.bolivar.ms.us

Chancery Clerk

Office of the Chancery Clerk
P.O. Box 238, Rosedale, MS 38769
Tel: (662) 759-3762 Fax: (662) 759-3467

Chancery Clerk **Brenett Haynes** . . . . (662) 759-3762
  E-mail: bnhaynes@co.bolivar.ms.us

Calhoun County

Circuit Clerk

Third Judicial District
One Courthouse Square, Oxford, MS 38655

Circuit Clerk, Calhoun County **Carlton Baker** . . . . (662) 412-3101
  P.O. Box 25, Pittsboro, MS 38951   Fax: (662) 412-3103

Chancery Clerk

Office of the Chancery Clerk
P.O. Box 8, Pittsboro, MS 38951-0008
Tel: (662) 412-3117 Fax: (662) 412-3111

Chancery Clerk **Romona Tillman** . . . . (662) 412-3117
  E-mail: rtillman@calhouncoms.com

Carroll County

Circuit Clerk

Fifth Judicial District
P.O. Box 721, Kosciusko, MS 39090

Circuit Clerk, Carroll County
  Durward Stanton . . . . (662) 237-9274 (First District)
  P.O. Box 60, Carrollton, MS 38917 (First District)   Tel: (662) 464-5476
  P.O. Box 6, Vaiden, MS 39176 (Second District)   (Second District)
                                                          Fax: (662) 464-5407
                                                          (Second District)

Chancery Clerk

Office of the Chancery Clerk
P.O. Box 60, Carrollton, MS 38917
Tel: (662) 237-9274 Fax: (662) 237-9642

Chancery Clerk **Stanley "Sugar" Mullins** . . . . (662) 237-9274

Chickasaw County

Circuit Clerk

Third Judicial District
One Courthouse Square, Oxford, MS 38655

Circuit Clerk, Chickasaw County
  Cassandra Pulliam . . . . (662) 456-2331 (First District)
  One Pinson Square, Room 2,   Tel: (662) 447-2838
  Houston, MS 38851 (First District)   (Second District)
  234 West Main Street, Room 203,   Fax: (662) 447-5024
  Okolona, MS 38860 (Second District)   (Second District)
  E-mail: cpulliam@courts.ms.gov

Chancery Clerk

Office of the Chancery Clerk
One Pinson Square, Houston, MS 38851
Tel: (662) 456-2513 Fax: (662) 456-5295

Chancery Clerk **Wanda Sweeney** . . . . (662) 456-2513
  E-mail: wanda.sweeney@sos.ms.gov

Choctaw County

Circuit Clerk

Fifth Judicial District
P.O. Box 721, Kosciusko, MS 39090

Circuit Clerk, Choctaw County **Peggy Miller** . . . . (662) 285-6245
  P.O. Box 34, Ackerman, MS 39735   Fax: (662) 285-2196

Chancery Clerk

Office of the Chancery Clerk
P.O. Box 250, Ackerman, MS 39735
Tel: (662) 285-6329 Fax: (662) 285-3444

Chancery Clerk **Steve Montgomery** . . . . (662) 285-6329
   E-mail: steve.montgomery@choctawcountyms.com

Claiborne County

Circuit Clerk

Twenty-Second Judicial District
P.O. Box 310, Hazlehurst, MS 39083

Circuit Clerk, Claiborne County **Sammie Lee Good** . . . . . (601) 437-5841
   P.O. Box 549, Port Gibson, MS 39150   Fax: (601) 437-4543

Chancery Clerk

Office of the Chancery Clerk
410 Market Street, Port Gibson, MS 39150-2000
Tel: (601) 437-4992 Fax: (601) 437-3137

Chancery Clerk **Gloria Kelly Dotson** . . . . (601) 437-4992
   E-mail: gloriadotson@ccmsgov.us

Clarke County

Circuit Clerk

Tenth Judicial District
P.O. Box 1167, Meridian, MS 39302

Circuit Clerk, Clarke County **Beth Doggett Jordan** . . . . . (601) 776-3111
   P.O. Box 216, Quitman, MS 39355   Fax: (601) 776-1001

Chancery Clerk

Office of the Chancery Clerk
P.O. Box 689, Quitman, MS 38355
Tel: (601) 776-2126 Fax: (601) 776-2756

Chancery Clerk **Angie Wade Chisholm** . . . . (601) 776-2126
   E-mail: chancery@clarkecountyms.gov

Clay County

Circuit Clerk

Sixteenth Judicial District
P.O. Box 1679, Starkville, MS 39760

Circuit Clerk, Clay County
   Robert D. "Bob" Harrell, Jr. . . . . (662) 494-3384
   205 Court Street, West Point, MS 39773   Fax: (662) 495-2057
   P.O. Box 364, West Point, MS 39773
   E-mail: rharrell@claycounty.ms.gov

Chancery Clerk

Office of the Chancery Clerk
205 Court Street, West Point, MS 39773
P.O. Box 815, West Point, MS 39773
Tel: (662) 494-3124 Fax: (662) 492-4059

Chancery Clerk **Amy G. Berry** . . . . (662) 494-3124
   E-mail: aberry@claycounty.ms.gov

Coahoma County

Circuit Clerk

Eleventh Judicial District
P.O. Box 478, Cleveland, MS 38732

Circuit Clerk, Coahoma County **Charles A. Oakes** . . . . . . (662) 624-3014
   115 First Street, Clarksdale, MS 38614   Fax: (662) 624-3075
   P.O. Drawer 849, Clarksdale, MS 38614
   E-mail: coahomacirclrk@yahoo.com

Chancery Clerk

Office of the Chancery Clerk
115 First Street, Clarksdale, MS 38614
P.O. Box 98, Clarksdale, MS 38614
Tel: (662) 624-3000 Fax: (662) 624-3040

Chancery Clerk **Ed Peacock III** . . . . (662) 624-3000
   E-mail: chanceryclerkcoahoma@yahoo.com

Copiah County

Circuit Clerk

Twenty-Second Judicial District
P.O. Box 310, Hazlehurst, MS 39083

Circuit Clerk, Copiah County **Edna E. Stevens** . . . . (601) 894-1241
   P.O. Box 467, Hazlehurst, MS 39083   Fax: (601) 894-3026
   E-mail: estevens@copiahcountyms.gov

Chancery Clerk

Office of the Chancery Clerk
122 South Lowe Street, Hazlehurst, MS 39083
Tel: (601) 894-3021 Fax: (601) 894-4081

Chancery Clerk **Steve Amos** . . . . (601) 894-3021
   E-mail: amos39083@aol.com

Covington County

Circuit Clerk

Thirteenth Judicial District
P.O. Box 545, Raleigh, MS 39153

Circuit Clerk, Covington County **Melissa Duckworth** . . . . (601) 765-6506
   P.O. Box 667, Collins, MS 39428   Fax: (601) 765-5012

Chancery Clerk

Office of the Chancery Clerk
P.O. Drawer 1679, Collins, MS 39428
Tel: (601) 765-4242 Fax: (601) 765-5016

Chancery Clerk **Jimmie Baggett** . . . . (601) 765-4242
   E-mail: jimmie.baggett@osa.ms.gov

DeSoto County

Circuit Clerk

Seventeenth Judicial District
P.O. Box 280, Hernando, MS 38632

Circuit Clerk, Desoto County **Dale K. Thompson** . . . . (662) 429-1325
   2535 Highway 51 South, Room 201,   Fax: (662) 449-1416
   Hernando, MS 38632

(continued on next page)

Mississippi Court Clerks and Courthouses *continued*

Chancery Clerk

Office of the Chancery Clerk
2535 Highway 51 South, Room 104, Hernando, MS 38632
Tel: (662) 469-8005 Fax: (662) 469-8308

Chancery Clerk **William E. "Sluggo" Davis** . . . . (662) 469-8005
 E-mail: wdavis@desotocountyms.gov

Forrest County

Circuit Clerk

Twelfth Judicial District
P.O. Box 309, Hattiesburg, MS 39403

Circuit Clerk, Forrest County **Lou Ellen Adams** . . . . (601) 582-3213
 P.O. Drawer 992, Hattiesburg, MS 39403   Fax: (601) 545-6065
 E-mail: ladams@co.forrest.ms.us

Chancery Clerk

Office of the Chancery Clerk
P.O. Box 951, Hattiesburg, MS 39401
Fax: (601) 545-6017

Chancery Clerk **Jimmy C. Havard** . . . . (601) 545-6013

Franklin County

Circuit Clerk

Sixth Judicial District
P.O. Box 1383, Natchez, MS 39121

Circuit Clerk, Franklin County **Millie Thornton** . . . . (601) 384-2320
 P.O. Box 267, Meadville, MS 39653   Fax: (601) 384-8244

Chancery Clerk

Office of the Chancery Clerk
P.O. Box 297, Meadville, MS 39653-0297
Tel: (601) 384-2330 Fax: (601) 384-5864

Chancery Clerk **Jill Jordan Gilbert** . . . . (601) 384-2330
 E-mail: jill.gilbert@sos.ms.gov

George County

Circuit Clerk

Nineteenth Judicial District
P.O. Box 998, Pascagoula, MS 39568

Circuit Clerk, George County **Chad Welford** . . . . (601) 947-4881
 355 Cox Street, Suite C, Lucedale, MS 39452   Fax: (601) 947-8804

Chancery Clerk

Chancery Clerk
355 Cox Street, Suite A, Lucedale, MS 39452
Fax: (601) 947-1300

Chancery Clerk **Cammie B. Byrd** . . . . (601) 947-4801

Mississippi Court Clerks and Courthouses *continued*

Greene County

Circuit Clerk

Nineteenth Judicial District
P.O. Box 998, Pascagoula, MS 39568

Circuit Clerk, Greene County **Cecelia Bounds** . . . .(601) 394-2379
 P.O. Box 310, Leakesville, MS 39451   Fax: (601) 394-2334

Chancery Clerk

Chancery Clerk
400 Main Street, Leakesville, MS 39451
Fax: (601) 394-4445

Chancery Clerk **Michelle Eubanks** . . . . (601) 394-2377

Grenada County

Circuit Clerk

Fifth Judicial District
P.O. Box 721, Kosciusko, MS 39090

Circuit Clerk, Grenada County **Michele Redditt** . . . . (662) 226-1941
 P.O. Box 1517, Grenada, MS 38902   Fax: (662) 227-2865
 E-mail: lbcirclk@ayrix.net

Chancery Clerk

Office of the Chancery Clerk
P.O. Box 1208, Grenada, MS 38902
Tel: (662) 226-1821 Fax: (662) 227-2860

Chancery Clerk **Johnny L. Hayward** . . . . (662) 226-1821
 E-mail: jhayward@grenadacountyms.org

Hancock County

Circuit Clerk

Second Judicial District
P.O. Box 1461, Gulfport, MS 39502

Circuit Clerk, Hancock County **Karen Ladner Ruhr** . . . . . (228) 467-5265
 152 Main Street, Suite B,   Fax: (228) 467-2779
 Bay Saint Louis, MS 39520

Chancery Clerk

Chancery Clerk
152 Main Street, Suite A, Bay Saint Louis, MS 39520

Chancery Clerk **Tim Kellar** . . . .(228) 467-5406

Harrison County

Circuit Clerk

Second Judicial District
P.O. Box 1461, Gulfport, MS 39502

Circuit Clerk, Harrison County
 Gayle Parker . . . . (228) 865-4051 (First District)
 P.O. Box 998, Gulfport, MS 39502 (First District)   Tel: (228) 435-8233
 P.O. Box 235, Biloxi, MS 39533   (Second District)
 E-mail: gkparker@co.harrison.ms.us   Fax: (228) 435-8270
          (Second District)

Chancery Clerk

Office of the Chancery Clerk
1801 23rd Avenue, Gulfport, MS 39501
Fax: (228) 214-1513
E-mail: chanceryclerk@co.harrison.ms.us

Chancery Clerk **John McAdams** . . . . (228) 865-4117

Hinds County

Circuit Clerk

Seventh Judicial District
P.O. Box 327, Jackson, MS 39205

Circuit Clerk, Hinds County
  Barbara Dunn . . . . (601) 968-6628 (First District)
  P.O. Box 327, Jackson, MS 39205 (First District)   Tel: (601) 857-8038
  P.O. Box 999, Raymond, MS 39154 (Second   (Second District)
  District)   Fax: (601) 857-0535
                                 (Second District)

Chancery Clerk

Chancery Clerk
P.O. Box 686, Jackson, MS 39205
316 South President Street, Jackson, MS 39201

Chancery Clerk **Eddie Jean Carr** . . . . (601) 968-6508

Holmes County

Circuit Clerk

Twenty-First Judicial District
P.O. Box 149, Lexington, MS 39095

Circuit Clerk, Holmes County **Earline Wright-Hart** . . . . . . (662) 834-2476
  P.O. Box 718, Lexington, MS 39095   Fax: (662) 834-3870

Chancery Clerk

Office of the Chancery Clerk
P.O. Box 239, Lexington, MS 39095
Tel: (662) 834-2508 Fax: (662) 834-1872

Chancery Clerk **Henry Luckett** . . . . (662) 834-2508
  E-mail: hluckett@holmescountyms.org

Humphreys County

Circuit Clerk

Twenty-First Judicial District
P.O. Box 149, Lexington, MS 39095

Circuit Clerk, Humphreys County **Timaka J. Jones** . . . . . (662) 247-3065
  P.O. Box 696, Belzoni, MS 39038   Fax: (662) 247-3906

Chancery Clerk

Office of the Chancery Clerk
P.O. Box 547, Belzoni, MS 39038
Tel: (662) 247-1740 Fax: (662) 247-0101

Chancery Clerk **Lawrence D. Browder** . . . . (662) 247-1740
  E-mail: lbrowder@courts.ms.gov

Issaquena County

Circuit Clerk

Ninth Judicial District
P.O. Box 351, Vicksburg, MS 39181

Circuit Clerk, Issaquena County **Erline Fortner** . . . . (601) 873-2761
  P.O. Box 27, Mayersville, MS 39113   Fax: (601) 873-2061

Chancery Clerk

Office of the Chancery Clerk
P.O. Box 27, Mayersville, MS 39113
Tel: (662) 873-2761 Fax: (662) 873-2061

Chancery Clerk **Erline Fortner** . . . . (662) 873-2761
  E-mail: clerk@issaquenacountyms.gov

Itawamba County

Circuit Clerk

First Judicial District
P.O. Drawer 1100, Tupelo, MS 38802

Circuit Clerk, Itawamba County **Carol Gates** . . . . (662) 862-3511
  201 West Main Street, Fulton, MS 38843   Fax: (662) 862-4006

Chancery Clerk

Office of the Chancery Clerk
P.O. Box 776, Fulton, MS 38843
Tel: (662) 862-3421

Chancery Clerk **James E. "Jim" Witt** . . . . (662) 862-3421
  E-mail: jwitt@itawambacoms.com

Jackson County

Circuit Clerk

Nineteenth Judicial District
P.O. Box 998, Pascagoula, MS 39568

Circuit Clerk, Jackson County **Joe W. Martin, Jr.** . . . . (228) 769-3040
  P.O. Box 998, Pascagoula, MS 39568   Fax: (228) 769-3180
  E-mail: joe_martin@co.jackson.ms.us

Chancery Clerk

Office of the Chancery Clerk
P.O. Box 998, Pascagoula, MS 39568
Fax: (228) 769-3397

Chancery Clerk **Terry Miller** . . . . (228) 769-3124
  E-mail: terry_miller@co.jackson.ms.us

Jasper County

Circuit Clerk

Thirteenth Judicial District
P.O. Box 545, Raleigh, MS 39153

Circuit Clerk, Jasper County
  Billy G. Rayner . . . . (601) 727-4941 (First District)
  P.O. Box 58, Paulding, MS 39348 (First District)   Tel: (601) 764-2245
  P.O. Box 447, Bay Springs, MS 39422 (Second   (Second District)
  District)   Fax: (601) 764-3078
  E-mail: brayner@co.jasper.ms.us   (Second District)

(continued on next page)

Chancery Clerk

Office of the Chancery Clerk
P.O. Box 1047, Bay Springs, MS 39422
Tel: (601) 764-3368 Fax: (601) 764-3999

Chancery Clerk **Barbara D. Ravenhorst** . . . . (601) 764-3368
   E-mail: bravenhorst@co.jasper.ms.us

Jefferson County

Circuit Clerk

Twenty-Second Judicial District
P.O. Box 310, Hazlehurst, MS 39083

Circuit Clerk, Jefferson County **Arnell Harried** . . . . (601) 786-3422
   1483 Main Street, Fayette, MS 39069   Fax: (601) 786-9676
   P.O. Box 305, Fayette, MS 39069

Chancery Clerk

Office of the Chancery Clerk
1483 Main Street, Fayette, MS 39069
P.O. Box 145, Fayette, MS 39063
Tel: (601) 786-3021 Fax: (601) 786-6009

Chancery Clerk **Delorise Frye** . . . . (601) 786-3021
   E-mail: delorisef@jeffersoncountyms.gov

Jefferson Davis County

Circuit Clerk

Fifteenth Judicial District
P.O. Box 488, Purvis, MS 39475

Circuit Clerk, Jefferson Davis County
   Clint W. Langley . . . . (601) 792-4231
   P.O. Box 1090, Prentiss, MS 39474   Fax: (601) 792-4957

Chancery Clerk

Office of the Chancery Clerk
P.O. Box 1137, Prentiss, MS 39474-1137
Tel: (601) 792-4204 Fax: (601) 792-2894

Chancery Clerk **John William Davies** . . . . (601) 792-4204
   E-mail: jwdavies53@hotmail.com

Jones County

Circuit Clerk

Eighteenth Judicial District
P.O. Box 685, Laurel, MS 39441

Circuit Clerk, Jones County
   Wendell Bart Gavin, Jr. . . . . (601) 477-8538 (First District)
   101 Court Street, Suite B,   Tel: (601) 425-2556
   Ellisville, MS 39437 (First District)   (Second District)
   P.O. Box 1336, Laurel, MS 39441 (Second District)   Fax: (601) 399-4774
              (Second District)

Chancery Clerk

Office of the Chancery Clerk
101 North Court Street, Ellisville, MS 39437 (First Judicial District)
415 North Fifth Avenue, Laurel, MS 39441 (Second Judicial District)
P.O. Box 248, Ellisville, MS 39437 (First Judicial District)
P.O. Box 1468, Laurel, MS 39441 (Second Judicial District)
Tel: (601) 477-3307 (First Judicial District)
Tel: (601) 428-0527 (Second Judicial District)
Fax: (601) 477-1240 (First Judicial District)
Fax: (601) 428-3610 (Second Judicial District)

Chancery Clerk **Concetta Brooks** . . . . (601) 428-0527
   E-mail: cbrooks@co.jones.ms.us

Kemper County

Circuit Clerk

Tenth Judicial District
P.O. Box 1167, Meridian, MS 39302

Circuit Clerk, Kemper County **Tracey Murray** . . . . (601) 743-2224
   P.O. Box 130, DeKalb, MS 39328   Fax: (601) 743-4173

Chancery Clerk

Office of the Chancery Clerk
P.O. Box 188, DeKalb, MS 39328
Tel: (601) 743-2560 Fax: (601) 743-2789

Chancery Clerk **Shirlene Watkins** . . . . (601) 743-2560
   E-mail: swatkins@kemper.k12.ms.us

Lafayette County

Circuit Clerk

Third Judicial District
One Courthouse Square, Oxford, MS 38655

Circuit Clerk, Lafayette County **Baretta J. Mosley** . . . . . . (662) 234-4951
   One Courthouse Square, Suite 101,   Fax: (662) 236-0238
   Oxford, MS 38655
   E-mail: bmosley@lafayettecoms.com

Chancery Clerk

Office of the Chancery Clerk
300 North Lamar Boulevard, Oxford, MS 38655
P.O. Box 1240, Oxford, MS 38655
Tel: (662) 234-2131 Fax: (662) 234-5038

Chancery Clerk **Sherry Wall** . . . . (662) 234-2131
   E-mail: swall@lafayettecoms.com

Lamar County

Circuit Clerk

Fifteenth Judicial District
P.O. Box 488, Purvis, MS 39475

Circuit Clerk, Lamar County **Leslie Wilson** . . . . (601) 794-8504
   P.O. Box 369, Purvis, MS 39475   Fax: (601) 794-3905

Chancery Clerk

Chancery Clerk
P.O. Box 247, Purvis, MS 39475

Chancery Clerk **Wayne Smith** . . . . (601) 794-8504

Lauderdale County

Circuit Clerk

Tenth Judicial District
P.O. Box 1167, Meridian, MS 39302

Circuit Clerk, Lauderdale County **Donna Jill Johnson** . . . (601) 482-9731
  500 Constitution Avenue, 1st Floor,   Fax: (601) 482-9734
  Meridian, MS 39301
  P.O. Box 1005, Meridian, MS 39302
  E-mail: circuitclerk@lauderdalecounty.org

Chancery Clerk

Office of the Chancery Clerk
500 Constitution Avenue, Meridian, MS 39301
Tel: (601) 482-9701   Fax: (601) 482-9744

Chancery Clerk **Carolyn Mooney** . . . . (601) 482-9701
  E-mail: chanceryclerk@lauderdalecounty.org

Lawrence County

Circuit Clerk

Fifteenth Judicial District
P.O. Box 488, Purvis, MS 39475

Circuit Clerk, Lawrence County
  James "Sandy" Brister . . . . (601) 587-4791
  P.O. Box 1249, Monticello, MS 39654   Fax: (601) 587-4405

Chancery Clerk

Office of the Chancery Clerk
P.O. Box 1160, Monticello, MS 39654
Tel: (601) 587-7162   Fax: (601) 587-0767

Chancery Clerk **Kevin Rayborn** . . . . (601) 587-7162
  E-mail: krayborn@co.lawrence.ms.us

Leake County

Circuit Clerk

Eighth Judicial District
P.O. Box 220, Decatur, MS 39327

Circuit Clerk, Leake County **Kathy G. Henderson** . . . . . . (601) 267-8357
  P.O. Box 67, Carthage, MS 39051   Fax: (601) 267-8889

Chancery Clerk

Office of the Chancery Clerk
P.O. Box 72, Carthage, MS 39051
Tel: (601) 267-7371   Fax: (601) 267-6137

Chancery Clerk **Dot Merchant** . . . . (601) 267-7371
  E-mail: dmerchant@co.leake.ms.us

Lee County

Circuit Clerk

First Judicial District
P.O. Drawer 1100, Tupelo, MS 38802

Circuit Clerk, Lee County **Joyce Roberts Loftin** . . . . (662) 432-2200
  P.O. Box 762, Tupelo, MS 38802   Fax: (662) 680-6079

Chancery Clerk

Office of the Chancery Clerk
P.O. Box 7127, Tupelo, MS 38802
Tel: (662) 432-2100   Fax: (662) 680-6091

Chancery Clerk **Bill Benson** . . . . (662) 432-2100
  E-mail: bbenson@co.lee.ms.us

Leflore County

Circuit Clerk

Fourth Judicial District
P.O. Box 244, Greenwood, MS 38935

Circuit Clerk, Leflore County **Elmus Stockstill** . . . . (662) 453-1435
  P.O. Box 1953, Greenwood, MS 38935   Fax: (662) 455-1278

Chancery Clerk

Office of the Chancery Clerk
P.O. Box 250, Greenwood, MS 38935-0250
Tel: (662) 453-6203   Fax: (601) 455-7965

Chancery Clerk **Sam Abraham** . . . . (662) 453-6203
  E-mail: sabraham@leflorecounty.net

Lincoln County

Circuit Clerk

Fourteenth Judicial District
P.O. Drawer 1350, Brookhaven, MS 39602

Circuit Clerk, Lincoln County **Dustin Bairfield** . . . . (601) 835-3435
  301 South First Street, Room 205,   Fax: (601) 835-3482
  Brookhaven, MS 39601
  E-mail: dbairfield@co.lincoln.ms.us

Chancery Clerk

Office of the Chancery Clerk
P.O. Box 555, Brookhaven, MS 39602
Tel: (601) 835-3411   Fax: (601) 835-3423

Chancery Clerk **Tillmon Bishop** . . . . (601) 835-3411
  E-mail: btbishop@co.lincoln.ms.us

Lowndes County

Circuit Clerk

Sixteenth Judicial District
P.O. Box 1679, Starkville, MS 39760

Circuit Clerk, Lowndes County
  Mahala Nickles "Haley" Salazar . . . . (662) 329-5900
  505 Second Avenue North, Room 264,   Fax: (662) 329-5935
  Columbus, MS 39701
  P.O. Box 31, Columbus, MS 39703

Chancery Clerk

Office of the Chancery Clerk
505 Second Avenue North, Columbus, MS 39701
P.O. Box 684, Columbus, MS 39703
Tel: (662) 329-5800

Chancery Clerk **Lisa Neese** . . . . (662) 329-5800
  E-mail: lisayn315@yahoo.com

(continued on next page)

Madison County

Circuit Clerk

Twentieth Judicial District
P.O. Box 1626, Canton, MS 39046

Circuit Clerk, Madison County **Lee Westbrook** . . . . (601) 859-4365
  128 West North Street, Canton, MS 39046   Fax: (601) 859-8555
  P.O. Drawer 1626, Canton, MS 39046

Chancery Clerk

Office of the Chancery Clerk
146 West Center Street, Canton, MS 39046
Tel: (601) 855-5526 Fax: (601) 859-0337

Chancery Clerk **Ronny Lott** . . . . (601) 855-5526
  E-mail: ronny.lott@madison-co.com

Marion County

Circuit Clerk

Fifteenth Judicial District
P.O. Box 488, Purvis, MS 39475

Circuit Clerk, Marion County **Janette Nolan** . . . . (601) 736-8246
  250 Broad Street, Suite 1,   Fax: (601) 731-6344
  Columbia, MS 39429

Chancery Clerk

Office of the Chancery Clerk
215 Broad Street, Columbia, MS 39429

Chancery Clerk **Cass Barnes** . . . . (601) 736-2691
  E-mail: cbarnes@co.marion.ms.us

Marshall County

Circuit Clerk

Third Judicial District
One Courthouse Square, Oxford, MS 38655

Circuit Clerk, Marshall County **Lucy Carpenter** . . . . (662) 252-3434
  P.O. Box 459, Holly Springs, MS 38635   Fax: (662) 252-5951

Chancery Clerk

Office of the Chancery Clerk
P.O. Box 219, Holly Springs, MS 38635
Tel: (662) 252-4431 Fax: (662) 551-3302

Chancery Clerk **Chuck Thomas** . . . . (662) 252-4431
  E-mail: chancery@marshallcoms.org

Monroe County

Circuit Clerk

First Judicial District
P.O. Drawer 1100, Tupelo, MS 38802

Circuit Clerk, Monroe County **Judy K. Butler** . . . . (662) 369-8695
  P.O. Box 843, Aberdeen, MS 39730   Fax: (662) 369-3684

Chancery Clerk

Office of the Chancery Clerk
P.O. Box 578, Aberdeen, MS 39730
Tel: (662) 369-8143 Fax: (662) 369-7928

Chancery Clerk **Ronnie Boozer** . . . . (662) 369-8143
  E-mail: rboozer@monroecoms.com

Montgomery County

Circuit Clerk

Fifth Judicial District
P.O. Box 721, Kosciusko, MS 39090

Circuit Clerk, Montgomery County
  Lanelle Garrett Martin . . . . (662) 283-4161
  P.O. Box 765, Winona, MS 38967   Fax: (662) 283-3363

Chancery Clerk

Office of the Chancery Clerk
P.O. Box 71, Winona, MS 38967
Tel: (662) 283-2333 Fax: (662) 283-2233

Chancery Clerk **Talmadge "Tee" Golding** . . . . (662) 283-2333
  E-mail: tgolding@montgomerycountyms.com

Neshoba County

Circuit Clerk

Eighth Judicial District
P.O. Box 220, Decatur, MS 39327

Circuit Clerk, Neshoba County **Patti Lee** . . . . (601) 656-4781
  401 East Beacon Street, Suite 110,   Fax: (601) 650-3997
  Philadelphia, MS 39350
  E-mail: circuitclerk@neshobacounty.net

Chancery Clerk

Office of the Chancery Clerk
401 Beacon Street, Suite 107, Philadelphia, MS 39350
Tel: (601) 656-3581 Fax: (601) 656-5915
E-mail: chanceryclerk@neshobacounty.net

Chancery Clerk **Guy Nowell** . . . . (601) 656-3581
  E-mail: chanceryclerk@neshobacounty.net

Newton County

Circuit Clerk

Eighth Judicial District
P.O. Box 220, Decatur, MS 39327

Circuit Clerk, Newton County **Mike Butler** . . . . (601) 635-2368
  P.O. Box 447, Decatur, MS 39327   Fax: (601) 635-3210

Chancery Clerk

Office of the Chancery Clerk
P.O. Box 68, Decatur, MS 39327
Tel: (601) 635-2367 Fax: (601) 635-3479

Chancery Clerk **George Hayes, Jr.** . . . . (601) 635-2367
  E-mail: gthayes@yahoo.com

Noxubee County

Circuit Clerk

Sixteenth Judicial District
P.O. Box 1679, Starkville, MS 39760

Circuit Clerk, Noxubee County (Acting) **Freda Phillips** . . . (662) 726-5737
505 South Jefferson, Macon, MS 39341   Fax: (662) 726-6041
E-mail: fphillips@courts.ms.gov

Chancery Clerk

Office of the Chancery Clerk
505 South Jefferson, Macon, MS 39341
Tel: (662) 726-4243 Fax: (662) 726-2272

Chancery Clerk **Mary Washington** . . . . (662) 726-4243
E-mail: mwashington@mdoc.state.ms.us

Oktibbeha County

Circuit Clerk

Sixteenth Judicial District
P.O. Box 1679, Starkville, MS 39760

Circuit Clerk, Oktibbeha County **Glenn Hamilton** . . . . (662) 323-1356
108 West Main Street, Starkville, MS 39759   Fax: (662) 323-1121

Chancery Clerk

Office of the Chancery Clerk
101 East Main Street, Starkville, MS 39759
Tel: (662) 323-5834 Fax: (662) 338-1064

Chancery Clerk **Monica W. Banks** . . . . (662) 323-5834
E-mail: monicawbanks@hotmail.com

Panola County

Circuit Clerk

Seventeenth Judicial District
P.O. Box 280, Hernando, MS 38632

Circuit Clerk, Panola County
  Melissa Meek Phelps . . . . (662) 487-2073 (First District)
215 Pocahontas Street, Sardis, MS 38666 (First   Tel: (662) 563-6210
District)   (Second District)
P.O. Box 346, Batesville, MS 38606 (Second   Fax: (662) 563-8233
District)   (Second District)

Chancery Clerk

Office of the Chancery Clerk
151 Public Square, Batesville, MS 38606
Tel: (662) 563-6205 Fax: (662) 563-6277

Chancery Clerk **Jim Pitcock** . . . . (662) 563-6205
E-mail: jrp@panola.com

Pearl River County

Circuit Clerk

Fifteenth Judicial District
P.O. Box 488, Purvis, MS 39475

Circuit Clerk, Pearl River County **Vickie P. Hariel** . . . . (601) 403-2300
200 South Main Street, Poplarville, MS 39470   Fax: (601) 403-2327

Chancery Clerk

Chancery Clerk
200 South Main Street, Poplarville, MS 39470
Fax: (601) 403-2317
Internet: http://www.pearlrivercounty.net/chancery/index.htm

Chancery Clerk **David Earl Johnson** . . . . (601) 403-2312

Perry County

Circuit Clerk

Twelfth Judicial District
P.O. Box 309, Hattiesburg, MS 39403

Circuit Clerk, Perry County **Martha F. Clark** . . . . (601) 964-8663
P.O. Box 198, New Augusta, MS 39642   Fax: (601) 964-8740

Chancery Clerk

Chancery Clerk
103 South Main Street, New Augusta, MS 39462
Fax: (601) 964-7646

Chancery Clerk **Vickie Walters** . . . . (601) 964-8398

Pike County

Circuit Clerk

Fourteenth Judicial District
P.O. Drawer 1350, Brookhaven, MS 39602

Circuit Clerk, Pike County **Roger A. Graves** . . . . (601) 783-2581
P.O. Box 31, Magnolia, MS 39652   Fax: (601) 783-6322
218 East Bay Street, Magnolia, MS 39652
E-mail: rogerg@co.pike.ms.us

Chancery Clerk

Office of the Chancery Clerk
P.O. Box 309, Magnolia, MS 39652
Tel: (601) 783-3362 Fax: (601) 783-5982
E-mail: dougt@co.pike.ms.us

Chancery Clerk **Doug Touchstone** . . . . (601) 783-3362
E-mail: dougt@co.pike.ms.us

Pontotoc County

Circuit Clerk

First Judicial District
P.O. Drawer 1100, Tupelo, MS 38802

Circuit Clerk, Pontotoc County **Melinda Nowicki** . . . . (662) 489-3908
P.O. Box 430, Corinth, MS 38835   Fax: (662) 489-2318

Chancery Clerk

Office of the Chancery Clerk
P.O. Box 209, Pontotoc, MS 38863
Tel: (662) 489-3900 Fax: (662) 489-3940

Chancery Clerk **Gary Moorman** . . . . (662) 489-3900
E-mail: gmoorman@pontotoccoms.com

(continued on next page)

Prentiss County

Circuit Clerk

First Judicial District
P.O. Drawer 1100, Tupelo, MS 38802

Circuit Clerk, Prentiss County **Mike Kelley** . . . . (662) 728-4611
   101-A North Main Street, Booneville, MS 38829   Fax: (662) 728-2006
   P.O. 727, Booneville, MS 38829

Chancery Clerk

Office of the Chancery Clerk
P.O. Box 477, Booneville, MS 38829-0477
Tel: (662) 728-8151 Fax: (662) 728-2007

Chancery Clerk **David "Bubba" Pounds** . . . . (662) 728-8151
   E-mail: bubba@co.prentiss.ms.us

Quitman County

Circuit Clerk

Eleventh Judicial District
P.O. Box 478, Cleveland, MS 38732

Circuit Clerk, Quitman County **Brenda A. Wiggs** . . . . (601) 326-8003
   220 Chestnut Street, Suite 4,   Fax: (601) 326-8004
   Marks, MS 38646

Chancery Clerk

Office of the Chancery Clerk
220 Chestnut Street, Suite 2, Marks, MS 38646
Tel: (662) 326-2661 Fax: (662) 326-8004

Chancery Clerk **Butch Scipper** . . . . (662) 326-2661

Rankin County

Circuit Clerk

Twentieth Judicial District
P.O. Box 1626, Canton, MS 39046

Circuit Clerk, Rankin County **Becky Boyd** . . . . (601) 825-1466
   215 East Government Street, Suite A,   Fax: (601) 825-1465
   Brandon, MS 39042
   P.O. Drawer 1599, Brandon, MS 39043
   E-mail: rdnboyd@rankincounty.org

Chancery Clerk

Office of the Chancery Clerk
211 East Government Street, Suite D, Brandon, MS 39042
Tel: (601) 825-1469 Fax: (601) 824-7116

Chancery Clerk **Larry Swales** . . . . (601) 825-1469
   E-mail: lswales@rankincounty.org

Scott County

Circuit Clerk

Eighth Judicial District
P.O. Box 220, Decatur, MS 39327

Circuit Clerk, Scott County **Joe Rigby** . . . . (601) 469-3601
   P.O. Box 371, Forest, MS 39074   Fax: (601) 469-5188

Chancery Clerk

Office of the Chancery Clerk
P.O. Box 630, Forest, MS 39074
Tel: (601) 469-1922 Fax: (601) 469-5180

Chancery Clerk **Lee Anne Livingston Palmer** . . . . (601) 469-1922
   E-mail: lee@fairoilco.com

Sharkey County

Circuit Clerk and Chancery Clerk

Ninth Judicial District
P.O. Box 351, Vicksburg, MS 39181

Circuit Clerk and Chancery Clerk, Sharkey County
   Murindia Williams . . . . (601) 636-8327
   P.O. Box 218, Rolling Fork, MS 39159   Fax: (601) 873-8327
   E-mail: mwilliams@stonecountyms.gov

Simpson County

Circuit Clerk

Thirteenth Judicial District
P.O. Box 545, Raleigh, MS 39153

Circuit Clerk, Simpson County **Steve Womack** . . . . (601) 847-2474
   P.O. Box 307, Mendenhall, MS 39114   Fax: (601) 847-4011

Chancery Clerk

Office of the Chancery Clerk
P.O. Box 367, Mendenhall, MS 39114
Tel: (601) 847-2626 Fax: (601) 847-7016

Chancery Clerk **Tommy Joe Harvey** . . . . (601) 847-2626
   E-mail: tjharvey@co.simpson.ms.us

Smith County

Circuit Clerk

Thirteenth Judicial District
P.O. Box 545, Raleigh, MS 39153

Circuit Clerk, Smith County **Anthony Grayson** . . . . (601) 782-4751
   P.O. Box 517, Raleigh, MS 39153   Fax: (601) 782-4007

Chancery Clerk

Office of the Chancery Clerk
P.O. Box 39, Raleigh, MS 39153
Tel: (601) 782-9811 Fax: (601) 782-4690

Chancery Clerk **Cindy Austin** . . . . (601) 782-9811
   E-mail: chanceryclerk@co.smith.ms.us

Stone County

Circuit Clerk

Second Judicial District
P.O. Box 1461, Gulfport, MS 39502

Circuit Clerk, Stone County **Kenny Hatten** . . . . (662) 928-5246
   323 East Cavers Avenue, Wiggins, MS 39577   Fax: (662) 286-7767
   E-mail: khatten@stonecountyms.gov

Chancery Clerk

Office of the Chancery Clerk
323 East Cavers Avenue, Wiggins, MS 39577
P.O. Box 7, Wiggins, MS 39577
Tel: (601) 928-5266 Fax: (601) 928-6464

Chancery Clerk **Gerald W. Bond** . . . . (601) 928-5266
  E-mail: gbond@stonecountyms.gov

Sunflower County

Circuit Clerk

Fourth Judicial District
P.O. Box 244, Greenwood, MS 38935

Circuit Clerk, Sunflower County **Sharon McFadden** . . . . . (662) 887-1252
  P.O. Box 880, Indianola, MS 38751   Fax: (662) 887-7077

Chancery Clerk

Office of the Chancery Clerk
P.O. Box 988, Indianola, MS 38751
Tel: (662) 887-4703 Fax: (662) 887-7054

Chancery Clerk **Paula S. Sykes** . . . . (662) 887-4703
  E-mail: psykes@co.sunflower.ms.us

Tallahatchie County

Circuit Clerk

Seventeenth Judicial District
P.O. Box 280, Hernando, MS 38632

Circuit Clerk, Tallahatchie County
  Stephanie D. Sims . . . . (662) 647-8758 (First District)
  P.O. Box 86, Charleston, MS 38921 (First District)   Tel: (662) 375-8515
  P.O. Box 96, Sumner, MS 38957 (Second District)   (Second District)
                                                          Fax: (662) 375-7252
                                                          (Second District)

Chancery Clerk

Office of the Chancery Clerk
P.O. Box 350, Charleston, MS 38921 (First District)
P.O. Box 180, Sumner, MS 38957 (Second District)
Tel: (662) 647-5551 (First District)
Tel: (662) 375-8731 (Second District)
Fax: (662) 647-3702 (First District)
Fax: (662) 375-7252 (Second District)

Chancery Clerk **Anita Greenwood** . . . . (662) 647-5551
  E-mail: agreenwood@courts.ms.gov

Tate County

Circuit Clerk

Seventeenth Judicial District
P.O. Box 280, Hernando, MS 38632

Circuit Clerk, Tate County **Edward Hadskey** . . . . (662) 562-5211
  201 Ward Street, Senatobia, MS 38868   Fax: (662) 562-7486

Chancery Clerk

Office of the Chancery Clerk
201 Ward Street, Senatobia, MS 38668
P.O. Box 309, Senatobia, MS 38668
Tel: (662) 562-5661 Fax: (662) 560-6205

Chancery Clerk **Wayne Crockett** . . . . (662) 562-5661

Tippah County

Circuit Clerk

Third Judicial District
One Courthouse Square, Oxford, MS 38655

Circuit Clerk, Tippah County **Randy Graves** . . . . (662) 837-7370
  102-A North Main, Ripley, MS 38663   Fax: (662) 837-1030

Chancery Clerk

Office of the Chancery Clerk
101 East Spring Street, Ripley, MS 38663
P.O. Box 99, Ripley, MS 38663
Tel: (662) 837-7374 Fax: (662) 837-7148

Chancery Clerk **Rodney McBryde** . . . . (662) 837-7374

Tishomingo County

Circuit Clerk

First Judicial District
P.O. Drawer 1100, Tupelo, MS 38802

Circuit Clerk, Tishomingo County **Donna Henry Dill** . . . . (662) 423-7026
  1008 Battleground, Iuka, MS 38852   Fax: (662) 423-1667

Chancery Clerk

Office of the Chancery Clerk
1008 Battleground Drive, Iuka, MS 38852
Tel: (662) 423-7010 Fax: (662) 423-7005

Chancery Clerk **Peyton Cummings** . . . . (662) 423-7010
  E-mail: pcummings@co.tishomingo.ms.us

Tunica County

Circuit Clerk

Eleventh Judicial District
P.O. Box 478, Cleveland, MS 38732

Circuit Clerk, Tunica County
  Sharon Granberry Reynolds . . . . (662) 363-2842
  1300 School Street, 1st Floor,   Fax: (662) 363-2413
  Tunica, MS 38676
  P.O. Box 184, Tunica, MS 38676

Chancery Clerk

Office of the Chancery Clerk
P.O. Box 217, Tunica, MS 38676
Tel: (662) 363-2451 Fax: (662) 357-5934

Chancery Clerk **Rechelle Siggers** . . . . (662) 363-2451
  E-mail: rechelle.siggers@tunicagov.com

Union County

Circuit Clerk

Third Judicial District
One Courthouse Square, Oxford, MS 38655

Circuit Clerk, Union County **Phyllis Stanford** . . . . (662) 534-1910
  P.O. Box 298, New Albany, MS 38652   Fax: (662) 534-2059

(continued on next page)

Chancery Clerk

Office of the Chancery Clerk
P.O. Box 847, New Albany, MS 38652
Tel: (662) 534-1900 Fax: (662) 534-1907

Chancery Clerk **Annette Hickey** . . . . (662) 534-1900
  E-mail: ahickey@courts.ms.gov

Walthall County

Circuit Clerk

Fourteenth Judicial District
P.O. Drawer 1350, Brookhaven, MS 39602

Circuit Clerk, Walthall County **Vernon E. Alford** . . . . (601) 876-5677
  200 Ball Avenue, Tylertown, MS 39667   Fax: (601) 876-4077

Chancery Clerk

Office of the Chancery Clerk
PO Box 351, Tylertown, MS 39667-0351
Fax: (601) 876-6026

Chancery Clerk **Bob A. Bracey** . . . . (601) 876-3553

Warren County

Circuit Clerk

Ninth Judicial District
P.O. Box 351, Vicksburg, MS 39181

Circuit Clerk, Warren County **Jan Hyland-Daigre** . . . . (601) 636-3961
  1009 Cherry Street, Vicksburg, MS 39183   Fax: (601) 630-4100
  P.O. Box 351, Vicksburg, MS 39181
  E-mail: circlk@co.warren.ms.us

Chancery Clerk

Office of the Chancery Clerk
1009 Cherry Street, Vicksburg, MS 39183-2539
P.O. Box 351, Vicksburg, MS 39183
Tel: (601) 636-4415 Fax: (601) 630-8016

Chancery Clerk **Donna Hardy** . . . . (601) 636-4415
  E-mail: dhardy@co.warren.ms.us

Washington County

Circuit Clerk

Fourth Judicial District
P.O. Box 244, Greenwood, MS 38935

Circuit Clerk, Washington County
  Barbara Esters Parker . . . . (662) 378-2747
  P.O. Box 1276, Greenville, MS 38702   Fax: (662) 334-2698
  E-mail: besters@co.washington.ms.us

Chancery Clerk

Office of the Chancery Clerk
P.O. Box 309, Greenville, MS 38701
Tel: (662) 332-1595 Fax: (662) 334-2725

Chancery Clerk **Marilyn Hansell** . . . . (662) 332-1595
  E-mail: mhansell@co.washington.ms.us

Wayne County

Circuit Clerk

Tenth Judicial District
P.O. Box 1167, Meridian, MS 39302

Circuit Clerk, Wayne County **Rose M. Bingham** . . . . (601) 735-1171
  609 Azalea Drive, Waynesboro, MS 39367   Fax: (601) 735-6261

Chancery Clerk

Office of the Chancery Clerk
609 Azalea Drive, Waynesboro, MS 39367
Tel: (601) 735-2873 Fax: (601) 735-6224

Chancery Clerk **Geary Jackson** . . . . (601) 735-2873
  E-mail: gearyjackson@waynecountyms.gov

Webster County

Circuit Clerk

Fifth Judicial District
P.O. Box 721, Kosciusko, MS 39090

Circuit Clerk, Webster County **Deborah Hood Neal** . . . . . (601) 258-6287
  P.O. Box 308, Walthall, MS 39771   Fax: (601) 258-7686

Chancery Clerk

Office of the Chancery Clerk
P.O. Box 398, Walthall, MS 39771
Tel: (662) 258-4131 Fax: (662) 258-9635

Chancery Clerk **Russell S. Turner** . . . . (662) 258-4131

Wilkinson County

Circuit Clerk

Sixth Judicial District
P.O. Box 1383, Natchez, MS 39121

Circuit Clerk, Wilkinson County
  Lynn Tolliver-Delaney . . . . (601) 888-6697
  P.O. Box 327, Woodville, MS 39669   Fax: (601) 888-6984

Chancery Clerk

Office of the Chancery Clerk
525 Main Street, Woodville, MS 39669
P.O. Box 516, Woodville, MS 39669
Tel: (601) 888-4381 Tel: (601) 888-6776

Chancery Clerk **Thomas C. Tolliver, Jr.** . . . . (601) 888-4381

Winston County

Circuit Clerk

Fifth Judicial District
P.O. Box 721, Kosciusko, MS 39090

Circuit Clerk, Winston County **Kim T. Ming** . . . . (662) 773-3581
  P.O. Drawer 785, Louisville, MS 39339   Fax: (662) 773-7192

Chancery Clerk

Office of the Chancery Clerk
P.O. Box 69, Louisville, MS 39339
Tel: (662) 773-3631 Fax: (662) 773-8814

Chancery Clerk **Julie Cunningham** . . . . (662) 773-3631
E-mail: jcunningham@lg.k12.ok.us

Yalobusha County

Circuit Clerk

Seventeenth Judicial District
P.O. Box 280, Hernando, MS 38632

Circuit Clerk, Yalobusha County
Daryl Burney . . . . (662) 675-8187 (First District)
P.O. Box 260, Coffeeville, MS 38922 (First District)   Tel: (662) 473-1341
P.O. Box 1431, Water Valley, MS 38965 (Second   (Second District)
District)   Fax: (662) 473-5020
                                                        (Second District)

Chancery Clerk

Office of the Chancery Clerk
P.O. Box 260, Coffeeville, MS 38922 (1st District)
P.O. Box 664, Water Valley, MS 38965 (2nd District)
Tel: (662) 675-2716 (First District)
Tel: (662) 473-2091 (Second District)
Fax: (662) 675-8004 (First District)
Fax: (662) 473-3622 (Second District)
E-mail: chanceryclerk@yaloshubacounty.net

Chancery Clerk **Amy McMinn** . . . . (662) 675-2716

Yazoo County

Circuit Clerk

Twenty-First Judicial District
P.O. Box 149, Lexington, MS 39095

Circuit Clerk, Yazoo County **Robert Coleman** . . . . (662) 746-1872
P.O. Box 108, Yazoo City, MS 39194   Fax: (662) 716-0113

Chancery Clerk

Office of the Chancery Clerk
P.O. Box 68, Yazoo City, MS 39194
Tel: (662) 746-2661 Fax: (662) 746-3893

Chancery Clerk **Quint Carver** . . . . (662) 746-2661
E-mail: qcarver@courts.ms.gov

Counties Within Judicial Districts

1st District
Areas Covered: Alcorn, Itawamba, Lee, Monroe, Pontotoc, Prentiss, and Tishomingo Counties.

2nd District
Areas Covered: Hancock, Harrison, and Stone Counties.

3rd District
Areas Covered: Benton, Calhoun, Chickasaw, Lafayette, Marshall, Tippah, and Union Counties.

4th District
Areas Covered: Leflore, Sunflower, and Washington Counties.

5th District
Areas Covered: Attala, Carroll, Choctaw, Grenada, Montgomery, Webster, and Winston Counties.

6th District
Areas Covered: Adams, Amite, Franklin, and Wilkinson Counties.

7th District
Areas Covered: Hinds County.

8th District
Areas Covered: Leake, Neshoba, Newton, and Scott Counties.

9th District
Areas Covered: Issaquena, Sharkey, and Warren Counties.

10th District
Areas Covered: Clarke, Kemper, Lauderdale, and Wayne Counties.

11th District
Areas Covered: Bolivar, Coahoma, Quitman, and Tunica Counties.

12th District
Areas Covered: Forrest and Perry Counties.

13th District
Areas Covered: Covington, Jasper, Simpson, and Smith Counties.

14th District
Areas Covered: Lincoln, Pike, and Walthall Counties.

15th District
Areas Covered: Jefferson Davis, Lamar, Lawrence, Marion, and Pearl River Counties.

16th District
Areas Covered: Clay, Lowndes, Noxubee, and Oktibbeha Counties.

17th District
Areas Covered: Desoto, Panola, Tallahatchie, Tate, and Yalobusha Counties.

18th District
Areas Covered: Jones County.

19th District
Areas Covered: George, Greene, and Jackson Counties.

20th District
Areas Covered: Madison and Rankin Counties.

(continued on next page)

Mississippi Court Clerks and Courthouses *continued*

21st District

Areas Covered: Holmes, Humphreys, and Yazoo Counties.

22nd District

Areas Covered: Claiborne, Copiah, and Jefferson Counties.

Missouri Court Clerks and Courthouses

The trial courts of general jurisdiction in Missouri are called circuit courts, which consist of several divisions. There are 45 judicial circuits, each circuit consisting of at least one county. Each county has a county clerk and a circuit court clerk. The circuit court clerks are listed below.

Missouri Supreme Court

Supreme Court Building, 207 West High Street, Jefferson City, MO 65101
P.O. Box 150, Jefferson City, MO 65102
Tel: (573) 751-4144 Fax: (573) 751-7514
Internet: www.courts.mo.gov

The Supreme Court consists of a chief justice and six judges who are appointed by the Governor from a list of candidates submitted by a nonpartisan Appellate Judicial Commission. Appointed judges face a retention vote in the next general election occurring after one year in office for a twelve-year term. The chief justice is elected by peer vote for a two-year term. Retirement is mandatory at age seventy; however, retired judges may be assigned to serve in state courts. The Supreme Court has exclusive appellate jurisdiction in all cases involving federal or Missouri constitutional law, federal treaties or statutes, Missouri revenue laws, and in any case involving the death penalty or life imprisonment. The Court exercises appellate jurisdiction over cases transferred from the Missouri Court of Appeals. The Court has rule-making authority over the lower courts and regulates admission to the state bar.

Court Staff

Fax: (573) 751-7514

Clerk of Court **Bill L. Thompson** . . . . (573) 751-4144
    E-mail: bill.thompson@courts.mo.gov

Missouri Court of Appeals

Tel: (417) 895-6811 Fax: (417) 895-6817

The judges of the Court of Appeals are initially appointed by the Governor from a list of candidates submitted by a nonpartisan Appellate Judicial Commission. They must then stand for retention in the next general election occurring at least one year after their appointment. Retention elections are held every twelve years. The chief judges are elected by peer vote in each district for a term determined by the district. The method of selection varies with each district, as does the length of term. Retirement is at age seventy, but retired judges may serve as senior judges in any Missouri court, as assigned by the Supreme Court. The Court of Appeals has appellate jurisdiction over civil and criminal cases, except those within the exclusive jurisdiction of the Missouri Supreme Court.

Missouri Court of Appeals, Eastern District

One Post Office Square, 815 Olive Street, St. Louis, MO 63101
Tel: (314) 539-4300 Fax: (314) 539-4324
Internet: www.courts.mo.gov

Areas Covered: Counties of Audrain, Cape Girardeau, Clark, Franklin, Gasconade, Jefferson, Knox, Lewis, Lincoln, Madison, Marion, Monroe, Montgomery, Osage, Perry, Pike, Ralls, St. Charles, St. Francois, St. Genevieve, St. Louis, St. Louis City, Scotland, Shelby, Warren and Washington

Court Staff

Clerk of Court **Laura Thielmeier Roy** . . . . (314) 539-4300
    E-mail: laura.roy@courts.mo.gov

Missouri Court of Appeals, Southern District

John Q. Hammons Building, 300 Hammons Parkway, Springfield, MO 65806
Tel: (417) 895-6811 Fax: (417) 895-6817
Internet: www.courts.mo.gov

Areas Covered: Counties of Barry, Barton, Bollinger, Butler, Camden, Carter, Cedar, Christian, Crawford, Dade, Dallas, Dent, Douglas, Dunklin, Greene, Hickory, Howell, Iron, Jasper, Laclede, Lawrence, McDonald, Maries, Mississippi, New Madrid, Newton, Oregon, Ozark, Pemiscot, Phelps, Polk, Pulaski, Reynolds, Ripley, Scott, Shannon, Saint Clair, Stoddard, Stone, Taney, Texas, Wayne, Webster and Wright

Court Staff

Clerk of Court **Sandra L. Skinner** . . . . (417) 895-6811
    E-mail: sandra.skinner@courts.mo.gov

Missouri Court of Appeals, Western District

1300 Oak Street, Kansas City, MO 64106-2970
Tel: (816) 889-3600 Fax: (816) 889-3668

Areas Covered: Counties of Adair, Andrew, Atchison, Bates, Benton, Boone, Buchanan, Caldwell, Callaway, Cass, Chariton, Clay, Clinton, Carroll, Cole, Cooper, Daviess, DeKalb, Gentry, Grundy, Henry, Holt, Howard, Harrison, Jackson, Johnson, Lafayette, Linn, Livingston, Macon, Mercer, Miller, Moniteau, Morgan, Nodaway, Platte, Putnam, Pettis, Randolph, Ray, Saline, Schuyler, Sullivan, Vernon and Worth

Court Staff

Clerk of Court **Terence G. Lord** . . . . (816) 889-3600
    E-mail: tlord@courts.mo.gov

County-By-County

Adair County

Circuit Clerk

2nd Judicial Circuit Court
Circuit Clerk, Adair County **Linda S. Decker** . . . . (660) 665-2552
    106 West Washington Street,   Fax: (660) 665-3420
    Kirksville, MO 63501

Andrew County

Circuit Clerk

5th Judicial Circuit Court
Circuit Clerk, Andrew County **Tena Christmas** . . . . (816) 324-4221
    Main Street, Savannah, MO 64485   Fax: (816) 324-5667

Atchison County

Circuit Clerk

4th Judicial Circuit Court
Circuit Clerk, Atchison County **Lorie Hall** . . . . (660) 744-2700
    P.O. Box 280, Rock Port, MO 64482   Fax: (660) 744-6100

(continued on next page)

Missouri Court Clerks and Courthouses *continued*

Audrain County

Circuit Clerk

12th Judicial Circuit Court
Circuit Clerk, Audrain County
Penny J. Creed-Craghead . . . . (573) 473-5840
101 North Jefferson, Mexico, MO 65265   Fax: (573) 581-3237

Barry County

Circuit Clerk

39th Judicial Circuit Court
Circuit Clerk, Barry County **Craig Williams** . . . .(417) 847-3133
102 West Street, Cassville, MO 65625   Fax: (417) 847-6298

Barton County

Circuit Clerk

28th Judicial Circuit Court
Circuit Clerk, Barton County **Janet Maupin** . . . . (417) 682-2444
1004 Gulf, Room 204, Lamar, MO 64759   Fax: (417) 682-2960

Bates County

Circuit Clerk

27th Judicial Circuit Court
100 West Franklin, Clinton, MO 64735

Circuit Clerk, Bates County **Diana Rich** . . . . (660) 679-5171
One North Delaware, Butler, MO 64730   Fax: (660) 679-4446

Benton County

Circuit Clerk

30th Judicial Circuit Court
Circuit Clerk, Benton County **Cheryl Schultz** . . . . (660) 438-7712
P.O. Box 37, Warsaw, MO 65355   Fax: (660) 438-5755

Bollinger County

Circuit Clerk

32nd Judicial Circuit Court
Circuit Clerk, Bollinger County
Jeaneal Vandeven . . . . (573) 238-1900 ext. 6
204 High Street, Suite 6, Marble Hill, MO 63764   Fax: (573) 238-2773

Boone County

Circuit Clerk

13th Judicial Circuit Court
Circuit Clerk, Boone County **Christy Blakemore** . . . .(573) 886-4000
705 East Walnut Street, Columbia, MO 65201   Fax: (573) 886-4274

Buchanan County

Circuit Clerk

5th Judicial Circuit Court
Circuit Clerk, Buchanan County **Mary Beattie** . . . .(816) 271-1462
411 Jules Street, St. Joseph, MO 64501

Missouri Court Clerks and Courthouses *continued*

Butler County

Circuit Clerk

36th Judicial Circuit Court
Circuit Clerk, Butler County
Cynthia "Cindi" Bowman . . . . (573) 686-8082
100 North Main, Poplar Bluff, MO 63901   Fax: (573) 686-8094

Caldwell County

Circuit Clerk

43rd Judicial Circuit Court
Circuit Clerk, Caldwell County **Carrie Miller** . . . . (816) 586-2581
49 East Main Street, Kingston, MO 64650   Fax: (816) 586-2333

Callaway County

Circuit Clerk

13th Judicial Circuit Court
Circuit Clerk, Callaway County **Judy Groner** . . . .(573) 642-0780
10 East Fifth Street, Fulton, MO 65251   Fax: (573) 642-0700

Camden County

Circuit Clerk

26th Judicial Circuit Court
Circuit Clerk, Camden County **Jo McElwee** . . . .(573) 346-3130
1 Court Circle, Camdenton, MO 65020   Fax: (573) 346-5422

Cape Girardeau County

Circuit Clerk

32nd Judicial Circuit Court
Circuit Clerk, Cape
Girardeau County
Patti Wibbenmeyer . . . . (573) 335-8253 (Cape Girardeau - Civil)
44 North Lorimier, Suite 1,   Tel: (573) 243-1755
Cape Girardeau, MO 63701 (Civil)   (Jackson - Criminal)
100 Court Street, Suite 301,   Fax: (573) 204-2405
Jackson, MO 63755 (Criminal)   (Jackson - Criminal)

Carroll County

Circuit Clerk

8th Judicial Circuit Court
Circuit Clerk, Carroll County **Cheryl A. Mansur** . . . .(660) 542-1466
8 South Main, Carrollton, MO 64633   Fax: (660) 542-1444

Carter County

Circuit Clerk

37th Judicial Circuit Court
Circuit Clerk, Carter County **Mary Godsy** . . . . (573) 323-4513
P.O. Box 578, Van Buren, MO 63965   Fax: (573) 323-8914

Cass County

Circuit Clerk

17th Judicial Circuit Court
Circuit Clerk, Cass County **Kim York** . . . . (816) 380-8227
2501 West Mechanic, Harrisonville, MO 64701   Fax: (816) 380-8225

Cedar County

Circuit Clerk

28th Judicial Circuit Court
Circuit Clerk, Cedar County **Melinda Gumm** . . . (417) 276-6700 ext. 234
P.O. Box 665, Stockton, MO 65785   Fax: (417) 276-5001

Chariton County

Circuit Clerk

9th Judicial Circuit Court
Circuit Clerk, Chariton County **Eric Stallo** . . . . (660) 288-3602
306 South Cherry Street, Keytesville, MO 65261   Fax: (660) 288-3763

Christian County

Circuit Clerk

38th Judicial Circuit Court
Circuit Clerk, Christian County **Barb Barnett-Stillings** . . . (417) 581-5120
110 West Elm, Room 202,   Fax: (417) 581-0391
Ozark, MO 65721

Clark County

Circuit Clerk

1st Judicial Circuit Court
Circuit Clerk, Clark County **Kim Schantz** . . . . (660) 727-3292
111 East Court Street, Suite 210,   Fax: (660) 727-1051
Kahoka, MO 63445

Clay County

Circuit Clerk

7th Judicial Circuit Court
Circuit Clerk, Clay County **Lee Bucksath** . . . .(816) 407-3900
11 South Water, Liberty, MO 64068   Fax: (816) 407-3888

Clinton County

Circuit Clerk

43rd Judicial Circuit Court
Circuit Clerk, Clinton County **Molly Livingston** . . . . (816) 539-3731
207 North Main Street, Plattsburg, MO 64477   Fax: (816) 539-3893

Cole County

Circuit Clerk

19th Judicial Circuit Court
Circuit Clerk, Cole County **Dawnel Davidson** . . . .(573) 634-9150
P.O. Box 1870, Jefferson City, MO 65102   Fax: (573) 635-0796

Cooper County

Circuit Clerk

18th Judicial Circuit Court
Circuit Clerk, Cooper County **Nancy Fisher** . . . . (660) 882-2232
200 Main Street, Booneville, MO 65233   Fax: (660) 882-2043

Crawford County

Circuit Clerk

42nd Judicial Circuit Court
Circuit Clerk, Crawford County **Karen Harlan** . . . . (573) 775-2866
P.O. Box 1550, Steelville, MO 65565   Fax: (573) 775-2452

Dade County

Circuit Clerk

28th Judicial Circuit Court
Circuit Clerk, Dade County **Mary McGee** . . . .(417) 637-2271
300 West Water, Greenfield, MO 65661   Fax: (417) 637-5055

Dallas County

Circuit Clerk

30th Judicial Circuit Court
Circuit Clerk, Dallas County **Susan Potter** . . . .(417) 345-2243
P.O. Box 1910, Buffalo, MO 65622   Fax: (417) 345-5539

Daviess County

Circuit Clerk

43rd Judicial Circuit Court
Circuit Clerk, Daviess County **Pam Howard** . . . . (660) 663-2932
Highway 13, Gallatin, MO 64640   Fax: (660) 663-2646

DeKalb County

Circuit Clerk

43rd Judicial Circuit Court
Circuit Clerk, DeKalb County **Julie Whitsell** . . . . (816) 449-2602
109 West Main, Maysville, MO 64469   Fax: (816) 449-2440
P.O. Box 248, Maysville, MO 64469

Dent County

Circuit Clerk

42nd Judicial Circuit Court
Circuit Clerk, Dent County **Becky Swiney** . . . . (573) 729-3931
112 East Fifth Street, Salem, MO 65560   Fax: (573) 729-9414

Douglas County

Circuit Clerk

44th Judicial Circuit Court
Circuit Clerk, Douglas County **Kim Hathcock** . . . . (417) 683-4713
P.O. Box 249, Ava, MO 65608   Tel: (417) 683-2794

Dunklin County

Circuit Clerk

35th Judicial Circuit Court
Circuit Clerk, Dunklin County **Paula Gargus** . . . . (573) 888-2456
P.O. Box 567, Kennett, MO 63857   Fax: (573) 888-2832

(continued on next page)

Franklin County

Circuit Clerk

20th Judicial Circuit Court
Circuit Clerk, Franklin County **Bill D. Miller** . . . . (636) 583-7378
401 East Main Street, Union, MO 63084

Gasconade County

Circuit Clerk

20th Judicial Circuit Court
Circuit Clerk, Gasconade County **Pamela Greunke** . . . . . . (573) 486-2632
Hermann, MO 65041   Fax: (573) 486-5812

Gentry County

Circuit Clerk

4th Judicial Circuit Court
Circuit Clerk, Gentry County **Janet Parsons** . . . . (660) 726-3618
200 West Clay Street, Albany, MO 64402   Fax: (660) 726-4102
P.O. Box 32, Albany, MO 64402

Greene County

Circuit Clerk

31st Judicial Circuit Court
Circuit Clerk, Greene County **Thomas Barr** . . . . (417) 868-4074
1010 North Boonville, Second Floor,
Springfield, MO 65802

Grundy County

Circuit Clerk

3rd Judicial Circuit Court
Circuit Clerk, Grundy County **Becky Stanturf** . . . . (660) 359-4040
700 Main, Trenton, MO 64683   Fax: (660) 359-6604
P.O. Box 196, Trenton, MO 64683

Harrison County

Circuit Clerk

3rd Judicial Circuit Court
Circuit Clerk, Harrison County **C. Sherece Eivins** . . . . (660) 425-6425
P.O. Box 189, Bethany, MO 64424   Fax: (660) 425-6390

Henry County

Circuit Clerk

27th Judicial Circuit Court
100 West Franklin, Clinton, MO 64735

Circuit Clerk, Henry County **Marsha Abbott** . . . . (660) 885-7230
100 West Franklin, Clinton, MO 64735   Fax: (660) 885-8247
P.O. Box 487, Clinton, MO 64735

Hickory County

Circuit Clerk

30th Judicial Circuit Court
Circuit Clerk, Hickory County **Cee Cee Smith** . . . . (417) 745-6421
P.O. Box 345, Hermitage, MO 65668   Fax: (417) 745-6670

Holt County

Circuit Clerk

4th Judicial Circuit Court
Circuit Clerk, Holt County **Vickie Book** . . . . (660) 446-3301
102 West Nodaway, Oregon, MO 64473   Fax: (660) 446-3328
P.O. Box 318, Oregon, MO 64473

Howard County

Circuit Clerk

14th Judicial Circuit Court
Circuit Clerk, Howard County **Charles J. Flaspohler** . . . . (660) 248-2194
1 Courthouse Square, Fayette, MO 65248

Howell County

Circuit Clerk

37th Judicial Circuit Court
Circuit Clerk, Howell County **Cindy Weeks** . . . . (417) 256-3741
P.O. Box 967, West Plains, MO 65775   Fax: (417) 256-4650

Iron County

Circuit Clerk

42nd Judicial Circuit Court
Circuit Clerk, Iron County **Sammye "Gail" White** . . . . . . (573) 546-2511
250 South Main Street, Suite 220,   Fax: (573) 546-6006
Ironton, MO 63650

Jackson County

Court Administrator

16th Judicial Circuit Court
Internet: www.courts.mo.gov/page.jsp?id=1901

Court Administrator **Jeffrey A. Eisenbeis** . . . . (816) 881-3658
415 East 12th Street, Third Floor, Suite 303,   Fax: (816) 881-3681
Kansas City, MO 64106

Jasper County

Circuit Clerk

29th Judicial Circuit Court
Circuit Clerk, Jasper County
Melissa Holcomb . . . . (417) 358-0441 (Carthage)
601 South Pearl, Carthage, MO 64836   Tel: (417) 625-4310
302 South Main, Joplin, MO 64801   (Joplin)
                                                   Fax: (417) 358-0461
                                                            (Carthage)

Jefferson County

Circuit Clerk

23rd Judicial Circuit Court
Internet: http://www.courts.mo.gov/page.jsp?id=1911

Circuit Clerk, Jefferson County **Michael Reuter** . . . . (636) 797-5443
P.O. Box 100, Hillsboro, MO 63050   Fax: (636) 797-5073

© Leadership Directories, Inc.

Johnson County

Circuit Clerk

17th Judicial Circuit Court
Circuit Clerk, Johnson County **Stephanie Elkins** . . . . (660) 422-7413
    101 West Market, Warrensburg, MO 64093   Fax: (660) 422-7417

Knox County

Circuit Clerk

2nd Judicial Circuit Court
Circuit Clerk, Knox County **Roma March** . . . . (660) 397-2305
    107 North Fourth Street, Edina, MO 63537   Fax: (660) 397-3331
    P.O. Box 116, Edina, MO 63537

Laclede County

Circuit Clerk

26th Judicial Circuit Court
Circuit Clerk, Laclede County **Wanda Tyre** . . . .(417) 532-2471
    Government Center, 200 North Adams,
    Lebanon, MO 65536

Lafayette County

Circuit Clerk

15th Judicial Circuit Court
Circuit Clerk, Lafayette County **Deana Aversman** . . . .(660) 259-6101
    P.O. Box 10, Lexington, MO 64067

Lawrence County

Circuit Clerk

39th Judicial Circuit Court
Circuit Clerk, Lawrence County **Steven W. Kahre** . . . . . . (417) 466-2471
    240 North Main, Suite 110,   Fax: (417) 466-7899
    Mount Vernon, MO 65712

Lewis County

Circuit Clerk

2nd Judicial Circuit Court
Circuit Clerk, Lewis County **Jan Geisendorfer** . . . . (573) 767-5352
    101 East Lafayette, Monticello, MO 63457   Fax: (573) 767-5342

Lincoln County

Circuit Clerk

45th Judicial Circuit Court
Circuit Clerk, Lincoln County **Grace Sinclair** . . . .(636) 528-6300
    45 Business Park Drive, Troy, MO 63379   Tel: (636) 528-9168

Linn County

Circuit Clerk

9th Judicial Circuit Court
Circuit Clerk, Linn County **Mary S. Enyeart** . . . . (660) 895-5212
    108 North High, Linneus, MO 64653   Fax: (660) 895-5277
    P.O. Box 84, Linneus, MO 64653

Livingston County

Circuit Clerk

43rd Judicial Circuit Court
Circuit Clerk, Livingston County
    Brenda Wright . . . .(660) 646-8000 ext. 305
    700 Webster, Chillicothe, MO 64601   Fax: (660) 646-2734

Macon County

Circuit Clerk

41st Judicial Circuit Court
Circuit Clerk, Macon County **Twila Halley** . . . . (660) 385-4631
    Building 2, 101 East Washington Street, Suite 2,   Tel: (660) 385-4235
    Macon, MO 63552

Madison County

Circuit Clerk

24th Judicial Circuit Court
Circuit Clerk, Madison County **Eileen Provow** . . . . (573) 783-2102
    P.O. Box 470, Fredericktown, MO 63645   Fax: (573) 783-5920

Maries County

Circuit Clerk

25th Judicial Circuit Court
Circuit Clerk, Maries County **Mark Buschmann** . . . .(573) 422-3338
    211 Fourth Street, Vienna, MO 65582   Fax: (573) 422-3976
    P.O. Box 490, Vienna, MO 65582
    E-mail: mark.buschmann@courts.mo.gov

Marion County, District One

Circuit Clerk

10th Judicial Circuit Court
Circuit Clerk, Marion County, District One
    Valerie Munzlinger . . . . (573) 769-2550
    100 South Main, Palmyra, MO 63461   Fax: (573) 769-4558
    P.O. Box 431, Palmyra, MO 63461

Marion County, District Two

Circuit Clerk

10th Judicial Circuit Court
Circuit Clerk, Marion County, District Two
    Carolyn Conners . . . . (573) 221-0198
    906 Broadway, Hannibal, MO 63401   Fax: (573) 221-9328

McDonald County

Circuit Clerk

40th Judicial Circuit Court
Circuit Clerk, McDonald County **Jennifer Mikeska** . . . . . .(417) 223-7515
    P.O. Box 157, Pineville, MO 64856   Fax: (417) 223-4125

(continued on next page)

Mercer County

Circuit Clerk

3rd Judicial Circuit Court
Circuit Clerk, Mercer County **Tammy Crouse** . . . . (660) 748-4335
  802 East Main, Princeton, MO 64673   Fax: (660) 748-4339

Miller County

Circuit Clerk

26th Judicial Circuit Court
Circuit Clerk, Miller County **Genise Buechter** . . . .(573) 369-1980
  P.O. Box 11, Tuscumbia, MO 65082

Mississippi County

Circuit Clerk

33rd Judicial Circuit Court
Circuit Clerk, Mississippi County
Dottie McKenzie . . . .(573) 683-2146 ext. 225
  200 North Main Street, Charleston, MO 63834   Fax: (573) 683-7696
  P.O. Box 369, Charleston, MO 63834

Moniteau County

Circuit Clerk

26th Judicial Circuit Court
Circuit Clerk, Moniteau County **Michele Higgins** . . . . (573) 796-2071
  200 East Main Street, California, MO 65018

Monroe County

Circuit Clerk

10th Judicial Circuit Court
Circuit Clerk, Monroe County **Heather Wheeler** . . . . (660) 327-5204
  300 North Main, Suite 201,   Fax: (660) 327-5781
  Paris, MO 65275

Montgomery County

Circuit Clerk

12th Judicial Circuit Court
Circuit Clerk, Montgomery County **Robyn Schmidt** . . . . . (573) 564-3341
  211 East Third Street,   Fax: (573) 564-3914
  Montgomery City, MO 63361

Morgan County

Circuit Clerk

26th Judicial Circuit Court
Circuit Clerk, Morgan County **Cheryl Morris** . . . . (573) 378-4413
  211 East Newton Street, Versailles, MO 65084

New Madrid County

Circuit Clerk

34th Judicial Circuit Court
Circuit Clerk, New Madrid County **Marsha Holiman** . . . . (573) 748-2228
  450 Main Street, New Madrid, MO 63869   Fax: (573) 748-5409
  E-mail: marsha.holiman@courts.mo.gov

Newton County

Circuit Clerk

40th Judicial Circuit Court
Circuit Clerk, Newton County **Patricia Krueger** . . . .(417) 451-8210
  101 South Wood, Neosho, MO 64850   Fax: (417) 451-8298
  P.O Box 130, Neosho, MO 64850

Nodaway County

Circuit Clerk

4th Judicial Circuit Court
Circuit Clerk, Nodaway County **Elaine M. Wilson** . . . . (660) 582-5431
  305 North Main Street, Maryville, MO 64468   Fax: (660) 582-2047

Oregon County

Circuit Clerk

37th Judicial Circuit Court
Circuit Clerk, Oregon County **Ronda Hall** . . . . (417) 778-7460
  P.O. Box 406, Alton, MO 65606   Fax: (417) 778-7206

Osage County

Circuit Clerk

20th Judicial Circuit Court
Circuit Clerk, Osage County **Charlene Eisterhold** . . . . (573) 897-2136
  P.O. Box 825, Linn, MO 65051   Fax: (573) 897-4075

Ozark County

Circuit Clerk

44th Judicial Circuit Court
Circuit Clerk, Ozark County **Becki Strong** . . . . (417) 679-4232
  P.O. Box 869, Gainesville, MO 65655   Tel: (417) 679-4554

Pemiscot County

Circuit Clerk

34th Judicial Circuit Court
Circuit Clerk, Pemiscot County **Kelly Maners** . . . . (573) 333-0187
  610 Ward Avenue, Caruthersville, MO 63830   Fax: (573) 333-1272

Perry County

Circuit Clerk

32nd Judicial Circuit Court
Circuit Clerk, Perry County **Becky Paulus** . . . . (573) 547-6581 ext. 0
  15 West Sainte Marie, Suite 2,   Fax: (573) 547-9323
  Perryville, MO 63775

Pettis County

Circuit Clerk

18th Judicial Circuit Court
Circuit Clerk, Pettis County **Susan Sadler** . . . . . . (660) 826-5000 ext. 453
  415 South Ohio, Sedalia, MO 65301   Fax: (660) 826-4520

Phelps County

Circuit Clerk

25th Judicial Circuit Court
Circuit Clerk, Phelps County **Sue Brown** . . . . (573) 458-6210
200 North Main Street, Rolla, MO 65401   Fax: (573) 458-6224

Pike County

Circuit Clerk

45th Judicial Circuit Court
Circuit Clerk, Pike County **Jerri Harrelson** . . . . (573) 324-5582
115 West Main, Bowling Green, MO 63334   Fax: (573) 324-6297

Platte County

Circuit Clerk

6th Judicial Circuit Court
Circuit Clerk, Platte County **Sandra Dowd** . . . . (816) 858-2232
415 Third Street, Platte City, MO 64079   Fax: (816) 858-3392

Polk County

Circuit Clerk

30th Judicial Circuit Court
Circuit Clerk, Polk County **Tiffany Phillips** . . . . (417) 326-4912
102 East Broadway, Room 14,   Fax: (417) 326-4194
Bolivar, MO 65613

Pulaski County

Circuit Clerk

25th Judicial Circuit Court
Circuit Clerk, Pulaski County **Rachelle K. Beasley** . . . . . . (573) 774-4755
301 Historic Route 66 East,   Fax: (573) 774-6967
Waynesville, MO 65583

Putnam County

Circuit Clerk

3rd Judicial Circuit Court
Circuit Clerk, Putnam County **Mitzi Shipley** . . . . (660) 947-2071
1601 West Main Street, Room 204,   Fax: (660) 947-2320
Unionville, MO 63565

Ralls County

Circuit Clerk

10th Judicial Circuit Court
Circuit Clerk, Ralls County **Gina Jameson** . . . . (573) 985-5633
P.O. Box 466, New London, MO 63459   Fax: (573) 985-3446

Randolph County

Circuit Clerk

14th Judicial Circuit Court
Circuit Clerk, Randolph County **Michelle Chapman** . . . . . (660) 277-4601
372 Highway JJ, Huntsville, MO 65259   Fax: (660) 277-4636

Ray County

Circuit Clerk

8th Judicial Circuit Court
Circuit Clerk, Ray County **Carolyne Conner** . . . . (816) 776-3377
100 West Main Street, Richmond, MO 64085   Fax: (816) 776-6016

Reynolds County

Circuit Clerk

42nd Judicial Circuit Court
Circuit Clerk, Reynolds County **Randy Cowin** . . . . (573) 648-2494
P.O. Box 76, Centerville, MO 63633   Fax: (573) 648-2503

Ripley County

Circuit Clerk

36th Judicial Circuit Court
Circuit Clerk, Ripley County **Sharon Richmond** . . . . (573) 996-2818
100 Courthouse Square, Suite 3,   Fax: (573) 996-5014
Doniphan, MO 63935

Saline County

Circuit Clerk

15th Judicial Circuit Court
Circuit Clerk, Saline County **Sharon Crawford** . . . . (660) 886-2300
P.O. Box 670, Marshall, MO 65340   Fax: (660) 831-5360

Schuyler County

Circuit Clerk

1st Judicial Circuit Court
Circuit Clerk, Schuyler County **Judy L. Keim** . . . . (660) 457-3784
Schuyler County Courthouse, Highway 136 East,   Tel: (660) 457-3016
Lancaster, MO 63548
P.O. Box 417, Lancaster, MO 63548

Scotland County

Circuit Clerk

1st Judicial Circuit Court
Circuit Clerk, Scotland County **Anita Watkins** . . . . (660) 465-8605
117 South Market Street, Suite 200,   Tel: (660) 465-2404
Memphis, MO 63555   Fax: (660) 465-8673

Scott County

Circuit Clerk

33rd Judicial Circuit Court
Circuit Clerk, Scott County **Christy M. Hency** . . . . (573) 545-3596
P.O. Box 587, Benton, MO 63736   Fax: (573) 545-3597

Shannon County

Circuit Clerk

37th Judicial Circuit Court
Circuit Clerk, Shannon County **Melany Williams** . . . . (573) 226-3315
P.O. Box 148, Eminence, MO 65466   Fax: (573) 226-5321

(continued on next page)

Shelby County

Circuit Clerk

41st Judicial Circuit Court
Circuit Clerk, Shelby County **Rose Shively** . . . . (573) 633-2151
P.O. Box 176, Shelbyville, MO 63469   Tel: (573) 633-2142

St. Charles County

Circuit Clerk

11th Judicial Circuit Court
Circuit Clerk, St. Charles County **Judy Zerr** . . . . (636) 949-3080
300 North Second Street, Suite 216,   Fax: (636) 949-7390
Saint Charles, MO 63301

St. Clair County

Circuit Clerk

27th Judicial Circuit Court
100 West Franklin, Clinton, MO 64735

Circuit Clerk, St. Clair County **Karen Hubbard** . . . . (417) 646-2226
655 Second Street, Osceola, MO 64776   Fax: (417) 646-2401

St. Francois County

Circuit Clerk

24th Judicial Circuit Court
Circuit Clerk, St. Francois County **Vicki Weible** . . . . (573) 756-4551
1 North Washington Street,   Fax: (573) 756-3733
Farmington, MO 63640

St. Louis City

Circuit Clerk

22nd Judicial Circuit Court
Circuit Clerk, St. Louis City County
  Thomas Kloeppinger . . . . (314) 622-4433
1114 Market Street, St. Louis, MO 63101

St. Louis County

Circuit Clerk

21st Judicial Circuit Court
Circuit Clerk, St. Louis County **Joan Gilmer** . . . . (314) 615-8029
7900 Carondelet, Clayton, MO 63105   Fax: (314) 615-8739

Ste. Genevieve County

Circuit Clerk

24th Judicial Circuit Court
Circuit Clerk, Ste. Genevieve County **Diana Grass** . . . . . . (573) 883-2705
55 South Third Street, Sainte Genevieve, MO 63670   Fax: (573) 883-9351

Stoddard County

Circuit Clerk

35th Judicial Circuit Court
Circuit Clerk, Stoddard County **Paula Yancey** . . . . (573) 568-4640
P.O. Box 30, Bloomfield, MO 63825   Fax: (573) 568-2271

Stone County

Circuit Clerk

39th Judicial Circuit Court
Circuit Clerk, Stone County **Deborah Scobee** . . . . (417) 357-6115
P.O. Box 18, Galena, MO 65656   Fax: (417) 357-6163

Sullivan County

Circuit Clerk

9th Judicial Circuit Court
Circuit Clerk, Sullivan County **Sherry Brinkley** . . . . (660) 265-4717
109 North Main, Milan, MO 63556   Fax: (660) 265-5071

Taney County

Circuit Clerk

38th Judicial Circuit Court
Circuit Clerk, Taney County **Beth Wyman** . . . . (417) 546-7230
P.O. Box 335, Forsyth, MO 65653   Fax: (417) 546-6133

Texas County

Circuit Clerk

25th Judicial Circuit Court
Circuit Clerk, Texas County **Marci Mosley** . . . . (417) 967-3742
210 North Grand, Houston, MO 65483   Fax: (417) 967-4220

Vernon County

Circuit Clerk

28th Judicial Circuit Court
Circuit Clerk, Vernon County **Carrie Poe** . . . . (417) 448-2525
100 West Cherry Street, Suite 15,   Fax: (417) 448-2512
Nevada, MO 64772

Warren County

Circuit Clerk

12th Judicial Circuit Court
Circuit Clerk, Warren County **Brenda Eggering** . . . . (636) 456-3363
104 West Main Street, Warrenton, MO 63383   Fax: (636) 456-2422

Washington County

Circuit Clerk

24th Judicial Circuit Court
Circuit Clerk, Washington County **Patty Boyer** . . . . (573) 438-4171
102 North Missouri Street,   Fax: (573) 438-7900
Potosi, MO 63664

Wayne County

Circuit Clerk

42nd Judicial Circuit Court
Circuit Clerk, Wayne County **Darren Garrison** . . . . (573) 224-3014
P.O. Box 47, Greenville, MO 63944   Tel: (573) 224-3225

Missouri Court Clerks and Courthouses *continued*

Webster County

Circuit Clerk

30th Judicial Circuit Court
Circuit Clerk, Webster County **Jill Peck** . . . . (417) 859-2006
P.O. Box B, Marshfield, MO 65706   Fax: (417) 468-3786

Worth County

Circuit Clerk

4th Judicial Circuit Court
Circuit Clerk, Worth County **Jana Findley** . . . . (660) 564-2210
P.O. Box 350, Grant City, MO 64456   Fax: (660) 564-3394

Wright County

Circuit Clerk

44th Judicial Circuit Court
Circuit Clerk, Wright County **Joe Chadwell** . . . . (417) 741-7121
P.O. Box 39, Hartville, MO 65667   Tel: (417) 741-7504

Counties Within Judicial Circuits

Circuit Court, 1st Circuit
Areas Covered: Clark, Schuyler, and Scotland Counties.

Circuit Court, 2nd Circuit
Areas Covered: Adair, Knox, and Lewis Counties.

Circuit Court, 3rd Circuit
Areas Covered: Grundy, Harrison, Mercer, and Putnam Counties.

Circuit Court, 4th Circuit
Areas Covered: Atchison, Gentry, Holt, Nodaway, and Worth Counties.

Circuit Court, 5th Circuit
Areas Covered: Andrew and Buchanan Counties.

Circuit Court, 6th Circuit
Areas Covered: Platte County.

Circuit Court, 7th Circuit
Areas Covered: Clay County.

Circuit Court, 8th Circuit
Areas Covered: Carroll and Ray Counties.

Circuit Court, 9th Circuit
Areas Covered: Chariton, Linn, and Sullivan Counties.

Circuit Court, 10th Circuit
Areas Covered: Marion, Monroe, and Ralls Counties.

Circuit Court, 11th Circuit
Areas Covered: St. Charles County.

Missouri Court Clerks and Courthouses *continued*

Circuit Court, 12th Circuit
Areas Covered: Audrain, Montgomery, and Warren Counties.

Circuit Court, 13th Circuit
Areas Covered: Boone and Callaway Counties.

Circuit Court, 14th Circuit
Areas Covered: Howard and Randolph Counties.

Circuit Court, 15th Circuit
Areas Covered: Lafayette and Saline Counties.

Circuit Court, 16th Circuit
Areas Covered: Jackson County.

Circuit Court, 17th Circuit
Areas Covered: Cass and Johnson Counties.

Circuit Court, 18th Circuit
Areas Covered: Cooper and Pettis Counties.

Circuit Court, 19th Circuit
Areas Covered: Cole County.

Circuit Court, 20th Circuit
Areas Covered: Franklin, Gasconade, and Osage Counties.

Circuit Court, 21st Circuit
Areas Covered: St. Louis County.

Circuit Court, 22nd Circuit
Areas Covered: City of St. Louis.

Circuit Court, 23rd Circuit
Areas Covered: Jefferson County.

Circuit Court, 24th Circuit
Areas Covered: Madison, Sainte Genevieve, Saint Francois, and Washington Counties.

Circuit Court, 25th Circuit
Areas Covered: Maries, Phelps, Pulaski, and Texas Counties.

Circuit Court, 26th Circuit
Areas Covered: Camden, Laclede, Miller, Moniteau, and Morgan Counties.

Circuit Court, 27th Circuit
Areas Covered: Bates, Henry, and St. Clair Counties.

Circuit Court, 28th Circuit
Areas Covered: Barton, Cedar, Dade, and Vernon Counties.

(continued on next page)

Missouri Court Clerks and Courthouses *continued*

Circuit Court, 29th Circuit
Areas Covered: Jasper County.

Circuit Court, 30th Circuit
Areas Covered: Benton, Dallas, Hickory, Polk, and Webster Counties.

Circuit Court, 31st Circuit
Areas Covered: Greene County.

Circuit Court, 32nd Circuit
Areas Covered: Bollinger, Cape Girardeau, and Perry Counties.

Circuit Court, 33rd Circuit
Areas Covered: Mississippi and Scott Counties.

Circuit Court, 34th Circuit
Areas Covered: New Madrid and Pemiscot Counties.

Circuit Court, 35th Circuit
Areas Covered: Dunklin and Stoddard Counties.

Circuit Court, 36th Circuit
Areas Covered: Butler and Ripley Counties.

Circuit Court, 37th Circuit
Areas Covered: Carter, Howell, Oregon, and Shannon Counties.

Circuit Court, 38th Circuit
Areas Covered: Christian and Taney Counties.

Circuit Court, 39th Circuit
Areas Covered: Barry, Lawrence, and Stone Counties.

Circuit Court, 40th Circuit
Areas Covered: McDonald and Newton Counties.

Circuit Court, 41st Circuit
Areas Covered: Macon and Shelby Counties.

Circuit Court, 42nd Circuit
Areas Covered: Crawford, Dent, Iron, Reynolds, and Wayne Counties.

Circuit Court, 43rd Circuit
Areas Covered: Caldwell, Clinton, Daviess, DeKalb, and Livingston Counties.

Circuit Court, 44th Circuit
Areas Covered: Douglas, Ozark, and Wright Counties.

Circuit Court, 45th Circuit
Areas Covered: Lincoln and Pike Counties.

Montana Court Clerks and Courthouses

The trial courts of general jurisdiction in Montana are called district courts. There are 22 judicial circuits, each district consisting of at least one county. The court clerk and the county clerk (recorder) are separate positions. The court clerk and recorder for each county are listed below. There is no intermediate appellate court in the State of Montana.

Montana Supreme Court

323 Justice Building, 215 North Sanders, Helena, MT 59620
P.O. Box 203003, Helena, MT 59620-3001
Tel: (406) 444-3858 Fax: (406) 444-5705

The Supreme Court consists of a chief justice and six justices who are elected in statewide, nonpartisan elections for eight-year terms. Vacancies are filled by appointment by the Governor from a list of nominees submitted by the Judicial Nominations Commission and confirmed by the Montana State Senate. The chief justice is elected to the position by the electorate in a statewide general election. The Supreme Court has appellate jurisdiction over cases from the Montana District Court, has supervisory control over all state courts, and has authority to regulate admission to the state bar and the conduct of its members.

Court Staff

Clerk of Court **Ed Smith** . . . . (406) 444-3858

County-By-County

Beaverhead County

District Court Clerk

Fifth Judicial District
Two South Pacific Street, Dillon, MT 59725

Clerk of District Court, Beaverhead County
  Carly Jay Anderson . . . . (406) 683-3725
  Two South Pacific Street, Suite Five,   Fax: (406) 683-3728
  Dillon, MT 59725

Clerk and Recorder

Office of the Clerk and Recorder
Two South Pacific Street, Suite 3, Dillon, MT 59725
Tel: (406) 683-3720 Fax: (406) 683-3781

Clerk and Recorder **Debbie Scott** . . . . (406) 683-3720
  E-mail: dscott@beaverheadcounty.org

Big Horn County

District Court Clerk

Twenty-Second Judicial District
809A East Fourth Avenue, Columbus, MT 59019

Clerk of District Court, Big Horn County
  Karen Jean Yarlott . . . . (406) 665-9750
  121 West Third Street, Hardin, MT 59034   Fax: (406) 665-9755
  E-mail: kyarlott@mt.gov

Montana Court Clerks and Courthouses *continued*

Clerk and Recorder

Office of the Clerk and Recorder
121 West Third Street, 2nd Floor, Room 203, Hardin, MT 59034
P.O. Box 908, Hardin, MT 59034
Tel: (406) 665-9730 Fax: (406) 665-9738

Clerk and Recorder **Kimberly Yarlott** . . . . (406) 665-9730
  E-mail: kyarlott@co.bighorn.mt.us

Blaine County

District Court Clerk

Seventeenth Judicial District
314 Second Avenue West, Malta, MT 59538

Clerk of District Court, Blaine County
  Kay O'Brien Johnson . . . . (406) 357-3230
  400 Ohio Street, Chinook, MT 59523   Fax: (406) 357-2199
  E-mail: kjohnson@mt.gov

Clerk and Recorder

Office of the Clerk and Recorder
420 Ohio Street, Chinook, MT 59523
P.O. Box 78, Chinook, MT 59523
Tel: (406) 357-3240 Fax: (406) 357-2199

Clerk and Recorder **Sandra L. Boardman** . . . . (406) 357-3240
  E-mail: sboardman@blainecounty-mt.gov

Broadwater County

District Court Clerk

First Judicial District
228 Broadway Street, Helena, MT 59604-4263

Clerk of District Court, Broadwater County
  Valerie Middlemas . . . . (406) 266-9236
  515 Broadway Street, Townsend, MT 59644-2397   Fax: (406) 266-4720
  E-mail: vmiddlemas@mt.gov

Clerk and Recorder

Office of the Clerk and Recorder
515 Broadway Street, Townsend, MT 59644
Tel: (406) 266-3445 Fax: (406) 266-3674

Clerk and Recorder **Doug Ellis** . . . . (406) 266-3445
  E-mail: dellis@co.broadwater.mt.us

Carbon County

District Court Clerk

Twenty-Second Judicial District
809A East Fourth Avenue, Columbus, MT 59019

Clerk of District Court, Carbon County
  Rochelle Loyning . . . . (406) 446-1225
  102 North Broadway, Red Lodge, MT 59068   Fax: (406) 446-1911
  E-mail: rloyning@mt.gov

Clerk and Recorder

Office of the Clerk and Recorder
17 West 11th Street, Red Lodge, MT 59068
P.O. Box 887, Red Lodge, MT 59068
Tel: (406) 446-1220 Fax: (406) 446-2640

Clerk and Recorder **Marcia Henigman** . . . . (406) 446-1220
  E-mail: recorder@co.carbon.mt.us

(continued on next page)

Carter County

District Court Clerk

Sixteenth Judicial District
1200 Main Street, Forsyth, MT 59327

Clerk of District Court, Carter County **Tracey Walker** .... (406) 775-8714
  214 Park Street, Ekalaka, MT 59324   Fax: (406) 775-8703

Clerk and Recorder

Office of the Clerk and Recorder
214 Park Street, Ekalaka, MT 59324
P.O. Box 315, Ekalaka, MT 59324
Tel: (406) 775-8749 Fax: (406) 775-8750

Clerk and Recorder **Pamela J. Castleberry** .... (406) 775-8749
  E-mail: cccnrc@midrivers.com

Cascade County

District Court Clerk

Eighth Judicial District
415 Second Avenue North, Great Falls, MT 59401

Clerk of District Court, Cascade County
  Faye McWilliams .... (406) 454-6780
  415 Second Avenue North,   Fax: (406) 454-6907
  Great Falls, MT 59401
  E-mail: fmcwilliams@mt.gov

Clerk and Recorder

Office of the Clerk and Recorder
121 Fourth Street North, Room 1B-1, Great Falls, MT 59401
Tel: (406) 454-6801 Fax: (406) 454-6703

Clerk and Recorder **Rina Moore** .... (406) 454-6801
  E-mail: rmoore@cascadecountymt.gov

Chouteau County

District Court Clerk

Twelfth Judicial District
315 Fourth Street, Havre, MT 59501

Clerk of District Court, Chouteau County **Rick Cook** ..... (406) 622-5024
  1308 Franklin Street, Fort Benton, MT 49442   Fax: (406) 622-3028
  E-mail: rcook@mt.gov

Clerk and Recorder

Office of the Clerk and Recorder
1308 Franklin Street, Fort Benton, MT 59442
Tel: (406) 622-5151 Fax: (406) 622-3012

Clerk and Recorder **Lana K. Claassen** .... (406) 622-5151
  E-mail: claassen@itstriangle.com

Custer County

District Court Clerk

Sixteenth Judicial District
1200 Main Street, Forsyth, MT 59327

Clerk of District Court, Custer County **Hazel Parker** ..... (406) 874-3326
  1010 Main Street, Miles City, MT 59301   Fax: (406) 874-3451
  E-mail: hparker@mt.gov

Clerk and Recorder

Office of the Clerk and Recorder
1010 Main Street, Miles City, MT 59301
Tel: (406) 874-3343 Fax: (406) 874-3452

Clerk and Recorder **Linda Corbett** .... (406) 874-3343
  E-mail: l.corbett@co.custer.mt.us

Daniels County

District Court Clerk

Fifteenth Judicial District
100 West Laurel, Plentywood, MT 59254

Clerk of District Court, Daniels County **Joan Bjarko** ..... (406) 487-2651
  213 Main Street, Scobey, MT 59263   Fax: (406) 487-5432
  E-mail: jbjarko@mt.gov

Clerk and Recorder

Office of the Clerk and Recorder
213 Main Street, Scobey, MT 59263
P.O. Box 247, Scobey, MT 59263
Tel: (406) 487-5561 Fax: (406) 487-5583

Clerk and Recorder **Kristy Jones** .... (406) 487-5561
  E-mail: clerkrec@danielsco.mt.gov

Dawson County

District Court Clerk

Seventh Judicial District
207 West Bell Street, Glendive, MT 59330

Clerk of District Court, Dawson County
  Tammy Helmuth .... (406) 377-2666
  207 West Bell Street, Glendive, MT 59330   Fax: (406) 377-7280
  E-mail: thelmuth@mt.gov

Clerk and Recorder

Office of the Clerk and Recorder
207 West Bell Street, Glendive, MT 59330
Tel: (406) 377-3058 Fax: (406) 377-1717

Clerk and Recorder **Shirley Kreiman** .... (406) 377-3058
  E-mail: kreimans@dawsoncountymail.com

Deer Lodge County

District Court Clerk

Third Judicial District
800 South Main Street, Anaconda, MT 59711-2999

Clerk of District Court, Deer Lodge County
  Susie Krueger .... (406) 563-4040
  800 South Main Street, Anaconda, MT 59711-2999   Fax: (406) 563-4077
  E-mail: skrueger@mt.gov

Clerk and Recorder

Office of the Clerk and Recorder
800 South Main, Second Floor, Anaconda, MT 59711
Tel: (406) 563-4058 Fax: (406) 563-4001

Clerk and Recorder **Joey Blodnick** .... (406) 563-4058
  E-mail: jblodnick@anacondadeerlodge.mt.gov

Fallon County

District Court Clerk

Sixteenth Judicial District
1200 Main Street, Forsyth, MT 59327

Clerk of District Court, Fallon County
Jeraldine A. Newell . . . . (406) 778-7114
10 West Fallon Avenue, Baker, MT 69313   Fax: (406) 778-2815
E-mail: jnewell@mt.gov

Clerk and Recorder

Office of the Clerk and Recorder
10 West Fallon Avenue, Baker, MT 59313
P.O. Box 846, Baker, MT 59313
Tel: (406) 778-7106 Fax: (406) 778-2048

Clerk and Recorder **Brenda J. Wood** . . . . (406) 778-7106
E-mail: falloncc@midrivers.com

Fergus County

District Court Clerk

Tenth Judicial District
712 West Main Street, Lewistown, MT 59457

Clerk of District Court, Fergus County
Phyllis D. Smith . . . . (406) 535-5026
712 West Main Street, Lewistown, MT 59457   Fax: (406) 535-6076
E-mail: psmith@mt.gov

Clerk and Recorder

Office of the Clerk and Recorder
712 West Main Street, Lewistown, MT 59457
Tel: (406) 535-5242 Fax: (406) 535-9023

Clerk and Recorder **Rana J. Wichman** . . . . (406) 535-5242
E-mail: clerkrecorder@co.fergus.mt.us

Flathead County

District Court Clerk

Eleventh Judicial District
920 South Main Street, Kalispell, MT 59901

Clerk of District Court, Flathead County **Peg Allison** . . . . (406) 758-5665
920 South Main Street, Kalispell, MT 59901   Fax: (406) 758-5857

Clerk and Recorder

Office of the Clerk and Recorder
800 South Main Street, Room 114, Kalispell, MT 59901
Tel: (406) 758-5526 Fax: (406) 758-5865

Clerk and Recorder **Debbie Pierson** . . . . (406) 758-5526
E-mail: Debbie.pierson@flathead.mt.gov

Gallatin County

District Court Clerk

Eighteenth Judicial District
615 South 16th Avenue, Bozeman, MT 59715

Clerk of District Court, Gallatin County
Jennifer Brandon . . . . (406) 582-2165
615 South 16th Avenue, Room 302,   Fax: (406) 582-2176
Bozeman, MT 59715
E-mail: jbrandon@mt.gov

Clerk and Recorder

Office of the Clerk and Recorder
311 West Main, Room 203, Bozeman, MT 59715
Tel: (406) 582-3050 Fax: (406) 582-3196
E-mail: clerkandrecorder@gallatin.mt.gov

Clerk and Recorder **Charlotte Mills** . . . . (406) 582-3050
E-mail: charlotte.mills@gallatin.mt.gov

Garfield County

District Court Clerk

Sixteenth Judicial District
1200 Main Street, Forsyth, MT 59327

Clerk of District Court, Garfield County
Jennifer Crawford . . . . (406) 557-6254
P.O. Box 8, Jordan, MT 59337   Fax: (406) 557-2625
E-mail: jcrawford@mt.gov

Clerk and Recorder

Office of the Clerk and Recorder
Garfield County Courthouse, Jordan, MT 59041
P.O. Box 7, Jordan, MT 59337
Tel: (406) 557-2760 Fax: (406) 557-2765

Clerk and Recorder **Janet Sherer** . . . . (406) 557-2760
E-mail: gccr@midrivers.com

Glacier County

District Court Clerk

Ninth Judicial District
226 First Street South, Shelby, MT 59474

Clerk of District Court, Glacier County
Janine R. Scott . . . . (406) 873-3619
512 East Main Street, Cut Bank, MT 59427   Fax: (406) 873-5627
E-mail: jscott@mt.gov

Clerk and Recorder

Office of the Clerk and Recorder
512 East Main Street, Cut Bank, MT 59427
Fax: (406) 873-3613

Clerk and Recorder **Glenda Hall** . . . . (406) 873-5063
E-mail: gmhall@glaciercountymt.org

Golden Valley County

District Court Clerk

Fourteenth Judicial District
506 Main Street, Roundup, MT 59072

Clerk of District Court and Recorder, Golden Valley
County **Mary Lu Berry** . . . . (406) 568-2231
P.O. Box 10, Ryegate, MT 59074   Fax: (406) 568-2428
E-mail: mberry@mt.gov

(continued on next page)

Granite County

District Court Clerk

Third Judicial District
800 South Main Street, Anaconda, MT 59711-2999

Clerk of District Court, Granite County
Carol Bohrnsen . . . . (406) 859-3712
220 North Sansome, Philipsburg, MT 59858   Fax: (406) 859-3817
E-mail: cbohrnsen@mt.gov

Clerk and Recorder

Office of the Clerk and Recorder
P.O. Box 925, Philipsburg, MT 59858
220 North Sansome Street, Missoula, MT 59801
Tel: (406) 859-3771   Fax: (406) 859-3817

Clerk and Recorder **Blanche McLure** . . . . (406) 859-3771
E-mail: graclerk@co.granite.mt.us

Hill County

District Court Clerk

Twelfth Judicial District
315 Fourth Street, Havre, MT 59501

Clerk of District Court, Hill County
Kathie Vigliotti . . . . (406) 265-5481 ext. 225
315 Fourth Street, Havre, MT 59501   Fax: (406) 265-3693
E-mail: kvigliotti@mt.gov

Clerk and Recorder

Office of the Clerk and Recorder
315 Fourth Street, Havre, MT 59501
Tel: (406) 265-5481 ext. 223 Fax: (406) 265-2445

Clerk and Recorder **Susan Armstrong** . . . . (406) 265-5481 ext. 223
E-mail: armstrongs@co.hill.mt.us

Jefferson County

District Court Clerk

Fifth Judicial District
Two South Pacific Street, Dillon, MT 59725

Clerk of District Court, Jefferson County
Marilyn A. Craft . . . . (406) 225-4042
201 Centennial Street, Boulder, MT 59632   Fax: (406) 225-4044
E-mail: mcraft@mt.gov

Clerk and Recorder

Office of the Clerk and Recorder
201 West Centennial, Boulder, MT 59632
P.O. Box H, Boulder, MT 59632
Tel: (406) 225-4020 Fax: (406) 225-4149

Clerk and Recorder **Bonnie Ramey** . . . . (406) 225-4020
E-mail: bramey@jeffersoncounty-mt.gov

Judith Basin County

District Court Clerk

Tenth Judicial District
712 West Main Street, Lewistown, MT 59457

Clerk of District Court, Judith Basin County
Julie Anderson Peevey . . . . (406) 566-2277 ext. 113
11 Third Street North, Stanford, MT 59479   Fax: (406) 566-2211
E-mail: jpeevey@mt.gov

Clerk and Recorder

Office of the Clerk and Recorder
91 Third Street North, Stanford, MT 59479
P.O. Box 427, Stanford, MT 59479
Tel: (406) 566-2277 ext. 109 Fax: (406) 566-2211

Clerk and Recorder **Amanda H. Kelly** . . . . (406) 566-2277 ext. 109
E-mail: akelly@co.judith-basin.mt.us

Lake County

District Court Clerk

Twentieth Judicial District
106 Fourth Avenue East, Polson, MT 59860

Clerk of District Court, Lake County **Lyn Fricker** . . . . (406) 883-7254
106 Fourth Avenue East, Polson, MT 59860   Fax: (406) 883-7343
E-mail: lfricker@mt.gov

Clerk and Recorder

Office of the Clerk and Recorder
106 Fourth Avenue East, Polson, MT 59860
Tel: (406) 883-7268 Fax: (406) 883-7283

Clerk and Recorder **Paula Holle** . . . . (406) 883-7215
E-mail: pholle@lakemt.gov

Lewis and Clark County

District Court Clerk

First Judicial District
228 Broadway Street, Helena, MT 59604-4263

Clerk of District Court, Lewis and Clark County
Nancy Sweeney . . . . (406) 447-8216
228 Broadway Street, Helena, MT 59604-4263   Fax: (406) 447-8275

Clerk and Recorder

Office of the Clerk and Recorder
316 North Park Avenue, Room 168, Helena, MT 59623
Tel: (406) 447-8334 Fax: (406) 457-8598

Clerk and Recorder **Paulette DeHart** . . . . (406) 447-8334
E-mail: pdehart@lccountymt.gov

Liberty County

District Court Clerk

Twelfth Judicial District
315 Fourth Street, Havre, MT 59501

Clerk of District Court, Liberty County
Anne Seidlitz-Melton . . . . (406) 759-5615
111 First Street East, Chester, MT 59522   Fax: (406) 759-5996
E-mail: aseidlitzmelton@mt.gov

Clerk and Recorder

Office of the Clerk and Recorder
111 First Street East, Chester, MT 59522
P.O. Box 459, Chester, MT 59522
Tel: (406) 759-5365 Fax: (406) 759-5395

Clerk and Recorder **Angel Colbry** . . . . (406) 759-5365
E-mail: clerk@co.liberty.mt.gov

Lincoln County

District Court Clerk

Nineteenth Judicial District
512 California Avenue, Libby, MT 59923

Clerk of District Court, Lincoln County **Susan Farmer** . . . (406) 293-7781
512 California Avenue, Libby, MT 59923
E-mail: sfarmer@mt.gov

Clerk and Recorder

Office of the Clerk and Recorder
512 California Avenue, Libby, MT 59923
Tel: (406) 283-2301 Fax: (406) 293-8577

Clerk and Recorder **Robin Benson** . . . . (406) 283-2301
E-mail: lcclerk@libby.org

Madison County

District Court Clerk

Fifth Judicial District
Two South Pacific Street, Dillon, MT 59725

Clerk of District Court, Madison County **Karen Miller** . . . (406) 843-4230
100 Wallace Street, Virginia City, MT 59755   Fax: (406) 843-5207

Clerk and Recorder

Office of the Clerk and Recorder
P.O. Box 366, Virginia City, MT 59755
100 West Wallace Street, Virginia City, MT 59755
Tel: (406) 843-4270 Fax: (406) 843-5264

Clerk and Recorder **Peggy Kaatz** . . . . (406) 843-4270
E-mail: pkaatz@madison.mt.gov

McCone County

District Court Clerk

Seventh Judicial District
207 West Bell Street, Glendive, MT 59330

Clerk of District Court, McCone County
Trudy Kirkegard . . . . (406) 485-3410
1004 C Avenue, Circle, MT 59215

Clerk and Recorder

Office of the Clerk and Recorder
1004 C Avenue, Circle, MT 59215
P.O. Box 199, Circle, MT 59215
Tel: (406) 485-3505 Fax: (406) 485-2689

Clerk and Recorder **Maridel L. Kassner** . . . . (406) 485-3505
E-mail: clerk@midrivers.com

Meagher County

District Court Clerk

Fourteenth Judicial District
506 Main Street, Roundup, MT 59072

Clerk of District Court, Meagher County
Donna Morris . . . . (406) 547-3612 ext. 110
15 Main Street, White Sulphur Springs, MT 59645   Fax: (406) 547-3836
E-mail: dmorris@mt.gov

Clerk and Recorder

Office of the Clerk and Recorder
15 West Main Street, White Sulphur Springs, MT 59645
Tel: (406) 547-3612 ext. 3021 Fax: (406) 547-3388

Clerk and Recorder **Dayna Ogle** . . . . (406) 547-3612 ext. 3021
E-mail: dogle@meaghercounty.mt.gov

Mineral County

District Court Clerk

Fourth Judicial District
200 West Broadway, Missoula, MT 59802

Clerk of District Court, Mineral County
Kathleen M. Brown . . . . (406) 822-3538
300 River Street, Superior, MT 59872   Fax: (406) 822-3822
E-mail: kbrown@mt.gov

Clerk and Recorder

Office of the Clerk and Recorder
300 River Street, Superior, MT 59872
P.O. Box 550, Superior, MT 59872
Tel: (406) 822-3521 Fax: (406) 822-3579

Clerk and Recorder **Staci Hayes** . . . . (406) 822-3521
E-mail: shayes@co.mineral.mt.us

Missoula County

District Court Clerk

Fourth Judicial District
200 West Broadway, Missoula, MT 59802

Clerk of District Court, Missoula County
Shirley E. Faust . . . . (406) 258-4780
200 West Broadway, Missoula, MT 59802   Fax: (406) 258-4899
E-mail: sfaust@mt.gov

Clerk and Recorder

Office of the Clerk and Recorder
200 West Broadway, Missoula, MT 59802
Tel: (406) 258-4752 Fax: (406) 258-3913
E-mail: recording@co.missoula.mt.us

Clerk and Recorder **Tyler Reed Gernant** . . . . (406) 258-4752
E-mail: tgernant@co.missoula.mt.us

(continued on next page)

Musselshell County

District Court Clerk

Fourteenth Judicial District
506 Main Street, Roundup, MT 59072

Clerk of District Court, Musselshell County
Connie Mattfield . . . . (406) 323-1413
506 Main Street, Roundup, MT 59072   Fax: (406) 323-1710
E-mail: cmattfield@mt.gov

Clerk and Recorder

Office of the Clerk and Recorder
506 Main, Roundup, MT 59072
Tel: (406) 323-1104 Fax: (406) 323-3303

Clerk and Recorder **Cheryl Tomassi** . . . . (406) 323-1104
E-mail: ctomassi@co.musselshell.mt.us

Park County

District Court Clerk

Sixth Judicial District
414 East Callender Street, Livingston, MT 46047

Clerk of District Court, Park County **June Little** . . . . (406) 222-4125
414 East Callender Street,   Fax: (406) 222-4128
Livingston, MT 46047

Clerk and Recorder

Office of the Clerk and Recorder/Surveyor
414 East Callender Street, Livingston, MT 59047
Tel: (406) 222-4110 Fax: (406) 222-4193

Clerk and Recorder/Surveyor **Denise Nelson** . . . . (406) 222-4110
E-mail: clerkrecorder@parkcounty.org

Petroleum County

District Court Clerk

Tenth Judicial District
712 West Main Street, Lewistown, MT 59457

Clerk of District Court, Petroleum County
Leslie Mitchell . . . . (406) 429-5311
201 East Main Street, Winnett, MT 59087   Fax: (406) 429-6328
E-mail: lmitchell@mt.gov

Clerk and Recorder

Office of the Clerk and Recorder
302 East Main, Winnett, MT 59087
P.O. Box 226, Winnett, MT 59087
Fax: (406) 429-6328

Clerk and Recorder **Leslie Mitchell** . . . . (406) 429-5331
E-mail: leslies@midrivers.com

Phillips County

District Court Clerk

Seventeenth Judicial District
314 Second Avenue West, Malta, MT 59538

Clerk of District Court, Phillips County
Tami Christofferson . . . . (406) 654-1023
314 Second Avenue WEst,   Fax: (406) 654-1023
Malta, MT 59538

Clerk and Recorder

Office of the Clerk and Recorder
314 South Second Avenue West, Malta, MT 59538
P.O. Box 360, Malta, MT 59538
Tel: (406) 654-2423 Fax: (406) 654-2429

Clerk and Recorder **Marian Ereaux** . . . . (406) 654-2423
E-mail: mereaux@phillipscounty.mt.gov

Pondera County

District Court Clerk

Ninth Judicial District
226 First Street South, Shelby, MT 59474

Clerk of District Court, Pondera County
Laurie Eisenzimer . . . . (406) 271-4026
20 Fourth Avenue SW, Conrad, MT 59425   Fax: (406) 271-4081
E-mail: lauriee@mt.gov

Clerk and Recorder

Office of the Clerk and Recorder
20 Fourth Avenue SW, Conrad, MT 59425
Tel: (406) 271-4001 Fax: (406) 271-4070

Clerk and Recorder **Kody Farkell** . . . . (406) 271-4001
E-mail: clerkrec@3rivers.net

Powder River County

District Court Clerk

Sixteenth Judicial District
1200 Main Street, Forsyth, MT 59327

Clerk of District Court, Powder River County
Aletta Shannon . . . . (406) 436-2320
P.O. Box 200, Broadus, MT 59317   Fax: (406) 436-2325
E-mail: ashannon@mt.gov

Clerk and Recorder

Office of the Clerk and Recorder
119 North Park Avenue, Broadus, MT 59317
P.O. Box 200, Broadus, MT 59317
Tel: (406) 436-2361 Fax: (406) 436-2151

Clerk and Recorder **Carole Richards** . . . . (406) 436-2361
E-mail: crichards@prco.mt.gov

Powell County

District Court Clerk

Third Judicial District
800 South Main Street, Anaconda, MT 59711-2999

Clerk of District Court, Powell County **Joan Burke** . . . . . . (406) 846-9787
409 Missouri Avenue, Deer Lodge, MT 59722   Fax: (406) 846-1031
E-mail: jburke@mt.gov

Clerk and Recorder

Office of the Clerk and Recorder
409 Missouri Avenue, Suite 203, Deer Lodge, MT 59722
Tel: (406) 846-9786 Fax: (406) 846-3891

Clerk and Recorder **Jody Walker** . . . . (406) 846-9786
E-mail: jwalker@powellcountymt.gov

Prairie County

District Court Clerk

Seventh Judicial District
207 West Bell Street, Glendive, MT 59330

Clerk of District Court and Recorder, Prairie County
Tammy Helmuth . . . . (406) 635-5575
217 West Park Street, Terry, MT 59349   Fax: (406) 635-5576
E-mail: tkalfell@mt.gov

Ravalli County

District Court Clerk

Twenty-First Judicial District
205 Bedford Street, Hamilton, MT 59840

Clerk of District Court, Ravalli County
Paige Trautwein . . . .(406) 375-6710
205 Bedford Street, Suite D,   Fax: (406) 375-6721
Hamilton, MT 59840

Clerk and Recorder

Office of the Clerk and Recorder
215 South Fourth Street, Suite C, Hamilton, MT 59840
Tel: (406) 375-6555   Fax: (406) 375-6554

Clerk and Recorder **Regina Plettenberg** . . . .(406) 375-6555
E-mail: rplettenberg@rc.mt.gov

Richland County

District Court Clerk

Seventh Judicial District
207 West Bell Street, Glendive, MT 59330

Clerk of District Court, Richland County
Janice Klempel . . . . (406) 433-1709
300 12th Avenue NW, Suite Three,   Fax: (406) 433-6945
Sidney, MT 59270
E-mail: jklempel@mt.gov

Clerk and Recorder

Office of the Clerk and Recorder
201 West Main, Sidney, MT 59270
Tel: (406) 433-1708   Fax: (406) 433-3731

Clerk and Recorder **Stephanie Verhasselt** . . . .(406) 433-1708
E-mail: sverhasselt@richland.org

Roosevelt County

District Court Clerk

Fifteenth Judicial District
100 West Laurel, Plentywood, MT 59254

Clerk of District Court, Roosevelt County **Jeri Toavs** . . . . (406) 653-6266
400 Second Avenue South,   Fax: (406) 653-6203
Wolf Point, MT 59201
E-mail: jtoavs@mt.gov

Clerk and Recorder

Office of the Clerk and Recorder
400 Second Avenue South, Wolf Point, MT 59201
Tel: (406) 653-6229   Fax: (406) 653-6289

Clerk and Recorder **Cheryl A. Hansen** . . . . (406) 653-6229
E-mail: chansen@rooseveltcounty.org

Rosebud County

District Court Clerk

Sixteenth Judicial District
1200 Main Street, Forsyth, MT 59327

Clerk of District Court, Rosebud County
Elizabeth Ball-Mavity . . . . (406) 346-7322
1200 Main Street, Forsyth, MT 59327   Fax: (406) 346-7551

Clerk and Recorder

Office of the Clerk and Recorder
1200 Main Street, Forsyth, MT 59327
P.O. Box 47, Forsyth, MT 59327
Tel: (406) 346-7318   Fax: (406) 346-7551

Clerk and Recorder **Joan K. Duffield** . . . . (406) 346-7318
E-mail: jduffield@rosebudcountymt.com

Sanders County

District Court Clerk

Twentieth Judicial District
106 Fourth Avenue East, Polson, MT 59860

Clerk of District Court, Sanders County
Candace "Candy" Fisher . . . .(406) 827-6962
P.O. Box 519, Thompson Falls, MT 59873   Fax: (406) 827-0094

Clerk and Recorder

Office of the Clerk and Recorder
1111 Main Street, Thompson Falls, MT 59873
P.O. Box 519, Thompson Falls, MT 59873
Tel: (406) 827-6922   Fax: (406) 827-6970

Clerk and Recorder **Nichol Scribner** . . . . (406) 827-6922
E-mail: nscribner@sanderscounty.mt.gov

Sheridan County

District Court Clerk

Fifteenth Judicial District
100 West Laurel, Plentywood, MT 59254

Clerk of District Court, Sheridan County
Teresa McCauley . . . . (406) 765-3404
100 West Laurel Avenue, Plentywood, MT 59254   Fax: (406) 765-2602
E-mail: tmccauley@mt.gov

Clerk and Recorder

Office of the Clerk and Recorder
100 West Laurel Avenue, Plentywood, MT 59254
Tel: (406) 765-3403   Fax: (406) 765-2609

Clerk and Recorder **June Johnson** . . . . (406) 765-3403
E-mail: record_supt@co.sheridan.mt.us

Silver Bow County

District Court Clerk

Second Judicial District
155 West Granite Street, Butte, MT 59701

Clerk of District Court, Silver Bow County
Lori Maloney . . . . (406) 497-6350
155 West Granite Street, Butte, MT 59701   Fax: (406) 497-6358
E-mail: lmaloney@mt.gov

(continued on next page)

Montana Court Clerks and Courthouses *continued*

Clerk and Recorder

Office of the Clerk and Recorder
155 West Granite Street, Room 208, Butte, MT 59701
Tel: (406) 497-6335 Fax: (406) 497-6328

Clerk and Recorder **Sally Hollis**.....................(406) 497-6335
E-mail: shollis@bsb.mt.gov

Stillwater County

District Court Clerk

Twenty-Second Judicial District
809A East Fourth Avenue, Columbus, MT 59019

Clerk of District Court, Stillwater County **Sandy Fox** .... (406) 322-8030
400 Third Avenue North, Columbus, MT 59019   Fax: (406) 322-8048

Clerk and Recorder

Office of the Clerk and Recorder
400 East Third Avenue North, 2nd Floor, Columbus, MT 59019
P.O. Box 149, Columbus, MT 59019
Tel: (406) 322-8000 Fax: (406) 322-8069

Clerk and Recorder **Heidi Stadel**.....................(406) 322-8000
E-mail: hstadel@stillwater.mt.gov

Sweet Grass County

District Court Clerk

Sixth Judicial District
414 East Callender Street, Livingston, MT 46047

Clerk of District Court, Sweet Grass County
   Deanna Novotny...............................(406) 932-5154
   200 West First Avenue, Big Timber, MT 59011   Fax: (406) 932-5433

Clerk and Recorder

Office of the Clerk and Recorder
115 West Fifth Avenue, Big Timber, MT 59011
P.O. Box 888, Big Timber, MT 59011
Tel: (406) 932-5152 Fax: (406) 932-3026

Clerk and Recorder **Vera Pederson**...................(406) 932-5152
E-mail: sgclerk1@itstriangle.com

Teton County

District Court Clerk

Ninth Judicial District
226 First Street South, Shelby, MT 59474

Clerk of District Court, Teton County **Lisa J. Sinton** .... (406) 466-2909
One Main Avenue South, Choteau, MT 59422   Fax: (406) 466-2910
E-mail: lsinton@mt.gov

Clerk and Recorder

Office of the Clerk and Recorder
One Main Avenue South, Choteau, MT 59422
P.O. Box 610, Choteau, MT 59422
Tel: (406) 466-2693 Fax: (406) 466-2138

Clerk and Recorder **Paula J. Jaconetty** ....(406) 466-2693
E-mail: paula@3rivers.net

Montana Court Clerks and Courthouses *continued*

Toole County

District Court Clerk

Ninth Judicial District
226 First Street South, Shelby, MT 59474

Clerk of District Court, Toole County **Debra Munson**....(406) 424-8330
226 First Street South, Shelby, MT 59474   Fax: (406) 424-8331
E-mail: dmunson3@mt.gov

Clerk and Recorder

Office of the Clerk and Recorder
226 First Street South, Shelby, MT 59474
Tel: (406) 424-8300 Fax: (406) 424-8301

Clerk and Recorder **Treva Nelson** ....(406) 424-8300
E-mail: tnelson@toolecountymt.gov

Treasure County

District Court Clerk

Sixteenth Judicial District
1200 Main Street, Forsyth, MT 59327

Clerk of District Court and Recorder, Treasure County
   Ruth L. Baker...................................(406) 342-5547
   307 Rapelje Avenue, Hysham, MT 59038   Fax: (406) 342-5445
   E-mail: rbaker@mt.gov

Valley County

District Court Clerk

Seventeenth Judicial District
314 Second Avenue West, Malta, MT 59538

Clerk of District Court, Valley County **Shelley Bryan** .... (406) 228-6268
501 Court Square, Suite Six,   Fax: (406) 228-6212
Glasgow, MT 59230
E-mail: sbryan@mt.gov

Clerk and Recorder

Office of the Clerk and Recorder
501 Court Square, Box 2, Glasgow, MT 59230
Tel: (406) 228-6220 Fax: (406) 228-9027

Clerk and Recorder **Lynne Nyquist**...................(406) 228-6220
E-mail: lnyquist@valleycountymt.net

Wheatland County

District Court Clerk

Fourteenth Judicial District
506 Main Street, Roundup, MT 59072

Clerk of District Court, Wheatland County **Janet Hill** .... (406) 632-4893
201 A Avenue NW, Harlowton, MT 59036   Fax: (406) 632-4873
E-mail: jhill@mt.gov

Clerk and Recorder

Office of the Clerk and Recorder
201 A Avenue, NW, Harlowton, MT 59036
P.O. Box 1903, Harlowton, MT 59036
Tel: (406) 632-4891 Fax: (406) 632-4880

Clerk and Recorder **Mary E. Miller**...................(406) 632-4891
E-mail: wccr@mtintouch.net

Montana Court Clerks and Courthouses *continued*

Wibaux County

District Court Clerk

Seventh Judicial District
207 West Bell Street, Glendive, MT 59330

Clerk of District Court, Wibaux County
Michael W. Schneider . . . . (406) 796-2484
203 Wibaux Street, Wibaux, MT 59353
E-mail: mschneider@mt.gov

Clerk and Recorder

Office of the Clerk and Recorder
203 Wibaux Street South, Wibaux, MT 59353
P.O. Box 199, Wibaux, MT 59353
Tel: (406) 796-2481 Fax: (406) 796-2625

Clerk and Recorder **Patricia Zinda** . . . . (406) 796-2481
E-mail: wibauxco@midrivers.com

Yellowstone County

District Court Clerk

Thirteenth Judicial District
217 North 27th Street, Billings, MT 59107

Clerk of District Court, Yellowstone County
Kristie Lee Boelter . . . . (406) 256-2851
217 North 27th Street, Billings, MT 59107   Fax: (406) 256-2995
E-mail: kboelter@mt.gov

Clerk and Recorder

Office of the Clerk and Recorder/Surveyor
P.O. Box 35001, Billings, MT 59107
Fax: (406) 256-2736
Internet: www.co.yellowstone.mt.gov/clerk

Clerk and Recorder/Surveyor **Jeff Martin** . . . . (406) 256-2785
E-mail: jmartin@co.yellowstone.mt.gov

Counties Within Judicial Districts

District Court, 1st District
Areas Covered: Broadwater and Lewis and Clark Counties.

District Court, 2nd District
Areas Covered: Silver Bow County.

District Court, 3rd District
Areas Covered: Deer Lodge, Granite, and Powell Counties.

District Court, 4th District
Areas Covered: Mineral and Missoula Counties.

District Court, 5th District
Areas Covered: Beaverhead, Jefferson, and Madison Counties.

District Court, 6th District
Areas Covered: Park and Sweet Grass Counties.

Montana Court Clerks and Courthouses *continued*

District Court, 7th District
Areas Covered: Dawson, McCone, Prairie, Richland, and Wibaux
Counties.

District Court, 8th District
Areas Covered: Cascade County.

District Court, 9th District
Areas Covered: Glacier, Pondera, Teton, and Toole Counties.

District Court, 10th District
Areas Covered: Fergus, Judith Basin, and Petroleum Counties.

District Court, 11th District
Areas Covered: Flathead County.

District Court, 12th District
Areas Covered: Chouteau, Hill, and Liberty Counties.

District Court, 13th District
Areas Covered: Yellowstone County.

District Court, 14th District
Areas Covered: Golden Valley, Meagher, Musselshell, and Wheatland
Counties.

District Court, 15th District
Areas Covered: Daniels, Sheridan, and Roosevelt Counties.

District Court, 16th District
Areas Covered: Carter, Custer, Fallon, Garfield, Powder River, Rosebud,
and Treasure Counties.

District Court, 17th District
Areas Covered: Blaine, Phillips, and Valley Counties.

District Court, 18th District
Areas Covered: Gallatin County.

District Court, 19th District
Areas Covered: Lincoln County.

District Court, 20th District
Areas Covered: Lake and Sanders Counties.

District Court, 21st District
Areas Covered: Ravalli County.

District Court, 22nd District
Areas Covered: Big Horn, Carbon, and Stillwater Counties.

Nebraska Court Clerks and Courthouses

The trial court of general jurisdiction in Nebraska is called the District Court. There are 12 judicial districts, each district including at least one county. Listed below are district court clerks for each county. In many counties the position of district court clerk and county clerk are combined.

Nebraska Supreme Court

2413 State Capitol Building, 1445 K Street, Lincoln, NE 68509
Tel: (402) 471-3731 Fax: (402) 471-3480
Internet: http://supremecourt.ne.gov

The Supreme Court consists of a chief justice and six associate justices who are appointed by the Governor from a list submitted by a judicial nominating commission. Justices run for retention in the next general election occurring more than three years after the appointment for a six-year term. The chief justice is elected on a statewide ballot, while the six associate justices are elected in six separate judicial districts throughout the state. The judicial districts are approximately equal in population and are redistricted by the State Legislature after every census. The Supreme Court has discretionary review of cases from the Nebraska Court of Appeals and hears cases regarding constitutional issues. The Court also has jurisdiction over all appeals dealing with the death penalty and the sentence of life imprisonment. Appeals are brought to the Court from the Nebraska District Courts, Juvenile Courts, Workers' Compensation Court, and administrative agencies. The Court is responsible for the regulation of the practice of law in the state and oversees the admission of attorneys to the state bar.

Court Staff

Clerk of Supreme Court and Court of Appeals
Teresa A. "Terri" Brown..........................(402) 471-3731

Nebraska Court of Appeals

State Capitol Building, 1445 K Street, Lincoln, NE 68508
P.O. Box 98910, Lincoln, NE 68509
Tel: (402) 471-3731 Fax: (402) 471-2197
Internet: court.nol.org/judges/appealsjudges.htm

The Court of Appeals, established in September 1991 as a result of a constitutional amendment, consists of a chief judge and five judges who are appointed by the Governor from a list submitted by judicial nominating commissions. Judges run for retention in the next general election occurring more than three years after appointment for a six-year term. The chief judge is selected by the Nebraska Supreme Court to serve a one-year renewable term. The districts from which the Court's judges are appointed are the same as those used for the six Supreme Court associate judges. The Court is divided into two panels consisting of three judges each. The Court of Appeals hears all appeals from lower courts, except cases involving the death penalty and life imprisonment and cases involving the constitutionality of a statute. In cases appealed to the Court, a petition to bypass may be filled with the Nebraska Supreme Court. If the Supreme Court deems it necessary, the petition will be granted and the case will be moved to the Supreme Court docket without first being heard by the Court of Appeals. A petition for further review may also be filed. This petition is filed after a case has been decided by the Court of Appeals and one of the parties involved is not satisfied with the ruling. The Supreme Court may also grant or deny this petition.

Court Staff

Clerk of Supreme Court and Court of Appeals
Teresa A. "Terri" Brown..........................(402) 471-3731
Fax: (402) 471-3480

County-By-County

Adams County

District Court Clerk

Tenth Judicial District
426 North Colorado Avenue, Minden, NE 68959

Clerk of the District Court, Adams County
Chrystine Setlik..................................(402) 461-7264
500 West Fourth Street, Room 200,   Fax: (402) 461-7269
Hastings, NE 68901
E-mail: csetlik@adamscounty.org

Antelope County

District Court Clerk

Seventh Judicial District
1313 North Main Street, Madison, NE 68748

Clerk of the District Court, Antelope County
Judy Cole..(402) 887-4508
501 Main Street, Neligh, NE 68756   Fax: (402) 887-4870
E-mail: judy.cole@nebraska.gov

Arthur County

District Court Clerk

Eleventh Judicial District
301 North Jeffers Street, North Platte, NE 69101

Clerk of the District Court, Arthur County
Becky Swanson..................................(308) 764-2203
P.O. Box 126, Arthur, NE 69121   Fax: (308) 764-2216
E-mail: becky.swanson@nebraska.gov

Banner County

District Court Clerk

Twelfth Judicial District
1725 10th Street, Gering, NE 69341

Clerk of the District Court, Banner County
Lori Hostetler..................................(308) 436-5265
P.O. Box 67, Harrisburg, NE 69345   Fax: (308) 436-4180
E-mail: lori.hostetler@nebraska.gov

Blaine County

District Court Clerk

Eighth Judicial District
148 West Fourth Street, Ainsworth, NE 69210

Clerk of the District Court, Blaine County
April Wescott..................................(308) 547-2222
145 Lincoln Avenue, Brewster, NE 68821   Fax: (308) 547-2228
E-mail: april.wescott@nebraska.gov

(continued on next page)

Nebraska Court Clerks and Courthouses *continued*

Boone County

District Court Clerk

Fifth Judicial District
2610 14th Street, Columbus, NE 68601

Clerk of the District Court, Boone County
Kathy Thorberg . . . . (402) 395-2057
222 South Fournth Street, Albion, NE 68620   Fax: (402) 395-6592
E-mail: kathy.thorberg@nebraska.gov

Box Butte County

District Court Clerk

Twelfth Judicial District
1725 10th Street, Gering, NE 69341

Clerk of the District Court, Box Butte County
Kevin Horn . . . . (308) 762-6293
515 Box Butte Avenue, Suite 300,   Fax: (308) 762-5700
Alliance, NE 69301
E-mail: kevin.horn@nebraska.gov

Boyd County

District Court Clerk

Eighth Judicial District
148 West Fourth Street, Ainsworth, NE 69210

Clerk of the District Court, Boyd County **Tracy Reiser** . . . (402) 775-2391
P.O. Box 26, Butte, NE 68722   Fax: (402) 775-2146
E-mail: tracy.reiser@nebraska.gov

Brown County

District Court Clerk

Eighth Judicial District
148 West Fourth Street, Ainsworth, NE 69210

Clerk of the District Court, Brown County
Travis D. Hobbs . . . . (402) 387-2705
148 West Fourth Street, Ainsworth, NE 69210   Fax: (402) 387-0918
E-mail: travis.hobbs@threeriver.net

Buffalo County

District Court Clerk

Ninth Judicial District
111 West First Street, Grand Island, NE 68801

Clerk of the District Court, Buffalo County
Sharon K. Mauler . . . . (308) 236-1246
P.O. Box 520, Kearney, NE 68848   Fax: (308) 233-3693
E-mail: sharon.mauler@nebraska.gov

Burt County

District Court Clerk

Sixth Judicial District
1555 Colfax Street, Blair, NE 68008

Clerk of the District Court, Burt County
Michele Quick . . . . (402) 374-2905
111 North 13th Street, Suite 11,   Fax: (402) 374-2906
Tekamah, NE 68061
E-mail: michele.quick@nebraska.gov

Nebraska Court Clerks and Courthouses *continued*

Butler County

District Court Clerk

Fifth Judicial District
2610 14th Street, Columbus, NE 68601

Clerk of the District Court, Butler County
Nancy Prochaska . . . . (402) 367-7460
451 Fifth Street, David City, NE 68632   Fax: (402) 367-3249
E-mail: nancy.prochaska@nebraska.gov

Cass County

District Court Clerk

Second Judicial District
1210 Golden Gate Drive, Papillion, NE 68046

Clerk of the District Court, Cass County
Barbara L. "Barb" Prokupek . . . . (402) 296-9339
346 Main Street, Room 303,   Fax: (402) 296-9345
Plattsmouth, NE 68048
E-mail: barb.prokupek@nebraska.gov

Cedar County

District Court Clerk

Sixth Judicial District
1555 Colfax Street, Blair, NE 68008

Clerk of the District Court, Cedar County
Janet Wiechelman . . . . (402) 254-6957
101 South Broadway Avenue, Second Floor,   Fax: (402) 254-6954
Hartington, NE 68739
E-mail: janet.wiechelman@nebraska.gov

Chase County

District Court Clerk

Eleventh Judicial District
301 North Jeffers Street, North Platte, NE 69101

Clerk of the District Court, Chase County **Debra Clark** . . . (308) 882-7500
P.O. Box 1299, Imperial, NE 69033   Fax: (308) 882-7552
E-mail: debra.clark@nebraska.gov

Cherry County

District Court Clerk

Eighth Judicial District
148 West Fourth Street, Ainsworth, NE 69210

Clerk of the District Court, Cherry County
Maedeane Rodgers . . . . (402) 376-1840
365 North Main Street, Valentine, NE 69201   Fax: (402) 376-3830
E-mail: maedeane.rodgers@nebraska.gov

Cheyenne County

District Court Clerk

Twelfth Judicial District
1725 10th Street, Gering, NE 69341

Clerk of the District Court, Cheyenne County
Debra Hume . . . . (308) 254-2814
1000 10th Avenue, Sidney, NE 69162   Fax: (308) 254-7832
E-mail: debra.hume@nebraska.gov

Clay County

District Court Clerk

First Judicial District
612 Grant Street, Beatrice, NE 68310

Clerk of the District Court, Clay County **Joni Skalka** . . . . (402) 762-3595
111 West Fairfield Street, Clay Center, NE 68933   Fax: (402) 762-3604
E-mail: joni.skalka@nebraska.gov

Colfax County

District Court Clerk

Fifth Judicial District
2610 14th Street, Columbus, NE 68601

Clerk of the District Court, Colfax County
Dori Kroeger . . . . (402) 352-8506
411 East 11th Street, Schuyler, NE 68661   Fax: (402) 352-8550
E-mail: dori.kroeger@nebraska.gov

Cuming County

District Court Clerk

Seventh Judicial District
1313 North Main Street, Madison, NE 68748

Clerk of the District Court, Cuming County
Laura Wagner . . . . (402) 372-6004
200 South Lincoln Street, West Point, NE 68788   Fax: (402) 372-6017
E-mail: laura.wagner@nebraska.gov

Custer County

District Court Clerk

Eighth Judicial District
148 West Fourth Street, Ainsworth, NE 69210

Clerk of the District Court, Custer County
Amy Oxford . . . . (308) 872-2121
431 South 10th Street, Broken Bow, NE 68822   Fax: (308) 872-5826
E-mail: amy.oxford@nebraska.gov

Dakota County

District Court Clerk

Sixth Judicial District
1555 Colfax Street, Blair, NE 68008

Clerk of the District Court, Dakota County
Phyllis Obermeyer . . . .(402) 987-2115
P.O. Box 66, Dakota City, NE 68731   Fax: (402) 987-2117
E-mail: phyllis.obermeyer@nebraska.gov

Dawes County

District Court Clerk

Twelfth Judicial District
1725 10th Street, Gering, NE 69341

Clerk of the District Court, Dawes County
Sharon Harrison . . . . (308) 432-0109
451 Main Street, Suite B, Chadron, NE 69337   Fax: (308) 432-0110
E-mail: sharon.harrison@nebraska.gov

Dawson County

District Court Clerk

Eleventh Judicial District
301 North Jeffers Street, North Platte, NE 69101

Clerk of the District Court, Dawson County
Becky Boryca . . . .(308) 324-4261
700 North Washington Street, Third Floor,   Fax: (308) 324-9876
Lexington, NE 68550
E-mail: becky.boryca@nebraska.gov

Deuel County

District Court Clerk

Twelfth Judicial District
1725 10th Street, Gering, NE 69341

Clerk of the District Court, Deuel County **Polly Olson** . . . (308) 874-3308
P.O. Box 327, Chappell, NE 69129   Fax: (308) 874-3472
E-mail: polly.olson@nebraska.gov

Dixon County

District Court Clerk

Sixth Judicial District
1555 Colfax Street, Blair, NE 68008

Clerk of the District Court, Dixon County
Jackie King-Coughlin . . . . (402) 755-5604
P.O. Box 395, Ponca, NE 68770   Fax: (402) 755-5651
E-mail: jackie.kingcoughlin@nebraska.gov

Dodge County

District Court Clerk

Sixth Judicial District
1555 Colfax Street, Blair, NE 68008

Clerk of the District Court, Dodge County
Linda Nelson . . . . (402) 727-2780
428 North Broad Street, Fremont, NE 68025   Fax: (402) 727-2773
E-mail: linda.strand.nelson@nebraska.gov

Douglas County

District Court Clerk

Fourth Judicial District
1701 Farnam Street, Omaha, NE 68183

Clerk of the District Court, Douglas County
John Friend . . . . (402) 444-7018
1701 Farnam Street, Third Floor,   Fax: (402) 444-1757
Omaha, NE 68183
E-mail: john.friend@douglascounty-ne.gov

Dundy County

District Court Clerk

Eleventh Judicial District
301 North Jeffers Street, North Platte, NE 69101

Clerk of the District Court, Dundy County **Tony Lutz** . . . . (308) 423-2058
P.O. Box 506, Benkelman, NE 69021   Fax: (308) 423-2325
E-mail: tony.lutz@nebraska.gov

(continued on next page)

Fillmore County

District Court Clerk

First Judicial District
612 Grant Street, Beatrice, NE 68310

Clerk of the District Court, Fillmore County
Peggy Birky . . . . (402) 759-3811
900 G Street, Geneva, NE 68361   Fax: (402) 759-4440
E-mail: Peggy.Birky@nebraska.gov

Franklin County

District Court Clerk

Tenth Judicial District
426 North Colorado Avenue, Minden, NE 68959

Clerk of the District Court, Franklin County
Marcia Volk . . . . (308) 425-6202
P.O. Box 146, Franklin, NE 68939   Fax: (308) 425-6203
E-mail: clerk@franklin.nacone.org

Frontier County

District Court Clerk

Eleventh Judicial District
301 North Jeffers Street, North Platte, NE 69101

Clerk of the District Court, Frontier County
Darla M. Walther . . . .(308) 367-8641
P.O. Box 40, Stockville, NE 69042   Fax: (308) 367-8730
E-mail: darla.walther@nebraska.gov

Furnas County

District Court Clerk

Eleventh Judicial District
301 North Jeffers Street, North Platte, NE 69101

Clerk of the District Court, Furnas County
Victoria Barnett . . . .(308) 268-4015
912 R Street, Beaver City, NE 68926   Fax: (308) 268-4700
E-mail: victoria.barnett@nebraska.gov

Gage County

District Court Clerk

First Judicial District
612 Grant Street, Beatrice, NE 68310

Clerk of the District Court, Gage County
Diane G. Wells . . . . (402) 223-1332
612 Grant Street, Room 11,   Fax: (402) 223-1313
Beatrice, NE 68310
E-mail: diane.wells@nebraska.gov

Garden County

District Court Clerk

Twelfth Judicial District
1725 10th Street, Gering, NE 69341

Clerk of the District Court, Garden County
Teresa McKeeman . . . .(308) 772-3924
611 Main Street, Oshkosh, NE 69154   Fax: (308) 772-9926
E-mail: teresa.mckeeman@nebraska.gov

Garfield County

District Court Clerk

Eighth Judicial District
148 West Fourth Street, Ainsworth, NE 69210

Clerk of the District Court, Garfield County
Stacia Quinn . . . .(308) 346-4161
P.O. Box 218, Burwell, NE 68823   Fax: (308) 346-4651
E-mail: stacia.quinn@nebraska.gov

Gosper County

District Court Clerk

Eleventh Judicial District
301 North Jeffers Street, North Platte, NE 69101

Clerk of the District Court, Gosper County
Cynthia Evans . . . .(308) 785-2611
507 Smith Avenue, Elwood, NE 68937   Fax: (308) 785-2300
E-mail: cynthia.evans@nebraska.gov

Grant County

District Court Clerk

Twelfth Judicial District
1725 10th Street, Gering, NE 69341

Clerk of the District Court, Grant County
Christee Haney . . . . (308) 458-2488
P.O. Box 139, Hyannis, NE 69350   Fax: (308) 458-2485
E-mail: christee.haney@nebraska.gov

Greeley County

District Court Clerk

Eighth Judicial District
148 West Fourth Street, Ainsworth, NE 69210

Clerk of the District Court, Greeley County
Mindy A. Grossart . . . . (308) 428-3625
P.O. Box 287, Greeley, NE 68842   Fax: (308) 428-3022
E-mail: mindy.grossart@nebraska.gov

Hall County

District Court Clerk

Ninth Judicial District
111 West First Street, Grand Island, NE 68801

Clerk of the District Court, Hall County
Valorie Bendixen . . . .(308) 385-5144
111 West First Street, Suite Four,   Fax: (308) 385-5110
Grand Island, NE 68801
E-mail: valorieb@hcgi.org

Hamilton County

District Court Clerk

Fifth Judicial District
2610 14th Street, Columbus, NE 68601

Clerk of the District Court, Hamilton County
Wendy C. Dethlefs . . . . (402) 694-3533
P.O. Box 201, Aurora, NE 68818   Fax: (402) 694-2250
E-mail: wendy.thomsen@nebraska.gov

Harlan County

District Court Clerk

Tenth Judicial District
426 North Colorado Avenue, Minden, NE 68959

Clerk of the District Court, Harlan County
Janet Dietz . . . .(308) 928-2173
P.O. Box 698, Alma, NE 68920   Fax: (308) 928-2079
E-mail: janet.dietz@nebraska.gov

Hayes County

District Court Clerk

Eleventh Judicial District
301 North Jeffers Street, North Platte, NE 69101

Clerk of the District Court, Hayes County
Susan Messersmith . . . . (308) 286-3413
505 Troth Street, Hayes Center, NE 69032   Fax: (308) 286-3208
E-mail: clerk@hayes.nacone.org

Hitchcock County

District Court Clerk

Eleventh Judicial District
301 North Jeffers Street, North Platte, NE 69101

Clerk of the District Court, Hitchcock County
Margaret Pollmann . . . .(308) 334-5646
P.O. Box 248, Trenton, NE 69044   Fax: (308) 334-5398
E-mail: margaret.pollmann@nebraska.gov

Holt County

District Court Clerk

Eighth Judicial District
148 West Fourth Street, Ainsworth, NE 69210

Clerk of the District Court, Holt County **Junior Young** . . . .(402) 336-2840
P.O. Box 755, O'Neill, NE 68763   Fax: (402) 336-3601
E-mail: junior.young@nebraska.gov

Hooker County

District Court Clerk

Eleventh Judicial District
301 North Jeffers Street, North Platte, NE 69101

Clerk of the District Court, Hooker County
David Sullivan . . . .(308) 546-2244
P.O. Box 184, Mullen, NE 69152   Fax: (308) 546-2490
E-mail: dave.sullivan@nebraska.gov

Howard County

District Court Clerk

Eighth Judicial District
148 West Fourth Street, Ainsworth, NE 69210

Clerk of the District Court, Howard County **Bev Sack** . . . .(308) 754-4343
P.O. Box 25, Saint Paul, NE 68873   Fax: (308) 754-4266
E-mail: bev.sack@nebraska.gov

Jefferson County

District Court Clerk

First Judicial District
612 Grant Street, Beatrice, NE 68310

Clerk of the District Court, Jefferson County
Shawna Taylor . . . .(402) 729-6807
411 Fourth Street, Fairbury, NE 68352   Fax: (402) 729-6808
E-mail: shawna.taylor@nebraska.gov

Johnson County

District Court Clerk

First Judicial District
612 Grant Street, Beatrice, NE 68310

Clerk of the District Court, Johnson County
Kathleen M. Nieveen . . . . (402) 335-6300
P.O. Box 416, Tecumseh, NE 68450   Fax: (402) 335-6311
E-mail: kathleen.nieveen@nebraska.gov

Kearney County

District Court Clerk

Tenth Judicial District
426 North Colorado Avenue, Minden, NE 68959

Clerk of the District Court, Kearney County
Jill L. Fritson . . . . (308) 832-1742
P.O. Box 208, Minden, NE 68949   Fax: (308) 832-0636
E-mail: jill.fritson@nebraska.gov

Keith County

District Court Clerk

Eleventh Judicial District
301 North Jeffers Street, North Platte, NE 69101

Clerk of the District Court, Keith County **Tina Devoe** . . . .(308) 284-3849
511 North Spruce Street, Room 202,   Fax: (308) 284-3978
Ogallala, NE 69153

Keya Paha County

District Court Clerk

Eighth Judicial District
148 West Fourth Street, Ainsworth, NE 69210

Clerk of the District Court, Keya Paha County
Suzy Wentworth . . . .(402) 497-3791
P.O. Box 349, Springview, NE 68778   Fax: (402) 497-3799
E-mail: suzy.wentworth@nebraska.gov

Kimball County

District Court Clerk

Twelfth Judicial District
1725 10th Street, Gering, NE 69341

Clerk of the District Court, Kimball County
Deb Diemoz . . . .(308) 235-3591
114 East Third Street, Suite Seven,   Fax: (308) 235-3654
Kimball, NE 69145
E-mail: cathleen.sibal@nebraska.gov

(continued on next page)

Knox County

District Court Clerk

Seventh Judicial District
1313 North Main Street, Madison, NE 68748

Clerk of the District Court, Knox County
Matthew Fischer . . . . (402) 288-5606
P.O. Box 126, Center, NE 68724   Fax: (402) 288-5609
E-mail: matthew.fischer@nebraska.gov

Lancaster County

District Court Clerk

Third Judicial District
575 South 10th Street, Lincoln, NE 68508

Clerk of the District Court, Lancaster County
Troy L. Hawk . . . . (402) 441-7328
575 South 10th Street, Lincoln, NE 68508   Fax: (402) 441-6190
E-mail: clerkdistct@lancaster.ne.gov

Lincoln County

District Court Clerk

Eleventh Judicial District
301 North Jeffers Street, North Platte, NE 69101

Clerk of the District Court, Lincoln County
Debra McCarthy . . . . (308) 535-3504
P.O. Box 1616, North Platte, NE 69103   Fax: (308) 535-3527
E-mail: debra.mccarthy@nebraska.gov

Logan County

District Court Clerk

Eleventh Judicial District
301 North Jeffers Street, North Platte, NE 69101

Clerk of the District Court, Logan County
Debbie Myers . . . . (308) 636-2311
P.O. Box 8, Stapleton, NE 69163   Fax: (308) 636-2333

Loup County

District Court Clerk

Eighth Judicial District
148 West Fourth Street, Ainsworth, NE 69210

Clerk of the District Court, Loup County
Debbie Postany . . . . (308) 942-3135
P.O. Box 187, Taylor, NE 68879   Fax: (308) 942-6015
E-mail: debbie.postany@nebraska.gov

Madison County

District Court Clerk

Seventh Judicial District
1313 North Main Street, Madison, NE 68748

Clerk of the District Court, Madison County
Marjorie Schaffer . . . . (402) 454-3311
1313 North Main Street, Madison, NE 68748   Fax: (402) 454-6528
E-mail: marjorie.schaffer@nebraska.gov

McPherson County

District Court Clerk

Eleventh Judicial District
301 North Jeffers Street, North Platte, NE 69101

Clerk of the District Court, McPherson County
Judy Dailey . . . . (308) 587-2363
P.O. Box 122, Tryon, NE 69167
E-mail: clerk@mcpherson.nacone.org

Merrick County

District Court Clerk

Fifth Judicial District
2610 14th Street, Columbus, NE 68601

Clerk of the District Court, Merrick County
Theresa Good . . . . (308) 946-2461
P.O. Box 27, Central City, NE 68826   Fax: (308) 946-3692
E-mail: theresa.good@nebraska.gov

Morrill County

District Court Clerk

Twelfth Judicial District
1725 10th Street, Gering, NE 69341

Clerk of the District Court, Morrill County
Julie Schildt . . . . (308) 262-1261
P.O. Box 824, Bridgeport, NE 69336   Fax: (308) 262-1799
E-mail: julie.schildt@nebraska.gov

Nance County

District Court Clerk

Fifth Judicial District
2610 14th Street, Columbus, NE 68601

Clerk of the District Court, Nance County
Danette Zarek . . . . (308) 536-2365
209 Esther Street, Fullerton, NE 68638   Fax: (308) 536-2742
E-mail: danette.zarek@nebraska.gov

Nemaha County

District Court Clerk

First Judicial District
612 Grant Street, Beatrice, NE 68310

Clerk of the District Court, Nemaha County
Amy Hector . . . . (402) 274-3616
1824 N Street, Auburn, NE 68305   Fax: (402) 274-4478
E-mail: amy.hector@nebraska.gov

Nuckolls County

District Court Clerk

First Judicial District
612 Grant Street, Beatrice, NE 68310

Clerk of the District Court, Nuckolls County
Royce Gonzales . . . . (402) 225-4341
P.O. Box 362, Nelson, NE 68961   Fax: (402) 225-2373
E-mail: royce.gonzales@nebraska.gov

© Leadership Directories, Inc.   *State Court Clerks and County Courthouses*

Otoe County

District Court Clerk

Second Judicial District
1210 Golden Gate Drive, Papillion, NE 68046

Clerk of the District Court, Otoe County **Janis Riege** .... (402) 873-9550
   P.O. Box 726, Nebraska City, NE 68410   Fax: (402) 873-9583
   E-mail: janis.riege@nebraska.gov

Pawnee County

District Court Clerk

First Judicial District
612 Grant Street, Beatrice, NE 68310

Clerk of the District Court, Pawnee County
   Candi Nichols .... (402) 852-2963
   P.O. Box 431, Pawnee City, NE 68420
   E-mail: candi.nichols@nebraska.gov

Perkins County

District Court Clerk

Eleventh Judicial District
301 North Jeffers Street, North Platte, NE 69101

Clerk of the District Court, Perkins County **Rita Long** ....(308) 352-4643
   P.O. Box 156, Grant, NE 69140   Fax: (308) 352-2455
   E-mail: rita.long@nebraska.gov

Phelps County

District Court Clerk

Tenth Judicial District
426 North Colorado Avenue, Minden, NE 68959

Clerk of the District Court, Phelps County
   Jennifer Nelson ....(308) 995-2281
   715 Fifth Avenue, Holdrege, NE 68949   Fax: (308) 995-2282
   E-mail: jennifer.nelson@nebraska.gov

Pierce County

District Court Clerk

Seventh Judicial District
1313 North Main Street, Madison, NE 68748

Clerk of the District Court, Pierce County
   Vickie Prince .... (402) 329-4335
   111 West Court Street, Room 12,   Fax: (402) 329-6412
   Pierce, NE 68767
   E-mail: vickie.prince@nebraska.gov

Platte County

District Court Clerk

Fifth Judicial District
2610 14th Street, Columbus, NE 68601

Clerk of the District Court, Platte County
   Marlene Vetick ....(402) 563-4906
   2610 14th Street, Columbus, NE 68601   Fax: (402) 562-6718
   E-mail: marlene.vetick@nebraska.gov

Polk County

District Court Clerk

Fifth Judicial District
2610 14th Street, Columbus, NE 68601

Clerk of the District Court, Polk County **Beth Pullen** .... (402) 747-3487
   P.O. Box 276, Osceola, NE 68651   Fax: (402) 747-8299
   E-mail: debra.girard@nebraska.gov

Red Willow County

District Court Clerk

Eleventh Judicial District
301 North Jeffers Street, North Platte, NE 69101

Clerk of the District Court, Red Willow County
   Lori O'Dea .... (308) 345-4583
   502 Norris Avenue, McCook, NE 69001   Fax: (308) 345-7907

Richardson County

District Court Clerk

First Judicial District
612 Grant Street, Beatrice, NE 68310

Clerk of the District Court, Richardson County
   Pamela S. "Pam" Scott ....(402) 245-2023
   1700 Stone Street, Falls City, NE 68355   Fax: (402) 245-3725
   E-mail: pam.scott@nebraska.gov

Rock County

District Court Clerk

Eighth Judicial District
148 West Fourth Street, Ainsworth, NE 69210

Clerk of the District Court, Rock County **Joyce Stahl** ... (402) 684-3933
   P.O. Box 367, Bassett, NE 68714   Fax: (402) 684-2741
   E-mail: clerk@rock.nacone.org

Saline County

District Court Clerk

First Judicial District
612 Grant Street, Beatrice, NE 68310

Clerk of the District Court, Saline County
   Joyce A. Wusk ....(402) 821-2823
   215 South Court Street, Wilber, NE 68465   Fax: (402) 821-3179
   E-mail: joyce.wusk@nebraska.gov

Sarpy County

District Court Clerk

Second Judicial District
1210 Golden Gate Drive, Papillion, NE 68046

Clerk of the District Court, Sarpy County
   Carol Kremer .... (402) 593-2267
   1210 Golden Gate Drive, Suite 3141,   Fax: (402) 593-4403
   Papillion, NE 68046
   E-mail: carol.kremer@nebraska.gov

(continued on next page)

Saunders County

District Court Clerk

Fifth Judicial District
2610 14th Street, Columbus, NE 68601

Clerk of the District Court, Saunders County
Patty J. McEvoy .... (402) 443-8113
387 North Chestnut Street, Suite Six,   Fax: (402) 443-8170
Waterloo, NE 68066
E-mail: patty.mcevoy@nebraska.gov

Scotts Bluff County

District Court Clerk

Twelfth Judicial District
1725 10th Street, Gering, NE 69341

Clerk of the District Court, Scotts Bluff County
Ann Rosenberry .... (308) 436-6641
1725 10th Street, Second Level,   Fax: (308) 436-6759
Gering, NE 69341
E-mail: ann.rosenberry@nebraska.gov

Seward County

District Court Clerk

Fifth Judicial District
2610 14th Street, Columbus, NE 68601

Clerk of the District Court, Seward County
Jacquelyn "Jacque" Stewart .... (402) 643-4895
P.O. Box 36, Seward, NE 68434   Fax: (402) 643-2950
E-mail: jacquelyn.stewart@nebraska.gov

Sheridan County

District Court Clerk

Twelfth Judicial District
1725 10th Street, Gering, NE 69341

Clerk of the District Court, Sheridan County
Carol Stouffer .... (308) 327-5654
P.O. Box 581, Rushville, NE 69360   Fax: (308) 327-5618
E-mail: carol.stouffer@nebraska.gov

Sherman County

District Court Clerk

Eighth Judicial District
148 West Fourth Street, Ainsworth, NE 69210

Clerk of the District Court, Sherman County
Marcy L. Sekutera ....(308) 745-1513
P.O. Box 456, Loup City, NE 68853   Fax: (308) 745-0157
E-mail: marcy.sekutera@nebraska.gov

Sioux County

District Court Clerk

Twelfth Judicial District
1725 10th Street, Gering, NE 69341

Clerk of the District Court, Sioux County
Michelle Zimmerman ....(308) 668-2443
P.O. Box 158, Harrison, NE 69346   Fax: (308) 668-2401
E-mail: michelle.zimmerman@nebraska.gov

Stanton County

District Court Clerk

Seventh Judicial District
1313 North Main Street, Madison, NE 68748

Clerk of the District Court, Stanton County
Wanda Heermann ....(402) 439-2222
804 Ivy Street, Stanton, NE 68779   Fax: (402) 439-2200
E-mail: wanda.heermann@nebraska.gov

Thayer County

District Court Clerk

First Judicial District
612 Grant Street, Beatrice, NE 68310

Clerk of the District Court, Thayer County
Stacey L. McLaughlin..........................(402) 768-6116
225 North Fourth Street, Room 302,   Fax: (402) 768-6128
Hebron, NE 68370
E-mail: stacey.mclaughlin@nebraska.gov

Thomas County

District Court Clerk

Eleventh Judicial District
301 North Jeffers Street, North Platte, NE 69101

Clerk of the District Court, Thomas County
Lorissa Hartman .... (308) 645-2261
503 Main Street, Thedford, NE 69166   Fax: (308) 645-2623
E-mail: lorissa.hartman@nebraska.gov

Thurston County

District Court Clerk

Sixth Judicial District
1555 Colfax Street, Blair, NE 68008

Clerk of the District Court, Thurston County
Gina Roth ....(402) 385-3318
106 Fifth Street, Pender, NE 68047   Fax: (402) 385-2762
E-mail: gina.roth@nebraska.gov

Valley County

District Court Clerk

Eighth Judicial District
148 West Fourth Street, Ainsworth, NE 69210

Clerk of the District Court, Valley County
Jenette G. Lindsey .... (308) 728-3700
125 South 15th Street, Ord, NE 68862   Fax: (308) 728-7725
E-mail: jenette.lindsey@nebraska.gov

Washington County

District Court Clerk

Sixth Judicial District
1555 Colfax Street, Blair, NE 68008

Clerk of the District Court, Washington County
Susan Paulsen ....(402) 426-6899
P.O. Box 431, Blair, NE 68008   Fax: (402) 426-6898
E-mail: susan.paulsen@nebraska.gov

Wayne County

District Court Clerk

Seventh Judicial District
1313 North Main Street, Madison, NE 68748

Clerk of the District Court, Wayne County
Debra "Deb" Alleman .... (402) 375-2260
510 Pearl Street, Wayne, NE 68787   Fax: (402) 375-0103
E-mail: deb.alleman@nebraska.gov

Webster County

District Court Clerk

Tenth Judicial District
426 North Colorado Avenue, Minden, NE 68959

Clerk of the District Court, Webster County
Lonnie Knehans .... (402) 746-2716
621 North Cedar Street, Red Cloud, NE 68970   Fax: (402) 746-2710
E-mail: clerk@webster.nacone.org

Wheeler County

District Court Clerk

Eighth Judicial District
148 West Fourth Street, Ainsworth, NE 69210

Clerk of the District Court, Wheeler County
Cara Snider .... (308) 654-3235
Third and Main Street, Bartlett, NE 68622   Fax: (308) 654-3470
E-mail: cara.snider@nebraska.gov

York County

District Court Clerk

Fifth Judicial District
2610 14th Street, Columbus, NE 68601

Clerk of the District Court, York County
Sharilyn Steube .... (402) 362-4038
510 Lincoln Avenue, York, NE 68467   Fax: (402) 362-2577
E-mail: sharilyn.ramsey@nebraska.gov

Counties Within Judicial Districts

District Court, 1st District

Areas Covered: Clay, Fillmore, Gage, Jefferson, Johnson, Nemaha, Nuckolls, Pawnee, Richardson, Aline, and Thayer Counties.

District Court, 2nd District

Areas Covered: Cass, Otoe, and Sarpy Counties.

District Court, 3rd District

Areas Covered: Lancaster County.

District Court, 4th District

Areas Covered: Douglas County.

District Court, 5th District

Areas Covered: Boone, Butler, Colfax, Hamilton, Merrick, Nance, Platte, Polk, Saunders, Seward, and York Counties.

District Court, 6th District

Areas Covered: Burt, Cedar, Dakota, Dixon, Dodge, Thurston, and Washington Counties.

District Court, 7th District

Areas Covered: Antelope, Cuming, Knox, Madison, Pierce, Stanton, and Wayne Counties.

District Court, 8th District

Areas Covered: Blaine, Boyd, Brown, Cherry, Custer, Garfield, Greeley, Holt, Howard, Keya Paha, Loup, Rock, Sherman, Valley, and Wheeler Counties.

District Court, 9th District

Areas Covered: Buffalo and Hall Counties.

District Court, 10th District

Areas Covered: Adams, Franklin, Harlan, Kearney, Phelps, and Webster Counties.

District Court, 11th District

Areas Covered: Arthur, Chase, Dawson, Dundy, Frontier, Furnas, Gosper, Hayes, Hitchcock, Hooker, Keith, Lincoln, Logan, McPherson, Perkins, Red Willow, and Thomas Counties.

District Court, 12th District

Areas Covered: Banner, Box Butte, Cheyenne, Dawes, Deuel, Garden, Grant, Kimball, Morrill, Scotts Bluff, Sheridan, and Sioux Counties.

Nevada Court Clerks and Courthouses

The trial courts of general jurisdiction in Nevada are called district courts. There are nine judicial districts, each district consisting of at least one county. In most counties the Clerk functions both as Court Clerk and County Clerk. In a few counties, the positions are separate. The intermediate appellate court in the State of Nevada is the Court of Appeals.

Nevada Supreme Court

Supreme Court Building, 201 South Carson Street, Suite 201,
Carson City, NV 89701-4702
Tel: (775) 684-1600
Internet: www.nevadajudiciary.us

The Supreme Court consists of a chief justice and six justices who run in nonpartisan elections for six-year terms. Appointees, who serve until the next general election, are selected by the Governor from nominees of the Commission on Judicial Selection to fill temporary vacancies. The chief justice is selected on the basis of seniority and serves a two-year term. The Supreme Court has appellate jurisdiction in all civil cases arising in district courts, and on questions of law alone in all criminal cases of the district courts. The court has power to issue writs of mandamus, certiorari, prohibition, quo warranto, and habeas corpus and all writs necessary or proper to the complete exercise of its appellate jurisdiction. The court also exercises administrative control over the lower courts and adopts rules governing the legal profession in the state.

Court Staff
Clerk of the Court **Tracie Lindeman** . . . . (775) 684-1600

Nevada Court of Appeals

200 Lewis Avenue, 17th Floor, Las Vegas, NV 89101
201 South Carson Street, Suite 250, Carson City, NV 89701-4702
Tel: (702) 486-9300

On November 4, 2014, Nevada voters approved an amendment to Article 6 of the Nevada Constitution in order to create an intermediate appellate court also known as the Nevada Court of Appeals. As a result of the approval, all appeals will still be filed with the Nevada Supreme Court, which will then assign cases to the three-judge Court of Appeals. This court will hear roughly one-third of all cases submitted to the Nevada Supreme Court.

Court Staff
Assistant Clerk, Court of Appeals
  Thomas "Tom" Harris . . . . (702) 486-9300

County-By-County

Carson City (Independent Municipality)

Clerk of Court

First Judicial District
885 East Musser Street, Carson City, NV 89701

Clerk-Recorder, Carson City **Sue Merriwether** . . . . (775) 887-2260
  885 East Musser Street, Suite 1025,   Tel: (775) 887-2146
  Carson City, NV 89701
  E-mail: districtcourtclerk@ci.carson-city.nv.us

Nevada Court Clerks and Courthouses *continued*

Churchill County

Clerk of Court

Tenth Judicial District
73 North Maine Street, Suite B, Fallon, NV 89406

Clerk of Court, Churchill County **Sue Sevon** . . . . (775) 423-6088
  73 North Maine Street, Suite B,   Fax: (775) 423-8578
  Fallon, NV 89406
  E-mail: ssevon@churchillcounty.org

Clark County

Clerk of Court

Eighth Judicial District
200 Lewis Avenue, Las Vegas, NV 89101

Court Executive Officer/Clerk of the Court
  Steven D. Grierson . . . . (702) 671-4528
  200 Lewis Avenue, Las Vegas, NV 89101   Tel: (702) 671-4548

Douglas County

Clerk of Court

Ninth Judicial District
1038 Buckeye Road, Minden, NV 89423

Clerk-Treasurer, Douglas County **Ted Thran** . . . . (775) 782-6273
  1038 Buckeye Road, Second Floor,   Fax: (775) 782-9016
  Minden, NV 89423
  E-mail: tthran@co.douglas.nv.us

Elko County

Clerk of Court

Fourth Judicial District
571 Idaho Street, Elko, NV 89801

Clerk, Elko County **Carol Fosmo** . . . . (775) 753-4600 ext. 326
  550 Court Street, Elko, NV 89801   Fax: (775) 753-4610
  E-mail: clerk@elkocountynv.net

Esmeralda County

Clerk of Court

Fifth Judicial District
1520 East Basin Avenue, Pahrump, NV 89060

Clerk/Treasurer, Esmeralda County
  LaCinda "Cindy" Elgan . . . . (775) 485-6309
  PO Box 547, Goldfield, NV 89013   Fax: (775) 485-6376
  E-mail: celgan@citlink.net

Eureka County

Clerk of Court

Seventh Judicial District
801 Clark Street, Ely, NV 89301

Clerk and Treasurer, Eureka County
  Beverly "Bev" Conley . . . . (775) 237-5262
  P.O. Box 677, Eureka, NV 89316   Fax: (775) 237-6015
  E-mail: bconley.ecct@eurekanv.org

(continued on next page)

Nevada Court Clerks and Courthouses *continued*

Humboldt County

Clerk of Court

Sixth Judicial District
400 Main Street, Lovelock, NV 89419

Clerk, Humboldt County **Tami Rae Spero** . . . . (775) 623-6343
  50 West Fifth Street, Room 207,   Fax: (775) 623-6309
  Winnemucca, NV 89445
  E-mail: coclerk@hcnv.us

Lander County

Clerk of Court

Sixth Judicial District
400 Main Street, Lovelock, NV 89419

Clerk, Lander County **Sadie Sullivan** . . . . (775) 635-5738
  315 South Humboldt Street,   Fax: (775) 635-0394
  Battle Mountain, NV 89820
  E-mail: landercountyclerk@gmail.com

Lincoln County

Clerk of Court

Seventh Judicial District
801 Clark Street, Ely, NV 89301

Clerk, Lincoln County **Lisa C. Lloyd** . . . . (775) 962-5390
  181 North Main Street, Suite 201,   Fax: (775) 962-5180
  Pioche, NV 89043
  E-mail: llloyd@lincolnnv.com

Lyon County

Clerk of Court

Office of the County Clerk
27 South Main Street, Yerington, NV 89447
Tel: (775) 463-6501 Fax: (775) 463-5305

County Clerk **Nikki A. Bryan** . . . . (775) 463-6501
  E-mail: nbryan@lyon-county.org

Mineral County

Clerk of Court

Fifth Judicial District
1520 East Basin Avenue, Pahrump, NV 89060

Clerk-Treasurer, Mineral County **Cherrie A. George** . . . . . (775) 945-2446
  105 South "A" Street, Suite One,   Fax: (775) 945-0706
  Hawthorne, NV 89415

Nye County

Clerk of Court

Fifth Judicial District
1520 East Basin Avenue, Pahrump, NV 89060

Clerk, Nye County **Sandra L. "Sam" Merlino** . . . . (775) 482-8127
  101 Radar Road, Tonopah, NV 89049   Fax: (775) 482-8133
  E-mail: smerlino@co.nye.nv.us

Nevada Court Clerks and Courthouses *continued*

Pershing County

Clerk of Court

Sixth Judicial District
400 Main Street, Lovelock, NV 89419

Clerk-Treasurer, Pershing County **Lacey Donaldson** . . . . . (775) 273-2410
  398 Main Street, Lovelock, NV 89419   Fax: (775) 273-2434
  E-mail: ldonaldson@pershingcounty.net

Storey County

Clerk of Court

First Judicial District
885 East Musser Street, Carson City, NV 89701

Clerk-Treasurer, Storey County **Vanessa Stephens** . . . . . . (775) 847-0969
  26 South B Street, Virginia City, NV 89440   Tel: (775) 847-0921
  E-mail: clerk@storeycounty.org

Washoe County

Clerk of Court

Second Judicial District
75 Court Street, Reno, NV 89501

Court Administrator and Clerk of Court, Washoe
  County **Jacqueline Bryant** . . . . (775) 328-3194
  75 Court Street, Reno, NV 89501   Fax: (775) 328-3194

White Pine County

Clerk of Court

Seventh Judicial District
801 Clark Street, Ely, NV 89301

Clerk, White Pine County **Nichole Baldwin** . . . . (775) 293-6509
  801 Clark Street, Suite Four,   Fax: (775) 289-2544
  Ely, NV 89301
  E-mail: wpclerk@mwpower.net

Counties Within Judicial Districts

District Court, 1st District
Areas Covered: City of Carson City and Storey County.

District Court, 2nd District
Areas Covered: Washoe County.

District Court, 3rd District
Areas Covered: Lyon County.

District Court, 4th District
Areas Covered: Elko County.

District Court, 5th District
Areas Covered: Esmeralda, Mineral, and Nye Counties.

District Court, 6th District
Areas Covered: Humboldt, Lander, and Pershing Counties.

Nevada Court Clerks and Courthouses *continued*

District Court, 7th District

Areas Covered: Eureka, Lincoln, and White Pine Counties.

District Court, 8th District

Areas Covered: Clark County.

District Court, 9th District

Areas Covered: Douglas County.

District Court, 10th District

Areas Covered: Churchill County.

New Hampshire Court Clerks and Courthouses

The trial courts of general jurisdiction in New Hampshire are called superior courts. There is one superior court site in nine counties and two superior court sites in Hillsborough County. The official title of the clerk in each county is the Clerk of the Superior Court. There is no intermediate appellate court in the State of New Hampshire.

New Hampshire Supreme Court

Supreme Court Building, One Charles Doe Drive,
Concord, NH 03301-6160
Tel: (603) 271-2646 Tel: (603) 271-3777 (Law Library)
Fax: (603) 513-5475 Fax: (603) 271-2168 (Law Library)
Internet: www.courts.state.nh.us/supreme/index.htm

The Supreme Court consists of a chief justice and four associate justices who are appointed by the Governor and Executive Council to serve until age seventy when retirement is mandatory. The Supreme Court has final appellate jurisdiction over all questions of law and over decisions or appeals of all trial courts and several administrative agencies. The Court exercises administrative control over all lower courts in the state.

Court Staff
Clerk of Court **Eileen Fox** . . . . (603) 271-2646
   E-mail: efox@courts.state.nh.us

County-By-County

Belknap County

Court Clerk
Belknap Superior Court
64 Court Street, Laconia, NH 03246
Tel: (855) 212-1234

Clerk of the Superior Court **Abigail Albee** . . . . (855) 212-1234
   E-mail: aalbee@courts.state.nh.us

Carroll County

Court Clerk
Carroll Superior Court
96 Water Village Road, Ossipee, NH 03864
Tel: (855) 212-1234

Clerk of the Superior Court **Abigail Albee** . . . . (855) 212-1234
   E-mail: aalbee@courts.state.nh.us

Cheshire County

Court Clerk
Cheshire Superior Court
33 Winter Street, Keene, NH 03431-0444
Tel: (855) 212-1234

Clerk of the Superior Court **James I. Peale** . . . . (855) 212-1234
   E-mail: jpeale@courts.state.nh.us

Coos County

Court Clerk
Coos Superior Court
55 School Street, Suite 301, Lancaster, NH 03584
Tel: (855) 212-1234

Clerk of the Superior Court **David P. Carlson** . . . . (855) 212-1234
   E-mail: dcarlson@courts.state.nh.us

Grafton County

Court Clerk
Grafton Superior Court
3785 Dartmouth College Highway, Haverhill, NH 03774
Tel: (855) 212-1234

Clerk of the Superior Court **David P. Carlson** . . . . (855) 212-1234
   E-mail: dcarlson@courts.state.nh.us

Hillsborough County (North)

Court Clerk
Hillsborough Superior Court - North
Hillsborough County Superior Court North, 300 Chestnut Street,
Manchester, NH 03101
Tel: (855) 212-1234

Clerk of Superior Court **W. Michael Scanlon** . . . . (855) 212-1234
   E-mail: mscanlon@courts.state.nh.us

Hillsborough County (South)

Court Clerk
Hillsborough Superior Court - South
30 Spring Street, Nashua, NH 03060
Tel: (855) 212-1234

Clerk of the Superior Court **Marshall Buttrick** . . . . (855) 212-1234
   30 Spring Street, Nashua, NH 03060
   E-mail: mbuttrick@courts.state.nh.us

Merrimack County

Court Clerk
Merrimack Superior Court
Merrimack Superior Court, 163 North Main Street,
Concord, NH 03302-2880
P.O. Box 2880, Concord, NH 03302-2880
Tel: (855) 212-1234

Clerk of the Superior Court **Tracy Uhrin** . . . . (855) 212-1234
   E-mail: tuhrin@courts.state.nh.us

Rockingham County

Court Clerk
Rockingham Superior Court
Rockingham County Courthouse, 10 Route 125, Brentwood, NH 03833
P.O Box 1258, Kingston, NH 03848-1258
Tel: (855) 212-1234

Clerk of the Superior Court **Raymond Taylor** . . . . (855) 212-1234
   E-mail: rtaylor@courts.state.nh.us

(continued on next page)

New Hampshire Court Clerks and Courthouses *continued*

Strafford County

Court Clerk

Strafford Superior Court
William A. Grimes Justice & Administration Building, 259 County Farm
Road, Suite 301, Dover, NH 03820
Tel: (855) 212-1234

Clerk of the Superior Court **Kimberly T. Myers** . . . . (855) 212-1234

Sullivan County

Court Clerk

Sullivan Superior Court
22 Main Street, Newport, NH 03773
Tel: (855) 212-1234

Clerk of the Superior Court **James I. Peale** . . . . (855) 212-1234
  E-mail: jpeale@courts.state.nh.us

New Jersey Court Clerks and Courthouses

The trial courts of general jurisdiction in New Jersey are called Superior Courts. There are 15 districts of Superior Court, each district (called a Vicinage) consisting of at least one county. County Clerks and Trial Court Administrators are listed below.

Supreme Court of New Jersey

25 West Market Street, Trenton, NJ 08625
P.O. Box 970, Trenton, NJ 08625-0970
Tel: (609) 984-7791 Fax: (609) 396-9056
Internet: www.judiciary.state.nj.us

The Supreme Court consists of a chief justice and six associate justices who are initially appointed by the Governor with consent of the New Jersey State Senate for seven-year terms with tenure granted upon reappointment. Retirement is mandatory at age seventy; however, retired justices may be recalled by the Court. The Supreme Court has final appellate jurisdiction on all constitutional questions, cases of dissent from the Appellate Division of the New Jersey Superior Court, and petitions for certification. The Court also has rule-making authority and regulates admission and discipline of attorneys and judges.

Court Staff
Clerk of the Court **Mark Neary** . . . . (609) 292-4837
  E-mail: mark.neary@judiciary.state.nj.us

New Jersey Superior Court, Appellate Division

Richard J. Hughes Justice Complex, 25 West Market Street,
Trenton, NJ 08625
P.O. Box 006, Trenton, NJ 08625-0006
Tel: (609) 292-4822 Fax: (609) 292-9806
Internet: www.judiciary.state.nj.us/appdiv/index.htm

The Appellate Division of the Superior Court consists of thirty-three judges who are assigned to parts of four or five judges. Appellate Division judges, including the presiding judge for administration and the presiding judge for each part, are selected from the Superior Court and assigned to the Division by the Supreme Court chief justice. All Superior Court judges are initially appointed by the Governor with consent of the New Jersey State Senate for seven-year terms with tenure granted upon reappointment. Retirement is mandatory at age seventy; however, retired judges may be recalled by the New Jersey Supreme Court. The Appellate Division of the Superior Court is the intermediate appellate court and hears appeals from the Law and Chancery Divisions of the Superior Court, Tax Court and state administrative agencies.

Court Staff
Clerk, Appellate Division **Joseph H. Orlando** . . . . (609) 292-6995
  E-mail: joe.orlando@judiciary.state.nj.us   Fax: (609) 292-9806

Tax Court of New Jersey

P.O. Box 972, Trenton, NJ 08625-0972
25 Market Street, Seventh Floor, North Wing, Trenton, NJ 08625-0037
Tel: (609) 292-5082 Tel: (609) 292-6989

Court Staff
Tax Court Clerk/Administrator **Cheryl A. Ryan** . . . . (609) 292-5082
  E-mail: cheryl.ryan@judiciary.state.nj.us

County-By-County

Atlantic County

County Clerk

Office of the County Clerk
5901 Main Street, Mays Landing, NJ 08330
County Office Building, 1333 Atlantic Avenue, 1st Floor,
Atlantic City, NJ 08401 (Atlantic City Satellite Office)
Tel: (609) 641-7867 Tel: (609) 343-2358 (Atlantic City Satellite Office)
Fax: (609) 909-5111 Fax: (609) 343-2167 (Atlantic City Satellite Office)
Web Form: www.atlanticcountyclerk.org/office.php
Internet: www.atlanticcountyclerk.org

County Clerk **Edward P. "Ed" McGettigan** . . . . (609) 645-5858
  E-mail: mcgettigan_ed@aclink.org

Trial Court Administrator

Vicinage 1
Atlantic County Civil Courts Building, 1201 Bacharach Boulevard,
Atlantic City, NJ 08401-4510
Cape May County Courthouse, Nine North Main Street,
Cape May, NJ 08210
Mays Landing Criminal Courts Complex, 4997 Unami Boulevard,
Mays Landing, NJ 08330
Tel: (609) 345-6700 (Atlantic City) Tel: (609) 465-1000 (Cape May)
Tel: (609) 909-8154 (Mays Landing) Fax: (609) 343-2232
Internet: www.judiciary.state.nj.us/atlantic/index.htm

Trial Court Administrator **Howard H. Berchtold, Jr.** . . . . . (609) 594-3400
  Atlantic County Civil Courts Building,   Fax: (609) 343-2232
  1201 Bacharach Boulevard,
  Atlantic City, NJ 08401-4510
  E-mail: howard.berchtold@judiciary.state.nj.us

Bergen County

County Clerk

Office of the County Clerk
One Bergen County Plaza, Room 122, Hackensack, NJ 07601
Tel: (201) 336-7000 Fax: (201) 336-7002
Internet: www.co.bergen.nj.us/countyclerk

County Clerk **John S. Hogan** . . . . (201) 336-7000
  E-mail: countyclerk@co.bergen.nj.us

Trial Court Administrator

Vicinage 2
Bergen County Justice Center, 10 Main Street, Hackensack, NJ 07601
Tel: (201) 527-2700
Internet: www.judiciary.state.nj.us/bergen/index.htm

Trial Court Administrator **Laura Simoldoni** . . . . (201) 527-2265
  E-mail: laura.simoldoni@judiciary.state.nj.us

Burlington County

County Clerk

Office of the County Clerk
Courts Facility, 49 Rancocas Road, Room 104, Mount Holly, NJ 08060
Fax: (609) 265-0696

County Clerk **Timothy Tyler** . . . . (609) 265-5122
  E-mail: ttyler@co.burlington.nj.us

(continued on next page)

New Jersey Court Clerks and Courthouses *continued*

Trial Court Administrator

Vicinage 3
49 Rancocas Road, Mount Holly, NJ 08060
P.O. Box 6555, Mount Holly, NJ 08060
Tel: (609) 518-2600 Fax: (609) 518-2539
Internet: www.judiciary.state.nj.us/burlington/index.htm

Trial Court Administrator **Jude Del Preore** . . . . (609) 518-2510
  49 Rancocas Road, Mount Holly, NJ 08060   Fax: (609) 518-2539
  E-mail: jude.delpreore@judiciary.state.nj.us

Camden County

County Clerk

Office of the County Clerk
Courthouse, 520 Market Street, Room 102, Camden, NJ 08102-1375
Tel: (856) 225-5300 Fax: (856) 225-7100

County Clerk **Joseph Ripa** . . . . (856) 225-5324
  E-mail: jripa@camdencounty.com

Trial Court Administrator

Vicinage 4
Hall of Justice, 101 South Fifth Street, Camden, NJ 08103
Tel: (856) 379-2200 Fax: (856) 379-2278
Internet: www.judiciary.state.nj.us/camden/index.htm

Trial Court Administrator **Kelly A. Law** . . . . (856) 379-2231
  Hall of Justice, 101 South Fifth Street, Suite 680,   Fax: (856) 379-2278
  Camden, NJ 08103
  E-mail: kelly.law@judiciary.state.nj.us

Cape May County

County Clerk

Office of the County Clerk
Seven North Main Street, DN 109,
Cape May Court House, NJ 08210-5000
P.O. Box 5000, Cape May Court House, NJ 08210-5000
Tel: (609) 465-1010 Fax: (609) 465-8625

County Clerk **Rita Marie Fulginiti** . . . . (609) 465-1010
  E-mail: coclerk@co.cape-may.nj.us

Trial Court Administrator

Vicinage 1
Atlantic County Civil Courts Building, 1201 Bacharach Boulevard,
Atlantic City, NJ 08401-4510
Cape May County Courthouse, Nine North Main Street,
Cape May, NJ 08210
Mays Landing Criminal Courts Complex, 4997 Unami Boulevard,
Mays Landing, NJ 08330
Tel: (609) 345-6700 (Atlantic City) Tel: (609) 465-1000 (Cape May)
Tel: (609) 909-8154 (Mays Landing) Fax: (609) 343-2232
Internet: www.judiciary.state.nj.us/atlantic/index.htm

Trial Court Administrator **Howard H. Berchtold, Jr.** . . . . . (609) 594-3400
  Atlantic County Civil Courts Building,   Fax: (609) 343-2232
  1201 Bacharach Boulevard,
  Atlantic City, NJ 08401-4510
  E-mail: howard.berchtold@judiciary.state.nj.us

New Jersey Court Clerks and Courthouses *continued*

Cumberland County

County Clerk

Office of the County Clerk
60 West Broad Street, Bridgeton, NJ 08302
Tel: (856) 453-4860 Fax: (856) 455-1410

County Clerk **Celeste M. Riley** . . . . (856) 453-4860
  E-mail: celesteri@co.cumberland.nj.us

Trial Court Administrator

Vicinage 15
60 West Broad Street, Bridgeton, NJ 08302
92 Market Street, Salem, NJ 08079
One North Broad Street, Woodbury, NJ 08096
Tel: (856) 451-8000 (Cumberland County)
Tel: (856) 853-3200 (Gloucester County)
Tel: (856) 935-7510 (Salem County)

Trial Court Administrator **Mark Sprock** . . . . (856) 453-4365
  60 West Broad Street, Bridgeton, NJ 08302   Fax: (856) 455-9490
  E-mail: mark.sprock@judiciary.state.nj.us

Essex County

County Clerk

Office of the County Clerk
Hall of Records, 465 Dr. Martin L. King, Jr. Blvd., Room 247,
Newark, NJ 07102
Tel: (973) 621-4921 Fax: (973) 621-2537
E-mail: info@essexclerk.com
Internet: www.essexclerk.com

County Clerk **Christopher J. "Chris" Durkin** . . . (973) 621-4921 ext. 223
  E-mail: cdurkin@essexcountynj.org

Trial Court Administrator

Vicinage 5
Veterans Courthouse, 50 West Market Street, Newark, NJ 07102
Hall of Records, 465 Dr. Martin Luther King Jr. Boulevard,
Newark, NJ 07102
Tel: (973) 693-5701
Internet: www.judiciary.state.nj.us/essex/index.htm

Trial Court Administrator **Amy K. DePaul** . . . . (973) 693-5704
  Veterans Courthouse, 50 West Market Street,
  Room 514, Newark, NJ 07102
  E-mail: amy.depaul@judiciary.state.nj.us

Gloucester County

County Clerk

Office of the County Clerk
Old Courthouse, 1 North Broad Street, Woodbury, NJ 08096
Tel: (856) 853-3237 Fax: (856) 853-3327

County Clerk **James N. "Jim" Hogan** . . . . (856) 853-3237
  E-mail: jhogan@co.gloucester.nj.us

Trial Court Administrator

Vicinage 15
60 West Broad Street, Bridgeton, NJ 08302
92 Market Street, Salem, NJ 08079
One North Broad Street, Woodbury, NJ 08096
Tel: (856) 451-8000 (Cumberland County)
Tel: (856) 853-3200 (Gloucester County)
Tel: (856) 935-7510 (Salem County)

Trial Court Administrator **Mark Sprock** . . . . (856) 453-4365
   60 West Broad Street, Bridgeton, NJ 08302   Fax: (856) 455-9490
   E-mail: mark.sprock@judiciary.state.nj.us

Hudson County

County Clerk

Office of the County Clerk
257 Cornelison Avenue, Fourth Floor, Jersey City, NJ 07302
Tel: (201) 369-3470 Fax: (201) 369-3478

County Clerk **Barbara A. Netchert** . . . . (201) 369-3470
   E-mail: countyclerk@hcnj.us   Fax: (201) 369-3478

Trial Court Administrator

Vicinage 6
Hudson County Administration Building, 595 Newark Avenue,
Jersey City, NJ 07306
William J. Brennan, Jr. Courthouse, 583 Newark Avenue,
Jersey City, NJ 07306-2395
Tel: (201) 795-6600 Fax: (201) 795-6603
Internet: www.judiciary.state.nj.us/hudson/index.htm

Trial Court Administrator **Silvia I. Gonzalez** . . . . (201) 795-6604
   Hudson County Administration Building,   Fax: (201) 795-6603
   595 Newark Avenue, Room 403,
   Jersey City, NJ 07306
   E-mail: silvia.gonzalez@judiciary.state.nj.us

Hunterdon County

County Clerk

Office of the County Clerk
Hall of Records, 71 Main Street, Flemington, NJ 08822-2900
Tel: (908) 788-1221 Fax: (908) 782-4068

County Clerk **Mary H. Melfi** . . . . (908) 788-1214
   E-mail: mmelfi@co.hunterdon.nj.us

Trial Court Administrator

Vicinage 13
20 North Bridge Street, Somerville, NJ 08876-1262 (Somerset County)
65 Park Avenue, Flemington, NJ 08822 (Hunterdon County)
413 2nd Street, Belvidere, NJ 07823 (Warren County)
Tel: (908) 231-7000 (Somerset)
Tel: (908) 237-5800 (Hunterdon) Tel: (908) 475-6150 (Warren)
Internet: www.judiciary.state.nj.us/somerset/index.html

Trial Court Administrator **Eugene Farkas** . . . . (908) 203-6151
   20 North Bridge Street, Somerville, NJ 08876-1262
   E-mail: eugene.farkas@judiciary.state.nj.us

Mercer County

County Clerk

County Clerk's Office
209 South Broad Street, Room 100, Trenton, NJ 08650
Tel: (609) 989-6820 Fax: (609) 989-1111
Internet: www.state.nj.us/counties/mercer/officials/clerk/

County Clerk **Paula Sollami Covello** . . . . (609) 989-6464
   E-mail: pscovello@mercercounty.org

Trial Court Administrator

Vicinage 7
209 South Broad Street, Trenton, NJ 08650-0068
P.O. Box 8068, Trenton, NJ 08650
Tel: (609) 571-4000
Internet: www.judiciary.state.nj.us/mercer/index.htm

Trial Court Administrator **Sue Regan** . . . . (609) 571-4910
   175 South Broad Street, Trenton, NJ 08650 (Civil
   Court)
   400 South Warren Street, Trenton, NJ 08650
   (Criminal Court)
   E-mail: sue.regan@judiciary.state.nj.us

Middlesex County

County Clerk

Office of the County Clerk
County Administration Building, 75 Bayard Street, 4th Floor,
New Brunswick, NJ 08903
Tel: (732) 745-3005 Fax: (732) 745-3642

County Clerk **Elaine M. Flynn** . . . . (732) 745-3005
   E-mail: elaine.flynn@co.middlesex.nj.us

Trial Court Administrator

Vicinage 8
56 Paterson Street, New Brunswick, NJ 08903
Tel: (732) 519-3200
Internet: www.judiciary.state.nj.us/middlesex/index.htm

Trial Court Administrator **Gregory Edwards** . . . . (732) 519-3428
   56 Paterson Street, First Floor,
   New Brunswick, NJ 08903
   E-mail: gregory.edwards@judiciary.state.nj.us

Monmouth County

County Clerk

Office of the County Clerk
33 Mechanic Street, Freehold, NJ 07728
Fax: (732) 409-7566

County Clerk **M. Claire French** . . . . (732) 431-7324

Trial Court Administrator

Vicinage 9
71 Monument Park, Freehold, NJ 07728
Tel: (732) 677-4300
Internet: www.judiciary.state.nj.us/monmouth/index.htm

Trial Court Administrator **Andrew M. Graubard** . . . . (732) 677-4580
   71 Monument Park, Freehold, NJ 07728
   E-mail: andrew.graubard@judiciary.state.nj.us

(continued on next page)

New Jersey Court Clerks and Courthouses *continued*

Morris County

County Clerk

Office of the County Clerk
Administration and Records Bldg., 10 Court Street, Morristown, NJ 07963
Tel: (973) 285-6059 Fax: (973) 285-5233

County Clerk **Ann Grossi**............................(973) 285-6125
E-mail: agrossi@co.morris.nj.us

Trial Court Administrator

Vicinage 10
Washington & Courts Streets, Morristown, NJ 07960-0910 (Morris County)
43-47 High Street, Newton, NJ 07860 (Sussex County)
Tel: (973) 656-4000 (Morris County)
Tel: (973) 579-0675 (Sussex County) Fax: (973) 656-3949
Internet: www.judiciary.state.nj.us/morris/index.htm

Trial Court Administrator **Rashad Shabaka-Burns** ...... (973) 656-3999
Washington & Courts Streets,   Fax: (973) 656-3949
Morristown, NJ 07960-0910

Ocean County

County Clerk

Office of the County Clerk
Court House, 118 Washington Street, Toms River, NJ 08754
P.O. Box 2191, Toms River, NJ 08754-2191
Tel: (732) 929-2018 Fax: (732) 349-4336
Internet: www.oceancountyclerk.com

County Clerk **Scott M. Colabella** ....(732) 929-2018
E-mail: scolabella@co.ocean.nj.us

Trial Court Administrator

Vicinage 14
118 Washington Street, Toms River, NJ 08754
Tel: (732) 929-2042
Internet: www.judiciary.state.nj.us/ocean/index.htm

Trial Court Administrator **Kenneth W. Kerwin** .... (732) 929-2042
118 Washington Street, Toms River, NJ 08754

Passaic County

County Clerk

Office of the County Clerk
Administrative/Courthouse Complex, 401 Grand St., Room 130,
Paterson, NJ 07505
Tel: (973) 225-3632 Fax: (973) 754-1920
Internet: www.passaiccountynj.org/countyclerk

County Clerk **Kristin Corrado** ....(973) 225-3632
E-mail: kcorrado@passaiccountynj.org

Trial Court Administrator

Vicinage 11
77 Hamilton Street, Paterson, NJ 07505
Tel: (973) 247-8000
Internet: www.judiciary.state.nj.us/passaic/index.htm

Trial Court Administrator **Robert D. Tracy** ....(973) 247-8001
77 Hamilton Street, 6th Floor,
Paterson, NJ 07505

New Jersey Court Clerks and Courthouses *continued*

Salem County

County Clerk

Office of the County Clerk
110 Fifth Street, Suite 200, Salem, NJ 08079
Tel: (856) 935-7510 Fax: (856) 935-8882

County Clerk **Gilda T. Gill** ....(856) 935-7510 ext. 8300
E-mail: info@salemcountyclerk.org

Trial Court Administrator

Vicinage 15
60 West Broad Street, Bridgeton, NJ 08302
92 Market Street, Salem, NJ 08079
One North Broad Street, Woodbury, NJ 08096
Tel: (856) 451-8000 (Cumberland County)
Tel: (856) 853-3200 (Gloucester County)
Tel: (856) 935-7510 (Salem County)

Trial Court Administrator **Mark Sprock** ....(856) 453-4365
60 West Broad Street, Bridgeton, NJ 08302   Fax: (856) 455-9490
E-mail: mark.sprock@judiciary.state.nj.us

Somerset County

County Clerk

Office of the County Clerk
20 Grove Street, Somerville, NJ 08876-1262
Tel: (908) 231-7013 Fax: (908) 253-8853
Internet: www.co.somerset.nj.us/clerk/

County Clerk **Brett A. Radi** ....(908) 231-7013
E-mail: radi@co.somerset.nj.us

Trial Court Administrator

Vicinage 13
20 North Bridge Street, Somerville, NJ 08876-1262 (Somerset County)
65 Park Avenue, Flemington, NJ 08822 (Hunterdon County)
413 2nd Street, Belvidere, NJ 07823 (Warren County)
Tel: (908) 231-7000 (Somerset)
Tel: (908) 237-5800 (Hunterdon) Tel: (908) 475-6150 (Warren)
Internet: www.judiciary.state.nj.us/somerset/index.html

Trial Court Administrator **Eugene Farkas** ....(908) 203-6151
20 North Bridge Street, Somerville, NJ 08876-1262
E-mail: eugene.farkas@judiciary.state.nj.us

Sussex County

County Clerk

Office of the County Clerk
83 Spring Street, Suite 304, Newton, NJ 07860
Tel: (973) 579-0900 Fax: (973) 383-7493

County Clerk **Jeffrey M. "Jeff" Parrott** ....(973) 579-0900
E-mail: jparrott@sussexcountyclerk.org

Trial Court Administrator

Vicinage 10
Washington & Courts Streets, Morristown, NJ 07960-0910 (Morris County)
43-47 High Street, Newton, NJ 07860 (Sussex County)
Tel: (973) 656-4000 (Morris County)
Tel: (973) 579-0675 (Sussex County) Fax: (973) 656-3949
Internet: www.judiciary.state.nj.us/morris/index.htm

Trial Court Administrator **Rashad Shabaka-Burns** ...... (973) 656-3999
Washington & Courts Streets,   Fax: (973) 656-3949
Morristown, NJ 07960-0910

New Jersey Court Clerks and Courthouses *continued*

Union County

County Clerk

Office of the County Clerk
Court House, Two Broad Street, 1st Floor, Room 115,
Elizabeth, NJ 07207
Fax: (908) 558-2589
Internet: clerk.ucnj.org

County Clerk **Joanne Rajoppi** ....(908) 527-4787
  E-mail: jrajoppi@ucnj.org

Trial Court Administrator

Vicinage 12
2 Broad Street, Elizabeth, NJ 07207
Tel: (908) 659-4600
Internet: www.judiciary.state.nj.us/union/index.htm

Trial Court Administrator (Acting) **James Agro** ....(908) 659-4640
  2 Broad Street, Elizabeth, NJ 07207   Fax: (908) 659-4641

Warren County

County Clerk

Office of the County Clerk
413 Second Street, Belvidere, NJ 07823
Tel: (908) 475-6211 Fax: (908) 475-6208

County Clerk **Patricia J. Kolb** ....(908) 475-6211
  E-mail: pkolb@co.warren.nj.us

Trial Court Administrator

Vicinage 13
20 North Bridge Street, Somerville, NJ 08876-1262 (Somerset County)
65 Park Avenue, Flemington, NJ 08822 (Hunterdon County)
413 2nd Street, Belvidere, NJ 07823 (Warren County)
Tel: (908) 231-7000 (Somerset)
Tel: (908) 237-5800 (Hunterdon) Tel: (908) 475-6150 (Warren)
Internet: www.judiciary.state.nj.us/somerset/index.html

Trial Court Administrator **Eugene Farkas** ....(908) 203-6151
  20 North Bridge Street, Somerville, NJ 08876-1262
  E-mail: eugene.farkas@judiciary.state.nj.us

Counties Within Judicial Districts

Superior Court, 1st Vicinage
Areas Covered: Atlantic and Cape May Counties.

Superior Court, 2nd Vicinage
Areas Covered: Bergen County.

Superior Court, 3rd Vicinage
Areas Covered: Burlington County.

Superior Court, 4th Vicinage
Areas Covered: Camden County.

Superior Court, 5th Vicinage
Areas Covered: Essex County.

Superior Court, 6th Vicinage
Areas Covered: Hudson County.

New Jersey Court Clerks and Courthouses *continued*

Superior Court, 7th Vicinage
Areas Covered: Mercer County.

Superior Court, 8th Vicinage
Areas Covered: Middlesex County.

Superior Court, 9th Vicinage
Areas Covered: Monmouth County.

Superior Court, 10th Vicinage
Areas Covered: Morris and Sussex Counties.

Superior Court, 11th Vicinage
Areas Covered: Passaic County.

Superior Court, 12th Vicinage
Areas Covered: Union County.

Superior Court, 13th Vicinage
Areas Covered: Hunterdon, Somerset, and Warrant Counties.

Superior Court, 14th Vicinage
Areas Covered: Ocean County.

Superior Court, 15th Vicinage
Areas Covered: Cumberland, Gloucester, and Salem Counties.

New Mexico Court Clerks and Courthouses

The trial courts of general jurisdiction in New Mexico are called District Courts. There are 13 such courts in the State. The listing that follows is divided into two sections. The first section gives the county clerks; the second section gives for each judicial district the telephone number of the court and the clerks for the counties within that district.

New Mexico Supreme Court

Supreme Court Building, 237 Don Gaspar Avenue, Santa Fe, NM 87501
P.O. Box 848, Santa Fe, NM 87504-0848
Tel: (505) 827-4860 Tel: (505) 827-4850 (Library Information)
Fax: (505) 827-4837
Internet: http://nmsupremecourt.nmcourts.gov

The Supreme Court consists of a chief justice and four associate justices who are elected in general elections to eight-year terms. Vacancies are filled by the Governor from a list submitted by the constitutionally created Judicial Selection Commission. Appointees serve until the next general election. The chief justice is elected by peer vote to a two-year term each January of odd-numbered years. The Supreme Court has appellate jurisdiction over all New Mexico District Court decisions in criminal cases imposing a death penalty or life imprisonment and in appeals from the Public Regulation Commission. All other cases are appealed to the New Mexico Court of Appeals. The Court has supervisory and administrative control over all lower courts and exercises disciplinary control over judges and attorneys in the state.

Court Staff

Chief Clerk of the Court **Joey Moya**.................(505) 827-4860

New Mexico Court of Appeals

Supreme Court Building, 237 Don Gaspar Avenue, Santa Fe, NM 87501
P.O. Box 2008, Santa Fe, NM 87504-2008
Tel: (505) 827-4925 Fax: (505) 827-4946
Internet: http://coa.nmcourts.com/

The Court of Appeals consists of ten judges who are elected in general elections for eight-year terms. Vacancies are filled by the Governor and appointees serve until December 31 following the next general election or for the remainder of the unexpired term, whichever is longer. The chief judge is elected by peer vote to serve a two-year term. The Court of Appeals has appellate jurisdiction over most civil cases, all actions under the Workers' Compensation Act, the Occupational Disease Disablement Law, the Health Care Provider Act, the Subsequent Injury Act and the Federal Employers' Liability Act. The Court also has appellate jurisdiction over criminal cases and post-conviction remedy proceedings (except where a sentence of death or life imprisonment has been imposed), decisions of administrative agencies as provided by law, municipal or county ordinance violations involving a fine or imprisonment and tort actions.

Court Staff

Chief Clerk of the Court **Mark Reynolds** .... (505) 827-4925

County-By-County

Bernalillo County

County Clerk

Office of the County Clerk
One Civic Center Plaza, NW, 6th Floor, Albuquerque, NM 87102
P.O. Box 542, Albuquerque, NM 87102
Tel: (505) 468-1290 (Recording & Filing) Fax: (505) 468-1293
Fax: (505) 468-1294 (Recording and Filing)
E-mail: clerk@bernco.gov
Internet: www.bernco.gov/clerk

County Clerk **Maggie Toulouse Oliver** .... (505) 468-1231

Catron County

County Clerk

Office of the County Clerk
100 Main Street, Reserve, NM 87830
P.O. Box 197, Reserve, NM 87830
Tel: (575) 533-6400 Fax: (575) 533-6453

County Clerk **M. Keith Riddle**.....................(575) 533-6400
E-mail: keith.riddle@catroncountynm.gov

Chaves County

County Clerk

Office of the County Clerk
One Street Mary's Place, Suite 110, Roswell, NM 88203
Tel: (575) 624-6614 Fax: (575) 624-6523

County Clerk **Dave Kunko** ....(575) 624-6614
E-mail: dkunko@co.chaves.nm.us

Cibola County

County Clerk

Office of the County Clerk
515 West High Street, Grants, NM 87020
Tel: (505) 285-2535 Fax: (505) 285-2562

County Clerk **Elisa "Lisa" Bro** .... (505) 285-2535
E-mail: elisa.bro@co.cibola.nm.us

Colfax County

County Clerk

Office of the County Clerk
230 North Third Street, Raton, NM 87740
P.O. Box 159, Raton, NM 87740
Tel: (575) 445-5551 Fax: (575) 445-4031

County Clerk **Freda L. Baca**.......................(575) 445-5551
E-mail: clerk@co.colfax.nm.us

(continued on next page)

Curry County

County Clerk

Office of the County Clerk
700 North Main Street, Suite 7, Clovis, NM 88101
Tel: (575) 763-5591   Fax: (575) 763-4232

County Clerk **Rosalie Riley** . . . . (575) 763-5591
   E-mail: rriley@currycounty.org

De Baca County

County Clerk

Office of the County Clerk
P.O. Box 347, Fort Sumner, NM 88119
Tel: (505) 355-2601   Fax: (505) 355-2441

County Clerk **Rosalie A. Gonzales-Joiner** . . . . (505) 355-2601
   E-mail: rosaliej@plateautel.net

Doña Ana County

County Clerk

Office of the County Clerk
845 North Motel Boulevard, Las Cruces, NM 88007
Tel: (575) 647-7421   Fax: (575) 525-6159

County Clerk **Lynn Ellins** . . . . (575) 647-7421 ext. 6156

Eddy County

County Clerk

Office of the County Clerk
325 South Main Street, Carlsbad, NM 88220
Tel: (575) 885-3383   Fax: (575) 234-1793

County Clerk **Robin VanNatta** . . . . (575) 885-3383
   E-mail: eddyclerk@co.eddy.nm.us

Grant County

County Clerk

Office of the County Clerk
1400 Highway 180 East, Silver City, NM 88061
P.O. Box 898, Silver City, NM 88062
Tel: (575) 574-0042   Fax: (575) 574-0073

County Clerk **Robert Zamarripa** . . . . (575) 574-0046
   E-mail: grantrzamari@cybermesa.com

Guadalupe County

County Clerk

Office of the County Clerk
1448 Historic Route 66, Suite 1, Santa Rosa, NM 88435
Tel: (505) 472-3791   Fax: (505) 472-4791

County Clerk **Patrick Z. Martinez** . . . . (575) 472-3791
   E-mail: pmartinez@guadco-nm.us

Harding County

County Clerk

Office of the County Clerk
35 Pine Street, Mosquero, NM 87733
P.O. Box 1002, Mosquero, NM 87733
Tel: (575) 673-2301   Fax: (575) 673-2922

County Clerk **Barbara Shaw** . . . . (575) 673-2301
   E-mail: bshaw@hardingcounty.org

Hidalgo County

County Clerk

Office of the County Clerk
300 Shakespeare, Lordsburg, NM 88045
Tel: (575) 542-9213   Fax: (575) 542-3193

County Clerk **Melissa DeLaGarza** . . . . (575) 542-9213
   E-mail: hidclk@aznex.net

Lea County

County Clerk

Office of the County Clerk
100 North Main, Lovington, NM 88260
P.O. Box 1507, Lovington, NM 88260
Tel: (575) 396-8619   Fax: (575) 396-3293

County Clerk **Pat Chappelle** . . . . (575) 396-8619
   E-mail: pchappelle@leacounty.net

Lincoln County

County Clerk

Office of the County Clerk
300 Central Avenue, Carrizozo, NM 88301
P.O. Box 338, Carrizozo, NM 88301
Tel: (575) 648-2394 ext. 6   Fax: (575) 648-2576

County Clerk **Rhonda Burrows** . . . . (575) 648-2394 ext. 6
   E-mail: rburrows@lincolncountynm.net

Los Alamos County

County Clerk

Office of the County Clerk
1000 Central Avenue, Suite 240, Los Alamos, NM 87544
Tel: (505) 662-8010   Fax: (505) 662-8008

County Clerk **Sharon Stover** . . . . (505) 662-8010
   E-mail: clerks@lacnm.us

Luna County

County Clerk

Office of the County Clerk
700 South Silver Avenue, Deming, NM 88030
P.O. Box 1838, Deming, NM 88030
Tel: (575) 546-0491   Fax: (575) 543-6617

County Clerk **Andrea Rodriguez** . . . . (575) 546-0491
   E-mail: andrea_rodriguez@lunacountynm.us

New Mexico Court Clerks and Courthouses *continued*

McKinley County

County Clerk

Office of the County Clerk
207 West Hill Street, Gallup, NM 87301
Tel: (505) 863-6866 Fax: (505) 863-1419

County Clerk **Harriett K. Becenti** . . . . (505) 863-6866
  E-mail: clerk@co.mckinley.nm.us

Mora County

County Clerk

Office of the County Clerk
Mora County Courthouse, Mora, NM 87732
P.O. Box 360, Mora, NM 87732
Tel: (505) 387-2448 Fax: (575) 387-9023

County Clerk **Joanne E. Padilla-Salas** . . . . (505) 387-2448
  E-mail: jpadilla-salas@countyofmora.com

Otero County

County Clerk

Office of the County Clerk
1101 New York Avenue, Alamogordo, NM 88310
Tel: (575) 437-4942 Fax: (575) 443-2928

County Clerk **Denise Guerra** . . . . (575) 437-4942
  E-mail: dguerra@co.otero.nm.us

Quay County

County Clerk

Office of the County Clerk
300 South Third Street, Tucumcari, NM 88401
P.O. Box 1246, Tucumcari, NM 88401
Tel: (575) 461-0510 Fax: (575) 461-0513

County Clerk **Veronica Marez** . . . . (575) 461-0510
  E-mail: veronica.marez@quaycounty-nm.gov

Rio Arriba County

County Clerk

Office of the County Clerk
Tierra Amarilla Court House, 7 Main Street, Tierra Amarilla, NM 87575
Tel: (575) 588-7724 Fax: (575) 588-7418

County Clerk **Moises A. Morales, Jr.** . . . . (575) 588-7724
  E-mail: mamorales@rio-arriba.org

Roosevelt County

County Clerk

Office of the County Clerk
109 West First Street, Lobby Box 4, Portales, NM 88130
Tel: (575) 356-8562 Fax: (575) 356-3560

County Clerk **DeAun Searl** . . . . (575) 356-8562
  E-mail: dsearl@rooseveltcounty.com

New Mexico Court Clerks and Courthouses *continued*

San Juan County

County Clerk

Office of the County Clerk
100 South Oliver Drive, Suite 200, Aztec, NM 87410
P.O. Box 550, Aztec, NM 87410
Tel: (505) 334-9471 Fax: (505) 334-3635

County Clerk **Debbie Holmes** . . . . (505) 334-9471
  E-mail: dholmes@sjcounty.net

San Miguel County

County Clerk

Office of the County Clerk
500 West National Avenue, Suite 113, Las Vegas, NM 87701
Tel: (505) 425-9331 Fax: (505) 454-1799
E-mail: mrivera@smcounty.net

County Clerk **Geraldine Gutierrez** . . . . (505) 425-9331 ext. 501
  E-mail: geraldineg@smcounty.net

Sandoval County

County Clerk

Office of the County Clerk
1500 Idalia Road, Bernalillo, NM 87004
P.O. Box 40, Bernalillo, NM 87004
Tel: (505) 867-7572 Fax: (505) 771-8610

County Clerk **Eileen Garbagni** . . . . (505) 867-7572
  E-mail: clerk@sandovalcountynm.gov

Santa Fe County

County Clerk

Office of the County Clerk
102 Grant Avenue, Santa Fe, NM 87501
Tel: (505) 986-6280 Fax: (505) 995-2767

County Clerk **Geraldine Salazar** . . . . (505) 986-6280
  E-mail: gsalazar@santafecountynm.gov

Sierra County

County Clerk

Office of the County Clerk
100 North Date, Truth or Consequences, NM 87901
Tel: (575) 894-2840 Fax: (505) 894-2516

County Clerk **Connie Greer** . . . . (575) 894-2840
  E-mail: cgreer@sierraco.org

Socorro County

County Clerk

Office of the County Clerk
200 Church Street, Socorro, NM 87801
Tel: (505) 835-0423 Fax: (505) 835-1043

County Clerk **Rebecca Vega** . . . . (505) 835-0423
  E-mail: rvega@co.socorro.nm.us

(continued on next page)

Taos County

County Clerk

Office of the County Clerk
105 Albright Street, Suite D, Taos, NM 87571
Tel: (575) 737-6380 Fax: (575) 737-6390

County Clerk **Anna Martinez** . . . . (575) 737-6381
    E-mail: anna.martinez@taoscounty.org

Torrance County

County Clerk

Office of the County Clerk
205 Ninth Street, Estancia, NM 87016
P.O. Box 767, Estancia, NM 87016
Tel: (505) 246-4735 Fax: (505) 384-4080

County Clerk **Linda Jaramillo** . . . . (505) 246-4735
    E-mail: ljaramillo@tcnm.us

Union County

County Clerk

Office of the County Clerk
100 Court Street, Clayton, NM 88415
P.O. Box 430, Clayton, NM 88415
Tel: (575) 374-9491 Fax: (575) 374-9591

County Clerk **Mary Lou Harkins** . . . . (575) 374-9491
    E-mail: unioncountyclerk@hotmail.com

Valencia County

County Clerk

Office of the County Clerk
444 Luna Avenue, Los Lunas, NM 87031
P.O. Box 969, Los Lunas, NM 87031
Tel: (505) 866-2073 Fax: (505) 866-2023

County Clerk **Peggy Carabajal** . . . . (505) 866-2073
    E-mail: peggy.carabajal@co.valencia.nm.us

District-By-District

First Judicial District

P.O. Box 2268, Santa Fe, NM 87504-2268
225 Montezuma Avenue, Santa Fe, NM 87501
Tel: (505) 455-8250 Fax: (505) 455-8280

Areas Covered: Los Alamos, Rio Arriba, and Santa Fe Counties.

Court Staff

District Clerk **Stephen T. Pacheco** . . . . (505) 455-8200
                                                                Fax: (505) 455-8207

Second Judicial District

400 Lomas NW, Albuquerque, NM 87102
P.O. Box 488, Albuquerque, NM 87103-0488
Tel: (505) 841-8400

Areas Covered: Bernalillo County.

Court Staff

District Clerk **James A. Noel** . . . . (505) 841-8400

Third Judicial District

201 West Picacho Avenue, Las Cruces, NM 88005
Tel: (575) 523-8200 Tel: (575) 528-8343

Areas Covered: Doña Ana County.

Court Staff

District Clerk **Claude Bowman** . . . .(575) 523-8283
                                                                Tel: (575) 528-8343

Fourth Judicial District

496 West National Street, Las Vegas, NM 87701-5402
Guadalupe County Courthouse, 420 Parker Avenue,
Santa Rosa, NM 88435
Tel: (505) 425-7281

Areas Covered: Guadalupe, Mora, and San Miguel Counties.

Court Staff

District Clerk **Aurora Lopez** . . . .(505) 425-7281

Fifth Judicial District

100 North Main, Lovington, NM 88260

Areas Covered: Chaves, Eddy, and Lea Counties.

Court Staff

District Clerk, Chaves County **Kennon Crowhurst** . . . . . . (575) 622-2212
    400 North Virginia, Roswell, NM 88202-1776
District Clerk, Eddy County **Eric Ellis** . . . . (575) 885-4740
    102 North Canal, Carlsbad, NM 88220
District Clerk, Lea County **Nelda Cuellar** . . . . (575) 396-8571

Sixth Judicial District

201 North Cooper Street, Silver City, NM 88062

Areas Covered: Grant, Hidalgo, and Luna Counties.

Court Staff

District Clerk, Grant County **Michael M. Medina** . . . . (575) 538-3250
District Clerk, Hidalgo County **Melissa Frost** . . . . (575) 542-3411
    300 Shakespeare, Lordsburg, NM 88045
District Clerk, Luna County **Angelic C. Gutierrez** . . . . (575) 546-9611
    855 South Platinum Avenue,
    Deming, NM 88030

Seventh Judicial District

200 Church Street, Socorro, NM 87801

Areas Covered: Catron, Sierra, Socorro, and Torrance Counties.

Court Staff

District Clerk, Catron County **Rachel Gonzales** . . . .(575) 835-0050
    101 Main Street, Reserve, NM 87830
District Clerk, Sierra County **(Vacant)** . . . .(575) 835-0050
    311 North Date Street,
    Truth or Consequences, NM 87901
District Clerk, Socorro County **Rachel Gonzales** . . . .(505) 835-0050
District Clerk, Torrance County **Angela Simpson** . . . .(575) 835-0050
    903 North Fifth Street, Estancia, NM 87016

New Mexico Court Clerks and Courthouses *continued*

Eighth Judicial District

105 Albright Street, Taos, NM 87571

Areas Covered: Colfax, Taos, and Union Counties.

Court Staff

District Clerk **Bernabe Struck** . . . . (575) 445-5585
   1413 South Second Street,
   Raton, NM 87740

Ninth Judicial District

700 North Main, Clovis, NM 88101
Internet: www.nmcourts9thjdc.com

Areas Covered: Curry and Roosevelt Counties.

Court Staff

District Clerk, Curry County **Shelly Burger** Suite 11 . . . . . (575) 742-7500
District Clerk, Roosevelt County **Vicki J. Wilkerson** . . . . . (575) 359-6920
   109 West First Street, Portales, NM 88130

Tenth Judicial District

300 South Third, Tucumcari, NM 88401

Areas Covered: De Baca, Harding, and Quay Counties.

Court Staff

District Clerk **Diane Ulibari** . . . . (575) 461-2764
   P.O. Box 1067, Tucumcari, NM 88401

Eleventh Judicial District

103 South Olive Drive, Aztec, NM 87410
207 West Hill Avenue, Room 200, Gallup, NM 87301
851 Andrea Drive, Farmington, NM 87401
Tel: (505) 334-6151 (Aztec) Tel: (505) 863-6816 (Gallup)
Tel: (505) 326-2256 (Farmington)

Areas Covered: McKinley and San Juan Counties.

Court Staff

District Clerk **Weldon J. Neff** . . . . (505) 334-6151

Twelfth Judicial District

1000 New York Avenue, Alamogordo, NM 88310

Areas Covered: Lincoln and Otero Counties.

Court Staff

District Clerk, Lincoln County (Acting) **Darla Goar** . . . . . . (575) 648-2432
   300 Central Avenue, Carrizozo, NM 88301   Fax: (575) 648-2581
   P.O. Box 725, Carrizozo, NM 88301
District Clerk, Otero County **Darla Goar** Room 108 . . . . . . (575) 437-7310
                                     Fax: (575) 434-8886

Thirteenth Judicial District

1500 Idalia Road, Bernalillo, NM 87004
P.O. Box 600, Bernalillo, NM 87004
Internet: www.13districtcourt.com

Areas Covered: Cibola, Sandoval, and Valencia Counties.

New Mexico Court Clerks and Courthouses *continued*

Court Staff

District Clerk, Cibola County **Kathy Gallegos** . . . . (575) 287-8831
   515 West High, Grants, NM 87020   Fax: (575) 285-5755
   P.O. Box 758, Grants, NM 87020
District Clerk, Sandoval County **Theresa Valencia**
   Building A . . . . (575) 867-2376
                                     Fax: (575) 867-5161
District Clerk, Valencia County **Philip Romero** . . . . (575) 865-4639
   1835 Highway 314 Southwest,   Fax: (575) 865-8801
   Los Lunas, NM 87031
   P.O. Box 1089, Los Lunas, NM 87031

New York Court Clerks and Courthouses

The trial courts of general jurisdiction in New York are called supreme courts. The State's highest court is called the Court of Appeals. There are 12 judicial districts of Supreme Court, each district consisting of at least one county. The county-by-county listing below, in addition to giving Supreme Court Clerk and County Clerk information, also includes the Clerk of the County Court, which is a court of limited jurisdiction.

New York Court of Appeals

Court of Appeals Hall, 20 Eagle Street, Albany, NY 12207-1095
Tel: (518) 455-7700
Internet: www.courts.state.ny.us/ctapps

The Court of Appeals, which is New York's court of last resort, consists of a chief judge and six associate judges who are appointed to fourteen-year terms. Judges are appointed by the Governor with the advice and consent of the New York State Senate from a list of candidates provided by the Commission on Judicial Nominations. The Court of Appeals hears both civil and criminal appeals. The jurisdiction of the Court is limited by Section 3 of Article VI of the New York Constitution to the review of questions of law, except in a criminal case in which the judgment includes a penalty of death or a case in which the Appellate Division of the Supreme Court, in reversing or modifying a final or interlocutory judgment or order, finds new facts and a final judgment or order is entered pursuant to that finding. An appeal may be taken directly from the court of original jurisdiction to the Court of Appeals from a final judgment or order in a civil action or proceeding in which the only question is the constitutionality of a state or federal statute. The Court also reviews determinations of the New York State Commission on Judicial Conduct.

Court Staff
Clerk of the Court **Andrew W. Klein** . . . . (518) 455-7700
Note: Clerk of the Court Andrew Klein announced he will retire from the court effective September 1, 2015.
E-mail: coa@courts.state.ny.us

New York Supreme Court, Appellate Division

Tel: (585) 530-3100 Fax: (585) 530-3247

The four Supreme Court Appellate Divisions located in Albany, Brooklyn, Manhattan and Rochester are courts of intermediate appellate jurisdiction hearing appeals from judgment and intermediate orders as well as certain original proceedings arising from the Supreme and County Courts, the Court of Claims, Surrogate's Court and Family Court. Additionally, the Appellate Divisions have original jurisdiction over applications to practice law and attorney disciplinary matters. Each Supreme Court Appellate Division consists of a Presiding Justice and Associate Justices appointed from the ranks of elected Supreme Court Justices by the Governor. The Appellate Divisions sit in panels of four to five justices to hear and determine those proceedings.

New York Supreme Court, Appellate Division, First Department

27 Madison Avenue, New York, NY 10010
Tel: (212) 340-0400 Fax: (212) 952-6580

Areas Covered: Counties of Bronx and New York

Court Staff
Clerk of the Court **Susanna Rojas** . . . . (212) 340-0400
E-mail: srojas@nycourts.gov

New York Supreme Court, Appellate Division, Second Department

45 Monroe Place, Brooklyn, NY 11201
Tel: (718) 875-1300 Fax: (718) 858-2446

Areas Covered: Counties of Dutchess, Kings, Nassau, Orange, Putnam, Queens, Richmond, Rockland, Suffolk and Westchester

Court Staff
Clerk of the Court **Aprilanne Agostino** . . . . (718) 722-6307
E-mail: aagostino@courts.state.ny.us

New York Supreme Court, Appellate Division, Third Department

P.O. Box 7288, Capitol Station, Albany, NY 12224-0288
Tel: (518) 471-4777 Fax: (518) 471-4750

Areas Covered: Counties of Albany, Broome, Chemung, Chenango, Clinton, Columbia, Cortland, Delaware, Essex, Franklin, Fulton, Greene, Hamilton, Madison, Montgomery, Otsego, Rensselaer, St. Lawrence, Saratoga, Schenectady, Schoharie, Schuyler, Sullivan, Tioga, Tompkins, Ulster, Warren and Washington

Court Staff
Clerk of the Court **Robert D. Mayberger** . . . . (518) 471-4777
E-mail: rmayberg@courts.state.ny.us

New York Supreme Court, Appellate Division, Fourth Department

50 East Avenue, Suite 200, Rochester, NY 14604
Tel: (585) 530-3100 Fax: (585) 530-3247
Internet: http://www.nycourts.gov/courts/ad4/

Areas Covered: Counties of Allegany, Cattaraugus, Cayuga, Chautauqua, Erie, Genesee, Herkimer, Jefferson, Lewis, Livingston, Monroe, Niagara, Oneida, Onondaga, Ontario, Orleans, Oswego, Seneca, Steuben, Wayne, Wyoming and Yates

Court Staff
Clerk of the Court **Frances Cafarell** . . . . (585) 530-3101
E-mail: fcafarell@courts.state.ny.us   Fax: (585) 530-3246

New York State Court of Claims

Robert Abrams Building for Law and Justice, Capitol Station, Albany, NY 12224
P.O. Box 7344, Albany, NY 12224
Tel: (518) 432-3411

Court Staff
Chief Clerk (Acting) **Scott M. Murphy** . . . . (518) 432-3411

(continued on next page)

New York Court Clerks and Courthouses *continued*

County-By-County

Albany County

Supreme and County Courts Chief Clerk

Third Judicial District
40 Steuben Street, 6th Floor, Albany, NY 12207
Tel: (518) 285-8300   Fax: (518) 426-1604
Internet: www.courts.state.ny.us/courts/3jd/index.shtml

Supreme and County Courts Chief Clerk, Albany
  County **Charles E. Diamond** . . . .(518) 285-8989
  Albany County Courthouse, 16 Eagle Street,   Fax: (518) 487-5020
  Albany, NY 12207
  E-mail: cdiamond@courts.state.ny.us

County Clerk

Office of the County Clerk
County Court House, 16 Eagle Street, Room 128, Albany, NY 12207
Fax: (518) 487-5099
Internet: www.albanycounty.com/clerk

County Clerk **Bruce A. Hidley** . . . .(518) 487-5100

Allegany County

Supreme and County Courts Chief Clerk

Eighth Judicial District
92 Franklin Street, 3rd Floor, Buffalo, NY 14202
Tel: (716) 845-2505   Fax: (716) 858-4828
Internet: www.courts.state.ny.us/courts/8jd/index.shtml

Supreme and County Courts Chief Clerk, Allegany
  County **Laura Gabler** . . . .(585) 268-5941
  Seven Court Street, Belmont, NY 14813-1084
  E-mail: lgabler@nycourts.gov

County Clerk

Office of the County Clerk
7 Court Street, Belmont, NY 14813
Tel: (585) 268-9270   Fax: (585) 268-5881

County Clerk **Robert L. Christman** . . . .(585) 268-9270
  E-mail: christr@alleganyco.com

Bronx County

Criminal Term Chief Clerk

Criminal Term
265 East 161st Street, Criminal Division, Bronx, NY 10451
Tel: (718) 618-3100   Fax: (718) 618-3585
Internet: www.nycourts.gov/courts/12jd/criminal.shtml

Chief Clerk, Bronx County Criminal Term
  Michelle Foggie . . . .(718) 618-3000
  265 East 161st Street, Bronx, NY 10451
  E-mail: mfoggie@courts.state.ny.us

Civil Term Chief Clerk

Civil Term
851 Grand Concourse, Bronx, NY 10451
Tel: (718) 618-1200   Fax: (718) 618-3545
Internet: www.nycourts.gov/courts/12jd/civil/civil.shtml

Chief Clerk, Bronx County Civil Term **Tracy Pardo** . . . . . .(718) 618-1200
  851 Grand Concourse, Bronx, NY 10451
  E-mail: tpardo@courts.state.ny.us

New York Court Clerks and Courthouses *continued*

County Clerk

Bronx County Clerk
851 Grand Concourse, Room 118, Bronx, NY 10451
Tel: (866) 797-7214   Fax: (718) 590-8122

County Clerk **Luis M. Diaz** . . . .(866) 797-7214
  E-mail: ldiaz@cityclerk.nyc.gov

Broome County

Supreme and County Courts Chief Clerk

Sixth Judicial District
31 Lewis Street, 5th Floor, Binghamton, NY 13901
Tel: (607) 240-5350   Fax: (212) 295-4927
Internet: www.courts.state.ny.us/courts/6jd/index.shtml

Supreme and County Courts Chief Clerk, Broome
  County **Karen K. Stephens** . . . .(607) 240-5800
  P.O. Box 1766, Binghamton, NY 13902   Fax: (607) 240-5940
  92 Court Street, Binghamton, NY 13901
  E-mail: karen.stephens@nycourts.gov

County Clerk

Office of the County Clerk
Broome County Office Building, 60 Hawley Street, 3rd Floor,
Binghamton, NY 13901
P.O. Box 2062, Binghamton, NY 13902-2062
Tel: (607) 778-2255   Fax: (607) 778-2243

County Clerk **Richard R. Blythe** . . . .(607) 778-2255
  E-mail: clerkinfo@co.broome.ny.us

Cattaraugus County

Supreme and County Courts Chief Clerk

Eighth Judicial District
92 Franklin Street, 3rd Floor, Buffalo, NY 14202
Tel: (716) 845-2505   Fax: (716) 858-4828
Internet: www.courts.state.ny.us/courts/8jd/index.shtml

Supreme and County Courts Chief Clerk, Cattaraugus
  County **Verna Dry** . . . .(716) 938-2388
  Cattaraugus County Courthouse, 303 Court Street,
  Little Valley, NY 14755
  E-mail: vdry@nycourts.gov

County Clerk

Office of the County Clerk
303 Court Street, Little Valley, NY 14755-1084
Tel: (716) 938-2297   Fax: (716) 938-2773

County Clerk **James Griffith** . . . .(716) 938-2297
  E-mail: jkgriffith@cattco.org

Cayuga County

Supreme and County Courts Chief Clerk

Seventh Judicial District
99 Exchange Boulevard, Rochester, NY 14614
Tel: (585) 371-3266   Fax: (585) 428-2190
Internet: www.courts.state.ny.us/courts/7jd/index.shtml

Supreme and County Courts Chief Clerk, Cayuga
  County **Kelly Wejko** . . . .(315) 237-6450
  152 Genesee Street, Auburn, NY 13021   Fax: (315) 237-6451
  E-mail: kwejko@courts.state.ny.us

New York Court Clerks and Courthouses *continued*

County Clerk

Office of the County Clerk
160 Genesee Street, 1st Floor, Auburn, NY 13021
Tel: (315) 253-1271 Fax: (315) 253-1653

County Clerk **Susan Dwyer** . . . .(315) 253-1271
   E-mail: sdwyer@cayugacounty.us

Chautauqua County

Supreme and County Courts Chief Clerk

Eighth Judicial District
92 Franklin Street, 3rd Floor, Buffalo, NY 14202
Tel: (716) 845-2505 Fax: (716) 858-4828
Internet: www.courts.state.ny.us/courts/8jd/index.shtml

Supreme and County Courts Chief Clerk, Chautauqua
   County **Kathleen Krauza** . . . .(716) 753-4835
   3 North Erie Street, Mayville, NY 14757-0292
   E-mail: kkrauza@nycourts.gov

County Clerk

Office of the County Clerk
One North Erie Street, Mayville, NY 14757
Tel: (716) 753-4331 Fax: (716) 753-4293

County Clerk **Larry Barmore** . . . .(716) 753-4331
   E-mail: barmorel@co.chautauqua.ny.us

Chemung County

Supreme and County Courts Chief Clerk

Sixth Judicial District
31 Lewis Street, 5th Floor, Binghamton, NY 13901
Tel: (607) 240-5350 Fax: (212) 295-4927
Internet: www.courts.state.ny.us/courts/6jd/index.shtml

Supreme and County Courts Chief Clerk, Chemung
   County **Nancy Kreisler** . . . . (607) 873-9450
   Chemung County Courthouse, 224 Lake Street,   Fax: (646) 963-6605
   Elmira, NY 14902-0588
   E-mail: nancy.kreisler@nycourts.gov

County Clerk

Office of the County Clerk
210 Lake Street, Elmira, NY 14905
Tel: (607) 737-2920

County Clerk **Catherine K. Hughes** . . . . (607) 737-2920
   E-mail: chughes@co.chemung.ny.us

Chenango County

Supreme and County Courts Chief Clerk

Sixth Judicial District
31 Lewis Street, 5th Floor, Binghamton, NY 13901
Tel: (607) 240-5350 Fax: (212) 295-4927
Internet: www.courts.state.ny.us/courts/6jd/index.shtml

Supreme and County Courts Chief Clerk, Chenango
   County **Catherine A. Schell** . . . . (607) 337-1457
   Chenango County Courthouse, West Park Place,   Fax: (917) 522-3477
   Norwich, NY 13815
   E-mail: cschell@courts.state.ny.us

New York Court Clerks and Courthouses *continued*

County Clerk

Office of the County Clerk
5 Court Street, Norwich, NY 13815
Tel: (607) 337-1450

County Clerk **Mary C. Weidman** . . . .(607) 337-1450
   E-mail: countyclerk@co.chenango.ny.us

Clinton County

Supreme and County Courts Chief Clerk

Fourth Judicial District
65 South Broadway, Suite 101, Saratoga Springs, NY 12866
Tel: (518) 285-5099 Fax: (518) 587-3179
E-mail: swinkle@courts.state.ny.us
Internet: www.courts.state.ny.us/courts/4jd/index.shtml

Supreme and County Courts Chief Clerk, Clinton
   County **Jan Lavigne** . . . . (518) 565-4715
   137 Margaret Street, Plattsburgh, NY 12901   Fax: (518) 285-8504
   E-mail: jlavigne@courts.state.ny.us

County Clerk

Office of the County Clerk
137 Margaret Street, 1st Floor, Plattsburgh, NY 12901
Tel: (518) 565-4700 Fax: (518) 565-4718

County Clerk **John Zurlo** . . . .(518) 565-4700
   E-mail: zurloj@co.clinton.ny.us

Columbia County

Supreme and County Courts Chief Clerk

Third Judicial District
40 Steuben Street, 6th Floor, Albany, NY 12207
Tel: (518) 285-8300 Fax: (518) 426-1604
Internet: www.courts.state.ny.us/courts/3jd/index.shtml

Supreme and County Courts Chief Clerk, Columbia
   County **David Cardona** . . . . (518) 285-8989
   621 State Route, Suite 23B,   Fax: (518) 487-5020
   Claverack, NY 12513

County Clerk

Office of the County Clerk
560 Warren Street, Hudson, NY 12534
Tel: (518) 828-3339 Fax: (518) 828-5299

County Clerk **Holly C. Tanner** . . . .(518) 828-3339
   E-mail: htanner@govt.co.columbia.ny.us

Cortland County

Supreme and County Courts Chief Clerk

Sixth Judicial District
31 Lewis Street, 5th Floor, Binghamton, NY 13901
Tel: (607) 240-5350 Fax: (212) 295-4927
Internet: www.courts.state.ny.us/courts/6jd/index.shtml

Supreme and County Courts Chief Clerk, Cortland
   County **Karen Jordan** . . . . (607) 753-5013
   46 Greenbush Street, Suite 301,   Fax: (646) 963-6452
   Cortland, NY 13045-2772
   E-mail: kjordan@courts.state.ny.us

(continued on next page)

County Clerk

Office of the County Clerk
46 Greenbush Street, Suite 105, Cortland, NY 13045
Tel: (607) 753-5021 Fax: (607) 756-3492

County Clerk **Elizabeth Larkin** . . . . (607) 753-5021
E-mail: elarkin@cortland-co.org

Delaware County

Supreme and County Courts Chief Clerk

Sixth Judicial District
31 Lewis Street, 5th Floor, Binghamton, NY 13901
Tel: (607) 240-5350 Fax: (212) 295-4927
Internet: www.courts.state.ny.us/courts/6jd/index.shtml

Supreme and County Courts Chief Clerk, Delaware
County **Kelly Sanfilippo** . . . . (607) 746-2131
Delaware County Courthouse, Three Court Street,   Fax: (646) 963-6402
Delhi, NY 13753
E-mail: ksanfilippo@courts.state.ny.us

County Clerk

Office of the County Clerk
3 Court Street, Delhi, NY 13753

County Clerk **Sharon A. O'Dell** . . . . (607) 746-2123
E-mail: sharon.odell@co.delaware.ny.us

Dutchess County

Supreme and County Courts Chief Clerk

Ninth Judicial District
111 Dr. Martin Luther King Jr. Blvd., 11th Floor,
White Plains, NY 10601
Tel: (914) 824-5100 Fax: (914) 995-4111
E-mail: 9thjdadministration@nycourts.gov
Internet: www.nycourts.gov/courts/9jd/

Supreme and County Courts Chief Clerk, Dutchess
County **Michael Thompson** . . . . (845) 431-1710
10 Market Street, Poughkeepsie, NY 12601   Fax: (845) 473-5403
E-mail: mthompson@courts.state.ny.us

County Clerk

Office of the County Clerk
22 Market Street, Poughkeepsie, NY 12601-3222
Tel: (845) 486-2120 Fax: (845) 486-2138

County Clerk **Bradford Kendall** . . . . (845) 486-2120

Erie County

Supreme and County Courts Chief Clerk

Eighth Judicial District
92 Franklin Street, 3rd Floor, Buffalo, NY 14202
Tel: (716) 845-2505 Fax: (716) 858-4828
Internet: www.courts.state.ny.us/courts/8jd/index.shtml

Supreme and County Courts Chief Clerk, Erie County
Ellis W. Bozzolo . . . . (716) 845-9301
25 Delaware Avenue, Buffalo, NY 14202
E-mail: ebozzolo@courts.state.ny.us

County Clerk

Office of the County Clerk
92 Franklin Street, Buffalo, NY 14202
Fax: (716) 858-6550
E-mail: eriecountyclerkoffice@erie.gov
Internet: www2.erie.gov/clerk

County Clerk **Christopher L. Jacobs** . . . . (716) 858-8866

Essex County

Supreme and County Courts Chief Clerk

Fourth Judicial District
65 South Broadway, Suite 101, Saratoga Springs, NY 12866
Tel: (518) 285-5099 Fax: (518) 587-3179
E-mail: swinkle@courts.state.ny.us
Internet: www.courts.state.ny.us/courts/4jd/index.shtml

Supreme and County Courts Chief Clerk, Essex
County **Terry Stoddard** . . . . (518) 873-3370
Essex County Courthouse, 7559 Court Street,   Fax: (518) 451-8738
Elizabethtown, NY 12932
E-mail: terry.stoddard@nycourts.gov

County Clerk

Office of the County Clerk
7559 Court Street, Elizabethtown, NY 12932
Tel: (518) 873-3600 Fax: (518) 873-3548

County Clerk **Joseph A. Provoncha** . . . . (518) 873-3601
E-mail: jprovon@co.essex.ny.us

Franklin County

Supreme and County Courts Chief Clerk

Fourth Judicial District
65 South Broadway, Suite 101, Saratoga Springs, NY 12866
Tel: (518) 285-5099 Fax: (518) 587-3179
E-mail: swinkle@courts.state.ny.us
Internet: www.courts.state.ny.us/courts/4jd/index.shtml

Supreme and County Courts Chief Clerk, Franklin
County **Bruce Cox** . . . . (518) 481-1749
Franklin County Courthouse, 355 West Main Street,   Fax: (518) 481-5456
Malone, NY 12953
E-mail: bcox@courts.state.ny.us

County Clerk

Office of the County Clerk
355 West Main Street, Suite 248, Malone, NY 12953
Tel: (518) 481-1681 Fax: (518) 483-9143

County Clerk **Kip Cassavaw** . . . . (518) 481-1684
E-mail: kcassava@co.franklin.ny.us

Fulton County

Supreme and County Courts Chief Clerk

Fourth Judicial District
65 South Broadway, Suite 101, Saratoga Springs, NY 12866
Tel: (518) 285-5099 Fax: (518) 587-3179
E-mail: swinkle@courts.state.ny.us
Internet: www.courts.state.ny.us/courts/4jd/index.shtml

Supreme and County Courts Chief Clerk, Fulton
County **Patricia Eschler** . . . . (518) 736-5662
223 West Main Street, Johnstown, NY 12095   Fax: (518) 762-5078
E-mail: peschler@courts.state.ny.us

New York Court Clerks and Courthouses *continued*
County Clerk

Office of the County Clerk
223 West Main Street, Johnstown, NY 12095
Tel: (518) 736-5555   Fax: (518) 762-9214

County Clerk **Ann L. Nickloy**........................(518) 736-5555
E-mail: ann.nickloy@ny.gov

Genesee County

Supreme and County Courts Chief Clerk

Eighth Judicial District
92 Franklin Street, 3rd Floor, Buffalo, NY 14202
Tel: (716) 845-2505   Fax: (716) 858-4828
Internet: www.courts.state.ny.us/courts/8jd/index.shtml

Supreme and County Courts Chief Clerk,
Genesee County **Mary Lou Strathearn**......(585) 344-2550 ext. 2239
One West Main Street, Batavia, NY 14020   Fax: (585) 344-8517
E-mail: mstrathe@nycourts.gov

County Clerk

Office of the County Clerk
15 Main Street, Batavia, NY 14020
Tel: (585) 815-7802   Fax: (585) 344-8521

County Clerk **Don M. Read**.........................(585) 815-7802
E-mail: coclerk@co.genesee.ny.us

Greene County

Supreme and County Courts Chief Clerk

Third Judicial District
40 Steuben Street, 6th Floor, Albany, NY 12207
Tel: (518) 285-8300   Fax: (518) 426-1604
Internet: www.courts.state.ny.us/courts/3jd/index.shtml

Supreme and County Courts Chief Clerk, Greene
County **Ellen Brower**..............................(518) 625-3160
320 Main Street, Catskill, NY 12414
E-mail: ebrower@courts.state.ny.us

County Clerk

Office of the County Clerk
411 Main Street, Catskill, NY 12414
Tel: (518) 719-3255   Fax: (518) 719-3284

County Clerk **Michael Flynn**.......................(518) 719-3255
E-mail: mflynn@discovergreene.com

Hamilton County

Supreme and County Courts Chief Clerk

Fourth Judicial District
65 South Broadway, Suite 101, Saratoga Springs, NY 12866
Tel: (518) 285-5099   Fax: (518) 587-3179
E-mail: swinkle@courts.state.ny.us
Internet: www.courts.state.ny.us/courts/4jd/index.shtml

Supreme and County Courts Chief Clerk, Hamilton
County **Araina Eldridge**............................(518) 648-5411
102 County View Drive, Lake Pleasant, NY 12108   Fax: (518) 453-8687
E-mail: araina.eldridge@nycourts.gov

New York Court Clerks and Courthouses *continued*
County Clerk

Office of the County Clerk
102 County View Drive, Lake Pleasant, NY 12108
Tel: (518) 548-7111   Fax: (518) 548-9740

County Clerk **Jane S. Zarecki**.....................(518) 548-7111
E-mail: countyclerk@hamiltoncountyny.gov

Herkimer County

Supreme and County Courts Chief Clerk

Fifth Judicial District
Onondaga County Office Building, 600 South State Street,
Syracuse, NY 13202
Tel: (315) 671-2111   Fax: (315) 671-1175
E-mail: amitche2@courts.state.ny.us
Internet: www.courts.state.ny.us/courts/5jd/index.shtml

Supreme and County Courts Chief Clerk, Herkimer
County **Paul B. Heintz**............................(315) 867-1346
Herkimer Couty Office and Court Facility,
301 North Washington Street,
Herkimer, NY 13350
E-mail: pheintz@courts.state.ny.us

County Clerk

Office of the County Clerk
109 Mary Street, Suite 1111, Herkimer, NY 13350
Tel: (315) 867-1129   Fax: (315) 866-4396

County Clerk **Sylvia Rowan** ....(315) 867-1129
E-mail: herkimercounty@herkimercounty.org

Jefferson County

Supreme and County Courts Chief Clerk

Fifth Judicial District
Onondaga County Office Building, 600 South State Street,
Syracuse, NY 13202
Tel: (315) 671-2111   Fax: (315) 671-1175
E-mail: amitche2@courts.state.ny.us
Internet: www.courts.state.ny.us/courts/5jd/index.shtml

Supreme and County Courts Chief Clerk, Jefferson
County **Deanna L. Morse**..........................(315) 785-7906
317 Washington Street, Watertown, NY 13601   Fax: (315) 266-4779
E-mail: dmorse@courts.state.ny.us

County Clerk

Office of the County Clerk
175 Arsenal Street, Watertown, NY 13601
Tel: (315) 785-3081   Fax: (315) 785-5145

County Clerk **Gizelle J. Meeks**....................(315) 785-3081
E-mail: gizellem@co.jefferson.ny.us

Kings County

Criminal Term Chief Clerk

Criminal Term
320 Jay Street, Brooklyn, NY 11201
Tel: (646) 386-4500
Internet: www.nycourts.gov/courts/2jd/kings/Criminal/index.shtml

Chief Clerk, Kings County Criminal Term
Daniel M. Alessandrino ....(347) 296-1100
320 Jay Street, Brooklyn, NY 11201
E-mail: daniel.alessandrino@nycourts.gov

(continued on next page)

New York Court Clerks and Courthouses *continued*

Civil Term Chief Clerk

Civil Term
360 Adams Street, Brooklyn, NY 11201
Tel: (718) 675-7699
Internet: www.nycourts.gov/courts/2jd/kings/Civil/index.shtml

Chief Clerk, Kings County Civil Term
  Charles A. Small . . . . (718) 675-7699
  360 Adams Street, Brooklyn, NY 11201
  E-mail: csmall@courts.state.ny.us

Lewis County

Supreme and County Courts Chief Clerk

Fifth Judicial District
Onondaga County Office Building, 600 South State Street,
Syracuse, NY 13202
Tel: (315) 671-2111 Fax: (315) 671-1175
E-mail: amitche2@courts.state.ny.us
Internet: www.courts.state.ny.us/courts/5jd/index.shtml

Supreme and County Courts Chief Clerk, Lewis
  County **Bart R. Pleskach** . . . . (315) 376-5347
  Lewis County Courthouse, 7660 State Street,   Fax: (315) 376-5398
  Lowville, NY 13367
  E-mail: bpleskach@courts.state.ny.us

County Clerk

Office of the County Clerk
7660 North State Street, Lowville, NY 13367
Tel: (315) 376-5333 Fax: (315) 376-3768

County Clerk **Douglas P. Hanno** . . . . (315) 376-5333
  E-mail: Clerk@lewiscountyny.org

Livingston County

Supreme and County Courts Chief Clerk

Seventh Judicial District
99 Exchange Boulevard, Rochester, NY 14614
Tel: (585) 371-3266 Fax: (585) 428-2190
Internet: www.courts.state.ny.us/courts/7jd/index.shtml

Supreme and County Courts Chief Clerk, Livingston
  County **Jose Cruzado** . . . . (585) 371-3920
  Two Court Street, Geneseo, NY 14454-1030   Fax: (585) 371-3935
  E-mail: jcruzado@courts.state.ny.us

County Clerk

Office of the County Clerk
6 Court Street, Room 201, Geneseo, NY 14454
Tel: (585) 243-7010

County Clerk **Mary Strickland** . . . . (585) 243-7010
  E-mail: mstrickland@co.livingston.ny.us

Madison County

Supreme and County Courts Chief Clerk

Sixth Judicial District
31 Lewis Street, 5th Floor, Binghamton, NY 13901
Tel: (607) 240-5350 Fax: (212) 295-4927
Internet: www.courts.state.ny.us/courts/6jd/index.shtml

Supreme and County Courts Chief Clerk, Madison
  County **Marianne Kincaid** . . . . (315) 366-2267
  Madison County Courthouse, North Court Street,   Fax: (646) 963-6588
  Wampsville, NY 13163
  E-mail: mkincaid@courts.state.ny.us

New York Court Clerks and Courthouses *continued*

County Clerk

Office of the County Clerk
P.O. Box 668, Wampsville, NY 13163
Tel: (315) 366-2261

County Clerk **Denise A. Roe** . . . . (315) 366-2261
  E-mail: denise.roel@madisoncounty.ny.gov

Monroe County

Supreme and County Courts Chief Clerk

Seventh Judicial District
99 Exchange Boulevard, Rochester, NY 14614
Tel: (585) 371-3266 Fax: (585) 428-2190
Internet: www.courts.state.ny.us/courts/7jd/index.shtml

Supreme and County Courts Chief Clerk, Monroe
  County **Bill Deninger** . . . . (585) 371-3758
  Monroe County Hall of Justice,   Fax: (585) 371-3780
  99 Exchange Boulevard, Rochester, NY 14614

County Clerk

Office of the County Clerk
County Office Building, 39 West Main Street, Room 101,
Rochester, NY 14614
Fax: (585) 753-1624
Internet: www.monroecounty.gov/clerk-index.php

County Clerk **Cheryl Dinolfo** . . . . (585) 753-1600
  E-mail: mcclerk@monroecounty.gov

Montgomery County

Supreme and County Courts Chief Clerk

Fourth Judicial District
65 South Broadway, Suite 101, Saratoga Springs, NY 12866
Tel: (518) 285-5099 Fax: (518) 587-3179
E-mail: swinkle@courts.state.ny.us
Internet: www.courts.state.ny.us/courts/4jd/index.shtml

Supreme and County Courts Chief Clerk, Montgomery
  County **Timothy Riley** . . . . (518) 853-4516
  58 Broadway, Fonda, NY 12068   Fax: (518) 853-3596
  E-mail: triley@courts.state.ny.us

County Clerk

Office of the County Clerk
Fonda, NY 12068-1500
Tel: (518) 853-8111 Fax: (518) 853-8220

County Clerk **Helen A. Bartone** . . . . (518) 853-8111

Nassau County

Supreme and County Courts Chief Clerk

Nassau County Court
100 Supreme Court Drive, Mineola, NY 11501
Tel: (516) 493-3000 Fax: (516) 571-3563

Supreme and County Courts Chief Clerk, Nassau
  County **Kathryn Driscoll Hopkins** . . . . (516) 493-3400
  100 Supreme Court Drive,
  Mineola, NY 11501
  E-mail: khopkins@courts.state.ny.us

County Clerk

Office of the County Clerk
240 Old Country Road, Mineola, NY 11501
Fax: (516) 742-4099

County Clerk **Maureen O'Connell** . . . . (516) 571-2660
    E-mail: moconnell@nassaucountyny.gov

New York County

County Clerk and Clerk of the Supreme Court Civil Branch

First Judicial District
100 Centre Street, New York, NY 10007

County Clerk and Clerk of the Supreme Court, Civil
    Branch **Milton Tingling, Jr.** . . . . (646) 386-5955
    60 Centre Street, New York, NY 10007   Fax: (212) 374-5790

New York County Criminal Term Chief Clerk

Criminal Term
100 Centre Street, New York, NY 10013
Tel: (646) 386-4000 Fax: (212) 374-0667
Internet: www.nycourts.gov/courts/1jd/criminal/

Chief Clerk, New York County Criminal Term
    Barry Clarke . . . . (646) 386-3900
    100 Centre Street, Room 1008,   Fax: (212) 374-3177
    New York, NY 10013
    E-mail: bclarke@courts.state.ny.us

New York County Courts Public Access Law Library

80 Centre Street, Room 468, New York, NY 10013
Tel: (646) 386-3715

Niagara County

Supreme and County Courts Chief Clerk

Eighth Judicial District
92 Franklin Street, 3rd Floor, Buffalo, NY 14202
Tel: (716) 845-2505 Fax: (716) 858-4828
Internet: www.courts.state.ny.us/courts/8jd/index.shtml

Supreme and County Courts Chief Clerk, Niagara
    County **Michael C. Veruto** . . . . (716) 371-4000
    775 Third Street, Niagara Falls, NY 14301   Fax: (716) 278-1809
    E-mail: mveruto@nycourts.gov

County Clerk

Office of the County Clerk
Courthouse, 175 Hawley Street, Lockport, NY 14094-2740
P.O. Box 461, Lockport, NY 14095-0461
Fax: (716) 439-7035
E-mail: niagaracounty.clerk@niagaracounty.com

County Clerk **Wayne F. Jagow** . . . . (716) 439-7022
    E-mail: wayne.jagow@niagaracounty.com

Oneida County

Supreme and County Courts Chief Clerk

Fifth Judicial District
Onondaga County Office Building, 600 South State Street,
Syracuse, NY 13202
Tel: (315) 671-2111 Fax: (315) 671-1175
E-mail: amitche2@courts.state.ny.us
Internet: www.courts.state.ny.us/courts/5jd/index.shtml

Supreme and County Courts Chief Clerk, Oneida
    County **Kathleen Aiello** . . . .(315) 266-4200
    Oneida County Courthouse, 200 Elizabeth Street,   Fax: (315) 798-6436
    Utica, NY 13501
    E-mail: kaiello@courts.state.ny.us

County Clerk

Office of the County Clerk
Oneida County Office Building, 800 Park Avenue, 2nd Floor,
Utica, NY 13501
Tel: (315) 798-5794 Fax: (315) 798-6440
E-mail: countyclerk@ocgov.net
Internet: www.ocgov.net/countyclerk

County Clerk **Sandra J. DePerno** . . . . (315) 798-5776

Onondaga County

Supreme and County Courts Chief Clerk

Fifth Judicial District
Onondaga County Office Building, 600 South State Street,
Syracuse, NY 13202
Tel: (315) 671-2111 Fax: (315) 671-1175
E-mail: amitche2@courts.state.ny.us
Internet: www.courts.state.ny.us/courts/5jd/index.shtml

Supreme and County Courts Chief Clerk, Onondaga
    County **Patricia J. Noll** . . . . (315) 671-1030
    Onondaga County Courthouse,   Fax: (315) 671-1176
    401 Montgomery Street, Syracuse, NY 13202
    E-mail: pnoll@courts.state.ny.us

County Clerk

Office of the County Clerk
Court House, 401 Montgomery Street, Room 200,
Syracuse, NY 13202-2171
Fax: (315) 435-3455
Internet: www.ongov.net/clerk

County Clerk **Sandra A. Schepp** . . . .(315) 435-2229

Ontario County

Supreme and County Courts Chief Clerk

Seventh Judicial District
99 Exchange Boulevard, Rochester, NY 14614
Tel: (585) 371-3266 Fax: (585) 428-2190
Internet: www.courts.state.ny.us/courts/7jd/index.shtml

Supreme and County Courts Chief Clerk, Ontario
    County **Marcilyn Morrisey** . . . . (585) 396-4239
    27 North Main Street, Canandaigua, NY 14424   Fax: (585) 396-4576
    E-mail: marcilyn.morrisey@nycourts.gov

(continued on next page)

County Clerk

Office of the County Clerk
20 Ontario Street, Canandaigua, NY 14424
Tel: (585) 396-4200

County Clerk **Matthew J. Hoose** . . . . (585) 396-4200
    E-mail: matthew.hoose@co.ontario.ny.us

Orange County

Supreme and County Courts Chief Clerk

Ninth Judicial District
111 Dr. Martin Luther King Jr. Blvd., 11th Floor,
White Plains, NY 10601
Tel: (914) 824-5100 Fax: (914) 995-4111
E-mail: 9thjdadministration@nycourts.gov
Internet: www.nycourts.gov/courts/9jd/

Supreme and County Courts Chief Clerk, Orange
   County **Lynn McKelvey** . . . .(845) 476-3500
285 Main Street, Goshen, NY 10924
    E-mail: lynn.mckelvey@nycourts.gov

County Clerk

Office of the County Clerk
Parry Building, 4 Glenmere Cove Road, Goshen, NY 10924
Fax: (845) 291-2691

County Clerk **Ann G. Rabbitt** . . . . (845) 291-2690
    E-mail: occrabbitt@orangecountygov.com

Orleans County

Supreme and County Courts Chief Clerk

Eighth Judicial District
92 Franklin Street, 3rd Floor, Buffalo, NY 14202
Tel: (716) 845-2505 Fax: (716) 858-4828
Internet: www.courts.state.ny.us/courts/8jd/index.shtml

Supreme and County Courts Chief Clerk, Orleans
   County **Kristin Nicholson** . . . . (585) 589-5458
Orleans County Courthouse,
One South Main Street, Suite 3,
Albion, NY 14411-1497
    E-mail: knichols@nycourts.gov

County Clerk

Office of the County Clerk
3 South Main Street, Suite 1, Albion, NY 14411
Tel: (585) 589-5334 Fax: (585) 589-0181

County Clerk **Karen Lake-Maynard** . . . . (585) 589-5334
    E-mail: Karen.Lake-Maynard@orleansny.com

Oswego County

Supreme and County Courts Chief Clerk

Fifth Judicial District
Onondaga County Office Building, 600 South State Street,
Syracuse, NY 13202
Tel: (315) 671-2111 Fax: (315) 671-1175
E-mail: amitche2@courts.state.ny.us
Internet: www.courts.state.ny.us/courts/5jd/index.shtml

Supreme and County Courts Chief Clerk, Oswego
   County **Sonya Malone** . . . . (315) 349-3277
Oswego County Courthouse, 25 East Oneida Street,   Fax: (315) 349-8513
Oswego, NY 13126
    E-mail: smalone@courts.state.ny.us

County Clerk

Office of the County Clerk
46 East Bridge Street, Oswego, NY 13126
Tel: (315) 349-8621

County Clerk **Michael C. Backus** . . . . (315) 349-8621
    E-mail: mbackus@oswegocounty.com

Otsego County

Supreme and County Courts Chief Clerk

Sixth Judicial District
31 Lewis Street, 5th Floor, Binghamton, NY 13901
Tel: (607) 240-5350 Fax: (212) 295-4927
Internet: www.courts.state.ny.us/courts/6jd/index.shtml

Supreme and County Courts Chief Clerk, Otsego
   County **Christy Bass** . . . . (607) 547-4364
Otsego County Courthouse, 197 Main Street,   Fax: (646) 963-6663
Cooperstown, NY 13326
    E-mail: cbass@courts.state.ny.us

County Clerk

Office of the County Clerk
197 Main Street, Cooperstown, NY 13326
Tel: (607) 547-4276 Fax: (607) 547-7544

County Clerk **Kathy Sinnott Gardner** . . . . (607) 547-4276
    E-mail: gardnerk@otsegocounty.com

Putnam County

Supreme and County Courts Chief Clerk

Ninth Judicial District
111 Dr. Martin Luther King Jr. Blvd., 11th Floor,
White Plains, NY 10601
Tel: (914) 824-5100 Fax: (914) 995-4111
E-mail: 9thjdadministration@nycourts.gov
Internet: www.nycourts.gov/courts/9jd/

Supreme and County Courts Chief Clerk, Putnam
   County **Karen O'Connor** . . . . (845) 208-7830
20 County Center, Carmel, NY 10512   Fax: (845) 208-7869
    E-mail: koconnor@courts.state.ny.us

County Clerk

Office of the County Clerk
40 Gleneida Avenue, Room 100, Carmel, NY 10512
Tel: (845) 808-1142

County Clerk **Michael Bartolotti** . . . .(845) 808-1142
    E-mail: michael.bartolotti@putnamcountyny.gov

Queens County

Supreme and County Courts Chief Clerk

Eleventh Judicial District
88-17 Sutphin Boulevard, Jamaica, NY 11435
Tel: (718) 298-1150 Fax: (718) 298-1183
Internet: www.nycourts.gov/courts/11jd/index.shtml

County Clerk and Clerk of the Supreme Court
   Audrey I. Pheffer . . . . (718) 298-0601
88-17 Sutphin Boulevard, Jamaica, NY 11435
    E-mail: apheffer@nycourts.gov

County Clerk

Queens County Clerk
88-11 Sutphin Boulevard, 1st Floor, Jamaica, NY 11439
Tel: (718) 298-0605

County Clerk **Audrey I. Pheffer** . . . . (718) 298-0601
E-mail: apheffer@nycourts.gov

Rensselaer County

Supreme and County Courts Chief Clerk

Third Judicial District
40 Steuben Street, 6th Floor, Albany, NY 12207
Tel: (518) 285-8300 Fax: (518) 426-1604
Internet: www.courts.state.ny.us/courts/3jd/index.shtml

Supreme and County Courts Chief Clerk, Rensselaer
County **Richard F. Reilly, Jr.** . . . . (518) 285-5025
Rensselaer County Courthouse, 80 Second Street,   Fax: (518) 270-3714
Troy, NY 12180
E-mail: rreilly@courts.state.ny.us

County Clerk

Office of the County Clerk
105 Third Street, Troy, NY 12180
Tel: (518) 270-4080 Fax: (518) 271-7998

County Clerk **Frank Merola** . . . . (518) 270-4080
E-mail: fmerola@rensco.com

Richmond County

Supreme and County Courts Chief Clerk

Thirteenth Judicial District
18 Richmond Terrace, Staten Island, NY 10301
Tel: (718) 675-8700 Fax: (718) 390-5435

Chief Clerk, Richmond County **Joseph Como** . . . . (718) 675-8701
18 Richmond Terrace, Staten Island, NY 10301
E-mail: jcomo@courts.state.ny.us

County Clerk

Richmond County Clerk
130 Stuyvesant Place, 2nd Floor, Staten Island, NY 10301
Tel: (718) 675-7700

County Clerk **Stephen J. Fiala** . . . . (718) 675-7700
E-mail: stephen.fiala@rcda.nyc.gov

Rockland County

Supreme and County Courts Chief Clerk

Ninth Judicial District
111 Dr. Martin Luther King Jr. Blvd., 11th Floor,
White Plains, NY 10601
Tel: (914) 824-5100 Fax: (914) 995-4111
E-mail: 9thjdadministration@nycourts.gov
Internet: www.nycourts.gov/courts/9jd/

Supreme and County Courts Chief Clerk, Rockland
County **John Hussey** . . . . (845) 483-8310
One South Main Street, New City, NY 10956   Fax: (845) 638-5312
E-mail: jhussey@courts.state.ny.us

County Clerk

Office of the County Clerk
One S. Main St., New City, NY 10956
Fax: (845) 638-5647

County Clerk **Paul Piperato** . . . . (845) 638-5076

Saratoga County

Supreme and County Courts Chief Clerk

Fourth Judicial District
65 South Broadway, Suite 101, Saratoga Springs, NY 12866
Tel: (518) 285-5099 Fax: (518) 587-3179
E-mail: swinkle@courts.state.ny.us
Internet: www.courts.state.ny.us/courts/4jd/index.shtml

Supreme and County Courts Chief Clerk, Saratoga
County **Carianne Brimhall** . . . . (518) 451-8888
Saratoga County Municipal Center,   Fax: (518) 453-5942
30 McMaster Street, Building 3,
Ballston Spa, NY 12020
E-mail: carianne.brimhall@nycourts.gov

County Clerk

Office of the County Clerk
40 McMaster Street, Ballston Spa, NY 12020
Tel: (518) 885-2213 Fax: (518) 884-4726
E-mail: countyclerk@saratogacountyny.gov

County Clerk **Craig A. Hayner** . . . . (518) 885-2213 ext. 4420

Schenectady County

Supreme and County Courts Chief Clerk

Fourth Judicial District
65 South Broadway, Suite 101, Saratoga Springs, NY 12866
Tel: (518) 285-5099 Fax: (518) 587-3179
E-mail: swinkle@courts.state.ny.us
Internet: www.courts.state.ny.us/courts/4jd/index.shtml

Supreme and County Courts Chief Clerk, Schenectady
County **Robin Farmer** . . . . (518) 285-8401
Schenectady County Judicial Building,   Fax: (518) 451-8731
612 State Street, Schenectady, NY 12305
E-mail: rfarmer@courts.state.ny.us

County Clerk

Office of the County Clerk
620 State Street, Schenectady, NY 12305
Tel: (518) 388-4220 Fax: (518) 388-4224

County Clerk **John J. Woodward** . . . . (518) 381-4220
E-mail: john.woodward@schenectadycounty.com

Schoharie County

Supreme and County Courts Chief Clerk

Third Judicial District
40 Steuben Street, 6th Floor, Albany, NY 12207
Tel: (518) 285-8300 Fax: (518) 426-1604
Internet: www.courts.state.ny.us/courts/3jd/index.shtml

Supreme and County Courts Chief Clerk, Schoharie
County **F. Christian Spies** . . . . (518) 453-6998
290 Main Street, Schoharie, NY 12157

(continued on next page)

New York Court Clerks and Courthouses *continued*

County Clerk

Office of the County Clerk
284 Main Street, 1st Floor, Schoharie, NY 12157
Tel: (518) 295-8316 Fax: (518) 295-8338

County Clerk and Records Management Officer and
   Commissioner of Motor Vehicles **M. Indica Jaycox** .... (518) 295-8316
   E-mail: millerk@co.schoharie.ny.us

Schuyler County

Supreme and County Courts Chief Clerk

Sixth Judicial District
31 Lewis Street, 5th Floor, Binghamton, NY 13901
Tel: (607) 240-5350 Fax: (212) 295-4927
Internet: www.courts.state.ny.us/courts/6jd/index.shtml

Supreme and County Courts Chief Clerk, Schuyler
   County **Rita S. Decker** ....(607) 535-7760
   105 Ninth Street, Unit 35,   Fax: (646) 963-6590
   Watkins Glen, NY 14891
   E-mail: rdecker@courts.state.ny.us

County Clerk

Office of the County Clerk
105 9th Street, Unit 8, Watkins Glen, NY 14891
Tel: (607) 535-8133 Fax: (607) 535-8130

County Clerk **Linda M. Compton** ....(607) 535-8133
   E-mail: lcompton@co.schuyler.ny.us

Seneca County

Supreme and County Courts Chief Clerk

Seventh Judicial District
99 Exchange Boulevard, Rochester, NY 14614
Tel: (585) 371-3266 Fax: (585) 428-2190
Internet: www.courts.state.ny.us/courts/7jd/index.shtml

Supreme and County Courts Chief Clerk, Seneca
   County **(Vacant)** ....(315) 539-7021
   48 West Williams Street, Waterloo, NY 13165   Fax: (315) 539-3267

County Clerk

Office of the County Clerk
1 DiPronio Drive, Waterloo, NY 13165
Tel: (315) 539-1771 Fax: (315) 539-3789

County Clerk **Christina L. Lotz** ....(315) 539-1771
   E-mail: clotz@co.seneca.ny.us

St. Lawrence County

Supreme and County Courts Chief Clerk

Fourth Judicial District
65 South Broadway, Suite 101, Saratoga Springs, NY 12866
Tel: (518) 285-5099 Fax: (518) 587-3179
E-mail: swinkle@courts.state.ny.us
Internet: www.courts.state.ny.us/courts/4jd/index.shtml

Supreme and County Courts Chief Clerk, St. Lawrence
   County **Mary Curran** ....(315) 379-2219
   St. Lawrence County Courthouse, 48 Court Street,   Fax: (315) 379-2423
   Canton, NY 13617
   E-mail: mcurran@courts.state.ny.us

New York Court Clerks and Courthouses *continued*

County Clerk

Office of the County Clerk
48 Court Street, Canton, NY 13617-1169
Tel: (315) 379-2237 Fax: (315) 379-2302

County Clerk **Mary Lou Rupp** ....(315) 379-2237
   E-mail: mrupp@stlawco.org

Steuben County

Supreme and County Courts Chief Clerk

Seventh Judicial District
99 Exchange Boulevard, Rochester, NY 14614
Tel: (585) 371-3266 Fax: (585) 428-2190
Internet: www.courts.state.ny.us/courts/7jd/index.shtml

Supreme and County Courts Chief Clerk, Steuben
   County **Betty Gerych**...........................(607) 776-7879
   3 East Pulteney Square, Bath, NY 14810   Fax: (607) 776-5226
   E-mail: bgerych@courts.state.ny.us

County Clerk

Office of the County Clerk
3 East Pulteney Square, Bath, NY 14810
Tel: (607) 664-2563 Fax: (607) 664-2157

County Clerk **Judith M. Hunter** ....(607) 664-2563

Suffolk County

Supreme and County Courts Chief Clerk

Suffolk County Court
400 Carleton Avenue, Central Islip, NY 11722
Tel: (631) 853-7740 Fax: (631) 853-7741

Supreme and County Courts Chief Clerk, Suffolk
   County **Frank L. Tropea**.........................(631) 852-2120
   210 Center Drive, Riverhead, NY 11901   Fax: (631) 852-2568
   E-mail: ftropea@courts.state.ny.us

County Clerk

Office of the County Clerk
310 Center Dr., Riverhead, NY 11901-3392
Tel: (631) 852-2000 Fax: (631) 852-2004
E-mail: countyclerk@suffolkcountyny.gov

County Clerk **Judith A. Pascale** ....(631) 852-2000
   E-mail: judith.pascale@suffolkcountyny.gov

Sullivan County

Supreme and County Courts Chief Clerk

Third Judicial District
40 Steuben Street, 6th Floor, Albany, NY 12207
Tel: (518) 285-8300 Fax: (518) 426-1604
Internet: www.courts.state.ny.us/courts/3jd/index.shtml

Supreme and County Courts Chief Clerk, Sullivan
   County **Sarah Katzman**..........................(845) 794-4066
   Sullivan County Courthouse, 414 Broadway,   Fax: (845) 791-6170
   Monticello, NY 12701
   E-mail: skatzman@courts.state.ny.us

New York Court Clerks and Courthouses *continued*

County Clerk

Office of the County Clerk
100 North Street, Monticello, NY 12701
Tel: (845) 807-0411   Fax: (845) 807-0434

County Clerk **Daniel L. Briggs**......................(845) 807-0411
E-mail: daniel.briggs@co.sullivan.ny.us

Tioga County

Supreme and County Courts Chief Clerk

Sixth Judicial District
31 Lewis Street, 5th Floor, Binghamton, NY 13901
Tel: (607) 240-5350   Fax: (212) 295-4927
Internet: www.courts.state.ny.us/courts/6jd/index.shtml

Supreme and County Courts Chief Clerk, Tioga County
JoAnn Peet................................... (607) 689-6102
Court Annex Building, 20 Court Street,   Fax: (212) 401-5970
Owego, NY 13827
E-mail: jpeet@courts.state.ny.us

County Clerk

Office of the County Clerk
16 Court Street, Owego, NY 13827
Tel: (607) 687-8660   Fax: (607) 687-8686

County Clerk **Robert L. Woodburn** .... (607) 687-8660
E-mail: woodburnr@co.tioga.ny.us

Tompkins County

Supreme and County Courts Chief Clerk

Sixth Judicial District
31 Lewis Street, 5th Floor, Binghamton, NY 13901
Tel: (607) 240-5350   Fax: (212) 295-4927
Internet: www.courts.state.ny.us/courts/6jd/index.shtml

Supreme and County Courts Chief Clerk, Tompkins
County **Paula M. Nichols**...................... (607) 272-0466
320 North Tioga Street, Ithaca, NY 14850   Fax: (212) 401-9071
E-mail: pnichols@courts.state.ny.us

County Clerk

Office of the County Clerk
320 North Tioga Street, Ithaca, NY 14850
Tel: (607) 274-5431

County Clerk **Maureen Reynolds**................... (607) 274-5431
E-mail: countyclerkmail@tompkins-co.org

Ulster County

Supreme and County Courts Chief Clerk

Third Judicial District
40 Steuben Street, 6th Floor, Albany, NY 12207
Tel: (518) 285-8300   Fax: (518) 426-1604
Internet: www.courts.state.ny.us/courts/3jd/index.shtml

Supreme and County Courts Chief Clerk, Ulster
County **Claudia Jones**..........................(845) 340-3377
Ulster County Courthouse, 285 Wall Street,
Kingston, NY 12401
E-mail: cjones@courts.state.ny.us

New York Court Clerks and Courthouses *continued*

County Clerk

Office of the County Clerk
244 Fair Street, Kingston, NY 12402
Tel: (845) 340-3228   Fax: (845) 340-3299

County Clerk **Nina Postupack**......................(845) 340-3288
E-mail: countyclerk@co.ulster.ny.us

Warren County

Supreme and County Courts Chief Clerk

Fourth Judicial District
65 South Broadway, Suite 101, Saratoga Springs, NY 12866
Tel: (518) 285-5099   Fax: (518) 587-3179
E-mail: swinkle@courts.state.ny.us
Internet: www.courts.state.ny.us/courts/4jd/index.shtml

Supreme and County Courts Chief Clerk, Warren
County **Joanne Mann**......................... (518) 761-6431
Warren County Municipal Center,   Fax: (518) 761-6253
1340 State Route 9, Lake George, NY 12845
E-mail: jmann@courts.state.ny.us

County Clerk

Office of the County Clerk
1340 State Route 9, Lake George, NY 12845
Fax: (518) 761-6551

County Clerk **Pamela J. Vogel** .... (518) 761-6429
E-mail: vogelp@warrencountyny.gov

Washington County

Supreme and County Courts Chief Clerk

Fourth Judicial District
65 South Broadway, Suite 101, Saratoga Springs, NY 12866
Tel: (518) 285-5099   Fax: (518) 587-3179
E-mail: swinkle@courts.state.ny.us
Internet: www.courts.state.ny.us/courts/4jd/index.shtml

Supreme and County Courts Chief Clerk, Washington
County **Tricia Robarge**..........................(518) 746-2521
Washington County Courthouse, 383 Broadway,   Fax: (518) 746-2519
Fort Edward, NY 12828
E-mail: trobarge@courts.state.ny.us

County Clerk

Office of the County Clerk
383 Broadway, Fort Edward, NY 12828
Tel: (518) 746-2170   Fax: (518) 746-2177

County Clerk **Donna Crandall**......................(518) 746-2170
E-mail: dcrandall@co.washington.ny.us

Wayne County

Supreme and County Courts Chief Clerk

Seventh Judicial District
99 Exchange Boulevard, Rochester, NY 14614
Tel: (585) 371-3266   Fax: (585) 428-2190
Internet: www.courts.state.ny.us/courts/7jd/index.shtml

Supreme and County Courts Chief Clerk, Wayne
County **Julie R. Brooks**..........................(315) 946-5459
Wayne County Hall of Justice, 54 Broad Street,   Fax: (315) 946-5456
Lyons, NY 14489
E-mail: jbrooks@courts.state.ny.us

(continued on next page)

New York Court Clerks and Courthouses *continued*

County Clerk

Office of the County Clerk
9 Pearl Street, Lyons, NY 14489
Tel: (315) 946-7470 Fax: (315) 946-5978

County Clerk **Michael Jankowski** . . . .(315) 946-7470
    E-mail: mjankowski@co.wayne.ny.us

Westchester County

Supreme and County Courts Chief Clerk

Ninth Judicial District
111 Dr. Martin Luther King Jr. Blvd., 11th Floor,
White Plains, NY 10601
Tel: (914) 824-5100 Fax: (914) 995-4111
E-mail: 9thjdadministration@nycourts.gov
Internet: www.nycourts.gov/courts/9jd/

Supreme and County Courts Chief Clerk, Westchester
  County **Nancy J. Barry** . . . . (914) 824-5400
  111 Dr. Martin Luther King Jr. Boulevard,   Fax: (914) 995-4323
  White Plains, NY 10601
  E-mail: nbarry@courts.state.ny.us

County Clerk

Office of the County Clerk
110 Dr. Martin Luther King, Jr. Blvd., White Plains, NY 10601
Tel: (914) 995-3081 Fax: (914) 995-4030
Internet: http://www.westchesterclerk.com

County Clerk **Timothy C. Idoni** . . . .(914) 995-3081
    E-mail: tci2@westchestergov.com

Wyoming County

Supreme and County Courts Chief Clerk

Eighth Judicial District
92 Franklin Street, 3rd Floor, Buffalo, NY 14202
Tel: (716) 845-2505 Fax: (716) 858-4828
Internet: www.courts.state.ny.us/courts/8jd/index.shtml

Supreme and County Courts Chief Clerk, Wyoming
  County **Rebecca Miller** . . . . (585) 786-3148
  147 North Main Street, Warsaw, NY 14569   Fax: (585) 786-2818
  E-mail: rmmiller@nycourts.gov

County Clerk

Office of the County Clerk
143 North Main Street, Suite 104, Warsaw, NY 14569
Tel: (585) 786-8810 Fax: (585) 786-3703

County Clerk **Rhonda Pierce** . . . .(585) 786-8810
    E-mail: county.clerk@wyomingco.net

Yates County

Supreme and County Courts Chief Clerk

Seventh Judicial District
99 Exchange Boulevard, Rochester, NY 14614
Tel: (585) 371-3266 Fax: (585) 428-2190
Internet: www.courts.state.ny.us/courts/7jd/index.shtml

Supreme and County Courts Chief Clerk, Yates County
  Margaret Dimartino . . . . (315) 536-5126
  415 Liberty Street, Penn Yan, NY 14527   Fax: (315) 536-5190
  E-mail: margaret.dimartino@nycourts.gov

New York Court Clerks and Courthouses *continued*

County Clerk

Office of the County Clerk
417 Liberty Street, Suite 1107, Penn Yan, NY 14527
Tel: (315) 536-5120 Fax: (315) 536-5545

County Clerk **Julie D. Betts** . . . .(315) 536-5120
    E-mail: countyclerk@yatescounty.org

Counties Within Judicial Districts

Note: The Supreme Court (trial court) is divided into four departments, which are subdivided into 12 districts. Listings below are arranged numerically by district with the department number given in parenthesis.

Supreme Court, 1st Judicial District (1st Department)
Areas Covered: New York County (Manhattan).

Supreme Court, 2nd Judicial District (2nd Department)
Areas Covered: Kings County.

Supreme Court, 3rd Judicial District (3rd Department)
Areas Covered: Albany, Columbia, Green, Rensselaer, Schoharie, Sullivan, and Ulster Counties.

Supreme Court, 4th Judicial District (3rd Department)
Areas Covered: Clinton, Essex, Franklin, Fulton, Hamilton, Montgomery, St. Lawrence, Saratoga, Schenectady, Warren, and Washington Counties.

Supreme Court, 5th Judicial District (4th Department)
Areas Covered: Herkimer, Jefferson, Lewis, Oneida, Onondaga, and Oswego Counties.

Supreme Court, 6th Judicial District (3rd Department)
Areas Covered: Broome, Chemung, Chenango, Cortland, Delaware, Madison, Otsego, Schuyler, Tioga, and Tompkins Counties.

Supreme Court, 7th Judicial District (4th Department)
Areas Covered: Cayuga, Livingston, Monroe, Ontario, Seneca, Steuben, Wayne, and Yates Counties.

Supreme Court, 8th Judicial District (4th Department)
Areas Covered: Allegany, Cattaraugus, Chautauqua, Erie, Genesee, Niagara, Orleans, and Wyoming Counties.

Supreme Court, 9th Judicial District (2nd Department)
Areas Covered: Dutchess, Orange, Putnam, Rockland, and Westchester Counties.

Supreme Court, 10th Judicial District (2nd Department)
Areas Covered: Nassau and Suffolk Counties.

Supreme Court, 11th Judicial District (2nd Department)
Areas Covered: Queens County.

Supreme Court, 12th Judicial District (1st Department)
Areas Covered: Bronx County.

New York Court Clerks and Courthouses *continued*

Supreme Court, 13th Judicial District (2nd Department)

Areas Covered: Richmond County

North Carolina Court Clerks and Courthouses

The trial courts of general jurisdiction in North Carolina are called superior courts. The 100 counties of the State of North Carolina are divided into 46 judicial districts of Superior Court for administrative purposes and 62 districts for electoral purposes. Listed below is the Clerk of Court for each county.

North Carolina Supreme Court

100 Justice Building, Two East Morgan Street, Raleigh, NC 27601
P.O. Box 2170, Raleigh, NC 27602
Tel: (919) 831-5700 Fax: (919) 831-5720
Internet: www.nccourts.org

The Supreme Court consists of a chief justice and six associate justices who are elected in statewide elections for eight-year terms. Vacancies may be filled by the Governor. Retirement is mandatory at age seventy-two; however, retired justices may be recalled to serve as needed. The Supreme Court exercises exclusive appellate jurisdiction over first degree murder cases in which the defendant is sentenced to death and over final orders by the North Carolina Utilities Commission for general rate cases. The Court also has appellate jurisdiction over cases involving substantial constitutional issues, cases of dissent in the North Carolina Court of Appeals, and cases which have been granted a review at the Court's discretion. The Court exercises original jurisdiction over the censure and removal of judges and has supervisory control and rule-making authority over the lower courts.

Court Staff
Clerk of the Court **Christie Speir Cameron Roeder** . . . . . (919) 831-5700

North Carolina Court of Appeals

One West Morgan Street, Raleigh, NC 27601
P.O. Box 2779, Raleigh, NC 27602-2779
Tel: (919) 831-3600
Tel: (919) 831-5708 (Electronic Access Registration)
Fax: (919) 831-3615
Internet: www.nccourts.org/courts/appellate/appeal

The Court of Appeals, established in 1967, consists of a chief judge and fourteen judges who are elected in statewide elections for eight-year terms. The chief judge is selected by the North Carolina Supreme Court chief justice. Judges sit in panels of three judges each. Retirement is mandatory at age seventy-two, but retired judges may be recalled to serve as needed. The Court of Appeals has appellate jurisdiction over cases appealed from the trial courts except those cases heard directly by the Supreme Court. The Court also hears appeals from the North Carolina Industrial Commission, Commissioner of Insurance, State Board of Contract Appeals, State Bar, Property Tax Commission, Department of Human Resources, Commissioner of Banks, Administrator of Savings and Loans, Governor's Waste Management Board and Utilities Commission in cases other than those concerning general rates.

Court Staff
Clerk of the Court **John H. Connell** . . . . (919) 831-3600
  E-mail: jhc@coa.state.nc.us

County-By-County

Alamance County

Court Clerk

Judicial District 15 A
212 West Elm Street, Graham, NC 27253
Tel: (336) 570-5216 Fax: (336) 570-5217

Clerk of Court, Alamance County **David J. Barber** . . . . . . (336) 570-5282
  212 West Elm Street, Graham, NC 27253
  E-mail: david.j.barber@nccourts.org

Alexander County

Court Clerk

Judicial District 22 A
221 East Water Street, Statesville, NC 28677
Tel: (704) 832-6618 Fax: (704) 832-6617

Clerk of Court, Alexander County **Danny Dyson** . . . . (828) 632-2215
  29 West Main Avenue, Taylorsville, NC 28681   Fax: (828) 632-3550

Alleghany County

Court Clerk

Judicial District 23
500 Courthouse Drive, Wilkesboro, NC 28697
Tel: (336) 651-4416 Fax: (336) 651-4417

Clerk of Court, Alleghany County **Susie J. Gambill** . . . . . (336) 372-8949
  12 North Main Street, Sparta, NC 28675   Fax: (336) 372-4899

Anson County

Court Clerk

Judicial District 20 A
114 North Greene Street, Wadesboro, NC 28170
Tel: (704) 994-3816 Fax: (704) 994-3817

Clerk of Court, Anson County **Marcus D. Hammonds** . . . (704) 994-3800
  P.O. Box 1064, Wadesboro, NC 28170   Fax: (704) 994-3801

Ashe County

Court Clerk

Judicial District 23
500 Courthouse Drive, Wilkesboro, NC 28697
Tel: (336) 651-4416 Fax: (336) 651-4417

Clerk of Court, Ashe County **Pam W. Barlow** . . . . (336) 219-1400
  150 Government Circle, Jefferson, NC 28640   Fax: (336) 219-1401

Avery County

Court Clerk

Judicial District 24
842 West King Street, Suite 13, Boone, NC 28607
Tel: (828) 268-6616 Fax: (828) 268-6617

Clerk of Court, Avery County **Lisa F. Daniels** . . . . (828) 737-6700
  P.O. Box 115, Newland, NC 28657   Fax: (828) 737-6701

(continued on next page)

Beaufort County

Court Clerk

Judicial District 2
P.O. Box 575, Washington, NC 27889
Tel: (252) 940-4016 Fax: (252) 940-4088

Clerk of Court, Beaufort County **V. Martin Paramore** . . . .(252) 940-4000
112 West Second Street, Washington, NC 27877   Fax: (252) 940-4001

Bertie County

Court Clerk

Judicial District 6 B
119 Justice Drive, Winton, NC 27986
Tel: (252) 358-7120 Fax: (252) 358-7121

Clerk of Court, Bertie County **Vasti F. James** . . . . (252) 794-6800
108 Dundee Street, Windsor, NC 27983

Bladen County

Court Clerk

Judicial District 13 A
100 Courthouse Square, Whiteville, NC 28472
Tel: (910) 641-4416 Fax: (910) 641-4417

Clerk of Court, Bladen County **Niki S. Dennis** . . . . (910) 872-7201
166 East Broad Street, Elizabethtown, NC 28337   Fax: (910) 872-7218

Brunswick County

Court Clerk

Judicial District 13 B
310 Government Center Drive, NE, Bolivia, NC 28422
Tel: (910) 253-3916 Fax: (910) 253-3917

Clerk of Court, Brunswick County **James MacCallum** . . .(910) 253-8502
310 Government Center Drive, NE,
Bolivia, NC 28422

Buncombe County

Court Clerk

Judicial District 28
60 Court Plaza, Asheville, NC 28801

Clerk of Court, Buncombe County
Steven D. Cogburn . . . . (828) 232-2605
60 Court Plaza, Asheville, NC 28801   Fax: (828) 232-2646

Burke County

Court Clerk

Judicial District 25 A
201 South Green Street, Morganton, NC 28655
Tel: (828) 433-3200 Fax: (828) 433-3217

Clerk of Court, Burke County **Mabel H. Lowman** . . . .(828) 432-2806
201 South Green Street, Morganton, NC 28655   Fax: (828) 438-5460

Cabarrus County

Court Clerk

Judicial District 19 A
77 Union Street South, Concord, NC 28025
Tel: (704) 786-4279 Fax: (704) 788-2587

Clerk of Court, Cabarrus County **William Baggs** . . . .(704) 786-4137
P.O. Box 70, Concord, NC 28026   Fax: (704) 792-2285

Caldwell County

Court Clerk

Judicial District 25 A
201 South Green Street, Morganton, NC 28655
Tel: (828) 433-3200 Fax: (828) 433-3217

Clerk of Court, Caldwell County
Kim E. Clark . . . .(828) 759-8403 ext. 8376
216 Main Street NW, Lenoir, NC 28645   Fax: (828) 757-1479

Camden County

Court Clerk

Judicial District 1
P.O. Box 1761, Manteo, NC 27954
Tel: (252) 475-5216 Fax: (252) 473-5217

Clerk of Court, Camden County **Paula Harrison** . . . . (252) 331-4871
P.O. Box 219, Camden, NC 27921   Fax: (252) 331-4827
E-mail: paula.harrison@nccourts.org

Carteret County

Court Clerk

Judicial District 3 B
302 Broad Street, New Bern, NC 28560
Tel: (252) 639-3012 Fax: (252) 639-3151

Clerk of Court, Carteret County **Pamela Hanson** . . . . (252) 504-4400
300 Courthouse Square, Beaufort, NC 28516   Fax: (252) 504-4401

Caswell County

Court Clerk

Judicial District 9 A
144 Court Square, Yanceyville, NC 27379
Tel: (336) 459-4016 Fax: (336) 459-4017

Clerk of Court, Caswell County **John Satterfield** . . . . (336) 459-4000
144 Court Square, Yanceyville, NC 27379   Fax: (336) 459-4001

Catawba County

Court Clerk

Judicial District 25 B
100 South West Boulevard, Newton, NC 28658
P.O. Box 1292, Newton, NC 28658
Tel: (828) 695-6116 Fax: (828) 695-6117

Clerk of Court, Catawba County **Al Jean M. Bogle** . . . . . (828) 695-6100
P.O. Box 790, Newton, NC 28658   Fax: (828) 465-8975
E-mail: coc@catawbacountync.gov

Chatham County

Court Clerk

Judicial District 15 B
104 East King Street, Hillsborough, NC 27278
Tel: (919) 644-4747 Fax: (919) 732-4497

Clerk of Court, Chatham County
David Samuel Cooper . . . . (919) 545-3500
Chatham County Justice Center,   Fax: (919) 545-3501
40 East Chatham Street, Pittsboro, NC 27312
E-mail: sam.cooper@nccourts.org

Cherokee County

Court Clerk

Judicial District 30 A
100 West Main Street, Franklin, NC 28734
Tel: (828) 524-6414 Fax: (828) 349-9835

Clerk of Court, Cherokee County **Roger D. Gibson** . . . . . (828) 837-2522
75 Peachtree Street, Murphy, NC 28906   Fax: (828) 837-8178

Chowan County

Court Clerk

Judicial District 1
P.O. Box 1761, Manteo, NC 27954
Tel: (252) 475-5216 Fax: (252) 473-5217

Clerk of Court, Chowan County **Michael J. McArthur** . . . (252) 368-5000
P.O. Box 588, Edenton, NC 27932   Fax: (252) 368-5001
E-mail: Michael.J.McArthur@nccourts.org

Clay County

Court Clerk

Judicial District 30 A
100 West Main Street, Franklin, NC 28734
Tel: (828) 524-6414 Fax: (828) 349-9835

Clerk of Court, Clay County **J. Tim Barrett** . . . . (828) 389-2300
261 Courthouse Drive, Hayesville, NC 28904   Fax: (828) 389-2301

Cleveland County

Court Clerk

Judicial District 27 B
100 Justice Place, Shelby, NC 28150
Fax: (704) 476-7817

Clerk of Court, Cleveland County **Mitzi M. Johnson** . . . . (704) 476-7800
100 Justice Place, Shelby, NC 28150   Fax: (704) 476-7801

Columbus County

Court Clerk

Judicial District 13 A
100 Courthouse Square, Whiteville, NC 28472
Tel: (910) 641-4416 Fax: (910) 641-4417

Clerk of Court, Columbus County **Jess H. Hill** . . . . (910) 641-4400
100 Courthouse Square, Whiteville, NC 28472   Fax: (910) 641-4401

Craven County

Court Clerk

Judicial District 3 B
302 Broad Street, New Bern, NC 28560
Tel: (252) 639-3012 Fax: (252) 639-3151

Clerk of Court, Craven County **Terri Sharpe** . . . . (252) 639-3000
302 Broad Street, New Bern, NC 28560   Fax: (252) 639-3030

Cumberland County

Court Clerk

Judicial District 12
117 Dick Street, Fayetteville, NC 28302
Tel: (910) 475-3000 Fax: (910) 475-3017

Clerk of Court, Cumberland County
Kimbrell Kelly-Tucker . . . . (910) 475-3000
117 Dick Street, Fayetteville, NC 28302

Currituck County

Court Clerk

Judicial District 1
P.O. Box 1761, Manteo, NC 27954
Tel: (252) 475-5216 Fax: (252) 473-5217

Clerk of Court, Currituck County **Ray Matusko** . . . . (252) 232-6200
P.O. Box 175, Currituck, NC 27929   Fax: (252) 232-6201
E-mail: ray.matusko@nccourts.org

Dare County

Court Clerk

Judicial District 1
P.O. Box 1761, Manteo, NC 27954
Tel: (252) 475-5216 Fax: (252) 473-5217

Clerk of Court, Dare County (Acting) **Dean M. Tolson** . . . (252) 475-5200
962 Marshall C. Collins Drive,   Fax: (252) 473-1620
Manteo, NC 27954
P.O. Box 1849, Manteo, NC 27954

Davidson County

Court Clerk

Judicial District 22 B
110 West Center Street, Lexington, NC 27292
Tel: (336) 242-6712 Fax: (336) 242-6869

Clerk of Court, Davidson County **Brian L. Shipwash** . . . . (336) 242-6701
110 West Center Street, Lexington, NC 27292   Fax: (336) 242-6759

Davie County

Court Clerk

Judicial District 22 B
110 West Center Street, Lexington, NC 27292
Tel: (336) 242-6712 Fax: (336) 242-6869

Clerk of Court, Davie County **Ellen Drechsler** . . . . (336) 751-3507
140 South Main Street, Mocksville, NC 27028   Fax: (336) 721-4720

(continued on next page)

Duplin County

Court Clerk

Judicial District 4 A
118 Duplin Street, Kenansville, NC 28349
Tel: (910) 478-3618　Fax: (910) 455-6710

Clerk of Court, Duplin County **Katie Harrell** . . . . (910) 275-7000
　118 Duplin Street, Kenansville, NC 28349　　　Fax: (910) 275-7001

Durham County

Court Clerk

Judicial District 14
201 East Main Street, Durham, NC 27701
Tel: (919) 808-3002　Fax: (919) 560-6877

Clerk of Court, Durham County **Archie L. Smith III** . . . . . (919) 808-3002
　201 East Main Street, Durham, NC 27701　　　Fax: (919) 564-3341

Edgecombe County

Court Clerk

Judicial District 7 B/C
115 Nash Street East, Wilson, NC 27893
301 Saint Andrew Street, Tarboro, NC 27886

Clerk of Court, Edgecombe County **Carol A. White** . . . . . (252) 823-3200
　301 St. Andrew Street, Tarboro, NC 27886　　　Fax: (252) 823-3201

Forsyth County

Court Clerk

Judicial District 21
200 North Main Street, Winston-Salem, NC 27101
Tel: (336) 779-6316　Fax: (336) 779-6301

Clerk of Court, Forsyth County **Susan S. Frye** . . . .(336) 779-6300
　200 North Main Street, Winston-Salem, NC 27101　　Fax: (336) 779-6301

Franklin County

Court Clerk

Judicial District 9
102 South Main Street, Louisburg, NC 27549
Tel: (919) 497-4300　Fax: (919) 497-1638

Clerk of Court, Franklin County
　Patricia Burnette-Chastain . . . .(919) 497-4200
　102 South Main Street, Louisburg, NC 27549

Gaston County

Court Clerk

Judicial District 27 A
325 North Marietta Street, Gastonia, NC 28052
Tel: (704) 852-3400　Fax: (704) 852-3335

Clerk of Court, Gaston County
　Lawrence N. Brown, Jr. . . . .(704) 852-3100
　325 North Marietta Street,　　　　　　　　Fax: (704) 852-3267
　Gastonia, NC 28052

Gates County

Court Clerk

Judicial District 1
P.O. Box 1761, Manteo, NC 27954
Tel: (252) 475-5216　Fax: (252) 473-5217

Clerk of Court, Gates County **Nell F. Wiggins** . . . . (252) 357-1365
　P.O. Box 31, Gatesville, NC 27938　　　　Tel: (252) 357-1047
　E-mail: Nell.F.Wiggins@nccourts.org

Graham County

Court Clerk

Judicial District 30 A
100 West Main Street, Franklin, NC 28734
Tel: (828) 524-6414　Fax: (828) 349-9835

Clerk of Court, Graham County **Tammy H. Holloway** . . . .(828) 479-7000
　12 Court Street, Robbinsville, NC 28771　　　Fax: (828) 479-7001

Granville County

Court Clerk

Judicial District 9
102 South Main Street, Louisburg, NC 27549
Tel: (919) 497-4300　Fax: (919) 497-1638

Clerk of Court, Granville County **JoAnn C. Averette** . . . . (919) 690-4800
　101 Main Street, Oxford, NC 27565

Greene County

Court Clerk

Judicial District 8 A
130 South Queen Street, Kinston, NC 28502
Tel: (252) 520-5420　Fax: (252) 520-5421

Clerk of Court, Greene County **Sandra Beaman** . . . .(252) 747-6200
　P.O. Box 675, Snow Hill, NC 28580　　　　Fax: (252) 747-2700

Guilford County

Court Clerk

Judicial District 18
201 South Eugene Street, Greensboro, NC 27401
Tel: (336) 412-7900　Fax: (336) 412-7901

Clerk of Court, Guilford County
　Lisa Johnson-Tomkins . . . . (336) 412-7300
　201 South Eugene Street, Greensboro, NC 27401　　Fax: (336) 412-7302

Halifax County

Court Clerk

Judicial District 6 A
357 Ferrell Lane, Halifax, NC 27839
Tel: (252) 593-3016　Fax: (252) 593-3013

Clerk of Court, Halifax County
　Rebecca C. "Becky" Spragins . . . . (252) 593-3000
　　　　　　　　　　　　　　　　　　　　Fax: (252) 593-3001

Harnett County

Court Clerk

Judicial District 11 A
P.O. Box 1045, Lillington, NC 27546
Fax: (910) 814-4487

Clerk of Court, Harnett County **Marsha L. Johnson** . . . . . (910) 814-4630
  301 West Cornelius Harnett Boulevard, Suite 100,   Fax: (910) 814-4560
  Lillington, NC 27546
  E-mail: marsha.l.johnson@nccourts.org

Haywood County

Court Clerk

Judicial District 30 B
285 North Main Street, Suite 3300, Waynesville, NC 28786
Fax: (828) 454-6490

Clerk of Court, Haywood County **June L. Ray** . . . . (828) 454-6501
  285 North Main Street, Suite 1500,   Fax: (828) 456-6333
  Waynesville, NC 28786

Henderson County

Court Clerk

Judicial District 29B
200 North Grove Street, Suite 163, Hendersonville, NC 28792
Tel: (828) 694-4230

Clerk of Court, Henderson County
  Kimberly Gasperson-Justice . . . . (828) 694-4100
  200 North Grove Street, Suite 163,   Fax: (828) 694-4107
  Hendersonville, NC 28792

Hertford County

Court Clerk

Judicial District 6 B
119 Justice Drive, Winton, NC 27986
Tel: (252) 358-7120 Fax: (252) 358-7121

Clerk of Court, Hertford County **Shirley Johnson** . . . . . . (252) 358-7100
  119 Justice Drive, Winton, NC 27986

Hoke County

Court Clerk

Judicial District 16 A
212 Biggs Street, Laurinburg, NC 28352
Tel: (910) 266-4575 Fax: (910) 266-4578

Clerk of Court, Hoke County **Evelyn McLeod** . . . . (910) 878-4100
  227 North Main Street, Raeford, NC 28376   Fax: (910) 878-4101

Hyde County

Court Clerk

Judicial District 2
P.O. Box 575, Washington, NC 27889
Tel: (252) 940-4016 Fax: (252) 940-4088

Clerk of Court, Hyde County **Brandy Pugh** . . . . (252) 926-4101
  30 Oyster Creek Road, Swan Quarter, NC 27885   Fax: (252) 926-1002
  E-mail: brandy.pugh@nccourts.org

Iredell County

Court Clerk

Judicial District 22 A
221 East Water Street, Statesville, NC 28677
Tel: (704) 832-6618 Fax: (704) 832-6617

Clerk of Court, Iredell County **James L. Mixon III** . . . . . . (704) 832-6600
  221 East Water Street, Statesville, NC 28677   Fax: (704) 832-6601

Jackson County

Court Clerk

Judicial District 30 B
285 North Main Street, Suite 3300, Waynesville, NC 28786
Fax: (828) 454-6490

Clerk of Court, Jackson County **Ann D. Melton** . . . . (828) 631-6400
  401 Grindstaff Cove Road,   Fax: (828) 631-6401
  Sylva, NC 28779

Johnston County

Court Clerk

Judicial District 11 B
207 East Johnston Street, Smithfield, NC 27577
Tel: (919) 209-5510 Fax: (919) 934-1760

Clerk of Court, Johnston County
  Michelle Ball . . . . (919) 209-5400 ext. 5442
  207 East Johnston Street, Smithfield, NC 27577   Fax: (919) 209-5401

Jones County

Court Clerk

Judicial District 4 A
118 Duplin Street, Kenansville, NC 28349
Tel: (910) 478-3618 Fax: (910) 455-6710

Clerk of Court, Jones County **Charles C. Henderson** . . . . (252) 448-7351
  101 Market Street, Trenton, NC 28585   Fax: (252) 448-1607

Lee County

Court Clerk

Judicial District 11 A
P.O. Box 1045, Lillington, NC 27546
Fax: (910) 814-4487

Clerk of Court, Lee County **Susie K. Thomas** . . . . (919) 708-4414
  1400 Horner Boulevard, Sanford, NC 27330
  E-mail: d.susie.thomas@nccourts.org

Lenoir County

Court Clerk

Judicial District 8 A
130 South Queen Street, Kinston, NC 28502
Tel: (252) 520-5420 Fax: (252) 520-5421

Clerk of Court, Lenoir County **Dawn G. Stroud** . . . . (252) 520-5300
  130 South Queen Street, Kinston, NC 28502   Fax: (252) 520-5385
  E-mail: dawn.g.stroud@nccourts.org

(continued on next page)

North Carolina Court Clerks and Courthouses *continued*

Lincoln County

Court Clerk

Judicial District 27 B
100 Justice Place, Shelby, NC 28150
Fax: (704) 476-7817

Clerk of Court, Lincoln County **Fred R. Hatley** . . . . (704) 742-7830
One Courthouse Square, Columbus, NC 28722   Fax: (704) 742-7801

Macon County

Court Clerk

Judicial District 30 A
100 West Main Street, Franklin, NC 28734
Tel: (828) 524-6414 Fax: (828) 349-9835

Clerk of Court, Macon County **Victor H. Perry** . . . . (828) 349-7200
100 West Main Street, Franklin, NC 28734   Fax: (828) 349-7201

Madison County

Court Clerk

Judicial District 24
842 West King Street, Suite 13, Boone, NC 28607
Tel: (828) 268-6616 Fax: (828) 268-6617

Clerk of Court, Madison County **Mark A. Cody** . . . . (828) 649-2531
P.O. Box 217, Marshall, NC 28753   Fax: (828) 649-2829

Martin County

Court Clerk

Judicial District 2
P.O. Box 575, Washington, NC 27889
Tel: (252) 940-4016 Fax: (252) 940-4088

Clerk of Court, Martin County **Tonya C. Leggett** . . . . (252) 809-5100
305 East Main Street, Williamston, NC 27892   Fax: (252) 809-5101

McDowell County

Court Clerk

Judicial District 29A
P.O. Box 188, Rutherfordton, NC 28139
Tel: (828) 288-8116

Clerk of Court, McDowell County **Melissa Adams** . . . . . . (828) 655-4100
21 South Main Street, Marion, NC 28752

Mecklenburg County

Court Clerk

Judicial District 26
832 East Fourth Street, Charlotte, NC 28202
Tel: (704) 686-0260 Fax: (704) 686-0340

Clerk of Court, Mecklenburg County
 Elisa Chinn-Gary . . . . (704) 686-0420
 832 East Fourth Street, Charlotte, NC 28202   Fax: (704) 686-0410

North Carolina Court Clerks and Courthouses *continued*

Mitchell County

Court Clerk

Judicial District 24
842 West King Street, Suite 13, Boone, NC 28607
Tel: (828) 268-6616 Fax: (828) 268-6617

Clerk of Court, Mitchell County **Janet L. Cook** . . . .(828) 688-2161
328 lONGVIEW dRIVE, Bakersville, NC 28705   Fax: (828) 688-2168

Montgomery County

Court Clerk

Judicial District 19 B
176 East Salisbury Street, Suite 405, Asheboro, NC 27203
Tel: (336) 328-3000 Fax: (336) 328-3185

Clerk of Court, Montgomery County **John Deaton** . . . . . .(910) 571-3700
108 East Main Street, Troy, NC 27371   Fax: (910) 576-5020

Moore County

Court Clerk

Judicial District 19 D
P.O. Box 1957, Carthage, NC 28327-1957
Tel: (910) 722-5016 Fax: (910) 722-5017

Clerk of Court, Moore County **Susan A. Hicks** . . . . (910) 722-5000
102 Monroe Street, Carthage, NC 28327   Fax: (910) 722-5001

Nash County

Court Clerk

Judicial District 7 A
234 West Washington Street, Nashville, NC 27856
Tel: (252) 220-3016 Fax: (252) 220-3017

Clerk of Court, Nash County **Rachel Joyner** . . . . (252) 220-3000
          Fax: (252) 220-3001

New Hanover County

Court Clerk

Judicial District 5
316 Princess Street, Wilmington, NC 28401
Tel: (910) 772-6616 Fax: (910) 772-6632

Clerk of Court, New Hanover County **Jan Kennedy** . . . . .(910) 772-6600
316 Princess Street, Wilmington, NC 28401

Northampton County

Court Clerk

Judicial District 6 B
119 Justice Drive, Winton, NC 27986
Tel: (252) 358-7120 Fax: (252) 358-7121

Clerk of Court, Northampton County
 LaQuitta Green-Cooper . . . . (252) 574-3100
 102 West Jefferson Streetn,   Fax: (252) 574-3101
 Jackson, NC 27845

Onslow County

Court Clerk

Judicial District 4 B
625 Court Street, Jacksonville, NC 28540
Tel: (910) 938-3552 Fax: (910) 455-2543

Clerk of Court, Onslow County **Bettie Gurganus** . . . . (910) 478-3600
   625 Court Street, Jacksonville, NC 28540   Fax: (910) 455-6285

Orange County

Court Clerk

Judicial District 15 B
104 East King Street, Hillsborough, NC 27278
Tel: (919) 644-4747 Fax: (919) 732-4497

Clerk of Court, Orange County **James C. Stanford** . . . . . (919) 644-4500
   106 East Margaret Lane, Hillsborough, NC 27278   Fax: (919) 644-4501
   E-mail: james.c.stanford@nccourts.org

Pamlico County

Court Clerk

Judicial District 3 B
302 Broad Street, New Bern, NC 28560
Tel: (252) 639-3012 Fax: (252) 639-3151

Clerk of Court, Pamlico County **Steven E. Hollowell** . . . . (252) 745-6600
   P.O. Box 776, Bayboro, NC 28515   Fax: (252) 745-6018
   E-mail: steven.e.hollowell@nccourts.org

Pasquotank County

Court Clerk

Judicial District 1
P.O. Box 1761, Manteo, NC 27954
Tel: (252) 475-5216 Fax: (252) 473-5217

Clerk of Court, Pasquotank County **Cathy Cartwright** . . . (252) 331-4600
   P.O. Box 449, Elizabeth City, NC 27907   Fax: (252) 331-4680
   E-mail: Connie.J.Thornley@nccourts.org

Pender County

Court Clerk

Judicial District 5
316 Princess Street, Wilmington, NC 28401
Tel: (910) 772-6616 Fax: (910) 772-6632

Clerk of Court, Pender County **Robert W. Kilroy** . . . . (910) 663-3900
   100 North Wright Street, Burgaw, NC 28425   Fax: (910) 663-3901

Perquimans County

Court Clerk

Judicial District 1
P.O. Box 1761, Manteo, NC 27954
Tel: (252) 475-5216 Fax: (252) 473-5217

Clerk of Court, Perquimans County **Todd W. Tilley** . . . . . . (252) 404-5000
   128 North Church Street, Hertford, NC 27944   Fax: (252) 404-5001
   E-mail: Todd.W.Tilley@nccourts.org

Person County

Court Clerk

Judicial District 9 A
144 Court Square, Yanceyville, NC 27379
Tel: (336) 459-4016 Fax: (336) 459-4017

Clerk of Court, Person County **Deborah Barker** . . . . (336) 503-5200
   304 South Morgan Street, Roxboro, NC 27573   Fax: (336) 503-5229

Pitt County

Court Clerk

Judicial District 3 A
100 West Third Street, Greenville, NC 27858
Tel: (252) 695-7260 Fax: (252) 830-3376

Clerk of Court, Pitt County
   Sara Beth Fulford Rhodes . . . . (252) 695-7100
   P.O. Box 6067, Greenville, NC 27835   Fax: (252) 830-3144

Polk County

Court Clerk

Judicial District 29B
200 North Grove Street, Suite 163, Hendersonville, NC 28792
Tel: (828) 694-4230

Clerk of Court, Polk County **Pamela Hyder** . . . . (828) 894-4900
   One Courthouse Square, Columbus, NC 28722   Fax: (828) 894-4901
   P.O. Box 38, Columbus, NC 28722

Randolph County

Court Clerk

Judicial District 19 B
176 East Salisbury Street, Suite 405, Asheboro, NC 27203
Tel: (336) 328-3000 Fax: (336) 328-3185

Clerk of Court, Randolph County **Pamela L. Hill** . . . . (336) 328-3001
   176 East Salisbury Street, Asheboro, NC 27203   Fax: (336) 328-3131

Richmond County

Court Clerk

Judicial District 20 A
114 North Greene Street, Wadesboro, NC 28170
Tel: (704) 994-3816 Fax: (704) 994-3817

Clerk of Court, Richmond County **Vickie B. Daniel** . . . . . . (910) 419-7400
   105 West Franklin Street, Rockingham, NC 28379   Fax: (910) 419-7401

Robeson County

Court Clerk

Judicial District 16 B
500 North Elm Street, Lumberton, NC 28358
Tel: (910) 272-5927 Fax: (910) 272-5917

Clerk of Court, Robeson County **Shelena Smith** . . . . (910) 272-5944
   500 North Elm Street, Lumberton, NC 28358   Fax: (910) 272-5901

(continued on next page)

Rockingham County

Court Clerk

Judicial District 17 A
P.O. Box 127, Wentworth, NC 27375
Tel: (336) 634-6016

Clerk of Court, Rockingham County **J. Mark Pegram** . . . . (336) 634-6000
P.O. Box 127, Wentworth, NC 27375   Fax: (336) 634-6001

Rowan County

Court Clerk

Judicial District 19 C
232 North Main Street, Suite 222, Salisbury, NC 28144
Tel: (704) 797-3012 Fax: (704) 797-3154

Clerk of Court, Rowan County **Jeffrey R. Barger** . . . . (704) 797-3001
210 North Main Street, Salisbury, NC 28144   Fax: (704) 797-3050

Rutherford County

Court Clerk

Judicial District 29A
P.O. Box 188, Rutherfordton, NC 28139
Tel: (828) 288-8116

Clerk of Court, Rutherford County **Steve H. Owens** . . . . . (828) 288-6100
229 North Main Street, Rutherfordton, NC 28139   Fax: (828) 288-6101
P.O. Box 630, Rutherfordton, NC 28139

Sampson County

Court Clerk

Judicial District 4 A
118 Duplin Street, Kenansville, NC 28349
Tel: (910) 478-3618 Fax: (910) 455-6710

Clerk of Court, Sampson County
Norman Wayne Naylor . . . . (910) 596-6600
101 East Main Street, Clinton, NC 28328   Fax: (910) 596-6601
E-mail: norman.w.naylor@nccourts.org

Scotland County

Court Clerk

Judicial District 16 A
212 Biggs Street, Laurinburg, NC 28352
Tel: (910) 266-4575 Fax: (910) 266-4578

Clerk of Court, Scotland County **W. Phillip McRae** . . . . . . (910) 266-4402
212 Biggs Street, Laurinburg, NC 28352   Fax: (910) 266-4466

Stanly County

Court Clerk

Judicial District 20 A
114 North Greene Street, Wadesboro, NC 28170
Tel: (704) 994-3816 Fax: (704) 994-3817

Clerk of Court, Stanly County **Michael E. Honeycutt** . . . . (704) 986-7000
201 South Second Street, Albemarle, NC 28002   Fax: (704) 986-7001

Stokes County

Court Clerk

Judicial District 17 B
201 East Kapp Street, Dobson, NC 27017
Tel: (336) 386-3700 Fax: (336) 386-9879

Clerk of Court, Stokes County **Jason Tuttle** . . . . (336) 593-4400
P.O. Box 250, Danbury, NC 27016   Fax: (336) 593-4401
E-mail: p.jason.tuttle@nccourts.org

Surry County

Court Clerk

Judicial District 17 B
201 East Kapp Street, Dobson, NC 27017
Tel: (336) 386-3700 Fax: (336) 386-9879

Clerk of Court, Surry County **Teresa O'Dell** . . . . (336) 386-3700
201 East Kapp Street, Dobson, NC 27017   Fax: (336) 386-9879

Swain County

Court Clerk

Judicial District 30 A
100 West Main Street, Franklin, NC 28734
Tel: (828) 524-6414 Fax: (828) 349-9835

Clerk of Court, Swain County **Hester G. Sitton** . . . . (828) 488-7400
101 Mitchell Road, Bryson City, NC 28713   Fax: (828) 488-7401

Transylvania County

Court Clerk

Judicial District 29B
200 North Grove Street, Suite 163, Hendersonville, NC 28792
Tel: (828) 694-4230

Clerk of Court, Transylvania County **Rita A. Ashe** . . . . . . (828) 885-3000
Seven East Main Street, Brevard, NC 28712   Fax: (828) 885-3001

Tyrrell County

Court Clerk

Judicial District 2
P.O. Box 575, Washington, NC 27889
Tel: (252) 940-4016 Fax: (252) 940-4088

Clerk of Court, Tyrrell County **Angie Sexton** . . . . (252) 796-6282
103 Main Street, Columbia, NC 27925   Fax: (252) 796-0008

Union County

Court Clerk

Judicial District 20 B
400 North Main Street, Monroe, NC 28112
Tel: (704) 698-3116 Fax: (704) 698-3117

Clerk of Court, Union County **Jeffrey L. Rowell** . . . . (704) 698-3100
400 North Main Street, Monroe, NC 28112   Fax: (704) 698-3101

Vance County

Court Clerk

Judicial District 9
102 South Main Street, Louisburg, NC 27549
Tel: (919) 497-4300 Fax: (919) 497-1638

Clerk of Court, Vance County **Deborah W. Finch** . . . . (252) 430-5100
156 Church Street, Henderson, NC 27536   Fax: (252) 492-6666

Wake County

Court Clerk

Judicial District 10
316 Fayetteville Street, Raleigh, NC 27601
Tel: (919) 792-4950 Fax: (919) 792-4951

Clerk of Court, Wake County **Jennifer Knox** . . . . (919) 792-4005
                                                              Fax: (919) 792-4601

Warren County

Court Clerk

Judicial District 9
102 South Main Street, Louisburg, NC 27549
Tel: (919) 497-4300 Fax: (919) 497-1638

Clerk of Court, Warren County **Richard E. Hunter, Jr.** . . . . (252) 257-3261
109 South Main Street, Warrenton, NC 27589

Washington County

Court Clerk

Judicial District 2
P.O. Box 575, Washington, NC 27889
Tel: (252) 940-4016 Fax: (252) 940-4088

Clerk of Court, Washington County
Denise M. Moulden . . . . (252) 791-4000
120 Adams Street, Plymouth, NC 27962   Fax: (252) 791-4001
E-mail: denise.m.moulden@nccourts.org

Watauga County

Court Clerk

Judicial District 24
842 West King Street, Suite 13, Boone, NC 28607
Tel: (828) 268-6616 Fax: (828) 268-6617

Clerk of Court, Watauga County **Diane Cornett Deal** . . . . (828) 268-6600
842 West King Street, Boone, NC 28607   Fax: (828) 268-6601

Wayne County

Court Clerk

Judicial District 8 B
224 East Walnut Street, Goldsboro, NC 27530
Tel: (919) 722-6100

Clerk of Court, Wayne County **Pam Minshew** . . . . (919) 722-6100
224 East Walnut Street, Room 230,
Goldsboro, NC 27530

Wilkes County

Court Clerk

Judicial District 23
500 Courthouse Drive, Wilkesboro, NC 28697
Tel: (336) 651-4416 Fax: (336) 651-4417

Clerk of Court, Wilkes County **Janet D. Handy** . . . . (336) 651-4400
500 Courthouse Drive, Wilkesboro, NC 28697   Fax: (336) 651-4401

Wilson County

Court Clerk

Judicial District 7 B/C
115 Nash Street East, Wilson, NC 27893
301 Saint Andrew Street, Tarboro, NC 27886

Clerk of Court, Wilson County **Andrew J. Whitley** . . . . . .(252) 291-7502
115 Nash Street East, Wilson, NC 27893   Fax: (252) 291-8635

Yadkin County

Court Clerk

Judicial District 23
500 Courthouse Drive, Wilkesboro, NC 28697
Tel: (336) 651-4416 Fax: (336) 651-4417

Clerk of Court, Yadkin County **Beth W. Holcomb** . . . . . . (336) 679-3600
101 South State Street, Yadkinville, NC 27055   Fax: (336) 679-3601

Yancey County

Court Clerk

Judicial District 24
842 West King Street, Suite 13, Boone, NC 28607
Tel: (828) 268-6616 Fax: (828) 268-6617

Clerk of Court, Yancey County **Tammy McEntyre** . . . .(828) 678-5700
110 Town Square, Burnville, NC 28714   Fax: (828) 678-5701

Counties Within Judicial Districts

Judicial District 1
Areas Covered: Camden, Chowan, Currituck, Dare, Gates, Pasquotanik
and Perquimans Counties.

Judicial District 2
Areas Covered: Beaufort, Hyde, Martin, Tyrrell and Washington
Counties.

Judicial District 3 A
Areas Covered: Pitt County.

Judicial District 3 B
Areas Covered: Carteret, Craven and Pamlico Counties.

Judicial District 4
Areas Covered: Duplin, Jones, Onslow and Sampson Counties.

Judicial District 5
Areas Covered: New Hanover and Pender Counties.

(continued on next page)

Judicial District 6 A
Areas Covered: Halifax County.

Judicial District 6 B
Areas Covered: Bertie, Hertford and Northampton Counties.

Judicial District 7
Areas Covered: Edgecombe, Nash and Wilson Counties.

Judicial District 8
Areas Covered: Greene, Lenoir and Wayne Counties.

Judicial District 9
Areas Covered: Franklin, Granville, Vance and Warren Counties.

Judicial District 9 A
Areas Covered: Caswell and Person Counties.

Judicial District 10
Areas Covered: Wake County.

Judicial District 11
Areas Covered: Harnett, Johnston Lee Counties.

Judicial District 12
Areas Covered: Cumberland County.

Judicial District 13
Areas Covered: Bladen, Brunswick and Columbus Counties.

Judicial District 14
Areas Covered: Durham County.

Judicial District 15 A
Areas Covered: Alamance County.

Judicial District 15 B
Areas Covered: Chatham and Orange Counties.

Judicial District 16 A
Areas Covered: Anson, Hoke, Richmond, and Scotland Counties.

Judicial District 16 B
Areas Covered: Robeson County.

Judicial District 17 A
Areas Covered: Rockingham County.

Judicial District 17 B
Areas Covered: Stokes and Surry Counties.

Judicial District 18
Areas Covered: Guilford County.

Judicial District 19 A
Areas Covered: Cabarrus County.

Judicial District 19 B
Areas Covered: Montgomery, Moore and Randolph Counties.

Judicial District 19 C
Areas Covered: Rowan County.

Judicial District 20 A
Areas Covered: Stanly County.

Judicial District 20 B
Areas Covered: Union County.

Judicial District 21
Areas Covered: Forsyth County.

Judicial District 22 A
Areas Covered: Alexander and Iredell Counties.

Judicial District 22 B
Areas Covered: Davidson and Davie Counties.

Judicial District 23
Areas Covered: Alleghany, Ashe, Wilkes and Yadkin Counties.

Judicial District 24
Areas Covered: Avery, Madison, Mitchell, Watauga and Yancey Counties.

Judicial District 25
Areas Covered: Burke, Caldwell and Catawba Counties.

Judicial District 26
Areas Covered: Mecklenburg County.

Judicial District 27 A
Areas Covered: Gaston County.

Judicial District 27 B
Areas Covered: Cleveland and Lincoln Counties.

Judicial District 28
Areas Covered: Buncombe County.

Judicial District 29 A
Areas Covered: McDowell and Rutherford Counties.

Judicial District 29 B
Areas Covered: Henderson, Polk, and Transylvania Counties.

Judicial District 30
Areas Covered: Cherokee, Clay, Graham, Haywood, Jackson, Macon and Swain Counties.

North Dakota Court Clerks and Courthouses

The trial courts of general jurisdiction in North Dakota are called district courts. There are seven judicial districts, each district consisting of several counties. The clerks listed in the county-by-county listing below are the clerks of the District Courts. There is no intermediate appellate court in the State of North Dakota.

North Dakota Supreme Court

State Capitol, Judicial Wing, 600 East Boulevard Avenue,
1st Floor, Bismarck, ND 58505-0530
Tel: (701) 328-2221 Fax: (701) 328-4480
E-mail: supclerkofcourt@ndcourts.gov
Internet: www.ndcourts.gov Tel: (800) 366-6888 (TTY)

The Supreme Court consists of a chief justice and four justices who are elected in nonpartisan elections for ten-year terms. Vacancies are filled by the Governor from a list provided by the Judicial Nomination Commission or by special election called by the Governor. Appointees serve at least two years and until the next general election thereafter. The subsequent term for that judgeship may be reduced to allow for the minimum two-year term and for the staggering of judicial elections. The chief justice is selected by justices of the Supreme Court and judges of the District Court for a five-year term or until the end of the elected term. The Supreme Court has final appellate jurisdiction over cases from the North Dakota District Courts. The Court has original jurisdiction with authority to issue, hear and determine such original and remedial writs as maybe necessary to properly exercise its jurisdiction. The Court is responsible for the discipline, admissions and licensing of attorneys and administration of the court system.

Court Staff
Clerk of Courts **Penny Miller**.......................(701) 328-2221
   E-mail: pmiller@ndcourts.gov

County-By-County

Adams County

Clerk of Court

Southwest Judicial District
Stark County Courthouse, 51 3rd Street East, Suite 202,
Dickinson, ND 58601

District Clerk, Adams County **Ginger Dangerud** ....(701) 567-2460
   P.O. Box 469, Hettinger, ND 58639-0469   Fax: (701) 567-2910
   E-mail: gdangeru@nd.gov

Barnes County

Clerk of Court

Southeast Judicial District
511 2nd Avenue, SE, Jamestown, ND 58401
Internet: http://www.ndcourts.gov/court/bios/Greenwood.htm

District Clerk, Barnes County **Wanda Auka** ....(701) 845-8512
   Barnes County Courthouse, 230 4th Street NW,   Fax: (701) 845-1341
   Room 303, Valley City, ND 58072
   E-mail: WAuka@ndcourts.gov

Benson County

Clerk of Court

Northeast Judicial District
301 Dakota Street West, #3, Cavalier, ND 58220-4100
Internet: http://www.ndcourts.gov/court/DISTRICTS/NE.htm

District Clerk, Benson County **Lana Johnson** ....(701) 473-5345
   P.O. Box 213, Minnewaukan, ND 58351-0213   Fax: (701) 473-5571
   E-mail: lkjohnso@nd.gov

Billings County

Clerk of Court

Southwest Judicial District
Stark County Courthouse, 51 3rd Street East, Suite 202,
Dickinson, ND 58601

District Clerk, Billings County **Donna Adams** ....(701) 623-4492
   P.O. Box 138, Medora, ND 58645   Fax: (701) 623-4896
   E-mail: dadams@nd.gov

Bottineau County

Clerk of Court

Northeast Judicial District
301 Dakota Street West, #3, Cavalier, ND 58220-4100
Internet: http://www.ndcourts.gov/court/DISTRICTS/NE.htm

District Clerk, Bottineau County **Rhonda Langehaug** ....(701) 228-3983
   314 West 6th Street, Suite 12,   Fax: (701) 228-2336
   Bottineau, ND 58318
   E-mail: RLangehaug@ndcourts.gov

Bowman County

Clerk of Court

Southwest Judicial District
Stark County Courthouse, 51 3rd Street East, Suite 202,
Dickinson, ND 58601

District Clerk, Bowman County **Jan Werre** ....(701) 523-3450
   104 1st Street NW, Suite #3,   Fax: (701) 523-5443
   Bowman, ND 58623
   E-mail: 06Clerk@ndcourts.gov

Burke County

Clerk of Court

Northwest Judicial District
P.O. Box 5005, Minot, ND 58702-5005

District Clerk, Burke County **Bonnie Bohnsack** ....(701) 377-2718
   P.O. Box 219, Bowbells, ND 58721-0219   Fax: (701) 377-2020
   E-mail: blbohnsack@nd.gov

Burleigh County

Clerk of Court

South Central Judicial District
P.O. Box 1013, Bismarck, ND 58502-1013
Internet: http://www.ndcourts.gov/court/DISTRICTS/SC.htm

District Clerk, Burleigh County **Michele Bring** ....(701) 222-6690
   P.O. Box 1055, Bismarck, ND 58502-1055   Fax: (701) 222-6758
   E-mail: mbring@ndcourts.gov

(continued on next page)

Cass County

Clerk of Court

East Central Judicial District
P.O. Box 2806, Fargo, ND 58108-2806

District Clerk, Cass County **Kathryn Ouren** . . . . (701) 451-6900
  P.O. Box 2806, Fargo, ND 58108-2806   Fax: (701) 451-6937
  E-mail: KOuren@ndcourts.gov

Cavalier County

Clerk of Court

Northeast Judicial District
301 Dakota Street West, #3, Cavalier, ND 58220-4100
Internet: http://www.ndcourts.gov/court/DISTRICTS/NE.htm

District Clerk, Cavalier County **Anita Beauchamp** . . . . . . (701) 256-2124
  901 3rd Street, Langdon, ND 58249   Fax: (701) 256-3468
  E-mail: 10Clerk@ndcourts.gov

Dickey County

Clerk of Court

Southeast Judicial District
511 2nd Avenue, SE, Jamestown, ND 58401
Internet: http://www.ndcourts.gov/court/bios/Greenwood.htm

District Clerk, Dickey County **Andi Schimke** . . . . . (701) 349-3249 ext. 4
  P.O. Box 336, Ellendale, ND 58436-0336   Fax: (701) 349-3560
  E-mail: ASchimke@ndcourts.gov

Divide County

Clerk of Court

Northwest Judicial District
P.O. Box 5005, Minot, ND 58702-5005

District Clerk, Divide County **Christina Running** . . . . (701) 965-6831
  P.O. Box 68, Crosby, ND 58730   Fax: (701) 965-6943
  E-mail: 12Clerk@ndcourts.gov

Dunn County

Clerk of Court

Southwest Judicial District
Stark County Courthouse, 51 3rd Street East, Suite 202,
Dickinson, ND 58601

District Clerk, Dunn County **Lisa Guenther** . . . . (701) 573-4447
  Dunn County Courthouse, 205 Owens Street,   Fax: (701) 573-4444
  Manning, ND 58642
  E-mail: 13Clerk@ndcourts.gov

Eddy County

Clerk of Court

Southeast Judicial District
511 2nd Avenue, SE, Jamestown, ND 58401
Internet: http://www.ndcourts.gov/court/bios/Greenwood.htm

District Clerk, Eddy County **Patty Hilbert** . . . . (701) 947-2813
  Eddy County Courthouse, 524 Central Avenue,   Fax: (701) 947-2067
  New Rockford, ND 58356
  E-mail: PHilbert@ndcourts.gov

Emmons County

Clerk of Court

South Central Judicial District
P.O. Box 1013, Bismarck, ND 58502-1013
Internet: http://www.ndcourts.gov/court/DISTRICTS/SC.htm

District Clerk, Emmons County **Anita Ilbach** . . . . (701) 254-4812
  P.O. Box 905, Linton, ND 58552-0905   Fax: (701) 254-4012
  E-mail: aibach@nd.gov

Foster County

Clerk of Court

Southeast Judicial District
511 2nd Avenue, SE, Jamestown, ND 58401
Internet: http://www.ndcourts.gov/court/bios/Greenwood.htm

District Clerk, Foster County **Tamara Becker** . . . . (701) 652-1001
  P.O. Box 257, Carrington, ND 58421   Fax: (701) 652-2173
  E-mail: tbecker@nd.gov

Golden Valley County

Clerk of Court

Southwest Judicial District
Stark County Courthouse, 51 3rd Street East, Suite 202,
Dickinson, ND 58601

District Clerk, Golden Valley County
  Patty Thompson . . . . (701) 872-3713
  P.O. Box 67, Beach, ND 58621-0067   Fax: (701) 872-4383
  E-mail: patthompson@nd.gov

Grand Forks County

Clerk of Court

Northeast Central Judicial District
124 South 4th Street, Grand Forks, ND 58206

District Clerk, Grand Forks County **Rebecca Absey** . . . . . (701) 787-2715
  P.O. Box 5939, Grand Forks, ND 58206-5939   Fax: (701) 787-2716
  E-mail: RAbsey@ndcourts.gov

Grant County

Clerk of Court

South Central Judicial District
P.O. Box 1013, Bismarck, ND 58502-1013
Internet: http://www.ndcourts.gov/court/DISTRICTS/SC.htm

District Clerk, Grant County **Joyce Stern** . . . . (701) 622-3615
  P.O. Box 258, Carson, ND 58529-0258   Fax: (701) 622-3717
  E-mail: jstern@nd.gov

Griggs County

Clerk of Court

Southeast Judicial District
511 2nd Avenue, SE, Jamestown, ND 58401
Internet: http://www.ndcourts.gov/court/bios/Greenwood.htm

District Clerk, Griggs County **Kelly Vincent** . . . . (701) 797-2772
  P.O. Box 326, Cooperstown, ND 58425-0326   Fax: (701) 797-3587
  E-mail: kelly.vincent@griggsnd.com

North Dakota Court Clerks and Courthouses *continued*

Hettinger County

Clerk of Court

Southwest Judicial District
Stark County Courthouse, 51 3rd Street East, Suite 202,
Dickinson, ND 58601

District Clerk, Hettinger County **Sylvia Gion** . . . . (701) 824-2645
P.O. Box 157, Mott, ND 58646-0668   Fax: (701) 824-2717
E-mail: sgion@nd.gov

Kidder County

Clerk of Court

South Central Judicial District
P.O. Box 1013, Bismarck, ND 58502-1013
Internet: http://www.ndcourts.gov/court/DISTRICTS/SC.htm

District Clerk, Kidder County **Barbara A. Steinke** . . . . . . (701) 475-2632
P.O. Box 66, Steele, ND 58482   Fax: (701) 475-2202
E-mail: 22Clerk@ndcourts.gov

LaMoure County

Clerk of Court

Southeast Judicial District
511 2nd Avenue, SE, Jamestown, ND 58401
Internet: http://www.ndcourts.gov/court/bios/Greenwood.htm

District Clerk, LaMoure County **Karin Boom** . . . . (701) 883-5301
P.O. Box 128, LaMoure, ND 58458   Fax: (701) 883-4240
E-mail: karin.boom@co.lamoure.nd.us

Logan County

Clerk of Court

South Central Judicial District
P.O. Box 1013, Bismarck, ND 58502-1013
Internet: http://www.ndcourts.gov/court/DISTRICTS/SC.htm

District Clerk, Logan County **Dawne Marquart** . . . . (701) 754-2751
Logan County Courthouse, 301 Broadway,   Fax: (701) 754-2270
Napoleon, ND 58561
E-mail: damarqua@nd.gov

McHenry County

Clerk of Court

Northeast Judicial District
301 Dakota Street West, #3, Cavalier, ND 58220-4100
Internet: http://www.ndcourts.gov/court/DISTRICTS/NE.htm

District Clerk, McHenry County **Lorraine Myers** . . . . (701) 537-5729
407 Main Street South, Room 203,   Fax: (701) 537-0555
Towner, ND 58788
E-mail: lmyers@nd.gov

North Dakota Court Clerks and Courthouses *continued*

McIntosh County

Clerk of Court

South Central Judicial District
P.O. Box 1013, Bismarck, ND 58502-1013
Internet: http://www.ndcourts.gov/court/DISTRICTS/SC.htm

District Clerk, McIntosh County **Carol Fey** . . . . (701) 288-3450
P.O. Box 179, Ashley, ND 58413-0179   Fax: (701) 288-3671
E-mail: 26Clerk@ndcourts.gov

McKenzie County

Clerk of Court

Northwest Judicial District
P.O. Box 5005, Minot, ND 58702-5005

District Clerk, McKenzie County **Jodee Lawlar** . . . . (701) 444-3616
201 5th Street, NW, Suite 524,   Fax: (701) 444-3916
Watford City, ND 58854

McLean County

Clerk of Court

South Central Judicial District
P.O. Box 1013, Bismarck, ND 58502-1013
Internet: http://www.ndcourts.gov/court/DISTRICTS/SC.htm

District Clerk, McLean County **Cathy Bailey** . . . . (701) 462-8541
P.O. Box 1108, Washburn, ND 58577-0139   Fax: (701) 462-8212
E-mail: CBailey@ndcourts.gov

Mercer County

Clerk of Court

South Central Judicial District
P.O. Box 1013, Bismarck, ND 58502-1013
Internet: http://www.ndcourts.gov/court/DISTRICTS/SC.htm

District Clerk, Mercer County **Wanda J. Knutson** . . . . (701) 745-3262
P.O. Box 39, Stanton, ND 58571   Fax: (701) 745-3710
E-mail: WKnutson@ndcourts.gov

Morton County

Clerk of Court

South Central Judicial District
P.O. Box 1013, Bismarck, ND 58502-1013
Internet: http://www.ndcourts.gov/court/DISTRICTS/SC.htm

District Clerk, Morton County **Lois Scharnhorst** . . . . (701) 667-3358
Morton County Courthouse, 210 2nd Avenue NW,   Fax: (701) 667-3474
Mandan, ND 58554-0186

Mountrail County

Clerk of Court

Northwest Judicial District
P.O. Box 5005, Minot, ND 58702-5005

District Clerk, Mountrail County **Traci Hysjulien** . . . . (701) 628-2915
P.O. Box 69, Stanley, ND 58784-0340   Fax: (701) 628-2276
E-mail: 31Clerk@ndcourts.gov

(continued on next page)

North Dakota Court Clerks and Courthouses *continued*

Nelson County

Clerk of Court

Northeast Central Judicial District
124 South 4th Street, Grand Forks, ND 58206

District Clerk, Nelson County **Ruth Stevens** . . . . (701) 247-2462
   210 B Avenue West, Suite 203,   Fax: (701) 247-2412
   Lakota, ND 58344-7410
   E-mail: rstevens@nd.gov

Oliver County

Clerk of Court

South Central Judicial District
P.O. Box 1013, Bismarck, ND 58502-1013
Internet: http://www.ndcourts.gov/court/DISTRICTS/SC.htm

District Clerk, Oliver County **Kim Wilkens** . . . . (701) 794-8777
   P.O. Box 125, Center, ND 58530   Fax: (701) 794-3476
   E-mail: kwilkens@nd.gov

Pembina County

Clerk of Court

Northeast Judicial District
301 Dakota Street West, #3, Cavalier, ND 58220-4100
Internet: http://www.ndcourts.gov/court/DISTRICTS/NE.htm

District Clerk, Pembina County **Kay N. Braget** . . . . (701) 265-4373
   301 Dakota Street West, #6,   Fax: (701) 265-4876
   Cavalier, ND 58220-4100
   E-mail: knbraget@nd.gov

Pierce County

Clerk of Court

Northeast Judicial District
301 Dakota Street West, #3, Cavalier, ND 58220-4100
Internet: http://www.ndcourts.gov/court/DISTRICTS/NE.htm

District Clerk, Pierce County **Colleen Stutrud** . . . . (701) 776-6161
   240 SE 2nd Street, Suite 8,   Fax: (701) 776-5707
   Rugby, ND 58368-1830
   E-mail: 35Clerk@ndcourts.gov

Ramsey County

Clerk of Court

Northeast Judicial District
301 Dakota Street West, #3, Cavalier, ND 58220-4100
Internet: http://www.ndcourts.gov/court/DISTRICTS/NE.htm

District Clerk, Ramsey County **Kari Landsem** . . . . (701) 662-1309
   524 4th Avenue NE, Unit 4,   Fax: (701) 662-1303
   Devils Lake, ND 58301
   E-mail: 36Clerk@ndcourts.gov

North Dakota Court Clerks and Courthouses *continued*

Ransom County

Clerk of Court

Southeast Judicial District
511 2nd Avenue, SE, Jamestown, ND 58401
Internet: http://www.ndcourts.gov/court/bios/Greenwood.htm

District Clerk, Ransom County **Bernadine Roach** . . . . (701) 683-5823
   P.O. Box 626, Lisbon, ND 58054-0626   Fax: (701) 683-5827
   E-mail: broach@nd.gov

Renville County

Clerk of Court

Northeast Judicial District
301 Dakota Street West, #3, Cavalier, ND 58220-4100
Internet: http://www.ndcourts.gov/court/DISTRICTS/NE.htm

District Clerk, Renville County **Jerene A. Bender** . . . . (701) 756-6398
   P.O. Box 68, Mohall, ND 58761   Fax: (701) 756-6398
   E-mail: 38Clerk@ndcourts.gov

Richland County

Clerk of Court

Southeast Judicial District
511 2nd Avenue, SE, Jamestown, ND 58401
Internet: http://www.ndcourts.gov/court/bios/Greenwood.htm

District Clerk, Richland County **Cindy Schmitz** . . . . (701) 671-1524
   Richland County Courthouse,   Fax: (701) 671-4444
   418 2nd Avenue North, Wahpeton, ND 58075
   E-mail: CSchmitz@ndcourts.gov

Rolette County

Clerk of Court

Northeast Judicial District
301 Dakota Street West, #3, Cavalier, ND 58220-4100
Internet: http://www.ndcourts.gov/court/DISTRICTS/NE.htm

District Clerk, Rolette County **Tracy Davis** . . . . (701) 477-3816
   P.O. Box 460, Rolla, ND 58367   Fax: (701) 477-8594
   E-mail: tdavis@ndcourts.gov

Sargent County

Clerk of Court

Southeast Judicial District
511 2nd Avenue, SE, Jamestown, ND 58401
Internet: http://www.ndcourts.gov/court/bios/Greenwood.htm

District Clerk, Sargent County **Gina Hillestad** . . . . (701) 724-6241
   Sargent County Courthouse,   Fax: (701) 724-6244
   355 Main Street South, Suite 2,
   Forman, ND 58032-4149
   E-mail: GHillest@nd.gov

Sheridan County

Clerk of Court

South Central Judicial District
P.O. Box 1013, Bismarck, ND 58502-1013
Internet: http://www.ndcourts.gov/court/DISTRICTS/SC.htm

District Clerk, Sheridan County **Joyce Dockter** . . . . (701) 363-2207
  P.O. Box 410, McClusky, ND 58463-0410   Fax: (701) 363-2953
  E-mail: jodockte@nd.gov

Sioux County

Clerk of Court

South Central Judicial District
P.O. Box 1013, Bismarck, ND 58502-1013
Internet: http://www.ndcourts.gov/court/DISTRICTS/SC.htm

District Clerk, Sioux County **Sandi Waliser** . . . . (701) 854-3853
  P.O. Box L, Fort Yates, ND 58538   Fax: (701) 854-3854
  E-mail: swaliser@nd.gov

Slope County

Clerk of Court

Southwest Judicial District
Stark County Courthouse, 51 3rd Street East, Suite 202,
Dickinson, ND 58601

District Clerk, Slope County **Marguerite Schatz** . . . . (701) 879-6275
  P.O. Box JJ, Amidon, ND 58620   Fax: (701) 879-6278
  E-mail: 44Clerk@ndcourts.gov

Stark County

Clerk of Court

Southwest Judicial District
Stark County Courthouse, 51 3rd Street East, Suite 202,
Dickinson, ND 58601

District Clerk, Stark County **Linda Splichal** . . . . (701) 227-3184
  Stark County Courthouse, 51 3rd Street East,   Fax: (701) 227-3185
  Suite 106, Dickinson, ND 58601
  E-mail: 45Clerk@ndcourts.gov

Steele County

Clerk of Court

East Central Judicial District
P.O. Box 2806, Fargo, ND 58108-2806

District Clerk, Steele County **Michelle Newman** . . . . (701) 524-2152
  P.O. Box 296, Finley, ND 58230-0296   Fax: (701) 524-1325
  E-mail: mnewman@nd.gov

Stutsman County

Clerk of Court

Southeast Judicial District
511 2nd Avenue, SE, Jamestown, ND 58401
Internet: http://www.ndcourts.gov/court/bios/Greenwood.htm

District Clerk, Stutsman County **Barb Hill** . . . . (701) 252-9042
  Stutsman County Courthouse,   Fax: (701) 251-6319
  Jamestown, ND 58401
  E-mail: BHill@ndcourts.gov

Towner County

Clerk of Court

Northeast Judicial District
301 Dakota Street West, #3, Cavalier, ND 58220-4100
Internet: http://www.ndcourts.gov/court/DISTRICTS/NE.htm

District Clerk, Towner County **Jolene D. Hoffert** . . . . (701) 968-4345
  P.O. Box 517, Cando, ND 58324-0517   Fax: (701) 968-4344
  E-mail: jhoffert@nd.gov

Traill County

Clerk of Court

East Central Judicial District
P.O. Box 2806, Fargo, ND 58108-2806

District Clerk, Traill County **Paulette Bowersox** . . . . (701) 636-4454
  P.O. Box 805, Hillsboro, ND 58045   Fax: (701) 636-5124
  E-mail: pbowerso@nd.gov

Walsh County

Clerk of Court

Northeast Judicial District
301 Dakota Street West, #3, Cavalier, ND 58220-4100
Internet: http://www.ndcourts.gov/court/DISTRICTS/NE.htm

District Clerk, Walsh County **Beverly Stremick** . . . . (701) 352-0350
  600 Cooper Avenue, Grafton, ND 58237   Fax: (701) 352-4466
  E-mail: Bstremick@ndcourts.gov

Ward County

Clerk of Court

Northwest Judicial District
P.O. Box 5005, Minot, ND 58702-5005

District Clerk, Ward County **Susan Hoffer** . . . . (701) 857-6600
  P.O. Box 5005, Minot, ND 58702-5005   Fax: (701) 857-6623
  E-mail: 51Clerk@ndcourts.gov

Wells County

Clerk of Court

Southeast Judicial District
511 2nd Avenue, SE, Jamestown, ND 58401
Internet: http://www.ndcourts.gov/court/bios/Greenwood.htm

District Clerk, Wells County **Carla Widiger** . . . . (701) 547-3122
  P.O. Box 155, Fessenden, ND 58438   Fax: (701) 547-3719
  E-mail: 52Clerk@ndcourts.gov

Williams County

Clerk of Court

Northwest Judicial District
P.O. Box 5005, Minot, ND 58702-5005

District Clerk, Williams County **Jody Fixen** . . . . (701) 774-4375
  P.O. Box 2047, Williston, ND 58802-2047   Fax: (701) 774-4379
  E-mail: JFixen@ndcourts.gov

(continued on next page)

North Dakota Court Clerks and Courthouses *continued*

Counties Within Judicial Districts

North Central Judicial District

Areas Covered: Burke, Mountrail, and Ward Counties.

Northeast Judicial District

Areas Covered: Benson, Bottineau, Cavalier, McHenry, Pembina, Pierce, Ramsey, Renville, Rolette, Towner, and Walsh Counties.

Northeast Central Judicial District

Areas Covered: Grand Forks and Nelson Counties.

Northwest Judicial District

Areas Covered: Divide, McKenzie and Williams Counties.

East Central Judicial District

Areas Covered: Cass, Steele, and Traill Counties.

Southeast Judicial District

Areas Covered: Barnes, Dickey, Eddy, Foster, Griggs, Kidder, LaMoure, Logan, McIntosh, Ransom, Richland, Sargent, Stutsman, and Wells Counties.

South Central Judicial District

Areas Covered: Burleigh, Emmons, Grant, McLean, Mercer, Morton, Oliver, Sheridan, and Sioux Counties.

Southwest Judicial District

Areas Covered: Adams, Billings, Bowman, Dunn, Golden Valley, Hettinger, Slope and Stark Counties.

Ohio Court Clerks and Courthouses

The trial courts of general jurisdiction in Ohio are called courts of common pleas. There is a court of common pleas in each county. The clerk of each common pleas court, given below, functions both as court clerk and county clerk. The Recorder's Office for each county is a separate office.

Supreme Court of Ohio

65 South Front Street, Columbus, OH 43215-3431
Tel: (614) 387-9000 Fax: (614) 387-9539
E-mail: constituent@sconet.state.oh.us
Internet: www.supremecourtofohio.gov

The Supreme Court consists of a chief justice and six justices who are nominated in partisan primaries but run on nonpartisan ballots in general elections for six-year terms. The Governor may appoint justices to temporarily fill vacancies which occur between general elections. Retirement is mandatory at the end of the term during which the justice turns seventy; however, retired justices may be recalled for assignment by the chief justice. The Supreme Court has appellate jurisdiction over cases which originate in the Ohio Courts of Appeals, involve the death penalty, involve state or federal constitutional law and cases which are significant or of public interest from any lower court. The Court has exclusive appellate jurisdiction over appeals from the Ohio Public Utilities Commission and concurrent appellate jurisdiction with the Ohio Courts of Appeals over appeals from the Ohio Board of Tax Appeals. The Court has original jurisdiction over matters related to the practice of law and admission to the bar in Ohio.

Court Staff
Clerk of Court **Sandra Grosko** . . . . (614) 387-9530
Fax: (614) 387-9539

Ohio Court of Appeals

Ohio Court of Appeals serves as the intermediate appellate court for the state. The Court of Appeals exercises two types of jurisdiction: appellate jurisdiction and original jurisdiction. The twelve districts of the Court of Appeals hear from cases arising in the Courts of Common Pleas, County District Courts, and Municipal Courts within their respective districts. The court has concurrent jurisdiction with the Ohio Supreme Court to hear appeals from a County Board of Tax Appeals. Decisions of the Court of Appeals may be reviewed by the Ohio Supreme Court. The appellate court also has limited original jurisdiction in quo warranto, mandamus, habeas corpus, prohibition and procedendo, and any cause on review as may be necessary to complete its determination. Judgments are subject to review by the Ohio Supreme Court. Each appellate district has a minimum of three judges. These judges are nominated in partisan primaries but run on nonpartisan ballots in general elections for six-year terms. The governor may appoint judges to temporarily fill vacancies that occur between general elections. Retirement is mandatory at the age of seventy; however, retired judges may be recalled for assignment by the Chief Justice of the Ohio Supreme Court. The clerks of court are independently elected officials.

Ohio Court of Appeals, First District

William H. Taft Law Center, 230 East Ninth Street, 12th Floor, Cincinnati, OH 45202-2138
Tel: (513) 946-3500 Fax: (513) 946-3411
Internet: www.hamilton-co.org/appealscourt

Areas Covered: County of Hamilton

Note: The Clerks of the Courts of Ohio are elected officials.

Court Staff
Administrator **Margaret M. "Molly" Leonard** . . . . (513) 946-3488
E-mail: mleonard@cms.hamilton-co.org

Ohio Court of Appeals, Second District

41 North Perry Street, Dayton, OH 45422-2170
Tel: (937) 225-4464 Tel: (800) 608-4652 (Toll-free in Ohio)
Fax: (937) 496-7724
Internet: www.mcohio.org/SecondDistrictAppeals

Areas Covered: Counties of Champaign, Clark, Darke, Greene, Miami and Montgomery

Note: The Clerks of the Courts of Ohio are elected officials.

Court Staff
Court Administrator **Erin Scanlon** . . . . (937) 225-4464

Ohio Court of Appeals, Third District

204 North Main Street, Lima, OH 45801
Tel: (419) 223-1861 Fax: (419) 224-3828
Internet: http://www.third.courts.state.oh.us/

Areas Covered: Counties of Allen, Auglaize, Crawford, Defiance, Hancock, Hardin, Henry, Logan, Marion, Mercer, Paulding, Putnam, Seneca, Shelby, Union, Van Wert and Wyandot

Note: The Clerks of the Courts of Ohio are elected officials.

Court Staff
Court Administrator **Gregory B. Miller** . . . . (419) 223-1861
E-mail: gmiller@third.courts.state.oh.us

Ohio Court of Appeals, Fourth District

Pickaway County Court House, 207 South Court Street, Circleville, OH 43113
Tel: (740) 474-5233 Fax: (740) 477-3976
Internet: www.4thdistrictappeals.com

Areas Covered: Counties of Adams, Athens, Gallia, Highland, Hocking, Jackson, Lawrence, Meigs, Pickaway, Pike, Ross, Scioto, Vinton and Washington

Note: The Clerks of the Courts of Ohio are elected officials.

Court Staff
Court Administrator **Sharon Maerten-Moore** . . . . (740) 779-6662

Ohio Court of Appeals, Fifth District

110 Central Plaza South, Suite 320, Canton, OH 44702-1411
Tel: (330) 451-7765 Tel: (800) 369-4528
Tel: (800) 750-0750 (TTY) Fax: (330) 451-7249
Internet: www.fifthdist.org

Areas Covered: Counties of Ashland, Coshocton, Delaware, Fairfield, Guernsey, Holmes, Knox, Licking, Morgan, Morrow, Muskingum, Perry, Richland, Stark and Tuscarawas

Note: The Clerks of the Courts of Ohio are elected officials.

Court Staff
Court Administrator **Melinda S. Cooper** . . . . (330) 451-7765
E-mail: mscooper@co.stark.oh.us

(continued on next page)

Ohio Court of Appeals, Sixth District

One Constitution Avenue, Toledo, OH 43604-1681
Tel: (419) 213-4755 Fax: (419) 213-4844
E-mail: 6thca@co.lucas.oh.us
Internet: http://www.co.lucas.oh.us/Appeals/

Areas Covered: Counties of Erie, Fulton, Huron, Lucas, Ottawa, Sandusky, Williams and Wood

Note: The Clerks of the Courts of Ohio are elected officials.

Court Staff
Court Administrator **Jason A. Hill** . . . . (419) 213-4755

Ohio Court of Appeals, Seventh District

131 West Federal Street, Youngstown, OH 44503-1710
Tel: (330) 740-2180 Fax: (330) 740-2182
Internet: http://www.seventh.courts.state.oh.us/

Areas Covered: Counties of Belmont, Carroll, Columbiana, Harrison, Jefferson, Mahoning, Monroe and Noble

Note: The Clerks of the Courts of Ohio are elected officials.

Court Staff
Court Administrator **Robert Budinsky** . . . . (330) 740-2180
 E-mail: seventhdistricto@aol.com

Ohio Court of Appeals, Eighth District

Cuyahoga County Courthouse, One Lakeside Avenue,
Cleveland, OH 44113
Tel: (216) 443-6350 Fax: (216) 443-2044
Internet: http://appeals.cuyahogacounty.us

Areas Covered: County of Cuyahoga

Note: The Clerks of the Courts of Ohio are elected officials.

Court Staff
Court Administrator **Ute Lindenmaier Vilfroy** . . . . (216) 443-6396
 E-mail: ulv@8thappeals.com

Ohio Court of Appeals, Ninth District

161 South High Street, Suite 504, Akron, OH 44308-1671
Tel: (330) 643-2250 Fax: (330) 643-2091
Internet: http://www.ninth.courts.state.oh.us/

Areas Covered: Counties of Lorain, Medina, Summit and Wayne

Note: The Clerks of the Courts of Ohio are elected officials.

Court Staff
Magistrate/Court Administrator **C. Michael Walsh** . . . . (330) 643-2250
 E-mail: cmwalsh@ninth.courts.state.oh.us

Ohio Court of Appeals, Tenth District

373 South High Street, 24th Floor, Columbus, OH 43215-6313
Tel: (614) 525-3580 Fax: (614) 525-7249
Internet: www.franklincountyohio.gov/appeals

Areas Covered: County of Franklin

Note: The Clerks of the Courts of Ohio are elected officials.

Court Staff
Court Administrator **Douglas W. Eaton** . . . . (614) 525-3580
 E-mail: dweaton@franklincountyohio.gov

Ohio Court of Appeals, Eleventh District

111 High Street, NE, Warren, OH 44481
Tel: (330) 675-2650 Fax: (330) 675-2655
Internet: www.11thcourt.co.trumbull.oh.us

Areas Covered: Counties of Ashtabula, Geauga, Lake, Portage and Trumbull

Note: The Clerks of the Courts of Ohio are elected officials.

Court Staff
Court Administrator **Shibani Sheth-Massacci** . . . . (330) 675-2650

Ohio Court of Appeals, Twelfth District

1001 Reinartz Boulevard, Middletown, OH 45042
Tel: (513) 425-6609 Tel: (800) 824-1883 (Toll-Free Ohio)
Fax: (513) 425-8751
Internet: www.twelfth.courts.state.oh.us

Areas Covered: Counties of Brown, Butler, Clermont, Clinton, Fayette, Madison, Preble and Warren

Note: The Clerks of the Courts of Ohio are elected officials.

Court Staff
Court Administrator **Bennett A. Manning** . . . . (513) 425-6609

County-By-County

Adams County

Clerk of Courts

Adams County
110 West Main Street, West Union, OH 45693
Tel: (937) 544-2921 Fax: (937) 544-8911

Clerk of Court **Larry Heller** . . . . (937) 544-2344
 E-mail: lheller@adamscountycourts.com

Allen County

Clerk of Courts

Allen County
301 North Main Street, Lima, OH 45802
P.O. Box 1243, Lima, OH 45802
Tel: (419) 223-8525 Fax: (419) 224-9269
Internet: www.co.allen.oh.us/ccom.php

Clerk of the Court **Margie J. Miller** . . . . (419) 223-8512
 Allen County Courthouse, 301 N. Main St.,   Fax: (419) 222-8427
 Lima, OH 45801
 P.O. Box 1243, Lima, OH 45802
 E-mail: mmiller@allencountyohio.com

Ashland County

Clerk of Courts

Ashland County
142 West Second Street, Ashland, OH 44805
Tel: (419) 282-4291 Fax: (419) 281-8315
Internet: www.ashlandcommonpleas.com

Clerk of the Court **Annette Shaw** . . . . (419) 282-4242
 Ashland County Courthouse, 142 W. Second St.,
 Ashland, OH 44805
 E-mail: clerkofcourts@ashlandcounty.org

Ashtabula County

Clerk of Courts

Ashtabula County
25 West Jefferson Street, Jefferson, OH 44047
Tel: (440) 576-3686 Fax: (440) 576-1426
Internet: www.court.co.ashtabula.oh.us

Clerk of the Court **Tami Pentek** . . . .(440) 576-3637
Ashtabula County Courthouse, 25 W. Jefferson St.,   Fax: (440) 576-2819
Jefferson, OH 44047

Athens County

Clerk of Courts

Athens County
One South Court Street, Athens, OH 45701
Tel: (740) 592-3242 Fax: (740) 592-3282
Internet: www.athensoh.org

Clerk of the Court **Ann C. Trout** . . . . (740) 592-3244
Athens County Courthouse, Court Street, 4th Floor,   Fax: (740) 592-3282
Athens, OH 45701-0290
E-mail: atrout@athensoh.org

Auglaize County

Clerk of Courts

Auglaize County
201 South Willipie Street, Suite 207, Wapakoneta, OH 45895
Tel: (419) 739-6770 Fax: (419) 739-6771
Internet: www2.auglaizecounty.org/courts/common-pleas

Clerk of the Court **Jean Meckstroth** . . . . (419) 739-6769
P.O. Box 409, Wapakoneta, OH 45895   Fax: (419) 739-6768
E-mail: jmeckstroth@auglaizecounty.org

Belmont County

Clerk of Courts

Belmont County
101 West Main Street, Saint Clairsville, OH 43950
Tel: (740) 699-2138

Clerk of the Court **Cynthia McGee** . . . .(740) 699-2169
Belmont County Courthouse,
Saint Clairsville, OH 43950
E-mail: cmcgee@belmontcountycoc.com

Brown County

Clerk of Courts

Brown County
Brown County Courthouse, 101 South Main, Georgetown, OH 45121
Tel: (937) 378-3100
Internet: www.browncountyclerkofcourts.org

Clerk of the Court **L. Clark Gray** . . . . (937) 378-6358
Brown County Courthouse, 101 South Main,
Georgetown, OH 45121

Butler County

Clerk of Courts

Butler County
Butler County Government Service Center, 315 High Street,
Third Floor, Hamilton, OH 45011
Tel: (513) 785-6550 Fax: (513) 785-5719
Internet: www.bccommonpleas.org

Clerk of the Courts **Mary L. Swain** . . . .(513) 887-3278
Butler County Government Service Center,   Fax: (513) 887-3966
315 High Street, Hamilton, OH 45011

Carroll County

Clerk of Courts

Carroll County
119 South Lisbon, Suite 400, Carrollton, OH 44615
P.O. Box 367, Carrollton, OH 44615
Tel: (330) 627-2450 Fax: (330) 627-0985

Clerk of the Courts **William "Bill" Wohlwend** . . . . (330) 627-4886
P.O. Box 367, Carrollton, OH 44615
E-mail: bwohlwend@carrollcountyohio.us

Champaign County

Clerk of Courts

Champaign County
200 North Main Street, Urbana, OH 43078
Tel: (937) 484-1000 Fax: (937) 484-1025

Clerk of the Courts **Penny S. Underwood** . . . .(937) 484-1047
Champaign County Courthouse, 200 N. Main St.,
Urbana, OH 43078

Clark County

Clerk of Courts

Clark County
101 North Limestone Street, Springfield, OH 45502
Tel: (937) 521-1760 Fax: (937) 328-2436

Clerk of the Court **Ronald Vincent** . . . .(937) 521-1680
P.O. Box 1008, Springfield, OH 45502   Fax: (937) 328-2436
E-mail: clerkofcourts@clarkcountyohio.gov

Clermont County

Clerk of Courts

Clermont County
270 Main Street, Batavia, OH 45103
Tel: (513) 732-8188 Fax: (513) 732-7987
Internet: www.clermontcommonpleas.com

Clerk of the Courts **Barbara Wiedenbein** . . . .(513) 732-8119
Clermont County Courthouse, 270 East Main Street,   Fax: (513) 732-7050
Batavia, OH 45103

(continued on next page)

Clinton County

Clerk of Courts

Clinton County
46 South South Street, 3rd Floor, Wilmington, OH 45177
Tel: (937) 382-3640 Fax: (937) 383-3455
E-mail: commonpleas@clintoncountycourts.org

Clerk of the Court **Cynthia R. Bailey** . . . . (937) 382-2316
Clinton County Courthouse, 46 S. South St.,   Fax: (937) 383-3455
Third Floor, Wilmington, OH 45177
E-mail: cbailey@clintoncountycourts.org

Columbiana County

Clerk of Courts

Columbiana County
105 South Market Street, Lisbon, OH 44432
Tel: (330) 424-7777 Fax: (330) 424-3960
Internet: www.ccclerk.org/common_pleas.htm

Clerk of the Court **Anthony J. Dattilio** . . . .(330) 424-7777
Columbiana County Courthouse, 105 S. Market St.,
Lisbon, OH 44432
E-mail: tdattilio@ccclerk.org

Coshocton County

Clerk of Courts

Coshocton County
318 Main Street, 2nd Floor, Coshocton, OH 43812
Tel: (740) 622-1456 Fax: (740) 295-0020
Internet: www.coshoctoncounty.net/agency/coc/

Clerk of the Court **Janet Mosier** . . . . (740) 622-1456
E-mail: janetmosier@coshoctoncounty.net   Fax: (740) 295-0020

Crawford County

Clerk of Courts

Crawford County
112 East Mansfield Street, Suite 200, Bucyrus, OH 44820
Tel: (419) 562-5771 Fax: (419) 562-8011

Clerk of the Court **Sheila Lester** . . . . (419) 562-2766
112 East Mansfield Street, Suite 204,   Fax: (419) 562-8011
Bucyrus, OH 44820
E-mail: clerk@crawford-co.org

Cuyahoga County

Clerk of Courts

Cuyahoga County
1200 Ontario Street, Cleveland, OH 44113-1678
Tel: (216) 443-8560 Fax: (216) 443-5424
Internet: http://cp.cuyahogacounty.us/internet/index.aspx

Clerk of the Court **Nailah K. Byrd** . . . .(216) 443-7952
E-mail: clerk_of_courts@cuyahogacounty.us

Darke County

Clerk of Courts

Darke County
504 South Broadway, Greenville, OH 45331
Tel: (937) 547-7337 Fax: (937) 547-6104

Clerk of the Court **Cindy Pike** . . . .(937) 547-7336
Darke County Courthouse,   Fax: (419) 782-2734
Greenville, OH 45331
E-mail: cpike@co.darke.oh.us

Defiance County

Clerk of Courts

Defiance County
221 Clinton Street, Third Floor, Defiance, OH 43512
P.O. Box 386, Defiance, OH 43512
Tel: (419) 782-5931 Fax: (419) 782-2437
E-mail: cpcourt@defiance-county.com
Internet: www.defiance-county.com/commonpleas/index.html

Clerk of the Court **Amy M. Galbraith** . . . .(419) 782-1936
Defiance County Courthouse, 221 Clinton St.,   Fax: (419) 784-2739
2nd Floor, Defiance, OH 43512
E-mail: clerk@defiance-county.com

Delaware County

Clerk of Courts

Delaware County
91 North Sandusky Street, Delaware, OH 43015
Tel: (740) 833-2550 Fax: (740) 833-2549
Internet: www.co.delaware.oh.us/court/index.asp

Clerk of the Court **Jan Antonoplos** . . . . (740) 833-2500
Delaware County Courthouse, 1st Fl.,   Fax: (740) 833-2499
91 N. Sandusky St., Delaware, OH 43015
E-mail: jana@co.delaware.oh.us

Erie County

Clerk of Courts

Erie County
323 Columbus Avenue, Sandusky, OH 44870
Tel: (419) 627-7731 Fax: (419) 627-6602

Clerk of the Court **Luvada Wilson** . . . . (419) 627-7708
Erie County Courthouse, 323 Columbus Ave.,   Fax: (419) 624-6873
Sandusky, OH 44870
E-mail: lwilson@eriecounty.oh.gov

Fairfield County

Clerk of Courts

Fairfield County
224 East Main Street, Lancaster, OH 43130
Tel: (740) 652-7387

Clerk of the Court **Branden C. Meyer** . . . . (740) 652-7387
Hall of Justice, 224 E. Main St.,   Fax: (740) 687-0158
Lancaster, OH 43130
P.O. Box 370, Lancaster, OH 43130-0370
E-mail: bmeyer@co.fairfield.oh.us

Ohio Court Clerks and Courthouses *continued*

Fayette County

Clerk of Courts

Fayette County
110 East Court Street, Washington Court House, OH 43160
Tel: (740) 335-4750 Fax: (740) 333-3557
Internet: www.fayette-co-oh.com/commplea/index.html

Clerk of the Court **Evelyn A. Pentzer** . . . . (614) 335-6371
Fayette County Courthouse, 110 E. Court St.,   Fax: (740) 333-3522
Washington Court House, OH 43160
E-mail: evelyn.pentzer@fayette-co-oh.com

Franklin County

Clerk of Courts

Franklin County
345 South High Street, 2nd Floor, Columbus, OH 43215
Tel: (614) 525-7492 Fax: (614) 525-4480

Clerk of Courts **Maryellen O'Shaughnessy** . . . . (614) 525-3600
373 South High Street, 23rd Floor,
Columbus, OH 43215-6313

Fulton County

Clerk of Courts

Fulton County
210 South Fulton Street, Wauseon, OH 43567
Tel: (419) 337-9260 Fax: (419) 337-9293

Clerk of the Court **Paul MacDonald** . . . . (419) 337-9230
Fulton County Courthouse, 210 S. Fulton St.,   Fax: (419) 337-9199
Wauseon, OH 43567
E-mail: pmacdonald@fultoncountyoh.com

Gallia County

Clerk of Courts

Gallia County
Gallia County Courthouse, 18 Locust Street, Gallipolis, OH 45631-1290
Tel: (740) 446-4612 Fax: (740) 441-2051
Internet: www.gallianet.net/Gallia/common_pleas.htm

Clerk of the Court **Noreen M. Saunders** . . . . (740) 446-4612 ext. 223
Gallia County Courthouse, 18 Locust Street,   Fax: (740) 441-2932
Room 1290, Gallipolis, OH 45631-1290
E-mail: clerkofcourts@gallianet.net

Geauga County

Clerk of Courts

Geauga County
100 Short Court Street, Chardon, OH 44024
Tel: (440) 279-1960 Fax: (440) 286-2127
Internet: www.geaugacourts.org

Clerk of the Court **Denise M. Kaminski** . . . . (440) 279-1960
Geauga County Courthouse,
Chardon, OH 44024
E-mail: dkaminski@geaugacourts.org

Ohio Court Clerks and Courthouses *continued*

Greene County

Clerk of Courts

Greene County
45 North Detroit Street, Xenia, OH 45385
Tel: (937) 562-5300
Internet: www.co.greene.oh.us/CPC/default.asp

Clerk of the Court **Terri A. Mazur** . . . . (937) 562-5295
Greene County Courthouse, 45 N. Detroit St.,   Fax: (937) 562-5309
Xenia, OH 45385
E-mail: tmazur@co.greene.oh.us

Guernsey County

Clerk of Courts

Guernsey County
801 Wheeling Avenue, Cambridge, OH 43725
Tel: (740) 432-9230 Fax: (740) 432-7807

Clerk of the Court **Teresa A. Dankovic** . . . . (740) 432-9230
Guernsey County Courthouse, 801 Wheeling Ave.,   Fax: (740) 432-7807
Cambridge, OH 43725
E-mail: tdankovic@guernseycounty.org

Hamilton County

Clerk of Courts

Hamilton County
1000 Main Street, Room 410, Cincinnati, OH 45202
Tel: (513) 946-5800 Fax: (513) 946-5808
Internet: www.hamilton-co.org/common_pleas

Clerk of the Court **Tracy Winkler** . . . . (513) 946-5656
                                                          Fax: (513) 946-3744

Hancock County

Clerk of Courts

Hancock County
300 South Main Street, Findlay, OH 45840
Tel: (419) 424-7008 Fax: (419) 424-7878
Internet: www.co.hancock.oh.us/commonpleas

Clerk of the Court **Cathy Prosser Wilcox** . . . . (419) 424-7037
300 South Main Street, Findlay, OH 45840   Fax: (419) 424-7801
E-mail: cawilcox@co.hancock.oh.us

Hardin County

Clerk of Courts

Hardin County
One Courthouse Square, Kenton, OH 43326
Tel: (419) 674-2256 Fax: (419) 674-2264
E-mail: commonpleas@hardincourts.com
Internet: www.hardincourts.com/CPSite

Clerk of the Court **Carrie L. Haudenschield** . . . . (419) 674-2282
One Courthouse Square, Suite 310,   Fax: (419) 674-2273
Kenton, OH 43326
E-mail: clerkofcourts@hardincourts.com

(continued on next page)

Harrison County

Clerk of Courts

Harrison County
100 West Market Street, Cadiz, OH 43907
Tel: (740) 942-8500   Fax: (740) 942-3006

Clerk of the Court **Leslie Milliken** . . . . (740) 942-8863
E-mail: lamilliken@frontier.com

Henry County

Clerk of Courts

Henry County
660 North Perry Street, Suite 301, Napoleon, OH 43545
Tel: (419) 592-5926   Fax: (419) 599-0803
E-mail: common.pleas@henrycountyohio.com
Internet: www.henrycountyohio.com/judgegeneralprobate.htm

Clerk of the Court **Connie Schnitkey** . . . . (419) 592-5886
Henry County Courthouse, 660 N. Perry St.,   Fax: (419) 592-5888
Suite 302, Napoleon, OH 43545
E-mail: connie.schnitkey@henrycountyohio.com

Highland County

Clerk of Courts

Highland County
105 North High Street, Hillsboro, OH 45133
Tel: (937) 393-2161   Fax: (937) 393-2989
E-mail: commonpleas@co.highland.oh.us

Clerk of the Court **Dwight "Ike" Hodson** . . . . (937) 393-9957
Highland County Courthouse, 105 N. High Street,   Fax: (937) 393-9878
Hillsboro, OH 45133
P.O. Box 821, Hillsboro, OH 45133
E-mail: clerkofcourts@co.highland.oh.us

Hocking County

Clerk of Courts

Hocking County
One East Main Street, Logan, OH 43138
Tel: (740) 385-4027
Internet: www.hockingcountycommonpleascourt.com

Clerk of the Court **Sharon Edwards** . . . . (740) 385-2616
Hocking County Courthouse, 1 E. Main Street,   Fax: (740) 385-1822
Logan, OH 43138
P.O. Box 108, Logan, OH 43138
E-mail: clerkofcourts@co.hocking.oh.us

Holmes County

Clerk of Courts

Holmes County
One East Jackson Street, Millersburg, OH 44654
Tel: (330) 674-5086   Fax: (330) 674-0289

Clerk of the Court **Ronda P. Steimel** . . . . (330) 674-1876
Holmes County Courthouse,   Fax: (330) 674-0289
One East Jackson St., Suite 306,
Millersburg, OH 44654
E-mail: rsteimel@co.holmes.oh.us

Huron County

Clerk of Courts

Huron County
Two East Main Street, Suite 202, Norwalk, OH 44857
Tel: (419) 668-6162   Fax: (419) 663-4048
Internet: www.huroncountycommonpleas.org

Clerk of the Court **Susan S. Hazel** . . . . (419) 668-5113
Huron County Courthouse, Two E. Main St.,   Fax: (419) 663-4048
Suite 207, Norwalk, OH 44857
E-mail: clerk@huroncountyclerk.com

Jackson County

Clerk of Courts

Jackson County
Jackson County Courthouse, 226 East Main Street,
Jackson, OH 45640-1791
Tel: (740) 286-3601

Clerk of the Court **Seth I. Michael** . . . . (740) 286-2006
Jackson County Courthouse, 226 East Main Street,   Fax: (740) 286-5186
Jackson, OH 45640-1791

Jefferson County

Clerk of Courts

Jefferson County
301 Market Street, Steubenville, OH 43952
Tel: (740) 283-8543

Clerk of the Court **John A. Corrigan** . . . . (740) 283-8583
P.O. Box 1326, Steubenville, OH 43952   Fax: (740) 283-8597

Knox County

Clerk of Courts

Knox County
111 East High Street, Second Floor, Mount Vernon, OH 43050
Tel: (740) 393-6777   Fax: (740) 393-5096
E-mail: commonpleas@co.knox.oh.us

Clerk of the Court **Mary Jo Hawkins** . . . . (740) 393-6788
Knox County Courthouse, 117 E. High St., 2nd Fl.,   Fax: (740) 392-3533
Mount Vernon, OH 43050
E-mail: clerkofcourts@co.knox.oh.us

Lake County

Clerk of Courts

Lake County
47 North Park Place, Painesville, OH 44077
Tel: (440) 350-2708

Clerk of the Court **Maureen G. Kelly** . . . . (440) 350-2657
Lake County Courthouse, 52 N. Park Pl.,   Fax: (440) 350-2958
Painesville, OH 44077
E-mail: maureen.kelly@lakecountyohio.gov

Lawrence County

Clerk of Courts

Lawrence County
111 South 4th Street, 3rd Floor, Ironton, OH 45638
Tel: (740) 533-4329 Fax: (740) 533-4377

Clerk of the Court **Michael P. Patterson** . . . .(740) 533-4355
Lawrence County Courthouse, 111 S. 4th Street,   Fax: (740) 533-4383
Ironton, OH 45638
P.O. Box 208, Ironton, OH 45638

Licking County

Clerk of Courts

Licking County
75 East Main Street, Newark, OH 43055
Tel: (740) 670-5797 Fax: (740) 670-5886

Clerk of the Court **Gary R. Walters** . . . . (740) 670-5794
Licking County Courthouse, 2nd Fl.,   Fax: (740) 670-5886
Newark, OH 43055
P.O. Box 4370, Newark, OH 43058-4370

Logan County

Clerk of Courts

Logan County
101 South Main Street, Bellefontaine, OH 43311
Tel: (937) 599-7260 Fax: (937) 292-4175
Internet: www.co.logan.oh.us/commonpleas

Clerk of the Court **Barb McDonald** . . . .(937) 599-7258
Logan County Courthouse,   Fax: (937) 599-7281
101 South Main Street, 2nd Floor, Room 12,
Bellefontaine, OH 43311
E-mail: bmcdonald@co.logan.oh.us

Lorain County

Clerk of Courts

Lorain County
225 Court Street, Elyria, OH 44035
Tel: (440) 329-5536 Fax: (440) 328-2416

Clerk of Court **Tom Orlando** . . . . (440) 329-5542
225 Court Street, Elyria, OH 44035   Fax: (440) 328-2163

Lucas County

Clerk of Courts

Lucas County
700 Adams Street, Toledo, OH 43604-5658
Tel: (419) 213-4777 Fax: (419) 213-4181

Clerk of the Court **J. Bernie Quilter** . . . .(419) 213-4484
E-mail: bquilter@co.lucas.oh.us   Fax: (419) 213-4487

Madison County

Clerk of Courts

Madison County
One North Main Street, London, OH 43140
Tel: (740) 845-1780 Fax: (740) 852-7144

Clerk of the Court **Renae Zabloudil** . . . . (740) 852-9776
Madison County Courthouse, One N. Main St.,   Fax: (740) 845-1778
London, OH 43140
E-mail: clerkofcourts@co.madison.oh.us

Mahoning County

Clerk of Courts

Mahoning County
120 Market Street, Youngstown, OH 44503
Tel: (330) 740-2158 Fax: (330) 740-2088

Clerk of the Courts **Anthony Vivo, Jr.** . . . . (330) 740-2104
  Fax: (330) 740-2105

Marion County

Clerk of Courts

Marion County
100 North Main Street, Marion, OH 43302
Tel: (740) 223-4000

Clerk of the Court **Julie M. Kagel** . . . .(740) 223-4270
Marion County Courthouse, 100 North Main Street,   Fax: (740) 223-4279
Marion, OH 43302
E-mail: jkagle@co.marion.oh.us

Medina County

Clerk of Courts

Medina County
93 Public Square, Second Floor, Medina, OH 44256
Tel: (330) 725-9131 Fax: (330) 764-8791
Internet: www.medinacommonpleas.com

Clerk of Court **David Wadsworth** . . . .(330) 725-9722
93 Public Square, Medina, OH 44256   Fax: (330) 764-8454
E-mail: dwadsworth@medinaco.org

Meigs County

Clerk of Courts

Meigs County
100 East Second Street, Pomeroy, OH 45769
Tel: (740) 992-5290 Fax: (740) 992-3828
E-mail: meigscommonpleascourt@yahoo.com

Clerk of the Court **Diane Lynch** . . . .(740) 992-5290
Meigs County Courthouse, 100 Second Street,   Fax: (740) 992-4429
Pomeroy, OH 45769
P.O. Box 151, Pomeroy, OH 45769

(continued on next page)

Mercer County

Clerk of Courts

Mercer County
Mercer County Courthouse, 101 North Main Street, Room 301,
Celina, OH 45822
Tel: (419) 586-2122 Fax: (419) 586-4000
Internet: www.mercercountyohio.org

Clerk of the Court **Kevin McKirnan** . . . . (419) 586-6461
Mercer County Courthouse,   Fax: (419) 586-5826
101 North Main Street, Room 205,
Celina, OH 45822
P.O. Box 28, Celina, OH 45822
E-mail: clerk@mercercountyohio.org

Miami County

Clerk of Courts

Miami County
201 West Main Street, Troy, OH 45373
Tel: (937) 440-6010 Fax: (937) 440-6011
Internet: http://co.miami.oh.us/A55969/mcounty.nsf/All/
Common%20Pleas-main

Clerk of the Court **Jan A. Mottinger** . . . . (937) 440-6010
Miami County Safety Bldg., 201 W. Main St.,   Fax: (937) 440-6011
Troy, OH 45373
E-mail: jmottinger@co.miami.oh.us

Monroe County

Clerk of Courts

Monroe County
101 North Main Street, Woodsfield, OH 43793
P.O. Box 563, Woodsfield, OH 43793
Tel: (740) 472-0841 Fax: (740) 472-2518

Clerk of the Court **Beth Ann Rose** . . . . (740) 472-0761
Monroe County Courthouse, 101 Main St.,   Fax: (740) 472-2549
Woodsfield, OH 43793
E-mail: monroecountyclerkofcourts@yahoo.com

Montgomery County

Clerk of Courts

Montgomery County
41 North Perry Street, Dayton, OH 45422-2170
Tel: (937) 225-6000 Fax: (937) 496-7389
Internet: http://montcourt.org/

Clerk of the Court **Gregory A. Brush** . . . . (937) 225-6118

Morgan County

Clerk of Courts

Morgan County
19 East Main Street, McConnelsville, OH 43756
Tel: (740) 962-3371

Clerk of the Courts, Morgan County **Carma Johnson** . . . . (740) 962-1386
                                            Fax: (740) 962-4522

Morrow County

Clerk of Courts

Morrow County
48 High Street, Mount Gilead, OH 43338
Tel: (419) 947-4515 Fax: (419) 947-4406
Internet: www.morrowcommonpleas.com

Clerk of the Court **Vanessa K. Mills** . . . . (419) 947-2085
                                            Fax: (419) 947-5421

Muskingum County

Clerk of Courts

Muskingum County
401 Main Street, Zanesville, OH 43701
Tel: (740) 455-7142 Fax: (740) 455-7177

Clerk of the Court **Todd Bickle** . . . . (740) 455-7104
Muskingum County Courthouse, 401 Main St.,   Fax: (740) 455-7177
Zanesville, OH 43701
E-mail: tabickle@muskingumcounty.org

Noble County

Clerk of Courts

Noble County
350 Court House, Caldwell, OH 43724
Tel: (740) 732-4408

Clerk of the Court **Karen S. Starr** . . . . (740) 732-5604
Noble County Courthouse,
Caldwell, OH 43724
E-mail: clerkofcourtsnoble@yahoo.com

Ottawa County

Clerk of Courts

Ottawa County
315 Madison Street, Room 301, Port Clinton, OH 43452
Tel: (419) 734-6790 Fax: (419) 734-6852
Internet: www.ottawacocpcourt.com/index.htm

Clerk of the Court **Gary Kohli** . . . . (419) 734-6755
Ottawa County Courthouse, 315 Madison St.,   Fax: (419) 734-6875
Room 304, Port Clinton, OH 43452

Paulding County

Clerk of Courts

Paulding County
Paulding County Courthouse, 115 North Williams Street,
Paulding, OH 45879
Tel: (419) 399-8220 Fax: (419) 399-8224

Clerk of the Court **Ann E. Pease** . . . . (419) 399-8210
Paulding County Courthouse,   Fax: (419) 399-8248
115 North Williams Street,
Paulding, OH 45879
E-mail: clerk@pauldingcountyoh.com

Ohio Court Clerks and Courthouses *continued*

Perry County

Clerk of Courts

Perry County
105 North Main Street, New Lexington, OH 43764
P.O. Box 7, New Lexington, OH 43764
Tel: (740) 342-1204 Fax: (740) 342-5500

Clerk of the Court **Timothy J. Wollenberg** . . . . (740) 342-1022
  Perry County Courthouse, 105 N. Main St.,   Fax: (740) 342-5527
  New Lexington, OH 43764
  P.O. Box 67, New Lexington, OH 43764

Pickaway County

Clerk of Courts

Pickaway County
207 South Court Street, Circleville, OH 43113
Tel: (740) 474-6026 Fax: (740) 477-6334
Internet: www.pickaway.org/cpcourt.htm

Clerk of the Court **James W. Dean** . . . . (740) 474-5231
  Pickaway County Courthouse, 207 S Court Street,   Fax: (740) 477-3976
  Circleville, OH 43113
  P.O. Box 270, Circleville, OH 43113

Pike County

Clerk of Courts

Pike County
100 East Second Street, Waverly, OH 45690
Tel: (740) 947-2212

Clerk of the Court **John E. Williams** . . . . (740) 947-2715
  Pike County Courthouse, 100 E. Second Street,   Fax: (740) 947-1729
  Waverly, OH 45690
  E-mail: pikecountycourt@yahoo.com

Portage County

Clerk of Courts

Portage County
203 West Main Street, Ravenna, OH 44266
Tel: (330) 297-3878 Fax: (330) 297-5370
Internet: www.co.portage.oh.us/commonpleas.htm

Clerk of the Court **Linda Fankhauser** . . . . (330) 297-3644
  Portage County Courthouse, 203 W. Main St.,   Fax: (330) 297-4554
  Ravenna, OH 44266
  E-mail: lfankhauser@portageco.com

Preble County

Clerk of Courts

Preble County
101 East Main Street, 3rd Floor, Eaton, OH 45320
Tel: (937) 456-8165 Fax: (937) 456-9548
Internet: www.preblecountyohio.net

Clerk of the Court **Christopher B. Washington** . . . . (513) 456-8160
  Preble County Courthouse, 101 E. Main St.,
  Eaton, OH 45320
  E-mail: cwashington@preblecountyohio.net

Ohio Court Clerks and Courthouses *continued*

Putnam County

Clerk of Courts

Putnam County
245 East Main Street, Ottawa, OH 45875
Tel: (419) 523-6200
Internet: http://courts.putnamcountyohio.gov/

Clerk of the Court **Teresa Lammers** . . . . (419) 523-3110
  Putnam County Courthouse,   Fax: (419) 523-5284
  245 East Main Street, Suite 301,
  Ottawa, OH 45875
  E-mail: tlammers@nwbright.net

Richland County

Clerk of Courts

Richland County
50 Park Avenue East, Mansfield, OH 44902
Tel: (419) 774-5570
Internet: www.richlandcountyoh.us/cpc.htm

Clerk of the Court **Linda H. Frary** . . . . (419) 774-5655
  Richland County Courthouse, 50 Park Ave.,   Fax: (419) 774-5547
  Mansfield, OH 44901
  P.O. Box 127, Mansfield, OH 44901
  E-mail: frary.l@cpcnet.co.richland.oh.us

Ross County

Clerk of Courts

Ross County
Two North Paint Street, Chillicothe, OH 45601
Tel: (740) 775-0333 Fax: (740) 775-2695

Clerk of the Court **Ty D. Hinton** . . . . (740) 775-0333
  Ross County Courthouse, 2 North Paint Street,   Fax: (740) 702-3018
  Chillicothe, OH 45601
  E-mail: rcclerk@bright.net

Sandusky County

Clerk of Courts

Sandusky County
100 North Park Avenue, Second Floor, Fremont, OH 43420
Tel: (419) 334-6170 Fax: (419) 334-6171

Clerk of the Court **Tracy Overmyer** . . . . (419) 334-6151
  Sandusky County Courthouse, 100 N. Park Ave.,   Fax: (419) 334-6164
  Fremont, OH 43420
  E-mail: clerk.of.courts@co.sandusky.oh.us

Scioto County

Clerk of Courts

Scioto County
602 Seventh Street, Portsmouth, OH 45662
Tel: (740) 355-8207

Clerk of the Court **Lisa D. Novinger** . . . . (740) 355-8210
  205 Scioto County Courthose,   Fax: (740) 354-2057
  602 Seventh Street, Room 205,
  Portsmouth, OH 45662
  E-mail: lwhite@sciotocounty.net

(continued on next page)

Seneca County

Clerk of Courts

Seneca County
Seneca County Courthouse, 117 East Market Street, Tiffin, OH 44883
Tel: (419) 448-1302
Internet: www.senecacocourts.org

Clerk of the Court **Mary K. Ward** . . . . (419) 447-0671
Seneca County Courthouse,   Fax: (419) 443-7919
117 East Market Street, Suite 4101,
Tiffin, OH 44883
E-mail: mward@acctiffin.com

Shelby County

Clerk of Courts

Shelby County
129 East Court Street, Third Floor, Sidney, OH 45365
P.O. Box 947, Sidney, OH 45365
Tel: (937) 498-7808   Fax: (937) 498-7824

Clerk of the Court **Michele K. Mumford** . . . . (937) 498-7221
Shelby County Courthouse, 100 East Court Street,   Fax: (937) 498-4840
Sidney, OH 45365
P.O. Box 809, Sidney, OH 45365
E-mail: mmumford@shelbycountyclerkofcourts.com

Stark County

Clerk of Courts

Stark County
115 Central Plaza North, Canton, OH 44702
Tel: (330) 451-7931   Fax: (330) 451-7740

Clerk of the Court **Nancy S. Reinbold** . . . . (330) 451-7792
County Office Building, 110 Central Plz. S.,   Fax: (330) 451-7852
Canton, OH 44702
E-mail: nsreinbold@co.stark.oh.us

Summit County

Clerk of Courts

Summit County
209 South High Street, Akron, OH 44308
Tel: (330) 643-2162   Fax: (330) 643-7791
Internet: www.summitcpcourt.net

Clerk of Court **Daniel M. Horrigan** . . . . (330) 643-2208
161 South High Street, Suite 502,   Fax: (330) 643-8307
Akron, OH 44308
E-mail: dhorrigan@summitoh.net

Trumbull County

Clerk of Courts

Trumbull County
161 High Street, Warren, OH 44481
Tel: (330) 675-2577

Clerk of the Court **Karen Infante Allen** . . . . (330) 675-2559
Trumbull County Courthouse, 160 High St., NW,
Warren, OH 44481
E-mail: clallen@co.trumbull.oh.us

Tuscarawas County

Clerk of Courts

Tuscarawas County
101 East High Avenue, New Philadelphia, OH 44663
Tel: (330) 365-3217   Fax: (330) 602-8811

Clerk of the Court **Jeanne M. Stephen** . . . . (330) 365-3243 ext. 3116
Tuscarawas County Courthouse,   Fax: (330) 343-4682
125 E. High Ave., Rm. 230,
New Philadelphia, OH 44663
E-mail: stephen@co.tuscarawas.oh.us

Union County

Clerk of Courts

Union County
215 West Fifth Street, Marysville, OH 43040
Tel: (937) 645-3015   Fax: (937) 645-3149

Clerk of the Court **Teresa L. Nickle** . . . . (937) 645-3006
215 West Fifth Street, Marysville, OH 43040   Fax: (937) 645-3162
E-mail: tnickle@co.union.oh.us

Van Wert County

Clerk of Courts

Van Wert County
121 East Main Street, Room 305, Van Wert, OH 45891
Tel: (419) 238-6935   Fax: (419) 238-2874
Internet: www.vwcommonpleas.org

Clerk of the Court **Cindy Mollenkopf** . . . . (419) 238-1022
121 East Main Street, 3rd Floor,   Fax: (419) 238-4760
Van Wert, OH 45891

Vinton County

Clerk of Courts

Vinton County
100 East Main Street, McArthur, OH 45651
Tel: (740) 596-4319
E-mail: clerkofcourts@co.vinton.oh.us
Internet: www.vintoncounty.com/Court_of_Common_Pleas.htm

Clerk of the Court **Lisa Gilliland** . . . . (740) 596-3001
Vinton County Courthouse, 100 E. Main St.,   Fax: (740) 596-9611
McArthur, OH 45651

Warren County

Clerk of Courts

Warren County
500 Justice Drive, Lebanon, OH 45036
Tel: (513) 695-1346   Fax: (513) 695-1757
Internet: www.co.warren.oh.us/commonpleas/index.htm

Clerk of the Court **James L. Spaeth** . . . . (513) 695-1869
Warren County Courthouse, 500 Justice Dr.,   Fax: (513) 695-2965
Lebanon, OH 45036
P.O. Box 238, Lebanon, OH 45036
E-mail: james.spaeth@co.warren.oh.us

Washington County

Clerk of Courts

Washington County
Washington County Courthouse, 205 Putnam Street, Marietta, OH 45750
Tel: (740) 373-6623 Fax: (740) 373-5713
Internet: www.washingtongov.org/cl-commonpleas.htm

Clerk of the Court **Brenda L. Wolfe** . . . . (740) 373-6623 ext. 365
  Washington County Courthouse, 205 Putnam Street,   Fax: (740) 374-3758
  Marietta, OH 45750
  E-mail: clerkofcourts@washingtongov.org

Wayne County

Clerk of Courts

Wayne County
107 West Liberty Street, Wooster, OH 44691
Tel: (330) 287-5590
Internet: www.wayneohio.org/public_access.php

Clerk of Court **Tim Neal** . . . . (330) 287-5590
  P.O. Box 507, Wooster, OH 44691-0113   Fax: (330) 287-5416
  E-mail: tneal@waynecountycourthouse.com

Williams County

Clerk of Courts

Williams County
One Courthouse Square, Bryan, OH 43506
Tel: (419) 636-2644 Fax: (419) 636-9886

Clerk of the Court **Kimberly L. Herman** . . . . (419) 636-1551
  Williams County Courthouse, One Courthouse Sq.,   Fax: (419) 636-7877
  Bryan, OH 43506

Wood County

Clerk of Courts

Wood County
One Courthouse Square, Bowling Green, OH 43402
Tel: (419) 354-9042

Clerk of the Court **Cindy Hofner** . . . . (419) 354-9280
  Wood County Courthouse, One Courthouse Sq.,   Fax: (419) 354-9241
  Bowling Green, OH 43402
  E-mail: clerkofcourts@co.wood.oh.us

Wyandot County

Clerk of Courts

Wyandot County
Wyandot County Courthouse, 109 South Sandusky Avenue,
Room 34, Upper Sandusky, OH 43351
Tel: (419) 294-1727 Fax: (419) 209-0251

Clerk of the Court **Ann Dunbar** . . . . (419) 294-1432
  Wyandot County Courthouse,   Fax: (419) 294-6414
  109 South Sandusky Avenue, Room 31,
  Upper Sandusky, OH 43351
  E-mail: akdunbar@co.wyandot.oh.us

Counties Within Appellate Districts

Court of Appeals, 1st District
Areas Covered: Hamilton County.

Court of Appeals, 2nd District
Areas Covered: Champaign, Clark, Darke, Greene, Miami, and
Montgomery Counties.

Court of Appeals, 3rd District
Areas Covered: Allen, Auglaize, Crawford, Defiance, Hancock, Hardin,
Henry, Logan, Marion, Mercer, Paulding, Putnam, Seneca, Shelby, Union,
Van Wert, and Wyandot Counties.

Court of Appeals, 4th District
Areas Covered: Adams, Athens, Gallia, Highland, Hocking, Jackson,
Lawrence, Meigs, Pickaway, Pike, Ross, Scioto, Vinton, and Washington
Counties.

Court of Appeals, 5th District
Areas Covered: Ashland, Coshocton, Delaware, Fairfield, Guernsey,
Holmes, Knox, Licking, Morgan, Morrow, Muskingum, Perry, Richland,
Stark, and Tuscarawas Counties.

Court of Appeals, 6th District
Areas Covered: Erie, Fulton, Huron, Lucas, Ottawa, Sandusky, Williams,
and Wood Counties.

Court of Appeals, 7th District
Areas Covered: Belmont, Carroll, Columbiana, Harrison, Jefferson,
Mahoning, Monroe, and Noble Counties.

Court of Appeals, 8th District
Areas Covered: Cuyahoga County.

Court of Appeals, 9th District
Areas Covered: Lorain, Medina, Summit, and Wayne Counties.

Court of Appeals, 10th District
Areas Covered: Franklin County.

Court of Appeals, 11th District
Areas Covered: Ashtabula, Geauga, Lake, Portage, and Trumbull
Counties.

Court of Appeals, 12th District
Areas Covered: Brown, Butler, Clermont, Clinton, Fayette, Madison,
Preble, and Warren Counties.

Oklahoma Court Clerks and Courthouses

The trial courts of general jurisdiction in Oklahoma are called district courts. There are 26 judicial districts, each district consisting of at least one county. Each county has a District Court Clerk and a County Clerk. District Court Clerks are given below.

Supreme Court of Oklahoma

2100 North Lincoln Boulevard, Suite 1, Oklahoma City, OK 73105
Tel: (405) 556-9300 Fax: (405) 528-1607

The Supreme Court consists of a chief justice, vice chief justice, and seven justices, one from each of the nine Supreme Court judicial districts, serving six-year terms. At the general election preceding the expiration of a term of office, a justice who wants to remain in office must file a candidacy to succeed himself. If a majority of those voters casting ballots in a nonpartisan election vote in favor of retention, the justice will serve another term. A vacancy occurring on the court during a term of office is filled by gubernatorial appointment. The Judicial Nominating Commission provides the Governor with a list of nominees which have been selected by the Commission from applicants living in the appropriate Supreme Court judicial district. The chief justice and vice chief justice are elected by peer vote to two-year terms. The Supreme Court has appellate jurisdiction over all civil cases at law and in equity. The Court has superintending control over all lower courts, agencies, commissions and boards created by law as well as administrative authority over all courts in the state, except the Court on the Judiciary and a Senate Court of Impeachment. The Court has exclusive jurisdiction over admission to the bar and the conduct of its members.

Court Staff
Clerk of the Court **Michael S. Richie** . . . . (405) 556-9400
   E-mail: michael.richie@oscn.net

Oklahoma Court of Civil Appeals

1915 North Stiles Avenue, Suite 357, Oklahoma City, OK 73105
601 State Office Building, 440 South Houston Avenue, Tulsa, OK 74127
Tel: (405) 521-3751 Tel: (918) 581-2711 (Tulsa Office)
Internet: www.oscn.net

The Court of Civil Appeals consists of a chief judge and eleven judges who are elected from the six judicial districts in nonpartisan retention elections for six-year terms. Two judges are elected from each district. Vacancies are filled by the Governor from a list submitted by the Judicial Nominating Commission. The chief judge is elected by peer vote to a one-year term. The Court sits in four divisions consisting of three judge panels. Divisions one and three sit in Oklahoma City and divisions two and four sit in Tulsa. The Court of Civil Appeals has jurisdiction over all civil cases as assigned to it by the Oklahoma Supreme Court.

Court Staff
Clerk of the Court **Michael S. Richie** . . . . (405) 556-9400
   E-mail: michael.richie@oscn.net

Oklahoma Court of Criminal Appeals

Oklahoma Judicial Center, 2100 North Lincoln Boulevard,
Suite 2, Oklahoma City, OK 73105-4907
Tel: (405) 556-9600 Fax: (405) 556-9130
Internet: www.okcca.net

The Court of Criminal Appeals is composed of five electoral districts represented by five judges who are initially appointed by the Governor from a list submitted by the Judicial Nominating Commission and thereafter, retained in statewide, nonpartisan elections for six-year terms. The positions of presiding judge and vice presiding judge rotate among the judges every two years. The Court of Criminal Appeals has exclusive appellate jurisdiction in criminal cases appealed from the Oklahoma District Courts and Municipal Criminal Courts of Record.

Court Staff
Fax: (405) 556-9130

Clerk of the Court **Michael S. Richie** . . . . (405) 556-9400
   E-mail: michael.richie@oscn.net

County-By-County

Adair County

District Court Clerk

Fifteenth Judicial District
220 West Division Street, Stilwell, OK 74960

Clerk of Court, Adair County **Nichole Cooper** . . . . (918) 696-7633
   220 West Division Street, Stilwell, OK 74960   Fax: (918) 696-5365

Alfalfa County

District Court Clerk

Fourth Judicial District
407 Government Street, Suite 30, Alva, OK 73717

Clerk of Court, Alfalfa County **Lori Irwin** . . . . (580) 596-3523
   300 South Grand Avenue,   Fax: (580) 596-2556
   Cherokee, OK 73728-2548
   E-mail: lori.irwin@oscn.net

Atoka County

District Court Clerk

Twenty-Fifth Judicial District
200 East Court Street, Atoka, OK 74525-2045

Clerk of Court, Atoka County **April Maxey** . . . . (580) 889-3565
   200 East Court Street, Atoka, OK 74525-2045   Fax: (580) 889-5075
   E-mail: april.maxey@oscn.net

Beaver County

District Court Clerk

First Judicial District
319 North Main Street, Guymon, OK 73942
P.O. Box 551, Guymon, OK 73942

Clerk of Court, Beaver County **Tammie Patzkowsky** . . . . (580) 625-3191
   111 West Second Street, Beaver, OK 73932
   E-mail: tammie.patzkowsky@oscn.net

(continued on next page)

Oklahoma Court Clerks and Courthouses *continued*

Beckham County

District Court Clerk

Second Judicial District
603 B Street, Arapaho, OK 73620
P.O. Box 180, Arapaho, OK 73620

Clerk of Court, Beckham County **Donna Howell** . . . . (580) 928-3330
  302 East Main Street, Sayre, OK 73662   Fax: (580) 928-9278
  P.O. Box 520, Sayre, OK 73662
  E-mail: donna.howell@oscn.net

Blaine County

District Court Clerk

Fourth Judicial District
407 Government Street, Suite 30, Alva, OK 73717

Clerk of Court, Blaine County **Cynthia Scheffler** . . . . (580) 623-5970
  212 North Weigel Street, Watonga, OK 73772-1286   Fax: (580) 623-4781
  E-mail: cynthia.scheffler@oscn.net

Bryan County

District Court Clerk

Nineteenth Judicial District
402 West Evergreen Street, Durant, OK 74701

Clerk of Court, Bryan County **Donna Alexander** . . . . (580) 924-1446
  402 West Evergreen Street,   Fax: (580) 931-0577
  Durant, OK 74701

Caddo County

District Court Clerk

Sixth Judicial District
Fourth and Choctaw Street, Chickasha, OK 73023-0605
P.O. Box 605, Chickasha, OK 73023-0605

Clerk of Court, Caddo County **Patti Barger** . . . . (405) 247-3393
  201 West Oklahoma Avenue,   Fax: (405) 247-4127
  Anadarko, OK 73005-3430
  P.O. Box 10, Anadarko, OK 73305-3430

Canadian County

District Court Clerk

Twenty-Sixth Judicial District
301 North Choctaw Street, El Reno, OK 73036-0730
P.O. Box 730, El Reno, OK 73036-0730

Clerk of Court, Canadian County **Marie Ramsey-Hirst** . . . (405) 262-1070
  301 North Choctaw Street,   Fax: (405) 262-1522
  El Reno, OK 73036-0730
  P.O. Box 730, El Reno, OK 73036-0730

Carter County

District Court Clerk

Twentieth Judicial District
P.O. Box 58, Madill, OK 73446

Clerk of Court, Carter County **Karen Volino** . . . . (580) 223-5253
  20 B Street SW, Ardmore, OK 73402-0037
  P.O. Box 37, Ardmore, OK 73402-0037
  E-mail: karen.volino@oscn.net

Oklahoma Court Clerks and Courthouses *continued*

Cherokee County

District Court Clerk

Fifteenth Judicial District
220 West Division Street, Stilwell, OK 74960

Clerk of Court, Cherokee County **Shelly Kissinger** . . . . . . (918) 456-0691
  213 West Delaware Street,   Fax: (918) 458-6587
  Tahlequah, OK 74464-3639
  E-mail: shelly.kissinger@oscn.net

Choctaw County

District Court Clerk

Seventeenth Judicial District
108 North Central Avenue, Idabel, OK 74745-3835
P.O. Box 1378, Idabel, OK 74745-3835

Clerk of Court, Choctaw County **Laura Sumner** . . . . (580) 326-7554
  300 East Jefferson Street, Hugo, OK 74743-4406   Fax: (580) 326-0291
  E-mail: laura.sumner@oscn.net

Cimarron County

District Court Clerk

First Judicial District
319 North Main Street, Guymon, OK 73942
P.O. Box 551, Guymon, OK 73942

Clerk of Court, Cimarron County **Debbie Kincannon** . . . . (580) 544-2221
  P.O. Box 788, Boise City, OK 73933   Fax: (580) 544-2006
  E-mail: debbie.kincannon@oscn.net

Cleveland County

District Court Clerk

Twenty-First Judicial District
200 South Peters Avenue, Norman, OK 73069-6070

Clerk of Court, Cleveland County **Rhonda Hall** . . . . (405) 321-6402
  200 South Peters Avenue, Norman, OK 73069-6070
  E-mail: rhonda.hall@oscn.net

Coal County

District Court Clerk

Twenty-Fifth Judicial District
200 East Court Street, Atoka, OK 74525-2045

Clerk of Court, Coal County **Rachel Nix** . . . . (580) 927-2281
  Four Main Street, Coalgate, OK 74538-2844   Fax: (580) 927-2339
  E-mail: rachel.nix@oscn.net

Comanche County

District Court Clerk

Fifth Judicial District
315 SW Fifth Street, Lawton, OK 73501-4327

Clerk of Court, Comanche County **Robert Morales** . . . . . . (580) 355-4017
  315 SW Fifth Street, Lawton, OK 73501-4327   Fax: (580) 248-5068
  E-mail: robert.morales@oscn.net

Cotton County

District Court Clerk

Fifth Judicial District
315 SW Fifth Street, Lawton, OK 73501-4327

Clerk of Court, Cotton County **Janet Shively** . . . . (580) 875-3137
  301 North Broadway, Walters, OK 73572
  E-mail: janet.shively@oscn.net

Craig County

District Court Clerk

Twelfth Judicial District
200 South Lynn Riggs Boulevard, Claremore, OK 74017

Clerk of Court, Craig County **Debbie Mason** . . . . (918) 256-6451
  201 West Delaware, Vinita, OK 74301   Fax: (918) 256-7606

Creek County

District Court Clerk

Twenty-Fourth Judicial District
222 East Dewey Avenue, Suite 201, Sapulpa, OK 74066-4237

Clerk of Court, Creek County **Amanda Vanorsdol** . . . . . . (918) 227-2525
  222 East Dewey Avenue, Sapulpa, OK 74066-4237   Fax: (918) 227-5030
  E-mail: amanda.vanorsdol@oscn.net

Custer County

District Court Clerk

Second Judicial District
603 B Street, Arapaho, OK 73620
P.O. Box 180, Arapaho, OK 73620

Clerk of Court, Custer County **Staci Hunter** . . . . (580) 323-3233
  603 B Street, Arapaho, OK 73620   Tel: (580) 331-1121
  P.O. Box D, Arapaho, OK 73620
  E-mail: staci.hunter@oscn.net

Delaware County

District Court Clerk

Thirteenth Judicial District
102 East Central Avenue, Miami, OK 74354-7030

Clerk of Court, Delaware County **Caroline Weaver** . . . . . . (918) 253-4420
  P.O. Box 407, Jay, OK 74346   Fax: (918) 253-5739
  E-mail: caroline.weaver@oscn.net

Dewey County

District Court Clerk

Fourth Judicial District
407 Government Street, Suite 30, Alva, OK 73717

Clerk of Court, Dewey County **Rachelle Rogers** . . . . (580) 328-5521
  P.O. Box 278, Taloga, OK 73667   Tel: (580) 328-5658
  Broadway and Ruble, Taloga, OK 73667
  E-mail: rachelle.rogers@oscn.net

Ellis County

District Court Clerk

Second Judicial District
603 B Street, Arapaho, OK 73620
P.O. Box 180, Arapaho, OK 73620

Clerk of Court, Ellis County **Sally Wayland** . . . .(580) 885-7255
  100 South Washington Street,   Fax: (580) 885-7506
  Arnett, OK 73832
  P.O. Box 217, Arnett, OK 73832
  E-mail: sally.wayland@oscn.net

Garfield County

District Court Clerk

Fourth Judicial District
407 Government Street, Suite 30, Alva, OK 73717

Clerk of Court, Garfield County **Margaret Jones** . . . . (580) 237-0232
  114 West Broadway Avenue,   Fax: (580) 548-2430
  Enid, OK 73701-4024
  E-mail: margaret.jones@oscn.net

Garvin County

District Court Clerk

Twenty-First Judicial District
200 South Peters Avenue, Norman, OK 73069-6070

Clerk of Court, Garvin County **Cindy Roberts** . . . . (405) 238-5596
  201 West Grant Street, Pauls Valley, OK 73075   Fax: (405) 238-1138
  P.O. Box 239, Pauls Valley, OK 73075-3248
  E-mail: cindy.roberts@oscn.net

Grady County

District Court Clerk

Sixth Judicial District
Fourth and Choctaw Street, Chickasha, OK 73023-0605
P.O. Box 605, Chickasha, OK 73023-0605

Clerk of Court, Grady County **Lisa Hannah** . . . . (405) 224-7446
  Fourth and Choctaw Street,   Fax: (405) 224-0514
  Chickasha, OK 73023-0605
  P.O. Box 605, Chickasha, OK 73023-0605
  E-mail: lisa.hannah@oscn.net

Grant County

District Court Clerk

Fourth Judicial District
407 Government Street, Suite 30, Alva, OK 73717

Clerk of Court, Grant County **Deana Kilian** . . . . (580) 395-2828
  112 East Guthrie Street, Room 202,
  Medford, OK 73759-1224
  E-mail: deana.kilian@oscn.net

(continued on next page)

Oklahoma Court Clerks and Courthouses *continued*

Greer County

District Court Clerk

Third Judicial District
101 North Main, Altus, OK 73521

Clerk of Court, Greer County **Rhonda Henry** . . . . (580) 782-3665
  106 East Jefferson, Mangum, OK 73554   Fax: (580) 782-4026
  P.O. Box 216, Mangum, OK 73554

Harmon County

District Court Clerk

Third Judicial District
101 North Main, Altus, OK 73521

Clerk of Court, Harmon County **Stacy Macias** . . . . (580) 688-3617
  114 West Hollis Street, Hollis, OK 73550   Fax: (580) 688-2900
  E-mail: stacy.macias@oscn.net

Harper County

District Court Clerk

First Judicial District
319 North Main Street, Guymon, OK 73942
P.O. Box 551, Guymon, OK 73942

Clerk of Court, Harper County **RaeJean Burke** . . . . (580) 735-2010
  311 S.E. First Street, Buffalo, OK 73834   Fax: (580) 735-2787
  E-mail: raejean.burke@oscn.net

Haskell County

District Court Clerk

Sixteenth Judicial District
110 Front Street, Poteau, OK 74953
P.O. Box 688, Poteau, OK 74953-0688

Clerk of Court, Haskell County **Robin Rea** . . . .(918) 967-3323
  202 East Main Street, Suite 9,   Fax: (918) 967-2819
  Stigler, OK 74462-2439
  E-mail: robin.rea@oscn.net

Hughes County

District Court Clerk

Twenty-Second Judicial District
120 South Wewoka Avenue, Wewoka, OK 74884-2638
P.O. Box 130, Wewoka, OK 74884-2638

Clerk of Court, Hughes County **Patty Tilley** . . . .(405) 379-3384
  200 North Broadway, Holdenville, OK 74848-0032   Tel: (405) 379-3204
  P.O. Box 32, Holdenville, OK 74848-0032
  E-mail: patty.tilley@oscn.net

Jackson County

District Court Clerk

Third Judicial District
101 North Main, Altus, OK 73521

Clerk of Court, Jackson County **Rhonda Stepanovich** . . . (580) 482-0448
  P.O. Box 616, Altus, OK 73521   Fax: (580) 482-0920
  E-mail: rhonda.stepanovich@oscn.net

Oklahoma Court Clerks and Courthouses *continued*

Jefferson County

District Court Clerk

Fifth Judicial District
315 SW Fifth Street, Lawton, OK 73501-4327

Clerk of Court, Jefferson County **Kimberly Berry** . . . . (580) 228-2961
  220 North Main Street, Third Floor,   Fax: (580) 228-3242
  Waurika, OK 73573-2235
  E-mail: kimberly.berry@oscn.net

Johnston County

District Court Clerk

Twentieth Judicial District
P.O. Box 58, Madill, OK 73446

Clerk of Court, Johnston County **Cassandra Slover** . . . . . (580) 371-3281
  403 West Main, Suite 201,   Fax: (580) 371-2199
  Tishomingo, OK 73460
  E-mail: cassandra.slover@oscn.net

Kay County

District Court Clerk

Eighth Judicial District
300 Courthouse Drive, Room 14, Perry, OK 73077

Clerk of Court, Kay County **Marilee Thornton** . . . . (580) 362-3350
  201 South Main Street, Newkirk, OK 74647-0428   Fax: (580) 632-1129
  E-mail: marilee.thornton@oscn.net

Kingfisher County

District Court Clerk

Fourth Judicial District
407 Government Street, Suite 30, Alva, OK 73717

Clerk of Court, Kingfisher County **Lisa Markus** . . . .(405) 375-3813
  101 South Main Street, Kingfisher, OK 73750-3241   Fax: (405) 375-4249
  P.O. Box 328, Kingfisher, OK 73750
  E-mail: lisa.markus@oscn.net

Kiowa County

District Court Clerk

Third Judicial District
101 North Main, Altus, OK 73521

Clerk of Court, Kiowa County **Chris Sanders** . . . . (580) 726-5125
  P.O. Box 854, Hobart, OK 73651   Fax: (580) 726-2340

Latimer County

District Court Clerk

Sixteenth Judicial District
110 Front Street, Poteau, OK 74953
P.O. Box 688, Poteau, OK 74953-0688

Clerk of Court, Latimer County **Melinda Brinlee** . . . .(918) 465-2011
  109 North Central Street,   Fax: (918) 465-3328
  Wilburton, OK 74578-9998
  E-mail: melinda.brinlee@oscn.net

Le Flore County

District Court Clerk

Sixteenth Judicial District
110 Front Street, Poteau, OK 74953
P.O. Box 688, Poteau, OK 74953-0688

Clerk of Court, Le Flore County **Melba Hall** . . . . (918) 647-3181
110 Front Street, Poteau, OK 74953
P.O. Box 688, Poteau, OK 74953-0688
E-mail: melba.hall@oscn.net

Lincoln County

District Court Clerk

Twenty-Third Judicial District
325 North Broadway Street, Shawnee, OK 74801-6938

Clerk of Court, Lincoln County **Cindy Kirby** . . . . (405) 258-1309
P.O. Box 307, Chandler, OK 74834-0307   Fax: (405) 258-3067
E-mail: cindy.kirby@oscn.net

Logan County

District Court Clerk

Ninth Judicial District
606 South Husband Street, Suite 206, Stillwater, OK 74074-4044

Clerk of Court, Logan County **ReJeania Zmek** . . . . (405) 282-0123
301 East Harrison Street, Room 201,   Tel: (405) 282-7661
Guthrie, OK 73044-4939
E-mail: rejeania.zmek@oscn.net

Love County

District Court Clerk

Twentieth Judicial District
P.O. Box 58, Madill, OK 73446

Clerk of Court, Love County **Kim Jackson** . . . . (580) 276-2235
405 West Main Street, Marietta, OK 73448-2848
E-mail: kim.jackson@oscn.net

Major County

District Court Clerk

Fourth Judicial District
407 Government Street, Suite 30, Alva, OK 73717

Clerk of Court, Major County **Shauna Hoffman** . . . . (580) 227-4690
500 East Broadway Street,   Fax: (580) 227-1275
Fairview, OK 73737-2243
E-mail: shauna.hoffman@oscn.net

Marshall County

District Court Clerk

Twentieth Judicial District
P.O. Box 58, Madill, OK 73446

Clerk of Court, Marshall County **Wanda Pearce** . . . . (580) 795-3278
P.O. Box 58, Madill, OK 73446   Fax: (580) 795-2169
E-mail: wanda.pearce@oscn.net

Mayes County

District Court Clerk

Twelfth Judicial District
200 South Lynn Riggs Boulevard, Claremore, OK 74017

Clerk of Court, Mayes County **Rita Harrison** . . . . (918) 825-2185
One Court Place, Suite 200,
Pryor, OK 74361-1018

McClain County

District Court Clerk

Twenty-First Judicial District
200 South Peters Avenue, Norman, OK 73069-6070

Clerk of Court, McClain County **Lynda Baker** . . . . (405) 527-3221
121 North Second Street, Suite 231,   Fax: (405) 527-1856
Purcell, OK 73080-0648
E-mail: lynda.baker@oscn.net

McCurtain County

District Court Clerk

Seventeenth Judicial District
108 North Central Avenue, Idabel, OK 74745-3835
P.O. Box 1378, Idabel, OK 74745-3835

Clerk of Court, McCurtain County **Vicki Justus** . . . . (580) 286-4950
108 North Central Avenue,   Fax: (580) 286-7095
Idabel, OK 74745-3835
P.O. Box 1378, Idabel, OK 74745
E-mail: vicki.justus@oscn.net

McIntosh County

District Court Clerk

Eighteenth Judicial District
115 East Carl Albert Parkway, McAlester, OK 74501-5020

Clerk of Court, McIntosh County **Carrie Pittman** . . . . (918) 689-2282
110 North First Street, Eufaula, OK 74432-0426   Fax: (918) 689-2995
P.O. Box 426, Eufaula, OK 74432-0426
E-mail: carrie.pittman@oscn.net

Murray County

District Court Clerk

Twentieth Judicial District
P.O. Box 58, Madill, OK 73446

Clerk of Court, Murray County **Christie Pittman** . . . . (580) 622-3223
Tenth and Wyandotte Stret,   Fax: (580) 622-2979
Sulphur, OK 73086-0578
P.O. Box 578, Sulphur, OK 73086
E-mail: christie.pittman@oscn.net

Muskogee County

District Court Clerk

Fifteenth Judicial District
220 West Division Street, Stilwell, OK 74960

Clerk of Court, Muskogee County **Paula Sexton** . . . . (918) 682-7873
220 State Street, Muskogee, OK 74402-6642   Fax: (918) 684-1696
P.O. Box 1350, Muskogee, OK 74402
E-mail: paula.sexton@oscn.net

(continued on next page)

Noble County

District Court Clerk

Eighth Judicial District
300 Courthouse Drive, Room 14, Perry, OK 73077

Clerk of Court, Noble County **Hillary Vorndran** . . . . (580) 336-5187
300 Courthouse Drive, Room 14,
Perry, OK 73077
E-mail: hillary.vorndran@oscn.net

Nowata County

District Court Clerk

Eleventh Judicial District
420 South Johnstone Avenue, Bartlesville, OK 74003-6602

Clerk of Court, Nowata County **Sarah Ewers** . . . . (918) 273-0127
229 North Maple Street, Nowata, OK 74048   Fax: (918) 273-2207
E-mail: sarah.ewers@oscn.net

Okfuskee County

District Court Clerk

Twenty-Fourth Judicial District
222 East Dewey Avenue, Suite 201, Sapulpa, OK 74066-4237

Clerk of Court, Okfuskee County **Sherri Foreman** . . . . . . (918) 623-0525
Third and Atlanta Street, Okemah, OK 74859-0106   Tel: (918) 623-2687
E-mail: sherri.foreman@oscn.net

Oklahoma County

District Court Clerk

Seventh Judicial District
County Office Building, 320 Robert S. Kerr Avenue, Room 409,
Oklahoma City, OK 73102

Clerk of Court, Oklahoma County **Tim Rhodes** . . . . (405) 713-1722
County Office Building,
320 Robert S. Kerr Avenue, Room 409,
Oklahoma City, OK 73102
E-mail: tim.rhodes@oscn.net

Okmulgee County

District Court Clerk

Twenty-Fourth Judicial District
222 East Dewey Avenue, Suite 201, Sapulpa, OK 74066-4237

Clerk of Court, Okmulgee County **Linda Beaver** . . . . (918) 756-3042
314 West Seventh Street, Suite 305,   Fax: (918) 758-1237
Okmulgee, OK 74447-5012
E-mail: linda.beaver@oscn.net

Osage County

District Court Clerk

Tenth Judicial District
600 Grandview Avenue, Pawhuska, OK 74056-4259

Clerk of Court, Osage County **Jennifer Burd** . . . . (918) 287-4104
600 Grandview Avenue, Pawhuska, OK 74056-4259
E-mail: jennifer.burd@oscn.net

Ottawa County

District Court Clerk

Thirteenth Judicial District
102 East Central Avenue, Miami, OK 74354-7030

Clerk of Court, Ottawa County **Cassie Key** . . . . (918) 542-2801
102 East Central Avenue, Suite 203,   Fax: (918) 540-3278
Miami, OK 74354-7030
E-mail: cassie.key@oscn.net

Pawnee County

District Court Clerk

Fourteenth Judicial District
500 South Denver Avenue, Tulsa, OK 74103-3861

Clerk of Court, Pawnee County **Janet Dallas** . . . . (918) 762-2547
500 Harrison Street, Suite 300,
Pawnee, OK 74058-2567
E-mail: janet.dallas@oscn.net

Payne County

District Court Clerk

Ninth Judicial District
606 South Husband Street, Suite 206, Stillwater, OK 74074-4044

Clerk of Court, Payne County **Lori Allen** . . . . (405) 372-4774
606 South Husband Street,   Fax: (405) 372-2654
Stillwater, OK 74074-4044
E-mail: lori.allen@oscn.net

Pittsburg County

District Court Clerk

Eighteenth Judicial District
115 East Carl Albert Parkway, McAlester, OK 74501-5020

Clerk of Court, Pittsburg County **Cindy Eller** . . . . (918) 423-4859
115 East Carl Albert Parkway,   Fax: (918) 426-1886
McAlester, OK 74501-5020
E-mail: cindy.eller@oscn.net

Pontotoc County

District Court Clerk

Twenty-Second Judicial District
120 South Wewoka Avenue, Wewoka, OK 74884-2638
P.O. Box 130, Wewoka, OK 74884-2638

Clerk of Court, Pontotoc County **Karen Dunnigan** . . . . . . (580) 332-5763
120 West 13th Street, Ada, OK 74820   Fax: (580) 332-5766
E-mail: karen.dunnigan@oscn.net

Pottawatomie County

District Court Clerk

Twenty-Third Judicial District
325 North Broadway Street, Shawnee, OK 74801-6938

Clerk of Court, Pottawatomie County **Valerie Ueltzen** . . . . (405) 273-3624
325 North Broadway Street,   Fax: (405) 878-5525
Shawnee, OK 74801-6938
E-mail: valerie.ueltzen@oscn.net

Pushmataha County

District Court Clerk

Seventeenth Judicial District
108 North Central Avenue, Idabel, OK 74745-3835
P.O. Box 1378, Idabel, OK 74745-3835

Clerk of Court, Pushmataha County **Tina Freeman** . . . . . . (580) 298-2274
  203 SW Third Street, Antlers, OK 74523-3899   Fax: (580) 298-3696
  E-mail: tina.freeman@oscn.net

Roger Mills County

District Court Clerk

Second Judicial District
603 B Street, Arapaho, OK 73620
P.O. Box 180, Arapaho, OK 73620

Clerk of Court, Roger Mills County **Jan Bailey** . . . . (580) 497-3361
  480 L.L. Males Avenue and Broadway Street,   Fax: (580) 497-2167
  Cheyenne, OK 73628
  E-mail: jan.bailey@oscn.net

Rogers County

District Court Clerk

Twelfth Judicial District
200 South Lynn Riggs Boulevard, Claremore, OK 74017

Clerk of Court, Rogers County **Kim Henry** . . . . (918) 923-4961
  200 South Lynn Riggs Boulevard,   Fax: (918) 923-4567
  Claremore, OK 74017
  E-mail: kim.henry@oscn.net

Seminole County

District Court Clerk

Twenty-Second Judicial District
120 South Wewoka Avenue, Wewoka, OK 74884-2638
P.O. Box 130, Wewoka, OK 74884-2638

Clerk of Court, Seminole County **Kimberly Davis** . . . . (405) 257-6236
  120 South Wewoka Avenue,   Fax: (405) 257-2631
  Wewoka, OK 74884-2638
  P.O. Box 130, Wewoka, OK 74884-2638
  E-mail: kimberly.davis@oscn.net

Sequoyah County

District Court Clerk

Fifteenth Judicial District
220 West Division Street, Stilwell, OK 74960

Clerk of Court, Sequoyah County **Vicki Beaty** . . . . (918) 775-4411
  120 East Chickasaw Street, Suite 205,   Fax: (918) 775-1223
  Sallisaw, OK 74955-4623
  E-mail: vicki.beaty@oscn.net

Stephens County

District Court Clerk

Fifth Judicial District
315 SW Fifth Street, Lawton, OK 73501-4327

Clerk of Court, Stephens County
  Margaret Cunningham . . . . (580) 470-2000
  101 South Eleventh Street,
  Duncan, OK 73533-4758

Texas County

District Court Clerk

First Judicial District
319 North Main Street, Guymon, OK 73942
P.O. Box 551, Guymon, OK 73942

Clerk of Court, Texas County **M. Renee Ellis** . . . . (580) 338-3003
  319 North Main Street, Suite 301,   Fax: (580) 338-3819
  Guymon, OK 73942
  P.O. Box 551, Guymon, OK 73942

Tillman County

District Court Clerk

Third Judicial District
101 North Main, Altus, OK 73521

Clerk of Court, Tillman County **Kevin Stevens** . . . . (580) 335-3023
  P.O. Box 116, Frederick, OK 73542   Fax: (580) 335-5613

Tulsa County

District Court Clerk

Fourteenth Judicial District
500 South Denver Avenue, Tulsa, OK 74103-3861

Clerk of Court, Tulsa County **Sally Howe Smith** . . . . (918) 596-5000
  500 South Denver Avenue,   Fax: (918) 596-5402
  Tulsa, OK 74103-3861
  E-mail: sally.smith@oscn.net

Wagoner County

District Court Clerk

Fifteenth Judicial District
220 West Division Street, Stilwell, OK 74960

Clerk of Court, Wagoner County **Jim Hight** . . . . (918) 485-4508
  307 East Cherokee Street, Wagoner, OK 74467   Fax: (918) 485-5836
  P.O. Box 249, Wagoner, OK 74467-4705
  E-mail: jim.hight@oscn.net

Washington County

District Court Clerk

Eleventh Judicial District
420 South Johnstone Avenue, Bartlesville, OK 74003-6602

Clerk of Court, Washington County **Jill Spitzer** . . . . (918) 337-2870
  420 South Johnstone Avenue,   Fax: (918) 337-2897
  Bartlesville, OK 74003-6602
  E-mail: jill.spitzer@oscn.net

(continued on next page)

Oklahoma Court Clerks and Courthouses *continued*

Washita County

District Court Clerk

Second Judicial District
603 B Street, Arapaho, OK 73620
P.O. Box 180, Arapaho, OK 73620

Clerk of Court, Washita County **Carol Corbett** . . . . (580) 832-3836
101 Main Street, Cordell, OK 73632   Fax: (580) 832-4123
P.O. 397, Cordell, OK 73632
E-mail: carol.corbett@oscn.net

Woods County

District Court Clerk

Fourth Judicial District
407 Government Street, Suite 30, Alva, OK 73717

Clerk of Court, Woods County **Della Dunnigan** . . . .(580) 327-3119
407 Government Street, Alva, OK 73717
E-mail: della.dunnigan@oscn.net

Woodward County

District Court Clerk

Fourth Judicial District
407 Government Street, Suite 30, Alva, OK 73717

Clerk of Court, Woodward County **Tammy Roberts** . . . . . (580) 256-3413
1600 Main Street, Woodward, OK 73801   Fax: (580) 254-6807
E-mail: tammy.roberts@oscn.net

Counties Within Judicial Districts

District Court, 1st Judicial District
Areas Covered: Beaver, Cimarron, Harper and Texas Counties.

District Court, 2nd Judicial District
Areas Covered: Beckham, Custer, Ellis, Roger Mills, and Washita Counties.

District Court, 3rd Judicial District
Areas Covered: Greer, Harmon, Jackson, Kiowa, and Tillman Counties

District Court, 4th Judicial District
Areas Covered: Alfalfa, Blaine, Dewey, Garfield, Grant, Kingfisher, Major, Woods and Woodward Counties.

District Court, 5th Judicial District
Areas Covered: Comanche, Cotton, Jefferson, and Stephens Counties.

District Court, 6th Judicial District
Areas Covered: Caddo and Grady Counties.

District Court, 7th Judicial District
Areas Covered: Oklahoma County.

District Court, 8th Judicial District
Areas Covered: Kay and Noble Counties.

Oklahoma Court Clerks and Courthouses *continued*

District Court, 9th Judicial District
Areas Covered: Logan and Payne counties.

District Court, 10th Judicial District
Areas Covered: Osage County.

District Court, 11th Judicial District
Areas Covered: Nowata and Washington Counties.

District Court, 12th Judicial District
Areas Covered: Craig, Mayes and Rogers Counties.

District Court, 13th Judicial District
Areas Covered: Delaware and Ottawa Counties.

District Court, 14th Judicial District
Areas Covered: Tulsa County.

District Court, 15th Judicial District
Areas Covered: Adair, Cherokee, Muskogee, Sequoyah and Wagoner Counties.

District Court, 16th Judicial District
Areas Covered: Haskell, Latimer, and Le Flore Counties.

District Court, 17th Judicial District
Areas Covered: Choctaw, McCurtain and Pushmataha Counties.

District Court, 18th Judicial District
Areas Covered: McIntosh and Pittsburg Counties.

District Court, 19th Judicial District
Areas Covered: Bryan County.

District Court, 20th Judicial District
Areas Covered: Carter, Johnston, Love, Marshall and Murray Counties.

District Court, 21st Judicial District
Areas Covered: Cleveland, Garvin and McClain Counties.

District Court, 22nd Judicial District
Areas Covered: Hughes, Pontotoc and Seminole Counties.

District Court, 23rd Judicial District
Areas Covered: Lincoln and Pottawatomie Counties.

District Court, 24th Judicial District
Areas Covered: Creek, Okfuskee and Okmulgee Counties.

District Court, 25th Judicial District
Areas Covered: Atoka and Coal Counties.

District Court, 26th Judicial District
Areas Covered: Canadian County.

Oregon Court Clerks and Courthouses

The trial courts of general jurisdiction in Oregon are called circuit courts. There are 36 such courts in 27 judicial districts throughout the State. Each county has a county clerk (generally handling deeds and records) and trial court clerk, sometimes referred to as the circuit clerk or the trial court administrator. The county clerks are listed below.

Oregon Supreme Court

Supreme Court Building, 1163 State Street, Salem, OR 97301-2563
Tel: (503) 986-5555 Fax: (503) 986-5560
Internet: courts.oregon.gov/supreme

The Supreme Court consists of a chief justice and six justices who are elected in statewide nonpartisan elections for six-year terms. The Governor may appoint a justice to temporarily fill a vacancy until the next general election. The Chief Justice is elected by peer vote for a six-year term. The Supreme Court may review any decision of the Oregon Court of Appeals and hears all appeals from the Oregon Tax Court. The court has general administrative and supervisory authority over the courts of the state and admission to the state bar.

Court Staff
Appellate Courts Records Administrator
Rebecca J. "Becky" Osborne . . . . (503) 986-5589
E-mail: rebecca.j.osborne@ojd.state.or.us

Oregon Court of Appeals

Supreme Court Building, 1163 State Street, Salem, OR 97301-2563
Tel: (503) 986-5555 Fax: (503) 986-5560
Internet: www.ojd.state.or.us

The Court of Appeals consists of a chief judge and nine judges who are elected in statewide, nonpartisan elections for six-year terms. Vacancies are filled by the Governor until a successor can be elected at the next general election. The Chief Judge is appointed by the Supreme Court Chief Justice for a two-year term. Cases are heard by panels of three judges. The Oregon Court of Appeals has appellate jurisdiction over all matters from the state's circuit courts, and review of most state administrative agency actions.

Court Staff
Appellate Courts Records Administrator
Rebecca J. "Becky" Osborne . . . . (503) 986-5550
E-mail: rebecca.j.osborne@ojd.state.or.us

Oregon Tax Court

1241 State Street, Salem, OR 97301-2563
Tel: (503) 986-5645 Fax: (503) 986-5507
E-mail: tax.court@ojd.state.or.us

Court Staff
Statutory Clerk **Rocco Lieuallen** . . . . (503) 986-5645
1241 State Street, Salem, OR 97301

Oregon Court Clerks and Courthouses *continued*

County-By-County

Baker County

County Clerk

Office of the County Clerk
1995 Third Street, Suite 150, Baker City, OR 97814
Tel: (541) 523-8207 Fax: (541) 523-8240

County Clerk **Cindy Carpenter** . . . . (541) 523-8207
E-mail: ccarpenter@bakercounty.org

Benton County

County Clerk

Office of the County Clerk
120 NW Fourth Street, Room 4, Corvallis, OR 97339
Tel: (541) 766-6831 Fax: (541) 766-6675

County Clerk **James Morales** . . . . (541) 766-6831
E-mail: james.morales@co.benton.or.us

Clackamas County

County Clerk

Office of the County Clerk
2051 Kaen Road, Second Floor, Oregon City, OR 97045
Tel: (503) 650-5686 Fax: (503) 650-5687
Internet: www.clackamas.us/clerk

County Clerk **Sherry Hall** . . . . (503) 655-8698
E-mail: sherryhal@co.clackamas.or.us

Clatsop County

County Clerk

Office of the County Clerk
820 Exchange Street, Suite 220, Astoria, OR 97103
Tel: (503) 325-8511 Fax: (503) 325-9307

County Clerk **Valerie Crafard** . . . . (503) 325-8511
E-mail: clerk@co.clatsop.or.us

Columbia County

County Clerk

Office of the County Clerk
230 Strand Street, Saint Helens, OR 97051
Tel: (503) 397-3796 Fax: (503) 397-7266

County Clerk and Recorder
Elizabeth E. "Betty" Huser . . . . (503) 397-3796
E-mail: betty.huser@co.columbia.or.us

Coos County

County Clerk

Office of the County Clerk
250 North Baxter, Coquille, OR 97423
Tel: (541) 396-7600 Fax: (541) 396-1013

County Clerk **Terri Turi** . . . . (541) 396-7600
E-mail: coosclerk@co.coos.or.us

(continued on next page)

Crook County

County Clerk

Office of the County Clerk
300 NE Third Street, Room 23, Prineville, OR 97754
Tel: (541) 447-6553 Fax: (541) 416-2145
E-mail: cc_clerk@co.crook.or.us

County Clerk **Cheryl Seely** .... (541) 447-6553
  E-mail: cheryl.seely@co.crook.or.us

Curry County

County Clerk

Office of the County Clerk
94235 Moore Street, Suite 212, Gold Beach, OR 97444
Tel: (541) 247-3297 Fax: (541) 247-9361
E-mail: clerk@co.curry.or.us

County Clerk **Renee' Kolen** .... (541) 247-3297
  E-mail: kolenr@co.curry.or.us

Deschutes County

County Clerk

Office of the County Clerk
1300 NW Wall Street, Suite 202, Bend, OR 97701
P.O. Box 6005, Bend, OR 97708-6005
Tel: (541) 388-6549 Fax: (541) 383-4424

County Clerk **Nancy Blankenship** .... (541) 388-6549
  E-mail: nancyb@deschutes.org

Douglas County

County Clerk

Office of the County Clerk
1036 SE Douglas Avenue, Room 124, Roseburg, OR 97470
P.O. Box 10, Roseburg, OR 97470
Tel: (541) 440-4324 Fax: (541) 440-4408

County Clerk **Patricia "Patty" Hitt** .... (541) 440-4324
  E-mail: pkhitt@co.douglas.or.us

Gilliam County

County Clerk

Office of the County Clerk
221 South Oregon Street, Room 200, Condon, OR 97823
P.O. Box 427, Condon, OR 97823
Tel: (541) 384-2311 Fax: (541) 384-2166

County Clerk **Ellen Wagenaar** .... (541) 384-2311
  E-mail: ellen.wagenaar@co.gilliam.or.us

Grant County

County Clerk

Office of the County Clerk
201 South Humbolt Street, Suite 290, Canyon City, OR 97820
Tel: (541) 575-1675 Fax: (541) 575-2248

County Clerk **Brenda Percy** .... (541) 575-1675
  E-mail: percyb@grantcounty-or.gov

Harney County

County Clerk

Office of the County Clerk
450 North Buena Vista Avenue, Room 14, Burns, OR 97720
Tel: (541) 573-6641 Fax: (541) 573-8370
E-mail: clerk@co.harney.or.us

County Clerk **Derrin "Dag" Robinson** .... (541) 573-6641
  E-mail: derrin.robinson@co.harney.or.us

Hood River County

County Clerk

Department of Records and Assessment
601 State Street, Hood River, OR 97031
Tel: (541) 386-1442 Fax: (541) 387-6864

Director/Assessor/Clerk **Brian D. Beebe** .... (541) 386-1442
  E-mail: brian.beebe@co.hood-river.or.us

Jackson County

County Clerk

Office of the County Clerk
10 South Oakdale, Room 114, Medford, OR 97501
Tel: (541) 774-6152 Fax: (541) 774-6714

County Clerk **Christine D. "Chris" Walker** .... (541) 774-6147
  E-mail: walkercd@jacksoncounty.org

Jefferson County

County Clerk

Office of the County Clerk
66 SE D Street, Suite C, Madras, OR 97741
Tel: (541) 475-4451 Fax: (541) 325-5018

County Clerk **Kathleen B. "Kathy" Marston** .... (541) 475-4451
  E-mail: kathy.marston@co.jefferson.or.us

Josephine County

County Clerk

Office of the County Clerk
500 NW Sixth Street, Room 170, Grants Pass, OR 97528
P.O. Box 69, Grants Pass, OR 97526
Tel: (541) 474-5240 Fax: (541) 474-5246
E-mail: clerk@co.josephine.or.us

County Clerk **Art Harvey** .... (541) 474-5240
  E-mail: aharvey@co.josephine.or.us

Klamath County

County Clerk

Office of the County Clerk
305 Main Street, Klamath Falls, OR 97601
Tel: (541) 883-5134 Fax: (541) 885-6757

County Clerk **Linda Smith** .... (541) 883-5134
  E-mail: lsmith@co.klamath.or.us

Lake County

County Clerk

Office of the County Clerk
513 Center Street, Lakeview, OR 97630
Tel: (541) 947-6006 Fax: (541) 947-0905
E-mail: clerk@co.lake.or.us

County Clerk **Stacie Geaney** . . . . (541) 947-6006
  E-mail: smgeaney@co.lake.or.us

Lane County

County Clerk

Office of the County Clerk
125 East Eighth Avenue, Eugene, OR 97401 (Deeds and Records)
275 West Tenth Avenue, Eugene, OR 97401 (Elections)
Tel: (541) 682-3654 (Deeds and Records)
Tel: (541) 682-4234 (Elections) Tel: (541) 682-3653 (Marriage Licenses)

County Clerk **Cheryl Betschart** . . . . (541) 682-4328
  E-mail: cheryl.betschart@co.lane.or.us

Lincoln County

County Clerk

Office of the County Clerk
225 West Olive Street, Room 201, Newport, OR 97365
Tel: (541) 265-4131 Fax: (541) 265-4950
E-mail: countyclerk@co.lincoln.or.us

County Clerk **Dana W. Jenkins** . . . . (541) 265-4131
  E-mail: djenkins@co.lincoln.or.us

Linn County

County Clerk

Office of the County Clerk
300 Fourth Avenue SW, Room 205, Albany, OR 97321
P.O. Box 100, Albany, OR 97321
Tel: (541) 967-3829 Fax: (541) 926-5109

County Clerk **Steve Druckenmiller** . . . . (541) 967-3829
  E-mail: sdruckenmiller@co.linn.or.us

Malheur County

County Clerk

Office of the County Clerk
251 B Street West, Suite 4, Vale, OR 97918
Tel: (541) 473-5151 Fax: (541) 473-5523
E-mail: countyclerk@malheurco.org

County Clerk **Deborah R. DeLong** . . . . (541) 473-5151
  E-mail: ddelong@malheurco.org

Marion County

County Clerk

County Clerk's Office
555 Court Street NE, Suite 2130, Salem, OR 97301
Tel: (503) 588-5225 Tel: (503) 588-5490 (Records Center and Archives)
Fax: (503) 373-4408
Internet: www.co.marion.or.us/co

County Clerk **Bill Burgess** . . . . (503) 588-5225
  E-mail: bburgess@co.marion.or.us

Morrow County

County Clerk

Office of the County Clerk
100 South Court Street, Suite 102, Heppner, OR 97836
P.O. Box 338, Heppner, OR 97836
Tel: (541) 676-5604 Fax: (541) 676-9876

County Clerk **Bobbi Childers** . . . . (541) 676-5604
  E-mail: bchilders@co.morrow.or.us

Multnomah County

Director of Elections

Elections Division
1040 SE Morrison Street, Portland, OR 97214
Fax: (503) 988-3719

Director **Tim Scott** . . . . (503) 988-3720

Polk County

County Clerk

Office of the County Clerk
850 Main Street, Dallas, OR 97338
Tel: (503) 623-9217 Fax: (503) 623-0717

County Clerk **Valerie "Val" Unger** . . . . (503) 623-9217
  E-mail: unger.valerie@co.polk.or.us

Sherman County

County Clerk

Office of the County Clerk
500 Court Street, Moro, OR 97039
P.O. Box 365, Moro, OR 97039
Tel: (541) 565-3606 Fax: (541) 565-3771

County Clerk **Jenine McDermid** . . . . (541) 565-3606
  E-mail: countyclerk@shermancounty.net

Tillamook County

County Clerk

Office of the County Clerk
201 Laurel Avenue, Tillamook, OR 97141
Tel: (503) 842-3402 Fax: (503) 842-1599
E-mail: clerk@co.tillamook.or.us

County Clerk **Tassi O'Neil** . . . . (503) 842-3402
  E-mail: toneil@co.tillamook.or.us

(continued on next page)

Oregon Court Clerks and Courthouses *continued*

Umatilla County

Office of County Records

Office of County Records
216 SE Fourth Street, Pendleton, OR 97801
Tel: (541) 278-6236 Fax: (541) 278-6345

Manager **Steve Churchill** . . . . (541) 278-6236
    E-mail: steve.churchill@co.umatilla.or.us

Union County

County Clerk

Office of the County Clerk
1001 Fourth Street, Suite D, La Grande, OR 97850
Tel: (541) 963-1006 Fax: (541) 963-1013

County Clerk **Robin A. Church** . . . . (541) 963-1006
    E-mail: rchurch@union-county.org

Wallowa County

County Clerk

Office of the County Clerk
101 South River Street, Room 100, Enterprise, OR 97828
Tel: (541) 426-4543 ext. 158 Fax: (541) 426-5901

County Clerk **Dana Roberts** . . . . (541) 426-4543 ext. 158
    E-mail: wcclerk@co.wallowa.or.us

Wasco County

County Clerk

Office of the County Clerk
511 Washington Street, Room 201, The Dalles, OR 97058
Tel: (541) 506-2530 Fax: (541) 506-2531
E-mail: countyclerk@co.wasco.or.us

County Clerk **Linda Brown** . . . . (541) 506-2530
    E-mail: lindab@co.wasco.or.us

Washington County

County Clerk

Assessment and Taxation Department
155 North First Avenue, Suite 230, Hillsboro, OR 97124-3072
Tel: (503) 846-8741 Fax: (503) 846-3909

Director **Richard W. Hobernicht** . . . . (503) 846-8741
    E-mail: richard_hobernicht@co.washington.or.us

Wheeler County

County Clerk

Office of the County Clerk
701 Adams Street, Room 204, Fossil, OR 97830
P.O. Box 327, Fossil, OR 97830
Tel: (541) 763-2400 Fax: (541) 763-2026

County Clerk **Barbara S. Sitton** . . . . (541) 763-2400
    E-mail: bsitton@co.wheeler.or.us

Oregon Court Clerks and Courthouses *continued*

Yamhill County

County Clerk

Office of the County Clerk
414 NE Evans Street, McMinnville, OR 97128
Tel: (503) 434-7518 Fax: (503) 434-7520

County Clerk **Brian Van Bergen** . . . . (503) 434-7518
    E-mail: vanbergenb@co.yamhill.or.us

Counties Within Judicial Circuits

Circuit Court, 1st Judicial District
Areas Covered: Jackson County.

Circuit Court, 2nd Judicial District
Areas Covered: Lane County.

Circuit Court, 3rd Judicial District
Areas Covered: Marion County.

Circuit Court, 4th Judicial District
Areas Covered: Multnomah County.

Circuit Court, 5th Judicial District
Areas Covered: Clackamas County.

Circuit Court, 6th Judicial District
Areas Covered: Umatilla and Morrow Counties.

Circuit Court, 7th Judicial District
Areas Covered: Gilliam, Hood River, Sherman, Wasco and Wheeler Counties.

Circuit Court, 8th Judicial District
Areas Covered: Baker County.

Circuit Court, 9th Judicial District
Areas Covered: Malheur County.

Circuit Court, 10th Judicial District
Areas Covered: Wallowa and Union Counties.

Circuit Court, 11th Judicial District
Areas Covered: Deschutes County.

Circuit Court, 12th Judicial District
Areas Covered: Polk County.

Circuit Court, 13th Judicial District
Areas Covered: Klamath County.

Circuit Court, 14th Judicial District
Areas Covered: Josephine County.

Oregon Court Clerks and Courthouses *continued*
Circuit Court, 15th Judicial District
Areas Covered: Coos and Curry Counties.

Circuit Court, 16th Judicial District
Areas Covered: Douglas County.

Circuit Court, 17th Judicial District
Areas Covered: Lincoln County.

Circuit Court, 18th Judicial District
Areas Covered: Clatsop County.

Circuit Court, 19th Judicial District
Areas Covered: Columbia County.

Circuit Court, 20th Judicial District
Areas Covered: Washington County.

Circuit Court, 21st Judicial District
Areas Covered: Benton County.

Circuit Court, 22nd Judicial District
Areas Covered: Jefferson and Crook Counties.

Circuit Court, 23rd Judicial District
Areas Covered: Linn County.

Circuit Court, 24th Judicial District
Areas Covered: Harney and Grant Counties.

Circuit Court, 25th Judicial District
Areas Covered: Yamhill County.

Circuit Court, 26th Judicial District
Areas Covered: Lake County.

Circuit Court, 27th Judicial District
Areas Covered: Tillamook County.

Pennsylvania Court Clerks and Courthouses

The trial court of general jurisdiction in Pennsylvania is called the Court of Common Pleas, of which there are 60 judicial districts in 67 counties. Each county has a Prothonotary (Keeper of the Civil Record) and a Recorder of Deeds. Many counties also have Clerks of Court (Keeper of the Criminal Record).

Supreme Court of Pennsylvania

1515 Market Street, Suite 1414, Philadelphia, PA 19102
Tel: (215) 560-6300

The Supreme Court consists of a chief justice and six justices who are initially elected in statewide, partisan elections for ten-year terms, and who then run for retention for additional ten-year terms. The Governor may, with the consent of the State Senate, appoint a justice to temporarily fill a vacancy until the next general election. The senior justice on the Court is designated as chief justice. Retirement is mandatory at age seventy; however, retired judges may be recalled for temporary assignment by the chief justice. The Supreme Court has exclusive appellate jurisdiction over appeals involving the Pennsylvania Court of Common Pleas in cases involving the imposition of capital punishment, right to public office, supersession of a district attorney, suspension or disbarment, public indebtedness and the constitutionality of any law. The Court has exclusive jurisdiction over all appeals of cases originating in the Commonwealth Court of Pennsylvania and over appeals from orders of the Commonwealth Court in cases originating in the Pennsylvania Board of Finance and Revenue. The Court may review decisions of the Pennsylvania Superior Court and Commonwealth Court. The Court exercises general supervisory control and rule-making authority over the court system.

Court Staff

Prothonotary **Irene Bizzoso** . . . . (717) 787-6181
Areas Covered: The Supreme Court Prothonotary is responsible for all court districts.
Pennsylvania Judicial Center,
601 Commonwealth Avenue, Suite 4500,
Harrisburg, PA 17106
P.O. Box 62575, Harrisburg, PA 17106
E-mail: irene.bizzoso@pacourts.us

Deputy Prothonotary, Harrisburg Office
Amy Dreibelbis . . . . (717) 787-6181
Areas Covered: Middle District - Adams, Bradford, Berks, Bucks, Carbon, Centre, Chester, Clinton, Columbia, Cumberland, Dauphin, Delaware, Franklin, Fulton, Huntingdon, Juniata, Lancaster, Lebanon, Lehigh, Luzerne, Lycoming, Mifflin, Montgomery, Montour, Northampton, Northumberland, Perry, Pike, Shuykill, Snyder, Sullivan, Susquehanna, Tioga, Union, Wayne, Wyoming, and York Counties.
601 Commonwealth Avenue,
Harrisburg, PA 17106
P.O. Box 62575, Harrisburg, PA 17106

Deputy Prothonotary, Philadelphia District Office
John W. Person, Jr. . . . . (215) 560-6370
Areas Covered: Eastern District – Pennsylvania County
468 City Hall, Philadelphia, PA 19107
E-mail: john.person@pacourts.us

Deputy Prothonotary, Pittsburgh District Office
John Vaskov . . . . (412) 565-2816
Areas Covered: Western District – Allegheny, Armstrong, Beaver, Bedford, Blair, Butler, Cambria, Cameron, Clarion, Clearfield, Crawford, Elk, Erie, Fayette, Forest, Greene, Indiana, Jefferson, Lawrence, McKean, Mercer, Potter, Somerset, Venango, Warren, Washington, and Westmoreland counties
801 City-County Bldg., Pittsburgh, PA 15219
E-mail: john.vaskov@pacourts.us

Superior Court of Pennsylvania

530 Walnut Street, Suite 315, Philadelphia, PA 19106
Tel: (215) 560-5800   Fax: (215) 560-6279

The Superior Court is comprised of three judicial districts and consists of a president judge and fourteen judges who are initially elected in statewide, partisan elections for ten-year terms and who then run for retention for additional ten-year terms. The Governor may, with the consent of the State Senate, appoint a justice to temporarily fill a vacancy until the next general election. The president judge is elected by the Court's commissioned (non-senior) judges for a five year term. Retirement is mandatory at age seventy; however, retired judges may be recalled for temporary assignments by the Supreme Court president judge. The Superior Court has exclusive jurisdiction over all cases at law and equity from Pennsylvania Courts of Common Pleas, except those cases which are under the exclusive jurisdiction of the Pennsylvania Supreme Court or Commonwealth Court. The Court hears appeals involving matters of contract, tort, domestic relations, nongovernment equity except for eminent domain and nonprofit corporation matters and most criminal cases.

Court Staff

Prothonotary **Joseph Seletyn** . . . . (215) 560-5800
Areas Covered: The Superior Court Prothonotary is responsible for all court districts
E-mail: joseph.seletyn@pacourts.us

Deputy Prothonotary, Philadelphia Office
Michael DiPasquale . . . . (215) 560-5800
Areas Covered: Eastern District – Pennsylvania County

Deputy Prothonotary, Harrisburg Office
Jennifer Traxler . . . . (717) 772-1294
Areas Covered: Middle District – Adams,   Fax: (717) 772-1297
Bradford, Berks, Bucks, Carbon, Centre, Chester, Clinton, Columbia, Cumberland, Dauphin, Delaware, Franklin, Fulton, Huntingdon, Juniata, Lancaster, Lebanon, Lehigh, Lycoming, Mifflin, Montgomery, Montour, Northampton, Northumberland, Perry, Pike, Shuykill, Snyder, Sullivan, Susquehanna, Tioga, Union, Wayne, Wyoming, and York Counties.
100 Pine Street, Suite 400,
Harrisburg, PA 17101
E-mail: jennifer.traxler@pacourts.us

Deputy Prothonotary, Pittsburgh Office
Nicholas V. Corsetti . . . . (412) 565-7592
Areas Covered: Western District – Allegheny,   Fax: (412) 565-7711
Armstrong, Beaver, Bedford, Blair, Butler, Cambria, Cameron, Clarion, Clearfield, Crawford, Elk, Erie, Fayette, Forest, Greene, Indiana, Jefferson, Lawrence, McKean, Mercer, Potter, Somerset, Venango, Warren, Washington, and Westmoreland counties
310 Grant Street, Suite 600,
Pittsburgh, PA 15219
E-mail: nicholas.corsetti@pacourts.us

(continued on next page)

Commonwealth Court of Pennsylvania

Pennsylvania Judicial Center, 601 Commonwealth Avenue,
Suite 2100, Harrisburg, PA 17120
P.O. Box 69185, Harrisburg, PA 17106
Tel: (717) 255-1600

The Commonwealth Court consists of nine judges who are elected for ten-year terms in partisan elections and who may be retained for additional ten-year terms in retention elections. Vacancies are filled by the Governor with the consent of the State Senate. Those appointed to vacant positions serve until the next general election. The president judge of the court is elected by members of the court and serves a five year, non-renewable term. Elected judges must retire at the age of seventy. Senior judges, appointed by the Supreme Court, serve in various capacities. The Commonwealth Court is primarily an intermediate appellate court. It hears appeals from orders of the courts of common pleas, usually involving government-related parties and issues, and petitions for review from orders of state agencies. The court also has limited jurisdiction to hear some civil actions by and against the Commonwealth government and its officers. Significant exceptions to the grant of original jurisdiction place most actions against the Commonwealth in the court of common pleas or an administrative tribunal. The court also has original jurisdiction to hear election matters involving statewide offices.

Court Staff
Prothonotary **Kristen W. Brown** . . . . (717) 255-1600
  E-mail: kristen.brown@pacourts.us
Chief Clerk **Michael F. Krimmel** . . . . (717) 255-1661
  E-mail: michael.krimmel@pacourts.us

County-By-County

Adams County

Clerk of Court

Fifty-First Judicial District
117 Baltimore Street, Gettysburg, PA 17325
Tel: (717) 337-9846 Fax: (717) 334-8817

Clerk of Court **Kelly A. Ruff Lawver** . . . . (717) 337-9806
  117 Baltimore Street, Room 103,   Fax: (717) 334-9333
  Gettysburg, PA 17325
  E-mail: klawver@adamscounty.us

Prothonotary

Office of the Prothonotary
117 Baltimore Street, Room 104 , Gettysburg, PA 17325
Tel: (717) 337-9834 Fax: (717) 334-0532

Prothonotary **Beverly Boyd** . . . . (717) 337-9834
  E-mail: bboyd@adamscounty.us

Recorder

Office of the Register of Wills and Recorder of Deeds
117 Baltimore Street, Room 102 , Gettysburg, PA 17325
Tel: (717) 337-9826 Fax: (717) 334-1758
E-mail: registerrecorder@adamscounty.us

Register of Wills and Recorder of Deeds
  Linda K. Myers . . . . (717) 337-9826
  E-mail: registerrecorder@adamscounty.us

Allegheny County

Court Records

Department of Court Records
Allegheny County Court House, 436 Grant Street, Room 114,
Pittsburgh, PA 15219
Internet: http://www.alleghenycounty.us/Civil/index.aspx

Director **Kate Barkman** . . . . (412) 350-5729
  E-mail: civil@alleghenycounty.us

Real Estate

Department of Real Estate
542 Forbes Avenue, Room 101, Pittsburgh, PA 15219-2904
Tel: (412) 350-4226 Fax: (412) 350-6877
E-mail: deptrealestate@alleghenycounty.us

Manager (Acting) **Jerry Tyskiewicz** . . . . (412) 350-4226

Armstrong County

Clerk of Court and Prothonotary

Thirty-Third Judicial Circuit
500 East Market Street, Suite 200, Kittanning, PA 16201
Tel: (724) 548-3284 Fax: (724) 548-3310
Internet: www.accourts.com

Clerk of Courts and Prothonotary **Brenda C. George** . . . . (724) 548-3251
  500 East Market Street, Suite 103,
  Kittanning, PA 16201
  E-mail: brenda.george@pacourts.us

Recorder

Office of the Register of Wills and Recorder of Deeds
500 East Market Street, Suite 102 , Kittanning, PA 16201
Tel: (724) 548-3220 Fax: (724) 548-3236

Register of Wills and Recorder of Deeds
  Marianne Hileman . . . . (724) 548-3220
  E-mail: mhileman@co.armstrong.pa.us

Beaver County

Clerk of Court

Thirty-Sixth Judicial District
Beaver County Courthouse, 810 Third Street, Beaver, PA 15009
Tel: (724) 770-4700 Fax: (724) 728-8708
Internet: www.beavercountycourts.org

Clerk of Court **Judy R. Enslen** . . . . (724) 728-5700
  Beaver County Courthouse, 810 Third Street,   Fax: (724) 728-8853
  Beaver, PA 15009
  E-mail: jenslen@beavercountypa.gov

Prothonotary

Office of the Prothonotary
810 Third Street, Beaver, PA 15009
Tel: (724) 770-4570 Fax: (724) 728-3360

Prothonotary **Nancy Cozzucoli Werme** . . . . (724) 770-4570
  E-mail: nwerme@beavercountypa.gov

Recorder

Office of the Recorder of Deeds
810 Third Street, Beaver, PA 15009
Tel: (724) 770-4560 Fax: (724) 728-8479

Recorder of Deeds **Janice Jeschke Beall** . . . . (724) 770-4560
  E-mail: jbeall@beavercountypa.gov

Bedford County

Clerk of Court and Prothonotary

Fifty-Seventh Judicial District
200 South Juliana Street, Bedford, PA 15522
Tel: (814) 623-4812 Fax: (814) 623-3858

Clerk of Court and Prothonotary **Cathy J. Fetter** . . . .(814) 623-4833
  200 South Juliana Street, Bedford, PA 15522
  E-mail: cfetter@bedfordcountypa.org

Recorder

Office of the Register of Wills and Recorder of Deeds
200 South Juliana Street,, Bedford, PA 15522
Tel: (814) 623-4836 Fax: (814) 624-0488

Register of Wills and Recorder of Deeds
  Faith A. Zembower. . . . . (814) 623-4836
  E-mail: fzembower@bedfordcountypa.org

Berks County

Clerk of Court

Twenty-Third Judicial District
Berks County Courthouse, 633 Court Street, 7th Floor,
Reading, PA 19601
Tel: (610) 478-6208 Fax: (610) 478-6366
Internet: www.co.berks.pa.us/courts/site/default.asp

Clerk of Court **James P. Troutman**. . . . .(610) 478-6550
  Berks County Courthouse, 633 Court Street,   Fax: (610) 478-6570
  Reading, PA 19601
  E-mail: jtroutman@co.berks.pa.us

Prothonotary

Office of the Prothonotary
633 Court Street, Second Floor, Reading, PA 19601
Tel: (610) 478-6970 Fax: (610) 478-6969
E-mail: prothonotary@countyofberks.com
Internet: www.co.berks.pa.us/prothonotary/site/default.asp

Prothonotary **Marianne Sutton** . . . . (610) 478-6970
  E-mail: msutton@countyofberks.com

Recorder

Office of the Recorder of Deeds
633 Court Street, Third Floor, Reading, PA 19601
Tel: (610) 478-3380 Fax: (610) 478-3359
E-mail: recorder@countyofberks.com

Recorder of Deeds **Frederick C. Sheeler** . . . . (610) 478-3380
  E-mail: fsheeler@countyofberks.com

Blair County

Clerk of Court and Prothonotary

Twenty-Fourth Judicial District
Blair County Courthouse, 423 Allegheny Street, Suite 239,
Hollidaysburg, PA 16648
Tel: (814) 693-3050

Clerk of Court and Prothonotary **Carol A. Newman** . . . . . (814) 693-3080
  Blair County Courthouse, 423 Allegheny Street,   Tel: (814) 317-1600
  Hollidaysburg, PA 16648
  E-mail: cnewman@blairco.org

Recorder

Office of the Register of Wills and Recorder of Deeds
423 Allegheny Street, Hollidaysburg, PA 16648
Tel: (814) 693-3097 Fax: (814) 693-3093

Register of Wills and Recorder of Deeds
  Mary Ann Bennis . . . . (814) 693-3097
  E-mail: mbennis@blairco.org

Bradford County

Clerk of Court and Prothonotary

Forty-Second Judicial District
Bradford County Courthouse, 301 Main Street, Towanda, PA 18848
Tel: (570) 265-1707
Internet: www.bradfordcountypa.org/Courts

Clerk of Court and Prothonotary **Sally F. Vaughn** . . . . (570) 265-1705
  Bradford County Courthouse, 301 Main Street,   Fax: (570) 265-1788
  Towanda, PA 18848
  E-mail: vaughns@bradfordco.org

Recorder

Office of the Register of Wills and Recorder of Deeds
301 Main Street, Towanda, PA 18848
Tel: (570) 265-1702 Fax: (570) 265-1721

Register of Wills and Recorder of Deeds
  Shirley Rockefeller . . . . (570) 265-1702
  E-mail: bcregrec@bradfordco.org

Bucks County

Clerk of Court

Seventh Judicial District
Bucks County Justice Center, 100 North Main Street,
Doylestown, PA 18901
Tel: (215) 348-6040 Fax: (215) 348-6386
Internet: www.buckscounty.org/courts/CourtInfo/CommonPleas.aspx

Clerk of Court **Mary K. Smithson** . . . . (215) 348-6389
  Bucks County Courthouse, 100 North Main Street,   Fax: (215) 348-6740
  Doylestown, PA 18901
  E-mail: cocassociates@co.bucks.pa.us

Prothonotary

Office of the Prothonotary
Bucks County Administration Building, 55 East Court Street,
2nd Floor, Doylestown, PA 18901
Bucks County Justice Center, 100 N. Main Street, Doylestown, PA 18901
Tel: (215) 348-6191 Fax: (215) 348-6184
Internet: www.buckscounty.org/government/rowofficers/prothonotary

Prothonotary **Patricia L. Bachtle** . . . . (215) 348-6191
  E-mail: plbachtle@co.bucks.pa.us

(continued on next page)

Recorder

Office of the Recorder of Deeds
Administration Building, 55 East Court Street, 2nd Floor,
Doylestown, PA 18901
Fax: (215) 340-8157
E-mail: recorderdeeds@co.bucks.pa.us

Recorder **Joseph J. Szafran, Jr.** . . . . (215) 348-6209

Butler County

Clerk of Court

Fiftieth Judicial District
Butler County Courthouse, 124 West Diamond Street, Butler, PA 16003
P.O. Box 1208, Butler, PA 16003
Tel: (724) 284-5200

Clerk of Courts **Lisa Weiland Lotz** . . . . (724) 284-5233
Butler County Courthouse,
124 West Diamond Street,
Butler, PA 16003
P.O. Box 1208, Butler, PA 16003
E-mail: llotz@co.butler.pa.us

Prothonotary

Office of the Prothonotary
300 South Main Street, 1st Floor, Butler, PA 16003-1208
Tel: (724) 284-5214

Prothonotary **Glenna Walters** . . . . (724) 284-5214
E-mail: gwalters@co.butler.pa.us

Recorder

Office of the Recorder of Deeds
124 West Diamond Street, Floor L, Butler, PA 16001
Tel: (724) 284-5340 Fax: (724) 285-9099

Recorder of Deeds **Michele Mustello** . . . . (724) 284-5340
E-mail: mmustell@co.butler.pa.us

Cambria County

Clerk of Court

Forty-Seventh Judicial District
Cambria County Courthouse, 200 South Center Street,
Ebensburg, PA 15931
Tel: (814) 472-1501 Fax: (814) 472-0761

Clerk of Court **Susan M. Kuhar** . . . . (814) 472-1540
Cambria County Courthouse,   Fax: (814) 472-0761
200 South Center Street, Ebensburg, PA 15931
E-mail: skuhar@cambriacountypa.gov

Prothonotary

Office of the Prothonotary
200 South Center Street, Ebensburg, PA 15931
Tel: (814) 472-1638 Fax: (814) 472-5632

Prothonotary **Debbie Martella** . . . . (814) 472-1638
E-mail: dmartella@co.cambria.pa.us

Recorder

Office of the Recorder of Deeds
200 South Center Street, Ebensburg, PA 15931
Tel: (814) 472-1473 Fax: (814) 472-1412

Recorder of Deeds **Andrea Sims** . . . . (814) 472-1473
E-mail: asims@co.cambria.pa.us

Cameron County

Clerk of Court, Prothonotary, and Recorder

Fifty-Ninth Judicial District
250 Main Street, Ridgway, PA 15853
P.O. Box 416, Ridgway, PA 15853
Tel: (814) 776-6144 Fax: (814) 772-7780

Prothonotary, Cameron County **Mary Grace Olay** . . . . (814) 486-3355
20 East Fifth Street, Emporium, PA 15834
E-mail: mgraceolay@yahoo.com

Carbon County

Clerk of Court

Fifty-Sixth Judicial District
Carbon County Courthouse, Four Broadway, Jim Thorpe, PA 18229
P.O. Box 131, Jim Thorpe, PA 18229
Tel: (570) 325-8556 Fax: (570) 325-9449
Internet: www.carboncourts.com

Clerk of Court **William C. McGinley** . . . . (570) 325-3637
Carbon County Courthouse, Four Broadway,   Fax: (570) 325-5705
Jim Thorpe, PA 18229
P.O. Box 107, Jim Thorpe, PA 18229
E-mail: bmcginley@carboncourts.com

Prothonotary

Office of the Prothonotary
P.O. Box 130, Jim Thorpe, PA 18229
Tel: (570) 325-2481 Fax: (570) 325-8047

Prothonotary **Joann M. Behrens** . . . . (570) 325-2481

Recorder

Office of the Recorder of Deeds
PO Box 89, Jim Thorpe, PA 18229
Tel: (570) 325-2651 Fax: (570) 325-2726

Recorder of Deeds **Emmett P. McCall** . . . . (570) 325-2651

Centre County

Clerk of Court and Prothonotary

Forty-Ninth Judicial District
Centre County Courthouse, 102 Allegheny Street,
Bellefonte, PA 16823-1488
Tel: (814) 355-6727 Fax: (814) 355-6707
Internet: www.co.centre.pa.us/271.asp

Clerk of Courts and Prothonotary **Debra C. Immel** . . . . . . (814) 355-6796
Centre County Courthouse,   Fax: (814) 355-8686
Allegheny and High Streets,
Bellefonte, PA 16823
E-mail: dimmel@centrecountypa.gov

Recorder

Office of the Recorder of Deeds
420 Holmes Street, Bellefonte, PA 16823-1488
Tel: (814) 355-6801 Fax: (814) 355-8680

Recorder of Deeds **Joseph L. Davidson** . . . . (814) 355-6801
414 Holmes Street, Bellefonte, PA 16823-1488
E-mail: rodinfo@centrecountypa.gov

Chester County

Clerk of Court

Fifteenth Judicial District
201 West Marker Street, Suite 4100, West Chester, PA 19380-0989
Tel: (610) 344-6170 Fax: (610) 344-6127
Internet: http://dsf.chesco.org/courts/site/default.asp

Clerk of Court **Robin Marcello** . . . . (610) 344-6135
  Chester County Courthouse,   Fax: (610) 344-6605
  201 West Market Street, Suite 1400,
  West Chester, PA 19380-0989
  P.O. Box 2746, West Chester, PA 19380-0989
  E-mail: rmarcello@chesco.org

Prothonotary

Office of the Prothonotary
201 West Market Street, Suite 1425, West Chester, PA 19380
P.O. Box 2746, West Chester, PA 19380-0989
Fax: (610) 344-5903

Prothonotary **Bryan D. Walters** . . . . (610) 344-6300
  E-mail: bwalters@chesco.org

Recorder

Office of the Recorder of Deeds
313 West Market Street, Suite 3302, West Chester, PA 19380-0991
P.O. Box 2748, West Chester, PA 19380-0991
Tel: (610) 344-6330 Fax: (610) 344-6408
Internet: www.chesco.org/recorder

Recorder of Deeds **Rick Loughery** . . . . (610) 344-6330

Clarion County

Clerk of Court and Prothonotary

Eighteenth Judicial District
Clarion County Courthouse, 421 Main Street, Suite 34, Clarion, PA 16214
Tel: (814) 226-9351 Fax: (814) 226-1097

Clerk of Court and Prothonotary
  Jeffrey A. Himes . . . . (814) 226-4000 ext. 2402
  Clarion County Courthouse, 421 Main Street,   Fax: (814) 227-2501
  Clarion, PA 16214
  E-mail: jhimes@co.clarion.pa.us

Recorder

Office of the Register of Wills and Recorder of Deeds
421 Main Street, 1st Floor, Suite 24, Clarion, PA 16214
Tel: (814) 226-4000 Fax: (814) 226-1117

Register of Wills and Recorder of Deeds
  Greg Mortimer . . . . (814) 226-4000 ext. 2500
  E-mail: gmortimer@co.clarion.pa.us

Clearfield County

Clerk of Court and Prothonotary

Forty-Sixth Judicial District
Clearfield County Courthouse, 230 East Market Street, Suite 228,
Clearfield, PA 16830
Tel: (814) 765-2641 Fax: (814) 765-7649
E-mail: courtadmin@clearfieldco.org
Internet: www.clearfieldco.org/courts.htm

Clerk of Court and Prothonotary
  Brian Spencer . . . . (814) 765-2641 ext. 5980
  Clearfield County Courthouse,   Fax: (814) 765-7659
  230 East Market Street, Clearfield, PA 16830
  P.O. Box 549, Clearfield, PA 16830

Recorder

Office of the Register of Wills and Recorder of Deeds
P.O. Box 361, Clearfield, PA 16830
Tel: (814) 765-2641 ext. 5012 Fax: (814) 765-6089

Register of Wills and Recorder of Deeds
  Maurene E. Inlow . . . . (814) 765-2641 ext. 5012
  E-mail: minlow@clearfieldco.org

Clinton County

Clerk of Court and Prothonotary

Twenty-Fifth Judicial District
Clinton County Courthouse, 230 East Water Street,
Lock Haven, PA 17745
Tel: (570) 893-4016 Fax: (570) 893-4145
Internet: www.clintoncountypa.com/courts.htm

Clerk of Court and Prothonotary **Marie J. Vilello** . . . . (570) 893-4007
  Clinton County Courthouse, 230 East Water Street,   Fax: (570) 893-4288
  Lock Haven, PA 17745
  E-mail: mvilello@clintoncountypa.com

Recorder

Office of the Register of Wills and Recorder of Deeds
230 East Water Street, Lock Haven, PA 17745
Tel: (570) 893-4010 Fax: (570) 893-4273

Register and Recorder **Jennifer L. Hoy** . . . . (570) 893-4010
  E-mail: regrec@clintoncountypa.com

Columbia County

Clerk of Court and Prothonotary

Twenty-Sixth Judicial District
Columbia County Courthouse, 35 West Main Street,
Bloomsburg, PA 17815
Tel: (570) 389-5667 Fax: (570) 389-5621
Internet: www.columbiapa.org/courts/index.php

Clerk of Court and Prothonotary (Columbia County)
  Barbara Silvetti . . . . (570) 389-5618
  Columbia County Courthouse, 35 West Main Street,   Fax: (570) 389-5620
  Bloomsburg, PA 17815
  P.O. Box 380, Bloomsburg, PA 17815
  E-mail: barbara.silvetti@pacourts.us

Recorder

Office of the Register of Wills and Recorder of Deeds
35 West Main Street, Bloomsburg, PA 17815
Tel: (570) 389-5632 Fax: (570) 389-5636

Register of Wills and Recorder of Deeds
  Brenda Lupini . . . . (570) 389-5632
  E-mail: blupini@columbiapa.org

Crawford County

Clerk of Court

Thirtieth Judicial District
Crawford County Courthouse, 903 Diamond Park, Meadville, PA 16335
Tel: (814) 333-7498 Fax: (814) 333-7489

Clerk of Court **Patricia A. "Patti" Wetherbee** . . . . (814) 333-7442
  Crawford County Courthouse, 903 Diamond Park,   Fax: (814) 333-7349
  Meadville, PA 16335
  E-mail: pwetherbee@crawfordcountypa.net

(continued on next page)

Prothonotary

Office of the Prothonotary
903 Diamond Park, 1st Floor, Meadville, PA 16335
Tel: (814) 333-7324   Fax: (814) 337-5416

Prothonotary **Emmy Arnett** . . . . (814) 333-7324
E-mail: earnett@co.crawford.pa.us

Recorder

Office of the Register of Wills and Recorder of Deeds
903 Diamond Park, Meadville, PA 16335
Tel: (814) 373-2537   Fax: (814) 337-5296

Register of Wills and Recorder of Deeds
Deborah Curry . . . . (814) 373-2537
E-mail: dcurry@co.crawford.pa.us

Cumberland County

Clerk of Court

Ninth Judicial District
Cumberland County Courthouse, One Courthouse Square,
Tunkhannock, PA 18657
Tel: (717) 240-6200   Fax: (717) 240-6460
E-mail: courtadmin@ccpa.net

Clerk of Court **Dennis E. Lebo** . . . . (717) 240-7748
Cumberland County Courthouse,   Fax: (717) 240-6571
One Courthouse Square, Tunkhannock, PA 18657
E-mail: clerkofcourts@ccpa.net

Prothonotary

Office of the Prothonotary
1 Courthouse Square, Suite 100, Carlisle, PA 17013
Tel: (717) 240-6195   Fax: (717) 240-6573

Prothonotary **David D. Buell** . . . . (717) 240-6195
E-mail: dbuell@ccpa.net

Recorder

Office of the Recorder of Deeds
1 Courthouse Square, Carlisle, PA 17013
Tel: (717) 240-6370
E-mail: recorderofdeeds@ccpa.net

Recorder of Deeds **Tammy Shearer** . . . . (717) 240-6370

Dauphin County

Clerk of Court

Twelfth Judicial District
Market and Front Streets, Harrisburg, PA 17101
Tel: (717) 780-6624   Fax: (717) 780-6465

Clerk of Court **Dale Elise Klein** . . . . (717) 780-6530
Dauphin County Courthouse, 101 Market Street,
Harrisburg, PA 17101
E-mail: dklein@dauphincounty.org

Prothonotary

Office of the Prothonotary
101 Market Street, Room 101, Harrisburg, PA 17101
Tel: (717) 780-6520

Prothonotary **Stephen E. Farina** . . . . (717) 780-6520
E-mail: sfarina@dauphinc.org

Recorder

Office of the Recorder of Deeds
101 Market Street, Room 102, Harrisburg, PA 17101
Tel: (717) 780-6560
Internet: www.dauphinc.org/deeds

Recorder of Deeds **James M. Zugay** . . . . (717) 780-6560
E-mail: jzugay@dauphinc.org

Delaware County

Judicial Support

Office of Judicial Support
Courthouse, 210 West Front Street, Media, PA 19063

Director **Angela L. Martinez** . . . . (610) 891-4370
E-mail: martineza@co.delaware.pa.us

Recorder

Office of the Recorder of Deeds
Government Center Bldg., 201 West Front Street, Room 107,
Media, PA 19063
Tel: (610) 891-4152

Recorder **Thomas J. Judge, Sr.** . . . . (610) 891-4152
E-mail: judget@co.delaware.pa.us

Elk County

Clerk of Court and Prothonotary

Fifty-Ninth Judicial District
250 Main Street, Ridgway, PA 15853
P.O. Box 416, Ridgway, PA 15853
Tel: (814) 776-6144   Fax: (814) 772-7780

Clerk of Court and Prothonotary, Elk County
Susanne Straub Schneider . . . . (814) 776-5344
240 Main Street, Ridgway, PA 15853   Fax: (814) 776-5303
P.O. Box 416, Ridgway, PA 15853
E-mail: sschneider@co.elk.pa.us

Recorder

Office of the Register of Wills and Recorder of Deeds
250 Main Street, Ridgway, PA 15853
Tel: (814) 776-5349   Fax: (814) 776-5382

Register of Wills and Recorder of Deeds
Pete Weidenboerner . . . . (814) 776-5349
E-mail: pete@countyofelkpa.com

Erie County

Clerk of Records

Office of the Clerk of Records
140 West Sixth Street, Room 120, Erie, PA 16501-1029
Tel: (814) 451-6250   Fax: (814) 451-6213

Clerk of Records **Kenneth J. "Ken" Gamble** . . . . (814) 451-6080
E-mail: kgamble@eriecountygov.org

Fayette County

Clerk of Court

Fourteenth Judicial District
Fayette County Courthouse, 61 East Main Street, Uniontown, PA 15401
Tel: (724) 430-1230 Fax: (724) 430-1001

Clerk of Court **Janice Snyder** . . . . (724) 430-1253
Fayette County Courthouse, 61 East Main Street,   Fax: (724) 438-8410
Uniontown, PA 15401
E-mail: janice.snyder@pacourts.us

Prothonotary

Office of the Prothonotary
61 East Main Street, Uniontown, PA 15401
Tel: (724) 430-1272 Fax: (724) 430-4555

Prothonotary **Nina Frankhouser** . . . . (724) 430-1272
E-mail: nfrankhouser@fayettepa.org

Recorder

Office of the Recorder of Deeds
61 East Main Street, Uniontown, PA 15401
Tel: (724) 430-1238 Fax: (724) 430-1458

Recorder of Deeds **David G. Malosky** . . . . (724) 430-1238

Forest County

Clerk of Court

Thirty-Seventh Judicial District
Warren County Courthouse, 204 Fourth Avenue, Warren, PA 16365
Tel: (814) 728-3530 Fax: (814) 728-3452
Internet: www.warrenforestcourt.org

Clerk of Court, Prothonotary, Register of Wills and
Recorder of Deeds, Forest County **Dawn M. Millin** . . . . (814) 755-3526
526 Elm Street, Suite 2, Tionesta, PA 16353   Fax: (814) 755-8837
E-mail: dmillin@co.forest.pa.us

Franklin County

Clerk of Court

Thirty-Ninth Judicial District
157 Lincoln Way East, Chambersburg, PA 17201
Tel: (717) 261-3848 Fax: (717) 261-3854

Clerk of Court, Franklin County **William E. Vandrew** . . . . (717) 261-3805
157 Lincoln Way East, Chambersburg, PA 17201

Prothonotary

Office of the Prothonotary
157 Lincoln Way East, Chambersburg, PA 17201
Tel: (717) 261-3858 Fax: (717) 264-6772

Prothonotary **Linda L. Beard** . . . . (717) 261-3858
E-mail: lbeard@franklincountypa.gov

Recorder

Office of the Register of Wills and Recorder of Deeds
157 Lincoln Way East, Chambersburg, PA 17201
Tel: (717) 261-3872 Fax: (717) 709-7211

Register of Wills and Recorder of Deeds **Linda Miller** . . . . (717) 261-3872
E-mail: lmiller@co.franklin.pa.us

Fulton County

Clerk of Court, Prothonotary, and Recorder

Thirty-Ninth Judicial District
157 Lincoln Way East, Chambersburg, PA 17201
Tel: (717) 261-3848 Fax: (717) 261-3854

Prothonotary, Fulton County **Patty Suders Fix** . . . . (717) 485-4212
Fulton County Courthouse,
201 North Second Street,
McConnellsburg, PA 17233
E-mail: prothonotary@co.fulton.pa.us

Greene County

Clerk of Court

Thirteenth Judicial District
Greene County Courthouse, 10 East High Street, Waynesburg, PA 15370
Tel: (724) 852-5237 Fax: (724) 627-4716

Clerk of Court **Sherry Wise** . . . . (724) 852-5281
Greene County Courthouse, 10 East High Street,   Fax: (724) 852-5316
Room 103, Waynesburg, PA 15370

Prothonotary

Office of the Prothonotary
10 East High Street, 1st Floor, Waynesburg, PA 15370
Tel: (724) 852-5288 Fax: (724) 852-5353

Prothonotary **Susan Kartley White** . . . . (724) 852-5288
E-mail: swhite@co.greene.pa.us

Recorder

Office of the Register of Wills and Recorder of Deeds
10 East High Street, Room 101, Waynesburg, PA 15370
Greene County Courthouse, 10 East High Street, Room 100,
Waynesburg, PA 15370
Tel: (724) 852-5283

Register of Wills and Recorder of Deeds (Acting)
Donna J. Tharp . . . . (724) 852-5284
E-mail: dtharp@co.greene.pa.us

Huntingdon County

Clerk of Court and Prothonotary

Twentieth Judicial District
223 Penn Street, Huntingdon, PA 16652
Tel: (814) 643-5078 Fax: (814) 643-8177

Clerk of Court and Prothonotary **Kay Coons** . . . . (814) 643-1610
P.O. Box 39, Huntingdon, PA 16652   Fax: (814) 643-4271
E-mail: kcoons@huntingdoncounty.net

Recorder

Office of the Register of Wills and Recorder of Deeds
223 Penn Street, Huntingdon, PA 16652
Tel: (814) 643-2740 Fax: (814) 643-6849

Register of Wills and Recorder of Deeds
Virginia Cooper . . . . (814) 643-2740
E-mail: regrec@huntingdoncounty.net

(continued on next page)

Indiana County

Clerk of Court and Prothonotary

Fortieth Judicial District
825 Philadelphia Street, Fourth Floor, Indiana, PA 15701
Tel: (724) 465-3955 Fax: (724) 463-2532
Internet: www.countyofindiana.org/courts

Clerk of Court and Prothonotary **Randy Degenkolb** . . . . . (724) 465-3855
825 Philadelphia Street, First Floor,
Indiana, PA 15701
E-mail: pcc@countyofindiana.org

Recorder

Office of the Register of Wills and Recorder of Deeds
825 Philadelphia Street, Indiana, PA 15701
Tel: (724) 465-3860 Fax: (724) 465-3863

Register of Wills and Recorder of Deeds
Patricia "Patty" Streams-Warman . . . . (724) 465-3860
E-mail: pswarman@countyofindiana.org

Jefferson County

Clerk of Court and Prothonotary

Fifty-Fourth Judicial District
Jefferson County Courthouse, 200 Main Street, Brookville, PA 15825
Tel: (814) 849-1631
E-mail: admin.court@jeffersoncountypa.com

Clerk of Court and Prothonotary **Tonya S. Geist** . . . . (814) 849-1606
Jefferson County Courthouse, 200 Main Street,   Fax: (814) 849-1625
Brookville, PA 15825

Recorder

Office of the Register of Wills and Recorder of Deeds
200 Main Street, Brookville, PA 15825
Tel: (814) 849-1610 Fax: (814) 849-1677

Register of Wills and Recorder of Deeds
Diane Maihle Kiehl . . . . (814) 849-1610
E-mail: dkiehl@co.jefferson.pa.us

Juniata County

Clerk of Court and Prothonotary

Forty-First Judicial District
2 East Main Street, New Bloomfield, PA 17068
P.O. Box 668, New Bloomfield, PA 17068
Tel: (717) 582-2131 Fax: (717) 582-5166

Clerk of Court and Prothonotary, Juniata County
Lori A. Ferry . . . . (717) 436-7715
Juniata County Courthouse,   Fax: (717) 436-7734
Bridge and Main Streets, Mifflintown, PA 17059
P.O. Box 68, Mifflintown, PA 17059
E-mail: lferry@juniataco.org

Recorder

Office of the Register of Wills and Recorder of Deeds
One North Main Street, Mifflintown, PA 17059
Tel: (717) 436-7709 Fax: (717) 436-7756

Register of Wills and Recorder of Deeds
Alicia A. Seigler . . . . (717) 436-7709
E-mail: aseigler@juniataco.org

Lackawanna County

Clerk of Court and Prothonotary

Forty-Fifth Judicial District
200 North Washington Avenue, Scranton, PA 18503
Tel: (570) 963-6773 Fax: (570) 963-6477

Clerk of Court and Prothonotary **Mary F. Rinaldi** . . . . (570) 963-6723
Brooks Building, 436 Spruce Street,   Fax: (570) 963-6387
Scranton, PA 18503
E-mail: rinaldim@lackawannacounty.org

Recorder

Office of the Recorder of Deeds
Lackawanna County Gateway Center, 135 Jefferson Avenue,
Scranton, PA 18503
Tel: (570) 963-6775 Fax: (570) 963-6390

Recorder of Deeds **Evie Rafalko-McNulty** . . . . (570) 963-6775
E-mail: mcnultye@lackawannacounty.org

Lancaster County

Clerk of Court

Second Judicial District
Lancaster County Courthouse, 50 North Duke Street, Lancaster, PA 17608
Tel: (717) 299-8041 Fax: (717) 295-3599
Internet: www.co.lancaster.pa.us/courts/site/default.asp

Clerk of Court **Joshua G. Parsons** . . . . (717) 299-8275
Lancaster County Courthouse,   Fax: (717) 295-3686
50 North Duke Street, Lancaster, PA 17608
P.O. Box 83480, Lancaster, PA 17608

Prothonotary

Office of the Prothonotary
50 N. Duke St., Lancaster, PA 17608-3480
Fax: (717) 293-7210

Prothonotary
The Honorable Katherine Wood-Jacobs . . . . (717) 299-8282
E-mail: kwoodjacobs@co.lancaster.pa.us

Recorder

Office of the Recorder of Deeds
150 North Queen Street, Suite 315, Lancaster, PA 17603
Fax: (717) 299-8393

Recorder of Deeds **Bonnie Bowman** . . . . (717) 299-8238

Lawrence County

Clerk of Court and Prothonotary

Fifty-Third Judicial District
Lawrence County Government Center, 430 Court Street,
New Castle, PA 16101
Tel: (724) 656-1930 Fax: (724) 656-2476
Internet: www.co.lawrence.pa.us/courts/index.html

Clerk of Court and Prothonotary **Helen I. Morgan** . . . . (724) 656-2143
Lawrence County Government Center,   Fax: (724) 656-1988
430 Court Street, New Castle, PA 16101
E-mail: helen.morgan@pacourts.us

Pennsylvania Court Clerks and Courthouses *continued*

Recorder

Office of the Register of Wills and Recorder of Deeds
430 Court Street, New Castle, PA 16101
Tel: (724) 656-2128   Fax: (724) 656-1966

Register of Wills and Recorder of Deeds
  Janet L. Kalajainen . . . . (724) 656-2128
  E-mail: jkalajainen@co.lawrence.pa.us

Lebanon County

Clerk of Court

Fifty-Second Judicial District
Lebanon County Municipal Building, 400 South Eighth Street,
Lebanon, PA 17042
Tel: (717) 274-2801   Fax: (717) 228-4457

Clerk of Court and Prothonotary
  Barb Smith . . . . (717) 274-2801 ext. 2118
  Lebanon County Municipal Building,   Fax: (717) 228-4467
  400 South Eighth Street, Lebanon, PA 17042
  E-mail: clerkofcourts102@lebcnty.org

Recorder

Office of the Recorder of Deeds
400 South Eighth Street, Room 107, Lebanon, PA 17042-6794
Tel: (717) 228-4447   Fax: (717) 228-4456

Recorder of Deeds **Donna J. Lutz** . . . . (717) 228-4447
  E-mail: dlutz@lebcnty.org

Lehigh County

Clerk of Judicial Records

Thirty-First Judicial District
Lehigh County Courthouse, 455 West Hamilton Street,
Allentown, PA 18101
Tel: (610) 782-3014   Fax: (610) 820-3093
Internet: www.lccpa.org

Clerk of Judicial Records **Andrea E. Naugle** . . . . (610) 782-3148
  Lehigh County Courthouse,
  455 West Hamilton Street,
  Allentown, PA 18101

Luzerne County

Clerk of Court and Prothonotary

Eleventh Judicial District
Luzerne County Courthouse, 200 North River Street,
Wilkes Barre, PA 18711
Tel: (570) 825-1500
Internet: www.luzernecountycourts.com

Clerk of Courts and Prothonotary **James Haddock** . . . . . . (570) 825-1585
  Luzerne County Courthouse,   Fax: (570) 825-1757
  200 North River Street, Wilkes Barre, PA 18711

Judicial Services and Records

Division of Judicial Services and Records
200 North River Street, Wilkes Barre, PA 18711
Fax: (570) 970-4580

Director **Joan Hoggarth** . . . . (570) 706-8412

Pennsylvania Court Clerks and Courthouses *continued*

Recorder

Office of the Recorder of Deeds
200 North River Street, Wilkes Barre, PA 18711
Fax: (570) 970-4580

Register of Wills and Recorder of Deeds
  Mary Dysleski . . . . (570) 825-1641

Lycoming County

Clerk of Court and Prothonotary

Twenty-Ninth Judicial District
Lycoming County Courthouse, 48 West Third Street, 4th Floor,
Williamsport, PA 17701
Tel: (570) 327-2330   Fax: (570) 327-2293

Clerk of Court and Prothonotary **Suzanne M. Fedele** . . . . (570) 327-2256
  Lycoming County Courthouse,   Fax: (570) 327-2505
  48 West Third Street, Williamsport, PA 17701
  E-mail: sfedele@lyco.org

Recorder

Office of the Register of Wills and Recorder of Deeds
48 West Third Street, 1st floor, Williamsport, PA 17701
Tel: (570) 327-2263   Fax: (570) 327-6790

Register of Wills and Recorder of Deeds
  Annabel Miller . . . . (570) 327-2263
  E-mail: amiller@lyco.org

McKean County

Clerk of Court and Prothonotary

Forty-Eighth Judicial District
McKean County Courthouse, 500 West Main Street, Smethport, PA 16749
Tel: (814) 887-3323   Fax: (814) 887-2712

Clerk of Court and Prothonotary
  Bonnie Moore Howard . . . . (814) 887-3270
  McKean County Courthouse, 500 West Main Street,   Fax: (814) 887-3219
  Smethport, PA 16749
  E-mail: bmhoward@mckeancountypa.org

Recorder

Office of the Recorder of Deeds
500 West Main Street, Smethport, PA 16749
Tel: (814) 887-3250   Fax: (814) 887-3255

Recorder of Deeds **Anne Bosworth** . . . . (814) 887-3250
  E-mail: acbosworth@mckeancountypa.org

Mercer County

Clerk of Court

Thirty-Fifth Judicial District
103 North Diamond Street, Suite 205, Mercer, PA 16137
Tel: (724) 662-3800

Clerk of Court **Kathleen M. Kloos** . . . . (724) 662-7548
  112 Mercer County Courthouse,   Fax: (724) 662-1530
  Mercer, PA 16137
  E-mail: kkloos@mcc.co.mercer.pa.us

(continued on next page)

Pennsylvania Court Clerks and Courthouses *continued*

Prothonotary

Office of the Prothonotary
Mercer County Courthouse, Room 105, Mercer, PA 16137
Tel: (724) 662-7561 Fax: (724) 662-2021

Prothonotary **Ruth Bice** . . . . (724) 662-7561
   E-mail: rbice@mcc.co.mercer.pa.us

Recorder

Office of the Recorder of Deeds
Mercer County Courthouse, Room 109, Mercer, PA 16137
Tel: (724) 662-3800 Fax: (724) 662-2096

Recorder of Deeds **Dee Dee Zickar** . . . . (724) 662-3800
   E-mail: dzickar@mcc.co.mercer.pa.us

Mifflin County

Clerk of Court and Prothonotary

Fifty-Eighth Judicial District
Mifflin County Courthouse, 20 North Wayne Street, Lewistown, PA 17044
Tel: (717) 248-4613 Fax: (717) 248-8337

Clerk of Court and Prothonotary **Tammy Stuck** . . . . (717) 248-8146
   Mifflin County Courthouse, 20 North Wayne Street,   Fax: (717) 248-5275
   Lewistown, PA 17044
   E-mail: prothonotary@co.mifflin.pa.us

Recorder

Office of the Register of Wills and Recorder of Deeds
20 North Wayne Street, Second Floor, Wayne, PA 17044
Tel: (717) 242-1449 Fax: (717) 248-2503

Register of Wills and Recorder of Deeds
   Barbara A. Stringer . . . . (717) 242-1449
   E-mail: bstringer@co.mifflin.pa.us

Monroe County

Clerk of Court and Prothonotary

Forty-Third Judicial District
Monroe County Courthouse, 610 Monroe Street, Stroudsburg, PA 18360
Tel: (570) 517-3009 Fax: (570) 517-3866

Clerk of Court and Prothonotary **George J. Warden** . . . . . (570) 517-3390
   Monroe County Courthouse, 610 Monroe Street,   Fax: (570) 420-3582
   Stroudsburg, PA 18360
   E-mail: gwarden@co.monroe.pa.us

Recorder

Office of the Register of Wills and Recorder of Deeds
Monroe County Courthouse, Seventh and Monroe Streets,
Stroudsburg, PA 18360
Tel: (570) 517-3969 Fax: (570) 517-3873

Register of Wills and Recorder of Deeds
   Helen Diecidue . . . . (570) 517-3969
   E-mail: hdiecidue@monroecountypa.gov

Pennsylvania Court Clerks and Courthouses *continued*

Montgomery County

Clerk of Court

Thirty-Eighth Judicial District
P.O. Box 311, Norristown, PA 19404
Tel: (610) 278-3224 Fax: (610) 292-2027
Internet: http://courts.montcopa.org/courts/site/default.asp

Clerk of Court **Ann Thornburg Weiss** . . . . (610) 278-3346
   P.O. Box 311, Norristown, PA 19404   Fax: (610) 278-5188
   E-mail: ann.weiss@pacourts.us

Prothonotary

Office of the Prothonotary
Airy and Swede Streets, Norristown, PA 19404
Office of the Prothonotary, P.O. Box 311, Norristown, PA 19404-0311
Fax: (610) 278-5994

Prothonotary **Mark Levy** . . . . (610) 278-3360

Recorder

Recorder of Deeds
One Montgomery Plaza, 425 Swede Street, Third Floor,
Norristown, PA 19404
P.O. Box 311, Norristown, PA 19404-0311
Fax: (610) 278-3869

Recorder of Deeds **Nancy J. Becker** . . . . (610) 278-3289

Montour County

Clerk of Court

Twenty-Sixth Judicial District
Columbia County Courthouse, 35 West Main Street,
Bloomsburg, PA 17815
Tel: (570) 389-5667 Fax: (570) 389-5621
Internet: www.columbiapa.org/courts/index.php

Clerk of Court and Prothonotary (Montour County)
   Susan M. Kauwell . . . . (570) 271-3010
   29 Mill Street, Danville, PA 17821

Recorder

Office of the Register of Wills and Recorder of Deeds
29 Mill Street, Danville, PA 17821
Tel: (570) 271-3012

Register of Wills and Recorder of Deeds
   Linda Weaver . . . . (570) 271-3012
   E-mail: montourregrec@yahoo.com

Northampton County

Clerk of Court

Third Judicial District
Northampton County Government Center, 669 Washington Street,
Easton, PA 18042
Tel: (610) 559-6700 Fax: (610) 559-6702
Internet: www.nccpa.org

Clerk of Court (Criminal) **Leigh Ann Fisher** . . . . (610) 559-3097
   Northampton County Government   Fax: (610) 252-4391
   Center, 669 Washington Street,
   Easton, PA 18042
   E-mail: lfisher@northamptoncounty.org

Prothonotary

Civil Division
Northampton County Courthouse, 669 Washington Street,
Easton, PA 18042-7475
Tel: (610) 559-3060

Clerk of Court and Prothonotary **Holly Ruggiero** . . . . (610) 559-3060

Recorder

Recorder of Deeds Division
Northampton County Courthouse, 669 Washington Street,
Easton, PA 18042-7475
Tel: (610) 559-3226

Recorder of Deeds **Andrea F. Suter** . . . . (610) 559-3226

Northumberland County

Clerk of Court and Prothonotary

Eighth Judicial District
201 West Market Street, Sunbury, PA 17801
Tel: (570) 988-4167 Fax: (570) 988-4497

Clerk of Court and Prothonotary **Justin Dunkelberger** . . . (570) 988-4148
Northumberland County Courthouse,
201 Market Street, Sunbury, PA 17801

Recorder

Office of the Register of Wills and Recorder of Deeds
201 Market Street, Sunbury, PA 17801
Tel: (570) 988-4143 Fax: (570) 988-4141

Register of Wills and Recorder of Deeds
Mary L. Zimmerman . . . . (570) 988-4143
E-mail: regrecmz@norrycopa.net

Perry County

Clerk of Court and Prothonotary

Forty-First Judicial District
2 East Main Street, New Bloomfield, PA 17068
P.O. Box 668, New Bloomfield, PA 17068
Tel: (717) 582-2131 Fax: (717) 582-5166

Clerk of Court and Prothonotary, Perry County
Brenda J. Albright . . . . (717) 582-2131
P.O. Box 668, New Bloomfield, PA 17068   Fax: (717) 582-5167
E-mail: brenda.albright@pacourts.us

Recorder

Office of the Register of Wills and Recorder of Deeds
Two East Main Street, New Bloomfield, PA 17068
Tel: (717) 582-2131 Fax: (717) 582-5149

Register of Wills and Recorder of Deeds
Wendy M. Welfley . . . . (717) 582-2131
E-mail: wwelfley@perryco.org

Philadelphia County

Clerk of Court and Prothonotary

First Judicial District
386 City Hall, Philadelphia, PA 19107
Tel: (215) 686-7000 Fax: (215) 686-7967
Internet: http://fjd.phila.gov

Clerk of Courts and Prothonotary **Eric Feder** . . . . (215) 683-7700
310 Criminal Justice Center, 1301 Filbert Street,
Philadelphia, PA 19107
E-mail: eric.feder@pacourts.us

Recorder

Department of Records
City Hall, Room 154, Philadelphia, PA 19107
Tel: (215) 686-2268 Fax: (215) 686-2273
Internet: www.phila.gov/records/
E-mail: records.info@phila.gov

Commissioner/Recorder of Deeds **Joan T. Decker** . . . . (215) 686-2268
E-mail: Joan.Decker@phila.gov

Pike County

Clerk of Court and Prothonotary

Sixtieth Judicial District
410 Broad Street, Milford, PA 18337
Tel: (570) 296-3556 Fax: (570) 296-6054

Clerk of Court and Prothonotary **Denise Fitzpatrick** . . . . . (570) 296-7231
Pike County Courthouse, 412 Broad Street,   Fax: (570) 296-1931
Milford, PA 18337
E-mail: dfitzpatrick@pikepa.org

Recorder

Office of the Recorder of Deeds
506 Broad Street, Milford, PA 18337
Tel: (570) 296-3508 Fax: (570) 296-3514

Recorder of Deeds **Sharon Schroeder** . . . . (570) 296-3508
E-mail: sschroeder@pikepa.org

Potter County

Clerk of Court and Prothonotary

Fifty-Fifth Judicial District
One East Second Street, Room 30, Coudersport, PA 16915
Tel: (814) 274-9720 Fax: (814) 274-3363

Clerk of Court and Prothonotary **Kathy Schroeder** . . . . . . (814) 274-9740
One East Second Street, Room 23,   Fax: (814) 274-3361
Coudersport, PA 16915
E-mail: kschroeder@pottercountypa.net

Recorder

Office of the Register of Wills and Recorder of Deeds
One North Main Street, 1st Floor, Coudersport, PA 16915
Tel: (814) 274-8370 Fax: (814) 274-3360

Register of Wills and Recorder of Deeds
Gary E. Kelsey . . . . (814) 274-8370
E-mail: gkelsey@pottercountypa.net

(continued on next page)

Schuylkill County

Clerk of Court

Twenty-First Judicial District
Schuykill County Courthouse, 401 North Second Street,
Pottsville, PA 17901
Tel: (570) 628-1333

Clerk of Court **Thomas Campion, Jr.** . . . . (570) 628-1140
 Schuykill County Courthouse,   Fax: (570) 628-1143
 401 North Second Street, Pottsville, PA 17901

Prothonotary

Office of the Prothonotary
401 North Second Street, 1st Floor, Pottsville, PA 17901
Tel: (570) 628-1270 Fax: (570) 628-1210

Prothonotary **David J. Dutcavich** . . . . (570) 628-1270
 E-mail: ddutcavich@co.schuylkill.pa.us

Recorder

Office of the Recorder of Deeds
401 North Second Street, Pottsville, PA 17901
Tel: (570) 628-1481 Fax: (570) 628-1210

Recorder of Deeds **Ann Dudish** . . . . (570) 628-1481
 E-mail: adudish@co.schuylkill.pa.us

Snyder County

Clerk of Court and Prothonotary

Seventeenth Judicial District
Snyder County Courthouse, Nine West Market Street,
Middleburg, PA 17842 (Snyder County Address)
Union County Courthouse, 103 South Second Street,
Lewisburg, PA 17837 (Union County Address)
P.O. Box 217, Middleburg, PA 17842
Tel: (570) 837-4344 Tel: (570) 524-8641 (Union County contact)
Fax: (570) 524-8644 (Union County contact)

Clerk of Court and Prothonotary (Snyder County)
 Teresa J. Berger . . . . (570) 837-4202
 Snyder County Courthouse,   Fax: (570) 837-4299
 Nine West Market Street, Middleburg, PA 17842
 P.O. Box 217, Middleburg, PA 17842

Recorder

Office of the Register of Wills and Recorder of Deeds
Nine West Market Street, Middleburg, PA 17842
Tel: (570) 837-4224 Fax: (570) 837-4299

Register of Wills and Recorder of Deeds
 Stacey L. Zerbe . . . . (570) 837-4224
 E-mail: szerbe@snydercounty.org

Somerset County

Clerk of Court

Sixteenth Judicial District
111 East Union Street, Suite 200, Somerset, PA 15501
Tel: (814) 445-1473 Fax: (814) 445-1455

Clerk of Court **Rose Svonavec** . . . . (814) 445-1435
 111 East Union Street, Suite 110,
 Somerset, PA 15501
 E-mail: svonavecr@co.somerset.pa.us

Prothonotary

Office of the Prothonotary
111 East Union Street, Suite 165, Somerset, PA 15501
Tel: (814) 445-1428 Fax: (814) 444-9270

Prothonotary **Angie Svonavec** . . . . (814) 445-1428
 E-mail: prothonotary@co.somerset.pa.us

Recorder

Office of the Recorder of Deeds
300 North Center Avenue, Suite 400, Somerset, PA 15501
Tel: (814) 445-1547 Fax: (814) 445-1563

Recorder of Deeds **Patricia A. Peifer** . . . . (814) 445-1547
 E-mail: peiferp@co.somerset.pa.us

Sullivan County

Clerk of Court, Prothonotary, and Recorder

Forty-Fourth Judicial District
One Courthouse Square, Tunkhannock, PA 18657
Tel: (570) 836-3151

Clerk of Court and Prothonotary/Recorder, Sullivan
 County **Kellie Carpenter** . . . . (570) 946-7351
 Sullivan County Courthouse,   Fax: (570) 946-4075
 Maine and Muncy Streets,
 Laporte, PA 18626
 E-mail: kcarpenter@sullivancounty-pa.org

Susquehanna County

Clerk of Court and Prothonotary

Thirty-Fourth Judicial District
P.O. Box 218, Montrose, PA 18801
Tel: (570) 278-4600

Clerk of Court and Prothonotary **Susan Eddleston** . . . . . . (570) 278-4600
 Susquehanna County Courthouse, 11 Maple Street,
 Montrose, PA 18801
 P.O. Box 218, Montrose, PA 18801

Recorder

Office of the Register of Wills and Recorder of Deeds
105 Maple Street, Montrose, PA 18801
Tel: (570) 278-4600 Fax: (570) 278-2963

Register of Wills and Recorder of Deeds
 Mary F. Evans . . . . (570) 278-4600
 E-mail: regrec@susqco.com

Tioga County

Clerk of Court and Prothonotary

Fourth Judicial District
118 Main Street, Wellsboro, PA 16901
Tel: (570) 723-8380 Fax: (570) 723-1633

Clerk of Court and Prothonotary **Marie Seymour** . . . . (570) 724-9281
 Tioga County Courthouse, 116 Main Street,
 Wellsboro, PA 16901

Recorder

Office of the Register of Wills and Recorder of Deeds
116 Main Street, Wellsboro, PA 16901
Tel: (570) 724-9260

Register of Wills and Recorder of Deeds
Jane E. Wetherbee ....(570) 724-9260
E-mail: jwetherbee@tiogacountypa.us

Union County

Clerk of Court and Prothonotary

Seventeenth Judicial District
Snyder County Courthouse, Nine West Market Street,
Middleburg, PA 17842 (Snyder County Address)
Union County Courthouse, 103 South Second Street,
Lewisburg, PA 17837 (Union County Address)
P.O. Box 217, Middleburg, PA 17842
Tel: (570) 837-4344 Tel: (570) 524-8641 (Union County contact)
Fax: (570) 524-8644 (Union County contact)

Clerk of Court and Prothonotary (Union County)
Linda Richards ....(570) 524-8751
Union County Courthouse,   Fax: (570) 524-8628
103 South Second Street, Lewisburg, PA 17837
E-mail: lrichards@unionco.org

Recorder

Office of the Register of Wills and Recorder of Deeds
103 South Second Street, Lewisburg, PA 17837
Tel: (570) 524-8762

Register of Wills and Recorder of Deeds (Acting)
Lisa A. Seward .... (570) 524-8767
E-mail: lseward@unionco.org

Venango County

Clerk of Court and Prothonotary

Twenty-Eighth Judicial District
Venango County Courthouse, 1168 Liberty Street, Franklin, PA 16323
Tel: (814) 432-9610 Fax: (814) 432-3149

Clerk of Court and Prothonotary **Paula Palmer** .... (814) 432-9577
Venango County Courthouse, 1168 Liberty Street,   Fax: (814) 432-9573
Franklin, PA 16323
E-mail: ppalmer@co.venango.pa.us

Recorder

Office of the Register of Wills and Recorder of Deeds
1168 Liberty Street, 1st Floor, Franklin, PA 16323
Tel: (814) 432-9539 Fax: (814) 432-9569

Register of Wills and Recorder of Deeds **Sue Hannon** ... (814) 432-9539
E-mail: shannon@co.venango.pa.us

Warren County

Clerk of Court and Prothonotary

Thirty-Seventh Judicial District
Warren County Courthouse, 204 Fourth Avenue, Warren, PA 16365
Tel: (814) 728-3530 Fax: (814) 728-3452
Internet: www.warrenforestcourt.org

Clerk of Court and Prothonotary, Warren County
Susan Kosinski ....(814) 728-3440
Warren County Courthouse, 204 Fourth Avenue,   Fax: (814) 728-3459
Warren, PA 16365
E-mail: skosinski@warren-county.net

Recorder

Office of the Register of Wills and Recorder of Deeds
204 Fourth Avenue, Warren, PA 16365
Tel: (814) 728-3430

Register of Wills and Recorder of Deeds **Lori Bimber** .... (814) 728-3430
E-mail: labimber@warren-county.net

Washington County

Clerk of Court

Twenty-Seventh Judicial District
Washington County Courthouse, One South Main Street,
Washington, PA 15301
Tel: (724) 228-6797
Internet: www.washingtoncourts.us/pages/home.aspx

Clerk of Court **Barbara Gibbs** ....(724) 228-6787
Washington County Courthouse,   Fax: (570) 253-0687
One South Main Street, Washington, PA 15301
E-mail: barbara.gibbs@pacourts.us

Prothonotary

Office of the Prothonotary
1 South Main Street, Suite 1001, Washington, PA 15301
Tel: (724) 228-6770
E-mail: mathenyp@co.washington.pa.us

Prothonotary **Phyllis Ranko-Matheny** ....(724) 228-6770

Recorder

Office of the Recorder of Deeds
100 West Beau Street, Room 204, Washington, PA 15301
Tel: (724) 228-6806 Fax: (724) 228-6737

Recorder of Deeds **Deborah "Debbie" Bardella** ....(724) 228-6806

Wayne County

Clerk of Court and Prothonotary

Twenty-Second Judicial District
Wayne County Courthouse, 925 Court Street, Honesdale, PA 18431
Tel: (570) 253-5970 Fax: (570) 253-2919
Internet: www.co.wayne.pa.us/?pageid=6

Clerk of Court and Prothonotary
Edward G. "Ned" Sandercock ....(570) 253-5970
Wayne County Courthouse, 925 Court Street,   Fax: (570) 253-0687
Honesdale, PA 18431
E-mail: esandercock@waynecountypa.gov

Recorder

Office of the Register of Wills and Recorder of Deeds
925 Court Street, Honesdale, PA 18431
Tel: (570) 253-5970 ext. 4040

Register of Wills and Recorder of Deeds
Ginger Golden .... (570) 253-5970 ext. 4040
E-mail: ggolden@co.wayne.pa.us

(continued on next page)

Pennsylvania Court Clerks and Courthouses *continued*

Westmoreland County

Clerk of Court

Tenth Judicial District
Westmoreland County Courthouse, Two North Main Street,
Greensburg, PA 15601
Tel: (724) 830-3818 Fax: (724) 830-3680

Clerk of Court **Bryan L. Kline** . . . . (724) 830-3734
    Westmoreland County Courthouse,   Fax: (724) 850-3979
    Two North Main Street, Suite 203,
    Greensburg, PA 15601
    E-mail: wcclkcrt@co.westmoreland.pa.us

Prothonotary

Office of the Prothonotary
2 North Main Street, Suite 501, Greensburg, PA 15601
Fax: (724) 830-3517

Prothonotary **Christina O'Brien** . . . . (724) 830-3502
    E-mail: prothon@co.westmoreland.pa.us

Recorder

Office of the Recorder of Deeds
2 North Main Street, Suite 503, Greensburg, PA 15601
Fax: (724) 853-4647

Recorder of Deeds **Frank Schiefer** . . . . (724) 830-3518

Wyoming County

Clerk of Court and Prothonotary

Forty-Fourth Judicial District
One Courthouse Square, Tunkhannock, PA 18657
Tel: (570) 836-3151

Clerk of Court and Prothonotary, Wyoming County
    Karen Bishop . . . . (570) 996-2234
    One Courthouse Square, Tunkhannock, PA 18657   Fax: (570) 996-0193
    E-mail: kbishop@wycopa.org

Recorder

Office of the Register of Wills and Recorder of Deeds
One Courthouse Square, Tunkhannock, PA 18657
Tel: (570) 996-2361

Register of Wills and Recorder of Deeds
    Dennis L. Montross . . . . (570) 996-2237
    E-mail: dmontross@wycopa.org

York County

Clerk of Court

Nineteenth Judicial District
York County Judicial Center, 45 North George Street, York, PA 17401
Tel: (717) 771-9234

Clerk of Court **Donald O'Shell** . . . . (717) 771-9612
    York County Judicial Center,   Fax: (717) 771-9096
    45 North George Street, York, PA 17401
    E-mail: droshell@yorkcountypa.gov

Prothonotary

Office of the Prothonotary
45 North George Street, York, PA 17401
Tel: (717) 771-9611

Prothonotary **Pamela S. Lee** . . . . (717) 771-9611
    E-mail: pslee@yorkcountypa.gov

Pennsylvania Court Clerks and Courthouses *continued*

Recorder

Office of the Recorder of Deeds
28 East Market Street, York, PA 17401
Tel: (717) 771-9608 Fax: (717) 771-9582

Recorder of Deeds **Randi L. Reisinger** . . . . (717) 771-9608
    E-mail: rlreisinger@yorkcountypa.gov

Counties Within Judicial Circuits

1st District
Areas Covered: Philadelphia County.

2nd District
Areas Covered: Lancaster County.

3rd District
Areas Covered: Northampton County.

4th District
Areas Covered: Tioga County.

5th District
Areas Covered: Allegheny County.

6th District
Areas Covered: Erie County.

7th District
Areas Covered: Bucks County.

8th District
Areas Covered: Northumberland County.

9th District
Areas Covered: Cumberland County.

10th District
Areas Covered: Westmoreland County.

11th District
Areas Covered: Luzerne County.

12th District
Areas Covered: Dauphin County.

13th District
Areas Covered: Greene County.

14th District
Areas Covered: Fayette County.

15th District
Areas Covered: Chester County.

Pennsylvania Court Clerks and Courthouses *continued*

16th District
Areas Covered: Somerset County.

17th District
Areas Covered: Snyder County and Union County.

18th District
Areas Covered: Clarion County.

19th District
Areas Covered: York County.

20th District
Areas Covered: Huntingdon County.

21st District
Areas Covered: Schuylkill County.

22nd District
Areas Covered: Wayne County.

23rd District
Areas Covered: Berks County.

24th District
Areas Covered: Blair County.

25th District
Areas Covered: Clinton County.

26th District
Areas Covered: Columbia County and Montour County.

27th District
Areas Covered: Washington County.

28th District
Areas Covered: Venango County.

29th District
Areas Covered: Lycoming County.

30th District
Areas Covered: Crawford County.

31st District
Areas Covered: Lehigh County.

32nd District
Areas Covered: Delaware County.

33rd District
Areas Covered: Armstrong County.

Pennsylvania Court Clerks and Courthouses *continued*

34th District
Areas Covered: Susquehanna County.

35th District
Areas Covered: Mercer County.

36th District
Areas Covered: Beaver County.

37th District
Areas Covered: Forest County and Warren County.

38th District
Areas Covered: Montgomery County.

39th District
Areas Covered: Franklin County and Fulton County.

40th District
Areas Covered: Indiana County.

41st District
Areas Covered: Juniata County and Perry County.

42nd District
Areas Covered: Bradford County.

43rd District
Areas Covered: Monroe County.

44th District
Areas Covered: Sullivan County and Wyoming County.

45th District
Areas Covered: Lackawanna County.

46th District
Areas Covered: Clearfield County.

47th District
Areas Covered: Cambria County.

48th District
Areas Covered: McKean County.

49th District
Areas Covered: Centre County.

50th District
Areas Covered: Butler County.

51st District
Areas Covered: Adams County.

(continued on next page)

Pennsylvania Court Clerks and Courthouses *continued*

52nd District
Areas Covered: Lebanon County.

53rd District
Areas Covered: Lawrence County.

54th District
Areas Covered: Jefferson County.

55th District
Areas Covered: Potter County.

56th District
Areas Covered: Carbon County.

57th District
Areas Covered: Bedford County.

58th District
Areas Covered: Mifflin County.

59th District
Areas Covered: Cameron County and Elk County.

60th District
Areas Covered: Pike County.

Puerto Rico Court Clerks and Courthouses

Puerto Rico is divided into 13 judicial regions. At the head of each region there is a Judicial Center under the administration of a Regional Presiding Judge. Each Judicial Center has a Chief Clerk.

Supreme Court of Puerto Rico

Ponce de Leon Avenue, Stop #8, San Juan, PR 00902
P.O. Box 9022392, San Juan, PR 00902-2392
Tel: (787) 723-6033 Fax: (787) 723-9199
Internet: www.ramajudicial.pr

Court Staff

Administrative Director of the Courts
Sonia Colon Velez Ivette. . . . . (787) 641-6600

Puerto Rico Courts of First Instance

Judicial Region Aguadilla

P.O. Box 1010, Aguadilla, PR 00605-1010
Tel: (787) 891-5555 Fax: (787) 882-2575

Areas Covered: Aguadilla.

Judicial Region Aibonito

150 Turquoise Street, Aibonito, PR 00705
P.O. Box 1449, Aibonito, PR 00705
Tel: (787) 735-8549 Fax: (787) 735-1879

Areas Covered: Aibonito.

Judicial Region Arecibo

535 Jose A. Cedeno Avenue, Arecibo, PR 00613-6005
P.O. Box 6005, Arecibo, PR 00613-6005
Tel: (787) 878-7530 Fax: (787) 878-8282

Areas Covered: Arecibo.

Judicial Region Bayamón

P.O. Box 60619, Bayamon, PR 00960-0619
Tel: (787) 785-3300 Fax: (787) 740-2700

Areas Covered: Bayamón.

Judicial Region Caguas

P.O. Box 491, Caguas, PR 00726-0491
Tel: (787) 653-0070 Fax: (787) 744-0505

Areas Covered: Caguas.

Judicial Region Carolina

P.O. Box 267, Carolina, PR 00986-0267
Tel: (787) 653-0070 Fax: (787) 744-0505

Areas Covered: Carolina.

Judicial Region Fajardo

P.O. Box 70009, Fajardo, PR 00738-7009
Tel: (787) 655-0620 Fax: (787) 655-0560

Areas Covered: Fajardo.

Judicial Region Guayama

P.O. Box 300, Guayama, PR 00785-0300
Tel: (787) 686-2000 Fax: (787) 864-2001

Areas Covered: Guayama.

Judicial Region Humacao

P.O. Box 885, Humacao, PR 00792-0885
Tel: (787) 656-0010

Areas Covered: Humacao.

Judicial Region Mayagüez

P.O. Box 1210, Mayaguez, PR 00681-1210
Tel: (787) 652-5555 Fax: (787) 833-1550

Areas Covered: Mayagüez.

Judicial Region Ponce

P.O. Box 7185, Ponce, PR 00732-7185
Tel: (787) 841-1510

Areas Covered: Ponce.

Judicial Region San Juan

P.O. Box 190887, San Juan, PR 00919-0887
Tel: (787) 641-6363 Fax: (787) 250-1697

Areas Covered: San Juan.

Judicial Region Utuado

P.O. Box 2555, Utuado, PR 00641-2555
Tel: (787) 894-2525 Fax: (787) 894-4958

Areas Covered: Utuado.

Rhode Island Court Clerks and Courthouses

The trial court of general jurisdiction in Rhode Island is called the Superior Court, of which there are four divisions. The Clerk in each county functions both as County Clerk and Trial Court Clerk. There is no intermediate appellate court in the State of Rhode Island.

Rhode Island Supreme Court

Frank Licht Judicial Complex, 250 Benefit Street, Providence, RI 02903
Tel: (401) 222-3272 TTY: (401) 222-3269 Fax: (401) 222-3599
Internet: www.courts.state.ri.us

The justices of the Supreme Court are appointed to life terms by the Governor and confirmed by the state legislature. All appointments are first nominated by the Judicial Review Committee. The Supreme Court exercises final appellate jurisdiction over all courts, determines the constitutionality of legislation and issue writs necessary to the exercise of proper jurisdiction. The Court has general supervision over all lower court and regulates admission to the bar and discipline of its members.

Court Staff
Clerk of Court **Debra Saunders** . . . . (401) 222-3272

County-By-County

Bristol/Providence County

Clerk of Court

Bristol/Providence County Superior Court
Licht Judicial Complex, 250 Benefit Street, Providence, RI 02903

Clerk **Henry S. Kinch, Jr.** . . . .(401) 222-3230
Fax: (401) 822-2701

Kent County

Clerk of Court

Kent County Superior Court
Leighton Judicial Complex, 222 Quaker Lane, West Warwick, RI 02886

Clerk **Nancy Striuli** . . . .(401) 822-6900
Leighton Judicial Complex, 222 Quaker Lane,   Fax: (401) 822-6905
West Warwick, RI 02886

Newport County

Clerk of Court

Newport County Superior Court
Florence K. Murray Judicial Complex, 45 Washington Square, Newport, RI 02840

Clerk **Jane M. Anthony** . . . .(401) 841-8330
Florence K. Murray Judicial Complex,   Fax: (401) 846-1673
45 Washington Square, Newport, RI 02840

Washington County

Clerk of Court

Washington County Superior Court
McGrath Judicial Complex, 4800 Tower Hill Road, Wakefield, RI 02879

Clerk **Edward P. Morrone** . . . . (401) 782-4121
McGrath Judicial Complex, 4800 Tower Hill Road,   Fax: (401) 782-4190
Wakefield, RI 02879

South Carolina Court Clerks and Courthouses

The trial courts of general jurisdiction in South Carolina are called circuit courts. There are 16 judicial circuits, each circuit consisting of at least two counties. The Clerk of the Court for each county functions both as the Clerk of the Circuit Court and the County Clerk.

South Carolina Supreme Court

1231 Gervais Street, Columbia, SC 29201
P.O. Box 11330, Columbia, SC 29211
Tel: (803) 734-1080 Fax: (803) 734-1499
Internet: www.sccourts.org

The Supreme Court consists of a chief justice and four associate justices who are elected by the South Carolina General Assembly for ten-year terms. The Governor may fill vacancies for unexpired terms not exceeding one year. The Supreme Court has appellate jurisdiction over cases involving the death penalty, public utility rates, significant constitutional issues, public bond issues and the elections laws. The Court may review decisions of the South Carolina Court of Appeals and has administrative control over all lower courts in the state. The Court also regulates the admission to the state bar and the practice of law in the state.

Court Staff
Clerk **Daniel E. Shearouse** . . . . (803) 734-1080
E-mail: dshearouse@sccourts.org

South Carolina Court of Appeals

1015 Sumter Street, Columbia, SC 29201
P.O. Box 11629, Columbia, SC 29211
Tel: (803) 734-1890 Fax: (803) 734-1839
Internet: www.sccourts.org

The Court of Appeals, which was established in 1983, consists of a chief judge and eight associate judges elected by the South Carolina General Assembly for six-year terms. The Governor may fill vacancies for unexpired terms not exceeding one year. The Court of Appeals exercises appellate jurisdiction over cases from the South Carolina Circuit Court and Family Court, except cases over which the Supreme Court has exclusive jurisdiction.

Court Staff
Clerk **Jenny Abbott Kitchings** . . . . (803) 734-1890
E-mail: jkitchings@sccourts.org   Fax: (803) 734-1839

County-By-County

Abbeville County

Court Clerk

Eighth Judicial District
1226 College Street, Newberry, SC 29108

Clerk of Court, Abbeville County
Emily Y. McMahan . . . . (864) 366-5312 ext. 55
P.O. Box 99, Abbeville, SC 29620-0099
E-mail: emcmahan@abbevillecountysc.com

Aiken County

Court Clerk

Second Judicial District
P.O. Box 90, Bamberg, SC 29003

Clerk of Court, Aiken County **Liz Godard** . . . . (803) 642-1587
P.O. Box 583, Aiken, SC 29802-0583   Fax: (803) 642-1718
E-mail: lgodard@aikencountysc.gov

Allendale County

Court Clerk

Fourteenth Judicial District
101 Hampton Street, Walterboro, SC 29488

Clerk of Court, Allendale County **Elaine Sabb** . . . . (803) 584-2737
P.O. Box 126, Allendale, SC 29810-0126   Fax: (803) 584-7046
E-mail: esabb@allendalecounty.com

Anderson County

Court Clerk

Tenth Judicial Circuit
P.O. Box 428, Walhalla, SC 29691

Clerk of Court, Anderson County **Richard A. Shirley** . . . . (864) 260-4053
P.O. Box 8002, Anderson, SC 29622-8002   Fax: (864) 260-4715
E-mail: rshirley@andersoncountysc.org   (Anderson)

Bamberg County

Court Clerk

Second Judicial District
P.O. Box 90, Bamberg, SC 29003

Clerk of Court, Bamberg County **James B. Hiers** . . . . (803) 245-3025
P.O. Drawer 150, Bamberg, SC 29003-0150   Fax: (803) 245-3088
E-mail: bambergc@bellsouth.net

Barnwell County

Court Clerk

Second Judicial District
P.O. Box 90, Bamberg, SC 29003

Clerk of Court, Barnwell County
Rhonda Dale McElveen . . . . (803) 541-1020
P.O. Box 723, Barnwell, SC 29812-0723   Fax: (803) 541-1025
E-mail: rmcelveen@barnwellsc.com

Beaufort County

Court Clerk

Fourteenth Judicial District
101 Hampton Street, Walterboro, SC 29488

Clerk of Court, Beaufort County **Jerri Ann Roseneau** . . . (843) 255-5050
P.O. Box 1128, Beaufort, SC 29901-1128   Fax: (843) 255-9412
E-mail: jroseneau@bcgov.net

(continued on next page)

Berkeley County

Court Clerk

Ninth Judicial Circuit
100 Broad Street, Suite 427, Charleston, SC 29401

Clerk of Court, Berkeley County **Mary P. Brown** . . . . (843) 719-4400
   P.O. Box 219, Moncks Corner, SC 29461-0219   Fax: (843) 719-4511
   E-mail: mbrown@berkeleycountysc.gov

Calhoun County

Court Clerk

First Judicial Circuit
P.O. Box 1949, Orangeburg, SC 29116-1949

Clerk of Court, Calhoun County **Kenneth Hasty** . . . . (803) 874-3524
   P.O. Box 709, St. Matthews, SC 29135   Fax: (803) 874-1942
   E-mail: khasty@calhouncounty.sc.gov

Charleston County

Court Clerk

Ninth Judicial Circuit
100 Broad Street, Suite 427, Charleston, SC 29401

Clerk of Court, Charleston County **Julie J. Armstrong** . . . (843) 958-5000
   100 Broad Street, Suite 106,   Fax: (843) 958-5020
   Charleston, SC 29401
   E-mail: jarmstrong@charlestoncounty.org

Cherokee County

Court Clerk

Seventh Judicial Circuit
180 Magnolia Street, Spartanburg, SC 29306

Clerk of Court, Cherokee County **Brandy McBee** . . . . (864) 487-2571
   P.O. Drawer 2289, Gaffney, SC 29342-2289
   E-mail: brandy.mcbee@cherokeesc.com

Chester County

Court Clerk

Sixth Judicial Circuit
1121 Broad Street, Camden, SC 29021-1707

Clerk of Court, Chester County **Sue K. Carpenter** . . . . (803) 385-2605
   P.O. Drawer 580, Chester, SC 29706-0580
   E-mail: scarpenter@chestercounty.org

Chesterfield County

Court Clerk

Fourth Judicial Circuit
531 East Caroline Avenue, Hartsville, SC 29550-4311

Clerk of Court, Chesterfield County **Faye L. Sellers** . . . . . (843) 623-2574
   P.O. Box 529, Chesterfield, SC 29709-0529
   E-mail: clerkofcc@shtc.net

Clarendon County

Court Clerk

Third Judicial Circuit
P.O. Box 1716, Sumter, SC 29510

Clerk of Court, Clarendon County **Beulah G. Roberts** . . . (803) 435-4443
   P.O. Box 136, Manning, SC 29102
   E-mail: clerkofcourt@clarendoncountygov.org

Colleton County

Court Clerk

Fourteenth Judicial District
101 Hampton Street, Walterboro, SC 29488

Clerk of Court, Colleton County **Patricia C. Grant** . . . . . . (843) 549-5791
   P.O. Box 620, Walterboro, SC 29488-0028   Fax: (843) 549-6857
   E-mail: pgrant@colletoncounty.org

Darlington County

Court Clerk

Fourth Judicial Circuit
531 East Caroline Avenue, Hartsville, SC 29550-4311

Clerk of Court, Darlington County **Scott B. Suggs** . . . . . . (843) 398-4330
   One Public Square, Room B4,
   Darlington, SC 29532
   E-mail: clerk@darcosc.com

Dillon County

Court Clerk

Fourth Judicial Circuit
531 East Caroline Avenue, Hartsville, SC 29550-4311

Clerk of Court, Dillon County **Gwen T. Hyatt** . . . . (843) 774-1425
   P.O. Box 1220, Dillon, SC 29536-1220
   E-mail: dilloncoc@bellsouth.net

Dorchester County

Court Clerk

First Judicial Circuit
P.O. Box 1949, Orangeburg, SC 29116-1949

Clerk of Court, Dorchester County **Cheryl Graham** . . . . . . (843) 563-0160
   5200 East Jim Bilton Boulevard,   Fax: (843) 563-0178
   St. George, SC 29477-8020
   E-mail: cgraham@dorchestercounty.net

Edgefield County

Court Clerk

Eleventh Judicial Circuit
129 Courthouse Square, Edgefield, SC 29824

Clerk of Court, Edgefield County **Charles L. Reel** . . . . (803) 637-4080
   P.O. Box 34, Edgefield, SC 29824-0034   Fax: (803) 637-4117
   E-mail: creel@edfieldcounty.sc.gov

Fairfield County

Court Clerk

Sixth Judicial Circuit
1121 Broad Street, Camden, SC 29021-1707

Clerk of Court, Fairfield County **Betty Jo Beckham** . . . . . (803) 712-6526
 P.O. Drawer 299, Winnsboro, SC 29180-0299
 E-mail: bbeckham@fairfieldsc.com

Florence County

Court Clerk

Twelfth Judicial Circuit
180 North Irby Street, Florence, SC 29501

Clerk of Court, Florence County **Connie Reel-Shearin** . . . (843) 665-3031
 108 North Irby Street, Room B11, Fax: (843) 665-3097
 Florence, SC 29501-3456

Georgetown County

Court Clerk

Fifteenth Judicial Circuit
401 Cleland Street, Georgetown, SC 29442

Clerk of Court, Georgetown County **Alma White** . . . . (843) 545-3036
 P.O. Box 479, Georgetown, SC 29442-0479 Fax: (843) 545-3204
 E-mail: awhite@gtcounty.org

Greenville County

Court Clerk

Thirteenth Judicial Circuit
305 East - North Street, Suite 318, Greenville, SC 29601

Clerk of Court, Greenville County **Paul Wickensimer** . . . . (864) 467-8551
 305 East North Street, Greenville, SC 29601-2121 Fax: (864) 467-8540
 E-mail: clerkofcourt@greenvillecounty.org

Greenwood County

Court Clerk

Eighth Judicial District
1226 College Street, Newberry, SC 29108

Clerk of Court, Greenwood County
 Angela M. Woodhurst . . . . (864) 942-8546
 528 Monument Street, Room 114, Fax: (864) 942-8693
 Greenwood, SC 29646-2634
 E-mail: awoodhurst@sccourts.org

Hampton County

Court Clerk

Fourteenth Judicial District
101 Hampton Street, Walterboro, SC 29488

Clerk of Court, Hampton County **Mylinda D. Nettles** . . . . (803) 914-2250
 P.O. Box 7, Hampton, SC 29924-0007 Fax: (803) 914-2258
 E-mail: mnettles@hamptoncountysc.org

Horry County

Court Clerk

Fifteenth Judicial Circuit
401 Cleland Street, Georgetown, SC 29442

Clerk of Court, Horry County **Melanie Huggins-Ward** . . . (843) 915-5080
 P.O. Box 677, Conway, SC 29528-0677 Fax: (843) 545-6801
 E-mail: hugginsm@horrycounty.org

Jasper County

Court Clerk

Fourteenth Judicial District
101 Hampton Street, Walterboro, SC 29488

Clerk of Court, Jasper County **Margaret Bostick** . . . . (843) 726-7710
 P.O. Box 126, Allendale, SC 29810-0126 Fax: (843) 726-7785
 E-mail: mbostick@jaspercountysc.gov

Kershaw County

Court Clerk

Fifth Judicial Circuit
1701 Main Street, Columbia, SC 29202

Clerk of Court, Kershaw County **Joyce McDonald** . . . . . . (803) 425-7223
 P.O. Box 1557, Camden, SC 29021-1557
 E-mail: joyce.mcdonald@kershaw.sc.gov

Lancaster County

Court Clerk

Sixth Judicial Circuit
1121 Broad Street, Camden, SC 29021-1707

Clerk of Court, Lancaster County **Jeff L. Hammond** . . . . . (803) 285-1581
 P.O. Box 1809, Lancaster, SC 29721-1809
 E-mail: jhammond@lancastercountysc.net

Laurens County

Court Clerk

Eighth Judicial District
1226 College Street, Newberry, SC 29108

Clerk of Court, Laurens County **Lynn Lancaster** . . . . (864) 984-3538
 P.O. Box 287, Laurens, SC 29360-0287 Fax: (864) 984-7023
 E-mail: llancaster@co.laurens.sc.us

Lee County

Court Clerk

Third Judicial Circuit
P.O. Box 1716, Sumter, SC 29510

Clerk of Court, Lee County **James I. Davis** . . . . (803) 484-5341
 P.O. Box 387, Bishopville, SC 29010-0387
 E-mail: jdavis@leecountysc.org

(continued on next page)

Lexington County

Court Clerk

Eleventh Judicial Circuit
129 Courthouse Square, Edgefield, SC 29824

Clerk of Court, Lexington County **Beth Carrigg** . . . . (803) 785-8212
  205 East Main Street, Suite 146,   Fax: (803) 785-8314
  Lexington, SC 29072-3557
  E-mail: bcarrigg@lex-co.com

Marion County

Court Clerk

Twelfth Judicial Circuit
180 North Irby Street, Florence, SC 29501

Clerk of Court, Marion County **Sherry R. Rhodes** . . . . . . (843) 423-8240
  P.O. Box 295, Marion, SC 29571-0295   Fax: (843) 423-8242
  E-mail: rhodess@marionsc.org

Marlboro County

Court Clerk

Fourth Judicial Circuit
531 East Caroline Avenue, Hartsville, SC 29550-4311

Clerk of Court, Marlboro County **William Funderburk** . . . (843) 479-5613
  P.O. Drawer 996, Bennettsville, SC 29512-0996
  E-mail: bfunderburk@bellsouth.net

McCormick County

Court Clerk

Eleventh Judicial Circuit
129 Courthouse Square, Edgefield, SC 29824

Clerk of Court, McCormick County
  Gwendolyn D. Chiles . . . . (864) 852-2195
  133 South Mine Street, Suite 102,   Fax: (864) 852-0071
  McCormick, SC 29835-8357
  E-mail: gchiles@mccormickcountysc.org

Newberry County

Court Clerk

Eighth Judicial District
1226 College Street, Newberry, SC 29108

Clerk of Court, Newberry County **Jackie S. Bowers** . . . . . (803) 321-2110
  P.O. Drawer 10, Newberry, SC 29108-0010   Fax: (803) 321-2111

Oconee County

Court Clerk

Tenth Judicial Circuit
P.O. Box 428, Walhalla, SC 29691

Clerk of Court, Oconee County **Beverly Whitfield** . . . . . . (864) 638-4280
  P.O. Box 678, Walhalla, SC 29691-0678   Fax: (864) 638-4282
  E-mail: bwhitfield@oconeesc.com

Orangeburg County

Court Clerk

First Judicial Circuit
P.O. Box 1949, Orangeburg, SC 29116-1949

Clerk of Court, Orangeburg County **Winnifa B. Clark** . . . . (803) 533-6260
  P.O. Box 9000, Orangeburg, SC 29115-9000
  E-mail: famcrt@orangeburgcounty.org

Pickens County

Court Clerk

Thirteenth Judicial Circuit
305 East - North Street, Suite 318, Greenville, SC 29601

Clerk of Court, Pickens County **Harold P. Welborn, Jr.** . . . (864) 898-5857
  P.O. Box 215, Pickens, SC 29671-0215   Fax: (864) 898-5863
  E-mail: pwelborn@co.pickens.sc.us

Richland County

Court Clerk

Fifth Judicial Circuit
1701 Main Street, Columbia, SC 29202

Clerk of Court, Richland County
  Jeanette W. McBride . . . . (803) 576-1951
  P.O. Box 2766, Columbia, SC 29202-2766
  E-mail: mcbridej@rcgov.us

Saluda County

Court Clerk

Eleventh Judicial Circuit
129 Courthouse Square, Edgefield, SC 29824

Clerk of Court, Saluda County **Doris B. Holmes** . . . . (864) 445-4500
  101 East Church Street, Suite 6,   Fax: (864) 445-3772
  Saluda, SC 29138-1444
  E-mail: db.holmes@saludacounty.sc.gov

Spartanburg County

Court Clerk

Seventh Judicial Circuit
180 Magnolia Street, Spartanburg, SC 29306

Clerk of Court, Spartanburg County
  Meredith Hope Blackley . . . . (864) 596-2591
  P.O. Box 3483, Spartanburg, SC 29304-3483
  E-mail: clerksoffice@spartanburgcounty.org

Sumter County

Court Clerk

Third Judicial Circuit
P.O. Box 1716, Sumter, SC 29510

Clerk of Court, Sumter County **James C. Campbell** . . . . . (803) 436-2227
  114 North Main Street, Room 308,
  Sumter, SC 29150-4965
  E-mail: JACampbell@sumtercountysc.org

Union County

Court Clerk

Sixteenth Judicial Circuit
Moss Justice Center, 1675-1H York Highway, Second Floor,
York, SC 29745-7434

Clerk of Court, Union County **William F. Gault**.........(864) 429-1630
P.O. Box 703, Union, SC 29379-0703   Fax: (864) 429-1715
E-mail: fgault@countyofunion.com

Williamsburg County

Court Clerk

Third Judicial Circuit
P.O. Box 1716, Sumter, SC 29510

Clerk of Court, Williamsburg County
Sharon Staggers...............................(803) 355-9321
125 West Main Street, Kingstree, SC 29556-3343
E-mail: sharon.staggers@williamsburgcounty.sc.gov

York County

Court Clerk

Sixteenth Judicial Circuit
Moss Justice Center, 1675-1H York Highway, Second Floor,
York, SC 29745-7434

Clerk of Court, York County **David Hamilton** .... (803) 684-8507
P.O. Box 649, York, SC 29745-0649   Fax: (803) 628-3226
E-mail: david.hamilton@yorkcountygov.com

Counties Within Judicial Circuits

Circuit Court, 1st Circuit
Areas Covered: Calhoun, Dorchester, and Orangeburg Counties.

Circuit Court, 2nd Circuit
Areas Covered: Aiken, Bamberg, and Barnwell Counties.

Circuit Court, 3rd Circuit
Areas Covered: Clarendon, Lee, Sumter, and Williamsburg Counties.

Circuit Court, 4th Circuit
Areas Covered: Chesterfield, Darlington, Dillon, and Marlboro Counties.

Circuit Court, 5th Circuit
Areas Covered: Kershaw and Richland Counties.

Circuit Court, 6th Circuit
Areas Covered: Chester, Fairfield and Lancaster Counties.

Circuit Court, 7th Circuit
Areas Covered: Cherokee and Spartanburg Counties.

Circuit Court, 8th Circuit
Areas Covered: Abbeville, Greenwood, Laurens and Newberry Counties.

Circuit Court, 9th Circuit
Areas Covered: Berkeley and Charleston Counties.

Circuit Court, 10th Circuit
Areas Covered: Oconee and Anderson Counties.

Circuit Court, 11th Circuit
Areas Covered: Edgefield, McCormick and Saluda Counties.

Circuit Court, 12th Circuit
Areas Covered: Florence and Marion Counties.

Circuit Court, 13th Circuit
Areas Covered: Greenville and Pickens Counties.

Circuit Court, 14th Circuit
Areas Covered: Allendale, Beaufort, Colleton, Hampton and Jasper Counties.

Circuit Court, 15th Circuit
Areas Covered: Georgetown and Horry Counties

Circuit Court, 16th Circuit
Areas Covered: Union and York Counties.

South Dakota Court Clerks and Courthouses

The trial courts of general jurisdiction in South Dakota are called circuit courts, of which there are seven judicial circuits. The Clerk in each county functions both as County Clerk and Clerk of the Circuit Court for that county. There is no intermediate appellate court in the State of South Dakota.

South Dakota Supreme Court

State Capitol Building, 500 East Capitol Avenue, Pierre, SD 57501
Tel: (605) 773-3511 Fax: (605) 773-6128
Internet: www.sdjudicial.com

The Supreme Court consists of a chief justice and four justices who are appointed by the Governor from one of five electoral districts throughout the state for initial three-year terms and then run for retention in statewide general elections for eight-year terms. The chief justice is elected by peer vote for a four-year term. Retirement is mandatory at age seventy; however, retired justices may be recalled for temporary assignment. The Supreme Court has original jurisdiction in cases involving interests of the state and exclusive appellate jurisdiction over the South Dakota Circuit Court. The Court may render advisory opinions to the Governor involving the exercise of his or her executive powers. The Court has authority to supervise admission to the state bar and the conduct of its members and the Court has general administrative and rule-making authority over the lower courts.

Court Staff
Clerk of the Court **Shirley A. Jameson-Fergel** . . . . (605) 773-3511
  E-mail: shirley.jameson-fergel@ujs.state.sd.us

County-By-County

Aurora County

Clerk of Court

First Judicial Circuit
209 East Main Street, Elk Point, SD 57025-2327

Circuit Clerk, Aurora County **Deb Thiry** . . . . (605) 942-7165
  P.O. Box 366, Plankinton, SD 57368-0366   Fax: (605) 942-7170
  401 North Main Street, Plankinton, SD 57368

Beadle County

Clerk of Court

Third Judicial Circuit
314 Sixth Avenue, Brookings, SD 57006-2085

Circuit Clerk, Beadle County **Anita Hasek** . . . . (605) 353-7165
  450 Third Street South West,
  Huron, SD 57350
  E-mail: anita.hasek@ujs.state.sd.us

Bennett County

Clerk of Court

Sixth Judicial Circuit
104 East Capitol Avenue, Pierre, SD 57501
Tel: (605) 773-3971

Circuit Clerk, Bennett County **Linda Larson** . . . . (605) 685-6969
  PO Box 281, Martin, SD 57551-0281   Fax: (605) 685-1075
  205 State Street, Martin, SD 57551
  E-mail: linda.larson@ujs.state.sd.us

Bon Homme County

Clerk of Court

First Judicial Circuit
209 East Main Street, Elk Point, SD 57025-2327

Circuit Clerk, Bon Homme County
  Heather Humphrey . . . . (605) 589-4215
  P.O. Box 6, Tyndall, SD 57066-0006   Fax: (605) 589-4245
  300 West 18th Avenue, Tyndall, SD 57066-0006

Brookings County

Clerk of Court

Third Judicial Circuit
314 Sixth Avenue, Brookings, SD 57006-2085

Circuit Clerk, Brookings County **Emily Mosley** . . . . (605) 688-4200
  314 Sixth Avenue, Brookings, SD 57006-2085
  E-mail: emily.mosley@ujs.state.sd.us

Brown County

Clerk of Court

Fifth Judicial Circuit
101 South East First Avenue, Aberdeen, SD 57402-1087

Circuit Clerk, Brown County **Marla R. Zastrow** . . . . (605) 626-2451
  101 South East First Avenue,   Fax: (605) 626-2280
  Aberdeen, SD 57402-1087
  P.O. Box 1087, Aberdeen, SD 57402-1087
  E-mail: 5thcircuit@ujs.state.sd.us

Brule County

Clerk of Court

First Judicial Circuit
209 East Main Street, Elk Point, SD 57025-2327

Circuit Clerk, Brule County **Doris Juhnke** . . . . (605) 734-4580
  300 South Courtland, Room 111,   Fax: (605) 734-4582
  Chamberlain, SD 57325-1599
  E-mail: doris.juhnke@ujs.state.sd.us

Buffalo County

Clerk of Court

First Judicial Circuit
209 East Main Street, Elk Point, SD 57025-2327

Circuit Clerk, Buffalo County **Doris Juhnke** . . . . (605) 734-4580
  300 South Courtland, Room 111,   Fax: (605) 734-4582
  Chamberlain, SD 57325-1599
  E-mail: doris.juhnke@ujs.state.sd.us

(continued on next page)

Butte County

Clerk of Court

Fourth Judicial Circuit
78 Sherman Street, Deadwood, SD 57732-0626
P.O. Box 626, Deadwood, SD 57732-0626

Circuit Clerk, Butte County **Shawn Sorenson** . . . . (605) 892-2516
839 Fifth Avenue, Belle Fourche, SD 57717
E-mail: shawn.sorenson@ujs.state.sd.us

Campbell County

Clerk of Court

Fifth Judicial Circuit
101 South East First Avenue, Aberdeen, SD 57402-1087

Circuit Clerk, Campbell County **Ann Byre** . . . . (605) 955-3536
P.O. Box 146, Mound City, SD 57646-0146   Fax: (605) 955-3580
111 Second Street North East,
Mound City, SD 57646
E-mail: ann.byre@ujs.state.sd.us

Charles Mix County

Clerk of Court

First Judicial Circuit
209 East Main Street, Elk Point, SD 57025-2327

Circuit Clerk, Charles Mix County **Deb Pfeffer** . . . . (605) 487-7511
P.O. Box 640, Lake Andes, SD 57356-0640   Fax: (605) 487-7547
400 Main Street, Lake Andes, SD 57356-0640
E-mail: deb.pfeffer@ujs.state.sd.us

Clark County

Clerk of Court

Third Judicial Circuit
314 Sixth Avenue, Brookings, SD 57006-2085

Circuit Clerk, Clark County **Tracy Aguayo** . . . . (605) 532-5851
P.O. Box 294, Clark, SD 57225-0294   Fax: (605) 532-4257
200 North Commercial Street,
Clark, SD 57225
E-mail: tracie.aguayo@ujs.state.sd.us

Clay County

Clerk of Court

First Judicial Circuit
209 East Main Street, Elk Point, SD 57025-2327

Circuit Clerk, Clay County **Jessica Bosse** . . . . (605) 677-6755
P.O. Box 377, Vermillion, SD 57069-0377   Fax: (605) 677-8885
211 West Main, Room 300,
Vermillion, SD 57069-0377
E-mail: jessica.bosse@ujs.state.sd.us

Codington County

Clerk of Court

Third Judicial Circuit
314 Sixth Avenue, Brookings, SD 57006-2085

Circuit Clerk, Codington County **Connie Hartley** . . . . (605) 882-5095
14 First Avenue South East,
Watertown, SD 57201
E-mail: connie.hartley@ujs.state.sd.us

Corson County

Clerk of Court

Fourth Judicial Circuit
78 Sherman Street, Deadwood, SD 57732-0626
P.O. Box 626, Deadwood, SD 57732-0626

Circuit Clerk, Corson County **Carey Arnold** . . . . (605) 273-4201
P.O. Box 175, Mc Intosh, SD 57641-0175   Fax: (605) 273-4597
108 First Street East, Mc Intosh, SD 57641
E-mail: carey.arnold@ujs.state.sd.us

Custer County

Clerk of Court

Seventh Judicial Circuit
P.O. Box 230, Rapid City, SD 57709

Circuit Clerk, Custer County **Debbie K. Salzsieder** . . . . . . (605) 673-4816
420 Mount Rushmore Road, Suite Six,
Custer, SD 57730
E-mail: debbie.salzsieder@ujs.state.sd.us

Davison County

Clerk of Court

First Judicial Circuit
209 East Main Street, Elk Point, SD 57025-2327

Circuit Clerk, Davison County **Barb McKean** . . . . (605) 995-8105
P.O. Box 927, Mitchell, SD 57301-0927   Fax: (605) 995-8112
200 East Fourth Ave, Mitchell, SD 57301-0927

Day County

Clerk of Court

Fifth Judicial Circuit
101 South East First Avenue, Aberdeen, SD 57402-1087

Circuit Clerk, Day County **Claudette Opitz** . . . . (605) 345-3771
711 West First Street, Room 201,   Fax: (605) 345-3818
Webster, SD 57274-1359
E-mail: claudette.opitz@ujs.state.sd.us

Deuel County

Clerk of Court

Third Judicial Circuit
314 Sixth Avenue, Brookings, SD 57006-2085

Circuit Clerk, Deuel County **Sandy Reichling** . . . . (605) 874-2120
P.O. Box 308, Clear Lake, SD 57226   Fax: (605) 874-3305
E-mail: sandy.reichling@ujs.state.sd.us

South Dakota Court Clerks and Courthouses *continued*

Dewey County

Clerk of Court

Fourth Judicial Circuit
78 Sherman Street, Deadwood, SD 57732-0626
P.O. Box 626, Deadwood, SD 57732-0626

Circuit Clerk, Dewey County **Ann LaCompte** . . . . (605) 865-3566
   P.O. Box 96, Timber Lake, SD 57656-0096   Fax: (605) 865-3641
   710 C Street, Timber Lake, SD 57656

Douglas County

Clerk of Court

First Judicial Circuit
209 East Main Street, Elk Point, SD 57025-2327

Circuit Clerk, Douglas County **Dorene Winckler** . . . . (605) 724-2585
   P.O. Box 36, Armour, SD 57313-0036   Fax: (605) 724-2508
   706 Braddock, Armour, SD 57313-0036
   E-mail: dorene.winckler@ujs.state.sd.us

Edmunds County

Clerk of Court

Fifth Judicial Circuit
101 South East First Avenue, Aberdeen, SD 57402-1087

Circuit Clerk, Edmunds County **Jean Hutson** . . . . (605) 426-6671
   210 Second Avenue, Ipswich, SD 57451   Fax: (605) 426-6323
   P.O. Box 384, Ipswich, SD 57451
   E-mail: jean.hutson@ujs.state.sd.us

Fall River County

Clerk of Court

Seventh Judicial Circuit
P.O. Box 230, Rapid City, SD 57709

Circuit Clerk, Fall River County **Carol Foster** . . . . (605) 745-5131
   906 North River Street, Hot Springs, SD 57747
   E-mail: carol.foster@ujs.state.sd.us

Faulk County

Clerk of Court

Fifth Judicial Circuit
101 South East First Avenue, Aberdeen, SD 57402-1087

Circuit Clerk, Faulk County **Marilyn Hadrick** . . . . (605) 598-6223
   P.O. Box 357, Faulkton, SD 57438-0357   Fax: (605) 598-6252
   110 Ninth Avenue, Faulkton, SD 57438
   E-mail: marilyn.hadrick@ujs.state.sd.us

Grant County

Clerk of Court

Third Judicial Circuit
314 Sixth Avenue, Brookings, SD 57006-2085

Circuit Clerk, Grant County **Julie Anderson** . . . . (605) 432-5482
   210 East Fifth Avenue, Milbank, SD 57252   Fax: (605) 432-5328
   E-mail: julie.anderson@ujs.state.sd.us

South Dakota Court Clerks and Courthouses *continued*

Gregory County

Clerk of Court

Sixth Judicial Circuit
104 East Capitol Avenue, Pierre, SD 57501
Tel: (605) 773-3971

Circuit Clerk, Gregory County **Sandy Teigen** . . . . (605) 775-2665
   8th and Washington, Burke, SD 57523   Fax: (605) 775-2766
   P.O. Box 430, Burke, SD 57523
   E-mail: sandy.teigen@ujs.state.sd.us

Haakon County

Clerk of Court

Sixth Judicial Circuit
104 East Capitol Avenue, Pierre, SD 57501
Tel: (605) 773-3971

Circuit Clerk, Haakon County **Janet Magelky** . . . . (605) 859-2627
   140 South Howard, Philip, SD 57567   Fax: (605) 859-2257
   P.O. Box 70, Philip, SD 57567
   E-mail: janet.magelky@ujs.state.sd.us

Hamlin County

Clerk of Court

Third Judicial Circuit
314 Sixth Avenue, Brookings, SD 57006-2085

Circuit Clerk, Hamlin County **Amy Keimig** . . . . (605) 783-3751
   P.O. Box 256, Hayti, SD 57241-0256   Fax: (605) 783-2157
   350 4th Street, Room Two,
   Hayti, SD 57241

Hand County

Clerk of Court

Third Judicial Circuit
314 Sixth Avenue, Brookings, SD 57006-2085

Circuit Clerk, Hand County **Marci Stevens** . . . . (605) 853-3337
   415 West First Avenue, Miller, SD 57362   Fax: (605) 853-3779
   E-mail: marci.stevens@ujs.state.sd.us

Hanson County

Clerk of Court

First Judicial Circuit
209 East Main Street, Elk Point, SD 57025-2327

Circuit Clerk, Hanson County **Pam Koupal** . . . . (605) 239-4446
   P.O. Box 127, Alexandria, SD 57311-0127   Fax: (605) 239-9446
   440 Main Street, Alexandria, SD 57311

Harding County

Clerk of Court

Fourth Judicial Circuit
78 Sherman Street, Deadwood, SD 57732-0626
P.O. Box 626, Deadwood, SD 57732-0626

Circuit Clerk, Harding County **Karen L. Teigen** . . . . (605) 375-3351
   P.O. Box 534, Buffalo, SD 57720   Fax: (605) 375-3432
   E-mail: karen.teigen@ujs.state.sd.us

(continued on next page)

Hughes County

Clerk of Court

Sixth Judicial Circuit
104 East Capitol Avenue, Pierre, SD 57501
Tel: (605) 773-3971

Circuit Clerk, Hughes County **Kelli Sitzman** . . . . (605) 773-3713
  104 East Capitol Avenue, Pierre, SD 57501   Fax: (605) 773-3875
  P.O. Box 1238, Pierre, SD 57501-1238
  E-mail: kelli.sitzman@ujs.state.sd.us

Hutchinson County

Clerk of Court

First Judicial Circuit
209 East Main Street, Elk Point, SD 57025-2327

Circuit Clerk, Hutchinson County **Dorene Winckler** . . . . . (605) 387-4215
  140 Euclid, Room 36, Olivet, SD 57052-2103   Fax: (605) 387-5035

Hyde County

Clerk of Court

Sixth Judicial Circuit
104 East Capitol Avenue, Pierre, SD 57501
Tel: (605) 773-3971

Circuit Clerk, Hyde County **Marilyn Hanson** . . . . (605) 852-2512
  412 Commerical South East,   Fax: (605) 852-2767
  Highmore, SD 57345
  P.O. Box 306, Highmore, SD 57345
  E-mail: marilyn.hanson@ujs.state.sd.us

Jackson County

Clerk of Court

Sixth Judicial Circuit
104 East Capitol Avenue, Pierre, SD 57501
Tel: (605) 773-3971

Circuit Clerk, Jackson County **Carol Schofield** . . . . (605) 837-2122
  P.O. Box 128, Kadoka, SD 57543-0128   Fax: (605) 837-2120
  One Main Street South, Kadoka, SD 57543
  E-mail: carol.schofield@ujs.state.sd.us

Jerauld County

Clerk of Court

Third Judicial Circuit
314 Sixth Avenue, Brookings, SD 57006-2085

Circuit Clerk, Jerauld County **April Grubb** . . . . (605) 539-1202
  P.O. Box 435, Wessington Springs, SD 57382   Fax: (605) 539-1203
  205 South Wallace, Wessington Springs, SD 57382
  E-mail: april.grubb@ujs.state.sd.us

Jones County

Clerk of Court

Sixth Judicial Circuit
104 East Capitol Avenue, Pierre, SD 57501
Tel: (605) 773-3971

Circuit Clerk, Jones County **Judy Feddersen** . . . .(605) 669-2361
  310 Main Street, Murdo, SD 57559   Fax: (605) 669-2641
  P.O. Box 448, Murdo, SD 57559
  E-mail: judy.feddersen@ujs.state.sd.us

Kingsbury County

Clerk of Court

Third Judicial Circuit
314 Sixth Avenue, Brookings, SD 57006-2085

Circuit Clerk, Kingsbury County **Wendy Sand** . . . . (605) 854-3811
  P.O. Box 176, De Smet, SD 57231-0176   Fax: (605) 854-9080
  202 Second Street, De Smet, SD 57231
  E-mail: wendy.sand@ujs.state.sd.us

Lake County

Clerk of Court

Third Judicial Circuit
314 Sixth Avenue, Brookings, SD 57006-2085

Circuit Clerk, Lake County **Linda Klosterman** . . . .(605) 256-5644
  200 East Center, Madison, SD 57042-2941   Fax: (605) 256-5080
  E-mail: linda.klosterman@ujs.state.sd.us

Lawrence County

Clerk of Court

Fourth Judicial Circuit
78 Sherman Street, Deadwood, SD 57732-0626
P.O. Box 626, Deadwood, SD 57732-0626

Circuit Clerk, Lawrence County **Carol Latuseck** . . . . (605) 578-2040
  P.O. Box 626, Deadwood, SD 57732   Fax: (605) 578-1571
  E-mail: carol.latuseck@ujs.state.sd.us

Lincoln County

Clerk of Court

Second Judicial Circuit
425 North Dakota Avenue, Sioux Falls, SD 57104

Circuit Clerk, Lincoln County **Christe Torgerson** . . . . (605) 987-5891
  104 North Main Street, Canton, SD 57013-1732

Lyman County

Clerk of Court

Sixth Judicial Circuit
104 East Capitol Avenue, Pierre, SD 57501
Tel: (605) 773-3971

Circuit Clerk, Lyman County **Rebecca Altman** . . . . (605) 869-2277
  300 South Main, Kennebec, SD 57544   Fax: (605) 869-2177
  P.O. Box 235, Kennebec, SD 57544
  E-mail: rebecca.altman@ujs.state.sd.us

Marshall County

Clerk of Court

Fifth Judicial Circuit
101 South East First Avenue, Aberdeen, SD 57402-1087

Circuit Clerk, Marshall County **Kim A. Burger** .... (605) 448-5213
  911 Vander Horck, Britton, SD 57430   Fax: (605) 448-5201
  P.O. Box 130, Britton, SD 57430
  E-mail: kim.burger@ujs.state.sd.us

McCook County

Clerk of Court

First Judicial Circuit
209 East Main Street, Elk Point, SD 57025-2327

Circuit Clerk, McCook County **Cheryl Miiller** .... (605) 425-2781
  P.O. Box 504, Salem, SD 57058-0504   Fax: (605) 425-3144
  130 West Essex Avenue, Salem, SD 57058
  E-mail: cheryl.miiller@ujs.state.sd.us

McPherson County

Clerk of Court

Fifth Judicial Circuit
101 South East First Avenue, Aberdeen, SD 57402-1087

Circuit Clerk, McPherson County **Ronda Geffre** .... (605) 439-3361
  P.O. Box 248, Leola, SD 57456-0248   Fax: (605) 439-3297
  706 Main Street, Leola, SD 57456
  E-mail: ronda.geffre@ujs.state.sd.us

Meade County

Clerk of Court

Fourth Judicial Circuit
78 Sherman Street, Deadwood, SD 57732-0626
P.O. Box 626, Deadwood, SD 57732-0626

Circuit Clerk, Meade County **Lane Keil** .... (605) 347-4411
  1425 Sherman Street, Sturgis, SD 57785-0939   Fax: (605) 347-3526
  P.O. Box 939, Sturgis, SD 57785-0939

Mellette County

Clerk of Court

Sixth Judicial Circuit
104 East Capitol Avenue, Pierre, SD 57501
Tel: (605) 773-3971

Circuit Clerk, Mellette County **Andrea Wade** .... (605) 259-3230
  P.O. Box 257, White River, SD 57579-0257   Fax: (605) 259-3030
  First and McKinley Street,
  White River, SD 57579
  E-mail: andrea.wade@ujs.state.sd.us

Miner County

Clerk of Court

Third Judicial Circuit
314 Sixth Avenue, Brookings, SD 57006-2085

Circuit Clerk, Miner County **Diane Keimig** .... (605) 772-4612
  P.O. Box 265, Howard, SD 57349-0265   Fax: (605) 772-4412
  North Main Street and Park Avenue,
  Howard, SD 57349
  E-mail: diane.keimig@ujs.state.sd.us

Minnehaha County

Clerk of Court

Second Judicial Circuit
425 North Dakota Avenue, Sioux Falls, SD 57104

Circuit Clerk, Minnehaha County **Angie Gries** .... (605) 367-5900
  425 North Dakota Avenue,
  Sioux Falls, SD 57104

Moody County

Clerk of Court

Third Judicial Circuit
314 Sixth Avenue, Brookings, SD 57006-2085

Circuit Clerk, Moody County **Lisa Johnson** .... (605) 997-3181
  P.O. Box 226, Flandreau, SD 57028   Fax: (605) 997-3861
  101 East Pipestone Avenue,
  Flandreau, SD 57028
  E-mail: lisa.johnson@ujs.state.sd.us

Pennington County

Clerk of Court

Seventh Judicial Circuit
P.O. Box 230, Rapid City, SD 57709

Circuit Clerk, Pennington County **Ranae Truman** .... (605) 394-2688
  P.O. Box 230, Rapid City, SD 57709
  E-mail: ranae.truman@ujs.state.sd.us

Perkins County

Clerk of Court

Fourth Judicial Circuit
78 Sherman Street, Deadwood, SD 57732-0626
P.O. Box 626, Deadwood, SD 57732-0626

Circuit Clerk, Perkins County **Trish Peck** .... (605) 244-5626
  100 East Main, Bison, SD 57620   Fax: (605) 244-7110
  P.O. Box 426, Bison, SD 57620-0426
  E-mail: trish.peck@ujs.state.sd.us

Potter County

Clerk of Court

Sixth Judicial Circuit
104 East Capitol Avenue, Pierre, SD 57501
Tel: (605) 773-3971

Circuit Clerk, Potter County **Cathy Westphal** .... (605) 765-9472
  201 South Exene, Gettysburg, SD 57442   Fax: (605) 765-9670
  P.O. Box 67, Gettysburg, SD 57442

(continued on next page)

Roberts County

Clerk of Court

Fifth Judicial Circuit
101 South East First Avenue, Aberdeen, SD 57402-1087

Circuit Clerk, Roberts County **Cindy Marohl** . . . . (605) 698-3395
   411 Second Avenue East, Sisseton, SD 57262   Fax: (605) 698-7894
   E-mail: cindy.marohl@ujs.state.sd.us

Sanborn County

Clerk of Court

Third Judicial Circuit
314 Sixth Avenue, Brookings, SD 57006-2085

Circuit Clerk, Sanborn County **Susan Johannsen** . . . . (605) 796-4515
   P.O. Box 56, Woonsocket, SD 57385-0056   Fax: (605) 796-4502
   604 West Sixth Street, Woonsocket, SD 57385
   E-mail: susan.johannsen@ujs.state.sd.us

Shannon County

Clerk of Court

Seventh Judicial Circuit
P.O. Box 230, Rapid City, SD 57709

Circuit Clerk, Shannon County **Carol Foster** . . . . (605) 745-5131
   906 North River Street, Hot Springs, SD 57747
   E-mail: carol.foster@ujs.state.sd.us

Spink County

Clerk of Court

Fifth Judicial Circuit
101 South East First Avenue, Aberdeen, SD 57402-1087

Circuit Clerk, Spink County **Elisha Kuhfield** . . . . (605) 472-4535
   210 East Seventh Avenue, Redfield, SD 57469   Fax: (605) 472-4352

Stanley County

Clerk of Court

Sixth Judicial Circuit
104 East Capitol Avenue, Pierre, SD 57501
Tel: (605) 773-3971

Circuit Clerk, Stanley County **Kelli Sitzman** . . . . (605) 223-7735
   Eight East Second Avenue,   Fax: (605) 223-7738
   Fort Pierre, SD 57532-0758
   P.O. Box 758, Fort Pierre, SD 57532-0758
   E-mail: kelli.sitzman@ujs.state.sd.us

Sully County

Clerk of Court

Sixth Judicial Circuit
104 East Capitol Avenue, Pierre, SD 57501
Tel: (605) 773-3971

Circuit Clerk, Sully County **Larash Nola** . . . . (605) 258-2535
   700 Ash Avenue, Onida, SD 57564   Fax: (605) 258-2270
   P.O. Box 188, Onida, SD 57564

Todd County

Clerk of Court

Sixth Judicial Circuit
104 East Capitol Avenue, Pierre, SD 57501
Tel: (605) 773-3971

Circuit Clerk, Todd County **Marsha Hodge** . . . . (605) 842-2266
   200 Third Street, Winner, SD 57580-0311   Fax: (605) 842-2267
   P.O. Box 311, Winner, SD 57580-0311
   E-mail: marsha.hodge@ujs.state.sd.us

Tripp County

Clerk of Court

Sixth Judicial Circuit
104 East Capitol Avenue, Pierre, SD 57501
Tel: (605) 773-3971

Circuit Clerk, Tripp County **Marsha Hodge** . . . . (605) 842-2266
   200 Third Street, Winner, SD 57580-0311   Fax: (605) 842-2267
   P.O. Box 311, Winner, SD 57580-0311
   E-mail: marsha.hodge@ujs.state.sd.us

Turner County

Clerk of Court

First Judicial Circuit
209 East Main Street, Elk Point, SD 57025-2327

Circuit Clerk, Turner County **Colleen Dunn** . . . . (605) 297-3115
   P.O. Box 446, Parker, SD 57053-0446   Fax: (605) 297-2115
   400 South Main, Parker, SD 57053-0446
   E-mail: colleen.dunn@ujs.state.sd.us

Union County

Clerk of Court

First Judicial Circuit
209 East Main Street, Elk Point, SD 57025-2327

Circuit Clerk, Union County **Melissa Larsen** . . . . (605) 356-2132
   209 East Main Street, Suite 230,   Fax: (605) 356-3687
   Elk Point, SD 57025-2327
   E-mail: melissa.larsen@ujs.state.sd.us

Walworth County

Clerk of Court

Fifth Judicial Circuit
101 South East First Avenue, Aberdeen, SD 57402-1087

Circuit Clerk, Walworth County **Ann Byre** . . . . (605) 649-7311
   4304 Fourth Avenue, Selby, SD 57472   Fax: (605) 649-7624
   P.O. Box 328, Selby, SD 57472
   E-mail: ann.byre@ujs.state.sd.us

Yankton County

Clerk of Court

First Judicial Circuit
209 East Main Street, Elk Point, SD 57025-2327

Circuit Clerk, Yankton County **Jody Johnson** . . . . (605) 668-3080
   410 Walnut, Suite 205, Yankton, SD 57078   Fax: (605) 668-5411
   E-mail: jody.johnson@ujs.state.sd.us

Ziebach County

Clerk of Court

Fourth Judicial Circuit
78 Sherman Street, Deadwood, SD 57732-0626
P.O. Box 626, Deadwood, SD 57732-0626

Circuit Clerk, Ziebach County **Judy Anderson** . . . . (605) 365-5159
  P.O. Box 306, Dupree, SD 57623-0306   Fax: (605) 365-5652
  601 Main Street, Dupree, SD 57623
  E-mail: judy.anderson@ujs.state.sd.us

Counties Within Judicial Districts

1st Circuit

Areas Covered: Aurora, Bon Homme, Brule, Buffalo, Charles Mix, Clay, Davison, Douglas, Hanson, Hutchinson, McCook, Turner, Union, and Yankton Counties.

2nd Circuit

Areas Covered: Lincoln and Minnehaha Counties.

3rd Circuit

Areas Covered: Beadle, Brookings, Clark, Codington, Deuel, Grant, Hamlin, Hand, Jerauld, Kingsbury, Lake, Miner, Moody, and Sanborn Counties.

4th Circuit

Areas Covered: Butte, Corson, Dewey, Harding, Lawrence, Meade, Perkins, and Ziebach Counties.

5th Circuit

Areas Covered: Brown, Campbell, Day, Edmunds, Faulk, Marshall, McPherson, Roberts, Spink, and Walworth Counties.

6th Circuit

Areas Covered: Bennett, Gregory, Haakon, Hughes, Hyde, Jackson, Jones, Lyman, Mellette, Potter, Stanley, Sully, Todd, and Tripp Counties.

7th Circuit

Areas Covered: Custer, Fall River, Pennington, and Shannon Counties.

Tennessee Court Clerks and Courthouses

The trial courts of general jurisdiction in Tennessee are called circuit courts. There are 31 districts of circuit court, each consisting of at least one county. Each county includes a County Clerk and a Clerk of the Circuit Court.

Tennessee Supreme Court

Supreme Court Building, 401 Seventh Avenue North,
Nashville, TN 37219-1407 (Middle Division)
Supreme Court Building, 505 Main Street, Suite 200,
Knoxville, TN 37902 (Eastern Division)
Six Highway 45 By-Pass, Jackson, TN 38301 (Western Division)
Tel: (615) 741-2681 (Middle Division)
Tel: (865) 594-6700 (Eastern Division)
Tel: (731) 423-5840 (Western Division)
Fax: (615) 532-8757 (Middle Division)
Fax: (865) 594-6497 (Eastern Division)
Fax: (731) 423-6453 (Western Division)
Internet: www.tncourts.gov

The Supreme Court is comprised of three judicial divisions and consists of a chief justice and four justices who are elected in statewide, partisan elections for eight-year terms. The chief justice is elected by peer vote to a four-year term. Retirement is usually at age seventy; however, retired justices may be recalled by the Supreme Court chief justice to serve temporary assignments. The Supreme Court hears direct appeals from the state's trial courts in cases involving a question of the constitutionality of a state law or municipal ordinance, the right to hold public office and other public law issues, workers' compensation, state revenue and death penalty convictions. The Court may review decisions of the state's two intermediate appellate courts by writ of certiorari. The Court exercises rule-making and supervisory control over the lower courts and disciplinary authority over members of the state bar.

Court Staff
Clerk of the Court **James M. Hivner** . . . . (615) 253-1470
   E-mail: james.hivner@tncourts.gov

Tennessee Court of Appeals

Internet: www.tsc.state.tn.us

The three divisions of the Court of Appeals each consists of a presiding judge and three judges who are elected in nonpartisan elections for eight-year terms. Vacancies are filled by the Governor from a list of candidates provided by the Appellate Court Nominating Commission; newly-appointed judges stand for retention in the first August biennial election occurring more than thirty days after their appointment. The presiding judges are elected by peer vote to a one-year term. Retirement is at age seventy. However, retired judges may be recalled by the Tennessee Supreme Court Chief Justice to serve temporary assignments. The Court of Appeals has direct appellate jurisdiction over all civil cases, except when the Supreme Court has exclusive jurisdiction or as provided by law.

Tennessee Court of Appeals, Eastern Grand Division

505 Main Street, Suite 200, Knoxville, TN 37902
P.O. Box 444, Knoxville, TN 37901-0444
Tel: (865) 594-6700 Fax: (865) 594-6497

Areas Covered: Counties of Anderson, Bledsoe, Blount, Bradley, Campbell, Carter, Claiborne, Cocke, Cumberland, Grainger, Greene, Hamblen, Hamilton, Hancock, Hawkins, Jefferson, Johnson, Knox, Loudon, McMinn, Meigs, Monroe, Morgan, Polk, Rhea, Roane, Scott, Sevier, Sullivan, Unicoi, Union and Washington

Court Staff
Chief Deputy Clerk **Joanne Newsome** . . . . (865) 594-6700
   E-mail: joanne.newsome@tncourts.gov

Tennessee Court of Appeals, Middle Grand Division

Supreme Court Building, 401 Seventh Avenue North,
Nashville, TN 37219-1407
Tel: (615) 741-2681 Fax: (615) 532-8757

Areas Covered: Counties of Bedford, Cannon, Cheatham, Clay, Coffee, Davidson, DeKalb, Dickson, Fentress, Franklin, Giles, Grundy, Hickman, Houston, Humphreys, Jackson, Lawrence, Lewis, Lincoln, Macon, Marion, Marshall, Maury, Montgomery, Moore, Overton, Perry, Pickett, Putnam, Robertson, Rutherford, Sequatchie, Smith, Summer, Stewart, Trousdale, Van Buren, Warren, Wayne, White, Williamson and Wilson

Court Staff
Chief Deputy Clerk **Lisa Marsh** . . . . (615) 741-2681
   E-mail: lisa_marsh@tncourts.gov

Tennessee Court of Appeals, Western Grand Division

Supreme Court Building, Six Highway 45 Bypass, Jackson, TN 38301
P.O. Box 909, Jackson, TN 38302-0909
Tel: (731) 423-5840 Fax: (731) 423-6453

Areas Covered: Counties of Benton, Carroll, Chester, Crockett, Decatur, Dyer, Fayette, Gibson, Hardeman, Hardin, Haywood, Henderson, Henry, Lake, Lauderdale, McNairy, Madison, Obion, Shelby, Tipton and Weakley

Court Staff
Chief Deputy Clerk **Nancy Acred** . . . . (731) 423-5840
   E-mail: nancy.acred@tncourts.gov

County-By-County

Anderson County

Circuit Clerk

Seventh Judicial Circuit
100 North Main, Clinton, TN 37716

Circuit Clerk, Anderson County **William T. Jones** . . . . (865) 463-6842
   100 Main Street, Room 301,
   Clinton, TN 37716

(continued on next page)

County Clerk

Office of the County Clerk
100 North Main Street, Room 111, Clinton, TN 37716-3617
Tel: (865) 457-6228 Fax: (865) 463-6892

County Clerk **Jeff Cole** . . . . (865) 457-6228
  E-mail: jcole@anderson-county.org

Bedford County

Circuit Clerk

Seventeenth Judicial Circuit
402 Belmont Avenue, Shelbyville, TN 37160

Circuit Clerk, Bedford County **Michelle Murray** . . . . (931) 684-3223
  One Public Square, Room 200,
  Shelbyville, TN 37160

County Clerk

Office of the County Clerk
104 North Side Square, Shelbyville, TN 37160
Tel: (931) 684-1921 Fax: (931) 685-9590

County Clerk **Donna Thomas** . . . . (931) 684-1921
  E-mail: donna.thomas@tn.gov

Benton County

Circuit Clerk

Twenty-Fourth Judicial Circuit
21460 East Main Street, Huntingdon, TN 38344

Circuit Clerk, Benton County **Sam Rainwaters** . . . . (731) 584-6711
  One East Court Square, Room 210,
  Camden, TN 38320
  E-mail: sam.rainwaters@tncourts.gov

County Clerk

Office of the County Clerk
One East Court Square, Suite 101, Camden, TN 38320
Tel: (731) 584-6053 Fax: (731) 584-4640

County Clerk **Wanda Malin** . . . . (731) 584-6053
  E-mail: wanda.malin@tn.gov

Bledsoe County

Circuit Clerk

Twelfth Judicial Circuit
P.O. Box 428, Winchester, TN 37398-0428

Circuit Clerk, Bledsoe County **Michael Walker** . . . . (423) 447-6488
  P.O. Box 455, Pikeville, TN 37367-0455
  E-mail: michael.walker@tncourts.gov

County Clerk

Office of the County Clerk
31 Main Street, Pikeville, TN 37367
P.O. Box 21, Pikeville, TN 37367
Tel: (423) 447-2137 Fax: (423) 447-6581

County Clerk **Carolyn M. Terry** . . . . (423) 447-2137
  E-mail: carolyn.terry@tn.gov

Blount County

Circuit Clerk

Fifth Judicial Circuit
942 East Lamar Alexander Parkway, Maryville, TN 37804

Circuit Clerk, Blount County **Tom Hatcher** . . . . (865) 273-5400
  Blount County Justice Center,
  926 East Lamar Alexander Parkway,
  Maryville, TN 37804-6201
  E-mail: thomas.hatcher@tncourts.gov

County Clerk

Office of the County Clerk
345 Court Street, Maryville, TN 27804-5906
Tel: (865) 273-5800 Fax: (865) 273-5815

County Clerk **Roy Crawford, Jr.** . . . . (865) 273-5800
  E-mail: rcrawford@blounttn.org

Bradley County

Circuit Clerk

Tenth Judicial Circuit
P.O. Box 846, Cleveland, TN 37311

Circuit Clerk, Bradley County **Gayla Harris Miller** . . . . . . (423) 728-7220
  155 North Ocoee Street, Room 205,
  Cleveland, TN 37311-5068

County Clerk

Office of the County Clerk
155 Ocoee Street, Room 101, Cleveland, TN 37311
Tel: (423) 728-7226 Fax: (423) 478-8845

County Clerk **Donna A. Simpson** . . . . (423) 728-7226
  E-mail: asimpson@bradleyco.net

Campbell County

Circuit Clerk

Eighth Judicial Circuit
241 Myers Street, Jacksboro, TN 37757

Circuit Clerk, Campbell County **Bobby Vann** . . . . (423) 562-2624
  P.O. Box 26, Jacksboro, TN 37757-0026

County Clerk

Office of the County Clerk
590 Main Street, Suite A-21, Jacksboro, TN 37757
705 West Central Avenue, LaFollette, TN 37766
321 South Main Street, Jellico, TN 37762
Tel: (423) 562-4985 (Jacksboro Office)
Tel: (423) 566-8130 (LaFollette Office)
Tel: (423) 784-8608 (Jellico Office) Fax: (423) 566-3852

County Clerk **Alene Baird** . . . . (423) 562-4985
  E-mail: alene.baird@tn.gov

Cannon County

Circuit Clerk

Sixteenth Judicial Circuit
20 Public Square, Murfreesboro, TN 37130

Circuit Clerk, Cannon County **Lynne D. Foster** . . . . (615) 563-4461
  One Public Square, Woodbury, TN 37190

County Clerk

Office of the County Clerk
200 West Main Street, Woodbury, TN 37190
Tel: (615) 563-4278 Fax: (615) 563-1289

County Clerk **Bobby P. Smith** . . . . (615) 563-4278
  E-mail: bobby.p.smith@tn.gov

Carroll County

Circuit Clerk

Twenty-Fourth Judicial Circuit
21460 East Main Street, Huntingdon, TN 38344

Circuit Clerk, Carroll County **Bertha Taylor** . . . . (731) 986-1932
  99 Court Square, Suite 103,
  Huntingdon, TN 38344-3726

County Clerk

Office of the County Clerk
625 High Street, Suite 103, Huntingdon, TN 38344
Tel: (731) 986-1960 Fax: (731) 986-1978

County Clerk **Darlene Kirk** . . . . (731) 986-1960
  E-mail: darlene.kirk@tn.gov

Carter County

Circuit Clerk

First Judicial Circuit
Washington County Justice Center, 108 West Jackson Boulevard,
Suite 2141, Jonesborough, TN 37659

Circuit Clerk, Carter County **Johnny Blankenship** . . . . . . (423) 542-1835
  Courthouse Annex, 900 East Elk Avenue,
  Elizabethton, TN 37643

County Clerk

Office of the County Clerk
801 East Elk Avenue, Elizabethton, TN 37643
Tel: (423) 542-1814 Fax: (423) 547-1502
E-mail: clerk@cartercountytn.gov

County Clerk **Mary Gouge** . . . . (423) 542-1814
  E-mail: mary.gouge@tn.gov

Cheatham County

Circuit Clerk

Twenty-Third Judicial Circuit
Humphreys County Courthouse, Waverly, TN 37185

Circuit Clerk, Cheatham County **Julie Hibbs** . . . . (615) 792-3272
  Criminal Justice Center, 100 Public Square,
  Room 225, Ashland City, TN 37015
  E-mail: julie.hibbs@tncourts.gov

County Clerk

Office of the County Clerk
264 South Main Street, Suite 108, Ashland City, TN 37015
Tel: (615) 792-5179 Fax: (615) 792-2094

County Clerk **Teresa Gupton** . . . . (615) 792-5179
  E-mail: teresa.gupton@tn.gov

Chester County

Circuit Clerk

Twenty-Sixth Judicial Circuit
515 South Liberty Street, Jackson, TN 38301

Circuit Clerk, Chester County **Justin Emerson** . . . . (731) 989-2454
  333 Eric Bell Drive, Suite D,
  Henderson, TN 38340

County Clerk

Office of the County Clerk
133 East Main Street, Henderson, TN 38340
Tel: (731) 989-2233 Fax: (731) 989-9602

County Clerk **Stacy Smith** . . . . (731) 989-2233

Claiborne County

Circuit Clerk

Eighth Judicial Circuit
241 Myers Street, Jacksboro, TN 37757

Circuit Clerk, Claiborne County **Jackie Rosenbalm** . . . . . (423) 626-3334
  Criminal Justice Center, 415 Straight Creek Road,
  New Tazewell, TN 37825

County Clerk

Office of the County Clerk
P.O. Box 318, Tazewell, TN 37879
Tel: (423) 626-3283 Fax: (423) 626-1661

County Clerk **Evelyn Hill** . . . . (423) 626-3283
  E-mail: evelyn.hill@tn.gov

Clay County

Circuit Clerk

Thirteenth Judicial Circuit
228 East Broad Street, Cookeville, TN 38501

Circuit Clerk, Clay County **Susan Birdwell** . . . . (931) 243-2557
  P.O. Box 749, Celina, TN 38551-0749
  E-mail: susan.birdwell@tncourts.gov

County Clerk

Office of the County Clerk
145 Cordell Hull Drive, Celina, TN 38551
P.O. Box 218, Celina, TN 38551
Tel: (931) 243-2249 Fax: (931) 243-3231

County Clerk **Donna Watson** . . . . (931) 243-2249
  E-mail: donna.watson@tn.gov

Cocke County

Circuit Clerk

Fourth Judicial Circuit
8554 South Highway 92, Dandridge, TN 37725

Circuit Clerk, Cocke County **Peggy Lane** . . . . (423) 623-6124
  111 Court Avenue, Newport, TN 37821

(continued on next page)

Tennessee Court Clerks and Courthouses *continued*

County Clerk

Office of the County Clerk
111 Court Avenue, Room 101, Newport, TN 37821
Tel: (423) 623-6176 Fax: (423) 623-6178

County Clerk **Jan Brockwell** . . . . (423) 623-6176
E-mail: jan.brockwell@tn.gov

Coffee County

Circuit Clerk

Fourteenth Judicial Circuit
300 Hillsboro Boulevard, Manchester, TN 37349

Circuit Clerk, Coffee County **Heather H. Duncan** . . . . (931) 723-5110
300 Hillsboro Boulevard, Manchester, TN 37349

County Clerk

Office of the County Clerk
1327 McArthur Street, Manchester, TN 37355
Tel: (931) 723-5106 Fax: (931) 723-8248

County Clerk **Teresa McFadden** . . . . (931) 723-5106
E-mail: teresa.mcfadden@tn.gov

Crockett County

Circuit Clerk

Twenty-Eighth Judicial Circuit
204 North Court Square, Trenton, TN 38382

Circuit Clerk, Crockett County **Kim Kail** . . . . (731) 696-5462
One South Bells Street, Suite 6,
Alamo, TN 38001
E-mail: kim.kail@tncourts.gov

County Clerk

Office of the County Clerk
One South Bells Street, Suite 1, Alamo, TN 38001
Tel: (731) 696-5452 Fax: (731) 696-3261

County Clerk **Ernest Bushart** . . . . (731) 696-5452
E-mail: ernest.bushart@tn.gov

Cumberland County

Circuit Clerk

Thirteenth Judicial Circuit
228 East Broad Street, Cookeville, TN 38501

Circuit Clerk, Cumberland County **Larry Sherrill** . . . . (931) 484-6647
60 Justice Center Drive, Suite 300,
Crossville, TN 38555

County Clerk

Office of the County Clerk
Two North Main Street, Suite 206, Crossville, TN 38555
Tel: (931) 484-6442 Fax: (931) 484-6440

County Clerk **Jule Bryson** . . . . (931) 484-6442
E-mail: jule.bryson@tn.gov

Tennessee Court Clerks and Courthouses *continued*

Davidson County

Circuit Clerk

Twentieth Judicial Circuit
One Public Square, Nashville, TN 37217

Circuit Clerk, Davidson County **Richard R. Rooker** . . . . . .(615) 862-5181
One Public Square, Suite 302,
Nashville, TN 37217
E-mail: circuit@nashville.gov

County Clerk

Office of the County Clerk
700 Second Avenue, South, Suite 101, Nashville, TN 37210
Tel: (615) 862-6050 (Auto Licenses and Titles)
E-mail: countyclerk@nashville.gov
Internet: http://nashvilleclerk.com/

County Clerk **Brenda P. Wynn** . . . .(615) 862-6250
E-mail: brenda.wynn@nashville.gov

Decatur County

Circuit Clerk

Twenty-Fourth Judicial Circuit
21460 East Main Street, Huntingdon, TN 38344

Circuit Clerk, Decatur County **Danny Tanner** . . . .(731) 852-3125
P.O. Box 488, Decaturville, TN 38329-0488
E-mail: danny.tanner@tncourts.gov

County Clerk

Office of the County Clerk
22 West Main Street, Decaturville, TN 38329
Tel: (731) 852-3417 Fax: (731) 852-3152

County Clerk **Melinda Broadway** . . . .(731) 852-3417

DeKalb County

Circuit Clerk

Thirteenth Judicial Circuit
228 East Broad Street, Cookeville, TN 38501

Circuit Clerk, DeKalb County **Katherine Pack** . . . .(615) 597-5711
Dekalb County Courthouse, One Public Square,
Room 303, Smithville, TN 37166
E-mail: katherine.pack@tncourts.gov

County Clerk

Office of the County Clerk
732 South Congress Boulevard, Smithville, TN 37166
Tel: (615) 597-5177 Fax: (615) 597-1404

County Clerk **James L. "Jimmy" Poss** . . . .(615) 597-5177
E-mail: jimmy.poss@tn.gov

Dickson County

Circuit Clerk

Twenty-Third Judicial Circuit
Humphreys County Courthouse, Waverly, TN 37185

Circuit Clerk, Dickson County **Pam Myatt** . . . .(615) 789-7010
Four Court Square, Charlotte, TN 37036
E-mail: pam.myatt@tncourts.gov

County Clerk

Office of the County Clerk
Four Court Square, Charleston, TN 37036
P.O. Box 220, Charlotte, TN 37036
106 North Main Street, Dickson, TN 37055
Tel: (615) 789-5093 (Charlotte Office)
Tel: (615) 446-2543 (Dickson Office)
Fax: (615) 789-0128 (Charlotte Office)
Fax: (615) 446-4495 (Dickson Office)

County Clerk **Luanne Greer** . . . . (615) 789-5093
    E-mail: luanne.greer@tn.gov

Dyer County

Circuit Clerk

Twenty-Ninth Judicial Circuit
106 West Court, Dyersburg, TN 38024

Circuit Clerk, Dyer County **Tom "T.J." Jones** . . . . (731) 286-7809
    P.O. Box 1360, Dyersburg, TN 38024-1360

County Clerk

Office of the County Clerk
115 West Market Street, Dyersburg, TN 38024
P.O. Box 1360, Dyersburg, TN 38024
Tel: (731) 286-7814 Fax: (731) 288-7719

County Clerk **Diane Moore** . . . . (731) 286-7814
    E-mail: diane.moore@tn.gov

Fayette County

Circuit Clerk

Twenty-Fifth Judicial Circuit
104 Lafayette Avenue, Ripley, TN 38063

Circuit Clerk, Fayette County **Ed Pulliam** . . . . (901) 465-5205
    705 Justice Drive, Somerville, TN 38068
    E-mail: ed.pulliam@tncourts.gov

County Clerk

Office of the County Clerk
One Court Square, Room 101, Somerville, TN 38068
P.O. Box 218, Somerville, TN 38068
Tel: (901) 465-5213 Fax: (901) 465-5293

County Clerk **Sue Culver** . . . . (901) 465-5213
    E-mail: sue.culver@tn.gov

Fentress County

Circuit Clerk

Eighth Judicial Circuit
241 Myers Street, Jacksboro, TN 37757

Circuit Clerk, Fentress County **Gina Mullinix** . . . . (931) 879-7919
    P.O. Box 699, Jamestown, TN 38556-0699

County Clerk

Office of the County Clerk
101 Main Street South, Jamestown, TN 38556
Tel: (931) 879-8014 Fax: (931) 879-8438

County Clerk **Marilyn Stephens** . . . . (931) 879-8014
    E-mail: marilyn.l.stephens@tn.gov

Franklin County

Circuit Clerk

Twelfth Judicial Circuit
P.O. Box 428, Winchester, TN 37398-0428

Circuit Clerk, Franklin County **Robert Baggett** . . . . (931) 967-2923
    360 Wilton Circle, Room 157,
    Winchester, TN 37398
    E-mail: robert.baggett@tncourts.gov

County Clerk

Office of the County Clerk
One South Jefferson Street, Winchester, TN 37398
Tel: (931) 967-2541 Fax: (931) 962-3364

County Clerk **Phillip Custer** . . . . (931) 967-2541
    E-mail: phillip.custer@franklincotn.us

Gibson County

Circuit Clerk

Twenty-Eighth Judicial Circuit
204 North Court Square, Trenton, TN 38382

Circuit Clerk, Gibson County **Janice Jones** . . . . (731) 855-7615
    295 North College Street, Trenton, TN 38382
    E-mail: janice.jones@tncourts.gov

County Clerk

Office of the County Clerk
One Court Square, Trenton, TN 38382
Tel: (731) 855-7642 Fax: (731) 855-7643

County Clerk **Joyce Brown** . . . . (731) 855-7642
    E-mail: joyce.brown@tn.gov

Giles County

Circuit Clerk

Twenty-Second Judicial Circuit
14 Public Square North, Columbia, TN 38401

Circuit Clerk, Giles County **Crystal Greene** . . . . (931) 363-5311
    P.O. Box 678, Pulaski, TN 38478-0678

County Clerk

Office of the County Clerk
One Public Square, Pulaski, TN 38478
Tel: (931) 363-1509 Fax: (931) 424-4795

County Clerk **Carol Wade** . . . . (931) 363-1509
    E-mail: carol.wade@state.tn.us

Grainger County

Circuit Clerk

Fourth Judicial Circuit
8554 South Highway 92, Dandridge, TN 37725

Circuit Clerk, Grainger County **Sherry Clifton** . . . . (865) 828-3605
    P.O. Box 157, Rutledge, TN 37861-0157
    E-mail: sherry.clifton@tncourts.gov

(continued on next page)

County Clerk

Office of the County Clerk
P.O. Box 116, Rutledge, TN 37861
Tel: (865) 828-3511 Fax: (865) 828-3203

County Clerk **Angie Lamb** . . . . (865) 828-3511
  E-mail: angie.lamb@tn.gov

Greene County

Circuit Clerk

Third Judicial Circuit
101 South Main Street, Greeneville, TN 37743

Circuit Clerk, Greene County **Pam Venerable** . . . . (423) 798-1760
  101 South Main Street, Greeneville, TN 37743

County Clerk

Office of the County Clerk
204 North Cutler Street, Suite 200, Greeneville, TN 37745
Tel: (423) 798-1708 Fax: (423) 798-1822

County Clerk **Lori Bryant** . . . . (423) 798-1708
  E-mail: lori.bryant@tn.gov

Grundy County

Circuit Clerk

Twelfth Judicial Circuit
P.O. Box 428, Winchester, TN 37398-0428

Circuit Clerk, Grundy County **Melody Oliver** . . . . (931) 692-3368
  P.O. Box 161, Altamont, TN 37301-0161
  E-mail: melody.oliver@tncourts.gov

County Clerk

Office of the County Clerk
P.O. Box 215, Altamont, TN 37301
Tel: (931) 692-3622 Fax: (931) 692-3659

County Clerk **Tammy Sholey** . . . . (931) 692-3622
  E-mail: tammy.sholey@tn.gov

Hamblen County

Circuit Clerk

Third Judicial Circuit
101 South Main Street, Greeneville, TN 37743

Circuit Clerk, Hamblen County **Teresa West** . . . . (423) 586-5640
  Justice Center, 510 Allison Street,
  Morristown, TN 37814

County Clerk

Office of the County Clerk
511 West Second North Street, Morristown, TN 37814
Tel: (423) 586-1993 Fax: (423) 585-2015

County Clerk **Linda Wilder** . . . . (423) 586-1993
  E-mail: lwilder@co.hamblen.tn.us

Hamilton County

Circuit Clerk

Eleventh Judicial Circuit
Hamilton County Courthouse, 625 Georgia Avenue, Suite 311,
Chattanooga, TN 37405

Circuit Clerk, Hamilton County **Larry Henry** . . . . (423) 209-6700
  625 Georgia Avenue, Chattanooga, TN 37402

County Clerk

Office of the County Clerk
County Courthouse, 201 East 7th Street, Chattanooga, TN 37402
Fax: (423) 209-6501
Internet: http://www.countyclerkanytime.com

County Clerk **William F. Knowles** . . . . (423) 209-6500
  E-mail: countyclerk@hamiltontn.gov

Hancock County

Circuit Clerk

Third Judicial Circuit
101 South Main Street, Greeneville, TN 37743

Circuit Clerk, Hancock County **Bill McMurry** . . . . (423) 733-2954
  P.O. Box 347, Sneedville, TN 37869-0347
  E-mail: bill.mcmurry@tncourts.gov

County Clerk

Office of the County Clerk
418 Harrison Street, Suite 96, Sneedville, TN 37869
P.O. Box 575, Sneedville, TN 37869
Tel: (423) 733-2519 Fax: (423) 733-4509

County Clerk **Jessie Royston** . . . . (423) 733-2519
  E-mail: jessie.royston@tn.gov

Hardeman County

Circuit Clerk

Twenty-Fifth Judicial Circuit
104 Lafayette Avenue, Ripley, TN 38063

Circuit Clerk, Hardeman County **Linda Fulghum** . . . . (731) 658-6524
  505 South Main Street, Suite A,
  Bolivar, TN 38008
  E-mail: linda.fulghum@tncourts.gov

County Clerk

Office of the County Clerk
100 North Main Street, Bolivar, TN 38008
Tel: (731) 658-3541 Fax: (731) 658-3482

County Clerk **Jerry Armstrong** . . . . (731) 658-3541
  E-mail: jerry.armstrong@tn.gov

Hardin County

Circuit Clerk

Twenty-Fourth Judicial Circuit
21460 East Main Street, Huntingdon, TN 38344

Circuit Clerk, Hardin County **Diane B. Polk** . . . . (731) 925-3583
  465 Main Street, Savannah, TN 38372
  E-mail: diane.polk@tncourts.gov

County Clerk

Office of the County Clerk
65 Court Street, Suite 1, Savannah, TN 38372
Tel: (731) 925-3921 Fax: (731) 926-4313

County Clerk **Connie S. Stephens** . . . . (731) 925-3921
E-mail: connie.s.stephens@tn.gov

Hawkins County

Circuit Clerk

Third Judicial Circuit
101 South Main Street, Greeneville, TN 37743

Circuit Clerk, Hawkins County **Sarah Davis** . . . . (423) 272-3397
115 Justice Center Drive, Suite 1237,
Rogersville, TN 37857
E-mail: sarah.davis@tncourts.gov

County Clerk

Office of the County Clerk
110 East Main Street, Room 204, Rogersville, TN 37857
Tel: (423) 272-7002 Fax: (423) 272-5801

County Clerk **Nancy Davis** . . . . (423) 272-7002
E-mail: nancy.davis@tn.gov

Haywood County

Circuit Clerk

Twenty-Eighth Judicial Circuit
204 North Court Square, Trenton, TN 38382

Circuit Clerk, Haywood County **Mary Bond London** . . . . (731) 772-1112
100 South Dupree Street, Brownsville, TN 38012

County Clerk

Office of the County Clerk
One North Washington, Brownsville, TN 38012
Tel: (731) 772-2362 Fax: (731) 772-1213

County Clerk **Sonya Castellaw** . . . . (731) 772-2362
E-mail: sonya.castellaw@tn.gov

Henderson County

Circuit Clerk

Twenty-Sixth Judicial Circuit
515 South Liberty Street, Jackson, TN 38301

Circuit Clerk, Henderson County **Beverly Dunaway** . . . . . (731) 968-2031
17 Monroe Avenue, Suite 9,
Lexington, TN 38351

County Clerk

Office of the County Clerk
17 Monroe Street, Lexington, TN 38351
Tel: (731) 968-2856 Fax: (731) 968-6644

County Clerk **Carolyn Holmes** . . . . (731) 968-2856
E-mail: carolyn.holmes@tn.gov

Henry County

Circuit Clerk

Twenty-Fourth Judicial Circuit
21460 East Main Street, Huntingdon, TN 38344

Circuit Clerk, Henry County **Mike Wilson** . . . . (731) 642-0461
101 West Washington Street, Second Floor,
Paris, TN 38242
E-mail: mike.wilson@tncourts.gov

County Clerk

Office of the County Clerk
101 West Washington Street, Suite 102, Paris, TN 38242
Tel: (731) 642-2412 Fax: (731) 644-0947

County Clerk **Donna Craig** . . . . (731) 642-2412
E-mail: donna.craig@tn.gov

Hickman County

Circuit Clerk

Twenty-First Judicial Circuit
135 Fourth Avenue, Franklin, TN 37064

Circuit Clerk, Hickman County **Dana Nicholson** . . . . (931) 729-2211
104 College Avenue, Suite 204,
Centerville, TN 37033
E-mail: dana.nicholson@tncourts.gov

County Clerk

Office of the County Clerk
114 North Central Avenue, Suite 202, Centerville, TN 37033
Tel: (931) 729-2621 Fax: (931) 729-9951

County Clerk **Casey Dorton** . . . . (931) 729-2621
E-mail: casey.dorton@hickmanco.com

Houston County

Circuit Clerk

Twenty-Third Judicial Circuit
Humphreys County Courthouse, Waverly, TN 37185

Circuit Clerk, Houston County **Sharon Tomlinson** . . . . . . (931) 289-4673
P.O. Box 414, Erin, TN 37061-0414
E-mail: sharon.tomlinson@tncourts.gov

County Clerk

Office of the County Clerk
4725 East Main Street, Erin, TN 37061
Tel: (931) 289-3141 Fax: (931) 289-2603

County Clerk **Robert R. Brown** . . . . (931) 289-3141
E-mail: robert.reed.brown@tn.gov

Humphreys County

Circuit Clerk

Twenty-Third Judicial Circuit
Humphreys County Courthouse, Waverly, TN 37185

Circuit Clerk, Humphreys County **Elaine Choate** . . . . (931) 296-2461
100 North Court Square, Room 106,
Waverly, TN 37185
E-mail: elaine.choate@tncourts.gov

(continued on next page)

County Clerk

Office of the County Clerk
102 Thompson Street, Room 2, Waverly, TN 37185
Tel: (931) 296-7671 Fax: (931) 296-2308

County Clerk **Cindy Wilson** ....(931) 296-7671
E-mail: cindy.wilson@tn.gov

Jackson County

Circuit Clerk

Fifteenth Judicial Circuit
228 East Broad Street, Cookeville, TN 38501

Circuit Clerk, Jackson County **Jeff Hardy** ....(931) 268-9314
P.O. Box 205, Gainesboro, TN 38562-0205
E-mail: jeff.hardy@tncourts.gov

County Clerk

Office of the County Clerk
P.O. Box 346, Gainesboro, TN 38562
Tel: (931) 268-9212 Fax: (931) 268-4149

County Clerk **Amanda Ward Stafford** ....(931) 268-9212
E-mail: amanda.stafford@tn.gov

Jefferson County

Circuit Clerk

Fourth Judicial Circuit
8554 South Highway 92, Dandridge, TN 37725

Circuit Clerk, Jefferson County **Penny Murphy** ....(865) 397-2786
765 Justice Center Drive,
Dandridge, TN 37725-0671

County Clerk

Office of the County Clerk
214 West Main Street, Dandridge, TN 37725
P.O. Box 710, Dandridge, TN 37725
Tel: (865) 397-2935 Fax: (865) 397-3839

County Clerk **Frank Herndon** ....(865) 397-2935
E-mail: frank.herndon@tn.gov

Johnson County

Circuit Clerk

First Judicial Circuit
Washington County Justice Center, 108 West Jackson Boulevard,
Suite 2141, Jonesborough, TN 37659

Circuit Clerk, Johnson County
Carolyn Wilson Hawkins ....(423) 727-9012
P.O. Box 73, Mountain City, TN 37683

County Clerk

Office of the County Clerk
222 West Main Street, Mountain City, TN 37683
Tel: (423) 727-9633 Fax: (423) 727-3133

County Clerk **Tammie Fenner** ....(423) 727-9633
E-mail: tammie.fenner@tn.gov

Knox County

Circuit Clerk

Sixth Judicial Circuit
400 Main Avenue, Knoxville, TN 37901

Circuit Clerk, Knox County
Catherine F. "Cathy" Shanks ....(865) 215-3637
400 Main Avenue, Room M-30,
Knoxville, TN 37901

County Clerk

County Clerk's Office
Old Courthouse, 300 Main Street, Knoxville, TN 37902
Tel: (865) 215-2385 Fax: (865) 215-3655
Internet: www.knoxcounty.org/clerk

County Clerk **Foster D. Arnett, Jr.** ....(865) 215-2385
E-mail: county.clerk@knoxcounty.org

Lake County

Circuit Clerk

Twenty-Ninth Judicial Circuit
106 West Court, Dyersburg, TN 38024

Circuit Clerk, Lake County **Debbie Beasley** ....(731) 253-7137
229 Church Street, Box 11,
Tiptonville, TN 38079

County Clerk

Office of the County Clerk
116 South Court Street, Tiptonville, TN 38079
Tel: (731) 253-7582 Fax: (731) 253-6815

County Clerk **Jo Ann Mills** ....(731) 253-7582
E-mail: joann.mills@tn.gov

Lauderdale County

Circuit Clerk

Twenty-Fifth Judicial Circuit
104 Lafayette Avenue, Ripley, TN 38063

Circuit Clerk, Lauderdale County **Richard Jennings** .....(731) 635-0101
675 Highway 51 South, Ripley, TN 38063-0509
E-mail: richard.jennings@tncourts.gov

County Clerk

Office of the County Clerk
100 Court Square, Ripley, TN 38063
Tel: (731) 635-2561 Fax: (731) 635-4301

County Clerk **Linda Summar** ....(731) 635-2561
E-mail: linda.summar@tn.gov

Lawrence County

Circuit Clerk

Twenty-Second Judicial Circuit
14 Public Square North, Columbia, TN 38401

Circuit Clerk, Lawrence County **Debbie Riddle** ....(931) 762-4398
240 West Gaines Street, Lawrenceburg, TN 38464
E-mail: debbie.riddle@tncourts.gov

County Clerk

Office of the County Clerk
200 West Gaines, Lawrenceburg, TN 38464
Tel: (931) 766-4176   Fax: (931) 766-4146

County Clerk **Chuck Kizer** .... (931) 766-4176
 E-mail: ckizer@lawcotn.org

Lewis County

Circuit Clerk

Twenty-First Judicial Circuit
135 Fourth Avenue, Franklin, TN 37064

Circuit Clerk, Lewis County **Barbara Hinson** .... (931) 796-3724
 110 Park Avenue North, Room 201,
 Hohenwald, TN 38462
 E-mail: barbara.hinson@tncourts.gov

County Clerk

Office of the County Clerk
110 North Park Avenue, Room 105, Hohenwald, TN 38462
Tel: (931) 796-2200   Fax: (931) 796-6010

County Clerk **Sandra Clayton** .... (931) 796-2200
 E-mail: sandra.clayton@tn.gov

Lincoln County

Circuit Clerk

Seventeenth Judicial Circuit
402 Belmont Avenue, Shelbyville, TN 37160

Circuit Clerk, Lincoln County **Lisa Corder-Simmons** .... (931) 433-2334
 112 Main Avenue, Room 203,
 Fayetteville, TN 37334

County Clerk

Office of the County Clerk
112 Main Avenue South, Suite 102, Fayetteville, TN 37334
Tel: (931) 433-2454   Fax: (931) 433-9304

County Clerk **Phyllis F. Counts** .... (931) 433-2454
 E-mail: phyllis.counts@tn.gov

Loudon County

Circuit Clerk

Ninth Judicial Circuit
1000 Bradford Way, Suite 400, Kingston, TN 37763

Circuit Clerk, Loudon County **Lisa Niles** .... (865) 458-2042
 P.O. Box 280, Loudon, TN 37774-0280
 E-mail: lisa.niles@tncourts.gov

County Clerk

Office of the County Clerk
101 Mulberry Street, Loudon, TN 37774
Tel: (865) 458-2726   Fax: (865) 458-9891

County Clerk **Darlene Russell** .... (865) 458-2726
 E-mail: darlene.russell@tn.gov

Macon County

Circuit Clerk

Fifteenth Judicial Circuit
228 East Broad Street, Cookeville, TN 38501

Circuit Clerk, Macon County **Rick Gann** .... (615) 666-2354
 Macon County Justice Center,
 904 Highway 52 Bypass East,
 Lafayette, TN 37083
 E-mail: rick.gann@tncourts.gov

County Clerk

Office of the County Clerk
104 County Courthouse, Lafayette, TN 37083
Tel: (615) 666-2333   Fax: (615) 666-2202

County Clerk **Connie Blackwell** .... (615) 666-2333
 E-mail: connie.blackwell@tn.gov

Madison County

Circuit Clerk

Twenty-Sixth Judicial Circuit
515 South Liberty Street, Jackson, TN 38301

Circuit Clerk, Madison County **Kathy Blount** .... (731) 423-6035
 515 South Liberty Street, Suite 200,
 Jackson, TN 38301
 E-mail: kathy.blount@tncourts.gov

County Clerk

Office of the County Clerk
100 East Main, Suite 105, Jackson, TN 38301
Tel: (731) 423-6022   Fax: (731) 424-4903

County Clerk **Fred Birmingham** .... (731) 423-6022
 E-mail: fbirmingham@co.madison.tn.us

Marion County

Circuit Clerk

Twelfth Judicial Circuit
P.O. Box 428, Winchester, TN 37398-0428

Circuit Clerk, Marion County **Lonna Henderson** .... (423) 942-8020
 Marion County Justice Center,
 Jasper, TN 37347

County Clerk

Office of the County Clerk
24 Courthouse Square, Room 101, Jasper, TN 37357
P.O. Box 789, Jasper, TN 37347
Tel: (423) 942-2515   Fax: (423) 942-0815

County Clerk **Dwight Minter** .... (423) 942-2515
 E-mail: dwight.minter@tn.gov

Marshall County

Circuit Clerk

Seventeenth Judicial Circuit
402 Belmont Avenue, Shelbyville, TN 37160

Circuit Clerk, Marshall County **Courtney Boatright** ..... (931) 359-0536
 Marshall County Courthouse, Room 302,
 Lewisburg, TN 37091
 E-mail: courtney.boatright@tncourts.gov

(continued on next page)

County Clerk

Office of the County Clerk
1107 Courthouse Annex, Lewisburg, TN 37091
Tel: (931) 359-1072 Fax: (931) 359-0559

County Clerk **Daphne Fagan** . . . . (931) 359-1072
E-mail: daphne.fagan@tn.gov

Maury County

Circuit Clerk

Twenty-Second Judicial Circuit
14 Public Square North, Columbia, TN 38401

Circuit Clerk, Maury County **Sandy McLain** . . . . (931) 375-1100
41 Public Square, Room 202,
Columbia, TN 38401

County Clerk

Office of the County Clerk
10 Public Square, Columbia, TN 38401
Tel: (931) 375-5200 Fax: (931) 375-5219

County Clerk **Joey Allen** . . . . (931) 375-5200
E-mail: JAllen@maurycounty-tn.gov

McMinn County

Circuit Clerk

Tenth Judicial Circuit
P.O. Box 846, Cleveland, TN 37311

Circuit Clerk, McMinn County **Rhonda J. Cooley** . . . . . . (423) 745-1923
Six East Madison Avenue, Room 211,
Athens, TN 37303
E-mail: rhonda.cooley@tncourts.gov

County Clerk

Office of the County Clerk
Five South Hill Street, Suite A, Athens, TN 37303
Tel: (423) 745-4440 Fax: (423) 744-1657

County Clerk **Evonne Hoback** . . . . (423) 745-4440
E-mail: evonne.hoback@tn.gov

McNairy County

Circuit Clerk

Twenty-Fifth Judicial Circuit
104 Lafayette Avenue, Ripley, TN 38063

Circuit Clerk, McNairy County **Byron Maxedon** . . . . (731) 645-1015
McNairy County Criminal Justice
Center, 300 Industrial Park Drive,
Selmer, TN 38375
E-mail: byron.maxedon@tncourts.gov

County Clerk

Office of the County Clerk
170 West Court Avenue, Selmer, TN 38375
Tel: (731) 645-3511 Fax: (731) 646-1414

County Clerk **Ronnie Price** . . . . (731) 645-3511
E-mail: ronnie.price@tn.gov

Meigs County

Circuit Clerk

Ninth Judicial Circuit
1000 Bradford Way, Suite 400, Kingston, TN 37763

Circuit Clerk, Meigs County **Darrell Davis** . . . . (423) 334-5821
17214 Highway 58, Second Floor,
Decatur, TN 37322-0205
E-mail: darrell.davis@tncourts.gov

County Clerk

Office of the County Clerk
17214 State Highwaty 58 North, Decatur, TN 37322
Tel: (423) 334-5747 Fax: (423) 334-2687

County Clerk **Janie Myers** . . . . (423) 334-5747
E-mail: janie.myers@tn.gov

Monroe County

Circuit Clerk

Tenth Judicial Circuit
P.O. Box 846, Cleveland, TN 37311

Circuit Clerk, Monroe County **Martha Cook** . . . . (423) 442-2396
105 College Street, Suite 103,
Madisonville, TN 37354

County Clerk

Office of the County Clerk
105 College Street, Madisonville, TN 37354-2400
Tel: (423) 442-2220 Fax: (423) 442-9542

County Clerk **Larry Sloan** . . . . (423) 442-2220
E-mail: monroeclerk@bellsouth.net

Montgomery County

Circuit Clerk

Nineteenth Judicial Circuit
Two Millennium Plaza, Clarksville, TN 37040

Circuit Clerk, Montgomery County **Cheryl J. Castle** . . . . . (931) 648-5700
Two Millennium Plaza, Suite 115,
Clarksville, TN 37040

County Clerk

Office of the County Clerk
350 Pageant Lane, Suite 502, Clarksville, TN 37040
Tel: (931) 648-5711 Fax: (931) 553-5160
E-mail: cclerk@montgomerycountytn.org

County Clerk **Kellie Jackson** . . . . (931) 648-5711
E-mail: kajackson@montgomerycountytn.org

Moore County

Circuit Clerk

Seventeenth Judicial Circuit
402 Belmont Avenue, Shelbyville, TN 37160

Circuit Clerk, Moore County **Christy Millsaps** . . . . (931) 759-7208
196 Main Street, Suite 404,
Lynchburg, TN 37352
E-mail: christy.millsaps@tncourts.gov

County Clerk

Office of the County Clerk
196 Main Street, Lynchburg, TN 37352
P.O. Box 206, Lynchburg, TN 37352
Fax: (931) 759-6394

County Clerk **Nancy Hatfield** . . . . (931) 759-7346
E-mail: nancy.hatfield@tn.gov

Morgan County

Circuit Clerk

Ninth Judicial Circuit
1000 Bradford Way, Suite 400, Kingston, TN 37763

Circuit Clerk, Morgan County **Pam Keck** . . . . (423) 346-3503
415 North Kingston, Wartburg, TN 37887-0163

County Clerk

Office of the County Clerk
415 South Kingston Street, Wartburg, TN 37887
Tel: (423) 346-3480 Fax: (423) 346-4161

County Clerk **Cheryl Collins** . . . . (423) 346-3480
E-mail: cheryl.collins@tn.gov

Obion County

Circuit Clerk

Twenty-Seventh Judicial Circuit
208 West Church Street, Union City, TN 38261

Circuit Clerk, Obion County **Harry Johnson** . . . . (731) 885-1372
Seven Bill Burnett Circle, Union City, TN 38261
E-mail: harry.johnson@tncourts.gov

County Clerk

Office of the County Clerk
Two Bill Burnett Circle, Union City, TN 37261
Tel: (731) 885-0945 Fax: (731) 885-0287

County Clerk **Vollie Jean Boehms** . . . . (731) 885-3831
E-mail: vollie.boehms@tn.gov

Overton County

Circuit Clerk

Thirteenth Judicial Circuit
228 East Broad Street, Cookeville, TN 38501

Circuit Clerk, Overton County **Barbara Matthews** . . . . . . (931) 823-2312
1000 John T. Poindexter Drive,
Livingston, TN 38570
E-mail: barbara.matthews@tncourts.gov

County Clerk

Office of the County Clerk
317 University Street, Room 22, Livingston, TN 38570
Tel: (931) 823-2631 Fax: (931) 823-2696

County Clerk **Victoria Looper** . . . . (931) 823-2631
E-mail: victoria.looper@tn.gov

Perry County

Circuit Clerk

Twenty-First Judicial Circuit
135 Fourth Avenue, Franklin, TN 37064

Circuit Clerk, Perry County **Peggy Smotherman** . . . . (931) 589-2218
P.O. Box 91, Linden, TN 37096-0091
E-mail: peggy.smotherman@tncourts.gov

County Clerk

Office of the County Clerk
121 East Main Street, Linden, TN 37096
Tel: (931) 589-2219 Fax: (931) 589-5107

County Clerk **Glenda Leegan** . . . . (931) 589-2219
E-mail: glenda.leegan@tn.gov

Pickett County

Circuit Clerk

Thirteenth Judicial Circuit
228 East Broad Street, Cookeville, TN 38501

Circuit Clerk, Pickett County **Larry Brown** . . . . (931) 864-3958
P.O. Box 188, Byrdstown, TN 38549-0188
E-mail: larry.brown@tncourts.gov

County Clerk

Office of the County Clerk
One Courthouse Square, Suite 201, Byrdstown, TN 38549
Tel: (931) 864-3879 Fax: (931) 864-7087

County Clerk **Charlie Lee** . . . . (931) 864-3879
E-mail: robert.e.lee@tn.gov

Polk County

Circuit Clerk

Tenth Judicial Circuit
P.O. Box 846, Cleveland, TN 37311

Circuit Clerk, Polk County **Connie H. Clark** . . . . (423) 338-4524
6239 Highway 411, Benton, TN 37307
E-mail: connie.clark@tncourts.gov

County Clerk

Office of the County Clerk
6239 Highway 411, Office 102, Benton, TN 37307
Tel: (423) 338-4526 Fax: (423) 338-4551

County Clerk **Angie Sanford** . . . . (423) 338-4526
E-mail: angie.sanford@tn.gov

Putnam County

Circuit Clerk

Thirteenth Judicial Circuit
228 East Broad Street, Cookeville, TN 38501

Circuit Clerk, Putnam County **Marcia Borys** . . . . (931) 528-1508
421 East Spring Street, Room 1C, Suite 49A,
Cookeville, TN 38501

(continued on next page)

County Clerk

Office of the County Clerk
121 South Dixie Avenue, Cookeville, TN 38501
Tel: (931) 526-7106 Fax: (931) 372-8201

County Clerk **Wayne Nabors**.......................(931) 526-7106
E-mail: wayne.nabors@tn.gov

Rhea County

Circuit Clerk

Twelfth Judicial Circuit
P.O. Box 428, Winchester, TN 37398-0428

Circuit Clerk, Rhea County **Jamie Holloway**...........(423) 775-7805
1475 Market Street, Suite 104,
Dayton, TN 37321
E-mail: jamie.holloway@tncourts.gov

County Clerk

Office of the County Clerk
375 Church Street, Suite 101, Dayton, TN 37321
Tel: (423) 775-7808 Fax: (423) 775-7898

County Clerk **Linda Shaver**........................(423) 775-7808
E-mail: linda.shaver@tn.gov

Roane County

Circuit Clerk

Ninth Judicial Circuit
1000 Bradford Way, Suite 400, Kingston, TN 37763

Circuit Clerk, Roane County **Ann Goldston**............(865) 376-2390
200 East Race Street, Suite 11,
Kingston, TN 37763
E-mail: ann.goldston@tncourts.gov

County Clerk

Office of the County Clerk
200 East Race Street, Suite 2, Kingston, TN 37763
P.O. Box 546, Kingston, TN 37763
Tel: (865) 376-5556 Fax: (865) 717-4121

County Clerk **Barbara Anthony**.....................(865) 376-5556
E-mail: banthonyclerk@roanegov.org

Robertson County

Circuit Clerk

Nineteenth Judicial Circuit
Two Millennium Plaza, Clarksville, TN 37040

Circuit Clerk, Robertson County **Lisa M. Cavender**.....(615) 384-7864
Robertson County Courthouse,
501 South Main Street, Room 109,
Springfield, TN 37172
E-mail: lisa.cavender@tncourts.gov

County Clerk

Office of the County Clerk
511 South Brown Street, Springfield, TN 37172
Tel: (615) 384-5895 Fax: (615) 384-2218

County Clerk **Susan K. Atchley**....................(615) 384-5895
E-mail: susan.atchley@tn.gov

Rutherford County

Circuit Clerk

Sixteenth Judicial Circuit
20 Public Square, Murfreesboro, TN 37130

Circuit Clerk, Rutherford County **Melissa Harrell**.......(615) 898-7820
20 Public Square North, Murfreesboro, TN 37130

County Clerk

Office of the County Clerk
319 North Maple Street, Suite 121, Murfreesboro, TN 37130
(Murfreesboro Office)
205 I Street, Smyrna, TN 37167 (Smyrna Office)
Tel: (615) 898-7800 (Murfreesboro Office)
Tel: (615) 459-9692 (Smyrna Office)
Fax: (615) 898-7830 (Murfreesboro Office)
Fax: (615) 355-4118 (Smyrna Office)

County Clerk **Lisa Crowell**........................(615) 898-7800
E-mail: lcrowell@rutherfordcountytn.gov

Scott County

Circuit Clerk

Eighth Judicial Circuit
241 Myers Street, Jacksboro, TN 37757

Circuit Clerk, Scott County **Donnie Phillips**...........(423) 663-2440
575 Scott High Drive, Huntsville, TN 37756-0330
E-mail: donnie.phillips@tncourts.gov

County Clerk

Office of the County Clerk
282 Court Street, Huntsville, TN 37756
P.O. Box 87, Huntsville, TN 37756
Tel: (423) 663-2588 Fax: (423) 663-3969

County Clerk **Patricia "Pat" Phillips**.................(423) 663-2588
E-mail: patricia.phillips@tn.gov

Sequatchie County

Circuit Clerk

Twelfth Judicial Circuit
P.O. Box 428, Winchester, TN 37398-0428

Circuit Clerk, Sequatchie County **Karen Millsaps**.......(423) 949-2618
Sequatchie County Justice Center,
351 Fredonia Road, Suite B,
Dunlap, TN 37327
E-mail: karen.millsaps@tncourts.gov

County Clerk

Office of the County Clerk
22 Cherry Street, Dunlap, TN 37327
P.O. Box 248, Dunlap, TN 37327
Tel: (423) 949-2522 Fax: (423) 949-6316

County Clerk **Charlotte Cagle**.....................(423) 949-2522
E-mail: charlotte.cagle@tn.gov

Tennessee Court Clerks and Courthouses *continued*

Sevier County

Circuit Clerk

Fourth Judicial Circuit
8554 South Highway 92, Dandridge, TN 37725

Circuit Clerk, Sevier County **Rita D. Ellison** . . . . (865) 453-5536
125 Court Square, Suite 204E,
Sevierville, TN 37862

County Clerk

Office of the County Clerk
125 Court Avenue, Suite 202E, Sevierville, TN 37862
Tel: (865) 453-5502   Fax: (865) 774-3954

County Clerk **Karen Cotter** . . . . (865) 453-5502
E-mail: karen.cotter@tn.gov

Shelby County

Circuit Clerk

Thirtieth Judicial Circuit
140 Adams Avenue, Memphis, TN 38151

Circuit Clerk, Shelby County **Jimmy Moore** . . . . (901) 222-3800
140 Adams Avenue, Room 324,
Memphis, TN 38151

County Clerk

Office of the County Clerk
150 Washington Avenue, Memphis, TN 38103
Fax: (901) 545-3779
E-mail: shelbycountyclerk@shelbycountytn.gov

County Clerk **Wayne Mashburn** . . . . (901) 222-3000
E-mail: wayne.mashburn@shelbycountytn.gov

Smith County

Circuit Clerk

Fifteenth Judicial Circuit
228 East Broad Street, Cookeville, TN 38501

Circuit Clerk, Smith County **Tommy Turner** . . . . (615) 735-0500
Smith County Courthouse, 211 North Main Street,
Carthage, TN 37030
E-mail: tommy.turner@tncourts.gov

County Clerk

Office of the County Clerk
122 Turner High Circle, Suite 101, Carthage, TN 37030
Tel: (615) 735-9833   Fax: (615) 735-8252

County Clerk **Clifa Norris** . . . . (615) 735-9833 ext. 5
E-mail: clifa.norris@tn.gov

Stewart County

Circuit Clerk

Twenty-Third Judicial Circuit
Humphreys County Courthouse, Waverly, TN 37185

Circuit Clerk, Stewart County **Jason Wallace** . . . . (931) 232-7042
P.O. Box 193, Dover, TN 37058-0193
E-mail: jason.wallace@tncourts.gov

Tennessee Court Clerks and Courthouses *continued*

County Clerk

Office of the County Clerk
225 Donelson Parkway, First Floor, Dover, TN 37058
P.O. Box 67, Dover, TN 37058
Tel: (931) 232-7616   Fax: (931) 232-4934

County Clerk **Jimmy Fitzhugh** . . . . (931) 232-7616
E-mail: jimmy.fitzhugh@tn.gov

Sullivan County

Circuit Clerk

Second Judicial Circuit
225 West Center Street, Kingsport, TN 37662

Circuit Clerk, Sullivan County **Tommy Kerns** . . . . (423) 279-2752

County Clerk

Office of the County Clerk
3528 Highway 126, Suite 101, Blountville, TN 37617
Tel: (423) 323-6428   Fax: (423) 279-2725

County Clerk **Jeanie Gammon** . . . . (423) 323-6428
E-mail: jeanie.gammon@tn.gov

Sumner County

Circuit Clerk

Eighteenth Judicial Circuit
Public Square, Gallatin, TN 37066

Circuit Clerk, Sumner County **Kathryn Strong** . . . . (615) 451-3209
Public Square, Gallatin, TN 37066
E-mail: kathryn.strong@tncourts.gov

County Clerk

Office of the County Clerk
355 North Belvedere Drive, Room 111, Gallatin, TN 37066
Tel: (615) 452-4063   Fax: (615) 452-9371
E-mail: clerk@sumnertn.org

County Clerk **Bill Kemp** . . . . (615) 452-4063
E-mail: bkemp@sumnertn.org

Tipton County

Circuit Clerk

Twenty-Fifth Judicial Circuit
104 Lafayette Avenue, Ripley, TN 38063

Circuit Clerk, Tipton County **Mike Forbess** . . . . (901) 475-3310
1801 South College Street, Suite 102,
Covington, TN 38019
E-mail: mike.forbess@tncourts.gov

County Clerk

Office of the County Clerk
220 Highway 51 North, Covington, TN 38019
Tel: (901) 476-0207   Fax: (901) 476-0297
E-mail: mgaither@tiptonco.com

County Clerk **Mary Gaither** . . . . (901) 476-0207
E-mail: mgaither@tiptonco.com

(continued on next page)

Trousdale County

Circuit Clerk

Fifteenth Judicial Circuit
228 East Broad Street, Cookeville, TN 38501

Circuit Clerk, Trousdale County **Kim Taylor** . . . . (615) 374-3411
200 East Main Street, Room 5,
Hartsville, TN 37074

County Clerk

Office of the County Clerk
200 East Main Street, Room 2, Hartsville, TN 37074
Tel: (615) 374-2906 Fax: (615) 374-1100

County Clerk **Rita Crowder** . . . . (615) 374-2906
E-mail: rita.crowder@tn.gov

Unicoi County

Circuit Clerk

First Judicial Circuit
Washington County Justice Center, 108 West Jackson Boulevard,
Suite 2141, Jonesborough, TN 37659

Circuit Clerk, Unicoi County **Darren Shelton** . . . . (423) 743-3541
P.O. Box 2000, Erwin, TN 37650-2000

County Clerk

Office of the County Clerk
100 North Main Street, Suite 100, Erwin, TN 37650
Tel: (423) 743-3381 Fax: (423) 743-5430

County Clerk **Mitzi Bowen** . . . . (423) 743-3381
E-mail: mitzi.bowen@tn.gov

Union County

Circuit Clerk

Eighth Judicial Circuit
241 Myers Street, Jacksboro, TN 37757

Circuit Clerk, Union County **Barbara J. Williams** . . . . (865) 992-5493
901 Main Street, Suite 220,
Maynardville, TN 37807
E-mail: barbara.williams@tncourts.gov

County Clerk

Office of the County Clerk
901 Main Street, Maynardville, TN 37807
Tel: (865) 992-8043 Fax: (865) 992-4992

County Clerk **Pam Ailor** . . . . (865) 992-8043
E-mail: pam.ailor@tn.gov

Van Buren County

Circuit Clerk

Thirty-First Judicial Circuit
111 South Court Square, McMinnville, TN 37110

Circuit Clerk, Van Buren County **(Vacant)** . . . . (931) 946-2153
179 Veterans Square, Spencer, TN 38585

County Clerk

Office of the County Clerk
500 College Street, Spencer, TN 38585
Tel: (931) 946-7171 Fax: (931) 946-2876

County Clerk **Lisa Rigsby** . . . . (931) 946-2121

Warren County

Circuit Clerk

Thirty-First Judicial Circuit
111 South Court Square, McMinnville, TN 37110

Circuit Clerk, Warren County **Bernie Morris** . . . . (931) 473-2373
P.O. Box 639, McMinnville, TN 37111-0639

County Clerk

Office of the County Clerk
201 Locust Street, Suite 2P, McMinnville, TN 37111
Tel: (931) 473-2623 Fax: (931) 473-8622

County Clerk **Lesa Scott** . . . . (931) 473-2623
E-mail: lesa.scott@tn.gov

Washington County

Circuit Clerk

First Judicial Circuit
Washington County Justice Center, 108 West Jackson Boulevard,
Suite 2141, Jonesborough, TN 37659

Circuit Clerk, Washington County **Karen Guinn** . . . . (423) 753-1736
108 West Jackson Boulevard, Suite 1210,
Jonesborough, TN 37659

County Clerk

Office of the County Clerk
103 East Main Street, Jonesborough, TN 37659
Tel: (423) 753-1621 Fax: (423) 753-1647

County Clerk **Kathy Storey** . . . . (423) 753-1621
E-mail: kathy.storey@tn.gov

Wayne County

Circuit Clerk

Twenty-Second Judicial Circuit
14 Public Square North, Columbia, TN 38401

Circuit Clerk, Wayne County **Billy G. Crews** . . . . (931) 722-5519
P.O. Box 869, Waynesboro, TN 38485-0869

County Clerk

Office of the County Clerk
100 Court Circle, Suite 200, Waynesboro, TN 38485
Tel: (931) 722-5544 Fax: (931) 722-6410

County Clerk **Stan Horton** . . . . (931) 722-5544
E-mail: stan.horton@tn.gov

Weakley County

Circuit Clerk

Twenty-Seventh Judicial Circuit
208 West Church Street, Union City, TN 38261

Circuit Clerk, Weakley County **Pam Belew** . . . . (731) 364-2456
116 West Main Street, Room 203,
Dresden, TN 38225-1164
E-mail: pam.belew@tncourts.gov

County Clerk

Office of the County Clerk
116 Main Street, Room 104, Dresden, TN 38225
Tel: (731) 364-2285 Fax: (731) 364-5236

County Clerk **Kim Hughey** . . . . (731) 364-2285
E-mail: kimhughey@weakleycountytn.gov

White County

Circuit Clerk

Thirteenth Judicial Circuit
228 East Broad Street, Cookeville, TN 38501

Circuit Clerk, White County **Beverly Templeton** . . . . (931) 836-3205
111 Depot Street, Suite 1,
Sparta, TN 38583
E-mail: beverly.templeton@tncourts.gov

County Clerk

Office of the County Clerk
One East Bockman Way, Sparta, TN 38583
Tel: (931) 836-3712 Fax: (931) 836-2601

County Clerk **Connie S. Jolley** . . . . (931) 836-3712
E-mail: connie.jolley@tn.gov

Williamson County

Circuit Clerk

Twenty-First Judicial Circuit
135 Fourth Avenue, Franklin, TN 37064

Circuit Clerk, Williamson County
Debra McMillan Barrett . . . . (615) 790-5454
135 Fourth Avenue South, Room 203,
Franklin, TN 37064

County Clerk

Office of the County Clerk
1320 West Main Street, Suite 135, Franklin, TN 37064
Tel: (615) 790-5712 Fax: (615) 790-5610

County Clerk **Elaine Anderson** . . . . (615) 790-5712
E-mail: elaine.anderson@tn.gov

Wilson County

Circuit Clerk

Fifteenth Judicial Circuit
228 East Broad Street, Cookeville, TN 38501

Circuit Clerk, Wilson County **Debbie Moss** . . . . (615) 444-2042
134 South College Street, Lebanon, TN 37088
E-mail: debbie.moss@tncourts.gov

County Clerk

Office of the County Clerk
Wilson County Judicial Center, 228 East Main Street, Room 101,
Lebanon, TN 37087
Tel: (615) 444-0314 Fax: (615) 443-2615

County Clerk **Jim Goodall** . . . . (615) 444-0314
E-mail: jim.goodall@tn.gov

Counties Within Judicial Circuits

Circuit Court, 1st Judicial Circuit
Areas Covered: Carter, Johnson, Unicoi, and Washington Counties.

Circuit Court, 2nd Judicial Circuit
Areas Covered: Sullivan County.

Circuit Court, 3rd Judicial Circuit
Areas Covered: Greene, Hamblen, Hancock, and Hawkins Counties.

Circuit Court, 4th Judicial Circuit
Areas Covered: Blount, Cocke, Grainger, Jefferson, and Sevier Counties.

Circuit Court, 5th Judicial Circuit
Areas Covered: Blount County.

Circuit Court, 6th Judicial Circuit
Areas Covered: Knox County.

Circuit Court, 7th Judicial Circuit
Areas Covered: Anderson County.

Circuit Court, 8th Judicial Circuit
Areas Covered: Campbell, Claiborne, Fentress, Scott, and Union Counties.

Circuit Court, 9th Judicial Circuit
Areas Covered: Loudon, Meigs, Morgan, and Roane Counties.

Circuit Court, 10th Judicial Circuit
Areas Covered: Bradley, McMinn, Monroe, and Polk Counties.

Circuit Court, 11th Judicial Circuit
Areas Covered: Hamilton County.

Circuit Court, 12th Judicial Circuit
Areas Covered: Bledsoe, Franklin, Grundy, Marion, Rhea, and Sequatchie Counties.

Circuit Court, 13th Judicial Circuit
Areas Covered: Clay, Cumberland, DeKalb, Overton, Pickett, Putnam, and White Counties.

Circuit Court, 14th Judicial Circuit
Areas Covered: Coffee County.

(continued on next page)

Tennessee Court Clerks and Courthouses *continued*

Circuit Court, 15th Judicial Circuit

Areas Covered: Jackson, Macon, Smith, Trousdale, and Wilson Counties.

Circuit Court, 16th Judicial Circuit

Areas Covered: Cannon and Rutherford Counties.

Circuit Court, 17th Judicial Circuit

Areas Covered: Bedford, Lincoln, Marshall, and Moore Counties.

Circuit Court, 18th Judicial Circuit

Areas Covered: Sumner County.

Circuit Court, 19th Judicial Circuit

Areas Covered: Montgomery and Robertson Counties.

Circuit Court, 20th Judicial Circuit

Areas Covered: Davidson County.

Circuit Court, 21st Judicial Circuit

Areas Covered: Hickman, Lewis, Perry, and Williamson Counties.

Circuit Court, 22nd Judicial Circuit

Areas Covered: Giles, Lawrence, Maury, and Wayne Counties.

Circuit Court, 23rd Judicial Circuit

Areas Covered: Cheatham, Dickson, Houston, Humphreys, and Stewart Counties.

Circuit Court, 24th Judicial Circuit

Areas Covered: Benton, Carroll, Decatur, Hardin, and Henry Counties.

Circuit Court, 25th Judicial Circuit

Areas Covered: Fayette, Hardeman, Lauderdale, McNairy, and Tipton Counties.

Circuit Court, 26th Judicial Circuit

Areas Covered: Chester, Henderson, and Madison Counties.

Circuit Court, 27th Judicial Circuit

Areas Covered: Obion and Weakley Counties.

Circuit Court, 28th Judicial Circuit

Areas Covered: Crockett, Gibson, and Haywood Counties.

Circuit Court, 29th Judicial Circuit

Areas Covered: Dyer and Lake Counties.

Circuit Court, 30th Judicial Circuit

Areas Covered: Shelby County.

Circuit Court, 31st Judicial Circuit

Areas Covered: Van Buren and Warren Counties.

Texas Court Clerks and Courthouses

The trial courts of general jurisdiction in Texas are called district courts. There are 456 separate district courts. Each county must be served by at least one district court. In a number of areas, the geographical jurisdiction of two or more district courts overlaps.

Supreme Court of Texas

Supreme Court Building, 201 West 14th Street, Room 104, Austin, TX 78701
P.O. Box 12248, Austin, TX 78711-2248
Tel: (512) 463-1312 Fax: (512) 463-1365
Internet: www.supreme.courts.state.tx.us

The Supreme Court consists of a chief justice and eight justices who are elected in statewide, partisan elections for six-year terms. Vacancies between elections are filled by the Governor with the advice and consent of the State Senate, and newly appointed justices serve until the next general election. The Supreme Court has final appellate jurisdiction over all civil and juvenile cases and authority to determine certain legal matters when no other court has jurisdiction. The Court has the authority to conduct proceedings for the involuntarily retirement or removal of judges and to make rules for the administration of justice, including rules of civil practice and procedure.

Court Staff
Clerk of the Court **Blake A. Hawthorne** . . . . (512) 463-1312
E-mail: blake.hawthorne@txcourts.gov

Texas Court of Criminal Appeals

Supreme Court Building, 201 West 14th Street, Room 106, Austin, TX 78701
P.O. Box 12308, Capitol Station, Austin, TX 78711
Tel: (512) 463-1551 Fax: (512) 463-7061
Internet: www.cca.courts.state.tx.us

The Court of Criminal Appeals consists of a presiding judge and eight judges who are elected in statewide, partisan elections for six-year terms. Vacancies between elections are filled by the Governor with the advice and consent of the State Senate, and newly-appointed judges serve until the next general election. The Court of Criminal Appeals has final appellate jurisdiction over all criminal cases except as provided by law and exclusive jurisdiction over automatic appeals in death penalty cases.

Court Staff
Clerk of the Court **Abel Acosta** . . . . (512) 936-1620
E-mail: abel.acosta@cca.courts.state.tx.us

Texas Court of Appeals

Internet: www.courts.state.tx.us/appcourt.asp

The Court of Appeals is comprised of fourteen judicial districts with between three and thirteen justices each. Each district has a chief justice who is elected to a six-year term by the voters of the district. Justices are also elected from the fourteen districts in partisan elections for six-year terms. Vacancies between elections are filled by the Governor with the advice and consent of the State Senate. The districts of the Court of Appeals have appellate jurisdiction within their respective districts over civil and criminal cases decided in the Texas District or County Courts.

Texas Court of Appeals, First District

301 Fannin Street, Houston, TX 77002
Tel: (713) 274-2700 Fax: (713) 755-9060
E-mail: 1stcoa@courts.state.tx.us
Internet: www.1stcoa.courts.state.tx.us

Areas Covered: Counties of Austin, Brazoria, Chambers, Colorado, Fort Bend, Galveston, Grimes, Harris, Waller and Washington

Court Staff
Clerk of the Court **Christopher A. Prine** . . . . (713) 274-2700
E-mail: christopher.prine@txcourts.gov

Texas Court of Appeals, Second District

Tim Curry Criminal Justice Center, 401 West Belknap, Suite 9000, Fort Worth, TX 76196
Tel: (817) 884-1900 Fax: (817) 884-1932
Internet: www.2ndcoa.courts.state.tx.us

Areas Covered: Counties of Archer, Clay, Cooke, Denton, Hood, Jack, Montague, Parker, Tarrant, Wichita, Wise and Young

Court Staff
Clerk of the Court **Debra Spisak** . . . . (817) 884-1900 ext. 226
E-mail: debra.spisak@txcourts.gov

Texas Court of Appeals, Third District

101 Price Daniel, Sr. Building, 209 West 14th Street, Austin, TX 78701
P.O. Box 12547, Austin, TX 78711
Tel: (512) 463-1733 Fax: (512) 463-1685
Internet: www.3rdcoa.courts.state.tx.us

Areas Covered: Counties of Bastrop, Bell, Blanco, Burnet, Caldwell, Coke, Comal, Concho, Fayette, Hays, Irion, Lampasas, Lee, Llano, McCulloch, Milam, Mills, Runnels, San Saba, Schleicher, Sterling, Tom Green, Travis and Williamson

Court Staff
Clerk of the Court **Jeffrey D. Kyle** . . . . (512) 463-1709
E-mail: jeff.kyle@3rdcoa.courts.state.tx.us

Texas Court of Appeals, Fourth District

Cadena-Reeves Justice Center, 300 Dolorosa, Room 3200, San Antonio, TX 78205-3037
Tel: (210) 335-2635 Fax: (210) 335-2762
Internet: www.4thcoa.courts.state.tx.us

Areas Covered: Counties of Atascosa, Bandera, Bexar, Brooks, Dimmit, Duval, Edwards, Frio, Gillespie, Guadalupe, Jim Hogg, Jim Wells, Karnes, Kendall, Kerr, Kimble, Kinney, LaSalle, Mason, Maverick, McMullen, Medina, Menard, Real, Starr, Sutton, Uvalde, Val Verde, Webb, Wilson, Zapata and Zavala

Court Staff
Clerk of Court **Keith E. Hottle** . . . . (210) 335-2510
E-mail: keith.hottle@txcourts.gov

(continued on next page)

Texas Court of Appeals, Fifth District

George L. Allen, Sr. Courts Building, 600 Commerce Street,
Suite 200, Dallas, TX 75202-4653
Tel: (214) 712-3400 Fax: (214) 745-1083
E-mail: clerk@5th.txcourts.gov
Internet: www.5thcoa.courts.state.tx.us

Areas Covered: Counties of Collin, Dallas, Grayson, Hunt, Kaufman, and Rockwall

Court Staff
Clerk of the Court **Lisa Matz** . . . . (214) 712-0199
    E-mail: lisa.matz@5th.txcourts.gov

Texas Court of Appeals, Sixth District

Bi-State Justice Building, 100 North State Line Avenue,
Texarkana, TX 75501
Tel: (903) 798-3046 Fax: (903) 798-3034
Internet: www.6thcoa.courts.state.tx.us

Areas Covered: Counties of Bowie, Camp, Cass, Delta, Fannin, Franklin, Gregg, Harrison, Hopkins, Hunt, Lamar, Marion, Morris, Panola, Red River, Rusk, Titus, Upshur and Wood

Court Staff
Clerk of the Court **Debbie Autrey** . . . . (903) 798-3046
    E-mail: debbie.autrey@txcourts.gov

Texas Court of Appeals, Seventh District

2-A Potter County Courts Building, 501 South Fillmore Street,
Amarillo, TX 79101-2449
P.O. Box 9540, Amarillo, TX 79105-9540
Tel: (806) 342-2650 Fax: (806) 342-2675
Internet: www.7thcoa.courts.state.tx.us

Areas Covered: Counties of Armstrong, Bailey, Briscoe, Carson, Castro, Childress, Cochran, Collingsworth, Cottle, Crosby, Dallam, Deaf Smith, Dickens, Donley, Floyd, Foard, Garza, Gray, Hale, Hall, Hansford, Hardeman, Hartley, Hemphill, Hockley, Hutchinson, Kent, King, Lamb, Lipscomb, Lubbock, Lynn, Moore, Motley, Ochiltree, Oldham, Parmer, Potter, Randall, Roberts, Sherman, Swisher, Terry, Wheeler, Wilbarger and Yoakum

Court Staff
Clerk of the Court **Vivian Long** . . . . (806) 342-2652

Texas Court of Appeals, Eighth District

1203 County Courthouse, 500 East San Antonio Avenue,
El Paso, TX 79901
Tel: (915) 546-2240 Fax: (915) 546-2252
E-mail: clerk@8thcoa.courts.state.tx.us
Internet: www.8thcoa.courts.state.tx.us

Areas Covered: Counties of Andrews, Brewster, Crane, Crockett, Culberson, El Paso, Hudspeth, Jeff Davis, Loving, Pecos, Presidio, Reagan, Reeves, Terrell, Upton, Ward and Winkler

Court Staff
Clerk of Court **Denise Pacheco** . . . . (915) 546-2240
    E-mail: clerk@8thcoa.courts.state.tx.us

Texas Court of Appeals, Ninth District

Jefferson County Courthouse, 1001 Pearl Street, Suite 330,
Beaumont, TX 77701-3352
Tel: (409) 835-8402 Fax: (409) 835-8497
Internet: www.9thcoa.courts.state.tx.us

Areas Covered: Counties of Hardin, Jasper, Jefferson, Liberty, Montgomery, Newton, Orange, Polk, San Jacinto and Tyler

Court Staff
Clerk of the Court **Carol Anne Harley** . . . . (409) 835-8402
    E-mail: charley@courts.state.tx.us

Texas Court of Appeals, Tenth District

McLennan County Courthouse, 501 Washington Avenue, Room 415,
Waco, TX 76701-1373
Tel: (254) 757-5200 Fax: (254) 757-2822
Internet: www.10thcoa.courts.state.tx.us

Areas Covered: Counties of Bosque, Brazos, Burleson, Coryell, Ellis, Falls, Freestone, Hamilton, Hill, Johnson, Leon, Limestone, McLennan, Madison, Navarro, Robertson, Somervell and Walker

Court Staff
Clerk of the Court **Sharri Roessler** . . . . (254) 757-5200
    E-mail: sharri.roessler@txcourts.gov

Texas Court of Appeals, Eleventh District

Eastland County Courthouse, 100 West Main Street, 3rd Floor,
Eastland, TX 76448
P.O. Box 271, Eastland, TX 76448
Tel: (254) 629-2638 Fax: (254) 629-2191
Internet: www.11thcoa.courts.state.tx.us

Areas Covered: Counties of Baylor, Borden, Brown, Callahan, Coleman, Comanche, Dawson, Eastland, Ector, Erath, Fisher, Gaines, Glasscock, Haskell, Howard, Jones, Knox, Martin, Midland, Mitchell, Nolan, Palo Pinto, Scurry, Shackelford, Stephens, Stonewall, Taylor and Throckmorton

Court Staff
Clerk of the Court **Sherry Williamson** . . . . (254) 629-2638
    E-mail: sherry.williamson@txcourts.gov

Texas Court of Appeals, Twelfth District

1517 West Front Street, Suite 354, Tyler, TX 75702
Tel: (903) 593-8471 Fax: (903) 593-2193
Internet: www.12thcoa.courts.state.tx.us

Areas Covered: Counties of Anderson, Angelina, Cherokee, Gregg, Henderson, Houston, Nacogdoches, Rains, Rusk, Sabine, Smith, San Augustine, Shelby, Trinity, Upshur, Van Zandt and Wood

Court Staff
Clerk of the Court **Cathy S. Lusk** . . . . (903) 593-8471
    E-mail: cathy.lusk@txcourts.gov

Texas Court of Appeals, Thirteenth District

Nueces County Courthouse, 901 Leopard Street, 10th Floor,
Corpus Christi, TX 78401
Hidalgo County Administration Building, 100 East Cano Street,
5th Floor, Edinburg, TX 78539
Tel: (361) 888-0416 Tel: (956) 318-2405 (Edinburg Office)
Fax: (361) 888-0794 Fax: (956) 318-2403 (Edinburg Office)
Internet: www.13thcoa.courts.state.tx.us

Areas Covered: Counties of Aransas, Bee, Calhoun, Cameron, De Witt,
Goliad, Gonzales, Hidalgo, Jackson, Kenedy, Kleberg, Lavaca, Live Oak,
Matagorda, Nueces, Refugio, San Patricio, Victoria, Wharton and Willacy

Court Staff

Clerk of the Court **Dorian Ramirez** . . . . (361) 888-0697
  E-mail: dorian.ramirez@courts.state.tx.us

Texas Court of Appeals, Fourteenth District

301 Fannin Street, Suite 245, Houston, TX 77002
Tel: (713) 274-2800 Fax: (713) 650-8550
Internet: www.14thcoa.courts.state.tx.us

Areas Covered: Counties of Austin, Brazoria, Chambers, Colorado, Fort
Bend, Galveston, Grimes, Harris, Waller and Washington

Court Staff

Clerk of the Court **Christopher A. Prine** . . . . (713) 274-2800

County-By-County

Anderson County

District Clerk

First Administrative Judicial Region
133 North Riverfront Boulevard, 5th Floor, Dallas, TX 75207
Tel: (214) 653-2943 Fax: (214) 653-2957
Internet: www.firstadmin.com

District Clerk, Anderson County **Janice G. Staples** . . . . . (903) 723-7412
  500 North Church Street, Room 18,
  Palestine, TX 75801

County Clerk

Office of the County Clerk
500 North Church, Room 10, Palestine, TX 75801
Fax: (903) 723-4625

County Clerk **Mark Staples** . . . . (903) 723-7402
  E-mail: mstaples@co.anderson.tx.us

Andrews County

District Clerk

Seventh Administrative Judicial Region
Midland County Courthouse, 500 North Loraine Street, Suite 502,
Midland, TX 79701
Tel: (432) 688-4370 Fax: (432) 688-4933
Internet: www.courts.state.tx.us/7ajr/7ajr.asp

District Clerk, Andrews County **Cynthia Jones** . . . . (432) 524-1417
  201 North Main, Andrews, TX 79714

County Clerk

Office of the County Clerk
215 Northwest First Street, Andrews, TX 79714

County Clerk **Kenda Heckler** . . . . (432) 524-1426
  E-mail: kheckler@co.andrews.tx.us

Angelina County

District Clerk

Second Administrative Judicial Region
301 North Thompson, Suite 102, Conroe, TX 77301
Tel: (936) 538-8176 Fax: (936) 538-8167
Internet: www.mctx.org/courts/second_administrative_judicial_region

District Clerk, Angelina County **Reba Squyres** . . . . (936) 634-4312
  P.O. Box 908, Lufkin, TX 75902-0908

County Clerk

Office of the County Clerk
215 East Lufkin Avenue, 1st Floor, Lufkin, TX 75901
Fax: (936) 634-8460
Internet: www.angelinacounty.net/coclerk

County Clerk **Amy Fincher** . . . . (936) 634-8339

Aransas County

District Clerk

Fourth Administrative Judicial Region
100 Dolorosa, 5th Floor, San Antonio, TX 78205
Tel: (210) 335-3954 Fax: (210) 335-3955
Internet: www.courts.state.tx.us/4ajr/4ajr.asp

District Clerk, Aransas County **Pam Heard** . . . . (361) 790-0128
  301 North Live Oak, Rockport, TX 78382-2798

County Clerk

Office of the County Clerk
301 North Live Oak, Room 101, Rockport, TX 78382
Fax: (361) 790-0119
Internet: http://www.aransascountytx.gov/clerk/

County Clerk **Valerie K. Amason** . . . . (361) 790-0122
  E-mail: vamason@aransascounty.org

Archer County

District Clerk

Eighth Administrative Judicial Region
401 West Belknap, 5th Floor, Fort Worth, TX 76196
Tel: (817) 884-1558 Fax: (817) 884-1560
E-mail: 8thadmin@8thjudicialregion.com

District Clerk, Archer County **Lori Rutledge** . . . . (940) 574-4615
  P.O. Drawer 815, Archer City, TX 76351-0815

County Clerk

Office of the County Clerk
P.O. Box 427, Archer City, TX 76351
Fax: (940) 574-2876

County Clerk **Karren Winter** . . . . (940) 574-4302
  E-mail: karren.winter@co.archer.tx.us

(continued on next page)

Texas Court Clerks and Courthouses *continued*

Armstrong County

District Clerk

Ninth Administrative Judicial Region
500 West Main, Room 204W, Brownfield, TX 79316
Tel: (806) 637-1329 Fax: (806) 637-8918
E-mail: kmoore@terrycounty.org

District and County Clerk, Armstrong County
Patricia Sherrill .... (806) 226-2081
P.O. Box 309, Claude, TX 79019-0309

Atascosa County

District Clerk

Fourth Administrative Judicial Region
100 Dolorosa, 5th Floor, San Antonio, TX 78205
Tel: (210) 335-3954 Fax: (210) 335-3955
Internet: www.courts.state.tx.us/4ajr/4ajr.asp

District Clerk, Atascosa County **Margaret Littleton** ..... (830) 769-3011
One Courthouse Circle Drive, Suite 4B,
Jourdanton, TX 78026-3446

County Clerk

Office of the County Clerk
One Courthouse Circle, Suite 102, Jourdanton, TX 78026
Fax: (830) 769-1021

County Clerk **Diane Gonzales** .... (830) 767-2511
E-mail: atascosacoclk@verizon.net

Austin County

District Clerk

Third Administrative Judicial Region
405 M.L.K Boulevard Drive, Georgetown, TX 78626
Tel: (512) 943-3777 Fax: (512) 943-3767
E-mail: presidingjudge3@wilco.org
Internet: www.courts.state.tx.us/3ajr/3ajr.asp

District Clerk, Austin County **Sue Murphy** .... (979) 865-5911
One East Main Street, Bellville, TX 77418-1598

County Clerk

Office of the County Clerk
One East Main Street, Bellville, TX 77418
Fax: (979) 865-0336

County Clerk **Carrie Gregor** .... (979) 865-5911
E-mail: countyc@industryinet.com

Bailey County

District Clerk

Ninth Administrative Judicial Region
500 West Main, Room 204W, Brownfield, TX 79316
Tel: (806) 637-1329 Fax: (806) 637-8918
E-mail: kmoore@terrycounty.org

District Clerk, Bailey County **Elaine Parker** .... (806) 272-3165
300 South First Street, Suite 130,
Muleshoe, TX 79347-0815

Texas Court Clerks and Courthouses *continued*

County Clerk

Office of the County Clerk
300 South First Street, Muleshoe, TX 79347
Fax: (806) 272-3538

County Clerk **Paula Benton** .... (806) 272-3044

Bandera County

District Clerk

Sixth Administrative Judicial Region
700 Main Street, Kerrville, TX 78028
Tel: (830) 792-2290 Fax: (830) 792-2294
E-mail: beckyh@co.kerr.tx.us
Internet: www.courts.state.tx.us/6ajr/6ajr.asp

District Clerk, Bandera County **Tammy Kneuper** .... (830) 796-4606
P.O. Box 2688, Bandera, TX 78003-2688

County Clerk

Office of the County Clerk
P.O. Box 823, Bandera, TX 78003
Fax: (830) 796-8323

County Clerk **Candy Wheeler** .... (830) 796-3332
E-mail: candyw@indian-creek.net

Bastrop County

District Clerk

Second Administrative Judicial Region
301 North Thompson, Suite 102, Conroe, TX 77301
Tel: (936) 538-8176 Fax: (936) 538-8167
Internet: www.mctx.org/courts/second_administrative_judicial_region

District Clerk, Bastrop County **Sarah Loucks** .... (512) 332-7244
P.O. Box 770, Bastrop, TX 78602

County Clerk

Office of the County Clerk
803 Pine, Room 112, Bastrop, TX 78602
Fax: (512) 332-7241

County Clerk **Rose Pietsch** .... (512) 332-7234
E-mail: rose.pietsch@co.bastrop.tx.us

Baylor County

District Clerk

Ninth Administrative Judicial Region
500 West Main, Room 204W, Brownfield, TX 79316
Tel: (806) 637-1329 Fax: (806) 637-8918
E-mail: kmoore@terrycounty.org

District Clerk, Baylor County **Chris Jakubicek** .... (940) 889-3322
101 South Washington Street,
Seymour, TX 76380-2566

County Clerk

Office of the County Clerk
101 South Washington, Seymour, TX 76380
Fax: (940) 889-4300

County Clerk **Chris Jakubicek** .... (940) 889-3322

Bee County

District Clerk

Fourth Administrative Judicial Region
100 Dolorosa, 5th Floor, San Antonio, TX 78205
Tel: (210) 335-3954   Fax: (210) 335-3955
Internet: www.courts.state.tx.us/4ajr/4ajr.asp

District Clerk, Bee County **Zenaida Silva**..............(361) 362-3242
   P.O. Box 666, Beeville, TX 78104-0666

County Clerk

Office of the County Clerk
105 West Corpus Christi, Beeville, TX 78102
Fax: (361) 492-5985

County Clerk **Mirella Escamilla Davis**................(361) 621-1557
   E-mail: mirella.davis@co.bee.tx.us

Bell County

District Clerk

Third Administrative Judicial Region
405 M.L.K Boulevard Drive, Georgetown, TX 78626
Tel: (512) 943-3777   Fax: (512) 943-3767
E-mail: presidingjudge3@wilco.org
Internet: www.courts.state.tx.us/3ajr/3ajr.asp

District Clerk, Bell County **Shelia Norman**............(254) 933-5197
   P.O. Box 909, Belton, TX 76513

County Clerk

Office of the County Clerk
1201 Huey Road, Belton, TX 76513
P.O. Box 480, Belton, TX 76513
Tel: (254) 933-5160   Fax: (254) 933-5176
E-mail: deed.recording@co.bell.tx.us
E-mail: vital.statistics@co.bell.tx.us

County Clerk **Shelley Coston**......................(254) 933-5160
   E-mail: shelley.coston@co.bell.tx.us

Bexar County

District Clerk

Fourth Administrative Judicial Region
100 Dolorosa, 5th Floor, San Antonio, TX 78205
Tel: (210) 335-3954   Fax: (210) 335-3955
Internet: www.courts.state.tx.us/4ajr/4ajr.asp

District Clerk, Bexar County **Donna Kay McKinney**.....(210) 335-2113
   101 West Nueva, Suite 217,
   San Antonio, TX 78205

County Clerk

Office of the County Clerk
County Courthouse, 100 Dolorosa, Suite 104,
San Antonio, TX 78205-3883
Fax: (210) 335-2197

County Clerk **Gerard C. "Gerry" Rickhoff**............(210) 335-2216
   E-mail: grickhoff@bexar.org

Blanco County

District Clerk

Third Administrative Judicial Region
405 M.L.K Boulevard Drive, Georgetown, TX 78626
Tel: (512) 943-3777   Fax: (512) 943-3767
E-mail: presidingjudge3@wilco.org
Internet: www.courts.state.tx.us/3ajr/3ajr.asp

District Clerk, Blanco County **Debby Elsbury**..........(830) 868-0973
   P.O. Box 382, Johnson City, TX 78636-0065

County Clerk

Office of the County Clerk
101 East Cypress, Johnson City, TX 78636
Fax: (830) 868-4158

County Clerk **Laura Walla**.........................(830) 868-7357

Borden County

District Clerk

Seventh Administrative Judicial Region
Midland County Courthouse, 500 North Loraine Street, Suite 502,
Midland, TX 79701
Tel: (432) 688-4370   Fax: (432) 688-4933
Internet: www.courts.state.tx.us/7ajr/7ajr.asp

District Clerk, Borden County **Jana Underwood**.......(830) 756-4312
   P.O. Box 124, Gail, TX 79738
   E-mail: jana.underwood@co.borden.tx.us

County Clerk

Office of the County Clerk
P.O. Box 124, Gail, TX 79738
Fax: (806) 756-4324

County Clerk **Jana Underwood**.....................(806) 756-4312
   E-mail: jana.underwood@co.borden.tx.us

Bosque County

District Clerk

Third Administrative Judicial Region
405 M.L.K Boulevard Drive, Georgetown, TX 78626
Tel: (512) 943-3777   Fax: (512) 943-3767
E-mail: presidingjudge3@wilco.org
Internet: www.courts.state.tx.us/3ajr/3ajr.asp

District Clerk, Bosque County **Betty Outlaw**...........(254) 435-2201
   P.O. Box 617, Meridian, TX 76665-0617

County Clerk

Third Administrative Judicial Region
405 M.L.K Boulevard Drive, Georgetown, TX 78626
Tel: (512) 943-3777   Fax: (512) 943-3767
E-mail: presidingjudge3@wilco.org
Internet: www.courts.state.tx.us/3ajr/3ajr.asp

District Clerk, Bosque County **Betty Outlaw**...........(254) 435-2201
   P.O. Box 617, Meridian, TX 76665-0617

(continued on next page)

Bowie County

District Clerk

First Administrative Judicial Region
133 North Riverfront Boulevard, 5th Floor, Dallas, TX 75207
Tel: (214) 653-2943 Fax: (214) 653-2957
Internet: www.firstadmin.com

District Clerk, Bowie County **Billy Fox** . . . . (903) 628-6775
710 James Bowie Drive, New Boston, TX 75570

County Clerk

Office of the County Clerk
710 James Bowie Drive, New Boston, TX 75570
Fax: (903) 628-6729

County Clerk **Tina Petty**. . . . . (903) 628-6740
E-mail: tina.petty@txkusa.org

Brazoria County

District Clerk

Second Administrative Judicial Region
301 North Thompson, Suite 102, Conroe, TX 77301
Tel: (936) 538-8176 Fax: (936) 538-8167
Internet: www.mctx.org/courts/second_administrative_judicial_region

District Clerk, Brazoria County **Rhonda Barchak** . . . . (979) 864-1316
111 East Locust, Room 500,
Angleton, TX 77515-4678

County Clerk

Office of the County Clerk
111 East Locust Street, Suite 200, Angleton, TX 77515
Fax: (979) 864-1358

County Clerk **Joyce Hudman** . . . . (979) 864-1355
E-mail: joyceh@brazoria-county.com

Brazos County

District Clerk

Second Administrative Judicial Region
301 North Thompson, Suite 102, Conroe, TX 77301
Tel: (936) 538-8176 Fax: (936) 538-8167
Internet: www.mctx.org/courts/second_administrative_judicial_region

District Clerk, Brazos County **Marc Hamlin** . . . . (979) 361-4228
300 East 26th Street, Suite 216,
Bryan, TX 77803-5360
E-mail: mhamlin@co.brazos.tx.us

County Clerk

Office of the County Clerk
300 East 26th Street, Suite 120, Bryan, TX 77803
Tel: (979) 361-4128 Fax: (979) 361-4312

County Clerk **Karen McQueen** . . . . (979) 361-4128
E-mail: kmcqueen@brazoscountytx.gov

Brewster County

District Clerk

Sixth Administrative Judicial Region
700 Main Street, Kerrville, TX 78028
Tel: (830) 792-2290 Fax: (830) 792-2294
E-mail: beckyh@co.kerr.tx.us
Internet: www.courts.state.tx.us/6ajr/6ajr.asp

District Clerk, Brewster County **Jo Ann Salgado** . . . . (432) 837-6216
P.O. Drawer 1024, Leakey, TX 78873

County Clerk

Office of the County Clerk
P.O. Drawer 119, Alpine, TX 79831
Fax: (432) 837-6217

County Clerk **Berta Rios Martinez** . . . . (432) 837-3366
E-mail: bmartinez@co.brewster.tx.us

Briscoe County

District Clerk and County Clerk

Ninth Administrative Judicial Region
500 West Main, Room 204W, Brownfield, TX 79316
Tel: (806) 637-1329 Fax: (806) 637-8918
E-mail: kmoore@terrycounty.org

District and County Clerk, Briscoe County
Bena Hester . . . . (806) 823-2134
P.O. Box 555, Silverton, TX 79257   Fax: (806) 823-2076

Brooks County

District Clerk

Fifth Administrative Judicial Region
200 North Almond Street, Alice, TX 78332
Tel: (361) 668-5766 Fax: (512) 367-5788
E-mail: fifth.region@yahoo.com
Internet: www.courts.state.tx.us/5ajr/5ajr.asp

District Clerk, Brooks County **Noe Guerra, Jr.** . . . . (361) 325-5604
P.O. Box 534, Falfurrias, TX 78355-0534

County Clerk

Office of the County Clerk
100 East Miller Street, Falfurrias, TX 78355
Fax: (361) 325-4944

County Clerk **Frutoso "Pepe" Garza** . . . . (361) 325-5604 ext. 150
E-mail: fgarza@co.brooks.tx.us

Brown County

District Clerk

Seventh Administrative Judicial Region
Midland County Courthouse, 500 North Loraine Street, Suite 502,
Midland, TX 79701
Tel: (432) 688-4370 Fax: (432) 688-4933
Internet: www.courts.state.tx.us/7ajr/7ajr.asp

District Clerk, Brown County **Cheryl Jones** . . . . (325) 643-2594
200 South Broadway, Room 101,
Brownwood, TX 76801-3192

County Clerk

Office of the County Clerk
200 South Broadway Street, Suite 101, Brownwood, TX 76801

County Clerk **Sharon Ferguson** . . . . (325) 643-2594
   E-mail: sharon.ferguson@browncountytx.org

Burleson County

District Clerk

Second Administrative Judicial Region
301 North Thompson, Suite 102, Conroe, TX 77301
Tel: (936) 538-8176 Fax: (936) 538-8167
Internet: www.mctx.org/courts/second_administrative_judicial_region

District Clerk, Burleson County **Dana Fritsche** . . . . (979) 567-2336
   100 West Buck Street, Suite 203,
   Caldwell, TX 77836

County Clerk

Office of the County Clerk
100 West Buck, Suite 203, Caldwell, TX 77836
Fax: (979) 567-2376

County Clerk **Anna L. Schielack** . . . . (979) 567-2329
   E-mail: coclerk@burlesoncounty.org

Burnet County

District Clerk

Third Administrative Judicial Region
405 M.L.K Boulevard Drive, Georgetown, TX 78626
Tel: (512) 943-3777 Fax: (512) 943-3767
E-mail: presidingjudge3@wilco.org
Internet: www.courts.state.tx.us/3ajr/3ajr.asp

District Clerk, Burnet County **Casie Walker** . . . . (512) 756-5450
   1701 East Polk Street, Suite 90,
   Burnet, TX 78611-2757

County Clerk

Office of the County Clerk
220 South Pierce, Burnet, TX 78611
Fax: (512) 756-5410

County Clerk **Janet Parker** . . . . (512) 756-5406
   E-mail: ctyclk@burnetcountytexas.org

Caldwell County

District Clerk

Third Administrative Judicial Region
405 M.L.K Boulevard Drive, Georgetown, TX 78626
Tel: (512) 943-3777 Fax: (512) 943-3767
E-mail: presidingjudge3@wilco.org
Internet: www.courts.state.tx.us/3ajr/3ajr.asp

District Clerk, Caldwell County **Tina Morgan** . . . . (512) 398-1806
   P.O. Box 749, Lockhart, TX 78644-0749

County Clerk

Office of the County Clerk
Caldwell County Justice Center, 1703 South Colorado Street,
Box 1, Suite 1200, Lockhart, TX 78644
Fax: (512) 398-9925

County Clerk **Carol Holcomb** . . . . (512) 398-1804
   E-mail: carol.holcomb@co.caldwell.tx.us

Calhoun County

District Clerk

Fourth Administrative Judicial Region
100 Dolorosa, 5th Floor, San Antonio, TX 78205
Tel: (210) 335-3954 Fax: (210) 335-3955
Internet: www.courts.state.tx.us/4ajr/4ajr.asp

District Clerk, Calhoun County
   Pamela Martin Hartgrove . . . . (361) 553-4630
   211 South Ann Street, Port Lavaca, TX 77979

County Clerk

Office of the County Clerk
211 South Ann Street, Port Lavaca, TX 77979
Fax: (361) 553-4420

County Clerk **Anna Goodman** . . . . (361) 553-4411
   E-mail: anna.goodman@calhouncotx.org

Callahan County

District Clerk

Seventh Administrative Judicial Region
Midland County Courthouse, 500 North Loraine Street, Suite 502,
Midland, TX 79701
Tel: (432) 688-4370 Fax: (432) 688-4933
Internet: www.courts.state.tx.us/7ajr/7ajr.asp

District Clerk, Callahan County **Amber Tinsley** . . . . (325) 854-5825
   100 West Fourth Street, Suite 104,
   Baird, TX 79504-5396

County Clerk

Office of the County Clerk
100 West Fourth Street, Suite 104, Baird, TX 79504
Fax: (325) 854-5816

County Clerk **Donna Bell** . . . . (325) 854-5815
   E-mail: clerk.info@callahancounty.org

Cameron County

District Clerk

Fifth Administrative Judicial Region
200 North Almond Street, Alice, TX 78332
Tel: (361) 668-5766 Fax: (512) 367-5788
E-mail: fifth.region@yahoo.com
Internet: www.courts.state.tx.us/5ajr/5ajr.asp

District Clerk, Cameron County **Aurora De La Garza** . . . . (956) 544-0838
   974 East Harrison, Brownsville, TX 78520-7123

(continued on next page)

Texas Court Clerks and Courthouses *continued*

County Clerk

Office of the County Clerk
964 East Harrison Street, Brownsville, TX 78520
Tel: (956) 544-0815
Internet: www.co.cameron.tx.us/countyclerk

County Clerk **Sylvia Garza Perez** . . . . (956) 544-0815

Camp County

District Clerk

First Administrative Judicial Region
133 North Riverfront Boulevard, 5th Floor, Dallas, TX 75207
Tel: (214) 653-2943 Fax: (214) 653-2957
Internet: www.firstadmin.com

District Clerk, Camp County **Teresa Bockmon** . . . . (903) 856-3221
  126 Church Street, Room 204,
  Pittsburg, TX 75686-1357

County Clerk

Office of the County Clerk
126 Church Street, Room 102, Pittsburg, TX 75686
Fax: (903) 856-6112

County Clerk **Elaine Young** . . . . (903) 856-2731

Carson County

District and County Clerk

Ninth Administrative Judicial Region
500 West Main, Room 204W, Brownfield, TX 79316
Tel: (806) 637-1329 Fax: (806) 637-8918
E-mail: kmoore@terrycounty.org

District and County Clerk, Carson County
  Celeste Bichsel . . . . (806) 537-3873
  P.O. Box 487, Panhandle, TX 79068   Fax: (806) 537-3623

Cass County

District Clerk

First Administrative Judicial Region
133 North Riverfront Boulevard, 5th Floor, Dallas, TX 75207
Tel: (214) 653-2943 Fax: (214) 653-2957
Internet: www.firstadmin.com

District Clerk, Cass County **Becky Wilbanks** . . . . (903) 756-7514
  P.O. Box 510, Linden, TX 75563-0510

County Clerk

Office of the County Clerk
P.O. Box 449, Linden, TX 75563
100 East Houston, Linden, TX 75563
Fax: (903) 756-8057

County Clerk **Jamie A. O'Rand** . . . . (903) 756-5071
  E-mail: orand.countyclerk@casscountytx.org

Texas Court Clerks and Courthouses *continued*

Castro County

District and County Clerk

Ninth Administrative Judicial Region
500 West Main, Room 204W, Brownfield, TX 79316
Tel: (806) 637-1329 Fax: (806) 637-8918
E-mail: kmoore@terrycounty.org

District and County Clerk, Castro County
  JoAnna Blanco . . . . (806) 647-3338
  100 East Bedford, Room 101,   Fax: (806) 647-5438
  Dimmitt, TX 79027-2643

Chambers County

District Clerk

Second Administrative Judicial Region
301 North Thompson, Suite 102, Conroe, TX 77301
Tel: (936) 538-8176 Fax: (936) 538-8167
Internet: www.mctx.org/courts/second_administrative_judicial_region

District Clerk, Chambers County **Patti L. Henry** . . . . (409) 267-2432
  P.O. Box NN, Anahuac, TX 77514-1739

County Clerk

Office of the County Clerk
P.O. Box 728, Anahuac, TX 77514
Fax: (409) 267-8405

County Clerk **Heather Hawthorne** . . . . (409) 267-2418
  E-mail: hhawthorne@co.chambers.tx.us

Cherokee County

District Clerk

First Administrative Judicial Region
133 North Riverfront Boulevard, 5th Floor, Dallas, TX 75207
Tel: (214) 653-2943 Fax: (214) 653-2957
Internet: www.firstadmin.com

District Clerk, Cherokee County **Janet Gates** . . . . (903) 683-4533
  P.O. Drawer C, Rusk, TX 75785-0505

County Clerk

Office of the County Clerk
135 South Main, Rusk, TX 75785
Fax: (903) 683-2457

County Clerk **Laverne Lusk** . . . . (903) 683-2350
  E-mail: coclerk@cocherokee.org

Childress County

District and County Clerk

Ninth Administrative Judicial Region
500 West Main, Room 204W, Brownfield, TX 79316
Tel: (806) 637-1329 Fax: (806) 637-8918
E-mail: kmoore@terrycounty.org

District and County Clerk, Childress County
  Zona Prince . . . . (940) 937-6143
  100 Avenue East NW, Box 4,
  Childress, TX 79201

Clay County

District Clerk

Eighth Administrative Judicial Region
401 West Belknap, 5th Floor, Fort Worth, TX 76196
Tel: (817) 884-1558 Fax: (817) 884-1560
E-mail: 8thadmin@8thjudicialregion.com

District Clerk, Clay County **Dan Slagle** . . . . (940) 538-4561
P.O. Drawer 568, Henrietta, TX 76365-0568

County Clerk

Office of the County Clerk
214 North Main Street, Henrietta, TX 76365
Fax: (940) 264-4160

County Clerk **Sasha Kelton** . . . . (940) 538-4631
E-mail: ccclerk@claycountytx.com

Cochran County

District and County Clerk

Ninth Administrative Judicial Region
500 West Main, Room 204W, Brownfield, TX 79316
Tel: (806) 637-1329 Fax: (806) 637-8918
E-mail: kmoore@terrycounty.org

District and County Clerk, Cochran County
Shanna Dewbre . . . . (806) 266-5450
100 North Main Street, Room 102,   Fax: (806) 266-9027
Morton, TX 79346-2500

Coke County

District and County Clerk

Seventh Administrative Judicial Region
Midland County Courthouse, 500 North Loraine Street, Suite 502,
Midland, TX 79701
Tel: (432) 688-4370 Fax: (432) 688-4933
Internet: www.courts.state.tx.us/7ajr/7ajr.asp

District Clerk, Coke County **Mary Grim** . . . . (325) 453-2631
13 East Seventh, Robert Lee, TX 76945-5077

Coleman County

District Clerk

Seventh Administrative Judicial Region
Midland County Courthouse, 500 North Loraine Street, Suite 502,
Midland, TX 79701
Tel: (432) 688-4370 Fax: (432) 688-4933
Internet: www.courts.state.tx.us/7ajr/7ajr.asp

District Clerk, Coleman County **Margie Mayo** . . . .(325) 625-2568
100 West Live Oak Street, Suite 201,
Coleman, TX 76834-3858

County Clerk

Office of the County Clerk
100 West Live Oak Street, Suite 105, Coleman, TX 76834
Fax: (325) 625-2889

County Clerk **Stacey Mendoza** . . . . (325) 625-2889
E-mail: cclerk@web-access.net

Collin County

District Clerk

First Administrative Judicial Region
133 North Riverfront Boulevard, 5th Floor, Dallas, TX 75207
Tel: (214) 653-2943 Fax: (214) 653-2957
Internet: www.firstadmin.com

District Clerk, Collin County
Andrea Stroh Thompson . . . .(972) 548-4320
2100 Bloomdale Road, Suite 12132,
McKinney, TX 75071

County Clerk

County Clerk's Office
2300 Bloomdale Road, Room 2106, McKinney, TX 75071
Tel: (972) 548-4185 Fax: (972) 547-5731
E-mail: ctyclerks@collincountytx.gov
Internet: www.co.collin.tx.us/county_clerk/index.jsp

County Clerk **Stacey Kemp** . . . .(972) 548-4133
E-mail: ctyclerks@collincountytx.gov

Collingsworth County

District and County Clerk

Ninth Administrative Judicial Region
500 West Main, Room 204W, Brownfield, TX 79316
Tel: (806) 637-1329 Fax: (806) 637-8918
E-mail: kmoore@terrycounty.org

District and County Clerk, Collingsworth County
Jackie Johnson . . . . (806) 447-2408
800 West Avenue, Box 10,   Fax: (806) 447-2409
Wellington, TX 79095-3039

Colorado County

District Clerk

Third Administrative Judicial Region
405 M.L.K Boulevard Drive, Georgetown, TX 78626
Tel: (512) 943-3777 Fax: (512) 943-3767
E-mail: presidingjudge3@wilco.org
Internet: www.courts.state.tx.us/3ajr/3ajr.asp

District Clerk, Colorado County **Harvey Vornsand** . . . . . . (979) 732-2536
400 Spring Street, Room 210E,
Columbus, TX 78934

County Clerk

Office of the County Clerk
Colorado County Courthouse Annex, 318 Spring Street, Room 103,
Columbus, TX 78934
Fax: (979) 732-8852

County Clerk **Kimberly Menke** . . . . (979) 732-6860
E-mail: kimberly.menke@co.colorado.tx.us

(continued on next page)

Comal County

District Clerk

Third Administrative Judicial Region
405 M.L.K Boulevard Drive, Georgetown, TX 78626
Tel: (512) 943-3777 Fax: (512) 943-3767
E-mail: presidingjudge3@wilco.org
Internet: www.courts.state.tx.us/3ajr/3ajr.asp

District Clerk, Comal County **Kathy H. Faulkner** . . . .(830) 221-1250
150 North Seguin, Suite 304,
New Braunfels, TX 78130-5160

County Clerk

Office of the County Clerk
178 E. Mill Street, Suite 101, New Braunfels, TX 78130
Fax: (830) 620-3410

County Clerk **Bobbie Koepp** . . . . (830) 221-1230

Comanche County

District Clerk

Third Administrative Judicial Region
405 M.L.K Boulevard Drive, Georgetown, TX 78626
Tel: (512) 943-3777 Fax: (512) 943-3767
E-mail: presidingjudge3@wilco.org
Internet: www.courts.state.tx.us/3ajr/3ajr.asp

District Clerk, Comanche County **Brenda Dickey** . . . .(325) 356-2342
P.O. Box 206, Comanche, TX 76442-3297

County Clerk

Office of the County Clerk
101 West Central, Comanche, TX 76442
Fax: (325) 356-3710

County Clerk **Ruby Lesley** . . . .(325) 356-2655
E-mail: rlesley@comanchetx.com

Concho County

District and County Clerk

Seventh Administrative Judicial Region
Midland County Courthouse, 500 North Loraine Street, Suite 502,
Midland, TX 79701
Tel: (432) 688-4370 Fax: (432) 688-4933
Internet: www.courts.state.tx.us/7ajr/7ajr.asp

District Clerk, Concho County **Phyllis Lovell** . . . .(325) 732-4322
P.O. Box 98, Paint Rock, TX 76866-0098

Cooke County

District Clerk

Eighth Administrative Judicial Region
401 West Belknap, 5th Floor, Fort Worth, TX 76196
Tel: (817) 884-1558 Fax: (817) 884-1560
E-mail: 8thadmin@8thjudicialregion.com

District Clerk, Cooke County **Susan Hughes** . . . .(940) 668-5450
101 South Dixon Street,
Gainesville, TX 76240-4796

County Clerk

Office of the County Clerk
Cooke County Courthouse, 101 South Dixon, Gainesville, TX 76240
Fax: (940) 668-5522

County Clerk **Rebecca Lawson** . . . .(940) 668-5521
E-mail: rebecca.lawson@co.cooke.tx.us

Coryell County

District Clerk

Third Administrative Judicial Region
405 M.L.K Boulevard Drive, Georgetown, TX 78626
Tel: (512) 943-3777 Fax: (512) 943-3767
E-mail: presidingjudge3@wilco.org
Internet: www.courts.state.tx.us/3ajr/3ajr.asp

District Clerk, Coryell County **Janice M. Gray** . . . . (254) 865-5911
P.O. Box 187, Gatesville, TX 76528

County Clerk

Office of the County Clerk
620 East Main Street, First Floor, Gatesville, TX 76528
Fax: (254) 865-8631

County Clerk **Barbara Simpson** . . . .(254) 865-5911 ext. 2235
E-mail: county_clerk@coryellcounty.org

Cottle County

District and County Clerk

Ninth Administrative Judicial Region
500 West Main, Room 204W, Brownfield, TX 79316
Tel: (806) 637-1329 Fax: (806) 637-8918
E-mail: kmoore@terrycounty.org

District and County Clerk, Cottle County **Jan Irons** . . . . . .(806) 492-3823
P.O. Box 717, Paducah, TX 79248-0717   Fax: (806) 492-2625

Crane County

District and County Clerk

Seventh Administrative Judicial Region
Midland County Courthouse, 500 North Loraine Street, Suite 502,
Midland, TX 79701
Tel: (432) 688-4370 Fax: (432) 688-4933
Internet: www.courts.state.tx.us/7ajr/7ajr.asp

District Clerk, Crane County **Judy Crawford** . . . .(432) 558-3581
P.O. Box 578, Crane, TX 79731-0578

Crockett County

District and County Clerk

Sixth Administrative Judicial Region
700 Main Street, Kerrville, TX 78028
Tel: (830) 792-2290 Fax: (830) 792-2294
E-mail: beckyh@co.kerr.tx.us
Internet: www.courts.state.tx.us/6ajr/6ajr.asp

District and County Clerk, Crockett County
Ninfa Preddy . . . .(325) 392-2022
P.O. Drawer C, Ozona, TX 76943   Fax: (325) 392-3742

Crosby County

District Clerk

Ninth Administrative Judicial Region
500 West Main, Room 204W, Brownfield, TX 79316
Tel: (806) 637-1329 Fax: (806) 637-8918
E-mail: kmoore@terrycounty.org

District Clerk, Crosby County **Shari Smith** . . . . (806) 675-2071
  201 West Aspen, Suite 207,
  Crosbyton, TX 79322-0207

County Clerk

Office of the County Clerk
201 West Aspen, Suite 102, Crosbyton, TX 79322
Fax: (806) 675-2980

County Clerk **Tammy Marshall** . . . . (806) 675-2334
  E-mail: tammy.marshall@sos.state.tx.us

Culberson County

District and County Clerk

Sixth Administrative Judicial Region
700 Main Street, Kerrville, TX 78028
Tel: (830) 792-2290 Fax: (830) 792-2294
E-mail: beckyh@co.kerr.tx.us
Internet: www.courts.state.tx.us/6ajr/6ajr.asp

District and County Clerk, Culberson County
  Linda McDonald . . . . (432) 283-2058
  P.O. Box 158, Van Horn, TX 79855-0158   Fax: (432) 283-9234

Dallam County

District and County Clerk

Ninth Administrative Judicial Region
500 West Main, Room 204W, Brownfield, TX 79316
Tel: (806) 637-1329 Fax: (806) 637-8918
E-mail: kmoore@terrycounty.org

District and County Clerk, Dallam County **Terri Banks** . . . (806) 244-4751
  P.O. Box 1352, Dalhart, TX 79022
  E-mail: clerk@dallam.org

Dallas County

District Clerk

First Administrative Judicial Region
133 North Riverfront Boulevard, 5th Floor, Dallas, TX 75207
Tel: (214) 653-2943 Fax: (214) 653-2957
Internet: www.firstadmin.com

District Clerk, Dallas County **Gary Fitzsimmons** . . . . (214) 653-7301
  600 Commerce, Dallas, TX 75202-4606

County Clerk

Office of the County Clerk
Records Bldg., 509 Main Street, 2nd Floor, Dallas, TX 75202
Fax: (214) 653-7176 Tel: (214) 653-7099

County Clerk **John Warren** . . . . (214) 653-7131
  E-mail: jwarren@dallascounty.org

Dawson County

District Clerk

Seventh Administrative Judicial Region
Midland County Courthouse, 500 North Loraine Street, Suite 502,
Midland, TX 79701
Tel: (432) 688-4370 Fax: (432) 688-4933
Internet: www.courts.state.tx.us/7ajr/7ajr.asp

District Clerk, Dawson County **Pam Huse** . . . . (830) 796-4606
  P.O. Box 1268, Lamesa, TX 79331-1268

County Clerk

Office of the County Clerk
P.O. Box 1268, Lamesa, TX 79331
Fax: (806) 872-2473

County Clerk **Gloria Vera** . . . . (806) 872-3778
  E-mail: dawsonclerk@windstream.net

Deaf Smith County

District Clerk

Ninth Administrative Judicial Region
500 West Main, Room 204W, Brownfield, TX 79316
Tel: (806) 637-1329 Fax: (806) 637-8918
E-mail: kmoore@terrycounty.org

District Clerk, Deaf Smith County **Jean Coody** . . . . (806) 364-3901
  235 East Third, Room 304,
  Hereford, TX 79045-5542

County Clerk

Office of the County Clerk
235 East Third Street, Hereford, TX 79045
Fax: (806) 363-7023

County Clerk **Imelda DeLaCerda** . . . . (806) 363-7077
  E-mail: dscclerk@wtrt.net

Delta County

District Clerk

First Administrative Judicial Region
133 North Riverfront Boulevard, 5th Floor, Dallas, TX 75207
Tel: (214) 653-2943 Fax: (214) 653-2957
Internet: www.firstadmin.com

District Clerk, Delta County **Jane Jones** . . . . (903) 395-4400
  200 West Dallas Avenue, Cooper, TX 75432

County Clerk

Office of the County Clerk
200 West Dallas Avenue, Cooper, TX 75432
Fax: (903) 395-4260

County Clerk **Jane Jones** . . . . (903) 395-4400 ext. 222
  E-mail: jjones@sos.state.tx.us

(continued on next page)

Denton County

District Clerk

Eighth Administrative Judicial Region
401 West Belknap, 5th Floor, Fort Worth, TX 76196
Tel: (817) 884-1558 Fax: (817) 884-1560
E-mail: 8thadmin@8thjudicialregion.com

District Clerk, Denton County **Sherri Adelstein** . . . . (940) 349-2200
P.O. Drawer 2146, Denton, TX 76202-2146

County Clerk

Office of the County Clerk
1450 East McKinney Street, Denton, TX 76209-4524
Tel: (940) 349-2012 Fax: (940) 349-2013

County Clerk **Juli Anne Luke** . . . . (940) 349-2012

DeWitt County

District Clerk

Fourth Administrative Judicial Region
100 Dolorosa, 5th Floor, San Antonio, TX 78205
Tel: (210) 335-3954 Fax: (210) 335-3955
Internet: www.courts.state.tx.us/4ajr/4ajr.asp

District Clerk, DeWitt County **Tabeth Gardner** . . . . (361) 275-0931
P.O. Box 845, Cuero, TX 77594

County Clerk

Office of the County Clerk
307 North Gonzales Street, Cuero, TX 77954
Fax: (361) 275-0866

County Clerk **Natalie Carson** . . . . (361) 275-0864
E-mail: natalie.carson@co.dewitt.tx.us

Dickens County

District Clerk

Ninth Administrative Judicial Region
500 West Main, Room 204W, Brownfield, TX 79316
Tel: (806) 637-1329 Fax: (806) 637-8918
E-mail: kmoore@terrycounty.org

District Clerk, Dickens County **Winona Humphreys** . . . . . (806) 623-5531
P.O. Box 120, Dickens, TX 79229-0120

County Clerk

Office of the District and County Clerk
P.O. Box 120, Dickens, TX 79229
Fax: (806) 623-5240

County Clerk **Winnona Humphreys** . . . . (806) 623-5531
E-mail: coclerk@caprock-spur.com

Dimmit County

District Clerk

Fourth Administrative Judicial Region
100 Dolorosa, 5th Floor, San Antonio, TX 78205
Tel: (210) 335-3954 Fax: (210) 335-3955
Internet: www.courts.state.tx.us/4ajr/4ajr.asp

District Clerk, Dimmit County **Maricela G. Gonzalez** . . . . (830) 876-4243
103 North Fifth Street, Carrizo Springs, TX 78834

County Clerk

Office of the County Clerk
103 North Fifth Street, Carrizo Springs, TX 78834
Fax: (830) 876-4205

County Clerk **Mario Z. Garcia** . . . . (830) 876-4238

Donley County

District and County Clerk

Ninth Administrative Judicial Region
500 West Main, Room 204W, Brownfield, TX 79316
Tel: (806) 637-1329 Fax: (806) 637-8918
E-mail: kmoore@terrycounty.org

District and County Clerk, Donley County **Fay Vargas** . . . (806) 874-3436
P.O. Drawer U, Clarendon, TX 79226   Fax: (806) 874-3351
E-mail: doncoclerk@windstream.net

Duval County

District Clerk

Fifth Administrative Judicial Region
200 North Almond Street, Alice, TX 78332
Tel: (361) 668-5766 Fax: (512) 367-5788
E-mail: fifth.region@yahoo.com
Internet: www.courts.state.tx.us/5ajr/5ajr.asp

District Clerk, Duval County **Richard Barton** . . . . (361) 279-6272
P.O. Drawer 428, San Diego, TX 78384

County Clerk

Office of the County Clerk
400 East Gravis, San Diego, TX 78384
Fax: (361) 279-3159

County Clerk **Elodia M. Garza** . . . . (361) 279-6272
E-mail: elodia.garza@co.duval.tx.us

Eastland County

District Clerk

Eighth Administrative Judicial Region
401 West Belknap, 5th Floor, Fort Worth, TX 76196
Tel: (817) 884-1558 Fax: (817) 884-1560
E-mail: 8thadmin@8thjudicialregion.com

District Clerk, Eastland County **Carol Ann Brittain** . . . . . . (254) 629-2664
100 West Main, Suite 206,
Eastland, TX 76448-2700

County Clerk

Office of the County Clerk
100 West Main, Suite 102, Eastland, TX 76448
Fax: (254) 629-8125

County Clerk **Cathy Jentho** . . . . (254) 629-1583
E-mail: ecco@eastlandcountytexas.com

Ector County

District Clerk

Seventh Administrative Judicial Region
Midland County Courthouse, 500 North Loraine Street, Suite 502,
Midland, TX 79701
Tel: (432) 688-4370 Fax: (432) 688-4933
Internet: www.courts.state.tx.us/7ajr/7ajr.asp

District Clerk, Ector County **Clarissa Webster** . . . . (432) 498-4290
300 North Grant, Room 301,
Odessa, TX 79761-5158

County Clerk

Office of the County Clerk
P.O. Box 707, Odessa, TX 79760
Fax: (432) 498-4177

County Clerk **Linda Haney** . . . . (432) 498-4130
E-mail: haneyld@co.ector.tx.us

Edwards County

District and County Clerk

Sixth Administrative Judicial Region
700 Main Street, Kerrville, TX 78028
Tel: (830) 792-2290 Fax: (830) 792-2294
E-mail: beckyh@co.kerr.tx.us
Internet: www.courts.state.tx.us/6ajr/6ajr.asp

District and County Clerk, Edwards County
Olga Lydia Reyes . . . . (830) 683-2235
P.O. Box 184, Rocksprings, TX 78880-0184   Fax: (830) 683-5376
E-mail: clerk@swtexas.net

El Paso County

District Clerk

Sixth Administrative Judicial Region
700 Main Street, Kerrville, TX 78028
Tel: (830) 792-2290 Fax: (830) 792-2294
E-mail: beckyh@co.kerr.tx.us
Internet: www.courts.state.tx.us/6ajr/6ajr.asp

District Clerk, El Paso County **Norma L. Favela** . . . . (915) 546-2021
500 East San Antonio, Room 103,
El Paso, TX 79901-2489

County Clerk

Office of the County Clerk
County Courthouse, 500 East San Antonio Avenue, Room 105,
El Paso, TX 79901-2496
Fax: (915) 546-2012
E-mail: countyclerk@epcounty.com
Internet: www.epcounty.com/clerk

County Clerk **Delia Briones** . . . . (915) 546-2071

Ellis County

District Clerk

First Administrative Judicial Region
133 North Riverfront Boulevard, 5th Floor, Dallas, TX 75207
Tel: (214) 653-2943 Fax: (214) 653-2957
Internet: www.firstadmin.com

District Clerk, Ellis County **Melanie Reed** . . . . (972) 825-5091
109 South Jackson Street,
Waxahachie, TX 75165-3745

County Clerk

Office of the County Clerk
109 South Jackson Street, Second Floor, Waxahachie, TX 75165
P.O. Box 250, Waxahachie, TX 75168
Fax: (972) 825-5075

County Clerk **Cindy Polley** . . . . (972) 825-5070
E-mail: cindy.polley@co.ellis.tx.us

Erath County

District Clerk

Eighth Administrative Judicial Region
401 West Belknap, 5th Floor, Fort Worth, TX 76196
Tel: (817) 884-1558 Fax: (817) 884-1560
E-mail: 8thadmin@8thjudicialregion.com

District Clerk, Erath County **Wanda Pringle** . . . . (254) 965-1486
112 West College Street, Stephenville, TX 76401

County Clerk

Office of the County Clerk
100 West Washington, Stephenville, TX 76401
Fax: (254) 965-5732

County Clerk **Gwinda Jones** . . . . (254) 965-1482
E-mail: countyclerk@co.erath.tx.us

Falls County

District Clerk

Third Administrative Judicial Region
405 M.L.K Boulevard Drive, Georgetown, TX 78626
Tel: (512) 943-3777 Fax: (512) 943-3767
E-mail: presidingjudge3@wilco.org
Internet: www.courts.state.tx.us/3ajr/3ajr.asp

District Clerk, Falls County **Christy Wideman** . . . . (254) 883-1419
P.O. Box 229, Marlin, TX 76661-0229

County Clerk

Office of the County Clerk
P.O. Box 458, Marlin, TX 76661
Fax: (254) 883-2260

County Clerk **Linda Watkins** . . . . (254) 883-1408
E-mail: linda.watkins@co.falls.tx.us

(continued on next page)

Fannin County

District Clerk

First Administrative Judicial Region
133 North Riverfront Boulevard, 5th Floor, Dallas, TX 75207
Tel: (214) 653-2943 Fax: (214) 653-2957
Internet: www.firstadmin.com

District Clerk, Fannin County **Nancy Young** . . . . (903) 583-7459
  101 East Sam Rayburn Drive, Suite 201,
  Bonham, TX 75418-4346

County Clerk

Office of the County Clerk
101 East Sam Rayburn Drive, Suite 102, Bonham, TX 75418
Fax: (903) 640-4241

County Clerk **Tammy Biggar** . . . . (903) 583-7486
  E-mail: countyclerk@fanninco.net

Fayette County

District Clerk

Third Administrative Judicial Region
405 M.L.K Boulevard Drive, Georgetown, TX 78626
Tel: (512) 943-3777 Fax: (512) 943-3767
E-mail: presidingjudge3@wilco.org
Internet: www.courts.state.tx.us/3ajr/3ajr.asp

District Clerk, Fayette County **Virginia Wied** . . . . (903) 473-5000
  151 North Washington, Room 102,
  La Grange, TX 75440

County Clerk

Office of the County Clerk
P.O. Box 59, La Grange, TX 78945
246 West Colorado Street, La Grange, TX 78945
Fax: (979) 968-8531

County Clerk **Julie Karstedt** . . . . (979) 968-3251
  E-mail: julie.karstedt@co.fayette.tx.us

Fisher County

District Clerk

Seventh Administrative Judicial Region
Midland County Courthouse, 500 North Loraine Street, Suite 502,
Midland, TX 79701
Tel: (432) 688-4370 Fax: (432) 688-4933
Internet: www.courts.state.tx.us/7ajr/7ajr.asp

District Clerk, Fisher County **Tammy Haley** . . . . (325) 776-2401
  P.O. Box 88, Roby, TX 79543-0088

County Clerk

Office of the County Clerk
112 North Concho Street, Roby, TX 79543
Fax: (325) 776-3274

County Clerk **Pat Thomson** . . . . (325) 776-2401
  E-mail: fishercountyclerk@yahoo.com

Floyd County

District Clerk

Ninth Administrative Judicial Region
500 West Main, Room 204W, Brownfield, TX 79316
Tel: (806) 637-1329 Fax: (806) 637-8918
E-mail: kmoore@terrycounty.org

District Clerk, Floyd County **Patty Davenport** . . . . (806) 983-4923
  105 Main Street, Room 207,
  Floydada, TX 79235-0067

County Clerk

Office of the County Clerk
105 South Main Street, Room 101, Floydada, TX 79235

County Clerk **Ginger Morgan** . . . . (806) 983-4900

Foard County

District Clerk

Ninth Administrative Judicial Region
500 West Main, Room 204W, Brownfield, TX 79316
Tel: (806) 637-1329 Fax: (806) 637-8918
E-mail: kmoore@terrycounty.org

District and County Clerk, Foard County
  Debra Hopkins . . . . (940) 684-1365
  P.O. Drawer 815, Vernon, TX 79227-0539

Fort Bend County

District Clerk

Second Administrative Judicial Region
301 North Thompson, Suite 102, Conroe, TX 77301
Tel: (936) 538-8176 Fax: (936) 538-8167
Internet: www.mctx.org/courts/second_administrative_judicial_region

District Clerk, Fort Bend County **Annie R. Elliott** . . . . (281) 633-7632
  1422 Eugene Heimann Circle,
  Richmond, TX 77469-3110

County Clerk

Office of the County Clerk
301 Jackson Street, Suite 101, Richmond, TX 77469
Fax: (281) 341-8697

County Clerk **Laura Richard** . . . . (281) 341-8652

Franklin County

District Clerk

First Administrative Judicial Region
133 North Riverfront Boulevard, 5th Floor, Dallas, TX 75207
Tel: (214) 653-2943 Fax: (214) 653-2957
Internet: www.firstadmin.com

District Clerk, Franklin County **Ellen Jaggers** . . . . (903) 537-8337
  P.O. Box 750, Mount Vernon, TX 75457

County Clerk

Office of the County Clerk
200 North Kaufman Street, Mount Vernon, TX 75457
Fax: (903) 537-2962

County Clerk **Betty Crane** . . . . (903) 537-2342 ext. 2
  E-mail: bcrane@co.franklin.tx.us

Freestone County

District Clerk

Second Administrative Judicial Region
301 North Thompson, Suite 102, Conroe, TX 77301
Tel: (936) 538-8176 Fax: (936) 538-8167
Internet: www.mctx.org/courts/second_administrative_judicial_region

District Clerk, Freestone County
Janet Haydon Chappell . . . . (903) 389-2534
P.O. Box 722, Fairfield, TX 75840-0722

County Clerk

Office of the County Clerk
103 East Main, Fairfield, TX 75840
Fax: (903) 389-6956

County Clerk **Linda Jarvis** . . . . (903) 389-2635
E-mail: linda.jarvis@co.freestone.tx.us

Frio County

District Clerk

Fourth Administrative Judicial Region
100 Dolorosa, 5th Floor, San Antonio, TX 78205
Tel: (210) 335-3954 Fax: (210) 335-3955
Internet: www.courts.state.tx.us/4ajr/4ajr.asp

District Clerk, Frio County **Ramona B. Rodriguez** . . . . . . (830) 334-8073
500 East San Antonio, Suite 8,
Pearsall, TX 78061-3100

County Clerk

Office of the County Clerk
500 East San Antonio Street, Box 6, Pearsall, TX 78061
Fax: (830) 334-0021

County Clerk **Angie Tullis** . . . . (830) 334-2214
E-mail: angietulliscountyclerk@yahoo.com

Gaines County

District Clerk

Seventh Administrative Judicial Region
Midland County Courthouse, 500 North Loraine Street, Suite 502,
Midland, TX 79701
Tel: (432) 688-4370 Fax: (432) 688-4933
Internet: www.courts.state.tx.us/7ajr/7ajr.asp

District Clerk, Gaines County **Sharon Taylor** . . . . (432) 758-4013
101 South Main, Room 311,
Seminole, TX 79360-4341

County Clerk

Office of the County Clerk
101 South Main, Room 206, Seminole, TX 79360
Fax: (432) 758-1442

County Clerk **Vicki Phillips** . . . . (432) 758-4003 ext. 221
E-mail: vicki.phillips@co.gaines.tx.us

Galveston County

District Clerk

Second Administrative Judicial Region
301 North Thompson, Suite 102, Conroe, TX 77301
Tel: (936) 538-8176 Fax: (936) 538-8167
Internet: www.mctx.org/courts/second_administrative_judicial_region

District Clerk, Galveston County **John D. Kinard** . . . . (409) 766-2424
600 59th Street, Room 4001,
Galveston, TX 77551-2388

County Clerk

Office of the County Clerk
600 59th Street, Suite 2001, Galveston, TX 77551
Fax: (409) 765-3160

County Clerk **Dwight Sullivan** . . . . (409) 766-2200

Garza County

District and County Clerk

Seventh Administrative Judicial Region
Midland County Courthouse, 500 North Loraine Street, Suite 502,
Midland, TX 79701
Tel: (432) 688-4370 Fax: (432) 688-4933
Internet: www.courts.state.tx.us/7ajr/7ajr.asp

District Clerk, Garza County **Jim Plummer** . . . . (806) 495-4430
P.O. Box 366, Post, TX 79356-0366

Gillespie County

District Clerk

Sixth Administrative Judicial Region
700 Main Street, Kerrville, TX 78028
Tel: (830) 792-2290 Fax: (830) 792-2294
E-mail: beckyh@co.kerr.tx.us
Internet: www.courts.state.tx.us/6ajr/6ajr.asp

District Clerk, Gillespie County **Jan Davis** . . . . (830) 997-6517
101 West Main Street, Room 204,
Fredericksburg, TX 78624-3700

County Clerk

Office of the County Clerk
101 West Main Street, Mail Unit 13, Fredericksburg, TX 78624
Fax: (830) 997-9958

County Clerk **Mary Lynn Rusche** . . . . (830) 997-6515
E-mail: mlrusche@gillespiecounty.org

Glasscock County

District and County Clerk

Seventh Administrative Judicial Region
Midland County Courthouse, 500 North Loraine Street, Suite 502,
Midland, TX 79701
Tel: (432) 688-4370 Fax: (432) 688-4933
Internet: www.courts.state.tx.us/7ajr/7ajr.asp

District Clerk, Glasscock County **Rebecca Batla** . . . . (830) 796-4606
P.O. Box 190, Garden City, TX 79739-0190

(continued on next page)

Texas Court Clerks and Courthouses *continued*

Goliad County

District Clerk

Fourth Administrative Judicial Region
100 Dolorosa, 5th Floor, San Antonio, TX 78205
Tel: (210) 335-3954 Fax: (210) 335-3955
Internet: www.courts.state.tx.us/4ajr/4ajr.asp

District Clerk, Goliad County **Mary Ellen Flores** . . . . (361) 645-3294
  P.O. Box 50, Goliad, TX 77963-0050

County Clerk

Office of the County Clerk
P.O. Box 50, Goliad, TX 77963
Fax: (361) 645-3474

County Clerk **Mary Ellen Flores** . . . . (361) 645-3294
  E-mail: mflores@goliadcountytx.gov

Gonzales County

District Clerk

Third Administrative Judicial Region
405 M.L.K Boulevard Drive, Georgetown, TX 78626
Tel: (512) 943-3777 Fax: (512) 943-3767
E-mail: presidingjudge3@wilco.org
Internet: www.courts.state.tx.us/3ajr/3ajr.asp

District Clerk, Gonzales County **Sandra Baker** . . . . (830) 672-2326
  414 Saint Joseph Street, Suite 300,
  Gonzales, TX 78629

County Clerk

Office of the County Clerk
Courthouse Annex, 1709 Sarah DeWitt Drive, Gonzales, TX 78629
Fax: (830) 672-2636

County Clerk **Lee Riedel** . . . . (830) 672-2801
  E-mail: lriedel@co.gonzales.tx.us

Gray County

District Clerk

Ninth Administrative Judicial Region
500 West Main, Room 204W, Brownfield, TX 79316
Tel: (806) 637-1329 Fax: (806) 637-8918
E-mail: kmoore@terrycounty.org

District Clerk, Gray County **Sandra Burkett** . . . . (806) 669-8010
  P.O. Box 1139, Pampa, TX 79066-1139

County Clerk

Office of the County Clerk
P.O. Box 1902, Pampa, TX 79066
Fax: (806) 669-8054

County Clerk **Susan Winborne** . . . . (806) 669-8004
  E-mail: susan.winborne@graycch.com

Texas Court Clerks and Courthouses *continued*

Grayson County

District Clerk

First Administrative Judicial Region
133 North Riverfront Boulevard, 5th Floor, Dallas, TX 75207
Tel: (214) 653-2943 Fax: (214) 653-2957
Internet: www.firstadmin.com

District Clerk, Grayson County **Kelly Ashmore** . . . . (903) 813-4355
  200 South Crockett, Suite 120A,
  Sherman, TX 75090

County Clerk

Office of the County Clerk
100 West Houston, Suite 17, Sherman, TX 75090
Fax: (903) 870-0829

County Clerk **Wilma Bush** . . . . (903) 813-4236
  E-mail: bushw@co.grayson.tx.us

Gregg County

District Clerk

First Administrative Judicial Region
133 North Riverfront Boulevard, 5th Floor, Dallas, TX 75207
Tel: (214) 653-2943 Fax: (214) 653-2957
Internet: www.firstadmin.com

District Clerk, Gregg County **Barbara Duncan** . . . . (903) 237-2663
  P.O. Box 711, Longview, TX 75606-0711

County Clerk

Office of the County Clerk
101 East Methvin, Suite 200, Longview, TX 75601
Fax: (903) 237-2574

County Clerk **Connie Wade** . . . . (903) 236-8430
  E-mail: connie.wade@co.gregg.tx.us

Grimes County

District Clerk

Second Administrative Judicial Region
301 North Thompson, Suite 102, Conroe, TX 77301
Tel: (936) 538-8176 Fax: (936) 538-8167
Internet: www.mctx.org/courts/second_administrative_judicial_region

District Clerk, Grimes County **Gay Wells** . . . . (936) 873-4430
  P.O. Box 234, Anderson, TX 77830-0234   Fax: (936) 873-2514

County Clerk

Office of the County Clerk
P.O. Box 209, Anderson, TX 77830
Fax: (936) 873-3308

County Clerk **David Pasket** . . . . (936) 873-4410

Guadalupe County

District Clerk

Third Administrative Judicial Region
405 M.L.K Boulevard Drive, Georgetown, TX 78626
Tel: (512) 943-3777 Fax: (512) 943-3767
E-mail: presidingjudge3@wilco.org
Internet: www.courts.state.tx.us/3ajr/3ajr.asp

District Clerk, Guadalupe County **Debra Crow** . . . . (903) 473-5000
101 East Court Street, Room 308,
Seguin, TX 78155-5742

County Clerk

Office of the County Clerk
211 West Court Street, Seguin, TX 78155
Fax: (830) 401-0300

County Clerk **Teresa Kiel** . . . . (830) 303-8859
E-mail: tkiel@co.guadalupe.tx.us

Hale County

District Clerk

Ninth Administrative Judicial Region
500 West Main, Room 204W, Brownfield, TX 79316
Tel: (806) 637-1329 Fax: (806) 637-8918
E-mail: kmoore@terrycounty.org

District Clerk, Hale County **Carla Cannon** . . . . (806) 291-5226
225 Broadway, Suite 4, Plainview, TX 79072-8050

County Clerk

Office of the County Clerk
500 Broadway, Room 140, Plainview, TX 79072
Fax: (806) 291-9810

County Clerk **Latrice Kemp** . . . . (806) 291-5261
E-mail: lkemp@halecounty.org

Hall County

District and County Clerk

Ninth Administrative Judicial Region
500 West Main, Room 204W, Brownfield, TX 79316
Tel: (806) 637-1329 Fax: (806) 637-8918
E-mail: kmoore@terrycounty.org

District and County Clerk, Hall County **Raye Bailey** . . . . . (806) 259-2627
512 West Main Street, Suite 8,
Memphis, TX 79245-3343

Hamilton County

District Clerk

Third Administrative Judicial Region
405 M.L.K Boulevard Drive, Georgetown, TX 78626
Tel: (512) 943-3777 Fax: (512) 943-3767
E-mail: presidingjudge3@wilco.org
Internet: www.courts.state.tx.us/3ajr/3ajr.asp

District Clerk, Hamilton County **Leoma Larance** . . . . (254) 386-1241
P.O. Box 187, Emory, TX 75440

County Clerk

Office of the County Clerk
102 North Rice Street, Suite 107, Hamilton, TX 76531
Fax: (254) 386-8727

County Clerk **Debbie Rudolph** . . . . (254) 386-1205
E-mail: countyclerk@hamiltoncountytx.org

Hansford County

District and County Clerk

Ninth Administrative Judicial Region
500 West Main, Room 204W, Brownfield, TX 79316
Tel: (806) 637-1329 Fax: (806) 637-8918
E-mail: kmoore@terrycounty.org

District and County Clerk, Hansford County **Kim Vera** . . . (806) 659-4110
15 NW Court, Spearman, TX 79081   Fax: (806) 659-4168
E-mail: kvera.cdc@co.hansford.tx.us

Hardeman County

District Clerk

Ninth Administrative Judicial Region
500 West Main, Room 204W, Brownfield, TX 79316
Tel: (806) 637-1329 Fax: (806) 637-8918
E-mail: kmoore@terrycounty.org

District and County Clerk, Hardeman County
Ellen London . . . . (940) 663-2961
P.O. Box 30, Quanah, TX 79252-0030

Hardin County

District Clerk

Second Administrative Judicial Region
301 North Thompson, Suite 102, Conroe, TX 77301
Tel: (936) 538-8176 Fax: (936) 538-8167
Internet: www.mctx.org/courts/second_administrative_judicial_region

District Clerk, Hardin County **Dana Hogg** . . . . (409) 246-5150
P.O. Box 2997, Kountze, TX 77625-2997

County Clerk

Office of the County Clerk
300 Monroe Street, Kountze, TX 77625
Fax: (409) 246-3208

County Clerk **Glenda Alston** . . . . (409) 246-5185

Harris County

District Clerk

Second Administrative Judicial Region
301 North Thompson, Suite 102, Conroe, TX 77301
Tel: (936) 538-8176 Fax: (936) 538-8167
Internet: www.mctx.org/courts/second_administrative_judicial_region

District Clerk, Harris County
Christopher "Chris" Daniel . . . . (713) 755-5749
P.O. Box 4651, Houston, TX 77210-4651

(continued on next page)

Texas Court Clerks and Courthouses *continued*

County Clerk

Office of the County Clerk
201 Caroline Street, 4th Floor, Houston, TX 77002
P.O. Box 1525, Houston, TX 77251-1525
Fax: (713) 755-4977
Internet: www.cclerk.hctx.net

County Clerk **Stan Stanart** . . . . (713) 755-6411
E-mail: sstanart@cco.hctx.net

Harrison County

District Clerk

First Administrative Judicial Region
133 North Riverfront Boulevard, 5th Floor, Dallas, TX 75207
Tel: (214) 653-2943 Fax: (214) 653-2957
Internet: www.firstadmin.com

District Clerk, Harrison County **Melinda Craig** . . . . (903) 935-8409
200 West Houston, Suite 234,
Marshall, TX 75671

County Clerk

Office of the County Clerk
200 West Houston, Suite 143, Marshall, TX 75670
Fax: (903) 935-4877

County Clerk **Patsy Cox** . . . . (903) 935-8403 ext. 1030

Hartley County

District Clerk

Ninth Administrative Judicial Region
500 West Main, Room 204W, Brownfield, TX 79316
Tel: (806) 637-1329 Fax: (806) 637-8918
E-mail: kmoore@terrycounty.org

District Clerk, Hartley County **Melissa Mead** . . . . (806) 235-3582
P.O Box Q, Channing, TX 79018-0189

County Clerk

Office of the County Clerk
P.O. Box 189, Channing, TX 79018
Fax: (806) 235-2316

County Clerk **Melissa Mead** . . . . (806) 235-3582 ext. 101
E-mail: melissa.mead@co.hartley.tx.us

Haskell County

District Clerk

Seventh Administrative Judicial Region
Midland County Courthouse, 500 North Loraine Street, Suite 502,
Midland, TX 79701
Tel: (432) 688-4370 Fax: (432) 688-4933
Internet: www.courts.state.tx.us/7ajr/7ajr.asp

District Clerk, Haskell County
Penny Young Anderson . . . . (940) 864-2030
P.O. Box 27, Haskell, TX 79521-0027

Texas Court Clerks and Courthouses *continued*

County Clerk

Office of the County Clerk
P.O. Box 725, Haskell, TX 79521
Fax: (940) 864-6164

County Clerk **Belia Abila** . . . . (940) 864-2451
E-mail: belia.abila@co.haskell.tx.us

Hays County

District Clerk

Third Administrative Judicial Region
405 M.L.K Boulevard Drive, Georgetown, TX 78626
Tel: (512) 943-3777 Fax: (512) 943-3767
E-mail: presidingjudge3@wilco.org
Internet: www.courts.state.tx.us/3ajr/3ajr.asp

District Clerk, Hays County **Beverly Crumley** . . . . (512) 393-7660
712 South Stagecoach Trail, Suite 2211,
San Marcos, TX 78666-5542

County Clerk

Office of the County Clerk
Hays County Government Center, 712 South Stagecoach Trail,
Suite 2008, San Marcos, TX 78666
Fax: (512) 393-7735

County Clerk **Liz Gonzalez** . . . . (512) 393-7738
E-mail: ccsearches@co.hays.tx.us

Hemphill County

District Clerk and County Clerk

Ninth Administrative Judicial Region
500 West Main, Room 204W, Brownfield, TX 79316
Tel: (806) 637-1329 Fax: (806) 637-8918
E-mail: kmoore@terrycounty.org

District and County Clerk, Hemphill County
Lisa Johnson . . . . (806) 323-6212
P.O. Box 867, Canadian, TX 79014-0867   Fax: (806) 323-9745
E-mail: lisaj@hemphill-clerk.com

Henderson County

District Clerk

First Administrative Judicial Region
133 North Riverfront Boulevard, 5th Floor, Dallas, TX 75207
Tel: (214) 653-2943 Fax: (214) 653-2957
Internet: www.firstadmin.com

District Clerk, Henderson County **Jean Godwin** . . . . (903) 675-6115
100 East Tyler, Room 203,
Athens, TX 75751

County Clerk

Office of the County Clerk
125 North Prairieville Street, Room 101, Athens, TX 75751
Fax: (903) 675-6105

County Clerk **Mary Margaret Wright** . . . . (903) 675-6140
E-mail: mwright@co.henderson.tx.us

Hidalgo County

District Clerk

Fifth Administrative Judicial Region
200 North Almond Street, Alice, TX 78332
Tel: (361) 668-5766 Fax: (512) 367-5788
E-mail: fifth.region@yahoo.com
Internet: www.courts.state.tx.us/5ajr/5ajr.asp

District Clerk, Hidalgo County **Laura Hinojosa** . . . . (956) 318-2200
100 North Closner, First Floor,
Edinburg, TX 78539

County Clerk

Office of the County Clerk
100 North Closner, 1st Floor, Edinburg, TX 78539
P.O. Box 58, Edinburg, TX 78540
Fax: (956) 318-2105
Internet: www.hidalgocountyclerk.us

County Clerk **Arturo Guajardo, Jr.** . . . . (956) 318-2100
E-mail: aguajardo@hidalgocountyclerk.us

Hill County

District Clerk

Third Administrative Judicial Region
405 M.L.K Boulevard Drive, Georgetown, TX 78626
Tel: (512) 943-3777 Fax: (512) 943-3767
E-mail: presidingjudge3@wilco.org
Internet: www.courts.state.tx.us/3ajr/3ajr.asp

District Clerk, Hill County **Angelia Orr** . . . . (254) 582-4042
P.O. Box 634, Hillsboro, TX 76645-0634

County Clerk

Office of the County Clerk
P.O. Box 398, Hillsboro, TX 76645
Fax: (254) 582-4003

County Clerk **Nicole Tanner** . . . . (254) 582-4030
E-mail: countyclerk@co.hill.tx.us

Hockley County

District Clerk

Ninth Administrative Judicial Region
500 West Main, Room 204W, Brownfield, TX 79316
Tel: (806) 637-1329 Fax: (806) 637-8918
E-mail: kmoore@terrycounty.org

District Clerk, Hockley County **Dennis Price** . . . . (806) 894-8527
802 Houston Street, Suite 316,
Levelland, TX 79336-4545

County Clerk

Office of the County Clerk
802 Houston Street, Suite 213, Levelland, TX 79336

County Clerk **Irene Gumula** . . . . (806) 894-3185
E-mail: igumula@hockleycounty.org

Hood County

District Clerk

Eighth Administrative Judicial Region
401 West Belknap, 5th Floor, Fort Worth, TX 76196
Tel: (817) 884-1558 Fax: (817) 884-1560
E-mail: 8thadmin@8thjudicialregion.com

District Clerk, Hood County **Tonna Trumble Hitt** . . . . (817) 579-3236
1200 West Pearl Street, Granbury, TX 76048

County Clerk

Office of the County Clerk
P.O. Box 339, Granbury, TX 76048
Fax: (817) 579-3441

County Clerk **Katie Lang** . . . . (817) 579-3222
E-mail: klang@co.hood.tx.us

Hopkins County

District Clerk

First Administrative Judicial Region
133 North Riverfront Boulevard, 5th Floor, Dallas, TX 75207
Tel: (214) 653-2943 Fax: (214) 653-2957
Internet: www.firstadmin.com

District Clerk, Hopkins County **Patricia Dorner** . . . . (903) 438-4082
P.O. Box 391, Sulphur Springs, TX 75483

County Clerk

Office of the County Clerk
128 Jefferson Street, Suite C, Sulphur Springs, TX 75482
Fax: (903) 438-4110

County Clerk **Debbie Shirley** . . . . (903) 438-4074
E-mail: cclerk@hopkinscountytx.org

Houston County

District Clerk

First Administrative Judicial Region
133 North Riverfront Boulevard, 5th Floor, Dallas, TX 75207
Tel: (214) 653-2943 Fax: (214) 653-2957
Internet: www.firstadmin.com

District Clerk, Houston County **Carolyn Rains** . . . . (936) 544-3255
P.O. Box 1186, Crockett, TX 75835-1186

County Clerk

Office of the County Clerk
P. O. Box 370, Crockett, TX 75835
401 East Houston Avenue, First Floor, Crockett, TX 75835
Fax: (936) 544-1954

County Clerk **Bridget Lamb** . . . . (936) 544-3255 ext. 240
E-mail: bridget.lamb@co.houston.tx.us

(continued on next page)

Howard County

District Clerk

Seventh Administrative Judicial Region
Midland County Courthouse, 500 North Loraine Street, Suite 502,
Midland, TX 79701
Tel: (432) 688-4370   Fax: (432) 688-4933
Internet: www.courts.state.tx.us/7ajr/7ajr.asp

District Clerk, Howard County **Colleen Barton** .... (432) 264-2223
  P.O. Drawer 2138, Big Spring, TX 79721-2138

County Clerk

Office of the County Clerk
P.O. Box 1468, Big Spring, TX 79721
Fax: (432) 264-2215

County Clerk **Donna Wright** .... (432) 264-2213
  E-mail: donna.wright@howardcountytx.com

Hudspeth County

District and County Clerk

Sixth Administrative Judicial Region
700 Main Street, Kerrville, TX 78028
Tel: (830) 792-2290   Fax: (830) 792-2294
E-mail: beckyh@co.kerr.tx.us
Internet: www.courts.state.tx.us/6ajr/6ajr.asp

District and County Clerk, Hudspeth County
  Virginia Doyal .... (915) 369-2301
  P.O. Drawer 58, Sierra Blanca, TX 79851-0058

Hunt County

District Clerk

First Administrative Judicial Region
133 North Riverfront Boulevard, 5th Floor, Dallas, TX 75207
Tel: (214) 653-2943   Fax: (214) 653-2957
Internet: www.firstadmin.com

District Clerk, Hunt County **Stacey Landrum** .... (903) 408-4172
  P.O. 1437, Greenville, TX 75403-1437

County Clerk

Office of the County Clerk
2507 Lee Street, Second Floor, Greenville, TX 75401
Fax: (903) 408-4287

County Clerk **Jennifer Lindenzweig** .... (903) 408-4130
  E-mail: jlindenzweig@huntcounty.net

Hutchinson County

District Clerk

Ninth Administrative Judicial Region
500 West Main, Room 204W, Brownfield, TX 79316
Tel: (806) 637-1329   Fax: (806) 637-8918
E-mail: kmoore@terrycounty.org

District Clerk, Hutchinson County **Robin Stroud** .... (806) 878-4017
  P.O. Box 580, Stinnett, TX 79083-1186

County Clerk

Office of the County Clerk
P.O. Box 1186, Stinnett, TX 79083
Fax: (806) 878-3497

County Clerk **Jan Barnes** .... (806) 878-4002
  E-mail: co.clerk@hutchinsoncnty.com

Irion County

District and County Clerk

Seventh Administrative Judicial Region
Midland County Courthouse, 500 North Loraine Street, Suite 502,
Midland, TX 79701
Tel: (432) 688-4370   Fax: (432) 688-4933
Internet: www.courts.state.tx.us/7ajr/7ajr.asp

District Clerk, Irion County **Molly Criner** .... (325) 835-2421
  P.O. Box 736, Mertzon, TX 76941-0736

Jack County

District Clerk

Eighth Administrative Judicial Region
401 West Belknap, 5th Floor, Fort Worth, TX 76196
Tel: (817) 884-1558   Fax: (817) 884-1560
E-mail: 8thadmin@8thjudicialregion.com

District Clerk, Jack County **Tracie Pippin** .... (940) 567-2141
  100 North Main Street, Suite 310,
  Jacksboro, TX 76458

County Clerk

Office of the County Clerk
100 Main Street, Suite 208, Jacksboro, TX 76458
Fax: (940) 567-6441

County Clerk **Janice "Jan" Robinson** .... (940) 567-2111
  E-mail: jrobinson@jackcounty.org

Jackson County

District Clerk

Fourth Administrative Judicial Region
100 Dolorosa, 5th Floor, San Antonio, TX 78205
Tel: (210) 335-3954   Fax: (210) 335-3955
Internet: www.courts.state.tx.us/4ajr/4ajr.asp

District Clerk, Jackson County **Sharon Mathis** .... (361) 782-3812
  115 West Main, Room 203,
  Edna, TX 77957

County Clerk

Office of the County Clerk
115 West Main, Room 101, Edna, TX 77957
Fax: (361) 782-3132

County Clerk **Barbara Williams** .... (361) 782-3563
  E-mail: jcclerk@co.jackson.tx.us

Jasper County

District Clerk

Second Administrative Judicial Region
301 North Thompson, Suite 102, Conroe, TX 77301
Tel: (936) 538-8176 Fax: (936) 538-8167
Internet: www.mctx.org/courts/second_administrative_judicial_region

District Clerk, Jasper County **Kathy Kent** . . . . (409) 384-2721
121 North Austin, Room 202,
Jasper, TX 75951

County Clerk

Office of the County Clerk
P.O. Box 2070, Jasper, TX 75951
Fax: (409) 384-7198

County Clerk **Debbie Newman** . . . .(409) 384-2632
E-mail: debbie.newman@co.jasper.tx.us

Jeff Davis County

District and County Clerk

Sixth Administrative Judicial Region
700 Main Street, Kerrville, TX 78028
Tel: (830) 792-2290 Fax: (830) 792-2294
E-mail: beckyh@co.kerr.tx.us
Internet: www.courts.state.tx.us/6ajr/6ajr.asp

District and County Clerk, Jeff Davis County
Jennifer Wright . . . . (432) 426-3251
P.O. Box 398, Fort Davis, TX 79734   Fax: (432) 426-3760

Jefferson County

District Clerk

Second Administrative Judicial Region
301 North Thompson, Suite 102, Conroe, TX 77301
Tel: (936) 538-8176 Fax: (936) 538-8167
Internet: www.mctx.org/courts/second_administrative_judicial_region

District Clerk, Jefferson County **Jamie Smith** . . . . (409) 835-8580
1001 Pearl Street, Suite 203,
Beaumont, TX 77701-3551

County Clerk

Office of the County Clerk
P.O. Box 1151, Beaumont, TX 77704
Fax: (409) 839-2394

County Clerk **Carolyn L. Guidry** . . . . (409) 835-8475

Jim Hogg County

District and County Clerk

Fifth Administrative Judicial Region
200 North Almond Street, Alice, TX 78332
Tel: (361) 668-5766 Fax: (512) 367-5788
E-mail: fifth.region@yahoo.com
Internet: www.courts.state.tx.us/5ajr/5ajr.asp

District Clerk, Jim Hogg County
Zonia Garza Morales . . . . (361) 527-4031
P.O. Box 878, Hebbronville, TX 78361

Jim Wells County

District Clerk

Fifth Administrative Judicial Region
200 North Almond Street, Alice, TX 78332
Tel: (361) 668-5766 Fax: (512) 367-5788
E-mail: fifth.region@yahoo.com
Internet: www.courts.state.tx.us/5ajr/5ajr.asp

District Clerk, Jim Wells County **R. David Guerrero** . . . . . (361) 668-5717
P.O. Drawer 2219, Alice, TX 78333-2219

County Clerk

Office of the County Clerk
P.O. Box 1459, Alice, TX 78333
Fax: (361) 661-1372

County Clerk **J.C. Perez III** . . . .(361) 668-5702
E-mail: jc.perez@co.jim-wells.tx.us

Johnson County

District Clerk

Eighth Administrative Judicial Region
401 West Belknap, 5th Floor, Fort Worth, TX 76196
Tel: (817) 884-1558 Fax: (817) 884-1560
E-mail: 8thadmin@8thjudicialregion.com

District Clerk, Johnson County **David Lloyd** . . . . (817) 556-6839
P.O. Drawer 495, Cleburne, TX 76033-0495

County Clerk

Office of the County Clerk
PO Box 662, Cleburne, TX 76033
Guinn Justice Center, 204 South Buffalo Ave, Room 407,
Cleburne, TX 76033
Fax: (817) 556-6710

County Clerk **Becky Ivey** . . . . (817) 556-6323
E-mail: becky@johnsoncountytx.org

Jones County

District Clerk

Seventh Administrative Judicial Region
Midland County Courthouse, 500 North Loraine Street, Suite 502,
Midland, TX 79701
Tel: (432) 688-4370 Fax: (432) 688-4933
Internet: www.courts.state.tx.us/7ajr/7ajr.asp

District Clerk, Jones County **Lacey Hansen** . . . . (325) 823-3731
P.O. Box 308, Anson, TX 79501-0308

County Clerk

Office of the County Clerk
P.O. Box 552, Anson, TX 79501
Fax: (325) 823-3979

County Clerk **LeeAnn Jennings** . . . . (325) 823-3762
E-mail: leeann.jennings@co.jones.tx.us

(continued on next page)

Karnes County

District Clerk

Fourth Administrative Judicial Region
100 Dolorosa, 5th Floor, San Antonio, TX 78205
Tel: (210) 335-3954 Fax: (210) 335-3955
Internet: www.courts.state.tx.us/4ajr/4ajr.asp

District Clerk, Karnes County **Denise Rodriguez** . . . . (830) 780-2562
   210 West Calvert, Room 180,
   Karnes City, TX 78118-2959

County Clerk

Office of the County Clerk
210 West Calvert, Suite 100, Karnes City, TX 78118
Fax: (830) 780-4576

County Clerk **Carol Swize** . . . . (830) 780-3938
   E-mail: carol.swize@co.karnes.tx.us

Kaufman County

District Clerk

First Administrative Judicial Region
133 North Riverfront Boulevard, 5th Floor, Dallas, TX 75207
Tel: (214) 653-2943 Fax: (214) 653-2957
Internet: www.firstadmin.com

District Clerk, Kaufman County **Rhonda Hughey** . . . . (972) 932-0279
   100 West Mulberry, Kaufman, TX 75142

County Clerk

Office of the County Clerk
100 West Mulberry, Kaufman, TX 75142
Fax: (972) 962-8018

County Clerk **Laura Hughes** . . . . (972) 932-4331 ext. 1104
   E-mail: countyclerk@kaufmancounty.net

Kendall County

District Clerk

Sixth Administrative Judicial Region
700 Main Street, Kerrville, TX 78028
Tel: (830) 792-2290 Fax: (830) 792-2294
E-mail: beckyh@co.kerr.tx.us
Internet: www.courts.state.tx.us/6ajr/6ajr.asp

District Clerk, Kendall County **Susan Jackson** . . . . (830) 249-9343
   201 East San Antonio Street, Suite 201,
   Boerne, TX 78006-2032

County Clerk

Office of the County Clerk
201 East San Antonio Drive, Suite 127, Boerne, TX 78006
Fax: (830) 249-3472

County Clerk **Darlene Herrin** . . . . (830) 249-9343 ext. 230
   E-mail: darlene.herrin@co.kendall.tx.us

Kenedy County

District and County Clerk

Fifth Administrative Judicial Region
200 North Almond Street, Alice, TX 78332
Tel: (361) 668-5766 Fax: (512) 367-5788
E-mail: fifth.region@yahoo.com
Internet: www.courts.state.tx.us/5ajr/5ajr.asp

District Clerk, Kenedy County **Veronica Vela** . . . . (361) 294-5220
   101 Mallory Street, Sarita, TX 78385

Kent County

District and County Clerk

Seventh Administrative Judicial Region
Midland County Courthouse, 500 North Loraine Street, Suite 502,
Midland, TX 79701
Tel: (432) 688-4370 Fax: (432) 688-4933
Internet: www.courts.state.tx.us/7ajr/7ajr.asp

District Clerk, Kent County **Craig Harrison** . . . . (806) 237-3881
   P.O. Box 9, Jayton, TX 79528-0009

Kerr County

District Clerk

Sixth Administrative Judicial Region
700 Main Street, Kerrville, TX 78028
Tel: (830) 792-2290 Fax: (830) 792-2294
E-mail: beckyh@co.kerr.tx.us
Internet: www.courts.state.tx.us/6ajr/6ajr.asp

District Clerk, Kerr County **Robbin Burlew** . . . . (830) 792-2281
   700 Main Street, Kerrville, TX 78028

County Clerk

Office of the County Clerk
700 East Main Street, Suite 122, Kerrville, TX 78028
Fax: (830) 792-2274

County Clerk **Rebecca Bolin** . . . . (830) 792-2255
   E-mail: bbolin@co.kerr.tx.us

Kimble County

District and County Clerk

Sixth Administrative Judicial Region
700 Main Street, Kerrville, TX 78028
Tel: (830) 792-2290 Fax: (830) 792-2294
E-mail: beckyh@co.kerr.tx.us
Internet: www.courts.state.tx.us/6ajr/6ajr.asp

District Clerk, Kimble County **Haydee Torres** . . . . (325) 446-3353
   501 Main Street, Junction, TX 76849-4763

King County

District and County Clerk

Ninth Administrative Judicial Region
500 West Main, Room 204W, Brownfield, TX 79316
Tel: (806) 637-1329 Fax: (806) 637-8918
E-mail: kmoore@terrycounty.org

District Clerk, King County **Jammye D. Timmons** . . . . . . (806) 596-4412
   P.O. Box 135, Guthrie, TX 79236-0135

Kinney County

District and County Clerk

Sixth Administrative Judicial Region
700 Main Street, Kerrville, TX 78028
Tel: (830) 792-2290 Fax: (830) 792-2294
E-mail: beckyh@co.kerr.tx.us
Internet: www.courts.state.tx.us/6ajr/6ajr.asp

District Clerk, Kinney County **Dora Elia Sandoval** . . . . . . (830) 563-2521
P.O. Drawer 9, Brackettville, TX 78832-0009

Kleberg County

District Clerk

Fifth Administrative Judicial Region
200 North Almond Street, Alice, TX 78332
Tel: (361) 668-5766 Fax: (512) 367-5788
E-mail: fifth.region@yahoo.com
Internet: www.courts.state.tx.us/5ajr/5ajr.asp

District Clerk, Kleberg County **Jennifer Whittington** . . . . (361) 595-8561
P.O. Box 312, Kingsville, TX 78364-0312

County Clerk

Office of the County Clerk
P.O. Box 1327, Kingsville, TX 78364
Fax: (361) 593-1355

County Clerk **Stephanie G. Garza** . . . . (361) 595-8548
E-mail: sagrza@klebergco.com

Knox County

District and County Clerk

Ninth Administrative Judicial Region
500 West Main, Room 204W, Brownfield, TX 79316
Tel: (806) 637-1329 Fax: (806) 637-8918
E-mail: kmoore@terrycounty.org

District Clerk, Knox County **Annette Offutt** . . . . (940) 459-2441
P.O. Box 196, Benjamin, TX 79505-0196

La Salle County

District and County Clerk

Fourth Administrative Judicial Region
100 Dolorosa, 5th Floor, San Antonio, TX 78205
Tel: (210) 335-3954 Fax: (210) 335-3955
Internet: www.courts.state.tx.us/4ajr/4ajr.asp

District Clerk, La Salle County **Margarita A. Esqueda** . . . (830) 879-4432
101 Courthouse Square, Suite 107,
Cotulla, TX 78014

Lamar County

District Clerk

First Administrative Judicial Region
133 North Riverfront Boulevard, 5th Floor, Dallas, TX 75207
Tel: (214) 653-2943 Fax: (214) 653-2957
Internet: www.firstadmin.com

District Clerk, Lamar County **Marvin Ann Patterson** . . . . (903) 737-2427
119 North Main, Room 405,
Paris, TX 75460

County Clerk

Office of the County Clerk
119 North Main, Paris, TX 75460
Fax: (903) 782-1100

County Clerk **Russ Towers** . . . . (903) 737-2420

Lamb County

District Clerk

Ninth Administrative Judicial Region
500 West Main, Room 204W, Brownfield, TX 79316
Tel: (806) 637-1329 Fax: (806) 637-8918
E-mail: kmoore@terrycounty.org

District Clerk, Lamb County **Stephanie Chester** . . . . (806) 385-4222
100 Sixth Drive, Room 212,
Littlefield, TX 79339-3366

County Clerk

Office of the County Clerk
100 Sixth Drive, Room 103, Littlefield, TX 79339
Fax: (806) 385-6485

County Clerk **Tonya Elaine Ritchie** . . . . (806) 385-4222 ext. 210
E-mail: tonyaritchie@nts-online.net

Lampasas County

District Clerk

Third Administrative Judicial Region
405 M.L.K Boulevard Drive, Georgetown, TX 78626
Tel: (512) 943-3777 Fax: (512) 943-3767
E-mail: presidingjudge3@wilco.org
Internet: www.courts.state.tx.us/3ajr/3ajr.asp

District Clerk, Lampasas County **Terri Cox** . . . . (512) 556-8271
P.O. Box 327, Lampasas, TX 76550-0324

County Clerk

Office of the County Clerk
P.O. Box 347, Lampasas, TX 76550
Tel: (512) 556-8271 Fax: (512) 556-8966

County Clerk **Connie Hartmann** . . . . (512) 556-8271
E-mail: chartmann@co.lampasas.tx.us

Lavaca County

District Clerk

Third Administrative Judicial Region
405 M.L.K Boulevard Drive, Georgetown, TX 78626
Tel: (512) 943-3777 Fax: (512) 943-3767
E-mail: presidingjudge3@wilco.org
Internet: www.courts.state.tx.us/3ajr/3ajr.asp

District Clerk, Lavaca County **Sherry Henke** . . . . (361) 798-2351
109 North La Grange Street,
Hallettsville, TX 77964

County Clerk

Office of the County Clerk
P.O. Box 326, Hallettsville, TX 77964
Fax: (361) 798-1610

County Clerk **Elizabeth A. Kouba** . . . . (361) 798-3612
E-mail: elizabethk@co.lavaca.tx.us

(continued on next page)

Lee County

District Clerk

Second Administrative Judicial Region
301 North Thompson, Suite 102, Conroe, TX 77301
Tel: (936) 538-8176   Fax: (936) 538-8167
Internet: www.mctx.org/courts/second_administrative_judicial_region

District Clerk, Lee County **Lisa Teinert** . . . . (979) 542-3684
   P.O. Box 176, Giddings, TX 78942-0176

County Clerk

Office of the County Clerk
P.O. Box 419, Giddings, TX 78942
Fax: (979) 542-2623

County Clerk **Sharon Blasig** . . . . (979) 542-3684
   E-mail: sharon.blasig@co.lee.tx.us

Leon County

District Clerk

Second Administrative Judicial Region
301 North Thompson, Suite 102, Conroe, TX 77301
Tel: (936) 538-8176   Fax: (936) 538-8167
Internet: www.mctx.org/courts/second_administrative_judicial_region

District Clerk, Leon County **Diane Oden Davis** . . . . (903) 536-2227
   P.O. Box 39, Centerville, TX 75833-0039

County Clerk

Office of the County Clerk
P.O. Box 98, Centerville, TX 75833
Fax: (903) 536-7581

County Clerk **Christie Wakefield** . . . . (903) 536-2352
   E-mail: christie.wakefield@co.leon.tx.us

Liberty County

District Clerk

Second Administrative Judicial Region
301 North Thompson, Suite 102, Conroe, TX 77301
Tel: (936) 538-8176   Fax: (936) 538-8167
Internet: www.mctx.org/courts/second_administrative_judicial_region

District Clerk, Liberty County **Donna G. Brown** . . . . (936) 336-4682
   1923 Sam Houston, Room 115,
   Liberty, TX 77575-4847

County Clerk

Office of the County Clerk
P.O. Box 369, Liberty, TX 77575
Fax: (936) 334-8174

County Clerk **Paulette Shivers Williams** . . . . (936) 336-4670

Limestone County

District Clerk

Second Administrative Judicial Region
301 North Thompson, Suite 102, Conroe, TX 77301
Tel: (936) 538-8176   Fax: (936) 538-8167
Internet: www.mctx.org/courts/second_administrative_judicial_region

District Clerk, Limestone County **Carol Sue Jenkins** . . . . (254) 729-3206
   P.O. Box 230, Groesbeck, TX 76642-0230

County Clerk

Office of the County Clerk
P.O. Box 350, Groesbeck, TX 76642
Fax: (254) 729-2951

County Clerk **Peggy Beck** . . . . (254) 729-5504
   E-mail: coclerk@co.limestone.tx.us

Lipscomb County

District and County Clerk

Ninth Administrative Judicial Region
500 West Main, Room 204W, Brownfield, TX 79316
Tel: (806) 637-1329   Fax: (806) 637-8918
E-mail: kmoore@terrycounty.org

District and County Clerk, Lipscomb County **Kim Blau** . . . (806) 862-3091
   P.O. Box 70, Lipscomb, TX 79056-0070

Live Oak County

District Clerk

Fourth Administrative Judicial Region
100 Dolorosa, 5th Floor, San Antonio, TX 78205
Tel: (210) 335-3954   Fax: (210) 335-3955
Internet: www.courts.state.tx.us/4ajr/4ajr.asp

District Clerk, Live Oak County **Melanie Matkin** . . . . (361) 449-2733
   P.O. Box 440, George West, TX 78022-0440

County Clerk

Office of the County Clerk
P.O. Box 280, George West, TX 78022
Fax: (361) 449-1616

County Clerk **Ida Vasquez** . . . . (361) 449-2733
   E-mail: cclerk@co.live-oak.tx.us

Llano County

District Clerk

Third Administrative Judicial Region
405 M.L.K Boulevard Drive, Georgetown, TX 78626
Tel: (512) 943-3777   Fax: (512) 943-3767
E-mail: presidingjudge3@wilco.org
Internet: www.courts.state.tx.us/3ajr/3ajr.asp

District Clerk, Llano County **Joyce Gillow** . . . . (325) 247-5036
   832 Ford Street, Llano, TX 78643-1920

County Clerk

Office of the County Clerk
P.O. Box 40, Llano, TX 78643
107 West Sandstone, Llano, TX 78643
Fax: (325) 247-2406

County Clerk **Marci Hadeler** . . . . (325) 247-4455
   E-mail: coclerk@co.llano.tx.us

Loving County

District and County Clerk

Seventh Administrative Judicial Region
Midland County Courthouse, 500 North Loraine Street, Suite 502,
Midland, TX 79701
Tel: (432) 688-4370 Fax: (432) 688-4933
Internet: www.courts.state.tx.us/7ajr/7ajr.asp

District Clerk, Loving County **Mozelle Carr** . . . . (432) 377-2441
  100 Bell Street, Mentone, TX 79754

Lubbock County

District Clerk

Ninth Administrative Judicial Region
500 West Main, Room 204W, Brownfield, TX 79316
Tel: (806) 637-1329 Fax: (806) 637-8918
E-mail: kmoore@terrycounty.org

District Clerk, Lubbock County **Barbara M. Sucsy** . . . . . . (806) 775-1310
  P.O. Box 10536, Lubbock, TX 79408-3536

County Clerk

County Clerk's Office
904 Broadway, Room 207, Lubbock, TX 79401
Tel: (806) 775-1076 Fax: (806) 775-1660

County Clerk **Kelly J. Pinion** . . . . (806) 775-1076
  E-mail: kpinion@co.lubbock.tx.us

Lynn County

District Clerk

Seventh Administrative Judicial Region
Midland County Courthouse, 500 North Loraine Street, Suite 502,
Midland, TX 79701
Tel: (432) 688-4370 Fax: (432) 688-4933
Internet: www.courts.state.tx.us/7ajr/7ajr.asp

District Clerk, Lynn County **Sandra Laws** . . . . (806) 561-4274
  P.O. Box 2688, Tahoka, TX 79373-0939

County Clerk

Office of the County Clerk
P.O. Box 937, Tahoka, TX 79373
Fax: (806) 561-4988

County Clerk **Susan Tipton** . . . . (806) 561-4750
  E-mail: susan.tipton@co.lynn.tx.us

Madison County

District Clerk

Second Administrative Judicial Region
301 North Thompson, Suite 102, Conroe, TX 77301
Tel: (936) 538-8176 Fax: (936) 538-8167
Internet: www.mctx.org/courts/second_administrative_judicial_region

District Clerk, Madison County **Rhonda Savage** . . . . (936) 348-9203
  101 West Main, Room 226,
  Madisonville, TX 77864-1901

County Clerk

Office of the County Clerk
103 West Main Street, Room 104, Madisonville, TX 77864
Fax: (936) 241-6211

County Clerk **Susanne Morris** . . . . (936) 241-6210
  E-mail: susanne.morris@madisoncountytx.org

Marion County

District Clerk

First Administrative Judicial Region
133 North Riverfront Boulevard, 5th Floor, Dallas, TX 75207
Tel: (214) 653-2943 Fax: (214) 653-2957
Internet: www.firstadmin.com

District Clerk, Marion County **Janie McCay** . . . . (903) 665-2441
  P.O. Box 628, Jefferson, TX 75657-0628

County Clerk

Office of the County Clerk
102 West Austin Street, Room 206, Jefferson, TX 75657
Fax: (903) 665-7936

County Clerk **Vickie Wray Smith** . . . . (903) 665-3971
  E-mail: vickie.smith@co.marion.tx.us

Martin County

District Clerk

Seventh Administrative Judicial Region
Midland County Courthouse, 500 North Loraine Street, Suite 502,
Midland, TX 79701
Tel: (432) 688-4370 Fax: (432) 688-4933
Internet: www.courts.state.tx.us/7ajr/7ajr.asp

District Clerk and County Clerk, Martin County
  Sharon Jones . . . . (432) 756-3412
  P.O. Box 906, Stanton, TX 79782-0906

Mason County

District and County Clerk

Sixth Administrative Judicial Region
700 Main Street, Kerrville, TX 78028
Tel: (830) 792-2290 Fax: (830) 792-2294
E-mail: beckyh@co.kerr.tx.us
Internet: www.courts.state.tx.us/6ajr/6ajr.asp

District and County Clerk, Mason County
  Pam G. Beam . . . . (325) 347-5253
  P.O. Box 702, Mason, TX 76856-0702

Matagorda County

District Clerk

Second Administrative Judicial Region
301 North Thompson, Suite 102, Conroe, TX 77301
Tel: (936) 538-8176 Fax: (936) 538-8167
Internet: www.mctx.org/courts/second_administrative_judicial_region

District Clerk, Matagorda County **Jamie Bludau** . . . . (979) 244-7621
  1700 Seventh, Room 307, Bay City, TX 77414

(continued on next page)

Texas Court Clerks and Courthouses *continued*

County Clerk

Office of the County Clerk
1700 Seventh Street, Room 202, Bay City, TX 77414
Fax: (979) 244-7688

County Clerk **Janet Hickl** . . . . (979) 244-7680
  E-mail: pjmahickl@sbcglobal.net

Maverick County

District Clerk

Fourth Administrative Judicial Region
100 Dolorosa, 5th Floor, San Antonio, TX 78205
Tel: (210) 335-3954 Fax: (210) 335-3955
Internet: www.courts.state.tx.us/4ajr/4ajr.asp

District Clerk, Maverick County **Irene Rodriguez** . . . . (830) 773-2629
  500 Quarry Street, Suite 5,
  Eagle Pass, TX 78852-2798

County Clerk

Office of the County Clerk
500 Quarry Street, Suite Two, Eagle Pass, TX 78852
Fax: (830) 752-4479

County Clerk **Sara Montemayor** . . . . (830) 773-2829
  E-mail: sara.montemayor@co.maverick.tx.us

McCulloch County

District Clerk

Sixth Administrative Judicial Region
700 Main Street, Kerrville, TX 78028
Tel: (830) 792-2290 Fax: (830) 792-2294
E-mail: beckyh@co.kerr.tx.us
Internet: www.courts.state.tx.us/6ajr/6ajr.asp

District Clerk, McCulloch County
  Michelle Pitcox . . . . (325) 597-0733 ext. 1
  199 Courthouse Square, Room 103,   Fax: (325) 597-0606
  Brady, TX 76825

County Clerk

Office of the County Clerk
101 North High, Brady, TX 76825
Fax: (325) 597-1731

County Clerk **Tina Smith** . . . . (325) 597-2400 ext. 2
  E-mail: mccoclerk1@verizon.net

McLennan County

District Clerk

Third Administrative Judicial Region
405 M.L.K Boulevard Drive, Georgetown, TX 78626
Tel: (512) 943-3777 Fax: (512) 943-3767
E-mail: presidingjudge3@wilco.org
Internet: www.courts.state.tx.us/3ajr/3ajr.asp

District Clerk, McLennan County **Karen Matkin** . . . . (254) 757-5054
  P.O. Box 2451, Waco, TX 76703-2451

Texas Court Clerks and Courthouses *continued*

County Clerk

Office of the County Clerk
215 North 5th Street, Room 223-A, Waco, TX 76701
Tel: (254) 757-5078 Fax: (254) 757-5146

County Clerk **J. A. "Andy" Harwell** . . . . (254) 757-5078

McMullen County

District and County Clerk

Fourth Administrative Judicial Region
100 Dolorosa, 5th Floor, San Antonio, TX 78205
Tel: (210) 335-3954 Fax: (210) 335-3955
Internet: www.courts.state.tx.us/4ajr/4ajr.asp

District Clerk, McMullen County **Dorairene Garza** . . . . . . (361) 274-3215
  P.O. Box 235, Tilden, TX 78072-0235

Medina County

District Clerk

Sixth Administrative Judicial Region
700 Main Street, Kerrville, TX 78028
Tel: (830) 792-2290 Fax: (830) 792-2294
E-mail: beckyh@co.kerr.tx.us
Internet: www.courts.state.tx.us/6ajr/6ajr.asp

District Clerk, Medina County **Cindy Fowler** . . . . (830) 741-6070
  1100 16th Street, Room 209,
  Hondo, TX 78861-1841

County Clerk

Office of the County Clerk
1100 16th Street, Room 109, Hondo, TX 78861
Fax: (830) 741-6015

County Clerk **Lisa Wernette** . . . . (830) 741-6040
  E-mail: countyclerk@medinacountytexas.org

Menard County

District and County Clerk

Sixth Administrative Judicial Region
700 Main Street, Kerrville, TX 78028
Tel: (830) 792-2290 Fax: (830) 792-2294
E-mail: beckyh@co.kerr.tx.us
Internet: www.courts.state.tx.us/6ajr/6ajr.asp

District and County Clerk, Menard County
  Ann Kothman . . . . (325) 396-4682
  P.O. Box 1038, Menard, TX 76859   Fax: (325) 396-2047

Midland County

District Clerk

Seventh Administrative Judicial Region
Midland County Courthouse, 500 North Loraine Street, Suite 502,
Midland, TX 79701
Tel: (432) 688-4370 Fax: (432) 688-4933
Internet: www.courts.state.tx.us/7ajr/7ajr.asp

District Clerk, Midland County **Ross Bush** . . . . (432) 688-4500
  500 North Lorraine, Suite 300,
  Midland, TX 79701

County Clerk

Office of the County Clerk
500 North Loraine Street, Fourth Floor, Midland, TX 79701
Fax: (432) 688-4926

County Clerk **Alison Haley** . . . . (432) 688-4403
E-mail: alison_haley@co.midland.tx.us

Milam County

District Clerk

Third Administrative Judicial Region
405 M.L.K Boulevard Drive, Georgetown, TX 78626
Tel: (512) 943-3777 Fax: (512) 943-3767
E-mail: presidingjudge3@wilco.org
Internet: www.courts.state.tx.us/3ajr/3ajr.asp

District Clerk, Milam County **Cindy Fechner** . . . .(254) 697-7052
102 South Fannin Street, Suite 5,
Cameron, TX 76520-4200

County Clerk

Office of the County Clerk
107 West Main Street, Cameron, TX 76520
Fax: (254) 697-7055

County Clerk **Barbara Vansa** . . . .(254) 697-7049
E-mail: milamcoclk@milamcounty.net

Mills County

District and County Clerk

Seventh Administrative Judicial Region
Midland County Courthouse, 500 North Loraine Street, Suite 502,
Midland, TX 79701
Tel: (432) 688-4370 Fax: (432) 688-4933
Internet: www.courts.state.tx.us/7ajr/7ajr.asp

District Clerk, Mills County **Carolyn Foster** . . . .(325) 648-2711
P.O. Box 646, Goldthwaite, TX 76844-0646

Mitchell County

District Clerk

Seventh Administrative Judicial Region
Midland County Courthouse, 500 North Loraine Street, Suite 502,
Midland, TX 79701
Tel: (432) 688-4370 Fax: (432) 688-4933
Internet: www.courts.state.tx.us/7ajr/7ajr.asp

District Clerk, Mitchell County **Belinda Blassingame** . . . (325) 728-5918
349 Oak Street, Room 302,
Colorado City, TX 79373-0939

County Clerk

Office of the County Clerk
349 Oak Street, Room 103, Colorado City, TX 79512
Fax: (325) 728-5322

County Clerk **Debby Carlock** . . . .(325) 728-3481
E-mail: dscarlock@co.mitchell.tx.us

Montague County

District Clerk

Eighth Administrative Judicial Region
401 West Belknap, 5th Floor, Fort Worth, TX 76196
Tel: (817) 884-1558 Fax: (817) 884-1560
E-mail: 8thadmin@8thjudicialregion.com

District Clerk, Montague County **Lesia Darden** . . . . (940) 894-2461
P.O. Drawer 155, Montague, TX 76251-0155

County Clerk

Office of the County Clerk
P.O. Box 77, Montague, TX 76251
Fax: (940) 894-6601

County Clerk **Glenda Henson** . . . .(940) 894-2461
E-mail: mcoclerk@windstream.net

Montgomery County

District Clerk

Second Administrative Judicial Region
301 North Thompson, Suite 102, Conroe, TX 77301
Tel: (936) 538-8176 Fax: (936) 538-8167
Internet: www.mctx.org/courts/second_administrative_judicial_region

District Clerk, Montgomery County
Barbara Gladden Adamick . . . . (936) 539-7855
P.O. Box 2985, Conroe, TX 77305-2985

County Clerk

Office of the County Clerk
210 West Davis, Conroe, TX 77301
Tel: (936) 539-7885 Fax: (936) 760-6990 (Courts)
Fax: (936) 760-6927 (Records)

County Clerk **Mark Turnbull** . . . . (936) 539-7885

Moore County

District Clerk

Ninth Administrative Judicial Region
500 West Main, Room 204W, Brownfield, TX 79316
Tel: (806) 637-1329 Fax: (806) 637-8918
E-mail: kmoore@terrycounty.org

District Clerk, Moore County **Diane Hoefling** . . . . (806) 935-4218
715 South Dumas Avenue, Room 109,
Dumas, TX 79029-4326

County Clerk

Office of the County Clerk
715 South Dumas Avenue, Room 107, Dumas, TX 79029
Fax: (806) 935-9004

County Clerk **Brenda McKanna** . . . . (806) 935-2009
E-mail: bmckanna@moore-tx.com

(continued on next page)

Morris County

District Clerk

First Administrative Judicial Region
133 North Riverfront Boulevard, 5th Floor, Dallas, TX 75207
Tel: (214) 653-2943 Fax: (214) 653-2957
Internet: www.firstadmin.com

District Clerk, Morris County **Gwen Oney** . . . . (903) 645-2321
  500 Broadnax Street, Daingerfield, TX 75638-1337

County Clerk

Office of the County Clerk
500 Broadnax, Suite D, Daingerfield, TX 75638
Fax: (903) 645-4026

County Clerk **Scott Sartain** . . . . (903) 645-3911
  E-mail: scott.sartain@co.morris.tx.us

Motley County

District and County Clerk

Ninth Administrative Judicial Region
500 West Main, Room 204W, Brownfield, TX 79316
Tel: (806) 637-1329 Fax: (806) 637-8918
E-mail: kmoore@terrycounty.org

District Clerk, Motley County **Kate Hurt** . . . . (806) 347-2621
  P.O. Box 660, Matador, TX 79244-0660

Nacogdoches County

District Clerk

First Administrative Judicial Region
133 North Riverfront Boulevard, 5th Floor, Dallas, TX 75207
Tel: (214) 653-2943 Fax: (214) 653-2957
Internet: www.firstadmin.com

District Clerk, Nacogdoches County
  Loretta Cammack . . . . (936) 560-7740
  101 West Main, Room 210,
  Nacogdoches, TX 75961-4832

County Clerk

Office of the County Clerk
101 West Main Street, Suite 110, Nacogdoches, TX 75961
Fax: (936) 559-5926

County Clerk **June Clifton** . . . . (936) 560-7733
  E-mail: county.clerk@co.nacogdoches.tx.us

Navarro County

District Clerk

Third Administrative Judicial Region
405 M.L.K Boulevard Drive, Georgetown, TX 78626
Tel: (512) 943-3777 Fax: (512) 943-3767
E-mail: presidingjudge3@wilco.org
Internet: www.courts.state.tx.us/3ajr/3ajr.asp

District Clerk, Navarro County **Joshua B. Tackett** . . . . (903) 654-3040
  P.O. Box 1439, Corsicana, TX 75151-1439

County Clerk

Office of the County Clerk
800 North Main, Corsicana, TX 75110
Tel: (903) 654-3035 Fax: (903) 654-3097

County Clerk **Sherry Dowd** . . . . (903) 654-3035
  E-mail: countyclerk@navarrocounty.org

Newton County

District Clerk

Second Administrative Judicial Region
301 North Thompson, Suite 102, Conroe, TX 77301
Tel: (936) 538-8176 Fax: (936) 538-8167
Internet: www.mctx.org/courts/second_administrative_judicial_region

District Clerk, Newton County **Bree Allen** . . . . (409) 379-3951
  P.O. Box 535, Newton, TX 75966-0535

County Clerk

Office of the County Clerk
115 Court Street, Newton, TX 75966
PO Box 484, Newton, TX 75966
Fax: (409) 379-9049

County Clerk **Sandra K. Duckworth** . . . . (409) 379-5341
  E-mail: sandra.duckworth@co.newton.tx.us

Nolan County

District Clerk

Seventh Administrative Judicial Region
Midland County Courthouse, 500 North Loraine Street, Suite 502,
Midland, TX 79701
Tel: (432) 688-4370 Fax: (432) 688-4933
Internet: www.courts.state.tx.us/7ajr/7ajr.asp

District Clerk, Nolan County **Jamie Clem** . . . . (325) 235-2111
  100 East Third, Suite 200,
  Sweetwater, TX 79373-0939

County Clerk

Office of the County Clerk
100 East Third Street, Suite 108, Sweetwater, TX 79556
Tel: (325) 235-2462 Fax: (325) 235-4635

County Clerk **Pat McGowan** . . . . (325) 235-2462
  E-mail: pat.mcgowan@co.nolan.tx.us

Nueces County

District Clerk

Fifth Administrative Judicial Region
200 North Almond Street, Alice, TX 78332
Tel: (361) 668-5766 Fax: (512) 367-5788
E-mail: fifth.region@yahoo.com
Internet: www.courts.state.tx.us/5ajr/5ajr.asp

District Clerk, Nueces County **Patsy Perez** . . . . (361) 888-0450
  901 Leopard, Suite 313, Corpus Christi, TX 78401

County Clerk

Office of the County Clerk
P.O Box 2627, Corpus Christi, TX 78403
Tel: (361) 888-0580 Fax: (361) 888-0329

County Clerk **Kara Sands** . . . . (361) 888-0580
E-mail: nueces.countyclerk@nuecesco.com

Ochiltree County

District Clerk

Ninth Administrative Judicial Region
500 West Main, Room 204W, Brownfield, TX 79316
Tel: (806) 637-1329 Fax: (806) 637-8918
E-mail: kmoore@terrycounty.org

District Clerk, Ochiltree County **Shawn Bogard** . . . . (806) 435-8054
511 South Main, Perryton, TX 79070

County Clerk

Office of the County Clerk
511 South Main, Perryton, TX 79070
Tel: (806) 435-8039 Fax: (806) 435-2081

County Clerk **Stacey Brown** . . . . (806) 435-8039

Oldham County

District and County Clerk

Ninth Administrative Judicial Region
500 West Main, Room 204W, Brownfield, TX 79316
Tel: (806) 637-1329 Fax: (806) 637-8918
E-mail: kmoore@terrycounty.org

District Clerk, Oldham County **Darla Lookingbill** . . . . (806) 267-2667
P.O. Box 360, Vega, TX 79092-0360

Orange County

District Clerk

Second Administrative Judicial Region
301 North Thompson, Suite 102, Conroe, TX 77301
Tel: (936) 538-8176 Fax: (936) 538-8167
Internet: www.mctx.org/courts/second_administrative_judicial_region

District Clerk, Orange County **Vickie Edgerly** . . . . (409) 882-7028
801 West Division, Orange, TX 77630-6364

County Clerk

Office of the County Clerk
123 South Sixth Street, Orange, TX 77630
Fax: (409) 882-7012

County Clerk **Brandy Robertson** . . . . (409) 882-7055
E-mail: brobertson@co.orange.tx.us

Palo Pinto County

District Clerk

Eighth Administrative Judicial Region
401 West Belknap, 5th Floor, Fort Worth, TX 76196
Tel: (817) 884-1558 Fax: (817) 884-1560
E-mail: 8thadmin@8thjudicialregion.com

District Clerk, Palo Pinto County **Janie Glover** . . . . (940) 659-1224
P.O. Drawer 189, Palo Pinto, TX 76484-0189

County Clerk

Office of the County Clerk
P.O. Box 219, Palo Pinto, TX 76484
Tel: (940) 659-1277 Fax: (940) 659-2289

County Clerk **Janette K. Green** . . . . (940) 659-1277
E-mail: janette.green@co.palo-pinto.tx.us

Panola County

District Clerk

First Administrative Judicial Region
133 North Riverfront Boulevard, 5th Floor, Dallas, TX 75207
Tel: (214) 653-2943 Fax: (214) 653-2957
Internet: www.firstadmin.com

District Clerk, Panola County **Debra Johnson** . . . . (903) 693-0306
101 South Sycamore Street, Room 201,
Carthage, TX 75633

County Clerk

Office of the County Clerk
110 South Sycamore, Room 201, Carthage, TX 75633
Tel: (903) 693-0302 Fax: (903) 693-0328

County Clerk **Paul Brevard** . . . . (903) 693-0302
E-mail: paul.brevard@co.panola.tx.us

Parker County

District Clerk

Eighth Administrative Judicial Region
401 West Belknap, 5th Floor, Fort Worth, TX 76196
Tel: (817) 884-1558 Fax: (817) 884-1560
E-mail: 8thadmin@8thjudicialregion.com

District Clerk, Parker County **Sharena Gilliland** . . . . (817) 598-6114
117 Fort Worth Highway,
Weatherford, TX 76086-4302

County Clerk

Office of the County Clerk
1112 Santa Fe Drive, Weatherford, TX 76086
Tel: (817) 594-7461 Fax: (817) 594-9540

County Clerk **Jeane Brunson** . . . . (817) 594-7461
E-mail: jeane.brunson@parkercountytx.com

Parmer County

District Clerk

Ninth Administrative Judicial Region
500 West Main, Room 204W, Brownfield, TX 79316
Tel: (806) 637-1329 Fax: (806) 637-8918
E-mail: kmoore@terrycounty.org

District Clerk, Parmer County **Sandra Warren** . . . . (806) 481-3419
P.O. Box 195, Farwell, TX 79325-0195

County Clerk

Office of the County Clerk
401 Third Street, Farwell, TX 79325
Tel: (806) 481-3691 Fax: (806) 481-9548

County Clerk **Geri Bowers** . . . . (806) 481-3691
E-mail: pcclerk@parmercounty.net

(continued on next page)

Texas Court Clerks and Courthouses *continued*

Pecos County

District Clerk

Sixth Administrative Judicial Region
700 Main Street, Kerrville, TX 78028
Tel: (830) 792-2290 Fax: (830) 792-2294
E-mail: beckyh@co.kerr.tx.us
Internet: www.courts.state.tx.us/6ajr/6ajr.asp

District Clerk, Pecos County **Gayle Henderson** . . . . (432) 336-3503
    400 South Nelson, Fort Stockton, TX 79735-7132

County Clerk

Office of the County Clerk
200 South Nelson, Fort Stockton, TX 79735
Tel: (432) 336-7555 Fax: (432) 336-7557

County Clerk **Liz Chapman** . . . . (432) 336-7555
    E-mail: liz.chapman@co.pecos.tx.us

Polk County

District Clerk

Second Administrative Judicial Region
301 North Thompson, Suite 102, Conroe, TX 77301
Tel: (936) 538-8176 Fax: (936) 538-8167
Internet: www.mctx.org/courts/second_administrative_judicial_region

District Clerk, Polk County **Kathy E. Clifton** . . . . (936) 327-6814
    101 West Mill, Suite 216,
    Livingston, TX 77351-3233

County Clerk

Office of the County Clerk
P.O. Drawer 2119, Livingston, TX 77351
Tel: (936) 327-6805 Fax: (936) 327-6855

County Clerk **Schelana Hock** . . . . (936) 327-6805

Potter County

District Clerk

Ninth Administrative Judicial Region
500 West Main, Room 204W, Brownfield, TX 79316
Tel: (806) 637-1329 Fax: (806) 637-8918
E-mail: kmoore@terrycounty.org

District Clerk, Potter County **Caroline Woodburn** . . . . (806) 379-2300
    P.O. Box 9570, Amarillo, TX 79105-9570

County Clerk

Office of the County Clerk
500 South Fillmore, Room 201, Amarillo, TX 79101
Tel: (806) 379-2275 Fax: (806) 379-2296

County Clerk **Julie Smith** . . . . (806) 379-2275
    E-mail: countyclerk@co.potter.tx.us

Texas Court Clerks and Courthouses *continued*

Presidio County

District and County Clerk

Sixth Administrative Judicial Region
700 Main Street, Kerrville, TX 78028
Tel: (830) 792-2290 Fax: (830) 792-2294
E-mail: beckyh@co.kerr.tx.us
Internet: www.courts.state.tx.us/6ajr/6ajr.asp

District Clerk, Presidio County **Virginia Pallarez** . . . . (432) 729-4812
    P.O. Box 789, Marfa, TX 79843

Rains County

District Clerk

First Administrative Judicial Region
133 North Riverfront Boulevard, 5th Floor, Dallas, TX 75207
Tel: (214) 653-2943 Fax: (214) 653-2957
Internet: www.firstadmin.com

District Clerk, Rains County **Deborah Traylor** . . . . (903) 473-5000
    P.O. Box 187, Emory, TX 75440

County Clerk

Office of the County Clerk
County Courthouse Annex, 220 West Quitman Street, Emory, TX 75440
Tel: (903) 473-5000 Fax: (903) 473-5086

County Clerk **Linda Wallace** . . . . (903) 473-5000 ext. 103
    E-mail: linda.wallace@co.rains.tx.us

Randall County

District Clerk

Ninth Administrative Judicial Region
500 West Main, Room 204W, Brownfield, TX 79316
Tel: (806) 637-1329 Fax: (806) 637-8918
E-mail: kmoore@terrycounty.org

District Clerk, Randall County **Jo Carter** . . . . (806) 468-5600
    2309 Russell Long Boulevard, Suite 110,
    Canyon, TX 79015-1096

County Clerk

Office of the County Clerk
2309 Russell Long Boulevard, Canyon, TX 79015
Tel: (806) 468-5505 Fax: (806) 468-5509

County Clerk **Renee Calhoun** . . . . (806) 468-5505
    E-mail: countyclerk@randallcounty.org

Reagan County

District Clerk

Sixth Administrative Judicial Region
700 Main Street, Kerrville, TX 78028
Tel: (830) 792-2290 Fax: (830) 792-2294
E-mail: beckyh@co.kerr.tx.us
Internet: www.courts.state.tx.us/6ajr/6ajr.asp

District and County Clerk, Reagan County **Terri Curry** . . . . (325) 884-2442
    P.O. Box 100, Big Lake, TX 76932

Real County

District and County Clerk

Sixth Administrative Judicial Region
700 Main Street, Kerrville, TX 78028
Tel: (830) 792-2290 Fax: (830) 792-2294
E-mail: beckyh@co.kerr.tx.us
Internet: www.courts.state.tx.us/6ajr/6ajr.asp

District Clerk, Real County **Bella A. Rubio** . . . . (830) 232-5202
P.O. Box 750, Leakey, TX 78873

Red River County

District Clerk

First Administrative Judicial Region
133 North Riverfront Boulevard, 5th Floor, Dallas, TX 75207
Tel: (214) 653-2943 Fax: (214) 653-2957
Internet: www.firstadmin.com

District Clerk, Red River County **Janice Gentry** . . . . (903) 427-3761
400 North Walnut Street, Clarksville, TX 75426

County Clerk

Office of the County Clerk
200 North Walnut Street, Clarksville, TX 75426
Tel: (903) 427-2401 Tel: (903) 427-3589

County Clerk **Shawn Weemes** . . . . (903) 427-2401

Reeves County

District Clerk

Seventh Administrative Judicial Region
Midland County Courthouse, 500 North Loraine Street, Suite 502,
Midland, TX 79701
Tel: (432) 688-4370 Fax: (432) 688-4933
Internet: www.courts.state.tx.us/7ajr/7ajr.asp

District Clerk, Reeves County **Pat Tarin** . . . . (432) 445-2714
P.O. Box 848, Pecos, TX 79772-0848

County Clerk

Office of the County Clerk
100 East Fourth Street, Room 101, Pecos, TX 79772
Tel: (432) 445-5467 Fax: (432) 445-3997

County Clerk **Dianne O. Florez** . . . . (432) 445-5467
E-mail: dfclerk@yahoo.com

Refugio County

District Clerk

Fourth Administrative Judicial Region
100 Dolorosa, 5th Floor, San Antonio, TX 78205
Tel: (210) 335-3954 Fax: (210) 335-3955
Internet: www.courts.state.tx.us/4ajr/4ajr.asp

District Clerk, Refugio County **Ruby Garcia** . . . . (361) 526-2721
P.O. Box 736, Refugio, TX 78377

County Clerk

Office of the County Clerk
P.O. Box 704, Refugio, TX 78377
Tel: (361) 526-2233 Fax: (361) 526-1325

County Clerk **Ida Ramirez** . . . . (361) 526-2233
E-mail: iramirez@atcog.org

Roberts County

District and County Clerk

Ninth Administrative Judicial Region
500 West Main, Room 204W, Brownfield, TX 79316
Tel: (806) 637-1329 Fax: (806) 637-8918
E-mail: kmoore@terrycounty.org

District Clerk, Roberts County **Toni Rankin** . . . . (806) 868-2341
P.O. Box 477, Miami, TX 79059-0477

Robertson County

District Clerk

Second Administrative Judicial Region
301 North Thompson, Suite 102, Conroe, TX 77301
Tel: (936) 538-8176 Fax: (936) 538-8167
Internet: www.mctx.org/courts/second_administrative_judicial_region

District Clerk, Robertson County **Barbara Axtell** . . . . (979) 828-3636
P.O. Box 250, Franklin, TX 77856-0250

County Clerk

Office of the County Clerk
P.O. Box 1029, Franklin, TX 77856
Tel: (979) 828-4130 Fax: (979) 828-1260

County Clerk **Kathryn Brimhall** . . . . (979) 828-4130

Rockwall County

District Clerk

First Administrative Judicial Region
133 North Riverfront Boulevard, 5th Floor, Dallas, TX 75207
Tel: (214) 653-2943 Fax: (214) 653-2957
Internet: www.firstadmin.com

District Clerk, Rockwall County **Kay McDaniel** . . . . (972) 204-6500
1111 East Yellowjacket Lane, Suite 200,
Rockwall, TX 75087

County Clerk

Office of the County Clerk
1111 East Yellowjacket Lane, Suite 100, Rockwall, TX 75087
Tel: (972) 204-6300 Fax: (972) 204-6319

County Clerk **Shelli Miller** . . . . (972) 204-6300
E-mail: smiller@rockwallcountytexas.com

(continued on next page)

Runnels County

District Clerk

Seventh Administrative Judicial Region
Midland County Courthouse, 500 North Loraine Street, Suite 502,
Midland, TX 79701
Tel: (432) 688-4370 Fax: (432) 688-4933
Internet: www.courts.state.tx.us/7ajr/7ajr.asp

District Clerk, Runnels County **Tammy Burleson** . . . . (325) 365-2638
  P.O. Box 166, Ballinger, TX 76821-0166

County Clerk

Office of the County Clerk
613 Hutchings Avenue, Room 106, Ballinger, TX 76821
Tel: (325) 365-2720 Fax: (325) 365-3408

County Clerk **Julia Miller** . . . .(325) 365-2720
  E-mail: julia.miller@co.runnels.tx.us

Rusk County

District Clerk

First Administrative Judicial Region
133 North Riverfront Boulevard, 5th Floor, Dallas, TX 75207
Tel: (214) 653-2943 Fax: (214) 653-2957
Internet: www.firstadmin.com

District Clerk, Rusk County **Jean Hodges** . . . . (903) 657-0353
  P.O. Box 1687, Henderson, TX 75653

County Clerk

Office of the County Clerk
115 North Main Street, Suite 206, Henderson, TX 75653-0758
Tel: (903) 657-0330 Fax: (903) 657-2387

County Clerk **Trudi McGill** . . . . (903) 657-0330

Sabine County

District Clerk

Second Administrative Judicial Region
301 North Thompson, Suite 102, Conroe, TX 77301
Tel: (936) 538-8176 Fax: (936) 538-8167
Internet: www.mctx.org/courts/second_administrative_judicial_region

District Clerk, Sabine County **Tanya Walker** . . . .(409) 787-2912
  P.O. Box 850, Hemphill, TX 75948-0850

County Clerk

Office of the County Clerk
P.O. Box 580, Hemphill, TX 75948

County Clerk **Janice McDaniel** . . . . (409) 787-3786
  E-mail: sabinecc@yahoo.com

San Augustine County

District Clerk

Second Administrative Judicial Region
301 North Thompson, Suite 102, Conroe, TX 77301
Tel: (936) 538-8176 Fax: (936) 538-8167
Internet: www.mctx.org/courts/second_administrative_judicial_region

District Clerk, San Augustine County **Jean Steptoe** . . . . . (936) 275-2231
  100 West Columbia, Room 202,
  San Augustine, TX 75972

County Clerk

Office of the County Clerk
203 Courthouse, San Augustine, TX 75972
Fax: (936) 275-2263

County Clerk **Margo Noble** . . . . (936) 275-2452

San Jacinto County

District Clerk

Second Administrative Judicial Region
301 North Thompson, Suite 102, Conroe, TX 77301
Tel: (936) 538-8176 Fax: (936) 538-8167
Internet: www.mctx.org/courts/second_administrative_judicial_region

District Clerk, San Jacinto County **Rebecca Capers** . . . . . (936) 653-2909
  One State Highway 150, Room 4,
  Coldspring, TX 77331-7755

County Clerk

Office of the County Clerk
1 State Highway 150, Room 2, Coldspring, TX 77331
Tel: (936) 653-5804 (Elections Office) Fax: (936) 653-8312

County Clerk **Dawn Wright** . . . . (936) 653-2324

San Patricio County

District Clerk

Fourth Administrative Judicial Region
100 Dolorosa, 5th Floor, San Antonio, TX 78205
Tel: (210) 335-3954 Fax: (210) 335-3955
Internet: www.courts.state.tx.us/4ajr/4ajr.asp

District Clerk, San Patricio County **Laura Miller** . . . . (361) 364-9377
  P.O. Box 1084, Sinton, TX 78387

County Clerk

Office of the County Clerk
400 West Sinton Street, Room 124, Sinton, TX 78387
P.O. Box 578, Sinton, TX 78387
Tel: (361) 364-9350 Fax: (361) 364-6112

County Clerk **Gracie Alaniz-Gonzales** . . . . (361) 364-9350
  E-mail: ggonzales@co.san-patricio.tx.us

San Saba County

District and County Clerk

Third Administrative Judicial Region
405 M.L.K Boulevard Drive, Georgetown, TX 78626
Tel: (512) 943-3777 Fax: (512) 943-3767
E-mail: presidingjudge3@wilco.org
Internet: www.courts.state.tx.us/3ajr/3ajr.asp

District Clerk, San Saba County **Kim Wells** . . . . (325) 372-3375
  500 East Wallace Street, San Saba, TX 76877

Schleicher County

District Clerk

Seventh Administrative Judicial Region
Midland County Courthouse, 500 North Loraine Street, Suite 502,
Midland, TX 79701
Tel: (432) 688-4370 Fax: (432) 688-4933
Internet: www.courts.state.tx.us/7ajr/7ajr.asp

District Clerk, Schleicher County **Mary Ann Gonzalez** . . .(325) 853-2833
  P.O. Drawer 580, Eldorado, TX 76936

County Clerk

Office of the County Clerk
P.O. Box 536, Eldorado, TX 76936
Tel: (325) 853-2833

County Clerk **Mary Ann Gonzalez** . . . .(325) 853-2833

Scurry County

District Clerk

Seventh Administrative Judicial Region
Midland County Courthouse, 500 North Loraine Street, Suite 502,
Midland, TX 79701
Tel: (432) 688-4370 Fax: (432) 688-4933
Internet: www.courts.state.tx.us/7ajr/7ajr.asp

District Clerk, Scurry County **Candace Jones** . . . . (325) 573-5641
  1806 25th Street, Suite 402,
  Snyder, TX 79549

County Clerk

Office of the County Clerk
1806 25th Street, #300, Snyder, TX 79549
Tel: (325) 573-5332 Fax: (325) 573-7396

County Clerk **Melody Appleton** . . . . (325) 573-5332
  E-mail: melody.appleton@co.scurry.tx.us

Shackelford County

District and County Clerk

Seventh Administrative Judicial Region
Midland County Courthouse, 500 North Loraine Street, Suite 502,
Midland, TX 79701
Tel: (432) 688-4370 Fax: (432) 688-4933
Internet: www.courts.state.tx.us/7ajr/7ajr.asp

District Clerk, Shackelford County **Cheri Hawkins** . . . . . . (325) 762-2232
  P.O. Box 2109, Albany, TX 76430

Shelby County

District Clerk

First Administrative Judicial Region
133 North Riverfront Boulevard, 5th Floor, Dallas, TX 75207
Tel: (214) 653-2943 Fax: (214) 653-2957
Internet: www.firstadmin.com

District Clerk, Shelby County **Lori Oliver** . . . . (936) 598-4164
  P.O. Box 1953, Center, TX 75935

County Clerk

Office of the County Clerk
124 Austin Street, Center, TX 75935
Fax: (936) 598-3701

County Clerk **Jennifer Fountain** . . . .(936) 598-6361

Sherman County

District and County Clerk

Ninth Administrative Judicial Region
500 West Main, Room 204W, Brownfield, TX 79316
Tel: (806) 637-1329 Fax: (806) 637-8918
E-mail: kmoore@terrycounty.org

District Clerk, Sherman County **Gina Gray** . . . .(806) 366-2371
  P.O. Box 270, Stratford, TX 79084

Smith County

District Clerk

First Administrative Judicial Region
133 North Riverfront Boulevard, 5th Floor, Dallas, TX 75207
Tel: (214) 653-2943 Fax: (214) 653-2957
Internet: www.firstadmin.com

District Clerk, Smith County **Lois Rogers** . . . .(903) 590-1660
  100 North Broadway, Room 204,
  Tyler, TX 75702-7236

County Clerk

Office of the County Clerk
200 East Ferguson, Suite 300, Tyler, TX 75702
Tel: (903) 590-4670 Fax: (903) 590-4689

County Clerk **Karen Phillips** . . . . (903) 590-4670
  E-mail: kphillips@smith-county.com

Somervell County

District and County Clerk

Eighth Administrative Judicial Region
401 West Belknap, 5th Floor, Fort Worth, TX 76196
Tel: (817) 884-1558 Fax: (817) 884-1560
E-mail: 8thadmin@8thjudicialregion.com

District Clerk, Somervell County **Michelle Reynolds** . . . . (254) 897-4427
  P.O. Drawer 1098, Glen Rose, TX 76043-1098

Starr County

District Clerk

Fifth Administrative Judicial Region
200 North Almond Street, Alice, TX 78332
Tel: (361) 668-5766 Fax: (512) 367-5788
E-mail: fifth.region@yahoo.com
Internet: www.courts.state.tx.us/5ajr/5ajr.asp

District Clerk, Starr County **Eloy Ruben Garcia** . . . . (956) 716-4800
  401 North Britton Avenue, Room 304,
  Rio Grande City, TX 78582

(continued on next page)

Texas Court Clerks and Courthouses *continued*
County Clerk

Office of the County Clerk
401 North Britton Avenue, Room 201, Rio Grande City, TX 78582
Tel: (956) 716-4800 Fax: (956) 487-8674

County Clerk **Dennis D. Gonzalez** . . . . (956) 716-4800 ext. 8032
E-mail: dennis.gonzalez@co.starr.tx.us

Stephens County

District Clerk

Eighth Administrative Judicial Region
401 West Belknap, 5th Floor, Fort Worth, TX 76196
Tel: (817) 884-1558 Fax: (817) 884-1560
E-mail: 8thadmin@8thjudicialregion.com

District Clerk, Stephens County **Christie L. Coapland** . . . (254) 559-3151
200 West Walker, Second Floor,
Breckenridge, TX 76424-3590

County Clerk

Office of the County Clerk
200 West Walker, Breckenridge, TX 76424
Tel: (254) 559-3700 Fax: (254) 559-5892

County Clerk **Jackie Ensey** . . . . (254) 559-3700

Sterling County

District and County Clerk

Seventh Administrative Judicial Region
Midland County Courthouse, 500 North Loraine Street, Suite 502,
Midland, TX 79701
Tel: (432) 688-4370 Fax: (432) 688-4933
Internet: www.courts.state.tx.us/7ajr/7ajr.asp

District Clerk, Sterling County **Jerri McCutchen** . . . . (325) 378-5191
P.O. Box 55, Sterling City, TX 76951-0055

Stonewall County

District Clerk

Seventh Administrative Judicial Region
Midland County Courthouse, 500 North Loraine Street, Suite 502,
Midland, TX 79701
Tel: (432) 688-4370 Fax: (432) 688-4933
Internet: www.courts.state.tx.us/7ajr/7ajr.asp

District Clerk, Stonewall County **Holly McLaury** . . . . (940) 989-2272
P.O. Drawer P, Aspermont, TX 79502-0914

County Clerk

Office of the County Clerk
P.O. Box P, Aspermont, TX 79502-0914
Tel: (940) 989-2272

County Clerk **Patricia Hoy** . . . . (940) 989-2272
E-mail: hoy.stoco.clrk@srcaccess.net

Texas Court Clerks and Courthouses *continued*
Sutton County

District and County Clerk

Sixth Administrative Judicial Region
700 Main Street, Kerrville, TX 78028
Tel: (830) 792-2290 Fax: (830) 792-2294
E-mail: beckyh@co.kerr.tx.us
Internet: www.courts.state.tx.us/6ajr/6ajr.asp

District and County Clerk, Sutton County
    Rachel Chavez Duran . . . . (325) 387-3815
    300 East Oak, Suite 3, Sonora, TX 76950-2602

Swisher County

District and County Clerk

Ninth Administrative Judicial Region
500 West Main, Room 204W, Brownfield, TX 79316
Tel: (806) 637-1329 Fax: (806) 637-8918
E-mail: kmoore@terrycounty.org

District and County Clerk, Swisher County
    Brenda Hudson . . . . (806) 995-3294
    119 South Maxwell, Tulia, TX 79088-2297   Fax: (806) 995-4121
    E-mail: brenda.hudson@swisher-tx.net

Tarrant County

District Clerk

Eighth Administrative Judicial Region
401 West Belknap, 5th Floor, Fort Worth, TX 76196
Tel: (817) 884-1558 Fax: (817) 884-1560
E-mail: 8thadmin@8thjudicialregion.com

District Clerk, Tarrant County **Thomas A. Wilder** . . . . (817) 884-1574
    401 West Belknap, Fort Worth, TX 76196

County Clerk

Office of the County Clerk
100 W. Weatherford St., Fort Worth, TX 76196-0401

County Clerk **Mary Louise Garcia** . . . . (817) 884-1195
                                                            Fax: (817) 884-3295

Taylor County

District Clerk

Seventh Administrative Judicial Region
Midland County Courthouse, 500 North Loraine Street, Suite 502,
Midland, TX 79701
Tel: (432) 688-4370 Fax: (432) 688-4933
Internet: www.courts.state.tx.us/7ajr/7ajr.asp

District Clerk, Taylor County **Patricia Henderson** . . . . (325) 674-1316
    300 Oak Street, Suite 400,
    Abilene, TX 79373-0939

County Clerk

Office of the County Clerk
300 Oak Street, Suite 200, Abilene, TX 79602
Tel: (325) 674-1202 Fax: (325) 674-1279

County Clerk **Larry G. Bevill** . . . . (325) 674-1202
    E-mail: bevill@taylorcountytexas.org

Terrell County

District and County Clerk

Sixth Administrative Judicial Region
700 Main Street, Kerrville, TX 78028
Tel: (830) 792-2290 Fax: (830) 792-2294
E-mail: beckyh@co.kerr.tx.us
Internet: www.courts.state.tx.us/6ajr/6ajr.asp

District Clerk, Terrell County **Martha Allen** . . . . (432) 345-2391
P.O. Box 410, Sanderson, TX 79848-0410

Terry County

District Clerk

Ninth Administrative Judicial Region
500 West Main, Room 204W, Brownfield, TX 79316
Tel: (806) 637-1329 Fax: (806) 637-8918
E-mail: kmoore@terrycounty.org

District Clerk, Terry County **Paige Lindsey** . . . . (806) 637-4202
500 West Main, Room 209E,
Brownfield, TX 79316-4335

County Clerk

Office of the County Clerk
500 West Main, Room 105, Brownfield, TX 79316
Tel: (806) 637-8551 Fax: (806) 637-4874

County Clerk **Kim Carter** . . . . (806) 637-8551

Throckmorton County

District and County Clerk

Seventh Administrative Judicial Region
Midland County Courthouse, 500 North Loraine Street, Suite 502,
Midland, TX 79701
Tel: (432) 688-4370 Fax: (432) 688-4933
Internet: www.courts.state.tx.us/7ajr/7ajr.asp

District Clerk, Throckmorton County
Mary "Susie" Walraven . . . . (940) 849-2501
P.O. Box 309, Throckmorton, TX 76843-0309

Titus County

District Clerk

First Administrative Judicial Region
133 North Riverfront Boulevard, 5th Floor, Dallas, TX 75207
Tel: (214) 653-2943 Fax: (214) 653-2957
Internet: www.firstadmin.com

District Clerk, Titus County **Debra Abston** . . . . (903) 577-6724
P.O. Box 492, Mt. Pleasant, TX 75456-0492

County Clerk

Office of the County Clerk
100 West First Street, Suite 204, Mt. Pleasant, TX 75455
Tel: (903) 577-6796 Fax: (903) 572-5078

County Clerk **Joan Newman** . . . . (903) 577-6796
E-mail: jnewman@co.titus.tx.us

Tom Green County

District Clerk

Seventh Administrative Judicial Region
Midland County Courthouse, 500 North Loraine Street, Suite 502,
Midland, TX 79701
Tel: (432) 688-4370 Fax: (432) 688-4933
Internet: www.courts.state.tx.us/7ajr/7ajr.asp

District Clerk, Tom Green County **Sheri Woodfin** . . . . (325) 659-6579
112 West Beauregard, San Angelo, TX 76903-5850

County Clerk

Office of the County Clerk
124 West Beauregard, San Angelo, TX 76903
Tel: (325) 659-6553 Fax: (325) 659-3251

County Clerk **Elizabeth McGill** . . . . (325) 659-6553
E-mail: elizabeth.mcgill@co.tom-green.tx.us

Travis County

District Clerk

Third Administrative Judicial Region
405 M.L.K Boulevard Drive, Georgetown, TX 78626
Tel: (512) 943-3777 Fax: (512) 943-3767
E-mail: presidingjudge3@wilco.org
Internet: www.courts.state.tx.us/3ajr/3ajr.asp

District Clerk, Travis County
Amalia Rodriguez-Mendoza . . . . (512) 854-9737
P.O. Box 679003, Austin, TX 78767-9003

County Clerk

Office of the County Clerk
5501 Airport Boulevard, Austin, TX 78751
P.O. Box 149325, Austin, TX 78714
Tel: (512) 854-9188 (Information) TTY: (512) 854-9069
Fax: (512) 854-3942 Fax: (512) 854-9075 (Elections)

County Clerk **Dana DeBeauvoir** . . . . (512) 854-9188
E-mail: dana.debeauvoir@co.travis.tx.us

Trinity County

District Clerk

Second Administrative Judicial Region
301 North Thompson, Suite 102, Conroe, TX 77301
Tel: (936) 538-8176 Fax: (936) 538-8167
Internet: www.mctx.org/courts/second_administrative_judicial_region

District Clerk, Trinity County **Cheryl Cartwright** . . . . (936) 642-1118
P.O. Box 549, Groveton, TX 75845-0549

County Clerk

Office of the County Clerk
P.O. Box 456, Groveton, TX 75845
Fax: (936) 642-3004

County Clerk **Shasta Bergman** . . . . (936) 642-1208
E-mail: shasta.bergman@co.trinity.tx.us

(continued on next page)

Tyler County

District Clerk

Second Administrative Judicial Region
301 North Thompson, Suite 102, Conroe, TX 77301
Tel: (936) 538-8176 Fax: (936) 538-8167
Internet: www.mctx.org/courts/second_administrative_judicial_region

District Clerk, Tyler County **Kim Nagypal** . . . . (409) 283-2162
  100 West Bluff, Room 203,
  Woodville, TX 75979-5220

County Clerk

Office of the County Clerk
116 South Charlton Street, Woodville, TX 75979
Fax: (409) 283-8049
E-mail: countyclerk.cc@co.tyler.tx.us

County Clerk **Donece Gregory** . . . . (409) 283-2281

Upshur County

District Clerk

First Administrative Judicial Region
133 North Riverfront Boulevard, 5th Floor, Dallas, TX 75207
Tel: (214) 653-2943 Fax: (214) 653-2957
Internet: www.firstadmin.com

District Clerk, Upshur County **Carolyn Parrott** . . . . (903) 843-5031
  405 North Titus, Gilmer, TX 75440

County Clerk

Office of the County Clerk
P.O. Box 730, Gilmer, TX 75644
Tel: (903) 843-4015 Fax: (903) 843-4504

County Clerk **Terri Ross** . . . . (903) 843-4015
  E-mail: terri.ross@countyofupshur.com

Upton County

District and County Clerk

Sixth Administrative Judicial Region
700 Main Street, Kerrville, TX 78028
Tel: (830) 792-2290 Fax: (830) 792-2294
E-mail: beckyh@co.kerr.tx.us
Internet: www.courts.state.tx.us/6ajr/6ajr.asp

District Clerk, Upton County **LaWanda McMurray** . . . . . . (432) 693-2861
  P.O. Box 465, Rankin, TX 79778-0465

Uvalde County

District Clerk

Sixth Administrative Judicial Region
700 Main Street, Kerrville, TX 78028
Tel: (830) 792-2290 Fax: (830) 792-2294
E-mail: beckyh@co.kerr.tx.us
Internet: www.courts.state.tx.us/6ajr/6ajr.asp

District Clerk, Uvalde County **Christina Ovalle** . . . . (830) 278-3918
  100 North Getty, Suite 15,
  Uvalde, TX 78801-5299

County Clerk

Office of the County Clerk
P.O. Box 284, Uvalde, TX 78802-0284
Tel: (830) 278-6614 Fax: (830) 278-8692

County Clerk **Donna M. Williams** . . . . (830) 278-6614
  E-mail: dwilliams@uvaldecounty.com

Val Verde County

District Clerk

Sixth Administrative Judicial Region
700 Main Street, Kerrville, TX 78028
Tel: (830) 792-2290 Fax: (830) 792-2294
E-mail: beckyh@co.kerr.tx.us
Internet: www.courts.state.tx.us/6ajr/6ajr.asp

District Clerk, Val Verde County **Jo Ann Cervantes** . . . . . (830) 774-7538
  P.O. Box 1544, Del Rio, TX 78841-1544

County Clerk

Office of the County Clerk
400 Pecan Street, 1st Floor, Del Rio, TX 78840
Tel: (830) 774-7564 Fax: (830) 774-7608

County Clerk **Generosa "Janie" Gracia-Ramon** . . . . (830) 774-7564
  E-mail: gramon@valverdecounty.org

Van Zandt County

District Clerk

First Administrative Judicial Region
133 North Riverfront Boulevard, 5th Floor, Dallas, TX 75207
Tel: (214) 653-2943 Fax: (214) 653-2957
Internet: www.firstadmin.com

District Clerk, Van Zandt County **Karen Wilson** . . . . (903) 567-6576
  121 East Dallas, Room 302,
  Canton, TX 75103-1604

County Clerk

Office of the County Clerk
121 East Dallas Street, Room 202, Canton, TX 75103
Tel: (903) 567-7555 Fax: (903) 567-6722

County Clerk **Pam Pearman** . . . . (903) 567-7555
  E-mail: countyclerk@vanzandtcounty.org

Victoria County

District Clerk

Fourth Administrative Judicial Region
100 Dolorosa, 5th Floor, San Antonio, TX 78205
Tel: (210) 335-3954 Fax: (210) 335-3955
Internet: www.courts.state.tx.us/4ajr/4ajr.asp

District Clerk, Victoria County **Cathy Stuart** . . . . (361) 575-0581
  115 North Bridge Street, Third Floor,
  Victoria, TX 77901-6544

County Clerk

Office of the County Clerk
115 North Bridge Street, Room 103, Victoria, TX 77901
Tel: (361) 575-1478 Fax: (361) 575-6276

County Clerk **Robert S. Cortez** . . . . (361) 575-1478
  E-mail: rcortez@vctx.org

Walker County

District Clerk

Second Administrative Judicial Region
301 North Thompson, Suite 102, Conroe, TX 77301
Tel: (936) 538-8176 Fax: (936) 538-8167
Internet: www.mctx.org/courts/second_administrative_judicial_region

District Clerk, Walker County **Robyn Flowers** . . . . (936) 436-4972
1100 University Avenue, Suite 209,
Huntsville, TX 77340-4642

County Clerk

Office of the County Clerk
1100 University Avenue, Suite 201, Huntsville, TX 77340

County Clerk **Kari French** . . . . (936) 436-4922
E-mail: kfrench@co.walker.tx.us

Waller County

District Clerk

Second Administrative Judicial Region
301 North Thompson, Suite 102, Conroe, TX 77301
Tel: (936) 538-8176 Fax: (936) 538-8167
Internet: www.mctx.org/courts/second_administrative_judicial_region

District Clerk, Waller County **Pat Spadachene** . . . . (979) 826-7735
836 Austin Street, Room 318,
Hempstead, TX 77445-4673

County Clerk

Office of the County Clerk
836 Austin Street, Suite 217, Hempstead, TX 77445
Tel: (979) 826-7711 Fax: (979) 826-7771

County Clerk **Debbie Hollan** . . . . (979) 826-7711
E-mail: d.hollan@wallercounty.us

Ward County

District Clerk

Seventh Administrative Judicial Region
Midland County Courthouse, 500 North Loraine Street, Suite 502,
Midland, TX 79701
Tel: (432) 688-4370 Fax: (432) 688-4933
Internet: www.courts.state.tx.us/7ajr/7ajr.asp

District Clerk, Ward County **Dianna Moore** . . . . (432) 943-2751
P.O. Box 440, Monahans, TX 79756-0440

County Clerk

Office of the County Clerk
400 South Allen, Suite 101, Monahans, TX 79756
Tel: (432) 943-3294 Fax: (432) 943-6054

County Clerk **Natrell Cain** . . . . (432) 943-3294
E-mail: natrell.cain@co.ward.tx.us

Washington County

District Clerk

Second Administrative Judicial Region
301 North Thompson, Suite 102, Conroe, TX 77301
Tel: (936) 538-8176 Fax: (936) 538-8167
Internet: www.mctx.org/courts/second_administrative_judicial_region

District Clerk, Washington County **Tammy Brauner** . . . . . (979) 277-6200
100 East Main, Suite 304,
Brenham, TX 77833-3753

County Clerk

Office of the County Clerk
100 East Main, Suite 102, Brenham, TX 77833
Tel: (979) 277-6200 Fax: (979) 277-6278

County Clerk **Beth A. Rothermel** . . . . (979) 277-6200
E-mail: brothermel@wacounty.com

Webb County

District Clerk

Fourth Administrative Judicial Region
100 Dolorosa, 5th Floor, San Antonio, TX 78205
Tel: (210) 335-3954 Fax: (210) 335-3955
Internet: www.courts.state.tx.us/4ajr/4ajr.asp

District Clerk, Webb County **Esther Degollado** . . . . (956) 523-4268
1110 Victoria, Suite 203, Laredo, TX 78042-0669

County Clerk

Office of the County Clerk
1110 Victoria Street, Suite 201, Laredo, TX 78040
Tel: (956) 523-4266 Fax: (956) 523-5035
Internet: www.webbcountytx.gov/countyclerk

County Clerk **Margie Ibarra** . . . . (956) 523-4266

Wharton County

District Clerk

Second Administrative Judicial Region
301 North Thompson, Suite 102, Conroe, TX 77301
Tel: (936) 538-8176 Fax: (936) 538-8167
Internet: www.mctx.org/courts/second_administrative_judicial_region

District Clerk, Wharton County **Kendra Charbula** . . . . (979) 532-5542
P.O. Box 391, Wharton, TX 77488-0391

County Clerk

Office of the County Clerk
309 East Milam Street, Suite 700, Wharton, TX 77488
Tel: (979) 532-2381 Tel: (979) 532-8426

County Clerk **Sandra K. Sanders** . . . . (979) 532-2381
E-mail: sandra.sanders@co.wharton.tx.us

(continued on next page)

Wheeler County

District Clerk

Ninth Administrative Judicial Region
500 West Main, Room 204W, Brownfield, TX 79316
Tel: (806) 637-1329 Fax: (806) 637-8918
E-mail: kmoore@terrycounty.org

District Clerk, Wheeler County **Sherri Jones** . . . . (806) 826-5931
P.O. Box 528, Wheeler, TX 79096-0528

County Clerk

Office of the County Clerk
401 Main Street, Wheeler, TX 79096
Tel: (806) 826-5544 Fax: (806) 826-3282

County Clerk **Margaret Dorman** . . . . (806) 826-5544
E-mail: margaret.dorman@co.wheeler.tx.us

Wichita County

District Clerk

Eighth Administrative Judicial Region
401 West Belknap, 5th Floor, Fort Worth, TX 76196
Tel: (817) 884-1558 Fax: (817) 884-1560
E-mail: 8thadmin@8thjudicialregion.com

District Clerk, Wichita County **Patti Flores** . . . . (940) 766-8190
900 Seventh Street, Room 303,
Wichita Falls, TX 76301-2483

County Clerk

Office of the County Clerk
900 7th Street, Room 250, Wichita Falls, TX 76301
Tel: (940) 766-8195 Fax: (940) 716-8554

County Clerk **Lori Bohannon** . . . . (940) 766-8195
E-mail: Lori.Bohannon@co.wichita.tx.us

Wilbarger County

District Clerk

Ninth Administrative Judicial Region
500 West Main, Room 204W, Brownfield, TX 79316
Tel: (806) 637-1329 Fax: (806) 637-8918
E-mail: kmoore@terrycounty.org

District Clerk, Wilbarger County **Brenda Peterson** . . . . . . (940) 553-3411
1700 Wilbarger Street, Room 33,
Vernon, TX 76384-4749

County Clerk

Office of the County Clerk
1700 Wilbarger, Room 15, Vernon, TX 76384
Tel: (940) 552-5486 Fax: (940) 553-1202

County Clerk **Jana Kennon** . . . . (940) 552-5486
E-mail: jkennon@co.wilbarger.tx.us

Willacy County

District Clerk

Fifth Administrative Judicial Region
200 North Almond Street, Alice, TX 78332
Tel: (361) 668-5766 Fax: (512) 367-5788
E-mail: fifth.region@yahoo.com
Internet: www.courts.state.tx.us/5ajr/5ajr.asp

District Clerk, Willacy County **Gilbert Lozano** . . . . (956) 689-2532
546 West Hidalgo Avenue, First Floor,
Raymondville, TX 78580-3530

County Clerk

Office of the County Clerk
576 West Main Street, Raymondville, TX 78580
Tel: (956) 689-2710 Fax: (956) 689-9849

County Clerk **Terry Flores** . . . . (956) 689-2710
E-mail: terry.flores@co.willacy.tx.us

Williamson County

District Clerk

Third Administrative Judicial Region
405 M.L.K Boulevard Drive, Georgetown, TX 78626
Tel: (512) 943-3777 Fax: (512) 943-3767
E-mail: presidingjudge3@wilco.org
Internet: www.courts.state.tx.us/3ajr/3ajr.asp

District Clerk, Williamson County **Lisa David** . . . . (512) 943-1212
P.O. Box 24, Georgetown, TX 78627-0024

County Clerk

Office of the County Clerk
405 Martin Luther King Street, Georgetown, TX 78626
Tel: (512) 943-1515 Fax: (512) 943-1616

County Clerk **Nancy E. Rister** . . . . (512) 943-1515
E-mail: nrister@wilco.org

Wilson County

District Clerk

Fourth Administrative Judicial Region
100 Dolorosa, 5th Floor, San Antonio, TX 78205
Tel: (210) 335-3954 Fax: (210) 335-3955
Internet: www.courts.state.tx.us/4ajr/4ajr.asp

District Clerk, Wilson County **Deborah Bryan** . . . . (830) 393-7322
P.O. Box 812, Floresville, TX 78114-0812

County Clerk

Office of the County Clerk
P.O. Box 27, Floresville, TX 78114
Tel: (830) 393-7308 Fax: (830) 393-7334

County Clerk **Eva S. Martinez** . . . . (830) 393-7308
E-mail: eva.martinez@co.wilson.tx.us

Winkler County

District Clerk

Seventh Administrative Judicial Region
Midland County Courthouse, 500 North Loraine Street, Suite 502, Midland, TX 79701
Tel: (432) 688-4370 Fax: (432) 688-4933
Internet: www.courts.state.tx.us/7ajr/7ajr.asp

District Clerk, Winkler County **Sherry Terry** . . . . (432) 586-3359
P.O. Box 1065, Kermit, TX 79745-1065

County Clerk

Office of the County Clerk
100 East Winkler, Kermit, TX 79745
Tel: (432) 586-3401

County Clerk **Shethelia Reed** . . . . (432) 586-3401
E-mail: shethelia.reed@co.winkler.tx.us

Wise County

District Clerk

Eighth Administrative Judicial Region
401 West Belknap, 5th Floor, Fort Worth, TX 76196
Tel: (817) 884-1558 Fax: (817) 884-1560
E-mail: 8thadmin@8thjudicialregion.com

District Clerk, Wise County **Brenda Rowe** . . . . (940) 627-5535
P.O. Box 308, Decatur, TX 76234-0308

County Clerk

Office of the County Clerk
P.O. Box 359, Decatur, TX 76234
Tel: (940) 627-3351 Fax: (940) 627-2138

County Clerk **Sherry Lemon** . . . . (940) 627-3351
E-mail: countyclerk@co.wise.tx.us

Wood County

District Clerk

First Administrative Judicial Region
133 North Riverfront Boulevard, 5th Floor, Dallas, TX 75207
Tel: (214) 653-2943 Fax: (214) 653-2957
Internet: www.firstadmin.com

District Clerk, Wood County **Jenica Turner** . . . . (903) 763-2361
P.O. Box 1707, Quitman, TX 75783-1707

County Clerk

Office of the County Clerk
100 South Main Street, Quitman, TX 75783
Tel: (903) 763-2711 Fax: (903) 763-5641

County Clerk **Kelley Price** . . . . (903) 763-2711
E-mail: kprice@co.wood.tx.us

Yoakum County

District Clerk

Ninth Administrative Judicial Region
500 West Main, Room 204W, Brownfield, TX 79316
Tel: (806) 637-1329 Fax: (806) 637-8918
E-mail: kmoore@terrycounty.org

District Clerk, Yoakum County **Sandra Roblez** . . . . (806) 456-7491
P.O. Box 899, Plains, TX 79355-0899

County Clerk

Office of the County Clerk
P.O. Box 309, Plains, TX 79355
Tel: (806) 456-7491 Fax: (806) 456-2258

County Clerk **Deborah L. Rushing** . . . . (806) 456-7491 ext. 294
E-mail: drushing@yoakumcounty.org

Young County

District Clerk

Eighth Administrative Judicial Region
401 West Belknap, 5th Floor, Fort Worth, TX 76196
Tel: (817) 884-1558 Fax: (817) 884-1560
E-mail: 8thadmin@8thjudicialregion.com

District Clerk, Young County **Jamie Land** . . . . (940) 549-0029
516 Fourth Street, Room 201,
Graham, TX 76450-2964

County Clerk

Office of the County Clerk
516 Fourth Street, Room 104, Graham, TX 76450
Tel: (940) 549-8432 Fax: (940) 521-0305

County Clerk **Kay Hardin** . . . . (940) 549-8432
E-mail: k.hardin@youngcounty.org

Zapata County

District Clerk

Fourth Administrative Judicial Region
100 Dolorosa, 5th Floor, San Antonio, TX 78205
Tel: (210) 335-3954 Fax: (210) 335-3955
Internet: www.courts.state.tx.us/4ajr/4ajr.asp

District Clerk, Zapata County **Dora Rames** . . . . (956) 765-9930
P.O. Box 788, Zapata, TX 78076-0788

County Clerk

Office of the County Clerk
200 East 7th Avenue, Suite 138, Zapata, TX 78076
Tel: (956) 765-9915 Fax: (956) 765-9933

County Clerk **Mary Jayne Villarreal-Bonoan** . . . . (956) 765-9915
E-mail: mjbonoan@sbcglobal.net

(continued on next page)

Zavala County

District Clerk

Fourth Administrative Judicial Region
100 Dolorosa, 5th Floor, San Antonio, TX 78205
Tel: (210) 335-3954 Fax: (210) 335-3955
Internet: www.courts.state.tx.us/4ajr/4ajr.asp

District Clerk, Zavala County **Rachel P. Ramirez** . . . . (830) 374-3456
  P.O. Box 704, Crystal City, TX 78839-2798

County Clerk

Office of the County Clerk
200 East Uvalde Street, Suite 7, Crystal City, TX 78839
Tel: (830) 374-2331 Fax: (830) 374-5955

County Clerk **Oralia Trevino** . . . . (830) 374-2331

Counties Within Judicial Districts

1st District Court
Areas Covered: Jasper, Newton, Sabine, and San Augustine Counties.

1st District Court (2nd)
Areas Covered: Jasper, Newton, and Tyler Counties.

2nd District Court
Areas Covered: Cherokee County.

3rd District Court
Areas Covered: Anderson, Henderson, and Houston Counties.

4th District Court
Areas Covered: Rusk County.

5th District Court
Areas Covered: Bowie and Cass Counties.

6th District Court
Areas Covered: Lamar, Medina, and Red River Counties.

7th District Court
Areas Covered: Smith County.

8th District Court
Areas Covered: Delta, Franklin, Hopkins, and Rains Counties.

9th District Court
Areas Covered: Montgomery County.

10th District Court
Areas Covered: Galveston County.

11th District Court
Areas Covered: Harris County.

12th District Court
Areas Covered: Grimes, Leon, Madison and Walker Counties.

13th District Court
Areas Covered: Navarro County.

14th District Court
Areas Covered: Dallas County.

15th District Court
Areas Covered: Grayson County.

16th District Court
Areas Covered: Denton County.

17th District Court
Areas Covered: Tarrant County.

18th District Court
Areas Covered: Johnson and Somervell Counties.

19th District Court
Areas Covered: McLennan County.

20th District Court
Areas Covered: Milam County.

21st District Court
Areas Covered: Bastrop, Burleson, Lee and Washington Counties.

22nd District Court
Areas Covered: Caldwell, Comal and Hays Counties.

23rd District Court
Areas Covered: Brazoria, Matagorda and Wharton Counties.

24th District Court
Areas Covered: Calhoun, De Witt, Goliad, Jackson, Refugio and Victoria Counties.

25th District Court
Areas Covered: Colorado, Gonzales, Guadalupe and Lavaca Counties.

25th District Court (2nd)
Areas Covered: Colorado, Gonzales, Guadalupe and Lavaca Counties.

26th District Court
Areas Covered: Williamson County.

27th District Court
Areas Covered: Bell and Lampasas Counties.

28th District Court
Areas Covered: Nueces County.

Texas Court Clerks and Courthouses *continued*

29th District Court
Areas Covered: Palo Pinto County.

30th District Court
Areas Covered: Wichita County.

31st District Court
Areas Covered: Gray, Hemphill, Lipscomb, Roberts and Wheeler Counties.

32nd District Court
Areas Covered: Fisher, Mitchell and Nolan Counties.

33rd District Court
Areas Covered: Blanco, Burnet, Llano and San Saba Counties.

34th District Court
Areas Covered: El Paso County.

35th District Court
Areas Covered: Brown and Mills Counties.

36th District Court
Areas Covered: Aransas, Bee, Live Oak, McMullen and San Patricio Counties.

37th District Court
Areas Covered: Bexar County.

38th District Court
Areas Covered: Medina, Real and Uvalde Counties.

39th District Court
Areas Covered: Haskell, Kent, Stonewall and Throckmorton Counties.

40th District Court
Areas Covered: Ellis County.

41st District Court
Areas Covered: El Paso County.

42nd District Court
Areas Covered: Callahan, Coleman and Taylor Counties.

43rd District Court
Areas Covered: Parker County.

44th District Court
Areas Covered: Dallas County.

45th District Court
Areas Covered: Bexar County.

Texas Court Clerks and Courthouses *continued*

46th District Court
Areas Covered: Foard, Hardeman and Wilbarger Counties.

47th District Court
Areas Covered: Armstrong, Potter and Randall Counties.

48th District Court
Areas Covered: Tarrant County.

49th District Court
Areas Covered: Webb and Zapata Counties.

50th District Court
Areas Covered: Baylor, Cottle, King and Knox Counties.

51st District Court
Areas Covered: Coke, Irion, Schleicher, Sterling and Tom Green Counties.

52nd District Court
Areas Covered: Coryell County.

53rd District Court
Areas Covered: Travis County.

54th District Court
Areas Covered: McLennan County.

55th District Court
Areas Covered: Harris County.

56th District Court
Areas Covered: Galveston County.

57th District Court
Areas Covered: Bexar County.

58th District Court
Areas Covered: Jefferson County.

59th District Court
Areas Covered: Grayson County.

60th District Court
Areas Covered: Jefferson County.

61st District Court
Areas Covered: Harris County.

62nd District Court
Areas Covered: Delta, Franklin, Hopkins and Lamar Counties.

63rd District Court
Areas Covered: Edwards, Kinney, Terrell and Val Verde Counties.

(continued on next page)

64th District Court
Areas Covered: Castro, Hale and Swisher Counties.

65th District Court
Areas Covered: El Paso County.

66th District Court
Areas Covered: Hill County.

67th District Court
Areas Covered: Tarrant County.

68th District Court
Areas Covered: Dallas County.

69th District Court
Areas Covered: Dallam, Hartley, Moore and Sherman Counties.

70th District Court
Areas Covered: Ector County.

71st District Court
Areas Covered: Harrison County.

72nd District Court
Areas Covered: Crosby and Lubbock Counties.

73rd District Court
Areas Covered: Bexar County.

74th District Court
Areas Covered: McLennan County.

75th District Court
Areas Covered: Liberty County.

76th District Court
Areas Covered: Camp, Morris and Titus Counties.

77th District Court
Areas Covered: Freestone and Limestone Counties.

78th District Court
Areas Covered: Wichita County.

79th District Court
Areas Covered: Brooks and Jim Wells Counties.

80th District Court
Areas Covered: Harris County.

81st District Court
Areas Covered: Atascosa, Frio, Karnes, La Salle and Wilson Counties.

82nd District Court
Areas Covered: Falls and Robertson Counties.

83rd District Court
Areas Covered: Pecos, Terrell and Val Verde Counties.

84th District Court
Areas Covered: Hansford, Hutchinson and Ochiltree Counties.

85th District Court
Areas Covered: Brazos County.

86th District Court
Areas Covered: Kaufman County.

87th District Court
Areas Covered: Anderson, Freestone, Leon and Limestone Counties.

88th District Court
Areas Covered: Hardin and Tyler Counties.

89th District Court
Areas Covered: Wichita County.

90th District Court
Areas Covered: Stephens and Young Counties.

91st District Court
Areas Covered: Eastland County.

92nd District Court
Areas Covered: Hidalgo County.

93rd District Court
Areas Covered: Hidalgo County.

94th District Court
Areas Covered: Nueces County.

95th District Court
Areas Covered: Dallas County.

96th District Court
Areas Covered: Tarrant County.

97th District Court
Areas Covered: Archer, Clay and Montague Counties.

98th District Court
Areas Covered: Travis County.

99th District Court
Areas Covered: Lubbock County.

100th District Court
Areas Covered: Carson, Childress, Collingsworth, Donley and Hall Counties.

101st District Court
Areas Covered: Dallas County.

102nd District Court
Areas Covered: Bowie and Red River Counties.

103rd District Court
Areas Covered: Cameron County.

104th District Court
Areas Covered: Taylor County.

105th District Court
Areas Covered: Kenedy, Kleberg and Nueces Counties.

106th District Court
Areas Covered: Dawson, Gaines, Garza and Lynn Counties.

107th District Court
Areas Covered: Cameron County.

108th District Court
Areas Covered: Potter County.

109th District Court
Areas Covered: Andrews, Crane and Winkler Counties.

110th District Court
Areas Covered: Briscoe, Dickens, Floyd and Motley Counties.

111th District Court
Areas Covered: Webb County.

112th District Court
Areas Covered: Crockett, Pecos, Reagan, Sutton and Upton Counties.

113th District Court
Areas Covered: Harris County.

114th District Court
Areas Covered: Smith County.

115th District Court
Areas Covered: Marion and Upshur Counties.

116th District Court
Areas Covered: Dallas County.

117th District Court
Areas Covered: Nueces County.

118th District Court
Areas Covered: Glasscock, Howard and Martin Counties.

119th District Court
Areas Covered: Concho, Runnels and Tom Green Counties.

120th District Court
Areas Covered: El Paso and Terry Counties.

121st District Court
Areas Covered: Yoakum County.

122nd District Court
Areas Covered: Galveston County.

123rd District Court
Areas Covered: Panola and Shelby Counties.

124th District Court
Areas Covered: Gregg County.

125th District Court
Areas Covered: Harris County.

126th District Court
Areas Covered: Travis County.

127th District Court
Areas Covered: Harris County.

128th District Court
Areas Covered: Orange County.

129th District Court
Areas Covered: Harris County.

130th District Court
Areas Covered: Matagorda County.

131st District Court
Areas Covered: Bexar County.

132nd District Court
Areas Covered: Borden and Scurry Counties.

133rd District Court
Areas Covered: Harris County.

134th District Court
Areas Covered: Dallas County.

135th District Court
Areas Covered: Calhoun, De Witt, Goliad, Jackson, Refugio and Victoria Counties.

(continued on next page)

136th District Court
Areas Covered: Jefferson County.

137th District Court
Areas Covered: Lubbock County.

138th District Court
Areas Covered: Cameron County.

139th District Court
Areas Covered: Hidalgo County.

140th District Court
Areas Covered: Lubbock County.

141st District Court
Areas Covered: Tarrant County.

142nd District Court
Areas Covered: Midland County.

143rd District Court
Areas Covered: Loving, Reeves and Ward Counties.

144th District Court
Areas Covered: Bexar County.

145th District Court
Areas Covered: Nacogdoches County.

146th District Court
Areas Covered: Bell County.

147th District Court
Areas Covered: Travis County.

148th District Court
Areas Covered: Nueces County.

149th District Court
Areas Covered: Brazoria County.

150th District Court
Areas Covered: Bexar County.

151st District Court
Areas Covered: Harris County.

152nd District Court
Areas Covered: Harris County.

153rd District Court
Areas Covered: Tarrant County.

154th District Court
Areas Covered: Lamb County.

155th District Court
Areas Covered: Austin, Fayette and Waller Counties.

156th District Court
Areas Covered: Aransas, Bee, Live Oak, McMullen and San Patricio Counties.

157th District Court
Areas Covered: Harris County.

158th District Court
Areas Covered: Denton County.

159th District Court
Areas Covered: Angelina County.

160th District Court
Areas Covered: Dallas County.

161st District Court
Areas Covered: Ector County.

162nd District Court
Areas Covered: Dallas County.

163rd District Court
Areas Covered: Orange County.

164th District Court
Areas Covered: Harris County.

165th District Court
Areas Covered: Harris County.

166th District Court
Areas Covered: Bexar County.

167th District Court
Areas Covered: Travis County.

168th District Court
Areas Covered: El Paso County.

169th District Court
Areas Covered: Bell County.

170th District Court
Areas Covered: McLennan County.

171st District Court
Areas Covered: El Paso County.

172nd District Court
Areas Covered: Jefferson County.

173rd District Court
Areas Covered: Henderson County.

174th District Court
Areas Covered: Harris County.

175th District Court
Areas Covered: Bexar County.

176th District Court
Areas Covered: Harris County.

177th District Court
Areas Covered: Harris County.

178th District Court
Areas Covered: Harris County.

179th District Court
Areas Covered: Harris County.

180th District Court
Areas Covered: Harris County.

181st District Court
Areas Covered: Randall and Potter Counties.

182nd District Court
Areas Covered: Harris County.

183rd District Court
Areas Covered: Harris County.

184th District Court
Areas Covered: Harris County.

185th District Court
Areas Covered: Harris County.

186th District Court
Areas Covered: Bexar County.

187th District Court
Areas Covered: Bexar County.

188th District Court
Areas Covered: Gregg County.

189th District Court
Areas Covered: Harris County.

190th District Court
Areas Covered: Harris County.

191st District Court
Areas Covered: Dallas County.

192nd District Court
Areas Covered: Dallas County.

193rd District Court
Areas Covered: Dallas County.

194th District Court
Areas Covered: Dallas County.

195th District Court
Areas Covered: Dallas County.

196th District Court
Areas Covered: Hunt County.

197th District Court
Areas Covered: Cameron and Willacy Counties.

198th District Court
Areas Covered: Kerr, Kimble, McCulloch, Mason and Menard Counties.

199th District Court
Areas Covered: Collin County.

200th District Court
Areas Covered: Travis County.

201st District Court
Areas Covered: Travis County.

202nd District Court
Areas Covered: Bowie County.

203rd District Court
Areas Covered: Dallas County.

204th District Court
Areas Covered: Dallas County.

205th District Court
Areas Covered: Culberson, El Paso and Hudspeth Counties.

206th District Court
Areas Covered: Hidalgo County.

207th District Court
Areas Covered: Caldwell, Comal and Hays Counties.

(continued on next page)

208th District Court
Areas Covered: Harris County.

209th District Court
Areas Covered: Harris County.

210th District Court
Areas Covered: El Paso County.

211th District Court
Areas Covered: Denton County.

212th District Court
Areas Covered: Galveston County.

213th District Court
Areas Covered: Tarrant County.

214th District Court
Areas Covered: Nueces County.

215th District Court
Areas Covered: Harris County.

216th District Court
Areas Covered: Bandera, Gillespie, Kendall and Kerr Counties.

217th District Court
Areas Covered: Angelina County.

218th District Court
Areas Covered: Atascosa, Frio, Karnes, La Salle and Wilson Counties.

219th District Court
Areas Covered: Collin County.

220th District Court
Areas Covered: Bosque, Comanche and Hamilton Counties.

221st District Court
Areas Covered: Montgomery County.

222nd District Court
Areas Covered: Deaf Smith and Oldham Counties.

223rd District Court
Areas Covered: Gray County.

224th District Court
Areas Covered: Bexar County.

225th District Court
Areas Covered: Bexar County.

226th District Court
Areas Covered: Bexar County.

227th District Court
Areas Covered: Bexar County.

228th District Court
Areas Covered: Harris County.

229th District Court
Areas Covered: Duval, Jim Hogg and Starr Counties.

230th District Court
Areas Covered: Harris County.

231st District Court
Areas Covered: Tarrant County.

232nd District Court
Areas Covered: Harris County.

233rd District Court
Areas Covered: Tarrant County.

234th District Court
Areas Covered: Harris County.

235th District Court
Areas Covered: Cooke County.

236th District Court
Areas Covered: Tarrant County.

237th District Court
Areas Covered: Lubbock County.

238th District Court
Areas Covered: Midland County.

239th District Court
Areas Covered: Brazoria County.

240th District Court
Areas Covered: Fort Bend County.

241st District Court
Areas Covered: Smith County.

242nd District Court
Areas Covered: Castro, Hale and Swisher Counties.

243rd District Court
Areas Covered: El Paso County.

Texas Court Clerks and Courthouses *continued*

244th District Court
Areas Covered: Ector County.

245th District Court
Areas Covered: Harris County.

246th District Court
Areas Covered: Harris County.

247th District Court
Areas Covered: Harris County.

248th District Court
Areas Covered: Harris County.

249th District Court
Areas Covered: Johnson and Somervell Counties.

250th District Court
Areas Covered: Travis County.

251st District Court
Areas Covered: Potter and Randall Counties.

252nd District Court
Areas Covered: Jefferson County.

253rd District Court
Areas Covered: Chambers and Liberty Counties.

254th District Court
Areas Covered: Dallas County.

255th District Court
Areas Covered: Dallas County.

256th District Court
Areas Covered: Dallas County.

257th District Court
Areas Covered: Harris County.

258th District Court
Areas Covered: Polk, San Jacinto and Trinity Counties.

259th District Court
Areas Covered: Jones and Shackelford Counties.

260th District Court
Areas Covered: Orange County.

261st District Court
Areas Covered: Travis County.

Texas Court Clerks and Courthouses *continued*

262nd District Court
Areas Covered: Harris County.

263rd District Court
Areas Covered: Harris County.

264th District Court
Areas Covered: Bell County.

265th District Court
Areas Covered: Dallas County.

266th District Court
Areas Covered: Erath County.

267th District Court
Areas Covered: Calhoun, De Witt, Goliad, Jackson, Refugio and Victoria Counties.

268th District Court
Areas Covered: Fort Bend County.

269th District Court
Areas Covered: Harris County.

270th District Court
Areas Covered: Harris County.

271st District Court
Areas Covered: Jack and Wise Counties.

272nd District Court
Areas Covered: Brazos County.

273rd District Court
Areas Covered: Sabine, San Augustine and Shelby Counties.

274th District Court
Areas Covered: Comal, Guadalupe and Hays Counties.

275th District Court
Areas Covered: Hidalgo County.

276th District Court
Areas Covered: Camp, Marion, Morris and Titus Counties.

277th District Court
Areas Covered: Williamson County.

278th District Court
Areas Covered: Leon, Madison and Walker Counties.

279th District Court
Areas Covered: Jefferson County.

(continued on next page)

280th District Court
Areas Covered: Harris County.

281st District Court
Areas Covered: Harris County.

282nd District Court
Areas Covered: Dallas County.

283rd District Court
Areas Covered: Dallas County.

284th District Court
Areas Covered: Montgomery County.

285th District Court
Areas Covered: Bexar County.

286th District Court
Areas Covered: Cochran and Hockley Counties.

287th District Court
Areas Covered: Bailey and Parmer Counties.

288th District Court
Areas Covered: Bexar County.

289th District Court
Areas Covered: Bexar County.

290th District Court
Areas Covered: Bexar County.

291st District Court
Areas Covered: Dallas County.

292nd District Court
Areas Covered: Dallas County.

293rd District Court
Areas Covered: Dimmit, Maverick and Zavala Counties.

294th District Court
Areas Covered: Van Zandt County.

295th District Court
Areas Covered: Harris County.

296th District Court
Areas Covered: Collin County.

297th District Court
Areas Covered: Tarrant County.

298th District Court
Areas Covered: Dallas County.

299th District Court
Areas Covered: Travis County.

300th District Court
Areas Covered: Brazoria County.

301st District Court
Areas Covered: Dallas County.

302nd District Court
Areas Covered: Dallas County.

303rd District Court
Areas Covered: Dallas County.

304th District Court
Areas Covered: Dallas County.

305th District Court
Areas Covered: Dallas County.

306th District Court
Areas Covered: Galveston County.

307th District Court
Areas Covered: Gregg County.

308th District Court
Areas Covered: Harris County.

309th District Court
Areas Covered: Harris County.

310th District Court
Areas Covered: Harris County.

311th District Court
Areas Covered: Harris County.

312th District Court
Areas Covered: Harris County.

313th District Court
Areas Covered: Harris County.

314th District Court
Areas Covered: Harris County.

315th District Court
Areas Covered: Harris County.

316th District Court
Areas Covered: Hutchinson County.

317th District Court
Areas Covered: Jefferson County.

318th District Court
Areas Covered: Midland County.

319th District Court
Areas Covered: Nueces County.

320th District Court
Areas Covered: Potter County.

321st District Court
Areas Covered: Smith County.

322nd District Court
Areas Covered: Tarrant County.

323rd District Court
Areas Covered: Tarrant County.

324th District Court
Areas Covered: Tarrant County.

325th District Court
Areas Covered: Tarrant County.

326th District Court
Areas Covered: Taylor County.

327th District Court
Areas Covered: El Paso County.

328th District Court
Areas Covered: Fort Bend County.

329th District Court
Areas Covered: Wharton County.

330th District Court
Areas Covered: Dallas County.

331st District Court
Areas Covered: Travis County.

332nd District Court
Areas Covered: Hidalgo County.

333rd District Court
Areas Covered: Harris County.

334th District Court
Areas Covered: Harris County.

335th District Court
Areas Covered: Bastrop, Burleson, Lee and Washington Counties.

336th District Court
Areas Covered: Fannin County.

337th District Court
Areas Covered: Harris County.

338th District Court
Areas Covered: Harris County.

339th District Court
Areas Covered: Harris County.

340th District Court
Areas Covered: Tom Green County.

341st District Court
Areas Covered: Webb County.

342nd District Court
Areas Covered: Tarrant County.

343rd District Court
Areas Covered: Aransas, Bee, Live Oak, McMullen and San Patricio Counties.

344th District Court
Areas Covered: Chambers County.

345th District Court
Areas Covered: Travis County.

346th District Court
Areas Covered: El Paso County.

347th District Court
Areas Covered: Nueces County.

348th District Court
Areas Covered: Tarrant County.

349th District Court
Areas Covered: Anderson and Houston Counties.

350th District Court
Areas Covered: Taylor County.

351st District Court
Areas Covered: Harris County.

(continued on next page)

352nd District Court
Areas Covered: Tarrant County.

353rd District Court
Areas Covered: Travis County.

354th District Court
Areas Covered: Hunt and Rains Counties.

355th District Court
Areas Covered: Hood County.

356th District Court
Areas Covered: Hardin County.

357th District Court
Areas Covered: Cameron County.

358th District Court
Areas Covered: Ector County.

359th District Court
Areas Covered: Montgomery County.

360th District Court
Areas Covered: Tarrant County.

361st District Court
Areas Covered: Brazos County.

362nd District Court
Areas Covered: Denton County.

363rd District Court
Areas Covered: Dallas County.

364th District Court
Areas Covered: Lubbock County.

365th District Court
Areas Covered: Dimmit, Maverick and Zavala Counties.

366th District Court
Areas Covered: Collin County.

367th District Court
Areas Covered: Denton County.

368th District Court
Areas Covered: Williamson County.

369th District Court
Areas Covered: Anderson and Cherokee Counties.

370th District Court
Areas Covered: Hidalgo County.

371st District Court
Areas Covered: Tarrant County.

372nd District Court
Areas Covered: Tarrant County.

377th District Court
Areas Covered: Victoria County.

378th District Court
Areas Covered: Ellis County.

379th District Court
Areas Covered: Bexar County.

380th District Court
Areas Covered: Collin County.

381st District Court
Areas Covered: Starr County.

382nd District Court
Areas Covered: Rockwall County.

383rd District Court
Areas Covered: El Paso County.

384th District Court
Areas Covered: El Paso County.

385th District Court
Areas Covered: Midland County.

386th District Court
Areas Covered: Bexar County.

387th District Court
Areas Covered: Fort Bend County.

388th District Court
Areas Covered: El Paso County.

389th District Court
Areas Covered: Hidalgo County.

390th District Court
Areas Covered: Travis County.

391st District Court
Areas Covered: Tom Green County.

392nd District Court
Areas Covered: Henderson County.

393rd District Court
Areas Covered: Denton County.

394th District Court
Areas Covered: Brewster, Culberson, Hudspeth, Jeff Davis and Presidio Counties.

395th District Court
Areas Covered: Williamson County.

396th District Court
Areas Covered: Tarrant County.

397th District Court
Areas Covered: Grayson County.

398th District Court
Areas Covered: Hidalgo County.

399th District Court
Areas Covered: Bexar County.

400th District Court
Areas Covered: Fort Bend County.

401st District Court
Areas Covered: Collin County.

402nd District Court
Areas Covered: Wood County.

403rd District Court
Areas Covered: Travis County.

404th District Court
Areas Covered: Cameron County.

405th District Court
Areas Covered: Galveston County.

406th District Court
Areas Covered: Webb County.

407th District Court
Areas Covered: Bexar County.

408th District Court
Areas Covered: Bexar County.

409th District Court
Areas Covered: El Paso County.

410th District Court
Areas Covered: Montgomery County.

411th District Court
Areas Covered: Polk, San Jacinto and Trinity Counties.

412th District Court
Areas Covered: Brazoria County.

413th District Court
Areas Covered: Johnson County.

414th District Court
Areas Covered: McLennan County.

415th District Court
Areas Covered: Parker County.

416th District Court
Areas Covered: Collin County.

417th District Court
Areas Covered: Collin County.

418th District Court
Areas Covered: Montgomery County.

419th District Court
Areas Covered: Travis County.

420th District Court
Areas Covered: Nacogdoches County.

421st District Court
Areas Covered: Caldwell County.

422nd District Court
Areas Covered: Kaufman County.

423rd District Court
Areas Covered: Bastrop County.

424th District Court
Areas Covered: Blanco, Burnet, Llano and San Saba Counties.

425th District Court
Areas Covered: Williamson County.

426th District Court
Areas Covered: Bell County.

427th District Court
Areas Covered: Travis County.

(continued on next page)

Texas Court Clerks and Courthouses *continued*

428th District Court
Areas Covered: Hays County.

429th District Court
Areas Covered: Collin County.

430th District Court
Areas Covered: Hidalgo County.

431st District Court
Areas Covered: Denton County.

432nd District Court
Areas Covered: Tarrant County.

433rd District Court
Areas Covered: Comal County.

434th District Court
Areas Covered: Fort Bend County.

435th District Court
Areas Covered: Montgomery County.

436th District Court
Areas Covered: Bexar County.

437th District Court
Areas Covered: Bexar County.

438th District Court
Areas Covered: Bexar County.

439th District Court
Areas Covered: Rockwall County.

441st District Court
Areas Covered: Midland County.

444th District Court
Areas Covered: Cameron County.

445th District Court
Areas Covered: Cameron County.

448th District Court
Areas Covered: El Paso County.

449th District Court
Areas Covered: Hidalgo County.

506th District Court
Areas Covered: Grimes and Waller Counties.

Utah Court Clerks and Courthouses

The trial courts of general jurisdiction in Utah are called district courts. There are eight judicial districts, each consisting of several counties. In the listing below, the court executive and court clerks for each district are given first, followed by a county-by-county listing of county clerks.

Utah Supreme Court

Scott M. Matheson Courthouse, 450 South State Street, 5th Floor, Salt Lake City, UT 84114
P.O. Box 140210, Salt Lake City, UT 84114-0210
Tel: (801) 238-7967 Tel: (801) 238-7990 (Supreme Court Law Library)
E-mail: supremecourt@utcourts.gov
Internet: courtlink.utcourts.gov

The Supreme Court consists of a chief justice, an associate chief justice and three justices who are initially appointed by the Governor upon recommendation of a Judicial Nominating Commission and then run unopposed for retention for a ten-year term in the first general election occurring not more than three years after appointment. The chief justice is elected by peer vote to a four-year term and the associate chief justice is elected by peer vote to a two-year term. The Supreme Court has exclusive appellate jurisdiction over first degree and capital felony convictions from the Utah District Court and civil judgments other than domestic relations. The Court also has exclusive appellate jurisdiction over cases where the Utah Court of Appeals does not have jurisdiction and over some administrative agencies. The Court exercises constitutional rule-making authority over procedure and evidence and regulates admission to the state bar and the conduct of its members.

Court Staff
Clerk of the Court **Andrea Martinez**..................(801) 238-7974
    E-mail: andrearm@utcourts.gov

Utah Court of Appeals

Scott M. Matheson Courthouse, 450 South State Street, 5th Floor, Salt Lake City, UT 84111
P.O. Box 140230, Salt Lake City, UT 84114-0230
Tel: (801) 578-3900
Tel: (801) 578-3923 (Electronic Bulletin Board Data)
Fax: (801) 578-3999
Internet: courtlink.utcourts.gov/

The Court of Appeals, established in 1987, consists of a presiding judge and six judges who are initially appointed by the Governor upon recommendation of a Judicial Nominating Commission and then run unopposed for retention for six-year terms at the first general election occurring not more than three years after appointment. The presiding judge is elected by peer vote to a two-year term. The Court sits in rotating panels of three judges each. The Court of Appeals exercises appellate jurisdiction over cases from the Utah Juvenile Courts, domestic relations cases, criminal cases (except those appealed directly to the Supreme Court) and cases from administrative agencies which are not appealed directly to the Supreme Court.

Court Staff
Clerk of the Court **Lisa A. Collins**....................(801) 578-3907
    E-mail: lisaac@email.utcourts.gov

Utah Court Clerks and Courthouses *continued*

District-By-District

First Judicial District
43 North Main, Brigham City, UT 84302-0873
Tel: (435) 734-4600 Fax: (435) 734-4610

Areas Covered: Box Elder County, Cache County, Rich County

Court Staff
Court Executive **Corrie Keller**........................(435) 750-1337
    135 North 100 West, Logan, UT 84321   Fax: (435) 750-1335
    E-mail: corriek@utcourts.gov
Clerk of Court **Chris Jeppesen**.....................(435) 734-4617
    E-mail: chrisj@utcourts.gov   Fax: (435) 734-4610

Second Judicial District
2525 Grant Avenue, Ogden, UT 84401
Tel: (801) 395-1079 Fax: (801) 395-1182

Areas Covered: Davis County, Morgan County, Weber County

Court Staff
Court Executive **Sylvester Daniels**.................. (801) 395-1107
    E-mail: sylvesterd@utcourts.gov   Fax: (801) 395-1182
Clerk of Court, Weber County **Maureen Magagna**......(801) 395-1060
      Fax: (801) 395-1182
Clerk of Court, Morgan County **Lynn Wiseman**........ (801) 845-4011
    48 Young Street, Morgan, UT 84050   Fax: (801) 829-6176
Clerk of Court, Davis County **Alyson Brown**...........(801) 479-3177
    1600 East South Weber Drive,   Fax: (801) 479-0066
    South Weber, UT 84405

Third Judicial District
450 South State Street, Salt Lake City, UT 84111
Tel: (801) 238-7300 Fax: (801) 238-7076

Areas Covered: Salt Lake County, Summit County, Tooele County

Court Staff
Court Executive **Peyton Smith**..................... (801) 238-7315
    E-mail: peytons@utcourts.gov   Fax: (801) 238-7074
Clerk of Court, Salt Lake County **Chris Davies**......... (801) 238-7334
    E-mail: chrisd@utcourts.gov   Fax: (801) 238-7430
Clerk of Court, Summit County (Acting) **Chris Davies**... (801) 233-9771
    8080 South Redwood Road, Suite 1701,   Fax: (801) 233-9760
    West Jordan, UT 84088
Clerk of Court, Tooele County (Acting) **Chris Davies**....(801) 233-9771
    8080 South Redwood Road,   Fax: (801) 233-9760
    West Jordan, UT 84088

Fourth Judicial District
125 North 100 West, Provo, UT 84601
Tel: (801) 429-1000 Fax: (801) 429-1033

Areas Covered: Juab County, Millard County, Utah County, Wasatch County

Court Staff
Court Executive **Shane Bahr**........................ (801) 429-1038
    E-mail: shaneb@utcourts.gov   Fax: (801) 489-1020
Clerk of Court **Lori Woffinden**..................... (801) 429-1176
    E-mail: loriw@utcourts.gov   Fax: (801) 429-1033

(continued on next page)

Fifth Judicial District

40 North 100 East, Cedar City, UT 84720
Tel: (435) 867-3250 Fax: (435) 867-3212

Areas Covered: Beaver County, Iron County, Washington County

Court Staff

Court Executive **Rick Davis** . . . . (435) 986-5722
   206 West Tabernacle, St. George, UT 84770   Fax: (435) 986-5723
   E-mail: rickd@utcourts.gov
Clerk of Court **Carolyn Bulloch** . . . .(435) 867-3201
   206 West Tabernacle, St. George, UT 84770   Fax: (435) 867-3212

Sixth Judicial District

845 East 300 North, Richfield, UT 84701
Tel: (435) 676-1104 Fax: (435) 676-8629

Areas Covered: Garfield County, Kane County, Piute County, Sanpete County, Sevier County, Wayne County

Court Staff

Court Executive **Wendell Roberts** . . . .(435) 896-2710
   E-mail: wendellr@utcourts.gov   Fax: (435) 896-2743
Clerk of the Court and County Clerk/Auditor
   Camille Moore . . . .(435) 676-1100
   P.O. Box 77, Panguitch, UT 84759   Fax: (435) 676-8239
Clerk of Court and County Clerk/Auditor, Kane
   County **Karla Johnson** . . . . (435) 644-2458
   Kane County Courthouse, 79 North Main Street,   Fax: (435) 644-2052
   Kanab, UT 84741
   E-mail: clerkkj@kanab.net
Clerk of the Court and County Clerk/Auditor, Piute
   County **Kali Gleave** . . . . (435) 577-2840
   Piute County Courthouse, 550 North Main,   Fax: (435) 577-2433
   Junction, UT 84740
   E-mail: valeenb@hotmail.com
Clerk of Court, Sanpete County **Keri Sargent** . . . . (435) 644-2706
     Fax: (435) 644-2743
Clerk of Court, Sevier County **Keri Sargent** . . . . (435) 644-2706
     Fax: (435) 644-2743
Clerk of Court, Wayne County **Ryan Torgerson** . . . .(435) 836-1300
   Wayne County Courthouse,   Fax: (435) 836-2479
   Loa, UT 84747-0189

Seventh Judicial District

149 East 100 South, Price, UT 84501
Tel: (435) 636-3400

Areas Covered: Carbon County, Emery County, Grand County, San Juan County

Court Staff

Court Executive **Terri Yelonek** . . . . (435) 636-3401
   E-mail: terriy@utcourts.gov   Fax: (435) 637-2102
Clerk of Court **Claudia Page** . . . . (435) 636-3400
   E-mail: claudiap@utcourts.gov

Eighth Judicial Circuit

920 East Highway 40, Vernal, UT 84078
Tel: (435) 781-9300 Fax: (435) 789-0564

Areas Covered: Daggett County, Duchesne County, Uintah County

Court Staff

Court Executive **Russell F. Pearson** . . . .(435) 781-9301
   E-mail: russellp@utcourts.gov   Fax: (435) 789-5639
Clerk of Court **Dawn Hautamaki** . . . . (435) 781-9303
   E-mail: dawnh@utcourts.gov   Fax: (435) 789-0564

County-By-County

Beaver County

County Clerk

Office of the County Clerk/Auditor
P.O. Box 392, Beaver, UT 84713
105 East Center Street, Beaver, UT 84713
Fax: (435) 438-6462

County Clerk/Auditor **Ginger McMullen** . . . . (435) 438-6463

Box Elder County

County Clerk

Office of the County Clerk/Auditor
One South Main Street, Suite 10, Brigham City, UT 84302
Fax: (435) 695-2502

County Clerk/Auditor **Marla Young** . . . .(435) 734-3393
   E-mail: myoung@boxeldercounty.org

Cache County

County Clerk

Office of the County Clerk
179 North Main Street, Suite 102, Logan, UT 84321
Fax: (435) 755-1980

County Clerk **Jill Zollinger** . . . .(435) 755-1460
   E-mail: jill.zollinger@cachecounty.org

Carbon County

County Clerk

Office of the County Clerk/Auditor
120 East Main, Price, UT 84501
Fax: (435) 636-3210

County Clerk/Auditor **Seth Oveson** . . . . (435) 636-3200
   E-mail: seth.oveson@carbon.utah.gov

Daggett County

County Clerk

Office of the County Clerk/Treasurer
P.O. Box 400, Manila, UT 84046
Fax: (435) 784-3335

County Clerk/Treasurer **Sue Olorenshaw** . . . .(435) 784-3154
   E-mail: solorenshaw@daggettcounty.org

Davis County

County Clerk

County Clerk/Auditor's Department
61 South Main Street, Room 136, Farmington, UT 84025
P.O. Box 618, Farmington, UT 84025
Tel: (801) 451-3213 Fax: (801) 451-3421
Internet: www.co.davis.ut.us/clerkauditor

County Clerk/Auditor **Curtis Koch** . . . .(801) 451-3324
   E-mail: ckoch@daviscountyutah.gov

Duchesne County

County Clerk

Office of the County Clerk/Auditor
P.O. Box 270, Duchesne, UT 84021
Fax: (435) 738-5522

County Clerk **JoAnn Evans**.........................(435) 738-1228
E-mail: jevans@duchesne.utah.gov

Emery County

County Clerk

Office of the County Clerk/Auditor
P.O. Box 907, Castle Dale, UT 84513
75 East Main, Castle Dale, UT 84513
Fax: (435) 381-5183

County Clerk/Auditor **Brenda Tuttle**.................(435) 381-3551
E-mail: clerk-auditor@emery.utah.gov

Garfield County

County Clerk

Sixth Judicial District
845 East 300 North, Richfield, UT 84701
Tel: (435) 676-1104 Fax: (435) 676-8629

Clerk of the Court and County Clerk/Auditor
Camille Moore....................................(435) 676-1100
P.O. Box 77, Panguitch, UT 84759   Fax: (435) 676-8239

Grand County

County Clerk

Office of the County Clerk/Auditor
125 East Center Street, Moab, UT 84532
Fax: (435) 259-2959

County Clerk/Auditor **Diana Carroll**.................(435) 259-1322
E-mail: dcarroll@grandcountyutah.net

Iron County

County Clerk

Office of the County Clerk/Auditor
P.O. Box 429, Parowan, UT 84761
Fax: (435) 477-8847

County Clerk **Jon Whittaker**.......................(435) 477-8341
E-mail: jon@ironcounty.net

Juab County

County Clerk

Office of the County Clerk/Auditor
160 North Main, Nephi, UT 84648
Fax: (435) 623-5936

County Clerk/Auditor **Alaina Lofgran**................(435) 623-3410
E-mail: alainal@juabcounty.com

Kane County

County Clerk

Sixth Judicial District
845 East 300 North, Richfield, UT 84701
Tel: (435) 676-1104 Fax: (435) 676-8629

Clerk of Court and County Clerk/Auditor, Kane
County **Karla Johnson** ....(435) 644-2458
Kane County Courthouse, 79 North Main Street,   Fax: (435) 644-2052
Kanab, UT 84741
E-mail: clerkkj@kanab.net

Millard County

County Clerk

Office of the County Clerk
765 South Highway 99, Suite Six, Fillmore, UT 84631
Fax: (435) 743-6923

County Clerk **Marki Rowley** ....(435) 743-6223
E-mail: mrowley@co.millard.ut.us

Morgan County

County Clerk

Office of the County Clerk/Auditor
48 West Young Street, Room 18, Morgan, UT 84050
Fax: (801) 829-6176

County Clerk/Auditor **Stacy Laffite**..................(801) 845-4011
E-mail: slafitte@morgan-county.net

Piute County

County Clerk

Sixth Judicial District
845 East 300 North, Richfield, UT 84701
Tel: (435) 676-1104 Fax: (435) 676-8629

Clerk of the Court and County Clerk/Auditor, Piute
County **Kali Gleave** ....(435) 577-2840
Piute County Courthouse, 550 North Main,   Fax: (435) 577-2433
Junction, UT 84740
E-mail: valeenb@hotmail.com

Rich County

County Clerk

Office of the County Clerk/Auditor
P.O. Box 218, Randolph, UT 84064
Fax: (435) 793-2410

County Clerk/Auditor **Becky Peart** ....(435) 793-2415
E-mail: bpeart@richcountyut.org

(continued on next page)

Utah Court Clerks and Courthouses *continued*

Salt Lake County

County Clerk

Office of the County Clerk
Salt Lake County Government Center, 2001 South State Street,
Suite S2200, Salt Lake City, UT 84190-1050
Tel: (385) 468-7399 Fax: (385) 468-7397
Internet: www.clerk.slco.org

County Clerk **Sherrie Swensen**......................(385) 468-7370
  E-mail: sswensen@slco.org

San Juan County

County Clerk

Office of the County Clerk/Auditor
P.O. Box 338, Monticello, UT 84535
Fax: (435) 587-2425

County Clerk/Auditor **John David Nielson** .... (435) 587-3223 ext. 4113
  E-mail: jdnielson@sanjuancounty.org

Sanpete County

County Clerk

Office of the County Clerk/Auditor
160 North Main, Suite 202, Manti, UT 84642
Fax: (435) 835-2144

County Clerk/Auditor **Sandy Neill**...................(435) 835-2131
  E-mail: sneill@sanpetecounty-ut.gov

Sevier County

County Clerk

Office of the County Clerk/Auditor
250 North Main Street, Richfield, UT 84701
Fax: (435) 896-8888

County Clerk/Auditor **Steven C. Wall**................(435) 893-0401

Summit County

County Clerk

Office of the County Clerk
P.O. Box 128, Coalville, UT 84017
Fax: (435) 336-3030

County Clerk **Kent Jones**..........................(435) 336-3203
  E-mail: kentjones@summitcounty.org

Tooele County

County Clerk

Office of the County Clerk/Auditor
47 South Main, Room 318, Tooele, UT 84074
Fax: (435) 882-7317

County Clerk/Auditor **Marilyn K. Gillette**..............(435) 843-3140
  E-mail: mgillette@co.tooele.ut.us

Utah Court Clerks and Courthouses *continued*

Uintah County

County Clerk

Office of the County Clerk/Auditor
147 East Main, Vernal, UT 84078
Fax: (435) 781-6701

County Clerk/Auditor **Michael Wilkins**................(435) 781-5361
  E-mail: mwilkins@co.uintah.ut.us

Utah County

County Clerk

County Clerk/Auditor's Office
100 East Center Street, Room 3600, Provo, UT 84606
Tel: (801) 851-8109 Fax: (801) 851-8232
Internet: www.utahcountyonline.org/Dept/clerkaud/index.asp

Clerk/Auditor **Bryan E. Thompson**...................(801) 851-8109
  E-mail: bryant@utahcounty.gov

Wasatch County

County Clerk

Office of the County Clerk/Auditor
25 North Main, Heber City, UT 84032
Fax: (435) 654-0834

County Clerk/Auditor **Brent Titcomb**.................(435) 657-3190
  E-mail: btitcomb@co.wasatch.ut.us

Washington County

County Clerk

Office of the County Clerk/Auditor
197 East Tabernacle Street, St. George, UT 84770
Fax: (435) 634-5763

County Clerk/Auditor **Kim M. Hafen**..................(435) 634-5712
  E-mail: kim.hafen@washco.utah.gov

Wayne County

County Clerk

Office of the County Clerk/Auditor
P.O. Box 189, Loa, UT 84747
Fax: (435) 836-2479

County Clerk/Auditor **Ryan Torgerson**................(435) 836-1300
  E-mail: ryan@wayne.utah.gov

Weber County

County Clerk

Office of the County Clerk/Auditor
2380 Washington Boulevard, Suite 320, Ogden, UT 84401
Tel: (801) 399-8400 Fax: (801) 399-8300
Internet: www.co.weber.ut.us/Clerk_Auditor

County Clerk/Auditor **Ricky D. Hatch**.................(801) 399-8613
  E-mail: rhatch@co.weber.ut.us

Vermont Court Clerks and Courthouses

The trial courts in Vermont include the superior courts (civil), the district courts (criminal), and the family courts. There is a superior court in each of the 14 counties of the State. The superior court clerks are given below. There is no intermediate appellate court in Vermont.

Vermont Supreme Court

111 State Street, Montpelier, VT 05609-0701
109 State Street, Montpelier, VT 05609-0801
Tel: (802) 828-3278 Tel: (802) 828-3234 (TTD)
Tel: (802) 828-2729 (Electronic Bulletin Board Data)
Fax: (802) 828-3457
Internet: www.vermontjudiciary.org

The Supreme Court consists of a chief justice and four associate justices who are initially appointed for six-year terms by the Governor with the advice and consent of the State Senate from a list of nominees submitted by the Judicial Nominating Board. Thereafter, the newly-appointed justices are subject to retention votes by the Vermont General Assembly for six-year terms. The chief justice is appointed by the Governor. Retirement is mandatory at age ninety; however, retired justices may be recalled by the chief justice to serve temporary assignments. The Supreme Court has appellate jurisdiction over the Vermont Superior Court, District Court, Family Court, Environmental Court and Judicial Bureau, as well as over the Vermont Probate Court when a question of law is involved. The Court also has appellate jurisdiction over certain administrative agency proceedings. The Court has administrative control over all courts, admittance to the state bar, and the regulation of the practice of law and disciplinary control over judges and attorneys.

Court Staff

Court Administrator and Clerk of the Court
Patricia Gabel . . . . (802) 828-3278
E-mail: patricia.gabel@state.vt.us

County-By-County

Addison County

Court Clerk

Addison Criminal Division
Seven Mahady Court, Middlebury, VT 05753

Superior Court Clerk (Interim) **Therese Corsones** . . . . . . (802) 388-4237
Seven Mahady Court, Middlebury, VT 05753
E-mail: therese.corsones@state.vt.us

Bennington County

Court Clerk

Bennington Criminal Division
200 Veterans Memorial Drive, Bennington, VT 05201

Superior Court Clerk **Mary Frost** . . . .(802) 447-2727
200 Veterans Memorial Drive,
Bennington, VT 05201
E-mail: mary.frost@state.vt.us

Caledonia County

Court Clerk

Caledonia Criminal Division
1126 Main Street, Suite One, St. Johnsbury, VT 05819

Superior Court Clerk **Kathleen Pearl** . . . . (802) 748-6600
1126 Main Street, Suite One,
St. Johnsbury, VT 05819
E-mail: kathleen.pearl@state.vt.us

Chittenden County

Court Clerk

Chittenden Criminal Division
32 Cherry Street, Suite 300, Burlington, VT 05401

Superior Court Clerk **Christine Brock** . . . .(802) 651-1950
32 Cherry Street, Suite 300,
Burlington, VT 05401
E-mail: christine.brock@state.vt.us

Essex County

Court Clerk

Essex Criminal Division
75 Courthouse Drive, Guildhall, VT 05905

Superior Court Clerk **Kathleen Pearl** . . . . (802) 676-3910
75 Courthouse Drive, Guildhall, VT 05905
E-mail: kathleen.pearl@state.vt.us

Franklin County

Court Clerk

Franklin Criminal Division
36 Lake Street, St. Albans, VT 05478

Superior Court Clerk **Gaye Paquette** . . . . (802) 524-7997
36 Lake Street, St. Albans, VT 05478
E-mail: gaye.paquette@state.vt.us

Grand Isle County

Court Clerk

Franklin Criminal Division
36 Lake Street, St. Albans, VT 05478

Superior Court Clerk **Gaye Paquette** . . . . (802) 524-7997
36 Lake Street, St. Albans, VT 05478
E-mail: gaye.paquette@state.vt.us

Lamoille County

Court Clerk

Lamoille Criminal Division
154 Main Street, Hyde Park, VT 05655

Superior Court Clerk **Kathleen Hobart** . . . . (802) 888-3887
154 Main Street, Hyde Park, VT 05655
E-mail: kathleen.hobart@state.vt.us

(continued on next page)

Vermont Court Clerks and Courthouses *continued*

Orange County

Court Clerk

Orange Criminal Division
Five Court Street, Chelsea, VT 05038

Superior Court Clerk **Theresa Scott** . . . . (802) 685-4610
  Five Court Street, Chelsea, VT 05038
  E-mail: theresa.scott@state.vt.us

Orleans County

Court Clerk

Orleans Criminal Division
217 Main Street, Newport, VT 05855

Superior Court Clerk **Tina de la Bruere** . . . . (802) 334-3325
  217 Main Street, Newport, VT 05855
  E-mail: tina.delabruere@state.vt.us

Rutland County

Court Clerk

Rutland Criminal Division
Nine Merchants Row, Rutland, VT 05701

Superior Court Clerk **Therese Corsones** . . . . (802) 786-5880
  Nine Merchants Row, Rutland, VT 05701
  E-mail: therese.corsones@state.vt.us

Washington County

Court Clerk

Washington Criminal Division
255 North Main Street, Barre, VT 05641

Superior Court Clerk (Acting) **Tina de la Bruere** . . . . (802) 479-4205
  255 North Main Street, Barre, VT 05641

Windham County

Court Clerk

Windham Criminal Division
30 Putney Road, Second Floor, Brattleboro, VT 05301

Superior Court Clerk **Anne Damone** . . . . (802) 257-2800
  30 Putney Road, Second Floor,
  Brattleboro, VT 05301
  E-mail: anne.damone@state.vt.us

Windsor County

Court Clerk

Orange Criminal Division
Five Court Street, Chelsea, VT 05038

Superior Court Clerk **Theresa Scott** . . . . (802) 685-4610
  Five Court Street, Chelsea, VT 05038
  E-mail: theresa.scott@state.vt.us

Virginia Court Clerks and Courthouses

The trial courts of general jurisdiction in Virginia are called circuit courts. There are circuit courts in every county and selected cities of the State. The listing below includes both cities and counties in which circuit courts preside. In addition to their circuit court duties, the clerks have general county clerk functions as well.

Supreme Court of Virginia

100 North Ninth Street, Richmond, VA 23219
Tel: (804) 786-2251
Tel: (804) 371-8611 (Electronic Bulletin Board Data)
Fax: (804) 786-6249
Internet: www.courts.state.va.us/scv

The Supreme Court consists of a chief justice and six justices who are elected by majority vote of the Virginia General Assembly for twelve-year terms. Vacancies on the Court occurring between sessions of the General Assembly may be filled by the Governor for a term expiring thirty days after the commencement of the next session of the General Assembly. The chief justice is elected by the Court for a four-year term. The Supreme Court has appellate jurisdiction over decisions of the lower courts. The Court exercises review over cases involving the death penalty, the disbarment of an attorney, or the State Corporation Commission. The Court has original jurisdiction in matters filed by the Judicial Inquiry and Review Commission relating to judicial censure, retirement and removal of judges. The Court exercises administrative control over the lower courts.

Court Staff
Clerk of Court **Patricia L. Harrington** . . . . (804) 786-2251
    E-mail: scvclerk@courts.state.va.us   Fax: (804) 786-6249

Court of Appeals of Virginia

109 North Eighth Street, Richmond, VA 23219-2321
Tel: (804) 371-8428
Internet: www.courts.state.va.us/coa/coa.htm

The Court of Appeals, established in 1985, consists of a chief judge and ten judges who are elected by majority vote of the Virginia General Assembly for eight-year terms. If a vacancy occurs while the General Assembly is not in session, the Governor may appoint a successor to serve until thirty days after the commencement of the next session of the General Assembly. The chief judge is elected by a majority vote of the judges of the Court to serve a term of four years. The Court of Appeals has authority to hear appeals as a matter of right from: (a) any final judgment, order, or decree of a circuit court involving affirmance or annulment of a marriage, divorce, custody, spousal or child support, or control or disposition of a child, as well as other domestic relations cases; (b) any final decision of the Workers' Compensation Commission; (c) any final decision of a circuit court on appeal from a decision of an administrative agency; and (d) any interlocutory order granting, dissolving, or denying an injunction or adjudicating the principles of a cause in any cases listed above. The Court also has authority to consider petitions for appeal from final orders of conviction in criminal and traffic matters except where a death penalty is imposed, final decisions of a circuit court on an application for a concealed weapons permit, and certain preliminary rulings in felony cases when requested by the Commonwealth.

Court Staff
Clerk of Court **Cynthia L. McCoy** . . . . (804) 371-8428
    E-mail: cmccoy@courts.state.va.us

Circuit-By-Circuit

Accomack Circuit Court

Circuit Clerk

Accomack Circuit Court
23316 Courthouse Avenue, Accomac, VA 23301-0126
P.O. Box 126, Accomac, VA 23301
Tel: (757) 758-5776 Fax: (757) 787-1849
Internet: http://www.courts.state.va.us/courts/circuit/Accomack/home.html

Clerk of Court **Samuel H. Cooper, Jr.** . . . . (757) 787-5776
    E-mail: shcooper@courts.state.va.us

Albemarle Circuit Court

Circuit Clerk

Albemarle Circuit Court
501 East Jefferson Street, Charlottesville, VA 22902-5110
Tel: (434) 972-4083 Tel: (434) 972-4085 Fax: (434) 293-0298

Clerk of Court **Debra Shipp** . . . . (434) 972-4083
    E-mail: dshipp@courts.state.va.us

Alexandria Circuit Court

Circuit Clerk

Alexandria Circuit Court
520 King Street, Alexandria, VA 22314
Tel: (703) 746-4044

Clerk of Court **Edward Semonian, Jr.** . . . . (703) 746-4044

Alleghany Circuit Court

Circuit Clerk

Alleghany Circuit Court
266 West Main Street, Covington, VA 24426-0670
P.O. Box 670, Covington, VA 24426-0670
Tel: (540) 965-1730 Fax: (540) 965-1737

Clerk of Court **Debra N. Byer** . . . . (540) 965-1730
    E-mail: dbyer@courts.state.va.us

Amelia Circuit Court

Circuit Clerk

Amelia Circuit Court
16441 Court Street, Amelia Court House, VA 23002-0237
P.O. Box 237, Amelia Court House, VA 23002-0237
Tel: (804) 561-2128 Fax: (804) 561-6364

Clerk of Court **Marilyn L. Wilson** . . . . (804) 561-2128
    E-mail: mwilson@courts.state.va.us

(continued on next page)

Virginia Court Clerks and Courthouses *continued*

Amherst Circuit Court

Circuit Clerk

Amherst Circuit Court
113 Taylor Street, Amherst, VA 24521
P.O. Box 462, Amherst, VA 24521
Tel: (434) 946-9321 Fax: (434) 946-9323

Clerk of Court **Roy C. Mayo III** . . . . (434) 946-9321
E-mail: rmayo@courts.state.va.us

Appomattox Circuit Court

Circuit Clerk

Appomattox Circuit Court
297 Court Street, Suite B, Appomattox, VA 24522-0672
Tel: (434) 352-5275 Fax: (434) 352-2781

Clerk of Courts **Janet A. Hix** . . . . (434) 352-5275
E-mail: jhix@courts.state.va.us

Arlington Circuit Court

Circuit Clerk

Arlington Circuit Court
1425 North Courthouse Road, Arlington, VA 22201
Tel: (703) 228-7010

Clerk of Court **Paul F. Ferguson** . . . . (703) 228-7010
E-mail: circuitcourt@arlingtonva.us

Augusta Circuit Court

Circuit Clerk

Augusta Circuit Court
1 East Johnson Street, Staunton, VA 24402-0689
Tel: (540) 245-5321 Fax: (540) 245-5318

Clerk of Court **Carol M. Brydge** . . . . (540) 245-5321

Bath Circuit Court

Circuit Clerk

Bath Circuit Court
P.O. Box 180, Warm Springs, VA 24484-0180
Tel: (540) 839-7226 Fax: (540) 839-7248

Clerk of Court **M. Wayne Winebriner** . . . . (540) 839-7226
E-mail: wwinebriner@courts.state.va.us

Bedford Circuit Court

Circuit Clerk

Bedford Circuit Court
123 East Main Street, Suite 201, Bedford, VA 24523
Tel: (540) 586-7632 Fax: (540) 586-6197

Clerk of Court **Cathy C. Hogan** . . . . (540) 586-7632
E-mail: chogan@courts.state.va.us

Virginia Court Clerks and Courthouses *continued*

Bland Circuit Court

Circuit Clerk

Bland Circuit Court
612 Main Street, Suite 104, Bland, VA 24315-0295
P.O. Box 295, Bland, VA 24315-0295
Tel: (276) 688-4562 Fax: (276) 688-2438

Clerk of Court **Rebecca I. Johnson** . . . . (276) 688-4562
E-mail: rijohnson@courts.state.va.us

Botetourt Circuit Court

Circuit Clerk

Botetourt Circuit Court
P.O. Box 219, Fincastle, VA 24090-0219
Tel: (540) 473-8274 Fax: (540) 473-8209

Clerk of Court **Tommy L. Moore** . . . . (540) 473-8274

Bristol Circuit Court

Circuit Clerk

Bristol Circuit Court
497 Cumberland Street, Bristol, VA 24201
Tel: (276) 645-7321 Fax: (276) 821-6097

Clerk of Court **Kelly Duffy** . . . . (276) 645-7321
E-mail: kduffy@courts.state.va.us

Brunswick Circuit Court

Circuit Clerk

Brunswick Circuit Court
216 North Main Street, Lawrenceville, VA 28368-0160
Tel: (434) 848-2215 Fax: (434) 848-4307
Internet: http://www.courts.state.va.us/courts/circuit/Brunswick/home.html

Clerk of Court **V. Earl Stanley, Jr.** . . . . (434) 848-2215
E-mail: vesjr@telpage.net

Buchanan Circuit Court

Circuit Clerk

Buchanan Circuit Court
101 East Main Street, Tazewell, VA 24651-1071
Tel: (276) 935-6567

Clerk of Court **Beverly S. Tiller** . . . . (276) 935-6567
E-mail: btiller@courts.state.va.us

Buckingham Circuit Court

Circuit Clerk

Buckingham Circuit Court
13061 W. James Anderson Highway, Buckingham, VA 23992-0107
P.O. Box 107, Buckingham, VA 23921-0107
Tel: (434) 969-4734 Fax: (434) 969-2043

Clerk of Court **Malcolm Booker, Jr.** . . . . (434) 969-4734
E-mail: mbooker@courts.state.va.us

Buena Vista Circuit Court

Circuit Clerk

Buena Vista Circuit Court
2039 Sycamore Avenue, Buena Vista, VA 24416
Tel: (540) 261-8627 Fax: (540) 261-8625

Clerk of Court **Christopher W. Coleman** . . . . (540) 261-8627
E-mail: ccoleman@courts.state.va.us

Campbell Circuit Court

Circuit Clerk

Campbell Circuit Court
732 Village Highway, Rustburg, VA 24588-0007
P.O. Box 7, Rustburg, VA 24588-0007
Tel: (434) 592-9517

Clerk of Court **Sheila Bosiger** . . . . (434) 592-9517

Caroline Circuit Court

Circuit Clerk

Caroline Circuit Court
112 Courthouse Lane, Suite A, Bowling Green, VA 22427-0309
Tel: (804) 633-5800

Clerk of Court **Ray S. Campbell, Jr.** . . . . (804) 633-5800
E-mail: rcampbell@courts.state.va.us

Carroll Circuit Court

Circuit Clerk

Carroll Circuit Court
605 Pine Street, Hillsville, VA 24343-0218
P.O. Box 218, Hillsville, VA 24343-0218
Tel: (276) 730-3070 Fax: (276) 730-3071

Clerk of Court (Acting) **Janice Jessup** . . . . (276) 730-3070

Charles City Circuit Court

Circuit Clerk

Charles City Circuit Court
10780 Courthouse Road, Charles City, VA 23030-0086
P.O. Box 86, Charles City, VA 23030-0086
Tel: (804) 652-2105 Tel: (804) 652-2107 Fax: (804) 829-5647
Internet: http://www.courts.state.va.us/courts/circuit/Charles_
City/home.html

Clerk of Court **Edith K. Holmes** . . . . (804) 652-2105
E-mail: ekholmes@courts.state.va.us

Charlotte Circuit Court

Circuit Clerk

Charlotte Circuit Court
125 David Bruce Avenue, Charlotte Court House, VA 23923-0038
P.O. Box 38, Charlotte Court House, VA 23923-0038
Tel: (434) 542-5147 Fax: (434) 542-4336

Clerk of Court **Stuart B. Fallen** . . . . (434) 542-5147
E-mail: sfallen@courts.state.va.us

Charlottesville Circuit Court

Circuit Clerk

Charlottesville Circuit Court
315 East High Street, Charlottesville, VA 22902
Tel: (434) 970-3766

Clerk of Court **Llezele Agustin Dugger** . . . . (434) 970-3766
E-mail: ldugger@courts.state.va.us

Chesapeake Circuit Court

Circuit Clerk

Chesapeake Circuit Court
307 Albermarle Drive, Suite 300A, Chesapeake, VA 23322-5579
Tel: (757) 382-3000 Fax: (757) 382-3034
Internet: http://www.courts.state.va.us/courts/circuit/Chesapeake/home.html

Clerk of Court **Faye W. Mitchell** . . . . (757) 382-3000
E-mail: fmitchell@courts.state.va.us

Chesterfield Circuit Court

Circuit Clerk

Chesterfield Circuit Court
9500 Courthouse Road, Chesterfield, VA 23832-0125
Tel: (804) 748-1241 Fax: (804) 796-5625

Clerk of Court **Wendy S. Hughes** . . . . (804) 748-1241

Clarke Circuit Court

Circuit Clerk

Clarke Circuit Court
102 North Church Street, Berryville, VA 22611-0189
P.O. Box 189, Berryville, VA 22611-0189
Tel: (540) 955-5116 Fax: (540) 955-0284

Clerk of Court **Helen Butts** . . . . (540) 955-5116
E-mail: hbutts@courts.state.va.us

Colonial Heights Circuit Court

Circuit Clerk

Colonial Heights Circuit Court
550 Boulevard, Colonial Heights, VA 23834-2841
P.O. Box 3401, Colonial Heights, VA 23834-2841
Tel: (804) 520-9364

Clerk of Court **Stacy L. Stafford** . . . . (804) 520-9364
E-mail: sstafford@courts.state.va.us

Craig Circuit Court

Circuit Clerk

Craig Circuit Court
182 Main Street, Suite 4, New Castle, VA 24127
Tel: (540) 864-6141 Fax: (540) 864-7471

Clerk of Court **Sharon P. Oliver** . . . . (540) 864-6141
E-mail: spoliver@courts.state.va.us

(continued on next page)

Culpeper Circuit Court

Circuit Clerk

Culpeper Circuit Court
135 West Cameron Street, Culpeper, VA 22701-3097
Tel: (540) 727-3438　Fax: (540) 727-3475

Clerk of Court **Janice J. Corbin** . . . . (540) 727-3438
　E-mail: jcorbin@courts.state.va.us

Cumberland Circuit Court

Circuit Clerk

Cumberland Circuit Court
1 Courthouse Circle, Cumberland, VA 23040-0008
P.O. Box 8, Cumberland, VA 23040-0008
Tel: (804) 492-4442　Fax: (804) 492-4876

Clerk of Court **Sarah A. Spry** . . . . (804) 492-4442

Danville Circuit Court

Circuit Clerk

Danville Circuit Court
401 Patton Street, Danville, VA 24543
Tel: (434) 799-5168　Fax: (434) 799-6502

Clerk of Court **Gerald A. Gibson** . . . . (434) 799-5168
　E-mail: ggibson@courts.state.va.us

Dickenson Circuit Court

Circuit Clerk

Dickenson Circuit Court
293 Clintwood Main Street, Clintwood, VA 24228-0190
P.O. Box 190, Clintwood, VA 24228-0190
Tel: (276) 926-1616　Fax: (276) 926-6465

Clerk of Court **Richard W. Edwards** . . . .(276) 926-1616
　E-mail: redwards@courts.state.va.us

Dinwiddie Circuit Court

Circuit Clerk

Dinwiddie Circuit Court
14008 Boydton Plank Road, Dinwiddie, VA 23841
P.O. Box 63, Dinwiddie, VA 23841-0063
Tel: (804) 469-4540

Clerk of Court **J. Barrett Chappell, Jr.** . . . .(804) 469-4540
　E-mail: bchappell@courts.state.va.us

Essex Circuit Court

Circuit Clerk

Essex Circuit Court
305 Prince Street, Tappahannock, VA 22560
P.O. Box 445, Tappahannock, VA 22560
Tel: (804) 443-3541　Fax: (804) 445-1216

Clerk of Court **Gayle Ashworth** . . . . (804) 443-3541
　E-mail: gashworth@courts.state.va.us

Fairfax Circuit Court

Circuit Clerk

Fairfax Circuit Court
4410 Chain Bridge Road, Fairfax, VA 22030
Tel: (703) 691-7320　Fax: (703) 273-6564

Clerk of Court **John T. Frey** . . . .(703) 246-4111

Fauquier Circuit Court

Circuit Clerk

Fauquier Circuit Court
29 Ashby Street, Warrenton, VA 20186-3202
Tel: (540) 422-8100

Clerk of Court **Gail H. Barb** . . . .(540) 422-8100
　E-mail: clerk@fauquiercounty.gov

Floyd Circuit Court

Circuit Clerk

Floyd Circuit Court
100 East Main Street, Floyd, VA 24091-0057
Tel: (540) 745-9330　Fax: (540) 745-9303

Clerk of Court **Wendell G. Peters** . . . .(540) 745-9330
　E-mail: wpeters@courts.state.va.us

Fluvanna Circuit Court

Circuit Clerk

Fluvanna Circuit Court
72 Main Street, Palmyra, VA 22963
P.O. Box 550, Palmyra, VA 22963
Tel: (434) 591-1970　Fax: (434) 591-1971

Clerk of Court **Bouson E. Peterson, Jr.** . . . .(434) 591-1970
　E-mail: bpeterson@courts.state.va.us

Franklin Circuit Court

Circuit Clerk

Franklin Circuit Court
275 South Main Street, Suite 212, Rocky Mount, VA 24151
P.O. Box 567, Rocky Mount, VA 24151
Tel: (540) 483-3065　Fax: (540) 483-3042

Clerk of Court **Teresa J. Brown** . . . . (540) 483-3065
　E-mail: tjbrown@courts.state.va.us

Frederick Circuit Court

Circuit Clerk

Frederick Circuit Court
5 North Kent Street, Winchester, VA 22601-5037
Tel: (540) 667-5770

Clerk of Court **Rebecca P. Hogan** . . . .(540) 667-5770
　E-mail: rhogan@courts.state.va.us

Fredericksburg Circuit Court

Circuit Clerk

Fredericksburg Circuit Court
701 Princess Anne Street, Fredericksburg, VA 22401
Tel: (540) 372-1066

Clerk of Court **Jeff Small** . . . . (540) 372-1066
　E-mail: jsmall@courts.state.va.us

Giles Circuit Court

Circuit Clerk

Giles Circuit Court
501 Wenonah Avenue, Pearisburg, VA 24134
P.O. Box 502, Pearisburg, VA 24134
Tel: (540) 921-1722　Fax: (540) 921-3825

Clerk of Court **Charles L. Fraley III** . . . . (540) 921-1722
　E-mail: cfraley@courts.state.va.us

Gloucester Circuit Court

Circuit Clerk

Gloucester Circuit Court
7400 Justice Drive, Room 327, Gloucester, VA 23061
Tel: (804) 693-2502　Fax: (804) 693-2186

Clerk of Court **Margaret F. Walker** . . . . (804) 693-2502
　E-mail: mwalker@courts.state.va.us

Goochland Circuit Court

Circuit Clerk

Goochland Circuit Court
2938 River Road West, Goochland, VA 23063
P.O. Box 196, Goochland, VA 23063
Tel: (804) 556-5353　Fax: (804) 556-4962

Clerk of Court **Dale W. Agnew** . . . . (804) 556-5353

Grayson Circuit Court

Circuit Clerk

Grayson Circuit Court
129 Davis Street, Independence, VA 24348-0130
P.O. Box 130, Independence, VA 24348-0130
Tel: (276) 773-2231　Fax: (276) 773-3338

Clerk of Court **Susan M. Herrington** . . . . (276) 773-2231
　E-mail: sherrington@courts.state.va.us

Greene Circuit Court

Circuit Clerk

Greene Circuit Court
P.O. Box 386, Stanardsville, VA 22973-0386
Tel: (434) 985-5208　Fax: (434) 985-6723

Clerk of Court **Brenda M. Compton** . . . . (434) 985-5208

Greensville Circuit Court

Circuit Clerk

Greensville Circuit Court
337 South Main Street, Emporia, VA 23847-0631
P.O. Box 631, Emporia, VA 23847-0631
Tel: (434) 348-4215　Fax: (434) 348-4020
Internet: http://www.courts.state.va.us/courts/circuit/Greensville/home.html

Clerk of Court **Robert C. Wrenn** . . . . (434) 348-4215

Halifax Circuit Court

Circuit Clerk

Halifax Circuit Court
8 South Main Street, Halifax, VA 24558-0729
P.O. Box 729, Halifax, VA 24558-0729
Tel: (434) 476-6211　Fax: (434) 476-2890

Clerk of Court **Cathy Cosby** . . . . (434) 476-6211
　E-mail: ccosby@courts.state.va.us

Hampton Circuit Court

Circuit Clerk

Hampton Circuit Court
101 King's Way Mall, Hampton, VA 23669-0040
P.O. Box 40, Hampton, VA 23669-0040
Tel: (757) 727-6105　Fax: (757) 728-3505
Internet: http://www.courts.state.va.us/courts/circuit/hampton/home.html

Clerk of Court **Linda Batchelor Smith** . . . . (757) 727-6105

Hanover Circuit Court

Circuit Clerk

Hanover Circuit Court
7507 Library Drive, Hanover, VA 23069-0039
Tel: (804) 365-6150　Fax: (804) 365-6278

Clerk of Court **Frank D. Hargrove, Jr.** . . . . (804) 365-6150
　E-mail: fhargrove@courts.state.va.us

Henrico Circuit Court

Circuit Clerk

Henrico Circuit Court
4301 East Parham Road, Henrico, VA 23273-0775
P.O. Box 90775, Henrico, VA 23273-0775
Tel: (804) 501-4202

Clerk of Court **Yvonne G. Smith** . . . . (804) 501-5334

Henry Circuit Court

Circuit Clerk

Henry Circuit Court
3160 Kings Mountain Road, Martinsville, VA 24112-3966
Tel: (276) 634-4880

Clerk of Court **Vickie Stone Helmstutler** . . . . (276) 634-4880
　E-mail: vhelmstutler@courts.state.va.us

(continued on next page)

Highland Circuit Court

Circuit Clerk

Highland Circuit Court
P.O. Box 190, Monterey, VA 24465-0190
Tel: (540) 468-2447 Fax: (540) 468-2047

Clerk of Court **Lois A. Showalter** . . . . (540) 468-2447

Hopewell Circuit Court

Circuit Clerk

Hopewell Circuit Court
100 East Broadway, Room 251, Hopewell, VA 23860-2715
Tel: (804) 541-2239 Fax: (804) 541-2438

Clerk of Court **Tamara J. Ward** . . . . (804) 541-2239
  E-mail: tward@courts.state.va.us

Isle of Wight Circuit Court

Circuit Clerk

Isle of Wight Circuit Court
17000 Josiah Parker Circle, Isle of Wight, VA 23397-0110
P.O. Box 110, Isle of Wight, VA 23397-0110
Tel: (757) 365-6233
Internet: http://www.courts.state.va.us/courts/circuit/Isle_of_
Wight/home.html

Clerk of Court **Sharon N. Jones** . . . . (757) 365-6233
  E-mail: sjones@courts.state.va.us

James City County/Williamsburg Circuit Court

Circuit Clerk

James City County/Williamsburg Circuit Court
5201 Monticello Avenue, Suite Six, Williamsburg, VA 23188-8218
Tel: (757) 564-2242 Fax: (757) 564-2329
Internet: http://www.courts.state.va.us/courts/circuit/James_City_
County~Williamsburg/home.html

Clerk of Court **Betsy B. Woolridge** . . . . (757) 564-2242
  E-mail: bwoolridge@courts.state.va.us

King and Queen Circuit Court

Circuit Clerk

King and Queen Circuit Court
234 Allen's Circle, King and Queen Court House, VA 23085
P.O. Box 67, King and Queen Court House, VA 23085
Tel: (804) 785-5984 Fax: (804) 785-5698
Internet: http://www.courts.state.va.us/courts/circuit/King_and_
Queen/home.html

Clerk of Court **Deborah F. Longest** . . . . (804) 785-5984
  E-mail: dlongest@courts.state.va.us

King George Circuit Court

Circuit Clerk

King George Circuit Court
9483 Kings Highway, Suite 3, King George, VA 22485-3444
Tel: (540) 775-3322

Clerk of Court **Charles V. Mason** . . . . (540) 775-3322
  E-mail: cmason@courts.state.va.us

King William Circuit Court

Circuit Clerk

King William Circuit Court
351 Courthouse Lane, Suite 130, King William, VA 23086-0216
P.O. Box 216, King William, VA 23086-0216
Tel: (804) 769-4936 Fax: (804) 769-4991
Internet: http://www.courts.state.va.us/courts/circuit/King_
William/home.html

Clerk of Court **Patricia M. Norman** . . . . (804) 769-4936
  E-mail: pnorman@courts.state.va.us

Lancaster Circuit Court

Circuit Clerk

Lancaster Circuit Court
8265 Mary Ball Road, Lancaster, VA 22503-2519
P.O. Box 99, Lancaster, VA 22503
Tel: (804) 462-5611 Fax: (804) 462-9978

Clerk of Court **Diane H. Mumford** . . . . (804) 462-5611
  E-mail: dmumford@courts.state.va.us

Lee Circuit Court

Circuit Clerk

Lee Circuit Court
Main Street, Jonesville, VA 24263-0326
P.O. Box 326, Jonesville, VA 24263-0326
Tel: (276) 346-7763 Fax: (276) 346-3440

Clerk of Court **Rene Lamey** . . . . (276) 346-7763
  E-mail: rlamey@courts.state.va.us

Loudoun Circuit Court

Circuit Clerk

Loudoun Circuit Court
18 East Market Street, Leesburg, VA 20178
P.O. Box 550, Leesburg, VA 20178
Tel: (703) 777-0270 Fax: (703) 777-0376

Clerk of Court **Gary M. Clemens** . . . . (703) 777-0270

Louisa Circuit Court

Circuit Clerk

Louisa Circuit Court
100 West Main Street, Louisa, VA 23093-0037
P.O. 37, Louisa, VA 23093-0037
Tel: (540) 967-5312 Fax: (540) 967-2705

Clerk of Court **Susan R. Hopkins** . . . . (540) 967-5312
  E-mail: shopkins@courts.state.va.us

Lunenberg Circuit Court

Circuit Clerk

Lunenberg Circuit Court
11435 Courthouse Road, Lunenburg, VA 23952
Tel: (434) 696-2132   Fax: (434) 696-3931

Clerk of Court **Gordon F. Erby** . . . . (434) 696-2132
E-mail: gerby@courts.state.va.us

Lynchburg Circuit Court

Circuit Clerk

Lynchburg Circuit Court
900 Court Street, Lynchburg, VA 24504
P.O. Box 4, Lynchburg, VA 24505-0004
Tel: (434) 455-2620   Fax: (434) 847-1864

Clerk of Court **Eugene C. Wingfield** . . . . (434) 455-2611
E-mail: eugene.wingfield@lynchburgva.gov

Madison Circuit Court

Circuit Clerk

Madison Circuit Court
1 Main Street, Madison, VA 22727-0220
P.O. Box 220, Madison, VA 22727-0220
Tel: (540) 948-6888   Fax: (540) 948-3759

Clerk of Court **Leeta D. Louk** . . . . (540) 948-6888

Martinsville Circuit Court

Circuit Clerk

Martinsville Circuit Court
55 West Church Street, Martinsville, VA 24114-1206
P.O. Box 1206, Martinsville, VA 24114-1206
Tel: (276) 403-5106   Fax: (276) 403-5232

Clerk of Court **Ashby R. Pritchett** . . . . (276) 403-5106
E-mail: apritchett@courts.state.va.us

Mathews Circuit Court

Circuit Clerk

Mathews Circuit Court
10622 Buckley Hall Road, Mathews, VA 23109
P.O. Box 463, Mathews, VA 23109
Tel: (804) 725-2550   Fax: (804) 725-7456
Internet: http://www.courts.state.va.us/courts/circuit/Mathews/home.html

Clerk of Court **Angela C. Ingram** . . . . (804) 725-2550
E-mail: aingram@courts.state.va.us

Mecklenburg Circuit Court

Circuit Clerk

Mecklenburg Circuit Court
1294 Jefferson Street, Boydton, VA 23917
P.O. 530, Boydton, VA 23917-0530
Tel: (434) 738-6191   Fax: (434) 738-6861

Clerk of Court **E.E. Coleman, Jr.** . . . . (434) 738-6191 ext. 4222
E-mail: ecoleman@courts.state.va.us

Middlesex Circuit Court

Circuit Clerk

Middlesex Circuit Court
73 Bowden Street, Saluda, VA 23149
P.O. Box 158, Saluda, VA 23149
Tel: (804) 758-5317   Fax: (804) 758-8637
Internet: http://www.courts.state.va.us/courts/circuit/Middlesex/home.html

Clerk of Court **Lynn L. Dunlevy** . . . . (804) 758-5317
E-mail: ldunlevy@courts.state.va.us

Montgomery Circuit Court

Circuit Clerk

Montgomery Circuit Court
55 East Main Street, Suite 1, Christiansburg, VA 24073
Tel: (540) 382-5760

Clerk of Court **Erica W. Williams** . . . . (540) 382-5760
E-mail: ewwilliams@courts.state.va.us

Nelson Circuit Court

Circuit Clerk

Nelson Circuit Court
84 Courthouse Square, 1st Floor, Lovingston, VA 22949-0010
P.O. Box 10, Lovingston, VA 22949-0010
Tel: (434) 263-7020   Fax: (434) 263-7027

Clerk of Court **Judy Stevens Smythers** . . . . (434) 263-7020
E-mail: jsmythers@courts.state.va.us

New Kent Circuit Court

Circuit Clerk

New Kent Circuit Court
12001 Courthouse Circle, New Kent, VA 23124-0098
P.O. Box 98, New Kent, VA 23124-0098
Tel: (804) 966-9520   Fax: (804) 966-9528
Internet: http://www.courts.state.va.us/courts/circuit/New_Kent/home.html

Clerk of Court **Karen A. Butler** . . . . (804) 966-9520
E-mail: kbutler@courts.state.va.us

Newport News Circuit Court

Circuit Clerk

Newport News Circuit Court
Courthouse Building, 2500 Washington Avenue,
Newport News, VA 23607-4307
Tel: (757) 926-8561   Fax: (757) 926-8531

Clerk of Court **(Vacant)** . . . . (757) 926-8561

Norfolk Circuit Court

Circuit Clerk

Norfolk Circuit Court
150 St. Paul's Boulevard, Norfolk, VA 23510-2773
Tel: (757) 664-4580
Internet: http://www.courts.state.va.us/courts/circuit/Norfolk/home.html

Clerk of Court **George E. Schaefer III** . . . . (757) 664-4393
E-mail: gschaefer@courts.state.va.us

(continued on next page)

Virginia Court Clerks and Courthouses *continued*

Northampton Circuit Court

Circuit Clerk

Northampton Circuit Court
5229 The Hornes, Eastville, VA 23347-0036
P.O. Box 36, Eastville, VA 23347
Tel: (757) 678-0465 Fax: (757) 678-5410
Internet: http://www.courts.state.va.us/courts/circuit/Northampton/home.html

Clerk of Court **Traci L. Johnson** . . . . (757) 678-0465
E-mail: tljohnson@courts.state.va.us

Northumberland Circuit Court

Circuit Clerk

Northumberland Circuit Court
39 Judicial Place, Heathsville, VA 22473-0217
Tel: (804) 580-3700 Fax: (804) 580-2261

Clerk of Court **Deborah Bingham** . . . . (804) 580-3700
E-mail: dbingham@courts.state.va.us

Nottoway Circuit Court

Circuit Clerk

Nottoway Circuit Court
328 West Courthouse Road, Nottoway, VA 23955-3619
Tel: (434) 645-9043 Fax: (434) 645-2201

Clerk of Court **Jane L. Brown** . . . . (434) 645-9043
E-mail: jlbrown@courts.state.va.us

Orange Circuit Court

Circuit Clerk

Orange Circuit Court
110 North Madison, Suite 300, Orange, VA 22960-0133
P.O. Box 230, Orange, VA 22960-0133
Tel: (540) 672-4030 Fax: (540) 672-2939

Clerk of Court **Teresa T. Carroll** . . . . (540) 672-4030
E-mail: tcarroll@courts.state.va.us

Page Circuit Court

Circuit Clerk

Page Circuit Court
116 South Court Street, Suite A, Luray, VA 22835-1200
Tel: (540) 743-4064 Fax: (540) 743-2338

Clerk of Court **C.R. Wilson** . . . . (540) 743-4064
E-mail: clerkwilson@hotmail.com

Patrick Circuit Court

Circuit Clerk

Patrick Circuit Court
Main Street, Stuart, VA 24171-0148
P.O. Box 148, Stuart, VA 24171-0148
Tel: (276) 694-7213 Fax: (276) 694-6943

Clerk of Court **Susan C. Gasperini** . . . . (276) 694-7213
E-mail: sgasperini@courts.state.va.us

Virginia Court Clerks and Courthouses *continued*

Petersburg Circuit Court

Circuit Clerk

Petersburg Circuit Court
One Courthouse Avenue, Petersburg, VA 23803
Tel: (804) 733-2367 Fax: (804) 732-5548

Clerk of Court **Shalva J. Braxton** . . . . (804) 733-2367
E-mail: sbraxton@courts.state.va.us

Pittsylvania Circuit Court

Circuit Clerk

Pittsylvania Circuit Court
3 North Main Street, Drawer 31, Chatham, VA 24531
Tel: (434) 432-7887 Fax: (434) 432-7913

Clerk of Court **H. F. Haymore, Jr.** . . . . (434) 432-7887
E-mail: hfhaymore@courts.state.va.us

Portsmouth Circuit Court

Circuit Clerk

Portsmouth Circuit Court
1345 Court Street, Portsmouth, VA 23705-1217
P.O. Box 1217, Portsmouth, VA 23705-1217
Tel: (757) 393-8671 Fax: (757) 399-4826
Internet: http://www.courts.state.va.us/courts/circuit/Portsmouth/home.html

Clerk of Court **Cynthia P. Morrison** . . . . (757) 393-8671
E-mail: cmorrison@courts.state.va.us

Powhatan Circuit Court

Circuit Clerk

Powhatan Circuit Court
3880 Old Buckingham Road, Suite C, Powhatan, VA 23139-0037
P.O. Box 37, Powhatan, VA 23139-0037
Tel: (804) 598-5660 Fax: (804) 598-5608

Clerk of Court **Teresa H. Dobbins** . . . . (804) 598-5660
E-mail: tdobbins@courts.state.va.us

Prince Edward Circuit Court

Circuit Clerk

Prince Edward Circuit Court
Courthouse Building, North Main Street, Farmville, VA 23901-0304
P.O. Box 304, Farmville, VA 23901
Tel: (434) 392-5145 Fax: (434) 392-3913

Clerk of Court **Machelle J. Eppes** . . . . (434) 392-5145
E-mail: meppes@courts.state.va.us

Virginia Court Clerks and Courthouses *continued*

Prince George Circuit Court

Circuit Clerk

Prince George Circuit Court
6601 Courts Drive, Prince George, VA 23875-0098
P.O. Box 98, Prince George, VA 23875-0098
Tel: (804) 733-2640 Fax: (804) 861-5721
Internet: http://www.courts.state.va.us/courts/circuit/Prince_George/home.html

Clerk of Court **Bishop Knott, Jr.** . . . .(804) 733-2640
   E-mail: circuitcourtclerk@princegeorgeva.org

Prince William Circuit Court

Circuit Clerk

Henrico Circuit Court
4301 East Parham Road, Henrico, VA 23273-0775
P.O. Box 90775, Henrico, VA 23273-0775
Tel: (804) 501-4202

Clerk of Court **Yvonne G. Smith** . . . . (804) 501-5334

Pulaski Circuit Court

Circuit Clerk

Pulaski Circuit Court
45 Third Street, NW, Suite 101, Pulaski, VA 24301
Tel: (540) 980-7825 Fax: (540) 980-7835

Clerk of Court **Maetta H. Crewe** . . . . (540) 980-7825
   E-mail: mcrewe@courts.state.va.us

Radford Circuit Court

Circuit Clerk

Radford Circuit Court
619 Second Street, West, Radford, VA 24141
Tel: (540) 731-3610 Fax: (540) 731-3612

Clerk of Court **Ann Howard** . . . . (540) 731-3610
   E-mail: ahoward@radford.va.us

Rappahannock Circuit Court

Circuit Clerk

Rappahannock Circuit Court
238 Gay Street, Washington, VA 22747-0517
P.O. Box 517, Washington, VA 22747-0517
Tel: (540) 675-5350 Fax: (540) 675-5351

Clerk of Court **Margaret Ralph** . . . .(540) 675-5350
   E-mail: mralph@courts.state.va.us

Richmond Circuit Court

Circuit Clerk

Richmond Circuit Court
400 North 9th Street, Richmond, VA 23219
Tel: (804) 646-6505

Clerk of Court **Edward F. Jewett** . . . . (804) 646-6505
   E-mail: circuitcourtclerkinformation@richmondgov.
   com

Virginia Court Clerks and Courthouses *continued*

Richmond County Circuit Court

Circuit Clerk

Richmond County Circuit Court
101 Court Circle, Warsaw, VA 22572-0956
P.O. Box 1000, Warsaw, VA 22572
Tel: (804) 333-3781 Fax: (804) 333-5396

Clerk of Court **Rosa S. Forrester** . . . . (804) 333-3781
   E-mail: rforrester@courts.state.va.us

Roanoke City Circuit Court

Circuit Clerk

Roanoke City Circuit Court
315 West Church Avenue, Roanoke, VA 24010-2610
P.O. Box 2610, Roanoke, VA 24010-2610
Tel: (540) 853-6702 Fax: (540) 853-1024

Clerk of Court **Brenda S. Hamilton** . . . . (540) 853-6702
   E-mail: brenda.hamilton@roanokeva.gov

Roanoke County Circuit Court

Circuit Clerk

Roanoke County Circuit Court
305 East Main Street, Salem, VA 24153-1126
P.O. Box 1126, Salem, VA 24153-1126
Tel: (540) 387-6205 Fax: (540) 387-6145

Clerk of Court **Steven A. McGraw, Sr.** . . . . (540) 387-6205
   E-mail: circlerk@roanokecountyva.gov

Rockbridge Circuit Court

Circuit Clerk

Rockbridge Circuit Court
20 South Randolph Street, Suite 101, Lexington, VA 24450-2552
Tel: (540) 463-2232 Fax: (540) 463-3850

Clerk of Court **D. Bruce Patterson** . . . . (540) 463-2232
                                                Fax: (540) 463-3850

Rockingham Circuit Court

Circuit Clerk

Rockingham Circuit Court
Court Square, Harrisonburg, VA 22801
Tel: (540) 564-3111 Fax: (540) 564-3127

Clerk of Court **Charles "Chaz" Evans-Haywood** . . . . (540) 564-3111
   E-mail: clerkchaz@rockinghamcountyva.gov

Russell Circuit Court

Circuit Clerk

Russell Circuit Court
53 East Main Street, Lebanon, VA 24266-0435
P.O. Box 435, Lebanon, VA 24266-0435
Tel: (276) 889-8023 Fax: (276) 889-8003

Clerk of Court **Ann Sword McReynolds** . . . . (276) 889-8023
   E-mail: amcreynolds@courts.state.va.us

(continued on next page)

Salem Circuit Court

Circuit Clerk

Salem Circuit Court
2 East Calhoun Street, Salem, VA 24153-7933
Tel: (540) 375-3067   Fax: (540) 375-4039

Clerk of Court **Chance Crawford** . . . . (540) 375-3067
   E-mail: ccrawford@courts.state.va.us

Scott Circuit Court

Circuit Clerk

Scott Circuit Court
202 West Jackson Street, Suite 102, Gate City, VA 24251-3012
Tel: (276) 386-3801   Fax: (276) 386-2430

Clerk of Court **Mark A. "Bo" Taylor** . . . .(276) 386-3801
   E-mail: mtaylor@courts.state.va.us

Shenandoah Circuit Court

Circuit Clerk

Shenandoah Circuit Court
112 South Main Street, Woodstock, VA 22664-1423
P.O. Box 406, Woodstock, VA 22664-1423
Tel: (540) 459-6150   Fax: (540) 459-6155

Clerk of Court **Denise F. Barb-Estep** . . . . (540) 459-6150

Smyth Circuit Court

Circuit Clerk

Smyth Circuit Court
109 West Main Street, Room 144, Marion, VA 24354
Tel: (276) 782-4044   Fax: (276) 782-4045

Clerk of Court **John H. Graham** . . . .(276) 782-4044
   E-mail: jgraham@courts.state.va.us

Southampton Circuit Court

Circuit Clerk

Southampton Circuit Court
22350 Main Street, Courtland, VA 23837
Tel: (757) 653-2200
Internet: http://www.courts.state.va.us/courts/
circuit/Southampton/home.html

Clerk of Court **Richard L. Francis** . . . . (757) 653-2200
   E-mail: rfrancis@courts.state.va.us

Spotsylvania Circuit Court

Circuit Clerk

Spotsylvania Circuit Court
9107 Judicial Center Lane, Spotsylvania, VA 22553
P.O. Box 96, Spotsylvania, VA 22553-0096
Tel: (540) 507-7600   Fax: (540) 582-2169

Clerk of Court **Christalyn M. Jett** . . . .(540) 507-7600
   E-mail: cjett@courts.state.va.us

Stafford Circuit Court

Circuit Clerk

Stafford Circuit Court
1300 Courthouse Road, Stafford, VA 22555-0069
P.O. Box 69, Stafford, VA 22555-2269
Tel: (540) 658-8750   Fax: (540) 658-4653

Clerk of Court **Barbara G. Decatur** . . . . (540) 658-8750
   E-mail: bdecatur@courts.state.va.us

Staunton Circuit Court

Circuit Clerk

Staunton Circuit Court
113 East Beverly Street, 2nd Floor, Staunton, VA 24401-4390
Tel: (540) 332-3874   Fax: (540) 332-3970

Clerk of Court **Thomas E. Roberts** . . . . (540) 332-3874
   E-mail: troberts@courts.state.va.us

Suffolk Circuit Court

Circuit Clerk

Suffolk Circuit Court
Mills E. Godwin, Jr. Courts Building, 150 North Main Street,
Suffolk, VA 23439-1604
P.O. Box 1604, Suffolk, VA 23439-1604
Tel: (757) 514-7800   Fax: (757) 514-7103
Internet: http://www.courts.state.va.us/courts/circuit/suffolk/home.html

Clerk of Court **W. Randolph Carter, Jr.** . . . .(757) 514-7800
   E-mail: wrcarter@courts.state.va.us

Surry Circuit Court

Circuit Clerk

Surry Circuit Court
28 Colonial Trail, East, Surry, VA 23883
Tel: (757) 294-3161   Fax: (757) 294-0471
Internet: http://www.courts.state.va.us/courts/circuit/surry/home.html

Clerk of Court **Gail P. Clayton** . . . .(757) 294-3161
   E-mail: gclayton@courts.state.va.us

Sussex Circuit Court

Circuit Clerk

Sussex Circuit Court
15088 Courthouse Road, Route 735, Sussex, VA 23884
P.O. Box 1337, Sussex, VA 23884
Tel: (434) 246-1012   Fax: (434) 246-2203
Internet: http://www.courts.state.va.us/courts/circuit/Sussex/home.html

Clerk of Court **Gary M. Williams** . . . . (434) 246-5511
   E-mail: gwilliams@courts.state.va.us

Tazewell Circuit Court

Circuit Clerk

Tazewell Circuit Court
101 East Main Street, Suite 202, Tazewell, VA 24651-1071
Tel: (276) 988-1222 Fax: (276) 988-7501

Clerk of Court **Tammy B. Allison** . . . . (276) 988-1222
 E-mail: tallison@courts.state.va.us

Virginia Beach Circuit Court

Circuit Clerk

Virginia Beach Circuit Court
2425 Nimmo Parkway, Building 10, 4th Floor,
Virginia Beach, VA 23456-9017
Tel: (757) 385-4501
Internet: http://www.courts.state.va.us/courts/circuit/Virginia_
Beach/home.html

Clerk of Court **Tina E. Sinnen** . . . . (757) 385-8817
 E-mail: tsinnen@courts.state.va.us

Warren Circuit Court

Circuit Clerk

Warren Circuit Court
1 East Main Street, Front Royal, VA 22630-3313
Tel: (540) 635-2435 Fax: (540) 636-3274

Clerk of Court **Jennifer R. Sims** . . . . (540) 635-2435
 E-mail: jsims@courts.state.va.us

Washington Circuit Court

Circuit Clerk

Washington Circuit Court
East Main Street, Abingdon, VA 24212-0289
Tel: (276) 676-6224 Fax: (276) 676-6218

Clerk of Court **Tricia S. Moore** . . . . (276) 676-6224
 E-mail: tmoore@courts.state.va.us

Waynesboro Circuit Court

Circuit Clerk

Waynesboro Circuit Court
250 South Wayne Avenue, Suite 202, Waynesboro, VA 22980-0910
P.O. Box 910, Waynesboro, VA 22980-0910
Tel: (540) 942-6616 Fax: (540) 942-6774

Clerk of Court **Nicole A. Briggs** . . . . (540) 942-6616

Westmoreland Circuit Court

Circuit Clerk

Westmoreland Circuit Court
P.O. Box 307, Montross, VA 22520-0307
Tel: (804) 493-0108 Fax: (804) 493-0393

Clerk of Court **Gwynne J. Chatham** . . . . (804) 493-0108
 E-mail: gchatham@courts.state.va.us

Winchester Circuit Court

Circuit Clerk

Winchester Circuit Court
The Judicial Center, 5 North Kent Street, Winchester, VA 22601
Tel: (540) 667-5770 Fax: (540) 667-6638

Clerk of Court **Terry H. Whittle** . . . .(540) 667-5770
 E-mail: twhittle@courts.state.va.us

Wise Circuit Court

Circuit Clerk

Wise Circuit Court
206 East Main Street, Wise, VA 24293-1248
P.O. Box 1248, Wise, VA 24293-1248
Tel: (276) 328-6111 Fax: (276) 328-0039

Clerk of Court **J. Jack Kennedy, Jr.** . . . . (276) 328-6111 ext. 246
 E-mail: jack@jackkennedy.net

Wythe Circuit Court

Circuit Clerk

Wythe Circuit Court
225 South Fourth Street, Room 105, Wytheville, VA 24382
Tel: (276) 223-6050 Fax: (276) 223-6057

Clerk of Court **Hayden H. Horney** . . . . (276) 223-6050
 E-mail: hhorney@courts.state.va.us

York County Poquoson Circuit Court

Circuit Clerk

York County Poquoson Circuit Court
300 Ballard Street, Yorktown, VA 23690-0371
P.O. Box 371, Yorktown, VA 23690-0371
Tel: (757) 890-3350 Fax: (757) 890-3364
Internet: http://www.courts.state.va.us/courts/circuit/York_County_
Poquoson/home.html

Clerk of Court **Kristen N. Nelson** . . . .(757) 890-3350

Virginia Cities and Counties Within Judicial Districts

Circuit Court, 1st Judicial Circuit
Areas Covered: Chesapeake.

Circuit Court, 2nd Judicial Circuit
Areas Covered: Virginia Beach, Accomack County and Northampton County.

Circuit Court, 3rd Judicial Circuit
Areas Covered: Portsmouth County.

Circuit Court, 4th Judicial Circuit
Areas Covered: Norfolk.

(continued on next page)

Circuit Court, 5th Judicial Circuit

Areas Covered: City of Franklin, Isle of Wight County, Southampton County and City of Suffolk.

Circuit Court, 6th Judicial Circuit

Areas Covered: Brunswick County, City of Emporia, Greensville County, City of Hopewell, Prince George County, Surry County, and Sussex County.

Circuit Court, 7th Judicial Circuit

Areas Covered: City of Newport News.

Circuit Court, 8th Judicial Circuit

Areas Covered: City of Hampton.

Circuit Court, 9th Judicial Circuit

Areas Covered: Charles City County, Gloucester County, James City County, City of Williamsburg, King William County, King and Queen County, Mathews County, Middlesex County, New Kent County and York County.

Circuit Court, 10th Judicial Circuit

Areas Covered: Appomattox County, Buckingham County, Charlotte County, Cumberland County, Halifax County, Lunenburg County, Mecklenburg County, and Prince Edward County.

Circuit Court, 11th Judicial Circuit

Areas Covered: Amelia County, Dinwiddie County, Nottoway County, City of Petersburg, and Powhatan County.

Circuit Court, 12th Judicial Circuit

Areas Covered: Chesterfield County and Colonial Heights.

Circuit Court, 13th Judicial Circuit

Areas Covered: City of Richmond.

Circuit Court, 14th Judicial Circuit

Areas Covered: Henrico County.

Circuit Court, 15th Judicial Circuit

Areas Covered: Caroline County, Essex County, City of Fredericksburg, Hanover County, King George County, Lancaster County, Northumberland County, Richmond County, Spotsylvania County, Stafford County, and Westmoreland County.

Circuit Court, 16th Judicial Circuit

Areas Covered: Albemarle County, City of Charlottesville, Culpeper County, Fluvanna County, Goochland County, Greene County, Louisa County, Madison County, and Orange County.

Circuit Court, 17th Judicial Circuit

Areas Covered: City of Arlington.

Circuit Court, 18th Judicial Circuit

Areas Covered: City of Alexandria.

Circuit Court, 19th Judicial Circuit

Areas Covered: Falls Church, City of Fairfax and Fairfax County.

Circuit Court, 20th Judicial Circuit

Areas Covered: Fauquier County, Loudoun County, and Rappahannock County.

Circuit Court, 21st Judicial Circuit

Areas Covered: Henry County, City of Martinsville, and Patrick County.

Circuit Court, 22nd Judicial Circuit

Areas Covered: City of Danville, Franklin County, and Pittsylvania County.

Circuit Court, 23rd Judicial Circuit

Areas Covered: City of Roanoke, Roanoke County, and City of Salem.

Circuit Court, 24th Judicial Circuit

Areas Covered: Amherst County, City of Bedford, Campbell County, City of Lynchburg, and Nelson County.

Circuit Court, 25th Judicial Circuit

Areas Covered: Alleghany County, City of Covington, Augusta County, Bath County, Botetourt County, City of Buena Vista, Craig County, Highland County, Rockbridge County, City of Staunton, and City of Waynesboro.

Circuit Court, 26th Judicial Circuit

Areas Covered: Clarke County, Frederick County, Page County, Rockingham County, Shenandoah County, Warren County, and City of Winchester.

Circuit Court, 27th Judicial Circuit

Areas Covered: Bland County, City of Carroll, Floyd, Giles, Grayson County, Montgomery County, Pulaski County, City of Radford, and Wythe County.

Circuit Court, 28th Judicial Circuit

Areas Covered: City of Bristol, Smyth County, and Washington County.

Circuit Court, 29th Judicial Circuit

Areas Covered: Buchanan County, Dickenson County, Russell County, and Tazewell County.

Circuit Court, 30th Judicial Circuit

Areas Covered: Lee County, Scott County, and Wise County.

Circuit Court, 31st Judicial Circuit

Areas Covered: Prince William County.

Washington Court Clerks and Courthouses

The trial courts of general jurisdiction in the state of Washington are called superior courts. There is one superior court per county, with the clerk in each county exercising both county clerk and trial court functions.

Washington Supreme Court

415 12th Avenue SW, Olympia, WA 98501-2314
P.O. Box 40929, Olympia, WA 98504-0929
Tel: (360) 357-2077
E-mail: supreme@courts.wa.gov
Internet: www.courts.wa.gov/court/supreme

The Supreme Court consists of a chief justice and eight justices who are elected in statewide nonpartisan elections to six-year terms. Vacancies are filled by the Governor and newly-appointed justices run for election on nonpartisan ballots in the next general election to complete the unexpired term. The position of chief justice is selected from the Court's own membership to serve a four-year term. Retirement is mandatory at age seventy-five; however, retired judges may be recalled to serve temporary assignments. The Supreme Court has original jurisdiction over petitions against state officers and can review decisions of lower courts if the money or value of property involved exceeds $200. (The $200 limitation is not in effect if the case involves a question of the legality of a tax, duty, assessment, toll, or municipal fine, or the validity of a statute.) Direct review by the Court of a trial court decision is permitted if the action involves a state officer, a trial court rules a statute or ordinance unconstitutional, conflicting statutes or rules of law are involved, or the issue is of broad public interest and requires prompt and ultimate determination. All cases in which the death penalty has been imposed are reviewed directly to the Court. The Court has discretionary review of decisions of the Washington Court of Appeals.

Court Staff
Clerk **Ronald R. Carpenter** . . . . (360) 357-2077
    E-mail: ronald.carpenter@courts.wa.gov

Washington Court of Appeals

Tel: (206) 753-3365 (Electronic Access Registration)
Internet: www.courts.wa.gov

Each Court of Appeals has a chief judge, and acting chief judge and two to seven judges who are elected on a nonpartisan ballot by the voters in their division for six-year terms. Vacancies are filled by the Governor, and newly-appointed judges run on the ballot in the next general election to complete the unexpired term. The judges in each division elect a chief judge and an acting chief judge for two-year terms. Retirement is mandatory at age seventy-five; however, retired judges may be recalled to serve temporary assignments. The Court of Appeals has exclusive appellate jurisdiction, except in those cases which are appealed directly to the Washington Supreme Court, and those over which the Supreme Court has asserted jurisdiction.

Washington Court of Appeals, Division I

One Union Square, 600 University Street, Seattle, WA 98101-4170
Tel: (206) 464-7750 Fax: (206) 389-2613

Areas Covered: Counties of Island, King, San Juan, Skagit, Snohomish and Whatcom

Court Staff
Court Administrator/Clerk of Court
    Richard D. Johnson . . . . (206) 464-5871
    E-mail: richard.johnson@courts.wa.gov

Washington Court of Appeals, Division II

950 Broadway, Suite 300, Tacoma, WA 98402
Tel: (253) 593-2970 Fax: (253) 593-2806
E-mail: coa2filing@courts.wa.gov

Areas Covered: Counties of Clallam, Clark, Cowlitz, Grays Harbor, Jefferson, Kitsap, Lewis, Mason, Pacific, Pierce, Skamania, Thurston and Wahkiakum

Court Staff
Clerk of the Court **David Ponzoha** . . . . (253) 593-2970
    E-mail: dave.ponzoha@courts.wa.gov

Washington Court of Appeals, Division III

500 North Cedar Street, Spokane, WA 99201-1905
Tel: (509) 456-3082 Fax: (509) 456-4288

Areas Covered: Counties of Adams, Asotin, Benton, Chelan, Columbia, Douglas, Ferry, Franklin, Garfield, Grant, Kittitas, Klickitat, Lincoln, Okanogan, Pend Oreille, Spokane, Stevens, Walla Walla, Whitman and Yakima

Court Staff
Fax: (509) 456-4288

Clerk/Administrator **Renee S. Townsley** . . . . (509) 456-3082
    E-mail: renee.townsley@courts.wa.gov

County-By-County

Adams County

Court Clerk
Adams County Superior Court
210 West Broadway, Ritzville, WA 99169-0216
P.O. Box 126, Ritzville, WA 99169-0216
Tel: (509) 659-3271 Fax: (509) 659-0118

Clerk of Court **Susie Kirkendall** . . . . (509) 953-3257

Asotin County

Court Clerk
Asotin County Superior Court
135 2nd Street, Asotin, WA 99402-0159
P.O. Box 159, Asotin, WA 99402-0159
Tel: (509) 243-2082 Fax: (509) 243-2072

Clerk of Court **Marie Eggart** . . . . (509) 243-2081
    E-mail: meggart@co.asotin.wa.us

Benton County

Court Clerk
Benton County Superior Court
Building A, 7122 West Okanogan Place, Kennewick, WA 99336-2359
Tel: (509) 736-3071 Fax: (509) 736-3057

Clerk of Court **Josie Delvin** . . . .(509) 735-8388
    E-mail: josie.delvin@co.benton.wa.us   Fax: (509) 783-1058

(continued on next page)

Chelan County

Court Clerk

Chelan County Circuit Court
401 Washington Street, Floor 5, Wenatchee, WA 98807-0880
Tel: (509) 667-6210 Fax: (509) 667-6588

Clerk of Court **Kim C. Morrison** . . . . (509) 667-6380
350 Orondo Ave, Wenatchee, WA 98801-2885
E-mail: kim.morrison@co.chelan.wa.us

Clallam County

Court Clerk

Clallam County Superior Court
223 East 4th Street, Sutie 9, Port Angeles, WA 98362-3015
Tel: (360) 417-2386 Fax: (360) 417-2581

Clerk of Court **Barbara J. Christensen** . . . . (360) 417-2231
223 East 4th Street, Suite 9,
Port Angeles, WA 98362-3015
E-mail: bchristensen@co.clallam.wa.us

Clark County

Court Clerk

Clark County Superior Court
1200 Franklin Street, Vancouver, WA 98666-5000
Tel: (360) 397-2150 Fax: (360) 397-6078

Clerk of Court **Scott G. Weber** . . . .(360) 397-2287
E-mail: countyclerk@clark.wa.gov   Fax: (360) 397-6099

Columbia County

Court Clerk

Columbia County Superior Court
341 East Main Street, Suite 2, Dayton, WA 99328-1361
Tel: (509) 382-4321 Fax: (509) 382-4830

Clerk of Court **Susan J. Marinella** . . . . (509) 382-4321
E-mail: sue_marinella@co.columbia.wa.us

Cowlitz County

Court Clerk

Cowlitz County Superior Court
312 SW 1st Avenue, Floor 2, Kelso, WA 98626-1739
Tel: (360) 577-3085 Fax: (360) 577-2323

Clerk of Court **Staci Myklebust** . . . . (360) 577-3016
E-mail: clerk@co.cowlitz.wa.us

Douglas County

Court Clerk

Douglas County Superior Court
203 South Rainier, Waterville, WA 98858
Tel: (509) 745-9063 Fax: (509) 745-8430

Clerk of Court **Tristen Worthen** . . . . (509) 745-8529
E-mail: tworthen@co.douglas.wa.us   Fax: (509) 745-8027

Ferry County

Court Clerk

Ferry County Superior Court
350 E Delaware Avenue, Republic, WA 99166-9747
Tel: (509) 684-7520

Clerk of Court **Jean Booher** . . . . (509) 775-5225 ext. 2505
E-mail: ferry-superior@co.ferry.wa.us

Franklin County

Court Clerk

Franklin County Superior Court
1016 North 4th Avenue, Suite 306, Pasco, WA 99301-3706
Tel: (509) 545-3525
Internet: http://www.co.franklin.wa.us/clerk

Clerk of Court **Michael J. Killian** . . . . (509) 545-3525
E-mail: mkillian@co.franklin.wa.us

Garfield County

Court Clerk

Garfield County Superior Court
789 Main Street, Pomeroy, WA 99347-0915
Tel: (509) 843-3731 Fax: (509) 843-1224

Court Administrator **Terrilie K. Cox** . . . . (509) 843-3731
E-mail: tcox@co.garfield.wa.us

Grant County

Court Clerk

Grant County Superior Court
35 C Street NW, Second Floor, Ephrata, WA 98823-0037
Tel: (509) 754-2011 Fax: (509) 754-6036

Clerk of Court **Kimberly A. Allen** . . . .(509) 754-2011 ext. 318

Grays Harbor County

Court Clerk

Grays Harbor County Superior Court
102 W Broadway Avenue, Montesano, WA 98563-3621
Tel: (360) 249-3842 Fax: (360) 249-6381

Clerk of Court **Cheryl Brown** . . . . (360) 249-3842

Island County

Court Clerk

Island County Superior Court
101 NE 6th Street, First Floor, Coupeville, WA 98239
P.O. Box 5000, Coupeville, WA 98239
Tel: (360) 679-7361 Fax: (360) 679-7383

Clerk of Court **Debra M. Van Pelt** . . . . (360) 679-7360
E-mail: debravanp@co.island.wa.us

Jefferson County

Court Clerk

Jefferson County Superior Court
1820 Jefferson Street, Port Townsend, WA 98368-6951
Tel: (360) 385-9360 Fax: (360) 385-9188

Clerk of Court **Ruth Gordon** . . . . (360) 385-9128
E-mail: rgordon@co.jefferson.wa.us

King County

Court Clerk

King County Superior Court
516 3rd Avenue, Seattle, WA 98104-2361
Tel: (206) 296-9100 Tel: (206) 205-5048 (TDD) Fax: (206) 296-0986

Director and Superior Court Clerk **Barbara Miner** . . . . (206) 296-7844
E-mail: barbara.miner@kingcounty.gov

Kitsap County

Court Clerk

Kitsap County Superior Court
614 Division Street, Port Orchard, WA 98366-4683
Tel: (360) 337-7140 Fax: (360) 337-4673

Clerk of Court **David "Dave" Peterson** . . . . (360) 337-7164
E-mail: dpeterso@co.kitsap.wa.us   Fax: (360) 337-4927

Kittitas County

Court Clerk

Kittitas County Superior Court
205 W 5th Avenue, Suite 207, Ellensburg, WA 98926-2887
Tel: (509) 962-7533 Fax: (509) 933-8223

Clerk of Court **Val Barschaw** . . . . (509) 962-7531
                                          Fax: (509) 962-7667

Klickitat County

Court Clerk

Klickitat County Superior Court
205 S Columbus Avenue, Goldendale, WA 98620-9279
Tel: (509) 773-5755 Fax: (509) 773-2496

Clerk of Court **Renea Campbell** . . . . (509) 773-5744
E-mail: reneac@klickitatcounty.org

Lewis County

Court Clerk

Lewis County Superior Court
345 W Main Street, 4th Floor, Chehalis, WA 98532-0336
Tel: (360) 740-1333 Fax: (360) 740-2603

Clerk of Court **Kathy A. Brack** . . . . (360) 740-1287

Lincoln County

Court Clerk

Lincoln County Superior Court
450 Logan Street, Davenport, WA 99122
Tel: (509) 725-3081 Fax: (509) 725-1150

Clerk of Court **Peggy Semprimoznik** . . . . (509) 725-1401
E-mail: psemprimoznik@co.lincoln.wa.us

Mason County

Court Clerk

Mason County Superior Court
419 N 4th Street, 2, Shelton, WA 98584-3419
Tel: (360) 427-9670 Fax: (360) 427-8443

Clerk of Court **Ginger Brooks** . . . . (360) 427-9670 ext. 346

Okanogan County

Court Clerk

Okanogan County Superior Court
149 3rd N, Okanogan, WA 98840
Tel: (509) 422-7130 Fax: (509) 422-7133

Clerk of Court **Charleen I. Groomes** . . . . (509) 422-7275
E-mail: cgroomes@co.okanogan.wa.us

Pacific County

Court Clerk

Pacific County Superior Court
300 Memorial Drive, South Bend, WA 98586
Tel: (360) 875-9327 Fax: (360) 875-9321

Clerk of Court **Virginia Leach** . . . . (360) 875-9320 ext. 2222
E-mail: vleach@co.pacific.wa.us

Pend Oreille County

Court Clerk

Pend Oreille County Superior Court
229 S Garden Avenue, Newport, WA 99156
Tel: (509) 447-2435 Fax: (509) 447-2734

Clerk of Court **Tammie Ownbey** . . . . (509) 447-2435
E-mail: townbey@pendoreille.org

Pierce County

Court Clerk

Pierce County Superior Court
930 Tacoma Avenue S, Tacoma, WA 98402-2108

Clerk of Court **Kevin Stock** . . . . (253) 798-7455
E-mail: kstock@co.pierce.wa.us   Fax: (253) 798-3428

(continued on next page)

San Juan County

Court Clerk

24th Judicial District
350 Court Street, Friday Harbor, WA 98250-7901

Clerk of Court **Joan P. White** . . . . (360) 378-2163
E-mail: joanw@co.san-juan.wa.us

Skagit County

Court Clerk

Skagit County Superior Court
205 W Kincaid Street, Mount Vernon, WA 98273-4225
Tel: (360) 336-9320 Fax: (360) 336-9340

Clerk of Court **Mavis Betz** . . . . (360) 336-9440
E-mail: supcrtclerk@co.skagit.wa.us

Skamania County

Court Clerk

Skamania County Superior Court
240 Vancouver Avenue, Stevenson, WA 98648-0790
Tel: (509) 427-3765 Fax: (509) 427-3768

Clerk of Court **Sharon Vance** . . . . (509) 427-3770
Fax: (509) 427-3777

Snohomish County

Court Clerk

26th Judicial District
3000 Rockefeller Avenue, MS 502, Everett, WA 98201-4046

Clerk of Court **Sonya Kraski** . . . . (425) 388-3466

Spokane County

Court Clerk

Spokane County Superior Court
1116 W Broadway Avenue, Spokane, WA 99260-0350
Tel: (509) 477-2211 Fax: (509) 477-5714

Clerk of Court **Thomas R. Fallquist** . . . . (509) 477-2211
E-mail: tfallquist@spokanecounty.org

Stevens County

Court Clerk

Stevens County Superior Court
215 S Oak Street, Rm 209, Colville, WA 99114-2862
Tel: (509) 684-7520 Fax: (509) 685-0679

Clerk of Court **Patty A. Chester** . . . . (509) 684-7575

Thurston County

Court Clerk

Thurston County Superior Court
2000 Lakeridge Drive SW, Building 2, Olympia, WA 98502
Tel: (360) 786-5560 Fax: (360) 754-4060

Clerk of Court **Betty J. Gould** . . . . (360) 786-5540 (Mon, Tues & Fri)
E-mail: gouldb@co.thurston.wa.us   Tel: (360) 709-3270
(Wed & Thur)
Fax: (360) 753-4033

Wahkiakum County

Court Clerk

Wahkiakum County Superior Court
64 Main Street, Cathlamet, WA 98612-0116
P.O. Box 116, Cathlamet, WA 98612-0116
Tel: (360) 795-3558 Fax: (360) 795-8813

Clerk of Court **Kay M. Holland** . . . . (360) 795-3558
E-mail: hollandk@co.wahkiakum.wa.us

Walla Walla County

Court Clerk

Walla Walla County Superior Court
315 W Main Street, Walla Walla, WA 99362-2864
Tel: (509) 524-2780 Fax: (509) 524-2779

Clerk of Court **Kathy A. Martin** . . . . (509) 524-2780
E-mail: kmartin@co.walla-walla.wa.us

Whatcom County

Court Clerk

Whatcom County Superior Court
311 Grand Avenue, Bellingham, WA 98225-4048
Tel: (360) 676-6777 Fax: (360) 676-6693

Court Administrator/ Clerk of Court **David Reynolds** . . . . (360) 676-6777
E-mail: dreynold@co.whatcom.wa.us

Whitman County

Court Clerk

Whitman County Superior Court
400 N Main Street, Colfax, WA 99111-2031
Tel: (509) 397-6244 Fax: (509) 397-2728

Clerk of Court **Jill Whelchel** . . . . (509) 397-6240
E-mail: clerk@co.whitman.wa.us

Yakima County

Court Clerk

Yakima County Superior Court
128 North Second Street, Room 314, Yakima, WA 98901
Tel: (509) 574-2710 Fax: (509) 574-2701
Internet: http://www.yakimacounty.us/superiorcourt/default.htm

Clerk of Court **Kim M. Eaton** . . . . (509) 574-1430
E-mail: kim.eaton@co.yakima.wa.us

West Virginia Court Clerks and Courthouses

The trial courts of general jurisdiction in West Virginia are called circuit courts. There are 31 judicial circuits, each circuit consisting of at least one county. Circuit Clerks are the clerk of the Circuit and Family Courts. Included below are Circuit Clerk and County Clerk listings. There is no intermediate appellate court in West Virginia.

West Virginia Supreme Court of Appeals

Capitol Complex, 1900 Kanawha Boulevard East, Room E-317, Charleston, WV 25305
Tel: (304) 558-2601 Tel: (304) 340-2324 (Supreme Court Library)
Fax: (304) 558-3815
Internet: www.courtswv.gov

The Supreme Court of Appeals consists of a chief justice and four justices who are elected in statewide, partisan elections for twelve-year terms. Vacancies are filled by the Gubernatorial appointment until the next general election. The position of chief justice alternates annually based on seniority among the justices. The Supreme Court of Appeals has appellate jurisdiction in all civil and criminal cases ruled upon by West Virginia's circuit courts. The Supreme Court has original jurisdiction in extraordinary writs (i.e. prohibition, mandamus, certiorari and habeas corpus) and in answering questions posited by federal courts. The Court has administrative authority over the circuit and magistrate courts.

Court Staff
Clerk **Rory L. Perry II** . . . . (304) 558-2601
  E-mail: rory.perry@courtswv.gov

County-By-County

Barbour County

Circuit Clerk

Nineteenth Judicial Circuit
Clerk of Court, Barbour County **Gerald M. Fogg** . . . . (304) 457-3454
  Eight North Main Street, Philippi, WV 26416   Fax: (304) 457-2790
  E-mail: gerald.fogg@courtswv.gov

County Clerk

Office of the County Clerk
26 North Main Street, Philippi, WV 26416
Tel: (304) 457-2232 Fax: (304) 457-5983

County Clerk **Macel Auvil** . . . . (304) 457-2232
  E-mail: barbourcounty@wvsos.com

Berkeley County

Circuit Clerk

Twenty-Third Judicial Circuit
Clerk of Court, Berkeley County **Virginia Sine** . . . . (304) 264-1918
  380 West South Street, Martinsburg, WV 25401   Fax: (304) 262-3139
  E-mail: virginia.sine@courtswv.gov

County Clerk

Office of the County Clerk
100 West King Street, Room 1, Martinsburg, WV 25401
Tel: (304) 264-1927 Fax: (304) 267-1794

County Clerk **John W. Small, Jr.** . . . . (304) 264-1927

Boone County

Circuit Clerk

Twenty-Fifth Judicial Circuit
Clerk of Court, Boone County **Sue Ann Zickefoose** . . . . . (304) 369-7321
  200 State Street, Madison, WV 25130   Fax: (304) 369-7326

County Clerk

Office of the County Clerk
200 State Street, Madison, WV 25130
Tel: (304) 369-7330 Fax: (304) 367-7329

County Clerk **Gary W. Williams** . . . . (304) 369-7330
  E-mail: gwilliams@boonecountywv.net

Braxton County

Circuit Clerk

Fourteenth Judicial Circuit
Clerk of Court, Braxton County **Susan Lemon** . . . . (304) 765-2837
  300 Main Street, Sutton, WV 26601   Fax: (304) 765-2947
  E-mail: susan.lemon@courtswv.gov

County Clerk

Office of the County Clerk
300 Main Street, Sutton, WV 26601
P.O. Box 486, Sutton, WV 26601
Tel: (304) 765-2833 Fax: (304) 765-2093

County Clerk **Susan K. Lunceford** . . . . (304) 765-2833

Brooke County

Circuit Clerk

First Judicial Circuit
Clerk of Court, Brooke County **Glenda Brooks** . . . . (304) 737-3662
  632 Main Street, Wellsburg, WV 26070   Fax: (304) 737-0352
  E-mail: glenda.brooks@courtswv.gov

County Clerk

Office of the County Clerk
201 Couthouse Square, Wellsburg, WV 26070
Tel: (304) 737-3661 Fax: (304) 737-4023

County Clerk **Sylvia Benzo** . . . . (304) 737-3661
  E-mail: sbenzo@mail.wvnet.edu

Cabell County

Circuit Clerk

Sixth Judicial Circuit
Clerk of Court, Cabell County **Jeffrey Hood** . . . . (304) 526-8622
  750 Fifth Avenue, Room 114,   Fax: (304) 526-8699
  Huntington, WV 25701

(continued on next page)

County Clerk

Office of the County Clerk
750 Fifth Avenue, Suite 108, Huntington, WV 25701-2072
Tel: (304) 526-8625 Fax: (304) 526-8632

County Clerk **Karen Cole** . . . . (304) 526-8625
E-mail: kcole@cabellcountyclerk.org

Calhoun County

Circuit Clerk

Fifth Judicial Circuit
Clerk of Court, Calhoun County **Sheila Garrettson** . . . . . (304) 354-6910
P.O. Box 266, Grantsville, WV 26147   Fax: (304) 354-6910

County Clerk

Office of the County Clerk
P.O. Box 230, Grantsville, WV 26147
Tel: (304) 354-6725 Fax: (304) 354-6447

County Clerk **Jean Simers** . . . . (304) 354-6725
E-mail: jean.simers@wv.gov

Clay County

Circuit Clerk

Fourteenth Judicial Circuit
Clerk of Court, Clay County **Mike Asbury** . . . . (304) 587-4256
P.O. Box 129, Clay, WV 25043   Fax: (304) 587-4346

County Clerk

Office of the County Clerk
P.O. Box 129, Clay, WV 25043-0129
Tel: (304) 587-4256 Fax: (304) 587-4346
E-mail: claycoclerk@hotmail.com

County Clerk **Connie Workman** . . . . (304) 587-4256
E-mail: cworkman@wvsos.com

Doddridge County

Circuit Clerk

Third Judicial Circuit
Clerk of Court, Doddridge County **Dwight Moore** . . . . . . (304) 873-2331
118 East Court Street, West Union, WV 26456   Fax: (304) 873-2260
E-mail: dwight.moore@courtswv.gov

County Clerk

Office of the County Clerk
135 Court Street, Room 102, West Union, WV 26456
Tel: (304) 873-2631 Fax: (304) 873-1840
E-mail: doddcoclerck@hotmail.com

County Clerk **Beth A. Rogers** . . . . (304) 873-2631

Fayette County

Circuit Clerk

Twelfth Judicial Circuit
Clerk of Court, Fayette County **Daniel Wright** . . . . (304) 574-4249
Fayette County Courthouse, 100 North Court Street,   Fax: (304) 574-4314
Fayetteville, WV 25840
E-mail: daniel.wright@courtswv.gov

County Clerk

Office of the County Clerk
100 Court Street, Fayetteville, WV 25840
P.O. Box 569, Fayetteville, WV 25840
Tel: (304) 574-4226 Fax: (304) 574-4335

County Clerk **Kelvin Holliday** . . . . (304) 574-4226
E-mail: keholliday@rocketmail.com

Gilmer County

Circuit Clerk

Fourteenth Judicial Circuit
Clerk of Court, Gilmer County **Karen Elkin** . . . . (304) 462-7241
10 Howard Street, Glenville, WV 26351   Fax: (304) 462-7038
E-mail: karen.elkin@courtswv.gov

County Clerk

Office of the County Clerk
10 Howard Street, Glenville, WV 26351
Tel: (304) 461-7641 Fax: (304) 462-8855

County Clerk **Jean Butcher** . . . . (304) 461-7641
E-mail: jbutcher8@frontier.org

Grant County

Circuit Clerk

Twenty-First Judicial Circuit
Clerk of Court, Grant County **Nancy Dayton** . . . . (304) 257-4545
5 Highland Avenue, Petersburg, WV 26847   Fax: (304) 257-2593
E-mail: nancy.dayton@courtswv.gov

County Clerk

Office of the County Clerk
5 Highland Avenue, Petersburg, WV 26847
Tel: (304) 257-4550 Fax: (304) 257-4207

County Clerk **Harold G. Hiser** . . . . (304) 257-4550

Greenbrier County

Circuit Clerk

Eleventh Judicial Circuit
Clerk of Court, Greenbrier County
Louvonne Arbuckle . . . . (304) 647-6626
200 North Court Street, Lewisburg, WV 24901   Fax: (304) 647-6666
E-mail: louvonne.arbuckle@courtswv.gov

County Clerk

Office of the County Clerk
200 Court Street North, Lewisburg, WV 24901
Tel: (304) 647-6602 Fax: (304) 647-6694

County Clerk **Robin Loudermilk** . . . . (304) 647-6602
E-mail: robinloudermilk.greenbrier@hotmail.com

Hampshire County

Circuit Clerk

Twenty-Second Judicial Circuit
Clerk of Court, Hampshire County **Sonja Embrey** . . . . (304) 822-5022
50 South High Street, Suite 2,   Fax: (304) 822-8257
Romney, WV 26757
E-mail: sonja.embrey@courtswv.gov

County Clerk

Office of the County Clerk
66 North High Street, Romney, WV 26757
P.O. Box 806, Romney, WV 26757
Tel: (304) 822-5112 Fax: (304) 822-4039
E-mail: hampcoclk@yahoo.com

County Clerk **Eric Strite** . . . . (304) 822-5112
E-mail: estrite@hampshirewv.com

Hancock County

Circuit Clerk

First Judicial Circuit
Clerk of Court, Hancock County
Brenda Jackson . . . . (304) 564-3311 ext. 261
P.O. Box 428, New Cumberland, WV 26047   Fax: (304) 564-5014
E-mail: brenda.jackson@courtswv.gov

County Clerk

Office of the County Clerk
P.O. Box 367, New Cumberland, WV 26047
Tel: (304) 564-3311 ext. 266 Fax: (304) 564-5941

County Clerk **George Foley** . . . . (304) 564-3311 ext. 266
E-mail: gfoley@hancockcountywv.org

Hardy County

Circuit Clerk

Twenty-Second Judicial Circuit
Clerk of Court, Hardy County **Kim Kimble Evans** . . . . (304) 530-0232
204 Washington Street, Room 237,   Fax: (304) 530-0231
Moorefield, WV 26836

County Clerk

Office of the County Clerk
204 Washington Street, Room 111, Moorefield, WV 26836
Tel: (304) 530-0250 Fax: (304) 530-0251

County Clerk **Gregory L. Ely** . . . . (304) 530-0250
E-mail: gely@k12.wv.us

Harrison County

Circuit Clerk

Fifteenth Judicial Circuit
Clerk of Court, Harrison County **Donald L. Kopp II** . . . . . (304) 624-8640
301 West Main Street, Clarksburg, WV 26301   Fax: (304) 624-8710
E-mail: donald.kopp@courtswv.gov

County Clerk

Office of the County Clerk
301 West Main Street, Clarksburg, WV 26301
Tel: (304) 624-8675 Fax: (304) 624-8575

County Clerk **Susan J. Thomas** . . . . (304) 624-8675
E-mail: sthomas@harrisoncountywv.com

Jackson County

Circuit Clerk

Fifth Judicial Circuit
Clerk of Court, Jackson County **Bruce DeWees** . . . . (304) 373-2210
100 Court Street, Ripley, WV 25271   Fax: (304) 372-6237
E-mail: bruce.dewees@courtswv.gov

County Clerk

Office of the County Clerk
100 Court Street North, Ripley, WV 25271
Tel: (304) 373-2250 Fax: (304) 372-1107

County Clerk **Jeff Waybright** . . . . (304) 373-2250
E-mail: jeff.waybright@jacksoncountywv.com

Jefferson County

Circuit Clerk

Twenty-Third Judicial Circuit
Clerk of Court, Jefferson County **Laura Storm** . . . . (304) 728-3231
P.O. Box 1234, Charles Town, WV 25414   Fax: (304) 728-3398
E-mail: laura.storm@courtswv.gov

County Clerk

Office of the County Clerk
100 East Washington Street, Charles Town, WV 25414
P.O. Box 208, Charles Town, WV 25414
Tel: (304) 728-3215 Fax: (304) 728-1957

County Clerk **Jennifer Maghan** . . . . (304) 728-3215
E-mail: jmaghan@jeffersoncountywv.org

Kanawha County

Circuit Clerk

Thirteenth Judicial Circuit
Clerk of Court, Kanawha County **Cathy S. Gaston** . . . . . . (304) 357-0440
111 Court Street, Charleston, WV 25301   Fax: (304) 357-0473

County Clerk

Office of the County Clerk
P.O. Box 3226, Charleston, WV 25332-3226
Fax: (304) 357-0585 Fax: (304) 357-0588 (Voters' Registration Fax)

County Clerk **Vera McCormick** . . . . (304) 357-0130
E-mail: veramccormick@kanawha.us

Lewis County

Circuit Clerk

Twenty-Sixth Judicial Circuit
Clerk of Court, Lewis County **John Hinzman** . . . . (304) 269-8210
117 Court Avenue, Weston, WV 26452   Fax: (304) 269-8249
E-mail: john.hinzman@courtswv.gov

County Clerk

Office of the County Clerk
110 Center Street, Weston, WV 26452-2129
Tel: (304) 269-8215 Fax: (304) 269-8202

County Clerk **Cynthia S. Rowan** . . . . (304) 269-8215
E-mail: crowan@lewiscountywv.org

Lincoln County

Circuit Clerk

Twenty-Fifth Judicial Circuit
Clerk of Court, Lincoln County
Charlie Brumfield . . . . (304) 824-7887 ext. 239
8000 Court Avenue, Hamlin, WV 25523   Fax: (304) 824-7310

(continued on next page)

County Clerk

Office of the County Clerk
P.O. Box 497, Hamlin, WV 25523
Tel: (304) 824-7990 ext. 233 Fax: (304) 824-2444

County Clerk **Direl Baker** . . . . (304) 824-7990 ext. 233
 E-mail: dgbclerk@gmail.com

Logan County

Circuit Clerk

Seventh Judicial Circuit
Clerk of Court, Logan County **Vickie "Vance" Kolota** . . . (304) 792-8550
 Logan County Courthouse, 300 Stratton Street,   Fax: (304) 792-8555
 Logan, WV 25601
 E-mail: vickie.kolota@courtswv.gov

County Clerk

Office of the County Clerk
300 Stratton Street, Logan, WV 25601
Tel: (304) 792-8600 Fax: (304) 792-8621

County Clerk **John A. Turner** . . . . (304) 792-8600
 E-mail: jturn4@yahoo.com

Marion County

Circuit Clerk

Sixteenth Judicial Circuit
Clerk of Court, Marion County **Rhonda L. Starn** . . . . (304) 367-5360
 219 Adams Street, Room 211,   Fax: (304) 367-5374
 Fairmont, WV 26554
 E-mail: rhonda.starn@courtswv.gov

County Clerk

Office of the County Clerk
219 Adams Street, Fairmont, WV 26554
Tel: (304) 367-5440 Fax: (304) 367-5448

County Clerk **Janice Cosco** . . . . (304) 367-5440
 E-mail: jcosco@wvsos.com

Marshall County

Circuit Clerk

Second Judicial Circuit
Clerk of Court, Marshall County **David Ealy** . . . . (304) 845-2130
 Marshall County Courthouse, 600 Seventh Street,   Fax: (304) 845-3948
 Moundsville, WV 26041
 E-mail: david.ealy@courtswv.gov

County Clerk

Office of the County Clerk
600 Seventh Street, Room 106, Moundsville, WV 26041
P.O. Box 459, Moundsville, WV 26041
Tel: (304) 845-1220 Fax: (304) 845-5891

County Clerk **Jan Pest** . . . . (304) 845-1220
 E-mail: countyclerk@marshallcountywv.org

Mason County

Circuit Clerk

Fifth Judicial Circuit
Clerk of Court, Mason County **Bill Withers** . . . . (304) 675-4400
 200 Sixth Street, Point Pleasant, WV 25550   Fax: (304) 675-7419
 E-mail: bill.withers@courtswv.gov

County Clerk

Office of the County Clerk
200 Sixth Street, Point Pleasant, WV 25550
Tel: (304) 675-1997 Fax: (304) 675-2521

County Clerk **Diana Cromley** . . . . (304) 675-1997
 E-mail: diana_crowley@yahoo.com

McDowell County

Circuit Clerk

Eighth Judicial Circuit
Clerk of Court, McDowell County **Francine Spencer** . . . . (304) 436-8535
 90 Wyoming Street, Suite 201,   Fax: (304) 436-6994
 Welch, WV 24801
 E-mail: francine.spencer@courtswv.gov

County Clerk

Office of the County Clerk
90 Wyoming Street, Suite 109, Welch, WV 24801
Tel: (304) 436-8544 Fax: (304) 436-8576

County Clerk **Donald L. Hicks** . . . . (304) 436-8544
 E-mail: dhicks@wvsos.com

Mercer County

Circuit Clerk

Ninth Judicial Circuit
Clerk of Court, Mercer County **Julie Ball** . . . . (304) 487-8323
 1501 Main Street, Princeton, WV 24740   Fax: (304) 425-1598
 E-mail: julie.ball@courtswv.gov

County Clerk

Office of the County Clerk
1501 West Main Street, Suite 121, Princeton, WV 24740
Tel: (304) 487-8312 Fax: (304) 487-9842

County Clerk **Verlin T. Moye** . . . . (304) 487-8466
 E-mail: vtmoye@mercercounty.org

Mineral County

Circuit Clerk

Twenty-First Judicial Circuit
Clerk of Court, Mineral County
 Krista Johnson Dixon . . . . (304) 788-1562
 150 Armstrong Street, Keyser, WV 26726   Fax: (304) 788-4109

County Clerk

Office of the County Clerk
150 Armstrong Street, Keyser, WV 26726
Tel: (304) 788-3924 Fax: (304) 788-4109

County Clerk **Lauren Ellifritz** . . . . (304) 788-3924
 E-mail: clerk2@mineralchamber.com

Mingo County

Circuit Clerk

Thirtieth Judicial Circuit
Clerk of Court, Mingo County **Grant Preece** . . . . (304) 235-0320
75 East Second Avenue, Williamson, WV 25661   Fax: (304) 235-0326
E-mail: grant.preece@courtswv.gov

County Clerk

Office of the County Clerk
75 East Second Avenue, Williamson, WV 25661
Tel: (304) 235-0330 Fax: (304) 235-0565

County Clerk **Jim Hatfield** . . . .(304) 235-0330

Monongalia County

Circuit Clerk

Seventeenth Judicial Circuit
Clerk of Court, Monongalia County **Jean Friend** . . . .(304) 291-7240
75 High Street, Morgantown, WV 26505   Tel: (304) 291-7273
E-mail: jean.friend@courtswv.gov

County Clerk

Office of the County Clerk
243 High Street, Morgantown, WV 26505
Tel: (304) 291-7230 Fax: (304) 291-7233

County Clerk **Carye Blaney** . . . .(304) 291-7230
E-mail: cblaney@monongaliacountyclerk.com

Monroe County

Circuit Clerk

Thirty-First Judicial Circuit
Clerk of Court, Monroe County **Leta Gullette-Coner** . . . . (304) 772-3017
Monroe County Courthouse, Main Street,   Fax: (304) 772-4497
Union, WV 24983
E-mail: leta.gullette@courtswv.gov

County Clerk

Office of the County Clerk
216 Main Street, Union, WV 24983
Tel: (304) 772-3096 Fax: (304) 772-4191

County Clerk **Donald J. Evans** . . . . (304) 772-3096
E-mail: devans@monroecountywv.net

Morgan County

Circuit Clerk

Twenty-Third Judicial Circuit
Clerk of Court, Morgan County **Kimberly J. Hanback** . . . (304) 258-8554
77 Fairfax Street, Berkeley Springs, WV 25411   Fax: (304) 258-7319
E-mail: kimberly.hanback@courtswv.gov

County Clerk

Office of the County Clerk
77 Fairfax Street, Room 102, Berkeley Springs, WV 25411
Tel: (304) 258-8547 Fax: (304) 258-8545
E-mail: morgancountyclerk@hotmail.com

County Clerk **Debra A. Kesecker** . . . . (304) 258-8547
E-mail: dkesecker@morgancountywv.gov

Nicholas County

Circuit Clerk

Twenty-Eighth Judicial Circuit
Clerk of Court, Nicholas County **Debbie Facemire** . . . . . .(304) 872-7810
700 Main Street, Summersville, WV 26651   Fax: (304) 872-7863

County Clerk

Office of the County Clerk
700 Main Street, Suite 2, Summersville, WV 26651
Tel: (304) 872-7820 Fax: (304) 872-9600

County Clerk **Audra Deitz** . . . .(304) 872-7820
E-mail: audra.deitz@nicholas.kyschools.us

Ohio County

Circuit Clerk

First Judicial Circuit
Clerk of Court, Ohio County **Brenda L. Miller** . . . .(304) 234-3611
1500 Chapline Street, Wheeling, WV 26003   Fax: (304) 232-0550
E-mail: brenda.miller@courtswv.gov

County Clerk

Office of the County Clerk
1500 Chapline Street, Wheeling, WV 26003
Tel: (304) 234-3656 Fax: (304) 234-3829

County Clerk **Patricia A. Fahey** . . . .(304) 234-3656
E-mail: ocpfahey@clerk.state.wv.us

Pendleton County

Circuit Clerk

Twenty-Second Judicial Circuit
Clerk of Court, Pendleton County **Shalee Wilburn** . . . . . . (304) 358-7067
P.O Box 846, Franklin, WV 26807   Fax: (304) 358-2152
E-mail: shalee.wilburn@courtswv.gov

County Clerk

Office of the County Clerk
100 South Main Strett, Franklin, WV 26807
P.O. Box 1167, Franklin, WV 26807
Tel: (304) 358-2505 Fax: (304) 358-2473

County Clerk **Linda Rexrode** . . . .(304) 358-2505
E-mail: countyclerk@pendletoncommission.com

Pleasants County

Circuit Clerk

Third Judicial Circuit
Clerk of Court, Pleasants County **Millie Farnsworth** . . . . .(304) 684-3513
301 Court Lane, Saint Mary's, WV 26170   Fax: (304) 684-3514
E-mail: millie.farnsworth@courtswv.gov

County Clerk

Office of the County Clerk
301 Court Lane, Saint Mary's, WV 26170
Tel: (304) 684-3542 Fax: (304) 684-7569

County Clerk **Sue E. Morgan** . . . . (304) 684-3542
E-mail: smorgan_clerk@yahoo.com

(continued on next page)

Pocahontas County

Circuit Clerk

Eleventh Judicial Circuit
Clerk of Court, Pocahontas County **Connie Carr** . . . . (304) 799-4604
  900 Tenth Avenue, Marlinton, WV 24954   Fax: (304) 799-0833
  E-mail: connie.carr@courtswv.gov

County Clerk

Office of the County Clerk
900 C Tenth Avenue, Marlinton, WV 24954
Tel: (304) 799-4549 Fax: (304) 799-6947
E-mail: pocahontascoclrk@aol.com

County Clerk **Melissa "Missy" Bennett** . . . . (304) 799-4549
  E-mail: pocahontascoclrk@aol.com

Preston County

Circuit Clerk

Eighteenth Judicial Circuit
Circuit Clerk **Betsy Castle** . . . . (304) 329-0047
  Preston County Courthouse,   Fax: (304) 329-1417
  101 West Main Street, Room 301,
  Kingwood, WV 26537
  E-mail: betsy.castle@courtswv.gov

County Clerk

Office of the County Clerk
106 West Main Street, Kingwood, WV 26537
Tel: (304) 329-0070 Fax: (304) 329-0198

County Clerk **Linda Huggins** . . . . (304) 329-0070
  E-mail: lhuggins@prestoncountywv.org

Putnam County

Circuit Clerk

Twenty-Ninth Judicial Circuit
Clerk of Court, Putnam County **Ronnie Matthews** . . . . . . (304) 586-0203
  3389 Winfield Road, Winfield, WV 25213   Fax: (304) 586-0221
  E-mail: ronnie.matthews@courtswv.gov

County Clerk

Office of the County Clerk
3389 Winfield Road, Winfield, WV 25213
Tel: (304) 586-0202 Fax: (304) 586-0200

County Clerk **Brian Wood** . . . . (304) 586-0202
  E-mail: b.wood@putnamcounty.org

Raleigh County

Circuit Clerk

Tenth Judicial Circuit
Clerk of Court, Raleigh County **Paul Flanagan** . . . . (304) 255-9135
  Raleigh County Courthouse, 222 Main Street,   Fax: (304) 255-9353
  Beckley, WV 25801
  E-mail: paul.flanagan@courtswv.gov

County Clerk

Office of the County Clerk
215 Main Street, Beckley, WV 25802
Tel: (304) 255-9123 Fax: (304) 255-9352

County Clerk **Betty Riffe** . . . . (304) 255-9123
  E-mail: bfriffe@hotmail.com

Randolph County

Circuit Clerk

Twentieth Judicial Circuit
Clerk of Court, Randolph County **Phil Riggleman** . . . . (304) 636-2765
  2 Randolph Avenue, Elkins, WV 26241   Fax: (304) 637-3700
  E-mail: phil.riggleman@courtswv.gov

County Clerk

Office of the County Clerk
2 Randolph Avenue, Elkins, WV 26241
Tel: (304) 636-0543 Fax: (304) 636-0544

County Clerk **Brenda D. Wiseman** . . . . (304) 363-0543
  E-mail: bwiseman@co.randolph.nc.us

Ritchie County

Circuit Clerk

Third Judicial Circuit
Clerk of Court, Ritchie County
  Rose Ellen Cox . . . . (304) 643-2164 ext. 229
  115 East Main Street, Harrisville, WV 26362   Fax: (304) 642-2534
  E-mail: rose.cox@courtswv.gov

County Clerk

Office of the County Clerk
115 East Main Street, Room 201, Harrisville, WV 26326
Tel: (304) 643-2164 Fax: (304) 643-2906

County Clerk **Tracy McDonald** . . . . (304) 643-2164 ext. 221
  E-mail: tdmcdona@clerk.state.wv.us

Roane County

Circuit Clerk

Fifth Judicial Circuit
Clerk of Court, Roane County **Andrea Stockner** . . . . (304) 927-2750
  200 Main Street, Spencer, WV 25276   Fax: (304) 927-2164
  E-mail: andrea.stockner@courtswv.gov

County Clerk

Office of the County Clerk
200 Main Street, Spencer, WV 25276
Tel: (304) 927-2860 Fax: (304) 927-2489

County Clerk **Charles B. White, Jr.** . . . . (304) 927-2860
  E-mail: cwhite2@clerk.state.wv.us

Summers County

Circuit Clerk

Thirty-First Judicial Circuit
Clerk of Court, Summers County **Linda Brumit** . . . . (304) 466-7103
  P.O. Box 1058, Hinton, WV 25951   Fax: (304) 466-7124
  E-mail: linda.brumit@courtswv.gov

County Clerk

Office of the County Clerk
120 Ballengee Street, Suite 106, Hinton, WV 25951
P.O. 97, Hinton, WV 25951
Tel: (304) 466-7104   Fax: (304) 466-7146

County Clerk **Mary Beth Merritt** . . . .(304) 466-7104

Taylor County

Circuit Clerk

Nineteenth Judicial Circuit
Clerk of Court, Taylor County **Vonda M. Reneman** . . . . . (304) 265-2480
  214 West Main Street, Room 105,   Fax: (304) 265-0459
  Grafton, WV 26354
  E-mail: vonda.reneman@courtswv.gov

County Clerk

Office of the County Clerk
214 West Main Street, Grafton, WV 26354
Tel: (304) 265-1401   Fax: (304) 265-5450

County Clerk **Georgianna Thompson** . . . . (304) 265-1401
  E-mail: georgianna.thompson@wvhouse.gov

Tucker County

Circuit Clerk

Twenty-First Judicial Circuit
Clerk of Court, Tucker County **Donna Jean Bava** . . . .(304) 478-2606
  Tucker County Courthouse, 271 First Street,   Fax: (304) 478-4464
  Suite 403, Parsons, WV 26287

County Clerk

Office of the County Clerk
215 First Street, Suite 3, Parsons, WV 26287
Tel: (304) 478-2414 ext. 201   Fax: (304) 478-2217

County Clerk **Sherry Simmons** . . . . (304) 478-2414 ext. 201
  E-mail: t.cclerk@hotmail.com

Tyler County

Circuit Clerk

Second Judicial Circuit
Clerk of Court, Tyler County **Candy Warner** . . . .(304) 758-4811
  600 Seventh Street, Moundsville, WV 26041   Fax: (304) 758-4008
  E-mail: candy.warner@courtswv.gov

County Clerk

Office of the County Clerk
P.O. Box 66, Middlebourne, WV 26149
Tel: (304) 758-2102   Fax: (304) 758-2126

County Clerk **Teresea R. Hamilton** . . . .(304) 758-2102

Upshur County

Circuit Clerk

Twenty-Sixth Judicial Circuit
Clerk of Court, Upshur County **Brian P. Gaudet** . . . .(304) 472-2370
  38 West Main Street, Room 304,   Fax: (304) 472-2168
  Buckhannon, WV 26201
  E-mail: brian.gaudet@courtswv.gov

County Clerk

Office of the County Clerk
40 West Main Street, Room 101, Buckhannon, WV 26201
Tel: (304) 472-1068   Fax: (304) 472-1029

County Clerk **Debbie Wilfong** . . . .(304) 472-1068
  E-mail: dtwilfong@upshurcounty.org

Wayne County

Circuit Clerk

Twenty-Fourth Judicial Circuit
Clerk of Court, Wayne County **M. "Jamie" Ferguson** . . . (304) 272-6360
  P.O. Box 38, Wayne, WV 25570   Fax: (304) 272-3496
  700 Hendricks Street, Wayne, WV 25570

County Clerk

Office of the County Clerk
P.O. Bos 248, Wayne, WV 25570
Tel: (304) 272-6362   Fax: (304) 272-5318

County Clerk **Renick Booth** . . . .(304) 272-6362
  E-mail: renickbooth@waynecountywv.org

Webster County

Circuit Clerk

Fourteenth Judicial Circuit
Clerk of Court, Webster County **Jeanie Moore** . . . .(304) 847-2421
  2 Court Square, Room G-4,   Fax: (304) 847-2062
  Webster Springs, WV 26288
  E-mail: jeanie.moore@courtswv.gov

County Clerk

Office of the County Clerk
Two Court Square, Room G1, Webster Springs, WV 26288
Tel: (304) 847-2508   Fax: (304) 847-5780

County Clerk **Eva R. Green** . . . .(304) 847-2508
  E-mail: webstercoclerk@frontiernet.net

Wetzel County

Circuit Clerk

Second Judicial Circuit
Clerk of Court, Wetzel County **Sharon Dulaney** . . . .(304) 455-8129
  P.O. Box 263, New Martinsville, WV 26155   Fax: (304) 455-1069
  E-mail: sharon.dulaney@courtswv.gov

County Clerk

Office of the County Clerk
P.O. Box 156, New Martinsville, WV 26155
Tel: (304) 455-8224   Fax: (304) 455-5256
E-mail: wetzelcoclk@hotmail.com

County Clerk **Carol S. Haught** . . . .(304) 455-8224
  E-mail: chaught@wvsos.com

Wirt County

Circuit Clerk

Fourth Judicial Circuit
Clerk of Court, Wirt County **Carol Frame** . . . .(304) 275-6597
  P.O. Box 465, Elizabeth, WV 26143   Fax: (304) 275-3230
  E-mail: carol.frame@courtswv.gov

(continued on next page)

West Virginia Court Clerks and Courthouses *continued*

County Clerk

Office of the County Clerk
P.O. Box 53, Elizabeth, WV 26143
Tel: (304) 275-4271 Fax: (304) 275-3418

County Clerk **Suellen Calebaugh** . . . .(304) 275-4271

Wood County

Circuit Clerk

Fourth Judicial Circuit
Clerk of Court, Wood County **Carole Jones** . . . .(304) 424-1700
  2 Government Square, Parkersburg, WV 26101   Fax: (304) 424-1747
  E-mail: carole.jones@courtswv.gov

County Clerk

Office of the County Clerk
One Court Square, Parkersburg, WV 26101
P.O. Box 1474, Parkersburg, WV 26102
Tel: (304) 424-1850 Fax: (304) 424-1982

County Clerk **Mark Rhodes** . . . .(304) 424-1850
  E-mail: mrhodes@woodcountywv.com

Wyoming County

Circuit Clerk

Twenty-Seventh Judicial Circuit
Clerk of Court, Wyoming County **David Stover** . . . .(304) 732-8000
  P.O. Box 190, Pineville, WV 24874   Fax: (304) 732-7262
  E-mail: david.stover@courtswv.gov

County Clerk

Office of the County Clerk
P.O. Box 309, Pineville, WV 24874
Tel: (304) 732-8000 Fax: (304) 732-9659

County Clerk **D. Michael Goode** . . . .(304) 732-8000
  E-mail: mikegoode@wyomingcounty.com

Counties Within Judicial Circuits

Circuit Court, 1st Judicial Circuit
Areas Covered: Hancock County, Brooke County, Ohio County.

Circuit Court, 2nd Judicial Circuit
Areas Covered: Marshall County, Tyler County, Wetzel County.

Circuit Court, 3rd Judicial Circuit
Areas Covered: Doddridge County, Pleasants County, Ritchie County.

Circuit Court, 4th Judicial Circuit
Areas Covered: Wood County, Wirt County.

Circuit Court, 5th Judicial Circuit
Areas Covered: Calhoun County, Jackson County, Mason County, Roane County.

Circuit Court, 6th Judicial Circuit
Areas Covered: Cabell County.

West Virginia Court Clerks and Courthouses *continued*

Circuit Court, 7th Judicial Circuit
Areas Covered: Logan County.

Circuit Court, 8th Judicial Circuit
Areas Covered: McDowell County.

Circuit Court, 9th Judicial Circuit
Areas Covered: Mercer County.

Circuit Court, 10th Judicial Circuit
Areas Covered: Raleigh County.

Circuit Court, 11th Judicial Circuit
Areas Covered: Greenbrier County, Pocahontas County.

Circuit Court, 12th Judicial Circuit
Areas Covered: Fayette County.

Circuit Court, 13th Judicial Circuit
Areas Covered: Kanawha County.

Circuit Court, 14th Judicial Circuit
Areas Covered: Braxton County, Clay County, Gilmer County, Webster County.

Circuit Court, 15th Judicial Circuit
Areas Covered: Harrison County.

Circuit Court, 16th Judicial Circuit
Areas Covered: Marion County.

Circuit Court, 17th Judicial Circuit
Areas Covered: Monongalia County.

Circuit Court, 18th Judicial Circuit
Areas Covered: Preston County.

Circuit Court, 19th Judicial Circuit
Areas Covered: Barbour County, Taylor County.

Circuit Court, 20th Judicial Circuit
Areas Covered: Randolph County.

Circuit Court, 21st Judicial Circuit
Areas Covered: Grant County, Mineral County, Tucker County.

Circuit Court, 22nd Judicial Circuit
Areas Covered: Hardy County, Hampshire County, Pendleton County.

Circuit Court, 23rd Judicial Circuit
Areas Covered: Berkeley County, Morgan County, Jefferson County.

Circuit Court, 24th Judicial Circuit
Areas Covered: Wayne County.

West Virginia Court Clerks and Courthouses *continued*

Circuit Court, 25th Judicial Circuit

Areas Covered: Boone County, Lincoln County.

Circuit Court, 26th Judicial Circuit

Areas Covered: Lewis County, Upshur County.

Circuit Court, 27th Judicial Circuit

Areas Covered: Wyoming County.

Circuit Court, 28th Judicial Circuit

Areas Covered: Nicholas County.

Circuit Court, 29th Judicial Circuit

Areas Covered: Putnam County.

Circuit Court, 30th Judicial Circuit

Areas Covered: Mingo County.

Circuit Court, 31st Judicial Circuit

Areas Covered: Monroe County, Summers County.

Wisconsin Court Clerks and Courthouses

The trial courts of general jurisdiction in Wisconsin are called circuit courts. There are 10 judicial districts of circuit court, each district consisting of at least one county.

Wisconsin Supreme Court

P.O. Box 1688, Madison, WI 53701-1688
16 East State Capitol, Madison, WI 53702
Tel: (608) 266-1880 Fax: (608) 267-0640
Internet: www.wicourts.gov

The Supreme Court consists of a chief justice and six justices who are elected at-large in nonpartisan elections for ten-year terms. Vacancies occurring between terms are filled by the Governor. The justice with the most seniority serves as chief justice. The Supreme Court exercises appellate jurisdiction over all courts and may hear original actions and proceedings. The Court may review judgments of, may remove cases from, and may accept certification by the Wisconsin Court of Appeals. The Court has general superintending control over all lower courts and may hear, determine and issue any writ relevant to its jurisdiction.

Court Staff

Clerk of Supreme Court **Diane Fremgen** . . . . (608) 266-1880
  110 E. Main St., Ste. 215,   Fax: (608) 267-0640
  Madison, WI 53703-3328
  E-mail: diane.fremgen@wicourts.gov

Wisconsin Court of Appeals

Ten East Doty Street, Suite 700, Madison, WI 53703
P.O. Box 1688, Madison, WI 53701-1688
Tel: (608) 266-1880 Fax: (608) 267-0640
Internet: www.wicourts.gov

The Court of Appeal is comprised of four districts and consists of a chief judge and fifteen judges who are elected for six-year terms. The Chief Judge is appointed by the Wisconsin Supreme Court to serve as the administrative head of the court for a three-year term. Presiding judges are appointed in each district by the Chief Judge to serve a two-year term. The Governor may appoint judges to the Court to temporarily fill vacancies that occur before a term has expired. The Court of Appeal has appellate jurisdiction over all final judgments and orders from Wisconsin circuit courts and has original jurisdiction to issue prerogative writs. The Court's decisions may be reviewed by the Wisconsin Supreme Court at its discretion, but there is no automatic appeal process. The Court exercises supervisory control over the lower courts.

Court Staff

Clerk of Court of Appeals **Diane Fremgen** . . . . (608) 266-1880
  110 E. Main St., Ste. 215,   Fax: (608) 267-0640
  Madison, WI 53703-3328
  E-mail: diane.fremgen@wicourts.gov

Wisconsin Court of Appeals, District I

330 East Kilbourn Avenue, Suite 1020, Milwaukee, WI 53202-3161
Tel: (414) 227-4680 Fax: (414) 227-4051
Internet: www.wicourts.gov/appeals

Areas Covered: County of Milwaukee

Wisconsin Court of Appeals, District II

2727 North Grandview Boulevard, Suite 300, Waukesha, WI 53188-1672
Tel: (262) 521-5230 Fax: (262) 521-5419
Internet: www.wicourts.gov/appeals

Areas Covered: Counties of Calumet, Fond du Lac, Green Lake, Kenosha, Manitowoc, Ozaukee, Racine, Sheboygan, Walworth, Washington, Waukesha and Winnebago

Wisconsin Court of Appeals, District III

2100 Stewart Avenue, Suite 310, Wausau, WI 54401-1700
Tel: (715) 848-1421 Fax: (715) 845-4523
Internet: www.wicourts.gov/appeals

Areas Covered: Counties of Ashland, Barron, Bayfield, Brown, Buffalo, Burnett, Chippewa, Door, Douglas, Dunn, Eau Claire, Florence, Forest, Iron, Kewaunee, Langlade, Lincoln, Marathon, Marinette, Menominee, Oconto, Oneida, Outagamie, Pepin, Pierce, Polk, Price, Rusk, Sawyer, Shawano, St. Croix, Taylor, Trempealeau, Vilas and Washburn

Wisconsin Court of Appeals, District IV

Ten East Doty Street, Suite 700, Madison, WI 53703-3397
Tel: (608) 266-9250 Fax: (608) 267-0432
Internet: www.wicourts.gov/appeals

Areas Covered: Counties of Adams, Clark, Columbia, Crawford, Dane, Dodge, Grant, Green, Iowa, Jackson, Jefferson, Juneau, LaCrosse, Lafayette, Marquette, Monroe, Portage, Richland, Rock, Sauk, Vernon, Waupaca, Waushara and Wood

County-By-County

Adams County

Court Clerk

Sixth Judicial District
210 West Center Street, Juneau, WI 53039

Circuit Clerk, Adams County **Kathleen R. Dye** . . . . (608) 339-4208
  P.O. Box 220, Friendship, WI 53934   Fax: (608) 339-4503
  E-mail: kathleen.dye@wicourts.gov

Ashland County

Court Clerk

Tenth Judicial District
1101 Carmichael Road, Hudson, WI 54016

Circuit Clerk, Ashland County **Kerrie Ferrando** . . . . (715) 682-7016
  201 West Main Street, Ashland, WI 54806   Fax: (715) 682-7919
  E-mail: kerrie.ferrando@wicourts.gov

Barron County

Court Clerk

Tenth Judicial District
1101 Carmichael Road, Hudson, WI 54016

Circuit Clerk, Barron County **Sharon Millermon** . . . . (715) 537-6265
  Barron County Justice Center,   Fax: (715) 537-6269
  1420 State Highway 25 North, Room 2201,
  Barron, WI 54812-3004
  E-mail: sharon.millermon@wicourts.gov

(continued on next page)

Wisconsin Court Clerks and Courthouses *continued*

Bayfield County

Court Clerk

Tenth Judicial District
1101 Carmichael Road, Hudson, WI 54016

Circuit Clerk, Bayfield County **Kay Cederberg** . . . . (715) 373-6108
117 East Fifth Street, Washburn, WI 54891   Fax: (715) 373-6317
P.O. Box 536, Washburn, WI 54891
E-mail: kay.cederberg@wicourts.gov

Brown County

Court Clerk

Eighth Judicial District
100 South Jefferson Street, Green Bay, WI 54305

Circuit Clerk, Brown County **John A. Vander Leest** . . . . . (920) 448-4155
100 South Jefferson Street,   Fax: (920) 448-4156
Green Bay, WI 54305
P.O. Box 23600, Green Bay, WI 54305-3600

Buffalo County

Court Clerk

Seventh Judicial District
222 North Iowa Street, Dodgeville, WI 53533

Circuit Clerk, Buffalo County **Roselle Schlosser** . . . . (608) 685-6212
407 South Second Street, Alma, WI 54610-0068   Fax: (608) 685-6211
P.O. Box 68, Alma, WI 54610-0068
E-mail: roselle.schlosser@wicourts.gov

Burnett County

Court Clerk

Tenth Judicial District
1101 Carmichael Road, Hudson, WI 54016

Circuit Clerk, Burnett County **Trudy Schmidt** . . . . (715) 349-2147
7410 County Road K, Room 115,   Fax: (715) 349-7659
Siren, WI 54872
E-mail: trudy.schmidt@wicourts.gov

Calumet County

Court Clerk

Fourth Judicial District
160 South Macy Street, Fond du Lac, WI 54935

Circuit Clerk, Calumet County **Barb VanAkkeren** . . . . (920) 849-1414
206 Court Street, Chilton, WI 53014   Fax: (920) 849-1483
E-mail: barb.vanakkeren@wicourts.gov

Chippewa County

Court Clerk

Tenth Judicial District
1101 Carmichael Road, Hudson, WI 54016

Circuit Clerk, Chippewa County **Karen Hepfler** . . . . (715) 726-7758
711 North Bridge Street, Room 220,   Fax: (715) 726-7786
Chippewa Falls, WI 54729
E-mail: karen.hepfler@wicourts.gov

Wisconsin Court Clerks and Courthouses *continued*

Clark County

Court Clerk

Sixth Judicial District
210 West Center Street, Juneau, WI 53039

Circuit Clerk, Clark County **Heather Bravener** . . . . (715) 743-5181
Clark County Courthouse, 517 Court Street,
Room 405, Neillsville, WI 54456
E-mail: heather.bravener@wicourts.gov

Columbia County

Court Clerk

Sixth Judicial District
210 West Center Street, Juneau, WI 53039

Circuit Clerk, Columbia County **Susan Raimer** . . . . (608) 742-9620
Carl Frederick Administration Building,   Fax: (608) 742-9601
400 DeWitt Street, Portage, WI 53901
P.O. Box 587, Portage, WI 53901
E-mail: susan.raimer@wicourts.gov

Crawford County

Court Clerk

Seventh Judicial District
222 North Iowa Street, Dodgeville, WI 53533

Circuit Clerk, Crawford County **Donna Steiner** . . . . (608) 326-0211
220 North Beaumont Road,   Fax: (608) 326-0288
Prairie Du Chien, WI 53821
E-mail: donna.steiner@wicourts.gov

Dane County

Court Clerk

Fifth Judicial District
215 South Hamilton Street, Madison, WI 53703

Circuit Clerk, Dane County **Carlo Esqueda** . . . . (608) 266-4311
Dane County Courthouse,   Fax: (608) 267-8859
215 South Hamilton Street, Room 1000,
Madison, WI 53703
E-mail: carlo.esqueda@wicourts.gov

Dodge County

Court Clerk

Sixth Judicial District
210 West Center Street, Juneau, WI 53039

Circuit Clerk, Dodge County **Lynn Hron** . . . . (920) 386-3570
210 West Center Street, Juneau, WI 53039
E-mail: lynn.hron@wicourts.gov

Door County

Court Clerk

Eighth Judicial District
100 South Jefferson Street, Green Bay, WI 54305

Circuit Clerk, Door County **Connie DeFere** . . . . (920) 746-2205
Door County Justice Center,   Fax: (920) 746-2520
1205 South Duluth Avenue,
Sturgeon Bay, WI 54235
E-mail: connie.defere@wicourts.gov

Douglas County

Court Clerk

Tenth Judicial District
1101 Carmichael Road, Hudson, WI 54016

Circuit Clerk, Douglas County **Michele Wick** . . . . (715) 395-1203
1313 Belknap Street, Room 309,
Superior, WI 54880

Dunn County

Court Clerk

Tenth Judicial District
1101 Carmichael Road, Hudson, WI 54016

Circuit Clerk, Dunn County **Clara D. Minor** . . . . (715) 232-2611
615 Stokke Parkway, Menomonie, WI 54751   Fax: (715) 232-6888
E-mail: clara.minor@wicourts.gov

Eau Claire County

Court Clerk

Tenth Judicial District
1101 Carmichael Road, Hudson, WI 54016

Circuit Clerk, Eau Claire County **Jodi Gobrecht** . . . . (715) 839-4816
721 Oxford Avenue, Suite 2220,   Fax: (715) 839-4817
Eau Claire, WI 54703

Florence County

Court Clerk

Ninth Judicial District
500 Forest Street, Wausau, WI 54403

Circuit Clerk, Florence County **Tanya Neuens** . . . . (715) 528-3205
P.O. Box 410, Florence, WI 54121   Fax: (715) 528-5470
E-mail: tanya.neuens@wicourts.gov

Fond du Lac County

Court Clerk

Fourth Judicial District
160 South Macy Street, Fond du Lac, WI 54935

Circuit Clerk, Fond Du Lac County **Ramona M. Geib** . . . (920) 929-3040
160 South Macy Street, Fond du Lac, WI 54935   Fax: (920) 929-3933
E-mail: ramona.geib@wicourts.gov

Forest County

Court Clerk

Ninth Judicial District
500 Forest Street, Wausau, WI 54403

Circuit Clerk, Forest County **Penny Carter** . . . . (715) 478-3323
200 East Madison, Crandon, WI 54520   Fax: (715) 478-3211
E-mail: penny.carter@wicourts.gov

Grant County

Court Clerk

Seventh Judicial District
222 North Iowa Street, Dodgeville, WI 53533

Circuit Clerk, Grant County **Tina McDonald** . . . . (608) 723-2752
130 West Maple Street, Lancaster, WI 53813   Fax: (608) 723-7370
P.O. Box 110, Lancaster, WI 53813
E-mail: tina.mcdonald@wicourts.gov

Green County

Court Clerk

Fifth Judicial District
215 South Hamilton Street, Madison, WI 53703

Circuit Clerk, Green County **Barbara Miller** . . . . (608) 328-9433
Green County Justice Center, 2841 Sixth Street,   Fax: (608) 328-9405
Monroe, WI 53566
E-mail: barbara.miller@wicourts.gov

Green Lake County

Court Clerk

Sixth Judicial District
210 West Center Street, Juneau, WI 53039

Circuit Clerk, Green Lake County **Susan J. Krueger** . . . . (920) 294-4142
571 County Road A, Green Lake, WI 54941
P.O. Box 3188, Green Lake, WI 54941
E-mail: susan.krueger@wicourts.gov

Iowa County

Court Clerk

Seventh Judicial District
222 North Iowa Street, Dodgeville, WI 53533

Circuit Clerk, Iowa County **Lia N. Gust** . . . . (608) 935-0395
222 North Iowa Street, Dodgeville, WI 53533
E-mail: lia.gust@wicourts.gov

Iron County

Court Clerk

Ninth Judicial District
500 Forest Street, Wausau, WI 54403

Circuit Clerk, Iron County **Karen Ransanici** . . . . (715) 561-4084
300 Taconite Street, Suite 207,
Hurley, WI 54534
E-mail: karen.ransanici@wicourts.gov

Jackson County

Court Clerk

Seventh Judicial District
222 North Iowa Street, Dodgeville, WI 53533

Circuit Clerk, Jackson County **Jan Moennig** . . . . (715) 284-0208
307 Main Street, Black River Falls, WI 54615   Fax: (715) 284-0270
E-mail: jan.moennig@wicourts.gov

(continued on next page)

Jefferson County

Court Clerk

Third Judicial District
515 West Moreland Boulevard, Waukesha, WI 53188

Circuit Clerk, Jefferson County **Carla Robinson** . . . . (920) 674-7150
  320 South Main Street, Room 115,   Fax: (920) 674-7425
  Jefferson, WI 53549
  E-mail: carla.robinson@wicourts.gov

Juneau County

Court Clerk

Sixth Judicial District
210 West Center Street, Juneau, WI 53039

Circuit Clerk, Juneau County **Loretta Roberts** . . . . (608) 847-9356
  200 Oak Street, Mauston, WI 53948   Fax: (608) 847-9360
  P.O. Box 246, Mauston, WI 53948
  E-mail: loretta.roberts@wicourts.gov

Kenosha County

Court Clerk

Second Judicial District
912 56th Street, Kenosha, WI 53140

Circuit Clerk, Kenosha County
  Rebecca Matoska-Mentink . . . . (262) 653-2664
  912 56th Street, Kenosha, WI 53140
  E-mail: rebecca.matoska-mentink@wicourts.gov

Kewaunee County

Court Clerk

Eighth Judicial District
100 South Jefferson Street, Green Bay, WI 54305

Circuit Clerk, Kewaunee County
  Rebecca A. Deterville . . . . (920) 388-7144
  613 Dodge Street, Kewaunee, WI 54216   Fax: (920) 388-7049
  E-mail: becky.deterville@wicourts.gov

La Crosse County

Court Clerk

Seventh Judicial District
222 North Iowa Street, Dodgeville, WI 53533

Circuit Clerk, La Crosse County **Pam Radtke** . . . . (608) 785-9590
  333 Vine Street, Room 1200,   Fax: (608) 789-7821
  La Crosse, WI 54601
  E-mail: pam.radtke@wicourts.gov

Lafayette County

Court Clerk

Fifth Judicial District
215 South Hamilton Street, Madison, WI 53703

Circuit Clerk, Lafayette County **Kitty McGowan** . . . . (608) 776-4832
  626 Main Street, Darlington, WI 53530
  P.O. Box 40, Darlington, WI 53530
  E-mail: kitty.mcgowan@wicourts.gov

Langlade County

Court Clerk

Ninth Judicial District
500 Forest Street, Wausau, WI 54403

Circuit Clerk, Langlade County **Marilyn Baraniak** . . . . (715) 627-6215
  800 Clermont Street, Antigo, WI 54409
  E-mail: marilyn.baraniak@wicourts.gov

Lincoln County

Court Clerk

Ninth Judicial District
500 Forest Street, Wausau, WI 54403

Circuit Clerk, Lincoln County **Cindy Kimmons** . . . . (715) 536-0319
  1110 East Main Street, Suite 205,   Fax: (715) 536-0361
  Merrill, WI 54452
  E-mail: cindy.kimmons@wicourts.gov

Manitowoc County

Court Clerk

Fourth Judicial District
160 South Macy Street, Fond du Lac, WI 54935

Circuit Clerk, Manitowoc County **Lynn Zigmunt** . . . . (920) 683-4025
  1010 South Eighth Street, First Floor, Room 105,   Fax: (920) 683-2733
  Manitowoc, WI 54221-2000
  P.O. Box 2000, Manitowoc, WI 54221-2000
  E-mail: lynn.zigmunt@wicourts.gov

Marathon County

Court Clerk

Ninth Judicial District
500 Forest Street, Wausau, WI 54403

Circuit Clerk, Marathon County **Shirley Lang** . . . . (715) 261-1300
  Marathon County Courthouse, 500 Forest Street, Fax: (715) 261-1319
  Wausau, WI 54403
  E-mail: shirley.lang@wicourts.gov

Marinette County

Court Clerk

Eighth Judicial District
100 South Jefferson Street, Green Bay, WI 54305

Circuit Clerk, Marinette County **Sheila Dudka** . . . . (715) 732-7450
  1926 Hall Avenue, Second Floor,   Fax: (715) 732-7461
  Marinette, WI 54143

Marquette County

Court Clerk

Sixth Judicial District
210 West Center Street, Juneau, WI 53039

Circuit Clerk, Marquette County
  Shari Rudolph . . . . (608) 297-3100 ext. 3005
  77 West Park Street, Montello, WI 53949
  P.O. Box 187, Montello, WI 53949
  E-mail: shari.rudolph@wicourts.gov

Wisconsin Court Clerks and Courthouses *continued*

Menominee County

Court Clerk

Ninth Judicial District
500 Forest Street, Wausau, WI 54403

Circuit Clerk, Menominee County **Pam Frechette** . . . . (715) 799-3313
 P.O. Box 279, Keshena, WI 54135   Fax: (715) 799-1322
 E-mail: pam.frechette@wicourts.gov

Milwaukee County

Court Clerk

First Judicial District
901 North 9th Street, Milwaukee, WI 53233

Circuit Clerk, Milwaukee County **John Barrett** . . . . (414) 278-5362
 Milwaukee County Courthouse,   Fax: (414) 223-1260
 901 North Ninth Street, Milwaukee, WI 53233
 E-mail: john.barrett@wicourts.gov

Monroe County

Court Clerk

Seventh Judicial District
222 North Iowa Street, Dodgeville, WI 53533

Circuit Clerk, Monroe County **Shirley K. Chapiewsky** . . . (608) 269-8745
 112 South Court Street, Room 203,
 Sparta, WI 54656
 E-mail: shirley.chapiewsky@wicourts.gov

Oconto County

Court Clerk

Eighth Judicial District
100 South Jefferson Street, Green Bay, WI 54305

Circuit Clerk, Oconto County **Michael C. Hodkiewicz** . . . (920) 834-6857
 301 Washington Street, Oconto, WI 54153   Fax: (920) 834-6867
 E-mail: michael.hodkiewicz@wicourts.gov

Oneida County

Court Clerk

Ninth Judicial District
500 Forest Street, Wausau, WI 54403

Circuit Clerk, Oneida County **Brenda Behrle** . . . . (715) 369-6120
 One South Oneida Avenue,
 Rhinelander, WI 54501
 P.O. Box 400, Rhinelander, WI 54501
 E-mail: brenda.behrle@wicourts.gov

Outagamie County

Court Clerk

Eighth Judicial District
100 South Jefferson Street, Green Bay, WI 54305

Circuit Clerk, Outagamie County **Lonnie Wolf** . . . . (920) 832-5131
 320 South Walnut, Appleton, WI 54911   Fax: (920) 832-5115
 E-mail: lonnie.wolf@wicourts.gov

Wisconsin Court Clerks and Courthouses *continued*

Ozaukee County

Court Clerk

Third Judicial District
515 West Moreland Boulevard, Waukesha, WI 53188

Circuit Clerk, Ozaukee County **Mary Lou Mueller** . . . . . . (262) 284-8409
 Ozaukee County Courthouse,   Fax: (262) 284-8491
 1201 South Spring Street,
 Port Washington, WI 53074

Pepin County

Court Clerk

Seventh Judicial District
222 North Iowa Street, Dodgeville, WI 53533

Circuit Clerk, Pepin County **Audrey Lieffring** . . . . (715) 672-8861
 740 Seventh Avenue West,   Fax: (715) 672-8521
 Durand, WI 54736
 E-mail: audrey.lieffring@wicourts.gov

Pierce County

Court Clerk

Seventh Judicial District
222 North Iowa Street, Dodgeville, WI 53533

Circuit Clerk, Pierce County **Peg Feuerhelm** . . . (715) 273-6741 ext. 6405
 414 West Main Street, Ellsworth, WI 54011-2000   Tel: (715) 273-6855

Polk County

Court Clerk

Tenth Judicial District
1101 Carmichael Road, Hudson, WI 54016

Circuit Clerk, Polk County **Jobie Bainbridge** . . . . (715) 485-9299
 Polk County Justice Center,   Fax: (715) 485-9262
 1005 West Main Street, Suite 300,
 Balsam Lake, WI 54810
 E-mail: jobie.bainbridge@wicourts.gov

Portage County

Court Clerk

Sixth Judicial District
210 West Center Street, Juneau, WI 53039

Circuit Clerk, Portage County **Patricia A. Baker** . . . . (715) 346-1364
 Portage County Courthouse, 1516 Church Street,   Fax: (715) 346-1236
 Stevens Point, WI 54481
 E-mail: clerkofcourts@co.portage.wi.us

Price County

Court Clerk

Ninth Judicial District
500 Forest Street, Wausau, WI 54403

Circuit Clerk, Price County **Chris Cress** . . . . (715) 339-3315
 126 Cherry Street, Phillips, WI 54555   Fax: (715) 339-3079
 E-mail: chris.cress@wicourts.gov

(continued on next page)

Racine County

Court Clerk

Second Judicial District
912 56th Street, Kenosha, WI 53140

Circuit Clerk, Racine County **Roseanne Lee** . . . . (262) 636-3146
730 Wisconsin Avenue, Racine, WI 53403
E-mail: roseanne.lee@wicourts.gov

Richland County

Court Clerk

Seventh Judicial District
222 North Iowa Street, Dodgeville, WI 53533

Circuit Clerk, Richland County **Stacy Kleist** . . . . (608) 647-3956
P.O. Box 655, Richland Center, WI 53581
E-mail: stacy.kleist@wicourts.gov

Rock County

Court Clerk

Fifth Judicial District
215 South Hamilton Street, Madison, WI 53703

Circuit Clerk, Rock County **Eldred Mielke** . . . . (608) 743-2200
51 South Main Street, Second Floor,   Fax: (608) 743-2223
Janesville, WI 53545
E-mail: eldred.mielke@wicourts.gov

Rusk County

Court Clerk

Tenth Judicial District
1101 Carmichael Road, Hudson, WI 54016

Circuit Clerk, Rusk County **Lyn Yotter** . . . . (715) 532-2108
311 Miner Avenue, Ladysmith, WI 54848

Sauk County

Court Clerk

Sixth Judicial District
210 West Center Street, Juneau, WI 53039

Circuit Clerk, Sauk County **Vicki Meister** . . . . (608) 355-3287
515 Oak Street, Room 204,   Fax: (608) 355-3480
Baraboo, WI 53913-2000
E-mail: vicki.meister@wicourts.gov

Sawyer County

Court Clerk

Tenth Judicial District
1101 Carmichael Road, Hudson, WI 54016

Circuit Clerk, Sawyer County **Claudia Burgan** . . . . (715) 634-4887
10610 Main, Suite 74, Hayward, WI 54843
E-mail: claudia.burgan@wicourts.gov

Shawano County

Court Clerk

Ninth Judicial District
500 Forest Street, Wausau, WI 54403

Circuit Clerk, Shawano County **Susan J. Krueger** . . . . (715) 526-9347
Shawano County Courthouse,   Fax: (715) 526-4915
311 North Main Street, Second Floor, Room 206,
Shawano, WI 54166
E-mail: susan.krueger@wicourts.gov

Sheboygan County

Court Clerk

Fourth Judicial District
160 South Macy Street, Fond du Lac, WI 54935

Circuit Clerk, Sheboygan County **Nan Todd** . . . . (920) 459-3068
615 North Sixth Street, Sheboygan, WI 53081   Tel: (920) 459-3921
E-mail: nan.todd@wicourts.gov

St. Croix County

Court Clerk

Tenth Judicial District
1101 Carmichael Road, Hudson, WI 54016

Circuit Clerk, St. Croix County **Kristi Severson** . . . . (715) 386-4633
1101 Carmichael Road, Hudson, WI 54016
E-mail: kristi.severson@wicourts.gov

Taylor County

Court Clerk

Ninth Judicial District
500 Forest Street, Wausau, WI 54403

Circuit Clerk, Taylor County **Rose Thums** . . . . (715) 748-1425
224 South Second Street, Medford, WI 54451   Fax: (715) 748-2465

Trempealeau County

Court Clerk

Seventh Judicial District
222 North Iowa Street, Dodgeville, WI 53533

Circuit Clerk, Trempealeau County
Michelle Weisenberger . . . . (715) 538-2311 ext. 240
36245 Main Street, Whitehall, WI 54773-0067   Fax: (715) 538-4400
E-mail: michelle.weisenberger@wicourts.gov

Vernon County

Court Clerk

Seventh Judicial District
222 North Iowa Street, Dodgeville, WI 53533

Circuit Clerk, Vernon County **Kathleen Buros** . . . . (608) 637-5340
400 Courthouse Square, Suite 115,   Fax: (608) 637-5554
Viroqua, WI 54665
E-mail: kathleen.buros@wicourts.gov

Vilas County

Court Clerk

Ninth Judicial District
500 Forest Street, Wausau, WI 54403

Circuit Clerk, Vilas County **Jean Numrich**. . . . .(715) 479-3632
  330 Court Street, Eagle River, WI 54521   Fax: (715) 479-3740
  E-mail: jean.numrich@wicourts.gov

Walworth County

Court Clerk

Second Judicial District
912 56th Street, Kenosha, WI 53140

Circuit Clerk, Walworth County **Sheila Reiff** . . . . (262) 741-7012
  Walworth County Judicial Center,
  1800 County Road NN, Elkhorn, WI 53121
  E-mail: sheila.reiff@wicourts.gov

Washburn County

Court Clerk

Tenth Judicial District
1101 Carmichael Road, Hudson, WI 54016

Circuit Clerk, Washburn County **Karen Nord** . . . .(715) 468-4677
  10 Fourth Avenue, Shell Lake, WI 54871   Fax: (715) 468-4678
  P.O. Box 339, Shell Lake, WI 54871
  E-mail: karen.nord@wicourts.gov

Washington County

Court Clerk

Third Judicial District
515 West Moreland Boulevard, Waukesha, WI 53188

Circuit Clerk, Washington County **Theresa M. Russell** . . .(262) 335-4341
  432 East Washington Street, Room 3151,   Tel: (262) 335-4776
  West Bend, WI 53095
  E-mail: washington.coc@wicourts.gov

Waukesha County

Court Clerk

Third Judicial District
515 West Moreland Boulevard, Waukesha, WI 53188

Circuit Clerk, Waukesha County **Kathleen A. Madden** . . .(262) 896-8525
  Waukesha County Courthouse,
  515 West Moreland Boulevard,
  Waukesha, WI 53188
  E-mail: kathleen.madden@wicourts.gov

Waupaca County

Court Clerk

Eighth Judicial District
100 South Jefferson Street, Green Bay, WI 54305

Circuit Clerk, Waupaca County **Terrie J. Tews** . . . .(715) 258-6460
  811 Harding Street, Waupaca, WI 54981   Fax: (608) 637-5554
  E-mail: terrie.tews@wicourts.gov

Waushara County

Court Clerk

Sixth Judicial District
210 West Center Street, Juneau, WI 53039

Circuit Clerk, Waushara County **Melissa Zamzow** . . . . . . (920) 787-0441
  209 South Saint Marie Street,
  Wautoma, WI 54982-0507
  P.O. Box 507, Wautoma, WI 54982-0507
  E-mail: melissa.zamzow@wicourts.gov

Winnebago County

Court Clerk

Fourth Judicial District
160 South Macy Street, Fond du Lac, WI 54935

Circuit Clerk, Winnebago County **Melissa Konrad** . . . . . . (920) 236-4848
  415 Jackson Street, Oshkosh, WI 54903-2808
  P.O. Box 2808, Oshkosh, WI 54903-2808
  E-mail: winnebago.coc@wicourts.gov

Wood County

Court Clerk

Sixth Judicial District
210 West Center Street, Juneau, WI 53039

Circuit Clerk, Wood County **Cindy Joosten**. . . . .(715) 421-8490
  P.O. Box 8095, Wisconsin Rapids, WI 54495-8095
  E-mail: cindy.joosten@wicourts.gov

Counties Within Judicial Districts

1st Judicial District
Areas Covered: Milwaukee County

2nd Judicial District
Areas Covered: Kenosha County, Racine County, Walworth County

3rd Judicial District
Areas Covered: Jefferson County, Ozaukee County, Washington County, Waukesha County

4th Judicial District
Areas Covered: Calumet County, Fond du Lac County, Manitowoc County, Sheboygan County, Winnebago County

5th Judicial District
Areas Covered: Dane County, Green County, Lafayette County, Rock County

6th Judicial District
Areas Covered: Adams County, Clark County, Columbia County, Dodge County, Green Lake County, Juneau County, Marquette County, Portage County, Sauk County, Waushara County, Wood County

7th Judicial District
Areas Covered: Buffalo County, Crawford County, Grant County, Iowa County, Jackson County, La Crosse County, Monroe County, Pepin County, Pierce County, Richland County, Trempealeau County, Vernon County

(continued on next page)

Wisconsin Court Clerks and Courthouses *continued*

8th Judicial District

Areas Covered: Brown County, Waupaca County, Outagamie County, Kewaunee County, Door County, Oconto County, Marinette County

9th Judicial District

Areas Covered: Florance County, Forest County, Iron County, Langlade County, Lincoln County, Marathon County, Menominee County, Oneida County, Price County, Shawano County, Taylor County, Vilas County

10th Judicial District

Areas Covered: Ashland County, Barron County, Bayfield County, Burnett County, Chippewa County, Douglas County, Dunn County, Eau Claire County, Polk County, Rusk County, St. Croix County, Sawyer County, Washburn County

Wyoming Court Clerks and Courthouses

The trial courts of general jurisdiction in Wyoming are called district courts. There are nine judicial districts of District Court, each district consists of at least one county. There is no intermediate appellate court in the State of Wyoming.

Wyoming Supreme Court

Supreme Court Building, 2301 Capitol Avenue, Cheyenne, WY 82002
Tel: (307) 777-7316 Fax: (307) 777-6129
Internet: www.courts.state.wy.us

The Supreme Court consists of a chief justice and four justices initially appointed by the Governor from a list of three nominees submitted by the Judicial Nominating Commission and subject to a retention vote one year after appointment. If retained, a justice serves for the remainder of the eight-year term and subsequent eight-year terms are by a nonpartisan retention vote. The chief justice is elected to serve a four-year term by peer vote. Retirement is mandatory at age seventy; however, retired justices may be recalled by the chief justice to serve temporary assignments. The Supreme Court has final appellate jurisdiction over all cases from the Wyoming District Courts and original jurisdiction to issue extradition writs. The Court exercises superintending control over inferior courts, regulates admission to the state bar and the practice of law, and may issue writs necessary to the exercise of proper jurisdiction.

Court Staff
Clerk of the Court **Carol Thompson** . . . . (307) 777-7316
   E-mail: cthompson@courts.state.wy.us

County-By-County

Albany County

District Court Clerk

Second Judicial District
525 Grand Avenue, Suite 305, Laramie, WY 82070

Clerk of Court, Albany County **Janice Sexton** . . . . (307) 721-2508
   525 Grand Avenue, Suite 305,
   Laramie, WY 82070
   E-mail: jsexton@co.albany.wy.us

County Clerk

Office of the County Clerk
525 East Grand Avenue, Suite 202, Laramie, WY 82070
Tel: (307) 721-2541 Fax: (307) 721-2544

County Clerk **Jackie R. Gonzales** . . . .(307) 721-2541
   E-mail: jgonzales@co.albany.wy.us

Big Horn County

District Court Clerk

Fifth Judicial District
1002 Sheridan Avenue, Cody, WY 82414
P.O. Box 1960, Cody, WY 82414
Tel: (307) 527-8690 Fax: (307) 527-8687

Clerk of Court, Big Horn County **Serena K. Lipp** . . . . (307) 568-2381
   420 West C Street, Basin, WY 82410   Fax: (307) 568-2791

County Clerk

Office of the County Clerk
P.O. Box 31, Basin, WY 82410
Tel: (307) 568-2357 Fax: (307) 568-9375

County Clerk **Lori Smallwood** . . . . (307) 568-2357
   E-mail: Lori.Smallwood@bighorncountywy.gov

Campbell County

District Court Clerk

Sixth Judicial District
500 South Gillette Avenue, Suite 2600, Gillette, WY 82716
P.O. Box 817, Gillette, WY 82716
Tel: (307) 682-3424 Fax: (307) 687-6209

Clerk of Court, Campbell County **Cheryl Chitwood** . . . . . (307) 682-3424
   500 South Gillette Avenue, Suite 2600,   Fax: (307) 687-6209
   Gillette, WY 82716
   P.O. Box 817, Gillette, WY 82716

County Clerk

Office of the County Clerk
500 South Gillette Avenue, Suite 1600, Gillette, WY 82716
Tel: (307) 682-7285 Fax: (307) 687-6455

County Clerk **Susan Saunders** . . . . (307) 682-7285
   E-mail: sfs02@ccgov.net

Carbon County

District Court Clerk

Second Judicial District
525 Grand Avenue, Suite 305, Laramie, WY 82070

Clerk of Court, Carbon County **Deborah D. Olson** . . . . . . (307) 328-2628
   415 West Pine Street, Rawlins, WY 82301   Fax: (307) 328-2629
   P.O. Box 67, Rawlins, WY 82301
   E-mail: deboraholson@carbonwy.com

County Clerk

Office of the County Clerk
P.O. Box 6, Rawlins, WY 82301
Tel: (307) 328-2668 Fax: (307) 328-2690

County Clerk **Gwynn Bartlett** . . . . (307) 328-2668
   E-mail: gwynnbartlett@carbonwy.com

Converse County

District Court Clerk

Eighth Judicial District
2125 East A Street, Torrington, WY 82240
P.O. Box 818, Torrington, WY 82240

Clerk of Court, Converse County **Pam McCullough** . . . . . (307) 358-3165
   107 North Fifth Street, Douglas, WY 82633   Fax: (307) 358-9783
   P.O. Box 189, Douglas, WY 82633

County Clerk

Office of the County Clerk
107 North Fifth Street, Suite 114, Douglas, WY 82633-2448
Tel: (307) 358-2244 Fax: (307) 358-5998

County Clerk **Lucile K. Taylor** . . . . (307) 358-2244
   E-mail: lucile.taylor@conversecountywy.gov

(continued on next page)

Crook County

District Court Clerk

Sixth Judicial District
500 South Gillette Avenue, Suite 2600, Gillette, WY 82716
P.O. Box 817, Gillette, WY 82716
Tel: (307) 682-3424 Fax: (307) 687-6209

Clerk of Court, Crook County
  Christina "Tina" Wood . . . . (307) 283-2523
  309 Cleveland, Sundance, WY 82729   Fax: (307) 283-2996
  P.O. Box 406, Sundance, WY 82729
  E-mail: tinaw@crookcounty.wy.gov

County Clerk

Office of the County Clerk
P.O. Box 37, Sundance, WY 82729
Tel: (307) 283-1323 Fax: (307) 283-3038

County Clerk **Linda Fritz** . . . . (307) 283-1323
  E-mail: lindaf@crookcounty.wy.gov

Fremont County

District Court Clerk

Ninth Judicial District
450 North Second Street, Lander, WY 82520
P.O. Box 370, Lander, WY 82520

Clerk of Court, Fremont County **Kristi H. Green** . . . . (307) 332-1134
  450 North Second Street, Lander, WY 82520
  P.O. Box 370, Lander, WY 82520

County Clerk

Office of the County Clerk
450 North 2nd Street, Lander, WY 82520
Tel: (307) 332-2405 Fax: (307) 332-1132

County Clerk **Julie Freese** . . . . (307) 332-2405
  E-mail: julie.freese@fremontcountywy.gov

Goshen County

District Court Clerk

Eighth Judicial District
2125 East A Street, Torrington, WY 82240
P.O. Box 818, Torrington, WY 82240

Clerk of Court, Goshen County **Kathi Rickard** . . . . (307) 532-2155
  2125 East A Street, Torrington, WY 82240   Fax: (307) 532-8608
  P.O. Box 818, Torrington, WY 82240

County Clerk

Office of the County Clerk
P.O. Box 160, Torrington, WY 82240
Tel: (307) 532-4051 Fax: (307) 532-7375

County Clerk **Cynthia Kenyon** . . . . (307) 532-4051
  E-mail: ckenyon@goshencounty.org

Hot Springs County

District Court Clerk

Fifth Judicial District
1002 Sheridan Avenue, Cody, WY 82414
P.O. Box 1960, Cody, WY 82414
Tel: (307) 527-8690 Fax: (307) 527-8687

Clerk of Court, Hot Springs County **Terri Cornella** . . . . . . (307) 864-3323
  415 Arapahoe Street, Thermopolis, WY 82443   Fax: (307) 864-3210

County Clerk

Office of the County Clerk
415 Arapahoe, Thermopolis, WY 82443
Tel: (307) 864-3515 Fax: (307) 864-3333

County Clerk **Nina Webber** . . . . (307) 864-3515
  E-mail: ninaw@hscounty.com

Johnson County

District Court Clerk

Fourth Judicial District
620 West Fetterman Street, Suite 208, Buffalo, WY 82834

Clerk of Court, Johnson County **Debra R. Vandel** . . . . (307) 684-7271
  620 West Fetterman Street, Suite 208,   Fax: (307) 684-5146
  Buffalo, WY 82834

County Clerk

Office of the County Clerk
76 North Main Street, Buffalo, WY 82834
Tel: (307) 684-7272 Tel: (307) 684-2708

County Clerk **Vicki Edelman** . . . . (307) 684-7272
  E-mail: clerk@johnsoncowy.us

Laramie County

District Court Clerk

First Judicial District
309 West 20th Street, Room 3205, Cheyenne, WY 82003
P.O. Box 787, Cheyenne, WY 82003

Clerk of Court, Laramie County **Diane Sanchez** . . . . (307) 633-4270
  309 West 20th Street, Room 3205,   Fax: (307) 633-4277
  Cheyenne, WY 82003
  P.O. Box 787, Cheyenne, WY 82003
  E-mail: districtcourtlc@laramiecounty.com

County Clerk

Office of the County Clerk
309 W. 20th St., Cheyenne, WY 82001
Fax: (307) 633-4240
Internet: http://www.laramiecountyclerk.com

County Clerk **Debbye Lathrop** . . . . (307) 633-4268
  E-mail: dlathrop@laramiecountyclerk.com

Lincoln County

District Court Clerk

Third Judicial District
80 West Flaming Gorge, Green River, WY 82935
P.O. Box 430, Green River, WY 82935

Clerk of Court, Lincoln County **Kenneth D. Roberts** .... (307) 877-3320
925 Sage Avenue, Kemmerer, WY 83101   Fax: (307) 877-6263
P.O. Drawer 510, Kemmerer, WY 83101
E-mail: kroberts@co.lincoln.wy.us

County Clerk

Office of the County Clerk
925 Sage Avenue, Suite 101, Kemmerer, WY 83101
Tel: (307) 877-9056 Fax: (307) 877-3101

County Clerk **Jeanne Wagner** .... (307) 877-9056 ext. 2020
E-mail: jwagner@lcwy.org

Natrona County

District Court Clerk

Seventh Judicial District
115 North Center Street, Suite 100, Casper, WY 82601

Clerk of Court, Natrona County **Gen Tuma** .... (307) 235-9243
115 North Center Street, Suite 100,   Fax: (307) 235-9493
Casper, WY 82601

County Clerk

Office of the County Clerk
200 North Center, 157, Casper, WY 82601
Tel: (307) 235-9206 Fax: (307) 235-9367

County Clerk **Renea Vitto** .... (307) 235-9206
E-mail: countyclerk@natronacounty-wy.gov

Niobrara County

District Court Clerk

Eighth Judicial District
2125 East A Street, Torrington, WY 82240
P.O. Box 818, Torrington, WY 82240

Clerk of Court, Niobrara County **Kayla Courtright** ...... (307) 334-2736
424 South Elm, Lusk, WY 82225   Fax: (307) 334-2703
P.O. Box 1318, Lusk, WY 82225

County Clerk

Office of the County Clerk
P.O. Box 420, Lusk, WY 82225
Tel: (307) 334-2211 Fax: (307) 334-3013

County Clerk **Becky Freeman** .... (307) 334-2211
E-mail: niocc@qwestoffice.net

Park County

District Court Clerk

Fifth Judicial District
1002 Sheridan Avenue, Cody, WY 82414
P.O. Box 1960, Cody, WY 82414
Tel: (307) 527-8690 Fax: (307) 527-8687

Clerk of Court, Park County **Patra Lindenthal** .... (307) 527-8690
1002 Sheridan Avenue, Cody, WY 82414   Fax: (307) 527-8687
P.O. Box 1960, Cody, WY 82414

County Clerk

Office of the County Clerk
1002 Sheridan Avenue, Cody, WY 82414
Tel: (307) 527-8600 Fax: (307) 527-8626

County Clerk **Colleen Renner** .... (307) 527-8600
E-mail: CRenner@ParkCounty.us

Platte County

District Court Clerk

Eighth Judicial District
2125 East A Street, Torrington, WY 82240
P.O. Box 818, Torrington, WY 82240

Clerk of Court, Platte County **Mona McAuley** .... (307) 322-3857
800 Ninth Street, Wheatland, WY 82201   Fax: (307) 322-5402
P.O. Box 158, Wheatland, WY 82201

County Clerk

Office of the County Clerk
P.O. Box 728, Wheatland, WY 82201
Tel: (307) 322-2315 Fax: (307) 322-2245

County Clerk **Chris Kanwischer** .... (307) 322-2315
E-mail: pcclerk@plattecountywyoming.com

Sheridan County

District Court Clerk

Fourth Judicial District
620 West Fetterman Street, Suite 208, Buffalo, WY 82834

Clerk of Court, Sheridan County **Nickie Arney** .... (307) 674-2960
224 South Main Street, Suite B11,   Fax: (307) 674-2589
Sheridan, WY 82801

County Clerk

Office of the County Clerk
224 South Main, B2, Sheridan, WY 82801
Tel: (307) 674-2500 Fax: (307) 675-2514

County Clerk **Eda Schunk Thompson** .... (307) 674-2500
E-mail: clerk@sheridancounty.com

Sublette County

District Court Clerk

Ninth Judicial District
450 North Second Street, Lander, WY 82520
P.O. Box 370, Lander, WY 82520

Clerk of Court, Sublette County **Janet Montgomery** .... (307) 367-4376
21 South Tyler, Pinedale, WY 82941   Fax: (307) 367-6474
P.O. Box 764, Pinedale, WY 82941

County Clerk

Office of the County Clerk
P.O. Box 250, Pinedale, WY 82941
Tel: (307) 367-4372 Fax: (307) 367-6396

County Clerk **Mary Lankford** .... (307) 367-4372
E-mail: mary.lankford@sublettewyo.com

(continued on next page)

Sweetwater County

District Court Clerk

Third Judicial District
80 West Flaming Gorge, Green River, WY 82935
P.O. Box 430, Green River, WY 82935

Clerk of Court, Sweetwater County **Donna Lee Bobak** . . . (307) 872-3820
  80 West Flaming Gorge, Green River, WY 82935   Fax: (307) 872-3986
  P.O. Box 430, Green River, WY 82935
  E-mail: bobakd@sweet.wy.us

County Clerk

Office of the County Clerk
80 West Flaming Gorge Way, Suite 150, Green River, WY 82935
Tel: (307) 872-3732 Fax: (307) 872-3994

County Clerk **Dale Davis** . . . . (307) 872-3732
  E-mail: davisd@sweet.wy.us

Teton County

District Court Clerk

Ninth Judicial District
450 North Second Street, Lander, WY 82520
P.O. Box 370, Lander, WY 82520

Clerk of Court, Teton County **Ann C. Sutton** . . . . (307) 733-2533
  180 South King Street, Jackson, WY 83001   Fax: (307) 734-1562
  P.O. Box 4460, Jackson, WY 83001

County Clerk

Office of the County Clerk
200 South Willow Street, Jackson, WY 83001
Tel: (307) 733-4430 Fax: (307) 739-8634

County Clerk **Sherry Daigle** . . . . (307) 733-4430
  E-mail: sdaigle@tetonwyo.org

Uinta County

District Court Clerk

Third Judicial District
80 West Flaming Gorge, Green River, WY 82935
P.O. Box 430, Green River, WY 82935

Clerk of Court, Uinta County **Kerri Bumgardner** . . . . (307) 783-0456
  80 West Flaming Gorge Way,   Fax: (307) 783-0400
  Green River, WY 82930
  P.O. Box 1906, Evanston, WY 82930

County Clerk

Office of the County Clerk and Recorder
225 9th Street, Evanston, WY 82930
Tel: (307) 783-0306 Fax: (307) 783-0511

County Clerk **Lana W. Wilcox** . . . . (307) 783-0306
  E-mail: lawilcox@uintacounty.com

Washakie County

District Court Clerk

Fifth Judicial District
1002 Sheridan Avenue, Cody, WY 82414
P.O. Box 1960, Cody, WY 82414
Tel: (307) 527-8690 Fax: (307) 527-8687

Clerk of Court, Washakie County **SuZann Whitlock** . . . . . (307) 347-4821
  1023 Big Horn Avenue, Worland, WY 82401   Fax: (307) 347-4325
  P.O. Box 862, Worland, WY 82401

County Clerk

Office of the County Clerk
P.O. Box 260, Worland, WY 82401
Tel: (307) 347-3131 Fax: (307) 347-9366

County Clerk **Mary Grace Strauch** . . . . (307) 347-3131
  E-mail: clerk@washakiecounty.net

Weston County

District Court Clerk

Sixth Judicial District
500 South Gillette Avenue, Suite 2600, Gillette, WY 82716
P.O. Box 817, Gillette, WY 82716
Tel: (307) 682-3424 Fax: (307) 687-6209

Clerk of Court, Weston County **Gidget Macke** . . . . (307) 746-4778
  One West Main, Newcastle, WY 82701   Fax: (307) 746-4778

County Clerk

Office of the County Clerk
1 West Main Street, Newcastle, WY 82701
Tel: (307) 746-4744 Fax: (307) 746-9505

County Clerk **Cheryl Kregel** . . . . (307) 746-4744
  E-mail: Cheryl@westongov.com

Counties Within Judicial Districts

District Court, 1st District
Areas Covered: Laramie County.

District Court, 2nd District
Areas Covered: Albany and Carbon Counties.

District Court, 3rd District
Areas Covered: Lincoln, Sweetwater, and Uinta Counties.

District Court, 4th District
Areas Covered: Johnson and Sheridan Counties.

District Court, 5th District
Areas Covered: Big Horn, Hot Springs, Park, and Washakie Counties.

District Court, 6th District
Areas Covered: Campbell, Crook, and Weston Counties.

District Court, 7th District
Areas Covered: Natrona County.

Wyoming Court Clerks and Courthouses *continued*

District Court, 8th District

Areas Covered: Converse, Goshen, Niobrara, and Platte Counties.

District Court, 9th District

Areas Covered: Fremont, Sublette, and Teton Counties.

State Probate, Recording, and Notary Offices

State Probate, Recording, and Notary Offices

This listing is intended to supplement the State clerk and county courthouse information. For county courthouse and Secretary of State addresses, phone numbers, and websites, please refer to the listing for that particular State.

Fees for the services listed below vary, and some States require checks to be certified. Also, when requesting a "Certificate of Notary" form, indicate whether certification is needed in a matter involving a foreign country observing the Hague Convention (Apostille Certification), which may require a special form.

Alabama

Estate & Wills Offices: County Probate Judge's Office

Deed & Mortgage Recording Offices: County Probate Judge's Office

Certificate of Notary: County Judge of Probate and Circuit Clerk in Jefferson County certified by Secretary of State

Alaska

Estate & Wills Offices: Superior Court for each judicial district

Deed & Mortgage Recording Offices: District Recorders Offices

Certificate of Notary: Office of Lieutenant Governor

Arizona

Estate & Wills Offices: Superior Court, each county

Deed & Mortgage Recording Offices: County Recorders Offices

Certificate of Notary: Secretary of State: Notary Division

Arkansas

Estate & Wills Offices: County Probate Clerks Offices

Deed & Mortgage Recording Offices: Circuit Clerks, each county

Certificate of Notary: Secretary of State: Notary Department

California

Estate & Wills Offices: County Clerks Offices

Deed & Mortgage Recording Offices: County Recorders Offices

Certificate of Notary: Secretary of State, Notary Public Division

Colorado

Estate & Wills Offices: District Probate Court Division

Deed & Mortgage Recording Offices: County Clerks & Recorders Offices

Certificate of Notary: Secretary of State, Notary Division

Connecticut

Estate & Wills Offices: District Probate Courts

Deed & Mortgage Recording Offices: Town Clerks Offices (Land Records)

Certificate of Notary: Secretary of State, Certification Unit

Delaware

Estate & Wills Offices: County Registers of Wills

Deed & Mortgage Recording Offices: County Recorders of Deeds Offices

Certificate of Notary: Secretary of State, Division of Corporations.

District of Columbia

Estate & Wills Offices: Superior Court, Register of Wills

Deed & Mortgage Recording Offices: Recorder of Deeds Offices

Certificate of Notary: Office of District of Columbia Secretary, Notary Public Section

Florida

Estate & Wills Offices: Circuit Court Clerks, each county

Deed & Mortgage Recording Offices: Circuit Court Clerks, each county

Certificate of Notary: Department of State, Bureau of Notaries

Georgia

Estate & Wills Offices: Judge of Probate Court, each county

Deed & Mortgage Recording Offices: Clerk of Superior Court, each county

Certificate of Notary: Clerk of Superior Court, each county

Hawaii

Estate & Wills Offices: Circuit Courts, each circuit

Deed & Mortgage Recording Offices: State Bureau of Conveyances

Certificate of Notary: Office of Lieutenant Governor

Idaho

Estate & Wills Offices: County District Courts

Deed & Mortgage Recording Offices: County Recorders Offices

Certificate of Notary: Secretary of State

Illinois

Estate & Wills Offices: Circuit Court Clerks Offices, each county

Deed & Mortgage Recording Offices: County Clerks or Recorders Offices

Certificate of Notary: Secretary of State, Index Department, Notary Section

Indiana

Estate & Wills Offices: Circuit or Probate Clerks, each county

Deed & Mortgage Recording Offices: County Recorders Offices

Certificate of Notary: Secretary of State, Attn: Authentications

Iowa

Estate & Wills Offices: Clerk of Court, each county

Deed & Mortgage Recording Offices: County Recorders Offices

Certificate of Notary: Secretary of State, Corporations Department

Kansas

Estate & Wills Offices: Probate Division of District Court

Deed & Mortgage Recording Offices: County Register of Deeds Offices

Certificate of Notary: Secretary of State, Notary Division

Kentucky

Estate & Wills Offices: District Courts (estates) and County Clerks (wills)

Deed & Mortgage Recording Offices: County Clerks Offices

Certificate of Notary: County Clerk where affidavit originated; Secretary of State (Apostille certification)

Louisiana

Estate & Wills Offices: Clerk of Court Offices, each parish

Deed & Mortgage Recording Offices: Clerk of Court Offices, each parish; Recorder of Mortgages in Orleans Parish

Certificate of Notary: Secretary of State, Commissions Department

Maine

Estate & Wills Offices: County Registers of Probate

Deed & Mortgage Recording Offices: County Registers of Deeds

Certificate of Notary: Secretary of State, Notary Division

Maryland

Estate & Wills Offices: Register of Wills, each county and Baltimore City

Deed & Mortgage Recording Offices: Circuit Court Clerk, each county and Baltimore City

Certificate of Notary: Clerk of Circuit Court in notary's place of authority

Massachusetts

Estate & Wills Offices: Register of probate, each county

Deed & Mortgage Recording Offices: County or District Registry of Deeds

Certificate of Notary: Secretary of State, Commission Section

Michigan

Estate & Wills Offices: County Probate Courts

Deed & Mortgage Recording Offices: County Register of Deeds

Certificate of Notary: Department of State, Great Seal Office

Minnesota

Estate & Wills Offices: County or District Probate Courts

Deed & Mortgage Recording Offices: County Recorders Offices

Certificate of Notary: Secretary of State

Mississippi

Estate & Wills Offices: Chancery Court Clerk Offices, each county

Deed & Mortgage Recording Offices: Chancery Court Clerk Offices, each county

Certificate of Notary: Secretary of State, Notary Division

Missouri

Estate & Wills Offices: Circuit Court, Probate Division, each county and St. Louis City

Deed & Mortgage Recording Offices: Recorder of Deeds each county and St. Louis City

Certificate of Notary: Secretary of State, Attn: Notary Clerk

Montana

Estate & Wills Offices: County District Court Clerks

Deed & Mortgage Recording Offices: County Clerks and Recorders

Certificate of Notary: Secretary of State, Notary Division

Nebraska

Estate & Wills Offices: County Court Clerks

Deed & Mortgage Recording Offices: County Register of Deeds

Certificate of Notary: Secretary of State, Notary Division

Nevada

Estate & Wills Offices: County Clerk Offices/Carson City Clerk

Deed & Mortgage Recording Offices: County Recorder Offices/Carson City Recorder

Certificate of Notary: Secretary of State, Notary Division

New Hampshire

Estate & Wills Offices: County Register of Probate

Deed & Mortgage Recording Offices: County Register of Deeds

Certificate of Notary: Secretary of State

New Jersey

Estate & Wills Offices: County Surrogate Offices & Superior Court

Deed & Mortgage Recording Offices: County Clerks or Registers Offices

Certificate of Notary: Department of Treasury, Division of Revenue and Enterprises Services

New Mexico

Estate & Wills Offices: Probate Court Clerk Offices, each county

Deed & Mortgage Recording Offices: County Clerk Offices

Certificate of Notary: Secretary of State, Attn: Notary Division

New York

Estate & Wills Offices: County Surrogate Offices

Deed & Mortgage Recording Offices: County Clerk Offices & New York City Registers Offices

Certificate of Notary: Clerk of County of Commission

North Carolina

Estate & Wills Offices: Clerk of Superior Court, each county

Deed & Mortgage Recording Offices: County Register of Deeds

Certificate of Notary: Secretary of State, Notaries Public Division

North Dakota

Estate & Wills Offices: County Courts

Deed & Mortgage Recording Offices: County Register of Deeds

Certificate of Notary: Secretary of State

Ohio

Estate & Wills Offices: Probate Court, each county

Deed & Mortgage Recording Offices: County Recorder Offices

Certificate of Notary: Clerk of Court of Common Pleas, County of Commission; Certified by Secretary of State.

Oklahoma

Estate & Wills Offices: County Court Clerks

Deed & Mortgage Recording Offices: County Clerks

Certificate of Notary: County Court Clerk in County of Notary's Commission; Certified by Secretary of State

Oregon

Estate & Wills Offices: Circuit Court Clerk, Probate Section, each county

Deed & Mortgage Recording Offices: County Clerks

Certificate of Notary: Secretary of State, Notary Section

Pennsylvania

Estate & Wills Offices: County Register of Wills

Deed & Mortgage Recording Offices: County Recorder of Deeds/ Philadelphia Commissioner of Records

Certificate of Notary: Department of State, Commission Bureau

Puerto Rico

Estate & Wills Offices: Clerk, Gen. Court of Justice, Supreme Court

Deed & Mortgage Recording Offices: Property Registry, Department of Justice

Certificate of Notary: Department of State, Certification Division

Rhode Island

Estate & Wills Offices: Probate Court Clerk Office, each city or town

Deed & Mortgage Recording Offices: Recorder or Land Records Office, each city or town

Certificate of Notary: Secretary of State, Notary Division

South Carolina

Estate & Wills Offices: County Probate Judge Offices

Deed & Mortgage Recording Offices: County Clerks of Courts

Certificate of Notary: Secretary of State, Notary Division

South Dakota

Estate & Wills Offices: County Clerk of Courts

Deed & Mortgage Recording Offices: County Register of Deeds

Certificate of Notary: Secretary of State

Tennessee

Estate & Wills Offices: County Clerk or Probate Court, each county

Deed & Mortgage Recording Offices: County Register of Deeds

Certificate of Notary: County Court Clerk of County of Notary's commission; Secretary of State, Notary Section (for Notaries-at-large).

Texas

Estate & Wills Offices: County Clerk Offices, Probate Section

Deed & Mortgage Recording Offices: County Clerk Offices

Certificate of Notary: Secretary of State, Notary Public Section.

Utah

Estate & Wills Offices: County Clerk Offices, Probate Division

Deed & Mortgage Recording Offices: County Recorders Offices

Certificate of Notary: Office of the Lieutenant Governor

Vermont

Estate & Wills Offices: District Probate Courts

Deed & Mortgage Recording Offices: Town or City Clerks Offices

Certificate of Notary: Secretary of State

Virginia

Estate & Wills Offices: Circuit Court Clerks, each county/city

Deed & Mortgage Recording Offices: Circuit Court Clerks, each county/city

Certificate of Notary: Secretary of Commonwealth

Washington

Estate & Wills Offices: Superior Court Clerk Offices, each county

Deed & Mortgage Recording Offices: County Auditor Offices

Certificate of Notary: Secretary of State

West Virginia

Estate & Wills Offices: Clerk of the County Commission

Deed & Mortgage Recording Offices: Clerk of the County Commission

Certificate of Notary: Secretary of State

Wisconsin

Estate & Wills Offices: County Register in Probate

Deed & Mortgage Recording Offices: County Register of Deeds

Certificate of Notary: Department of Financial Institutions, Notary Section

Wyoming

Estate & Wills Offices: County District Court Clerk Offices

Deed & Mortgage Recording Offices: County Clerk Offices

Certificate of Notary: Secretary of State, Notary Division

Offices of Vital Statistics

Offices of Vital Statistics

This section includes a listing for each state's office in charge of vital statistics—the official records of birth, death, marriage, and divorce. Contact information for each office is provided, including the website address. Also included are details on the availability and cost for ordering copies of vital records from each state.

Alabama
Center for Health Statistics
RSA Tower, 201 Monroe Street, Suite 1150, Montgomery, AL 36104

P.O. Box 5625, Montgomery, AL 36103-5625

Tel: (334) 206-5426

Fax: (334) 206-2659

Internet: www.adph.org/vitalrecords/

Vital Records
Cost of Birth Certificates: $15.00

Cost of Death Certificates: $15.00

Cost of Marriage Records: $15.00

Cost of Divorce Records: $15.00

Alaska
Bureau of Vital Statistics
3601 C Street, Suite 128, Anchorage, AK 99503 (Anchorage Office)

1648 South Cushman, Suite 203, Fairbanks, AK 99701 (Fairbanks Office)

5441 Commercial Boulevard, Juneau, AK 99801 (Juneau Office)

P.O. Box 110675, Juneau, AK 99801 (Juneau Office)

Tel: (907) 269-0091 (Anchorage Office)

Fax: (907) 269-0994 (Anchorage Office)

Tel: (907) 451-5060 (Fairbanks Office)

Fax: (907) 451-5093 (Fairbanks Office)

Tel: (907) 465-3391 (Juneau Office)

Fax: (907) 465-3618 (Juneau Office)

Email: bvsresearch@alaska.gov

Internet: www.dhss.alaska.gov/dph/VitalStats

Vital Records
Cost of Birth Certificates: $30.00; $25.00 for each additional copy

Cost of Death Certificates: $30.00; $25.00 for each additional copy

Cost of Marriage Records: $30.00; $25.00 for each additional copy

Cost of Divorce Records: $30.00; $25.00 for each additional copy

Arizona
Office of Vital Records
1818 West Adams Street, Phoenix, AZ 85007

P.O. Box 3887, Phoenix, AZ 85030-3887

Tel: (602) 542-2955

Tel: (888) 816-5907

Fax: (602) 249-3040

E-mail: webovr@azdhs.gov

Internet: www.azdhs.gov/vital-records/

Vital Records
Cost of Birth Certificates: Certified photocopy before 1997: $15.00; 1997-present: $10.00

Cost of Death Certificates: $20.00

Arkansas
Arkansas Department of Health [ADH]
4815 West Markham Street, Slot 44, Little Rock, AR 72205 (Vital Records)

Tel: (501) 661-2336 (Vital Records)

Fax: (501) 661-2717 (Vital Records)

http://www.healthyarkansas.com

Vital Records
Cost of Birth Certificates: $12.00; $10.00 each additional copy

Cost of Death Certificates: $10.00; $8.00 each additional copy

Cost of Marriage Records: $10.00; $10.00 each additional copy

Cost of Divorce Records: $10.00; $10.00 each additional cost

Cost of Credit Card Order: $9.75 additional charge

Cost of Fax Order: $9.75 additional charge

California
California Department of Public Health [CDPH]
1615 Capitol Avenue, MS 0500, Sacramento, CA 95814

P.O. Box 997377, MS 0500, Sacramento, CA 95899-7377

Tel: (510)-620-3129

http://www.cdph.ca.gov

Vital Records
Cost of Birth Certificates: $25.00

Cost of Death Certificates: $21.00

Cost of Divorce Records: $14.00

Cost of Marriage Records: $15.00

Colorado

Colorado Department of Public Health and Environment, Vital Records Section

4300 Cherry Creek Drive South, HSVRD-VR-A1, Denver, CO 80246-1530

Tel: (303) 692-2200

Fax: (800) 423-1108

Email: vital.records@state.co.us

Internet: www.colorado.gov/cdphe

Vital Records

Cost of Birth Certificates: $17.75; $10.00 each additional copy

Cost of Death Certificates: $20.00; $13.00 each additional copy

Cost of Marriage Records: $17.00; $10.00 each additional copy

Cost of Divorce Records: $17.00; $10.00 each additional copy

Cost of Credit Card Order: $21.00

Cost of Fax Order: $21.00

Connecticut

Department of Public Health [DPH]

410 Capitol Avenue, Hartford, CT 06106

P.O. Box 340308, Hartford, CT 06134-0308

Tel: (860) 509-7700 (Vital Records)

Fax: (860) 509-7964 (Vital Records)

Internet: www.ct.gov/dph

Vital Records

Cost of Birth Certificates: $30.00

Cost of Death Certificates: $20.00

Cost of Marriage Records: $20.00

Divorce Records: Obtain through county clerk

Delaware

Department of Health and Social Services [DHSS]

417 Federal Street, Dover, DE 19901 (Vital Records)

P.O. Box 637, Dover, DE 19903 (Vital Records)

Tel: (302) 739-4721 (Vital Records)

Internet: www.dhss.delaware.gov

Vital Records

Cost of Birth Certificates: $25.00 each

Cost of Death Certificates: $25.00 each

Cost of Marriage Records: $25.00 each

Cost of Divorce Records: Cost varies according to year and must be obtained from county court where divorce obtained.

District of Columbia

Department of Health [DOH]

899 North Capitol Street, NE, Washington, DC 20002

Tel: (202) 442-9298 (Vital Records)

Fax: (202) 442-4848

Internet: www.doh.dc.gov/service/vital-records

Vital Records

Cost of Birth Certificates: $23.00 long form (only)

Cost of Death Certificates: $18.00

Florida

Department of Health

P.O. Box 210, Jacksonville, FL 32231 (Vital Records)

Tel: (904) 359-6900 ext 9000 (Vital Records)

Fax: (904) 359-6993 (Vital Records)

Email: VitalStats@doh.state.fl.us (Vital Statistics)

Internet: www.doh.state.fl.us

Vital Records

Cost of Birth Certificates: $14:00; $9.00 each additional copy

Cost of Death Certificates: $5.00; $4.00 each additional copy

Cost of Marriage Records: $5.00; $4.00 each additional copy

Cost of Divorce Records: $5.00; $4.00 each additional copy

Cost of Credit Card Order: $5.00 additional charge

Georgia

Department of Public Health [DPH]

Two Peachtree Street, NW, Floor 15, Atlanta, GA 30303-3142

Tel: (404) 679-4702 (Vital Records)

Fax: (404) 657-2715

Internet: dph.georgia.gov

Vital Records

Cost of Birth Certificates: $25.00; $5.00 each additional copy

Cost of Death Certificates: $25.00; $5.00 each additional copy

Cost of Marriage Records: $10.00; $5.00 each additional copy

Cost of Fax Order: $10.00; $5.00 each additional copy

Hawaii
Office of Health Status Monitoring [OHSM]
1250 Punchbowl Street, Honolulu, HI 96813

P.O. Box 3378, Honolulu, HI 96801

Tel: (808) 586-4542 (Vital Records)

Tel: (808) 586-4533 (Vital Records Telephone System)

Fax: (808) 586-4606

Internet: www.health.hawaii.gov/vitalrecords/

Vital Records
Cost of Birth Certificates: $10.00; $4.00 each additional copy

Cost of Death Certificates: $10.00; $4.00 each additional copy

Cost of Marriage Records: $10.00; $4.00 each additional copy

Cost of Divorce Records: $10.00; $4.00 each additional copy

Idaho
Department of Health and Welfare
450 West State Street, Boise, ID 83702

P.O. Box 83720, Boise, ID 83720-0036

Tel: (208) 334-5980 (Vital Records)

TTY: (208) 334-4921

Fax: (208) 332-7260

Email: apsportal@dhw.idaho.gov

Internet: www.healthandwelfare.idaho.gov

Vital Records
Cost of Birth Certificates: $13.00

Cost of Death Certificates: $14.00

Cost of Marriage Records: $13.00

Cost of Divorce Records: $13.00

Illinois
Division of Vital Records
925 East Ridgely Avenue, Springfield, IL 62702

Tel: (217) 557-5163 (Vital Records)

Fax: (217) 785-3209 (Vital Records)

Internet: www.idph.state.il.us/vitalrecords

Vital Records
Cost of Birth Certificates: $15.00, $2.00 each additional copy; $10.00 computer generated copy

Cost of Death Certificates: $17.00 certified copy; $10.00 uncertified copy; $2.00 each additional copy

Cost of Marriage Records: $5.00 for verification

Cost of Divorce Records: $5.00 for verification

Indiana
Indiana State Department of Health [ISDH]
Two North Meridian Street, Indianapolis, IN 46204

P.O. Box 7125, Indianapolis, IN 46206 (Vital Records)

Tel: (317) 233-2700 (Vital Records)

TTY: (317) 233-7859

Fax: (317) 233-7387

Internet: www.in.gov/isdh

Vital Records
Cost of Birth Certificates: $10.00; $4.00 each additional copy

Cost of Death Certificates: $8.00; $4.00 each additional copy

Marriage Records: Obtained through county clerk

Divorce Records: Obtained through county clerk

Iowa
Iowa Department of Public Health [IDPH]
Lucas State Office Building, 321 East 12th Street, Des Moines, IA 50319-0075

Tel: (515) 281-4944 (Vital Records)

Fax: (515) 281-4958

TTY: (800) 735-2942

Email: webmaster@idph.state.ia.us

Internet: www.idph.state.ia.us

Vital Records
Cost of Birth Certificates: $20.00

Cost of Death Certificates: $20.00

Cost of Marriage Records: $20.00

Divorce Records: Obtained through county clerk

Kansas
Office of Vital Statistics
Curtis State Office Building, 1000 Southwest Jackson Street, Suite 120, Topeka, KS 66612-2221

Tel: (785) 296-1400

Fax: (785) 296-8075

E-mail: vital.records@kdheks.gov

Internet: www.kdheks.gov/vital

Vital Records
Cost of Birth Certificates: $15.00

Cost of Death Certificates: $15.00

Cost of Marriage Records: $15.00

Cost of Divorce Records: $15.00

Cost of Credit Card Order: $9.00 additional charge

Kentucky

Office of Vital Statistics

275 East Main Street, 1E-A, Frankfort, KY 40621

Tel: (502) 564-4212

Fax: (866) 283-7477

Internet: www.chfs.ky.gov/dph/vital/

Vital Records

Cost of Birth Certificates: $10.00

Cost of Death Certificates: $16.00

Cost of Marriage Records: $6.00

Cost of Divorce Records: $6.00

Cost of Credit Card Order: $10.00 additional charge

Louisiana

Center of State Registrar and Vital Records

1450 Poydras Street, Suite 400, New Orleans, LA 70112

P.O. Box 60630, New Orleans, LA 70160

Tel: (504) 593-5100

Fax: (504) 568-8716

E-mail: _dhh-vitalweb@la.gov

Internet: www.vitalrecords.dhh.la.gov/

Vital Records

Cost of Birth Certificates: $15.00 long form; $9.00 short form

Cost of Death Certificates: $7.00

Cost of Marriage Records: Cost varies by parish

Cost of Divorce Records: Cost varies by parish

Maine

Data, Research & Vital Statistics

11 State House Station, 220 Capitol Street, Augusta, ME 04333-0011

Tel: (207) 287-5500

Fax: (207) 287-5470

E-mail: maine.ODRVS@maine.gov

Vital Records

Cost of Birth Certificates: $15.00

Cost of Death Certificates: $15.00

Cost of Marriage Records: $15.00

Cost of Divorce Records: $15.00

Maryland

Department of Health and Mental Hygiene [DHMH]

6550 Reistertown Road, Baltimore, MD 21215 (Vital Records)

Tel: (410) 764-3038 (Vital Records)

Tel: (800) 832-3277 (Vital Records)

TTY: (800) 735-2258

Fax: (410) 767-6489

E-mail: dhmh.healthmd@maryland.gov

Internet: www.dhmh.state.maryland.gov/

Vital Records

Cost of Birth Certificates: $24.00

Cost of Death Certificates: $24.00

Cost of Marriage Records: $24.00

Cost of Divorce Records: $24.00

Massachusetts

Executive Office of Health and Human Services [EOHHS]

150 Mount Vernon Street, First Floor, Dorchester, MA 02125 (Vital Records)

Tel: (617) 740-2600 (Vital Records)

E-mail: vital.regulation@state.ma.us

Internet: www.mass.gov/dph/rvrs

Internet: http://www.state.ma.us/dph/bhsre/rvr/rvr.htm (Vital Records)

Vital Records

Cost of Birth Certificates: $20.00 at Registry counter; $50 via Internet, Telephone, Fax and Mail

Cost of Death Certificates: $20.00 at Registry counter; $50 via Internet, Telephone, Fax and Mail

Cost of Marriage Records: $20.00 at Registry counter; $50 via Internet, Telephone, Fax and Mail

Cost of Divorce Records: Cost varies according to county

Michigan

Department of Community Health [MDCH]

P.O. Box 30721, Lansing, MI 48909 (Vital Records)

Capitol View Building, 201 Townsend Street, Seventh Floor, Lansing, MI 48913

Tel: (517) 335-8656 (Vital Records)

TTY: (517) 373-3573

Fax: (517) 321-5884 (Vital Records)

Internet: www.michigan.gov/mdch

Vital Records

Cost of Birth Certificates: $34.00; $16.00 each additional copy; $12.00 additional charge for expedited service

Cost of Death Certificates: $26.00; $12.00 each additional copy; $10.00 additional charge for expedited service

Cost of Marriage Records: $26.00; $12.00 each additional copy; $10.00 additional charge for expedited service.

Cost of Divorce Records: $26.00; $12.00 each additional copy; $10.00 additional charge for expedited service.

Minnesota

Minnesota Department of Health [MDH]

Freeman Building, 625 Robert Street North, St. Paul, MN 55155

P.O. Box 64882, Saint Paul, MN 55164-0882

P.O. Box 64975, St. Paul, MN 55164-0975

Tel: (651) 201-5980 (Vital Records)

TTY: (651) 201-5797

Fax: (651) 201-5740 (Vital Records)

Fax: (651) 291-0101 (Vital Records, Credit Card Payments)

Email: health.issuance@state.mn.us

Internet: www.health.state.mn.us/

Vital Records

Cost of Birth Certificates: $26.00; $19.00 for each additional copy; $20.00 for expedited service; $16.00 for Federal Express

Cost of Death Certificates: $13.00; $6.00 each additional copy; $20.00 for expedited service; $16.00 for Federal Express

Marriage Records: Actual certificate must be obtained from county

Divorce Records: Actual certificate must be obtained from county

Cost of Credit Card Order: $6.00 additional charge

Mississippi

Mississippi State Department of Health [MSDH]

570 East Woodrow Wilson, Jackson, MS 39215-1700

P.O. Box 1700, Jackson, MS 39215-1700 (Vital Records

Tel: (601) 206-8200 (Vital Records)

Internet: www.msdh.state.ms.us

Vital Records

Cost of Birth Certificates: $15.00

Cost of Death Certificates: $15.00

Cost of Marriage Records: $15.00

Cost of Divorce Records: $15.00 [For County page/book number]; actual certificate must be obtained from county

Missouri

Department of Health and Senior Services [DHSS]

P.O. Box 570, Jefferson City, MO 65102

Tel: (573) 751-6387 (Vital Records)

Fax: (573) 751-6010

E-mail: info@health.mo.gov

Internet: www.health.mo.gov/

Vital Records

Cost of Birth Certificates: $15.00

Cost of Death Certificates: $13.00

Cost of Marriage Records: $15.00

Cost of Divorce Records: $15.00

Cost of Credit Card Order: $9.95 additional charge; $17.50 additional charge for UPS

Montana

Department of Public Health and Human Services [DPHHS]

P.O. Box 4210, Helena, MT 59620-4210

Tel: (406) 444-4228 (Vital Records)

TTY: (406) 444-2590

Fax: (406) 444-1803 (Vital Records)

Internet: www.dphhs.mt.gov

Vital Records

Cost of Birth Certificates: $12.00

Cost of Death Certificates: $12.00

Cost of Marriage Records: obtain through the clerk of district court

Cost of Divorce Records: obtain through the clerk of district court

Cost of Credit Card Order: $10.50 additional charge, $18.00 additional charge for UPS Express

Nebraska

Department of Health and Human Services [DHHS]

301 Centennial Mall South, Lincoln, NE 68509

1033 O Street, Suite 130, Lincoln, NE 68508 (Vital Records)

Tel: (402) 471-2871 (Vital Records)

Tel: (402) 471-6440 (Vitalchek for expedited service)

TTY: (402) 471-9570

Fax: (402) 471-9449

E-mail: dhhs.helpline@nebraska.gov

Internet: www.dhhs.ne.gov

Vital Records

Cost of Birth Certificates: $17.00

Cost of Death Certificates: $16.00

Cost of Marriage Records: $16.00

Cost of Divorce Records: $16.00

Nevada

Bureau of Health Statistics, Planning, Epidemiology and Response

4150 Technology Way, Suite 104, Carson City, Nevada 89706

Tel: (775) 684-4242 (Vital Records)

Fax: (775) 684-4156 (Vital Records)

Vital Records

Cost of Birth Certificates: $20.00

Cost of Death Certificates: $20.00

Cost of Marriage Records: cost varies according to county

New Hampshire

Division of Vital Records Administration

71 South Fruit Street, Concord, NH 03301-2410

Tel: (603) 271-4650

Fax: (601) 271-3447

E-mail: vitalrecords@sos.nh.gov

Internet: www.sos.nh.gov/vital_records.aspx

Vital Records

Cost of Birth Certificates: $15.00; $10.00 each additional copy

Cost of Death Certificates: $15.00; $10.00 each additional copy

Cost of Marriage Records: $15.00; $10.00 each additional copy

Cost of Divorce Records: $15.00; $10.00 each additional copy

New Jersey

Department of Health

Health and Agriculture Building, Trenton, NJ 08625

P.O. Box 370, Trenton, NJ 08625 (Vital Records)

Tel: (609) 292-4087 (Vital Records)

Tel: (877) 572-6342 (Vitalchek for check and Federal Express)

Fax: (609) 984-5474

Internet: www.state.nj.us/health

Vital Records

Cost of Birth Certificates: $25.00; $2.00 each additional copy

Cost of Death Certificates: $25.00; $2.00 each additional copy

Cost of Marriage Records: $25.00; $2.00 each additional copy

Cost of Divorce Records: Obtained through Superior Court (609)421-6100

New Mexico

Department of Health [DOH]

1190 South St. Francis Drive, Santa Fe, NM 87602

P.O. Box 26110, Santa Fe, NM 87502-6110 (Vital Records)

Tel: (505) 827-0121 (Vital Records)

Fax: (505) 827-2530

Internet: www.health.state.nm.us

Vital Records

Cost of Birth Certificates: $10.00

Cost of Death Certificates: $5.00

New York

New York State Department of Health [NYSDOH]

800 North Pearl Street, Menands, NY 12204 (Vital Records)

P.O. Box 2602, Albany, NY 12220-2602 (Vital Records)

Tel: (518) 474-3077 (Vital Records)

Tel: (212) 639-9675 (Vital Records [NYC])

Fax: (518) 474-9168 (Vital Records)

E-mail: vr@health.ny.gov (Vital Records)

Internet: www.health.ny.gov/

Vital Records

Cost of Birth Certificates: $30.00

Cost of Death Certificates: $30.00

Cost of Marriage Records: $30.00

Cost of Divorce Records: $30.00

Cost of Credit Card Order: $52.25; $66.25 for United Parcel Service (UPS)

North Carolina
Division of Public Health
1903 Mail Service Center (Vital Records), Raleigh, NC 27699-1903

Tel: (919)733-3000 (Vital Records)

Fax: (919) 733-1511

Internet: http://vitalrecords.nc.gov/vitalrecords (Vital Records)

Vital Records
Cost of Birth Certificates: $24.00; $15.00 each additional copy

Cost of Death Certificates: $24.00; $15.00 each additional copy

Cost of Marriage Records: $24.00; $15.00 each additional copy

Cost of Divorce Records: $24.00; $15.00 each additional copy

Cost of Credit Card Order: $71.70 for expedited service sent by Federal Express

North Dakota
Department of Health
State Capitol, 600 East Boulevard Avenue, Bismarck, ND 58505-0200

Tel: (701) 328-2360 (Vital Records)

Fax: (701) 328-1850 (Vital Records)

E-mail: vitalrec@nd.gov (Vital Records)

Internet: www.ndhealth.gov/vital (Vital Records)

Vital Records
Cost of Birth Certificates: $7.00; $4.00 each additional copy

Cost of Death Certificates: $5.00; $2.00 each additional copy

Cost of Marriage Records: Varies by county

Ohio
Department of Health [ODH]
246 North High Street, Columbus, OH 43215

P.O. Box 15098, Columbus, OH 43215-0098 (Vital Records)

Tel: (614) 466-2531 (Vital Records)

E-mail: vitalstat@odh.ohio.gov (Vital Records)

Internet: www.odh.ohio.gov/vitalstatistics/vitalstats.aspx (Vital Records)

Vital Records
Cost of Birth Certificates: $21.50

Cost of Death Certificates: $21.50

Cost of Marriage Records: Obtain certified copies from Probate Court where event occurred

Cost of Divorce Records: Obtain certified copies from Probate Court where event occurred

Oklahoma
Oklahoma State Department of Health [OSDH]
1000 N.E. 10th Street, Oklahoma City, OK 73117-1299

P.O. Box 53551, Oklahoma City, OK 73152 (Vital Records)

Tel: (405) 271-4040 (Vital Records)

E-mail: askvr@health.ok.gov (Vital Records)

Internet: http://www.ok.gov/health/Birth_and_Death_Certificates/

Vital Records
Cost of Birth Certificates: $15.00; $15.00 each additional copy

Cost of Death Certificates: $15.00; $15.00 each additional copy

Cost of Marriage Records: Cost varies by county

Cost of Divorce Records: Cost varies by county

Cost of Credit Card Order: Additional charge for credit card transactions varies

Oregon
Oregon Health Authority [OHA]
500 Summer Street NE, E-20, Salem, OR 97301

Tel: (971) 673-1222

E-mail: oha.directorsoffice@state.or.us

Internet: http://www.oregon.gov/oha

Vital Records
Cost of Birth Certificates: $20.00; $15.00 each additional copy

Cost of Death Certificates: $20.00; $15.00 each additional copy

Cost of Marriage Records: $20.00; $15.00 each additional copy

Cost of Divorce Records: $20.00; $15.00 each additional copy

Cost of Credit Card Order: $18.45 additional charge

Pennsylvania
Department of Health
Health and Welfare Building, Eighth Floor West, Harrisburg, PA 17120

P.O. Box 1528, New Castle, PA 16103 (Vital Records)

Tel: (724) 656-3100 (Vital Records)

TTY: (717) 783-6514

Fax: (717) 772-6959

E-mail: webmaster@health.state.pa.us

Internet: http://www.health.state.pa.us/vitalrecords/ (Vital Records)

Vital Records
Cost of Birth Certificates: $20.00

Cost of Death Certificates: $9.00

Cost of Marriage Records: Cost varies by county

Cost of Divorce Records: Cost varies by county

Puerto Rico

Health Department

P.O. Box 11854, Fernandez Juncos Station, San Juan, PR 00910 (Vital Records)

Tel: (787) 767-9120 (Vital Records)

Tel: (787) 753-5003 (Vital Records)

Fax: (787) 250-6547

Internet: www.salud.gov.pr

Vital Records

Cost of Birth Certificates: $5.00

Cost of Death Certificates: $5.00

Cost of Marriage Records: $5.00

Cost of Divorce Records: $5.00

Rhode Island

Department of Health

Cannon Building, Three Capitol Hill, Providence, RI 02908-5097

Tel: (401) 222-2812 (Divorce Records)

Tel: (401) 222-2812 (Vital Records)

TTY: (401) 222-2506

Fax: (401) 222-6548

Internet: http://www.health.ri.gov/

Vital Records

Cost of Birth Certificates: $20.00; $15.00 each additional copy

Cost of Death Certificates: $20.00; $15.00 each additional copy

Cost of Marriage Records: $20.00; $15.00 each additional copy

Cost of Divorce Records: Cost varies by county

South Carolina

Department of Health and Environmental Control [DHEC]

2600 Bull Street, Columbia, SC 29201

Tel: (803) 898-3630 (Vital Records)

Fax: (803) 898-3323

Internet: www.scdhec.gov

Vital Records

Cost of Birth Certificates: $12.00; $3.00 each additional copy

Cost of Death Certificates: $12.00; $3.00 each additional copy

Cost of Marriage Records: $12.00; $3.00 each additional copy

Cost of Divorce Records: $12.00; $3.00 each additional copy

South Dakota

Department of Health

600 East Capitol Avenue, Pierre, SD 57501-2536

Tel: (605) 773-4961 (Vital Records)

Fax: (605) 773-5683

Internet: www.state.sd.us/doh/vitalrec/vital.htm (Vital Records)

Vital Records

Cost of Birth Certificates: $15.00

Cost of Death Certificates: $15.00

Cost of Marriage Records: $15.00

Cost of Divorce Records: $15.00

Tennessee

Department of Health

Central Services Building, 421 Fifth Avenue North, First Floor, Nashville, TN 37243 (Vital Records)

Tel: (615) 741-1763 (Vital Records)

Fax: (615) 741-9860 (Vital Records)

Internet: http://www2.state.tn.us/health/vr/index.htm (Vital Records)

Vital Records

Cost of Birth Certificates: $15.00 long form; $8.00 short form; $5.00 each additional copy

Cost of Death Certificates: $7.00; $5.00 each additional copy

Cost of Marriage Records: $15.00; $5.00 each additional copy

Cost of Divorce Records: $15.00; $5.00 each additional copy

Texas

Department of State Health Services [DSHS]

1100 West 49th Street, Austin, TX 78756

P.O. Box 12040, Austin, TX 78711-2040 (Vital Records)

Tel: (888) 963-7111 (Vital Records)

Fax: (512) 776-7711 (Vital Records)

Email: registrar@dshs.state.tx.us

Internet: www.dshs.state.tx.us/vs/default.shtm (Vital Records)

Vital Records

Cost of Birth Certificates: $22.00

Cost of Death Certificates: $20.00; $3 each additional copy

Cost of Marriage Records: $20.00

Cost of Divorce Records: $20.00

Utah

Utah Department of Health [UDOH]

288 North 1460 West, Salt Lake City, UT 84116-0700 (Vital Records)

P.O. Box 141012, Salt Lake City, UT 84114-1000 (Vital Records)

Tel: (801) 538-6105 (Vital Records)

TTY: (801) 538-6622

Fax: (801) 538-7012 (Vital Records)

E-mail: vrequest@utah.gov (Vital Records)

Internet: www.health.utah.gov/vitalrecords (Vital Records)

Vital Records

Cost of Birth Certificates: $20.00; $8.00 each additional copy

Cost of Death Certificates: $18.00; $8.00 each additional copy

Cost of Marriage Records: cost varies by county

Cost of Divorce Records: cost varies by county

Cost of Credit Card Order: $15.50 additional charge

Vermont

Health Department

P.O. Box 70, Burlington, VT 05402

Tel: (802) 863-7275 (Vital Records)

Fax: (802) 863-7425

Internet: www.healthvermont.gov

Vital Records

Cost of Birth Certificates: $10.00

Cost of Death Certificates: $10.00

Cost of Marriage Records: $10.00

Cost of Divorce Records: $10.00

Virginia

Department of Health [VDH]

109 Governor's Street, Richmond, VA 23219

Tel: (804) 662-6200 (Vital Records)

Internet: www.vdh.virginia.gov

Vital Records

Cost of Birth Certificates: $12.00

Cost of Death Certificates: $12.00

Cost of Marriage Records: $12.00

Cost of Divorce Records: $12.00

Washington

Department of Health [DOH]

101 Israel Road, SE, Tumwater, WA 98501

P.O. Box 9709, Olympia, WA 98507-9709 (Vital Records)

Tel: (360) 236-4501

Tel: (360) 236-4300 (Vital Records)

Fax: (360) 586-7424

Internet: www.doh.wa.gov

Vital Records

Cost of Birth Certificates: $20.00

Cost of Death Certificates: $20.00

Cost of Marriage Records: $20.00

Cost of Divorce Records: $20.00

West Virginia

Department of Health and Human Resources [DHHR]

350 Capitol Street, Charleston, WV 25301 (Vital Records)

Tel: (304) 558-2931 (Vital Records)

Fax: (304) 558-8001 (Vital Records)

Internet: www.wvdhhr.org

Vital Records

Cost of Birth Certificates: $12.00; $12.00 each additional copy

Cost of Death Certificates: $12.00; $12.00 each additional copy

Cost of Marriage Records: $12.00; $12.00 each additional copy

Cost of Divorce Records: Cost varies by county

Wisconsin

Department of Health Services [DHS]

P.O. Box 309, Madison, WI 53701-0309 (Vital Records)

Tel: (608) 266-1371 (Vital Records)

TTY: (608) 266-3683

Fax: (608) 266-7882

Email: dhsvitalrecords@wisconsin.gov (Vital Records)

Internet: www.dhs.wisconsin.gov/vitalrecords (Vital Records)

Vital Records

Cost of Birth Certificates: $20.00; $3.00 each additional copy; $20.00 additional for expedited service

Cost of Death Certificates: $20.00; $3.00 each additional copy; $20.00 additional for expedited service

Cost of Marriage Records: $20.00; $3.00 each additional copy; $20.00 additional for expedited service

Cost of Divorce Records: $20.00; $3.00 each additional copy; $20.00 additional for expedited service

Wyoming

Wyoming Department of Health [WDH]

401 Hathaway Building, 2300 Capitol Avenue, Cheyenne, WY 82002

Tel: (307) 777-7264 (Vital Records)

Fax: (307) 777-7439

E-mail: wdh@wyo.gov

Internet: http://health.wyo.gov/rfhd/vital_records/NewGateway.html (Vital Records)

Vital Records

Cost of Birth Certificates: $13.00

Cost of Death Certificates: $10.00

Cost of Marriage Records: $13.00

Cost of Divorce Records: $13.00

Corporate and UCC Filings

Corporate and UCC Filings

Listed below are the phone numbers at State offices that provide information on corporate filings (e.g., domestic and foreign corporations registered in the state), annual reports issued by these corporations, UCC filings, limited partnerships and other financial information, trademark and tradename availabilities, and notaries. Names and addresses of Secretaries of State are given in the State Court Charts, beginning on page 1 of this directory.

Alabama

General Information: (334) 242-7200

Corporations Section: (334) 242-5324

Name Availabilities: (334) 242-5324

Limited Partnerships: (334) 242-5324

UCC: (334) 242-5324

Trademarks: (334) 242-5325

Notaries: (334) 242-7202

Alaska

UCC: (907) 269-8899

Corporation, Limited Partnership and Limited Liability Information: (907) 465-2550

Arizona

Secretary of State

General Information - UCC: (602) 542-4285

Limited Partnerships: (602) 542-6187

UCC: (602) 542-6187

Notaries: (602) 542-6187

Fax - UCC: (602) 542-7386

State Corporation Commission

General Information - Corporations: (602) 542-3026

Annual Reports: (602) 542-3285

Fax - Corporations: (602) 542-8813

Arkansas

General Information: (501) 682-3409

Name Availability: (501) 682-3409

UCC Searches & Inquiries: (501) 682-5078

UCC: (501) 682-5078

Franchise Tax/Annual Reports: (501) 682-3409

Limited Partnerships: (501) 682-3409

Notaries: (501) 682-3409

Trademarks, Boards and Commissions: (501) 682-3409

Fax - Corporations: (501) 682-3437

Fax - UCC (501) 682-3500

California

Business Programs: (916) 657-5448

UCC: (916) 653-3516

Annual Reports: (916) 657-3537

Partnerships/LLCs: (916) 653-3365

Colorado

Business Division: (303) 894-2200, #2

Annual Reports: (303) 894-2200, #2

Licensing/Notaries: (303) 894-2200, #4

UCC: (303) 894-2200, #2

Business Entities, Tradenames & Trademarks: (303) 894-2200, #3

Elections: (303) 894-2200, #3

Connecticut

General Information: (860) 509-6200

Business Information Line: (860) 509-6002

Forms - Automated Order Line: (860) 509-6079

Document Review (Business Filings Only) (860) 509-6003

Research and Response Unit (UCC, Copies, Certificates): (860) 509-6002

Delaware

Receptionist: (302) 739-3077

Corporate General Information: (302) 739-3073, #2

Name Reservation: (302) 739-3073

Franchise Tax Information: (302) 739-3073 #3

UCC: (302) 739-3073 #4

Expedited Services Information: (302) 739-3073

Limited Partnerships: (302) 739-3073

Fax: (302) 739-3812; (302) 739-3813

District of Columbia

Information: (202) 442-4434

Corporations Division: (202) 442-4432

Name Availabilities: (202) 442-4432

Florida

General Corporate Information: (850) 245-6500

Trademarks /LLCS /Partnerships: (850) 487-6051

Foreign Qualifications: (850) 487-6051

Fictitious Names: (850) 487-6058

Annual Reports: (850) 245-6056

Fax - Commercial Recording: (850) 245-6013

Domestic/Profit & Non-Profit: (850) 245-6052

Amendments/Dissolutions/Mergers: (850) 245-6050

Certification: (850) 245-6053

Reinstatements: (850) 245-6059

Fax - Director: (850) 245-6014

Georgia

Corporations Division

General Information: (404) 656-2817

UCC Information: (404) 327-9058

Hawaii

Business Registration Division

General Information: (808) 586-2727

Corporations Section: (808) 586-2727

Name Availabilities: (808) 586-2727

Annual Reports: (808) 586-2727

Limited Partnerships: (808) 586-2727

Brokers/Dealers: (808) 586-2722

Securities Offering/Franchise: (808) 586-2722

Fax: (808) 586-2733

Bureau of Conveyances

UCC Information: (808) 587-0147

Fax: (808) 587-0136

Idaho

General Information: (208) 334-2300

Corporations: (208) 334-2301

Limited Partnerships: (208) 334-2301

Trademarks: (208) 334-2300

Name Availability: (208) 334-2301

Annual Reports: (208) 334-2301

UCC: (208) 334-3191

Notaries: (208) 334-2300

Fax: (208) 334-2847

Illinois

General Information: (217) 782-7880

Corporations Section: (217) 782-6961

Name Availability: (217) 782-9521

Annual Reports: (217) 782-7808

Trademarks: (217) 524-0400

UCC: (217) 782-7518

Limited Partnerships: (217) 785-8960

Limited Liability Companies: (217) 524-8008

Fax: (217) 524-8281

Indiana

Corporate Information: (317) 232-6576

Fax: (317) 233-3387

UCC: (317) 233-3984

Notaries: (317) 232-6576

Iowa

General: (515) 281-5204

Corporations Section: (515) 281-5204

Name Availability: (515) 281-5204

Annual Reports: (515) 281-7796

Limited Partnerships: (515) 281-5204

Notaries: (515) 281-8363

Fax - Corporations: (515) 242-5953

UCC: (515) 281-5204

Fax - UCC: (515) 242-5953

Kansas

Corporations Section: (785) 296-4564

Name Availability: (785) 296-4564

Annual Reports: (785) 296-4564

Fax - Corporate: (785) 296-4570

General Information (UCC): (785) 296-4564

Fax – UCC: (785) 296-4570

Kentucky

Filing Information: (502) 564-3490

Records: (502) 564-3490

Name Availability: (502) 564-3490

Annual Reports: (502) 564-3490

UCC Branch: (502) 564-3490

Trademark, Service Mark: (502) 564-3490

Fax: (502) 564-5687

Corporate Records: (502) 564-3490

Louisiana

General Information: (225) 925-4704

Corporations Section: (225) 925-4704

Name Availabilities: (225) 925-4704

Annual Reports: (225) 925-4704

Limited Partnerships: (225) 925-4704

Trademarks: (225) 925-4704

Fax - Corporations: (225) 932-5314

UCC Information: (225) 922-1193

Fax - UCC: (225) 932-5318

Maine

General Information: (207) 624-7736

New Filings: (207) 624-7752

Annual Reports: (207) 624-7752

Notaries: (207) 624-7752

UCC: (207) 624-7760

Fax: (207) 287-5428

Maryland

General Information: (410) 767-1340

Corporations Section: (410) 767-1340

Name Availabilities & Resident Agent Information: (410) 767-1330

UCC: (410) 767-1459

Limited Partnerships: (410) 767-1340

Forms Line: (410) 767-1180

Fax: (410) 333-7097

Massachusetts

Corporations Section: (617) 727-9640

Name Availability: (617) 727-9640

Annual Reports: (617) 727-9640

UCC: (617) 727-2860

Limited Partnerships: (617) 727-2859

Trademarks: (617) 727-8329

Dissolutions: (617) 727-2850

Nonprofit: (617) 727-2850

Business Trusts: (617) 727-2587

Forms: (617) 727-9440

Michigan

Department of Labor & Economic Growth

General Information: (517) 241-6470

Trademark/Servicemark Forms: (517) 241-6470

Annual Reports: (517) 241-6470

Customer Service

Corporate Record or to order copies or certificates: (517) 241-6470

UCC: (517) 322-1144

Fax - UCC: (517) 322-5434

Minnesota

General Information: (651) 296-2803

Toll Free: (877) 551-6767

Name Availability: (651) 296-2803

Annual Reports: (651) 296-2803

Certified Copies and Certificates: (651) 296-2803

UCC Filings Information: (651) 296-2803

Fax-back Forms: (651) 296-7067

Mississippi

Corporations: (601) 359-1633

Notary Division: (601) 359-1633

UCC: (601) 359-1633

Fax: (601) 359-1607

Missouri

General Information: (573) 751-4153

Toll Free: (866) 223-6535

UCC Filings: (573) 751-4628

Montana

General Information: (406) 444-2034

Corporations Section: (406) 444-3665

Name Availability: (406) 444-3665

Annual Reports: (406) 444-5522

Limited Partnerships: (406) 444-3665

Notaries: (406) 444-5379

UCC: (406) 444-2468

Fax: (406) 444-3976

Nebraska

Information: (402) 471-4070

Corporations Section: (402) 471-4079

Annual Reports: (402) 471-4079

Limited Partnerships: (402) 471-4079

Notaries: (402) 471-2558

UCC: (402) 471-4080

Fax - Corporations: (402) 471-3666

Fax - UCC: (402) 471-4429

Nevada

General Information: (775) 684-5708

Corporations Section: (775) 684-5708

Name Availability: (775) 684-5708

Annual Reports: (775) 684-5708

Status: (775) 684-5708

UCC: (702) 684-5708

Limited Partnerships: (775) 684-5708

Notaries: (775) 684-5708

Fax: (775) 684-5725

Corporate Copies and Certification: (775) 684-5645

New Hampshire

Corporations Section: (603) 271-3244

Corporate Information: (603) 271-3246

Name Availabilities: (603) 271-3246

UCC: (603) 271-3276

Fax: (603) 271-6316

New Jersey

Information: (609) 292-9292

Corporations Section: (609) 292-9292

Name Availability: (609) 292-9292

Annual Reports: (609) 292-9292

UCC: (609) 292-9292

Limited Partnerships: (609) 292-9292

Notaries: (609) 292-9292

New Mexico

Secretary of State

UCC, Limited Partnerships, Notaries, Trademarks/Tradenames/Election Code: (505) 827-3614

Operations Section Tel: (505) 827-3614

Operations Section Fax: (505) 827-3611

Corporations Section Tel: (505) 827-34508

Corporations Section Fax: (505) 827-4387

New York

Corporate and Business Information: (518) 473-2492

Corporate & Business Records: (900) 835-2677 (Toll charge)

Corporations Fax: (518) 474-5173

UCC: (518) 474-4763

Fax – UCC: (518) 474-4478

North Carolina

Information: (919) 807-2000

Corporations Section: (919) 807-2225

Corporations Fax: (919) 807-2039

Name Availability: (919) 807-2225

Limited Partnerships: (919) 807-2225

Notaries: (919) 807-2219

Notaries Fax: (919) 807-2130

Trademarks: (919) 807-2162

UCC Information: (919) 807-2219

Fax – UCC: (919) 807-2120

North Dakota

Business Division: (701) 328-4284

Business Registration Documents Fax: (701) 328-2992

Business Information, Copies, and Certificates Fax: (701) 328-0106

UCC Central Indexing Tel: (701) 328-3662

UCC Central Indexing Fax: (701) 328-4219

Ohio

General Information: (614) 466-3910; (877) 767-3453
Corporations Section: (614) 466-3910; (877) 767-3453
Fax: (614) 466-2892

Oklahoma

Secretary of State General Information: (405) 521-3911
Certification Department: (405) 521-4211
Fax: (405) 521-3771

Oregon

General Information-Corporate & UCC: (503) 986-2200
Copies/Certificates: (503) 986-2317
Fax - UCC: (503) 373-1166
Fax - Notary Public: (503) 986-2300

Pennsylvania

General Information: (717) 787-1057
Automated Form Ordering: (717) 787-1057, Option 1
UCC: (717) 787-1057, Option 3
Customer Service: (717) 787-1057, Option 4
Fax: (717) 783-2244

Puerto Rico

General Information: (787) 722-2121
Corporations Section: (787) 722-2121, Ext. 6226
Annual Reports: (787) 722-2121
Notaries: (787) 722-2121, Ext. 6336

Rhode Island

Corporations: (401) 277-3040
Notaries: (401) 277-1487
Trademark Division: (401) 222-3040
UCC: (401) 277-3040
Fax: (401) 277-1309

South Carolina

Information: (803) 734-2170
Corporations Section: (803) 734-2158
Name Availabilities: (803) 734-2158
UCC: (803) 734-2175
Limited Partnerships: (803) 734-2158
Notaries: (803) 734-2512
Fax: (803) 734-2164

South Dakota

Information: (605) 773-4845
Corporations Section: (605) 773-4845
Name Availability: (605) 773-4845
Annual Reports: (605) 773-4845
Limited Partnerships: (605) 773-4845
Notaries: (605) 773-3539
Secretary of State's Office (605) 773-3537
UCC: (605) 773-4422
Fax: (605) 773-4550

Tennessee

Information: (615) 741-2286
Corporations Certification: (615) 741-6488
UCC: (615) 741-3276
Notaries: (615) 741-2650
Trademarks: (615) 741-0531
Service of Process: (615) 741-1799
Fax - Corporate: (615) 532-9870
Fax - UCC: (615) 532-2892

Texas

Corporations Section
General Information: (512) 463-5555
Name Availability: (512) 463-5555
Limited Partnerships: (512) 463-5578
Fax: (512) 463-5709
Certifying: (512) 463-5586
Trademarks: (512) 463-9760
Legal Staff: (512) 463-5586
Assumed Names: (512) 463-9760

UCC Section
UCC: (512) 475-2700
UCC Searches: (512) 475-2703
Fax: (512) 463-1423

Utah

Corporations: (801) 530-4849
UCC: (801) 530-4849
Toll-Free in State: (877) 526-3994

Vermont

General Information: (802) 828-2386
Fax: (802) 828-2853

Virginia

Information: (804) 371-9733
Corporations Section: (804) 371-9733
Name Availability: (804) 371-9733
Annual Reports: (804) 371-9733
UCC: (804) 371-9733
Business Entities: (804) 371-9733
Fax: (804) 371-9654

Washington

Business Information: (360) 725-0377
Corporations Section: (360) 725-0377
Annual Reports: (360) 725-0377
Charities Program: (360) 725-0738
Limited Partnerships/Trademarks: (360) 725-0377
UCC: (360) 664-1530
Fax – UCC: (360) 586-4414
Forms: (360) 725-0377

West Virginia

Information: (304) 558-6000
Corporations Section: (304) 558-8000
Name Availability: (304) 558-8000
UCC: (304) 558-6000
Limited Partnerships: (304) 558-8000
Notaries: (304) 558-6000
Fax: (304) 558-0900
Limited Liability Companies: (304) 558-8000

Wisconsin

Information: (608) 261-9555
Corporations Section: (608) 261-7577
Fax - Corporations: (608) 267-6813
Domestic Annual Reports: (608) 261-7577
Foreign Annual Reports: (608) 267-3218
Limited Partnerships: (608) 267-7107
Foreign Corporations: (608) 267-7107
Name Reservation by Phone: (608) 261-7577
UCC Section: (608) 261-9548
Fax - UCC: (608) 264-7965

Wyoming

Information: (307) 777-7311
Corporations Section:
(307) 777-7311
Name Availability: (307) 777-7311
Annual Reports: (307) 777-7311
UCC: (307) 777-7311
Notaries: (307) 777-7370
Fax: (307) 777-5339